Social Ethics in the Making

Books by Gary Dorrien

Logic and Consciousness

The Democratic Socialist Vision

Reconstructing the Common Good

The Neoconservative Mind: Politics, Culture, and the War of Ideology

Soul in Society: The Making and Renewal of Social Christianity

The Word as True Myth: Interpreting Modern Theology

The Remaking of Evangelical Theology

The Barthian Revolt in Modern Theology

The Making of American Liberal Theology: Imagining Progressive Religion, 1805–1900

The Making of American Liberal Theology: Idealism, Realism, and Modernity, 1900–1950

Imperial Designs: Neoconservatism and the New Pax Americana

The Making of American Liberal Theology: Crisis, Irony, and Postmodernity, 1950–2005

Social Ethics in the Making:
Interpreting an American Tradition

Gary Dorrien

Reinhold Niebuhr Professor of Social Ethics,
Union Theological Seminary
Professor of Religion, Columbia University

WILEY-BLACKWELL
A John Wiley & Sons, Ltd., Publication

This edition first published 2009
© 2009 Gary Dorrien

Blackwell Publishing was acquired by John Wiley & Sons in February 2007. Blackwell's publishing program has been merged with Wiley's global Scientific, Technical, and Medical business to form Wiley-Blackwell.

Registered Office
John Wiley & Sons Ltd, The Atrium, Southern Gate, Chichester, West Sussex, PO19 8SQ, United Kingdom

Editorial Offices
350 Main Street, Malden, MA 02148-5020, USA
9600 Garsington Road, Oxford, OX4 2DQ, UK
The Atrium, Southern Gate, Chichester, West Sussex, PO19 8SQ, UK

For details of our global editorial offices, for customer services, and for information about how to apply for permission to reuse the copyright material in this book please see our website at www.wiley.com/wiley-blackwell.

The right of Gary Dorrien to be identified as the author of this work has been asserted in accordance with the Copyright, Designs and Patents Act 1988.

Library of Congress Cataloging-in-Publication Data

Dorrien, Gary J.
   Social ethics in the making : interpreting an American tradition / Gary Dorrien.
      p. cm.
   Includes bibliographical references and index.
   ISBN 978-1-4051-8687-2 (hardcover : alk. paper)   1. Christian sociology–United States.   2. Social gospel–United States.   3. Social ethics–United States.   4. Christian ethics–United States.   I. Title.
   BT738.D655 2008 2009
   261.80973–dc22
                                                                          2008009057

A catalogue record for this book is available from the British Library.

Set in 10 on 12 Bembo by SNP Best-set Typesetter Ltd., Hong Kong
Printed in Singapore by Utopia Press Pte Ltd

1   2009

For James Cone
Eminent theologian and treasured friend

Contents

Plates   x

Acknowledgments   xiv

Introduction   1

1.   Inventing Social Ethics: Francis Greenwood Peabody,
William Jewett Tucker, and Graham Taylor   6

    Becoming Francis Greenwood Peabody   7
    Philosophies of Moral Philosophy   10
    Beyond Moral Philosophy: Social Ethics   15
    The Social Question, William Jewett Tucker, and Liberal Theology   20
    Jesus and the Social Question   25
    Up from Slavery: The Race Problem in the Social Question   29
    Retreating to the Seminaries   32
    Getting Peabody Right   35
    Christian Sociology: Graham Taylor   36
    The Social Gospel in the Classroom and Public Square   44

2.   The Social Gospel: Washington Gladden, Josiah Strong,
Walter Rauschenbusch, and Harry F. Ward   60

    Good Theology and the Social Good: Washington Gladden   61
    The Social Gospel Difference and the Challenge of Darwinism   69
    Manifest Destiny and the Crucible of Race: Fiske, Gladden, and
      Josiah Strong   73
    The Great War and the Social Gospel   79
    The Socialist Kingdom of God: Walter Rauschenbusch   83
    Asking the Social Question   87
    The Kingdom as Political Theology   89
    German America and the Wider Kingdom   92
    The Social Crisis and the Social Gospel   94

The Social Gospel Ascending   97
Christianizing the American Order   99
The Great War and the Social Gospel   104
Social Christianity and Radical Reconstruction: Harry F. Ward   109
Ward, Reinhold Niebuhr, and the Soviet Spirit   120

3. Lift Every Voice: Reverdy C. Ransom, Jane Addams, and
    John A. Ryan   146

    Becoming Reverdy C. Ransom   147
    Mainstreaming the Black Social Gospel   158
    Fostering Democratic Citizenship: Jane Addams   168
    Democracy, Social Ethics, and Pragmatism   175
    Social Doctrine in Action: John A. Ryan   185
    Mainstreaming the Catholic Social Gospel   199

4. Christian Realism: Reinhold Niebuhr, H. Richard Niebuhr,
    John C. Bennett, and Paul Ramsey   226

    Becoming Reinhold Niebuhr   226
    Rejecting Social Gospel Idealism   236
    H. Richard Niebuhr, Liberal Religion, and Radical Monotheism   239
    Christian Realism as Socialist Faith   244
    Niebuhrian Realism, World War II, and the Cold War   259
    The Niebuhrian Method and Legacy   271
    Making Sense of Niebuhrian Realism: John C. Bennett and
        Paul Ramsey   276
    A New Liberal Consensus?   287

5. Social Christianity as Public Theology: Walter G. Muelder,
    James Luther Adams, John Courtney Murray, and Dorothy Day   305

    Socializing Personalist Theory: Walter G. Muelder   306
    Moral Theory, Culture, and Christian Social Ethics   316
    Personalism Against the Current   320
    James Luther Adams and Unitarian Christianity   324
    Rethinking Religious Freedom and Pluralism:
        John Courtney Murray   334
    The American Idea and the Catholic Presence   349
    Dorothy Day and the Catholic Worker Movement   361

6. Liberationist Disruptions: Martin Luther King Jr, James H. Cone,
    Mary Daly, and Beverly W. Harrison   390

    Martin Luther King Jr and the Beloved Community   391
    James H. Cone and Black Liberation Theology   396
    Beyond Patriarchal Religion: Mary Daly and the Rebirth of
        Feminism   411
    Christian Feminist Liberation Ethics: Beverly W. Harrison   421

7. Disputing and Expanding the Tradition: Carl F. H. Henry,
    John Howard Yoder, Stanley Hauerwas, Michael Novak, and
    Jim Wallis   447

    Carl F. H. Henry and the New Evangelicalism   448
    John Howard Yoder and the Politics of Jesus   460
    Thinking Christian Pacifism Through: Stanley M. Hauerwas   474
    Ideological Americanism: The Neoconservative Reaction   488
    Michael Novak and Democratic Capitalism   489
    Interrogating Liberation Theology and the Catholic Bishops   503
    Progressive Evangelicalism: Jim Wallis   512

8. Dealing with Modernity and Postmodernity: Charles Curran,
    James M. Gustafson, Gibson Winter, Cornel West, Katie G. Cannon,
    and Victor Anderson   533

    Moral Theology and the Curran Controversy   534
    Naturalistic Theocentrism: James M. Gustafson   544
    Elements for a Social Ethic: Gibson Winter   549
    Prophetic Public Criticism: Cornel West   563
    Womanist Ethics: Katie Geneva Cannon   584
    Taking Postmodernity Seriously: Victor Anderson   592

9. Economy, Sexuality, Ecology, Difference: Max L. Stackhouse,
    Dennis P. McCann, Lisa Sowle Cahill, Marvin M. Ellison,
    John B. Cobb, Jr, Larry Rasmussen, Daniel C. Maguire,
    Sharon Welch, Emilie M. Townes, Ada María Isasi-Díaz,
    María Pilar Aquino, and David Hollenbach   611

    Capitalist Apologetics as Public Theology: Max Stackhouse and
        Dennis McCann   612
    Right Ordering and Sexual Difference   616
    Lisa Sowle Cahill: Sources, Norms, and Moral Reasoning   618
    Marvin M. Ellison: Sexual Justice   621
    Debating Economic Democracy   624
    Ecology as Political Economics and Theology   626
    Eco-Justice for the Sake of Everything: Larry Rasmussen and
        Daniel C. Maguire   630
    Sharon Welch: Toward an Ethic of Risk and Conflict   637
    Emilie Townes: Womanism and the Cultural Production of Evil   640
    Latina Feminisms: Ada María Isasi-Díaz and María Pilar Aquino   646
    Human Rights and Catholic Social Ethics: David Hollenbach   657

10. Borders of Possibility: The Necessity of "Discredited" Social
    Gospel Ideas   674

    Social Ethics and Racial Justice   677
    Foreign Policy Realism and American Empire   680
    Economic Democracy: The Future of a Discredited Vision   683

Index   692

Figure 1 Francis
Greenwood Peabody

Figure 2 William
Jewett Tucker

Figure 3
Graham Taylor

Figure 4
Washington Gladden

Figure 5
Josiah Strong

Walter Rauschenbusch

Figure 6 Walter
Rauschenbusch

Figure 7
Harry F. Ward

Figure 8 Reverdy
C. Ransom

Figure 9
Jane Addams

Figure 10
John A. Ryan

Figure 11
Reinhold Niebuhr

Figure 12
H. Richard Niebuhr

Figure 13
John C. Bennett

Figure 14
Paul Ramsey

Figure 15
Walter G. Muelder

Figure 16
James Luther Adams

Figure 17 John
Courtney Murray

Figure 18
Dorothy Day

Figure 19 Martin
Luther King, Jr

Figure 20
James H. Cone

Figure 21 Mary Daly

Figure 22
Beverly W. Harrison

Figure 23
Carl F. H. Henry

Figure 24
John Howard Yoder

Figure 25
Stanley Hauerwas

Figure 26
Michael Novak

Figure 27 Jim Wallis

Figure 28
Charles Curran

Figure 29
James. M. Gustafson

Figure 30 Gibson Winter

Figure 31
Cornel West

Figure 32
Katie G. Cannon

Figure 33 Victor Anderson

Figure 34
Max L. Stackhouse

Figure 35 Dennis P. McCann

Figure 36
Lisa Sowle Cahill

Figure 37
Marvin M. Ellison

Figure 38
John B. Cobb, Jr

Figure 39 Larry Rasmussen

Figure 40
Daniel C. Maguire

Figure 41
Sharon Welch

Figure 42
Emilie M. Townes

Figure 43
Ada María Isasi-Díaz

Figure 45
David Hollenbach

Figure 44
María Pilar Aquino

Acknowledgments

For the rights of access to and permission to quote from the unpublished letters and papers of Francis Greenwood Peabody, grateful acknowledgment is made to the Andover-Harvard Theological Library, Harvard Divinity School, Cambridge, Massachusetts, with special thanks to Curator Frances O'Donnell; for the unpublished letters and papers of Graham Taylor, grateful acknowledgment is made to the Midwest Manuscript Collection, The Newberry Library, Chicago, Illinois; Washington Gladden, grateful acknowledgment is made to the Archives/Library Edition of the Ohio Historical Society in Columbus, Ohio, with special thanks to Mr. Gary Arnold, Chief Bibliographer at the Ohio Historical Society; for the unpublished letters and papers of Walter Rauschenbusch, grateful acknowledgment is made to the Rauschenbusch Family Papers, American Baptist-Samuel Colgate Historical Library of the American Baptist Historical Society, Colgate-Rochester/Crozer Divinity School, Rochester, New York, with special thanks to Assistant Director Nancy Blostein; for the unpublished letters and papers of Harry F. Ward and Beverly W. Harrison, grateful acknowledgment is made to the Burke Library of Columbia University/Union Theological Seminary in New York, New York, with special thanks to Archivist Ruth Tonkiss Cameron, Archives of Women in Theological Scholarship; for the unpublished letters and papers of Reverdy C. Ransom, grateful acknowledgment is made to the Reverdy C. Ransom Papers, Payne Theological Seminary, Wilberforce, Ohio; for the unpublished letters and papers of Reinhold Niebuhr, grateful acknowledgment is made to the Manuscript Division, Library of Congress, Washington, DC, with special thanks to Archivist Fred Bauman, and the Columbia University Oral History Research Collection, Columbia University, New York, New York, with special thanks to Associate Director Jessica Wiederhorn; for the unpublished letters and papers of Walter G. Muelder, grateful acknowledgment is made to the Department of Library Research Collections, Boston University School of Theology, Boston, Massachusetts, with special thanks to Dawn Piscitello, Research Collections Librarian; for the unpublished letters and papers of John Courtney Murray, grateful acknowledgment is made to the Archives of the Woodstock College Library, Georgetown University, Washington, DC.

For the photo of Francis Greenwood Peabody, grateful acknowledgment is made to Manuscripts and Archives, Andover-Harvard Theological Library, Harvard Divinity School, Harvard University, Cambridge, Massachusetts, with special thanks to Curator Frances O'Donnell; for the photo of Graham Taylor, grateful acknowledgment is made to the Morrison-Shearer Foundation, Northbrook, Illinois (Photographs by Helen

Balfour Morrison used with permission by the Morrison-Shearer Foundation, Northbrook, Illinois), with special thanks to Program Manager Julia Mayer; for the photo of Washington Gladden, grateful acknowledgment is made to the Ohio Historical Society, Columbus, Ohio, with special thanks to Teresa Carstensen, Photoduplication/ Library Acquisitions Coordinator; for the photo of Walter Rauschenbusch, grateful acknowledgment is made to the American Baptist Archives Center, Valley Forge, Pennsylvania "Courtesy of the American Baptist Historical Society, American Baptist-Samuel Colgate Historical Library," with special thanks to Executive Director Deborah Van Broekhoven; for the photo of Harry F. Ward, grateful acknowledgment is made to his granddaughter, with special thanks to Ruth Tonkiss Cameron, Archivist, Union Theological Seminary Records, The Burke Library Archives, and Director of Publications and Media Relations Joann Anand, Union Theological Seminary, New York, New York, with credit to photographer Luke Nelson; for the cover photo of Reverdy C. Ransom, grateful acknowledgment is made to The Wilberforce University Archives, Wilberforce, Ohio, with special thanks to Associate Librarian Jacqueline Brown, and to Anthony B. Pinn, editor of *Making the Gospel Plain: The Writings of Bishop Reverdy C. Ransom* (Trinity Press International, 1999); for the inside photo of Reverdy C. Ransom, grateful acknowledgment is made to the African Methodist Episcopal Church Sunday School Union, Nashville, Tennessee, with special thanks to Andre' Wright, Administrative Assistant; for the photo of Jane Addams, grateful acknowledgment is made to Swarthmore College Peace Collection, Swarthmore, Pennsylvania, with special thanks to Technical Services Specialist Mary Beth Sigado and Curator Wendy Chmielewski; for the photo of John A. Ryan, grateful acknowledgment is made to "Monsignor John A. Ryan, ca. 1935, photograph from The American Catholic History Research Center and University Archives, The Catholic University of America, Washington, D.C.," with special thanks to Audiovisual Archivist Robin C. Pike and Administrative Assistant Jane Stoeffler; for the cover photo of Reinhold Niebuhr and the photos of Beverly W. Harrison and Larry Rasmussen, grateful acknowledgment is made to Union Communications Office, Union Theological Seminary, New York, New York, with special thanks to Joann Anand, Director of Publications and Media Relations; for the inside photo of Reinhold Niebuhr, grateful acknowledgment is made to Union Theological Seminary Records, The Burke Library Archives, with special thanks to Archivist Ruth Tonkiss Cameron, Associate Director of Development for Online Communications James J. Kempster and Director of Publications and Media Relations Joann Anand, Union Theological Seminary, New York, New York, with credit to Pan American World Airways Atlantic Division, LaGuardia Field; for the photo of H. Richard Niebuhr, grateful acknowledgment is made to Manuscripts and Archives, Yale University, New Haven, Connecticut, with special thanks to Public Services Manager Cynthia Ostroff, Library Services Assistant Stephen Ross and Technical Service Assistant Dika Goloweiko-Nussberg; for the photo of John C. Bennett, grateful acknowledgment is made to Union Theological Seminary Records, The Burke Library Archives, with special thanks to Archivist Ruth Tonkiss Cameron and Director of Publications and Media Relations Joann Anand, Union Theological Seminary, New York, New York, with credit to the photographic firm Blackstone-Shelburne, New York, New York; for the photo of Paul Ramsey, grateful acknowledgment is made to Princeton University Archives, Department of Rare Books and Special Collections, Princeton University Library, Princeton, New Jersey, with special thanks to Ben Primer, Associate University Librarian for Rare Books and Special Collections, to Jennifer M. Cole, Public Policy Papers Project

Archivist, and Christine W. Kitto, Seeley G. Mudd Manuscript Library, Princeton, New Jersey; for the photos of Walter G. Muelder and Martin Luther King Jr., grateful acknowledgment is made to Boston University Photo Services, with special thanks to Director Frederick Sway; for the photo of James Luther Adams, grateful acknowledgment is made to Harvard News Office, Harvard University, Cambridge, Massachusetts, with special thanks to Harvard Divinity School Office of Communications Staff Assistants Elizabeth Busky and Chris Bower; for the photo of John Courtney Murray, grateful acknowledgment is made to Catholic News Service, Washington, D.C., with credit to CNS Photographer Paul Haring; for the photo of Dorothy Day, grateful acknowledgment is made to "Photo by Fritz Kaeser, © University of Notre Dame," with special thanks to Steve Moriarty, The Fritz and Milly Kaeser Curator of Photography, The Snite Museum of Art, and Archivist William Kevin Cawley, University of Notre Dame, Notre Dame, Indiana, and Phillip M. Runkel, Archivist, Raynor Memorial Libraries, Marquette University, Milwaukee, Wisconsin with credit to "Milwaukee Journal photo, courtesy of the Marquette University Archives"; for the photo of James H. Cone, grateful acknowledgment is made to James H. Cone, with special thanks to Union Theological Seminary, New York, New York, and to Special Assistant to James H. Cone, Victoria Furio, with credit to photographer Charlotte Raymond; for the photo of Mary Daly, grateful acknowledgment is made to EnlightenNext, Inc. (Reprinted with permission from *What is Enlightenment?* magazine, Fall/Winter 1999, copyright 1999 EnlightenNext, Inc., all rights reserved, http://www.wie.org), with special thanks to Administrative Assistant Judy Fox; for the photo of Carl F. H. Henry, grateful acknowledgment is made to Christianity Today, International (photo credits, Christianity Today, International), with special thanks to Editorial Administrative Assistant Ashley Gieschen and Design Director Gary Gnidovic and with special thanks to Carol Henry Bates, William Bates, Senior Vice President for Institutional Advancement Paul J. Maurer, and University Librarian Rob Krapohl, Trinity International University, Deerfield, Illinois; for the photo of John Howard Yoder, grateful acknowledgment is made to the Mennonite Publishing House, Paul Schrock Photograph Collection, Mennonite Church USA Archives, Goshen, Indiana, with special thanks to Dennis Stoesz, Archivist, Goshen Office; for the photo of Stanley Hauerwas, grateful acknowledgment is made to Stanley Hauerwas, with credit to Duke University Photography, Duke University, Durham, North Carolina, and with special thanks to Duke Divinity School Research Associate Carole Baker and Associate Dean for Communications Jonathan Goldstein; for the photo of Michael Novak, grateful acknowledgment is made to Michael Novak, with special thanks to his Research Assistant, Ashley Morrow, American Enterprise Institute, Washington, D.C.; for the photo of Jim Wallis, grateful acknowledgment is made to Jim Wallis, with special thanks to Jason Gedeik, Press Secretary, *Sojourners* Magazine, Washington, D.C.; for the photo of Charles Curran, grateful acknowledgment is made to Charles Curran, with special thanks to Southern Methodist University/Perkins School of Theology, Dallas, Texas; for the photo of James M. Gustafson, grateful acknowledgment is made to the Office of Public Affairs, Yale University, New Haven, Connecticut (Photographs of Yale affiliated individuals maintained by the Office of Public Affairs, Yale University, 1879-1989 [RU 686], Manuscripts & Archives, Yale University Library), with special thanks to Chief Research Archivist Judith Ann Schiff, Associate University Librarian Ann Okerson and Public Services Archivist William Massa; for the photo of Gibson Winter, grateful acknowledgment is made to Special Collections, Princeton Theological Seminary, Princeton, New Jersey, with special thanks to Kenneth Woodrow Henke, Research Archivist; for the photo of Cornell West, grateful acknowledgment is made to Cornel West, with credit to photographer Brain Velenchencko, and with special thanks to Mary Ann Rodriguez, Assistant, Department of Religion, Princeton University, Princeton, New Jersey; for the photo of Katie G. Cannon, grateful acknowledgment is made to Katie G. Cannon, with special thanks to Union Theological Seminary & Presbyterian School of Christian Education, Richmond, Virginia; for the photo of Victor Anderson, grateful acknowledgment is made to Victor Anderson, with special thanks to Vanderbilt University, Nashville, Tennessee; for the photo of Max Stackhouse, grateful acknowledgment is made to Max Stackhouse, with special thanks to Princeton Theological Seminary, Princeton, New Jersey; for the photo of Dennis P. McCann, grateful acknowledgment is made to Dennis P. McCann; for the photo of Lisa Sowle Cahill, grateful acknowledgment is made to Lisa Sowle Cahill, with special thanks to Boston College, Boston, Massachusetts; for the photo of Marvin M. Ellison, grateful acknowledgment is made to Marvin M. Ellison, with special thanks to Bangor Theological Seminary, Portland, Maine; for the photo of John B. Cobb, Jr., grateful acknowledgment is made to the Center for Process Studies, Claremont School of Theology, Claremont, California, with special thanks to Communications Director J. R. Hustwit and Program Director John Quiring; for the photo of Daniel C. Maguire, grateful acknowledgment is made to Daniel C. Maguire, with special thanks to Marquette University, Milwaukee, Wisconsin; for the photo of Sharon Welch, grateful acknowledgment is made to Sharon Welch, with thanks to Meadville Lombard Theological School, Chicago, Illinois; for the photo of Emilie M. Townes, grateful acknowledgment is made to Emilie M. Townes, with special thanks to Yale Divinity School, New Haven, Connecticut; for the photo of Ada María Isasi-Díaz, grateful acknowledgment is made to Ada María Isasi-Díaz, with special thanks to Drew University Theological School, Madison, New Jersey; for the photo of María Pilar Aquino, grateful acknowledgment is made to María Pilar Aquino, with special thanks to the Office of Public Relations, the University of San Diego, San Diego, California; for the photo of David Hollenbach, grateful acknowledgment is made to David Hollenbach; for the back cover photo of Gary Dorrien, grateful acknowledgment is made to Union Theological Seminary, New York, New York, with special thanks to Director of Publications and Media Relations Joann Anand, with credit to photographer Lynn Saville.

The photo of William Jewett Tucker, which is taken from *My Generation* (Houghton Mifflin Company, 1919) by William Jewett Tucker, is in the Public Domain. The photo of Josiah Strong, which is taken from *The New Home Missions* (NY: Missionary Education Movement of the US and Canada, 1914) by Harlan Paul Douglas, is in the Public Domain; special thanks is given to Ralph E. Luker, author of *The Social Gospel in Black and White: American Racial Reform, 1885–1912* (The University of North Carolina Press, 1991).

This book is a byproduct of my work at Union Theological Seminary and Columbia University as a teacher to graduate students and, especially, a mentor to doctoral students. Shortly after I moved to New York in 2005 and began working with doctoral students in social ethics, it occurred to me that we lacked a history of the field they were entering. Every field should have an account of its origins, development, key figures, methodological options, and theoretical varieties, I thought. Meeting with one of my doctoral advisees, Christine Pae, I mused that perhaps my next project would be a history of social ethics; Christine replied, "Could you hurry up and write it? I'll be doing my comprehensive exams next year."

That suggested an impossibly ambitious timeline, but I soon plunged into the research for this book, and taught a course titled "Social Ethics as a Discipline" that mapped out the book's narrative structure. I am deeply grateful to all of the master's and doctoral degree students in that course for enriching my perspective on this subject. Above all, I am grateful to my current group of doctoral students – Lisa Anderson, Malinda Berry, Chloe Breyer, Ian Doescher, Babydoll Kennedy, Jeremy Kirk, Eboni Marshall, David Orr, Christine Pae, Gabriel Salguero, Charlene Sinclair, Joe Strife, Rima Veseley-Flad, and Demian Wheeler. The privilege of working with these gifted, fascinating, and promising scholars has been the most rewarding experience of my academic career.

Three faculty colleagues at Union Theological Seminary befriended me immediately upon my arrival in New York and helped me feel that I had found a new home. This book is dedicated to one of them, James Cone. The second was Christopher Morse, an accomplished theologian and extraordinary teacher whose greatest distinction is his genial gift for friendship. The third friend, Joe Hough, is retiring from the presidency of Union Seminary as this book goes to press. Union Theological Seminary in its long and noted history has never had a better president than Joe Hough, nor a more remarkable human being. All of us in the Union community wish him fond farewell and will miss him desperately.

I am grateful to numerous expert readers who reviewed the manuscript either in whole or in part, including John B. Cobb, Jr., James Cone, Charles Curran, Christopher Evans, Ada María Isasi-Díaz, Stanley Hauerwas, Charles Henderson, Jennifer Jesse, Daniel Maguire, Larry Rasmussen, Emilie M. Townes, and Sarah Winter. Many thanks to my editors at Blackwell for their friendly and skillful work, especially copy-editor Felicity Marsh, project manager Louise Spencely, and publisher Rebecca Harkin. Thanks to Diana Witt for another stellar index. As usual I end with a word of thanks to my incomparable friend Becca Kutz-Marks, now of Austin, Texas, whose gift of friendship is a constant grace in my life, and who marshaled the gallery of photographs in this book with her usual care and exuberance.

Introduction

In the early 1880s, proponents of what came to be called "the social gospel" founded what came to be called "social ethics." This book is a history of the tradition of social ethics of the USA, a tradition that began with the distinctly modern idea that Christianity has a social-ethical mission to transform the structures of society in the direction of social justice.

The simultaneous rise of the social gospel and social ethics was not coincidental, nor the fact that sociology, "social justice," social Darwinism, corporate capitalism, modern socialism, and the trade unions arose at the same time. For social ethics was essentially a departmental subset of the social gospel. The social gospel was novel for its idea of social salvation. Social salvation was based on the sociological idea of social structure. The term "social justice" gained currency in the literature of rising Socialist and union movements. And the social gospelers had to figure out how to affirm Darwinism as science while rejecting an ascending social Darwinism. By the 1890s the favored shorthand for all of this was "the social problem," to which social ethics brought the resources of a socially awakened Christianity.

This book describes the founding and development of social ethics as a discourse in the realms of the academy, church, and general public. It explains and analyzes the three major traditions of social ethics, offshoots of these traditions, evangelical and neoconservative alternatives, and various confessional and cultural standpoints from which religious thinkers have construed the social meaning of Christianity, all in a narrative fashion.

Nearly from the beginning, "social ethics" named a specific academic field and a way of thinking about Christian ethics that transcended the academy. This book pays attention to both meanings, featuring prominent academic voices *and* important exponents of social Christianity who had little or no relation to the social ethics guild. In the latter category, pastors and movement activists are prominent; on the other hand, after the book enters the postmodern era, the academics prevail almost without exception. In contemporary social ethics, even self-described "public intellectuals" and "public theologians" are academics.

Social Ethics in the Making emphasizes the role of the liberal-Progressive social gospel in giving birth to social ethics and establishing its disciplinary character. It describes the founders of social ethics whom history forgot, the liberal Protestant social gospelers whom history remembered, and the founders of African-American and Roman Catholic traditions of social Christianity. It devotes more attention to

Reinhold Niebuhr than to any other figure, analyzing his influential blend of realist politics and neo-Augustinian theology, while making room for H. Richard Niebuhr's ethic of the responsible self. It treats liberation theology as a third major tradition alongside the social gospel and Christian realism, interpreting liberationism fundamentally as an eruption of repressed and excluded voices. It examines various offshoots and hybrid blends of these traditions and gives extensive attention to evangelical and neoconservative alternatives. It emphasizes contemporary discussions of race, gender, sexuality, ecology, and cultural difference, and analyzes fundamental debates over the coherence and relevance of the social-ethical tradition.

Some of the latter debates have carried on for over a century. Is social Christianity a naturalistic and/or sociopolitical replacement for traditional Christian supernaturalism? Has social ethics addressed the appropriate topics? Was it fatally flawed from the beginning through its connection to social gospel Progressivism? How political or realistic can social ethics be without losing its basis in Christianity? Does social ethics need a specific social scientific method to be a field, or is it better off being the place in a theological curriculum where one directly takes up current social problems?

The founders of social ethics, notably Francis Greenwood Peabody, had no doubt that this new field needed a scientific method. Social ethics was established to expound the ethical dimension of a rising, ostensibly unified field of social science. Beginning as a successor to required courses in moral philosophy, it approached ethics inductively as the study of social movements addressing social problems. Social ethicists used social scientific methods to observe, generalize, and correlate their way to an account of the whole, including its ethical character. By attaching themselves to social science, the social-ethical founders won a place for their enterprise in theological education, and aspired to one in social science.

But the social sciences took the path of specialization and secularization, leaving social ethics to theology. Afterwards, the view that social ethics had to have a blood relationship to science became a minority one, while the field's greatest figures paid little attention to disciplinary concerns. What mattered to the great advocates of social Christianity was to change the world, not the university. The three towering figures in American Christian social ethics are Walter Rauschenbusch, the prophet of the social gospel; Reinhold Niebuhr, the theorist of Christian realism; and Martin Luther King, Jr, the leader of modern America's greatest liberation movement. But Rauschenbusch and King did not teach social ethics, and Niebuhr took little interest in disciplinary or methodological issues.

Niebuhr did not worry about the disciplinary standing of his field, nor did he share Peabody's fixation with social scientific validation. He ended up in social ethics because that was the place where liberal seminaries took up current social problems. That was what he cared about: the struggle for justice and a decent world order. To the extent that Niebuhr had a method, it was a dispositional one of determining the meaning of justice in the interaction of Christian love and concrete situation. For Niebuhr, justice was a contextual application of the law of love to the sociopolitical sphere, mediated by the principles of freedom, equality, and order.

A great deal of social ethics has been Niebuhrian in the sense of being essentially political, activist, and pragmatic. That did not start with Niebuhr, because in this respect he simply assumed the activist orientation of the social gospel movement that preceded him. Rauschenbusch had no field or doctorate; he taught in the German Department at Colgate Rochester Seminary and ended up, by accident, in church history. Niebuhr had no field or doctorate either, except for the social-ethical space that he inherited from the social gospel. Thus the major social ethicists have not been the ones that worried about the social scientific or methodological standing of their field.

But social ethics has not lacked method-minded caretakers of the discipline that Peabody, William Jewett Tucker, and Graham Taylor founded. In the second generation of the social gospel, Harry F. Ward and John A. Ryan were notable practitioners of a distinct method. Ward used a stripped down variant of Peabody's method, while Ryan fashioned a Roman Catholic version of the social gospel that blended policy arguments with Thomist philosophy. In the next generation field consciousness heightened, notably in the work of John C. Bennett, Walter G. Muelder, and James Luther Adams. Bennett developed the theory of "middle axioms" that Niebuhr partly adopted; Muelder developed a "synoptic" method that fit his personalist theory of the social mind as the total content of objective spirit; Adams developed an influential curriculum model at the University of Chicago Divinity School. At Chicago, a school with a tradition of naturalistic empiricism, students were trained to search for moral norms within the variegated life of society, integrating social scientific research with ethical reasoning. In recent social ethics, Gibson Winter and James Gustafson have been the leading advocates of binding ethics to social science. This book examines these figures and perspectives, in addition to social ethics as liberationist, womanist, *mujerista,* and feminist praxis, and to social ethics as communitarian narrative, biblical application, confessional discipline, ecumenical consensus, and postmodern carnival.

It would be enough to write a strictly disciplinary history of American social ethics. It would be enough, and more interesting, to write a book on social-ethical thinkers who made a public impact. A third possibility would focus on the social ethics of the Christian denominations and ecumenical movement. This book combines the first and second projects while telling an ample slice of the third story through its interpretation of ecumenical theologians such as Ward, Bennett, Muelder, both Niebuhrs, John Courtney Murray, John Howard Yoder, Max Stackhouse, and Larry Rasmussen. By giving equal weight to the disciplinary and public stories, I show that social ethics at its best has been a public discourse of the academy and church.

In addition to the field's usual cast of luminaries, this book tells the unknown story of the founders of social ethics, restores Harry Ward to his rightful place in social Christian history, and gives featured attention to streams of the social gospel that were not white-male-Protestant. Reverdy Ransom was a major black social gospeler of his time and a forerunner of the civil rights movement. A theological liberal, he was also a Socialist, a black nationalist, and in his later career, a bishop in the African Methodist Episcopal Church. He was a liberationist and Afrocentrist before these terms had currency. His rhetorical eloquence, for which he was renowned in his time, was stunning. Afterwards he was almost completely forgotten; the present work makes an argument for remembrance. Jane Addams, by contrast, was famous in her time and became more so afterwards, but she is rarely counted as a Christian social ethicist, a convention I argue against.

The Catholic figures discussed in the first half of this book had different kinds of careers from their Protestant counterparts. Catholic officials and intellectuals took a cautious attitude toward America's predominantly Protestant society, and they had to cope with the papal condemnations of modernism. Catholic institutions were also slow to recognize social ethics as a discipline. While all of that changed after Vatican II another significant difference remained: for most liberal Protestants, denominational identity was not very important, but for Catholics, the church and its tradition were centrally important. All three of the pre-Vatican II Catholics featured in this book – John A. Ryan, John Courtney Murray, and Dorothy Day – were theologically conservative, but each of them took edgy social-ethical positions that risked ecclesiastical censure. Ryan vigorously supported the New Deal, Murray defended religious freedom, and Day was a pacifist movement leader. Murray's stance led to ecclesiastical censure; at Vatican II he was vindicated.

After Vatican II, Catholic social-ethical thought was very much like liberal Protestant ethics in its diversity of perspectives and engagement with liberation theology. Mary Daly began her career as a Catholic theologian before opting for radical feminism. Michael Novak took a brief turn as a Catholic New Leftist before opting for Catholic neoconservatism. Charles Curran's influential arguments against Catholic teaching on sexual ethics led to his censure by the Vatican. David Hollenbach formulated a prominent Catholic position on human rights, defending economic rights in opposition to Novak. Dennis P. McCann was closer to Novak, criticizing typical social-ethical progressivism on political economics. Lisa Sowle Cahill espoused a liberal feminist perspective on sexual ethics. Daniel C. Maguire proposed an ethical "common creed" with a strongly liberationist bent. Ada María Isasi-Díaz and María Pilar Aquino advocated *mujerista* and Latina feminist perspectives, respectively, that reflected the influence of Latin American liberation theology. All of these perspectives were forged in dialogue with or as types of liberation theology, though negatively in Novak's case.

The influence of liberation theology as a third major tradition of social ethics shows through in most of the book's second half. Chapter 6 discusses liberationist founders Martin Luther King, Jr, James H. Cone, Mary Daly, and Beverly W. Harrison, describing Cone's founding of black liberation theology, Daly's origination of radical feminist theology, and Harrison's leading role in establishing feminist social ethics and queer theory.

Chapter 7 deals with evangelical and neoconservative perspectives, featuring Carl F. H. Henry, John Howard Yoder, Stanley Hauerwas, Michael Novak, and Jim Wallis. Henry, the major theologian of conservative evangelicalism, achieved godfather status in the Christian Right movement. Yoder championed the pacifism and Anabaptist evangelicalism of the radical Reformation. Hauerwas found a sizable audience as an evangelical Methodist proponent of a Yoder-style communal ethic. Novak's "theology of the corporation" wedded corporate capitalist apologetics to conservative Catholic ethics. Wallis achieved public prominence as the spokesperson for a neglected alternative, progressive evangelicalism. Yoder, Hauerwas and Wallis had little in common with the Christian Right and even less with neoconservatives, but all the thinkers featured in Chapter 7 had fundamental objections to the social-ethical tradition. For them, social ethics had begun badly by baptizing liberal modernism; afterward it made faulty course corrections; repeatedly, it was about the wrong things.

Chapters 8 and 9 describe the legacies of liberation theology and the concerns of late twentieth and early twenty-first century social ethicists to make sense of postmodernity, cultural difference, sexuality, and ecology. Except for James Gustafson, all the thinkers featured in Chapter 8 either adopted or interrogated key aspects of liberationist criticism, as did every ethicist featured in Chapter 9.

Chapter 8 mixes disciplinary, ecclesiological, and public concerns, analyzing Charles Curran's moderate liberalism, Gibson Winter's argument for social ethics as social scientific praxis, James Gustafson's theocentric ethics, Cornel West's publicly prominent social criticism, Katie G. Cannon's exposition of womanist ethics, and Victor Anderson's postmodern cultural criticism. With a focus on work contemporary with the writing of the book, Chapter 9 describes the state of the field in the early 2000s with reference to economy, sexuality, ecology, and difference, featuring Max Stackhouse and Dennis McCann on political economy; Stackhouse, Lisa Sowle Cahill, and Marvin M. Ellison on sexual ethics; John B. Cobb, Jr. and Larry Rasmussen on ecological ethics; Daniel Maguire's proposal for a common Christian ethical creed; Sharon Welch's feminist ethic of risk and solidarity; Emilie M. Townes's elaboration of womanist ethics; the Latina feminist perspectives of Ada María Isasi-Díaz and María Pilar Aquino; and David Hollenbach's defense of human rights. My concluding chapter makes an argument for the relevance of the social gospel vision of economic democracy, the limits and value of progressive realism, and the importance of liberationist and ecological criticism.

Even a large book devoted solely to contemporary social ethics would face very difficult problems of selection and emphasis. This book, dealing with the current scene only in its later chapters, can address only a fraction of the field's current debates. The book as a whole gives highest priority to racial justice, economic justice, war, and representing the field's diversity of perspectives, traditions, and theorists. The priority given to the ethics of war and violence drops back somewhat in the last two chapters to make room for ecological ethics and debates about gay and lesbian sexuality. Arguments about militarism and war are as important today as ever before; a substantial portion of my own work is devoted to this subject. But most of the arguments in this area are not new; ours is the generation to feature the ethics of difference.

This book makes a pitch, however, for the enduring relevance of the most "discredited" social gospel idea of all, economic democracy. Ernst Troeltsch, in his classic history of Christian social thought *The Social Teaching of the Christian Churches* (1912), observed that up to the late nineteenth century, Christianity had developed only two major social philosophies: medieval Catholicism and Calvinist Protestantism. The modern social gospel – specifically, Christian socialism – was significant for having developed the third one, he argued. Its goal was to make Christianity relevant to a nationalistic, capitalist, technological, and increasingly secular order, an ambitious project that Aquinas and Calvin could not have imagined. Troeltsch cautioned that the social problem was "vast and complicated," and that modern defenders of the traditional models offered little help in alleviating "all this distress which weighs on our hearts and minds like a perpetual menace." To move forward, Christianity had to build on the achievements of the Christian Socialists, who regained for the church the "Utopian and revolutionary character" of Christianity in modern form.[1]

A century later that is still what Christianity needs to do.

Note

1 Ernst Troeltsch, *The Social Teaching of the Christian Churches*, 2 vols., trans. Olive Wyon (1st edn.: 1912; Louisville: Westminster John Knox Press, 1992), 2: quotes, 1011, 728.

Chapter 1

Inventing Social Ethics

Francis Greenwood Peabody, William Jewett Tucker,
and Graham Taylor

The social gospelers who founded social ethics were not the ones whom history remembered. The social gospelers history remembered were bracing personalities with a missionary spirit who reached the general public: Washington Gladden, Richard Ely, Josiah Strong, George Herron, and Walter Rauschenbusch. Another renowned social gospeler, Shailer Mathews, was a half-exception by virtue of playing several roles simultaneously, but he operated primarily in the public square. All the renowned social gospelers came to be renowned by preaching the social gospel as a form of public homiletics.

The founders of social ethics also spoke to the general public, but as social ethicists they were absorbed by a cause that belonged to the academy: making a home for Christian ethics as a self-standing discipline of ethically grounded social science. They urged that society is a whole that includes an ethical dimension; thus, there needed to be something like social ethics. This discipline would be a central feature of liberal arts and seminary education. It would succeed the old moral philosophy, replacing an outmoded Scottish commonsense realism with a socially oriented idealism.

Intellectually the founders of social ethics belonged to the American generation that reconciled Christianity to Darwinism, accepted the historical critical approach to the Bible, and discovered the power of social ideas. As first generation social gospelers they believed that modern scholarship had rediscovered the social meaning of Christianity in the kingdom-centered faith of the historical Jesus. As early advocates of sociology, they also believed in the disciplinary unity of social science and its ethical character.

Francis Greenwood Peabody, a longtime professor at Harvard University, was the first to teach social ethics as an academic discipline, in 1880. William Jewett Tucker, an Andover Seminary professor who later achieved distinction as president of Dartmouth College, taught courses in the 1880s on "social economics." Graham Taylor, an indefatigable social activist and colleague of Jane Addams, chaired the first department of Christian Sociology, at Chicago Theological Seminary (CTS). These pioneers of social-ethical analysis were publicly prominent in their time, and did not belong wholly to the academy. But because they fought primarily in the academy, with limited success, they were not remembered as major social gospelers.

Peabody, Tucker, and Taylor proposed to study social conditions with a Christian ethical view toward what might be done about them. They shared Ely's concern that the emerging discipline of sociology needed to be informed by the ethical conscience of progressive religion. They updated the liberal third way between authoritarian orthodoxy and secular disbelief. They resisted an ascending social Darwinism in the social sciences and an ascending radicalism in the Socialist and labor movements. They were advocates of liberal reform, good government, cooperation, the common good, and the social gospel Jesus. Believing that social science had a great future in the academy and modern society, they did not want it to be lost to Christianity, or Christianity to it. Earnestly they sought to show that Christianity was descriptively and normatively relevant to modern society.

The founders of social ethics, to their regret, lived to witness the fragmentation of social science, the academic denial of its ethical character, and the marginalization of their intellectual enterprise. Having started something new, they lost the battle for social ethics as a university discipline, but won a place for it in theological education, establishing a theological discipline that outlived much of its social gospel basis. Social ethics survived, albeit on the fringe of the academy, because it was rooted in the nineteenth-century discovery that there is such a thing as social structure and that redemption always has a social dimension.

Becoming Francis Greenwood Peabody

Most of the early social gospelers came from evangelical backgrounds, but the first social ethicist, Francis Greenwood Peabody, was born into liberal Christianity as the son of a prominent Unitarian pastor, Ephraim Peabody, and a privileged Unitarian mother, Mary Ellen Derby. Ephraim Peabody spent his early pastoral career as a Unitarian missionary to the western United States (Cincinnati) and his later career as minister of King's Chapel in Boston. Highly regarded as a spiritual leader, he preached often on character development and personality, and was known for his dedication to the poor, organizing poor-relief projects. In 1856, when his son Francis was 9 years old, Ephraim Peabody died of tuberculosis; Francis later recalled that he was "nearly seven" at the time. Elsewhere he recalled, with stronger reliability, that his parents had contrasting but complementary personalities. His father was imbued with a radiant holiness and unworldly simplicity that made him a beloved pastor, while his mother, the granddaughter of America's first millionaire (Salem merchant Elias Haskett Derby), was a cultivated, worldly, impressive woman of confident charm. Peabody viewed his parents' happy marriage as a symbol of the two traditions of New England coming together: "the idealism of the hills and the commercialism of the cities."[1]

As a widow, Mary Ellen Peabody resolved to raise her four children in the spiritual seriousness of their departed father. "All was for his sake; each decision of school or play was as he would have desired," Peabody later recalled. The ebullient, "luxury-loving" mother became a disciplinarian, dispensing religion with a more rigorous hand than Peabody recalled as being in the nature of his father's gentle spirit. For many years the family did not celebrate Thanksgiving because Ephraim Peabody had died on Thanksgiving. Thrown into economic hardship by his death, the family continued to live in Boston's wealthy Beacon Hill, where, Peabody claimed, he felt no envy of privileged neighbors. Gradually he forgot his father's appearance and maxims, but another kind of paternal memory was instilled in him, one that stayed in his psyche and worldview.[2]

Peabody wrote affectionate recollections of his parents for the rest of his life, in addition to character portraits of the many friends and relatives who made up New England's close-knit circle of Unitarian leaders. His father's former congregation paid for his education, which Peabody took at Harvard College and Harvard Divinity School, graduating respectively in 1869 and 1872. In his telling, his schooling was unremittingly desultory. As a youth it had seemed to him that Harvard professors were remarkably insular and uninteresting. Huddled in a small, secluded world of texts and each other's company, they seemed to prize their detachment from the real world of politics, commerce, and Boston as though it were a virtue. Sadly, they did not improve after Peabody enrolled at the college. He allowed that Harvard professors were distinguished intellectually, dwelling high above others, where "the air was pure"; philosopher Francis Bowen, an able proponent of Scottish commonsense moralism, taught there, as did botanist Asa Gray, mathematician Benjamin Peirce, and rhetoric scholar Francis J. Child, all respected scholars with much to offer. But in Peabody's experience of them, Harvard professors took little interest in anything besides themselves and their subjects. They bored their students with deadly recitations and barely acknowledged that a school must have students. Peabody compared them to a monastic order.[3]

The Divinity School proved to be equally depressing. Peabody called his three years of divinity training "a disheartening experience of uninspiring study and retarded thought." In theory Harvard Divinity School was nondenominational, not Unitarian, but in reality, a fuddy-duddy brand of Unitarian orthodoxy prevailed. Formally the school contended that it sought the truth, rather than declaring it, in matters of divinity; in reality it remained so deeply attached to the embattled Unitarian orthodoxy of the National Conference of Unitarian Churches that university officials periodically debated a divorce from the Divinity School. During Peabody's years there historical criticism was practiced sparingly, philosophical idealism was spurned, classroom lectures seemed purposely dull, and theology and ethics were taught, in his phrase, as "subjects of ecclesiastical erudition and doctrinal desiccation." Reaching for the strongest way of conveying a bad memory, Peabody declared: "The fresh breeze of modern thought rarely penetrated the lecture-rooms . . . I cannot remember attaining in seven years of Harvard classrooms anything that could be fairly described as an idea."[4]

That was slightly hyperbolic. Harvard Divinity School declined steeply from 1840 to 1880, averaging four faculty members and 20 students. It reached its nadir in the year 1868–9, when dean Oliver Stearns was its only full-time, able-bodied professor in residence. But the school was always liberal by virtue of being Unitarian; in the 1850s, despite being neglected by the university, it had three able teachers (Convers Francis, George Rapall Noyes, and Frederic Henry Hedge) and one bad one (George E. Ellis). Moreover, the Divinity School's upward turn began in 1869, just as Peabody arrived, when Harvard's new president, Charles William Eliot, declared that a revamped Divinity School had a vital role to play in creating a model research university at Harvard. Three new faculty appointments were made: Charles Carroll Everett, the first Bussey Professor of Theology, who became a distinguished dean at the Divinity School; Ezra Abbott, the first Bussey Professor of New Testament Criticism and Interpretation, who achieved scholarly distinction; and Edward James Young, Hancock Professor of Hebrew and Old Testament, who flopped as a scholar and teacher and was forced to resign in 1880, ostensibly to make room for a non-Unitarian.[5]

These teachers schooled Peabody in German names, labels, and oracles. Despite his complaints that he heard no modern thoughts, Peabody also complained that his teachers idolized German scholars, settling disputed points with a word from a German authority. This species of reverence drove him straight to Germany. He later explained, "It seemed essential to peace of mind that one should determine whether the gods of German theology were infallible, or whether they might sometimes nod." Peabody owed his German education to his Harvard teachers, and his subsequent career would not have been possible without the changes that occurred at Harvard during his student days.[6]

In Germany he journeyed first to Heidelberg, which he didn't like for its arid rationalism, then to Leipzig, which was worse for its backward-looking orthodoxy. He found a brief reward in Halle, where, like many American students before him, notably Charles Briggs and Egbert Smyth, he luxuriated in the lectures and friendship of Friedrich August Tholuck. A legendary pietist scholar and theologian, equally renowned for his kindly manner, Tholuck welcomed Americans into his classroom and home. As a theologian he stressed religious experience in the fashion of Friedrich Schleiermacher while avoiding the radical aspects of Schleiermacher's thought. Tholuck taught that evangelical faith and historical criticism were natural allies because good scholarship construed biblical meaning within the circle of faith: "It must be remembered that the scientific apprehension of religious doctrines presupposes a religious experience. Without this moral qualification, it is impossible to obtain a true insight into theological dogmas."[7]

Peabody heard Tholuck lecture on historical and modern theology, and Tholuck offered to meet with him privately to study Schleiermacher's *Discourses on Religion*. But upon descending the stairway in his home to greet Peabody for their first session, Tholuck either stumbled or had a seizure, falling down the stairs. His health deteriorated rapidly afterwards. Though Tholuck lectured for seven more years until his death in 1877, Peabody and his wife Cora Weld were the last Americans to experience the Tholuck effect. For Peabody, Tholuck was the ideal: a rigorous scholar with a devout Christian spirit. Years later Peabody put it stronger, recalling that Tholuck showed him "that the career of a scholar might be consistent with the character of a saint." In Tholuck's classroom Peabody began his long association with German thought and his career as an American interpreter of German theology.[8]

His first idea came to him in a German bookshop in 1872. Perusing Otto Pfleiderer's book *Die Religion, ihr Wesen und ihre Geschichte* (1869) (*Religion, Its Nature and Its History*) it occurred to Peabody that he might spend his life doing the sort of thing that Pfleiderer did: validating a religious philosophy by its history. Instead of beginning with an a priori doctrine or tradition, one might derive a religious outlook from an inductive study of human nature and ethical activity. Peabody reasoned that if he studied religion inductively, through its historical development, he should be able to defend it in a way that rescued religion from provincialism.[9]

That was the seed of social ethics — at least, in his case. Peabody expected to write about such things as a pastor. After a brief stint as a chaplain at Antioch College in Ohio he came home to Boston as minister of the First Parish (Unitarian) in Cambridge. Peabody gave six years to parish ministry, although in practice, as he admitted, it was more like three. He aspired to a long career at Cambridge's flagship Unitarian parish, but was ill most of the time. Nineteenth-century New Englanders believed that long, arduous trips to California and Europe were the best remedy for chronic illnesses, so Peabody took two of them. His father had died of tuberculosis at the age of 49; many of Peabody's devoted parishioners feared that he was destined to a similar fate. In 1880, after returning from a second prolonged absence still in poor health, he resigned himself to a lower, less important, less taxing vocation: lecturer at Harvard Divinity School. To Peabody, giving up the ministry for the work of a seminary instructor seemed "a calamity." He consoled himself that perhaps he could teach seminarians "the lessons of my own defeat." Instead he found an unexpected calling at the take-off of the social gospel, the American liberal theology movement, and Harvard's drive to become a modern research university.[10]

Philosophies of Moral Philosophy

The social gospel happened for a confluence of reasons that impacted on each other. It was fed by the wellsprings of eighteenth-century Enlightenment humanitarianism and the postmillennialist passion for social redemption that fueled the evangelical anti-slavery movements. It took root as a response to the corruption and oppressive conditions of the Gilded Age, goaded by writers such as Edward Bellamy, Stephen Colwell, Richard Ely, and Henry Demarest Lloyd. It took inspiration from the existence of a Christian Socialist movement in England, and rode on the back of a rising sociological consciousness and literature.[11]

Above all, the social gospel was a response to a burgeoning labor movement. Union leaders blasted the churches for doing nothing for poor and working-class people. Liberal Christian leaders realized it was pointless to defend Christianity if the churches were indefensible on this issue. Defending Christianity and improving its social conscience went together.

Thus the first attempts by seminaries to link Christian ethics with social problems usually folded the enterprise into apologetics. Christianity had to be defended against the new challenges to Christian belief. In 1851 the earliest forerunner of the social gospel, Stephen Colwell, admonished Protestant ministers not to deride the stirrings of the poor for social justice. A Philadelphia manufacturer and trustee of Princeton Theological Seminary, Colwell had a prescient social conscience. His book *New Themes for the Protestant Clergy* (1851) urged that it was natural and a good thing for the working class to revolt against a predatory economic system. Colwell wanted American Protestantism to be known for speaking to the working class "in tones of kindness and encouragement." Instead of defending "selfishness to its highest limits" in the economic order Protestant ministers should demand an economy consistent with the teachings of Jesus: "This idea of considering men as mere machines for the purpose of creating and distributing wealth, may do well to round off the periods, syllogisms, and statements of political economists; but the whole notion is totally and irreconcilably at variance with Christianity."[12]

Colwell was an advocate of sharing and community, not socialism, but he credited Socialists for championing social justice: "We look upon the whole socialist movement as one of the greatest events of this age." He shook his head at ministers who attacked socialism as an enemy of Christianity, imploring them to stop embarrassing Christianity with such nonsense. Besides making a show of their ignorance, he admonished, the clergy betrayed "a stubborn and wicked conservatism which is rooted to one spot in this world of evil."[13]

Colwell was a lonely voice in Protestant polite society of the 1850s and 1860s, but in 1871 he became the principal founder of a chair in Christian ethics at Princeton

Theological Seminary, the first of its kind in the United States. Eventually named the Stephen Colwell Chair of Christian Ethics, it was originally called the chair of Christian Ethics and Apologetics. The seminary announced that its purpose was to explore "Christian ethics, theoretically, historically, and in living connection with various branches of the social sciences." That was an early definition of social ethics, although the chair's first occupant, Charles A. Aiken, emphasized apologetics and philosophical ethics, not the social sciences. He took a brief and apologetic pass at labor, assured that Christianity gave labor a new dignity, and stressed the history of philosophical ethics. Aiken's model was the old moral philosophy, not social ethics.[14]

The founders of social ethics conceived their invention as the successor to a fading, venerable, still-important moral philosophy. Nearly every American college put moral philosophy at the center of its required curriculum, usually as a capstone course taught by a clergyman college president. In most colleges theology was esteemed and daily chapel was compulsory. The unifying center of the curriculum, however, was a vaguely religious course in moral philosophy consisting of four parts. The first part expounded the method of a favored philosophy; the second part offered an account of human nature and its drives; the third part developed a general ethical system; and the fourth part applied moral principles to institutional and social concerns. Moral philosophy was a remarkably uniform enterprise in American schools because one school of philosophy dominated American education: Scottish commonsense realism.[15]

Until the late seventeenth century, the right philosophy in Western higher education was Aristotelianism. Harvard, founded in 1636, was colonial America's only school of higher education in the seventeenth century. It taught the classical *trivium* of grammar, rhetoric, and logic and the *quadrivium* of arithmetic, music, geometry, and astronomy. Critics protested that a Puritan college should put Calvinist theology at the center of its curriculum, but Harvard conducted classes in Latin, featured Aristotle in physics and metaphysics, and stuck with the pagan texts and forms of the Great Tradition. In the manner of medieval universities, Harvard surrounded and supplemented its classical curriculum with Christian texts (especially Puritan theologian William Ames' *Medulla Theologica*), a few recent authors, and a strongly Christian environment. School officials stressed that Puritan thought was fully compatible with natural science, which was called "natural philosophy." Reformed theology taught that creation could be known through reason; thus, Harvard's Puritan heritage had nothing to fear from the scientific study of creation.[16]

By the end of the seventeenth century, however, a more modern idea of natural philosophy had pushed Aristotle aside. Aristotle taught that objects acquire impetus or gravity, and virtue is an acquired skill that one develops through practice. The former notion, to Christian interpreters, left the universe open to supernatural agency, while Aristotle's open-ended concept of the moral life was amenable to Christian appropriation. Modern science, to the contrary, epitomized in Isaac Newton's physics, taught that the universe is a closed system with universal physical laws. Newton (1642–1727) discovered the generalized binomial theorem, the law of gravitation, and the principle of the composition of light, and invented calculus (though he did not publish until after Leibniz, decades later). Newton's masterwork, *Philosophiae Naturalis Principia Mathematica* (1687), modeled on Euclidean geometry, demonstrated its propositions mathematically from definitions and mathematical axioms. He taught that the world consists of material bodies that interact according to three laws of motion concerning the uniformity of motion, change of motion, and mutuality of action. Newton described the ultimate conditions of his system – absolute time, space, place, and motion – as independent quantities constituting an absolute framework for measure. His belief in God rested chiefly on his admiration for the mathematical order of creation. The *Principia* was hailed immediately as a revolutionary leap forward in understanding, making Newton famous. In the late seventeenth century "the new natural philosophy," as it was called at Harvard, was Newton's picture of nature as a universal system of mathematical order.[17]

Harvard president Increase Mather, fighting off a liberal surge, commended Newtonian students in a commencement address for savoring "a liberal mode of philosophizing." Since Aristotle was wrong about creation, resurrection, and the immortality of the soul, Mather allowed, it was not a bad thing to put Aristotle in his place. But the ideal was the true liberal one of seeking the truth through the old and new ways: "You who are wont to philosophize in a liberal spirit, are pledged to no particular master, yet I would have you hold fast to that one truly golden saying of Aristotle: *Find a friend in Plato, a friend in Socrates* (and I would say a friend in Aristotle), *but above all find a friend in Truth.*" That diplomatic maneuvering was not enough to prevent Mather's factional rivals from replacing him as Harvard's president in 1701, the same year that Connecticut Congregational clergy founded Yale. Connecticut pastors charged that Harvard was obviously backsliding from Puritan orthodoxy. In 1711, Harvard president John Leverett confirmed that Harvard had moved away from Aristotle, if not orthodoxy: "In philosophical matters, Harvardians philosophize in a sane and liberal manner, according to the manner of the century." Natural philosophy was the system in which true explanations about natural things were provided, he explained: "Without any manner of doubt whatever, all humane matters must be tested by Philosophy. But the same license is not permissible to Theologians."[18]

At Harvard, Newtonian physics defined "the manner of the century" in natural philosophy, while the works of Newton's friend and Royal Society colleague John Locke (1632–1704) acquired canonical status in epistemology, political philosophy, moral philosophy, and method. In Book 1 of his *Essay concerning Human Understanding* (1689), Locke argued that the mind has no innate ideas. In Book 2 he argued that all ideas are products of sensory experience or reflection on experience. In Book 3 he discussed how language gets in the way of the attempt to lay hold of reality. In Book 4 he described the empirical method of analyzing and making judgments about evidence. Locke argued that the mind works on its ideas of sensation and reflection through the operations of combination, division, generalization, and abstraction. On ideas he was an empiricist, seeming to argue that ideas are mental objects, though he inspired rival schools of interpretation on this point. On knowledge he was a rationalist, arguing that knowledge is a product of reason working out the connections between ideas, not something produced directly by our senses. On substance he seemed to believe that things possess a substratum that support their properties, though interpretations varied here as well. On matters religious he was a Puritan Enlightenment defender of the reasonableness of Christianity and the divine commands of God. Locke distinguished between belief and knowledge, arguing that something can be rationally believed as true, but not rightly counted as knowledge, if it is established without direct observation or reasoned deduction. A bare authority claim is never an adequate basis for knowledge, but revelation has its place in theology if it does not contradict reason. God's existence is knowable because it is a condition of human existence, but matters of revelation can be rational beliefs at most, not knowledge.[19]

These ideas had a vast influence in Western philosophy; following Locke, philosophers conceived epistemology as theorizing about the elements, combinations, and associations of experience, or differently, how perceptions are filtered through the mind's innate capacities that arrange them into ideas. Immanuel Kant, Frances Hutcheson, and James Mill philosophized in the Lockean mode, as did George Berkeley, the next great British philosopher after Locke, who set his extreme idealism against the ostensibly skeptical and atheistic implications of Locke's thought. In the colonial and postcolonial United States Locke was revered as a defender of private property and theorist of the "nightwatchman state." It helped that he was a public intellectual, not a university professor, and that in his later life he was perhaps the most famous intellectual in Europe.

But despite the great respect that Locke commanded in the USA, his thought was not the basis of American moral philosophy. Harvard gave pride of place to Locke, but in the eighteenth and early nineteenth centuries many newly founded church-related colleges did not. Colonial and postcolonial American educators looked to Great Britain for guidance in philosophy, but Locke was too skeptical to inspire confidence, and it was a dismal period for Oxford and Cambridge. Locke's denial of innate ideas, his thin theory of the self, his rationalistic reserve, and his non-Trinitarianism were cited against him by nervous American religious leaders and educators, who got their philosophical bearings from the Scottish Enlightenment.

Unitarian leader William Ellery Channing was a notable example of a religious leader who embraced Scottish moralism after turning from Locke. In the 1790s, when Channing was a student at Harvard, Locke's *Essay concerning Human Understanding* was a pillar of the Harvard curriculum. But Channing was appalled by Locke's denial of innate ideas. If human beings had a spiritual nature, it could not be that all ideas were products of sensory experience or reflection on experience; Channing smelled the materialism in Locke's sensationalist epistemology. Hollis professor David Tappan advised Channing that Frances Hutcheson was worth reading, at least outside class. By then American colleges were already turning to the Scottish moralists for philosophical guidance, a trend begun and maintained by the College of Philadelphia since its founding in 1755. Hutcheson contended that the soul has an innate capacity for altruism, which supported Channing's faith that human beings possess an innate spiritual nature and moral sense. On that basis Scottish commonsense philosophy captured the field of American moral philosophy and much of the Unitarian movement before it finally overtook Harvard too.[20]

The Scottish Enlightenment philosophers who mattered to American educators were not the ones who grew famous, David Hume and Adam Smith. The really significant Scottish thinkers, to Americans, were the commonsense realists: Francis Hutcheson (1694–1747), Adam Ferguson (1723–1816), Thomas Reid (1710–96), and Welsh intuitionist Richard Price (1723–91). These thinkers combined epistemological realism, intuitionism, moral idealism, and an appeal to commonsense universalism. They taught that the fundamental principles of reason and morals are self-evident intuitions. Even Locke, despite his denial of innate ideas, conceded the reality of one intuitive belief: self-consciousness of one's existence. To the commonsense moralists, that put into play the basis of a better philosophy than Lockean empiricism.[21]

They argued that self-consciousness contains fundamental principles that are prior to and independent of experience, such as substance, extension, mass, and the moral sense. All discoveries of reason are grounded on these innate principles. Scottish commonsense was not a monolith: Reid and Price judged that Hutcheson's ethical sentimentalism was too subjective; Price held that Hutcheson shortchanged the free agency of the self in making moral choices; against Hutcheson, Reid and Price held that the moral sense is educable. But all contended that virtue and vice belong to the nature of things. The fundamental principles of reason cannot be denied without self-contradiction, they argued; nobody seriously denies the reality of causality or an external world. In the same way, the very ideas of moral right and wrong are inherent in the process of reasoning. The way forward in philosophy was to affirm the verdict of common sense that sensation automatically causes true belief in external objects.

The greatest commonsense thinker, Reid, stressed that every ideal system eventually conflicts with the innate principles of conception and belief by which the mind works. Descartes, seeking an ideal system, launched philosophy down a blind alley; those that followed came to doubt that they knew anything for sure. Some denied the reality of mind and some denied matter; Hume even denied that he had a self. Reid urged deep thinkers to return to the mind's given furniture, which they took for granted in their everyday living. However many fundamental principles there may have been – Reid never developed a systematic account – they were divinely given and the answer to modern philosophy's embarrassing confusions: "They make up what is called *the common sense of mankind*; and, what is manifestly contrary to any of those first principles, is what we call *absurd*."[22]

Commonsense intuitionism was an alternative to religious dogmatism and the empiricist stricture that evidence about the things of sense is all that we have. It inferred universal moral laws from the common experience of conscience. It offered a unifying language and philosophy of virtue. It serviced the need of a broad moral philosophy that was not owned exclusively by any theological or ideological party. And it provided a basis for conceiving morality as an autonomous science.

The career of commonsense realism at Princeton was a bellwether of its success elsewhere. In the late 1750s, while Francis Bowen taught a commonsense blend of natural religion, moral philosophy, political economy, and civil polity at Harvard as the Alford Professor, Princeton president Jonathan Edwards contended that commonsense was too optimistic. Hutcheson's theory of a universal moral sense wrongly minimized original sin, Edwards argued; thus it wrongly supposed that human beings possessed the free ability to choose the good.

But even at Princeton commonsense was soon claimed for Calvinist orthodoxy. In 1768 John Witherspoon – the only cleric to sign the Declaration of Independence – became president of Princeton. To Witherspoon it was terribly important to establish ethics as a self-standing science. Hutcheson had shown how to do so, even if his theology fell short of robust orthodoxy. Human consciousness was a source of scientific data, and scientific examination disclosed the existence of a moral sense, from which the principles of a universal ethic could be derived. On that basis Witherspoon re-established moral philosophy at Princeton and later helped to organize the new American government along with his protégé, James Madison. For Witherspoon, as for hundreds of American clergy who served as college presidents and taught the required course on moral philosophy, the new science of morality served the cause of building up the new Republic. Religion and morality supported each other, but theologies were many, while morality was a common inheritance. That rendering of moral truth had a long career in the American academy.[23]

Beyond Moral Philosophy: Social Ethics

Moral philosophy was about nurturing moral values and serving the good of the Republic, vaguely in the name of religion. But the schoolmaster ethos of moral philosophy did not wear well in the Gilded Age. American colleges, having been founded to produce an educated clergy, tried to accommodate the needs of an expanding constituency by adding modern subjects to the classical model. By the mid-1860s the needs outstripped the model. American colleges and the growing number of universities had to change the model to give engineers, business executives, and scientists the education they needed. The universities, especially, gave higher priority to science. Brown University president Francis Wayland was a pioneer of the university model, under which inductive science grew stronger in the academy. Philosophical idealism also grew stronger in the American academy, reflecting, like the rise of science, the admiration of American educators for German universities. University of Michigan chancellor Henry P. Tappan was a leading advocate of fashioning American universities on the German model.[24]

To an academy that increasingly prized scientific induction as the golden road to truth, moral philosophy appeared quaint, and science no longer took a back seat to philosophy or theology. Universities changed to accommodate the needs of an industrial society and the increasing prestige of science. In the 1870s moral philosophy fell off its pedestal, derided for its emphasis on deductive reasoning. It was not yet out of a job, because American educational leaders still believed that knowledge had little worth if virtue decreased. Some discipline had to speak for the moral basis of the social order and the academy's search for truth. But the climate had changed, as the founders of social ethics perceived. If the unifying, moral, and spiritual efficacy of the old moral philosophy was to be recovered, it had to speak the language of science. The founders of social ethics also judged, however, that the new moral philosophy had to be more Christian than the old one.

The social gospelers who proposed to replace moral philosophy with social ethics made a shrewdly pious, though sincere, claim: their approach was more explicitly Christian than the old one, because it recovered the kingdom faith of Jesus for modern Christianity. It was the same argument they employed to defend biblical criticism. Moral philosophy, like historic Christianity, obscured the gospel with dubious accretions and traditions, but liberal Protestant scholarship stripped away the inventions of human mediators to regain the religion of Jesus.

In 1877, Union Theological Seminary took a step in the direction of social ethics, establishing a course in Christian ethics taught by George L. Prentiss. The idea that Christian ethics might be taught more or less on its own was gaining traction. Union and Princeton seminaries kept a wary eye on each other; thus Union noticed Princeton's precedent in establishing an ethics chair. At the college level Christian ethics was absorbed by moral philosophy; in seminaries it was a branch in the tree of systematic theology, usually called moral philosophy or "moral science." Years later Prentiss reflected that the crucial difference between the old moral philosophy and the new Christian ethics was the explicitly Christian character of the latter. Moral philosophy "had little to do with Christianity," he recalled, exaggerating to make a point. "Manuals and elementary treatises were based almost wholly upon the simple teaching of reason and conscience, irrespective of revelation or the Bible." To Prentiss the new

Christian ethics was better because it had a sharper theological identity, it offered a stronger apologetic, and it was more relevant socially: "Both Christian apology and Christian Ethics seem to me specially fitted to aid in the solution of some of the hardest present day problems concerning truth and duty, whether in the social, political or commercial sphere." In the academy, the apostle of that proposition was Peabody.[25]

Peabody recognized that his timing was highly fortunate, having come along when something really new was possible. By his reckoning, he got to play a leading role in three academic revolutions. The first was the transformation of a denominational seminary into a nondenominational, university school of theology. The second was the invention of social ethics. The third was the abolition of Harvard's chapel requirement. At Harvard, none of these "revolutions" would have occurred without president Charles Eliot's strong support of the Divinity School and his insistence that it outgrow its sectarian past. In each case, a strong-minded lesser player carried out the change. The agent of the Divinity School's transformation was Charles Carroll Everett, who served as dean from 1879 to 1900. The founder of social ethics was Peabody, though he gave the credit to his patron, New York philanthropist Alfred Tredway White. Peabody was also the one who alleviated Harvard students of compulsory chapel, but he gave the credit to legendary Episcopal rector and Harvard trustee Phillips Brooks.[26]

When Peabody began his teaching career, Harvard Divinity School was not much more than a training school for Unitarian pastors. All American seminaries were denominational training schools, while theology, being based in the seminaries, was only slightly less parochial. Peabody later recalled: "Theology as a science, correlated with law or medicine, with the same method of free research and the same spirit of singleminded devotion to truth, had practically no recognition among American seminaries." In 1879, just before he joined the faculty, he told Harvard's Board of Overseers that the Divinity School should aspire to be a thoroughly academic, "unsectarian school" modeled on the great German universities. Years later Peabody took pride that Unitarian Harvard was the first institution to set theology free from the church, by setting the Divinity School free from monolithic Unitarian influence. Formally at least, Harvard opted for university theology, which he called "the higher Unitarianism."[27]

Under Everett's leadership, the new Divinity School claimed to stand for objective theological scholarship, not a party interest. Hebrew was demoted to an elective, instruction in "social service" was added, an elective system was adopted, and the faculty made diversity hires. In 1880, Crawford Howell Toy, a Southern Baptist biblical scholar, replaced Edward Young in the Hancock chair, and Peabody was appointed lecturer in ethics and homiletics. The following year Peabody was appointed as Parkman Professor of Theology; David Gordon Lyon, a Southern Baptist protégé of Toy's, took the Hollis chair; and a lay Congregationalist with little religious background, Ephraim Emerton, took the Winn chair in church history. In 1883 the elective system was formally introduced and another Congregationalist, Joseph Henry Thayer, joined the faculty and subsequently gained the Bussey chair in New Testament Criticism. These six scholars, counting Everett, worked together at Harvard to the end of the century. All of them except Thayer had studied in Germany, and all believed in the ideal of objective scholarship – specifically, the practice of critical, genetic interpretation – which they called the scientific method.[28]

From the beginning of his career Peabody was keenly aware of, and troubled about, William Graham Sumner at Yale, who used Herbert Spencer's *Study of Sociology* as a textbook. Peabody also knew that the American Social Science Association was trying to hold together the vision of a unified scientific study of society. Both were public matters that helped to shape Peabody's sense of his enterprise. An optimistic, vaguely religious version of social Darwinism with a strong progress-motif was popular in American culture; libertarians and early Progressivists alike assured that American society was evolving in a good direction. Sumner, however, had a darker view of where social evolution was headed, and he played up the anti-theistic aspects of social Darwinism, which offended religious leaders.

In the 1860s Sumner had studied biblical criticism at Göttingen, which attracted him to social and historical analysis, but which ended his plans to become an Episcopal priest. In 1870 he read Spencer's essays, later collected as *The Study of Sociology*, which converted him to social Darwinism. Two years later he joined the Yale faculty to teach political and social science. An eccentric figure, riveting in the classroom, Sumner gave cheeky, opinionated lectures that propagandized for social Darwinism in the name of "the science of society," a phrase he preferred to sociology. He refused to teach women, railed against government, and exhorted his well-born male students to resist all schemes to lift up the poor and weak. His aggressive teaching sparked a public controversy over the boundaries of the new social science. Religious leaders deplored Sumner's bias against Christian ethics; his defenders replied that he studied society empirically and inductively just like nature. Sociology would not get anywhere as a science if it had to defer to religious objections.[29]

A few social Darwinists equivocated on whether social Darwinism and the scientific understanding of society were the same thing. Sumner replied that upholding a doctrine, even one as sound as social Darwinism, was not really the point. That was why he preferred not to speak of sociology, which sounded like a bundle of ideas or doctrines. What mattered was the disinterested, scientific pursuit of truth. On the other hand, he assured, the truth disclosed by science was Spencer's picture of a brutal struggle for survival, which made a mockery of fashionable sentimental humanism. Social evolution was about the competition of life for the limited resources of nature. Culture was the cultivation of physical and psycho-social traits that advanced the struggle for life.

Moralists, Sumner observed, spoke on behalf of "the weak" and "the poor," claiming that government existed "in some especial sense, for the sake of the classes so designated, and that the same classes (whoever they are) have some especial claim on the interest and attention of the economist and social philosopher." Some moralists even measured the moral health of society by how it treated its most vulnerable members. That was utter nonsense, Sumner replied; it was perverse to suppose that "the training of men is the only branch of human effort in which the labor and care should be spent, not on the best specimens but on the poorest." There was such a thing as progress in civilization, Sumner allowed; he was not a reactionary who believed in turning back the clock on universal (male) suffrage or education for the masses. But progress was extremely slow and slight, it always had a dark side, and it was easily wrecked by indulgent sentimentality toward the poor: "Under our so-called progress evil only alters its forms, and we must esteem it a grand advance if we can believe that, on the whole, and over a wide view of human affairs, good has gained a hair's breadth over evil in a century."[30]

This was a major voice in the contest to define the meaning of the new social science for American politics and society. Sumner's blend of *laissez-faire* economics and Darwinian natural selection made a strong bid to set sociology against the biblical and humanitarian command to remember the poor. In 1885 a small group of social gospelers led by Richard Ely and Washington Gladden founded the American Economics Association to oppose the ascending idea that survival of the fittest was the last word in social science. The group declared in its platform:

> We hold that the doctrine of *laissez-faire* is unsafe in politics and unsound in morals; and that it suggests an inadequate explanation of the relations between the state and the citizens . . . We hold that the conflict of labor and capital has brought to the front a vast number of social problems whose solution is impossible without the united efforts of the church, state and science.

At the founding conference of the Association in Saratoga, New York, Ely implored that good social science went hand in hand with good religion:

> We who have resolved to form an American Economics Association hope to do something toward the developing of a system of social ethics. We wish to accomplish certain practical results in the social and financial world, and believing that our work lies in the direction of practical Christianity, we appeal to the church, the chief of the social forces in this country, to help us, to support us, and to make our work a complete success, which it can by no possibility be without her assistance.

Good social science had an ethical conscience that opposed the predatory anarchy of unregulated capitalism, but it could not win the struggle for social influence in the USA without the active support of the churches.[31]

Peabody shared that conviction with a rising movement for "Applied Christianity," although he was ambivalent about the American Economics Association, since he also believed in the dream of a unified social science. In 1865 the American Social Science Association had been founded to promote social scientific analysis and solutions to social problems. Frank Sanborn, secretary of the group, noted that theology and "ecclesiastical polemics" were being overtaken by a better kind of literature consisting of "systems, essays, manuals, and illustrations of Social Science, which have little to do with heaven or hell, but aim to make this pitiful little globe of ours a better place for us while we inhabit its crust." Twenty years later Sanborn reaffirmed that good social science had a powerful ethical aim. To positivists, good social science dealt with facts, not with values. To social Darwinists, the ideal was a marriage of Darwinian natural selection to a rigorous Protestant work ethic. To traditional religionists, dogma trumped science. To Sanborn, the ideal was a unified social science that analyzed society and helped to solve its problems: "Methinks this expresses very well what our association has been doing in its broader field and with more miscellaneous activity, for the last twenty years. To learn patiently what *is* – and to promote diligently what *should* be – this is the double duty of all the social sciences."[32]

The founders of social ethics believed in that double duty. The crucial thing was to hold together the *is* and the *ought*. On the other hand, social scientists had very little social agency besides writing books. To make a real impact on American society, the social sciences and Christian ethics had to be fused together, mobilizing the churches to promote progressive social change.

That was the idea that Peabody took to his early classes at Harvard. In 1881 he was appointed to the Parkman chair and began teaching a course titled "Practical Ethics" at the Divinity School. Two years later he opened the course to undergraduates under the title, "Ethical Theories and Moral Reform." The title changed several times over the years, from "Philosophy 5" to "Ethical Theories and Social Reforms" to "The Practical Ethics of Social Reforms" to "The Ethics of the Social Question." Finally, after 20 years of name changes, Peabody's friend and colleague William James asked "Why not call it 'Social Ethics'?" That settled the name of this enterprise at Harvard. The topics, however, changed very little over the years; Peabody had a clear method from the beginning, and he divided his time between the Divinity School and the College. In 1886 he was appointed Plummer Professor of Christian Morals, a chair that better reflected his role at Harvard. Meanwhile the enrollments kept climbing. In 1883 he had eight students; by 1902 he had 112; in 1906 he topped out with 146 undergraduates. A faculty colleague jocularly dubbed the course "Drainage and Divorce," which morphed into the students' tag, rendered with a mixture of affection and whimsy: "Peabo's drainage, drunkenness, and divorce."[33]

In 1895 Peabody added a second course, "Sociological Seminaries," for divinity and other graduate students, which focused variously on the idea of a Christian social order, the ethics of Jesus and the New Testament, religion and society, Christian ethics and modern life, and the history of social ethics; in 1905 he changed the title to "Social Ethics Seminaries." By then the original course was an institution at Harvard. Until 1905 it was offered, at the College, in the Philosophy department, but in 1906 social ethics became a self-standing department funded by Alfred Tredway White. Peabody's dream for social ethics appeared to be coming true, at least at Harvard. After his friend Everett retired in 1901 – Peabody called him "both father-confessor and delightful companion" – Peabody served as dean of the Divinity School for five years, and when he retired in 1913, the Department of Social Ethics featured seven courses and several research seminars.[34]

From the beginning Peabody approached ethics inductively as the study of social movements addressing major social problems. Temperance and divorce were high on the list, befitting his connection to moral philosophy and the usual concerns of theological ethics, but he also featured the labor movement, "the Indian problem," and philanthropy. He stressed that from a social scientific standpoint, the principles of ethics had to be derived from the study of social problems and the movements to correct them. In 1886 Peabody explained to Sanborn

> I was led to my subject by a somewhat different road from most of those who deal with it. As a teacher of ethics I became aware of the chasm which exists between such abstract study and the practical application of moral ideals; and it seemed to me possible to approach the theory of ethics inductively, through the analyses of great moral movements, which could be easily characterized and from which principles could be deduced.[35]

In the footsteps of moral philosophy he began the course with a detailed outline of his method, but Peabody cautioned that the old moral philosophy was deductive and focused on the individual; the new Christian ethics was inductive and emphasized social problems. Moral philosophy was good at abstracting inferences from the common experience of conscience, but it was too removed from specific social problems to deal with them effectively. Emphasizing psychology and deduction, the moral philosophers "dissected and tabulated the impulses and emotions of life." They turned ethics into a "dull study" that deadened youthful minds. What was needed was a "science of life" that started with "the data and the problems of life." Sometimes Peabody stated explicitly that his project was to transform moral philosophy: "What moral philosophy needs is a new method of approach." On the other hand, the social sciences were in danger of losing the language of moral value. To prevent that calamity, a scientific approach to ethics was needed that found its moral principles "through the observation and analysis of moral facts."[36]

Peabody's method had three steps: observation, generalization, and correlation. Although he waited until the end of his teaching career to publish a thorough account of it – *The Approach to the Social Question* (1909) – he taught a rudimentary version of it from the beginning. The first step was to generate data; the second was to assemble and analyze the data; the third was to discern the underlying moral unity in nature. Somewhere between the second and third steps, he taught, science passed into philosophy. The hard part was the third step work of drawing ethical principles from the data: "The various social movements, which at first appeared so distinguishable and isolated – the problems of the family, of poverty, of industry, of drink – each with its own literature, experiments, programmes, and solutions, are yet correlated expressions of the unity of the social world." All social issues and events were interrelated. Thus, the hardest work of the social ethicist was to grasp the underlying unity of the whole, including its ethical character and principles.[37]

Certainly his students found it the hardest part. Peabody required them to study a philanthropic or reform organization and write a term paper that followed the social-ethical method. Most of the papers got stuck in step one. Only rarely did a student develop an ethical argument from the study and analysis of a social organization. Peabody realized that his course merely scratched the surface of what social ethics could be. Modestly he described his lectures as being merely "sound and just," not "original or interesting." In later life he recalled, "While many youths got little from their researches but an easy 'C,' here and there, I like to believe, a life was steadied or a career determined." He did not expect his students to manage step three; that was the teacher's role, to tease out the ethical principles and reflect on the interdependence of social forces. The course spurred many Harvard students to volunteer for social work organizations, however, and Peabody was ambitious for social ethics as a discipline, telling Sanborn: "There is in this department a new opportunity in university instruction. With us it has been quite without precedent. It summons the young men who have been imbued with the principles of political economy and of philosophy to the practical application of those studies. It ought to do what college work rarely does – bring a young man's studies near to problems of an American's life."[38]

The Social Question, William Jewett Tucker, and Liberal Theology

Peabody was in the twilight of his career at Harvard before he published his first book, *Jesus Christ and the Social Question*, in 1900. By then the social gospel movement was thriving, with an ample literature; Ely, Gladden, Strong, and Mathews were well-known authors; the founding social gospel organizations were established; and the Herron phenomenon had already peaked. The social gospelers were keenly aware that their generation marked a turning point in Christian history. Peabody's first book declared that the present age had "a special work to do" because it had seized upon "the social question." Already the movement was looking backward to recount its history. Advocates explained that the social gospel was essentially a recovery of the social teachings of the Hebrew prophets and Jesus. Sometimes they interpreted it as the next phase of the anti-slavery movement or an outgrowth of English Christian socialism. Founders were identified and heralded, sometimes stretching back to Theodore Parker, Horace Bushnell, or Henry Ward Beecher.[39]

Walter Rauschenbusch announced that the "wreath of the pioneer" in social ethics belonged to William Jewett Tucker and Andover Theological Seminary, which set two generations of historians and commentators on a mistaken path. Tucker was not quite the first to teach what came to be called social ethics, and he left the field too soon to make anywhere near the contribution that Peabody made to it. But he was a pioneer of the field, alongside the distinction for which he was better known in his middle career, being a member of the Andover Seminary group, which endured a six-year heresy proceeding over liberal theology.[40]

Tucker was an 1861 graduate of Dartmouth College, to which he returned as president after the Andover Controversy finally ended, and an 1866 graduate of Andover Seminary, to which he returned after an early career as a minister. For 13 years he ministered to Congregational and Presbyterian churches in New Hampshire and New York before joining the Andover faculty in 1880. His ministerial experiences convinced him, during the same period that Washington Gladden reached similar conclusions, that the church needed a more liberal theology and a relevant social ethic. Tucker later explained, "The religion of the previous generation had become largely introspective. The proof of its reality rested in certain experiences. It sent the religious man to his closet." The old evangelicalism had a strong belief in charity, he allowed, which impelled the evangelical Christian to do good works in the world, "but it did not send him into the shop or the factory. It was not a type of religion fitted to understand or to meet the problems involved in the rise of industrialism." The old evangelicalism was outward reaching and courageous in its missionary zeal, "but it shrank from contact with the growing material power of the modern world. It saw the religious peril of materialism, but not the religious opportunity for the humanizing of material forces." In that spirit Tucker returned to his second alma mater to teach sacred rhetoric, including pastoral theology and homiletics.[41]

Andover Seminary was founded in 1808 as a conservative Calvinist protest against the liberal turn at Harvard, although an earlier entity on which Andover was based, Phillips Academy, had been founded in 1778. New England Congregationalism, increasingly split between a growing Unitarian faction and an orthodox party of Old School Calvinists and New Divinity "Hopkinsians," needed a seminary for its orthodox party. Andover Seminary grew into a powerhouse institution on that basis; by the mid-nineteenth century it averaged 150 students, at a time when no other seminary except Princeton enrolled more than 100. For more than 70 years, Andover protected its conservative identity by requiring faculty to sign a strict creedal statement every year. But that did not stop the denomination's showcase orthodox seminary from turning liberal, causing the Andover Controversy.

Faculty members Tucker, Egbert Smyth, J. W. Churchill, Edward Y. Hincks, and George Harris made inviting targets of themselves by editing a mildly liberal journal, *Andover Review*. In 1886 the seminary's Board of Visitors launched heresy trials against them. *Andover Review* stood for a Christian accommodation of Darwinian theory, opposed "orthodoxism" and secular rationalism, called for a morally acceptable concept of Christ's atonement, questioned the logic of substitutionary atonement, and held out for a universalistic "future probation" after death. While conceding that there was probably such a thing as "novelty of doctrine without progress," the Andover theologians urged that believing in the possibility of genuine progress was part of what it meant to have faith in the ongoing work of the Holy Spirit. They called their perspective "progressive orthodoxy." The Board of Visitors replied that "progressive orthodoxy" was liberalism by an evasive name, and "future probation," in particular, was a disastrous heresy that cut the nerve of missions. The formal charges contained 16 items, beginning with biblical authority and Christology, moving on to moral atonement, a modal Trinity, and the future probation, and ending with the logical conclusion that, having taught liberal doctrines, the Andover professors had signed the Andover Creed in bad faith.[42]

Tucker's middle career, the professorial one, was consumed by two questions: Was Andover to be a liberal seminary? and Would the *Andover Review* editors keep their jobs? After long dispute, both questions were answered in the affirmative. In 1890 the Supreme Court of Massachusetts declared that the proceedings against the Andover professors were faulty, and in 1892 all five were acquitted. But the enterprise for which Tucker wanted to be known was his pioneering role in establishing social ethics as a discipline. Liberal theology and social Christianity were intimately related, but not quite the same thing; for Tucker, the crucial thing was to bring them together, humanizing theology and society. A seminary was not really progressive if it humanized theology but left the social question alone. According to Tucker, two seminaries led the fight to humanize theology – Union and Andover. Union liberalized the doctrine of Scripture, and Andover liberalized the doctrine of human destiny. Harvard had strayed too far from the Protestant mainstream to count as a creative force in theology. Tucker also overlooked Harvard when he told the story of the origins of social ethics. In his telling, as in Rauschenbusch's, social ethics as a discipline began at Andover Seminary.[43]

That was a slight exaggeration. In the early 1880s Tucker included social topics at the end of his courses on homiletics and pastoral theology, but he did not teach his social ethics course "Social Economics" until 1889. In the early 1880s he gave lectures on "The Church in its relation to the Indifferent and Prejudiced Classes." Years later he remarked, "The venture of the department into the field of sociological studies was an innovation in a theological field." That was certainly true, aside from Peabody and J. H. W. Stuckenberg. For that matter, few colleges taught sociology in 1880, although Miami University of Ohio philosopher Robert Hamilton Bishop was the first American to separate sociology from philosophy, in a course taught in 1834. Tucker stressed that American colleges and seminaries lacked the requisite scientific background to make professional use of the new knowledge in the social sciences. American churches were deeply involved in philanthropy and other charitable activities, which helped to spur interest in social science. But the central driving force behind the eruption of social consciousness and the rise of the social gospel, as Tucker recognized, was the emergence of a workers movement that demanded economic justice, not charity. A vast army of unskilled and increasingly organized laborers demanded to be treated as citizens with rights to decent wages and working conditions.[44]

The class struggles of 1886 comprised the nub of the story. By that year the Knights of Labor, founded in 1869, had one million members. In March 1886 the Knights struck against Jay Gould's Missouri–Pacific railroad system, tying up 5,000 miles of track. In April President Grover Cleveland gave the first presidential address dealing with trade union and labor issues, suggesting that government serve as an arbitrator in labor–capital disputes. On May 1 the Knights joined with the Black International anarchists, the Socialist unions and other trade unions in massive demonstrations for an eight-hour day. The march of 80,000 protesters down Michigan Avenue in Chicago was the first "May Day" demonstration. Two days later an attack on strikebreaking workers at the McCormick Reaper Manufacturing Company in Chicago led to a deadly police reaction that sparked a riot in Haymarket Square. On May 10 the Supreme Court ruled that a corporation was a legal person under the Fourteenth Amendment, giving corporations the privileges of citizenship. In June eight anarchists were convicted of conspiracy to murder in the Haymarket riot, despite a weak case against them. Later that month Congress passed legal authorization for the incorporation of trade unions. In October the Supreme Court ruled that states could not regulate interstate commerce passing through their borders, annulling the legal power of states over numerous trusts, railroads, and holding companies. In December the American Federation of Labor was organized out of the former Federation of Trades and Labor Unions, comprising a major new force in unionism.[45]

These events inspired, goaded, and frightened middle-class Protestants to take the social gospel theologians seriously; the interest of Protestant churches in the social question was overdue. Ely's *The Labor Movement in America* (1886) counseled Americans not to dread the rising of the working class; his best-selling *Aspects of Social Christianity* (1889) encouraged readers to send money to the American Economics Association, "a real legitimate Christian institution." In 1889 he observed that at least a few seminaries had begun to give "serious attention to social science," especially Hartford and Andover. At Hartford, Graham Taylor had warmed to the social gospel. At Andover, Tucker launched his course on "Social Economics."[46]

On occasion the social gospelers lauded University of Wisconsin president John Bascom as a treasured ally, but his books received little attention, one reason being that Bascom was a generation older than the social gospel founders. Lutheran theologian J. H. W. Stuckenberg was another able advocate of social Christianity whose book, *Christian Sociology* (1880), foreshadowed social gospel themes and arguments. He was the first to use the term "Christian Sociology," which he noted with pride and disappointment: "This whole subject has been greatly neglected; and this must surprise every one who feels its importance." Explaining the neglect, he observed that the subject was "so vast," its number of objects was "so great," and these objects were "so diverse" that organizing them into a single field of inquiry was extremely daunting. Stuckenberg made a strong beginning, but he was so little known that even the social gospelers ignored him. It didn't help that he was a Lutheran teaching at Pennsylvania College (later Gettysburg College). American Lutheranism was not a player in progressive Christian circles, and Stuckenberg's commitment to social Christianity cut against the grain of Lutheran two-kingdoms theology. He was too isolated to make a significant impact on his own group or to be noticed beyond it. During the Civil War he kept a diary of his experience as a chaplain with the Pennsylvania Volunteer Infantry; published posthumously, it was titled "I'm Surrounded by Methodists."[47]

Tucker, by contrast, had ready access to the rising social gospel and liberal theology movements. He titled his course "Social Economics" to make a point about what it meant to apply theology to life under modern conditions. Social economics had approximately the same relation to the church that political economics had to the state, he argued. Just as the state had economic obligations and functions, the church had social obligations and even functions, minus political functions. Because industrialism created new social conditions and classes, the ethical meaning of the gospel had changed. The entire social economy of the West was changed by modern capitalism, including the role of the church in society. Capitalism and modernity marginalized the church *and* heaped new moral responsibilities upon it. Tucker's course began with the transition from slavery to serfdom in medieval Europe; reviewed the rise of industrialism and the factory system in England; discussed English Chartism, trade union organizing, labor legislation, and democracy; traced the history of slavery, immigration, and labor legislation in the United States; discussed wages, profits, workplace issues, and the use of leisure; and compared the American socialist movement with German and English socialism. Seniors spent six weeks doing field research on the union movement, supported by a scholarship program. Like virtually all social gospel courses and literature of the late nineteenth century, Tucker's leaned on Ely's writings. He also assigned Herbert Spencer, Karl Marx, John Stuart Mill, and Henry George, and subsequently gave versions of the course that focused on crime, pauperism, and disease.[48]

Tucker took pride that his faculty colleagues wanted Andover to teach and support social Christianity. What surprised him was the overwhelming response by pastors and congregations. He struggled to keep up with an outpouring of mail and requests, including a heavy demand for extension courses. Many pastors recognized that they needed to learn something about political economics. Finally Tucker worked out an arrangement to publish three yearly courses in monthly installments of *Andover Review*, focusing on labor issues, poverty and disease, and crime.

Like most of the social gospelers, Tucker was a progressive reformer, not a socialist or revolutionary. He believed in clean government, graduated taxes, expanded democracy, and government as a custodian of the common good. In 1893 he returned to his collegiate alma mater, Dartmouth, to serve as its ninth president. At the time the school had a regional profile, 300 students, and a large debt. When Tucker retired in 1909 Dartmouth had a national reputation, 1,100 students, 20 new buildings, and a transformed curriculum. Grateful alumni called him "the great president" and "the president who refounded Dartmouth."[49]

In retirement he exulted at returning to politics and the social question. Like most progressives of his generation, Tucker voted Republican for most of his life, but by 1912 Republicans were the conservative party and many of Tucker's friends wanted the entire progressive movement to join the Progressive party, under Theodore Roosevelt's leadership. Tucker supported Roosevelt for the presidency, but was relieved when Roosevelt declined, after the election, to make a permanent home in the Progressive party. For Tucker, progressivism was the worldview and social ethic of the best Republicans, Democrats, Socialists, and independents. To identify it with a single political party was to cheapen and degrade it. He did not want all progressives to join the same party, just as he did not want all religious progressives to join the same denomination. To really believe in progressivism was to hope that it would win all the parties and denominations. For the social gospelers of Tucker's generation, that did not seem so wild a dream, at least until 1918.[50]

Jesus and the Social Question

Peabody was slow to produce a book, but at the turn of the century, when he was 53 years old, he produced one of the classics of the social gospel: *Jesus Christ and the Social Question*. After that he wrote six more books. His first was an introduction to social Christianity structured as an exposition of the teaching of Jesus. The book was optimistic, idealistic, and immanentalist, but it was none of these things in the sense that Niebuhrians later parodied. It stood in the tradition of the nineteenth-century liberal lives of Jesus literature, but was keenly aware of current German scholarship on the liberal Jesus and contained an intelligent response to it. It was sympathetic to the upsurge of the disinherited, but rejected socialism, radicalism, and all other isms that dismissed the necessity of cultivating virtue and moral character.

Peabody stressed that the current movements for social justice were signs of social health and vitality. The strongest movements existed in educated, comparatively prosperous nations, he noted. There were no movements for social justice in poor, repressive, dysfunctional nations like Egypt or Turkey. Putting it too strongly, partly because he could not resist a snappy aphorism, Peabody declared, "The problem of social justice does not grow out of the worst social conditions, but out of the best." Modernity was a good thing, but it could be made better, to benefit everyone. To Peabody, the radical socialist denigration of the family, private property, and the state was repugnant; on the other hand, he praised the party of revolution for pressing the social question: "Behind all the extraordinary achievements of modern civilization, its transformations of business methods, its miracles of scientific discovery, its mighty combinations of political forces, there lies at the heart of the present time a burdening sense of social mal-adjustment which creates what we call the social question."[51]

The nineteenth-century English Christian Socialists had no answer, he judged; their distinction was in facing up to the problem. Frederick Denison Maurice confessed that he could not see his way beyond the recognition that it was a lie to treat competition as the law of the universe. Christian socialism would have rested in that negation if English cooperativism had not come along to give Maurice and Charles Kingsley an answer. Peabody noted, pointedly, that the English cooperativists were humble handworkers, "without the counsel of the learned." Early English Christian socialism – the kind of socialism that Peabody liked – was an exemplary type of opportunism: "The English opportunists gave the strength of their leadership to the cooperative movement, and found satisfaction for their Christian socialism in a practical scheme which they themselves had not devised."[52]

Peabody admired common sense, as he understood it, and commended it to economists and theologians. In his view, too many prophets mistook themselves for economists or policy-makers, advocating schemes that were bound to fail: "Neither ethical passion nor rhetorical genius equip a preacher for economic judgments." In the same way he admonished readers to use their common sense in interpreting gospel maxims. The teaching of Jesus had prophetic social content, but "however weighty it may be, the mind of the Teacher was primarily turned another way." Contrary to otherworldly religion, the ethic of Jesus had a strong social dimension, but contrary to shallow renderings of the social gospel, the supreme concern of Jesus was not the transformation of society. Jesus was a revealer, not a reformer or revolutionary. He viewed the

world from above, not from the earth. His ultimate concern was to show the movement of God's life in human souls, not to become entangled in social problems.[53]

That was the pattern of Peabody's favorite kind of aphorism: this, not that. He
employed it repeatedly in characterizing the message of Jesus: "He was not primarily
the deviser of a social system, but the quickener of single lives. His gift is not that of
form, but that of life." Peabody aphorized in other forms, too, especially on this theme:
"His conversation was in heaven; therefore the world was at his feet . . . The prophets
wrestled with the waves of social agitation; Jesus walked upon them . . . The work of
a reformer is for his own age; that of a revealer for all ages." In Peabody's rendering,
Jesus approached the social question "from within" by inspiring individuals: "It is for
others to serve the world by organization; he serves it through inspiration." Sealing
the point, Peabody returned to "this, not that," but turned it around: "His contribution is not one of social organization or method, but of a point of view, a way of
approach, and an end to attain. His social gospel is not one of fact or doctrine, but
one of spirit and aim."[54]

That formulation helped Peabody deal with the German apocalyptic Jesus. A great
deal of social gospel preaching and theology described Jesus as the herald of an egalitarian, idealistic movement to build the kingdom of God on earth. To many social
gospelers, that was the core of the gospel. In the early 1890s, however, German
scholars Ernst Issel, Otto Schmoller, and Johannes Weiss began to argue that the mind
and teaching of Jesus were primarily eschatological and apocalyptic, not social. Jesus
was a herald of the imminent, cataclysmic end of the world by God's apocalyptic
action. Weiss put it sharply: "As Jesus conceived it, the Kingdom of God is a radically
superworldly entity which stands in diametric opposition to this world. This is to say
that there *can* be no talk of an *innerworldly* development of the Kingdom of God in
the mind of Jesus!" By the turn of the century this thesis was a powerful scholarly
trend, which gave the social gospelers heartburn. A few years later Albert Schweitzer
made it famous in his book *Quest of the Historical Jesus.*[55]

But Peabody did not claim that "thy Kingdom come" was about building a new
social order; neither did he claim, like Rauschenbusch and other social gospelers, that
the early church must have put its own apocalypticism into Jesus' mouth. To Peabody,
the crucial datum was that Jesus spoke of the kingdom as a present spiritual reality:
"the kingdom of God is within you." Whatever else was true about the kingdom
sayings, it made no sense to say that the church invented the spiritual and ethical
sayings, because the church was apocalyptic. Peabody liked the phrase of Matthew
Arnold, "Jesus above the heads of his reporters." To Peabody, the best rule of interpretation in this area was "The more spiritual and ethical a teaching is, the more likely
it is to have come from the Teacher's lips." As for the apocalyptic statements, he kept
an open mind. They may have come from Jesus, or from the church, or the church
may have heightened Jesus' eschatological tendency. But if they came from Jesus,
Peabody contended, what mattered was that these statements had to be integrated with
Jesus' more basic understanding of the kingdom as a spiritual, already present reality.
The eschatological thesis began at the wrong point, at the end; the true beginning
point for Jesus was the present reality of the kingdom.[56]

Since Peabody did not deny that Jesus might have described the kingdom in apocalyptical terms, he seemed to be left with a paradoxical Jesus who preached radically
contrasting things about his central concept. But Peabody argued that if Jesus viewed
the world from above, the paradox was more apparent than real. The kingdom had

already come, but it was not yet fulfilled. The present reality of the kingdom was somewhat comprehensible and expressible, but its fulfillment was beyond comprehension. The wild language of the New Testament for it was merely a marker for something that could not be expressed. The kingdom was already present in every life that welcomed God's Spirit, "and when at last that same spirit shall penetrate the whole world, then there will result a social future which language itself is hardly rich enough to describe." The key to Jesus' idea of the kingdom of God was Jesus' own religious consciousness:

> He looks on human life from above, and, seeing it slowly shaped and purified by the life of God, regards the future of human society with a transcendent and unfaltering hope. In the purposes of God the kingdom is already existent, and when his will is done on earth, then his kingdom, which is now spiritual and interior, will be as visible and as controlling as it is in heaven.[57]

Though Jesus looked on human life from above, Peabody stressed, he approached it from within, by inspiring individual souls. Thus, the kingdom was an unfolding process of social righteousness fueled by the progressive sanctification of individual souls, but at the same time, the individual was called to this better life by the kingdom ideal. Peabody's concept of social salvation was less robust and more individualistic than that of Gladden or Rauschenbusch, but he had a version of the social gospel thesis that personal salvation and social salvation were interdependent, mutually indispensable, and grew together. Like all religious liberals of his time, he used the idealist language of personality to explicate this idea: the social order was produced by the creative spiritual power of personality, and personality was fulfilled only in the collective quest for social righteousness. In Peabody's telling, that was the social teaching of Jesus expressed in modern language: "The world of social ethics, then, lies in the mind of Jesus like an island in the larger sea of the religious life; but the same principle of service controls one, whether he tills the field of his island or puts forth to the larger adventure of the sea." For Jesus there was no conflict between the spiritual life and the social good, for he conceived personal religion as the means to the end of social religion. Jesus viewed the social question from above, in the light of his spiritual vision; he approached the social question from within, through the development of every person's spiritual character or personality; he made judgments about social matters in accordance with their contribution to the kingdom of God.[58]

Although Peabody's beloved Unitarian tradition was increasingly post-Christian, he championed its Christian stream. Although he found certain trends in American life distressing he tried to be optimistic that it was headed in the right direction. Out of every 1,000 marriages 60 ended in divorce, which was awful, he acknowledged. But it was good to remember, while socialist garbage about the obsolescence of the family filled the air, that 940 marriages out of every 1,000 sustained "some degree of unity and love." Relatedly, a good deal of modern literature gave the impression "that licentious imaginings and adulterous joys have displaced in modern society pure romance and wholesome love." That was ominous, Peabody allowed, but it was still a marginal phenomenon in American culture: "The eddies of dirty froth which float on the surface of the stream of social life and mar its clearness are not the signs which indicate its current." Mainstream American culture still prized the Christian virtues: "Beneath these signs of domestic restlessness the main body of social life is yet untainted, and the teaching of Jesus concerning unselfishness and unworldliness is practically verified in multitudes of unobserved and unpolluted homes."[59]

On the moral problem of wealth, Peabody cautioned against simplistic prooftexting, as in camels going through the eye of a needle. Jesus was a "spiritual seer," not a social demagogue. He elevated social ideals rather than leveling social classes. He cared about how one lived, not about the extent of one's wealth. To Peabody, the relevant maxim was "A man does not own his wealth, he owes it." Jesus taught that all of one's gains were owed to the kingdom of God. As long as one did not acquire wealth by immoral means, or make an idol of moneymaking, it was possible for the "ministry of wealth" to serve the kingdom of God. Because wealth was notoriously corrupting, Peabody acknowledged, "the Christian man of wealth knows that it is hard for him to enter the kingdom of God." To avoid being corrupted, the wealthy Christian male administered his affairs "with watchfulness over himself and with hands clean of malice, oppression, or deceit." He did not use charity to atone for ill gains; he was not one person in business and someone else on Sunday, but the same morally responsible self at all times: "His business is a part of his religion, and his philanthropy is a part of his business." Rich Christian women had special moral challenges and virtues, too. They spurned "foolishness and vanity," maintaining homes of "simplicity and good sense." They were equally at ease among rich and poor persons. And they kept their hearts clean "from the temptations of self-indulgence."[60]

Peabody favored cooperative ownership in the industrial sector, because cooperatives subordinated profit to personality. Unlike unregulated capitalism and the soulless economism of the radical socialists, the cooperative approach passed the moral test of Jesus, the flourishing of personality. It recognized, at least implicitly, that the root of the industrial problem lay in character, not structural arrangements. On the other hand, Peabody argued, because the cooperative approach had the highest moral standing, it was also the most demanding morally, requiring special virtues. Cooperative workers had to be patient, self-sacrificing, and honorable, otherwise their enterprises failed. That was not a fault of the cooperative system, which he called "a striking illustration of the teaching of Jesus." From a Christian point of view, what was needed in the economic order was precisely the lifting of industrial life to the level of a moral opportunity. Peabody explained the connection between the Christian gospel and cooperative economics:

> A few plain people associate themselves in a cooperative enterprise, quite unconscious that they are in any degree bearing witness to the social principles of the gospel; they apply themselves to the simple problem of conducting a shop or factory with fidelity, self-sacrifice, and patience; and as their work expands they seem to themselves to have made a good commercial venture, while in fact, in one corner of the great industrial world they are illustrating the principle of the Christian religion, that industrial progress begins from within.[61]

Jesus Christ and the Social Question contained effusions about optimism on which a later generation pounced. In Peabody's telling, Jesus was "the most unfaltering of optimists," every step of his ministry "was guided by an unconquerable optimism," and despite the bigotry, stupidity, meanness, and hypocrisy that constantly confronted him, he remained a "consistent optimist, confident that the world about him is ready for his message." Optimism was transforming because it sustained hope for the world, Peabody urged. Socialism painted a bleak picture to heighten the contrast with its economic ideal, it robbed persons of their hope, and it did nothing to nurture the virtues of unselfishness, magnanimity, and simplicity of character. By contrast, "Jesus illuminates the real world and makes it the instrument of his ideal."[62]

In his closing pages Peabody briefly applied his version of the social gospel to his nation's recent foray into imperialism. In 1898 the United States took the Philippine Islands and formally annexed the Hawaiian Islands; the following year it partitioned the Samoan Islands; in 1900 it helped to suppress the Boxer Rebellion in China. Some Protestant leaders protested that imperialism was a bad thing even when the United States did it; they included Graham Taylor, George Herron, Henry van Dyke, Leonard Bacon, Henry C. Potter, and Charles R. Brown. Others contended that imperialism could be a good thing if the invader had benevolent intentions, especially if the conqueror in question was the USA. Gladden, Mathews, Josiah Strong, Lyman Abbott, and W. H. P. Faunce pressed the latter argument; Peabody lined up with them: "It is the moral quality of the conquest itself, and not that which may happen after the conquest, which represents the Christian energy of the conquering nation; and it is the motives which prompt and direct the original approach to a heathen civilization which are likely either to bring heathen to Christ or to repel them from him."[63]

Jesus Christ and the Social Question was lauded immediately as a major statement of the rising social gospel, and was soon translated into German, French, and Swedish. It might have won Peabody a high place in the remembered social gospel if Rauschenbusch had not come along. Besides lacking Rauschenbusch's blazing style, however, Peabody was too fixated on spiritualized ideals to compete with him for movement influence. Peabody stressed that social ideals were expressions of inward spirituality (personality), but that was no match for Rauschenbusch's prophetic language of social justice and solidarity. Peabody never quite absorbed the fact that the social gospel, to meet the challenge of the socialist and trade union movements, had to meet these movements on their level of historical struggle; workers and the disinherited were not looking for a more educated pietism. For them, Peabody-style social ethics was not much of an answer to the social problem.

It was ideally suited, however, for the generational task of finding a social scientific alternative to moral philosophy. Peabody interpreted modern industrial strife as a sign of progress indicating a rising idealism among American workers. Morally, his idealism prized the governing of one's actions by ideals; epistemologically and metaphysically, it held that mind was prior and superior to the things of sense; ontologically it believed in an evolutionary progress toward eventual perfection. Behind the egotism, hatred, greed, and violence of history there was a divine will that forged good from evil appearances. The world was redeemed by the interaction of divine will and human will pulling history forward. Thus, the central business of social ethics was to study reform movements that struggled for and expressed the progress of personality.

Up from Slavery: The Race Problem in the Social Question

Peabody judged that in the field of racial justice, the vehicle of progress was education. In this belief he had a great deal of social gospel company, though Northern white social gospelers disagreed over the priority that Peabody and Lyman Abbott gave to vocational education.

For the most part the social gospel was not outspoken on the dignity and rights of black Americans. Southern social gospelers Thomas Dixon Jr, Alexander McKelway and Edgar Gardner Murphy were outright racists in the precise sense of the term, believing that blacks were biologically inferior, as was Northern social gospeler Charles H. Parkhurst.[64] Dixon's writings on race consciousness and the necessity of segregation outsold the books of any Northern social gospeler. Closer to the mainstream of the Northern social gospel, Josiah Strong and Lyman Abbott were right-leaning cultural chauvinists, pressing strongly for black assimilation to an Anglo-Saxonist ideal. They lionized Booker T. Washington as a black American symbol of the ideal. Another mainstream group, the Left-leaning assimilationists, also lionized Washington and the educational path to black progress, but with a stronger recognition of the rights of blacks; they included Joseph Cook, Quincey Ewing, Benjamin Orange Flower, William Channing Gannett, Jenkin Lloyd Jones, Henry Demarest Lloyd, and William Hayes Ward. A small group, siding with the W. E. B. Du Bois side of the argument, was outspoken on the subjects of black dignity and rights; they included Algernon Sidney Crapsey, Herbert Seeley Bigelow, Harlan Paul Douglass, Newell Dwight Hillis, and Charles Spahr.[65]

In 1910 nearly 90 percent of American blacks still lived in the South. Most social gospel leaders had little acquaintance with African Americans; they felt awkward about addressing a problem that was remote from their experience; and only the bravest of them publicly repudiated the prevalent American assumption of black inferiority. Many social gospelers believed in the redeemer mission of their nation, which usually led to the belief that Anglo-Saxons were the leaders and saviors of the world. Moreover, evolutionary science was supposedly on their side; Darwinism was said to be a secular explanation of the Anglo-Saxonist mission to civilize the world.

Only rarely did a social gospel leader publicly question the Supreme Court's 1896 *Plessy v. Ferguson* ruling that "separate but equal" segregation was consistent with the Fourteenth Amendment's guarantee of equal protection under the law. The social gospelers had a conscience about the evils of slavery and white supremacism in America, and some of them fought rearguard battles against the restriction of black suffrage in the South; but for the most part their efforts to do something specific for racial justice were restricted to educational programs, such as those of the American Missionary Society. Peabody was a prominent example of that strategy, giving many years of service to the Hampton Institute, while speaking for glacial slowness on justice for blacks.

His father had opposed slavery and assisted fugitive slaves, including Frederick Douglass and a frequent visitor to the Peabody home who braved the communion rail at King's Church. But Ephraim Peabody did not roar against slavery like Theodore Parker or William Ellery Channing. He cautioned that some things were worse than slavery and worried that abolition might turn the slaves into "idle and sensual savages." Thus he believed in African colonization, which upheld the rule of law and had a chance of being acceptable to Southerners. His son later judged that the Civil War refuted the conservative temporizers and radical abolitionists alike, working out the divine will to free the slaves and save the Union simultaneously.[66]

Francis Greenwood Peabody had little acquaintance with blacks before 1890 when Robert Ogden, a trustee of Hampton Institute in Washington, DC, asked him to join Hampton's board of trustees. Founded in 1868 by a former lieutenant-colonel of the ninth US Colored Troops regiment of the Union army, Samuel Chapman

Armstrong, the Hampton Institute was a vocational school for blacks (and, by 1878, Native Americans) that stressed "hand, head, and heart" (vocation, academics, and faith). In the morning students attended academic classes and chapel; in the afternoon they were trained in blacksmithing, carpentry, cooking, dressmaking, farming, laundering, sewing, or shoemaking. Peabody fell in love with the school, believing it was exactly what blacks needed to become self-reliant and productive: "Hampton Institute is essentially a spiritual enterprise, conceived as a form of missionary service, perpetuated as a school of character, and maintained by a long series of self-sacrificing teachers." He liked the saying of Tuskagee principal Booker T. Washington, a Hampton graduate: "A country which was not safe with ignorant slaves cannot be safe with ignorant freemen."[67]

American liberal Protestantism played a large role in making Washington famous. In 1899 Lyman Abbott, editor of the *Outlook*, invited Washington to tell his personal story; the result, composed by Washington, Abbott, and ghostwriter Max Bennett Thrasher, became a classic of American autobiography: *Up from Slavery*. The book was serialized to the *Outlook's* 100,000 subscribers and established the model of a black leader for much of black and white America. *The Outlook* praised Washington effusively for years afterward, and took strong exception when Du Bois criticized him for selling out the rights of blacks to higher education and equal standing before the law.[68]

The key to the controversy, Abbott explained in the *Outlook*, was that Du Bois was ashamed of his race. Du Bois made the white man the standard, but Washington looked for a standard in the ideals of his own race. Du Bois sought social equality for blacks, but Washington was too self-respecting for that. Du Bois was university-oriented, but Washington emphasized industrial schools. Du Bois wanted blacks to read the Ten Commandments in Hebrew; Washington wanted blacks to obey them in English. Du Bois tried to push his race into a higher place; Washington sought to make the race stronger. Du Bois demanded the right to vote; Washington sought to make blacks competent for the duties of citizenship.[69]

Peabody was too gentlemanly to put it that stridently, but he stood with Abbott, Washington, and Hampton: the crucial task was to train "a backward race for citizenship." His many years of sincere effort on behalf of African-American advancement did not curtail his patronizing attitude toward black Americans. Peabody wrote that Americans of African descent were instilled with so much docility as to be easily exploited and a danger to themselves: "The habits of slavery had discouraged self-reliance, persistency, and initiative; false notions of liberty had encouraged the childlike impression that freedom meant freedom from work." In brief, black Americans suffered from debilitating "native and inbred deficiencies." Yet they also demonstrated "racial qualities" on which a "firm civilization" could be built, albeit very slowly: "Teachableness, gratitude, absence of resentment and animosity, a rare gift of playfulness and humor, and above all a dominant strain of genuine, even if emotional, religion – these were traits which had in them great possibilities both of character and of capacity." Peabody recalled that many slaves, remarkably, fought for the Confederacy. A race that remained loyal even to slave-owners "might be trusted to exhibit similar loyalty to teachers and friends." A race that was brave enough to make good soldiers "might be willing to wrestle with the rudiments of education." And a race that showed religious feeling "might be led to develop an unstable and intermittent piety into a rational and ethical faith."[70]

Peabody was willing to offend his white audiences when they denied that blacks were educable, or when they fantasized about colonizing African Americans in a

"Negro state" (Texas was the usual candidate). He could speak with feeling about the humanity of blacks, but always with a whiff of white supremacy and a stream of stereotypes. To him it was obvious that the justice issues pressed by Du Bois were distracting luxuries. Training for a trade was the overwhelming need: "There is but one way out of what is called the Negro Problem – it is the way that leads up." Peabody assured readers that he was against repression, which never ensured anyone's safety. The chief threats to American civilization were "those created either by a prevailing illiteracy or by an unassimilated culture." America needed to abolish black illiteracy without lurching to "top-heavy education," which was equally terrible in this case: "If a little knowledge is a dangerous thing, then a pretence of knowledge is, to the fertile imagination and ready tongue of the Negro, hardly less dangerous."[71]

Retreating to the Seminaries

Meanwhile at the citadels of top-heavy education, social science broke into a plethora of professions and scientific disciplines that went their own way. Instead of a unified social science operating on behalf of ethical reforms, the disciplines staked out their professional or scientific turf, usually with no ethics. In 1870 the National Prison Association broke away; in 1874 the National Conference of Charities and Corrections followed suit; in 1884 the American Historical Society declared its independence as a science; in 1885 the American Economic Association affirmed Ely's reform orientation at its founding, but, by the turn of the century, it had dropped ethics and reform. In 1888 the American Statistical Association was founded. The next year the American Academy of Social and Political Science was founded. In 1903 the American Sociological Society was founded. Two years later the American Sociological Association was launched, finishing off the American Social Science Association, which went out of business in 1909. All the new disciplines declared that they possessed the method, boundaries, and status of a science; thus they took leave of squishy ethical concerns. The phase in which the social sciences had a social philosophy was over; if sociology was really a science, it did not need a philosophy, even a moral one.[72]

This turn of events proved to be devastating for the original idea of social ethics, but at Harvard the social ethics idea seemed to be winning nonetheless. Peabody's courses were popular, by 1903 he had a wealthy benefactor, and by 1905 he had a department and a sprawling "Social Museum" of his own. His benefactor, Alfred Tredway White, owned innovative low-cost housing projects in Brooklyn, which provided 2,000 tenants with dwellings of unusually high quality. Peabody arranged a meeting with White after hearing of his work. He later recalled, "It was on my part a case of love at first sight, and on his part the beginning of forty years of devoted friendship." Peabody found a soulmate in the rich, gentlemanly, pious, Unitarian, philanthropic White:

> There were few incidents in my own religious life so appealing and tranquilizing as the family worship shared in his home before the busy day's work began. He was blessed with a most lovely and devoted wife, of the same rational faith and the same complete dedication to generous thoughts and deeds, and his home life has been to many a guest a lesson in the simplicity which is in Christ. Indeed, it was more than once a matter of playful discussion among friends whether Mr. or Mrs. White was the more perfect in character – a debate which never reached a conclusive decision.[73]

White was so humble and quiet that it took Peabody several years to realize "his vigor of thought or strength of will." That was the period in which White gave nearly $300,000 to Harvard. One morning in 1905, sitting by the fire after breakfast in White's home, White asked Peabody what he could do to help college students become stewards of the public good. Peabody replied that Harvard needed $50,000 to build Emerson Hall for the philosophy department, and if White provided the money, he could demand *pro rata* space for Peabody's enterprise. A few days later Harvard had the money, to the astonishment of the philosophy department. Successive gifts endowed the Social Ethics Department and Peabody's Social Museum, which contained charts, maps, photographs, and models illustrating social conditions and reform efforts in Europe and the USA. Housed on the second floor of Emerson Hall, the museum had a library of over 3,000 books when Peabody retired in 1913; by 1920 it held over 10,000 artifacts. Peabody's purpose in building the museum was to promote scientific understanding and ethical idealism, exemplifying social ethics. He explained: "To interpret nature one must, first of all, see, touch, scrutinize, and analyze. The laboratory, the dissecting table, the clinic, the microscope, the museum, are the instruments of sound learning." But mere knowledge was a mere beginning; inspiration leading to ethical commitment was also needed. Peabody hoped the museum would instill a sense of "companionship" and "sympathy" in students, verifying "the faith of ethical idealists."[74]

Some of Peabody's faculty colleagues, although grateful for Emerson Hall, found its second floor an embarrassment. Philosophy chair Hugo Münsterberg, an occupant of the ground floor, was anxious not to be linked with Peabody's "special department" above. To Münsterberg, social ethics and its museum were a waste of academic space; moreover, he disliked the flow of visitors to the museum, which disrupted the solitude of the philosophers. With as much tact as he could muster, he told Peabody that social ethics stood on the "periphery" of Harvard's real business, and that he worried that it gave "too much the real stamp to the whole building." Harvard economist Frank Taussig had similar misgivings. A bitter opponent of historical economics, which replaced the deductive classicism of David Ricardo and John Stuart Mill with inductive studies of how economies actually worked, Taussig contended that if economics was a science it had to have abstract laws of supply and demand, rent, wages, and value (although he allowed for marginalist corrections of classical theory). In departmental politics he lamented that Peabody's strange field held back the development of sociology at Harvard. For 40 years Harvard's only sociology course was taught in the economics department; Harvard had no sociology department until 1931. Taussig pointed to the "hortatory flavor" of social ethics, which undermined the "cold dry atmosphere of science." Because social ethics was so influential, Harvard was slow to develop a real discipline of sociology.[75]

There was also the fact that social ethics was Christian and theological. Peabody's signature work was an exposition of the teaching of Jesus, and his seminars bore such titles as "The Ethics of Jesus Christ," "The Ethical Teaching of the New Testament," and "Christian Ethics and Modern Life." *The Harvard Bulletin*, announcing White's major gift in 1905, noted gently that the Christian content of Peabody's teaching and scholarship was not universally admired on Harvard's faculty. For his part, Peabody made no apology for holding back the "cold dry" variety of sociology at Harvard. In *The Approach to the Social Question* he compared sociology to "dirigible ballooning," which, though attractive to inventive minds, still grappled confusedly with "great difficulties of balance and steering, and remains for the present very much in air."[76]

Eliot told White that his support of Peabody's work would make social ethics "permanent at Harvard University." Peabody trusted that was true. But permanence was a tall order, especially for an enterprise that grated on faculty colleagues. In his later career Peabody guided the social ethics department to emphasize professional social work, and when he retired he chose two specialists on social work and legislative reform, Robert F. Foerster and James Ford, to be his successors. From 1913 to 1920 the department of social ethics taught courses on welfare administration, housing, rural development, race and immigration, and temperance, in addition to Peabody's introductory course. All had a decidedly professional bent, including the introductory course. The program focused on the college; its approach to divorce and temperance dropped Peabody's Christian framework; the Christian origin of social ethics faded from view; even the ethical considerations were minimized. In the introductory course, ethics shrank to a single text by John Dewey and James Tufts.[77]

Harvard president A. Lawrence Lowell probably would have shipped the entire operation to the Divinity School if White had not insisted that college students needed ethical instruction. But if that was the point, the new social ethicists were failing to do their job. In 1918 Lowell took a half-step by splitting social ethics between the Divinity School and the college. The following year he appointed Harvard's charismatic professor of clinical medicine, Richard Clarke Cabot, to teach ethics to college students. In 1920 Cabot reorganized the department to restore its emphasis on the ethical *ought*. Cabot had recently returned from active duty in World War I, during which he had resolved that an education with no moral foundation was not a blessing. With enthusiasm he took over the social ethics department, pledging to restore its no longer fashionable mission to nurture moral feeling in Harvard undergraduates. Cabot invited overcomers to class who told their stories of triumph over adversity. He had students read biographies of heroic figures to inspire their own moral idealism. In 1927 Peabody enthused that Cabot's "fertile genius" revived the social ethics program and regained its emphasis on moral idealism, although Peabody surely understood that Cabot lacked his academic ambitions for the discipline. Peabody conceived social ethics as an inductive enterprise of ethical reflection within the organic processes of social evolution, but Cabot was an Emersonian individualist. Peabody taught his students an ethical system, but Cabot moved straight to concrete ethical challenges, assuming the existence of right and wrong.[78]

That approach regained some of the department's former popularity among Harvard undergraduates, but it was not a way to build a discipline of social ethics. Realizing that he was getting nowhere professionally, Foerster moved to Princeton in 1922 to teach economics, and Ford spent most of his time in Washington DC, directing Better Homes in America. Cabot attracted promising instructors, notably psychologist Gordon Allport, but they departed too. Cabot's success was personal, not academic, and in 1927 the faculty established a concentration in sociology and social ethics, stripping social ethics of its independence. Three years later Harvard hired a formidable sociologist, Pitirim Sorokin, to chair the committee on the sociology/social ethics concentration, who quickly disposed of social ethics. In 1930 the program still had a few faculty supporters: Cabot, Ford, Allport (who had joined the psychology department), and philosopher Ralph Barton Perry. The Divinity School looked the other way. Allport tried to persuade Sorokin that the Peabody tradition at Harvard had special value and charms, but Sorokin had no interest in sharing his department with it. Social ethics could go its own way or be absorbed by a new department, sociology. In 1931 the faculty opted for absorption, creating a self-standing sociology department. Some of the old social ethics courses hung on for a few years, but the social ethics department was no more, and soon the courses were gone too.[79]

Getting Peabody Right

The failure of Peabody's disciplinary dream and the flaws of his late Victorian, sometimes patronizing voice of privilege conspired against him after the social gospel era. Though he was an important and in many ways admirable champion of the social gospel, he received little mention when the social gospel was recalled. When his chief achievement was remembered, it was usually construed wrongly. Aaron I. Abell contended that social ethics was merely the faith of the social gospel in academic dress. Gladys Bryson contended that it was merely an extension of moral philosophy with a social scientific gloss. David Potts, in an otherwise valuable study of Peabody's career, extended Bryson's argument that Peabody merely renewed, not replaced, moral philosophy. The social sciences were out to discover new truths, Potts explained, but Peabody used these disciplines "to reaffirm traditional ethical and religious truths." That is, he used induction not to discover ethics, but to serve ethical beliefs that he assumed from the outset.[80]

Robert L. Church agreed that Peabody was a showcase example of the tendency to use social scientific rhetoric as a disguise for one's inability or refusal to take science seriously. Church took for granted that science was a disinterested, objective use of empirical method. By that standard, Peabody exemplified the confusion that many nineteenth-century academics found in switching from deductive to inductive reasoning. Church explained that "despite his use of the word 'inductive' and his introduction of 'scientific' methods, Francis G. Peabody sought no new principles from the facts he and his students examined but merely used the facts to reaffirm traditional *a priori* principles." In Church's telling, Peabody was significant as a prominent example of the confused, idealistic, not really academic social thought that "permeated student life in most American universities in the eighties and nineties." The social gospel skillfully captured and reflected the Progressive era. But yearning for a better society and understanding society were two different things; Church admonished, "Peabody's mixture of Paul's teachings in 1 Corinthians with the recent findings of social science merely exaggerated the kind of balance of old and new, of past and future, of realism and utopianism that existed in the minds of many progressives and in the Progressive Movement as a whole." The new sciences offered something new, an objective understanding of social relations, not a mixture of new and old ideas. Social ethics failed to win academic standing because it was short on "intellectual discipline" and the "new modes of thinking" that did prevail in the academy.[81]

Potts and Church wrote in the mid-1960s, when the layer-cake understanding of science still prevailed among historians. Illusions about scientific objectivity notwithstanding, they were not fair to Peabody's idea, or even his execution of it. James Dombrowski, writing in 1936, got it right, although Dombrowski immediately let his Marxism get in the way of fairly assessing what came of Peabody's method. Dombrowski observed that Peabody used the inductive method to develop general moral principles, not to isolate practical problems and solutions. Peabody did not assume his moral principles on a priori grounds; he worked seriously at finding them.

But he made no attempt to hide his apologetic intent in doing inductive research. For Peabody, Dombrowski explained rightly, the point was always to substantiate a moral interpretation of social evolution and to refute the pessimistic, degrading, reductionist view of the self of *laissez-faire* and socialist ideologies. All social facts were signs and expressions of a rational moral principle that Christianity called the divine will. Social reform movements were powered by the operation of this moral will. As a Marxist, Dombrowski rejected this idea of a grounding moral principle in the world, which smacked of "live and let live." If things really worked out for the better on their own, Dombrowski objected, there was no reason for a social ethicist not to be a social Darwinist. In the end, both views had the same "easy unwarranted optimism."[82]

But the social gospel had the gospel spirit too deeply to say that; Peabody's commitments to reform movements, activist government, cooperative economics, and moral idealism were the antithesis of social Darwinism. Always he espoused the Christian ideal of love as the motive power operative in reform movements and good religion. He worried about relativism, admitting that the social question was "as fluid and changeful, and often as turbid and violent as a rushing stream," but his ethical idealism was a bulwark against it. He perceived that the pragmatism of his friend William James shook the epistemological foundations of his own idealism, but contended that his emphasis on will, unlike that of James, did not lead to the poverty of mere empiricism, experimentalism, probabilism, and the denial of ideals. James, tied up in philosophical problems, stressed the will to believe and the authenticity of "first-hand" individual religion. Peabody, guided by his religious faith, stressed the will to help and the institutional character of social religion and ethical idealism.[83]

Though he took pride in launching social ethics and in eliminating Harvard's chapel requirement (coerced religion was bad religion, Peabody argued), he did not like the phrase "Christian sociology." To Peabody, "Christian sociology" cheapened both terms, in the manner of "Christian astronomy" or "Christian chemistry." For the same reason he did not care for "Christian economics" or "Christian socialism." But he was enormously fond of Graham Taylor, who wore "Christian sociology" as a hard-earned badge of honor. The idea that Peabody shared with Tucker and Taylor, social ethics, was a new thing. It grew out of moral philosophy and was deeply wedded to the social gospel, but it was something different from moral philosophy and it belonged to the academy, where it outlasted the social gospel.[84]

Christian Sociology: Graham Taylor

By religious background and temperament Graham Taylor was an unlikely candidate for liberal theology or social Christianity, yet he came to epitomize, for many, the liberal social gospel. He was born in 1851 in Schenectady, New York, where his father William Taylor was a fourth generation Dutch Reformed pastor. Taylor's mother died the following year, shortly afterward the family moved to Philadelphia, and William Taylor married his departed wife's sister. The family moved to what Taylor would always count as his childhood home, New Brunswick, New Jersey, when he was 11 years old; six years later it moved to Newark, New Jersey.

In his telling, his father practiced a gentle version of a forbidding and repressive family religion. Taylor found most Reformed preachers severe, a bearing that even his father assumed when mounting the pulpit. For years Taylor brooded over the contrast between his family's warm piety and the severity of its denominational theology; often he sought assurance from his father that God was a merciful father, not a wrathful judge. Thus he delayed joining the church until he was 15, when his father nudged him to affirm his infant baptism.[85]

Despite these youthful anxieties, which "might have repelled me from entering the ministry," Taylor never considered a different calling. Deeply bonded to his father, he followed William Taylor into the ministry and became his closest friend. Just as Jesus had come to show the Father, Taylor devoted his life to following Jesus, whom he knew through his father's preaching and example. Years later he recalled, "Thus my father became my theology, and his life and love the trellis over which the vine of mine grew upward."[86]

Taylor returned to New Brunswick for his college and seminary training, graduating from Rutgers College in 1870 and New Brunswick Theological Seminary in 1873. In college he studied botany indoors, chemistry with no laboratories, government with no mention of citizenship, and moral philosophy with no social dimension, all on the side; mostly he studied Latin, Greek, and Hebrew. Seminary was more of the same, with the liberal arts replaced by church government, homiletics, and Reformed Church constitution. As soon as he entered the ministry he felt that something terribly important was lacking in his education. Fifteen years later, upon beginning his academic career, Taylor felt it more acutely, "especially while initiating courses of study and practice that dealt with the social antecedents, surroundings, and relationships of fellow-men." Years later he reflected, "The failure of the then-prevalent classical curriculum to put the student in vital touch with his environment I have had reason very continuously to deplore ever since I was graduated."[87]

His first pastorate was in Hopewell, New York, a rural community where he was ordained shortly before marrying the daughter of a seminary professor. There he began to get social ideas, and a few liberal ones, mostly from reading the *Independent* (a popular Congregational newspaper) and Horace Bushnell, though Taylor's early preaching was conventionally evangelical. He gave revival sermons modeled on Dwight Moody's evangelism, and grew fond of saying that more heresy was lived than believed. Defying local custom he refused to make social distinctions between blacks and whites, and challenged his congregation's tight-fisted lack of benevolence giving and missionary work. But Taylor was not very good at "come to Jesus" preaching. He rationalized that he lacked the time to be an effective preacher; years later he implied that he choked on the Reformed emphasis on election and total depravity; in any case, his early sermons were laced with hellfire, his misgivings notwithstanding. Many years later, writing his memoir, Taylor read a few of his early sermons and burned them out of embarrassment. The memory of preaching such "red in tooth and claw" specimens to Hopewell farmers was painful to him, he wrote. His congregation had been at home in the natural world, but he had not comprehended that the world, being the object of God's love, was the subject of redemption.[88]

He gave seven years to Hopewell, gradually tempering his orthodoxy. Taylor could speak the language of election and imputation to believers, but not to seekers, outsiders, or troubled insiders. In 1880 he moved to Fourth Congregational Church of Hartford, Connecticut, which was nothing like the Dutch Reformed congregations of his youth. During his seminary years Taylor had enjoyed a close friendship with Chester Hartranft, a local pastor. After Hartranft became president of Hartford

Theological Seminary, he looked for a way to bring Taylor to Hartford; Fourth Church was the answer.

Hartford was the home of Pratt and Whitney tool and machine makers, the Samuel Colt firearms plant, and the nation's top insurance companies. Half of its population of 42,000 was foreign-born and mostly poor. Fourth Congregational, located on Main Street at the center of the city, had an illustrious past. A legendary pastor, William Patton, had preached against slavery from the pulpit, and the church had a heritage of temperance and women's suffrage activism. By 1880 Fourth Church shared in the pride of local Congregationalists that Horace Bushnell's lonely, embattled, prophetic career had taken place in Hartford, at North Congregational Church. Taylor felt immediately the theological influence of Bushnell, who died in 1875. He vowed to study German, hoping to impress his cosmopolitan congregation with the latest in German biblical criticism.[89]

But Fourth Church had declined precipitously, partly because it had no history of welcoming or helping the lower classes of Hartford, especially recent immigrants. Like its neighboring Protestant churches, Fourth Church had a long history of assuring itself that poverty went hand in hand with laziness, weakness, and crime. Bushnell had a conscience about class snobbery, as he showed occasionally from the pulpit, but he could be quoted the other way too, validating the prejudices of Hartford's polite society. This legacy had everything to do with the crisis of Hartford Protestantism, especially Fourth Church, in the decade before Taylor arrived.

In the 1870s wealthy Protestants fled to the suburbs, avoiding the rapidly growing industrialism and the foreign-born workers who toiled in the factories. The established congregations that remained in the city usually ignored their new neighbors, or ran from them, following the well-to-do to the suburbs. One of Taylor's predecessors at Fourth Church, Nathaniel Burton, took many parishioners with him in 1870 when he moved to a new structure on the edge of Bushnell Park. At least that was still in the city, although Burton, like his prominent Congregational colleagues Edwin Pond Parker (South Congregational Church) and Joseph Twichell (Asylum Hill Congregational Church) preached the gospel of avoiding the poor and lowly.

All three of Taylor's new Congregational colleagues were thoughtful, articulate, mannered, genial, and attuned to the Gilded Age. They took for granted that Fourth Church was dying. The sanctuary, built for 1,200, typically housed less than 50 worshippers on Sundays. Inheriting a church roll of 542 names, Taylor determined that 218 were real, few of them from the church's old guard. Most of Taylor's dwindling congregation consisted of firefighters, police officers, mechanics, day laborers, and small merchants. To them, and the old guard parishioners who remained, Taylor delivered a blunt message. The church had to evangelize the vast array of "poor and delinquent people" who lived there, otherwise it would die, deservedly. Taylor banked on the church's progressive legacy, reasoning that the remaining old guarders would recognize the necessity of reinventing their congregation. The central city district in which Fourth Church was located was home to 75 percent of the city's poor. He later recalled: "Their need to be served appealed to me so much more than serving the church that I challenged it to devote itself to the people surrounding it as the only hope of saving itself."[90]

Taylor launched a battery of prayer groups, Bible studies, discussion groups, and outreach activities to renew Fourth Church. He preached revival, inviting noted evangelists to Hartford. In 1880 it was still possible for a celebrity preacher like Moody to draw large crowds in Hartford; Moody conducted a successful Hartford revival in 1878. But Taylor was still a dismal revival preacher and the professionals that he brought to Hartford fared no better. Most Hartford ministers looked down on revival preaching and evangelical missions as a whole. To them it was a matter of self-respect; Hartford had outgrown "come to Jesus" religion. Undaunted, Taylor tried to forge an alliance with the City Missionary Society, a spin-off of Charles Finney's Hartford revival of 1852 that ministered to the city's poor. But his ambitions were too grandiose for the group's traditional street ministry; Taylor got nowhere with the YMCA and YWCA; and he struck out with an interdenominational gathering of Hartford pastors. As a last resort he returned to the Congregational ministers, proposing a Pastor's Mission to evangelize and serve the city's lower classes. Parker rudely told him to get lost, but Taylor persuaded Twichell to join him, and the two engendered enough support from the Congregational Pastors' Union to launch the mission at Fourth Church.[91]

Taylor later recalled, "To me the duty of the hour called for a democratic evangelism, in which my people were better prepared to follow than I was to lead. The more my preaching scaled to previous standards, the less it attracted those without." Hiring an evangelist, Henry Gillette, who had recently conducted a thorough canvass for the Connecticut Bible Society, Taylor and Gillette waged an exhausting campaign of door-to-door evangelism, making thousands of personal calls per year. They reached out to unchurched tenement-dwellers, shopkeepers, prostitutes, police officers, firefighters, local prisoners, state prisoners in nearby Wethersfield, and alcoholics. Most of the work consisted of pastoral counseling and evangelism, in addition to helping people find jobs and living quarters and deal with the city court. Taylor's hard work paid off for Fourth Church; by 1883 the congregation's average Sunday attendance was over 400. "We went out to find the people where they were," he recollected. He and Gillette conducted outdoor services on street corners, the local baseball stadium, and the church porch, taking pride that his stadium services rivaled local sporting events for attendance. They launched a Sunday evening service featuring personal testimonies. Reformed alcoholics, former prisoners, and ex-gamblers streamed into Fourth Church, causing appalled Hartford observers to call it "the church for ex-convicts."[92]

By 1884 Taylor was eager to compare notes with other social ministry pioneers. He traveled to New York to meet with Henry Schauffler of the Congregational Home Missionary Society and William Rainsford of St George's Episcopal Church. The following year he attended Josiah Strong's Inter-Denominational Congress in Cincinnati, savoring speeches by Strong, Ely, Gladden, and Lyman Abbott. On the same trip he studied the Congregational and YMCA social ministries in Chicago, exulting at Dwight Moody's Chicago Avenue Tabernacle. Back in Hartford he brought lost souls to his home, where his wife Leah Demarest Taylor cheerfully fed and clothed strangers alongside her four children. Taylor also rescued alcoholic backsliders at local saloons. Horace Bushnell's widow, Mary Bushnell, contributed generously to Taylor's projects and became a treasured friend; Charles E. Stowe, a Congregational pastor and son of Harriet Beecher Stowe, became another close friend. Taylor told his father that he received rather frosty treatment from polite society, and that most of his ministerial colleagues found it unseemly for a pastor to troll in the slums for members. One of his breakthrough ideas, encouraged by Chester Hartranft, was to recruit student volunteers from Hartford Seminary, which expanded the mission's programs and inadvertently put Taylor on a new career track.[93]

In 1888 Hartford Seminary offered him a professorship in practical theology. Taylor later called it the greatest surprise of his life, notwithstanding that he served as a seminary trustee, his friend was the president, his congregation employed many seminarians, and he was acquiring a national reputation as a social minister. Taylor worried that he lacked the academic training to be a seminary professor; Hartranft replied that he was actually doing practical theology, which made him uniquely qualified to teach it. Taylor had additional misgivings. Theologically he was more conservative than the Hartford Congregational ministers, which made him doubt that he could be a seminary professor in liberal New England. He later recalled that Hartford liberalism "seemed to me to be destructive to the very foundations of the faith 'once delivered.'" He had trouble even understanding liberal theology, much less accepting it. On the other hand, he was moving in that direction, he admired Horace Bushnell, Hartford Seminary had a reactionary past, and its current faculty was cool toward Taylor's democratic evangelism. Between the Hartford ministers and Hartford Seminary there was a vast gulf, charged with bitter feeling. Taylor doubted that he was called to bridge the gulf, and he was determined not to give up his ministry or base of support at Fourth Church.[94]

Mary Bushnell helped him decide, paying a call that Taylor described as motherly and angelic. She told him that even though Hartford Seminary had attacked her husband for decades, she liked the thought of Taylor having an impact on Hartford seminarians. Toward that end she gave him 12 copies of Bushnell's *Christian Nurture* to use with his students. Taylor accepted the post under the condition of being allowed to keep his pastorate; he wanted to use Fourth Church as a social ministry laboratory for his students. The Congregational ministers, however, vehemently opposed that solution, charging that Taylor lusted for power and influence. Even his colleagues in the Pastors' Mission admonished him harshly, threatening to withdraw their financial support. That strengthened Taylor's resolve to hold both positions, which he began in September 1888. Many years later he noted that his appointment reflected a significant turn in American Christianity, showing the rapidly growing influence of the social gospel.[95]

He taught courses in pastoral care, homiletics, pastoral administration, church polity, and Christian sociology, in addition to supervising the fieldwork program. In his inaugural address Taylor observed that the pulpit was "no longer the only fulcrum of the Church's power." Effective ministry also included religious education, evangelistic missions, temperance work, charity organizations, and other forms of social ministry: "The channel through which life is now sweeping is less individualistic than sociological in its formation. All human life and interests, industrial and political, intellectual and spiritual . . . contribute toward the pull of this social gravity." Heredity and social environment were major factors in personal and social redemption, he stressed. To understand the causes of poverty, alcoholism, and crime, one had to make use of the new social sciences. If the church wanted social science to be Christian, not godless, "she must formulate a Christian Sociology, and train her leaders and people in it."[96]

For Taylor, the essential thing was to use sociology for Christian purposes, thus advancing sociology and Christianity. The American Social Science Association's commitment to a unified and ethical social science was beyond his purview; what mattered was to Christianize sociology for theological education. He was vaguely aware that Peabody and Tucker had preceded him, but did not know how they went about it: "No syllabi came from these seminary or any other classrooms to guide me in the preparation of my own initial courses." Taylor expected to use Spencer's popular *Studies in Sociology*, which appeared in 1873, but upon reading it found that the book was "more of a foil against which to strike" than an aid to Christian sociology. Spencer was too mechanistic to be a guide to social relationality, process, and personal will, and his social Darwinism was morally repugnant.[97]

Fortunately, the literature of social Christianity was growing rapidly. Taylor relied on Ely's books, especially *Social Aspects of Christianity and Other Essays* (1889), and Gladden's books, especially *Working People and their Employers* (1876) and *Applied Christianity: The Moral Aspects of Social Questions* (1886). Gladden convinced him that one could embrace the liberal social gospel with no loss of evangelical faith. As an author, pastor, and movement leader, Gladden became Taylor's teacher and role model; later they also became friends; still later Taylor put Gladden in the category of William Taylor and Chester Hartranft: "He became a father in God to me." Taylor loved Gladden's hymn, "O Master, let me walk with thee," and he adopted Gladden's signature theme that personal and social salvation were indispensable to each other.[98]

In the category of "theology for preaching," Taylor favored Gladden, Bushnell, and Henry Ward Beecher. In his courses he assigned J. R. Seeley's *Ecce Homo: A Survey of the Life and Work of Jesus Christ* (1866), which humanized the gospel story; J. B. Mozley's *Ruling Ideas in Early Ages* (1877), which favored "the ancient race consciousness" over modern individualism; Josiah Strong's *Our Country* (1885), which combined social Christianity with manifest destiny; and English Anglican William H. Fremantle's *The World as the Subject of Redemption* (1885), which convinced Taylor that social salvation was biblical, not merely a modern viewpoint. Taylor played up Mozley's and Fremantle's solidaristic language of the "human race" while quietly straining out Strong's *apologia* for world conquering Anglo-Saxonism. He embraced Fremantle's thesis that "one soul at a time" evangelism fell short of the Christian ideal, exhorting his students to be "world-savers" like Fremantle.[99]

He was not a polished classroom performer, nor a careful scholar. Taylor often rushed late to class, always peppered his lectures with anecdotes from his pastoral experiences, and usually held his students' attention with stream of consciousness comments about ministering in the real world. One student remembered of Taylor's Hartford years that he was "the most irregular lecturer academically that I ever knew . . . but we learned something that we never could have learned in any other way."[100]

In 1892 Taylor was invited to speak at Chicago Theological Seminary (CTS), which proved to be a set-up. A wealthy benefactor had challenged CTS to raise $350,000, promising a $100,000 bequest for doing so. Samuel Ives Curtis, a professor of Old Testament and the seminary's finance committee chair, had a strategy: invite Taylor to establish the nation's first department of Christian sociology at CTS. On his way home from the lecture, Taylor wrote in his diary, "Xtn Sociology is God's door to all that can make the remainder of my life most effectual. Henceforth I seek that Kingdom of God first . . . But whither? E or W?" Back in Hartford, Taylor's colleagues and parishioners were incredulous that he might choose the West. Hartford was cultured, while Chicago was crude and half-civilized. How could there be any question? Faculty friend Clark Beardslee told him it would be a calamity for Hartford Seminary if he left. Hartranft started with guilt, admonishing Taylor that he owed much of his "present elevation" to Hartford Seminary; moved to a warning, that he would become lost in the "seething and chaotic mess" of Chicago; and ended with a counter-offer, a department of Christian sociology at Hartford.[101]

When he reread these letters 38 years later, Taylor marveled that his heart yielded to his head, after months of wavering. During the wavering Ives journeyed to Hartford to press the case for CTS, presenting over 100 pages of reasons why Taylor should choose the greater freedom, opportunity, and challenge of Chicago. Later he sent a telegram that pushed Taylor over the edge: "The Kingdom is one. God knows neither East nor West. The decisive question is where one can be most useful."[102]

Hartford Seminary was hampered by its reactionary heritage and conservative aftermath. Because the seminary's financial constituency was mostly conservative, it could move only so far in a liberal direction. Taylor chose the "unrestricted liberty" of Chicago, joining a vast surge of old and new Americans in moving there. The great fire of 1871 had destroyed the heart of the city and a large section of its north side, but by 1880 Chicago was roaring again. Streams of Slovaks, Poles, Italians and Russian Jews came to Chicago to compete with German and Irish settlers for jobs, compounding the city's volatile labor problems; by 1890 its population exceeded 1,000,000. Taylor arrived in 1892, witnessing the construction of buildings for the World's Fair and the launching of the University of Chicago, which established the world's first department of sociology. The gray Gothic towers of William Rainey Harper's university were erected on the same land – the Midway Plaisance – that housed the gigantic Ferris wheel and other attractions of the 1893 World's Columbian Exposition. Although Taylor was eager to immerse himself in the city, he spent his first year on the fund-raising trail, raising the $350,000 that the seminary needed to get the $100,000 that would pay for his new department.[103]

For 12 months he spoke in churches, state associations, and colleges across the USA, explaining why American Protestantism needed seminary departments of Christian sociology. The church could not build the kingdom of God if its pastors were not trained in Christian sociology, he implored. The emergence of Christian sociology reflected "the rise of a mighty social movement within the churches, which, while quiet, unrecognized, and hardly conscious of its own existence as yet, is deep, pervasive, intensely practical, eager to learn, and destined to prevail." Taylor vowed that if he were allowed to lead such a department at CTS, his primary texts would be "the street, the shop, the school, the mission." He also expected to establish a settlement house where seminarians would live among working-class people and understand the industrial revolution from their perspective. Within a year he had exceeded the fund-raising goal for his department, and he dreamed of establishing many settlement houses.[104]

Taylor had read about the first settlement house experiment (Toynbee Hall in England, founded in 1884) and probably knew that Stanton Coit, after living in Toynbee Hall, had founded the first American settlement house in the USA (Neighborhood Guild in New York) in 1886. Coit's subsequent book *Neighborhood Guilds: An Instrument of Social Reform* (1891) became a personal favorite of Taylor's. Upon moving to Chicago Taylor became friends with Jane Addams, who had founded Hull House in 1889 after visiting Toynbee Hall. He judged that she had the settlement idea exactly right: "In the personality of Jane Addams, living on the corner of Polk and Halsted streets, I found a personification of spiritual and social ideals, dwelling in simple, natural, neighborly, human relations with her cosmopolitan neighbors, and exerting far-flung influences over the more privileged classes." Addams was generous and idealistic, Taylor later recalled: "When I was a stranger she took me in, stranger though I was to her except in the fellowship of kindred faith. And I have never since gone out beyond the reach of her friendly counsel, or beyond the range of her varied experience and world-wide sympathies." But Addams was also tough-minded, strong, and realistic. She understood that Hull House struck its neighbors as a strange undertaking, and sometimes a threatening one. She worked diligently to overcome both impressions without allowing herself or her fellow residents to be bullied. She practiced cooperation, avoided using her class privileges to get her way, and called her neighbors "neighbors," not "the poor." That was the model that Taylor had in mind for CTS's settlement house.[105]

The seminary's trustees, however, told Taylor that he would have to wait for one, pleading lack of money. Taylor could not stand to wait, especially in the depression of 1893 and the desperate aftermath of the World's Fair. Huge numbers of homeless, hungry men and women, many of them former construction workers at the fair grounds, slept in the parks and begged for food, shivering from the freezing winds blowing off Lake Michigan. Taylor walked the streets and gazed at the haunting faces of poverty and neglect:

> I found them sleeping on the bare floors of miserable lodging-houses and barrel-house saloons, in the corridors of police-station cell rooms, on the stone floors and stairways of the old City Hall, as well as wandering about the streets begging for a dime, as the last chance to get under shelter for the night. Then for the first time I imagined what an inconceivable experience it must be not to have, or know how to find, a place to sleep through the night already darkening down upon one.[106]

In that mood he bought a settlement house of his own, declaring that he was determined to teach Christian sociology "from the ground up and not from the clouds down." Taylor decided that the house had to be large enough to accommodate a dozen residents, including his four children, and neighborhood gatherings. He settled on a run-down brick house in Chicago's Seventeenth Ward, a working-class district of congested tenements, unpaved alleys, and sporadically collected garbage. Located at the corner of Union Street and Milwaukee Avenue, the house was neighbored by boarding houses and small factories, in a district crowded with German, Irish, and Scandinavian immigrants. In the company of four seminary students, Taylor and his family moved into the house in October 1894. He later recalled that he took a missionary attitude, taking on "what missionaries' families had never failed to do in following the cross to any land or people. There we gathered successive groups of resident workers around our family circle to constitute a living link which might help relate more closely the classes so widely separated by the social cleavage."[107]

At first the house and community had no name, while CTS demanded one for its public relations. Taylor fumbled with variations on "commonwealth," the idea of "sharing what each can be to all and what all can be to each." In one of his versions of what happened, a business acquaintance named Edward Cragin blurted out to him in an elevator, on the day of CTS's deadline for a name, "Call it Chicago Commons!" In Taylor's other version, Cragin provided "commons" and Curtiss insisted on putting "Chicago" in the name. For Taylor the Chicago Commons was a personal sociological laboratory that, for 44 years, grounded his social Christian activism: teaching social ethics, establishing a training school for social workers, writing articles and a weekly column, winning the trust of puzzled neighbors in the Seventeenth Ward, arbitrating labor disputes, preaching progressive religion, and advocating civic reforms.[108]

By 1910 there were approximately 400 settlements in the USA, nearly a third of them in Chicago. For liberals seeking an alternative to bitter class politics, the settlement example of Addams and Taylor offered a compelling model. From 1896 to 1905 Taylor published a monthly magazine of settlement movement news and opinion, *The Commons*. In 1905 it merged with *Charities*, published by the New York Charity Organization Society, to form *Charities and The Commons*, for which Taylor served as associate editor. In 1909 the magazine evolved into a weekly, *The Survey*, for which Taylor served as Chicago director, associate editor, and frequent contributor. In addition, from 1902 to 1938 Taylor wrote a weekly column for the Chicago *Daily News*, dispensing his views on civic reform, politics, neighborhood issues, labor unions, and the rights of immigrants. In 1895 he founded the School of Social Economics, housed at the Chicago Commons, which offered the nation's first course offerings in social work. In 1903 this program evolved into the Social Science Center for Practical Training in Philanthropic and Social Work, the nation's first yearlong social work educational program, which trained young women and men for positions in settlements and social agencies. In 1908 Taylor changed the school's name to the Chicago School of Civics and Philanthropy, which was absorbed by the University of Chicago in 1920 and renamed the School of Social Service Administration. Taylor was also actively involved in the Chicago Civic Federation, the Municipal Voters' League, the Chicago Plan Commission, and the Vice Commission, as well as the Federal Council of Churches, the National Congregational Council, the International Congregational Council, the Chautauqua Society, the Men and Religion Forward Movement, the National Federation of Churches and Christian Workers, and the short-lived American Institute of Christian Sociology.[109]

The Social Gospel in the Classroom and Public Square

Taylor had begun moving toward social gospel theology when he started his academic career at Hartford; by the time that he arrived in Chicago he was a liberal social gospeler through and through. His two inaugural addresses showed the difference. At Hartford he stressed the distinctive importance of the church as a redemptive force in society; at CTS he stressed that all social, civic, political, and economic institutions were essentially religious, being charged with building the kingdom on earth. At Hartford he stressed building up the church out of the community and defended the supernatural authority of scripture; at CTS he stressed the building of redeemed communities and embraced biblical criticism.[110]

In the classroom Taylor taught students to study social conditions, classify and analyze the relevant facts, and draw their own conclusions. His chief theme was the interdependence of family, church, business, government, and civil society. Besides directing CTS's fieldwork program, he taught a first-year course on "Biblical Sociology," a second-year course on "Economics of the Kingdom," and a third-year course in sociology. He also taught elective courses on social institutions, dependency, ethical aspects of industry, municipal reform, and crime; in 1905 he changed the name of his department to Social Economics.

His concept of Christian sociology had five parts. In the opening section of Biblical Sociology, Taylor expounded the social-ethical method of observation, classification and analysis, and synthesis. In his second section he traced the development of the kingdom idea and social institutions in Hebrew scripture. His third section described the social ideals of Jesus; the fourth section described the social ideals of early Christianity; and the final section applied the social concepts of the Bible to modern life, correlating the kingdom of God to the five spheres of modern existence: family, neighborhood, economics, politics, and religion. To Taylor, the kingdom of God was "the progressive realization in human experience and history of the divine ideal of relationship between man and God and man and man" within the five spheres.[111]

His reading lists kept up with a burgeoning social gospel movement, notably Peabody's *Jesus Christ and the Social Question*, Mathews' *Social Teaching of Jesus* (1897), and George Herron's *The New Redemption* (1893) and *The Christian State* (1895). Taylor exulted at the publication of W. D. P. Bliss' *Encyclopedia of Social Reform* (1897), the first work of its kind in the USA, and he continued to assign Gladden, Ely, Fremantle, and Seeley. After Rauschenbusch electrified the field with *Christianity and the Social Crisis* (1907), Taylor had a new favorite, without converting to Rauschenbusch's radical politics. Taylor began every class with whatever caught his attention on the way from the Commons to the seminary, and he ended with a comment on society or the cosmos as a system. He explained,

> I tried to start each course on some common ground shared by my students. Usually it was the Christian "burden of the soul," which I interpreted as a personal concern for the whole self of each man, woman, and child. Gradually we worked back into the antecedents and out into the social conditions which relate many others to every one of us. This led us farther afield than the parish and its more or less arbitrarily organized societies and agencies.[112]

He was a popular teacher whom students called "Doc" and admired for his humor, generosity, buoyant spirit, and, above all, living what he taught. One student observed,

> He starts like a Ford on a cold morning – on one cylinder – he halts and feels around for words, but after about ten minutes he is hitting on all four and runs like a Packard Twelve with intellect, will, emotion, and body in action. He is a torrent and a whirlwind, a great soul always driving on to a big destiny.[113]

William Rainey Harper found it strange that the world's first department of sociology did not make use of Taylor's expertise despite his proximity. In 1902 he asked Taylor to join the sociology department at Chicago as a full-time lecturer, promising a professorship in two years. Taylor's seminary colleagues warned that the religious character of his work would be lost if he joined the "businessmen" at Harper's university. For three years Taylor split the difference, teaching half-time at the seminary and half-time at the university, where his sociology colleagues were Albion Small, Charles Henderson, and Charles Zueblin. Small founded the department after a distinguished career as a political scientist and college president at Colby College. Taylor taught courses in philanthropy, the labor movement, and civic reformism, but after three years he judged that the university was not a good fit for him. Harper's death in 1906 may have sealed Taylor's decision not to continue there.[114]

Christian sociology at a liberal Christian seminary was his academic calling, though Taylor lamented that even at CTS he spent most of his time counteracting the individualism of his students. Routinely, he had to assure students that his subjects belonged in a seminary curriculum. Taylor later recalled that getting the students to read Gladden and Ely helped to overcome their "conventionally individualistic, if not otherworldly" idea of religion, but what really worked was sending them into Chicago's jails, police stations, courts, hospitals, and asylums. Best of all, every year he initiated a handful of students into the world of the urban poor at Chicago Commons, where "my students met submerged classes of people with whose individuals they should deal."[115]

CTS stood by Taylor when reactionaries charged, inevitably, that "Christian sociology" was a euphemism for socialism, excusing criminal behavior, and destroying the moral fiber of society. Chicago's leading financial journal, the *Chicago Chronicle*, labored this theme for years, as did a right-wing Republican paper, *Inter-Ocean*. At CTS chapel services the seminary's president, Franklin W. Fisk, prayed for Taylor's protection. CTS struggled financially through these years, and Taylor realized that it paid a financial price for harboring a nettlesome do-gooder and reformer. The price became more personal after Fisk retired in 1906. Reeling from a financial crisis, the seminary implored Taylor to accept the presidency. Repeatedly he refused, though he served as acting president in 1907–8. Taylor told friends that reactionary criticism rolled off him, but not his captivity to administrative tasks. His work was teaching, writing, and activism, not running a seminary.[116]

Daily News editor and publisher Victor Lawson agreed heartily. In 1902, during an especially bad spate of attacks on Taylor's reformism, Lawson hired him as a weekly columnist. The following year he paid Taylor's entire salary at the seminary, telling Fisk to inform conservative alumni that Taylor cost the seminary nothing that year. For three decades Taylor and Lawson had an unlikely, mutually admiring, deeply bonded relationship. Lawson was politically and theologically conservative, but he ran an open shop journalistically and greatly respected Taylor. Only after the publisher died in 1925 did Taylor learn that Lawson had been the mystery benefactor whose gift brought him to Chicago. Every week, unfailingly, for 23 years Taylor sent a weekly column to Lawson, sometimes from afar, always making sense of current debates over economic policies, politics, public schools and libraries, relief and correctional institutions, and reform movements.[117]

Though he wrote constantly for publication, Taylor told Addams that he did not aspire to book writing. After Addams published her memoir, *Twenty Years at Hull House*, in 1910, Taylor's friends urged him to do the same; for many years he declined. His first book, *Religion in Social Action* (1913), was a collection of *Survey* articles that Taylor published only because the magazine's editorial board wanted to offer something to new subscribers. In her introduction to the book Addams described Taylor as "an 'expert' adviser in the best sense of the term," one whose expertise was based on "his long familiarity with the men who are 'down and out,' both the vagrant and the criminal."[118]

Modestly Taylor protested that he wrote journalistic commentary, not books. *Religion in Social Action*, however, won an appreciative audience for its message that religion and life were "one and the same." Religion and human life were essentially alike in being mostly about relationships, he explained. The Bible was the story of the relationships between God and the human race; it was the book of life because it gave life through its narration of living relationships. In the Bible, especially John, faith was the "verb of action," the doing of the truth through which the nations were saved. To Taylor, the Bible and Christianity sanctioned various theologies, but a single ideal,

Godly life, which was "always and everywhere the same." Good religion was always about the flourishing of life in community: "It is short-sighted to ask whether you should work for the individual or for his surroundings and relationships. You cannot work for one without working for the other. You are not shut up to such a dilemma. You ought to work both ends of the line at once if you expect to meet the real man in the middle."[119]

Taylor stressed that love involved caring about the life of the beloved. To love him was to care whether his wife had the opportunity to stay at home to care for their children, whether the children had good schooling, whether the family had a decent house to live in, and whether the local environment was free of corruption, offering a wholesome influence on his children. Like all liberals of his generation, Taylor stressed the importance of "personality," the self as a unified center of spiritual consciousness. But he played up the social character of the self. Personality was not just the divinity-inspired soul of romanticism, transcendentalism, or idealism, for "even our self-consciousness is due in such part to others that it cannot be accounted for apart from them." Personality consisted in that which one shared with others. Just as there was no self-educated person, the "self-made" person of American mythology was an idolatrous illusion: "Those who think they have made themselves generally worship their maker." The appropriate response to being educated and nurtured by others was to serve others.[120]

Taylor decried the prevalence of dualistic religion, "trying to be religious individually while collectively we are pagan." Each person lived one life, not two, he urged. It was ridiculous to assign religion to private piety lacking any bearing on taxes, education, immigration, the family, or war: "This awful dualism is the ethical tragedy of the age." Taylor had a favorite story on this theme. At a speaking engagement he tried to win over a group of radical workers by explaining what religion was really about. Religion was the expression of a person's ideals, he contended; therefore, every person was religious. The workers wailed in protest; they were not religious and had never heard such a "reasonable definition" of religion. Taylor allowed that the church usually did not describe religion reasonably; nonetheless, what mattered was that good religion was about the flourishing of life in relationship. One did not have to be a Christian to be religious, but Christianity, rightly understood, was the religion of the ideals of Jesus. In Taylor's telling, "this humanized definition of religion so overcame their objection that some of these very men offered to organize and join a church, 'if it could be called by another name.'" Christianity had ruined the word "Christian" for these workers, but not the ideals of Jesus.[121]

Persistently he preached that salvation was personal and social, "you cannot work for one without working for the other." The social interpretation of religious feeling and action was not new, he assured; it was as old as "Thou shall love thy neighbor as thyself." He did not worry about social religion eroding religious feeling, for every sphere of life was charged with the sacred. Religion was essential to *all* life. Putting it with a flourish that sounded like Rauschenbusch, Taylor declared, "The gospel of the kingdom is sociology with God left in it, with the Messianic spirit as the bond of unity, with the new birth of the individual for the regeneration of society, and the dynamic spirit of religion as the only power adequate to fulfill its social ideals." There was still time to reclaim the Christian inspiration of sociology, he urged. Just as Christians were wrong to leave the struggle for social justice to secular socialists, they were wrong to let secular sociologists own sociology. The study of social relations got its birthright from Judaism and Christianity; rightly understood, sociology was "the science of the kingdom." Taylor wanted the modern church to use sociology to help fulfill "the covenants of promise in both testaments."[122]

Christian sociology perceived the soul in society, beginning with the family, which Taylor called "the primary cell of the whole social organism." Of all things human, he wrote, nothing was as close to divinity as the family, "the visible sign of all the invisible sanctities of religion." The social gospelers were earnest late-Victorians, believing deeply in the especially sacred character of family life. One of their main arguments against capitalism was that it drove mothers into the labor market. Taylor, Rauschenbusch, and Gladden supported women's suffrage, but cringed at mothers aspiring to professional careers. Taylor argued that because life was reproduced and the human race was perpetuated through the family, it shared "the creative prerogative of the life-giver." Thus, the first duty of religion was to "safeguard and promote the family." That entailed supporting the "parental instinct," providing maternity benefits for mothers trapped in the necessity of industrial labor, teaching sex education in the churches and public schools, and promoting the active cooperation of church, government, school, and neighborhood.[123]

In political economy Taylor supported profit-sharing, cooperative experiments, workplace safety, the abolition of child labor, social insurance, and a minimum wage that was more than "a mere living wage." On the labor/capital struggle he clung to Gladden's view of the 1880s, that the church should be a mediating "honest broker," not a partisan, although Gladden was basically pro-unionist by the 1890s. Taylor wanted the minister to be known as "a mass-man not a class-man," standing in between the capitalist and working classes and declaring "all ye are brethren." The job of the church was to keep the class struggle from exploding into a class war. Taylor allowed that modern churches were too divided to succeed. But that was why the social gospelers were ardent ecumenists. They viewed the reunification of the churches as an aspect of their mission to Christianize society and save the world. In 1908 they founded the Federal Council of Churches of Christ in America. Taylor urged that if the Federal Council united American Protestants as a social force, and the united Protestants linked arms with the Jewish and Roman Catholic faiths, the social situation would be very different. Organized religion would have the power to deal with America's organized economic interests, although Taylor preferred to speak of cooperating "with the organized industry of the American people." When that occurred, he asserted, the cause of peace and progress in America's "great democracy" would make a giant leap toward the kingdom of God.[124]

Seventeen years later, Taylor still chuckled at the memory that his old nemesis with a superior attitude in Hartford, Edwin Pond Parker, wrote a respectful review of *Religion in Social Action*. By 1913 the social gospel was so strong that even snobs like Parker had to accommodate it. With gratitude he recalled that Rauschenbusch highlighted his agreements with Taylor instead of chiding him for timidity. Rauschenbusch reported that he filled his copy of Taylor's book with marginal notes and signs; the book had so many apt statements "that it is hard to pass them by without some physical act of approbation." Gladden also praised the book, noting, with a knowing suggestion of his role in the transition, that Taylor had not lost his evangelical faith in converting to the social gospel: "What happened with him was only a change of emphasis, due to the discovery that religion is not a department of life, but that it included the whole of life − man in all his relations."[125]

Despite being drenched in politics and surrounded by partisan types, Taylor was not politically partisan. For most of his career he steered clear of party commitments in national politics in order to protect his influence in Chicago politics, where he took positions on a case-by-case basis. He was consistently anti *laissez-faire*, pro immigration, anti imperialist, anti corruption, and pro neighborhood, and he prized the trust that Chicago readers placed in him. On racial and religious prejudice he stressed that in any single form it nearly always led to other forms, and that white racism against blacks was especially toxic.

In 1908 hundreds of marauding white rioters in Springfield, Illinois set off a race riot that killed nine black Americans and seriously wounded 100 others. Taylor found it a "sorry comment upon American civilization" to have produced a "new race of white barbarians" which believed it had no means of protecting itself from black Americans "except the blood and fire of extermination." There were "barbarians" on both sides of the racial divide in Springfield and America, he allowed; however, the root cause of America's continuing racial pathology was the insistence of white Americans on isolating and holding down blacks. America's policy of racial repression was bound to produce "a crucifixion of its justice, humanity, and religion," such as occurred in Springfield. The Springfield rioters had to be punished, but more important, the USA had to build a civilization that eliminated white racism and civilized "our barbarians, both white and black."[126]

Taylor worked with black church and community leaders during the Great Migration to forge that better civilization. In 1910 the African-American population of Chicago was just over 44,000; by 1920 it was 110,000. Taylor was amply acquainted with what he called "the scare-head alarms of the white race's danger from 'the rising tide of color.'" He lamented that Chicago's experience proved "how readily partisan demagogues may array racial elements in a cosmopolitan population against each other." Stressing that race prejudice was evil in itself, he added that it also damaged every other aspect of the social fabric. In Chicago, the "heedlessness of some citizens toward the racial self-respect of others" made them easy prey for racist demagoguery.[127]

World War I had a dampening effect on racist fear mongering, Taylor observed, but afterward "this primitive, elemental instinct asserted itself all over the world," including Chicago. In July 1919 a group of white bathers threw stones at blacks whom they deemed had crowded too close to their area. A black youth drowned; gunfire erupted; rival gangs battled in a race riot that killed 38 people, wounded over 500 others, and set fire to many black dwellings. Citizens representing 48 civic, professional, and religious organizations gathered to deal with the aftermath of the riot; Taylor was appointed to the group's "Committee of Six" that negotiated with local and state officials. A decade later he judged that Chicago made very slow, but real and continual progress in race relations, partly because the black community raised up a new generation of community leaders such as physician George C. Hall, legislator Edward Morris, lawyer Adelbert Roberts, and minister Lacy K. Williams.[128]

Most of Taylor's friends were progressives, and by 1912 they were Progressives, anxious to establish a new party; Jane Addams, Charles Crane, William Kent, Charles Merriam, Mary McDowell and Raymond Robins were prominent among them. Taylor undoubtedly voted for Theodore Roosevelt in 1912, but he disliked the intense partisanship of the social worker movement. He wished that more of his social work disciples followed his example of steering independents to the best candidates. There had to be a place in politics for citizens of conscience and independence.

But the demise of the Progressives after 1912 and Woodrow Wilson's talent for idealistic oratory caused Taylor to shed some of his cautiousness about national politics. In 1916 Lawson refused to publish Taylor's endorsement of Wilson; the following year Taylor rallied to Wilson's call to war. He admired Wilson's wartime leadership, especially his idealistic pledge to "make the world safe for democracy" and create a League of Nations that put an end to war. Writing to his son, Taylor opined that Wilson would rank next to Lincoln as a great president. Years later he acknowledged that America's war fever in 1917–18 "unbalanced all of us more or less."[129]

Though he grieved that Wilson had mediocre successors, James M. Cox in 1920 and John W. Davis in 1924, Taylor held his nose and voted for both of them; in 1924 Republican candidate Calvin Coolidge did not bother to campaign outside his house. Like most of the social worker movement Taylor switched to Herbert Hoover in 1928, praising his humanitarian relief work during World War I and his brilliant career as Commerce Secretary in the Harding administration; the social workers also appreciated Hoover's staunch support of prohibition. Four years later Taylor clung to Hoover against Franklin Roosevelt, then supported the New Deal after Roosevelt surprised him. In 1936 he voted in his last presidential election – for Roosevelt – still calling himself "a middle-of-the-road independent."[130]

Taylor's moderate temperament helped him take in stride the bitter disappointments of the 1920s and 1930s, although he found the dismal choice of 1924 especially hard to take. In 1912 three of the four presidential candidates vied for the progressive vote; a dozen years later Americans chose between a Republican throwback to 1880s *laissez-faire* and a Democrat who opposed anti-lynching legislation and women's suffrage, in addition to doubting that African Americans should be allowed to vote. Taylor sympathized with the generation that came of age in such a low period. Laboring on his memoirs in the 1920s, he took six years to write a plodding 450-page tome of long, twisting sentences that zigged and zagged between autobiography and history. The book stirred little reaction and he understood why. A real autobiography would have been more interesting, but he could not just write about himself; what mattered was the expanding social frontier. A friend pleaded for clean sentences with everyday words, but Taylor loved convoluted Victorian sentences with sesquipedalian words. In any case, by 1930 nobody was interested in the social gospel generation. Liberal Victorianism was decidedly out of fashion; its rhetoric of progress, idealism, moralism, and spirit overcoming nature was a quaint echo of a lost world. The 1930s were about crisis, realism, and collapsing civilizations. Near the end of his life Taylor reflected that he should have written the book sooner, before his generation died off: "The younger generations knew little and cared less about it all."[131]

Louise Wade, in her fine biography of Taylor, aptly noted that he was too optimistic to be a trailblazer. Taylor was immune to disappointment; when he lost a battle he simply bounced back and tried again. Instead of leading factional groups in new directions, he tried to bring them together. He liked to say that his life had three motifs, "a democratic faith, an educational purpose, and a religious hope." His friend Percy Alden put it more functionally, observing that Taylor's activism, teaching and preaching were always about the same thing: "to educate the civic conscience, to establish better social conditions, and to make it easier for people to live the true and pure life."[132]

Taylor did not think of the social gospel as something that had been surpassed, or that could be. The liberal social gospel was a recovery of the very spirit and faith of

Jesus in a modern context. It made Christianity relevant and credible in ways that were not outdated, however much the new pessimists claimed otherwise. Taylor enjoyed recalling with Peabody that Christian sociology did not exist before they came along. In the same vein, he recalled that when he started teaching he tried to find an encyclopedia definition of sociology, to no avail. The 1873 edition of the *American Encyclopedia* said nothing about sociology, nor did the 1887 edition of the *Universal Encyclopedia*, though a later edition explained: "The conception of a comprehensive social science we owe to Auguste Comte, who invented for it the objectionable name Sociology."[133]

To Taylor and Peabody the rise of social ethics was part of a permanent break-through in human consciousness. Sociology got off to a rocky and dangerous beginning, but the social ethicists created something better that deserved a permanent place in theological education. In 1899 Taylor put it bluntly in a speech to the International Congregational Council. *Laissez-faire* ideology was "the lisping of the infancy of economic science," he remarked, but it was too repugnant to Christianity and civilization to prevail: "For even civilization means human interference in the cosmic struggle for existence. The 'let alone theory' of society bears the mark of Cain. Its theological definition is hell." The church's social mission was to recognize the divine ideal of human life, initiate movements for its realization, and transmit the Spirit's power for social regeneration: "This is the church's social question. Will we reform ourselves in order to conform the world to Christ?"[134]

In that voice social ethics entered the academy and fought for the right to stay there.

Notes

1 Francis Greenwood Peabody, *Reminiscences of Present-Day Saints* (Boston: Houghton Mifflin, 1927), "nearly," 1; Robert Swain Peabody and Francis Greenwood Peabody, *A New England Romance: The Story of Ephraim Peabody and Mary Jane Peabody* (Boston: Houghton Mifflin, 1920).

2 Peabody, *Reminiscences of Present-Day Saints*, 2–3.

3 Francis Greenwood Peabody, *A Little Boy in Little Boston: Reminiscences of Childhood* (Cambridge: n.p., 1935), 17–19; Peabody, *Harvard in the Sixties: A Boy's Eye View* (Cambridge: n.p., 1935), "the air," 19–20; see Samuel Eliot Morison, *Three Centuries of Harvard* (Cambridge, MA: Harvard University Press, 1936).

4 Peabody, *Reminiscences of Present-Day Saints*, 65, 66.

5 See Sidney E. Ahlstrom, "The Middle Period (1840–80)," in *The Harvard Divinity School: Its Place in Harvard University and in American Culture*, ed. George Huntston Williams (Boston: Beacon Press, 1954), 78–116; Robert S. Morison, "The First Half Century of the Divinity School," *Addresses Delivered at the Observance of the 100th Anniversary of the Establishment of the Harvard Divinity School* (Cambridge, MA: Harvard University Press, 1917), 14–15.

6 Peabody, *Reminiscences of Present-Day Saints*, 68.

7 Friedrich August Gottreu Tholuck, "Theological Encyclopedia and Methodology," *Bibliotheca Sacra* 1 (1844), 194–5.

8 Peabody, *Reminiscences of Present-Day Saints*, quote 71.

9 Otto Pfleiderer, *Die Religion, ihr Wesen und ihre Geschichte : auf Grund des gegenwärtigen Standes der philosophischen und der historischen Wissenschaft* (Leipzig: Fues, 1869); Peabody, *Reminiscences of Present-Day Saints*, 67.

10 Peabody, *Reminiscences of Present-Day Saints*, quotes 114, 117.

11 See Edward Bellamy, *Looking Backward, 2000–1887* (1st edn., 1888; Cambridge, MA: Harvard University Press, 1967); Stephen Colwell, *New themes for the Protestant clergy: creeds without charity, theology without humanity, Protestantism without Christianity; with notes on the literature of charity, population, pauperism, political economy, and Protestantism* (Philadelphia: Lippincott, Grambo, & Co., 1851); Henry Demarest Lloyd, *Wealth Against Commonwealth* (New York: Harper & Brothers, 1894).

12 Colwell, *New themes for the Protestant clergy*, quotes 267, 240–1.

13 Ibid., 359–60; see Stephen Colwell, *Politics for American Christians: A Word upon Our Example as a Nation* (Philadelphia: Lippincott, Grambo, 1852); James Dombrowski, *The Early Days of Christian Socialism in America* (New York: Columbia University Press, 1936), 31–4.

14 Princeton Theological Seminary Catalogue, 1872, cited in Dombrowski, *The Early Days of Christian Socialism in America*, 60; C. A. Aiken, *Christian Ethics*, ed. Princeton Theological Seminary Class of 1879 (Princeton: Princeton University Press, 1879).

15 See Gladys Bryson, "The Emergence of the Social Sciences from Moral Philosophy," *International Journal of Ethics* 42 (April 1932), 304–7; Bryson, "Sociology Considered as Moral Philosophy," *Sociological Review* 24 (January 1932), 26–36; Bryson, "The Comparable Interests of the Old Moral Philosophy and the Modern Social Sciences," *Social Forces* 11 (October 1932), 19–27.

16 See John Van Engen, "Christianity and the University: The Medieval and Reformation Legacies," in *Making Higher Education Christian: The History and Mission of Evangelical Colleges in America*, eds. Joel A. Carpenter and Kenneth W. Shipps (Grand Rapids: Christian University Press, 1987), 23–34; Samuel Eliot Morison, *Harvard College in the Seventeenth Century* (Cambridge, MA: Harvard University Press, 1936), 169–266; George M. Marsden, *The Soul of the American University: From Protestant Establishment to Established Nonbelief* (New York: Oxford University Press, 1994), 33–44.

17 Isaac Newton, *Philosophiae Naturalis Principia Mathematica* (1689) (*Sir Isaac Newton's Mathematical Principles of Natural Philosophy and his System of the World*, trans. Florian Cajori [Berkeley: University of California Press, 1934]); H. S. Thayer, "Sir Isaac Newton," *Cambridge Dictionary of Philosophy* (Cambridge: Cambridge University Press, 1995), 529–30.

18 Mather and Leverett quoted in Morison, *Harvard College in the Seventeenth Century*, 167, 168; and Marsden, *The Soul of the American University: From Protestant Establishment to Established Nonbelief*, 49.

19 John Locke, *An Essay concerning Human Understanding*, ed. Peter H. Nidditch (1689; Oxford: Clarendon Press, 1975); Locke, *The Reasonableness of Christianity*, ed. George W. Ewing (1695; Washington, DC: Regnery Gateway, 1965); Locke, *Two Treatises of Government*, ed. Peter Laslett (1689; Cambridge: Cambridge University Press, 1988); see J. W. Yolton, *Locke and the Compass of the Human Understanding* (Cambridge: Cambridge University Press, 1970); R. S. Woolhouse, "John Locke," *Oxford Companion to Philosophy*, ed. Ted Honderich (Oxford: Oxford University Press, 1995), 493–6; Woolhouse, *Locke* (Minneapolis: University of Minnesota Press, 1983).

20 *Memoir of William Ellery Channing, with Extracts from His Correspondence and Manuscripts*, 2 vols., ed. William Henry Channing (London: George Routledge & Co., 1850), 1: 47–8; see Roger L. Emerson, "Science and Moral Philosophy in the Scottish Enlightenment," in *Studies in the Philosophy of the Scottish Enlightenment*, ed. M. A. Stewart (Oxford: Clarendon Press, 1990), 32–8; Mark A. Noll, "Common Sense Traditions and American Evangelical Thought," *American Quarterly* 37 (1985), 216–38; Daniel Walker Howe, *The Unitarian Conscience: Harvard Moral Philosophy, 1805–1861* (Cambridge, MA: Harvard University Press, 1970).

21 Thomas Reid, *An Inquiry into the Human Mind, on the principles of Common Sense*, 3rd edn. (Dublin: R. Marchbank, 1779); abridged edition reprinted in Reid, *Inquiry and Essays*,

ed. Ronald E. Beanblossom and Keith Lehrer (Indianapolis: Hackett Publishing Co., 1983); Adam Ferguson, *Principles of Moral and Political Science* (Edinburgh: A. Strahan & T. Cadell, 1792); Frances Hutcheson, *A System of Moral Philosophy in three books*, 2 vols. (Glasgow: R. & A. Foulis, 1755); Richard Price, *A Review of the Principal Questions and Difficulties in Morals*, 2nd edn. (London: T. Cadell, 1769).

22 Reid, *An Inquiry into the Human* Mind, 118; see Reid, "Essay Five: Of Morals," in *Essays on the Intellectual Powers of Man* (1785), reprinted in Reid, *Inquiry and Essays*, 351–68; see D. O. Thomas, *The Honest Mind: The Thought and Work of Richard Price* (Oxford: Oxford University Press, 1977).

23 See Marsden, *The Soul of the American University: From Protestant Establishment to Established Nonbelief*, 59–64; Mark A. Noll, *Princeton and the Republic, 1768–1822: The Search for a Christian Enlightenment in the Era of Samuel Stanhope Smith* (Princeton: Princeton University Press, 1989); Garry Wills, *Inventing America: Jeffersons' Declaration of Independence* (Garden City, NY: Doubleday, 1978), 176–80.

24 See Francis Wayland, *Thoughts on the Present Collegiate System of the United States* (Boston: Gould, Kendall and Lincoln, 1842); Henry P. Tappan, *University Education* (New York: G. P. Putnam, 1851); Laurence Veysey, *The Emergence of the American University* (Chicago: University of Chicago Press, 1965), 126–33; Marsden, *The Soul of the American University: From Protestant Establishment to Established Nonbelief*, 99–110.

25 George L. Prentiss, *The Bright Side of Life: Glimpses of It Through Fourscore Years*, 2 vols. (Asbury Park, NJ: Press of M., W., & C. Pennypacker, 1901), 2: 395; cited in Dombrowski, *The Early Days of Christian Socialism in America*, 61–2.

26 Peabody, *Reminiscences of Present-Day Saints*, 117–18.

27 Ibid., quotes 121; "Reports of Committees of the Board of Overseers, 1878–1879," 20–7, cited in Levering Reynolds, Jr, "The Later Years (1880–1953)," in *The Harvard Divinity School: Its Place in Harvard University and in American Culture*, "unsectarian school," 168.

28 Reynolds, "The Later Years (1880–1953)," 166–74; see Ephraim Emerton, *Living and Learning: Academic Essays* (Cambridge, MA: Harvard University Press, 1921); Charles Carroll Everett, "The Divinity School as It Is," *Harvard Graduates' Magazine* 5 (June 1897), 503.

29 See Robert G. McCloskey, *American Conservatism in the Age of Enterprise: A Study of William Graham Sumner, Stephen J. Field, and Andrew Carnegie* (Cambridge, MA: Harvard University Press, 1951); Bruce Curtis, *William Graham Sumner* (Boston: Twayne, 1981); William Thomas O'Connor, *Naturalism and the Pioneers of American Sociology* (Washington, DC, Catholic University of America Press, 1942).

30 William Graham Sumner, *Social Darwinism: Selected Essays*, ed. Albert Galloway Keller (Englewood Cliffs, NJ: Prentice-Hall, 1963), quotes 94, 95; see Sumner, *The Challenge of Facts and Other Essays* (New Haven: Yale University Press, 1914).

31 *Publication of the American Economics Association* (1886), quotes 2, 18, 43; cited in Dombrowski, *The Early Days of Christian Socialism in America*, 51.

32 L. L. Bernard and Jesse Bernard, *Origins of American Sociology: The Social Science Movement in the United States* (New York: Thomas Y. Crowell, 1943), quotes, 545, 559.

33 David B. Potts, "Social Ethics at Harvard, 1881–1931: A Study in Academic Activism," in *Social Sciences at Harvard, 1860–1920: From Inculcation to the Open Mind*, ed. Paul Buck (Cambridge, MA: Harvard University Press, 1965), 94–6, "Peabo's," 95; Peabody, *Reminiscences of Present-Day Saints*, "why not" and "drainage," 136–7; Grace Cumming Long, "The Ethics of Francis Greenwood Peabody: A Century of Christian Social Ethics," *Journal of Religious Ethics* 18 (Spring 1990), 56.

34 Long, "The Ethics of Francis Greenwood Peabody: A Century of Christian Social Ethics," 56; Potts, "Social Ethics at Harvard, 1881–1931: A Study in Academic Activism," 94–6; Peabody, *Reminiscences of Present-Day Saints*, "both father," 123.

35 Francis Greenwood Peabody to Franklin Sanborn, 1886, cited in Franklin Sanborn, "The Social Sciences: Their Growth and Future," *Journal of Social Science* 21 (September 1886), 7–8; and Potts, "Social Ethics at Harvard, 1881–1931: A Study in Academic Activism," 96.

36 Francis Greenwood Peabody, review of *The Theory of Morals*, by Paul Janet, *Science* 3 (March 21, 1884), 360–2, "so far" and "a science of," 361; Peabody, "The Philosophy of the Social Questions," *Andover Review* 8 (December 1887), 561–73, "dull study," "what moral," and "through," 565–6; Peabody, "Social Reforms as Subjects of University Study," *Independent* 40 (January 14, 1886), 5–6, "dissected," 5.

37 Francis Greenwood Peabody, *The Approach to the Social Question* (New York: Macmillan, 1909), quotes 34–5.

38 "Social Ethics," *Harvard Crimson* (October 13, 1892), "sound and just," 1; Peabody to Sanborn, cited in Sanborn, "The Social Sciences: Their Growth and Future," 7–8; both cited in Potts, "Social Ethics at Harvard, 1881–1931: A Study in Academic Activism," 96–7; "while many," 138.

39 Francis Greenwood Peabody, *Jesus Christ and the Social Question* (New York: Macmillan, 1900), quotes 1, 2.

40 Walter Rauschenbusch, *Christianizing the Social Order* (New York: Macmillan, 1912), 30.

41 See William Jewett Tucker, *The Making and Unmaking of the Preacher* (Boston: Houghton Mifflin, 1898); Tucker, *My Generation: An Autobiographical Interpretation* (Boston: Houghton Mifflin, 1919), 51–89, quote 97.

42 *Progressive Orthodoxy: A Contribution to the Christian Interpretation of Christian Doctrines*, ed. Egbert C. Smyth, William J. Tucker, J. W. Churchill, George Harris, Edward Y. Hincks (Boston: Houghton Mifflin, 1885), quote 9; see *The Andover Trial, Professor Smyth's Argument with the Statements of Professors Tucker, Harris, Hincks, and Churchill* (Boston: Houghton Mifflin, 1887); Gary Dorrien, *The Making of American Liberal Theology: Imagining Progressive Religion, 1805–1900* (Louisville: Westminster John Knox, 2001), 290–3. *The Andover Review, a Religious and Theological Monthly*, was published from 1884 to 1893.

43 Tucker, *My Generation: An Autobiographical Interpretation*, 99.

44 Ibid., quote 172; see L. L. Bernard, "The Social Sciences as Disciplines," *Encyclopedia of the Social Sciences*, 15 vols., eds. Edwin Robert Anderson Seligman and Alvin Saunders Johnson (New York: Macmillan, 1930), 1: 321–3; Dombrowski, *The Early Days of Christian Socialism in America*, 62.

45 See William Green, *Modern Trade Unionism* (Washington, DC: American Federation of Labor, 1925); *Almanac of American History*, ed. Arthur M. Schlesinger, Jr (New York: Barnes & Noble Books, 1993), 359–61.

46 Richard T. Ely, *The Labor Movement in America* (New York: Thomas Y. Crowell, 1886); Ely, *Social Aspects of Christianity and Other Essays* (New York: Thomas Y. Crowell, 1889), quotes 25, 27.

47 J. H. W. Stuckenberg *Christian Sociology* (New York: Funk, 1880; London: R. D. Dickinson, 1881), quotes 4; (Stuckenberg, *The Age and the Church; being a study of the age, and the adaptation of the church to its needs* (Hartford: The Student, 1893); Stuckenberg, *Sociology, the Science of Human Society* (New York: G. P. Putman's Sons, 1903); Stuckenberg, David T. Hedriick, and Gordon Barry, *I'm Surrounded by Methodists: Diary of John H. W. Stuckenberg, Chaplain of the 145th Pennsylvania Volunteer Infantry* (Gettysburg, PA: Thomas Publications, 1995); see John Bascom, *Sociology* (New York: G. P. Putnam's Sons, 1887); Bascom, *Ethics, or Science of Duty* (New York: G. P. Putnam's Sons, 1879); Bascom, *Social Theory: A Grouping of Social Facts and Principles* (New York: Thomas Crowell, 1895). For a typical note of fondness and regret about Bascom, see Washington Gladden, *Recollections* (Boston: Houghton Mifflin, 1909), 74.

48 William Jewett Tucker, "Social Economics," Course Syllabus, *Andover Review* 2 (1889); reprinted in Tucker, *My Generation: An Autobiographical Interpretation*, 175.

49 See Tucker, *My Generation: An Autobiographical Interpretation*, 249–413; Obituary notice for William Jewett Tucker, *New York City American* (September 30, 1926).

50 Tucker, *My Generation: An Autobiographical Interpretation*, 422; see William Jewett Tucker, *The Function of the Church in Modern Society* (Boston: Houghton Mifflin, 1911).

51 Peabody, *Jesus Christ and the Social Question*, quotes 2, 11.

52 Ibid., 36–8, quote 38.

53 Ibid., quotes 35, 77.

54 Ibid., quotes 87, 90, 110–11.

55 Ernst Issel, *Die Lehre vom Reiche Gottes im Neuen Testament* (Leiden: E. J. Brill, 1891); Otto Schmoller, *Die Lehre vom Reiche Gottes in den Schriften des Neuen Testament* (Leiden: E. J. Brill, 1891); Johannes Weiss, *Die Predigt Jesu vom Reiche Gottes* (1892; Göttingen : Vandenhoeck & Ruprecht, 1964), Weiss, *Jesus' Proclamation of the Kingdom of God*, trans. Richard H. Hiers and David L. Holland (Philadelphia: Fortress Press, 1971), quote 114; Albert Schweitzer, *Von Reimarus zu Wrede* (Tübingen: Mohr, 1906), Schweitzer, *Quest of the Historical Jesus*, trans. W. Montgomery (New York: Macmillan, 1910).

56 Peabody, *Jesus Christ and the Social Question*, 91–7.

57 Ibid., quotes 100, 101.

58 Ibid., 101–28, quotes 102, 103, 104.

59 Ibid., quotes 180.

60 Ibid., 183–225, quotes 208, 213, 224–5.

61 Ibid., 267–326, quotes 284.

62 Ibid., quotes 300, 301, 302, 308.

63 Ibid., 355.

64 See Edgar Gardner Murphy, *Problems of the Present South: A Discussion of the Educational, Industrial, and Political Issues in the Southern States* (New York: Macmillan, 1904); Murphy, *The Basis of Ascendancy: A Discussion of Certain Principles of Public Policy Involved in the Development of the Southern States* (New York: Longmans, Green, and Co., 1908); Thomas Dixon Jr, *The Clansman: An Historical Romance of the Ku Klux Klan* (New York: Double-day, Page and Co., 1905); Dixon, *Leopard's Spots: A Romance of the White Man's Burden, 1865–1900* (New York: Doubleday, Page, and Co., 1902); Dixon, *The Sins of the Father: A Romance of the South* (New York: D. Appleton and Co., 1912).

65 See Ralph E. Luker, *The Social Gospel in Black and White: American Racial Reform, 1885–1912* (Chapel Hill: University of North Carolina Press, 1991); Ronald C. White, Jr, *Liberty and Justice for All: Racial Reform and the Social Gospel (1877–1925)* (New York: Harper & Row, 1990); David M. Reimers, *White Protestantism and the Negro* (New York: Oxford University Press, 1965).

66 Francis Greenwood Peabody, "If Lincoln Came to Hampton," *Southern Workman* 51 (April 1922), 162; Ephraim Peabody, "Slavery in the United States: Its Evils, Alleviations, and Remedies," *North American Review* 73 (October 1851), 347–85; Robert Peabody and Francis Greenwood Peabody, *A New England Romance: The Story of Ephraim and Mary Jane Peabody*, 126–8; Luker, *The Social Gospel in Black and White: American Racial Reform, 1885–1912*, 128.

67 Francis Greenwood Peabody, *Education for Life: The Story of Hampton Institute* (Garden City: Doubleday, Page, and Co., 1918), quotes xii, xiii; see Booker T. Washington, *Up from Slavery, an Autobiography* (New York: Doubleday, Page, and Co., 1901).

68 These two paragraphs on Washington and the *Outlook* are adapted from Gary Dorrien, *The Making of American Liberal Theology: Imagining Progressive Religion, 1805–1900* (Louisville: Westminster John Knox Press, 2001), 328.

69 Editorial, "Two Typical Leaders," *The Outlook* 74 (May 23, 1903), 214–16; W. E. B. Du Bois, *The Souls of Black Folk* (Chicago: A. C. McClurg & Co., 1903), 53–4; Luker, *The Social Gospel in Black and White: American Racial Reform, 1885–1912*, 214–16.

70 Peabody, *Education for Life: The Story of Hampton Institute*, quotes 23, 24,

71 Ibid., 321.

72 Bernard and Bernard, *Origins of American Sociology: The Social Sciences Movement in the United States*, 559; Frank L. Tolman, "The Study of Sociology in Institutions of Learning in the United States," *American Journal of Sociology* 5 (May 1902), 797–8; George W. Pickering, "Theology as Social Ethics," *American Journal of Theology and Philosophy* 17 (January 1996), 16–17.

73 Peabody, *Reminiscences of Present-Day Saints*, 141.

74 Ibid., 141–7, "his vigor," 142; Potts, "Social Ethics at Harvard, 1881–1931: A Study in Academic Activism," 112–13; Francis Greenwood Peabody, *The Social Museum as an Instrument of University Teaching*, Publications of the Department of Social Ethics at Harvard University, 1 (Cambridge, MA: Harvard University, 1908), quotes 1–2, 6–7.

75 Potts, "Social Ethics at Harvard, 1881–1931: A Study in Academic Activism," quotes, 113–15; Robert L. Church, "The Economists Study Society: Sociology at Harvard, 1891–1902," *Social Sciences at Harvard, 1860–1920: From Inculcation to the Open Mind*, 18–90.

76 "A Significant Gift," *Harvard Bulletin* (June 21, 1905), 5; Potts, "Social Ethics at Harvard, 1881–1931: A Study in Academic Activism," 114; Peabody, *The Approach to the Social Question*, 5.

77 Peabody, *Reminiscences of Present-Day Saints*, quote 148; Potts, "Social Ethics at Harvard, 1881–1931: A Study in Academic Activism," 118–19; Reynolds, Jr, "The Later Years (1880–1953), 201.

78 Potts, "Social Ethics at Harvard, 1881–1931: A Study in Academic Activism," 120–3; Peabody, *Reminiscences of Present-Day Saints*, quote 148.

79 Potts, "Social Ethics at Harvard, 1881–1931: A Study in Academic Activism," 124–6; see Pitirim Sorokin, "Sociology as a Science," *Social Forces* 10 (October 1931), 21–7.

80 Aaron I. Abell, *The Urban Impact on American Protestantism, 1865–1900* (Cambridge, MA: Harvard University Press, 1943); Bryson, "The Emergence of the Social Sciences from Moral Philosophy," 304–23; Potts, "Social Ethics at Harvard, 1881–1931: A Study in Academic Activism," 97.

81 Robert L. Church, "Introduction," *Social Sciences at Harvard, 1860–1920: From Inculcation to the Open Mind*, 1–17, quotes 6, 13.

82 Dombrowski, *The Early Days of Christian Socialism in America*, 70.

83 Peabody, *The Approach to the Social Question*, 96–7, 135–9, 183–4, quote 4–5; Potts, "Social Ethics at Harvard, 1881–1931: A Study in Academic Activism," 116–17; William James, *The Will to Believe and Other Essays in Popular Philosophy* (New York: Longmans, Green & Co., 1897); James, *The Varieties of Religious Experience* (New York: Longmans, Green & Co., 1902).

84 Peabody, *Jesus Christ and the Social Question*, 174; Peabody, *Reminiscences of Present-Day Saints*, 157–68.

85 Graham Taylor, *Pioneering on Social Frontiers* (Chicago: University of Chicago Press, 1930), 340–4.

86 Ibid., 345–6.

87 Ibid., 348.

88 Ibid., 358; Graham Taylor, "The Heresy of Life," *Christian Intelligencer* 49 (May 23, 1878), 1–2; Louise C. Wade, *Graham Taylor: Pioneer for Social Justice, 1851–1938* (Chicago: University of Chicago Press, 1964), 11–15.

89 See Gary Dorrien, *The Making of American Liberal Theology: Imagining Progressive Religion, 1805–1900* (Louisville: Westminster John Knox Press, 2001), 111–78.

90 Taylor, *Pioneering on Social Frontiers*, quotes 362.

91 Graham Taylor, *Five Years' Growth: A Sketch of Evangelistic Work Centering at the Fourth Church* (Hartford, CT: Hartford Printing Co., 1889), 7–8; Taylor, "The Hartford Pastors' Mission," *The Congregationalist* 39 (April 28, 1887), 2; Taylor, *Pioneering on Social Frontiers*, 362–3; Wade, *Graham Taylor: Pioneer for Social Justice, 1851–1938*, 31–2.

92 Taylor, *Five Years' Growth: A Sketch of Evangelistic Work Centering at the Fourth Church*, 8–12; Graham Taylor, "An Evangelistic Church," *Religious Herald* (December 25, 1884); Taylor, *Pioneering on Social Frontiers*, quotes 363.

93 Wade, *Graham Taylor: Pioneer for Social Justice, 1851–1938*, 33; Taylor, *Five Years' Growth: A Sketch of Evangelistic Work Centering at the Fourth Church*, 12–13; C. Howard Hopkins, *The Rise of the Social Gospel in American Protestantism, 1865–1915* (New Haven: Yale University Press, 1940), 113–14.

94 Taylor, *Pioneering on Social Frontiers*, 378–9, quote 379.

95 Graham Taylor, Journal entries of February 6, 1888 and February 23, 1888; Taylor, Diary entries of February 16, 1888 and February 23, 1888, Graham Taylor Papers, Midwest Manuscript Collection, Roger and Julie Baskes Department of Special Collections, Newberry Library, Chicago; Wade, *Graham Taylor: Pioneer for Social Justice, 1851–1938*, 38–9; Taylor, *Pioneering on Social Frontiers*, 378–80.

96 Graham Taylor, *The Practical Training Needed for the Ministry of To-Day* (Hartford: Hartford Seminary Publications, 1888), quotes 12, 15, 17; Wade, *Graham Taylor: Pioneer for Social Justice, 1851–1938*, 41–2.

97 Taylor, *Pioneering on Social Frontiers*, quotes 393, 396.

98 Ibid., quotes 394; Washington Gladden, *Working People and their Employers* (Boston: Lockwood, Brooks, and Co., 1876; New York: Funk & Wagnalls Co., 1894).

99 J. R. Seeley, *Ecce Homo: A Survey of the Life and Work of Jesus Christ* (1866; New York: Macmillan, 1895); J. B. Mozley, *Ruling Ideas in Early Ages and their Relation to Old Testament Faith* (New York: E. P. Dutton, 1877); Josiah Strong, *Our Country, its Possible Future and its Present Crisis* (New York: Baker & Taylor for the American Home Missionary Society, 1885 William H. Fremantle, *The World as the Subject of Redemption: being an attempt to set forth the functions of the church as designed to embrace the whole race of mankind* (London: Rivington, 1885; New York: Longmans, Green, 1895); Taylor, *Pioneering on Social Frontiers*, quotes 389.

100 Ozora S. Davis, in "Addresses at Dinner in Honor of Dr. Graham Taylor, May 27, 1930," Graham Taylor Papers, cited in Wade, *Graham Taylor: Pioneer for Social Justice, 1851–1938*, 44.

101 Taylor, Diary, April 20, 1892, Graham Taylor Papers; Clark Beardslee to Graham Taylor, July 20, 1892; Chester D. Hartranft to Graham Taylor, 1892, cited in Wade, *Graham Taylor: Pioneer for Social Justice, 1851–1938*, 47–8; Taylor, *Pioneering on Social Frontiers*, 381.

102 Taylor, *Pioneering on Social Frontiers*, 381–3, quote 383.

103 Ibid., quote 381; Wade, *Graham Taylor: Pioneer for Social Justice, 1851–1938*, 51–4; Richard J. Storr, *Harper's University: The Beginnings* (Chicago: University of Chicago Press, 1966), 18–20; Bessie Louise Pierce, *A History of Chicago*, 3 vols., Vol. 3: *The Rise of a Modern City, 1871–1893* (New York: Knopf, 1957), 3–12.

104 Graham Taylor, *The Sociological Training of the Ministry, Address Delivered before the Evangelical Alliance Congress, at Chicago, October 13, 1893* (Chicago: n.p., 1893), 1–20, quotes 16, 8; Taylor, "Our New Professorship," *The Advance* 25 (September 8, 1892), 698; Wade, *Graham Taylor: Pioneer for Social Justice, 1851–1938*, 79.

105 Stanton Coit, *Neighborhood Guilds; An Instrument of Social Reform* (London: S. Sonnenschein, 1892); Taylor, *Pioneering on Social Frontiers*, quotes 6, 7; see Graham Taylor, "Jane Addams' Twenty Years of Industrial Democracy," *The Survey* 25 (25 (December 3, 1910), 405–9; Taylor, "Jane Addams – Interpreter," *American Review of Reviews* 40 (December 1909), 688–94; Robert A. Woods and Albert J. Kennedy, *The Settlement Horizon, A National Estimate* (New York: Russell Sage Foundation, 1922); J. A. R. Pimlott, *Toynbee Hall, Fifty Years of Social Progress, 1884–1934* (London: J. M Dent and Sons, 1935); Jane Addams, *Twenty Years at Hull House, with Autobiographical Notes* (New York: Macmillan, 1910).

106 Taylor, *Pioneering on Social Frontiers*, 110; Graham Taylor, "The Social Settlement and Its Suggestions to the Churches," *Hartford Seminary Record* 4 (December 1893), 55–63.

107   Graham Taylor, "Response of Graham Taylor," *Chicago Theological Seminary Register* 17 (January 1927), "from the ground," 8; cited in Wade, *Graham Taylor: Pioneer for Social Justice, 1851–1938*, 81; Taylor, *Pioneering on Social Frontiers*, "what missionaries' families," 7; Taylor, "The Commons – The Chicago Seminary Settlement," *The Advance* 29 (October 11, 1894), 60.

108   Taylor, *Pioneering on Social Frontiers*, 7–8; Graham Taylor, *Chicago Commons Through Forty Years* (Chicago: Chicago Commons Association, 1936), 9; Wade, *Graham Taylor: Pioneer for Social Justice, 1851–1938*, 81–2.

109   The School of Social Service Administration, University of Chicago, "About SSA: SSA's Origins," www.ssa.uchicago.edu, accessed March 15, 2006; Wade, *Graham Taylor: Pioneer for Social Justice, 1851–1938*, 3–4; Taylor, *Pioneering on Social Frontiers*, 9–10.

110   Taylor, *The Practical Training Needed for the Ministry of To-Day*, 2–17; Graham Taylor, "Address When Inaugurated Prof. of Christian Sociology in C.T.S.," April 18, 1893, unpublished manuscript, Graham Taylor Papers; Taylor, *Pioneering on Social Frontiers*, 398.

111   Graham Taylor, *Syllabus in Biblical Sociology* (Chicago: Desplaines Press, 1900), 1–29; Taylor, "Social Economics – Prescribed and Elective Courses," 1906, Graham Taylor Papers; Wade, *Graham Taylor: Pioneer for Social Justice, 1851–1938*, 96–7.

112   Graham Taylor, *Books for Beginners, in the Study of Christian Sociology and Social Economics* (Boston: Congregational Sunday-School and Publication Society, n.d.), 1–14; Shailer Mathews, *The Social Teaching of Jesus: An Essay in Christian Sociology* (New York: Macmillan, 1897); George Herron, *The New Redemption* (New York: T. Y. Crowell, 1893); Herron, *The Christian State: A Political Vision of Christ* (New York: T. Y. Crowell, 1895); William Dwight Porter Bliss, *Encyclopedia of Social Reform, including Political Economy, Political Science, Sociology, and Statistics* (New York: Funk and Wagnalls, 1897); Walter Rauschenbusch, *Christianity and the Social Crisis* (New York: Macmillan, 1907); Taylor, *Pioneering on Social Frontiers*, quote 398–9.

113   J. W. F. Davies, "Graham Taylor: A Tribute From the Alumni," *Chicago Theological Seminary Register* 18 (November 1928), quote 16, cited in Wade, *Graham Taylor: Pioneer for Social Justice, 1851–1938*, 98; see Robert W. Gammon, "Twenty Five Years of Chicago Commons: How Graham Taylor's Dreams Came True," *Congregationalist and Advance* CIV (May 15, 1919), 621; Gammon, "Graham Taylor: An Intimate Portrait," *Advance* 131 (January 1, 1939), 1.

114   Wade, *Graham Taylor: Pioneer for Social Justice, 1851–1938*, 99–100.

115   Taylor, *Pioneering on Social Frontiers*, 400.

116   Ibid., 401–3; Samuel Ives Curtiss, "Twenty-Five Years as a Seminary Professor 1878–1903," *Chicago Seminary Quarterly* 3 (July 1903), 13.

117   Taylor, *Pioneering on Social Frontiers*, 429–35.

118   Graham Taylor to Jane Addams, September 13, 1913, Graham Taylor Papers; Wade, *Graham Taylor: Pioneer for Social Justice, 1851–1938*, 106–7; Jane Addams, Introduction to Taylor, *Religion in Social Action* (New York: Dodd, Mead and Co., 1913), xxvii.

119   Taylor, *Religion in Social Action*, quotes 1, 6, 23.

120   Ibid., quotes 25, 47, 54.

121   Ibid., quotes 82, 86–7.

122   Ibid., quotes 100–1, 104.

123   Ibid., 120–39 quotes 120, 122, 123.

124   Ibid., 167–210, quotes 186, 202, 210; see Graham Taylor, "After Trades Unions – What? A Glance Behind for a Look Ahead," *The Commons* 9 (April 1904), 105–8; Taylor, "Between the Lines in Chicago's Industrial War," *The Commons* 5 (April 30, 1900), 1–4; Taylor, "The Church and Industrial Discontent," *Christian Century* 37 (March 18, 1920), 9–10; Taylor, "The Church for Industrial Brotherhood," *The Survey* 25 (November 5, 1910), 177–8; Taylor, "Church Members and the Industrial Conflict," *Congregationalist*

and Advance CIV (September 4, 1919), 296–7; Taylor, "Industrial Peace – With Honor and Democracy," *The Survey* 31 (March 7, 1914), 723–4; Taylor, "To Conquer the Industrial Situation," *Christian Register* 98 (September 4, 1919), 849–50.

125   Edwin Pond Parker, "The Optimist – Religion in Social Action," Hartford *Courant* (February 8, 1914); Walter Rauschenbusch, review of *Religion in Social Action*, by Graham Taylor, *The Survey* 31 (January 31, 1914), 527; Washington Gladden, review of ibid., *Congregationalist and Christian World* 99 (March 19, 1914), n.p.; Taylor, *Pioneering on Social Frontiers*, 427–8.

126   Graham Taylor, "The Race Riot in Lincoln's City," *Charities and the Commons* 20 (August 29, 1908), 627–8.

127   Graham Taylor, "Chicago in the Nation's Race Strife," *The Survey* 42 (August 9, 1919), 695–7; Taylor, "Foreign Born Citizens as Political Assets," National Conference of Social Work, *Proceedings, 1918*, 452–7; Taylor, "Routing the Segregationists in Chicago," *The Survey* 29 (November 30, 1912), 254–6; Taylor, *Pioneering on Social Frontiers*, quotes 240.

128   Taylor, *Pioneering on Social Frontiers*, quotes 240; see Reverdy Cassius Ransom, *The Pilgrimage of Harriet Ransom's Son* (Nashville: Sunday School Union, 1949); Monroe N. Work, "The Negro Church in the Negro Community," *Southern Workman* 38 (August 1908), 428–32; Luker, *The Social Gospel in Black and White: American Racial Reform, 1885–1912*, Richard R. Wright, *87 Years Behind the Black Curtain, An Autobiography* (Philadelphia: Rare Book Co., 1965).

129   Wade, *Graham Taylor: Pioneer for Social Justice, 1851–1938*, 193–5; Taylor to Graham Romeyn Taylor, January 19, 1919, cited in ibid., 195; Taylor, *Pioneering on Social Frontiers*, "unbalanced," 239.

130   Graham Taylor to Raymond Robins, July 4, 1936, quote cited in Wade, *Graham Taylor: Pioneer for Social Justice, 1851–1938*, 195; see Graham Taylor, "Voting for the Best in a Bad Situation," *Daily News* (October 30, 1920); Taylor, "Deciding Votes Between Candidates," *Daily News* (November 1, 1924); Taylor, "The Man for the Present Crisis," *Daily News* (October 22, 1932).

131   Wade, *Graham Taylor: Pioneer for Social Justice, 1851–1938*, 217–18; see Robert L. Duffus, "On Social Frontiers in Chicago," *New York Times Book Review* (July 6, 1930), 4.

132   Wade, *Graham Taylor: Pioneer for Social Justice, 1851–1938*, 224; Percy Alden, "Graham Taylor: An Appreciation," *The Commons* (August 1897), 2, cited in ibid., 225.

133   Taylor, *Pioneering on Social Frontiers*, 391.

134   Graham Taylor, "The Church in Social Reforms, An Address Delivered in Boston, Mass., September 23, 1899, Before the International Congregational Council" (n.p., n.d.); reprinted as Taylor, "The Church in Social Reforms," Proceedings, Second International Congregational Council (Boston: Samuel Usher, 1899), 143–50; and Taylor, "The Social Function of the Church," *American Journal of Sociology* 5 (November 1899), 305–21; Wade, *Graham Taylor: Pioneer for Social Justice, 1851–1938*, 111–12.

Chapter 2

The Social Gospel

Washington Gladden, Josiah Strong, Walter Rauschenbusch,
and Harry F. Ward

The faults of the social gospel movement were extensive. It was sentimental, moralistic, idealistic, and politically naive. It preached a gospel of cultural optimism and a Jesus of middle-class idealism. Its claims to prophesy were belied by its class interests and late-Victorian sensibility. It was culturally chauvinistic, spoke the language of triumphal missionary religion, baptized the Anglo-Saxon ideology of Manifest Destiny, and rationalized American imperialism. For several years it fixated on a radical spellbinder, George Herron, who flamed out as quickly as he arose. It fell short of demanding racial justice or even integration, and with exceptions it gave tepid support to women's rights. It opposed World War I until a liberal Protestant president took the USA into the war, whereupon the movement promptly dispatched its opposition to war. After the war many social gospelers overreacted by reducing the social gospel to pacifist idealism, while the movement's successor to Walter Rauschenbusch, Harry F. Ward, became enthralled with Soviet communism. Faced with a generation that did not believe the world was getting better, the social gospelers tried to make adjustments in the 1930s, but not very convincingly.[1]

For decades the social gospel was ridiculed on these counts, beginning with Reinhold Niebuhr's frosty proto-Marxist polemic of 1932, *Moral Man and Immoral Society*. Two generations of seminarians learned about the social gospel by reading its Niebuhrian critics, not Rauschenbusch or Washington Gladden, and the reputation of the social gospel improved only slightly after Niebuhr's generation had passed. Despite its faults, however, the social gospel movement produced a greater progressive religious legacy than any generation before or after it. Christian realism inspired no hymns and built no lasting institutions. It was not even a movement, but rather, a reaction to the social gospel centered on one person, Reinhold Niebuhr. The social gospel, by contrast, was a half-century movement and enduring perspective that paved for way for everything else in social ethics. It had prominent black church advocates such as Reverdy Ransom, Benjamin E. Mays, and Mordecai Johnson. It had anti-imperialist, socialist, and feminist advocates on its side in addition to the mushy reformers. And it created the ecumenical and social justice ministries that remain the heart of American social Christianity.[2]

The notion that Christianity has a social mission to transform the structures of society in the direction of equality, freedom, and community was something new in Christian history. Nineteenth-century evangelicalism was rich in abolitionist and temperance convictions, and sometimes, feminist ones, but it had no theology of social salvation. Until the social gospel, no Christian movement did. In the process of theorizing what it meant to save the world, the social gospel movement, never a monolith, produced a few leaders that liberal Protestantism later preferred to forget. Josiah Strong was an irrepressible movement activist, but American Protestants were belatedly embarrassed by his ardent defense of Anglo-Saxon superiority. George Herron preached a sensational gospel of national salvation by class, but American capitalists did not repent of being capitalists, and Herron's scandalous divorce in 1901 made him an embarrassment. Harry F. Ward sought to renew the social gospel after it plunged into the ditch of World War I, but he became smitten with communism, the ultimate embarrassment. The greatest leaders of the social gospel were the two that history remembered as such: Washington Gladden and Walter Rauschenbusch.[3]

Good Theology and the Social Good: Washington Gladden

For thirty years the Social Gospel was usually called "Applied Christianity" and its public leaders were the pathbreakers that Peabody, Tucker, and Taylor assigned to their classes: Washington Gladden, Richard Ely, Josiah Strong, Shailer Mathews, George Herron. Walter Rauschenbusch soared past all of them in 1907. By 1910 the movement was usually called the Social Gospel, and Gladden was justly tagged as its father.

The "father of the Social Gospel" was christened Solomon Washington Gladden in 1836 and born in Pottsgrove, Pennsylvania to Solomon and Amanda Gladden. Family tradition held that his great-grandfather was one of George Washington's bodyguards, hence the middle name by which he later chose to be called. When Gladden was 5 years old his father died and he was sent to live with an uncle in Owego, New York, where his formal schooling was restricted to four months per year due to the demands of farm work. That turned out to be just enough, given his talents and bookish habits, to qualify him for Williams College and the Congregational ministry. As a youth Gladden identified with the antislavery movement and the Republican party. In the 1850s he studied at Williams College, got a Congregational preaching license without attending seminary, and took his first ministerial post in Brooklyn, New York.[4]

The Brooklyn congregation had few members, no leaders, and no natural constituency. Calling itself the First Congregational Methodist Church, it was the product of an angry split-off from a local Methodist congregation, and burdened with a huge church-building debt. For Gladden, a product of quiet villages and farm communities, the congregation and its city were both traumatizing. Brooklyn's population in 1860 was approximately 275,000. To Gladden the city seemed "a thing stupendous and overpowering, a mighty monster, with portentous energies." Its god-like powers left him stupefied, especially its power "to absorb human personalities and to shape human destinies." He was bewildered by the rushing complexity of the city: "Everything was alive, yet there was a vivid sense of the impersonality and brutality of the whole movement, of the lack of coordinating intelligence." Overwhelmed by his environment, burdened with administrative problems, poorly compensated, anxious about his inadequacies, and frightened about his country's impending war, Gladden unraveled emotionally. He suffered a nervous breakdown and resigned his position in June 1861.[5]

His personal breakdown mirrored the trauma of a nation descending into civil war. Business was paralyzed, Brooklyn merchants stood idle in the marketplace, and church attendance dwindled to nothing. Gladden found rescue in Morrisania, New York, a secluded suburban village. The tiny congregation of Morrisania, located two miles north of the Harlem River (later it became part of the Bronx), invited Gladden to regain his health as their pastor in a low-pressure environment. There he found healing and enrichment. He wanted to study at Union Theological Seminary, but managed to attend only a few lectures. As in his youth, he made up for sparse circumstances through independent reading, finding his reward in the writings of Horace Bushnell and English Anglican cleric Frederick Robertson.[6]

In Gladden's telling, Robertson opened his eyes and Bushnell taught him how to use them. From Robertson he learned to preach with imagination and daring; to Bushnell he owed his deliverance from believing in eternal hellfire and capricious divine judgment. Bushnell's book *God in Christ* convinced Gladden that Christianity made sense only as a form of progressive, ethical religion. The gospel became good news to him under the force of Bushnell's conviction that God is morally just. To Gladden, Bushnell was an inspiring model because he had the courage to reject offensive teachings, such as "that men should be judged and doomed before they were born; that men should be held blameworthy and punishable for what was done by their ancestors; that justice could be secured by the punishment of one for the sin of another."[7]

To carry on the work of theology and preaching in Bushnell's spirit was to reformulate Christian teaching from an ethical standpoint, Gladden judged. Modern theology needed to harmonize Christian teaching "with the ethical convictions and the spiritual needs of men," not refurbish doctrines that Bushnell rightly left behind.[8]

To this straightforward task Gladden dedicated his long career of preaching, ministry, journalism, and social activism. He ministered for five years in Morrisania, developed his theology, and regained his health; in 1866 he moved to North Adams Congregational Church in North Adams, Massachusetts, where his ambitions and horizon expanded almost immediately. Morrisania was homogeneous and suburban, but North Adams was a New England factory town and democratic community. People of different social classes regularly interacted in North Adams, sometimes antagonistically; the strains of industrial conflict and disorder were part of its social makeup. In Morrisania, Gladden's influence was restricted to his suburbanized congregation, but in North Adams, he had access to an entire community. The opportunity to practice a genuinely social ministry lifted his spirits; he embraced the opportunity to reach a wider public.

From the beginning, Gladden's social ministry was linked to his ideals of simplicity, frugality, and the right of constructive work. He was slow to perceive the structural down side of New England's booming industrialization. Lacking any grasp of labor politics, he stressed the moral responsibilities of workers and the wonders of machine production. His 1869 travel guide *From the Hub to the Hudson* celebrated New England's growing industries without a whiff of concern about working conditions, child labor, or labor rights. From the beginning, however, as throughout his career, he emphasized the necessity of a strong work ethic and the dignity of constructive work. Gladden worried about the corroding effects of commercial society on the virtues of honesty, integrity, and frugal living; on the other hand, in response to a local YMCA dispute, he defended the right of workers to enjoy innocent amusements such as backgammon, checkers, bowling, billiards, and square dancing. The latter venture plunged Gladden into a bitter, long-running controversy within a few months of his arrival in North Adams. The following year, on the occasion of his installation service, he invited the notorious Bushnell to sermonize on the meaning of Christian faith, which offended the same people scandalized by his position on square dancing.[9]

Gladden was opinionated, verbal, and politically engaged; his aggressive civic and religious activism put off many of his new neighbors; but he was never an ideologue. Even after he became a sharp critic of capitalism, he took a pragmatic approach to economic policy and emphasized the primacy of individual responsibility. His moralism was more yielding than most ministers on the right to innocent recreation, but he condemned gambling, alcohol imbibing, polka-dancing and waltzes, asserting that sexualized dancing of the latter sorts derived from the gutter depravity of Paris.

He was sensitive to the antagonism he inspired; he may have been theologically liberal, he acknowledged, but that did not make him any less centered in the life and teaching of Christ. Less than a year after Gladden arrived in North Adams, he preached a very personal sermon that defended his morality from sensational rumors. At the low point of his social ostracism, when he feared that Jesus was his only sure friend, he wrote a yearning, wistful hymn, "Oh, Master Let Me Walk with Thee," that became a classic of liberal Christian piety. The qualities of Christ-following vulnerability and good will that it expressed struck deep chords of feeling in what became the American social gospel movement. On the strength of these qualities and his public ministry, Gladden won the respect and affection of his congregation. He shaped North Adams Congregational to his religious sensibility, while members took pride in his growing reputation as a writer.[10]

In the late 1860s he started writing for the *Independent*, a leading national Congregational newspaper based in Brooklyn; in 1870 he became a mainstay of a new, soon legendary magazine, *Scribner's Monthly*, which was later renamed *The Century*; and in 1871 he got a fantasy offer from the *Independent* to be its religion editor. The irony of returning to the monster-metropolis of Brooklyn gave Gladden pause, but only briefly. This time he had a sense of self and calling that made him eager to seize a larger public. When a churchly cleric chided him that God called ministers to preach, not edit, Gladden retorted that if printing presses had existed in the first century, the apostle Paul surely would have published a newspaper.[11]

For four years Gladden interpreted trends in modern American religion to a mass audience, never hiding his viewpoint. Horace Bushnell, William Cullen Bryant, William Lloyd Garrison, Henry James, William Dean Howells, and John Greenleaf Whittier wrote frequently for the *Independent*. The office traffic alone was fascinating. Frequent visitors included Schuyler Colfax, the Vice-President of the United States; Massachusetts Senator Henry Wilson, who succeeded Colfax as Vice-President; and Garrison, whose late-life serenity impressed Gladden greatly.

Surrounded by such company, Gladden thrived and dissented. He celebrated the progress of liberal Protestant religion and embraced his employer's slogan: "Right, Radical, and Religious." In religious matters he had a straightforward concept of the difference between good and bad theology, which he expressed frequently: good theology stood for the moral good, while bad theology identified God or Christianity with morally repugnant beliefs. Everything else in religion was secondary to this moral test, he believed. From his surveyor's perch at the *Independent*, Gladden judged that American Christianity was generally improving, but still contained sizable factions that taught immoral doctrines as sacred truths; to Gladden, that was the mission field for liberal Christianity.[12]

His tenure at the *Independent*, however, increasingly taxed his own moral integrity. Gladden shared the paper's general politics, agreeing that good Republicanism supported the Republicans currently in power. But *Independent* publisher Henry Bowen was anxious to curry favor with President Grant, which caused friction between Gladden and Bowen over the paper's one-sided coverage of the 1872 presidential election and its lax coverage of corruption problems in the Grant Administration. Gladden also wanted the *Independent* to deal with the failures of Reconstruction, and he protested that Bowen blurred the distinction between the paper's editorials and its advertisements. Upon realizing, in November 1874, that Bowen's commercialization of the *Independent* was not going to change, Gladden returned to the pastorate, in Springfield, Massachusetts. In later life he remembered the Gilded Age as a low period in which a war-ravaged nation yielded to selfishness and corruption. Grant's presidency was ruined by the cultural aftershocks of the Civil War, and American society suffered a "serious loss of national probity and honor."[13]

In Springfield Gladden began to write books for the progressive religious movement that he believed was overdue. A journalist by training and temperament, he had a knack for explaining religious issues in everyday language. Most of his early books were collections of sermons and adult education lectures. *Being a Christian* (1876) argued that the heart of religion is its effect on personal character, and that one becomes a Christian by choosing the Christian way of life. *The Christian Way* (1876) urged that truthfulness is the essential virtue in life, even in business and religion. Christians in business were called to be beacons of truthfulness, while in religion, one of the worst evils was to pretend to believe something, or be forced to do so.[14]

Gladden gave seven years to Springfield, defending the right of workers to form unions, and in 1882 made his last career move, although he didn't think of it that way at the time. Offered a position at *The Century* by his friend Roswell Smith, he considered returning to full-time journalism. At the same time he was invited to the pastorate of First Congregational Church in Columbus, Ohio. Gladden was hesitant to leave New England, but Smith convinced him to take the Columbus position, urging that "every man ought to go west" for a few years. "If God calls, you go to the largest Congregational church in the name of Congregationalism at the West," Smith exhorted. "You have no conception of the power of such a position in Ohio. You would tower up there, head and shoulders above other men, in influence." That was assurance enough for Gladden. "The areas were larger, and so were the opportunities," he later recalled. "I might want to come back to the East, some day, but for the next ten years, at least, that was the place for me." He stayed for the remaining 36 years of his life, and amply fulfilled his friend's prediction.[15]

Columbus, Ohio was a good place to conjure the social meaning of Christianity, although Gladden was slow to concede the point. A city of 53,000 in 1882, Columbus was crude, mostly unpaved, and poorly lit when Gladden arrived there. The city's domestic architecture was depressing to him; the flatness and monotony of the Ohio landscape, "a perpetual weariness . . . hard to bear," were even more so. Ohio State University barely existed, numbering just over 300 students. Gladden cheered himself that Columbus was Ohio's capital city, "pervaded by the atmosphere of politics," and that some of its wide streets contained "large possibilities of beauty." In his early years there he gave more attention to national Congregationalist controversies than to local social concerns. Congregationalists fiercely debated the liberalization of Andover Seminary, the "Creed of 1883," and the "New Theology" of Congregational pastors

Theodore Munger and Newman Smyth. Gladden defended the liberalism of his friends Munger and Smyth as an overdue reform in American theology.[16]

Gradually he became a midwesterner, while ministering to an upscale church standing across the street from Ohio's state capital. A product of the complex interrelationship of Central Ohio Congregationalism and Presbyterianism, First Congregational Church derived from a blended Congregational–Presbyterian congregation named First Presbyterian. In 1852, a group of antislavery Congregationalists and Presbyterians broke away from First Presbyterian; four years later, following the trend of similar splinterings involving antislavery sentiment, they changed their name from Third Presbyterian to First Congregational. Long accustomed to social activism and progressive religion, the Columbus Congregationalists welcomed Gladden warmly, well beyond the standard of New England cordiality. Gladden worked hard for them, visiting nearly every family each year. On Sunday mornings he preached about personal religion; on Sunday evenings and various weekday occasions he preached on social and theological topics. All but a few of his 38 books were collections of his favorite sermons. Gladden was kindly, genial, and somewhat shy, with a keen sense of irony. Beloved by his Columbus congregation, he maintained cordial relations with most parishioners, though with a definite formal reserve; his personal correspondence extended to only a handful of parishioners. Occasions of intimate self-revelation were extremely rare for Gladden in any context; his memoir barely mentioned his wife, it gave little insight into his inner life, and it said nothing at all about his personal life after the Civil War.[17]

Gladden's memoir and prolific writings were much longer on "the industrial problem," "the municipal problem," "the Negro problem," and the merits of America's recent presidents. He later recalled that although American churches were still very conservative in the 1880s, they were "getting ready for a forward movement." For Gladden, the strike against the Columbus and Hocking Valley Coal and Iron Company in 1884–5 was a major turning point, because most of the company's top executives were members of his congregation. Beginning as a demand for higher wages, the strike quickly became a battle for and against trade unionism. Two of the company's vice presidents, Walter Crafts and Thaddeus Longstreth, were members of Gladden's board of trustees. Longstreth was militantly hostile to unionism; Crafts was a milder personality, yet he vowed to Gladden, "We'll kill that union if it costs half a million dollars." In the end, both sides suffered heavy losses. The strike lasted 11 months, ending with an abject surrender by the miners, who reorganized shortly afterward, forced the company to submit to outside arbitration, and won an arbitrated wage-fixing agreement. Crafts later conceded to Gladden that the company was better off dealing with an organized union than a mob.[18]

Gladden's lectures during this period launched the explicitly social gospel phase of his career. With earnest confidence he proclaimed that the church had a great deal to say about wealth, inequality, labor, unions, socialism, and war, "and it is high time that the Church of God were saying it from hearts of flame with tongues of fire." The Puritan roots of the social gospel showed through whenever he warmed to the theme of Christian America: "We must make men believe that Christianity has a right to rule this kingdom of industry, as well as all the other kingdoms of this world." The gospel recognizes no political or national boundaries on its claims, he exhorted. Morally serious Christianity claimed "that her law is the only law on which any kind of society will rest in security and peace; that ways must be found of incorporating good-will as a regulative principle, as an integral element, into the very structure of industrial society."[19]

Nearly always he followed with a qualifying assurance. Gladden prized his reputation for objectivity and fairness. He wanted the church to be the conscience of an expanding industrial society without taking sides in the class struggle. He stressed that both sides of the labor–capital wars often bargained in bad faith, considered only their own interest, demonized their opponents, and resorted to unjustified coercion. A characteristic speech on these themes, his most significant lecture of the mid-1880s, sought to mediate an 1886 strike in Cleveland. Gladden called for a negotiated settlement and pledge of cooperation. He endorsed trade unionism while censuring the war-like tactics of both sides: "Is not this business of war a senseless, brutal, barbarous business, at best? Does either side expect to do itself any good by fighting the other?" He made personal appeals and assurances:

> Permit me to say that I know something about this war; I have been in the thick of it for thirty years, trying to make peace, and helping to care for the sick and the wounded; and I know that the wrong is not all on one side, and that the harsh judgments and the fierce talk of both sides are inexcusable.

He allowed that both sides had strong arguments. The working class could not win the class struggle without uniting, and "the masters" could not win without smashing the unions. The problem was the shared assumption that winning and warfare were necessary. Gladden ended with a blend of personal and religious appeals: "Is it well, brother men, is it well to fight? Is it not better to be friends? Are you not all children of one Father? Nay, are you not, as the great apostle said, members one of another? Your war is not only wholesale fratricide, it is social suicide."[20]

This speech was widely praised for showing that the church could be an honest broker of labor–capital conflict. Invited to deliver it to the upscale Law and Order League of Boston, at Tremont Temple, Gladden received a rousing ovation and an invitation to give it the following week to a working-class audience in the same auditorium, by which he was cheered heartily. Loading his speeches with figures and topical references, his message featured the Golden Rule, a dualistic view of human nature, and a plea for cooperation. In the 1880s Gladden's ideas of the good society and social salvation were still essentially individualistic. Just as individuals should practice the Golden Rule of loving one's neighbor as oneself, he urged, employers and their employees should practice cooperation, disagreements should be negotiated in a spirit of other-regarding fellowship, and society should be organized to serve human welfare rather than profits. He disliked business corporations and corporate unionism because the virtues of other-regarding cooperation were practicable only for individuals and small groups. Gladden taught that all individuals combined traits of egotism and altruism and that both were essential to the creation of a good society. There was such a thing as self-regarding virtue, he acknowledged; without it society would have no dynamism or vigor. The problem was that American capitalism ran on competitive vigor alone.[21]

He was fond of saying that capitalism amounted to a "social solecism," holding society together on an anti-social basis. That was economics as war, he protested, "a war in which the strongest will win." Because the wage system was inherently predatory and anti-social, it was immoral and anti-Christian. Gladden reasoned that there were three fundamental options in political economy: relations of labor and capital could be based on slavery, wages, or cooperation. The wage system was better than slavery, he allowed, but it was still far from anything that Christian morality could accept. The first stage of industrial progress featured the subjugation of labor by capital; the second stage was essentially a war between labor and capital; the third stage was the social and moral ideal, the cooperative commonwealth in which labor and capital shared a common interest and spirit.[22]

Gladden believed during his early and middle career that this ideal was imminently attainable. "It is not a difficult problem," he assured his listeners, speaking of the class struggle. "The solution of it is quite within the power of the Christian employer. All he has to do is admit his laborers to an *industrial partnership* with himself *by giving them a fixed share in the profits of production*, to be divided among them, in proportion to their earnings, at the end of the year." Profit sharing was the key to making a good society in the realm of political economy. It rewarded productivity and cooperative action; it channeled the virtues of self-regard and self-sacrifice; it socialized the profit motive and abolished the wage system; and it promoted mutuality, equality, and community. To the Christian, Gladden contended, the strongest argument for cooperative economics was its simple justice:

> Experience has shown him that the wage-receiving class are getting no fair share of the enormous increase of wealth; reason teaches that they never will receive an equitable proportion of it under a wage-system that is based on sheer competition; equity demands, therefore, that some modification of the wage-system be made in the interest of the laborer. If it is made, the employer must make it.[23]

To the respected Protestant pastor who preached every Sunday to the business class and very few workers, the crucial hearts and minds belonged to the employers. The ideal solution was to convince the capitalist class to set up profit-sharing enterprises, not to abolish capitalism from above or below. In an age of ascending socialist movements, Gladden repeatedly cautioned that most employers were no less moral than the laborers they employed. It was too soon to give up on a decentralized, cooperative alternative to the wage system. The best strategy was to mobilize good will and channel self-interest to good ends, bringing about "the Christianization of the present order," not its destruction. More broadly, the "principal remedy" for the evils of the prevailing system was "the application by individuals of Christian principles and methods to the solution of the social problem."[24]

Gladden was slow to acknowledge the structural limitations on social justice. He sought to appeal to the rationality and moral feelings of a capitalist class increasingly pressured by embittered workers; only gradually did he perceive the irony of his assurance that business executives were at least as moral as their employees. If that was true, it showed that the crisis of the prevailing order was about more than the morality of individuals. As late as 1893, he defended his basic strategy of appealing to the moral feelings of the business class. Calling for an "industrial partnership" model of profit sharing, Gladden wrote, "I would seek to commend this scheme to the captains of industry by appealing to their humanity and their justice; by asking them to consider the welfare of their workmen as well as their own. I believe that these leaders of business are not devoid of chivalry; that they are ready to respond to the summons of good-will." At the same time, he acknowledged that he was moving to a more explicitly pro-union perspective: "I confess that I am strongly inclined to take the working-man's view." Capitalist America should be capable of forming industrial partnerships, he urged, even if it was not capable of moving all the way to cooperative ownership. In any case, he stopped promising that the class struggle could be easily remedied. The deepening chasm between labor and capital that Gladden witnessed in the 1890s drove him to a more realistic, structural view of political economy. His judgment that working people were losing the class war made him a stronger unionist, though he still blasted union violence and featherbedding.[25]

Like most of the social gospel movement, he took pains to dissociate himself from "socialism," by which he meant centralized state ownership of all or most business enterprises. But, like much of the social gospel movement, he moved to a "monopoly enterprises" socialism combined with an economic democracy model of profit-sharing and cooperative enterprises. Gladden's critique of state socialism was sensible and pre-scient. He objected that it denigrated the spirit of individual creativity and invention, ignoring "the function of mind in production – the organizing mind and the inventive mind." He added that Marxism was wrong about labor creating all value: "It is not true that labor is the sole cause of value or wealth. Many substances and possessions have great value on which no labor has ever been expended." Gladden rejected the Marxist and utopian socialist promise of providing meaningful work for everyone: "Socialism takes away the burdens that are necessary for the development of strength. It undertakes too much. It removes from the individual the responsibilities and cares by which his mind is awakened and his will invigorated."[26]

Most importantly, socialism was too grandiose and bureaucratic to work. It required enormous governmental power and virtually infinite bureaucratic wisdom. "The theory that it proposes is too vast for human power," Gladden objected. "It requires the state to take possession of all the lands, the mines, the houses, the stores, the railroads, the furnaces, the factories, the ships, – all the capital of the country of every description." Under a socialist order, he noted with incredulity, American government bureaucrats would be vested with the power to set wages, prices, and production quotas for a sprawling continent of consumers and producers: "What an enormous undertaking it must be to discover all the multiform, the infinite variety of wants of sixty millions of people, and to supply all these wants, by governmental machinery! What a tremen-dous machine a government must be which undertakes, in a country like ours, to perform such a service as this!" Americans were not accustomed to viewing govern-ment as an agent of redemption, and Gladden, while believing that Americans were too individualistic, also believed they were right not to make government "the medium and minister of all social good."[27]

Gladden-style applied Christianity was essentially moralistic, cooperativist, and pre-disposed to make peace. It was allergic to Marxist rhetoric about smashing the capitalist state. It was skeptical even of European social democracy. The social gospelers sought to Christianize society through further progress, reforms, and evangelization, not through revolutionary schemes to collectivize the economic order. Yet for all of Gladden's determination to stand for a third way, he drifted to the Left in the 1890s. He recognized that the greatest threat to his social vision came from a burgeoning corporate capitalism. He counseled that socialists should be respected, and respectfully corrected, as long as they avoided unnecessary violence. He called himself "enough of a Socialist" to advocate a foreign policy opposed to war and based on international treaties with all nations. His judgment that working people were losing ground in the class struggle caused him to defend the union movement most of the time. He insisted that the right to property was subordinate to the rights of life and freedom. He also significantly qualified his opposition to socialism, making exceptions for the entire class of economic monopolies. In the early 1890s, these included the railroad, telegraph, gas, and electric companies; Gladden later judged that mines, watercourses, water-suppliers, and telephone services also belonged to this category. The railroad companies in particular were "gigantic instruments of oppression." In any industry in which no effective competition existed, he argued, the only just recourse was state control. The railroad and electric companies did not operate under the law of supply and demand, nor offer their commodities or services in an open market; in effect, they closed the market. "This is not, in any proper sense, trade; this is essentially taxation," Gladden argued. "And, therefore, I think that all virtual monopolies must eventually belong to the state."[28]

His realism on the labor–capital struggle steadily deepened. In *Social Facts and Forces* (1897), Gladden argued that unionists had legitimate reasons to intimidate scab-laborers, though he still argued that the goal of trade unionism had to be human solidarity, not proletarian solidarity. His memoir, *Recollections* (1909), judged that America was probably headed for an imminent plunge "into a Socialistic experiment," though he warned that socialism was inferior to cooperative strategies and that American society was insufficiently educated and socialized for either approach. By the time that he wrote *The Labor Question* (1911), the social gospel was at high tide, but Gladden did not share Rauschenbusch's faith that the last unchristianized sector of American society – the economy – was in the process of being Christianized. The triumph of corporate capitalism and the rise of aggressive labor organizations such as the National Association of Manufacturers and the revolutionary Industrial Workers of the World (IWW) ended Gladden's fantasy of a paternalistic share-economy. He realized that his hope of a non-socialist, decentralized economic democracy had little material basis in a society increasingly divided along class lines. Giving up on profit sharing and co-operatives, he took his stand with a flawed labor movement. Unorganized labor was "steadily forced down toward starvation and misery," he observed. Elsewhere he lamented that corporate capitalism was becoming utterly predatory and vengeful toward unions, "maintaining toward them an attitude of almost vindictive opposition." In this context, unionism was the only serious force of resistance against the corporate deg-radation of labor. If the dream of a cooperative economy was to be redeemed, Gladden argued, it would have to be redeemed as a form of union-gained industrial democracy. The partnership between labor and capital that America needed more desperately than ever would have to be gained through union-organized collective bargaining, gaining for workers their appropriate share of economic control.[29]

The Social Gospel Difference and the Challenge of Darwinism

Every social gospeler was a theorist of social salvation, but Gladden was its foremost proponent; most of the early social gospelers got it from him. "The end of Christianity is twofold, a perfect man in a perfect society," he wrote in 1893, giving a liberal twist to postmillennialism, "These purposes are never separated; they cannot be separated. No man can be redeemed and saved alone; no community can be reformed and ele-vated save as the individuals of which it is composed are regenerated." The message of the gospel was addressed to individuals, Gladden allowed, but the gospel addressed each individual as a member of a social organism, which created the medium through which individuals responded to the message: "This vital and necessary relation of the individual to society lies at the basis of the Christian conception of life. Christianity would create a perfect society, and to this end it must produce perfect men; it would bring forth perfect men, and to this end it must construct a perfect society."[30]

The social gospelers claimed to recover the meaning of Christ's petition "Thy kingdom come." For Jesus, as for genuine Christianity, the purpose of God's inbreaking kingdom was to regenerate individuals and society as coordinate interests. Gladden taught that neither form of regeneration was possible without the other: "Whatever the order of logic may be, there can be no difference in time between the two kinds of work; that we are to labor as constantly and as diligently for the improvement of the social order as for the conversion of man." Personal and social regeneration had to go together. Gladden urged that the church's social mission was to claim the kingdoms of this world for the kingdom of Christ, including "the kingdom of commerce, and the kingdom of industry, and the kingdom of fashion, and the kingdom of learning, and the kingdom of amusement; every great department of society is to be pervaded by the Christian spirit and governed by Christian law."[31]

To Christianize society was to suffuse its sentiments, doctrines, customs, institutions, and laws with the Christian spirit. "This is what is meant by the coming to earth of the kingdom of heaven," Gladden explained. "We pray every day that it may come, but we do not by this prayer imply that its advent is still to be awaited." For Christ, as for the Christ-following church, the kingdom of God had already broken into nature and history as the Spirit that inspired the fulfillment of the divine will: "It was present then, this divine society, this kingdom of truth and love; and the centuries have but enlarged its dominion and confirmed its peaceful sway."[32] Gladden stressed that the early Christians, being subjects, not citizens, had no political responsibilities. "To preach politics to them would be like preaching about dancing to people with amputated limbs." The early Christians did not ask themselves how they should exercise power in a morally responsible way, but to modern Christians that was the central ethical question.[33]

Gladden pioneered a new kind of social ministry in the course of addressing this question. In addition to his extensive involvements in the ecumenical movement and building educational institutions for black Americans, he served on the Columbus city council, the Columbus board of trade, and, for many years, the labor committee of the National Council of the Congregational Churches. He took part in nearly every organization launched by the social gospel movement, including the Inter-Denominational Congress, founded by Josiah Strong in 1885, and the Evangelical Alliance, which became a social gospel vehicle under Strong's leadership in the late 1880s. With Ely and economist John Bates Clark he was a cofounder of the American Economic Association. In the early 1890s he joined Ely and Lyman Abbott in building up the Chautauqua Society, which spawned the American Institute of Christian Sociology (led by Ely), which spawned the Summer School of Applied Christianity. Gladden wrote frequently for the *Dawn*, a Christian Socialist monthly founded by W. D. P. Bliss, and the *Kingdom*, a social gospel periodical founded by Congregationalists.[34]

Near the end of Gladden's long ministerial career, his successor in Columbus, Carl S. Patton, told him that he had two absorbing interests: liberal theology and the social gospel. Gladden looked at him quizzedly and asked, "Well, what else IS there?" His generation made that a plausible question. After liberal theology took over the elite divinity schools and seminaries, Gladden wrote books that introduced biblical criticism and liberal theology to lay readers, and that erased any remaining distinction between liberal theology and the social gospel. For Gladden these movements belonged together as two facets of the same faith. His effectiveness as an advocate of liberal theology owed much to his relatively conservative version of it. Holding a pastor's aversion to what he called "the fields of destructive criticism," Gladden appropriated biblical criticism with a light touch. To him, being a theological liberal meant coming to terms with modern scholarship on the Bible, the Enlightenment and modern humanitarian critiques of religious authoritarianism, and Darwinian evolution. Sorting out the last of these challenges would have been enough for any generation – for the social gospel liberals, it was only part of a many-layered crisis of belief holding creative possibilities and perils on all sides.[35]

The unavoidable thinker for Gladden's generation was Herbert Spencer, the theorist of a massive system of evolutionary philosophy that included social Darwinism. Every liberal theologian of the late nineteenth century struggled to accommodate Darwinism, which required coming to terms with Spencer's enormously influential system. In the Gilded Age, American historian Richard Hofstadter observed, "it was impossible to be active in any field of intellectual work without mastering Spencer." The architects of American philosophical pragmatism and idealism (especially William James, Josiah Royce, John Dewey, and Borden P. Bowne) all struggled with Spencer's system, as did the founders of American sociology (Lester Ward, Charles Cooley, Albion W. Small, and Spencer's apologist, William Graham Sumner). In essence, Spencerism was a mechanistic world-systems philosophy. It combined Darwinian natural selection theory with *laissez-faire* economic ideology, anarchist politics, early thermodynamics theory, Sir Charles Lyell's geology, Lamarckian developmental theory, Malthusian population theory, and Samuel Taylor Coleridge's idea of a universal pattern of evolution. As a philosophy of evolution it described life as a continuous process of development from incoherent homogeneity (protozoa) to coherent heterogeneity; as a political philosophy it opposed all state-supported poor laws, education, sanitary supervision and other measures that impeded the beneficent natural process that Spencer called "the survival of the fittest."[36]

The social gospel liberals were intimidated, attracted, and appalled by Spencer's system all at once. They took much of it as an authoritative scientific description of the way the world worked. Gladden found it inspiring as proof of the unity and rationality of nature even as he blasted the parts that were moral non-starters. Appealing to Scottish philosopher Henry Drummond and "mutual aid" theorist Prince Kropotkin, Gladden insisted that life was not, and never had been, a purely predatory struggle for existence. Evolutionary science demonstrated that life was also a struggle for the life of others, he argued. The ruling principle of life was cooperation, not individual competition. Even animals and pre-historic tribes were self-sacrificing and cooperative in some of their everyday practices. More importantly, Gladden contended, the spiritual force that built the kingdom of God was self-sacrificing love, not survival of the fittest. That conviction stood behind the confident pronouncements of Gladden and Ely in founding the American Economic Association. To them, the modern trade union was second only to the church as a force for community, moral inspiration, and social justice.[37]

Scientists and historians later distinguished sharply between Darwinian theory and Spencer's rendering of it, but the social gospelers did not have that working for them.

In their time Spencer had immense prestige. Even as they said "no" to social Darwinism they felt obliged to deal with the rest of his system, especially the parts that were plainly Darwinian. Darwin and Spencer raised for them with particular urgency the question of how theology should accept correction from science. Did natural selection leave room for God? The social gospel liberals took comfort that Darwin left room for God, but they were keenly aware that many Darwinists did not, and that the academy was leaving God behind. On this matter they took guidance from John Fiske, a brilliant polymath and America's leading popularizer of Darwinian theory.

Fiske allowed that Spencer got Darwin mostly right, but he rejected Spencer's claim that the reality behind the universe was unknowable. At a banquet in Spencer's honor he noted that even Spencer spoke of a "Power" in life that was revealed "in every throb of the mighty rhythmic life of the universe." Taking from Spencer the evolutionary concept of life as a continuous adjustment of inner relations to outer relations, Fiske argued that this outlook made a better fit with a religious worldview than with atheism, because evolutionary theory and religion were both concerned with the manifestations of a single, infinite, and eternal Power. Living things were fundamentally characterized by their response to external stimuli, he explained, just as Spencer said. The eye began with pigment grains in a dermal sac, making the spot sensitive to light, "then came, by slow degrees, the heightened translucence, the convexity of surface, the refracting humors, and the multiplication of nerve vesicles arranging themselves as retinal rods." The complex adjustment of inner relations to outer relations produced an immense expansion of life: "Then came into existence, moreover, for those with eyes to see it, a mighty visible world that for sightless creatures had been virtually non-existent."[38]

In Fiske's telling, the evolution of the eye was a paradigmatic process of preparation for the revelation of the glory of creation. It provided, like all examples of evolutionary process, a telling analogy of the constitutively human impulse to worship, the universal human response to the indwelling of human beings in creation. All the analogies of evolutionary science confirmed the existence of a human impulse to reach out to an unseen world, he argued. In every instance of expansion and as a whole, nature shouted against the atheistic assumption of a breach of continuity between human evolution and other evolution:

> So far as our knowledge of Nature goes the whole momentum of it carries us onward to the conclusion that the Unseen World, as the objective term in a relation of fundamental importance that has coexisted with the whole career of Mankind, has a real existence; and it is but following out the analogy to regard that Unseen World as the theatre where the ethical process is destined to reach its full consummation.[39]

The social gospel liberals took their bearings from that assurance. Gladden called Fiske's writings "a veritable evangel to many groping minds." Following Fiske, Gladden wrote that the "greatest fact" of human history "is this universal belief in an unseen world and in a God who is the Father of our spirits. *It is this fact, which evolution, through countless ages, has been producing.*" Fiske taught that immense variation was the first great truth of evolution, but the entire series, "in each and every one of its incidents," showed the divine creativity at work. Gladden replied with gratitude: "That is the last, the sanest, and the strongest word that evolution has to speak respecting the fundamental truth of evolution." Religion was too deeply insinuated in the nature and evolutionary history of humankind to be cast aside, Gladden asserted. Admittedly, science dismantled the old supernatural worldview, but that was a good thing; at the same time, science needed religion as a break on its tendency to merely rip things apart. Religion reminded science not to ignore the Power "by which all these fragments are knit together in unity." Gladden enthused that modern theology made Christianity stronger by making it more credible than ever before.[40]

Manifest Destiny and the Crucible of Race: Fiske, Gladden, and Josiah Strong

The legacy of John Fiske in liberal theology was more complex and ambiguous, however, than his apologetic service on theism. Fiske helped the liberals save a role for God in evolutionary process, but he belongs to history as the leading theorist of Manifest Destiny, a notion that infected much of the social gospel movement with a "scientific" rationale for Anglo-Saxon superiority and expansion. The same social gospelers who blasted social Darwinism as a morally repugnant basis for political economy had a tendency to invoke its authority on behalf of Anglo-Saxonism. That part of it was not morally repugnant to them, since it confirmed their prejudices and self-regard, and they had Fiske's authority for it. A generally pacific figure, Fiske embraced Spencer's claim that militarism and violence belonged to the pre-industrial stages of civilization, and he had global ambitions for the race that created industrial civilization.[41]

The "manifest destiny" of Anglo-Saxon America was a favorite theme of Fourth of July orators long before Fiske endorsed it. His contribution was to enlist evolutionary science on its behalf, and thus make it respectable and historic. In *The Descent of Man* Darwin predicted, and then hedged on his prediction, that the advance of higher civilizations would gradually extinguish the world's backward races. Fiske did not hedge. Brushing away Darwin's equivocations on social Darwinism, he nominated "the English race" (Fiske eschewed the term Anglo-Saxon) as the civilizing hope of the world. The imperial outreach of England and the out-populating power of the USA put the entire planet within reach of English civilization, he observed; by his "extremely moderate" estimate, America's population would exceed 700 million by the end of the twentieth century.[42]

In Fiske's view, American civilization had exactly the right combination of social factors to peaceably civilize the world: democracy, federal-system diversity, and industrialism. If only the USA were to drop its backward, shameful tariff system and openly compete with the rest of the world, it would transform the world through commerce and the power of its superior civilization. America and England possessed the power to remake the world in their own image. That was the hope of world peace and prosperity. As long as the world remained partly barbarous, Fiske argued, war was inevitable. For the barbarous races, war was "both a necessity and a favourite occupation." Thus, the civilized nations had to be willing to fight to keep the barbarians from destroying civilization. On the other hand, civilized Christian nations did not wage wars against each other; the very thought of it was "a wretched absurdity." Civilized peoples did not kill each other, and Christian civilization was the solution to war. Fiske taught that American civilization was the symbol and beginning of the world's salvation. Establishing American democracy and federalism over the entire

American continent was a good beginning; the goal was to establish it "over the world." The manifest destiny of the English race was to make all of humanity civilized and Christian.[43]

Fiske's signature oration on this theme, "Manifest Destiny," was first delivered to the Royal Institute of Great Britain and published in *Harper's Magazine* in 1885, and it made him famous. He gave the speech in cities across the USA, drawing huge crowds and acclaim. At the request of President Rutherford B. Hayes and General William T. Sherman he gave it in Washington and made a great success, all of which heightened his reputation among anglophile social gospelers. More importantly, all of this was a mere overture to the explosive impact of Josiah Strong's *Our Country*, also published in 1885, which mixed the same argument with a strong blend of rural Protestant virtues and prejudices.

In 1885 Josiah Strong was a restless, energetic, but little-accomplished ministerial activist whose career stops had led to a five-year stint as Secretary of the American Home Missionary Society in Ohio, Kentucky, West Virginia, and western Kentucky. In the latter capacity he produced an electrifying rewrite of a stock Home Missionary theme. For more than 40 years the American Home Missionary Society published a series of articles and booklets titled *Our Country*. Always it detailed the challenges to American missions posed by heathen Indians, Catholic immigrants, Mormons, rationalist infidels, and Wild West barbarism in general. Bushnell's *Barbarism the First Danger* was a staple of this series. Strong's contribution to the series culled information from a wide range of sources, including some that were quite new to missionary literature. *Our Country* was written to raise money for the mission movement. It also launched a sizable segment of the social gospel movement and turned Strong into the movement's organizational leader.[44]

Like its namesake publications, *Our Country* was long on the "perils" that stood in the way of a Christianized America, especially immigration, Romanism, Mormonism, intemperance, socialism, concentrated wealth, and cities. Though most of the social gospel literature was optimistic, a spirit of crisis pervaded *Our Country*. The American experiment showed signs of going seriously wrong, Strong warned: "Glory is departing from many a New England village, because men alien in blood, in religion, and in civilization, are taking possession." At the same time, he acknowledged that the "marked superiority" of the Anglo-Saxon race owed much to its "highly mixed origin." The Anglo-Saxons were Saxons, Normans, and Danes, but also Celts and Gauls, Irish and Welsh, Frisians and Flamands, French Huguenots and German Palatines. This fact explained a great deal about the vitality and superiority of the Anglo-Saxon race, Strong asserted. It was superior because it assimilated inferior races. Strong boasted that by Ralph Waldo Emerson's criterion – "the best nations are those most widely related" – the USA was already by far the world's best nation: "There is here a commingling of races; and, while the largest injections of foreign blood are substantially the same elements that constituted the original Anglo-Saxon admixture, so that we may infer the general type will be preserved, there are strains of other bloods being added." If America managed its immigration policy carefully, the Anglo-Saxon race was sure to rise to a "higher destiny" in America and the world.[45]

Strong explained that every great race was defined by one or two great ideas. For the Greeks, it was beauty; for the Hebrews, purity; for the Romans, law; for the Anglo-Saxons, the ruling ideas were civil liberty and pure spiritual Christianity. These ideas elevated the human race to its present state of achievement, Strong observed, and fortunately, the Anglo-Saxons were also "the great missionary race." In a single century the USA had increased its territory by ten-fold while the English built a global empire. Strong enthused, "This mighty Anglo-Saxon race, though comprising only one-thirteenth part of mankind, now rules more than one-third of the earth's surface, and more than one-fourth of its people." Moreover, by the end of the twentieth century, he expected Anglo-Saxons to outnumber "all the other civilized races of the world." Believing that the course of history reflected God's providential will for the world, he asserted that the meaning of the Anglo-Saxon ascendancy was theological: "Does it not look as if God were not only preparing in our Anglo-Saxon civilization the die with which to stamp the peoples of the earth, but as if he were also massing behind that die the mighty power with which to press it?"[46]

The Anglo-Saxons were the savior race, and America was destined to be "the great home of the Anglo-Saxon, the principal seat of his power, the center of his life and influence." England's "pretty island" was too small to transform the world. Anticipating Frederick Jackson Turner by a decade, Strong predicted that the approaching American settlement of the world's last great frontier would be an important turning point in American and world history. The American continent was enormous, with excellent resources and climate: "It lies in the pathway of the nations, it belongs to the zone of power, and already, among Anglo-Saxons, do we lead in population and wealth."[47]

Because the Americans were Anglo-Saxons, they possessed a fervent colonizing spirit; Strong called it "an instinct or genius for colonizing." The Anglo-Saxon was typically energetic, perseverant, and independent; "he excels all others in pushing his way into new countries." Strong allowed that there was a down side to all of this pushing and colonizing. The world's great races spent most of their time fighting wars, and the Anglo-Saxons were no exception. They had to kill a lot of people to get ahead. But the world was progressing beyond the stage of war and conquest, and it was making this advance through the progress of Anglo-Saxon Christianity and industrialism: "We are leaving behind the barbarism of war; as civilization advances, it will learn less of war, and concern itself more with the arts of peace, and for these the massive battle-ax must be wrought into tools of finer temper." Citing battlefield statistics from the Civil War, Strong showed that Americans were growing taller and stronger. The "superior vigor" of the American people confirmed Darwin's suggestion in *The Descent of Man* that the "wonderful progress of the United States, as well as the character of the people, are the results of natural selection."[48]

Strong's conclusion combined God and Darwin. Through the evolutionary process of natural selection, he explained, God was "training the Anglo-Saxon race for an hour sure to come in the world's future." Strong admonished his readers that Christianity was the crucial underpinning of Anglo-Saxon superiority; if the Anglo-Saxons discarded Christianity and rested on their racial advantages alone, the race would "speedily decay." But as long as the Anglo-Saxons remained Christian, the "dark problem of heathenism among many inferior peoples" had a divine solution. God's "final and complete solution" was contained in what Bushnell called "the out-populating power of the Christian stock." The divine solution to history was the Anglo-Saxon Christianization of America and then the world.[49]

Our Country struck a deep cultural nerve, setting off an intense reaction. As a reflection of American Gilded Age anxieties, it remains singularly revealing; Strong understood very well the mind and feelings of his country's dominant culture. His position at the right edge of the social gospel movement, theologically and politically, made him an effective proponent of the social gospel in mainstream church circles. The book sold 175,000 copies in English and made its author a major movement figure. In 1886 Strong became secretary of the American Evangelical Alliance (the organizational forerunner of the Federal Council of Churches). Under his leadership the Evangelical Alliance became an institutional vehicle of the social gospel, convening influential conferences in 1887, 1889, and 1893. The 1887 conference in Washington attracted nearly 1,500 delegates; the 1889 conference in Boston focused on urban problems and progress in industrial cooperation; the 1893 conference in Chicago, held in connection with the World's Columbian Exposition, featured new social gospel leaders George Herron and Jane Addams. In the same year Gladden, Ely, Peabody, and Albion Small represented the social gospel at the World's Parliament of Religions.[50]

Strong wanted the Protestant churches to pull together and stop competing with each other. His book *The New Era, or, The Coming Kingdom* (1893) protested that many towns had too many churches, especially in wealthy areas, while many poor communities had no church at all. That was no way to Christianize America. The moral crisis of American civilization had not passed, he warned. America had an immense capacity to advance the cause of righteousness on earth, and to hinder it. America's race-blending was a good thing within limits, Strong allowed, but its immigration policy ignored those limits, which ran down America's Anglo-Saxon stock: "There is now being injected into the veins of the nation a large amount of inferior blood every day of every year." Immigration was corrupting America, and so was alcohol. The cause of the kingdom required Americans to annihilate the saloon "and every other agency which is devitalizing and corrupting our population." If America was to Christianize the world, it had to begin with itself. In a single-sentence aside that cried out for a chapter, Strong declared, "I do not imagine than an Anglo-Saxon is dearer to God than a Mongolian or an African." Since Anglo-Saxonism was a cultural category for him, he did not regard himself as a racist, and was not taken as one by black associates such as Booker T. Washington. To Strong, the point of the social gospel was always the Christianization of the world: "My plea is not, Save America for America's sake, but, Save America for the world's sake."[51]

World events evoked further clarifications about what it meant to "Christianize the world." In the late 1890s, after the USA stepped dramatically onto the stage of empire, Strong and Lyman Abbott led the movement's pro-imperial faction; Taylor, George Herron, Edward Everett Hale, and Henry van Dyke led the anti-imperial resistance; Gladden carved a path between the two flanks. Strong urged that it was no longer possible for Americans to "drift with safety to our destiny." America was God's chosen nation, "shut up to a perilous alternative," and was now obliged to accept moral responsibility for its redeemer status. Abbott's *Outlook* took the same line, enthusing that "the army among Anglo-Saxon peoples is no longer a mere instrument of destruction. It is a great reconstructive organization." Abbott explained that the "function of the Anglo-Saxon race" was to confer the civilizing gifts of law, commerce, and education "on the uncivilized people of the world." Replying to dissident Republicans like Andrew Carnegie and George F. Hoar, "mugwump" anti-imperialists like William James and Charles Eliot Norton, and social gospelers like Taylor and Herron, Abbott pronounced: "It is said that we have no right to go to a land occupied by a barbaric people and interfere with their life. It is said that if they prefer barbarism they have a right to remain barbarians. I deny the right of a barbaric people to retain possession of any quarter of the globe. What I have already said I reaffirm: barbarism has no rights which civilization is bound to respect. Barbarians have rights which civilized people are bound to respect, but they have no right to their barbarism."[52]

Gladden took the same view while trying not to sound like an imperialist, holding out for the primacy of good intentions. Between 1888 and 1898 he traveled to England four times, and found that England and America were essentially alike. Continental Europe, on the other hand, felt truly alien and often repulsive to him, even in the Protestant countries. Civilized nations did not fight each other, Gladden asserted, but sometimes they could not escape fighting wars against barbarism. Thus, England and America needed to stand together to defend and extend Christian civilization. Shortly before the outbreak of the Spanish–American war, Gladden was repulsed by reports that Spanish soldiers were butchering Cubans involved in the Cuban rebellion. Though he judged that the Cubans were too "ignorant, superstitious, brutal and degraded" to be capable of self-government, he supported the Spanish–American war as a humanitarian commitment to repel their oppressors. His chief concerns in 1898 were that America needed to maintain pure motives in fighting the war and also maintain its friendship with England. He rejected imperialist and anti-imperialist rhetoric alike on the same ground; both groups assumed that American policy was based on selfish motives. "We are not going to be dragged into any war for purposes of conquest – neither for the acquisition of territory nor for the extension of trade," Gladden countered. "And those who are preaching this jingoism to-day should be warned that the Nation has a conscience that can speak and make itself heard, and that will paralyze its arm whenever it is lifted to do injustice to any weaker people."[53]

That was a mainstream social gospel perspective at the turn of the century. In the name of peace and humanitarianism, Gladden supported his country's imperial maneuvers in Latin America, the Philippines, the Middle East, Africa, and East Asia. Like Mathews and even (for a time) Rauschenbusch, he took it for granted that America intervened only to liberate and civilize. It was "morally unthinkable" to him that the United States might set free the Philippines, Puerto Rico, and Guam after Spain relinquished these colonial possessions. He lectured that "degraded races" never worked their way up to civilization: history showed that "inferior races" had to be lifted up to civilized standards of behavior by stronger races. Gladden exulted that his country was beginning to join England in this humanitarian mission. He supported America's suppression of the Philippine independence rebellion of 1899, contending that the Philippinos were too backward for independence; he judged that Cuba needed "many years" of careful guidance and sharply criticized President Theodore Roosevelt for withdrawing from Cuba; anxious for Christian access to "the vast mongolian population," he took pride in America's role in establishing an open door to China.[54]

At the beginning of each year Gladden preached a sermon on the ways that America and the world had improved over the past year. Equating divine providence with civilizational progress, he found ample evidence of progress. In his later career, before World War I made a terrible mockery of it, he dreamed that the world's progress towards civilization and its frightful new weapons were making war obsolete. Civilized nations did not fight each other, he reasoned, and the new machinery of mass destruction functioned as a deterrent to war. At the same time, he threw himself into a host of causes where progress lagged. Gladden advocated municipal ownership of public-service industries as an antidote to monopoly corruption; he supported numerous municipal and antipoverty reforms, as well as the municipal church movement; he persistently spoke against anti-Catholic prejudice, which cost him the presidency of Ohio State University in 1893; more than most social gospelers, he also welcomed African-American speakers to his pulpit and worked for many years to create new educational and industrial opportunities for American blacks.[55]

The primary vehicle for his outreach to blacks was the American Missionary Association (AMA), a consolidation of several Congregational antislavery missionary societies that was founded in 1846. Before the Civil War the AMA worked entirely among northern blacks, but after the war it moved into the south and established numerous schools and churches open to blacks. The schools included Hampton Institute, Fisk University, Berea College, Tillotson Institute, Atlanta University, Howard University, Tougaloo University, Straight University, and Talladega College, as well as scores of primary and secondary schools. In its early postwar ministries, the AMA fought against segregation; later it acquiesced to the demands of a dominant segregationist culture. Over the course of his long association with the organization, Gladden served in a variety of capacities, including vice-president and president. For nearly 30 years, he accepted the line on black development eventually identified with Booker T. Washington, telling wary audiences that the AMA did not seek integration or political equality for blacks; it was enough to help blacks get on their feet after the ravages of slavery.

Gladden believed that Reconstruction was a catastrophe that unnecessarily alienated white southerners; for years he insisted that genuine reconstruction had to begin with "civilizing" education programs and take into account the bruised feelings of southerners. He never fully absorbed the fact that white racism was the chief cause of America's terrible racial problems after the war. In the 1890s, however, his optimism that American race relations were improving was belatedly chastened by the persistence of violence against blacks. In 1895 Gladden urged the AMA to condemn racist lynchings; the following year he admonished the AMA that conditions for blacks in America were not much better than slavery. The public reaction to President Roosevelt's welcome of Booker T. Washington to the White House was a measure of white America's contempt for blacks. Roosevelt's hospitality to a black man set off a firestorm of criticism and ridicule. The AMA, at the same meeting that elected Gladden to its presidency in 1901, solemnly commended Roosevelt. Two years later, upon reading W. E. B. Du Bois's newly published book *The Souls of Black Folk* Gladden converted to an equality-seeking racial politics. He had met Du Bois at Atlanta University and was greatly impressed. *The Souls of Black Folk* pressed upon him the fact that blacks were oppressed in the south as a class and that Washington-style uplift programs wrongly denigrated the importance of higher education for blacks. Gladden heralded the book to Christian audiences. While affirming that the AMA stood "for no unnatural fusion of races, for no impracticable notions of social intercourse," he urged that political equality was another matter entirely. Social equality was negotiable, but justice was not. Christian morality and the demands of justice required nothing less than "perfect equality for the Negro before the law, and behind the law." With his conversion to this view, Gladden was administered a strong taste of the extent of American racism in reading his mail. He later admitted that the "bitter and violent" letters he received gave him a new realization of what blacks were up against in his beloved country.[56]

On this issue, as on others, Gladden landed in the middle of the social gospel movement, leaning Left. He urged that the Washington versus Du Bois debate presented a false choice. To him, *The Souls of Black Folk* was a singularly revealing work that illuminated the consciousness and subjection of an oppressed minority. Gladden accepted educational restrictions on the franchise, "but when one law is made for black men and another for white men, the injustice is so glaring that it cannot endure." He believed it was wrong to emphasize industrial education to the exclusion of higher education. Industrial education was appropriate for the masses, he reasoned, but America needed black leaders also: "I fear that Mr. Washington is putting too much weight on economic efficiency as the solvent of race prejudice. All that Booker Washington is doing we may heartily rejoice in, but there are other things that ought not be left undone." Gladden stuck to that "both–and" for the rest of his life: "There is no reason why there should be any quarrel between these two classes of educators; each needs the other's aid." He also praised "the glorious company" of his white southern allies, admonishing that cultivating the good will of white Americans was part of the struggle for racial justice. The saving work of the AMA was impossible without the good will of white southerners "whose eyes are open to the ethical principles involved in our most serious social question." Though he acknowledged in 1909 that most southerners did not yet share his view of the race problem, "it is the opinion that must prevail, because this is a moral universe."[57]

The Great War and the Social Gospel

His belief that the good was prevailing held firm until the year of his retirement, 1914. Gladden ended his autobiography with a stirring affirmation of the moral universe. The nations were piling up weapons, he allowed in 1909, and organized capital and labor were waging class war, but these were the last gasps of a discredited principle. It was not possible that the world would indulge the "howling farce" of violence for much longer. The civilized nations were converting the world to "the possibility of cooperation as the fundamental social law." The kingdom of God was growing under modernity. "It is impossible that the nations should go on making fools of themselves," Gladden averred. The world was getting better through the influence of the United States, which was growing more Christianized. Gladden exhorted his readers,

> We turn our faces to the future with good hope in our hearts. There are great industrial problems before us, but we shall work them out; there are battles to fight, but we shall win them. With all those who believe in justice and the square deal, in kindness and good will, in a free field and a fair chance for every man, the stars in their courses are fighting, and their victory is sure.[58]

Five years later he retired from First Church, Columbus, shortly before Europe descended into World War I. In a stream of sermons he condemned the war and tried to make sense of it. Gladden claimed at first that the world was still getting better, because the war showed the futility of war and the necessity of a federation of nations. Blaming the war on the corruption and privileged egotism of Europe's ruling classes, he charged that so-called war fever was nothing but ruling class manipulation of the hatred and nationalistic fears of ordinary people. Gladden's anglophilia did not extend to solidarity in war, at least not before 1917. Against Lyman Abbott, Harry Emerson Fosdick, and other early proponents of American preparedness and participation, Gladden campaigned against preparedness. He gave antiwar speeches and joined anti-interventionist organizations, including the American Peace Society, the Church Peace Union (founded by Andrew Carnegie), and the American Alliance for International Friendship. He even joined the League to Enforce Peace, holding his nose at associating with William Howard Taft. By 1915 Gladden was willing to take antiwar allies wherever he could find them.[59]

"I am a pacifist myself," he announced in the *New Republic*. "At the beginning of this war my pacifism was mild and moderate, but with every month it has grown more radical and more irreconcilable; the one lesson I have learned is the insanity of militarism." He allowed that self-sacrificial love was a beautiful virtue, "but to kill for one's country is neither sweet nor beautiful." He was ready to give his life for America, but would never be ready to kill for it – "that does not invite me." 'War is madness, Gladden cautioned; "it is the reversal of the nature of things; it is a social solecism." Not quite a pacifist, Gladden granted that fighting in self-defense to prevent a horrible outcome was morally justified. But the Great War was nothing like a last resort to avert a horrible outcome; it was fueled on all sides by aggression, corruption, and greed. It lacked a redeeming or justifying moral purpose. None of the warring parties showed any interest in brokering terms of peace. England and France entered the war ostensibly to prevent German conquest, he observed, but now both countries were clearly determined to conquer Germany. In the *Nation* Gladden bitterly lamented that war was great for science and technology, creating "new machinery for maiming and mangling and brutalizing men, new methods of inflicting torture" and new devices "for erasing the beauty of the earth and ruining its fairest monuments."[60]

Until December 1915 President Wilson was an ally of the "peace and unpreparedness" forces, but on December 7 Wilson announced in his State of the Union address that the cause of American peace could no longer afford American unpreparedness. Wilson's military build-up called for a standing army of 142,000 and a reserve force of 400,000. Three days later Wilson stroked familiar chords in a speech to the Federal Council of Churches: Christianity was not important as a body of doctrines, he told the liberal Protestant leaders; it was important as "a vital body of conceptions which can be translated into life for us." Just as cooperation was "the vital principle of social life," Christianity was "the most vitalizing thing in the world." Gladden took a diplomatic tack in responding to the President. In a letter he thanked and praised Wilson for commending the social gospel – "the best of it was that you knew what it was that you were trying to commend." He ended by asking the president to read his enclosed manifesto for pacifism: "It is not often that your policy fails of my hearty approval, but here is a matter in which I wish I might have a hearing." Wilson graciously replied that it gave him second thoughts to be opposed by someone like Gladden. He promised to read the pamphlet; in the meantime he assured Gladden that he was determined to conduct his policies in accordance with Gladden's ideals.[61]

Gladden feared that Wilson was set upon the path to war. From the pulpit he declared, "Just now it appears probable that our nation is going to be sucked into the maelstrom; and plunged into a conflict with a people with whom we have no legitimate quarrel. The people of the United States and the people of Germany are not enemies. We bear them no grudges." The following January he warned that public sentiment was shifting in the direction of intervening, even though Americans had no concept of what they might hope to accomplish. "What is going to happen at the close of this war?" he asked. "What will be the condition of the Great European nations when they stop fighting?" Setting himself against Wilson's military build-up,

Gladden joined forces with Jane Addams and Unitarian pacifist John Haynes Holmes, appearing before military affairs committees of the House and Senate and making antiwar speeches. For weeks he toured New England as a featured speaker of the anti-preparedness movement. War was abominable, he pleaded, America had no reason to attack Germany, and it lacked a coherent vision of postwar Europe. In a book, *The Forks of the Road* (1916), Gladden implored that it was not too late for America and other nations to accept the law of love as the governing law of the world.[62]

Every selfish act bred deeper selfishness, selfishness bred hate, and hate was murderous, Gladden admonished his readers, appealing to the spirit of Jesus. He refused to believe that humankind disagreed with him amid the carnage of the war: "I confess that I am unable to entertain such a benumbing conception. I cannot even imagine that this bloody lesson will be lost upon the world." At the same time he warned that a host of "sinister and infernal influences" were at work to push the USA into war. Some "hysterical alarmists" scared Americans with invasion fantasies; others, "a good many partly developed human beings," found the smell of blood exciting. They were anxious not to miss out on the thrill of killing. Then there was the sinister influence of war capitalism: "There are tremendous financial combinations involving billions of capital, which stand to make immense profits out of war, and out of the preparation for war, and they are moving heaven and earth today to drive this nation into the complications which will put money in their purses."[63]

Believing deeply in the cooperative psychology of civilization, Gladden pleaded against regressing to the "ape and tiger psychology" of barbarism and the animal world. Civilized relations were based on mutual trust, he observed; in civilized societies, people did not carry weapons or live by the law of retribution. Yet in the present war, civilized nations were reverting to animal violence and living by retribution. Meanwhile the United States moved steadily closer to this "Gehenna of militarism." The prospect of it filled Gladden with revulsion: "God grant that I may not live to see it!"[64] He implored Wilson to take the lead in organizing a "League of Peace" that outlawed war and enforced the moral law with international police power: "This war is the most astounding development of history; should not the reactions which follow the war be equally astounding?"[65]

Except for 1912, when he supported Theodore Roosevelt's Progressive ticket, Gladden had voted Republican all his life. Like most reformers, however, he supported Wilson in 1916, mostly because Wilson seemed closest to him on the peace issue. A month after the election, Wilson asked the warring powers to state their war aims. Gladden took heart that the President was determined to obtain conditions for peace negotiations and keep America out of the war. He met with Wilson shortly afterward, who apparently expressed his resolve to broker terms of peace. Appearing before the US Senate on January 22, Wilson called for the creation of a "League of Peace" and urged the warring parties to negotiate a "peace without victory." The war needed to be resolved in a way that did not produce bitter losers, and the proposed federation of peace-loving nations would keep the peace: "The equality of nations upon which peace must be founded if it is to last must be an equality of rights. Only a peace between equals can last. Only a peace the very principle of which is equality and a common participation in a common benefit."[66]

It was a stirring moment for social gospel progressives and liberal internationalists. Wilson's dramatic address was a page from the diplomatic sections of *The Forks of the Road*. He seemed to be sincere about living up to social gospel ideals. But the warring powers on both sides were determined to gain victory, and on January 31, Germany declared that it would resume unrestricted submarine warfare against all ships, armed or unarmed, that sailed into a German war zone. Three days later the American steamship *Housatonic* was sunk without warning. Wilson broke off diplomatic relations with Germany, declaring that Germany's resumption of unrestricted submarine warfare was an intolerable act of aggression.[67]

Gladden sadly accepted that Wilson had no alternative. In February the British Secret Service intercepted a telegram from the German Foreign Minister Zimmerman to the German Ambassador in Mexico in which the German Foreign Minister schemed for Mexican entrance into the war on the side of the Central Powers in return for New Mexico, Texas and Arizona. The following month five American ships were sunk without warning. Gladden struggled with his conscience while most Americans decided for war. He wrote a book titled "Killing Wrong-Doers as a Cure for Wrong-Doing." The title brought a smile to Rauschenbusch's face just before America went to war, but the book was never published. Gladden mused from the pulpit that perhaps this war – "the darkest cloud that has ever obscured the sky" – contained a glimmer of light. The world's leaders, to judge from their recent words, seemed to be sickening of the war: "All the great people in the world, the kings, kaisers, czars, emperors, chancellors, presidents, princes, foreign ministers – all the people who make wars – are now with one voice declaring and proclaiming that there are to be no more wars; that this is the last war." The idea of going to war to put an end to war was the kind of rationale that Gladden needed.[68]

On April 2 Wilson expressed this rationale in political terms, telling a joint session of Congress that America needed to join the war against Germany to serve the world's greater good: "The world must be made safe for democracy. Its peace must be planted upon the tested foundations of political liberty." Like most social gospelers, Gladden made a convincing reversal as soon as his nation went to war. The call of country and Wilson's soaring idealistic rhetoric were irresistible to him, and to them. Lyman Abbott, who converted early, called the war "a crusade to make this world a home in which God's children can live in peace and safety, a crusade far more in harmony with the spirit and will of Christ than the crusade to recover from the pagans the tomb in which the body of Christ was buried." Shailer Mathews, who traveled the same path as Gladden, soon exulted that America at war was proving to be "a glorious super-person, possessed of virtues, power, ideals, daring, and sacrifice."[69]

Gladden was never as jingoistic as Abbott, but he matched Mathews for wartime myth-making. He quoted Wilson's idealistic claims repeatedly and insistently in defending America's intervention. The other nations had gone to war for the sake of their material self-interests, he declared, but America intervened for the sake of democracy and world peace. This mission was necessary, though awful: "War, even when a nation accepts it with chagrin and without any expectation of exclusive gain, is a devilish business. He who sups with the devil must fish with a long spoon." Seeking additional assurance, Gladden claimed that Wilson's declaration of war against Germany was not really a declaration of war, it was merely a self-respecting recognition that Germany was already warring against the United States. America's entry into the war was "an acceptance of the belligerency which has been thrust upon us."[70]

Wilson pledged that America desired no conquest or dominion, that America acted out of concern for justice, peace and human rights, not for revenge, and that America had no selfish ends to serve: "We seek no indemnities for ourselves, no material compensation for the sacrifices we shall freely make. We are but one of the champions of the rights of mankind. We shall be satisfied when those rights have been made as secure as the faith and the freedom of nations can make them." These assurances became Gladden's scripture. "I believe that these words are true," he proclaimed,

> And I thank God that I have lived to hear them spoken. They can never be recalled. They can never be forgotten. They will live as long as freedom lives. They will be emblazoned on the banners of the Universal Brotherhood. And when their full meaning is grasped by the great nations of the earth war will be no more.

Americans had a "right to believe" that they intervened to put an end to war, he insisted, for Americans entered the war "to make the world safe for democracy, to defeat a monstrous aggression, [and] to create a new organization of mankind." To Gladden, Wilson's pledge to make the world safe for democracy was "the greatest word I think that this generation has heard. It defines our destiny."[71]

He preached continually on fighting for democracy and creating a League of Nations in the months that remained to him.[72] Gladden claimed never to doubt that his country sought to create a world order based on the golden rule: "All that is needed to bring permanent peace to earth is that every nation trust all other nations just as it wishes to be trusted by them." He seemed to forget his belief that war belonged to the jungle phase of human existence. "This war needn't be a curse; it may be the greatest blessing that has ever befallen this land," he declared. Asked near the end of his life if he knew of any reason not to be hopeful, Gladden replied, "Not one." His entire life had been a miracle, lived through eighty-three years of transforming American Christian progress.[73]

The Socialist Kingdom of God: Walter Rauschenbusch

The two greatest exponents of the social gospel died in 1918, but ended their days very differently. Gladden lived a full life and made his peace with the Great War. Walter Rauschenbusch was devastated by the war, which he saw as the death of social gospel idealism, and he died at the age of 56. In other ways, too, they were significantly different kinds of social gospelers. Rauschenbusch was a socialist and high-voltage prose stylist who condemned capitalism as unregenerate and sometimes blasted his opponents. He was more deeply pious and evangelical than much of the left wing of the social gospel movement, but he belonged unmistakably to the left wing. He was inspiring and challenging to pastors, but also dangerous. Gladden was never dangerous. He was not the type to ascertain wind direction before taking a position, yet he always ended up in the movement's mainstream, because he belonged there and others looked to him for guidance.

Near the end of his life Gladden wrote

> I have never doubted that the Kingdom I have always prayed for is coming; that the gospel I have always preached is true. I believe that the democracy is getting a new heart, and a new spirit, that the nation is being saved. It is not yet saved and its salvation depends on you and me, but it is being saved. There are signs that a *new way of thinking, a new social consciousness*, are taking possession of the nation.

To Gladden, cooperation, democracy, and progress were god-terms; he never lost faith that the kingdom of God was an ongoing American project. On these crucial counts he and Rauschenbusch were very much alike. Both were apostles of the social gospel idea that cooperation, democracy, and progress were the building blocks of Christian salvation in the social sphere. In Rauschenbusch the social gospel acquired its greatest champion, at the moment that Gladden's version of it became respectable and enfranchised.[74]

Walter Rauschenbusch was the only surviving son of a formidable and problematic father, August Rauschenbusch, and a mother, Caroline, who spent her adult life coping with a bad marriage decision. August was born to a prominent German family that claimed five successive generations of university-trained Lutheran pastors. He extended this unbroken family line to six generations, but later converted to the Baptist faith while serving as a missionary in the USA. On the rebound from a broken romance he married a former confirmation student, and soon regretted it; in America he became a prominent Baptist scholar and professor in the German Department at Rochester Theological Seminary. August Rauschenbusch was accomplished, headstrong, irritable, religiously zealous, a gifted teacher, and, to his family, prone to self-pitying meanness. His nervous bullying made him a bad husband and, at best, a difficult father; Walter Rauschenbusch spent his childhood sympathizing with his mother and trying to please his father. At his father's insistence Walter spent four years of his childhood in Germany, in the company of his mother and sisters; as a teenager he studied for three years at the Rochester Free Academy and had a conversion experience; after high school he returned to Germany for four years of classical education. August Rauschenbusch was determined that his son should acquire a cultured, classical, German education and not to be Americanized; he was also determined to arrange lengthy separations from his wife, whose death he sometimes asked God to arrange.[75]

August's fervent piety and demanding academic expectations pervaded the life of his family, even during lengthy periods of separation. Walter, the family's only surviving son, was the focal point of his father's ambitions, a fact that he mostly appreciated. Later he recalled of August: "He was a man of the old school and not to be trifled with. But I never doubted his love and care for me." As a student at the Gütersloh Gymnasium in Westphalia, Germany, Walter mastered Greek and Latin, learned French and Hebrew, and won the school's top prize. His later writings carefully refrained from commenting on August's bullying manner and bad temper; the family drama poked through only in a few letters. In one of them Walter wrote to August from Germany, interceding on his mother's behalf, "You cannot imagine how the quarrels at home have oppressed us children."[76]

Returning to the USA in 1883 after four years at Gütersloh, Rauschenbusch finished a college degree at the University of Rochester and began a seminary degree at his father's institution at the same time, aspiring to be a kinder version of his orthodox father. A physiology professor at the university, Harrison Webster, who became a treasured friend, assured Rauschenbusch that Darwinian evolution was compatible with Christianity; he also commended Henry George's "single tax" populism. Rochester Seminary, on the other hand, was slower to enter the modern age. Every member of the faculty was either conservative or very conservative. August Rauschenbusch was a commanding figure there, as was seminary president and evangelical icon Augustus Hopkins Strong, who taught a slightly updated version of Baptist Calvinist scholasticism. Old Testament scholar Howard Osgood was a fundamentalist, while the seminary's least conservative teacher, New Testament scholar William Arnold Stevens, earned his reputation as a liberal by rejecting fundamentalist inerrancy theory. Stevens taught that scripture was an inspired *record* of divine revelation, not revelation itself. It surprised Rauschenbusch that Stevens treated discrepancies in the Gospel narratives as discrepancies; eventually Rauschenbusch surprised himself by giving up the doctrine of biblical infallibility. From church historian Benjamin True, Rauschenbusch absorbed the incarnationalist historicism of German scholar August Neander, which conceived Christ as a divine power entering and progressively transforming history. Homiletics professor Thomas Harwood Pattison was another key influence, encouraging Rauschenbusch to study the sermons of liberal Anglican Frederick W. Robertson, which he found spiritually liberating in the same way as Gladden before him.[77]

Robertson's ethical concept of the way of the cross and his personal example of shedding an inherited conservative religion struck deep chords in Rauschenbusch, as did Bushnell's atonement theology. Though Rauschenbusch carefully avoided theological discussions with his father, by his senior year he was ready to stand up to Augustus Strong, whose *Lectures on Theology* (1876) and *Systematic Theology* (1886) defined Baptist orthodoxy.[78] To Strong, Bushnell's atonement theology was beyond the pale; to young Rauschenbusch, it was a ray of light that helped him believe more deeply in the gospel. In a paper for Strong's class Rauschenbusch argued that substitutionary doctrine turned salvation into an abstract Trinitarian transaction and taught a morally repugnant concept of divine justice, while Bushnell's theory of moral and spiritual influence was gospel-centered, intelligible to human experience, and morally uplifting. Alarmed by the paper, Strong spent several class sessions refuting it, as Rauschenbusch later recalled: "This paper was written with a good deal of heat and was felt by Dr. Strong to be subversive of Scriptural authority. He spent several lectures after it going over the ground."[79]

Rauschenbusch quietly held his ground that biblical statements were not true merely because they appeared in the Bible; they were true only if they appealed to critical readers as true in their own right. That was a theme of his favorite spiritual writers – Robertson, Bushnell, Samuel Taylor Coleridge, William Wordsworth, Phillips Brooks. Rauschenbusch filled a composition book with their spiritual sayings. Like Robertson, he found that the gospel became real to him in a new way after he preached a liberal version of it to working-class people. For two summers he ministered to a struggling Baptist congregation in Louisville, Kentucky. "I began with the determination to raise the spiritual standard of every Christian among them," he told his friend Munson Ford. Working door to door, Rauschenbusch sought to "awaken in their hearts the love of Christ as the only sure cure for their love of self and sin." That experience changed his mind about becoming an academic, convincing him that parish ministry was the best outlet for his religious idealism.[80]

The way of the cross became newly meaningful to Rauschenbusch after he stopped believing that Christ's saving death was imputed to believers. He told Ford,

> I am just beginning to believe in the Gospel of the Lord Jesus Christ, not exactly in the shape in which the average person proclaims it as the infallible truth of the Most High, but in a shape that suits my needs, that I have gradually constructed for myself in studying the person and teaching of Christ, and which is still in rapid progress of construction.

He was ready to "do hard work for God," living literally by the teaching and spirit of Jesus. Toward this end he avoided romantic entanglements: "On the whole I find myself better without." Years later he recalled his consuming determination "to follow

Jesus Christ in my personal life, and live over again his life, and die over again his death."[81]

Rauschenbusch's liberal turn had little sense of a social dimension, and it was socially isolating. He was lonely in seminary. His friends had moved on and his sisters Frida and Emma had married and departed while he stayed in school, living in his head. Later he recalled of his father, "He kept me at school till I was twenty-four." Though Walter embraced his father's vocational dream for him – to minister to the German Baptist community – his relations with his parents were tense and, at best, polite. August and Caroline Rauschenbusch were dismayed by their son's liberal turn. After Walter was called to the Second German Baptist Church of New York City, he told his parents, "I believe in the gospel of Jesus Christ with all my heart. What this gospel is, everyone has to decide for himself, in the face of his God."[82]

The Second German Baptist Church of New York City was located on West 45th Street near 10th Avenue on Manhattan's West Side. It bordered the northern edge of the notorious gang-ruled district known as Hell's Kitchen and was only a few blocks west of the Tenderloin district, where gambling and prostitution flourished. The church was barely functional when Rauschenbusch arrived. It numbered approximately 125 members, most of them factory-laboring German immigrants, and its building was ugly, run-down, and depressing, like its neighborhood. Rauschenbusch lacked any concept of the church as an instrument of social justice: "My idea then was to save souls, in the ordinarily accepted religious sense." On the other hand, from the beginning he vowed to live according to the way and spirit of Jesus, and he invoked Neander's idea of Christianity as the expansion of Christ's incarnation in history. Rauschenbusch conceived the Christian life as a kingdom-building journey from sin to salvation; his theology was historical and postmillennialist before it became socialist. He preached that the church existed to hasten and participate in the coming of God's kingdom: Christians were called to insinuate God's love and justice into the world.[83]

As a pastor, Rauschenbusch was diligent, faithful and inspiring. His sermonizing and energetic care gave an emotional lift to his long-dispirited congregation. Under his leadership, and with the assistance of John D. Rockefeller – who took a kindly interest in August Rauschenbusch's promising Baptist son – the church built an impressive new building a few blocks away, on West 43rd Street near 9th Avenue. Rauschenbusch took pride in this accomplishment, but worried that the new sanctuary might be too nice for the spiritual health of his congregation. By the time it was dedicated in March 1890 he also had ambivalent feelings on other matters, as well as feelings of distraction, frustration, and disappointment. In his last year of seminary his hearing diminished; in New York it worsened dramatically. Seeking medical treatment, Rauschenbusch was told he suffered from a neurological defect. He underwent treatments that failed to improve his hearing and he worried that he could not be a pastor if he went deaf.[84]

He also worried that his parents' marriage was finished. In 1888 August Rauschenbusch retired from teaching. Rochester Seminary offered his German Department position to Walter, who declined it with flattered gratitude; his work in New York City was just beginning. August gave himself a retirement gift by returning to Germany without his wife. On the pretext that Walter could use some household help, August deposited Caroline with her son just before he sailed from New York. His goodbye consisted of a handshake; afterwards Walter found his mother convulsed in tears. For two years they shared an apartment as August brushed off the admonishments of scandalized Baptist friends. Walter and his mother coped with the situation gamely, though there were strains between them. In 1890, strengthened by the assurance that his daughter Frida would look out for Caroline, August Rauschenbusch allowed his wife to join him in Hamburg, where they lived more agreeably until his death in 1899. Walter revered his father as the trailblazing German-American Baptist of his generation who set the standard for German Baptist education. He internalized his father's ambitions for his ministerial and, later, academic career, and its locus in the German Baptist community. But he became a determinately different kind of husband, father, and theologian. In his introduction to the half-autobiography, half-biography of August Rauschenbusch that Walter completed after his father's death, he allowed that August was known to be stern and even harsh with students and acquaintances. A heavy veil was cast over the family drama, however. The loyal son would not tarnish his father's memory, or hurt the feelings of relatives, or deprive German-American Baptists of their hero.[85]

Under these trying personal circumstances Walter Rauschenbusch found his way to the social gospel. He embraced his father's missionary ambitions, but not his father's authority-religion. He went deaf, but did not leave the ministry. He bore his loss of hearing bravely and adeptly, though without the saving grace of learning to laugh at it. In the course of coping with his deafness Rauschenbusch's gregarious personality became shy, sensitive, and somewhat lonely. At the same time, buoyed up by a happy marriage, a cadre of like-minded friends, and an upsurge of social idealism outside the churches, he dared to imagine the church as an agent of social transformation.

Asking the Social Question

Rauschenbusch had barely grasped that a social crisis existed before he began to relate the ethic of Jesus to it. In later years it bothered him greatly that he came to the social gospel from outside the church, because the church as he knew it had no social conscience. "This is one of the saddest things that I can say, but I cannot get it out of my mind," he recalled in 1913. "The church held down the social interest in me. It contradicted it; it opposed it; it held it down as far as it could; and when it was a question about giving me position or preferment, the fact that I was interested in the workingman was actually against me."[86] He came to New York with "no idea of social questions." To the downtrodden immigrants of Hell's Kitchen he brought the pious maxims of his inherited evangelicalism, and "discovered that they didn't fit." Rauschenbusch was driven to "social ideas" by the misery of his congregants and neighbors. "The world is hard and without feeling," he wrote to his cousin Maria Döring. "Here I see so much of this that my heart bleeds for the victims."[87]

His parishioners lived in squalid five-story tenements that pressed more than 20 families into each building. The malnutrition and diseases of the children, and their funerals, tore at him: "Oh, the children's funerals! They gripped my heart – that was one of the things I always went away thinking about – why did the children have to die?" Friends and clerical colleagues admonished Rauschenbusch to save souls, not waste his time and vocation on social work. A young missionary on his way to an early death in Africa "implored me almost with tears to dismiss these social questions and give myself to 'Christian work.'" These appeals were painfully upsetting to

Rauschenbusch, but not convincing: "All our inherited ideas, all theological literature, all the practices of church life, seemed to be against us." To him, politics became unavoidable. If people suffered because of politics and economics, gospel preaching had to deal with politics and economics. He found his first guides to "social ideas" in the economic journalist Henry George, who ran for mayor of New York in 1886, and Richard Ely.[88]

Henry George was a high school dropout whose Damascus-road moment occurred at the age of 30. Walking the streets of New York in 1869, he was overwhelmed by the contrast between the comforts of the city's upper class and the degradation of its poor. He resolved to devote his life to reforming the system that produced such extremes of wealth and poverty. Ten years later his major work, *Progress and Poverty*, argued for a "single tax" on the unearned increment in the value of land. As long as land values increased, he observed, those who worked the land had to pay more and more for the right to work. The most ethical and practical way to break the cycle of structural impoverishment was to appropriate the unearned increment in the value of land by taxing it. The tax would free up land held for speculation, stimulate construction, create new housing and jobs, and drive down the cost of rent, while the proceeds of the tax would fund government programs designed to help the needy.[89]

In October 1886, five months after Rauschenbusch moved to New York, George launched his campaign for mayor as the candidate of a reformist coalition of trade unionists and socialists. Rauschenbusch attended a rally for George at Cooper Union at which Fr Edward McGlynn, an ardent George supporter and Catholic priest, excited the crowd by exhorting, "Thy Kingdom come! Thy will be done on earth." Rauschenbusch was deeply stirred. The George campaign had Christian support, and it was about the right issues. While steering clear of socialism, it claimed that the existence of poverty and unearned wealth were structurally linked in the existing system. A progressive government was needed to reform capitalism. Rauschenbusch supported George's candidacy and devoured his writings. Though he later judged that George's single tax did not address key structural aspects of the economic problem, he drew on George's analysis for the rest of his career and expressed gratitude for the inspiring impact of "this single-minded apostle of a great truth."[90]

One of George's campaign workers, Baptist minister Leighton Williams, became a close friend to Rauschenbusch and introduced him to Ely's writings. The two ministers found a kindred spirit in Baptist pastor Nathaniel Schmidt; the threesome met every week for discussion and prayer. Eager to crystallize and disseminate their views, they drafted chapters for a book on the social meaning of the gospel, which they never completed.[91] Williams acted as the group's mentor; Rauschenbusch did most of the writing; Schmidt contributed some writing and a heavy editorial hand. For the next 20 years they wrote collaboratively in this manner. Rauschenbusch later recalled that during his early ministry he had six books in his head: five were scholarly, one was dangerous. Three times he tried to write the dangerous one, but never finished it, feeling compelled to start over with each attempt. Meanwhile he poured out sharply written, sometimes cheeky articles for a monthly newspaper, *For the Right*, that he and Williams launched in 1889.[92]

For the Right was launched during the very period that Rauschenbusch began to think of himself as a socialist. One of his models was the Society of Christian Social-ists, an ecumenical fellowship founded by W. D. P. Bliss in April 1889. Bliss leaned toward Fabian Socialism, but his group was ideologically diverse. Its founding statement of principles declared, "The teachings of Jesus Christ lead directly to some specific form or forms of socialism." *For the Right* had a similar idea. The editors promised to serve no party interest or ideology, but exempted Christian Socialism from these categories. In their reckoning Christian Socialism was broad-minded, wholesome, and ecumenical, like themselves: "To apply the ethical principles of Jesus Christ so that our industrial relationships may be humanized, our economic system moralized, justice pervade legislation, and the State grown into a true commonwealth – we band together as Christian Socialists."[93]

Rauschenbusch was a fire hydrant of opinions for the paper. He advocated an eight-hour workday, socialization of the railroads, municipal ownership of utilities, a city-owned underground transit system, the single tax, separation of church and state, government regulation of trusts and monopolies, ballot reform, and workplace safety. He also wrote about technology, strikes, labor and capital relations, good government, free trade, personal ethics, individualism, and the kingdom of God. He repeatedly gave his assurance that personal salvation and social salvation went together.[94]

For the Right lasted 18 months, folding in March 1891 during the same week that Rauschenbusch departed for a sabbatical in Germany and England. The paper was too radical for most of its desired audience and too Christian for disaffected workers who were already radicalized. The editors' earnest moralizing fell flat, some of their articles were patronizing (Rauschenbusch sometimes resorted to children's stories) and they never found a clear focus. By 1891 their seed money ran out and Rauschenbusch was ready to resign his pastorate. The surf-like roar in his ears had not abated. He was nearly deaf and felt unable to continue as a minister. Augustus Strong renewed his offer of a teaching position at Rochester Seminary, but Rauschenbusch doubted that he could teach, either. He proposed to resign from his pastorate, go abroad for a year of study, and pursue a literary career. His congregation pleaded with him to take a paid sabbatical instead. Gratefully Rauschenbusch accepted their offer and sailed to Europe, in search of a medical cure and a deeper grounding in Christian Socialism.

The Kingdom as Political Theology

In the company of his sister Emma, who longed for a European respite, Rauschenbusch traveled to England and Germany, studied socialist experiments, gave up on a medical cure, and labored on his dangerous book – the massive manuscript on the social meaning of Christianity. This was at least his second major pass at the book, which he continued to revise for six years. As his learning proceeded, so did the need for revisions. He titled the book "Revolutionary Christianity" and crammed it with his studies in biblical criticism, Christian history, and social analysis. Parts of it ended up in his blockbuster coming-out book *Christianity and the Social Crisis*, which Rauschenbusch published 16 years later; parts of it were published as separate essays; much of it was lost to readers until social ethicist Max Stackhouse discovered a misfiled manuscript in the 1960s in the archives of the American Baptist Historical Society, which he published as *The Righteousness of the Kingdom*; other manuscripts were lost.[95]

In Germany Rauschenbusch found the key to his theology and his life. The coming of the kingdom on earth was not a new theme for him, but now he grasped its centrality and symphonic totality for the first time. Previously he was content to repeat German theologian Albrecht Ritschl's image of Christianity as an ellipse with two centers: eternal life was the goal of individual existence and the kingdom of God was the goal of humanity. But in Germany it occurred to Rauschenbusch that the kingdom was not merely a major part of Jesus' teaching: it was the controlling center. *Revolutionary Christianity* proposed that Christianity was revolutionary in its nature because the ethic and example of Jesus were revolutionary. Historic Christianity lacked the very core of Jesus' teaching and meaning. Because Jesus proclaimed and initiated the kingdom, the church was supposed to be a new kind of community that transformed the world by the power of Christ's kingdom-bringing Spirit. The mission of the church was not merely to save people's souls for the heavenly world to come, but "to overcome the spirit dominant in the world and thus penetrate and transform the world."[96]

Rauschenbusch's realization of the centrality and totalizing coherence of the kingdom brought a new coherence to his thinking. Though he struggled with the manuscript, his controlling insight was in place. He stopped trying to fit his Christ-following social consciousness into his old Christianity, "my old religion." Later he recalled,

> And then the idea of the kingdom of God offered itself as the real solution for that problem. Here was a religious conception that embraced it all. Here was something so big that absolutely nothing that interested me was excluded from it. Was it a matter of personal religion? Why, the kingdom of God begins with that! The powers of the kingdom of God well up in the individual soul; that is where they are born, and that is where the starting point necessarily must be. Was it a matter of world-wide mission? Why, that is the kingdom of God, isn't it – carrying it out to the boundaries of the earth. Was it a matter of getting justice for the workingman? Is not justice part of the kingdom of God? Does not the kingdom of God simply consist of this – that God's will shall be done on earth, even as it is now in heaven? And so, wherever I touched, there was the kingdom of God. That was the brilliancy, the splendor of that conception – it touches everything with religion. It carries God into everything that you do, and there is nothing else that does it in the same way.[97]

It was not a question of fitting the ethic of the kingdom into the old Christianity, he reasoned. The kingdom was the heart of Christianity; it was a social reality that pervaded all humanity and nature. It was always working toward the realized life of God. In Rauschenbusch's rendering of it, the kingdom faith was decidedly evangelical. The kingdom stood at the center of Christianity not merely because it was beautifully symphonic or ethical, but because "you have the authority of the Lord Jesus Christ in it." It was Jesus' Word and idea. For years after the name "social gospel" came into vogue, Rauschenbusch had mixed feelings about it; the name seemed redundant to him. He hated to concede that any non-social faith deserved to be called a form of the Christian gospel. The kingdom of God "cannot be lived out by you alone," he demanded.

> You have to live it out with me, and with that brother sitting next to you. We together have to work it out. It is a matter of community life. The perfect community of men – that would be the kingdom of God! With God above them; with their brother next to them – clasping hands in fraternity, doing the work of justice – that is the kingdom of God![98]

Returning to his New York congregation, Rauschenbusch teamed up with Williams to infiltrate the Baptist Congress. In 1892 they organized a progressive caucus in it; the following year the caucus morphed into a formal organization, the Brotherhood of the Kingdom, which became Rauschenbusch's spiritual home.[99] The group's original members included Rauschenbusch, Williams, Schmidt, Philadelphia pastors Samuel Zane Batten and George Dana Boardman, Hamilton theologian William Newton Clarke, and six others. Like the Fabian Socialists, whom some of them admired, the Brotherhood Baptists were skilled pamphleteers. They disagreed about socialism, women's suffrage, and at first, accepting non-Baptist members; in common they believed in a Christ-following kingdom ideal: "Obeying the thought of our Master, and trusting in the power and guidance of the Spirit, we form ourselves into a Brotherhood of the Kingdom, in order to re-establish this idea in the thought of the church, and to assist in its practical realization in the life of the world." By 1894 Rauschenbusch's view of the membership issue prevailed, and the Brotherhood of the Kingdom opened its fellowship to women and non-Baptists.[100]

That year he wrote his most important Brotherhood tract, on the five dimensions of the kingdom. Rauschenbusch was not always careful to say that the kingdom of Christ was more than the building of God's cooperative commonwealth on earth. In his pamphlet, which set the matter straight, however, he was very careful. He observed that most Christians conceived the kingdom as the heavenly hope of life after death. A smaller group, mystical Christians, stressed the inward spiritual reality of the kingdom. A third group, often priestly, sometimes possessing ecclesiastical power, employed the words "kingdom" and "church" interchangeably. A fourth group, newly aroused in the nineteenth century, identified the kingdom with the second coming of Christ. A fifth group, also newly aroused in recent times, conceived the kingdom as "kingdom-building" work beyond the existing work of the church. Some believers of the latter sort were missionaries or pastors who called for new fields of Christian action, others reduced the work of the kingdom to social work alone.[101]

Rauschenbusch urged that all these views had a strong claim to a vital piece of the kingdom idea; the problem was that each of them tended to reduce the kingdom to only one or two of its constitutive elements. The true kingdom of God "stands for the sum of all divine and righteous forces on earth," he contended. "It is a synthesis combining all the conceptions mentioned above." Elsewhere he put it dialectically: "When taken as parts of that larger idea, and recognized in their relation to it, they are good and indispensable. When taken as a substitute for it, they work mischief."[102]

He stressed that the biblical idea of the kingdom had an apocalyptic aspect and an ethical aspect. It was wrong to sneer at premillennialists for fixating on the second coming of Jesus, for at least they grasped a neglected aspect of the kingdom idea: "They have it in a bizarre form often, but they have it." The kingdom idea included the end of history by an apocalyptic divine act. In Rauschenbusch's view, the champions of the ethical pole of the kingdom hope were the Socialists. Even though Socialists tended to struggle for the kingdom of God "with God left out," he acknowledged, "yet that fractional part of the idea of the kingdom which they have got casts a halo about their aims, and puts a religious enthusiasm into their propaganda." The Socialists were keepers of the biblical dream that society should be organized for the sake of all its people. Rauschenbusch called the church back to the prophetic vision of social justice and community that modern parlance called "Socialist."[103]

In the same years that the *Religionsgeschichtliche Schule* began to challenge the liberal picture of Jesus, Rauschenbusch held out for a comprehensive understanding of the kingdom. The kingdom was in heaven *and* on earth, he stressed. It began in the depths of the human heart, but was not meant to stay there; the church was an instrument for the advancement of the kingdom, but it did not embrace all the forces of the kingdom; though the perfection of the kingdom was reserved for a future epoch, the kingdom existed and was being developed in the here and now. The church was wrong to settle for less than the kingdom and the socialists were wrong to struggle for the kingdom with God left out. What was needed was to pull together the other-worldly, mystical, ecclesiastical, millennialist, and socialist fragments of the kingdom idea into an organic whole, wedding the Christian and socialist movements.[104]

German America and the Wider Kingdom

In 1889 Rauschenbusch met Pauline Rother, a Milwaukee schoolteacher, while he was attending a German Baptist convention in Milwaukee. They met again the following year, corresponded for two years, and were married in 1893. Their marriage became a sustained love affair, mutually supportive, affectionate and admiring, which produced five children. Pauline Rauschenbusch was devoted to her husband and supported his activist calling. She often made home visits with him, and in many ways helped him cope with his deafness. Rauschenbusch marveled at her love for him; expressions of gratitude and love passed easily between them throughout their marriage. Four years after their wedding Rochester Seminary called again, offering Rauschenbusch a position in the German Department; this time he was ready to become an academic. He reasoned that his deafness would be less of a handicap in the classroom than in the ministry, that Pauline would like Rochester more than New York, and that Rochester Seminary was shedding its rigid conservatism.[105]

Rochester was still a conservative seminary, however. It hired Rauschenbusch to carry on his father's legacy, not to espouse Christian Socialism. The German Department was a showcase institution; no American seminary or denomination could boast of a more ambitious attempt to keep alive the ideal of a non-assimilated, non-English speaking Protestantism with high academic standards. Most German Baptist leaders had no sympathy for Rauschenbusch's socialism or theological liberalism. By temperament and conviction they espoused a religion of otherworldly sectarianism, especially the German-Russian immigrants. They tolerated Rauschenbusch's politics and theology only as long as he labored in the cause of his father. For them, as for August Rauschenbusch, the cause of German-American Protestantism was all consuming. Many German Baptist leaders were not shy in expressing the view that northern European immigrants made the best Americans and Christians, and that German immigrants were the best Americans and Christians of all. America's openness to immigrants from southern and eastern Europe made them anxious; vehemently the German Baptist leaders drew the line at admitting non-Europeans. They worried that America's republican democratic experiment would fail if the United States opened itself to people from backward parts of the world.[106]

In his early career Rauschenbusch took a principled stand against these prejudices. He strongly supported open immigration, denounced racist arguments for immigration restrictions, and told the Baptist Congress that America should be open to all who came to it, "for I believe God made it for all." Two years before he was appointed to Rochester Seminary's German Department faculty, however, he repaired his credentials as a German Baptist leader by writing an ugly fundraising letter for the German Department. "Is the American stock so fertile that it will people this continent alone?" he asked. Not content to make a pitch for German immigrants, Rauschenbusch played to the racial fears of potential German Department donors: "Are the whites of this continent so sure of their possession against the blacks of the South and the seething yellow flocks beyond the Pacific that they need no reinforcement of men of their own blood while yet it is time?"[107]

Two years later, now as a member of the faculty, he toned down the racism, but made essentially the same appeal in another fundraising pamphlet for the German Department. The Germans "are of the same stock as the English, readily assimilated, and a splendid source of strength for America, physically, intellectually, and morally," he boasted. Neither of these fundraising appeals was publicly signed; only insiders knew it was Rauschenbusch who stooped to racist demagoguery to raise money for the German Department. In 1902, however, he stood before a commencement assembly at the German Department's Fiftieth Anniversary celebration and said the same thing with a new twist. Essentially he argued that Germans were first cousins of the Anglo-Saxons, they helped to build modern democracy, and thus they deserved to be included in Manifest Destiny. It was short sighted to give Anglo-Saxons exclusive credit for civilization. Rauschenbusch explained that modern democratic civilization was created by a single Teutonic racial stock consisting of Anglo-Saxons, Germans, and their American offspring. But the civilizational achievements of the race were imperiled by "alien strains" arriving from places like France, Spain, the Slavic lands, Bohemia, Poland, and the Russian Jewish territories. He had a vision: "Let the Teutons of the old home, the Teutons of the island and the Teutons of the farther continent look each other in the face and stand shoulder to shoulder in whatever mission for the world God has in store for us."[108]

Having championed a generous and enlightened view of immigration in the past, Rauschenbusch knew what was wrong with his subsequent tack. His alarm at the declining number of immigrants from Germany reduced him to making prejudiced appeals to promote his group. In addition, he worried that immigrants from authoritarian cultures posed a threat to America's fragile experiment in democracy. In his usage, "Teutonic" was a cultural signifier more than a literally racial one; it referred to a "tun"-oriented cultural tradition that was favorable to democratic values and institutions. He meant to promote democratic ends; moreover, on various occasions he lauded the United States for giving all races equality under the law (as though it did). Under the pressure of his ethnic and pro-democracy concerns, however, he claimed that immigrants from some racial groups were more equal than others, an odious claim that also undermined his argument for the universality of democratic rights and values. Despite his general inclination to resist the prevalent racism of his culture, he resorted to racist tactics in the service of his ethnic group.

Rauschenbusch's concern to carry on his father's legacy to German-American Baptists absorbed his early academic career. German Baptist leaders, faced with a declining number of German immigrants and serious questions about the viability of maintaining separate German institutions in the American Baptist Church, looked to August Rauschenbusch's son for leadership. By patrimony and training he seemed ideally suited for the task. Rauschenbusch was intimately acquainted with the languages and cultures of Germany and the United States, he praised the civilizational virtues of German Americans, and he accepted the burden of explaining Germany's new expansionist militancy to wary Americans.

He gave five years to the German Department. During the school year Rauschenbusch taught English and American literature, physiology, physics, civil government, political economy, astronomy, zoology, and a cluster of courses on the New

Testament; during vacations he raised money for the German Department on lengthy speaking tours. It was an exhausting regimen that left little time for his wider concerns. Increasingly he resented the demands of carrying on his father's work, especially after his father died in 1899. The German-American community was hostile to the social gospel, the demands of maintaining August's legacy were withering, and English-speaking America showed little interest in a three-way marriage of "Teutonic" nations. In 1902 Pauline remarked that while Rauschenbusch could certainly get along without the German Department, the German Department could not get along without him. That was an argument for staying put, which Rauschenbusch accepted as such. He cared deeply not to offend his German Baptist constituency. But a few months later the seminary's English Department position in church history became available, with the death of Benjamin True. Augustus Strong told Rauschenbusch it was time for him to serve the wider kingdom of God; Rauschenbusch gratefully agreed. Thus it was as a church historian that he wrote the classic works of the social gospel movement.[109]

As a German Department functionary he was short on time and a favorable audience for advocating the social gospel, though Rauschenbusch managed occasional articles and lectures on his favorite topics. At the turning point of his career he hoped for a sabbatical leave to make himself competent in church history, but the seminary made him wait five years. He had to learn a new field as he taught it, and thus found himself squeezed again for time. But Rauschenbusch found a way to make his job preparation serve his social gospel vocation. He felt acutely the historical implausibility of the basic social gospel argument. If he and Gladden were right about the kingdom basis of Christianity, why was social Christianity so novel? Why had no one preached the social gospel version of the gospel until very recently?

Rauschenbusch approached his courses and writing with these questions in mind. He made the unlikely field of church history an ally of the social gospel. He spoke at civic groups and churches, launched a local chapter of the Brotherhood of the Kingdom, and supported the proposed Federal Council of Churches, telling Brotherhood friends that the Federal Council might make their group unnecessary. And he returned to the dangerous book. Though chastened by his failure to turn *Revolutionary Christianity* into a polished work, Rauschenbusch incorporated parts of it and other previous writings into a mostly-new book on the social meaning of the gospel, *Christianity and the Social Crisis* (1907). The first part described the essential purpose of prophetic biblical religion as the transformation of human society into the kingdom of God; the second part explained why the Christian church had never carried out this mission; the third part urged that it was not too late for the church to follow Jesus. The second part was the key to the book, as Rauschenbusch realized, though he feared that the third part – a blazing argument for Christian socialism – would get him fired. For parts of his answer to the book's central question he leaned on German church historian Adolf von Harnack, citing him eight times, while contending that no one had given a satisfactory answer. Rauschenbusch implied, but was too modest to say, "no one until now."[110]

The Social Crisis and the Social Gospel

Revolutionary Christianity had patches of labored writing and clumsy connections, but all was smooth and sparkling in *Christianity and the Social Crisis*. The book enthralled readers with its graceful flow of short, clear sentences, its charming metaphors, and its vigorously paced argument. It was filled with sharp moral judgments, especially against priestly religion and social oppression, but the book showed a tender heart for individuals of all kinds.

Rauschenbusch argued that prophetic religion was the "beating heart" of scripture, the prophetic spirit "rose from the dead" in Jesus and the early church, and Christianity was supposed to be a prophetic Christ-following religion of the kingdom. Most religions were priestly and power worshipping, Rauschenbusch stressed. Religion typically sought to reconcile human beings, through ritual, with the powers of nature or force or wealth. But prophetic biblical religion eschewed the worship of power, condemned the evils of injustice and oppression, and insisted that "ethical conduct is the supreme and sufficient religious act."[111]

He conceived of Jesus as a prophet of the kingdom of God who "realized the life of God in the soul of man and the life of man in the love of God." This liberal formula – "the real secret of his life" – smacked of the modernist self-projections that Albert Schweitzer skewered the year before in *The Quest of the Historical Jesus*, but Rauschenbusch cautioned that Jesus was not a modern figure, and certainly not a modern social reformer: "Sociology and political economy were just as far outside of his range of thought as organic chemistry or the geography of America." The social aims of Jesus were comprehensible only if one interpreted Jesus in relation to his historical context, Rauschenbusch argued. The pertinent factors were the subjection of Jews under Roman tyranny and the resulting prevalence of apocalyptic expectation. The popular hope was for a "divine catastrophe" that smashed the power of Rome and raised Israel to new life, which the Jews of Jesus' time called the kingdom of God. Rauschenbusch acknowledged that Jesus evoked and drew upon this common understanding of the kingdom. Jesus shared the Jewish revulsion at Roman tyranny, he believed that the coming kingdom was to be God's creation – "it was not to be set up by man-made evolution" – and he believed in a divine consummation at the end of history.[112]

But more important were the things he did not share with his time. That was Harnack's principle, which Rauschenbusch invoked without mentioning Harnack. The more that Jesus came to believe in the spiritual and moral blessings of God's kingdom and in the power of these blessings to reshape human life, Rauschenbusch argued, "the more would the final act of consummation recede in importance and the present facts and processes grow more concrete and important to his mind." John the Baptist proclaimed that the kingdom had almost arrived; Jesus announced that it was already present, or at least, its kernel was already present. This was the essence of his novel and transcendent faith. Those who claimed that Jesus conceived the kingdom as a purely catastrophic-eschatological reality had some scriptural texts on their side, Rauschenbusch allowed, but there were other texts that supported a social, comprehensive, and developmental understanding of the kingdom. The parables of Jesus were nearly always polemical, he noted; Jesus told parables to subvert the worldview of his listeners. In the synoptic parables of the sower, the tares, the net, the mustard seed, and leaven, Jesus replaced a catastrophic-apocalyptic idea of the kingdom with a developmental, realistic idea. The parables were protests against the late Jewish apocalyptic worldview, not products of it. Jesus was sociable, he made ethics the test of religion, he said the kingdom was already present, and he compared the kingdom to the germinating and growing processes of natural life.[113]

Then how were the apocalyptic aspects of the synoptic gospels to be explained? Rauschenbusch allowed that first-century Judaism was apocalyptical, Jesus was probably influenced by it, and the early church was apocalyptical. But that was no reason to smash the ethical and developmental core of Jesus' teaching. Weiss and Schweitzer treated Mark 13 as a master-text of apocalyptic smashing; Rauschenbusch replied that Mark 13 sounded more like the early church than like Jesus. "We must allow that it is wholly probable that the Church which told and retold the sayings of Jesus insensibly molded them by its own ideas and hopes," he argued. The Jewish kingdom hope was apocalyptical, Jesus failed to wean his disciples from it, apocalypticism was the form of the kingdom hope "most congenial to cruder minds," and its fervid impatience with the world fit the needs of the early church. Rauschenbusch concluded: "It is thus exceedingly probable that the Church spilled a little of the lurid colors of its own apocalypticism over the loftier conceptions of its Master, and when we read his sayings to-day, we must allow for that and be on the watch against it."[114]

The notion that the gospel had a social meaning had been recovered only recently. Rauschenbusch feared that if the Weiss–Schweitzer reading of Jesus carried the day, or at least the field of theology, the social message would be lost again. He conceded as much as he could without giving up the liberal Jesus. Jesus shared the substance of an apocalyptical expectation with his community, "but by his profounder insight and his loftier faith he elevated and transformed the common hope." Jesus rejected violence of all kinds, including the apocalyptical violence of God, Rauschenbusch argued: "He postponed the divine catastrophe of judgment to the dim distance and put the emphasis on the growth of the new life that was now going on." Thus did the provincial Jewish hope of the kingdom by divine violence become "a human hope with universal scope," to be carried out by those who built the kingdom of the good.[115]

Rauschenbusch stressed that apocalypticism prevailed historically, not Jesus. Early Christianity was too pervaded by apocalyptic dreams to conceive the kingdom as a worldly social hope; moreover, it was too repressed by a dominating external power to think otherwise. The kingdom took a further beating after Christianity became thoroughly Hellenistic. Hellenistic Christianity was ascetic, it emphasized the dualism of spirit and matter, it fixated on salvation as the eternal life of an individual soul, and it accommodated a priestly, hierarchical, ecclesiastical notion of the church. All of this was a disaster for the Christian parts of Christianity, Rauschenbusch charged.

Christianity and the Social Crisis called for a politics of the cooperative commonwealth that steered America in the direction of democratic socialism. The crisis of capitalist civilization was an opportunity to recover the lost kingdom ideal of Jesus. If production could be organized on a cooperative basis, if distribution could be organized by principles of justice, if workers could be treated as valuable ends and not as dispensable means to a commercial end, if parasitic wealth and predatory commerce could be abolished . . . Rauschenbusch's fantasy of "ifs" went on for a half-page. If all these things could be realized, he dreamed,

> then there might be a chance to live such a life of gentleness and brotherly kindness and tranquility of heart as Jesus desired for men. It may be that the cooperative Common-wealth would give us the first chance in history to live a really Christian life without retiring from the world, and would make the Sermon on the Mount a philosophy of life feasible for all who care to try.[116]

That was the idealistic dream of the kingdom come, but Rauschenbusch warned that nothing close to it could be achieved by idealism alone. He was sentimental, to be sure, and moralistic, admonishing trade unionists and socialists against a merely class-driven politics. The moral vision of the kingdom was always paramount for him. He got as much mileage as he could from moral idealism, and tried to make socialism less frightening to middle-class readers. In the closing pages of his 420-page manifesto he observed that the three institutions closest to the hearts of ordinary Americans – the home, school, and church – were socialistic forms of organization. Individualism was neither warm nor saving, he argued; it was the social impulse that redeemed life and made it good. Thus, "there cannot really be any doubt that the spirit of Christianity has more affinity for a social system based on solidarity and human fraternity than for one based on selfishness and mutual antagonism." It followed that "one of the greatest services which Christianity could render to humanity in the throes of the present transition would be to aid those social forces which are making for the increase of communism."[117]

In 1907 "communism" was interchangeable with "communalism" or socialism, at least in Rauschenbusch's usage. Lacking any anticipation of Bolshevik totalitarianism, his rhetoric was innocent, but he was not naive about the power of middle-class moralism. Rauschenbusch was explicit that moral idealism alone would not create a good society: "We must not blink the fact that the idealists alone have never carried through any great social change. In vain they dash their fair ideas against the solid granite of human selfishness." The possessing classes ruled by force and cunning and long-standing monopoly power, he observed: "They control nearly all property. The law is on their side, for they have made it. They control the machinery of government and can use force under the form of law." For these reasons, the capitalist and aristo-cratic classes were nearly impervious to moral truth. For Rauschenbusch it was a good thing to be on the side of moral truth, but being morally right was never enough: "For a definite historical victory a given truth must depend on the class which makes that truth its own and fights for it."[118]

He ended with a flourish. Rauschenbusch's trump argument was the necessity of struggling for an ideal that could not be fully attained. "We shall never have a perfect social life, yet we must seek it with faith," he urged. Human beings would never create a perfect commonwealth, yet they could not discover how much of the co-operative ideal was attainable without struggling for the whole thing. To spurn the struggle for the ideal was to preempt otherwise attainable gains toward it: "At best there is always an approximation to a perfect social order. The kingdom of God is always but coming. But every approximation to it is worth while."[119]

The Social Gospel Ascending

Christianity and the Social Crisis was skillfully fashioned and perfectly timed. It sold 50,000 copies, going through 13 printings in five years, and boosted the social Chris-tian movement to new heights of recognition and influence. Nothing like its sprawling conflation of historical, theological, and political arguments had been published before. The book's bold arguments inspired social gospel leaders to be more daring in their religious and political claims. Rauschenbusch warned a churchly religious establish-ment, "If the Church tries to confine itself to theology and the Bible, and refuses its larger mission to humanity, its theology will gradually become mythology and its Bible a closed book." The book inspired hundreds of seminarians to join the social gospel vanguard and train for a social Christian ministry. Some reviewers, notably sociologist Albion Small, criticized Rauschenbusch for failing to delineate his brand of socialism, but *Christianity and the Social Crisis* gave ballast to the Progressive demand for state power to control capitalism and promote equality. Rauschenbusch later reflected that the book's fortunate timing allowed it to become "an expression of what thousands were feeling."[120]

Already beloved at Rochester Seminary, he became an object of pride there after his book became a national sensation. Rauschenbusch returned from his German sabbatical to find himself cast as a movement leader and religious celebrity, just in time to help launch the Federal Council of Churches and cheer the Methodist Social Creed.

The Federal Council of Churches was the fulfillment of an American Protestant dream. Nineteenth-century evangelicals, realizing that the cause of Christianizing an expanding American nation was beyond the scope of any denomination, founded the American Board of Commissioners for Foreign Missions (1810), the American Bible Society (1816), the American Sunday School Union (1824), and the American Home Missionary Society (1826). Service oriented, youth based forms of interdenominational cooperation were established in the 1850s and flourished after the Civil War, notably the Young Men's Christian Association and the American Ladies' Christian Association (later renamed the Young Women's Christian Association). These organizations cultivated a generation of ecumenically minded social gospelers, leading to the founding of a major service organization in 1895, the World's Student Christian Federation, and the Federal Council of Churches in 1908, representing 33 denominations. Social gospelers dominated the Federal Council: Frank Mason North, Shailer Mathews, Josiah Strong, Washington Gladden, William Adams Brown, Harry F. Ward, Charles S. Macfarland, Charles Stelzle, Graham Taylor, Robert E. Speer, and Walter Rauschenbusch. The council functioned as a kind of laboratory for social gospel ideas that infiltrated the churches and seminaries. Placing divisive Christian doctrines off limits, it sought to advance common social goals. Frank Mason North, chair of the council's executive committee, also chaired its committee on labor issues, which composed a social creed in 1908 modeled on the Methodist Social Creed of 1908. The Social Creed of the Churches called for "equal rights and complete justice for all men in all stations of life," abolition of child labor, safe working conditions, special provisions for female workers, a living wage in every industry, poverty abatement, old age insurance, and equitable distribution of wealth. Its principal author was Ward, who also wrote the Methodist version with help from North, and Rauschenbusch had a hand in the Federal Council text.[121]

He could see the kingdom coming. Rauschenbusch was sensitive to the charge that the social gospel reduced Christianity to socialism; thus, he looked for ways to show that it was rooted in personal piety. His prayers, he knew, were the best window on his personal faith. In addition to his personal devotions Rauschenbusch wrote prayers for worship services, conferences, Brotherhood retreats, and his seminary classes. Some were published in *The American Magazine*, a popular monthly; others were collected in a popular book, *For God and the People: Prayers of the Social Awakening* (1910), which revealed to many readers the possibility of real-life, socially engaged prayer. For some it was the reassuring word they needed to become social gospelers.[122]

At the same time Rauschenbusch constantly heard the demand for a sequel to his major work. *Christianity and the Social Crisis* commended democratic socialism, but did not explain what it was. It had an 80-page chapter titled "What To Do," but stinted on concrete proposals. These issues absorbed Rauschenbusch's attention after he unexpectedly became famous. His publisher, Macmillan, wanted a second installment of the same book; Rauschenbusch produced something better, a major work provocatively titled *Christianizing the Social Order*.[123]

Christianizing the American Order

He confessed at the outset that he had expected to write no more books on the social question. *Christianity and the Social Crisis* contained everything he had to say on the subject, so his sabbatical focused on Christian history, his professional field:

> But meanwhile the social awakening of our nation had set in like an equinoctial gale in March, and when I came home, I found myself caught in the tail of the storm. *Christianity and the Social Crisis* had won popular approval far beyond my boldest hopes, and the friends of the book drew me, in spite of myself, into the public discussion of social questions.[124]

Posing as a reluctant movement leader, Rauschenbusch apologized for burdening the public with another large tome on social Christianity, then took it back: "The subject of the book needs no such apology as is implied in the foregoing statements. If there is any bigger or more pressing subject for the mind of a Christian man to handle, I do not know of it." Before 1900, he recalled, he belonged to a handful of ministers who shouted in the wilderness: "It was always a happy surprise when we found a new man who had seen the light. We used to form a kind of flying wedge to support a man who was preparing to attack a ministers' conference with the social Gospel." But now the social gospel was sweeping ministers' conferences. A third great Awakening was occurring in American life, one that recovered the social spirit and kingdom goal of Jesus.[125]

Christianizing the Social Order reworked familiar Rauschenbusch themes, sometimes with heightened claims. The kingdom of God was not only "the lost social ideal of Christendom," but also "the first and the most essential dogma of the Christian faith." The Reformation revived Pauline theology, but "the present-day Reformation is a revival of the spirit and aims of Jesus himself." It was to be expected that Jesus retained certain unfortunate thought-forms of his background, Rauschenbusch advised; what mattered was the spirit and trajectory of Jesus' religion, not the dogmas he inherited. Instead of asking, "What did Jesus think?" the right question was, "In what direction were his thoughts working?" To follow Jesus was to follow "the line of his movement," not to swallow every aspect of his worldview.[126]

On the eclipse of the kingdom ideal in Christian history, Rauschenbusch dwelt longer this time on the shortcomings of the Reformation. Luther and Calvin had little feeling for the kingdom, they disliked the book of Revelation, and they had little democratic spirit. The Reformation broke the Catholic Church's imprisonment of the kingdom idea, but not to reclaim its true meaning. It took modern social idealism and historical criticism to recover Jesus and his kingdom; Rauschenbusch declared, "The eclipse of the Kingdom idea was an eclipse of Jesus. We had listened too much to voices talking about him, and not enough to his own voice. Now his own thoughts in their lifelike simplicity and open-air fragrance have become a fresh religious possession, and when we listen to Jesus, we cannot help thinking about the Kingdom of God."[127]

Even at the high tide of the social gospel, *Christianizing the Social Order* was a provocative title. Rauschenbusch appreciated that rhetoric about "Christianizing" society was unsettling to many. He tried to assure them that he had no theocratic hankerings. To speak of Christianizing the social order had nothing to do with putting Christ's name in the US Constitution or otherwise breaching the American wall between church and state, he argued. He was a Baptist who treasured the wall. The social gospel was about social and cultural transformation, not state religion: "Christianizing the social order means bringing it into harmony with the ethical convictions which we identify with Christ."[128]

Neither did "Christianizing" mean that the moral values of Christ were exclusive to Christianity. For Rauschenbusch it was very important to affirm the opposite. Christianity was historically particular, he reasoned, but the moral values of Christianity were universal, being shared by all people of good will regardless of religious creed or lack of one. The moral values defined the universal content of good will. At the same time, he believed, it was appropriate to identify the ethical ideal with Christ as its ultimate exemplar. The moral values of freedom, sacrificial love, compassion, justice, humility, fraternity, and equality found their highest expression in the life, teaching, and spirit of Jesus. It was better to risk speaking of Christ than to avoid speaking of him. The social gospel movement had more to lose than to gain by replacing Christ's name with common-denominator moral language: "To say that we want to moralize the social order would be both vague and powerless to most men. To say that we want to christianize it is both concrete and compelling."[129]

Thus Rauschenbusch used the words "Christianize," "moralize," "humanize," and "democratize" interchangeably, while reserving trump status for Christianize: "Christianizing means humanizing in the highest sense." *Christianizing the Social Order* argued that most of America's social order was already Christianized. An unchristian social order made good people do bad things; a Christian social order made bad people do good things. By his account, American society in 1912 was semi-Christian. America's families, churches, politics, and educational systems were Christian for the most part, but these moral gains were threatened by an economic system that militated against America's democratizing Christian spirit.[130]

The pre-modern family was despotic and exploitative, he explained; so were the pre-modern state and church, in ways that reinforced the repressive character of the family. As an institution, the church was reactionary, coercive, and politically cunning; as a moral power it conspired with society in condemning females to subservience. But the democratizing spirit of the modern age raised the legal status of women nearly to the point of equality with men, and Rauschenbusch looked forward to the next stage of women's progress: "The suffrage will abolish one of the last remnants of patriarchal autocracy by giving woman a direct relation to the political organism of society, instead of allowing man to exercise her political rights for her." Meanwhile the churches learned that coercion had the same relation to true religion that rape had to love. The churches did not welcome their salvation, Rauschenbusch observed; they had to be converted against their will, by their loss of temporal authority and unearned wealth. In his view, modern churches still fell short of being Christianized; for one thing, many of them took reactionary positions on "the public activities and the emancipation of women."[131]

Rauschenbusch was a good enough Victorian to feel substantial inner conflict on the latter issue. He supported the right of women to equal rights in society, but wanted wives and mothers to stay home and take care of their families. Though he supported the right of women to higher education, it disturbed him greatly that most college-educated women of his generation remained unmarried. Repeatedly he urged his reading and lecture audiences not to erode the (late Victorian) middle-class ideal of family life in the name of individual progress for women. What made the middle-class family ideal was precisely that it allowed women not to work outside the home. Rauschenbusch's tender feelings for the domestic cult of true womanhood inspired some of his most florid passages. "The health of society rests on the welfare of the home," he declared in *Christianity and the Social Crisis*. "What, then, will be the outcome if the unmarried multiply; if homes remain childless; if families are homeless; if girls do not know housework; and if men come to distrust the purity of women?" That was a vision of barbarism to Rauschenbusch. He blamed capitalism for emptying the home of its nurturing wives and mothers.[132]

Christian Socialism was the wholesome alternative. It lifted women to the level of equality that they deserved, while supporting the mother-nurtured family as the key to a healthy society. This crucial balancing act was a job distinctively suited for Christian Socialism, Rauschenbusch believed. Just as modern Christianity needed the socialist passion for justice to fulfill the social ideals of the gospel, the socialist movement needed the spiritual and moral conscience of Christianity to be saved from crude materialism, especially on the subject of family values.

In the family, the church, education, and the political sphere, democracy was gaining and nearly dominant. Education was the privilege of the few in a non-democratic society, Rauschenbusch noted; in a democracy it was the right of all: "Democracy stands for the cooperative idea applied to politics." Though democracy was not quite the same thing as Christianity, "in politics democracy is the expression and method of the Christian spirit." By this criterion America was nearly Christianized.[133]

The holdout was the economic system, "the unregenerate section of our social order." Rauschenbusch cautioned that the problem was systemic, not personal. He doubted that capitalists as individuals were less moral than others; the problem was that capitalism made even good people do bad things. The predatory anti-social spirit of capitalism was inimical to Christianity, he judged, yet Christian moralists timidly avoided the subject. Rauschenbusch admonished that the tests of Christian morality applied to the economic system: "Does it make it fairly easy to do right and hard to do wrong? Does it call men upward or tempt them downward? Does it reward or penalize fraternal action? Does it furnish the material basis for the Reign of God on earth?"[134]

He answered that capitalism was essentially corrupting and predatory, degrading every profession that it touched, turning people into small-minded consumers, and extending its reach to every sector of society. Thus it threatened to undermine the social gains of all other spheres of American society. Anticipating Daniel Bell's "cultural contradictions of capitalism" thesis by 60 years, Rauschenbusch argued that capitalism was "sapping its own foundations" by degrading the cultural capital on which America's economic success depended. "Religious frugality laid the foundations for capitalism and put civilization on its legs financially. Now capitalism is disintegrating that virtue in the descendants of the Calvinists and persuading them to buy the baubles that capital may make profit."[135]

The learned professions were not as commercialized as the rest of American society, he allowed, but the "rising tide of capitalistic profit making" eroded even this class of exceptions. The law was the most commercialized profession, which was the same thing as saying it was the most corrupt: "'Commercializing a profession' always means degrading it." Wherever it prevailed, the logic of capital caused "a surrender of the human point of view, a relaxing of the sense of duty, and a willingness to betray the public – if it pays."[136]

Rauschenbusch did not believe that profit was the key problem or that liberal reformism could tame the capitalist beast. Under the pressure of reformist movements, he acknowledged, the American state made the beast more tolerable "by pulling a few of the teeth and shortening the tether of greed." The problem was structural: the autocratic power "unrestrained by democratic checks" that capitalism gave to owners and managers. In his view, profit had a sound moral basis to the extent that it represented a fair return on one's useful labor and service. Even the wage system could be justified where free land was available, or a certain kind of labor was scarce, or an employer was especially generous. But in the real world, crowded labor markets and the capitalist control of the instruments of production allowed capitalists to make unearned profits off the exploited labors of the weak; Rauschenbusch called it "a tribute collected by power."[137]

The root problem was that workers had no property rights under capitalism; the solution was to democratize the process of investment: "Political democracy without economic democracy is an uncashed promissory note, a pot without the roast, a form without substance. But in so far as democracy has become effective, it has quickened everything it has touched." Democracy was needed in the economic sphere for the same reasons it was needed everywhere else in society. It promoted freedom and equality, legitimated the necessary exercise of authority, and served as a brake on the will-to-power of the privileged classes.[138]

Economic democracy was about the expansion of property rights under new forms, not the elimination of property rights, he argued. Under capitalism, the capitalist class wrote its own interests into the law; under a fully realized democracy, the nation's property laws would serve the interests of the public as a whole. Rauschenbusch's concept of fully realized economic democracy was a patchwork of themes from various socialist and reformist traditions that did not always fit together. He could be sloppy in failing to distinguish among direct workers' ownership, mixed forms of cooperative ownership, and public ownership of production. He offered no help in delineating various schools of socialism. Though he opposed centralized collectivism and accepted the necessity of the market in a democratic society, he claimed that in a socialist society prices would be based entirely on service rendered. Economic democracy ran straight from the farm to the kitchen, he promised: "It means the power to cut all monopoly prices out of business and to base prices solely on service rendered." Thus he retained the utopian Marxist vision of a cooperative society while assuming – against Marx – that markets could not be abolished in a free society.[139]

Rauschenbusch's weakness for idealistic rhetoric caused him to exaggerate the extent to which economic democracy could replace economic competition. He thought that economic democracy would ensure the elimination of the middleman's profits. While he rejected Marx's materialistic determinism and his contempt for liberal democracy, he accepted the Marxist theories of surplus value and the class struggle. In his view, the good parts of Marxism were salvageable by extending the democratizing logic of liberal democracy into the economic sphere. For all of his idealistic rhetoric and unassimilated borrowings from Marx, however, Rauschenbusch wisely urged that the mix of ownership modes in a democracy had to be a matter of contextual judgment. The blueprint dogmatism of the Marxist tradition was alien to him. John Stuart Mill's vision of decentralized socialism fitted Rauschenbusch better, as did Mill's claim that the logic of liberal democracy led to democratic socialism. Mills' *Principles of Political Economy* envisioned workers "collectively owning the capital with which they carry on their operations, and working under managers elected and removable by themselves." *Christianizing the Social Order* embraced this vision of pluralistic democratic socialism, claiming that only socialism had any prospect of competing with nationalistic militarism as a unifying social force in American life.[140]

Rauschenbusch tried to be optimistic that Americans were up to it. He knew that liberalism was too weak to compete with the spirit of capitalism or militarism. He tried to believe that Christianity linked with socialism could overcome America's assiduously cultivated egocentrism. "Capitalism has overdeveloped the selfish instincts in us all and left the capacity of devotion to larger ends shrunken and atrophied," he lamented.[141]

In 1912, however, Rauschenbusch believed he was witnessing the beginning of a new epoch in American life. Americans were low on cooperative consciousness, but they prized democracy, and real democracy led to democratic socialism, which was not a monolithic idea: "There is unity of movement, and yet endless diversity of life." He had the same hope for socialism that he held for Christianity: that it would become more truly itself. Rauschenbusch was keenly aware, as he told Peabody, that most socialists wanted nothing to do with Christianity. But if modern Christians could hope for the Christianization of China, why was it ridiculous to hope for the Christianization of a political movement that got its inspiration from Christianity? "The Socialists are hopeless about the social regeneration of the Church," Rauschenbusch observed. "Yet it has come faster than I dared to hope. At any rate I am not going to tell the Socialists that I expect them to remain atheists. I shall tell them that they are now religious in spite of themselves and that an increased approach to religion is inevitable as they emerge from the age of polemics and dogmatism."[142]

Christianizing the Social Order dispensed with the cautionary words about the class struggle that ended *Christianity and the Social Crisis*. The social gospel movement was soaring, churches were scrambling to get on the right side of the social question, and politicians were competing for the mantle of Progressivism. Rauschenbusch dared to hope that idealism might prevail without a class war after all. He counseled liberals and progressives to own up to the socialism in their creed: "Every reformer is charged with socialism, because no constructive reform is possible without taking a leaf from the book of socialism." He urged that it was better to wear the label as a badge of honor than to cower from it. Sensitive to the charge that his long discussions of political economy marked a falling away from "the high religious ground," Rauschenbusch replied that all 476 pages of *Christianizing the Social Order* were religious. The book's sole concern was the kingdom of God and its salvation. The social gospel was primarily a call for a revival of religion and a Christian transformation of society he pledged:

> We do not want less religion; we want more; but it must be a religion that gets its orientation from the Kingdom of God. To concentrate our efforts on personal salvation, as orthodoxy has done, or on soul culture, as liberalism has done, comes close to refined

selfishness. All of us who have been trained in egotistic religion need a conversion to Christian Christianity, even if we are bishops or theological professors. Seek ye first the Kingdom of God and God's righteousness, and the salvation of your souls will be added to you.[143]

The Great War and the Social Gospel

The peak years of the social gospel movement lasted almost two election cycles, from 1907 to 1914. These were the same years in which Rauschenbusch enjoyed his fame. Though he suffered "a sort of compressed anxiety" anticipating the reaction to *Christianizing the Social Order*, for a brief time he tapped the zeitgeist again. The book was widely reviewed and sold well. Brimming with idealism, it kept a vow of silence on German matters that Rauschenbusch fretted over, while saying many hopeful things about German reform legislation and German socialism. After Germany went to war, Rauschenbusch was among the first to recognize that the animating spirit of his book belonged to a bygone era.[144]

For 10 years he worried about Germany's military build-up and the hostile relations between Germany and England. A return visit to Germany in 1910 heightened his foreboding. On various occasions Rauschenbusch warned that even civilized nations could be driven to war by appeals to nationalist pride and greed. In January 1914 he cautioned a lecture audience in New York that historic opportunities rarely lasted for more than a few years. He could feel the passing of the social gospel moment. After Europe plunged into war, Rauschenbusch felt the threat of its carnage very personally. He feared for Westphalian relatives and friends who fought for Germany, and for his widowed sister Frida and her daughters in Germany. From several of them, including Frida, he received pro-German letters defending the Kaiser's invasion of Belgium and France. Above all he feared that the United States might intervene in the war and that his three teenage sons would be called to fight.[145]

Rauschenbusch was not an absolute pacifist. In 1898 he celebrated America's victory in the Spanish–American War; on various occasions he praised the Puritan Revolution, which produced "the ablest ruler England has ever had" (Oliver Cromwell); and the American Revolutionary War, because it gave birth to American democracy; and the American Civil War, because it abolished slavery. But he urged that most wars had nothing to do with creating democracy or liberating enslaved masses, and in the years that built up to world war in Europe, his revulsion for war deepened. *Christianizing the Social Order* stressed that wars were usually fought for conquest and exploitation; *For God and the People* lamented, "Ever the pride of kings and the covetousness of the strong has driven peaceful nations to slaughter." That was Rauschenbusch's feeling when Europe plunged into war in August 1914. His students and colleagues noticed an immediate change in him. His sparkling optimism and humor vanished. He battled a deep sadness, admitting to *The Congregationalist* that he felt overcome by "profound grief and depression of spirit." As a symbol of mourning he began to wear a piece of black crepe on his lapel. He asked American Baptists to aid afflicted Baptists on both sides of the war, and spoke out against American intervention.[146]

It pained him that American public opinion favored England. Rauschenbusch loved Germany only a little less than he loved the United States. In 1902 he told a commencement crowd that he was deeply bonded to both nations: "My cradle stood on

American soil, but my mother's cradle-song was German as her heart. Will you blame me if I love both countries and defend each in turn?" By 1914 that was not a tolerable perspective in American life. Rauschenbusch urged that Germany was no more militaristic than its neighbors and no more imperialist than England. The following year he protested against America's policy of selling armaments to the Allied powers, calling for a government prohibition of all arms shipments.[147]

That provoked a firestorm of outrage. Most social gospelers shared Rauschenbusch's view that the United States should not send troops to Europe, but opposing Allied arms shipments was another matter, as was the claim that Germany was no worse than England. Editorialists maligned Rauschenbusch's patriotism, his summer cottage in Ontario was repeatedly vandalized, and many of his friends and followers distanced themselves from him. After one of his lecture invitations was rescinded, a newspaper headlined, "Methodists Do Not Want to Hear Pro-German Divine." Longtime friends refused to attend his services and lectures. Others remained civil toward him, but cool; Rauschenbusch took their discrete silence as a rebuke.[148]

To friends he protested that his antimilitarism was a Christian conviction, it was not a recent phenomenon, and he did not favor Germany over the United States: "I have been a Christian supporter of the peace idea for some years. During the Spanish–American War I took the average attitude and voiced it effectively. But shortly afterward the peace movement got a strong grip on me." It grieved him to read that he was motivated by a "disloyal preference" for Germany: "I have always expressed strongly my preference for America."[149] As America's involvement in the war grew deeper and the charges of disloyalty rang in his ears, Rauschenbusch withdrew from the public debate over the war. He agonized over the militarization of his country and church. "It was hard enough to combine Christianity and capitalistic business," he remarked. "Now we are asked to combine Christianity and war." He told a friend that the spirits of Martin Luther and Oliver Cromwell were alien to him; they despised the lower classes and "cheerfully" supported mass killing, but he could not combine Christianity and war without losing his faith: "Don't ask me to combine religion and the war spirit. I don't want to lose my religion; it's all I've got."[150]

He told Gladden that the Allied conceit of an idealistic victory was the greatest illusion of all: "Their entire scheme of morality is based on the premise of a successful democratic termination. But under the table they will be making very different deals." To Episcopal social gospeler Algernon Crapsey he admitted, "I am glad I shall not live forever. I am afraid of those who want to drag our country in to satisfy their partisan hate, or because they think universal peace will result from the victory of the allies." In 1916 he joined the newly founded pacifist Fellowship of Reconciliation, telling a friend that he was delighted to find people more radical than himself.[151]

His last two books fought off his deepening sorrow and depression. Rauschenbusch cut back on his grueling lecture schedule in 1914, which had kept him from writing books that he had in mind, especially one on social salvation. In 1915 he turned to a project requested by the Sunday School Council of Evangelical Denominations: a fourth-year textbook on the social teaching of Jesus to be published in the Sunday School Council series, "College Voluntary Study Courses." Rauschenbusch was eager to reach young people with his version of the gospel message. His brief social gospel primer *The Social Principles of Jesus* was published in 1916 and sold over 27,000 copies in its first two years. It summarized the teachings of Jesus on poverty, property, compassion, violence, justice, and the kingdom of God, declaring that the kingdom "is a real thing, now in operation." The kingdom was within and among human beings he taught, "It overlaps and interpenetrates all existing organizations, raising them to a higher level when they are good, resisting them when they are evil, quietly revolutionizing the old social order and changing it into the new." At times the kingdom suffered terrible reversals – "we are in the midst of one now." But God wrought victory out of the wrecks of defeat: "The Kingdom of God is always coming; you can never lay your hand on it and say, 'It is here.' But such fragmentary realizations of it as we have, alone make life worth living."[152]

That was the tone of his final work as well. The social gospel was long on practical criticism and short on theological reflection; very late in his life, in 1917, Rauschenbusch sought to provide the missing theological basis in *A Theology for the Social Gospel*. From certain appearances, the social gospel movement was still doing very well. Many Protestant leaders were enthused by America's wartime solidarity and sense of moral purpose; to them, the war effort was an example of social gospel idealism. Rauschenbusch countered that it was nothing of the kind. To him the real social gospel movement was paralyzed and dispirited, if not disintegrating. It survived only on the hope that genuine social Christianity could be revived after the war was over. *A Theology for the Social Gospel* gave voice to this rather desperate hope: "The Great War has dwarfed and submerged all other issues, including our social problems. But in fact the war is the most acute and tremendous social problem of all."[153]

He called for a larger social gospel vision that dealt with international issues. The social gospel that was needed would address not only national inequality, injustice, and immorality but also nationalism, militarism, imperialism, and global interdependence: "The social problem and the war problem are fundamentally one problem, and the social gospel faces both. After the War the social gospel will 'come back' with pent-up energy and clearer knowledge."[154]

Rauschenbusch struggled to believe that assurance: "The era of prophetic and democratic Christianity has just begun." The social gospel movement was new, he allowed, but the social gospel was not. It was neither alien nor novel, being the religion of Jesus. Rauschenbusch wearied of reviewers who found his writings weak on sin, though the worst on this theme was yet to come. He granted that some liberals deserved to be criticized on this count. The social gospel emphasis on social environment had a tendency to unload personal responsibility for sin, he allowed, "and human nature is quick to seize the chance." On the other hand, traditional orthodoxy did the same thing with its doctrines of original sin and the divine decrees. The old theology prattled endlessly about sin, but it unloaded responsibility for sin on Adam, the devil, and predestination. More importantly, the old orthodoxy obsessed over small legalisms pertaining to personal habits while it ignored massive social evils that oppressed millions of victims. For century after century the great majorities of peasants and workers suffered the ravages of exploitation, war and repression, "sucked dry by the parasitic classes of society," yet when did the "great" theologians ever condemn "these magnificent manifestations of the wickedness of the human heart?"[155]

The social gospel conceived the essence of sin as selfishness, Rauschenbusch observed, but differently from orthodoxy: "If our will is so completely depraved, where do we get the freedom on which alone responsibility can be based?" Because it pressed an unreal doctrine of uniform corruption, the old orthodoxy overlooked the fact that sin was also transmitted through social tradition and institutions. Rauschenbusch stressed that society was at least as important as original sin and it was more amenable to moral correction.[156]

With Schleiermacher and Ritschl, the social gospel recognized the supernatural power of evil and the social reality of original sin. Human beings were bonded to each other in their bondage to sin, Rauschenbusch explained, but this bondage was not uniform essential depravity. Some people were more sinful than others; some traditions bore greater moral guilt than others. By exaggerating the biological transmission of evil as uniform depravity, traditional Christianity overlooked the equally destructive means by which evil was transmitted through social tradition. Rauschenbusch warned that this failing had reactionary consequences, because it undercut the theological basis of moral efforts to resist the spread of evil. It was through socialization, not heredity, that drug addiction, social cruelty, perversity, racism, and ethnic feuds were transmitted from one generation to the next:

> When negroes are hunted from a Northern city like beasts, or when a Southern city degrades the whole nation by turning the savage inhumanity of a mob into a public festivity, we are continuing to sin because our fathers created the conditions of sin by the African slave trade and by the unearned wealth they gathered from slave labour for generations.[157]

He called the sum of these evils the kingdom of evil. The concept of a kingdom of evil was very old, Rauschenbusch reflected, but he meant something a bit different in retrieving the name. Ancient and medieval Christianity believed in demons. The "kingdom of evil" for traditional Christianity was a kingdom of evil spirits headed by Satan. But modern people did not believe in demons, and Satan was nearly as unreal: "A vital belief in demon powers is not forthcoming in modern life." Rauschenbusch was fully modern on this count, feeling no nostalgia for devil mythology. His concept of the kingdom of evil was social and historical. What disturbed him was the prospect of a modern Christianity that also did not believe in the reality of evil, or that conceived evil only as "disjointed" events. He countered that evil was real, powerful, organic and solidaristic in modern life. All people were bound together in the condition of bearing the yoke of evil and suffering, but only the social gospel made sense of this fact.[158]

A Theology for the Social Gospel urged that it was not enough to democratize politics, the church, or even economics; modern Christianity needed to complete the task of democratizing God. If the kingdom of God was thoroughly democratizing in its ethical and spiritual character, he reasoned, so must be the God of the kingdom. God was a loving Creator, not the feudal monarch of classical theology: "The worst form of leaving the naked unclothed, the hungry unfed, and the prisoners uncomforted, is to leave men under a despotic conception of God and the universe." The God of the heavenly monarchy needed vice-regents, popes, and kings to manage his kingdom, but the indwelling, democratic God lived and moved in the lives of human beings, acting directly upon them:

> A God who strives within our striving, who kindles his flame in our intellect, sends the impact of his energy to make our will restless for righteousness, floods our sub-conscious mind with dreams and longings, and always urges the race on toward a higher combination of freedom and solidarity – that would be a God with whom democratic and religious men could hold converse as their chief fellow-worker, the source of their energies, the ground of their hopes.[159]

In the same month that *A Theology for the Social Gospel* was published, Rauschenbusch began to feel desperately tired. He experienced convulsions, numbness, and other ailments that his doctors diagnosed as "pernicious anemia." Rauschenbusch sur-mised that he was exhausted and violently depressed. He canceled his outside lectures, explaining, "I have overworked," but kept teaching until March 1918. To Clarence Barbour he reported in February, "I am not getting better." He had no strength, he couldn't type, and his legs were stiff. Sensing that he was dying, he wrote several final statements. One was a set of instructions that accepted his early death as God's will: "Since 1914 the world is full of hate, and I cannot expect to be happy again in my lifetime."[160]

Another statement, carefully crafted, tried to reconcile Rauschenbusch to his country and take wartime pressure off Rochester Seminary without violating his antiwar con-science. In response to a query from Cornelius Woelfkin, pastor of Fifth Avenue Baptist Church in New York City, Rauschenbusch drafted a public letter that nearly expressed hope for an Allied victory. He described Germany as "the champion of two hateful remnants of the past, autocracy and war," and observed that the "Russian, Austrian and Prussian governments have long been the chief reactionary and anti-democratic forces of European politics." Though he hated war above all, he declared "I heartily hope that out of all this suffering will come the downfall of all autocratic government in the central empires." He warned that if the Central Powers were to win the war, they would "doubtless fasten this philosophy of imperialism and milita-rism on the world. I should regard this as a terrible calamity to the world, and have always feared a German triumph." From the beginning he had felt that a German victory would be "a terrible calamity to the world."[161]

His position had not really changed, but his criticism of Germany had been muted throughout the war. Had he made his deathbed statement two years earlier, Rauschen-busch might have spared himself much of the hate mail that so deeply wounded him. Though the letter said less than Rochester Seminary wanted, Barbour avidly publicized it. Though he never quite endorsed America's intervention, Rauschenbusch could not die estranged from his friends and country.[162]

He died of brain cancer on July 25, 1918, during the last weeks of World War I, at the age of 56. After Rauschenbusch and Gladden died, and the war ended, Protes-tant leaders Shailer Mathews, Charles Macfarland, Kirby Page, Sherwood Eddy, Harry Emerson Fosdick, Charles Clayton Morrison, Justin Wroe Nixon and Francis J. McConnell tried to revive the social gospel. Forced to fight rearguard battles for control of the mainline denominations against a militant fundamentalist backlash, they tried to accentuate the positive. Social Christianity was not merely anti-fundamentalist, they argued; it stood for good things. It stood for peace, social justice, cooperative relations, healthy families, international order, and the spirit of Jesus.[163]

In the seminaries they had a respectful hearing. A peace-oriented version of the social gospel had a strong influence in the liberal Protestant seminaries and divinity schools of the 1920s and early 1930s. It fueled a sprawling network of denominational peace fellowships and social justice ministries, inspired a burgeoning antiwar move-ment, provided a basis for the ascending ecumenical movement, and influenced virtu-ally every prominent liberal theologian of the time.

But Americans in the 1920s were tired of social crusades, both foreign and domestic, and the labor unrest of the postwar aftermath scared them. Many cheered, and others looked the other way, while their government waged an ugly crackdown on leftists. They rejected the League of Nations and vowed to "return to normalcy." Female suffrage finally won through, as did temperance, but that ended the two great social movements of the late nineteenth century, and Americans rebelled against Prohibition. With the partial exception of the ecumenical movement – which was a project of clerics and academics – the only social gospel cause that attracted popular interest was the peace issue. Many mainline Protestants repented of their wartime jingoism. They pledged not to support the war business again. Reduced to this cause, the social gospelers who lived beyond the Great War did what they could to redeem the social gospel vision of a good society. They looked to a social ethicist and indefatigable movement activist, Harry F. Ward, to lead the postwar renewal of the social gospel. But Ward turned out to be in the mold of George Herron, in a generation when the religion of Communist salvation was very far from innocent.

Social Christianity and Radical Reconstruction: Harry F. Ward

Harry Frederick Ward was so ardently devoted to the class interests of working-class people that he was routinely described, wrongly, as having come from them. He was born to a family of middle-class English Methodist shopkeepers in Chiswick, a suburb of London, in 1873. His parents began their careers as cheesemongers, moved on to being proprietors of a butcher's shop, and sent Harry to a boarding school catering to the landed gentry and a rising middle class. The Wards were highly reticent, even among themselves, even by English standards; Ward later recalled, "I come of a breed that is stark in speech and used to stand[ing] mute when greatly moved." By 1887 the family had a second butcher's shop, and the shopkeepers' ethos of hard work and long hours was deeply instilled in young Harry. On the other hand, opportunities for higher education were very limited in England; thus Ward immigrated to the USA in 1891 to complete his education.[164]

As a youth Ward was afflicted with rheumatic fever, which cast a shadow over his entire health-challenged life, though he lived to be 93. He aspired to be a Wesleyan lay preacher like his father, who was also named Harry Ward. For the senior Ward, who gave outdoor revival sermons against laziness, worldly diversions, and establishment religion, preaching and business were a good balance. For his son, a voracious reader with a gift for public speaking, the life of a shopkeeper held little appeal. Young Harry Ward was already an accomplished street preacher when he immigrated to the USA, where he stayed with uncles in Utah, Illinois, and Idaho, and mourned the news of his mother's death. In 1893 he enrolled at the University of Southern California (USC), a new Methodist institution and not much of a school; Ward spent most of his time at fraternity parties. But he took one assignment seriously – the Methodist Church's accreditation exam for ministerial standing. The reading list for the exam included Ely's *Social Aspects of Christianity*. Ward devoured the book and was changed by it. In England he had an inkling of the social gospel – Methodist minister Hugh Price Hughes was renowned in London for his social evangelism – but Ely's book convinced Ward that the gospel really was social. It also explained why so many working-class people derided Christianity and Wesleyan street preaching.[165]

Ward's conversion to a social Christian outlook helped him decide for a more serious academic climate. He had wanted to study at Northwestern University in Evanston, Illinois, but judged that his frail health needed sunny California. Now the difference between the academic rigor of Methodist Northwestern and the barely-a-college frivolity of Methodist USC seemed too great not to risk his health. A further draw was the presence of a young, brilliant, religious philosopher at Northwestern, George Albert Coe, who had taught previously at USC. Transferring to Northwestern in 1894, Ward became a champion debater, was deeply influenced by Coe's interpretation of religion as a social phenomenon, and forged a close friendship with him. Coe's version of religious humanism drew on his training in Boston University personalism. By the mid-1890s he taught a doctrine that he called "salvation by education," which he later expounded in an influential book, *The Religion of a Mature Mind* (1902). In Coe's classroom, Ward relinquished what remained of his revivalist theme that the ultimate realities were God and the soul; Coe insisted that all religious experience was triadic, involving a social dimension. A Northwestern economics professor, John Gray, assured Ward that good economics was moral; meanwhile Ward met his future wife, Daisy Kendall, a fellow student and the daughter of a wealthy, Methodist, fervently moralistic family that made its fortune selling shoes and boots after the Civil War.[166]

Ward's conversion to the social gospel heightened his enthusiasm for academic study and relieved him of his former anxiety that one had to choose between knowledge and faith. He excelled as a philosophy major at Northwestern, won a scholarship to Harvard's master's program in philosophy, and discovered the limit of his enthusiasm for philosophy. Coe's teaching style was friendly and practical, but at Harvard, William James drilled students in the finer points of epistemology. In a seminar on German idealist Rudolf Hermann Lotze, James tracked the twists and turns of Lotze's metaphysical arguments, prompting Ward to complain, "Those German brains are built on such a plan that you have to organize a search party before you can find out what they mean." Ward wished that James would simply expound his own pragmatism. Like Reinhold Niebuhr after him, Ward's calling to social ethics was influenced by the experience of struggling with epistemological arguments that seemed hopelessly abstract and incomprehensible. He told Daisy in a letter that philosophy rarely grabbed him intellectually and it never grabbed him emotionally.[167]

Jamesian pragmatism made sense to Ward, but James gave little class time to it. Ward's interest in the ethics of Jesus took him to Peabody's classroom, which suited him perfectly. In 1898, when Ward earned his philosophy degree at Harvard, he had three intellectual heroes: Ely, who had converted him to social Christianity; Coe, who gave him a religious philosophical worldview; and Peabody, who taught him how to understand Jesus, the New Testament, and the relation of both to the social question. Ward soon moved beyond Ely and Peabody, but not beyond Coe. Years later, when he told his students that the social gospel was inadequate, he meant Ely and Peabody, not Coe or Rauschenbusch. The typical social gospel, in his telling, was reformist and dualistic, distinguishing between personal and social salvation. Good social Christianity, on the other hand, was radical and integral, conceiving salvation as inherently social. Ely and Peabody helped him get to the social gospel, but Ward and Coe moved to a vision of radical social reconstruction that eschewed mere reforms.[168]

Upon graduating from Harvard, Ward returned to Chicago to head Northwestern University's settlement house experiment, where he clashed with members of the governing council, formed friendships with Jane Addams and Graham Taylor – Addams called him "my little preacher" – and resigned after two years. His next stop was a ministerial post at Chicago's 47th Street Methodist Episcopal Church, where Ward came into his own. Every male adult in his congregation, except for a dentist, was a stockyard worker, many of them in the meatpacking industry. For Ward, ministering in this crowded, hellish, back-of-the-yards district was a searing experience, one that left a permanent mark. Historian David Nelson Duke aptly noted that Ward's early years in Chicago burned a hole in his psyche. Ward preached on poverty, property, moral economics, the rights of workers, and the right to a decent environment. The latter issue was personal, because his nine years in Chicago nearly killed him. The air pollution was dreadful; the stench was overwhelming. Ward was an extreme work-aholic and he battled chronic illnesses. Without his summer vacations at Lonely Lake in Canada, which became a yearly refuge, he might not have survived. On occasion he risked a word about racial justice, telling his parishioners they should empathize with the pain of black Americans, though Ward keenly understood that his embattled congregants identified African Americans with scabbing and strikebreaking. In 1902 he finally received a preaching certificate, without the benefit of seminary training; the following year he moved to Chicago's Union Avenue Church, where his parish-ioners still worked for the stockyards, but mostly in white-collar jobs.[169]

Ward became a locally and nationally prominent social gospel activist during his five years at Union Avenue Church. He joined the City Club of Chicago, a public welfare group that included Jane Addams and philosopher George Herbert Mead; took an active role in the Chicago Civic Federation, where the leaders included social gospelers Albion Small, Graham Taylor, and William T. Stead; and forged friendships with Frank Mason North and Walter Rauschenbusch, who spoke alongside him at labor rallies. Ward and North, lamenting that Methodists had little role in the social gospel, vowed to get their church into it. In 1907 Ward organized a national Methodist conference in Washington, DC that founded a new service organization, the Methodist Federation for Social Service. The group included ministers North and Worth Tippy, labor economist John Commons, Indiana governor Frank Hanley, social worker Mary McDowell, settlement house leader Edward Devine, and Denver judge Ben Lindsay, who founded the juvenile court. United States vice-president Charles Fairbanks attended the conference, afterwards taking the group to meet President Theodore Roosevelt. The Methodist social gospelers, feeling their rising status in American Christianity, struck immediately for a major role in the General Conference of the Methodist Episcopal Church, which met in May 1908.

The Social Creed of the Churches was a byproduct of that initiative. Ward jotted the first draft on a Western Union pad, listing 11 reforms; J. W. Magruder did a bit of editorial smoothening; and the Methodist General Council endorsed it:

> We deem it the duty of all Christian people to concern themselves directly with certain practical industrial problems. To us it seems that the churches must stand –
>
> For equal rights and complete justice for all men in all stations of life.
> For the principles of conciliation and arbitration in industrial relations.
> For the protection of the workers from dangerous machinery, occupational diseases, injuries, and mortality.
> For the abolition of child labor.
> For such regulation of the conditions of labor for women as shall safeguard the physical and moral health of the community.
> For the suppression of the 'sweating system.'
> For the gradual and reasonable reduction of the hours of labor to the lowest practical point, with work for all; and for that degree of leisure for all which is the condition of the highest human life.

> For the release from employment one day in seven.
>
> For a living wage in every industry.
>
> For the highest wage that each industry can afford, and for the most equitable division of the products of industry that can ultimately be devised.
>
> For the recognition of the Golden Rule, and the mind of Christ as the supreme law of society and the sure remedy for all social ills.

The original creed, despite being focused on workplace issues, stopped short of advocating cooperative ownership or profit sharing; its reference to the rights of women was restricted to the workplace; and it made no reference to racial justice. Neither did any of the creed's later versions assert a commitment to racial justice until the Federal Council's 1932 version. Consummating a 1905 Plan of Federation, the Federal Council of Churches was founded in December 1908 in Philadelphia, where North added four reforms to Ward's list and eliminated the "Golden Rule" statement. Thus the Federal Council's 1908 version of the Social Creed of the Churches contained 14 reforms, though North failed to mention that Ward had written most of them. For decades afterwards North was identified as the author of the creed.[170]

Ward resented the oversight. In February 1909 he told Daisy: "I am waiting to see whether he acknowledges any credit to anyone else. I suppose a man ought to be satisfied to do the thing and let other fellows get the credit." But Ward's stature grew in ecumenical circles, with or without the credit. Writing to Daisy from one of his speaking tours for the Federation, he vowed, "If I'm spared I hope to show those fellows something yet." His poor health made him doubt that he had many years left. By 1912, however, when the Federal Council asked him to produce a book on the Social Creed, Ward was known for his extensive speaking tours and radical politics. Rauschenbusch convinced him that the social gospel needed to be Socialist; Ward told his audiences to read Rauschenbusch above all others; and he told Rauschenbusch that he did so. In a 12-month period from 1912 to 1913 he gave 347 lectures and conducted 36 conferences in 17 states, including three months of constant speaking on the West Coast. Ward defended the labor movement, explained the social creed, praised the women's suffrage movement, and, in two of his favorite speeches, extolled the Socialist stream of the social gospel. Jesus and socialism had the same ethic, Ward argued. Both favored the weak and oppressed, conceived economics in moral terms, and envisioned a transformed order of peace and social justice. Socialism came about because Christianity abandoned its social mission; the hope of the world was to merge the Christian and socialist faiths. Christianity needed the practical idealism and "intense passion for justice" of the Socialist and labor movements; on the other hand, these movements needed "the God consciousness, the sense of eternal values, and the obligation of universal brotherhood" that Christianity at its best proclaimed.[171]

In 1913 Methodist bishop Francis McConnell secured a half-time teaching post for Ward at McConnell's alma mater Boston University. This position was the first chair of social service at an American seminary, which allowed Ward to spend the other half of his time directing the Methodist Federation of Social Service, a position he held from 1912 to 1944. In phrases close to those of Rauschenbusch, he taught that the Hebrew prophets were "the beating heart of the Old Testament," Jesus fulfilled the "social program" of the prophets, and the kingdom of God was "a collective conception involving the whole social life of man." Already Ward had the controlling idea of his political thought, which came to be called the "Popular Front" or "united front." In 1915 he declared that the "only possible way" to beat the class system was to "get the most of us together in the common cause, to get the great mass of workers and the more prominent members of society to join hands." That was always the point of his activist dealings with religious and non-religious liberals, progressives, radicals, Socialists, and Communists. Politically, Ward was an anti-capitalist revolutionary. In his first book, *Social Evangelism* (1915) he urged that every Christian was called to be a "social evangel," putting God into the life of the community, which could be done only through radical activism. Social evangelism endorsed no privileges, created no priests, and developed no hierarchy: "It puts all to work in the task of transforming life. Its goal cannot be reached except by the cooperation of all." Ward enthused that the social gospel made religion interesting again, bringing immigrants and the working class back to church. But gathering a crowd was not an end in itself, he cautioned – it was merely an opportunity to build the kingdom of God.[172]

He brought that rendering of the gospel faith to so many people that Charles Macfarland, general secretary of the Federal Council of Churches, declared in 1916 that the Federal Council regarded Ward as "the greatest prophet today," apparently forgetting Rauschenbusch. Meanwhile Boston University found it rather trying to have a prophet on its faculty. Ward blasted the Methodist Book Concern for using non-union labor. He condemned capitalism as predatory and corrupting, causing School of Theology dean L. J. Birney to protest that he never excoriated the sins of labor. And Ward opposed America's intervention in World War I, though he was careful to say it in a way that averted legal trouble. The nature of the war did not change after Wilson changed his mind, Ward argued. The war was still a product of the fatal link between capitalism and militarism, just as the social gospelers claimed repeatedly before 1917. In *The Christian Demand for Social Reconstruction* (1918) Ward put it bluntly, though in the broad context of opposing all wars for capitalist and imperial control. The spirit of society (its organizing principle) and the end of society (its goal) belonged together he urged: "If society seeks possession, then it must have force to protect the possessor. If it seeks power, it must have armies as the tool of the aggressor." The Christian spirit, construed as the religion of Jesus, harmonized with the end of demo-cratic cooperation; by contrast, capitalist industry and the militarist state were intrinsi-cally linked as predatory forces, working together to consolidate and sustain national and class power over the many. Ward declared, "If we would overthrow one, the other also must be destroyed, for they are inseparably joined." What mattered was nothing less than the complete "overthrow of militarism and of capitalistic industrial-ism." If the nations did not get rid of capitalism, "militarism will be continued and extended, blood and iron will continue to rule the world, and Christianity will struggle for its existence as a rebellious protest against the powers that be."[173]

These positions were too hard-edged for Boston University, but not for Union Theological Seminary, where Ward began lecturing part-time in 1916. Two years later Ward accepted the Christian ethics chair at Union, which had been vacated by its firing of ethicist Thomas C. Hall. A respected academic who had studied in Germany and married a German, Hall took anti-preparedness activism a step too far. In 1915, anxious to keep America out of the war, he defended Germany's sinking of the SS *Lusitania* as a tragic necessity of war. His statement outraged seminary trustees, and a month after America entered the war, Hall was sacked with no hearing or exchange of correspondence. Compared to Hall, Ward seemed restrained to the trustees. While

Ward packed for New York in July 1918, Rauschenbusch died; Ward wrote to Pauline Rauschenbusch: "The banner he so gallantly lifted will not fail. It will be carried forward by many of those whom he has taught by word and pen."[174]

That was what Ward thought the rest of his life would be about – carrying Rauschenbusch's banner. He heard it repeatedly when introduced as a speaker. In his inaugural address at Union, Ward declared that in some situations, such as the current postwar environment, the only possible defense was a strong offense. Merely holding on to progressive gains was not an option. If America did not advance to economic democracy, it would retreat to something worse than the status quo. Ward's book *The Gospel for a Working World* (1918) exhorted his readers to believe that the idealistic gospel of love, stripped of a radical commitment to social justice, was meaningless to oppressed people: "There are scant results to be gathered from preaching the gospel of love to groups of workers in whose lives injustice is continually breeding hate and revenge." As soon as Christians awoke to the ethical meaning of Christianity in the industrial world they discovered the limits of individualism, charity, and reform. As soon as they tried to change the structures of oppression they learned "that they must reckon with the whole practice of the industrial world." The industrial order was a structure of relations between persons, Ward observed. It was not a state of nature or the way things had to be, and it could be transformed by deliberate, convictional, collective effort: "The gospel requires tremendous transformations in modern industry; that is precisely its challenge to the modern Christian."[175]

Ward perceived that the aftermath of the war was disastrous for Christian socialism. It was hard to see a revolution brewing in the America of the Espionage Act, a burgeoning corporate sector that profited from the war, and escalating popular hysteria against radicalism and socialism. Americans despised the Socialist party for opposing the war; in March 1919 the Supreme Court upheld the Espionage Act, which sent Socialist leader Eugene Debs to the Atlanta Penitentiary; and Americans seethed at the perceived betrayal of the new Bolshevik regime in Russia, which negotiated a peace treaty with Germany eight months before the Armistice. Afterwards the Bolsheviks exhorted workers of the world to join them in smashing capitalism. Many Americans feared that it might be happening in their country. The IWW (founded in 1905) had struck hard in Lawrence, Massachusetts (1912) and Paterson, New Jersey (1913). After the war the Labor movement struck harder with pent-up demands. In May through August, 1919, the movement averaged over 350 strikes per month; in August an American branch of the Communist party was founded at a convention in Chicago; by the end of the year four million American workers had gone on strike during some part of the year. President Wilson, deciding not to negotiate the Versailles Treaty and the League of Nations Covenant with the US Senate, tried to win public support through an exhausting speaking tour, but lost political allies, suffered a devastating stroke, and lost the Senate battle for the Versailles Treaty. In September 1919, Massachusetts governor Calvin Coolidge attained national fame by busting a strike of Boston police officers; the following January US Attorney General A. Mitchell Palmer raided thousands of private homes and labor headquarters across the nation, lacking warrants and evidence, in the name of combating America's "Red Menace." A sensationalist press heaped adulation on Palmer and whipped up popular anxieties about socialist revolutions hatched in Moscow, all of which gave Union's new ethics professor much to oppose.[176]

Ward's first major work, *The New Social Order: Principles and Programs* (1919), fixed an excited eye on Russia. The beginnings of a new social order were already present, he declared – "Here and there parts of it may be seen breaking through the shell of the old, which has long been nourishing the embryo." He did not believe that the world was going Bolshevik, or that all roads led to state socialism, or that the League of Nations would inaugurate the kingdom of God. But he did believe that socialism was moving forward swiftly, which evoked reactionary attacks on all varieties of social-ism, communism, radicalism, internationalism, and progressivism. Ward told Americans not to fear the socialist tide. There was such a thing as socialism with democracy; in fact, the only true socialism was democratic. The Versailles Treaty seemed to leave the old order pretty much in tact, aside from punishing Germany, but Ward assured that "the good old days for the people of power and privilege are not coming back." A rising labor movement guaranteed that no ruling class of any nation would ever rest comfortably again: "The concentration of economic power is to be challenged as the concentration of military power has been challenged. The people throughout the world who toil for a mere living, a little less or a little more, are not going to remain quiescent in a subordinate and inferior social status."[177]

Ward allowed that the power brokers at the Paris Peace Conference had a different vision. To them the new world order was simply the old world order managed more efficiently for their interests. Making the world safe for democracy meant capitalizing the entire planet, so that "their descendants may draw perpetual interest." They were great advocates of extending "civilization," which meant imposing capitalism "upon every one of the 'backward peoples,' regardless of their wishes, ideals, and aspirations." The Paris dignitaries supported the League of Nations, Ward noted, but to them it represented merely "an opportunity to organize loot on a grander scale, to avoid inconvenient quarrels concerning the division of the spoils and to maintain the arrange-ment by combined force." Ward counseled that politically this marriage was a loser, and ethically it was repugnant. Americans were wrong to call it civilization, when most of the world's people were excluded from the benefits. And structurally it was unsustainable anyway. Even if the capitalist class got its way for a while, organizing the League of Nations on capitalist terms, the League would not last, because capital-ism subverted and corrupted everything it touched, including the sovereignty of nation states. Capitalism and international cooperation between nation states did not go together. For Ward, however, that was an argument against capitalism only, not against international cooperation. If capitalism prevailed, there would be no League of Nations in the long run; if international cooperation prevailed, it would be the death knell of a system that knew no value besides profit. Because the power of a rising international labor movement was terribly, wonderfully real, Ward contended, the days of capitalist hegemony were numbered.[178]

In the meantime American politics was in a bad way. Ward acknowledged that Americans were sore and stiff from the burdens of war, they were handicapped by their ignorance of the radical and socialist movements in Europe, they believed in American exceptionalism, and they were both liberated and deluded by the peculiari-ties of the American experience. To some degree the USA *was* an exception to history, he allowed, but Americans naively overestimated the difference. History was coming to the USA in the rise of the laboring classes. The American ruling class wanted to make the whole world capitalist; Ward observed that a different kind of missionary impulse was also spreading in the country. He respected the missionary impulse, since any faith, system, or ideology with a strong life force was bound to have one. But some causes were more worthy of being exported than others, and history was moving in a quite specific direction: "We all like to do it: first the kings, then the statesmen,

then the capitalists; now the professors and next the working men." The next stage
of history was an explosion of world democracy in which the overwhelming majority
populations of the world organized the factors of production and wrote their interests
into the laws: "In magnitude, nature and consequences, one of the greatest changes
in human history is now occurring, involving all humanity and all the institutions of
society and its customs. Men everywhere are seeking a way to live together so that
the nations may never again be drawn into war, so that there shall be freedom and
development for all peoples."[179]

He realized that that smacked of exaggeration in 1919; thus Ward filled his book
with long discussions of the British Labour party, the Russian Soviet Republic, the
League of Nations, Labor and radical movements in the USA, and the remarkable rise
of social Christianity. He hated violence, yet cautioned his readers that "no significant
change in human history has occurred without violence." He explained Fabian socialism, described the Labour party platform, and turned to the hot subject: the Bolshevik
revolution. The idea of a society organized for the sake of all its people, with no
privileged or subordinated classes, was not a modern ideal, Ward observed. It was the
dream of respected and derided idealists alike from ages past. With the Bolshevik revolution, this idea was getting its first serious test: "Now the Western nations must face
in the field of practical organization the question of whether or not they will accept
or reject this ideal."[180]

The Soviet Constitution nationalized the economy and instituted universal work
requirements. That was more sweeping than anything imagined by the British Labour
party, Ward observed. Moreover, the English Socialists had nothing like the Bolshevik
dictatorship of the proletariat, in which revolutionary leaders assumed dictatorial
powers to expropriate, disarm, and defeat opponents of the revolution. Ward judged
that the Soviet constitution was wrong to suppress minority rights – "an undue assertion of majority power" – and counseled that, as with the US Espionage Act, it was
too soon to say whether democracy could be fostered by the temporary denial of
democracy. Likewise it was too soon to say whether the Soviet regime would adopt a
more tolerant policy toward organized religion than its current repressive one. He
stressed, however, that Soviet democracy was already far ahead of England and the
USA on the ethics of the franchise. In the Western democracies, access was qualified
by property, literacy, and gender; in the Soviet state the disqualifying factor was productive energy. The right to vote in the Soviet Union, or be voted for, was denied to
all capitalists, private merchants, and commercial brokers, monks and clergy, and agents
of the former police and ruling dynasty. Ward advised Americans to hold their moral
censure; a nation that prized productive work was not inferior to one that disenfranchised blacks, women, people lacking education, or anyone lacking property.[181]

On the politics of the moment, *The New Social Order* pleaded for a change of policy,
one that stopped the British and American plots against a struggling Soviet government. Ward did not say explicitly that the Bolshevik regime pursued the biblical idea
of a good society more seriously than the Western democracies, but on the lecture
trail and in the Methodist Federation's newsletter he did say it, setting off a firestorm
of controversy in Methodist circles. Prominent Methodists demanded to know the
extent and depth of his sympathy for the Bolshevik revolution. A leading Methodist
publication, the *New York Christian Advocate*, blasted Ward for having "surrendered his
mind and heart" to Bolshevik communism. The Methodist Book Concern, seizing a
revenge opportunity, announced dramatically that it would stop printing one of Ward's

books and burn the plates for it. Ward replied that the Bolsheviks had neither his mind nor heart. He rejected their doctrine of the dictatorship of the proletariat, their vindictive treatment of past injustices, and their prohibitions against teaching religious doctrine.[182]

That was assurance enough for most social gospelers. In a bleak political moment, religious progressives were grateful to have a forceful, intelligent, passionate advocate, one they frequently compared to Rauschenbusch. A reviewer for the *Nation* put it plainly: "The mantle of Walter Rauschenbusch seems to have fallen on the shoulders of Harry Ward." Pauline Rauschenbusch said the same thing, telling Ward that she admired his brave stand against "the powerful," which gave him the stature of a prophet: "Walter has gone on and is out of this phase of the strife and so I'm doubly glad you are still here."[183]

In the 1920s the strongly anti-capitalist stream of social Christianity had numerous prominent advocates besides Ward, including Sherwood Eddy, Kirby Page, George Albert Coe, Norman Thomas, and Justin Wroe Nixon. Francis McConnell worked the boundary between the movement's radical and liberal streams, and virtually all social gospelers endorsed a cooperativist critique of capitalism. In addition, throughout the decade social gospel pastors, theologians, and repented of their wartime jingoism and pledged never to support another war. The memory of Ward's opposition to World War I strengthened his prophetic standing in a movement that became, above all, an antiwar enterprise. In 1919 the US Senate Committee Investigating German Propaganda asked Ward to account for his involvement with radical antiwar organizations. Ward replied that the pertinent issue was not German propaganda, his loyalty to the US, or his relationship to radical organizations; what mattered was that he hated militarism: "I was against militarism before the war; I was against it during the war; and if there is any of it left after a large part of the world has been trying to destroy it, I am still against it." Years later he recalled of this period of his life: "It is good for a man to find out early in life how many will be missing from roll call on the day of battle. Then he will discover in time that the few who will stand are sufficient."[184]

Ward treasured the democratic leftists who stood with him against the Red Scare. They included veterans of the American Union Against Militarism (Jane Addams, John Haynes Holmes, Oswald Garrison Villard, Norman Thomas), labor radicals (Elizabeth Gurley Flynn, William Z. Foster), liberal lawyers (Felix Frankfurter, Albert DeSilver), and independent radicals (James Weldon Johnson, Roger Baldwin). During the war, Thomas and Baldwin worked with Ward to help conscientious objectors; afterwards they asked him to lead the ACLU's board of directors. The founding members of the American Civil Liberties Union (ACLU) were a varied bunch, aside from their prominence on the democratic Left. Ward's stature among them was remarkable for a seminary professor. In an unprecedented crisis, the stars of America's democratic Left asked him to hold together their emergency effort to prevent the US government from destroying the American Left and American civil liberties. For the next 20 years Ward's work in that cause fueled most of his very large FBI file. In 1920 his role in the ACLU was cited with alarm by the New York State Legislative Joint Committee Investigating Seditious Acts, which identified Union Seminary as one of "two dangerous centers of Revolutionary Socialist teaching of a university type in ecclesiastical institutions." The committee topped that piece of hyperbole by warning that Ward's style of "Bolshevism" was "far worse than the Bolshevism of Russia." Two years later FBI Director William J. Burns described Ward as a typical leftist "alien" who, like most of his kind, "reviles our sanctuary, pollutes the temple, and spreads from the very sanctum itself the seeds of discord, envy, and strife."[185]

Ward's stock reply was that he belonged to no party or faction; he simply tried to follow the teaching of Jesus. In New York he was buoyed by Coe, who taught religious education and psychology at Union Seminary from 1909 to 1922 and at Teachers College, Columbia University from 1922 to 1927. At Union Seminary his mannered colleagues wished he were more like them, but defended his integrity and academic freedom. In the Methodist Church, McConnell defended Ward's controversial role as director of the Methodist Federation for Social Service for many years. Above all, Ward was strengthened by the unfailing support of his wife Daisy, who put up with his long speaking tours and assured him he was needed in the social struggle.

Contrary to the convention that the social gospel ended in 1918, the movement had its widest and deepest impact on American churches in the 1920s and 1930s. In 1910 it was just getting a toehold in the seminaries and churches; by 1925 it flowed routinely from the seminaries to the churches, or at least, to the pulpits and ministerial conferences. The social gospel was the dominant language of liberal Protestant pastors, which made it possible for so many of them to condemn war and even capitalism in the 1930s.

By the mid-1920s, however, Ward had stopped reciting the remarkable story of social Christianity. He was no longer impressed by its progress; even the language of progress was becoming ridiculous to him, at least with reference to anything American. By 1924 he was uncharacteristically dispirited. The constant attacks on his faith and ideology wore him down, he was frustrated with the church and appalled at American politics, his daughter Muriel suffered from a serious illness, and his torrent of writings slowed to a trickle. Ward could still lecture and write articles while feeling blue, but to write big books he had to have a big idea that he believed was being realized. Increasingly he mused that the essential thing was to be faithful to a good cause, not to be successful. It could not be wrong to struggle for the right things, even if one accomplished little. The only way to find out how much democracy could be attained was to struggle for it all the time. In that mood he and Daisy went to Russia in 1924–5 to see if all the bad things being said about Soviet communism were true.

To his disappointment quite a few of them were. Ward acknowledged that the Soviet Union had very little freedom of speech and assembly, and no freedom of the press: "The censor is still omnipotent if not omniscient." With so much political repression, "rank injustice and oppression" were inevitable. He remained hopeful and sympathetic toward the Soviet experiment, but cautioned American liberals to lower their expectations of it. The Soviet revolution was still imperiled by counter-revolutionary opposition for which reason its needed reforms were still being delayed, and the delay was likely to last for some time. Later in the same sabbatical Ward visited Gandhi in India and traveled through China. In both places he warned intellectuals against detaching themselves from the struggles of working people; in China he met radical intellectuals who had a hard time comprehending the concept of a Christian Socialist. Upon returning to the USA Ward could feel his former passion and another big book coming on, though he no longer spoke the optimistic social gospel language of divine providence, cultural progress, and the kingdom of God. His politics and person had taken too many beatings to sustain a progress narrative. Now he wrote scathing critiques of Western decadence, materialism, and imperialism, and he wrote more explicitly as a religious humanist with a radical pragmatic bent. In a 1928 symposium on "Recent Gains in American Civilization," Ward seethed against the liberal language of "progress" and "civilization." Merely to use these terms, he warned, was to risk reinforcing "our comfortable, middle-class religionists in the false security which emanates from the idea of automatic progress that left them so unprepared and helpless when the World War hit them." His grammar had hardened, but his surge of world-building conviction had returned.[186]

In 1928, taking his usual summer vacation at Lonely Lake in Canada, Ward built a six-foot writing table under a lean-to roof at the top of a bluff overlooking the lake, where he wrote *Our Economic Morality and the Ethic of Jesus* (1929). The book's point of origin explained its lack of footnotes, though Ward explained that footnoted books cost too much; he wanted to reach beyond the academy. Immediately he drew the contrast between his optimistic spirit of 1919 and the situation a decade later. *The New Social Order* was lifted by the wartime hope of new possibilities, but in 1929, if one aspired to be constructive and relevant, one had to be mostly critical, because American capitalism had become more entrenched and corrupt than ever: "Never in the story of mankind has any nation made as much money with as little consideration for moral values and social consequences as the United States in the last decade." In that exasperated mood Ward wrote his signature work.[187]

His signature theme, that good economics was moral, had not changed: "This modern attempt at economics without morals enlarges the historic monstrosity of the economic man." The myth of the "economic man" was that human beings were impervious to all factors besides economic gain. Ward protested that capitalism had advanced to the point of turning this myth into a social system "without heart or conscience." He wished that its academic priests would call their discipline "chrematistics" – the science of money-making – instead of corrupting the noble word, "economics." Many economists simply perpetuated the myths of *laissez-faire* ideology: "They repeat Smith and Ricardo as though the world had never moved since they died." Others made slight adjustments "to prove what incorrigible theologians they really are." Liberal economists, at least making contact with the real world, made larger adjustments for things that paid off – safety and health regulations, time limits, and higher wages. But that left the essential factors untouched, Ward objected. There was a story of progress to be told about the human experience, just as the progressives contended. In the historical struggle to shuck off war, slavery, exploitation, and empire, human beings gradually found their souls by recognizing there was such a thing as the common good. Modern capitalism, however, told people "to cease this striving in which man has been finding his soul." By enshrining selfishness as the generative principle and force of social existence, capitalism ensured "the dominion of those who have achieved power in the economic war and of their descendants."[188]

Ward allowed that the capitalist religion had many believers: "What was once a mystic faith of the few in the power of self-interest to achieve a social order is now a popular dogma, and true to form it acquires authority rather than evidence." Many people realized that capitalism was bad for their moral health, but judged that it "worked" as a prosperity machine. Ward acknowledged that many Americans were very well fed and housed. But the "back streets" of America's mill towns were filled with people who suffered long days of miserable, grinding work for little pay, he admonished. Did their lives count for nothing in assessing what worked? And even if capitalism worked, compared to feudalism, as a mode of production, how could it be wrong to strive for an economic system that did a better job of distributing economic gains? America had vast natural wealth on a large continent unhampered by centuries of feudal history, yet its vaunted economic system produced high rates of poverty and unemployment. How could that be counted as success? Noting that the unemployment problem was getting worse, Ward judged that so-called free enterprise was running out of steam. Early American capitalism had an expanding frontier to exploit and plenty of capacity to capitalize labor; now markets were occupied, all the property worth having in the USA was bought up, and corporate control and wealth were inherited.[189]

Liberal reformers contended that capitalism was great at production but lousy at just distribution; Ward refused to concede the first part. Production and distribution went together, the capitalist faith that distribution would take care of itself was refuted by reality, and, in recent years, even production had languished. Many big industries were running at less than 50 percent capacity. Ward urged that there had to be a better way to organize the economy than to divide the productive, distributive, and consumptive parts of the economic process from each other and set them against each other: "In its old age capitalistic society destroys its own morality of initiative, enterprise, and hard work. It operates for us finally only at the cost of other people. And if in the end it succeeds for them it will be at our cost." The key to a better system was the golden rule of Jesus, treating others as one would want others to treat one's self. In economic terms, that meant a system of reciprocal benefit.[190]

Ward allowed that it was a novel development in Christianity to take seriously the social ethic of Jesus, and that only the "left wing" of modern Christianity did so. Thus it was not surprising that Christianity rarely contributed much to the struggle for a good society, and in America there were distinctive national myths to overcome. In Russia the old order was gone; in Europe and China it was fading fast; "in this country alone is there stagnation." But even the USA had streams of progressives, radicals, and social gospelers who recognized that "the times are ripe and rotten ripe for change."[191]

He did not romanticize the existing socialist revolution. Soviet Communists parroted Nikolai Bukharin's dictum that the spiritual life of society depended on the material production of society; Ward replied that the reverse was equally true. The spiritual and material productive forces were interdependent; each of them operated constantly as both cause and effect. Criticizing Soviet restrictions on personal freedom, he rejected the denigration of the individual and glorification of force that paraded in Soviet Communist propaganda, all of which were as contrary to the ethic of Jesus as the capitalist religion of selfishness and empire. Translated into modern terms, Ward contended, Jesus stood for personality, cooperation, mutual aid, and peace: "The ethic of Jesus substitutes a spiritual warfare against the forces that hinder and destroy the common good, carried on in the spirit of renunciation. The choice is not between evolution and revolution, but between two kinds of revolution – one a voluntary transformation of economic society, the other its catastrophic overthrow." Ward wanted a radical democratic socialism by consent, not a dictatorial socialism governed by a new class of revolutionary rulers. The way of Jesus was, for him, the standard that rebuked capitalist civilization, but also a bulwark against the wrong kind of socialism.[192]

Ward, Reinhold Niebuhr, and the Soviet Spirit

Had he stuck with that formulation, Ward would have been remembered as a major social gospeler in the socialist tradition of Bliss, Herron, Rauschenbusch, and Walter Muelder. In 1929 he was 56 years old. Ward was too radical not to be controversial, but his brand of independent socialism was a respectable position in the social gospel movement, his theology belonged to its mainstream, and in the 1930s, reeling from the Depression, many religious intellectuals flocked to a radical perspective much like Ward's.

He seemed to have been ahead of the curve. In the mid-1930s nearly every mainline Protestant church officially declared that it would never support another war. Between 1934 and 1936 the Disciples of Christ, the Episcopal Church, the Northern Baptist Convention, the General Council of Congregational and Christian Churches, both of the major Presbyterian churches, and both of the major Methodist Episcopal churches categorically repudiated the war business. Many pastors and ministerial conferences were equally tough on capitalism, which seemed to have collapsed. In 1934 Kirby Page and a group of church leaders representing 10 Protestant denominations sent a questionnaire to 99,890 ministers and 609 rabbis, receiving 20,870 replies. Approximately 51 percent of the respondents declared that they favored a "drastically reformed capitalism," and 28 percent opted for socialism, defined as the democratic socialism of the Socialist party or something like it. Methodism had the highest number of Socialist clergy, at 34 percent, followed by Evangelical (33 percent), Congregational (33 percent), Reformed (32 percent), Disciples (30 percent), Episcopal (24 percent), Baptist (22 percent), Presbyterian (19 percent), and Lutheran (12 percent). Permission to be quoted on their economic position was given by 87 percent of the respondents, who apparently felt no need to hide it. Certainly, American Protestant clergy as a whole were not as left-wing as these results. Only 14 percent of the Lutheran pastors responded, and 9 percent of the Baptists, compared to the average of 21 percent; the pastors with liberal or socialist views were probably the ones most likely to respond. Still, in 1934, nearly 6,000 Protestant ministers declared themselves to be Socialists.[193]

The 1932 version of the Social Creed of the Churches reflected the increasingly radical views of Depression era clergy. Issued by the Federal Council of Churches, its demands included:

(2) Social planning and control of the credit and monetary systems and the economic processes of the common good.

(3) The right of all to the opportunity for self-maintenance; a wider and fairer distribution of wealth; a living wage, as a minimum, and above this a just share for the worker in the product of industry and agriculture.

(5) Social insurance against sickness, accident, want in old age, and unemployment.

(8) The right of employees and employers alike to organize for collective bargaining and social action; protection of both in the exercise of this right; the obligation of both to work for the public good; encouragement of cooperatives and other organizations among farmers and other groups.

(9) Abolition of child labor; adequate provision for the protection, education, spiritual nurture, and wholesome recreation of every child.

(14) Application of the Christian principle of redemption to the treatment of offenders; reform of penal and correctional methods and institutions and of criminal court procedure.

(15) Justice, opportunity, and equal rights for all; mutual goodwill and cooperation among racial, economic, and religious groups.

(16) Repudiation of war, drastic reduction of armaments, participation in international agencies for the peaceable settlement of all controversies; the building of a cooperative world order.

(17) Recognition and maintenance of the rights and responsibilities of free speech, free assembly, and a free press; the encouragement of free communication of mind with mind as essential to the discovery of truth.[194]

Much of the 1932 creed simply restated Ward's original version; the rest of it expanded significantly on the original, taking positions that Ward had advocated in ecumenical circles for years. No individual had done more than Ward to bring main-line Protestantism to the point of demanding social control of credit, a living wage, equal rights for all people, the repudiation of war, collective security, and the creation of a cooperative world order.

In the 1930s Ward's mainstream status was further burnished by his connection to an increasingly prominent colleague, Reinhold Niebuhr, whose politics seemed to be very much like Ward's. When Niebuhr joined the faculty in 1928 he got a frosty welcome from many colleagues who shuddered at his rough manners and lack of graduate training. Ward was his friend and ally. Many readers of their books found Ward and Niebuhr to be barely distinguishable. Ward was fond of saying that Christians had much to learn from Marxism, but in the 1930s Niebuhr said the same thing. Ward was prone to either/or dualisms about world-historical choices, but so was Niebuhr. In the 1930s both of them urged that history would either move forward to radical socialism or backward to capitalist barbarism. Niebuhr was active in the Socialist party, which was too stodgy and anti-Bolshevik for Ward's taste – but Niebuhr was never stodgy and for years he had a conflicted view of the Soviet Union. Even at Union, during Niebuhr's early years there, students thought the main difference between Niebuhr and Ward was that Niebuhr had an ebullient, charismatic personality.

In 1931 Ward published a book, *Which Way Religion?* that his younger colleague might have written a year or so earlier. Ward took for granted, as did Niebuhr, that he was witnessing a life-threatening crisis of capitalist civilization. American Protestantism had two options in 1931, he contended. It was the same choice that Protestantism faced in the 1920s, but unfortunately church leaders and theologians spent most of the decade fighting with fundamentalists. That was the wrong battle, because the religion of biblical inerrancy and literal interpretation was hopelessly backward and reactionary. History had already passed it by, as it deserved; treating fundamentalism as a serious foe was ridiculous. To Ward, the modernist–fundamentalist controversy was a diversion from the real struggle of the age between resurgent statism and ethical religion. The real threat to all things good was the gathering force of absolute states that crushed dissent and molded empires, "even under the slogan of democracy."[195]

Ward recalled that the Great War was supposed to end the religion of state power. Instead, the postwar period was all about building up powerful, militaristic, immoral states. Russia was an obvious example, but the same thing happened in Europe and the USA. Powerful interests were using growing, centralized governments to enhance their financial and imperial control. The old religion of biblical authority and orthodox literalism posed no threat to the new militarism, Ward observed. What was needed was a vibrant ethical religion that spoke for real democracy, peace, and the common good in opposition to the growing government monoliths: "Whether it be here or in Russia, those who need an absolute state to execute their designs find their real enemy to be not an infallible or superstitious church, but an ethical religion which is as antithetical to absolutism as it is to infallibility and superstition." American Protestantism needed to marshal its forces against the new nationalism before it was too late: "It is in this struggle between the state as a self-conscious, self-seeking economic organization and the larger, longer interests of man represented by a developing ethical religion that the question of the final moral authority for human society is to be worked out."[196]

Ward assured his readers that ethical religion was the true wellspring of Christianity, while modern nationalism was a repugnant ideology that all followers of Jesus had to resist: "American Protestantism has two choices simultaneously before it, one thrust from without and one arising within." The former spoke the language of security and power; the latter was the life-giving ethic of Jesus. Behind the drive for state power lay the mechanistic and imperial nature of the modern industrial system. Communist militarism was a variation of the same drive for state dominance and control that fueled the capitalist West: "These historic forces now join in conflict, and the two choices offer us only one decision. To submit to the state is to reject an ethical religion. To defy the political–economic order is to choose the ethical imperative." Ward acknowledged that most American Christians did not see that a stark either/or was at issue. If the issue were Jesus versus slavery, most contemporary Christians would recognize the either/or. He left the implication unspoken: most Christians got slavery wrong in its time, too. The task of the social gospel was to help Christians see that capitalism was like slavery; they could not have the capitalist state and Jesus too.[197]

Niebuhr blasted capitalism with essentially the same either/or, but by 1931 he was growing uneasy with ethical idealist ways of putting it, and he began to worry about Ward's fixation with communism. That summer, while Ward prepared for a sabbatical year in the Soviet Union, Niebuhr wrote to Ursula Keppel-Compton (whom he married in December) that some Union students showed "a curious lack of perspective." Niebuhr was clear that he admired the passion of Union students for social justice; he especially enjoyed working with the doctoral students that he and Ward shared, especially James Dombrowski. But Niebuhr noted that when these students plunged into politics "they become so excited about the class struggle that nothing but communism is good enough for them."[198]

That was an omen. Ward's polemic against ascending statism had always conflicted with his belief in scientific planning as the solution to the competitive chaos, predatory destructiveness, and breakdown of the capitalist system. In 1931 he was on the verge of betraying the former conviction without realizing it. Conditions in New York worsened just before Ward left for Russia, which heightened his desire to find that the Soviet revolution was working. Soviet communism, despite its obvious problems, stood alone as a real-world symbol of the dream of a post-capitalist order. Its leaders did not believe in God, but to Ward they stood for the actual meaning of "God," the realization of the historical kingdom of justice and peace. In that mood he found a more vibrant, optimistic spirit among Russians than he had experienced previously. Aided by one of his former students, Julius Hecker, Ward visited Soviet factories, agencies, and farm collectives, everywhere claiming to find buoyant, optimistic citizens determined to build a Communist utopia. He enthused, "The Communists are doing what the idealists have long desired, they are turning the battle spirit of man into constructive channels." Ward marveled that in only a few years, communism had transformed the culture and expectations of ordinary people: "The resultant change in the psychological atmosphere is one of the things that causes the visitor to realize that he is in a new world." Though the Soviet system still had serious problems, he was convinced that Russians now felt hopeful about their nation's direction and proud of its accomplishments.[199]

Back in New York, Niebuhr felt caught in a swirl of opinions. Union Seminary president Henry Sloane Coffin was alarmed that Niebuhr and Ward were turning their students into radical socialists, if not Communists; Niebuhr felt lonely on the faculty with Ward gone; at the same time he realized that some of their best students admired Ward's brand of radicalism over his own; now he fretted that Ward was taking a Communist plunge. In November he wrote to Kempton-Compton: "Had a letter from Ward today. He is a complete Communist by now and says that nothing he reads from us, that is in our magazines, interests him. It all seems to belong to an old world while he is in the world which represents the future. I just wonder what he will be like when he comes back."[200]

When Ward came back he was a fervent Communist fellow-traveler. The Soviet revolution was succeeding, he wrote, because it rested on the enthusiasm of an uncorrupted younger generation and the foundations of "a machine-making industry, a socialized agriculture, and a universal culture." His major work, *In Place of Profit: Social Incentives in the Soviet Union* (1933) touted the superiority of the Soviet system, adorned with supportive quotes from Joseph Stalin and V. M. Molotov. The Soviet Union was the first nation to organize its economy for use instead of profit, Ward explained; in ethical language, it was the first nation to replace the will to gain with the will to serve. It relieved workers of having to fear sickness and old age, covered all workers with a vast system of social insurance, and relieved workers of the fear of losing their jobs. That raised the question of lazy workers, but Ward showed assurance that communism overcame that problem through education. To the outside world the Soviet persecution of the kulaks (independent farmers) and speculators looked bad; Ward explained that cracking down on holdouts was a social necessity that helped to abolish the profit system. By making it impossible to own productive capital, the Soviets wisely cut the root of the profit motive. The Soviet state owned the industrial machine in its entirety and 90 percent of the machinery of distribution, and it rightly decreed that the right to use land belonged only to those who cultivated it with their own labor: "At every possible point the feeding ground for the possessive appetites is being occupied by other forces and they are growing feeble from lack of nourishment." The Bolshevik revolution got rid of a corrupt ruling family, Ward observed, but more importantly, it launched a "far-reaching change in economic habits and ethical values," showing the way to a classless society.[201]

In Place of Profit quoted numerous happy Russians from Ward's travels, as well as Americans who moved to the Soviet Union in order not to worry about old age, money, or losing their jobs. It gave Stalin the benefit of the doubt for luring workers to factories with pay incentives, while worrying that this policy undercut the Communist ideal of equality. In general, Soviet planning was faithful to the ideal, Ward judged. It rewarded ambition only in terms of social service and abolished the career ladder. He acknowledged that one could still meet plenty of selfish careerists in Moscow, but "the younger crowd is against them, and when their nature is manifest the penalty is swift and sufficient." That was the ideal, allowing only one path to success, "a social machine operating for social ends." A good society abolished the legal basis on which the possessive appetite fed, Ward argued, citing Lenin for support. A former American told him that in the USA he had worried about having a job and paying rent; in the Soviet Union he thought only about "how to produce better." Another former American remarked that those who looked out for themselves and were unwilling to sacrifice for a common future did not belong in the Soviet Union. In that spirit, Russians were creating funds for the nation's social purposes. The first generation of Communists had to pay a steep price to capitalize the nation's heavy industries, but in Ward's telling the factories were filled with determined workers who pledged "We must work for Stalin's fund."[202]

The battle imagery of Soviet propaganda now seemed more inspiring to him, dramatizing the building of communism as a great war. Ward explained that the Soviet regime had to wage constant warfare against Social Democrats, because they betrayed socialism during World War I, tried to cut political deals with the bourgeoisie, hindered the proletarian revolution, and opposed communism and revolution. Social Democrats also rejected the dictatorship of the proletariat, Ward explained, leaving unsaid whether he now considered this something to be held against them. In addition the regime had to fight constant battles against deviationists, Trotskyist leftists, Bukharinist opportunists, other kinds of opportunists, counter-revolutionaries, and, of course, capitalism. Ward took a brief pass at the Soviet war against religion, explaining that it was intertwined with the party's struggle against alcoholism. In Russian Orthodoxy the feast days and family ceremonies always involved getting drunk, and priests were usually first to get inebriated; the Communist Party, on the other hand, was determined to abolish alcoholism. In Ward's telling, Soviet communism represented the beginning of the last and greatest migration of human endeavor to a new world order. The real builders of human progress, the toilers, were "on the march in search of a new home for the spirit of man."[203]

In 1931 it was not obvious that Ward had crossed a line that would marginalize him or his subsequent reputation. Intellectuals stampeded to socialism in the 1930s, and many said wilder things than Ward. Niebuhr stumped for Marxist revolution in the 1930s yet managed to become a pillar of the Democratic Party establishment afterward. The negative reaction to Ward's fellow-traveling was delayed in liberal Protestant circles by the terrible uncertainties of the Depression. Capitalism was so battered and vulnerable that Ward's cheering for communism did not seem like career suicide. When Ward's closest friend, Coe, questioned why *In Place of Profit* was so relentlessly one-sided, Ward replied that too much was at stake to worry about appearances. Coe asked how he could ignore the brutal tactics of the Soviet General Public Administration in persecuting political opponents; Ward replied that despite its heavy-handedness, there would be no Soviet Union without it. The same thing was true of the Red Army. Ward claimed to oppose militarism, yet he apologized for the Red Army; he denigrated Norman Thomas, yet Thomas was consistently antimilitaristic. When Coe pressed him on these contradictions, Ward repeated that the Soviets had a right to defend their regime from counter-revolutionaries. Having faced up to his own either/or, he would not concede anything that blurred it.[204]

Meanwhile he joined no party and defended his right not to be labeled. Never a party joiner anyway (he refused to register to vote until 1940, and never actually voted in his life), Ward figured he could do more to advance an American version of communism by not joining any party, especially the American Communists. If people needed to call him something, he preferred something like "independent radical." In the 1930s, however, in addition to leading the Methodist Federation and chairing the ACLU, Ward chaired a major united front organization, the American League Against War and Fascism. All united front groups opposed war and fascism, but some operated on the basis of pacifism, and others antifascism; Ward's was the largest group of the latter type. His leadership of the most important pro-Soviet popular front organization of the Depression era made him a magnet for conservative Methodist criticism, especially since he brought the Methodist Federation into it. Often quizzed on his sympathy for Soviet communism, Ward explained that he had come down on the side of the world's only Communist experiment. He would not dwell on the faults of the one nation that tried to build an ethical economic system, though he never denied that the Soviet Union had some serious ones.

In his telling, the Soviets were much like the Jesuits of an earlier age, except the Soviets were better. The Jesuits "tortured and burned people for the good of their immortal souls," while the Communists merely banished people to "isolated communities" for the sake of a good society. Both used state power to protect their organizations, but the Jesuits used it to enhance the power of the church, while the Communists used it to achieve a social ideal. Ward stuck with that formula after Eugene Lyons and others documented Stalin's persecution of the kulaks. Had Stalin not liquidated the kulaks as a class, Ward contended, they would have created a capitalist state within the Soviet revolution, delayed collectivization, and slowed industrial development. The first phase of the offensive, admittedly, went too fast, but Stalin took control of the problem afterward. The kulaks had to be dealt with, as did the Bukharinist "right opportunists" who wanted to bring the kulaks along gradually, educating them into socialism. Ward commended Stalin and Molotov for preventing the independent farmers and Bukharinists from slowing "the whole movement." His sympathetic parsing of the 1929 "liquidation" announcement left an especially foul odor. Between 1930 and 1933 Molotov carried out a deportation and terror campaign that stuffed millions of kulaks into cattle cars, shipped them to arctic wastelands, and killed approximately 14 million of them.[205]

By the end of the Great Terror Ward was accustomed by conviction and habit to explaining the Stalinist perspective, which made his life at Union Seminary increasingly strained. He was known to castigate Coffin for his fuddy-duddy manners and liberalism, while Coffin protested repeatedly that Ward embarrassed the seminary and radicalized its students. On May Day 1934 a Union student group called the Agenda Club hoisted a red flag on the seminary flagpole, enraging Coffin, who pointed an accusing finger at Ward and Niebuhr. Coffin was slow to grasp the differences between Niebuhr's neo-Marxist realism and Ward's pro-Soviet radicalism, and he seemed not to realize that Ward and Niebuhr had become icy and competitive with each other beneath their veneer of public cordiality. Niebuhr told his wife in 1936 that he found Ward's sneering "almost as difficult to bear" as the superficial liberalism of Coffin and most of the seminary's faculty. Ward, while denying any personal antagonism, charged that Coffin-style liberalism was too squishy and compromised to fight for a just cause, especially in a crisis: "As long as they are only liberals they cannot help serving to deliver us into the hands of the Fascists."[206]

Ward and Niebuhr worked together effectively with their students, who perceived the differences between them. Myles Horton, who later founded the Highlander Folk School in Tennessee, sided with Niebuhr during his socialist period. To Ward's disciples, especially Dombrowski, Eugene Link, Sam Franklin, and Frank Herriott, Ward was the greater figure, despite his Old World reserve and Niebuhr's growing fame. They always knew where Ward stood on an issue, he taught for a verdict, and he was a stickler for social-ethical method, teaching his students to ask three questions: What are the facts? What do they mean? What should be done? That was a stripped-down version of Peabody's method. Ward stressed that social ethics was about holding together theory and practice, and he based class discussions on student field research. In the early and mid-1930s he had more doctoral students than Niebuhr, who bluntly explained that Ward was more radical, plainspoken, methodical, and concrete, whereas Niebuhr's students majored in Niebuhr. Eugene Link put it vividly: "Ward quietly permitted the students to talk over a burning question. At appropriate times he would interject facts or raise a Socratic kind of question. Niebuhr, in contrast, usually held center stage, tossing out wit and polysyllabic nouns."[207]

Niebuhr was often asked to lead worship services at Union, while Ward was rarely asked. Niebuhr was a sensational preacher, while many students judged that Ward's Christianity was a veneer for his real religion of advancing communism. Link subsequently recalled that caution toward Ward was "prevalent at Union." Ward's students shook their heads that Union and the public favored Niebuhr. To them, Ward was a model united-front radical who published thoroughly researched books directly relevant to the social struggle, while Niebuhr wrote thinly researched books that oscillated between otherworldliness and the real world. Link explained of Niebuhr, "He relieved the pressures to work for basic change in a harsh economic order by administering to troubled minds a charming array of cleverly turned theologisms, alluring Biblical anecdotes, and daring intellectual gymnastics."[208]

Coffin appreciated that Ward had devoted students. One of them told Coffin, "[Ward] made us plough deeper than our *status quo* minds had been wont to do. He was ruthlessly honest and painfully probing. That he was a prophet I never had any doubt." Another student came closer to Coffin's feeling about Ward: "He was distinctly a controversial figure – inordinately admired by some and equally disliked by others . . . He was too deeply sold on the idea that a change in the social order was the sole thing needed. Those who took his teaching as half-truth got more from it than those who took it as gospel." Coffin's own judgment was that Ward "made himself difficult to defend" by blasting the very liberalism for which Union was known: "Dr. Ward was a moving preacher and a devout spirit; but as the years passed he became more and more committed to extreme radical social views, and the administration of the Seminary had more protests from various Church groups concerning his utterances than concerning all the other members of the faculty combined."[209]

Yet Coffin allowed Ward to teach for three years beyond his retirement age of 65, and Link acknowledged that Coffin handled Ward with "stubborn grace," sometimes remarking jocularly that his radicals on the faculty had counterparts "to be found in the Bible." That was how Ward viewed himself. He believed in the simple social gospel, which led to his politics. To Ward, Niebuhr's blend of Augustine, Luther, Calvin, and Barth was a strange concoction of little value. It amazed him when Niebuhr became famous through it. Ward described Niebuhr's thought as "romanticism in reverse gear," meaning that it failed to deal with real things and was backward-looking too. Elsewhere he remarked that Niebuhr's combination of leftist politics and conservative theology was like having two horses pull a wagon in opposite directions; the misguided theological horse was sure to prevent him getting anywhere worth going. Niebuhr's disappointment with Ward was equally sharp. In 1936 the two ethicists spoke at the same banquet; Niebuhr was appalled: "He gave a pathetic defense of Russia. I thought he had learned a little more . . . I never thought Christianity could sink to such a farrago of nonsense . . . This is the straw to break the camel's back for me."[210]

But the earthquake was still to come. Niebuhr was usually respectful to fellow travelers in public, and in the late 1930s he was just beginning to question his own leftist dogmas. It was not inconceivable that he and Ward could have become allies again; by 1942 Niebuhr was on good terms with several former fellow-travelers. Ward was not one of them, however, because he refused to let any mere event diminish his devotion to the Soviet Union. In August 1939, Hitler and Stalin signed a nonaggression pact that gave Ward a fresh opportunity to face up to the evils of Soviet communism. Many American Communists repudiated the party, while liberals streamed out of the American League for Peace and Democracy, which had changed its name (in 1937) from the American League Against War and Fascism, and which Ward still chaired. Others gave up on communism after the Soviets invaded Finland on November 30.

But Ward clung to his defining either/or and its catch-phrases. He would not break faith with the world's hope of a new world order, even if it linked arms with Hitler and invaded its neighbors. Thus he became someone to be shunned by anti-Communist leftists like Niebuhr and Norman Thomas. In October Thomas told Ward that if he could not manage to criticize the terrible evils of Soviet tyranny he was obviously not the person to chair the ACLU. The ACLU was under pressure to prove that it was not a Communist front. Ward had been called to testify before the House Special Committee to Investigate Un-American Activities (HUAC), which wanted to know about Communist influence on the American League for Peace and Democracy. The ACLU leaders did not want their organization to go down with him, despite the fact that most of them had belonged to the League before the Nazi–Soviet Pact.[211]

In his testimony before HUAC on October 23, 1939, Ward was vague and evasive about the extent of Communist influence on the League. The hearing exposed his lack of direct contact with the Soviet Union since 1932. Aside from reading about it, he had spoken with only two travelers in the past seven years, which seemed to explain how he could keep saying the same things about the success of communism there. The League judged that HUAC was a Communist front, and the spotlight shifted to the ACLU. A bitter faction fight took place over the right of Communists and Fascists to hold leadership or staff positions in the ACLU. Some ACLU leaders, especially John Haynes Holmes, charged that Ward did not really care about civil liberties; he cared only about advancing communism. In February 1940 that sentiment prevailed, and the ACLU voted to exclude officers and staff allied with totalitarian movements. The ACLU explained that because it stood for civil liberties "in all aspects and all places," it could not have officers or staff that supported either fascism or communism, and it would be the judge of what "support" meant. That ousted Communist Party member Elizabeth Gurley Flynn, and it exposed Ward to the prospect of a private hearing and expulsion. He obliged with the expected response, resigning in disgust. It was absurd for an organization calling itself the American Civil Liberties Union to set up a doctrinal test for membership, Ward protested. For 20 years he had served as board president; now his name was to be erased from the organization's literature and its institutional memory. On Ward's way out, board member Holmes thanked him for his "unqualified fairness" during his board presidency.[212]

Ward's substantial role in the social gospel movement met the same fate. Allowed three extra years at Union, he retired in 1941, insisting that he regretted nothing and had nothing for which to apologize. The HUAC judgment against the American League for Peace and Democracy was ridiculous, he contended. It created a myth about Communist influence that scared people who did not understand the purpose or function of united fronts. Even if the Communists tried to use the League for their ends, so what? "We are using the Communist party, too." In February 1940 Ward and a few others disbanded the League quietly, without consulting its membership, and Ward tried to change the subject to American economic democracy, writing a book titled *Democracy and Social Change* (1940). But he had lost his liberal Christian audience; afterwards he wrote for leftist and pro-Soviet publishing houses that made his old audience shudder. In his later years Ward was reduced to the crowds that pro-Communist groups were capable of turning out. He recalled on the occasion of his retirement that at the outset of his career some of his socialist friends asked why he wasted his time with the church. "I replied, 'Here is the machinery and power dedicated to the achievement of the highest life for man; I will try to use it for that purpose." But that was a merely pragmatic basis for a ministry, reducing Christianity to a vehicle for his politics, and in the end he had no pragmatic basis.[213]

In 1941 he seemed to get a second chance at redeeming his reputation, when Germany declared war on the Soviet Union. Ward reasoned that the time was ripe to restore Stalin's reputation in the USA. The way he went about it, however, left the job to others, who played up the contributions of "Uncle Joe" to the Allied war effort. Ward tried to convince Americans that Stalin was right to make a pact with Hitler and invade Finland; both were acts of national self-preservation. That raised the question of whether Ward was capable of opposing any Soviet interest on moral, international, or American grounds. Ward explained why the answer, apparently, was negative: "The self-interest of the Soviet Union is more in the interest of world-wide democracy than the self-interest of the British and American financial-imperialists."[214]

That was the tone and line of his book *The Soviet Spirit* (1944), a rehash of Ward's celebration of Soviet communism and of his writings for the *New Masses* and *Daily Worker*. Often he rang the chimes on Soviet policy: the Soviets withdrew from World War I because they lacked resources; they bonded with Hitler because they had no options after the Allies sold out at Munich; they invaded Finland because they needed it to fight the Nazis. Later he explained that the Soviets took over Eastern Europe because they needed a defensible border. Ward lived long enough to witness the spectacle of a Soviet premier, Nikita Khrushchev, condemning Stalin's internal purges, but he could not bring himself to correctly summarize its content. He referred lamely to "the sudden revelation of the shocking violations of the Soviet constitution in the last years of Stalin." But the story was terribly old; it was shocking only to those who had willfully swallowed the Stalinist line; it was about mass murder, not mere violations of the Soviet constitution; and it was hardly confined to Stalin's last years.[215]

Ward treasured his protégés from Union seminary and basked in their appreciation at his retirement. A notable disciple was missing from the occasion, however. Julius Hecker was born in Leningrad, immigrated to the USA as a young man, became a US citizen, and studied under Ward at Union. He served briefly as a Methodist pastor in New York and earned a doctorate at Columbia University. Inspired by the Soviet revolution and the hope of a new world order, he returned to the Soviet Union in the 1920s, giving up his US citizenship. When Ward and his wife visited the Soviet Union in 1924 Hecker was their host; when they returned in 1931–2, Hecker made the arrangements that got Ward into workplaces and agencies that he wrote about. Hecker shared Ward's enthusiasm for the Soviet revolution and was eager to help his former teacher. In Moscow he and Ward had their picture taken while sitting in a car; in the picture, the usually reserved Ward wore a broad smile.

In 1938 Hecker was swept up in one of Stalin's purges and shot. David Nelson Duke, researching his biography of Ward, learned of Hecker by accident, in an offhand comment by Ward's daughter-in-law Mary McNeer Ward. In a soft voice, she wondered how Ward could have forgotten his former student. How could he go on rationalizing the Great Terror after it murdered his treasured friend? Duke's answer was, "holy war dualism," but he also noted that Ward kept the 1932 picture of himself and Hecker in his personal papers, not in the family photo albums. Did Ward look at the picture while writing about Stalin's purges and prison camps? Did the picture haunt him as he apologized for the largest mass murder in history? Did it raise the question that perhaps he should have vested his faith in something besides a particular, blood-soaked experiment in social engineering?[216]

The shame of the Ward episode exceeds its impact on the tradition of social ethics. Donald Meyer, in his book *The Protestant Search for Political Realism* (1960), aptly judged, "In Harry Ward the link between anxiety and total politics became absolute." Ward knew better than the line that he took; his own writings of the 1920s refuted the later ones. But he had to have a lodestar that transcended criticism, even if that required looking the other way and destroying his legacy.[217]

So far as the social ethics tradition is concerned, a large piece of the shame of the Ward episode is that he squandered his distinct opportunity to stand for and sustain a prophetic social gospel. Ward was significant, not merely as a major player in his time, but because he was not most of the things that were usually held against the social gospel. He was not a middle-class idealist or sentimentalist. He was not a reformer or political meliorist. He did not cheer for Anglo-Saxonism or American exceptionalism. He did not temporize about racial justice or women's rights. He did not believe that rationality and good will were enough to save society. He hated imperialism and war, aside from the Soviet exception. On the other hand, he shared the common social gospel fault of reducing Christianity to his social activism. Had Christianity meant anything to Ward besides a vehicle for his politics, he might have found a way back from the lie to which he devoted his life from 1918 to 1966.

Notes

1   For an earlier version of this framing statement, see Gary Dorrien, "Social Salvation: The Social Gospel as Theology and Economics," *The Social Gospel Today*, ed. Christopher H. Evans (Louisville: Westminster John Knox Press, 2001), 101–2.

2   See Ralph E. Luker, "Interpreting the Social Gospel: Reflections on Two Generations of Historiography," *Perspectives on the Social Gospel: Papers from the Inaugural Social Gospel Conference at Colgate Rochester Divinity School*, ed. Christopher H. Evans (Lewiston, NY: Edwin Mellen Press, 1999), 1–13; Christopher H. Evans, "Historical Integrity and Theological Recovery: A Reintroduction to the Social Gospel," *The Social Gospel Today*, 1–13.

3   See George Herron, *The New Redemption: A Call to the Church to Reconstruct Society According to the Gospel of Christ* (New York: T. Y. Crowell, 1893); Herron, *The Christian Society* (Chicago: Fleming H. Revell, 1894); Herron, *The Christian State: A Political Vision of Christ* (New York: T.Y. Crowell, 1895); Herron, *The Larger Christ* (Chicago: T.Y. Fleming H. Revell, 1891).

4   The Gladden section of this chapter is adapted from Gary Dorrien, *The Making of American Liberal Theology: Imagining Progressive Religion, 1805–1900* (Louisville: Westminster John Knox Press, 2001), 261–334.

5   Washington Gladden, *Fifty Years in the Ministry* (Columbus, Ohio: Lawrence Press Company, 1910), 2–3, 6–11; Gladden, *Recollections* (Boston: Houghton Mifflin Company, 1909), 1–15, 85–91, quotes 88, 90; see Jacob Henry Dorn, *Washington Gladden: Prophet of the Social Gospel* (Columbus: Ohio State University Press, 1967), 12–13, 31–2.

6   Gladden, *Recollections*, 114–16, 121–3, quote, 115.

7   Ibid., 119–20.

8   Washington Gladden, "Horace Bushnell and Progressive Orthodoxy," *Pioneers of Religious Liberty in America* (Boston: American Unitarian Association, 1903), 256, 260.

9   Washington Gladden, *Amusements: Their Uses and Their Abuses* (North Adams, MA: James T. Robinson & Company, 1866); Gladden, *Plain Thoughts on the Art of Living* (Boston: Ticknor and Fields, 1868), 140–7; Gladden, *From the Hub to the Hudson: With Sketches of Nature, History and Industry in North-Western Massachusetts* (Boston: New England News Company, 1869), 28–41.

10 Gladden, *Amusements: Their Uses and Their Abuses*, 5–11; Gladden, *Plain Thoughts on the Art of Living*, 169–86; Dorn, *Washington Gladden: Prophet of the Social Gospel*, 46–7; John W. Buckham, *Progressive Religious Thought in America: A Survey of the Enlarging Pilgrim Faith* (Boston: Houghton Mifflin Company, 1919), 250. Buckham noted that "Oh, Master, let me walk with thee" is a heretic's hymn – "a 'heretic of yesterday' and a saint of to-day."

11 Gladden, *Recollections*, 173–5, 182–3, quote, 183; Dorn, *Washington Gladden: Prophet of the Social Gospel*, 54.

12 Frank Luther Mott, *A History of American Magazines, 1741–1905*, 4 vols. (Cambridge, MA: Harvard University Press, 1938–1957), 3: 457–72; Editorial, *Independent* 23 (April 6, 1871), 6; Gladden, *Recollections*, 185–91, quote, 190; Dorn, *Washington Gladden: Prophet of the Social Gospel*, 55.

13 Gladden, *Recollections*, 192–222, quote, 221; Dorn, *Washington Gladden: Prophet of the Social Gospel*, 57.

14 Washington Gladden, *Being a Christian: What It Means and How to Begin* (Boston: Congregational Publishing Society, 1876); Gladden, *The Christian Way: Whither It Leads and How to Go On* (New York: Dodd, Mead & Company, 1877).

15 Roswell Smith letter to Gladden, October 2, 1882, Ohio State Historical Society, Gladden Papers; Gladden, *Recollections*, 283.

16 Gladden, *Recollections*, 284–90; see Alfred E. Lee, *History of the City of Columbus: Capital of Ohio*, 2 vols. (New York: Munsell & Company, 1892), 1: 830–6; Daniel Day Williams, *The Andover Liberals* (New York: Octagon Books, 1970); William Jewett Tucker, *My Generation: An Autobiographical Interpretation* (Boston: Houghton Mifflin Company, 1919), 101–247.

17 See Gaius Glenn Atkins, "Washington Gladden – And After," *Religion in Life: A Christian Quarterly* 5 (Winter, 1936), 599–600; Dorn, *Washington Gladden: Prophet of the Social Gospel*, 71–5; Wilbur A. Siebert, "A Reminiscence," *First Church News: The Gladden Centennial* 6 (February 1936), 10; Washington Gladden, *The Christian Pastor and the Working Church* (Edinburgh: T. & T. Clark, 1898), 50–1; Gladden, *Recollections*, 98; Peter Clark Macfarlane, "Washington Gladden, The First Citizen of Columbus," *Colliers* 49 (June 29, 1912), 20–4; Charles Reynolds Brown, *They Were Giants* (New York: Macmillan Company, 1935), 211–40. Gladden's wife, Jennie, was actively involved in church and community affairs, serving for many years as president of the Women's Missionary Society of First Church Congregational. After a prolonged illness, she died during the period that Gladden wrote his autobiography, an experience that undoubtedly heightened his strong sense of privacy.

18 Quotes in Gladden, *Recollections*, 291, 292; see Dorn, *Washington Gladden: Prophet of the Social Gospel*, 208–9; John L. Shover, "Washington Gladden and the Labor Question," *Ohio Historical Quarterly* 68 (October 1959), 337.

19 Washington Gladden, "The Wage-Workers and the Churches," in Gladden, *Applied Christianity: Moral Aspects of Social Questions* (Boston: Houghton, Mifflin and Company, 1889), 173.

20 Washington Gladden, "Is It Peace Or War?" in Gladden, *Applied Christianity: Moral Aspects of Social Questions*, 102–45, quotes, 131, 141, 145.

21 Washington Gladden, "Christianity and Wealth," in Gladden, *Applied Christianity: Moral Aspects of Social Questions*, 8–32; see Gladden, *Recollections*, 300–4.

22 Washington Gladden, *Working People and Their Employers* (New York: Funk & Wagnalls,1894), 44–5; Gladden, "Christianity and Wealth," quote 32–3.

23 Gladden, "Christianity and Wealth," 34–5. See Richard T. Ely, ed., *A History of Cooperation in America* (Baltimore: Johns Hopkins University Press, 1888); Nicholas Paine Gilman, *Profit Sharing Between Employer and Employee: A Study in the Evolution of the Wages System* (London: Macmillan Company, 1890); Gladden's thinking on profit-sharing was strongly influenced by Sedley Taylor, *Profit-Sharing Between Labor and Capital, Six Essays* (New York: Humboldt Publishing Company, 1886).

24 Washington Gladden, "The Strength and Weakness of Socialism," in Gladden, *Applied Christianity: Moral Aspects of Social Questions*, 53–101, quotes, 98, 100.

25 Washington Gladden, *Tools and the Man: Property and Industry under the Christian Law* (Boston: Houghton, Mifflin and Company, 1893), quotes, 214, 124; discussion of co-operative ownership, 190–203.

26 Ibid., 130, 271.

27 Ibid., 264–5; closing quote in Washington Gladden, *Christianity and Socialism* (New York: Eaton & Mains, 1905), 141.

28 Gladden, *Christianity and Socialism*, 102–38, right to property statement, 92; Washington Gladden, *Social Facts and Forces* (New York: G. P. Putnam's Sons, 1897), 80–6; Gladden, *Recollections*, 308–9; Gladden, *Tools and the Man*, 294–302, quotes, 299, 300.

29 Washington Gladden, *The Labor Question* (Boston: Pilgrim Press, 1911), 3–55, 98–110, quote, 55; Gladden, *Recollections*, 306–8; Gladden, *Social Facts and Forces*, 81–2; unidentified "vindictive opposition" quote in *Recollections*, 305; see John L. Shover, "Washington Gladden and the Labor Question," *Ohio Historical Quarterly* 68 (October 1959), 344–5.

30 Gladden, *Tools and the Man*, 1–2.

31 Ibid., 3–4, 6; see Washington Gladden, *Social Salvation* (Boston: Houghton, Mifflin and Company, 1902), 1–31; Gladden, "Where Is the Kingdom of God?" in Gladden, *Burning Questions of the Life That Now Is, and of That Which is to Come* (London: James Clarke & Company, 1890, 223–48; Gladden, *The Church and the Kingdom* (New York: Fleming H. Revell Company, 1894); Gladden, *The Lord's Prayer* (Boston: Houghton Mifflin, 1880), 59–81.

32 Gladden, *Tools and the Man*, quotes 18–19.

33 Ibid., "dismal and dreadful," 23; Gladden, *Social Salvation*, "no political responsibilities," 21.

34 Charles H. Hopkins, *The Rise of the Social Gospel in American Protestantism, 1865–1915* (New Haven: Yale University Press, 1940), 113–17, 175–6, 194–5, 260; Henry F. May, *Protestant Churches and Industrial America* (New York: Harper & Brothers, 1949), 254; Dorn, *Washington Gladden: Prophet of the Social Gospel*, 200–1; Richard T. Ely, *Ground Under Our Feet: An Autobiography* (New York: Macmillan Company, 1938), 140–3.

35 Washington Gladden, *Present Day Theology* (Columbus: McClelland & Company, 1913); Gladden, *Seven Puzzling Bible Books: A Supplement to "Who Wrote the Bible?"* (Boston: Houghton, Mifflin and Company, 1897); Gladden, *Who Wrote the Bible?: A Book for the People* (Boston: Houghton, Mifflin and Company, 1891), "fields of destructive criticism," 276; see Gladden, *Social Salvation*, 12–31; Gladden, *Ruling Ideas of the Present Age* (Boston: Houghton, Mifflin and Company, 1895), 3–16, 165–87.

36 Richard Hofstadter, *Social Darwinism in American Thought* (rev. edn., Boston: Beacon Press, 1955), 31–50, quote, 33; Herbert Spencer, *First Principles* (New York: D. Appleton & Company, 1864); Spencer, *The Man Versus the State*, ed. Truxton Beale (New York: Mitchell Kennerley, 1916); Spencer, *The Principles of Sociology*, 3 vols. (New York: D. Appleton & Company, 1876–97); Spencer, *The Principles of Ethics*, 2 vols. (New York: D. Appleton & Company, 1895–8); William Graham Sumner, *The Challenge of Facts and Other*

Essays (New Haven: Yale University Press, 1914); Sumner, *Essays of William Graham Sumner*, 2 vols., ed. Albert G. Keller and Maurice R. Davie (New Haven: Yale University Press, 1934).

37 Henry Drummond, *Natural Law in the Spiritual World* (Chicago: Donohue Brothers, 1881); Drummond, *The Ascent of Man* (New York: James Pott and Company, 1895); Peter Kropotkin, *Mutual Aid: A Factor in Evolution* (London: McClure, Phillips, 1902); American Economic Association statement of principles quoted in Ely, *Ground Under Our Feet: An Autobiography*, 140; Richard T. Ely, *The Labor Movement in America* (New York: Macmillan Company, 1905), 138; Ely, "The Past and Present of Political Economy," *Johns Hopkins University Studies in Historical and Political Science* (Baltimore: Johns Hopkins University Press, 1884), "tool in the hands," 202; Washington Gladden, "Why I Am Thankful," *The Congregationalist* 82 (November 18, 1897), 734–5; Gladden, *The Church and the Kingdom*, 46–67; Dorn, *Washington Gladden: Prophet of the Social Gospel*, 191–2; Hofstadter, *Social Darwinism in American Thought*, 108–9.

38 John Fiske, "Evolution and Religion," in Fiske, *Excursions of an Evolutionist* (Boston: Houghton, Mifflin and Company, 1891), 294–305, "mighty rhythmic" quote, 302; Fiske, *Through Nature to God* (Boston: Houghton, Mifflin and Company, 1899), 176–84, eye quote, 184; Washington Gladden, "Has Evolution Abolished God?" in Gladden, *Burning Questions of the Life that Now Is, and of That Which Is to Come*, 3–33; Washington Gladden, *How Much Is Left of the Old Doctrines?* (Boston: Houghton, Mifflin and Company, 1899), 1–45; Charles Darwin, *The Origin of Species* (London: J. Murray, 1859); Darwin, *The Descent of Man and Selection in Relation to Sex* (1st edn., London: J. Murray, 1871).

39 Fiske, *Through Nature to God*, 131–94, quotes, 190–1; see John Fiske, *The Destiny of Man Viewed in the Light of His Origin* (Boston: Houghton, Mifflin and Company, 1884), 108–19; Fiske, *A Century of Science and Other Essays* (Boston: Houghton, Mifflin and Company, 1899); Fiske, *Outlines of Cosmic Philosophy*, 2 vols. (Boston: Houghton, Mifflin and Company, 1874).

40 John Fiske, "Darwinism Verified," in Fiske, *Darwinism and Other Essays* (Boston: Houghton, Mifflin and Company, 1884), 1–31, quote, 7; Gladden, *How Much is Left of the Old Doctrines?* "veritable evangel" and "greatest fact" quotes, 19, 23; Gladden, "Has Evolution Abolished God?" closing quote, 28; see Fiske, "In Memoriam: Charles Darwin," in Fiske, *Excursions of an Evolutionist*, 337–69; Fiske, *The Idea of God as Affected by Modern Knowledge*, 135–57. Among Fiske's sizable corpus of writings, the key works, for Gladden, were *The Destiny of Man Viewed in the Light of His Origin*, *The Idea of God as Affected by Modern Knowledge* (Boston: Houghton Mifflin, 1893), and especially, *Through Nature to God*; Washington Gladden, *Where Does the Sky Begin?* (Boston: Houghton, Mifflin and Company, 1904), 50–1; Gladden, *How Much Is Left of the Old Doctrines?* 24–5.

41 See John Fiske, *American Political Ideas, Viewed from the Standpoint of Universal History* (New York: Harper & Brothers, 1885); Fiske, *Civil Government in the United States* (Boston: Houghton, Mifflin and Company, 1890); Lyman Abbott, *The Theology of an Evolutionist* (Boston: Houghton Mifflin Company, 1897).

42 John Fiske, "Manifest Destiny," originally delivered to the Royal Institute of Great Britain, 1880, reprinted in Fiske, "Manifest Destiny," *Harper's Magazine* 70 (March 1885), 578–90; and Fiske, *American Political Ideas, Viewed from the Standpoint of Universal History*, 101–52, quote, 131.

43 Fiske, "Manifest Destiny," 146, 148.

44 Josiah Strong, *Our Country, Its Possible Future and Its Present Crisis* (New York: American Home Missionary Society, 1886; rev. edn., New York: Baker & Taylor, 1891; reprint, Cambridge, MA: Harvard University Press, 1963, ed. Jurgen Herbst), x–xi; see Horace Bushnell, *Barbarism the First Danger: A Discourse for Home Missions* (New York: American Home Missionary Society, 1847); Edward T. Root, "Josiah Strong: A Modern Prophet of the Kingdom of God," *New Church Review* 29 (June 1922), 47–54; Shailer Mathews,

"The Development of Social Christianity in America," *Journal of Religion* 7 (July 1927), 376–86; Hofstadter, *Social Darwinism in American Thought*, 177–8.

45   Strong, *Our Country*, 210–11, see 41–58.

46   Ibid., 200–2, 205.

47   Ibid., 206, 208, see 195–9.

48   Ibid., 209, 210, 212; Darwin, *The Descent of Man and Selection in Relation to Sex* (rev. 2nd edn., New York: D. Appleton & Company, 1888), 142.

49   Darwin, *The Descent of Man and Selection in Relation to Sex* (1st edn., 1871), 154; Horace Bushnell, *Christian Nurture* (New York: Charles Scribner's Sons, 1861), 213; Strong, *Our Country*, 213–15.

50   Hopkins, *The Rise of the Social Gospel in American Protestantism, 1865–1915*, 113–16; *The Christian Union* 32 (December 17, 1885), 6–8; May, *Protestant Churches and Industrial America*, 194; Hofstadter, *Social Darwinism in American Thought*, 178; see Evangelical Alliance for the USA, *Christianity Practically Applied: The Discussions of the International Christian Conference held in Chicago, October 8–14, 1893*, 2 vols. (New York: Baker & Taylor Company, 1894); Aaron I. Abell, *The Urban Impact on American Protestantism, 1850–1900* (Cambridge, MA: Harvard University Press, 1943), 224–45; James Dombrowski, *The Early Days of Christian Socialism in America* (New York: Columbia University Press, 1936), 60–73; William Jewett Tucker, *My Generation: An Autobiographical Interpretation* (Boston: Houghton, Mifflin Company, 1919), 169–77; May, *Protestant Churches and Industrial America*, 194–5.

51   Josiah Strong, *The New Era, or, The Coming Kingdom* (New York: Baker & Taylor Company, 1893), 17–40, 41–53, 54–80, 178–202, 296–341, quotes, 77, 80.

52   Josiah Strong, *Expansion, Under New World-Conditions* (New York: Baker & Taylor Company, 1900), 280–1; editorial, *The Outlook* 70 (July 29, 1899), 699; Lyman Abbott, *The Rights of Man: A Study in Twentieth Century Problems* (Boston: Houghton, Mifflin and Company, 1901), quote 274; see Graham Taylor, "Social Under-Tow of the War," *The Commons* 3 (June 1898), 5–6; Taylor, "Social 'Overflow' of the War," *The Commons* 3 (August 1898), 2–3; Robert L. Beisner, *Twelve Against Empire: The Anti-Imperialists, 1898–1900* (New York: McGraw-Hill, 1968); Winthrop S. Hudson, "Protestant Clergy Debate the Nation's Vocation, 1898–1899," *Church History* 42 (1973), 110–18; Robert T. Handy, *A Christian America: Protestant Hopes and Historical Realities* (2nd edn., New York: Oxford University Press, 1984), 243.

53   Washington Gladden, "The Issues of the War," *The Outlook* 59 (July 16, 1898), 673–5; Gladden sermon on England and America standing together, "The Future of the Aristocracy," preached on October 11, 1891, Gladden Papers; discussion of Gladden's views of Anglo-American solidarity and the Spanish–American war in Dorn, *Washington Gladden: Prophet of the Social Gospel*, 402–12; quote on Cubans cited by Dorn from Gladden sermon reprinted in the *Ohio State Journal*, January 5, 1897.

54   "Morally unthinkable" and "degraded races" in Washington Gladden, "The Signing of the Treaty," sermon, December 18, 1898, Gladden Papers; Gladden, "The Problem of the Philippines," sermon, September 3, 1899, Gladden Papers; Gladden, "The People of the Philippines," sermon, September 10, 1899, Gladden Papers; Gladden, "The Chinese Mind," sermon, September 9, 1900, Gladden Papers; Gladden, "Good News from the Wide World," sermon, September 22, 1901; Gladden Papers; "Good News from the Wide World," sermon, December 27, 1908, Gladden Papers; Dorn, *Washington Gladden: Prophet of the Social Gospel*, 412–15.

55   In 1893, ex-President Rutherford B. Hayes interviewed Gladden and informed him that the Ohio State University Board of Trustees, of which Hayes was president, had selected Gladden to be the university's next president. The state legislature was controlled by anti-Catholic bigots, however, who blocked Gladden's appointment. See *Diary and Letters of Rutherfor Birchard Hayes: Nineteenth President of the United States*, 5 vols. (Columbus: Ohio

State Archaeological and Historical Society, 1922–6), 5: 81, 94; Gladden, *Recollections*, 414–15; Dorn, *Washington Gladde: Prophet of the Social Gospel*, 118–19.

56   "No unnatural fusion" and "perfect equality" quotes in Washington Gladden, *The Negro's Southern Neighbors and His Northern Friends* (New York: Congregational Rooms, [1903]); Gladden, "Sociological Aspects of A.M.A. Work," *The Congregationalist* 81 (October 29, 1896), 646–9; Gladden, "The Negro Crisis: Is the Separation of the Two Races to Become Necessary?", *American Magazine* 63 (January, 1907), 296–301; Gladden, *Recollections*, 366–76; citations and discussion in Dorn, *Washington Gladden: Prophet of the Social Gospel*, 293–302; see Ralph E. Luker, *The Social Gospel in Black and White: American Racial Reform, 1885–1912* (Chapel Hill: University of North Carolina Press, 1991), 211–16.

57   Washington Gladden, "Some Impressions Gained during a Visit to the Southern United States," sermon, May 31, 1903, Gladden Papers; "Even These Least," sermon, January 9, 1916, Gladden Papers; "no reason" and "moral universe" quotes in Gladden, *Recollections*, 375–6; see Luker *The Social Gospel in Black and White*, 215–16.

58   Gladden, *Recollections*, 419, 431.

59   Washington Gladden, *The Great War – Six Sermons* (Columbus, OH: McClelland and Company, 1915), corrupt rulers argument, 8–9; Gladden, *Is War a Moral Necessity? Sermon Preached before First Congregational Church of Detroit, April 18, 1915* (Detroit: Printed by Friends, 1915), 6–15; Gladden, "What War Must Bring," *War and Peace* (Columbus, OH: First Congregational Church, 1914), 30–1; Gladden, "Universal Righteousness," sermon, March 29, 1915, Gladden Papers; Gladden, "Nations Are Members One of Another," sermon, April 11, 1915, Gladden Papers; Gladden, "Does Human Nature Change?", sermon, May 30, 1915, Gladden Papers; Gladden, "Christ's Light in the World," sermon, December 26, 1915, Gladden Papers; Gladden, "Getting Ready for War," sermon, January [?] 1916, Gladden Papers; Charles S. Macfarland, *Pioneers for Peace through Religion: Based on the Records of the Church Peace Union (Founded by Andrew Carnegie), 1914–1945* (New York: Fleming H. Revell, Company, 1946), 46; Dorn, *Washington Gladden: Prophet of the Social Gospel*, 417–23; Richard D. Knudten, *The Systematic Thought of Washington Gladden* (New York: Humanities Press, 1968), 175–85.

60   Washington Gladden, "A Communication: A Pacifist's Apology," *The New Republic* 5 (November 20, 1915), 75–6; caveat against absolute pacifism in Gladden, *The Great War – Six Sermons*, 14; "new machinery" quote in Gladden, "A Plea for Pacifism," *The Nation*, Supplement to Vol. 103 (Columbus, OH: Champlin Press, 1916), 7.

61   Woodrow Wilson, "An Annual Message on the State of the Union," December 7, 1915, *The Papers of Woodrow Wilson* 69 vols., ed. Arthur S. Link (Princeton: Princeton University Press, 1980), 35: 293–310; Wilson, "An Address to the Federal Council of Churches," December 10, 1915, ibid., 35: 329–36, quotes, 329, 330, 332; Washington Gladden to Woodrow Wilson, December 11, 1915, ibid., 35: 344–5; Woodrow Wilson to Washington Gladden, December 14, 1915, ibid., 35: 353.

62   Woodrow Wilson to Washington Gladden, December 14, 1915, Gladden Papers; "Just Now it Appears," Gladden sermon, "Christ's Light in the World," December 26, 1915, Gladden Papers; "What is Going," Gladden sermon, "Getting Ready for War," January [?] 1916, Gladden Papers.

63   Washington Gladden, *The Forks of the Road* (New York: Macmillan Company, 1916), 31–2, 98, 106–7.

64   Gladden, "A Plea for Pacifism," 7.

65   Gladden, *The Forks of the Road*, 137–8.

66   Woodrow Wilson, "An Appeal for a Statement of War Aims," December 18, 1916, *The Papers of Woodrow Wilson*, 40: 273–6; Wilson, "An Address to the Senate," January 22, 1917, ibid., 40: 533–9, quotes, 536.

67   See Thomas J. Knock, *To End All Wars: Woodrow Wilson and the Quest for a New World Order* (Princeton: Princeton University Press, 1992), 108–22; Ronald Schaffer, *America in*

the Great War: The Rise of the Welfare State (New York: Oxford University Press, 1991), xiv–xvii; Henry F. May, *The End of American Innocence: A Study of the First Years of Our Own Time, 1912–1917* (New York: Alfred A. Knopf, 1959), 355–86.

68 "Darkest cloud" and "All the great people," Gladden sermon, 'High Lights of Mercy," February 11, 1917, Gladden Papers.

69 Woodrow Wilson, "An Address to a Joint Session of Congress," April 2, 1917, *The Papers of Woodrow Wilson*, 41: 519–27, quote, 525; Lyman Abbott, *The Twentieth Century Crusade* (New York: Macmillan Company, 1918), 62; Shailer Mathews, *Patriotism and Religion* (New York: Macmillan Company, 1918), 4; Ray H. Abrams, *Preachers Present Arms* (New York: Round Table Press, 1933), 54–5.

70 Washington Gladden, "America at War," sermon, April 29, 1917, Gladden Papers.

71 Wilson, "An Address to a Joint Session of Congress," 525; Gladden, "America at War."

72 Washington Gladden, "The Nation Is at School," July 1, 1917; Gladden, "Religion After the War," September 2, 1917; Gladden, "Industry After the War," September 12, 1917; Gladden, "Education After the War," September 19, 1917; Gladden, "The High Calling of America," September 23, 1917; Gladden, "The Family After the War," September 26, 1917; Gladden, "The Good Fight," November 4, 1917; Gladden, "The Crying Need for Religion," November 24, 1917; Gladden, "Wilson's Message to the Belligerants," [?] 1917; Gladden, "Where Are We?" 1917, Gladden Papers.

73 "All that is needed" in Washington Gladden, "Loyalty," reprinted in Gladden, *The Interpreter* (Boston: Pilgrim Press, 1918), 81–96, quote, 96; "this war" in Gladden, "America at War"; Gladden, "What Is Progress?" sermon, March 14, 1915, Gladden Papers.

74 Washington Gladden, "A New Heart for the Nation," in Gladden, *The Interpreter*, 131–47, quotes, 145.

75 See August Rauschenbusch, *Leben und Wirken von August Rauschenbusch*, completed and edited by Walter Rauschenbusch (Cassel: J. G. Oncken, 1901), 15–97; Dores Robinson Sharpe, *Walter Rauschenbusch* (New York: Macmillan Co., 1942), 20–2; Walter Rauschenbusch, "Augustus Rauschenbusch, D.D.," *Baptist Home Missions Monthly* (September 1898), 323–4; Paul M. Minus, *Walter Rauschenbusch: American Reformer* (New York: Macmillan Co., 1988), 2–4; August Rauschenbusch to Maria Ehrhardt, 24 July 1873, Archives, North American Baptist Conference, Sioux Falls, South Dakota. The Rauschenbusch section of this chapter is adapted from Gary Dorrien, *The Making of American Liberal Theology: Idealism, Realism, and Modernity, 1900–1950* (Louisville: Westminster John Knox Press, 2003), 73–150.

76 "He was," Walter Rauschenbusch to D. C. Vandercook, February 23, 1917, Box 32, Rauschenbusch Family Collection; Walter Rauschenbusch to August Rauschenbusch, October 15, 1882, Box 34, Rauschenbusch Family Collection, American Baptist–Samuel Colgate Historical Library, Rochester, New York.

77 Walter Rauschenbusch to Munson Ford, February 28, 1884, Box 23, Rauschenbusch Family Collection; Walter Rauschenbusch to Munson Ford, March 19, 1882, Box 23, Rauschenbusch Family Collection; Rauschenbusch to Munson Ford, March 18, 1883, Box 23, Rauschenbusch Family Collection; Sharpe, *Walter Rauschenbusch*, 40–52; Walter Rauschenbusch to D. C. Vandercook, February 23, 1917, Box 32, Rauschenbusch Family Collection; Walter Rauschenbusch, "The Kingdom of God," January 2, 1913 address at the Cleveland YMCA, excerpts reprinted in *Cleveland's Young Men* 27 (January 9, 1913); reported in *Rochester Democrat and Chronicle* (January 25, 1913); excerpts reprinted in Robert T. Handy, ed., *The Social Gospel in America, 1870–1920: Gladden, Ely, Rauschenbusch* (New York: Oxford University Press, 1966), 264–7.

78 Augustus Hopkins Strong, *Lectures on Theology* (Rochester: E. R. Andrews, 1876); Strong, *Systematic Theology: A Compendium and Commonplace Book Designed for the Use of Theological Students* (Rochester: E. R. Andrews, 1886; 7th edn., New York: A. C. Armstrong and Son, 1902); see Grant Wacker, *Augustus H. Strong and the Dilemma of Historical Consciousness* (Macon, GA: Mercer University Press, 1985).

79 Walter Rauschenbusch, "The Bushnellian Theory of the Atonement," November 17, 1885, Box 14, Rauschenbusch Family Collection; closing quote, Rauschenbusch's undated, handwritten cover note to this section of his collected materials.

80 "I began," Walter Rauschenbusch to Munson Ford, December 31, 1884, Box 23; Rauschenbusch to Ford, June 14, 1884, Box 23, Rauschenbusch Family Collection.

81 "Just beginning to believe," Walter Rauschenbusch to Munson Ford, May 30, 1885, Box 23, Rauschenbusch Family Collection; "on the whole," Rauschenbusch to Ford, December 31, 1884; "hard work for God" and "ought to follow Jesus Christ," Rauschenbusch, "The Kingdom of God," 1913 YMCA address, excerpts reprinted in Handy, ed., *The Social Gospel in America*, 265; see Sharpe, *Walter Rauschenbusch*, 52–7.

82 "He kept me at school," Rauschenbusch to Vandercook, February 23, 1917; Walter Rauschenbusch to Munson Ford, February 20, 1886, Box 23, Rauschenbusch Family Collection; Walter Rauschenbusch to Caroline Rauschenbusch, September 24, 1886, North American Baptist Conference Archives, cited in Minus, *Walter Rauschenbusch*, 53.

83 Walter Rauschenbusch to Munson Ford, June 30, 1886, Box 23, Rauschenbusch Family Collection; "My idea," Walter Rauschenbusch, "Genesis of 'Christianity and the Social Crisis,'" *Rochester Theological Seminary Bulletin: The Record* (November 1918), 51; Walter Rauschenbusch, Sermon Notebook 2, 1886, Box 150, Rauschenbusch Family Collection.

84 Dores Sharpe attributed Rauschenbusch's hearing problems to a relapse from the Russian grippe in the winter of 1888; Sharpe, *Walter Rauschenbusch*, 65–6.

85 Walter Rauschenbusch to Lina Döring, July 14, 1886, December 14, 1886, North American Baptist Conference Archives; Minus, *Walter Rauschenbusch*, 54; August Rauschenbusch, *Leben und Wirken von August Rauschenbusch*, iii–v.

86 Rauschenbusch, "The Kingdom of God," 1913 YMCA address, excerpts reprinted in Handy, ed., *The Social Gospel in America*, 266.

87 Rauschenbusch, "Genesis of 'Christianity and the Social Crisis,'" "no idea" and "didn't fit" quotes, 51; Walter Rauschenbusch to Maria Döring, January 14, 1887, North American Baptist Conference Archives, cited in Minus, *Walter Rauschenbusch*, 60.

88 "Children's funerals" in Rauschenbusch, "The Kingdom of God," Cleveland YMCA address, 265–6; "implored me almost" and "all our inherited ideas" in Walter Rauschenbusch, *Christianizing the Social Order* (New York: Macmillan, 1912), 92; "I went ahead" in Rauschenbusch, "The Genesis of 'Christianity and the Social Crisis,'" 51.

89 Henry George, *Progress and Poverty* (New York: Robert Schalkenbach Foundation, 1879, reprint 1955); Fred Nicklason, "Henry George, Social Gospeller," *American Quarterly* 22 (1970), 649–64; James Dombrowski, *The Early Days of Christian Socialism in America* (New York: Columbia University Press, 1936), 35–49.

90 Walter Rauschenbusch to "Madame," February 16, 1897, Box 23, Rauschenbusch Family Papers; Rauschenbusch, *Christianizing the Social Order*, 91–2, "I owe" quote, 394; see Stephen Bell, *Rebel, Priest, and Prophet: A Biography of Dr. Edward McGlynn* (New York: Devin-Adair, 1937), 33–8. Rauschenbusch may have served as a ward captain in George's campaign, though solid documentation is lacking thus far; see Minus, *Walter Rauschenbusch*, 209, n. 26.

91 See Leighton Williams, "The Brotherhood of the Kingdom and Its Work," Brotherhood Leaflet No. 10; reprinted in *The Kingdom* 1 (August 1907), no pagination; Williams, "The Reign of the New Humanity," *The Kingdom* 1 (December 1907); E. F. Merriam, "The Brotherhood of the Kingdom," *The Watchman* (August 13, 1908); Nathaniel Schmidt to Walter Rauschenbusch, April 18, 1889, Box 23, Rauschenbusch Family Collection; Minus, *Walter Rauschenbusch*, 57–8.

92 "Compelled to stop," Rauschenbusch, "The Kingdom of God," 1913 Cleveland YMCA Lecture, reported in *Rochester Democrat and Chronicle* (January 25, 1913); "We desire to make," Editorial, *For the Right* 1 (November 1889); see Sharpe, *Walter Rauschenbusch*, 86–7. The most representative example that we possess of Rauschenbusch's "dangerous book" is the text that Max L. Stackhouse discovered, reconstructed and published under

the title *The Righteousness of the Kingdom* (Nashville: Abingdon Press, 1968; reprint, Lewiston, NY: Edwin Mellen Press, 1999). The precise history of the manuscript is unknown; Schmidt evidently held onto it for lengthy periods of time, and Rauschenbusch continued to work on it in the early 1890s. For the history of the text, see the editor's introduction, *The Righteousness of the Kingdom*, 14–18.

93   "Declaration of Principles of the Society of Christian Socialism," *The Dawn* 1 (May 15, 1889), 3; Editorial, "Declaration of Principles of the Christian Socialist Society of New York City," *For the Right* (April 1890); see Walter Rauschenbusch, "Some Words about Socialism in America," *For the Right* 1 (April 1890); Dombrowski, *The Early Days of Christian Socialism in America*, 96–107; William Dwight Porter Bliss, *A Handbook of Socialism* (New York: S. Sonnenschein, C. Scribners, 1895); Christopher L. Webber, "William Dwight Porter Bliss (1856–1926: Priest and Socialist," *Historical Magazine of the Protestant Episcopal Church* 28 (March 1959), 9–39; Richard B. Dressner, "William Dwight Porter Bliss's Christian Socialism," *Church History* 47 (March 1978), 66–82. Bliss's periodical *The Dawn* was published from 1889 to 1896.

94   Walter Rauschenbusch, "Good Men and Good Government," *For the Right* 2 (August 1890).

95   Leighton Williams to Walter Rauschenbusch, July 3, 1891, Box 23, Rauschenbusch Family Collection; Minus, *Walter Rauschenbusch*, 75–9; editor's introduction, *The Righteousness of the Kingdom*, 17–20.

96   Rauschenbusch, *The Righteousness of the Kingdom*, quote 87; see Rauschenbusch, "Noch einmal die sociale Frage," *Der Sendbote*.

97   Rauschenbusch, "The Kingdom of God," 1913 Cleveland YMCA lecture, excerpts reprinted in Handy, ed., *The Social Gospel in America*, 267.

98   Ibid., 267.

99   Leighton Williams, *The Baptist Position: Its Experimental Basis* (New York: E. Scott & Co., 1892), 4–5, 13–15; Winthrop S. Hudson, ed., *Walter Rauschenbusch: Selected Writings* (New York: Paulist Press, 1984), 21–4; Minus, *Walter Rauschenbusch*, 83–4; Vernon Parker Bodein, *The Social Gospel of Walter Rauschenbusch and Its Relation to Religious Education*, Yale Studies in Religious Education, 16 (New Haven: Yale University Press, 1944), 22–4; Sharpe, *Walter Rauschenbusch*, 116–17.

100   "Spirit and Aims of the Brotherhood of the Kingdom," Preamble to the Constituting Document of the Brotherhood of the Kingdom; this statement was reproduced as a frontispiece to all annual reports of the Brotherhood of the Kingdom. See Leighton Williams, "The Brotherhood of the Kingdom and Its Work," *The Kingdom* (August 1907); Mitchell Bronk, "An Adventure in the Kingdom of God," *Crozer Quarterly* (January 1937), 21–8; C. Howard Hopkins, "Walter Rauschenbusch and the Brotherhood of the Kingdom," *Church History* 7 (June 1938), 138–56; Walter Rauschenbusch, Corresponding Secretary, undated, Box 23, Rauschenbusch Family Collection; Walter Rauschenbusch, "The Brotherhood of the Kingdom," Brotherhood Leaflet No. 2, 1893, reprinted in Hudson, ed., *Walter Rauschenbusch: Selected Writings*, 74–6.

101   Walter Rauschenbusch, "The Kingdom of God," Brotherhood Leaflet No. 4, 1894; reprinted in Hudson, ed., *Walter Rauschenbusch: Selected Writings*, 76–9.

102   Ibid., quote, 78.

103   Walter Rauschenbusch, "A Conquering Idea," *The Examiner* (July 31, 1892), reprinted in Hudson, ed., *Walter Rauschenbusch: Selected Writings*, 71–4, quotes 72; Walter Rauschenbusch, "Our Attitude Toward Millenarianism," *The Examiner* (September 24 and October 1, 1896), reprinted in Hudson, ed., *Walter Rauschenbusch: Selected Writings*, 79–94; see Rauschenbusch, "Some Words about Socialism in America," 3.

104   Rauschenbusch, "The Kingdom of God," Brotherhood Leaflet No. 4, 76–8; Walter Rauschenbusch, "The Ideals of Social Reformers," *American Journal of Sociology* 2 (July 1896), 202–19; reprinted in Handy, ed., *The Social Gospel in America*, 274–89.

105 Walter Rauschenbusch, class letter [to Rochester Seminary class of 1886], 1893, Box 153, Rauschenbusch Family Collection.

106 See James M. Berquist, "German-America in the 1890s: Illusions and Realities," *Germans in America: Aspects of German-American Relations in the Nineteenth Century*, ed. Allen McCormick (New York: Brooklyn College Press, 1983); Lawrence B. Davis, *Immigrants, Baptists, and the Protestant Mind in America* (Urbana, IL: University of Illinois Press, 1973).

107 *Annual Report of the Baptist Congress*, 1888, "for I believe" quote, 87; Walter Rauschenbusch (unsigned), "What Shall We Do with the Germans," (pamphlet, 1895); see Minus, *Walter Rauschenbusch*, 105; John R. Aiken, "Walter Rauschenbusch and Education for Reform," *Church History* 36 (December 1967), 459–60.

108 Walter Rauschenbusch (unsigned), "The German Seminary in Rochester," (pamphlet, 1897), Box 47, Rauschenbusch Family Collection; Walter Rauschenbusch, "The Contribution of Germany to the National Life of America," Commencement address, Fiftieth Anniversary of the Rochester Theological Seminary German Department, Box 92, Rauschenbusch Family Collection, quoted in *Rochester Democrat and Chronicle* (May 8, 1902). Sharpe devoted a single one-sentence aside to this issue, with no hint of controversy or racism; see Sharpe, *Walter Rauschenbusch*, 367.

109 Pauline Rauschenbusch to Walter Rauschenbusch, August 4, 1902, Box 35, Rauschenbusch Family Collection; Minus, *Walter Rauschenbusch*, 117–18, Pauline Rauschenbusch and Augustus Strong statements quoted, 117; Sharpe, *Walter Rauschenbusch*, 177–8.

110 Walter Rauschenbusch, *Christianity and the Social Crisis* (New York: Macmillan, 1907; reprint, Louisville: Westminster John Knox Press, 1991), xxxvii; citations of Harnack on 95, 112, 129, 130, 132, 156, 191, 298.

111 Rauschenbusch, *Christianity and the Social Crisis*, quote 3.

112 Ibid., quotes 47, 48, 63.

113 Ibid., 54–71, quote, 63.

114 Ibid., 62, 63.

115 Rauschenbusch, *Christianity and the Social Crisis*, quotes, 64, 65.

116 Rauschenbusch, *Christianity and the Social Crisis*, quote, 341.

117 Ibid., quotes, 397, 398.

118 Ibid., quotes, 400, 401.

119 Ibid., 420, 421.

120 "If the church" quote, Rauschenbusch, *Christianity and the Social Crisis*, 339; "an expression of," Rauschenbusch, "Genesis of 'Christianity and the Social Crisis,'" 53; Albion W. Small, review of *Christianity and the Social Crisis*, by Walter Rauschenbusch, *Unity* (December 12, 1907).

121 See Samuel McCrea Cavert, *The American Churches in the Ecumenical Movement, 1900–1968* (New York: Association Press, 1968); Charles Howard Hopkins, *History of the YMCA in North America* (New York: Association Press, 1951); Grace H. Wilson, *The Religious and Philosophical Works of the YWCA* (New York: Teachers College Press, 1933); Henry J. Pratt, *The Liberalization of American Protestantism: A Case Study in Complex Organizations* (Detroit: Wayne State University Press, 1972); Sidney E. Mead, *The Lively Experiment: The Shaping of Christianity in America* (New York: Harper & Row, 1963), 177–83; Martin E. Marty, *Righteous Empire: The Protestant Experience in America* (New York: Dial Press, 1970), 206–9; Frank Mason North to Walter Rauschenbusch, August 3, 1908, Box 25, Rauschenbusch Family Collection; *The Social Creed of the Churches*, ed. Harry F. Ward (Cincinnati: Eaton & Maine, 1912).

122 Walter Rauschenbusch, *For God and the People: Prayers of the Social Awakening* (Boston: Pilgrim Press, 1910), 45, 126.

123 Most of *Christianizing the Social Order* was delivered as the Earl Lectures at Pacific Theological Seminary in Berkeley, California in April 1910, and the Merrick Lectures at Ohio Wesleyan University in Delaware, Ohio in April 1911.

124 Rauschenbusch, *Christianizing the Social Order*, quote, vii.

125 Ibid., quotes, viii, 9.

126 Ibid., 48–60, quotes, 49, 58, 56.

127 Ibid., 89–90.

128 Ibid., 123–5, quote, 125.

129 Ibid., 124–5, quotes, 125.

130 Ibid., 125–30, quote, 125.

131 Ibid., 130–8, quotes, 131, 135. Janet Fishburn's early work claimed that Rauschenbusch opposed female suffrage and that he "abhorred feminism because it was potentially destructive of family and society." See Janet Forsythe Fishburn, *The Fatherhood of God and the Victorian Family: The Social Gospel in America* (Philadelphia: Fortress Press, 1981), 124. Martin E. Marty, among others, repeated Fishburn's claims; see Martin E. Marty, *Modern American Religion, Volume 1: The Irony of It all, 1893–1919* (Chicago: University of Chicago Press), 292.

132 Rauschenbusch, *Christianity and the Social Crisis*, quotes, 279, 276; see Walter Rauschenbusch, "Some Moral Aspects of the 'Woman Movement,'" *Biblical World* 42 (October 1913), 195–8; Walter Rauschenbusch, "What About the Woman?" Box 20, Rauschenbusch Family Papers; Peter Gabriel Filene, *Him Her Self: Sex Roles in Modern America* (New York: Harcourt Brace Jovanovich, 1974), 23–9; Fishburn, *The Fatherhood of God and the Victorian Family*, 120–7; Fishburn, "Walter Rauschenbusch and 'The Women Movement': A Gender Analysis"; Susan Curtis, *A Consuming Faith: The Social Gospel and Modern American Culture* (Baltimore: Johns Hopkins University Press, 1991), 107–8, 112.

133 Rauschenbusch, *Christianizing the Social Order*, 137–55, quotes 152, 153.

134 Ibid., quotes, 156, 157, 158.

135 Daniel Bell, *The Cultural Contradictions of Capitalism* (New York: Basic Books, 1976); Rauschenbusch, *Christianizing ther Social Order*, quote, 212.

136 Rauschenbusch, *Christianizing the Social Order*, 311–23, quotes, 317.

137 Ibid., quote 314.

138 Ibid., 341–3, 352–6.

139 Ibid., quote, 361.

140 John Stuart Mill, *Principles of Political Economy* 2 vols. (New York: Appleton & Co., 1884), 2: 357–9; Rauschenbusch, *Christianizing the Social Order*, 356–71; Walter Rauschenbusch, "Christian Socialism," *A Dictionary of Religion and Ethics*, eds. Shailer Mathews and Gerald Birney Smith (New York: Macmillan Company, 1923), 90–1.

141 Rauschenbusch, *Christianizing the Social Order*, quote, 369.

142 Ibid., quote 329; Walter Rauschenbusch to Francis G. Peabody, December 14, 1912, Box 26, Rauschenbusch Family Collection.

143 Rauschenbusch, *Christianizing the Social Order*, 458–66, quotes, 433, 464–5.

144 "Compressed anxiety," Walter Rauschenbusch to John Wright Buckham, December 24, 1912, Box 26, Rauschenbusch Family Collection.

145 Walter Rauschenbusch, Address to Religious Citizenship League, January 30, 1914; Rauschenbusch, "The Contribution of Germany to the National Life of America," Box 92; Rauschenbusch, *For God and the People*, 109; Walter Rauschenbusch to Hilmar Rauschenbusch, September 23, 1914, Box 37, Rauschenbusch Family Collection; Minus, *Walter Rauschenbusch*, 177–8.

146 Rauschenbusch, *Christianizing the Social Order*, 366, "ablest ruler" quote, 334; Rauschenbusch, *For God and the People*, "ever the pride" quote, 109; Walter Rauschenbusch to *The Congregationalist*, September 24, 1914.

147 "My cradle" quote, Rauschenbusch, "The Contribution of Germany to the National Life of America," Box 92; Walter Rauschenbusch to "a Friend," March 7, 1917, Box 32, Rauschenbusch Family Collection; Walter Rauschenbusch, "Be Fair to Germany: A Plea for Open-mindedness," *The Congregationalist*, October 15, 1914.

148 "Methodists Do Not Want to Hear Pro-German Divine," *Regina Morning Leader* (November 5, 1914).

149 Rauschenbusch to "A Friend," March 7, 1917.

150 Walter Rauschenbusch to John S. Phillips, May 16, 1917, Box 32, Rauschenbusch Family Collection.

151 Walter Rauschenbusch to Washington Gladden, January 17, 1917, Box 32, Rauschenbusch Family Collection; Walter Rauschenbusch to Algernon Crapsey, open letter published in *Rochester Herald*, August 23, 1915; Rauschenbusch to Dores Robinson Sharpe, April 21, 1916; Minus, *Walter Rauschenbusch*, 179–82; Sharpe, *Walter Rauschenbusch*, 378–9. Rauschenbusch was one of Crapsey's few defenders when he was tried a decade earlier for heresy; his letter to Crapsey in 1915 was a reply to a quite formal letter in which Crapsey questioned the soundness of his ideology and theology.

152 Walter Rauschenbusch, *The Social Principles of Jesus* (New York: Association Press, 1916), quotes, 196–7.

153 Walter Rauschenbusch, *A Theology for the Social Gospel* (New York: Macmillan, 1917; reprint, Louisville: Westminster John Knox Press, 1997), 4. This section adapts material from Gary Dorrien, *Soul in Society: The Making and Renewal of Social Christianity* (Minneapolis: Fortress Press, 1993), 52–4, and Dorrien, *Reconstructing the Common Good: Theology and the Social Order* (Maryknoll, NY: Orbis Books, 1992), 38–40.

154 Rauschenbusch, *A Theology for the Social Gospel*, 4.

155 Ibid., 7–30, quotes, 279; ibid., 31–7, quotes, 33, 34; Rauschenbusch, *Christianity and the Social Crisis*, 158.

156 Rauschenbusch, *A Theology for the Social Gospel*, 45–68, quotes, 53, 59, 60.

157 Albrecht Ritschl, *Die christliche Lehre von der Rechtfertigung und Versöhnung* 1 (4th edn.: Bonn: A. Marcus und Webers Verlag, 1903), 496, 555–6; Friedrich Schleiermacher, *The Christian Faith*, ed. H. R. Mackintosh and J. S. Stewart (2nd German edn., 1830; English trans., Edinburgh: T. & T. Clark, 1928), 287–9; Rauschenbusch, *A Theology for the Social Gospel*, 92–4, 79.

158 Rauschenbusch, *A Theology for the Social Gospel*, 81–92, quotes, 81–2, 86.

159 Ibid., 159–87, quotes, 174, 179.

160 L. Hamman to John R. Williams, May 28, 1918, Box 93; Hamman to Williams, June 3, 1918, Box 93; "I have overworked," Walter Rauschenbusch to Herbert White, January 18, 1918, Box 32; Walter Rauschenbusch to Clarence A. Barbour, 5 February 25, 1918, Box 32; Walter Rauschenbusch, "Instructions in Case of My Death," March 31, 1918, Box 87, Rauschenbusch Family Collection.

161 Walter Rauschenbusch to Cornelius Woelfkin, first draft, April 25, 1918; published version, May 1, 1918; Rochester Seminary press release version subtitled "ALWAYS AN AMERICAN," July 11, 1918, Box 91, Rauschenbusch Family Collection.

162 Walter Rauschenbusch to W. G. Ballantine, February 4, 1918, Box 93, Rauschenbusch Family Collection.

163 See Shailer Mathews, *The Faith of Modernism* (New York: Macmillan Co., 1924); Charles S. Macfarland, *Across the Years* (New York: Macmillan Co., 1936); Harry Emerson Fosdick, *Christianity and Progress* (New York: Fleming H. Revell Co., 1922); Justin Wroe Nixon, *The Moral Crisis in Christianity* (New York: Harper & Brothers, 1931); Francis J. McConnell, *Democratic Christianity* (New York: Macmillan Co., 1919).

164 Harry F. Ward to Daisy Kendall Ward, April 20, 1909, quote; Harry F. Ward Papers, Burke Library, Union Theological Seminary/Columbia University; David Nelson Duke, *In the Trenches with Jesus and Marx: Harry F. Ward and the Struggle for Social Justice* (Tuscaloosa: University of Alabama Press, 2003), 3–16; Eugene P. Link, *Labor–Religion Prophet: The Times and Life of Harry F. Ward* (Boulder, CO: Westview Press, 1984), 2–13.

165 James Dombrowski, *The Early Days of Christian Socialism in America* (New York: Columbia University Press, 1936), 50; Duke, *In the Trenches with Jesus and Marx: Harry F. Ward and*

the *Struggle for Social Justice*, 17–22; Link, *Labor–Religion Prophet: The Times and Life of Harry F. Ward*, 4–6.

166   See George Albert Coe, *The Religion of a Mature Mind* (Chicago: Fleming H. Revell, 1902); Coe, *Education in Religion and Morals* (New York: Fleming H. Revell, 1904); Coe, "The Religious Problems in Colleges," *Northwestern* (19 (April 13, 1899), 2–5; Harry F. Ward, "We Were Friends," *Religious Education* 47 (March–April 1952), 88–9.

167   Harry F. Ward to Daisy Kendall, October 15, 1897, "those German brains," Harry Ward Papers; Ward to Kendall, February 28, 1898, Harry Ward Papers; Duke, *In the Trenches with Jesus and Marx: Harry F. Ward and the Struggle for Social Justice*, 37–8.

168   James Dombrowski and Eugene P. Link were former students of Ward's who embraced his account of the difference in their writings; see Dombrowski, *The Early Days of Christian Socialism in America*, 56–9; Link, *Labor–Religion Prophet: The Times and Life of Harry F. Ward*, xix, 17.

169   Link, *Labor–Religion Prophet: The Times and Life of Harry F. Ward*, 16–21; David Nelson Duke, "Harry F. Ward, Social Gospel Warrior in the Trenches: The Social Gospel's Staying Power During the War and Its Aftermath," *Perspectives on the Social Gospel: Papers from the Inaugural Social Gospel Conference at Colgate Rochester Divinity School*, ed. Christopher H. Evans (Lewiston, NY: Edwin Mellen Press, 1999), 197–219, psyche remark, 200; Duke, *In the Trenches with Jesus and Marx: Harry F. Ward and the Struggle for Social Justice*, 44–58.

170   *The Social Creed of the Churches*, ed. Harry F. Ward (New York: Eaton & Mains, 1912); Link, *Labor–Religion Prophet: The Times and Life of Harry F. Ward*, 38–54; Eugene P. Link, "Latter Day Christian Rebel: Harry F. Ward," *Mid-America* 56 (1974), 225–7; Creighton Lacy, *Frank Mason North: His Social and Ecumenical Mission* (Nashville: Abingdon Press, 1967), 132–5; Hopkins, *The Rise of the Social Gospel in American Protestantism, 1865–1915*, 289–301; Donald K. Gorrell, *The Age of Social Responsibility: The Social Gospel in the Progressive Era, 1900–1920* (Macon, GA: Mercer University Press, 1988), 90–102.

171   Harry F. Ward to Daisy Kendall Ward, February 17, 1909, quotes, Harry F. Ward Papers; Harry F. Ward to Walter Rauschenbusch, December 29, 1913, Box 27, Walter Rauschenbusch Papers; Harry F. Ward, "The Challenge of Socialism to Christianity," *Ford Hall Folks* (March 22, 1914), 1–4, cited in Duke, *In the Trenches with Jesus and Marx: Harry F. Ward and the Struggle for Social Justice*, 78–80; Harry F. Ward, "The Labor Movement," in *Social Ministry: An Introduction to the Study and Practice of Social Service*, ed. Harry F. Ward (New York: Eaton & Mains, 1910), 107–31, closing quotes 131.

172   Harry F. Ward, "The Church and Social Service in the United States," 1914, in Ward, *The Harry F. Ward Sampler*, ed. Annette T. Rubinstein (New York: Methodist Federation for Social Action, 1963), "beating heart," 5–6; Harry F. Ward, *The Labor Movement from the Standpoint of Religious Values* (New York: Sturgis and Walton, 1917), "only possible way," 1915 speech, 70; Ward, *Social Evangelism* (New York: Missionary Education Movement of the United States and Canada, 1915), "it puts" 90. Harry F. Ward, "The Church and the Industrial Situation," Lecture Series Notes, Union Theological Seminary, November 15, 16, 17, 23, 24, 1916, Harry F. Ward Papers.

173   Charles Macfarland quoted from the *General Conference Journal* (1916), 803, cited in Richard D. Tholin, "Prophetic Action and Denominational Unity: The Function of Unofficial Social Action Groups in the Methodist Church and the Protestant Episcopal Church," ThD dissertation, Union Theological Seminary, New York, 1967, and Duke, *In the Trenches with Jesus and Marx: Harry F. Ward and the Struggle for Social Justice*, 85; L. J. Birney to Harry F. Ward, January 26, 1917, Harry F. Ward Papers; Harry F. Ward, *The Labor Movement from the Standpoint of Religious Values* (New York: Sturgis and Walton, 1917), 139–53; Ward, "Why Go to War?" Emergency Peace Committee of Massachusetts, Boston, MA, March 18, 1917, Harry F. Ward Papers; Ward, *The Christian Demand for Social Reconstruction* (Philadelphia: Walter H. Jenkins, 1918), quotes, 50–1; Ward, "The Abolition of Poverty," Ford Hall Union Lecture Series Notes, Boston University, March 13, 15, 20, 27, 29, 1917, Harry F. Ward Papers.

174 Harry F. Ward to Pauline Rauschenbusch, August 1, 1918, Box 91, Walter Rauschenbusch Papers; Robert T. Handy, *A History of Union Theological Seminary in New York* (New York: Columbia University Press, 1987), 140–1.

175 Harry F. Ward, "The Present Task of Christian Ethics," *Union Theological Seminary Bulletin* 2 (November 1918), 20–4; Ward, *The Gospel for a Working World* (New York: Missionary Education Movement of the United States and Canada, 1918), quotes, 229, 232–3, 238; Ward, "Address to the Methodist Minister's Meeting," First Methodist Episcopal Church, Chicago, IL, May 19, 1919, Harry F. Ward Papers.

176 Harry F. Ward, "Address to the Rock River Conference," Chicago, IL, October 6, 1921; Ward, "Challenge of [the] Social Crisis to Christianity," "The Present Social Crisis," and "The Answer of Christianity to the Social Crisis," Addresses to Student Summer Conferences, July 1921, Harry F. Ward Papers; see James Macregor Burns, *The Workshop of Democracy* (New York: Vintage Books, 1986), 448–68; Nick Salvatore, *Eugene V. Debs: Citizen and Socialist* (Urbana, IL: University of Illinois Press, 1982), 286–307; Thomas J. Knock, *To End All Wars: Woodrow Wilson and the Quest for a New World Order* (Princeton: Princeton University Press, 1992), 227–70; Duke, *In the Trenches with Jesus and Marx: Harry F. Ward and the Struggle for Social Justice*, 96–9; Daniel Bell, *Marxian Socialism in the United States* (Princeton: Princeton University Press, 1952), 105–6; Melvyn Dubofsky, *We Shall Be All: A History of the Industrial Workers of the World* (New York: Quadrangle, 1969), 423–68.

177 Harry F. Ward, *The New Social Order: Principles and Programs* (New York: Macmillan, 1920), quotes v, 5.

178 Ibid., 11–17, quotes 13.

179 Ibid., quotes 22, 30.

180 Ibid., quotes 376, 235.

181 Ibid., 225–71, quote 244.

182 Ibid., 380; "Bolshevism and the Methodist Church: An Account of the Controversy Precipitated by Professor Ward," *Current Opinion* 66 (June 1919), 380–1; Robert H. Craig, "An Introduction to the Life and Thought of Harry F. Ward," *Union Seminary Quarterly Review* 24 (Summer 1969), 339–40; Duke, *In the Trenches with Jesus and Marx: Harry F. Ward and the Struggle for Social Justice*, 101–3; Milton John Huber, "A History of the Methodist Federation for Social Action," PhD dissertation, Boston University, 1949, 132–8; James R. Joy, "An Account of the Controversy Precipitated by Professor Ward," *New York Christian Advocate* (March 13, 1919), n.p.; Gorrell, *The Age of Social Responsibility: The Social Gospel in the Progressive Era, 1900–1920*, 312–14; Harry F. Ward, "A Statement by Harry F. Ward," *Christian Advocate* (April 3, 1919), 434.

183 Review of *The Gospel for a Working World*, by Harry F. Ward, *Nation* 108 (March 15, 1919), 407; Pauline Rauschenbusch to Harry F. Ward, April 3, 1919, Harry F. Ward Papers.

184 Harry F. Ward to the Senate Committee Investigating German Propaganda, Washington, DC, January 28, 1919, Harry Ward Papers; Harry F. Ward, "Why I Have Found Life Worth Living," *Christian Century* (March 1, 1928), 281–3, quote 281; see Sherwood Eddy, *Religion and Social Justice* (New York: George H. Doran, 1927); Eddy and Kirby Page, *The Abolition of War: The Case against War and Questions and Answers Concerning War* (New York: George H. Doran Co., 1924); Walter G. Muelder, *Methodism and Society in the Twentieth Century* (Nashville: Abingdon Press, 1961); William McGuire King, "The Emergence of Social Gospel Radicalism: The Methodist Case," *Church History* 50 (December 1981), 437–45; King describes the anti-capitalist social gospelers as the movement's "reconstructionist" wing.

185 W. J. Burns, FBI Director, to the Honorable Martin B. Madden, House of Representatives, April 7, 1922, FBI files on Harry F. Ward, cited in Duke, *In the Trenches with Jesus and Marx: Harry F. Ward and the Struggle for Social Justice*, 110; *Revolutionary Radicalism: Its History, Purpose and Tactics with an Exposition and Discussion of the Steps Being Taken and Required to Curb It* (Albany, NY: J. B. Lyon, 1920), 115, cited in ibid., 115; Doug

Rossinow, "The Radicalization of the Social Gospel: Harry F. Ward and the Search for a New Social Order, 1898–1936," *Religion and American Culture: A Journal of Interpretation* 15 (2005), 85–6. The other institution cited was St. Stephens College at Annandale, New York.

186 Harry F. Ward to Gordon, Muriel, and Lynd Ward, September 15, 1924, and Ward to Gordon, Muriel, and Lynd Ward and Ward relatives, March 25, Harry F. Ward Papers; Harry F. Ward, "Civil Liberties in Russia," *Nation* 120 (March 1925), 234–7, quotes 236; Ward, "Will Religion Survive in Russia?" *Christian Century* 42 (February 12, 1925), 215–18; Ward, "China's Anti-Christian Movement," *Christian Century* 43 (April 15, 1926), 474–6; Ward, "China's Anti-Christian Temper," *Christian Century* 43 (May 13, 1926), 611–16; Ward, "The Future of Religion," *World Tomorrow* 8 (December 1925), 372–4; Ward, "Progress or Decadence?" *Recent Gains in American Civilization*, ed. Kirby Page (New York: Harcourt, Brace, 1928), 277–305, "our comfortable," 279.

187 Harry F. Ward, *Our Economic Morality and the Ethic of Jesus* (New York: Macmillan, 1929), v–vii, quote vi.

188 Ibid., quotes 4, 62, 21.

189 Ibid., 31–78, quote 67.

190 Ibid., 84–193, quote 100.

191 Ibid., quotes 11, 286.

192 Ibid., 286–323, quote 314–15.

193 Robert Moats Miller, *American Protestantism and Social Issues, 1919–1939* (Chapel Hill: University of North Carolina Press, 1958), 101–2; see Muelder, *Methodism and Society in the Twentieth Century*, 137–8.

194 Federal Council of the Churches of Christ in America, *Quadrennial Report* (1932).

195 Harry F. Ward, *Which Way Religion?* (New York: Macmillan, 1931), 11–54, quote 28.

196 Ibid., quotes 28.

197 Ibid., 30–5, quotes 34; Harry F. Ward, "Public Education: Assembling Constructive Forces for the Ideal Consummation," Address to the Teachers Union Auxiliary October Conference, October 2, 1932, Harry F. Ward Papers.

198 Reinhold Niebuhr to Ursula Kempton-Compton, August 8, 1931, Reinhold Niebuhr Papers, Library of Congress, cited in Duke, *In the Trenches with Jesus and Marx: Harry F. Ward and the Struggle for Social Justice*, 147.

199 Daisy Kendall Ward to her children, September 19, 1931, Harry Ward Papers; Harry F. Ward, *In Place of Profit: Social Incentives in the Soviet Union* (New York: Charles Scribner's Sons, 1933), quotes 107, 75.

200 Reinhold Niebuhr to Ursula Kempton-Compton, November 24, 1931, Reinhold Niebuhr Papers, cited in Duke, *In the Trenches with Jesus and Marx: Harry F. Ward and the Struggle for Social Justice*, 151.

201 Ward, *In Place of Profit: Social Incentives in the Soviet Union*, 3–17, quotes vii, 16, 17.

202 Ibid., quotes 53, 65, 58.

203 Ibid., 86–107, quote 107.

204 George Albert Coe to Harry F. Ward, February 26, 1933, George Albert Coe Papers, Yale Divinity School Library; Ward to Coe, May 5, 1933, Coe Papers; Coe to Ward, May 11, 1933, Coe Papers; Ward to Coe, June 25, 1933, Coe Papers, cited in Duke, *In the Trenches with Jesus and Marx: Harry F. Ward and the Struggle for Social Justice*, 158–60.

205 Ward, *In Place of Profit: Social Incentives in the Soviet Union*, 239, 411–12; Eugene Lyons, *Assignment in Utopia* (New York: Harcourt, Brace and Co., 1937); see Robert Conquest, *Harvest of Sorrow: Soviet Collectivization and the Terror-Famine* (New York: Oxford, 1987).

206 Reinhold Niebuhr to Ursula Niebuhr, May 19, 1936, Reinhold Niebuhr Papers; Harry F. Ward to George Albert Coe, June 3, 1936, George Albert Coe Papers, cited in Duke, *In the Trenches with Jesus and Marx: Harry F. Ward and the Struggle for Social Justice*, 173, 171; Handy, *A History of Union Theological Seminary in New York*, 185–6; "Can We Control

Foreign Policy by Legislation?" WCAO Radio Address, November 12, 1938, Harry F. Ward Papers; Ward, "Address to the League for Peace and Democracy," New York, NY, April 28, 1938, Harry F. Ward Papers.

207 Link, *Labor–Religion Prophet: The Times and Life of Harry F. Ward*, quote 234; see Aimee Isgrig Horton, *The Highlander Folk School: A History of Its Major Programs, 1932–1961* (Brooklyn, NY: Carlson, 1989); Frank T. Adams, *James A. Dombrowski: An American Heretic, 1897–1983* (Knoxville: University of Tennessee Press, 1992); Rossinow, "The Radicalization of the Social Gospel: Harry F. Ward and the Search for a New Social Order, 1898–1936," 93; Harry F. Ward, "Democracy in Danger," WNYC Radio Address, June 24, 1938, Harry F. Ward Papers.

208 Link, *Labor–Religion Prophet: The Times and Life of Harry F. Ward*, 235.

209 Henry Sloane Coffin, *A Half-Century of Union Theological Seminary, 1896–1945* (New York: Charles Scribner's Sons, 1954), 101–2.

210 Link, *Labor–Religion Prophet: The Times and Life of Harry F. Ward*, 243; Harry F. Ward to George Albert Coe, February 19, 1933, George Albert Coe Papers; Jack R. McMichael to David Nelson Duke, July 19, 1979, "two horses" image; Reinhold Niebuhr to Ursula Niebuhr, n.d. (1936), Reinhold Niebuhr Papers; citations in Duke, *In the Trenches with Jesus and Marx: Harry F. Ward and the Struggle for Social Justice*, 173–4.

211 Norman Thomas to Harry F. Ward, October 10, 1939, Harry F. Ward Papers; Harry F. Ward, "Statement by Dr. Harry F. Ward, National Chairman," American League for Peace and Democracy, November 1938, Harry F. Ward Papers.

212 *Investigation of Un-American Propaganda Activities in the United States, Hearings before a Special Committee on Un-American Activities, House of Representatives, Seventy-fifth Congress* (Washington, DC: United States Government Printing Office, 1938), 6262–318; Samuel Walker, *In Defense of American Liberties: A History of the ACLU* (New York: Oxford University Press, 1990), quotes, 131–2; *The Trial of Elizabeth Gurley Flynn by the American Civil Liberties Union*, ed. Corliss Lamont (New York: Horizon Press, 1968), 42–3; Doug Rossinow, " 'The Model of a Model Fellow Traveler': Harry F. Ward, the American League for Peace and Democracy, and the 'Russian Question' in American Politics, 1933–1956," *Peace & Change* 29 (April 2004), 199; Duke, *In the Trenches with Jesus and Marx: Harry F. Ward and the Struggle for Social Justice*, 181–3; Link, *Labor–Religion Prophet: The Times and Life of Harry F. Ward*, 215–26.

213 "Peace League Dies in Secret Session," *New York Times* (February 2, 1940), "we are," 1; Rossinow, " 'The Model of a Model Fellow Traveler': Harry F. Ward, the American League for Peace and Democracy, and the 'Russian Question' in American Politics, 1933–1956," 198; Harry F. Ward, *Democracy and Social Change* (New York: Modern Age, 1940); Ward, "Some Things I Have Learned While Teaching," *Alumni Bulletin of Union Theological Seminary* 16 (June 1941), "I replied," 12.

214 Harry F. Ward, "Protestants and the Anti-Soviet Front," *Protestant* 4 (December 1941–January 1942), 64–5; Duke, *In the Trenches with Jesus and Marx: Harry F. Ward and the Struggle for Social Justice*, 195; Ward, "Religion and War, "Address to the American People's Meeting, National Religious Committee of the American Peace Mobilization," New York, NY, April 6, 1941, Harry F. Ward Papers.

215 Harry F. Ward, *The Soviet Spirit* (New York: International Publishers, 1944); Ward, *The Story of American–Soviet Relations, 1917–1959* (New York: National Council of American–Soviet Relations, 1959), quote 58; see Ward, "Debs, Bourne, and Reed," *New Masses* 38 (March 4, 1941), 13; Ward, "The Lenin Spirit," *Daily Worker* (February 4, 1945), 5; Ward, "Pulpits in War," *New Masses* 47 (June 15, 1943), 15–17.

216 Duke, *In the Trenches with Jesus and Marx: Harry F. Ward and the Struggle for Social Justice*, 190–1, 271.

217 Donald Meyer, *The Protestant Search for Political Realism, 1919–1941* (1960; 2nd edn., Middletown, CT: Wesleyan University Press, 1988), 186.

Chapter 3

Lift Every Voice

Reverdy C. Ransom, Jane Addams, and John A. Ryan

There were other important voices in the early making of social Christianity and social ethics besides the dominant white, male, middle-class, Protestant ones. The black social gospel tradition began with the brave and eloquent preaching of Reverdy C. Ransom. Very few women had leadership roles in the early making of social ethics, but Jane Addams was an iconic figure. And American Catholicism produced a vital and influential form of social Christianity through the work of John A. Ryan.

To say that there were important proponents of African-American and Catholic versions of the social gospel is not quite the same thing as saying that because of these figures the social gospel movement was richer and more diverse than it seemed. The social gospel of the Progressive era was determinedly white and Protestant. It had a conscience about white America's mistreatment of African Americans, but was usually paternalist in its dealings with blacks, taking white superiority for granted. It had a passion for ecumenical cooperation, but usually viewed Catholicism as beyond the pale of ecumenical fellowship. The white social gospel had room for Addams, Vida Scudder (an Episcopal socialist and Wellesley College English professor), and Anna Howard Shaw (a feminist leader and Methodist minister). But its emphatic Protestantism and theological liberalism thwarted significant contact with Catholics, with the chief exception of Ryan, and its relationships with black social gospelers such as Ransom, Ida B. Wells (Barnett), Henry McNeal Turner, Monroe Work, and Richard R. Wright Jr. were not reciprocal. Ransom and Wright deeply absorbed social gospel theology and politics, forging personal relationships with white social gospelers. Yet they were not treated as equal counterparts in the development of social Christianity. The black social gospel tradition developed as a subordinated discourse, because the American social gospel was as segregated as its society.

The greatest social gospeler, Walter Rauschenbusch, had a typically meager acquaintance with black Americans. When Rauschenbusch returned to Rochester in 1897 to be a seminary professor, only 600 of Rochester's 162,000 residents were black. He realized that he lacked knowledge and moral authority on the subject of race. More importantly, what he did know was too depressing to mix into his books and articles on the forward march of the kingdom. Rauschenbusch waited until his last years to say anything about racial justice. In *Christianizing the Social Order* (1912) he finally managed to say that the spirit of Jesus "smites race pride and prejudice in the face in the name of humanity," and in *A Theology for the Social Gospel* (1917) he described racial lynching as the ultimate example of evil as a social inheritance. That was the sort of thing one might have expected to read in Rauschenbusch, yet these statements came from nowhere, raising, for him, a new subject. In 1914 he explained why it took him so long to give racial justice even a sentence or two: "For years, the problem of the two races in the South has seemed to me so tragic, so insoluble, that I have never yet ventured to discuss it in public."[1]

To Reverdy Ransom, that was an existentially plausible reaction, since he understood the difficulty of sustaining hope in a seemingly hopeless situation. He dealt with it every day in ministering to black Americans who had actually suffered the tragedy and often been defeated by it. But for Ransom the response of mute hopelessness was an ethical impossibility. If Christianity had any social-ethical meaning in the American context, it had to begin with the evils of white supremacism and hatred that oppressed black Americans.

Becoming Reverdy C. Ransom

Reverdy Cassius Ransom was deeply aware that he was not a self-made success; thus he titled his autobiography *The Pilgrimage of Harriet Ransom's Son* (1949). He was born in January 1861 in Flushing, Ohio, the only child of a powerful, loving woman who assured him that he was "let down from the skies." Ransom had red hair and never knew anything of his father, two facts that were probably related. A local member of Congress, John A. Bingham, paid Harriet Ransom five dollars in gold for the right to name her son after two politicians, Reverdy Johnson of Maryland (a prominent lawyer and subsequent Senate defender of President Andrew Johnson) and Cassius Marcellus Clay of Kentucky (an anti-slavery Whig and later Republican who served in the 1860s as Minister to Russia). He got his surname from the man who eventually married Harriet, George Warner Ransom, although Reverdy Ransom may have acquired the name before his mother married. During the Civil War he lived with his mother and maternal grandmother in the latter's two-room log house; in 1865 Harriet left her mother's house to work as a domestic servant in Washington, Ohio, placing Reverdy with George Ransom's parents, who owned a farm nearby. For Reverdy Ransom it was a difficult transition. Harriet paid the Ransoms to care for him; there were numerous Ransom children in the house, who did not welcome him; he was always hungry and plagued with scary voices in his head; and George Ransom's sister treated him badly, calling him "that little red-headed devil."[2]

At night Reverdy joined his mother in the unheated attic of a Washington merchant, one of the homes in which she worked. He dreaded the cold attic and the Ransom household; at the same time, he was deeply influenced by the Ransoms, his mother's religion, and his mother's white employers. Harriet and the Ransom family were active members of the African Methodist Episcopal Church (AME), which was organized in Ohio in the 1820s and surged with the migration of blacks to Ohio after the Civil War. In his later life Reverdy expressed gratitude for the model of hard work and faithful belief that the Ransom family gave him, though his stepfather remained unconverted for many years. Harriet's employers were prosperous, educated, articulate, pro-slavery Northern Democrats who took for granted that their children would go to college. In the early 1860s only five states permitted working-class black males to vote, and all were in New England, where only 4 percent of the nation's free blacks lived. Ohio, part of the Old Northwest Territory, was hostile terrain for

blacks, often resenting its rising black population. Yet it was a magnet for black migration, mainly because of geography, partly because abolitionist revival preaching made
deep inroads there. From her employers Harriet got her ideas about how her son
should speak and carry himself, and she vowed that he would go to college.[3]

Ransom was a long shot to make it to college, even with a determined mother.
In 1869 Harriet moved to nearby Cambridge, Ohio, a town of 2,500, with approximately 300 African Americans. Some were former slaves; others were the children of
former slaves; others were descendants of poor, rural Ohio blacks of the antebellum
period; virtually all scraped out a bare subsistence living. Ransom was sent to a segregated black school, housed in the local AME Church, where a single white man taught
all the classes, making little attempt at classroom management. Ransom was fascinated
with history and geography, but he heard the same lessons year after year. When he
was 13 years old his mother demanded that he be allowed to attend the local public
school; decades later Ransom recalled: "I can still see the finger of Professor McBurney
pointing and waving while he told my mother: 'You must take your child right down
there to the colored school where he belongs, we cannot admit him here.'" Thus he
returned for more years of the same fare, yearning for the Latin grammar textbooks
of his white friends. Ransom performed janitorial services for a shoe store proprietor
in exchange for private algebra lessons. His mother performed laundry services for a
succession of white people who tutored him in other subjects. "There was almost no
high aspiration among the colored youth of our community and nothing to inspire
it," Ransom later recalled. "Few books and papers were available. The Church was
the social centre of our life."[4]

Ransom braved the derision of friends for aspiring to college. Often he attended
the local Court of Common Pleas, where he watched lawyers interrogate witnesses
and craft legal arguments. Working as a "houseboy" in the home of a bank cashier,
he became a voracious reader and worked on his speaking skills:

> I was almost daily in the homes of our most cultured and wealthy white people, for
> whom my mother worked. I took note of their customs, manners, and conversation even
> to the form of their words and the modulation of their voices. I was ever trying to
> explain and reconcile their world to the one in which I lived among my own people.

Why was there such a chasm between the black and white Americas? Why couldn't
he go to school with his friends who happened to be white? Why were all black
people poor? Harriet replied that ignorance was almost always the answer; the solution
was to be educated. Her dream for him was an education at Wilberforce University,
an AME school in Wilberforce, Ohio named after the eighteenth-century abolitionist
William Wilberforce. Ransom took a summer normal school course to qualify for
admission to Wilberforce, and in 1881 he was admitted. But in the spring of 1881
Harriet Ransom had to overcome two crises to get her son to college.[5]

Her savings, it turned out, were considerably less than needed; Harriet Ransom
solved that problem by selling the family cow and mortgaging her house, with her
husband George Ransom's consent. The bigger crisis was that Reverdy impulsively
married Leanna Watkins in February and she immediately became pregnant. Many
years later he shuddered at the memory:

> It is a strange caprice of fate that most people, usually in youth, or at the threshold of
> their career, have an experience, or tragedy, that puts a mark upon the heart, mind, or

spirit, that one carries through life. In all such lives there is a sealed room, the privacy of which no one is permitted to tarry long upon the threshold of its poignant memories.

Ransom regretted that he came so close to breaking his mother's heart. He allowed himself the explanation that it was hard to watch others enjoy sexual relations when his religious scruples forbade sex before marriage: "We lived in a community of free morals. We were both in our teens. She was one of the finest and the best among us. She was comely to look upon, added to this, the correctness of her life and conduct caused her to stand apart from most all of the other girls in her group." Undaunted, Harriet Ransom declared that even teenaged fatherhood would not stand between her son and a college education. For eight years she took charge of the next George Ransom, named after her husband, while Reverdy headed for Wilberforce University.[6]

Wilberforce was the nation's oldest private, historically black university. It was founded in 1856 by the Cincinnati Conference of the Methodist Episcopal Church, North, and was located originally in Xenia, Ohio, a community settled in the 1840s by fugitive slaves, free blacks, and the racially mixed families of southern slaveowners. Its original constituency was primarily the planter class that needed a university for its mulatto children. The school closed in 1862 as a casualty of the Civil War, and the following year Bishop Daniel A. Payne, who had served on Wilberforce's board of trustees, bought the university for $10,000. Payne re-founded the school as an AME Church institution; in 1891 it spawned a seminary, Payne Theological Seminary.[7]

Bishop Payne, the AME Church's dominant figure, shaped Wilberforce firmly in his image. Wilberforce was a "praying school" that stressed learning, service to one's race and nation, and above all, Godly living. It held compulsory chapel services twice per day and reflected the middle-class worldview of a relatively affluent black elite, though by 1880 Payne was beleaguered by demands to make his university and church more closely tied to the African-American folk culture of an increasingly Southern denomination. Three of the church's bishops – Payne, J. A. Shorter, and Benjamin W. Arnett – lived at Wilberforce, reinforcing the school's earnest piety. Payne was intense, rigidly disciplined, scholarly, and theologically conservative. He inveighed against emotional religion, the spirituals (which he called "cornfield ditties") and disrespect for church law; he took a stringent view of episcopal authority, especially his own; and his favorite theologian was Charles Hodge, Princeton Seminary's guardian of Reformed orthodoxy. On the other hand, unlike Princeton Seminary, Payne's university reverberated with the language of racial equality and black progress. Wilberforce took seriously its role as the "intellectual center of the AME Church" and its commitment to racial integration. It took pride that its predominantly black male faculty included three white female professors and an interracial marriage of two beloved professors, William S. Scarborough and S. C. Scarborough. On academic grounds Wilberforce was a disappointment to Ransom; AME bishop and historian Richard R. Wright Jr later remarked that Wilberforce was "little more than a high school" in the late nineteenth century. But Ransom loved the school for preaching and practicing racial equality: "Racial self-confidence, self-respect, dignity, honor, the ambition to achieve in every line of endeavor, were taught and encouraged."[8]

In that environment he belatedly joined the church. As a youth Ransom had enjoyed watching others come forward to be saved, especially when mourners wailed and rolled on the floor, and he felt the call to follow Jesus. But the "mourner's bench" was not for him; if he had to become the object of a frenzied spectacle to join the church, he could wait. Wilberforce provided the quiet, orderly religious atmosphere that was better suited to convert him. As a freshman Ransom joined the church; as a sophomore he transferred to Oberlin College. Ransom wanted a more rigorous education with a "broader and more liberal" curriculum. Accepting a scholarship to Oberlin he found the academic environment that he wanted, but not the social climate that he expected, despite Oberlin's abolitionist legacy. Black students were excluded from most of the college's social life, and, in the year that Ransom arrived on campus, a new regulation segregating African-American girls was instituted in the women's dining hall. Ransom helped to organize a protest against the new policy, gave a speech against it, and promptly lost his scholarship by faculty action. That bruising reaction sent him back to Wilberforce, cutting him deeply; a few years later he wrote an upbeat memoir of his college days that made no mention of his year at Oberlin.[9]

In a chastened and appreciative mood Ransom made the best of being at Wilberforce. On his first try he had worried that "a Faculty composed of colored men" probably did not compare to the better white schools. Now he was grateful that Wilberforce practiced racial equality and wanted him. On his first try he had chafed at the school's regimented social relations. Males and females were not permitted to speak to each other on campus or even quietly walk together; games and dancing were forbidden; meetings between males and females were permitted once per month in chaperoned "socials" lasting two hours; and Ransom felt estranged from his uneducated bride. None of that improved for him on his second try. He chafed for two more years at Wilberforce, yet made a home there and in the AME Church. At Oberlin Ransom felt called to ministry; at Wilberforce he decided to complete his college and theological education at the same time. Always short of money, Ransom vowed not to stay in school any longer than necessary.[10]

To train for the ministry at Wilberforce, however, required Ransom to be highly circumspect, because he had two delicate problems. One was his troubled marriage; Ransom said as little as possible about it and divorced his wife shortly after graduating from Wilberforce. The other problem was his theological liberalism, the origin of which he never explained. At Oberlin Ransom may have heard of liberal theology, but Oberlin in the 1880s was an outpost of militant antiliberalism in theology, having acquired the old Andover Seminary journal *Bibliotheca Sacra* as a forum for defending orthodoxy. Perhaps a Wilberforce or Oberlin teacher piqued Ransom's curiosity by criticizing liberal theologians. Perhaps he read Bushnell or a Unitarian theologian on his own. In any case, as Ransom later recounted, he spent much of his time at Wilberforce concealing his personal beliefs from theologian T. H. Jackson, whose orthodoxy was rigid and emphatic. Jackson tolerated no sign of heresy and was assiduous in searching for it. For Ransom, that created intellectual, moral, and vocational problems. He rejected Trinitarian doctrine, accepted evolutionary theory, and reasoned that all doctrines were "man-made," not divine. Finding it difficult to keep Jackson from detecting his liberal views, he was sensitive to the dubious ethics of concealment, and thus doubted whether he belonged in the ministry.[11]

In his junior year Ransom was licensed to preach, which gave him the opportunity to improve his exceptional speaking skills. In his senior year he served a church in nearby Selma, Ohio, where he courted his second wife, a student named Emma Connor; by then Ransom was determined to see if a theological liberal could make it in the AME ministry. Poetically he wrote to himself that he would not "sneak" deceitfully into God's temple for the sake of winning fame or acclaim: "I'd rather dwell in poverty obscure, and all the pangs of poverty endure, than for the honors which the Church can give, through life a timorous hypocrite to live." His 1886 graduating class at Wilberforce consisted of eight men and one woman. For years afterward he lamented that most Wilberforce students did not make it to graduation. Ransom's stepfather, not yet a Christian, was appalled that he wasted his education on the ministry; George Ransom considered it ridiculous for an educated black man to beg his living off poor blacks. Harriet Ransom, on the other hand, made a memorable scene at her son's graduation. Every member of the graduating class delivered an oration or essay; Ransom's oration was wildly applauded. Harriet Ransom, sobbing with joy, forced her way onto the stage to embrace her son. A reporter wrote that the scene evoked tears throughout the crowd; for the rest of his life Ransom remarked that he and his mother graduated together: "She saw the fruit of her sacrifices, the fulfillment of her hopes, and with characteristic impulsiveness gave expression to the happiness that thrilled her."[12]

Although he struggled for years with a troubled conscience about pretending to be orthodox, Ransom entered the ministry as a disciple of Payne. In 1886, when Ransom took his first pastorate, Payne had been a bishop for 34 years. For Payne, the cause of keeping African Methodism ascetic and impeccably orthodox was a consuming passion. He opposed the 1880 election of two Southern bishops (Richard H. Cain and Henry McNeal Turner), fearing that the creation of new AME schools in the South would jeopardize Wilberforce's orthodox influence and its quest for excellence. In 1880 Allen University (formerly Payne Institute) was established in Columbia, South Carolina; in 1881 Paul Quinn College was founded in Waco, Texas; in 1883 Edward Waters College was founded in Jacksonville, Florida; in 1885 Morris Brown College opened its doors in Atlanta, Georgia. Many African Methodists exulted that Paine's vision of an educated church and clergy was being realized in the establishment of new AME schools; Paine saw it very differently. It was better to have one strong, orthodox school than to have several weak, compromised ones, he protested.[13]

Bishop J. P. Campbell assigned Ransom to a tiny congregation of 13 members, most of them elderly, in Altoona, Pennsylvania and another congregation of seven women, five of them widows, in Hollidaysburg. Ransom's next assignment was a mission parish in Allegheny City, Pennsylvania that had five members; he objected to Payne, who chastised him, "Begone! Leave my presence! There are people there!" Ransom found hundreds of people there, "living in wretched tenements in the alleys, and in shanty boats along the river front." With his new wife Emma Connor he visited the tenements and boats daily, building up his church. He bought a house in a white neighborhood, which the neighbors promptly stoned, nearly hitting his infant son Reverdy Junior. Ransom bitterly protested the AME custom of assigning young pastors to impossible posts without regarding their talents; it was wasteful and degrading to send the church's most promising ministers to places that crushed their spirit. Sixty years later he was still complaining: "There can be no virtue in being hungry, or in being deprived of the ordinary comforts of life."[14]

Ransom used his connections to Payne and Wilberforce to get on a better career track. In April 1890 he published a sharp attack on C. S. Smith, director of the AME Sunday School Union, for using a revised version of the Apostles' Creed. Smith eliminated the phrase about Christ's descent into hell; Ransom acidly replied that it was a very serious thing for a church functionary to break the "golden chain of faith" just because he did not believe some part of the church's creed. Invoking Princeton theologian A. A. Hodge's phrase, Ransom charged that Smith's revision was a "dreadful violation" of Christian solidarity that led to mysticism and pantheism. Elsewhere he supported Payne's view that the AME was building too many "so-called colleges" that diminished Wilberforce, and he published a glowing memoir of his Wilberforce days that described the school as the pride and intellectual showcase of the AME Church. In September 1890 Payne rewarded him with an attractive parish in Springfield, Ohio. North Street Church had "carpets on the floor, cushioned pews, stained glass windows, and a marble pulpit," Payne told Ransom. On the other hand, he dolefully cautioned Ransom, his successor would undoubtedly "mar or destroy all you have been able to build up."[15]

Ransom's gratitude to Wilberforce was genuine, though it masked misgivings that he freely expressed in later years, and he may have tried to talk himself into Payne-style orthodoxy, though he later reported that his personal beliefs were liberal throughout his career. He gave three years to Springfield, acquired a reputation as an outstanding preacher, and attended the World's Parliament of Religion in Chicago, which was held in connection with the Columbian Exposition of 1893. The parliament and exposition both impressed him as momentous signs of modern progress. Taking pride that AME bishop Benjamin W. Arnett spoke at the parliament, Ransom enthused that it was a good thing for the world's religions to grow in mutual respect and understanding. He also attended lectures by Josiah Strong and Washington Gladden, and was introduced to Ida B. Wells, the national president of the Anti-Lynching League. Later that year, after Ransom had been promoted to St John Church in Cleveland, he stressed that African Americans shared in the progress of American civilization.

"In these closing years of the nineteenth century, 'progress' is a word upon every tongue," he observed. "Men of every rank and calling conjure with this word." American science, invention, manufacture, statecraft, art, literature and religion were flourishing. But Ransom cautioned that the true mark of progress was spiritual renewal, not growth in machines or products. It was Martin Luther defying the Catholic hierarchy, AME founder Richard Allen taking a "manly stand for manhood Christianity," and Abraham Lincoln issuing the Emancipation Proclamation. Black Americans profoundly appreciated the church, school, and home, which were the pillars of high civilization, Ransom observed. Wherever blacks moved, they promptly built churches. Despite being deprived of education, they made greater efforts to become literate than any people in history. Despite having their families ripped apart by slavery, they built new families as circles of virtue. All of this counted in the tally of American progress, he asserted. Yet for all of America's progress, the year 1893 witnessed "no abatement of the barbarities" that blacks suffered at the hands of white Americans. The USA was still a nation in which innocent blacks were lynched or burned by racist mobs. Not all blacks were innocent, Ransom allowed; true criminals of every race had to be punished: "But for these lynchings and burnings there can be no excuse, for the law is on the side of the lynchers; the courts, juries, militia are in their hands."[16]

He warned that America could not be truly civilized and savagely terrorize blacks at the same time: "This epidemic of mob violence, of outrage, and crime is making deep inroads upon the nation's constitutional authority and moral strength." It was shameful that "the southern lyncher, backed by public sentiment, has no need to seek cover for his crimes." Northern newspapers reported lynchings and burnings with rarely a word of condemnation. Southern authors rationalized racist murder by depict-ing blacks as too dangerous and inhuman to be dealt with by mere law; thus the lynchers were praised as saviors of civilization. Ransom observed that many American blacks, being marked for denigration and abuse, had lost all hope: "The field of opportunity is largely closed against us." Others fantasized about returning to Africa. America was not that hopeless, he urged. African Americans were Americans, and they needed to be courageous: "The man or the race who falters and retreats because the door of opportunity and endeavor is slammed in his face is unworthy of the goal he seeks . . . Let the Negro continue to act the brave, the manly part."[17]

That was Ransom's prophetic voice of judgment and inspiration. He also had a pastoral voice that preached the gospel of clean, ethical, productive living. Ransom admonished black youths to be morally serious, spurning the indulgences of white youth: "The white boys and girls of this country have standing at their backs centuries of glorious achievements, and if they stop to play a little by the way, or if they stray from the way and give themselves to vices and follies, they have a foothold in the earth that you don't possess." White youths could afford to be frivolous, he explained, because they had power. Their fathers owned the banks and manufacturing companies. They stood to inherit the mansions on Cleveland's Euclid Avenue and Prospect Street, where John D. Rockefeller, Henry Payne, and other Standard Oil millionaires lived.[18]

Ministering to the city's largest black congregation, Ransom despaired of black fathers who gambled and black mothers who drank. He noted, with incredulity, that some mothers dispatched their children to buy alcohol: "No matter what excuse you frame for a woman that sends her child to a saloon, I say there is something the matter with the mother-heart in that woman." That must have been a painfully conflicted jeremiad. Ransom adored his mother and was grateful to her, but all the women in his family circle drank whiskey, as he recalled elsewhere: "Every two or three days, they would give us children ten or fifteen cents and a little tin bucket and send us for whiskey. Every morning before prayers and breakfast, they each drank a toddy and gave some to all the children." Throughout his career Ransom was noted for not being judgmental toward those who struggled with sexual moral lapses or alcoholism, a fact that was surely connected to his own embarrassing first marriage and his lifelong struggle with alcoholism. Near the end of his life he confessed with typical honesty that his alcoholism had been "a serious handicap to my reputation, my usefulness, and my spiritual power."[19]

In Cleveland, confronted by stark class divisions and increasingly drawn to national politics, Ransom decided that he was a Socialist. In this area he took a distinctive path. Payne avoided politics and racial justice activism, concentrating entirely on build-ing up the AME Church. Arnett, however, was deeply involved in Republican Party politics. He served one term in the Ohio legislature (1885–7), introduced a bill that ended school segregation in the state, and cultivated close ties with Ohio Republican Senator Mark Hanna and Ohio governor William McKinley. In the 1890s Hanna was the leading powerbroker in the national Republican party; McKinley was his protégé. Arnett worked hard at politics, which, for him, consisted mostly of winning patronage positions for his relatives and allies. His political ministry legitimized Ransom's political interests, and he became a close friend and protector to Ransom. Yet Ransom took little interest in patronage or building his own political machine. For him, the best kind of political ministry focused on electing people who advanced the interests of black Americans. He advocated a socialist-oriented politics of racial justice, not winning personal favors from establishment politicians. Thus he formed a local chapter of the Anti-Lynching League and served as its president. In 1896 Arnett placed him in the best city for that kind of ministry, Chicago, giving Ransom a choice between a relatively affluent parish on Wabash Avenue, Quinn Chapel and a large parish in the black section of town west of State Street, Bethel Church. Ransom chose Bethel Church, where Ida B. Wells was a member, and soon drew crowds that overflowed the sanctuary's seating capacity of 900.[20]

At first he flattered himself that the crowds were drawn to his spellbinding preaching, but then Ransom noticed that other black churches were overflowing too. The Great Migration was on, bringing huge numbers of blacks to Chicago from the South; Ransom later recalled, "The number of these people increased so rapidly that the colored clergymen of the city were bewildered. They were unprepared by training, experience and vision, to cope with the moral, social and economic conditions so suddenly thrust upon them." In that environment he got his first taste of local political activism, helped Wells establish a kindergarten at Bethel Church, and organized a "Men's Sunday Club" that became the prototype for AME "Sunday Forums" across the country. The Sunday club, which met weekly to discuss moral and social issues, swelled to over 500 members. Ransom also opened the church to the Manassa Society, an organization of biracial married couples that grew to include over 350 couples; during his eight years in Chicago Ransom wed 104 black males to white women and three white men to black women. Taking on the charged topic of heredity and environment, he contended that environment was far more important than heredity as a determinant of intelligence, character, and success. And he joined a new racial justice organization led by Wells, the Afro-American Council, which grew out of the old Afro-American League in which Wells had also played a leading role.[21]

The Afro-American League had begun as a militant racial justice group led by New York socialist T. Thomas Fortune and Cleveland journalist Harry C. Smith, but in the 1890s it swung toward Booker T. Washington-style accommodation and fizzled out, just as blacks were stripped of their rights throughout the South and the Supreme Court provided legal sanction for racial segregation in *Plessey v. Ferguson*. Meeting in 1898, the Afro-American Council's first order of business was to determine what kind of civil rights group it proposed to be in the face of disenfranchisement, lynching, and segregation. Would it take Washington's path of preaching bootstrap uplift, accepting segregation, keeping quiet about lynching, and denouncing black militancy?

Ransom pressed hard for a verdict on that question. Despite being in Chicago, Washington skipped the group's founding meeting, but he summoned its president, AME Zion bishop Alexander Waters, to meet with him in his hotel room, where he admonished Waters to restrain the group's militant wing. That infuriated the radicals, for whom Ransom, freshly appointed as a vice president of the council, stridently replied,

I know of no man who has received more advertising from his connection with the Negro race than has Booker T. Washington. He has posed as the leader of the colored people and the Moses who was to lead his people out of the wilderness. Yet he has hung around the outskirts of this council casting aspersions and contempt on its proceedings. He has refused to come inside. He sat in his room at the Palmer House and sent for our president to wait upon him. No such man ought to claim to be our leader. We went the country to know he is nothing to us. We hold him in contempt.

That brought a downpour of editorial condemnation on Ransom for denigrating the Moses of black America. He backed down, assuring his critics that he respected Washington and should not have spoken so harshly. Even W. E. B. Du Bois judged that Ransom had gone too far. Black and white moderates revered Washington; a radical faction led by William Monroe Trotter was bitterly anti-Washington; Du Bois wanted to establish a viable alternative to accommodation and radical belligerence. The Afro-American Council eventually swung in favor of Bookerism, causing Ransom to drop out. But Ransom had made a mark, serving notice that the cause of militant racial justice had a significant new voice in a surprising place, the AME ministry.[22]

He flourished in Chicago, which he later called the site of his golden years. Wright had the same impression, remarking that Ransom "fell under the influence of the 'Social Gospel'" during his Chicago ministry, though Wright may not have realized that Ransom was an ardent social gospeler when he got there. In Chicago Ransom forged friendships with Jane Addams, Graham Taylor, Mary MacDowell, superlawyer Clarence Darrow, and prominent social gospel minister Frank W. Gunsaulus, as well as black civic leaders Theodore Jones, Edward H. Morris, Edward H. Wright, and S. Lang Williams. His friendships with Darrow and Gunsaulus were especially close and trusting. Darrow, an agnostic humanist, was deeply involved in racial justice causes, often providing legal counsel for black organizations and individuals. Like Du Bois, Ransom was highly attuned to the varieties of white prejudice; both of them judged that Darrow did not have any.[23]

In political economics Ransom outflanked most of his friends to the left, urging that a strong commitment to social justice should lead to democratic socialism. Fundamentally, he argued, socialism was about democracy as a means and end. It opposed anarchic government and overcentralized government, seeking to make ordinary people the owners of their economic fate. It centered on the rights and needs of human beings, which were universal: "Socialism and industrial reform is not a question of race; it is not confined to the boundaries of any nation or continent; it is the question of man." Socialism was the sign and goal of the coming solidarity of the human race, Ransom urged. It had little following among American blacks, but that would change as blacks increasingly took account of the big picture. Until recently, blacks struggled merely to survive poverty, ignorance, homelessness, denigration, and violence. They had little occasion to reflect on "the deep questions that concern the destiny of nations or the welfare of mankind." Moreover, Ransom observed, it did not help the cause of black socialism that most of the Labor movement was racist. The Federation of Labor had no color line, but most labor organizations had the word "white" in their constitutions, and they despised blacks for taking jobs as strikebreakers. Ransom argued that the answer to this sorry picture was to include blacks in the universal struggle for economic justice and socialism:

> We shall see the steeples of a new civilization rising. A civilization which shall neither be Anglo-American, Asiatic, nor African; but one which, recognizing the unity of the race and the brotherhood of man, will accord to each individual the full reward which the free exercise of his powers has won, and the right to stand upon an equal plane and share all of the blessings of our common heritage.[24]

Bethel Church had a group called the IBW Woman's Club, named after Ida B. Wells, which Ransom addressed in 1897. He told the group that he took pride in being an American Christian, because American Christianity produced the "highest type of man" in the world. Confucianism, Buddhism, and Islam all produced estimable human beings, he allowed, but none compared to the American Christian, who had the largest heart and brain, the most productive economy, and the strongest civilization in the world. America's major drawback was that it degraded the manhood of black males and, even worse, the womanhood of black females:

> Our womanhood was degraded by the slave hut. No woman under heaven could develop and grow into large proportions under those conditions. The miserable hovel or hut which she was compelled to call her home and the conditions under which she was compelled to live meant stamping out the higher and nobler instincts in her nature and the degradation of womanhood. The springs of maternal affection were almost sapped by the abominable and damnable system. Wifely devotion was made almost impossible.

Ransom reminded his audience that all of this was "recent history," and thus affected the present. It was painful but necessary to recall this history, just as it was difficult but necessary to believe that a much better history lay ahead: "We find that we are not cultured yet, that social life among us is very crude; we have only the rudiments of it." But it was happening, undeniably: "There is coming a time – the day is almost at hand – when the better elements among us are beginning to class themselves together, and they are saying to those who are not fit for respectable association, 'If you want to stand on this plane, you must qualify yourself by virtue, by intelligence and culture so to stand.'"[25]

When America went to war in 1898 in the name of its manifest destiny, Ransom was eager to help the cause. His connection to President McKinley, through Arnett, was a factor, though Ransom resented McKinley's lack of political backbone on racial justice. Discovering that the only black American unit in the Illinois State Militia was a battalion headquartered in Chicago, Ransom campaigned for a black regiment led by black officers. Upon winning the Illinois governor's support, Ransom recruited the full quota of the regiment at his own expense, using Bethel Church as a sleeping quarter for volunteers. When soldiers returned from the Spanish–American War, he spoke for the city of Chicago at a huge celebration. For years afterward Ransom shook his head at anti-imperialists who protested that the republic was ending: "However loudly they may shout their notes of warning, the great mass of the nation is borne forward by the current of events. The step, once taken, cannot be retraced. In a new sense we have become a world power." Ransom stood squarely with the social gospel faction that wanted to Christianize imperialism. America at its best invaded only to liberate, he averred: "While other nations subjugate alien peoples, we must liberate them. While others exploit the material resources of foreign lands, we must develop them." It was a good thing to have a missionary spirit, if the goal was human solidarity and liberation. Christianity and socialism were inherently missionary faiths: "The necessity for coopera-tion among men, their mutual interests, and the common good are bounded by no race or clime. The destiny of our race is bound up with the destiny of humanity, even as the destiny of our nation is bound up with the destiny of the world."[26]

By 1900 Chicago was the national center of a rising settlement movement, but there were no settlement houses in black communities. Ransom asked Addams and Taylor what it would take to create one; Addams stressed it would take a lot of money. Through a California friend Addams made the first contribution to Ransom's center and helped him get financial backing from Mrs George Pullman (widow of the

Pullman railroad founder) and Robert L. Lincoln (Pullman company president and son of President Abraham Lincoln). Ransom moved into old railroad mission on Dearborn Street and named it the Institutional Church and Social Settlement. He had Arnett's blessing, but faced intense opposition from AME colleagues. The center featured a gymnasium, dining area, kitchen, eight large rooms, and an auditorium seating 1,200. Its program, largely modeled on Taylor's program at Chicago Commons, included boys and girls clubs, a nursery, a kindergarten, sewing and cooking classes, concerts, discussion groups, and lectures. Ransom contended that the center served vital needs that most black churches did not address. From the beginning his black clerical colleagues bitterly disagreed, especially AME pastors. They charged that Ransom replaced gospel evangelism with social work, copied white social gospelers, and took unfair advantage of his large following at Bethel Church. Sometimes they claimed that his work undermined their programs. Ransom replied that he preached and practiced the gospel, Bethel's support was a good thing, and the parallel church programs were fictional. Many years later he recalled: "It was entirely beyond their conception of what a church should be. Their only appeal was preaching, praying, singing, shouting, baptizing and Holy Communion, but going out into the street and highways, bearing a message of social, moral, economic and civic salvation they did not believe to be a function of the church."[27]

In 1903 he found a more dangerous kind of trouble by campaigning against the gambling racket on Chicago's South side. Infuriated by racketeers who preyed on black school children, Ransom implored the police to crack down, but was told they could not find the perpetrators. He persuaded a journalist to take photographs of the numbers offices out of which the racketeers operated, but the reporter was assaulted and his camera smashed. Finally Ransom preached a series of sermons against the gambling trade; in reply his Institutional Church building was dynamited, blowing out the windows and blasting cracks in the walls and foundation stones. The *Chicago Tribune* editorialized, "The colored clergyman against whom this attack was directed is doing a noble work and one much needed, for many of his own people are victims, but neither he nor all the clergymen in the city, acting alone, can break up this nefarious business."[28]

By the end of his Chicago ministry in 1904 Ransom had a national reputation for his preaching eloquence, the settlement ministry, taking on the numbers racket, mediating a stockyard strike, and his ongoing feud with Washington. In 1903 black militants in Boston led by William Monroe Trotter challenged Washington at a tumultuous public meeting that the press called "the Boston riot." The following Sunday Ransom declared from his pulpit that Washington was not a true leader or representative of black Americans. It was perverse to call Washington a black leader when he surrendered the rights of black Americans: "A colored man should have the right to vote, to own his own home, to transact his business, have a fair trial if he commits a crime, just as a white man does." That was what black Americans really believed, Ransom asserted. It looked otherwise from the black press only because Washington and his allies controlled the black press.[29]

That kind of argument went down very badly with most of Ransom's ministerial colleagues, who also resented his growing fame. Some of them spent ample time scheming to get rid of him. By 1904 they had convinced the AME's new presiding bishop of the Chicago area, C. T. Shaffer, to dispatch Ransom to the Indiana Conference as a presiding elder. A close ally of Washington, Bishop Abram Grant, played a key role in hatching the plan. Hearing of his imminent departure, Ransom confronted Shaffer, who responded coolly that he made appointments only at the denomination's annual conference. Ransom replied, "You are a liar." He knew that Shaffer had already cut a deal, and he informed the presiding bishop that he had no intention of going along. Knowing that he still had a protector in Arnett, who had become presiding bishop of the New England conference, Ransom resigned from the Institutional Church and transferred himself to New England, accepting Arnett's offer of a church in New Bedford, Massachusetts. Richard R. Wright Jr, who assisted Ransom at the Institutional Church and later became a bishop, recalled that Ransom's opponents were determined to make the settlement "a regular AME church, to cut out the social foolishness and bring religion back."[30]

Mainstreaming the Black Social Gospel

New Bedford was a shock for Ransom. He was used to large crowds, noise, and strenuous activities; in New Bedford all was small and tranquil: "Here I found the atmosphere and people so quaint, so subdued, so unlike the general forms of community life I have ever known, I sometimes thought I was like a disembodied spirit trying to get acquainted with the modes of life in the spirit world." He had met plenty of bland, colorless white people in the past, but in New Bedford even the black people were that way. Their worship was cold and formal, they had no spontaneity, and they spurned the spirituals; many were also kindly. Ransom made some friends in New Bedford, but was relieved, after one year, when Arnett found a better fit for him, at the Charles Street AME Church in Boston.[31]

That year, 1905, anti-Washington militants organized the all-black Niagara Movement to replace the politics of Bookerite accommodation. W. E. B. Du Bois, who tagged Washington as "the Great Accommodator," was the group's leader; William Monroe Trotter of the National Equal Rights League (NERL), a militant group, was another major player in the Niagara Movement; Ransom was a founding member. The Niagara Movement stood for "full manhood suffrage," the abolition of discrimination in public accommodation, freedom of speech and assembly, universal education, and equal rights regardless of race or class. In 1906 the group held its second conference at Harper's Ferry, West Virginia, to honor the centenary of John Brown's birth, 47 years after Brown's band of radical abolitionists had seized the Federal arsenal there. Ransom gave the featured address, on "The Spirit of John Brown."[32]

A person like Brown appeared only once or twice in a thousand years, Ransom declared. He towered above all others, like Mt Blanc, the king of the mountains, or like Melchizedek (Genesis 14), who had no predecessors or successors. Brown was a singular man of action who belonged to no party or school. The abolitionists had spellbinding speakers like Henry Ward Beecher and Wendell Phillips, but Brown felt called by God to *do* something: "God sent him to Harper's Ferry to become a traitor to the government in order that he might be true to the slave." Brown tried to spark the slaves to rise up and strike for their freedom. Spurning the slow trickle of the Underground Railroad, he set fire to the slave system in its homeland. That was still the point, Ransom urged: "The Negro will never enjoy the fruits of freedom in this country until he first demonstrates his manhood and maintains his rights here *in the South*, where they are the most violently protested and most completely denied."[33]

He stressed that 1906 was not much different from 1859. Before the Civil War, the Northern states and federal government allowed the South to treat blacks pretty much however it wanted, and that was still the case. President Roosevelt was "absolutely silent" about enforcing the Fifteenth Amendment, and his secretary of war, William Howard Taft, insultingly dismissed blacks as political children. Ransom allowed that Taft was right about one thing: American blacks had a "childlike faith" in the Republican party. But finally, "the scales are falling from the Negro's eyes. He is being disillusioned by the acts of a *Republican Congress*, the speeches of members of a *Republican cabinet*, and the silence of a *Republican president*." Politically awakened blacks realized that Republicans were very nearly as bad as Democrats on racial justice, Ransom observed. Despite contrary appearances, American blacks were not divided about what they wanted; all 10 million of them wanted an equal opportunity to "every avenue of American life." They were divided about how to get there. One group took the very slow road, counseling patient submission to humiliation and degradation; the other group refused to be "remanded to an inferior place." The second group recognized the importance of property and economic development, but refused to barter "its manhood for the sake of gain." It believed in hard work, but did not believe "in artisans being treated as industrial serfs."[34]

Ransom declared that the soul of John Brown marched on in the courageous resistance of the second group: "The Negroes who are aggressively fighting for their rights have the press against them and the weight of public opinion. They are branded as disturbers of the harmony between the races, but they have the same spirit that animated the founders of this nation." Ransom drew out the link to the founders. The Niagara Movement was not simply a fight for the rights of American blacks, he argued. It defended the American nation by calling the USA to its own best meaning, fighting on the ground of "our common manhood and equality." If the Declaration of Independence was not a lie, and a righteous God still ruled in heaven, it had to be that American blacks were on their way to taking their place in America's household as equal to all others.[35]

Ransom had a vision of American blacks and whites going forth "hand in hand" to teach the world how to build a democratic, interracial, Christian society. It was not an incidental theme for him, or something that he trotted out merely at wartime or on ceremonial occasions. It was fundamental to his black social gospel vision of a redeemed creation. He stressed that if American blacks attained their rights in the USA, they would be in a position to play a uniquely redemptive role in the world by virtue of being Americans:

> The Negro himself can perhaps do more than any other to silence confusion by proving for himself and for the blacks throughout the world that he is capable of attaining to the very highest and best within this civilization. For the Negro here is the only Negro on the face of the earth in vital daily contact with the white man within the same government on terms of equality. If he fails through ignorance, incapacity, laziness, shiftlessness, courage, in a sense the black race throughout the world has failed.

Ransom exhorted black and white Americans to show the world that color was superficial. What mattered was the "common humanity and manhood" of all human beings: "From the shores of this country the Negro and the white man should go forth, hand in hand, to teach Russia, Japan, England, India, Europe, and Africa how men of different races may live together upon terms of equality, of fraternity, and of peace."[36]

That vision of global transformation flew on the wings of the Progressivist belief in progress and the social gospel expectation of Christianizing and democratizing the world. Yet Ransom also watched the racial pathology of his country grow more insidious and hopeless. In 1911, at the height of white social gospel optimism, he observed that America's racial oppression had become so terrible that white progressives cowered even from mentioning it: "We have actually arrived at the place where it requires courage and may entail sacrifice – political, moral, or financial – for a man, black or white, to plead for justice for the Negro." The white person who spoke up for the rights of blacks was immediately denigrated as "a fanatic who would foist upon the white people social equality with the blacks, while making them in some sections politically dominant." For the black person who stood up for the selfhood and rights of black Americans, the social punishments ranged from a long list of epithets to physical violence. Remarking on President Taft's announcement that he would appoint no blacks to office in any community where white people objected, Ransom reminded his audience at Park Street Church in Boston that Taft belonged to the party that blacks routinely supported. He, on the other hand, supported Eugene Debs and the Socialists.[37]

Ransom's two years in Boston heightened his profile in the church and racial justice movements. The city took pride in its abolitionist legacy, and it remained the national center of radical thought and action on behalf of racial justice. It was the home of Trotter and the NERL, which outlasted the milder Niagara Movement. Ransom made many friendships there, deciding that he had found a home. It helped that his brief stay in Boston coincided with the centenaries honoring the birth of John Brown and William Lloyd Garrison.

He gave bravura speeches at both events. Ransom's speech at Harper's Ferry had a tumultuous reception; antislavery veterans exulted that they had heard nothing like it since the abolitionist stem-winders of the 1850s. His speech honoring Garrison at Fanuiel Hall in Boston received a similar reaction. The *Boston Herald* reported that "The applause was simply tremendous, frequently compelling the speaker to pause for several minutes. At its close the scene was indescribable. Women wept, men embraced each other. Guests on the platform rushed upon the orator with congratulations, the program was forgotten and only the playing of the band restored order and made it possible to proceed." Julia Ward Howe, composer of the "Battle Hymn of the Republic," caressed Ransom's hands and stared at him adoringly, which got a lot of newspaper play.[38]

But the AME Church in New England had many pastors who were not impressed with Ransom's press clippings, his radical friends, or Julia Ward Howe's admiration. Having been rescued by Arnett from his conservative detractors in Chicago, Ransom found similar trouble in New England, albeit mostly at the murmuring level. Getting to Boston was his last favor from Arnett, who died in 1906. After that Ransom was on his own in the church, as he soon realized. In 1907 Arnett's successor, Henry McNeal Turner, informed Ransom that he had received many complaints about him, enough to raise the question whether he should remove Ransom from Boston: "This is not saying that I am going to do it, but I fear I may want to do it, from the contingency of present apprehension." Ransom was incredulous; his ministry in Boston was a smashing success: "No minister belonging to my group was so much in demand for the various activities in the city of Boston, as I was." Two months later Turner moved him to Bethel Church in New York City. At least Bethel, located on West 25th Street, was a large and prestigious congregation; Ransom was too big to be shuffled off to Indiana. He took the transfer with a heavy heart, gave five years to Bethel Church, and plunged into local politics.[39]

Appalled that New York City had no black police officers to speak of, Ransom helped Tammany Hall win the mayoral race. His reward was to get blacks on the police force and involved in the Democratic party, which broke the Republican monopoly in New York in the black community. In 1909 he played an active role in cofounding the National Association for the Advancement of Colored People (NAACP), and he gave half-hearted aid to Booker T. Washington in a bizarre court case that ended in a hung jury. Two years later, at a centennial memorial for Wendell Phillips at Plymouth Church in Brooklyn, Ransom ferociously ripped into Washington for betraying black Americans. The first speaker at the centennial, scholar Charles Edward Russell, put the audience to sleep with an hour-long recitation. Plymouth pastor Newell Dwight Hillis asked Ransom if he would prefer to give his speech on a later occasion; Ransom assured Hillis that he would bring the crowd to life. In an electrifying address Ransom declared: "The traitors within the ranks of our race are known. They have neither our confidence nor our hearts." The Bookerites were taken seriously, he charged, only because they were bankrolled by white wealth, used by politicians for partisan advantage, and lionized by a newspaper establishment "whose approving voice is the mouthpiece of a decadent public opinion which would let the Negro question 'work itself out' under the baleful influence of the many degrading forms of Jim Crowism."[40]

For the rest of his life, accommodation and Jim Crow were linked inseparably in Ransom's mind. In 1906 he had a bruising encounter with Jim Crowism on a train to a speaking engagement in Alabama, where he was abused for sitting in the white section. Recalling the incident over 40 years later, what stuck with Ransom, as always, was the lesson that accommodating white bigotry or seeking to pacify it did nothing to reduce, much less eliminate, the oppression of American blacks. Hampton Institute poured out accommodating, vocationally trained blacks every year, but that did not stop the state of Virginia from tightening its Jim Crow restrictions. Atlanta had a black college on "every hill," yet blacks were murdered in Georgia "with more impunity than any man would dare to take the life of a good dog."[41]

Ransom's years in New York coincided with the establishment of the Federal Council of Churches, in which he was active for many years. He represented the AME on the Federal Council, served on the council's executive committee, and chaired its Race Relations Commission. On the religion and politics of social salvation apart from racial justice he was an unabashed admirer of the council, stating that it was the best and most effective institution in American Protestantism. On racial justice he appreciated that the council occasionally issued fine words – Ransom usually wrote them – but he protested that nothing changed in the council's member churches. One statement received a typically distressing reaction. The council observed,

> There is also among the Negroes an increasing distrust of the white race, and a growing contempt for its religion and its sense of justice – feelings which are breeding a new spirit of antagonism and aggression. And through all this tangle of suspicion and hatred, in this professedly Christian land, mob violence strikes unimpeded, deepening the Negro's distrust, and inflaming the worst passions of lawless Whites.

At the council's next meeting, a white minister from Texas denounced the statement, contending that lynching was a legitimate method of protecting white women. The

Federal Council, asked to repudiate the statement in the interest of "peace and harmony," responded by toning it down, declaring that lynching aggravated the crime problem, weakened the force of law, and threatened to destroy civilization. Ransom resigned himself to milder admonition: "It did not satisfy radicals like myself and others, but we realized that we were living in the United States and not in the millennium."[42]

Near the end of his New York ministry in 1912, after he had already accepted his next post, Ransom revealed that his passion for racial justice had belatedly tempered his enthusiasm for American manifest destiny. On June 5 the Taft administration invaded Cuba to protect American interests. Two weeks later, on the eve of the Republican National Convention, Ransom expanded on his stock theme that American blacks had lingered too long in a pathetic reliance on the Republican party while their rights were annulled. The USA was not the only place where blacks suffered under vicious racism, he observed. Wherever the white man roamed, he proclaimed his lordship over darker-skinned people. Now the US Marines were proclaiming it in Cuba. Ransom declared,

> We are against any American government in Cuba whose object is to set up a white man's government on that island. If this government by its might crushes the present revolt of the blacks of Cuba against injustice, it may by its intervention proclaim peace, but it will be the peace of despotism and everlasting disgrace to a nation whose chief claim to greatness rests upon the fact that it stands for free self-government without distinction of blood, religion, or race.

He was finished with enlisting black Americans to subdue people of color in foreign lands. Instead of putting down brown insurgents in the Philippines or black ones in Cuba, Ransom declared that he would prefer to see every black American soldier discharged, court-martialed, or imprisoned for desertion.[43]

By then he had made a career move that rescued him from the whims and politicking of bishops. In 1912 Ransom was elected editor of the *AME Church Review*, which gave him an independent base as a general officer of the denomination, responsible only to the General Conference. It also gave him a vehicle to convert many AME clergy to his viewpoint and legitimize himself, both of which he accomplished in his 12 years as the journal's editor. Founded in 1884, the *AME Review* was a quarterly journal with denominational backing, not a sectarian bulletin board, though it also covered denominational news. Open to writers and topics beyond the AME Church, it featured prominent black voices (Frederick Douglass and Frances Ellen Harper were early contributors) and, more importantly, provided an outlet for lesser known authors. Ransom's predecessor as editor, medical college professor C. V. Roman, looked down on preachers; losing the journal to Ransom was a shock to him. But Ransom sustained the journal's literary quality, widened its scope and audience, and was reelected by large majorities in 1916 and 1920.

Under his direction the *AME Review* had four objectives: to feature the best black scholarship in America; educate the church and its ministry; report on all major developments in theology, ethics, culture, science, and the arts; and advocate racial justice. Ransom aimed directly at what his friend Du Bois called "the talented tenth," the educated black elite. On his watch the journal contained scholarly articles by W. S. Scarborough and Kelly Miller, poetry by Georgia Douglas Johnson and James Weldon

Johnson, and activist pieces by William Monroe Trotter, T. Thomas Fortune, and Oswald Garrison Villard.[44]

Persistently Ransom expounded on what it meant, psychologically and morally, to be proud of one's blackness. "Find a man who has no pride and you have one whose past is inglorious and whose future is without hope," he wrote. Pride motivated human beings to adventure, risk, endure, and triumph. Ransom liked to say there was a "pride of race" that lifted the "gifted spirits" of a group to greatness, winning "a crown of fadeless immortality." There was also a pride of race that bred intolerance and contempt; whenever it prevailed in a dominant class, it produced shrunken souls, "like a withered leaf." The ideal was a pride of personality that transcended race. Grounded in the recognition of the divine light within each soul, "this pride becomes the highest form of meekness which inherits the earth and the heaven, too." It had peers, but no superiors "in a world which slowly, more and more, revolves from darkness into light."[45]

Though his later work skewered white supremacist versions of manifest destiny, Ransom retained his more inclusive idea of it, working both sides of a dialectics of manifest destiny and black consciousness. In 1920 he made sense of the USA's refusal to join the League of Nations by invoking a strained analogy between the American government and the AME Church. The Monroe Doctrine had no place in the US Constitution, he observed, yet it was "the most zealously guarded and sacredly cherished" statement of the principles by which the USA related to other nations. The AME Church had its own Monroe Doctrine, the principles of AME founder Richard Allen. In this doctrine, discrimination in the church of Christ on the basis of nationality or race was forbidden. Just as the USA stayed true to its anti-imperial identity by staying out of the League of Nations, the AME Church steered clear of all alliances and programs "that would invade or compromise the Negro's religious liberty, equality, and manhood."[46]

The situation for blacks in the USA was terrible and desperate, Ransom stressed, yet it was also distinctly promising, filled with redemptive possibilities that reverberated to the ends of the earth. On the one hand, "the white man yields nothing, even to his own poor laboring masses, through sympathy or love. He yields not to the persuasion of logic or the sanctity of his religious creeds. He only yields or compromises in the face of aggressive, determined, uncompromising power."[47] Ransom preached the necessity of gaining black power for redemptive ends. Yet, by virtue of being Americans, he usually added, black Americans had precious advantages over all other blacks in the world: "He is the best housed, the best fed, the most intelligent, the best educated, and enjoys more freedom in the United States of America than any other group of Negroes on the face of the earth."[48]

More than any other group, the black American "placed his faith in God and the brotherhood of man set forth in the principles of American democracy." Thus, the dialectic came together in the African-American quest for equal rights and social justice. America had what the world needed, but its redemptive power was diminished by white America's mistreatment of its black population, which stood for Americanism at its best. The more power and well-being that black Americans gained, the more the USA became the best version of itself: "We have it in our power to be foremost in the rank of the men and women who are the salt of the earth and the light of the world for all men everywhere who strive for peace on earth and goodwill among men."[49]

Ransom's tireless preaching of that message won a large following in the AME Church, which carried him to a bishop's chair. Editing a quarterly magazine was not a full-time vocation for him; thus he launched a mission church in New York's "Black Tenderloin" district that he named the Church of Simon of Cyrene. Here he ministered to what he called "the bad Negroes . . . the Negroes of the slums," often lamenting that mainline black denominations like the AME Church were just as middle class and cut off from the urban poor as the mainline white denominations. "The Negroes of character, intelligence and means have withdrawn themselves too far from the ignorant, the depraved and struggling mass," he observed, though he also sympathized: "These cannot rise without their aid, but the more neglected will tend to drag the upper stratum of the race down to the depth wherein they lie." Somehow, he urged, "these two extremes" had to be brought together, "until each stands uplifted under the inspiration of a quickening touch, girded with new power and strength and animated with unity of purpose."[50]

In the early stages his mission church was fiercely resented by AME clergy, who charged that Ransom was on another ego trip, one power base was not enough for him, and he was sure to steal members from them. The loudest complainer was Benjamin W. Arnett Jr, Ransom's successor at Bethel Church, who made Ransom promise not to poach members from him. Ransom and his wife Emma shared the life of the urban poor, toured the local saloons, gambling joints, and prostitution houses, and "said nothing about religion whatever" except to those who made their way to his church. In 1918 Ransom ran for Congress as an independent supported by the United Civic League of New York. Running mostly as a protest against Republican arrogance toward blacks, he got a visit from a Republican official who offered him a state office, then $5,000, to withdraw from the race; Ransom told the official to go to hell. The Republicans responded by successfully challenging his petitions, knocking his name off the ballot.[51]

Ransom did not really want to be a bishop, because that meant being a church administrator. But 12 years as a general officer of the church gave him a national base in the denomination, and he had spent his entire career trying to become as influential as possible. Thus he found it impossible to resist the "weight, authority, influence, and . . . power" that came with the position. In 1924 he was elected the forty-eighth bishop of the AME Church, overcoming a Southern block desperate not to have a radical Du Bois-type as a bishop. Shortly before the election he visited Harriet Ransom, who told him, "God has answered my prayer. He let His glory shine round about. When you are elected let me know."[52]

He lost none of his edge or fire during his 28 years as a bishop; on the other hand, it was true, as Ransom feared, that the job turned him into an administrative functionary. His best speeches and writings were his early ones; afterwards his life was consumed with committee work, financial planning, episcopal supervision, and personnel decisions. He supervised the AME churches of Kentucky, Louisiana, Ohio, Pennsylvania, South Carolina, Tennessee, and West Virginia; struggled valiantly, but failed, to merge the three black Methodist denominations; founded the Fraternal Council of Negro Churches, which he served as president; and chaired Wilberforce University's board of trustees. In a denomination plagued with factionalism and mediocre success at reaching across its class divide, Ransom found much of his administrative work grinding and emotionally draining. In his years at the *AME Review* he campaigned for a merger of the AME, AME Zion, and Colored Methodist Episcopal (derived from the old Methodist Episcopal Church, South) churches. In 1922, Union seemed within reach. But aspirants for the bishopric in both denominations did not like their chances for election in a united church, and by then there was too much history to overcome. Recognizing that merger was a lost cause for his generation, Ransom founded the Fraternal Council of Negro Churches, an association of 12 black denominations, in 1934. It met until 1939, lapsed for two years, and tried again in 1942, but never became a vital organization. The council lacked funding and leaders who had time for it. Ransom also played a major role in an emotionally grueling ecclesiastical court case against a bishop charged with defrauding the church; for months he fretted that the moral integrity of the denomination was at stake. In 1941 his beloved partner Emma died, after 44 years of sharing his ministerial work; two years later Ransom married a former Wilberforce dean, Georgia Myrtle Teal.[53]

In his last years the black nationalist strain of Ransom's thought was stronger than the socialist and social gospel strains. In the 1930s it amazed him that the same nation that demeaned and terrorized its own blacks could muster so much sympathy for persecuted Jews, Armenians, and Irish. Repeatedly Ransom protested that blacks in America had never been anything but loyal Americans and faithful Christians, but what did it get them? For generations American blacks believed that if they went to church, showed good character, got an education, and learned a trade, they would be granted equal rights in the USA, "but their disillusionment is almost complete, since they find Christ has not been able to break the American color line. If Jesus wept over Jerusalem, he should have for America an ocean of tears." Ransom observed that white Americans feared their precious culture would be Africanized; thus they repressed blacks viciously. But why were they so fearful? "We hear no fear expressed of our country being Germanized or Jewized; we hear no cry going up from North or South against Irish political ascendancy. Is there any evidence anywhere in a single page of American history where the Negro has been less patriotic and true to our institutions than any of these elements which we have named?"[54]

American blacks had many problems of their own to overcome, Ransom stressed; it was cruelly perverse that they also had to overcome a hateful, violent, fearful white majority that believed in its own superiority. Ignorance was a huge problem in the black community "because he is denied in every possible way any encouragement to learn." There was much poverty, "because he must receive always the lowest wage when permitted work." There were many slums, "because segregation forces him there, and studied policy denies him modern sanitation and health supervision." But some things were getting better Ransom observed: "He is recovering from a condition of promiscuous breeding and concubinage to one in which family life is being established and respected. He is learning to respect law, despite unlawful mobocracy both in certain courts and in the commonwealth . . . He is increasing in race-consciousness, racial self-respect, racial self-reliance."[55]

Speaking to the Second Parliament of Religion in 1933, Ransom took no interest in conference pieties that all religions were essentially alike, and made no pretense of disavowing theological imperialism of an ethical, liberal, inclusive sort. The religion of Jesus was the absolute religion, he asserted. Nothing else came close it: "Jesus taught that God is the father of all mankind; all people of every race are brothers and sisters, and are therefore equals. They should be united and governed by the Supreme Law of Love. Love God supremely; love your neighbor as you do yourself." Because he was committed to that idea of good religion, Ransom embraced the objective of

Christianity: "To supercede all other religious faiths and become the one universal and dominant kingdom of God from sea to sea and from river to the ends of the earth. With it there is neither accommodation nor compromise. Christ must be exalted over all and above all, God blessed forevermore." That was the real thing, Ransom admonished; there was nothing weak or compromised in the religion of Jesus: "He offers a way of salvation and life, and points to himself and his followers as witnesses to its truth. Take it or leave it. It is new wine and cannot be retained in old wine skins."[56]

As usual, that point led to Ransom's imminent eschatology of a Christianized world: "If Christianity is to be established on the earth and the brotherhood of man with peace, justice, righteousness, the stage for its consummation is completely set here in the United States of America." But in his later career he usually took it back shortly after saying it. It was hard to prophesy about black and white America saving the world together when white America kept its boot on the neck of black America, and thereby lost its soul. The later Ransom taught that the white nations and Asia were headed downward, while the future belonged to the children of Africa and their descendants. "Asia, Europe, and America have had their day, or are now standing at the zenith of their power," he explained. These powers did not represent any conceivable "spiritual and social future" for humanity. They stood for weapons, wealth, power, diplomacy, science, technology, logic, and philosophy, all of which had failed, or were failing: "The spiritual and social pathway of humanity is strewn with the debris of their inadequacy." The white world never created a great religion, and its substitutes were barren. The hope of the world was in the last place that white America thought to look: "The African and his descendants are the last spiritual reserves of humanity."[57]

Sometimes he put it in world-historical terms. The Pyramids, the Pantheon, and the Colosseum were the "tombstones" of Egypt, Greece, and Rome, Ransom observed. They marked the spots where grotesque civilizations destroyed themselves in materialistic celebrations of supremacy and power. Similarly in modern times, the ascendancy of the black race was served and prepared by "the colonizing, exploring, inventive, and materialistic white man."

Ransom explained that the black race lacked "natural aptitudes and special endowments" for success in "the realm of things material, scientific, or commercial." The black imagination was primarily literary, artistic, and spiritual. It was not controlling or grasping, but looked to the future, which was open. It brought mind and heart together, struggling to comprehend how white America could lynch 5,000 American blacks in 70 years. Ransom predicted that if ever a great epic poem were written about the American experience or a great American symphony composed, the author or composer would be an African American.[58]

That was still an echo of Ransom's early buoyancy, but only an echo. The tasks of church administration in a difficult church situation and the sheer torment of coping with a racist society wore him down. In his later career he could still give a strong speech or sermon, but his days of enthralling racially mixed audiences with scintillating oratory were long past. His later audiences were church and civic groups, not surging crowds of movement activists; Ransom felt the difference. He was keenly aware that for all his later eminence as a bishop, his world got smaller. In 1936 he told the AME General Conference, "The world has little interest in us or concern about us as to what we do and what we say here. To them, we are just a group of Negroes here legislating and voting on matters that concern our church." That was not the life he had sought before he took the bishop's chair. The older he got, the more fondly he remembered Chicago.[59]

As it was, Ransom's sense of shrinking despite ecclesiastical station was a harbinger of his fate, because long before he died in 1959 (he retired in 1952), he was forgotten. Du Bois ranked Ransom as an orator "in the category of Demosthenes," grandly assuring, "He has erected a monument in the history of African Methodism, America, and the world which shall last throughout time and eternity." On the contrary, the first great figure of the black social gospel was almost completely forgotten. Even the literature of the black church gave him scant notice, and he was ignored in histories of the social gospel and modern American Christianity. After Martin Luther King Jr had come and gone, the existence of the black social gospel tradition that influenced King had to be explained. Morehouse College president Benjamin E. Mays, Howard University president Mordecai Johnson, and Boston University chapel dean Howard Thurman were remembered. But, unlike them, Ransom had no connection to King, and Mays and Thurman had more clout with the white Protestant establishment. The activist organizations through which Ransom made a public impact in his early career folded, secularized, or let him down. The Socialist party self-destructed in the 1920s and was culturally alien to him. He quit the Afro-American Council after it opted for Bookerism. He lost his place in the settlement movement after leaving Chicago. The reincarnations of the old antislavery organizations faded away. The Niagara Movement was too radical to be pragmatic and too pragmatic for radicals like Trotter; thus it dissolved. The NAACP grew out of the Niagara Movement, but took a secular path. Along the way Ransom found an increasingly consuming home in the AME Church, despite his misgivings about it, where a limited context and his increasingly black nationalist rhetoric reinforced each other.

Ransom's vision did not really diminish in his later years. He would have preferred to work in large interracial organizations that struggled for the cooperative common-wealth for all people. But they did not exist, and the necessity of resisting the down-ward slide of unrelenting racial oppression prevailed in his daily choices. After 1912 he despaired over America's presidential choices. Woodrow Wilson or Charles Evan Hughes? Hughes offered nothing to blacks, and Wilson crushed what remained of blacks' rights. Ransom called Wilson's aggressive segregationism "unpatriotic, undemo-cratic, and fiendish." To him it was a bitter irony that Wilson's liberal politics, edu-cated intellect, and ethical bearing applied no brake on his deep-seated racism. To be sure, Ransom shared some racialist assumptions with some of his least favorite white people. He believed that the different races were genetically endowed with particular traits; thus he asserted that blacks were not suited for math, logic or science, but were "naturally" gifted at music, speaking, friendliness, feeling, and spirituality. But Ransom's deepest purpose was to abolish racist ordering, not perpetuate it, and his statements about racial traits bore the marks of one who came of age intellectually in the 1880s, when social Darwinism excited and traumatized many minds.[61]

In 1935 Ransom dedicated his book *The Negro: The Hope or the Despair of Christianity* to the memory of two champions of the true commonwealth whom he missed. One was William Monroe Trotter, the militant activist who founded the *Boston Guardian* newspaper in 1901, disrupted a Booker T. Washington event in 1903, co-founded the Niagara Movement in 1905, founded the NERL in 1908, and personally confronted Wilson in 1914. Trotter denounced Wilson for doing nothing about segregation or lynching; Wilson replied that segregation was good for blacks and Trotter's manner offended him. Editorialists across the nation were offended too. The following year Trotter led a nationwide protest against the film *Birth of a Nation*, which glorified the Ku Klux Klan; in 1919 he showed up at the Paris Peace Conference and exhorted the diplomats to outlaw racial discrimination; in the 1920s he and the NERL faded from prominence, tagged as impossibly belligerent; in 1934 he plunged to his death from the roof of his apartment building, apparently by suicide. Ransom felt his loss deeply; Trotter was his symbol of prophetic antiracist militancy. He hailed Trotter as "the consistent and uncompromising champion of Freedom, Justice, and Equality."[62]

The other late friend to whom Ransom dedicated his book was Jane Addams, who had died in May 1935. To Ransom, Addams symbolized the path of race-blind progressivism that he might have preferred for himself had he shared her privileges or had America taken a different path. He lauded her as one "who knew neither race, class, nor creed, in her long effort to build a better humanity and to make a better world." By noting that Addams had no creed, Ransom underscored that his heroes in social justice activism – Du Bois, Trotter, Addams – had not made their home in the church. But long after she was gone, Addams was often derided for not being sufficiently radical, interesting, or secular.[63]

Fostering Democratic Citizenship: Jane Addams

In her lifetime Jane Addams was famous and widely admired, then famous but less widely admired, then more famous and admired than ever, surpassed in fame among American women only by Eleanor Roosevelt, and by none in admiration. In 1931 she won the Nobel Peace Prize and was showered with approbation, which went on for 25 years after her death. Routinely Addams was lionized as an American saint, which set her up for a season of being forgotten by history, when she was not being dismissed as an over-rated, self-regarding moralist.

On the centennial of her birth, 1960, the lionizing was still occurring. Historian Henry Steele Commager, perpetuating the image of Addams as the Gandhi of American Progressivism, warmly recounted her establishment of Hull House, wrongly claimed that she "never thought of herself," nodded approvingly at her reputation as America's only saint, and concluded that "It was as Saint Jane that she was known to millions around the earth and none now will challenge her right to that name." That verdict, attached the following year as a foreword to Addams' memoir *Twenty Years at Hull House*, contributed greatly to her season of dismissal and backlash.[64]

To historians and cultural critics who came of age in the 1960s and after Addams registered as a boring, moralistic, charity worker – the church lady of Progressivism – or something worse. Her generation had to deal with lynching, massive strikes, a world war, and government repression, yet she seemed to fixate on her own virtue. To many critics Addams epitomized the hapless politics and conceits of the comfortable, Progressive do-gooders. Instead of supporting the radicals who tried to transform the structures of American society, she made a fetish of her own moral idealism and turned her working-class neighbors into clients of it. Long condemned by conservatives for launching the social work industry, Addams acquired academic critics who agreed for different reasons.

Historian Daniel Levine, in an otherwise positive assessment, was the first to raise the criticism that Addams sometimes "looked with condescension on her neighbors."

Two years later, in 1964, historian Jill Ker Conway contended that Addams combined a Victorian idea of "feminine excellence" with an "extreme drive to power." That opened the door to rougher treatments. In Conway's version, Addams became famous as a byproduct of her extraordinary public service and quest for power; historian Allen F. Davis countered that fame, not power, was always the point for Addams. In *American Heroine: The Life and Legend of Jane Addams* (1973), a book that ruled the field for three decades as the only scholarly biography of Addams, Davis portrayed his subject as an egotistical and manipulative guardian of her public image. Other scholars amplified the charge of cultural chauvinism. Historian T. J. Jackson Lears described Addams as a "manipulative" social-work prototype who projected her own longings for "intense experience" onto the working-class subjects of her ministrations. Literary historian Tom Lutz agreed that Addams epitomized the "haughty" social type that blamed its personal problems on an oversupply of upper-middle-class refinement and education yet imposed its civilizing schemes on working-class clients. Historian Rivka Shpak Lissak upped the ante on that reading, depicting Addams as an agent of American cultural homogeneity who disarmed her clients of their class consciousness to make them "passive" participants in American society.[65]

That was a deep plunge from the adulatory treatment that Addams got for decades, which she always claimed to dislike anyway. Her vast output of essays, letters, journals, and books were strewn with just enough condescending statements to fuel the derision of her debunkers, and they showed as much worldly ambition as saintliness. But Addams was a valiant defender of immigrants and immigration. She was constantly on guard against the trap of paternalism and self-critical when she fell into it. Her project was always to strengthen American democracy by fostering a republic of active citizens, not to engender a dependent class of welfare clients. As a Christian and a feminist she worked out self-understandings that worked for her, if not for later critics. She was an early exponent of American pragmatism and the "Deweyan" strategy of rebuilding the public. She anticipated multicultural criticism by decades. And in the early twenty-first century she acquired defenders and a bit of public recognition on these points. Contrary to the common judgment that as a thinker she was merely a publicist, Addams was an incisive thinker who made an important contribution to social ethics.[66]

Laura Jane Addams was born in 1860, the eighth child of John Huy Addams and Sarah Weber Addams, who called her Jenny. Only three of her siblings lived to adulthood, and her mother died when Addams was 2 years old. Pregnant with her ninth child, Sarah Addams took a bad fall on the way to helping a neighbor deliver a baby, and died from internal bleeding. John Addams waited six years to remarry; in the meantime he raised an adoring youngest child who inherited his intensely moral bearing. In later life Jane Addams was fond of recalling that her father was deeply compassionate and ethical, unfailingly honest, an abolitionist, a temperance man, an admirer and colleague of Abraham Lincoln, and a "self-made man." The latter designation, treasured in nineteenth-century America, was a bit of a stretch in his case, since John Addams's father owned extensive farmlands and an inn. Both of Jane Addams's parents were products of prosperous upper-middle-class families; when her father moved to northern Illinois he had capital in hand, which he invested successfully. Jane Addams grew up in Cedarville, Illinois, where her father owned two mills, a woolen factory, 1,800 acres of farmland and timberland, and a nearby opera house, in addition he founded a bank and several insurance companies.[67]

A Whig and then a Republican like Lincoln, John Addams served in the Illinois Senate from 1854 to 1870. In a notoriously corrupt environment he was noted for incorruptibility and his feeling of kinship with his fellow politician. He cherished their correspondence, one letter of which asked him to support Lincoln's run for the US Senate in 1855. Since Lincoln was still a Whig at the time, and married to a Southerner, many Illinois Republicans distrusted him. Years later John Addams showed the letter to his daughter; it began, "My dear Double-D'ed Addams," noted that Addams would surely vote with his conscience, and inquired which direction his conscience was moving. Addams voted for Lincoln; a few years later he adorned his home with portraits of the president. Many years later Addams observed, "I always tend to associate Lincoln with the tenderest thoughts of my father." The memory of seeing her father aid a runaway slave was a touchstone for her, as was his declaration that, despite appearing to be a Presbyterian, in his head and heart he was a Quaker. A believer in evangelical perfectionism, John Addams founded the local Sunday school movement and attended the Presbyterian Church. But when Jane asked him about theology, he explained that he was a Hicksite Quaker, believing in the inner light. John Addams did not belong to a church or accept a creed for the same reason that Lincoln did not: accepting a religious dogma violated his intellectual integrity. His children were not baptized because he and Sarah Addams wanted them to decide for themselves whether to be Christians. In Jane Addams's telling, her father urged her to be true always to what she felt and understood inside: "Mental integrity above everything else." For the rest of her life she revered him as the epitome of ethical and intellectual integrity.[68]

This reverence survived John Addams's marriage to a high-strung woman of wild mood swings, Anna Hostetter Haldeman Addams, with whom Jane had a conflicted relationship. Addams's stepmother had an explosive temper and a need to dominate; she was also lively and affectionate, attending to Addams in ways that she needed. John Addams was austere and not inclined to initiate a conversation with a child; Jane's discussions with him always began with a question from her. Often he replied that he lacked sufficient time to reply; on other occasions he delivered a single-sentence oracle and refused to elaborate. Jane did not have to pursue her stepmother, however, who was constantly engaged with the Addams children and her own. Had Jane not been forced to escape her family drama in her late twenties, her autobiography might have offered a word of gratitude to her stepmother. As it was, Anna Addams was left out of *Twenty Years at Hull-House.*

Instead of attending Smith College, as she wanted to, Jane Addams went to nearby Rockford Female Seminary, as her father wished. To her surprise she flourished there, studying voraciously and editing the school magazine. She wrote preachy articles about aspiring to high ideals and snobbish articles about coping with "stupid people" who lacked cultural sophistication. With a fretful premonition of her future she worried about what Rockford students would be able to do with their learning after they graduated. In the meantime she endured evangelical appeals to accept Jesus and be saved – very few students at Rockford had not done so. Addams later recalled, "We were the subject of prayer at the daily chapel exercise and the weekly prayer meeting, attendance upon which was obligatory." Keeping in mind her father's example of spiritual integrity, she held out. In 1881 Addams graduated at the top of her class of seven, although she had to wait an extra year to receive a bachelor's degree, because Rockford was not an accredited college until then. Her valedictory address exhorted her classmates to hold fast to the world-transforming ideals of beauty, genius, and courage. That summer several classmates wrote to her lamenting their lack of support from home for continuing their studies; further education for a female seemed pointless to their families. Addams's situation was a bit less bleak; her father, judging that she had overworked at Rockford, declared that she could study at Smith after she had rested for a year.[69]

Then her world exploded, as John Addams suddenly fell ill from appendicitis and died in a hotel room. For Jane, the death of her father was devastating. She told her friend and college classmate Ellen Gates Starr that losing him was the greatest sorrow that could have befallen her. Starr replied that Addams was too much like her father for her moral purposes "to be permanently shaken by anything, even the greatest sorrow." For eight years that assurance seemed mistaken as Addams suffered from depression, exhaustion, back pain, a gruesome back operation, aimlessness, and the paralyzing sense that her life had lost whatever meaning it once possessed. She admonished herself to take up her father's cause of loving and doing right, but grew sullen and depressed, floundering in what she later called "the snare of preparation." At the time Addams called it moral defeat. She took a brief pass at medical school, submitted to a regime of rest and electric shocks for nervous exhaustion, tried the nineteenth-century panacea – a Grand Tour of Europe – and had a breakthrough moment in London's East End. A city missionary offered to acquaint Addams with the "submerged tenth" of London. Gazing from a double-decker bus, she witnessed, with horror, a group of poor men and women bidding for rotten vegetables from two hucksters' carts. She later remembered her revulsion as a turning point.[70]

In Rome Addams was deeply impressed by the catacombs, where it amazed her to see cheerful spring flowers and lambs on the ceilings of underground burial grounds. To her surprise she felt drawn to Christianity as a personal faith, reflecting that it was ethical, communal, and devoted to helping hurting people. She told Starr that she believed increasingly in "keeping the events and facts of Christ's life before me and letting the philosophy go." On returning to the USA, Addams was baptized and joined the Presbyterian Church. Years later she explained that, undoubtedly, she was weary of herself and of asking what would become of her. But her conversion was more than a matter of getting over herself: "Something persuasive within made me long for an outward symbol of fellowship, some bond of peace, some blessed spot where unity of spirit might claim right of way over all differences." Her passion for democratic ideals was growing within her, she recalled, but it was not enough to embrace democracy without a moral and spiritual ground that bound all people together.[71]

In Addams's telling, she came to understand that women like her – "the first generation of college women" – were nearly ruined by their privileges. When they went to college they were not ready to leave their comfortable worlds of family and emotional engagement. Mistaking education with the mere acquisition of knowledge, they lost "that simple and almost automatic response to the human appeal, that old healthful reaction resulting in activity from the mere presence of suffering or of helplessness." Putting it bluntly, long after Addams had awoken from numbness and self-absorption, "they are so sheltered and pampered they have no chance even to make 'the great refusal.'" It was hard to realize what life was about when one was "smothered and sickened with advantages," Addams explained. Anna Addams pressed hard to marry her troubled son George off to Jane, but by 1887 Jane had realized that to get better, she had to break away from her suffocating family circle, leaving an embittered stepmother behind. In her words, she recovered when she renounced the assumption "that the sheltered, educated girl has nothing to do with the bitter poverty and the social maladjustment which is all about her."[72]

On a second European tour in 1888, excited by reports about Toynbee Hall, Addams first contemplated the possibility of starting a settlement of her own. The idea occurred to her in Spain; in Paris she parted with Starr, who had chaperoning duties in Italy; Addams went to London and found her calling. Toynbee Hall was managed by Anglican priest Samuel Barnett, a gentle soul and energetic reformer, and his wife Henrietta, a forceful personality and manager. He was humble and she was not, but both won the affection of their working-class neighbors. The Barnetts and their mostly college-boy residents practiced the evangelism of friendship and edification, offering concerts, literary seminars, recreation, and conversation to the poor of London's East End. Their style, like that of Anglican socialism and the American social gospel, was radical and conservative at the same time, blending an egalitarian spirit with hierarchical givens. To Addams, that was the right idea; the Barnetts were the kind of reformers who possessed common sense and got things done. Their deep involvement in union solidarity work surprised her; Addams knew nothing about trade unions, except that Americans of her class despised them. Someone at Toynbee Hall gave her a copy of Marx's *Capital*; quickly she discerned that Karl Marx was not her kind of thinker. For Addams the crucial things were ideas and moral truth, which Marx denigrated. She did not care for Marx's relentless focus on economics and the factors of production. John Addams had admired Giuseppe Mazzini, the leader of Italy's struggle against French rule. Mazzini was a moralist who appealed to human duties; to Jane Addams, as for her father, that was the right approach. Years later she wrote that upon leaving Toynbee Hall, she knew that "the period of mere passive receptivity had come to an end," and with it the snare of preparation, which, as Tolstoy observed, entangled young people in "a curious inactivity" at the very time of life when they were most anxious to make their mark on the world.[73]

In February 1889 she and Starr searched for a Chicago settlement house. The city was obvious: Chicago was the largest city of their native state and the second largest in the USA, Starr already lived there, and it was booming. From the beginning Addams was determined to teach by example, practice cooperation, and live by a democratic ethos that cut across class lines. Toynbee Hall was her model, with three crucial differences. First, the immigrant factor loomed much larger in Chicago. The Barnetts had immigrant neighbors, but nothing like Chicago's rising populations of northern, central, eastern, and southern Europeans. Addams and Starr were especially interested in Germans and Italians, because the two women spoke both languages and had traveled in Germany and Italy. Second, being women, they wanted most of their residents to be female like themselves. In seeking supporters they argued that women were distinctly suited to break down social barriers and forge interpersonal bonds. Third, the fact that the Barnetts talked so much about connecting with "the people" showed that even the most well-meaning reformers in a deeply class-based society had trouble doing it. Addams wanted her settlement house to be more naturally democratic, which she believed to be possible in the more democratic USA. Drawing on her inheritance, she bought a big house on Halsted Street, on the city's West Side, where Italian and German immigrants predominated, in addition to Poles, Bohemians, Irish, Russian Jews, French Canadians, and English. Hull House, the settlement, was named in honor of the building's original owner; by 1910 it consisted of 13 buildings.[74]

From the beginning the settlement performed, as Addams put it, "the humblest neighborhood services," especially taking care of babies and little children, nursing the sick, preparing the dead for burial, and providing garbage removal services. The doors were always open until 11:00 P.M. and never locked. Hull House was long on lectures, concerts, reading groups, and discussion groups; it bustled with children, police officers, ministers, trade union organizers, political activists, random neighbors looking for company, political activists, and intellectuals; and it won the affection of its neighbors by asking, week after week "What can we do to help?" On occasion, worship services were held at the settlement, in a variety of forms; sometimes Addams led a service of Bible reading and prayers. But no religious instruction took place. Addams was anxious not to offend the many Catholics and Jews who came to Hull House, a policy that offended conservative evangelicals; repeatedly she was blasted in the evangelical press for running a mission that left out Jesus. That was not how Addams viewed her work, however. She and Starr told visitors that their purpose was to serve God by following the way of Jesus, and Addams joined a Congregational church on Ewing Street. Her main reason for not offering religious instruction at Hull House was that she was serious about conceiving Jesus as a model to emulate, not the object of doctrine. Theology was secondary and divisive; what mattered was to live the gospel faith by serving human need and building healthy communities.[75]

Addams stressed that educated women were especially suited for settlement work; in fact, it was an answer to the problem of the privileged, educated, aimless woman, as it had been for her. By 1892 her inner circle at Hull House, in addition to Starr, included Mary McDowell, who became a prominent social worker; Julia Lathrop, who matched Addams's moral purposefulness, but with a sharp sense of humor; Mary Rozet Smith, who became Addams's special companion; and Florence Kelley, a temperamental, outspoken Marxist and sometime collaborator with Friedrich Engels. Addams thrived on the verbal fireworks between Lathrop and Kelley; meanwhile her "Boston marriage" of devoted partnership with Starr eventually gave way to a similar relationship with Smith. The three women maintained an assiduous silence on whether these relationships were sexual.

In 1892 Addams lectured on "the subjective necessity for social settlements," contending that settlement work delivered young people, especially women, from "the brunt of being cultivated into unnourished, oversensitive lives." It was a sad and unfortunately common thing for young women to sink straight into listless misery after graduating from college, she observed. Lacking meaningful work to do, they fell into a vague torpor. In childhood they heard missionaries speak about famines in India and China; they went to lectures on the suffering of the poor in Siberia and East London; repeatedly they were exhorted to be sensitive and self-sacrificing, considering the good of the many. But what was the point of cultivating so much altruism if the young woman, upon finishing college, had no opportunity to practice it? "We have in America a fast-growing number of cultivated young people who have no recognized outlet for their active faculties," Addams warned. "They hear constantly of the great social maladjustment, but no way is provided for them to change it, and their uselessness hangs about them heavily."[76]

It made sense that the settlement movement began in England instead of the USA, she judged, because England, being a class society, needed it more. But the need was growing rapidly in the United States as immigrants pored into American cities. Addams rejoiced that American Protestantism responded with the social gospel, which recovered the spirit and religion of Jesus: "The impulse to share the lives of the poor, the desire to make social service, irrespective of propaganda, express the spirit of Christ, is as old as Christianity itself." Jesus did not elaborate doctrines or identify faith with any particular set of them, she argued. He taught that all truth was one and to appropriate the truth was to be free: "His teaching had no dogma to mark it off from truth and action in general. He himself called it a revelation – a life." Early Christianity thrived on that spirit: "The spectacle of the Christians loving all men was the most astounding Rome had ever seen. They were eager to sacrifice themselves for the weak, for children, and for the aged; they identified themselves with slaves and did not avoid the plague; they longed to share the common lot that they might receive the constant revelation."[77]

That was the joy of Christ, in Addams's rendering – the joy of finding the Christ that resided in every person. She enthused that it was spreading in church and society; the settlement movement was merely an example: "I believe that this turning, this renaissance of the early Christian humanitarianism, is going on in America, in Chicago, if you please, without much speaking, but with a bent to express in social service and in terms of action the spirit of Christ." The new social activism in Christianity took little interest in theology, doctrine, or even itself; what mattered was to change the world in a Christly way. Addams observed that three motive forces gave rise to Hull House. She did not know, and was not terribly interested in figuring out, the precise relations of these motives, but she knew what they were, just as she knew that the new social Christianity was a recovery of the original Christian spirit. The first motive was the desire to advance the social meaning of democracy as an egalitarian movement. The second was the urge to assist in the progress of the human race. The third was "the Christian movement toward humanitarianism." Addams was sufficiently quiet about her religion for many observers to mistakenly believe she did not to have one. What she had, and never relinquished, was a vital faith that brought God quietly into all that she did.[78]

Hull House proved to be a magnet for the kind of gently raised, idealistic, female social worker that Addams described and epitomized. Most of them had no acquaintance with Socialists or radicals, which put them on a steep learning curve after they arrived at the settlement. Addams later recalled that her youthful residents were often "bewildered by the desire for constant discussion" that swirled around them. Kelley, on the other hand, was well suited for the settlement's chief venture in political discussion, the Working People's Social Science Club, which met on Wednesday nights. Lectures on socialism, anarchism, strikes, trade unions, and unemployment were standard fare, followed by a second hour of discussion that often grew very heated. Addams received much of her political education in this group, while gaining a reputation for holding her own with anarchists, Socialists, union organizers, and liberal intellectuals. Sometimes she weighed in to keep the group's strongest blocs – the Russian Jewish socialists and German anarchists – from dominating the discussion. In a non-dogmatic sense of the term she became a socialist, which, in this crowd, meant that she was not a socialist. "I should have been glad to have had the comradeship of that gallant company had they not firmly insisted that fellowship depends upon identity of creed," she later explained. Addams was not against creeds on principle; she yearned for the "comfort" of one in the social arena. But the card-carrying Socialists insisted that class consciousness was the key to everything, which struck Addams as an exaggeration. The ideology of class struggle did not explain her own burning desire to abolish poverty, or the class-obliviousness of many Americans. In her experience, even immigrants tended to lose their class consciousness after they lived in the USA for a few years. So Addams refused to substitute a dubious ideology for the certainties of her moral conviction.[79]

The social science club was a tough crowd. Political points were debated fiercely; in the club's first seven years it had only one meeting at which the whole group applauded the speaker. On the other hand, it evoked no lasting acrimony or temper tantrums from lecturers, except for one professor who was unaccustomed to being challenged. Addams observed, "Radicals are accustomed to hot discussion and sharp differences of opinion and take it all in a day's work." Hull House sponsored 14 discussion groups, in addition to courses in French, painting, literature, and college extension courses in Latin and Greek. It established many firsts, including the first social settlement in Chicago; the first US settlement with female and male residents; the first public playground, public bath, public kitchen, public gymnasium, and public swimming pool in Chicago; and the first citizenship preparation classes in the USA. Addams took special delight in the Hull House Labor Museum, where workers learned the historical and industrial significance of their jobs; she described the museum in Deweyan terms as a continuing interpretation and renewal of experience. And she took pride that the Women Shirt Makers, Dorcas Federal Labor Union, Women Cloak Makers, and Chicago Woman's Trade Union League were organized at Hull House. In 1892 Addams noted that the settlement averaged 1,000 guests per week, and that it was mainly in the business of practicing and nurturing citizenship: "I am always sorry to have Hull House regarded as philanthropy, although it doubtless has strong philanthropic tendencies."[80]

John Dewey was a frequent guest and lecturer. In 1892 he stayed for a week at Hull House; two years later he moved to Chicago to teach at the newly opened University of Chicago; afterward he and Addams deeply influenced each other, developing their concept of democracy as the work of continually building the public. Dewey loved Hull House and Addams, though he could not imagine how she managed to write there. By the mid-1890s Addams was so popular in reform circles that standing ovations were routine at her lectures. Usually she spoke on the necessity of helping immigrants and the urban poor flourish as individuals, citizens, and members of local communities, though sometimes she injected a political word. From the beginning she expounded the "Deweyan" theme that education is as broad as experience itself, because education *is* experience; rightly conceived, education needed to be in vital contact with life. In the later 1890s she became increasingly explicit on the "Deweyan" theme that Dewey regarded as original to Addams: Democracy is a way of life, not merely a political system. For Addams, as for Dewey, democracy and pragmatism fit together as the experimental enterprise of ordinary people working together to discern and achieve the common good. Morality is inherently social; subjectivity develops only through social relationships; knowledge and ethical values belong together; democracy and ethics belong together; and the tests of moral truth, like any other claim, are experimental.[81]

Democracy, Social Ethics, and Pragmatism

Contemplating her first book in 1898, a collection of her lectures and articles, Addams thought she would feature the theme of "ethical survivals." One of her central convictions, a frequent lecture topic, was that obsolete ideas were often disastrous in the ethical sphere. Addams found a great deal of obsolete thinking in corrupt city politics, American presumptions of moral superiority, and her own struggle to let go of idealistic moralism in favor of ethical pragmatism.

Nowhere in life was it more important to remain open-minded and experimental than in the ethical sphere, she urged. That argument played a prominent role, though not quite a unifying one, in the book that Addams put together, *Democracy and Social Ethics* (1902).[82]

A meditation on the impact of modern democracy on morality, the book was organized around six pairs of human relationships: the charity worker and the beneficiary, the parent and the adult daughter, the household employer and the servant, the employer and the working-class employee, the educator and the adult student, and the politician and the voter. In each case Addams argued that society was moving beyond an outmoded, individualistic ethic to a humanitarian, democratic ethic in which the perspectives of many cultures interacted to form a new social whole. The American working-class was not merely a "lower class" of unsuccessful and morally challenged individuals, she contended. Working-class Americans of different nationalities had their own cultures. They did not associate the saloon with danger and depravity, raise their children gently, or prize formal education. They rejected the bourgeois habits of temperance, thrift, modesty, and politeness that middle- and upper-middle-class Americans identified with moral character and goodness. Addams observed that even the "safest platitudes" of gently raised people like herself made little sense to poor families. To "the charity visitor," the poor had dysfunctional views of early marriage, child labor, and clothing options, but to the poor, Addams explained, working-class values made sense within their social and cultural contexts. Describing her own experience, she remarked: "She discovers how incorrigibly bourgeois her standards have been, and it takes but a little time to reach the conclusion that she cannot insist so strenuously upon the conventions of her own class, which fail to fit the bigger, more emotional, and freer lives of working people."[83]

Experience had relativized parts of her moral code, but Addams held fast to a social gospel rendering of the good. "Ethics" is nothing more or less than a substitute term for righteousness, she observed. In each age the test of what it means to be righteous changes. In ages past it was a mark of moral achievement not to steal; later, people aspired to a sense of family obligation; in the modern age, the test of personal morality included caring about society: "To attain individual morality in an age demanding social morality, to pride one's self on the results of personal effort when the time demands social adjustment, is utterly to fail to apprehend the situation." Addams was old enough to remember when "democracy" was not a treasured term in American politics and culture. To the propertied classes of her youth it was a synonym for "mob rule," or put more high-mindedly, a frightful "rule by faction." But in the closing years of the nineteenth century "democracy" acquired the glow of righteousness. It became a wish for the well being of all men and a creedal belief in the essential dignity and equality of all men; Addams subsumed women in that category. Most of all, democracy became "that which affords a rule of living as well as a test of faith."[84]

In addition to holding high ideals, she urged, it was important to pursue them in the right way. The process was social and the tests were pragmatic. The democratic spirit engendered new and greater social duties, bringing people of diverse backgrounds together to solve common problems. Addams enthused that it was growing tremendously in America, and the new duties were ascertained "by mixing on the thronged and common road where all must turn out for one another." When people associated only with others who shared their background, economic status, or beliefs, they assumed that their ways and beliefs were superior. That was a violation of the ideal of human unity, Addams contended; moreover, it morally damaged every provincial soul. The spirit of democracy engendered a wider reading of human life that mobilized an expansive consciousness and sympathy. She stressed that it was a recent historical phenomenon: "We find in ourselves a new affinity for all men, which probably never existed in the world before." It was a great advance in human progress to understand the roles played by ignorance and deprivation in causing criminal behavior; more importantly, further advances depended upon widening the scope of human understanding across cultures, social classes, and nations. Addams put it aptly in a sentence that capsulized her social ethic: "We are under a moral obligation in choosing our experiences, since the result of those experiences must ultimately determine our understanding of life."[85]

To be selfish was to fail the fundamental test of morality, choosing one's experiences within a narrow frame of perceived self-interest. To be saved from selfishness, in social-ethical terms, was to throw oneself into contact with the experiences of the many, giving rise to a feeling of affinity with all people and a willingness to practice the method of cooperation in dealing with others. Sympathetic cooperation mobilized the better angels of every human self, Addams argued, and it offered the best way to comprehend people who were different from one's self. Thus, the essential idea of democracy – human solidarity in a common project – was also the source and subject matter of social ethics: "It is as though we thirsted to drink at the great wells of human experience, because we knew that a daintier or less potent draught would not carry us to the end of the journey, going forward as we must in the heat and jostle of the crowd."[86]

Addams realized that social consciousness was not necessarily saving. Some strategies of social salvation failed the test of efficient action, and some were morally repugnant. In *Democracy and Social Ethics* she stressed the universality of true democracy and human solidarity to distinguish it from exclusivist and supremacist forms of social salvation. In *Newer Ideals of Peace* (1907) she added that social sentiments "must be enlightened, disciplined and directed by the fullest knowledge." The latter book was her plea for a civilized alternative to war. Addams was a believer in the Progressive faith that war would become obsolete as society advanced to higher levels of enlightenment and civilization. By 1907 she believed that her nation had nearly outgrown war. In the past, she argued, the cause of antimilitarism was carried forward by small groups of hardy pacifists preaching a "dovelike ideal" in the manner of creedal religion. Addams admired the pacifist idealists, but identified with a stronger social tide that proclaimed "the newer, more aggressive ideals of peace."[87]

Leo Tolstoy epitomized the former type in her rendering. For many years Tolstoy's religious writings had canonical status for Addams, and in 1896, two years after his book *The Kingdom of God is Within You* was published in England, Addams had an unsettling encounter with him at his ancestral estate Yasnaya Polyana, about 130 miles south of Moscow. Tolstoy wore peasant garb and a long gray beard; Addams wore a fashionable travel gown. Taking hold of her billowing silk upper sleeves – Addams later recalled ruefully that they were "monstrous in size" – Tolstoy remarked that he could make a frock from the sleeves alone. Did not such an outfit impose a barrier between her and working-class Americans? She replied, defensively, that working girls in Chicago wore similar outfits and that if she dressed like a peasant, she would have to choose among the 36 nationalities that lived in her ward. Tolstoy's wife added, supportively, that her attempts to make dresses from superfluous parts of her gowns had not worked. Tolstoy, backing off from female solidarity, switched to food and shelter. Who fed Addams and how did she obtain a roof over her head? Addams confessed that she was an absentee landlord of a farm 100 miles from Chicago, and, no, she did not bake her own bread. Tolstoy was appalled; did she really think she could help people more by adding herself to overcrowded Chicago than by tilling her own soil? Years later, recalling the scene, Addams stressed that Tolstoy subjected his entire family to his late-life "martyrdom of discomfort" and that all of them seemed quite depressed by it, although for a while after her encounter, Addams tried to bake her own bread.[88]

She had journeyed to Russia knowing that she disagreed with Tolstoy about the necessity of living the same life as the downtrodden, yet she had gone as a pilgrim hoping for an illuminating word or gesture. Tolstoy's reaction to her strengthened Addams's conviction that compassion had to mean something else in America; as she told Mary Rozet Smith, "a man cannot be a Christian by himself." Tolstoy was a prophet of martyrdom, seeking to purify himself through suffering and hardship. Standing against the way of the world, his penchant for antagonizing others became a sign of his moral purity. Addams later confessed that she felt mortified at the thought of rejecting Tolstoy. Who was she to disagree with him? But Addams did not believe the world was saved by antagonism and personal martyrdom. Letting go of her hero-worship of Tolstoy, she began to relinquish her own martyrdom complex. Repeatedly she told lecture audiences that he was a "seer" who offered a model of moral integrity, but not the only or best model. In *Newer Ideals of Peace*, she wrote that Tolstoy was the master of "reducing all life to personal experience," which gave his work its "relentless power." But martyrdom and antagonism would never put an end to war. Tolstoy raged against government as the oppressor of the poor. His moralism and anarchism were cut from the same cloth; Addams replied that modern democratic civilization was the answer, not the problem.[89]

"It is not so much by the teaching of moral theorems that virtue is to be promoted as by the direct expression of social sentiments and by the cultivation of practical habits," she wrote. Gradually, with the growth of democracy, humanitarianism, and the social understanding of religion, society was coming to grasp the sheer stupidity, uselessness, and self-destructiveness of war. In the past, Addams observed, people actually believed that the way to obtain peace was to prepare for war; now they recognized that militarization for peace was a *reductio ad absurdum*. War belonged to the jungle phase of civilization. Leaving behind Tolstoy's language of non-resistance, which suggested passivity, feebleness, and fixation with personal purity, Addams called for a peace movement that used proactive, transformative terms such as "overcoming," "substituting," "re-creating," "readjusting moral values," and, her favorite, "forming new centers of spiritual energy." In the past, the claims of blood, group, and nation prevailed in sending the poor to kill each other. In 1907, apologists for the war system still claimed that war stirred the "nobler blood" and "higher imagination" of the nation, liberating Americans from the bonds of moral torpor and consumerism. Addams replied: "We do not see that this is to borrow our virtues from a former age and to fail to utilize our own." Modern humanitarianism was too soft and idealistic. What was needed was a gritty, brave humanitarianism that arose through "a patient effort to work it out by daily experience."[90]

The more that the modern state grew into the full meaning of its democratic creed and mission, building up a cooperative commonwealth of equal citizens, the less it would tolerate militarism and war. Addams saw the beginning of a cosmopolitan international order in the multi-ethnic urban civilization of her neighborhood. A good government was the steward of the common good, whether at the local, state, or national level; Addams reasoned that international governing bodies would be no different. Nation states would relate to each other much like America's nation of immigrants already related to each other. For Addams, the modern, multi-ethnic, democratic state represented the nurturing principle, replacing coercion and authoritarianism with democratic cooperation. The state's monopoly on violence was a good thing if the state was democratic and good. Preaching what she knew from her experience of building peaceable, democratic communities, Addams added that if America was to become a fully realized democracy of peace, equality, cultural diversity, and freedom, it had to grant women the right to vote.

The cause of a civilized world order was linked directly to that of the growth of democracy and citizenship within nations, both of which demanded and depended upon the flourishing of women. Addams argued that extending suffrage to women would enable them to preserve their households and humanize the political sphere. As society grew more complex, women needed to extend their sense of responsibility beyond their own doorsteps to create a good society. Though politics was said to be too harsh for women, Addams replied that women could make it less harsh by bringing the "gentler side of life" into it. If women voted, the abolition of child labor would be a high priority in American politics, and the "ancient evil" of prostitution would surely be abolished. Addams took for granted that the loss of one's virtue was such a dreadful calamity that no woman would consent to it willingly. Pressing the analogy to America's enslavement of Africans, she called prostitution "white slavery." In her rendering, prostitutes were unwilling victims of economic exploitation who were usually lured or deadened by addiction to alcohol. "A surprising number of country girls have been either brought to Chicago under false pretenses, or have been decoyed into an evil life very soon after their arrival in the city," Addams observed in 1912. "From the point of view of the traffickers in white slaves, it is much cheaper and safer to procure country girls after they have reached the city." If America got rid of alcohol and allowed women to vote, urbanization would be less perilous, politicians would take prostitution more seriously as a crime against women, and the moral health of American society would increase tremendously. For Addams, the battle against "white slavery" was the abolitionism of the early twentieth century; repeatedly she admonished her lecture audiences that suffrage, child labor, temperance, and the abolition of prostitution were crucial causes that belonged together.[91]

In 1912 she lost a bit of her luster on the Left by helping to create Theodore Roosevelt's Progressive party. Campaigning hard for Roosevelt, Addams swallowed his militarism and the party's lily-white policy in the South, which mortified many of her progressive friends. She replied, citing Aristotle, that in politics, questions were studied for the sake of action, not knowledge. It was pointless to get involved in politics if one insisted on being pure. Addams believed in getting as much as possible through political involvement and then returning for more. She added that unlike the Republican and Democratic parties, the new Progressive party permitted women to be convention delegates. As for the party's backsliding on racial justice, liberals had to get political about the national politics of race. Republicans gave lip service to racial equality, which allowed Democrats to dominate the South, which meant there was no national party. Both parties were content to be regional entities, which made it easy for party managers to have their way and guaranteed that nothing changed on the politics of race. Addams contended it was better for the Progressives to say nothing about race in the hope of building a national party than to follow the Republicans in mouthing commitments they had no intention of fulfilling. The way to crack the Democratic hold on the South was to build a national party without directly challenging white supremacism in the South. At least the Progressives had the nerve to try something different; in Addams's words, they took "the color question away from sectionalism and put it in a national setting which might clear the way for a larger perspective. Possibly this is all we can do at the present moment."[92]

But the Progressive party proved to be little more than a vehicle for personal ambitions of Roosevelt, who returned to the Republicans in 1916, ending the fantasy of a two-party South. By then Addams was deeply involved in a larger controversy that considerably diminished her status for many years. From 1912 until her death in 1935, Addams lifted the cause of peace above all others. She led or supported virtually every notable peace organization to arise in the USA, spoke constantly on behalf of international cooperation and antimilitarism, and paid a huge personal price for it for over a decade. The scale of the slaughter in World War I horrified her; in the early years it averaged over 15,000 deaths per day. Speaking for several peace organizations, especially the Woman's Peace party, Addams pinned her hopes for a truce on President Wilson. At the founding of the Woman's Peace party in January 1915 she implored the USA to stay neutral in order to end the war. The American party joined the 15-nation Women's International Committee for Permanent Peace; later it evolved into the Women's International League for Peace and Freedom (WILPF). In April 1915 Addams chaired the group's International Congress of Women at The Hague, which, despite immense logistical and political difficulties in wartime, brought together 1,336 women from 12 nations, including belligerents and neutrals.[93]

The founding of the World Court of Conciliation and Arbitration at The Hague in 1899 was a potent symbol to Addams and the peace party of the road the world was supposed to be taking. In her keynote address she urged delegates not to forsake the solidarity of women as a peaceable political class transcending national boundaries. The cause of peace was badly battered, she acknowledged, but not hopelessly lost. The immediate imperative was to end the war, putting a stop to the self-perpetuating cycle of fighting, suffering, and revenge that bred new animosities. The International Congress of Women called for a permanent international court, an agreement not to ratify the fruits of conquest, universal disarmament, female suffrage, and the abolition of secret treaties. It also made Addams its organizational leader. At the time she was confident that Wilson would keep America out of the war. But the following month, after Germany sank the passenger ship *Lusitania*, Addams found herself in a very different political culture than the one she thought she was building.[94]

After the congress she toured Austro-Hungary, Belgium, Britain, France, Germany, Italy, and Switzerland as an amateur diplomat, meeting soldiers, religious leaders, foreign ministers, and even a few prime ministers, who treated her party with courtesy and respect. In July Addams returned to the USA, filled with determination to expand the antiwar movement. She gave a powerful antiwar address at Carnegie Hall that evoked thunderous applause, and was stunned by a furious backlash that knocked her off her public pedestal.

The speech began agreeably enough, disclaiming personal prominence and working Addams's familiar theme that women were naturally devoted to peace. Addams assured her listeners that she was not really the leader of the women's world peace movement. The European women wanted a president from a neutral nation, preferably one far away, so the American leader was chosen. As for female peacemaking, she acknowledged that most women were fervent war-boosters, just like men; Addams knew about the surging throngs of women at railroad stations who urged their sons, husbands, and neighbors to kill for their country. "But the women do have a sort of pang about it," she contended. Even the women who wished they had more than a half-dozen sons to give to the war often expressed, when pressed on the point, "a certain protest, a certain plaint against the whole situation which very few men, I think, are able to formulate." Addams vested much of her hope on that misgiving: "Now I submit that any, shall I say plain mother, any peasant woman who found two children fighting, not for any cause which they stated, but because he did that and I did this, and therefore he did that to me, that such a woman would say: That can't go on; that leads to continued hatred and quarreling."[95]

That was always the point, in a talk that featured Addams's typically measured, temperate prose. She stressed that foreign ministers and prime ministers on both sides routinely said the same thing, employing the same phrases about self-defense and preserving their civilization. Her theme was the tragic pointlessness of it all. When Addams met with Wilson that month, he seemed to agree with her about the tragic futility of the war and the necessity of brokering a truce. But at the end of her speech Addams sealed the point with a claim that enraged many Americans. Old men fought wars by sending young men to fight and die in them, she observed. Many soldiers did not believe in the war, or were traumatized at the thought of having to kill someone, or were terrified at the horror of the bayonet charges. So how did the officers get them to fight? Addams reported that the German, English, and French officers got soldiers intoxicated before sending them into battle. The Germans used a formula, the British used rum, and the French used absinthe: "They all have to give them the 'dope' before the bayonet charge is possible. Think of that. No one knows who is responsible. All the nations are responsible, and they indict themselves."[96]

That set off a firestorm of offended rage. Critics accused Addams of defaming and dishonoring the Allied soldiers. In their telling, Addams told orphaned children of Allied war heroes that their fathers died, not for their country, but because they were drunk. Richard Harding Davis, a popular militarist, described Addams as a "self-satisfied woman" who thought nothing of throwing hand grenades on the graves of fallen heroes. Throughout the controversy, it mattered little that Addams's report was factually accurate. What mattered, to her many accusers, was that she smeared Allied soldiers as cowards and drunks. In later years Addams wrote about the episode several times, but at the time she took only a pass at setting the record straight, explaining to a reporter after a speech at Chautauqua that the business about cowardice was made up. She had not claimed or implied that the soldiers lacked courage; her point was that modern men were too civilized to be savage killers, thus their horror at warfare had to be dulled with drugs. But the reporter garbled her statement; the condemnations continued to pile up as American identification with the Allies intensified; and Addams gave up trying to defend herself. Later she recalled that attacks on her character dragged on "for week after week in every sort of newspaper," and she received "an enormous number of letters, most of them abusive." In her account, the most abusive ones came from civilians who hated her for defaming the soldiers and from old men who wanted to remember their war experiences in a rosy light, while the letters she received from active soldiers thanked her for telling the truth.[97]

Addams was not a newcomer to criticism; for years she took steady fire from conservatives and radical leftists. But these attacks confirmed her self-image, and she was used to being admired. The wartime attacks were devastating to her feelings and self-image. She later reflected that by temperament and habit she had always kept "rather in the middle of the road." In politics and social reform she stood for "the best possible," but the war pushed her to the left politically, which was a more vulnerable place to be, setting her up for hostile rejoinders. Reeling from the outraged reactions that rained upon her, Addams fell into a wounded depression that lasted for the rest of the war. "It seemed to me at the time that there was no possibility of making any explanation," she later recalled. Having crossed a fateful line, damaging her reputation by seeming to impugn the nobility and heroism of the soldier, she avoided the spotlight, stunned by the fury of war psychology, and fell ill with pleuropneumonia: "I experienced a bald sense of social opprobrium and wide-spread misunderstanding which brought me very near to self pity, perhaps the lowest pit into which human nature can sink." In other words, "I gave up in despair."[98]

Her mode was to be with the people, urging them forward; it was painful to be alienated from the many who admired soldiering and fervently identified with the Allies against Germany. The charge that Addams smeared Allied soldiers followed her wherever she went. Some of her longtime friends shunned her or treated her coolly. Speeches were cancelled, and for the first time she heard herself booed when introduced. Addams waited for the storm to pass, but it only got worse after America entered the war. Had she reversed direction, like Gladden, and made her peace with America's intervention, all might have been forgiven. Addams fretted, sorrowed, and doubted herself, but refused to say that she had been wrong about the war; thus the social punishments worsened: "We were constantly told by our friends that to stand aside from the war mood of the country was to surrender all possibility of future influence, that we were committing intellectual suicide, and would never again be trusted as responsible people or judicious advisers." After the war ended, she wished she could look back and say that she had done all she could to oppose it. But the truth was that she fell into "faint-heartedness," failing to challenge the war psychology that raged all around her. Faced with the disapproval of old friends, the constant charge of lack of patriotism, and the futility of opposing something that had already happened, Addams lapsed into defeated silence: "We gradually ceased to state our position as we became convinced that it served no practical purpose, and worse than that, often found that the immediate result was provocative."[99]

Addams's second bout with emotional exhaustion, like her first, was linked to her inability to translate her moral ideals into practical action. She recovered her personality and some of her reputation only as the ending of the war yielded new humanitarian challenges. The war created food shortages in Europe by displacing farmers and destroying distribution networks; in addition, Germany and Austro-Hungary were starved by the Allied food blockade. After the war Addams joined Herbert Hoover's food relief campaign in Europe, in her case under the auspices of the American Red Cross and the American Friends' Service Committee. Though she did not think much of Wilson's League of Nations, which allowed too much room for war, she told herself and her audiences that the existence of an international food relief effort showed there was such a thing as humanitarian international cooperation.[100]

In the 1920s Addams focused almost exclusively on the peace issue, giving ballast to the social gospel turn to antiwar activism and building up the WILPF. Attacks on her baleful influence were commonplace for groups like the Daughters of the American Revolution, but gradually Addams regained much of her previous standing in American life, largely through the testimonials and awards that her many admirers showered upon her. In her second memoir, *The Second Twenty Years at Hull-House* (1930), she lamented the passing of Victorian duty and discretion, admonished her readers that "Victorian prudery" deserved better than its postwar reputation, shook her head at the anxiety of One Hundred Percent Americanism, and enthused that antiwar sentiment was rising. On Prohibition she lamented the "almost hypnotic influence of the slogans of the press." The slogans were that more people drank than ever before, Prohibition diminished America's respect for law in general, organized crime made Prohibition more trouble than it was worth, and Prohibition wrongly infringed personal liberty. Addams replied that truly great undertakings were difficult. The world was watching America's grand experiment in public moral health; if Prohibition were abandoned, the calamity would not just be for the USA.[101]

She took great satisfaction in living to see her gender achieve the vote, and Addams took pride that "many of the voting women have exhibited an intelligent and sustained interest in world affairs." On immigration, however, she witnessed a decline in America's public morality. Immigration froze during the war years, the quota acts followed, and in 1924 Congress rolled back immigration to admit only 2 percent of the immigrant nationality that was in the country in 1890, excluding Japanese entirely. Addams remarked that Americans were obviously "contemptuous" of immigrants "who differ from us." Not coincidentally, Americans also had an "exaggerated acceptance of standardization." There was nothing wrong in itself with wanting to be like one's neighbors, she allowed, but this sentiment had to be checked by moral criticism; otherwise it led to one of democracy's worst problems – "the tyranny of the herd mind." One might have expected a nation of immigrants to be tolerant and liberal, she observed ruefully, yet America's intolerance for dissent and difference blazed fiercely during the war and after it. Germany and Austro-Hungary were surely repressive, yet neither belligerent had anything like the Palmer raids or the Red scare. As usual, Addams called for calmness, moral probity, and practical intelligence in dealing with the immigration issue. Ethnic diversity was a fact of life in the USA; thus, America's different groups could not be judged by a single norm or cultural standard: "To be intelligent about them requires constant acquaintance and research."[102]

Near the end of her life she offered a toast to her favorite philosopher, Dewey, characteristically crediting him with her own ideas; Dewey was equally generous in crediting Addams. In Addams's rendering, Dewey was the great theorist and teacher of education as the experience of life: "His insistence upon an atmosphere of freedom and confidence between the teacher and pupil, of a common interest in the life they held together, profoundly affected all similar relationships, certainly those between the social worker and his client." This use of the term "client" was not quite what Addams meant, as the rest of her argument made clear. She did not regard her neighbors as "clients," any more than she thought of herself as dispensing "charity," though her writings used both terms. Hull House was always about creating citizens for a multi-ethnic democracy, of which Addams considered herself merely a well-known example. To her understanding, she had not created Hull House; Hull House created her. She recalled that at the beginning she liked to say that the welfare of the community was a mutual responsibility, "but John Dewey told us that the general intelligence is dormant, with its communications broken and faint, until it possesses the public as its medium." The business of Hull House was the civic work of continually renewing the public as a flourishing democracy.[103]

Besides having the same philosophy, Dewey and Addams nearly always agreed about politics. In her long career Addams could remember only one occasion when she and Dewey disagreed on a major issue. Dewey was her barometer of political wisdom, but, more importantly, he shared her temperament, and, most importantly of all to Addams, he had a method. Like her, Addams recalled, Dewey opposed war during wartime, not just between wars, which thrust him into a position he greatly disliked, "the position of the doctrinaire." Dewey's style was to bring people along, appealing to evidence, common sense, and the practical common good. He hated standing outside the gate in the self-righteous company of those who shouted, "Thus says the Lord," and so did she. Dewey was never an ideologue, because he held firmly to a pragmatic method in a democratic spirit. To the extent that she allowed herself to boast, Addams boasted that she operated in the public square in Dewey's fashion: "The Dewey teaching saved us from resorting to the infallible solace vouchsafed to the self-righteous, and as we struggled in one country after another for a foothold in reality and actually found it, we were grateful to him for having taught us a method."[104]

A great deal of liberal Protestant social ethics took that option, conflating the secular and the sacred as a single work of building democracy. Contrary to many interpreters, Addams did not become less Christian in her later life; a secularized version of the social gospel was always her mainstay. Her early writings mentioned Jesus only a bit more often than her later writings, which was not very much. For Addams, Jesus showed the way, but the point was to follow the way in a modern context, not theologize about Jesus. Many social gospelers in the generation after Rauschenbusch took that tack, rendering Christian meaning as social and practical virtually without remainder. Christianity was actualized as social progress, and social progress was actualized as democracy and cooperation.

Historian Catherine Peaden contended that although Addams used Christian language to explain herself and her work it rested increasingly on an Arnoldian concept of culture as a replacement for religion. Historian R. A. R. Edwards agreed that although Addams used Christian rhetoric to bolster faith, her concern was to promote faith in democracy, not God. These were plausible renderings if one assumed a conventional understanding of religion, but they did not quite describe the faith that was real and motivating to Addams. Neither did it do justice to the streams of social gospel Christianity and empirical theology that influenced Addams and played a large role in subsequent liberal theology. Peaden and Edwards came closer to grasping her faith than the interpreters who read it as mere window-dressing, but they judged Addams by a standard of "religious" seriousness that she rejected. Like Dewey and the Chicago school theologians whom she befriended, Addams did not believe in the sacred/secular distinction. To her, good religion was historical and naturalistic; it was about life on earth, not a transhistorical realm. Eschewing theology, she did not write it on the side, unlike Dewey and William James. Dewey had a pragmatic concept of God as the active relation between the ideal and the actual. The Chicago school theologians saved a bit more objectivity, conceiving God as a structured event within history or the creative matrix of the world process. Addams was no less religious than the theologians who developed the empirical and process traditions in theology; moreover, she was not non-religious merely for believing that the secular/sacred dichotomy was very bad for religion and the world. The secularizing stream of the social gospel that she represented should not be construed as lacking religiousness merely because it contended that the things of divinity and the social good went together inseparably.[105]

Yet in the real world of communities, institutions, religions, and consumer choices that Addams prized as the locus of religious meaning, the option that she represented seemed vital or even comprehensible only to a small number. Her residents and guest lecturers, sometimes, were religiously musical in her style, but most of her neighbors were traditional Catholics, Orthodox, and Protestants. Hull House religion was low church and discursive. On things of the spirit it was comfortable with art and drama, not liturgy. When pressed on the point, Addams maintained that her working-class neighbors should have been able to find spiritual meaning in her stripped-down ethical religion. But for most of her neighbors, religion was also about mystery, sacraments, saints, theology, and miracles. Here, Addams-style social Christianity made little attempt to evoke reciprocal relations. Religion, the mostly-unspoken mainstay of her moral universe, was a day-to-day barrier to sympathetic understanding at Hull House.

There was a social gospel that did not derive from Protestant revivalism, evangelicalism, liberalism, and secularism. It had a more robust sympathy than Addams for a great deal of immigrant religion, because like many immigrants, it was Catholic. In the USA the Catholic stream of modern social Christianity got a late start as a movement, yet, to many Catholics influenced by it, the social interpretation of Christianity began in 1891 with *Rerum Novarum*, not the unfamiliar organizations built by Josiah Strong. Its leading theorist was the Right Reverend Monsignor John A. Ryan, not the unfamiliar Walter Rauschenbusch. Through the writings and active public and ecclesiastical career of Ryan, the modern social gospel was legitimized in American Catholicism and welded into Catholic doctrine.

Social Doctrine in Action: John A. Ryan

John A. Ryan was a pioneer in Catholic social thought who viewed himself as having merely applied Catholic principles to a changing social order. He was born in 1869 on a farm in Vermillion, Dakota County, Minnesota, about 20 miles south of St Paul. His parents, William and Maria Ryan, both immigrated to Minnesota from Tipperary, Ireland before meeting and marrying in Minneapolis. The farm community in which Ryan was raised consisted entirely of Irish Catholic immigrants. Even at school he never met a non-Catholic, since the adjoining community to the south consisted entirely of German Catholics. Ryan later recalled that the two communities got along well, although the Irish took for granted their racial superiority over the Germans. From both sides of his family he was bred in the memories of Irish Catholic resistance to English Protestant domination.

Both of Ryan's parents told stories of landlord oppression in Ireland and an eventual flight to America; William Ryan's story was especially gripping, as it involved the death of a newborn baby on the roadside after his family was evicted from its farm in winter. In Vermillion the local Catholic parish had services only once per month; on the remaining Sundays the Ryans had to journey 10 miles in a lumber wagon to get to Mass. William and Maria Ryan were devoutly religious and fervently opposed to idleness and sloth; they prayed for the privilege of giving priests and nuns to the church. William held mortgages on two farms and Maria bore 11 children, of whom two became nuns and two became priests. Michael John was the oldest; in his school days he dropped the first name. For the rest of his life Ryan proudly cited the robust vitality and health of his large family as an argument against the "pestilential practice" of birth control.[106]

Besides devotional fare and the Bible, the Ryan home had no library, and Ryan attended an ungraded district school until the age of 17. His family subscribed to a weekly magazine, however, *The Irish World and American Industrial Liberator*, which reinforced the family narrative of oppression in Ireland. Ryan consumed the magazine, identifying with its Irish nationalism and its condemnations of English oppression. He later recalled that one could not read it on a regular basis "without acquiring an interest in and a love of economic justice, as well as political justice." From an early age he viewed the Irish struggle for liberation as political and economic, extending to a critique of the landlord system. Meanwhile he watched his parents eke out a subsistence living in a local economy wracked by monetary deflation coupled with high interest rates. William Ryan lived by the barter system, occasionally selling some pigs or eggs, and never had a bank account. For 20 years he paid 12 percent interest on one of his farm mortgages, living perpetually in debt. The Ryans were Democrats, viewing Republicans as hostile to farmers and the working class, though Ryan's father made an exception for Republican James Blaine in 1884, because Grover Cleveland was even worse for working people. Ryan grew up believing that Republicans were the wrong party on everything, except the rights of black Americans, because they catered to eastern business interests. In 1886 a charismatic populist, Ignatius Donnelly, caught Ryan's attention during his campaign for the Minnesota legislature. Ryan ardently followed Donnelly's career for many years afterward, devouring populist and trade union literature. As a student at the Christian Brothers' School in St Paul he attended so many sessions of the Minnesota legislature that his classmates called him "Senator."[107]

He had just enough schooling from the Christian Brothers to attend seminary. Having received barely a grade school education in Vermillion, Ryan qualified for a diploma by attending the Christian Brothers' School for a few months. Immersing himself in populist politics, he felt a call to the priesthood, graduated in 1887, and moved on to St Thomas Seminary in St Paul. Ryan grasped that his combination of interests made him unusual; years later he reflected that he was slightly ahead of the curve of Catholic social teaching. For him, the social question was consuming; even his diary was filled politics and economics, with barely a word about his inner life. His beliefs were straight out of the labor/populist playbook: a graduated income tax, expansion of the currency, an eight-hour work day, restrictions on immigration, prohibitions on speculative ownership and alien ownership of land, and government ownership of public utilities. In 1892 he cast his first vote in a national election for James B. Weaver of the Peoples' party. Ryan's classmates were incredulous that he opted for radicals; he told them that populists stood for nearly all the right things.[108]

For five years, 1887 to 1892, Ryan undertook preparatory studies at St Thomas Seminary, essentially completing his high school and junior college education; afterwards, for six years, he studied there and at the new St Paul Seminary as a seminarian. Ryan wanted to study sociology and economics, but had to do so on his own. For nineteenth-century American Catholic educators the struggle to build an immigrant church took priority; political economy was a luxury. The USA was too Protestant and culturally diverse for Catholics to build religiously exclusive trade unions, and in

1887 Baltimore's James Cardinal Gibbons barely dissuaded the Vatican from disallowing American Catholics to join the Knights of Labor. Ryan attended seminary when the difference between "liberal" and "conservative" American Catholicism became a matter of heated identity politics. The difference had very little to do with religious doctrine and everything to do with what it meant to be Catholic in the United States.

The first great battles against American anti-Catholicism were fought by the first large wave of Catholic immigrants – mostly Irish, with some Germans – in the 1840s and 1850s. The groups that battled hardest for respect and acceptance also led the effort to assimilate American Catholicism into American culture. Isaac Hecker, the son of German immigrants and a convert from Methodism and Unitarianism, was the leading advocate of Americanization. In 1857 he was expelled from the Redemptorists for overzealously advocating an American religious order; the following year Pope Pius IX approved Hecker's request to found the Paulist order, which specialized in converting Protestants, and which Hecker served as superior until his death in 1888. Hecker contended that American-style religious liberty and political democracy were potentially compatible with Roman Catholicism and that the church needed to be open to modern science as well. Constantly embattled, Hecker was consumed by controversy in his later life. Yet his cause gained respectability in the 1880s and 1890s, chiefly because Irish clerics dominated the church and some were committed liberals. The English-speaking, democratic, public-oriented Irish seemed more "American" to American Protestants than the foreign-speaking immigrants from continental Europe. In the 1880s and 1890s, when Ryan attended seminary, the split between the church's liberal and conservative leaders, nearly all of them Irish, pervaded the church. Conservatives battled constantly against American tendencies, while liberals warned that American Catholicism would be ghettoized if it held out against American liberalism and democracy. The liberals were led by Peoria, Illinois bishop John Lancaster Spalding and St Paul, Minnesota archbishop John Ireland; the conservatives were led by New York archbishop Michael A. Corrigan and Rochester, New York bishop Bernard J. McQuaid; Gibbons mediated between them while leaning toward the liberals. Ryan identified with his liberal bishop, Ireland, while fretting that his own economic populism was too radical for the church.[109]

The controversy over Fr Edward McGlynn was troubling to Ryan as he searched for Catholic writers and clergy who shared his politics. McGlynn's involvement in Henry George's 1886 New York mayoral campaign caught Walter Rauschenbusch's attention; it also alarmed the Vatican, which in 1887, at Corrigan's urging, excommunicated McGlynn for his role in the campaign. Five years later the excommunication was revoked. Ryan watched this episode with a wary eye, hoping there was a place in the church for economic populists like McGlynn and himself. Spalding's political idealism and opposition to American imperialism gave Ryan hope. English bishop William Francis Barry was another kindred spirit who urged the church to support the labor movement. Ryan's bishop, Ireland, was conservative on economics, treasuring his friendships with wealthy Catholics, yet he was liberal enough on politics and church politics to be something of a role model. Pressing to complete his preparatory training, Ryan had no inkling that the current pope, Leo XIII, was preparing an encyclical that would open a new chapter of Catholic doctrine. On May 15, 1891 the Vatican directly addressed the social question in *Rerum Novarum: The Condition of Labor*, a historic encyclical that made Ryan's career possible.[110]

Pope Leo XIII was not expected to be a bold leader. Cardinal Gioacchino Pecci, who became Leo XIII in 1878, was known for the seemingly backward-looking view that the church should anchor its teaching in a slightly modernized Thomism. He ascended to the papacy at a time when the church was besieged by hostile social forces and currents of opinion. The church of the nineteenth century was battered by anti-clerical and nationalist movements; the industrial revolution overturned the social landscape of Western Europe; the rise of biblical criticism, liberalism, capitalism, democracy, Marxism, and Darwinism challenged church teaching; the papal states were lost in 1870; and Leo's predecessor, Pius IX, died as a prisoner of the Vatican while the Italian government occupied Rome. By the late 1880s liberal capitalism was at the high tide of its transforming social power and prestige, while European Catholicism was identified with monarchy and feudal economics. In his first encyclical, *Aeterni Patris* (1879), Leo XIII urged Catholic bishops to immerse themselves in the "streams of wisdom flowing inexhaustibly from the precious fountainhead of the Angelic Doctor" [Thomas Aquinas]. In *Rerum Novarum* he launched the modern tradition of Catholic social teaching, using Thomistic theory as the standard for judging the modern world. Leo's purpose was essentially conservative, with reformist leanings – to apply traditional Catholic thought to the new social conditions created by the industrial revolution. By taking up the social question so directly, however, he legitimized social ethics as a field within Catholic theology, identified the church with a surprisingly definite viewpoint on political economy, and provoked Catholics in the USA to re-assess their relationship to American capitalism.[111]

Rerum Novarum was not as hostile to capitalism and the modern world as the church's substantial right flank, but it took an unmistakably dim view of liberal capitalist civilization. Over the past century, the pope observed, the ancient worker guilds had been destroyed, and the public authority of the church was savaged by nationalist, liberal and capitalist social forces: "Hence by degrees it has come to pass that working-men have been given over, isolated and defenseless, to the callousness of employers and the greed of unrestrained competition." Usury was practiced shamelessly by "avaricious and grasping men," the contract system prevailed, and a few people owned the major means of production, "so that a small number of very rich men have been able to lay upon the masses of the poor a yoke little better than slavery itself." In this situation, Leo XIII declared, the Catholic Church had to find and stand for a solution to the ravages of the modern disorder: "There can be no question whatever, that some remedy must be found, and quickly found, for the misery and wretchedness which press so heavily at this moment on the large majority of the very poor."[112]

Steering a careful path between capitalism and socialism, *Rerum Novarum* held out for the dual nature of the person and the institutional foundation of society in the family. Modern capitalism was morally repugnant on its face, the pope argued, because it released the individual from moral and social obligations. Socialism, on the other hand, was a collectivist overreaction to capitalist greed that disrespected the spiritual nature and rights of individuals. Leo observed: "To remedy these evils the *socialists*, working on the poor man's envy of the rich, endeavor to destroy private property, and maintain that individual possessions should become the common property of all, to be administered by the State or by municipal bodies." Destroying private property was a disastrously bad idea, because it stripped the worker of "the very reason and motive of his work," to obtain property. Besides robbing the "lawful possessor" of the fruit of his labor, it gave undue powers to the state and caused "complete confusion in the community." Appealing to natural law theory, Leo countered that society originated in the family, private property was a natural right, and a good society prized the spiritual and material needs of individuals.[113]

The father-ruled family was the basic unit of society, a "true society" of its own "governed by a power within itself, that is to say, by the father." Leo stressed that this social organism was anterior to the state and nation, and the means by which property was rightly transmitted from one generation to the next. Appealing to Thomas Aquinas, the pope urged the view that the right to property was essential for "the carrying on of human life," but at the same time, in a moral and spiritual sense, one's possessions were common to all. In extreme cases it was a duty to share one's possessions with others lacking the necessities of life; at all times it was a moral duty to be charitable, giving to the indigent "out of that which is left over." *Rerum Novarum* taught a strong view of the state's duty to uphold justice. Although the state had to be careful not to usurp the rights of individuals or families, it was obligated to "anxiously safeguard the community and all its parts." That meant that the poor and helpless held "a claim to special consideration," because they were most in need of the state's protection, and the state had to put down violent revolutionaries and others "imbued with bad principles." Breaking new ground, it also meant that the state had to regulate working conditions in the factories, where the "cruelty of grasping speculators" was a major problem. It meant that workers and employers needed to be free to set wages, that employers had to pay a "just wage," and that workers had the right to form trade unions or create associations of workers and employers. Leo remarked: "Such associations should be adapted to the requirements of the age in which we live – an age of greater instruction, of different customs, and of more numerous requirements in daily life."[114]

Rerum Novarum evoked praise, furious denunciations, and, in both cases, surprise in Europe, where no one expected the Vatican to weigh in so directly on political economics. In the USA it stirred little reaction among Catholic scholars and clergy besides quiet puzzlement and embarrassment. Catholic seminaries, anxious to preserve the faith in Protestant, capitalist America, did not dwell on the social question. The church had no tradition of addressing social issues and the US bishops had no national organization to do so. To theologians of an immigrant church in a roaringly successful capitalist nation, the pope's strident attacks on capitalist speculators seemed off-key at best. Ryan's teachers at St Thomas Seminary were typical, ignoring the encyclical. Finally in 1894, an English professor assigned it as an essay topic; Ryan fixed on Leo's discussion of the state, especially his rejection of *laissez-faire* ideology: "Whenever the general interest or any particular class suffers, or is threatened with, evils which can in no other way be met, the public authority must step in to meet them." That sentence surprised and delighted Ryan. After 10 years of hearing that his populist views were anathema to mainstream America and the Catholic Church, he told himself that at least the Catholic part was wrong: "The doctrine of state intervention which I had come to accept and which was sometimes denounced as 'socialistic' in those benighted days, I now read in a Papal encyclical. Only those who know the condition of American Catholic social thought before 1890 can understand how and why Leo's teaching on the state seemed almost revolutionary."[115]

In 1894 St Paul Seminary opened for business and St Thomas Seminary was renamed the College of St Thomas. Moving to the new seminary, Ryan took in his stride the fact that its founder was a railroad baron, James J. Hill; at the same time it bothered him that he was still on his own for economics and sociology. He found a favorite author in Richard Ely, whose books he devoured in the mid-1890s, and also read an economics textbook for the first time. Ryan liked Ely's emphasis on the ethical dimension of economics and his willingness to bring explicitly religious principles into political economy. He embraced Ely's reformist, economic democracy alternative to socialism, which advocated government ownership of natural monopolies, graduated taxes on unused land held for speculation, restrictions on the sale of publicly owned land, and the abolition of sweatshops and child labor.[116]

By the late 1890s, while making his way through required courses in theology, philosophy, scripture, and church history, Ryan was anxious to get on with his own work. He took little interest in theology, groused in his journal that there had to be some reward for years and years of studying philosophy, and worked hard at acquiring a clear and concrete writing style. If the real world of political economy was his subject, his style needed to be purged of literary indulgences: "I wanted to examine economic life in the light of Christian principles, with a view to making them operative in the realm of industry." He reasoned that this was "proper work for a priest," even though none of his friends or teachers agreed. How could it not be the church's business to apply the moral law to political economics? Ryan held fast to the pope's declaration, near the end of *Rerum Novarum*, that nothing was more important in the modern context. In 1898, at the age of 29, he was ordained to the priesthood. He gave three months to a small country parish, then consented happily to Archbishop Ireland's plan for him: graduate study at Catholic University, followed by a professorship at St Paul Seminary. Four years later Ryan had most of a dissertation in hand that made him an important player in social ethics and Catholic social theology.[117]

He was lucky to get four years of training for his field, which allowed him to write *A Living Wage* (1906). Ireland had meant to give him only two. Catholic University of America, established as a graduate and research center, was only 11 years old when Ryan enrolled there in 1898. From the beginning it was a battleground of the church's dispute over Americanism. Spalding and Ireland were leading supporters of the university, and its first rector, Bishop John Keane, favored the church's modernizing wing. But in 1896 the Vatican replaced Keane with an ecclesiastical middle-of-the-roader, Monsignor Thomas Conaty, and in January 1899 Leo XIII rocked the liberal wing with a stunning condemnation of Americanism in the encyclical *Testem benevolentiae*. The pope repudiated the view that "the church ought to adapt herself somewhat to our advanced civilization, and, relaxing her ancient rigor, show some indulgence to modern popular theories and methods." Ryan and most of his teachers tried to believe that somehow the pope's condemnation did not apply to American supporters of republican government like themselves.[118]

There was a back-story European basis for thinking so, or at least hoping so. *Testem benevolentiae* was, in part, a response to a bitter feud in French Catholicism between modernizers and reactionaries. French liberals pointed to the American church as proof that Catholicism was compatible with republican government; French conservatives, who opposed the French Republic, countered that the American church was selling out the ancient faith. With a large dose of special pleading, if not dissembling, Ryan and his superiors contended that the encyclical applied only to the French republicans, not American liberals like themselves, looking past the fact that it explicitly condemned "Americanism" and was addressed formally to Cardinal Gibbons.

Catholic University kept its head down during Conaty's rectorship and stuck to a quietly liberal course. Ryan studied sociology and moral theology, respectively, under two priests and liberal-leaning scholars, William Kerby and Thomas J. Bouquillon. In economics his teachers were W. J. Ashley, who covered the medieval guild system, and John A. Hobson, who taught that underconsumption and oversaving were the chief causes of depressions, a theory that Ryan adopted. Having finally received some formal instruction in economics, he was eager for a third year of graduate study, but lacked any word from Ireland, who was in Europe. Ryan gave himself the benefit of the doubt, returning to the university; a bit later he learned that Ireland had meant for him to begin teaching at St Paul's. In the end he got a third and fourth year of graduate study, wrote *A Living Wage*, and began his teaching career as a fully trained social ethicist, though it took him another four years to complete the requirements for his doctorate.[119]

A Living Wage was inspired by Leo XIII's statement in *Rerum Novarum* that "there is a dictate of nature more imperious and more ancient than any bargain between man and man, that the remuneration must be enough to support the wage earner in reasonable and frugal comfort." The book also showed the payoff of Ryan's years of philosophical instruction, developing the theory of rights on which all his subsequent work was based. Ryan argued that every individual had a personal and natural right to a wage that afforded a decent standard of living. As a *personal* reality, this right was absolute, not social; it belonged to the individual as an individual, not as a member of society, much less a particular kind of society. It was a *natural* right, not a positive one, because it was the endowment of every divinity-imprinted human being from birth, not something conferred by society or earned within it. In other words, the right to a living wage was an inviolable moral claim to a personal good that derived from each person's rational nature as a natural right, not a positive or legal right established by civil authority. Its validity depended on the will of no person except the one in whom it inhered.[120]

For Ryan it was crucial to insist on the absolute right to a living wage; otherwise it depended on the politics of particular societies. Critics of natural rights theory usually argued that rights came into existence and obtained their apparent necessity only in society. Since all rights derived from society, they existed for a social end, to serve the social welfare. Ryan replied that certain rights required no social organization or contact. As long as two human beings existed at the same time, their rights to life, liberty, and property were existent. These rights had no utility apart from social relationships, but that did not make them social creations. Natural rights were like evening gowns, Ryan analogized; they were worn only in certain contexts, but that did not make them products of the occasions. Since the right to a living wage was natural, not social, it was primarily about the right-bearer's welfare in society, not the welfare of society. For Ryan, as for Leo XIII, that was the key to the Catholic protection of the rights and absolute value of personhood.

In Catholic natural law theory, eternal law existed in God's mind from eternity, and natural law was the apprehension of God's eternal law by human reason. Theoretically, human beings were capable of knowing God's will and acting upon it, but because of sin, human action was corrupted. Aquinas argued, along Aristotelian lines, that it was possible to rationally discern the specific ends toward which human beings naturally tended (for example, to live, reproduce, acquire knowledge, maintain a good society, and worship God) and the general end for which God created human beings, to be with God in eternity. Catholic theologians differed over the relation of intellect and will, and the extent of human corruption by sin, but they agreed that because of sin, the state was needed to provide for the common good, especially by restraining evil. The church, being superior to the state by virtue of its divine origin and supernatural end, interpreted the implications of the natural law for individuals and the state.[121]

This tradition of natural right theory was more moderate and credible than the Enlightenment versions that nineteenty-century philosophers rejected, Ryan stressed. In the Catholic idea, the natural rights of the individual derived from the individual's essential nature, relations, and end. They proceeded from the natural law, the portion of God's eternal law that applied to human endeavor. In Catholic thought, the natural law referred to the essential and permanent aspects of human existence; thus it was readily intuited or observed. The Enlightenment radicals, however, fixed on a pre-social "state of nature," not the law of nature, fancifully playing up the primitive and unconventional. For Aquinas and the Catholic tradition, the law of nature was an ideal *for* human law; for Rousseau and the Enlightenment radicals it was an ideal to be reached by dispensing with human law. Ryan placed the Catholic idea between the positivist and Rousseauian primitivist ideas. It taught that individuals were endowed naturally by God with rights to the development of personality that the state must not overrule; at the same time it taught that the state had a duty to adjudicate individual claims for the sake of the just welfare of all its citizens. On the question of the limit of individual rights, Ryan rejected Kant's rule that a person could do anything that did not interfere with the equal liberty of others, since that opened the door to subjective relativism and abuse. The "true formula" was the Thomistic one, that the individual "has a right to all things that are essential to the reasonable development of his personality, consistently with the rights of others and the complete observance of the moral law." The right to a living wage had a stronger basis than the willingness of communities to acknowledge it, being inherent in the God-given dignity of every person.[122]

That did not mean that the right to a living wage was original and primary, inhering in all persons regardless of condition, like the right to live or to marry. The wage system was not universal like marriage, Ryan reasoned; thus the right to a living wage was derived and secondary, pertinent only for wage-earners. It was deduced from the right to subsist upon the earth's bounty, a biblical theme that Ryan described as a consistent, if vaguely formulated, principle of Christian ethics from the early Fathers onward. Ambrose and Basil were eloquent on the subject; Aquinas added that property should be owned privately but used in common, so that all persons could be sustained by the earth's bounty. Ryan noted that all titles of private ownership were particular, validating claims to particular things: "They show why the good in question belongs to the present claimant *rather than to any other owner,* but they do not prove the validity of private property as an *institution.* Private ownership of the earth's resources is right and reasonable not for its own sake – which would be absurd – but because it enables men to supply their wants more satisfactorily than would be possible in a regime of common property."[123]

A Living Wage offered a theory of minimal decency, not a theory of the just wage; justice was more complex. The minimum standard was a step beyond subsistence, Ryan argued. It was that a human being had the right to a decent livelihood that did not violate one's personhood: "He is to live as a man, not as an animal. He must have food, clothing and shelter. He must have opportunity to develop within reasonable limits all his faculties, physical, intellectual, moral and spiritual." The rational ground of the right was the dignity and essential needs of personhood. To hinder any person from obtaining access on reasonable terms to a decent existence was to violate that person's intrinsic worth as a person.[124]

For centuries the church repeated the same vague phrases about paying a "fair price" for human labor. Ryan stressed that not until 1891 did Catholic teaching on this point make a significant advance, though he acknowledged that *Rerum Novarum* built on the social democratic activism of German archbishop Wilhelm E. von Ketteler, who supported the labor movement of the 1860s and 1870s and eventually advocated state support of producer cooperatives. With *Rerum Novarum*, Ryan observed, the idea of a living wage became "an explicit principle of Catholic ethics." In addition to declaring that "reasonable and frugal comfort" was, by natural right, the minimum standard of compensation, the pope admonished that if a worker was driven by necessity or fear of a worse evil to accept worse conditions, "he is the victim of fraud and injustice."[125]

Ryan urged that *Rerum Novarum* shared the same social-ethical spirit as the English Anglican socialism of F. D. Maurice and Charles Kingsley, the German Christian socialism of Adolf Stöcker and Rudolf Todt, and the American social gospel of Gladden and Ely. In the second edition of *A Living Wage* (1920) he noted approvingly that the Federal Council of Churches of America gave priority to a living wage over dividends. In the original edition of 1906, he estimated that the minimal income needed for an average American family was $600, and that approximately 60 percent of adult male workers in the USA received less than this amount.[126]

Like his tradition, Ryan read his gender assumptions into the natural law; on the other hand, he took a tougher line than Leo XIII on the necessity of a family living wage as distinguished from a personal living wage. Leo, when asked whether the minimum standard should be a family wage, referred the question to Tommaso Cardinal Zigliara, who invoked the distinction between justice and morality: the minimum standard for justice was a wage sufficient for the personal maintenance of the worker, but an employer who paid only that much failed the test of charity. Ryan replied that if the idea of a living wage was about justice, it had to apply to the entire families of wage earners. It was not a moral ideal in the first place, and if it did not apply to the families for which wage earners labored, it was not terribly meaningful. Every man had the right to become the head of a family, Ryan reasoned; thus the right to a family wage derived from the primary rights to live and to marry. It was not a question merely of meeting the needs of the family, because on that ground one could make a similar argument that a minimum wage should cover the needs of one's ailing or dependent parents.

Ryan did not go that far. The right to the means of maintaining one's wife and children was not derived from the duty of maintaining them, but rather, from the laborer's dignity. Maintaining a wife and children was an essential need of the wage earner, belonging to a different category than that of supporting one's parents. If male wage earners did not, in "the normal order of things," maintain their families financially, they would not be entitled to the additional remunerations that distinguished a family living wage from a personal living wage. As it was, Ryan argued, the duty to provide for one's family was merely the occasion or condition of the right to a living wage, not its ultimate cause: "The right to the conditions of being the head of a family, which is obvious, implies the right to a family Living Wage, because nature and reason have decreed that the family should be supported by its head."[127]

His argument was straightforwardly patriarchal and essentialist. Since men were the heads of families by eternal and natural law, the right to a living wage was primarily about them and their dignity. Ryan said nothing about women who provided the sole support for their families, nor about women wage earners as a whole. He was emphatic that the welfare of the family and society made it "imperative that the wife and mother should not engage in any labor except that of the household." Supporting one's parents, on the other hand, was not an essential condition of a good life; thus it was not a component of the living wage: "In the normal order of things the parents themselves will have, or should have, taken precautions against such an emergency." Ryan counseled against pegging the living wage to the size of a man's family or even the existence of one. It was better to fix a uniform rate for wages and the cost of rearing a family than to pay the family wage situationally, he judged. The crucial thing was to establish the living wage principle as simply as possible, establishing a compulsory minimum wage sufficient for the decent maintenance of the average American family.[128]

A Living Wage was the first work in English to make a sustained argument for a minimum wage. When Ryan began teaching at St Paul Seminary in 1902 he hoped to finish the dissertation promptly and earn his doctorate. But teaching proved to be more demanding than he anticipated, and for two years he found that he had time only for preparing lectures. Besides teaching the usual courses in moral theology on right conduct, moral norms, moral law, conscience, virtue and vice, justice and right, and contracts (he was delighted to be spared from teaching the sacraments, especially penance and matrimony), Ryan taught the first courses offered in a Catholic seminary on economics and sociology. By 1905 he finally had a finished text in hand, and Ely convinced Macmillan to publish it, though Ryan had to pay for the plates because Macmillan anticipated weak sales. Ely urged, correctly, that the book was timely, important, and should sell.

At St Paul's, the only diocesan seminary formally affiliated with Catholic University of America, Ryan acquired the nickname "Fogy Ryan" for his distant manner and dull lectures. Disdaining class discussion, he filled his class time with detailed, formal lectures that showed his learning in sociology and social ethics. He took little interest in conversation or socializing outside class either. Though reasonably affable in everyday relations, Ryan guarded his study time zealously, which was virtually all of his non-sleeping time not claimed by classes and seminary business. One colleague, a German language professor, persisted in trying to establish a chatting relationship with him; repeatedly Ryan snapped, "What do you want?" which dissuaded others from trying. "Fogy Ryan," surrounded by sociable colleagues who acquired "character" status in seminary lore, did not become one. But he gained respect as a forward-looking teacher who focused on the big picture, especially after *A Living Wage* was reviewed widely, and mostly favorably, in the Catholic press. Several reviewers praised Ryan for showing that there was such a thing as a Catholic version of the social gospel. Ryan took particular delight in William Barry's enthusiastic review in the *Catholic Times* (Liverpool), and he appreciated that even the book's negative reviews usually had a respectful tone.[129]

As the reviews appeared, and Ryan saw himself described repeatedly as a promising scholar, he began to think of his work in movement terms, advancing Catholic thought on socioeconomic issues on which it offered little relevant teaching. On issues affecting wage earners, he advocated minimum wage legislation, an eight-hour workday, a minimum working age of 16, the creation of state employment agencies and formal labor arbitration boards, municipal housing, and state government unemployment, health, and old age insurance. On issues affecting consumers, he advocated national and state government ownership of railroads and telephone and telegraph companies, municipal ownership of gas and electric lighting, waterworks, and streetcars, and national ownership of mineral and forestlands. Regarding monopolies that were not public utilities, he advocated price controls on all firms except those demonstrating extraordinary efficiency. On tax policy he advocated progressive rates on incomes and inheritances, as well as the partial appropriation of increases in the value of land. Lecturing often on these subjects to church groups, seminaries, trade unions, and civic organizations, Ryan denied that workers on strike held a right to their jobs. It followed that workers had no right to use force to prevent strikebreakers from working in their place, even when employers sinned against charity and justice by hiring strikebreakers. Ryan allowed that in theory, coercion against strikebreakers might be justified, but in practical terms the benefits of labor violence never outweighed their evil social effects.[130]

Though Ryan firmly denied that he was a socialist, his opponents on the Catholic Right charged that he was one in all but name. *Der Wanderer*, a reactionary German-language newspaper based in St Paul, Minnesota, targeted him as a socialistic modernizer; prominent conservative Catholic lay leaders Edward McSweeney and Rome G. Brown charged that Ryan was a half-socialist leaning toward the whole thing; Ryan replied that he was no more radical than Leo XIII. One of his social gospel friends in the Federal Council of Churches remarked with a twinge of envy that at least Ryan was able to hang his radical pronouncements on a papal encyclical. Ryan agreed that it was a sizable advantage to have a pope on his side; at the same time he lamented his isolation on the social Christian frontier. The Protestant social gospelers had ample company, but where were his Catholic comrades? If his views were really as orthodox as he claimed, why did he not have bishops and priests at his side, or at least behind him? Before World War I Ryan became used to being castigated as a "dangerous agitator"; afterward "subversive" became the favored epithet. Ryan later acknowledged that he experienced some anxiety at being a pioneer, and especially at being accused by "prominent fellow Catholics" of teaching unorthodox views: "However, I never permitted myself to become discouraged, nor was I ever seriously tempted to lessen my activities or to compromise or soften the principles in which I believed."[131]

But for several years he did worry about his standing with the Vatican, especially after biblical scholar Francis E. C. Gigot gave Ryan a chilling warning of the "it could happen to you" variety. In 1907 Pope Pius X condemned the historical critical approach to scripture and 64 related modernist ideas in *Lamentabili Sane*; the same year, in *Pascendi Dominici Gregis*, he described modernism as the synthesis of all heresies. These encyclicals and the Vatican's subsequent institution of an anti-modernist oath for all Catholic clergy and theology professors crushed the beginnings of a modernist theological movement in the USA. For three years a handful of Sulpician priests at St Joseph's Seminary in Yonkers (Dunwoodie), New York had published a ground-breaking journal, *New York Review*, which advocated a mild historicist alternative to the church's regnant neo-scholasticism. Gigot was the group's leading Bible scholar. In 1908, shortly after the *New York Review* folded and a neo-scholastic curriculum was reinstated at the seminary, Ryan exhorted Gigot to cheer up. There had to be a way to do quality Bible scholarship despite the Vatican's condemnation of modern critical tools. Gigot told Ryan not to be so smug; his social ethic could very well be next in line for Vatican censure. That warning reverberated in Ryan's head for three years, stoking his fear that the Vatican might declare that his brand of American social democracy was beyond the pale. But in 1911 he was assured by Irish Franciscan Peter

Fleming, a cleric in Rome with Vatican connections, that he would be safe as long as he avoided the "stigma or implication" of socialism. Ryan trusted that Fleming knew what he was talking about. He later recalled that for the rest of his career he took assurance from Fleming's advice. In 1913 he tried to dispose of the stigma threat by debating with prominent New York socialist Morris Hillquit.[132]

Hillquit, a Russian immigrant, lawyer, Socialist party leader, and prolific author, focused on the actual Socialist movement, not the variety of literary socialisms. The real thing stood for collective ownership of the economy, and its major theorists included Marx, Engels, Ferdinand Lasalle, Jean Jaurés, Georges Plekhanoff, and H. M. Hyndman. On the other hand, Hillquit judged that "bastard offshoots" like "State Socialism" and "Christian Socialism" had no significance. That was fine with Ryan, who preferred a simple and straightforward definition of the subject. Hillquit claimed that under modern capitalism, anarchy reigned supreme, energy and resources were wasted on a monumental scale, pauperism was rampant, the working class was getting poorer, and the American nation stood helpless before the mighty economic trusts. Ryan replied that exaggeration and half-truths reigned supreme in Hillquit's typical socialist rhetoric. How could Hillquit know that reforming the trusts was pointless? The great trusts were barely 20 years old and American politics was just beginning to respond to them. Far from getting poorer, American workers had more discretionary income, leisure, recreation, and access to culture than their parents or grandparents; that was why socialism did not tempt them. The USA had about four million paupers in 1904, Ryan allowed, but that made them a small minority of the American population, and most of them were not paupers in the strict sense of the term, depending on charity permanently. Most of them relied on charity only for a brief time. Capitalism was undoubtedly wasteful and anarchic, Ryan acknowledged, but these were small evils by comparison to Hillquit's remedy of abolishing individual liberty and making everyone a servant of the state. It was much better to reform capitalism. Economic conditions for the masses were better in 1913 than for any previous generation, and the key to making America more just and good was to employ state power toward the end of attaining equality of opportunity.[133]

Ryan cautioned that many of America's social problems sprang directly from defects in human nature, such as ignorance and greed, which would exist under any system. Certain evils were more distinctive to capitalism, he argued: oppression of labor, excessive remuneration for the capitalist class, insufficient remuneration for most wage earners, and unjust distribution of productive property and capital ownership. But the answer was a reform politics that respected the right of individuals to use the bounty of nature toward the end of their self-development, not to "build up a bureaucracy more despotic than anything of the kind that the world has ever seen." He stressed that he hated the predatory and oppressive aspects of capitalist civilization as much as any Socialist: "I deplore the actual and removable evils of our social system quite as strongly as Mr. Hillquit." Ryan had no fondness for "the Capitalist Type," and he expected succeeding generations to judge that the greed, materialism, labor oppression, and "hideous" contrast between the rich and poor in the USA of his time amounted to "essential barbarism." But socialism had no substitute for the two "powerful springs of effort and efficiency" that it eliminated: the hope of reward and the fear of loss. It wrongly made social expediency the test of morality, instead of the other way around. The place to begin in political economy was with the indestructible rights of the individual, Ryan urged, but Hillquit and the Socialists wrongly believed that the individual had no rights against the state.[134]

The Ryan–Hillquit debate went on for four months and was published in *Every-body's Magazine* as a seven-part series. Both contestants were praised for their lucidity and intelligence. Although many Catholics agreed with the *Catholic Fortnightly Review* that Ryan made church teaching sound too much like socialism, the debate boosted his reputation in liberal Catholic circles. That was fortunate for his ambition, because Ryan had grown restless in St Paul. For years he dreamed of getting himself trans-ferred to New York, ideally to edit a magazine on Catholic social doctrine. Ryan lobbied the archbishop of New York, John Cardinal Farley, to launch a house organ for the National Conference of Catholic Charities, but Farley declined. Ryan later explained that most bishops considered him too radical. His isolation was another factor, as Ryan was often the only Catholic in the groups and conferences in which he took part.[135]

In 1914 he got a better offer, however, a political science position at Catholic University. Gibbons, the university chancellor, wanted Ryan at the nation's premier Catholic graduate institution, as did Ryan's former teacher Kerby. Ireland blocked the appointment, telling his friend Gibbons to stop poaching from his seminary, but the following year he relented, giving in to Ryan's fervent pleas to be released. It probably helped that Ireland's social circle included well-to-do locals who were eager for Ryan to leave; his departure was barely noted by the diocesan paper. Ryan returned to Catholic University in 1915 with his typical stern air and rumpled clothes, determined to raise the national profile of Catholic social ethics within and outside the church. His appointment to the political science department was a stopgap to hold him until a theology position opened up, which happened the following year.

Never an inspiring teacher, Ryan was routinely described by his students as dull, dry, phlegmatic, and a bit grumpy. Aside from an economics class that he taught at Trinity College, he taught only graduate students after moving to Catholic University, never more than 10 per class. His writings and public activism, however, immediately lifted the social-ethical profile of Catholic University. In 1917 Ryan launched his long dreamed-of magazine, *Catholic Charities Review*, for which he served as editor, business manager, and principal author.[136]

The year before that he published his major work, *Distributive Justice* (1916), which described the moral aspects of the distributive process of wages, interest, monopoly, and the land question. The problem of distributive justice was primarily about incomes, Ryan argued, not possessions, and it was about the distribution of the products of industry among four classes – landowners, capitalists, business people, and laborers – not the distribution of all the nation's goods among all people. *Distributive Justice* had a distinct argument, though readers had to plow through hundreds of pages of diffuse economic discussion to find it. Ryan's thesis was that the American system of political economy was gravely unjust in all four of its fundamental institutions – private land-ownership, private ownership of capital, business practices, and the wage system – but none of these institutions was essentially unjust.[137]

Ryan reviewed socialist and single tax arguments against private landownership, defended private ownership as a natural right and the best system of land tenure, and discussed the ethics of private capital and interest. Blasting Marx's labor theory of value as "arbitrary, unreal, and fantastic," he argued that private ownership and management of capital were superior to socialist collectivism and that the state needed to be the guardian of social justice, improving the industrial system. Marx taught that labor was the only explanation and determinant of value; Ryan replied that labor created some things lacking any value, some things (like land and minerals) had value with no labor, and some things (Renoir's paintings, for example) had far greater value than the labor expended upon them. The true determinants of value were utility and scarcity.[138]

On the ethics of interest, Ryan noted that numerous popes and church councils of the Middle Ages condemned all interest on loans. In the seventeenth century Catholic moralists began to make an exception for the legal rate of interest allowed by civil governments, and by the eighteenth century "usury" meant, in effect, charging a higher rate of interest than that authorized by the state. Since money had become virtually productive, readily exchangeable for productive property, what used to be called usury had become morally justified. Under capitalism money was the economic equivalent of productive capital. The church recognized the new social reality by dropping the subject of usury from its moral discourse and offering no new teaching on the subject, Ryan observed. The last formal pronouncement on it by a pope was Benedict XIV's encyclical, *Vix Pervenit*, in 1745, which refrained from condemning interest received from investments in productive property. Ryan judged that the church was right to adjust slowly to the logic of capitalism, and the modern church probably did not need a formal position on the subject:

> Evidently this is good logic and common sense. If it is right for the stockholder of a railway to receive dividends, it is equally right for the bondholder to receive interest. If it is right for a merchant to take from the gross returns of his business a sum sufficient to cover interest on his capital, it is equally right for the man from whom he has borrowed money for the enterprise to exact interest.[139]

Distributive Justice argued that private ownership was a fundamental and natural human right, and that landowners and capitalists had an equal right to take rent and interest, respectively, but that tenants and employees had a stronger right to a decent livelihood and a living wage. Ryan wanted reforms in the current system of land tenure that curtailed monopolies, limited the excessive gains of the landowner class, and made it possible for the laboring class to acquire land. All natural monopolies needed to belong to the state and nation, and progressive taxes were axiomatic. Ryan favored a supertax on estates, and he wanted the state and the banks to promote a greater diffusion of capital by expanding the cooperative sector: "Through co-operation the weaker farmers, merchants, and consumers can do business and obtain goods at lower costs, and save money for investment with greater facility, while the laborers can slowly but surely become capitalists and interest-receivers, as well as employees and wage-receivers."[140]

If a business company followed the rules of fair competition, it had a right to all the profits it could obtain. Similarly, landowners had a right to all the economic rent they could obtain, modified by the right of tenants and employees to a decent livelihood and the right of the state to tax the land up to the point of lowering its value. Ryan cautioned against the desire for a simple, clear, emotionally satisfying standard of distributive justice. Socialism was precise and inspiring, but wrong. The best approach to justice was complex, balanced, imprecise, and reformist: "Although the attainment of greater justice in distribution is the primary and most urgent need of our time, it is not the only one that is of great importance." America needed to conserve its natural resources, abolish its habits of wastefulness, and adopt scientific methods of soil cultivation. Above all, the building of a good society depended more upon personal regeneration than any collection of social reforms. Ryan took only a brief pass at the latter theme, but he ended with it:

The rich must cease to put their faith in material things, and rise to a simpler and saner plane of living; the middle classes and the poor must give up their envy and snobbish imitation of the false and degrading standards of the opulent classes; and all must learn the elementary lesson that the path to achievements worth while leads through the field of hard and honest labor, not of lucky "deals" or gouging the neighbor, and that the only life worth living is that in which one's cherished wants are few, simple, and noble. For the adoption and pursuit of these ideals the most necessary requisite is a revival of genuine religion.[141]

Mainstreaming the Catholic Social Gospel

Distributive Justice was widely praised as a work of distinct intelligence and rigor. Though deeply indebted to *Rerum Novarum*, the book mentioned the encyclical only three times, resting on Ryan's own mastery of economic argument from a natural law standpoint. It put an end to debates about Ryan's standing in Catholic social ethics, which freed him to devote his later writing to topical subjects. Though he wrote very little about international issues, Ryan supported the USA's intervention in World War I and Wilson's campaign for American participation in the League of Nations. In August 1917 Pope Benedict XV pleaded for a negotiated settlement to the war, which Ryan supported; 20 years later he stressed that if the Allies and Central Powers had ended the war in 1917 there would have been no Nazi ascendancy. The pope also called for an international organization for peace. Soon after Wilson launched his campaign for the League of Nations, Ryan judged that average American Catholics were in no mood to line up with Wilson or the pope. He admonished the bishops and Catholic press to provide leadership on the issue, to no avail. German-American Catholics were hostile to Wilson because of the war; Irish-American Catholics were alienated by America's alliance with England; American Catholics as a whole spurned Wilson's idealism and internationalism. Ryan lamented that they were as provincial and conservative on foreign policy as on economic policy. Although tagged as an "Americanizer," he spent much of his career trying to get American Catholics to be less American and more Catholic, taking his favorite papal statements as the definition of good Catholicism.[142]

At the same time he continued to battle the Socialist Left. In 1918 Ryan observed that the Socialist movement no longer insisted on state ownership of farmland and also backed off a bit on capital, allowing individuals to own the tools and machines with which they labored. But it still stood for government ownership and management of all land used for industrial purposes and of all large and medium-sized farms, and it wanted to abolish rent and interest. That turned every worker into a mere hireling of the state: "He must work for the state or starve." Repeatedly Ryan complained that Socialists enjoyed greater moral authority among progressives than they deserved, while the moral wisdom of Catholic teaching was ignored. How else could Eugene Debs have won 900,000 votes in 1912? Progressives and radicals voted for the social reforms that Debs stressed without thinking responsibly about the implications of his socialist program. Ryan urged that *Rerum Novarum* provided the basis of a better political ideology. Protestantism gave birth to the modern capitalist menace; Catholicism stood for the hope of salvation from it: "Thank God, we Catholics are in no degree responsible for the invention of the cold, ugly, soulless thing called modern capitalism, with its industrial autocracy at one extreme and its proletarian masses at the other.

Without the Reformation the capitalism that we now know would have been, humanly speaking, impossible."[143]

He also plunged into the immigration debate, siding with his union friends against fellow Catholics who, even if they belonged to unions, could not abide the implications or company of the anti-immigrant movement. In 1915 Wilson vetoed a bill requiring a literacy test for immigrants, but two years later, despite another Wilson veto, it became law. Wilson admonished that literacy was not a good test of character; Ryan, acknowledging the racist factor, agreed with the president that the character issue was a red herring. For Ryan the issue was the necessity of holding down the wage-diminishing supply of unskilled labor. It troubled him to be aligned with racists and against virtually the entire Catholic press; on the other hand, his commitment to the living wage prevailed. In 1914 the outbreak of World War I cut off the flow of immigrants to the USA, which set off a sharp rise in wages. Ryan and his union allies wanted to sustain that trend, and they feared an avalanche of immigrants after the war ended. If America prohibited unskilled foreigners from immigrating for 10 years, Ryan urged in 1917, the living wage would surely be written into American law.[144]

On prohibition and women's suffrage he came down on the side of tepid acceptance, sometimes emphasizing his reservations. Ryan wrote only once about prohibition in the years before it became law, judging that the right to drink was less important to human welfare than the social good that prohibiting alcohol would serve. Wherever prohibition had the support of 75 percent of the population, it was worth trying. On the other hand, he detested the strident moralism and undemocratic spirit of professional prohibitionists, a feeling he expressed freely in the classroom.[145]

He had the same problem with women's suffrage, partly because many of the same women were leaders in both causes. Ryan could not relate to them. "A very large proportion of the women agitators for suffrage have been and are of the radical type, or the advanced feminist type," he observed. These women were not mothers like most women, nor were they feminine. They tended to be women of leisure, who flocked to settlement work and philanthropy, or women in the professions or labor unions, who took an unwomanly interest in politics: "Their dissatisfaction with male political rule and their desire that women should share the business of government arise mainly from facts and considerations peculiar to their special classes, and sometimes to their personal conditions." To Ryan it was pathetic that female suffrage activists presumed to speak for all women, because "their ideas and psychology are remote from the mental habits and attitudes of the majority of women." To put it gently, "their theories and performances do not reflect the ideas and temper of women generally." To put it less gently, most women found fulfillment as housewives and mothers, but most feminists latched onto politics as compensation for their "lives of emptiness and aimlessness." That explained why their arguments were so lacking in common sense or attractiveness; the suffrage movement reflected the skewed perspectives of an odd minority, "considerably tainted with excessive radicalism of various kinds." Most women did not want or need to vote, Ryan asserted; if the suffrage question were put to them, it would lose resoundingly. In his telling, that was why feminists worked on the guilt feelings of men; they were too shrewd to let suffrage depend on women: "They have preferred to entrust their cause to the men rather than to the members of their own sex as a whole."[146]

Yet for all the strangeness and radicalism of the suffrage movement, the feminists were good at politics, Ryan acknowledged. They kept pushing the rock of suffrage up the mountain of American politics and Constitutional revision; they had a president – Wilson – on their side; and in 1917 they won a huge victory in New York State. Ryan believed that New York was a turning point for the movement, which he did not begrudge. He had long believed that women deserved to vote, even if he disliked the kind of women who campaigned for it. There was no reason why women could not understand the great issues that confronted their nation and community, he argued. Admittedly, most women would never be as politically knowledgeable as their husbands, because "woman's true and permanent place is the home." But with a reasonable amount of effort they were capable of "a fairly intelligent exercise of the voting privilege." On most issues they were likely to vote the same as their husbands, and on issues that affected the home and morals, they were likely to have better politics than their husbands. To Ryan, that was a net gain for the republic. It was a good thing for wives and mothers to speak for themselves, instead of letting radical feminists speak for them, and on some issues they were likely to make politics more friendly to families and morality.[147]

By the end of the war in December 1918 every group with social ambitions had either published a program for social reconstruction or had one cooking. Ryan had read nearly a dozen of them when he drafted his own in December. The British Labour Party and the US Chamber of Commerce had two of the stronger ones; Ryan was eager to show that Catholicism had a better idea. His 12-point agenda included minimum wage legislation, unemployment and health insurance, a minimum age (16) for working, legal enforcement of the right to organize, continuation of the National War Labor Board, a national employment service, public housing, continuation of wartime wages, excessive profits and incomes taxes, control of monopolies, support of worker ownership, and support of cooperative ownership. He had barely roughed out a first draft when Fr John O'Grady, secretary of the National Catholic War Council, saw it on Ryan's desk and demanded to have it for the council, which consisted of the Catholic Archbishops of the United States.[148]

O'Grady was in a hurry; the church needed a program and Ryan knew the issues better than anyone. For the US bishops, this was a novel undertaking. Having lacked a national organization that addressed social issues, the bishops had never issued a policy statement. But in 1917 the National Catholic War Council was formed to coordinate Catholic support for the war effort, and after the war O'Grady and others turned it into a policy organization. By 1919 it had four programmatic divisions, one of which, the Social Action Department, was directed by Ryan. In 1923 the group formally became the National Catholic Welfare Conference. At the turning point in February 1919 the bishops pared Ryan's 12 points to 11, making only slight revisions in his 16-page text. They retained his emphasis that most workers had insufficient income while the capitalist class made too much. Expressions of stunned delight and outrage poured in. The *National Civic Federation Review* set the tone and storyline for much of the hostile reaction, charging that radicals had deceived the bishops into calling for the overthrow of the American system and the inauguration of "a reign of chaos." Frank Walsh, chair of the War Labor Board and a Catholic progressive, exulted that suddenly he was proud to be a Catholic; the riches of a profound but hidden ethical tradition had been unveiled. Many sympathetic observers declared that the "Bishops' Program" launched a new era in American Catholicism. Ryan hoped that was true. He told his sister that the Bishops' Program vindicated his entire career; perhaps the church would find its social-ethical voice in the 1920s. Later he recalled sadly, "All

such hopeful forecasts met with disappointment. For more than a decade, social thinking and social action were chilled and stifled in an atmosphere of pseudo prosperity
and thinly disguised materialism."[149]

As director of the National Catholic Welfare Conference's Social Action Department Ryan worked an inside/outside strategy, trying to build a progressive constituency in the church and increase its public advocacy of social justice causes. Grimly he
battled the selfishness of the 1920s, which he called "this degeneration." By then his
major works were behind him. It was a full-time job to oppose the shallow hedonism
and cynicism of the time, plus an upsurge of anti-Catholic prejudice, especially of the
respectable sort. Ryan confronted anti-Catholic prejudice in scholarly and popular
forums, where, in both cases, the burning issue was the Catholic Church's view of
religious freedom. In 1922 he and Jesuit scholar Moorhouse F. X. Millar published a
reader for the National Catholic Welfare Council (NCWC), *The State and the Church*,
which sought to explain the church's teaching about the state, why it was correct and
necessary, and why it was not threatening to American religious freedom. For over
30 years this book was the standard text in the field, providing strong instruction and
apologetics. It was less successful, however, in providing assurance that Catholics could
be trusted in politics. For decades afterward critics of Catholic authoritarianism and
intolerance rested their case by quoting Ryan.[150]

The book's first chapter reprinted Pope Leo XIII's encyclical letter of November
1, 1885, *Immortale Dei*, on the "Christian Constitution of States," which reaffirmed
the church doctrine that the state was morally obligated to "have care for religion"
and recognize the "true" religion. Expounding the pope's teaching, Ryan moved
quickly to the heart of the matter, concerning the "true" religion:

> This means the form of religion professed by the Catholic Church. It is a thoroughly
> logical position. If the State is under moral compulsion to profess and promote religion,
> it is obviously obliged to profess and promote only the religion that is true; for no indi-
> vidual, no group of individuals, no society, no State is justified in supporting error or in
> according to error the same recognition as to truth.

Was it not better to trust truth to overcome error by its own power? Ryan replied
that history was chastening. Terribly destructive errors existed "side by side" with the
Catholic Church for centuries, and if the church had not forcefully opposed the Protestant Reformation, the destruction would have been monumental. Was it not better
to treat all religions as being equally sound? Ryan replied that two contradictory propositions could not be true. If Catholicism and Protestantism contradicted each other, at
least one of them had to be wrong. Was it not impossible to determine which religion
was the true one? Ryan replied that the evidence for Catholicism was overwhelming;
any person of good will who examined the evidence would find that Catholicism was
the true religion. Was it not better for the church's life and vitality to be separate from
the state? Ryan cautioned against the fallacy of the particular instance. In the USA the
separation of church and state worked well for the church, and in some nations the
union of church and state worked badly, but the church did not determine its teaching
on the basis of a few impressions about a few countries in a particular moment of time.
Church teaching had a logic and took a larger historical view.[151]

The heart of the matter concerning the union of church and state was easily summarized; he wrote, "The State should officially recognize the Catholic religion as the

religion of the commonwealth." That did not mean that the church did not tolerate other religions, he cautioned. The "best" evidence of the church's tolerance was that the popes of the Middle Ages, in their capacity as civil rulers of the Papal States, allowed Jews to worship freely. Ryan reasoned that the same principle applied to persons who were baptized into a Protestant sect: "For their participation in false worship does not necessarily imply a willful affront to the true Church nor a menace to public order or social welfare." It was possible to be a Protestant and not be in bad faith; moreover, a flourishing Catholic state could afford to be generous to unbelievers: "The religious performances of an insignificant and ostracized sect will constitute neither a scandal nor an occasion of perversion to Catholics." Ryan stressed that Catholic teaching drew the line at practices contravening natural law and at heresy within the church. In both cases the church's position was absolute, regardless of its relationship to a particular state. The church did not tolerate evils such as idolatry or sexual perversity, nor did it tolerate "false doctrine among Catholics," which was a "menace" to the spiritual welfare of true believers.[152]

Ryan knew how that sounded to American Protestants and some liberal Catholics. The church was straightforwardly intolerant about certain things, he affirmed, but it was never unreasonable, because error had no rights: "Since the profession and practice of error are contrary to human welfare, how can error have rights? How can the voluntary toleration of error be justified?" If only one religion could be true, and Catholicism was the one, there was no logical ground for universal toleration. Some critics, especially some of Ryan's nervous liberal Catholic friends, objected that Protestants might turn the Catholic argument for intolerance against Catholics; Ryan replied that in fact, Protestantism never worked as a state religion "because no Protestant sect claims to be infallible." Wherever the old Protestant states tried to replace the Catholic Church with an intolerant Protestant one, the experiment went badly, because Protestantism had nothing but private judgment, a variously interpreted Bible, and weak ecclesiology to offer. For a non-Catholic to recognize the truth of the Catholic faith, Ryan argued, good will was required, but every rational person could see that the church had logic on its side: "If there is only one true religion, and if its possession is the most important good in life for States as well as individuals, then the public profession, protection, and promotion of this religion and the legal prohibition of all direct assaults upon it, becomes one of the most obvious and fundamental duties of the State."[153]

That was the doctrine of the church, Ryan stressed; papal teaching on this subject was clear, logical, and not optional. But in practice it applied without exception only to the ideal, "the completely Catholic State," of which there were hardly any left, if any at all. In the real world Catholics had to deal with a variety of rival religions and worldviews, including rival theories of government. Ryan moved quickly to the upshot: the USA was nothing like a Catholic state. Did the ideal of a Catholic state give American Protestants a legitimate basis for resisting the growth of Catholicism in American life and politics? Ryan replied that the USA was too overwhelmingly Protestant for that to be a serious question. In theory Catholic teaching committed American Catholics to an ideal that, in fact, no Catholic expected to be realized. For that matter, the whole world was turning against Catholicism in this respect. Thus, the practical reality was "so remote" from the ideal "that no practical man will let it disturb his equanimity or affect his attitude toward those who differ from him in religious faith." Ryan allowed that in the USA, faced with the hostility of "zealots and bigots" who fanned the flames of anti-Catholicism, it was tempting for Catholics to relinquish "the principles of eternal and unchangeable truth" for a bit of civil peace. But that would never work anyway, "for they would not think us sincere," and denying the truth was the greatest evil. So American Catholics held fast to the vision of an American Catholic state, while Ryan assured non-Catholics that this vision was "so improbable and so far in the future that it should not occupy their time or attention."[154]

The latter assurance did not spare him from having to revisit this topic throughout the 1920s, especially after Al Smith was nominated for the presidency in 1928. By then Ryan had changed his position on Prohibition, which had a role in the presidential campaign. For 10 years Ryan made his support for Prohibition contingent on its efficacy, but in 1926 he judged that temperance advocates like him had aimed too high. Prohibition was simply not workable in the American context; thus, the infringement upon individual liberty and individual rights that it represented was not justified. The Eighteenth Amendment, Ryan wrote, was "an unnecessary, unwise and unjust enactment" that Americans needed to abolish. Two years later the Democrats nominated a Catholic governor and temperance opponent, Alfred E. Smith, for the presidency. As governor of New York, Smith had helped bring about the repeal of the New York State Enforcement Act, though he tried to soft-pedal his position on the presidential campaign trail. As the first Catholic nominated by a major party for president, his candidacy unleashed a flood of anti-Catholic propaganda, which Ryan did his best to correct.[155]

Did the Catholic Church not teach that it alone possessed divine sanction, and thus no other church had a natural right to exist? Ryan replied that this doctrine of the church did not conflict with the US Constitution, because the Constitution defined legal rights, not natural rights. But did the Catholic Church not claim the right to draw the line that separated its jurisdiction from the state on issues in which both the church and state had an interest? Ryan replied that the church's conflict with the American state was more apparent than real, since the Constitution recognized the right of Americans to practice any religious doctrine that did not infringe the rights or property of other Americans, and the Catholic Church taught no proscribed practices. The Supreme Court rightly prohibited Mormons from practicing polygamy, but Catholicism posed no such challenges to American law. But did the Catholic Church not condemn any state that granted equal favor to the Catholic and non-Catholic religions? Ryan replied that this was a genuine conflict, but not quite what it seemed. The church's doctrine in this area referred to the ideal, the Catholic state, but the church recognized that in the real world there were very few Catholic states, if any, and it did not condemn states that sanctioned religious pluralism. Moreover, the statements of the church and the American Constitution were not about the same thing, because the Constitution took no position on whether one religion was more true or good than any other.[156]

Virtually every critic brought up the *Syllabus of Errors*. Turning the usual accusation around, Ryan observed that nothing in the *Syllabus* was condemned "either explicitly or implicitly" in the Constitution. As for the usual accusation, that the Constitution affirmed and required things condemned in the *Syllabus*, Ryan argued that critics routinely blurred the difference between statements about ethical principles and political policies. The Constitution said nothing about moral rights, he stressed; it dealt with practical policies of government, not ethical principles. Some critics, such as *Atlantic Monthly* writer Charles C. Marshall, implored Catholic apologists to admit the "inevitable conflict" between the Catholic and American ideas. Ryan replied, "Well, we will not concede anything of the sort, for we know the teaching and spirit of our Church better than does Mr. Marshall, and we think we understand the provisions and implications of the Constitution. We even indulge the supposition that we have a better acquaintance than he with the rules of logic." American Catholics did not fantasize about fusing the church and state, despite the impressions of anti-Catholic critics.[157]

One such critic, Protestant pastor Charles H. Fountain, took a lower road, contending that no Catholic should be elected to any political office because that gave undeserved prestige to a religious dictatorship. Ryan replied, in that case, why not prohibit Catholics from serving in the US army or navy? Also, his liberal Protestant friends should stop associating with him, since that gave undeserved prestige to Catholicism too: "The sum of the matter is that Mr. Fountain would, from fear of a remote and hypothetical danger, sentence the Catholic people of America to be treated by their non-Catholic fellow-citizens as veritable Pariahs." Ryan smelled a witch-hunt in the "hideous prejudice" of Americans like Fountain, who, if left unchallenged, would consign Catholics to the Ku Klux Klan corner of American infamy: "It is all profoundly discouraging, not only to Catholics but to all lovers of justice and haters of intolerance."[158]

The election of 1928 proved dreadfully discouraging on that point. Ryan agreed with the saying that Hoover defeated Smith because of Prohibition, prejudice, and prosperity, but he stressed that anti-Catholic prejudice carried the day for Hoover. For months Americans were drenched in a downpour of anti-Catholic fear mongering that overwhelmed normal politics. Ryan professed no lasting grievance against average Americans who didn't know any better: "They are inheritors of a long anti-Catholic tradition, compact of misrepresentation and falsehood. They have never had adequate opportunity to learn the facts about the Catholic Church." But he seethed at the educated clergy and political professionals who smeared the church for political advantage: "I cannot feel so indulgent toward the men who have exploited religious intolerance in the campaign from their pulpits, from the platform and by the written and printed word. Most of these men know better or are culpably ignorant." *The Christian Century* was an especially painful example of the former. On October 18, 1928, *Century* editor Charles Clayton Morrison editorialized that Protestants should not "look with unconcern upon the seating of a representative of an alien culture, of a medieval Latin mentality, of an undemocratic hierarchy and of a foreign potentate in the great office of the President of the United States." Ryan recoiled at that string of bigotries: "If a high class journal, which prides itself as 'liberal' could conscientiously use this sort of argument, the same is probably true of thousands upon thousands of educated Protestants."[159]

Ryan fought against and for liberalism. In 1929 the *Nation* ran an editorial that claimed that the Catholic Church was "unalterably opposed to very nearly every tenet of the liberal creed." Ryan's "yes" and "no" were equally emphatic. A true Catholic could not be the kind of liberal who rejected the authority of the church or divine authority, he stressed; Ryan was disgusted by liberals who disobeyed the commands of the church and yet claimed to be Catholic. Discussions of this topic usually brought up the Index of Prohibited Books. Regarding the great literature that Catholics were deprived of reading, Ryan replied, in effect, "Give me a break." Clergy and teachers had no trouble obtaining the required permissions to do their work, he stated, and the "average educated Catholic" did not miss anything by being deprived of Gibbon's *Decline and Fall of the Roman Empire*, Kant's *Critique of Pure Reason*, or Darwin's *Origin of Species*. What about the *Book of Common Prayer* or the Protestant Bibles? Ryan responded: "It is difficult to see what benefit the ordinary Catholic would derive from their perusal. After all, we have incomparably better prayer books of our own, and the Church possessed and preserved the integral Scriptures for many centuries before the emergence of Martin Luther and King James I." A few things on the Index were poor imitations of the real thing, and most things on the Index were truly harmful, or trash, or both.[160]

But Ryan treasured his good standing in American liberal politics and economics, and he was zealous for his church to have a similar standing. He gave unstinting support to civil liberties causes, serving as the only Catholic priest on the national board of the American Civil Liberties Union (ACLU), and he worked tirelessly for the National Catholic Welfare Conference, serving as director of its Washington, DC division. To his colleagues in the ACLU and other progressive organizations Ryan was an invaluable link to a foreign world, Catholicism. Repeatedly they lauded his constructive, good-spirited cooperation and intellectual rigor. Ryan clashed with ACLU director Roger Baldwin over Baldwin's absolutist concept of free speech, and on occasion he got into political scrapes involving links to Communists that embarrassed him; Ryan had trouble keeping straight the profusion of groups that asked for his endorsement. But he took a stoic attitude to problems of this kind, reasoning that, in a reactionary time, doing civil liberties work involved taking a few lumps. He served on the ACLU board until 1935, when the group's aggressive adoption of academic freedom as a civil liberties issue drove him out. Ryan protested that defending *civil* liberties was enough for the ACLU, and that academic freedom was best handled by academic organizations. He could imagine the ACLU contending that Catholic universities had no right to fire professors for teaching heresy.[161]

The low point of his career occurred in 1923, when the Supreme Court declared in *Adkins v. Children's Hospital* that minimum wage legislation was unconstitutional. Ryan blasted the decision in an address to the Catholic Conference on Industrial Problems, and was gratified the following year when the court overruled most of the Adkins decision in a similar case upholding the state of Washington. It was not his last experience of seeing a cherished idea struck down by the Supreme Court. In the meantime, leaning on Hobson's theory of underconsumption, Ryan protested that the prosperity of the 1920s was a hollow phenomenon that left too many people behind. After he turned out to be right about the hollowness, he pressed hard on Hobson's theory to explain why the Depression occurred.[162]

In December 1928 Ryan disputed Hoover's "chicken in every pot, two cars in every garage" boilerplate by noting that America had over three million unemployed workers. Some of them lacked a job for seasonal, local, or technological reasons, Ryan observed, but there was also a growing problem of chronic unemployment caused by general overproduction and underconsumption. Most American industries were capable of producing more goods than they could sell at profitable prices. Because the capacity for overproduction had become chronic in the American economy, so had the problem of unemployment. The system excelled at turning out consumer goods, but a growing number of farmers and laborers were poor or unemployed, thus creating an insufficient demand for consumer goods that threatened to depress the economy. Right up to the great crash of October 1929, Ryan warned that modern capitalism had a chronic unemployment problem because machine production far outraced the buying power of consumers. Hoover declared that human wants were almost insatiable; Ryan replied that the invention of new commodities was unlikely to solve the unemployment problem, and that creating loads of new luxuries was not desirable anyway. What good was it to produce new vanity items and junk for the well off when others had nothing? Instead of more-of-the-same capitalism, Ryan wanted Hoover to create new programs in public works, push through a universal minimum-wage law, and establish a five-day workweek.[163]

The basic problem was "our old friend 'overproduction,'" he warned – the general, constant, systemic capacity for overproduction that more-of-the-same economic policy encouraged. In the summer of 1929 Ryan judged that the problem was most acute in agriculture, coalmining, textiles, and shoe manufacturing, and nearly as serious in the building trades. One symptom was a locked-out labor reserve suffering in the midst of seeming prosperity. Another was the dramatic increase in the cost of selling goods. Advertising was supposed to convey information, he argued, but America was witnessing an explosion of "high-power salesmanship" that had nothing to do with providing information. In Ryan's estimate, about 90 percent of advertising either promoted a certain brand that was no better than others or aroused a desire for something that nobody needed. He was not against advertising, he averred; on the other hand, the frenzy of the advertising industry struck Ryan as not a good thing, either for society's moral health or for what it said about the economy.[164]

He was mindful of sailing against the general public and the economics establishment. The public rewarded Republican "prosperity" at the polls, while economists assured that general overproduction was impossible. Neo-classical economic theory taught that a supply of any kind of goods was a demand for other goods. Ryan agreed that every supply of goods constituted a potential demand, "a power to call for some other kind of goods," but that was not necessarily an actual demand for something that existed. Textile owners and farmers both produced surpluses, but many farmers were poorer for it: "When two persons have a surplus of goods on their hands only one may desire the products of the other or neither may desire what the other has to offer." Ryan appreciated that his objections sounded carping and unappreciative in the context of the Roaring Twenties' economy. He made it worse by cautioning that the next generation was not likely to find its economic equivalent of the automobile industry. In that case, society would become even more dependent on the expanding consumption of luxuries, which was dangerous. Obsessing over frivolous things was not good for the well off, and "the masses ought not to be required to provide superfluous goods for the few, while they themselves are unable to obtain a reasonable amount of necessaries and comforts."[165]

In October 1929, writing in *Commonweal*, Ryan cautioned that a day of reckoning was approaching. It arrived while the magazine was still on the newsstands. Afterward he stressed that the crash of prices on Wall Street was an effect, not a cause. Even without the "orgy of speculation" that reached its peak in October, the Depression would have been general and devastating; the stock market crash simply made it "spectacularly obvious." Ryan wrote a flurry of speeches and articles in response to the Depression, contending that it was caused by overproduction of capital goods and underconsumption of consumer goods, and that government needed to respond by providing employment and lifting the economy. The economy's crash was not Hoover's fault, Ryan acknowledged; however, Hoover made it worse by refusing to make adequate public expenditures on public works. Ryan wanted an increase in income taxes for unemployment relief, and, by 1932, a $6 billion appropriation by Congress for public works. Repeatedly he made the case for Hobson's theory of underconsumption, advocated higher incomes for farmers and laborers, demanded lower interest rates, and insisted that the owners of capital should have a smaller share of the national income. Priming the economic pump through public works was not a permanent fix, he allowed; the ideal ratio of private to public employees was about two-and-one-half to one. But in the emergency context of the Depression, a massive program of public works and relief was an economic and moral necessity. In 1932 the USA elected a president who unexpectedly turned out to agree.[166]

Ryan was vacationing in Ireland when the Democratic Party nominated Franklin Roosevelt for president. The prospect of a Roosevelt presidency was a dismal one for him. Roosevelt had no discernible beliefs, his campaign flitted from one opportunistic posture to another, and he criticized Hoover for excessive spending, promising to cut government spending by 25 percent. That left Ryan with no one to vote for. He told his students that America was paralyzed by the greed of the few and the timidity of the many. When Roosevelt gave his inaugural address on March 4, 1933, Ryan, feeling ill, listened by radio. He felt a bit elevated by the president's opening statements, felt better as the speech rolled on, appreciated Roosevelt's ridiculous but hopeful "the only thing we have to fear is fear itself," and felt mildly enthused by Roosevelt's closing promise to provide "direct, vigorous" leadership. The next day Roosevelt declared a four-day bank holiday and slapped an embargo on the export of gold, silver, and currency. Ryan disliked the Economy Act of mid-March, which reduced the salaries of government employees and lowered veterans' benefits, and he shook his head at the Emergency Banking Act's currency manipulation. Neither measure put more money into the hands of poor and working-class people, which was the crucial thing.[167]

But as the New Deal got rolling, Ryan found himself approving nearly everything that Roosevelt proposed, and cultivating relationships with New Dealers. In the early going, Labor Secretary Frances Perkins invited him to the White House for a conference on labor issues, Democrats John McCormack and Hugo Black consulted him about upcoming legislation, Ryan helped the White House and National Recovery Administration (NRA) enlist support for the NRA, he joined the advisory council of the US Employment Service, and he later chaired the group. He also joined the National Advisory Committee of the Subsistence Homesteads Division. Amazed at the activist spirit of the Roosevelt administration and immediately identified with it, Ryan filled his calendar with meetings and conferences, and his writings defended New Deal programs.

His vindication in the political and ecclesiastical spheres happened at the same time and for closely related reasons, though each had its own center of gravity. In the political sphere Ryan's outspoken advocacy of Keynesian welfare economics before the New Deal existed made him a prophetic figure after the New Deal was launched. In the ecclesiastical sphere he was rewarded for anticipating a similar turn in Catholic social thought. Pope Pius XI, in 1933, conferred upon Ryan the honor of Domestic Prelate in the Papal Household, with the title of Right Reverend Monsignor. To Ryan these were signature achievements that he proudly called vindications of his entire career. But he had not sought the papal title, which was initiated by Catholic University to bring honor to itself and Ryan, and Ryan was mindful that his ascending reputation occurred against the backdrop of massive human suffering. By the time that he received a papal title, he was deeply absorbed in New Deal planning meetings and conferences. He told his students that what mattered to him was the social witness of the church and getting something done in the real world. Toward both ends he took deep satisfaction in having another papal encyclical on his side, Pius XI's *Quadragesimo Anno (After Forty Years*, 1931).

Quadragesimo Anno was an affirmation of the social-ethical legacy of *Rerum Novarum* and a step beyond it. The second great social encyclical of the modern papacy, it enthused that the first one "completely overthrew those tottering remains of liberalism which had long hampered effective intervention by the government." Pius XI praised Leo XIII for helping Catholics develop their social views "more intensely and on truer lines," encouraging "outstanding Catholics" to advocate government policies that conformed to Catholic principles of justice and morality. Extending the logic of *Rerum Novarum* to a vastly different historical context, Pius declared that the church was morally obligated to take positions on social and economic issues to the extent that these issues and positions carried moral implications. He repeated Leo XIII's principle that the right to property had to be distinguished from its use and strongly affirmed Leo's doctrine of the right to a just wage. In the 40 years since *Rerum Novarum*, the pope observed, important changes had occurred in capitalism and socialism. Early capitalism was primarily about free competition, but modern capitalism was primarily about the "despotic economic domination" of a ruling elite of owners and administrative directors of invested funds. Early capitalism, lacking sufficient intervention by the state and people, led to something worse: "This accumulation of power, a characteristic note of the modern economic order, is a natural result of unrestrained free competition which permits the survival of those only who are the strongest. This often means those who fight most relentlessly, who pay least heed to the dictates of conscience."[168]

The drive for increasingly concentrated power under modern capitalism led to a threefold struggle for domination, Pius wrote, "First, there is the struggle for dictatorship in the economic sphere itself; then, the fierce battle to acquire control of the State, so that its resources and authority may be abused in the economic struggles." Finally, the nations clashed between themselves, driven by the predatory logic of capitalism and its lust for economic advantage. In brief, the pope lamented, "Free competition has committed suicide; economic dictatorship has replaced a free market." On the other hand, since *Rerum Novarum* the Socialist movement had split into two bitterly hostile camps, though both were un-Christian. The pope observed that Communism, wherever it came to power, "shows itself cruel and inhuman in a manner unbelievable and monstrous." Social democratic socialism was much closer to the Christian worldview, and increasingly so, Pius allowed: "Its programs often strikingly approach the just demands of Christian social reformers." But democratic socialists could not bring themselves to repudiate the doctrines of class warfare and the abolition of private property, he observed. They mitigated and moderated these doctrines considerably, but clung to them, if only rhetorically. Pius XI looked forward to a merger of social democracy and Christian reform, which was possible if Socialists relinquished the bad parts of the old socialism.[169]

Quadragesimo Anno broke new ground in describing the politics and ethics of Catholic reformism, acknowledging that it was changing too. The crucial section of the encyclical was titled "The Reconstruction of the Social Order." The pope observed that under capitalism the law of supply and demand divided the labor market into two classes, and the struggle between them turned the market "into an arena where the two armies are engaged in combat." That was the class war in all but name, which he repudiated: "To this grave disorder which is leading society to ruin a remedy must evidently be applied as speedily as possible." His remedy was a version of syndicalism that he called "the syndicate." The basis of the new social order worth building was the integrated planning council or guild: "There cannot be question of any perfect cure, except this opposition be done away with, and well-ordered members of the social body come into being: functional 'groups'; namely binding men together not according to the position they occupy in the labor market, but according to the diverse functions which they exercise in society." In every industry the planning group needed to include all interested parties on both sides of the labor/capital divide.[170]

Focusing on the workplace, the pope did not include public representation in the syndicates, but stressed that the state exercised a supervisory role in the process that watched out for the public good and prevented bureaucratic dictatorships from forming. The goal was to maximize industrial self-government by bringing employers and employees together, enabling labor to share in all industrial policies and decisions: "In these associations the common interest of the whole 'group' must predominate: and among these interests the most important is the directing of the activities of the group to the common good." In this vision, he explained, "the State here grants legal recognition to the syndicate or union, and thereby confers on it some of the features of a monopoly." The decision to join a syndicate had to be optional for everyone, but the union fees and taxes that supported the syndicates were obligatory for all who belonged to given branches. Employers and employees retained the rights of separate assembly and voting; strikes and lockouts were forbidden; and if the contending parties in a planning council could not reach agreement, public authority had to intervene. For the first time, the Vatican endorsed the socialist phrase, "social justice." *Quadragesimo Anno* explained that it brought together the rights and good of every person with the common good: "The public institutions of the nations should be such as to make all human society conform to the requirements of the common good, that is, the norm of social justice."[171]

On May 15, 1931 Ryan listened to the radio transmission of this encyclical from the Vatican at the office of the *New York Times*. For weeks afterward he gladly accepted congratulations for having anticipated the direction of Catholic social ethics and advanced it. The following year he had a private audience with the pope, who encouraged him to spread the message of the encyclical. Often Ryan and R. A. McGowan, an official of the National Catholic Welfare Conference, corrected misrepresentations of the pope's syndicalism, explaining that it was not a papal version of fascism. Under fascism the government created and controlled the syndicates, but in the pope's vision the syndicates belonged to the people. Under fascism the government carried out most of the decisions and planning, but in the pope's vision the government played a merely supervisory role as the ultimate protector of the public good.

Above all, fascism was about national glory, war, and empire; Catholic syndicalism was about social justice, bringing about the integration of human rights and the common good. The Vatican envisioned decentralized planning councils that facilitated industrial self-government within the various occupational groups, Ryan explained. Since the term "syndicate" had a history in Socialist thought, and a connotatively overloaded one, he stressed that Pius XI called the planning councils "occupational groups." The Catholic ideal was not a form of socialism, because socialism remained an ideology of government collectivism even in its milder social democratic forms. But it was not really capitalist, either, unless "capitalism" was defined as private ownership and operation of the means of production. Historically, capitalism was about holding wages as low as possible, striving for as much profit and interest as possible, and maximizing economic domination. The Catholic model was a third way that ripped the collectivism and atheism out of social democracy and the predatory individualism and greed out of capitalism: "The new social order recommended by the Holy Father would exemplify neither individualism nor socialism."[172]

In December 1933 Ryan's political and ecclesiastical worlds conflated at a festive service at Catholic University's National Shrine of the Immaculate Conception and an elaborate banquet at the Willard Hotel celebrating his investiture as a monsignor. By then he had stopped complaining of being a voice in the wilderness or a lonely Catholic at progressive gatherings. At the service he donned the purple robes that marked his ecclesiastical rank and vindication. At the banquet he was lauded by a parade of religious and, especially, political figures that included Frances Perkins, cleric Patrick Healy, Nebraska senator George Norris, Minnesota senator Henrick Shipstead, and labor activist Edward Keating. All of them hailed Ryan as the pioneer and leader of a socially awakened American Catholicism, and Perkins stressed that Roosevelt was enacting Ryan's economic agenda.[173]

The New Deal program that meant the most to Ryan, the National Industrial Recovery Act of 1933, was the most short-lived. It advocated a 40-hour workweek, minimum wage rates, the right of labor to collective bargaining, a substantial measure of industrial self-government, and, at least implicitly, the purchasing-power theory of economic recovery. Ryan called it a weak version of Pius XI's occupational group system. Though Ryan stressed that the NRA fell short of the pope's radical democratic vision of employee representation, he stumped for it passionately as a huge leap forward. Later he argued that if the NRA had been allowed to continue, it would have evolved into the planning council scheme envisioned in *Quadragesimo Anno.*

The NRA was accused of being un-American, anti-capitalist, and un-Constitutional; more plausibly to Ryan, it was also charged with favoring large companies over small ones. In 1934 he was appointed by NRA administrator Hugh Johnson to a three-person committee, the Industrial Appeals Board, which responded to complaints about the operations of the NRA. Ryan took seriously the complaints from small producers, but judged repeatedly in favor of the large firms, which paid higher wages and were better equipped technologically. He reasoned that it was better to see some firms go out of business than to allow the nation's rising wage structure to collapse. In 1935 the Supreme Court ruled that the National Industrial Recovery Act was unconstitutional; two years later Roosevelt responded by going after the court.[174]

Ryan, having expected the court to overturn the NRA, implored Roosevelt to fight for it. The crucial thing was to subordinate capitalist greed to the nation's common welfare while spurning the "quack remedies" of right-wing populists like New Orleans senator Huey P. Long and radio priest Charles E. Coughlin. Ryan fretted that Roosevelt gave up too easily and lost the momentum of the early New Deal. Later that year, however, Roosevelt got the Social Security Act through Congress and rescued part of the NRA through the Wagner–Connery Act, which set up the National Labor Relations Board to encourage worker unionization. The Wagner–Connery Act of 1935 was the most far-reaching pro-union legislation ever enacted in the USA. Ryan, encouraged by the president's surprising mettle, urged him not to settle for half a loaf. In a personal letter he asked Roosevelt to rescue other parts of the NRA, by constitutional amendment if necessary, especially the measures dealing with wages and hours.[175]

He also ramped up his public defenses of Roosevelt, especially against Coughlin. A parish priest in Royal Oak, Michigan, and a sensational radio performer, Coughlin was adept at provoking xenophobic anxieties. He specialized in conspiracy rhetoric, routinely describing Roosevelt and his aides as Communists. His bigotry grew more explicit as the decade wore on; by the late 1930s he charged that American progressivism was a Jewish enterprise and that Jews in Germany provoked their own persecution. In 1936 he was wildly popular and still a bit coy in his prejudices. Claiming a populist mantle, he called his organization the National Union for Social Justice, and his newspaper *Social Justice*, all of which Ryan found appalling, embarrassing, and perplexing. Was it better to attack Coughlin and inflame his huge following, or ignore him as someone beneath debating? Coughlin's priestly status settled the question for Ryan. A month before the presidential election of 1936, Ryan decided that silence was intolerable. In a radio address he admonished Coughlin that lying was against God's law, denied indignantly that Roosevelt was a Communist, chided that Coughlin's economic analysis was at least 50 percent wrong, and declared that Coughlin was out of step with Catholic social thought. Coughlin replied with a tag that stuck, calling Ryan the "Right Reverend spokesman for the New Deal." As for lying, he insisted that the New Dealers were either Communist sympathizers or outright Communists.[176]

The reaction of the Catholic press was chastening for Ryan and Catholic liberalism. The two priests received roughly equal support, while some Catholic papers took a third option, admonishing both men to leave politics behind and return to being priests. Ryan got a sizable taste of the third reaction at Catholic University, where many students and faculty found his politicking unseemly. He received hundreds of infuriated and abusive letters from Coughlin's supporters, which made him shudder. Coughlin's skill at appealing to base instincts notwithstanding, how could so many people believe that he stood for the true Catholic faith? Ryan also received many grateful letters, however, including one from Attorney General Homer S. Cummings and another from Roosevelt that praised his "magnificent" speech. As usual, Ryan claimed in public that the controversy did not faze him personally. What mattered was to transform the American social order in the direction of Catholic social teaching; the Coughlin controversy was troubling mainly because Coughlin's demagoguery made the church look bad. Taking a cue from his friends, Ryan wore the tag "Right Reverend New Dealer" as a badge of honor, relishing that it symbolized the achievements of his two-track career.[177]

At the 1937 presidential inaugural Ryan gave the benediction; shortly afterward he learned that Roosevelt had a plan to alleviate himself of an anti-New Deal Supreme Court. The court had already nullified the NRA and the Guffey Coal Act, and the National Labor Relations Act was in jeopardy. This time Roosevelt surprised Ryan by going too far, asking Congress to authorize him to appoint one additional justice to the Supreme Court for every existing member of the court who had reached the age of 70, up to a total of six extra judges. Ryan took up the president's cause, though he dispensed with Roosevelt's smokescreen about heightening the efficiency of an elderly court. The problem was the court's conservative fixation, not its age, Ryan declared. Five of the justices were plainly hostile to government activism, and the crisis of the court had become intolerable. Much of the Catholic press was incredulous that Ryan defended even the president's court-packing abuse of power. The reaction was so harsh that Ryan's friends worried that he might be losing his leadership status in the field. Once again Ryan shrugged off the attacks and the fretting. A few years later he allowed that Roosevelt probably should have taken a different tack, but in the next breath he took it back, contending that the New Deal was worth defending by extreme measures. It was mere ideology and self-interested politics that struck down parts of the New Deal, he insisted, not anything in the Constitution that actually contradicted New Deal reforms: "The clauses in the Constitution upon which the Court based its unfavorable decisions are composed of general terms, which cannot be applied to a particular law without construction and interpretation."[178]

In 1939 Ryan turned 70, an occasion that 600 friends celebrated at the Willard Hotel, including Supreme Court justices Felix Frankfurter, Hugo Black, and William O. Douglas. Greetings from many others poured in, including a laudatory one from Roosevelt. The speeches went on for over three hours, to Ryan's delight; he later remarked that he enjoyed praise at least as much as the average person. Having reached the mandatory retirement age at Catholic University, his health began to fade shortly afterward. Ryan kept writing and lecturing, but he needed the disciplines of a day job. In 1940 he chafed at the decree of Monsignor Michael Ready, general secretary of the NCWC, that NCWC officials were to stay out of partisan politics during the election. Ryan wanted to stump for Roosevelt, but bit his tongue; dropping the NCWC was unthinkable for him. At the same time he cheered a 1940 statement by the American bishops, "The Church and the Social Order," that endorsed most of his signature reform proposals.

Having supported Roosevelt's naval buildup in the late 1930s, Ryan was an early proponent of stopping Nazi fascism by force. In October 1939 he urged in a radio address: "Hitler is a madman and a monster . . . In the present crisis our country is morally obliged to do all that it reasonably can to defeat Hitler and destroy Hitlerism." Ryan fumed at Irish Americans who saw little choice between England and Nazi Germany, which carried provincial resentments to a ridiculous extreme. He admonished Irish Americans to stop hiding behind American isolationism, which he also detested. Waging war was "practically never justified," he allowed in 1940, but isolationism was cowardly and immoral, and the present crisis was an emergency exception to the Christian predisposition against war: "I have no hesitation in saying that a successful war against this immoral Nazi program would be the lesser evil." At the time Ryan believed that direct American intervention was unnecessary, if the USA supplied England. Heeding Ready's admonition to pipe down about the war, at least until the November election, Ryan concentrated on his memoir. His brother Lawrence, a priest, urged him to drop his score-settling pages on Coughlin, his extravagant praise of Roosevelt, and his condemnations of Hitler. These were transient matters, out of place in a big-picture memoir, Lawrence argued. Reluctantly, Ryan agreed that Coughlin did not deserve a section, or any mention at all, in the permanent record of his career. His statements about Roosevelt and fascism belonged to another category, however. Ryan kept all of them, declaring that nations were subject to the moral law: "I reject and detest isolationism under any and every guise. For these reasons likewise, I desire and hope for a British victory over Hitler and Mussolini." *Social Doctrine in Action* was published in 1941. By then Ryan had given up believing that England could win the war by itself, and the constraints of an election season were behind him.[179]

In his long and prolific career Ryan had almost nothing to say about racial justice. He tried briefly in the 1930s to get an African-American settlement house started in southwest Washington, DC, and in 1939 he co-sponsored Marian Anderson's historic concert at Lincoln Memorial. In 1943 he gave a lecture at Howard University on racial discrimination, the first of his career. He meant to say a word against prejudice, but had only platitudes and an unintentionally patronizing tone for his audience, showing that he knew little about the subject. To his friends it was a singular embarrassment. Ryan's health was deteriorating rapidly, and he died two years later.[180]

To the end of his days he symbolized the possibility of a Catholic orthodoxy that struggled for a progressive transformation of the economic order. Most Catholic liberals of Ryan's generation were blocked by the Vatican's condemnations of modernism, but he skirted unpromising subjects, laying claim to the kernel of progressive social teaching in the modern papal tradition that was actually there. He knew he was lucky. Had he gravitated to another subject, he would have had to keep his head down, like many of his colleagues. Had he not lucked into a prelate, Ireland, who liked him and defended his right to speak, Ryan would have gone nowhere. In an age, however, when Catholic liberals usually had to speak cautiously, discerning wind direction before saying anything, Ryan spoke plainly and directly, never hiding behind a subterfuge. Where he stood was always obvious, and he avoided personal attacks. He fought his way through numerous controversies, but did not seek to provoke unnecessarily, and nearly always fought fairly. He benefited from the favorable attention of Ireland, Cushing, and other powerful prelates, but did not run to them for protection, standing on his own convictions. For most of his career, *Rerum Novarum* was all the protection that he needed.

In his last years he bristled at reviewers of his plodding memoir, who noted its stiffness. Ryan could be acidly short in social interactions, and even his memoir disclosed almost nothing about his inner life. When pressed on the issue, he explained that as a celibate he lacked the "love interest" and "glamour" that reviewers wanted in a memoir. That compounded the impression of a lack of inner feeling, which many of his colleagues and students considered obvious. But Ryan's ceaseless campaigning for social justice had to have some emotional wellspring. The one that he claimed was simple and powerful: to serve Christ by advancing Christ's cause of social justice: "Whatever I have accomplished in this field, I humbly thank Almighty God, Who inspired me with the desire to preach His social gospel and Who has sustained and guided me through all the years of my life."[181]

Ryan took for granted that the church's tradition of natural law reasoning was a tremendous advantage for Catholic social ethics and that it offered the best way to mediate Catholic convictions to the public square. He took only a rare pass at the language of faith, judging that it had little place in public discussion, and mentioned the Bible even less. His work had an inductive dimension in its use of economics and sociology, but it was firmly controlled by his adherence to the scholastic understanding of natural law as the expression of God's immutable plan. If God had an eternal plan, the point of ethics was to elucidate the universal principles that were based upon it. Good social ethics trusted in the capacity of reason to decipher the eternal laws of God in creation. It gave short shrift to the disabling ravages of sin, favored natural law over historical consciousness, and pressed for social reforms that were consistent with natural law and the church's normative teaching. Explaining his method, Ryan observed: "I ask myself, first, 'is this measure in conformity with right reason and Catholic teaching?' Second, 'is it wise and prudent to advocate the reform at this time?' "[182]

That approach took him far, creating a distinctly Catholic version of social Christianity. It also saddled Catholic social ethics, however, with claims about the church's "eternal and immutable" teaching concerning women, sexuality, the Catholic state, and the church itself that succeeding generations found highly problematic. The first of these issues to catch fire, after Ryan was gone, was religious freedom and the Catholic state.

Notes

1   Walter Rauschenbusch, *Christianizing the Social Order* (New York: Macmillan, 1912), 60; Rauschenbusch, *A Theology for the Social Gospel* (New York: Macmillan, 1917), 79; Rauschenbusch, "The Belated Races and the Social Problems," *Methodist Review* 40 (April 1914), 258.

2   Reverdy C. Ransom, *The Pilgrimage of Harriet Ransom's Son* (Nashville: A.M.E. Sunday School Union, 1949), 15–20, quote 15, 19; Richard R. Wright, Jr, *The Bishops of the African Methodist Episcopal Church* (Nashville: A.M.E. Sunday School Union, 1963), 287.

3   Alexander Keyssar, *The Right to Vote: The Contested History of Democracy in the United States* (New York: Basic Books, 200), 52.

4   Ransom, *The Pilgrimage of Harriet Ransom's Son*, quotes 22, 23.

5   Ibid., quote 24.

6   Ibid., quotes, 26, 26–7.

7   Wright, *The Bishops of the African Methodist Episcopal Church*, quote 287; Horace Talbert, *Sons of Allen: Together with a Sketch of the Rise and Progress of Wilberforce University* (Xenia, OH: Aldine Press, 1906), 266–8; John Hope Franklin and Alfred A. Moss, Jr, *From Slavery to Freedom: A History of Negro Americans* (6th edn., New York: Alfred A. Knopf, 1988), 150. Carter G. Woodson, *History of the Negro Church* (1921; reprint, Washington, DC: Associated Publishers), 181.

8   Daniel Alexander Payne, *Recollections of Seventy Years* (Nashville: A.M.E. Sunday School Union, 1888); Josephus R. Coan, *Daniel Alexander Payne: Christian Educator* (Philadelphia: A.M.E. Book Concern, 1935); David Wills, "Reverdy C. Ransom: The Making of an AME Bishop," *Black Apostles: Afro-American Clergy Confront the Twentieth Century*, eds. Richard Newman and Randall K. Burkett (Boston: G. K. Hall, 1978), reprinted in *Making the Gospel Plain: The Writings of Bishop Reverdy C. Ransom*, ed. Anthony B. Pinn (Harrisburg, PA: Trinity Press International, 1999), 9–43; Ransom, *The Pilgrimage of Harriet Ransom's Son*, "praying school" and "racial self-confidence," 31; Wright, *The Bishops of the African Methodist Episcopal Church*, "intellectual," 81; Reverdy C. Ransom, *School Days at Wilberforce* (Springfield, OH: New Era, 1890), 20–40; Hallie Q. Brown, *Pen Pictures of Pioneers of Wilberforce* (Xenia, OH: Aldine Publishing, 1937).

9   Ransom, *The Pilgrimage of Harriet Ransom's Son*, quote 33; Ransom, *School Days at Wilberforce*.

10   Ransom, *School Days at Wilberforce*, quote 19; Ransom, *The Pilgrimage of Harriet Ransom's Son*, 32–4, 39.

11   Ransom, *School Days at Wilberforce*, 37–42; Ransom, *The Pilgrimage of Harriet Ransom's Son*, 37–8, quote 38; on Oberlin, see Gary Dorrien, *The Making of American Liberal Theology: Idealism, Realism, and Modernity, 1900–1950* (Louisville: Westminster John Knox Press, 2003), 62–5.

12   Ransom, *The Pilgrimage of Harriet Ransom's Son*, 37–8, quotes 38–9, 41–2; John G. Brown, "Wilberforce University: Twenty-Third Commencement Exercises – A Brilliant Closing," *Christian Recorder* 24 (July 8, 1886), 1; Reverdy C. Ransom, "Why This Haste?" *Christian Recorder* 28 (August 28, 1890), 1; Will, "Reverdy C. Ransom: The Making of an AME Bishop," 20–1.

13   Daniel A. Payne, "Some Thoughts About the Past, Present and Future of the African M.E. Church," *AME Church Review* 1 (July 1884), 5–8; Daniel A. Payne, *A History of*

the African Methodist Episcopal Church (1891; reprint, New York: Arno Press, 1969); Payne and Charles Spencer Smith, *A History of the African Methodist Episcopal Church, Chronicling the Principal Events in the Advance of the African Methodist Episcopal Church from 1856 to 1922* (Philadelphia: Book Concern of the AME Church, 1922; New York: Johnson Reprint Corp., 1968); Will, "Reverdy C. Ransom: The Making of an AME Bishop," 16.

14 Ransom, *The Pilgrimage of Harriet Ransom's Son*, quotes 47, 50; see Reverdy C. Ransom, "Too Cultured for His Flock," *Christian Recorder* 24 (November 18, 1886), 2.

15 Reverdy C. Ransom, "Dr. C. S. Smith's Version of the Apostles' Creed," *Christian Recorder* 28 (April 24, 1890), quotes 1; Ransom, *The Pilgrimage of Harriet Ransom's Son*, "carpets" and "mar," 55; Will, "Reverdy C. Ransom: The Making of an AME Bishop," 24–5.

16 Reverdy C. Ransom, "Out of the Midnight Sky: A Thanksgiving Address," Thanksgiving address delivered November 30, 1893 in Mt Zion Congregational Church, Cleveland, Ohio (Cleveland: Fraternal Printing and Publishing, n.d.), Reverdy C. Ransom Collection, Payne Theological Seminary, Wilberforce, OH, reprinted in *Making the Gospel Plain: The Writings of Reverdy C. Ransom*, 59–67, quotes 61, 64, 65.

17 Ibid., quotes 65, 66.

18 Reverdy C. Ransom, "Lions by the Way," in *Disadvantages and Opportunities of the Colored Youth* (Cleveland: Thomas & Mattill, Printers, 1894), Reverdy C. Ransom Collection, reprinted in *Making the Gospel Plain: The Writings of Reverdy C. Ransom*, 67–74, quote 69.

19 Ibid., "no matter," 71; Ransom, *The Pilgrimage of Harriet Ransom's Son*, "every two or three," 20; Reverdy C. Ransom, "Confessions of a Bishop," *Ebony* 5 (March 1950), 73.

20 David A. Gerber, *Black Ohio and the Color Line* (Urbana: University of Illiinois Press, 1976), 345–70; Ransom, *The Pilgrimage of Harriet Ransom's Son*, 65–77; Will, "Reverdy C. Ransom: The Making of an AME Bishop," 32–3; Wright, *The Bishops of the African Methodist Episcopal Church*, 82.

21 Ransom, *The Pilgrimage of Harriet Ransom's Son*, 81–5, quote 82; Reverdy C. Ransom, "Heredity and Environment," Address to the Literacy Congress, Indianapolis, IN, 1898, published in Ransom, *The Spirit of Freedom and Justice: Orations and Speeches* (Nashville: AME Sunday School Union, 1926), 161–3; see Ida B. Wells, *Crusade for Justice: The Autobiography of Ida B. Wells*, ed. Alfreda M. Duster (Chicago: University of Chicago Press, 1970), 254–62.

22 Will, "Reverdy C. Ransom: The Making of an AME Bishop," quote 34; Reverdy C. Ransom, "Chicago Honored by the Race," *Christian Recorder* (September 7, 1899), 1, 6; Calvin S. Morris, *Reverdy C. Ransom: Black Advocate of the Social Gospel* (Lanham, MD: University Press of America, 1990), 134–8; Louis Harlan, *Booker T. Washington: The Making of a Black Leader, 1856–1901* (New York: Oxford University Press, 1972), 263–6.

23 Wright, *The Bishops of the African Methodist Episcopal Church*, quote 289; see Irving Stone, *Clarence Darrow for the Defense* (New York: Doubleday & Co., 1941), 96–101, 471; Ransom, *The Pilgrimage of Harriet Ransom's Son*, 86, 114.

24 Reverdy C. Ransom, "The Negro and Socialism," *AME Church Review* 13 (1896–7), reprinted in *Making the Gospel Plain: The Writings of Reverdy C. Ransom*, 183–9, quotes 187, 189, and *Black Socialist Preacher*, ed. Philip S. Foner (San Francisco: Synthesis Publications, 1983), 282–9.

25 Reverdy C. Ransom, "Deborah and Jael," Sermon to the IBW Woman's Club, at Bethel AME Church, Chicago, June 6, 1897 (Chicago: Crystal Print, n.d.), reprinted in *Making the Gospel Plain: The Writings of Reverdy C. Ransom*, 75–85, quotes 77, 80.

26 Reverdy C. Ransom, "Thanksgiving Address, 1904," Address delivered in Bethel AME Church, New Bedford, MA, reprinted in *Making the Gospel Plain: The Writings of Reverdy C. Ransom*, 85–91, quotes 89, 91; Ransom, *The Pilgrimage of Harriet Ransom's Son*, 85–6.

27 Ransom, *The Pilgrimage of Harriet Ransom's Son*, 88, 103–18; Reverdy C. Ransom to Claude A Barnett, May 14, 1945, Claude A. Barnett Papers, Chicago Historical Society, quote cited in Morris, *Reverdy C. Ransom: Black Advocate of the Social Gospel*, 112.

28 Editorial, "The Policy Swindle," *Chicago Tribune* (May 4, 1903); Ransom, *The Pilgrimage of Harriet Ransom's Son*, 119–35.

29 Reverdy C. Ransom, Sermon of August 2, 1903, Institutional Church and Settlement House, Chicago, *Literary Digest* 27 (1903), 188, cited in Wills, "Reverdy C. Ransom: The Making of an AME Bishop," 36; see "The Opposition to Booker T. Washington," *Literary Digest* 27 (August 15, 1903), 188–9; W. E. B. Du Bois, *Dusk of Dawn* (1940; reprint, New York: Schocken Books, 1970), 86–8.

30 Ransom, *The Pilgrimage of Harriet Ransom's Son*, 135; Richard R. Wright Jr, *Eighty-Seven Years Behind the Black Curtain: An Autobiography* (Philadelphia: Rare Book, 1965), 148.

31 Ransom, *The Pilgrimage of Harriet Ransom's Son*, 143–8, quote 143.

32 W. E. B. Du Bois, "The Niagara Movement: Address to the Country," (1906), in *W. E. B. Du Bois: A Reader*, ed. David Levering Lewis (New York: Henry Holt, 1995), 367–9.

33 Reverdy C. Ransom, "The Spirit of John Brown," Address delivered at the Second Annual Meeting of the Niagara Movement, Harper's Ferry, West Virginia, August 17, 1906, published in Ransom, *The Spirit of Freedom and Justice: Orations and Speeches* (Nashville: AME Sunday School Union, 1926), and reprinted in *Making the Gospel Plain: The Writings of Reverdy C. Ransom*, 92–102, quotes 94, 95.

34 Ibid., quotes 98, 99.

35 Ibid., quotes 100, 101.

36 Reverdy C. Ransom, Thanksgiving Sermon preached at Bethel AME Church, New York, November 25, 1909, published in Ransom, *The Spirit of Freedom and Justice: Orations and Speeches*, and reprinted in *Making the Gospel Plain: The Writings of Reverdy C. Ransom*, 102–11, quotes 111.

37 Reverdy C. Ransom, "Charles Sumner: A Plea for the Civil and Political Rights of Negro Americans," Boston Centennial Oration, January 6, 1911, at Park Street Church, Boston, reprinted in *Making the Gospel Plain: The Writings of Reverdy C. Ransom*, 112–22, quotes 117.

38 August Meier, *Negro Thought in America, 1880–1915: Racial Ideologies in the Age of Booker T. Washington* (Ann Arbor: University of Michigan Press, 1988), 182; Ransom, *The Pilgrimage of Harriet Ransom's Son*, 169–71, *Boston Herald* quote, 171.

39 H. M. Turner to R. C. Ransom, May 7, 1907; Ransom, *The Pilgrimage of Harriet Ransom's Son*, Turner letter, 200, Ransom quote 199.

40 Reverdy C. Ransom, "Wendell Phillips: Centennial Oration," Address delivered November 29, 1911, Plymouth Church, Brooklyn, New York, reprinted in *Making the Gospel Plain: The Writings of Reverdy C. Ransom*, 123–34, quotes 126; Ransom, *The Pilgrimage of Harriet Ransom's Son*, 215–16, 221–5.

41 Ransom, *The Pilgrimage of Harriet Ransom's Son*, 173–92, quotes 183, 184.

42 Wright, *The Bishops of the African Methodist Episcopal Church*, Federal Council quote, 290; Reverdy C. Ransom, "Editorial, the Federal Council," *AME Review* (January 1917), 159–60; Morris, *Reverdy C. Ransom: Black Advocate of the Social Gospel*, 60.

43 Reverdy C. Ransom, Remarks at Bethel AME Church, Chicago, June 12, 1912, published in Ransom, *The Spirit of Justice and Freedom: Orations and Speeches*, and reprinted in *Making the Gospel Plain: The Writings of Reverdy C. Ransom*, 139–45, quotes 141.

44 Reverdy C. Ransom, "Editorial, The Editor's Chair," *AME Church Review* (April 1920), 507–8; Ransom, "Editorial, The Preacher-Editor," *AME Church Review* (July 1912), 81; Ransom, *The Spirit of Justice and Freedom: Orations and Speeches*, 94–7; Morris, *Reverdy C. Ransom: Black Advocate of the Social Gospel*, 60–1.

45 Reverdy C. Ransom, "Race Pride," *AME Church Review*, reprinted in *Making the Gospel Plain: The Writings of Reverdy C. Ransom*, 181–2.

46 Reverdy C. Ransom, "The Coming Vision," Address to the AME General Conference of 1920, published in the *AME Church Review* (January 1921), 135–9, reprinted in *Making the Gospel Plain: The Writings of Reverdy C. Ransom*, 215–22, quotes 215.

47 Reverdy C. Ransom, "Crispus Attucks, a Negro, the First to Die for American Independence: An Address," Address to the Metropolitan Opera House, Philadelphia, PA, March 6, 1930, published in Ransom, *The Negro: The Hope or the Despair of Christianity* (Boston: Ruth Hill, 1935), 78–87; reprinted in *Making the Gospel Plain: The Writings of Reverdy C. Ransom*, 145–52, "the white man," 150.

48 Reverdy C. Ransom, "The Paraclete of God the Only Hope for Brotherhood and Peace," *Making the Gospel Plain: The Writings of Reverdy C. Ransom*, 166–70, quotes 169.

49 Ibid., 169.

50 Ransom, *The Pilgrimage of Harriet Ransom's Son*, quotes 230.

51 Ibid., 228–57, quote 231.

52 Ibid., quotes 261, 264; see Wright, *The Bishops of the African Methodist Episcopal Church*, 287–92.

53 Reverdy C. Ransom, "Editorial, A Step Toward Denominational Union," *AME Church Review* (July 1912), 85; Ransom, "Editorial, Organic Union," *AME Church Review* (January 1921), 155–6; Ransom, *The Pilgrimage of Harriet Ransom's Son*, 267–74, 303–19; George A. Singleton, *The Romance of African Methodism* (New York: Exposition Press, 1952), 86–8, 162–82; Morris, *Reverdy C. Ransom: Advocate of the Black Social Gospel*, 60–3; Wright, *Eighty-Seven Years Behind the Black Curtain: An Autobiography*, 219–22; Will, "Reverdy C. Ransom: The Making of an AME Bishop," 41–2; Wright, *The Bishops of the African Methodist Episcopal Church*, 291–92.

54 Reverdy C. Ransom, "The Negro, The Hope or the Despair of Christianity," Address to the World Fellowship of Faiths, Second Parliament of Religions, Chicago, IL, 1933, published in Ransom, *The Negro: The Hope or the Despair of Christianity*, 1–7, "but their," 55; Ransom, "The Race Problem in a Christian State," Address to the Women's International League and Fellowship of Faith, Dayton, Ohio, February 15, 1935, published in Ransom, *The Negro: The Hope or the Despair of Christianity*, 64–77, "we hear," 72–3.

55 Reverdy C. Ransom, "The Pulpit and the American Negro," published in Ransom, *The Negro: The Hope or the Despair of Christianity*, 41–7, quotes 44–5.

56 Ransom, "The Negro, the Hope or the Despair of Christianity," 2–3.

57 Ibid., quotes 3, 6.

58 Reverdy C. Ransom, "The Future of the Negro in the United States," published in Ransom, *The Negro: The Hope or the Despair of Christianity*, 88–98, quotes 95, 96.

59 Reverdy C. Ransom, "The Church That Shall Survive," Sermon to the AME General Conference, New York, May 6, 1936, reprinted in Singleton, *The Romance of African Methodism: A Study of the African Methodist Episcopal Church*, 146–56, and *Making the Gospel Plain: The Writings of Reverdy C. Ransom*, 152–61, quote 158.

60 W. E. B. Du Bois, "A Tribute to Reverdy Cassius Ransom," *AME Church Review* (April–June 1959), reprinted in *Making the Gospel Plain: The Writings of Bishop Reverdy C. Ransom*, xvii–xix, quote xix.

61 Reverdy C. Ransom, "Editorial, Segregation," *AME Church Review* (January 1913), 229–30.

62 Ransom, *The Negro: The Hope or the Despair of Christianity*, i; Stephen R. Fox, *The Guardian of Boston: William Monroe Trotter* (New York: Atheneum, 1970); see Reverdy C. Ransom, "Editorial, President Wilson, Trotter, and the American People," *AME Church Review* (January 1915), 309–18.

63 Ransom, *The Negro: The Hope or the Despair of Christianity*, i.

64 Jane Addams, *Twenty Years at Hull-House, with Autobiographical Notes* (New York: Macmillan, 1910; Signet Classics edition, New York: New American Library Signet Classics, 1961); Henry Steele Commager, "Jane Addams: 1860–1960," *Saturday Review* (December 24, 1960), reprinted as the foreword to the Signet Classics edition, ix–xix, quote xix.

65   Daniel Levine, "Jane Addams: Romantic Radical, 1889–1912," *Mid-America* 44 (October 1962), 195–210, quote 200; Jill Ker Conway, "Jane Addams: American Heroine," *Daedalus* 93 (Spring 1964), 761–80, reprinted in *The Woman in America*, ed. Robert J. Lifton (Boston: Houghton Mifflin, 1965), quote 250; Allen F. Davis, *American Heroine: The Life and Legend of Jane Addams* (New York: Oxford University Press, 1973); J. J. Jackson Lears, *No Place of Grace: Antimodernism and the Transformation of American Culture, 1880–1920* (Chicago: University of Chicago Press, 1983), 79–80; Tom Lutz, *American Nervousness: An Anecdotal History* (Ithaca: New York, 1991), 28; Rivka Shpak Lissak, *Pluralism and Progressives: Hull House and the New Immigrants, 1890–1919* (Chicago: University of Chicago Press, 1989), 20–3, quote 23; see Daniel Levine, *Jane Addams and the Liberal Tradition* (Madison, WI: State Historical Society of Wisconsin, 1971). For discussions of the Addams literature, see Louise K. Knight, *Citizen: Jane Addams and the Struggle for Democracy* (Chicago: University of Chicago Press, 2005), 405–12; Jean Bethke Elshtain, *Jane Addams and the Dream of American Democracy: A Life* (New York: Basic Books, 2002), 18–22.

66   See Victoria Brown, *The Education of Jane Addams* (Philadelphia: University of Pennsylvania, 2004); Knight, *Citizen: Jane Addams and the Struggle for Democracy*; Elshtain, *Jane Addams and the Dream of American Democracy: A Life*.

67   Knight, *Citizen: Jane Addams and the Struggle for Democracy*, 12–29; Addams, *Twenty Years at Hull-House, with Autobiographical Notes*, Signet Classics edition, 6–11, quote 8.

68   Addams, *Twenty Years at Hull-House, with Autobiographical Notes*, quotes 20, 20–1, 10; Knight, *Citizen: Jane Addams and the Struggle for Democracy*, 424.

69   Addams, *Twenty Years at Hull-House, with Autobiographical Notes*, quote 32; Knight, *Citizen: Jane Addams and the Struggle for Democracy*, 80–111.

70   Jane Addams to Ellen Gates Starr, September 3, 1881; Ellen Gates Starr to Jane Addams, September 10, 1881, cited in Knight, *Citizen: Jane Addams and the Struggle for Democracy*, 114, 115; Addams, *Twenty Years at Hull-House, with Autobiographical Notes*, 42–5, "submerged," 43.

71   Jane Addams to Ellen Gates Starr, March 30, 1885, cited in Knight, *Citizen: Jane Addams and the Struggle for Democracy*, 139; Addams, *Twenty Years at Hull-House, with Autobiographical Notes*, quote 51; Elshtain, *Jane Addams and the Dream of American Democracy: A Life*, 72–4.

72   Addams, *Twenty Years at Hull-House, with Autobiographical Notes*, quotes, 46, 47.

73   Knight, *Citizen: Jane Addams and the Struggle for Democracy*, 1166–73; Addams, *Twenty Years at Hull-House, with Autobiographical Notes*, quotes 57.

74   Addams, *Twenty Years at Hull-House, with Autobiographical Notes*, 58–64; Knight, *Citizen: Jane Addams and the Struggle for Democracy*, 179–98.

75   Addams, *Twenty Years at Hull-House, with Autobiographical Notes*, quote 72.

76   Jane Addams, "The Subjective Necessity for Social Settlements," Address to the Ethical Culture Societies Summer School, Plymouth, MA, 1892, published in *Philanthropy and Social Progress, Seven Essays by Miss Jane Addams, Robert A. Woods, Father J.O.S. Huntington, Professor Franklin H. Giddings and Bernard Bosanquet*, ed. Henry C. Adams (New York: Thomas Y. Crowell, 1893), reprinted in Addams, *Twenty Years at Hull-House, with Autobiographical Notes*, 74–85, quotes 75, 79.

77   Ibid., quotes 80–1.

78   Ibid., quotes 82, 83; see Knight, *Citizen: Jane Addams and the Struggle for Democracy*, 461–2.

79   Addams, *Twenty Years at Hull-House, with Autobiographical Notes*, 118–31, quotes 118, 124.

80   Ibid., 124–5, 155–62, "radicals," 125; Jane Addams, *The Spirit of Youth and the City Streets* (New York: Macmillan, 1909), 122–6; Addams, "The Objective Value of a Social Settlement," published in *Philanthropy and Social Progress, Seven Essays by Miss Jane Addams, Robert A. Woods, Father J.O.S. Huntington, Professor Franklin H. Giddings and Bernard*

Bosanquet, reprinted in *The Social Thought of Jane Addams*, ed. Christopher Lasch (Indianapolis: Bobbs-Merrill, 1965), 44–61, and *The Jane Addams Reader*, ed. Jean Bethke Elshtain (New York: Basic Books, 2002), 29–45, "I am," 45.

81 See *The Essential Dewey: Volume 1: Pragmatism, Education, Democracy*, ed. Larry A. Hickman and Thomas M. Alexander (Bloomington: Indiana University Press, 1998), 281–343; Robert B. Westbrook, *John Dewey and American Democracy* (Ithaca, NY: Cornell University Press, 1991); Jane M. Dewey, "Biography of John Dewey," *The Philosophy of John Dewey*, ed. Paul Arthur Schilpp (Evanston: Northwestern University Press, 1939), 30.

82 For the original versions of lectures and articles that Addams folded into *Democracy and Social Ethics*, see Jane Addams, "The Subtle Problems of Charity," *Atlantic Monthly* 84 (February 1899), 163–78; Addams, "The College Woman and the Family Claim," *The Commons* 3 (September 1898), 3–7; Addams, "A Belated Industry," *American Journal of Sociology* 1 (March 1896), 536–50; Addams, "Trade Unions and Public Duty," *American Journal of Sociology* 4 (January 1899), 448–62; Addams, "Foreign-Born Children in the Primary Grades," National Education Association, *Journal of Proceedings and Addresses* (1897), 104–12; Addams, "Ethical Survivals in Municipal Corruption," *International Journal of Ethics* 8 (April 1898), 273–91.

83 Jane Addams, *Democracy and Social Ethics* (1902; Urbana, IL: University of Illinois Press, 2002), quotes 18, 21.

84 Ibid., quotes 6, 7.

85 Ibid., quotes 7, 8.

86 Ibid., quote 9.

87 Jane Addams, *Newer Ideals of Peace* (New York: Macmillan, 1907), quotes 10, 3.

88 Addams, *Twenty Years at Hull-House*, 176–8.

89 Ibid., 178–9; Jane Addams to Mary Rozet Smith, September 4, 1895, cited in Knight, *Citizen: Jane Addams and the Struggle for Democracy*, 371; Jane Addams, "Tolstoi," *Chautauqua Assembly Herald* 23 (August 9, 1898), 3, 6–7; Addams, *Newer Ideals of Peace*, 3–4.

90 Addams, *Newer Ideals of Peace*, 7–8, 26, 27.

91 Jane Addams, "Woman Suffrage and the Protection of the Home," *Ladies' Home Journal* 27 (January 1910), "gentler," 22; Addams, "A New Conscience and an Ancient Evil," *McClure's Magazine* 38 (November 1911), 2–13; Addams, *A New Conscience and an Ancient Evil* (New York: Macmillan, 1912), "a surprising," 145; Addams, "Why Women Should Vote," *Woman's Journal* 43 (October 28, 1911), 337; Addams, "Stage Children," *Survey* 25 (December 3, 1910), 342–3; Addams, "Child Labor on the Stage," *Uniform Child Labor Laws, the Proceedings of the 7th Annual Conference of the National Child Labor Committee, Birmingham, Alabama, 9–12 March 1911* (New York: National Child Labor Committee, 1911), 60–5; Addams, "Votes for Women and Other Votes," *Survey* 28 (June 15, 1912), 191; Addams, "Indirect Influence," *Woman's Journal* 43 (November 23, 1912), 373; Addams, "Why Women Are Concerned with the Larger Citizenship," *Woman Citizen's Library*, ed. Shailer Mathews (Chicago: Woman Citizen's Library, 1913–1914), 9: 2123–42.

92 Jane Addams, "My Experiences as a Progressive Delegate," *McClure's Magazine* 40 (November 1912), 12–14; Addams, "The Progressive Party and the Negro," *Crisis; a Record of the Darker Races* 5 (November 1912), quote 31.

93 Jane Addams, "Is the Peace Movement a Failure?" *Ladies' Home Journal* 31 (November 1914), 5; Addams, *The Second Twenty Years at Hull-House, September 1909 to September 1929; With a Record of a Growing World Consciousness* (New York: Macmillan, 1930), 113–16; Elshtain, *Jane Addams and the Dream of American Democracy: A Life*, 221–4; John C. Farrell, *Beloved Lady: A History of Jane Addams' Ideas on Reform and Peace* (Baltimore, MD: Johns Hopkins University Press, 1967), 5.

94 Jane Addams, "Presidential Address," International Congress of Women at the Hague, April 28–May 1, 1915, *Report* (1915), 18–22; Farrell, *Beloved Lady: A History of Jane*

Addams' Ideas on Reform and Peace, 148–51; Gertrude Bussey and Margaret Tims, *Women's International League for Peace and Freedom, 1915–1965: A Record of Fifty Years' Work* (London: George Allen and Unwin, 1965), 8–9; Elshtain, *Jane Addams and the Dream of American Democracy: A Life*, 224–5; Addams, *The Second Twenty Years at Hull-House, September 1909 to September 1929; With a Record of a Growing World Consciousness*, 116–28; Jane Addams, Emily G. Balch, and Alice Hamilton, *Women at the Hague, the International Congress of Women and its Results* (New York: Macmillan, 1915); Addams, "What War is Destroying," *Advocate of Peace* 77 (March 1915), 64–5.

95 Jane Addams, "Address of Miss Addams at Carnegie Hall" (The Revolt Against War), *Survey* 34 (July 17, 1915), 355–9, reprinted in *The Jane Addams Reader*, 327–40, quotes 335, 337.

96 Ibid., quotes 339.

97 Jane Addams, *Peace and Bread in Time of War* (New York: Macmillan, 1922), 134–48; Addams, *The Second Twenty Years at Hull-House, September 1909 to September 1929; With a Record of a Growing World Consciousness*, 131–3, quote 133; Richard Harding Davis, letter to the *New York Times*, July 13, 1915.

98 Addams, *Peace and Bread in Time of War*, quotes 132–3, 139.

99 Ibid., quotes 140–1; see Jane Addams, "Patriotism and Pacifists in Wartime," *City Club of Chicago Bulletin* 10 (June 18, 1917), 184–90.

100 Jane Addams, "World's Food and World's Politics," National Conference of Social Work, *Proceedings* (1918), 650–6; Addams, "World's Food Supply and Woman's Obligation," General Federation of Women's Clubs, *Biennial Convention* 14 (1918), 251–63; Addams and Alice Hamilton, "After the Lean Years, Impressions of Food Conditions in Germany when Peace was Signed," *Survey* 42 (September 6, 1919), 793–7.

101 Addams, *The Second Twenty Years at Hull-House*, 188–262, quotes 193, 254.

102 Ibid., 80–114, 263–303, quotes 111, 289, 302–3.

103 Jane Addams, "A Toast to John Dewey," *Survey* 63 (November 15, 1929), 203–4, quotes 203.

104 Ibid., quotes 204.

105 Catherine Peaden, "Jane Addams and the Social Rhetoric of Democracy," *Oratorical Culture in Nineteenth-Century America*, eds. Gregory Clark and S. Michael Halloran (Carbondale, IL: Southern Illinois Press, 1993), 193; R. A. R. Edwards, "Jane Addams, Walter Rauschenbusch, and Dorothy Day: A Comparative Study of Settlement Theology," *Gender and the Social Gospel*, eds. Wendy J. Deichmann Edwards and Carolyn De Swarte Gifford (Urbana: University of Illinois Press, 2003), 154.

106 John A. Ryan, *Social Doctrine in Action: A Personal History* (New York: Harper & Brothers, 1941), 1–5, quote 4; Francis L. Broderick, *Right Reverend New Dealer: John A. Ryan* (New York: Macmillan, 1963), 1–3.

107 Ryan, *Social Doctrine in Action: A Personal History*, quote 8; Broderick, *Right Reverend New Dealer: John A. Ryan*, 8–9.

108 See J. D. Hicks, *The Populist Revolt* (Minneapolis: University of Minnesota Press, 1931); *The Populist Mind*, ed. Norman Pollack (Indianapolis: Bobbs Merrill 1967); Lawrence Goodwyn, *Democratic Promise: The Populist Movement in America* (New York: Oxford University Press, 1976).

109 See Joseph McSorley, *Isaac Hecker and His Friends* (New York: Paulist Press, 1972); David J. O'Brien, *Isaac Hecker: An American Catholic* (Mahwah, NJ: Paulist Press, 1992); Walter Elliott, *The Life of Father Hecker* (New York: Columbus Press, 1891); Robert D. Cross, *The Emergence of Liberal Catholicism in America* (Cambridge, MA: Harvard University Press, 1958), 19–21, 182–9; John Tracy Ellis, *The Life of James Cardinal Gibbons: Archbishop of Baltimore, 1834–1921* (Milwaukee: Bruce Publishing Company, 1952); James J. Hennesey, *American Catholics: A History of the Roman Catholic Community in the United States* (New York: Oxford University Press, 1981); Will Herberg, *Protestant–Catholic–Jew* (Garden City,

NJ: Doubleday, 1960), 145; Broderick, *Right Reverend New Dealer: John A. Ryan*, 12–15; John T. McGreevy, *Cathlicism and American Freedom: A History* (New York: W. W. Norton, 2003), 91–126.

110   See John Lancaster Spalding, *Education and the Higher Life* (Chicago: A. C. McClurg, 1890); Spalding, *Socialism and Labor, and Other Arguments, Social, Political, and Patriotic* (Chicago: A. C. McClurg, 1902); Spalding, *Religion, Agnosticism, and Education* (Chicago: A. C. McClurg, 1902); Spalding, *The Life of the Rev. M. J. Spalding, D.D., Archbishop of Baltimore* (New York: Christian Press Association, 1873); William Francis Barry, *The New Antigone* (New York: Macmillan, 1887); Barry, *The Two Standards* (New York: The Century Co., 1899); Barry, *Heralds of Revolt: Studies in Modern Literature and Dogma* (London: Hodder & Stoughton, 1904); John Ireland, *The Church and Modern Society*, 2 vols. (Chicago: D. H. McBride and Co., 1897).

111   McGreevy, *Cathlicism and American Freedom: A History*, 118–38, quote 127–8; David J. O'Brien, "A Century of Catholic Social Teaching," *One Hundred Years of Catholic Social Thought: Celebration and Change*, ed. John A. Coleman, SJ (Maryknoll, NY: Orbis Books, 1991), 13–24; Gerald A. McCool, *From Unity to Pluralism: The Internal Evolution of Thomism* (New York: Fordham University Press, 1989), 5–39.

112   Pope Leo XIII, *Rerum Novarum: The Condition of Labor* (1891), *Catholic Social Thought: The Documentary Heritage*, ed. David J. O'Brien and Thomas A. Shannon (Maryknoll, NY: Orbis Books, 1992), 14–39, quotes 15.

113   Ibid., quotes 15.

114   Ibid., quotes 18, 22–3, 27, 29, 30, 33; Thomas Aquinas, *Summa Theologiae*, 3 vols., trans. Fathers of the English Dominican Province (New York: Benziger Brothers, 1948), 1: 2a 2ae, Q. lxvi, art. 2.

115   Pope Leo XIII, *Rerum Novarum: The Condition of Labor*, quote 28; Ryan, *Social Doctrine in Action: A Personal History*, 44–5.

116   Richard T. Ely, *Socialism: An Examination of its Nature, its Strength and its Weakness, with Suggestions for Social Reform* (New York: Thomas Y. Crowell, 1894).

117   Ryan, *Social Doctrine in Action: A Personal History*, 58–60, quotes 59; Broderick, *Right Reverend New Dealer: John A. Ryan*, 16–17.

118   John Tracy Ellis, *The Formative Years of the Catholic University of America* (Washington, DC: American Catholic Historical Association, 1946); Peter E. Hogan, *The Catholic University of America, 1896–1903: The Rectorship of Thomas J. Conaty* (Washington, DC: Catholic University of America Press, 1949), 13–27; Broderick, *Right Reverend New Dealer: John A. Ryan*, 27–30; Pope Leo XIII, *Testem benevolentiae*, reprinted in *Documents of American Catholic History*, ed. John Tracy Ellis (Milwaukee: Bruce Publishing Company, 1956), 554–62.

119   See William J. Ashley, *An Introduction to English Economic History and Theory* (New York: G. P. Putnam's Sons, 1894); John A. Hobson, *The Evolution of Modern Capitalism: A Study of Machine Production* (New York: Scribner's, 1894); Hobson, *The Problem of the Unemployed: An Enquiry and an Economic Policy* (London: Methuen & Co., 1896); Ryan, *Social Doctrine in Action: A Personal History*, 62–71.

120   Pope Leo XIII, *Rerum Novarum: The Condition of Labor*, 31; John A. Ryan, *A Living Wage* (New York: Macmillan, 1906; rev. edn., New York: Macmillan, 1920), 3–26.

121   See Thomas Aquinas, *Summa Theologiae*, Ia IIae q.94, a.4, Ia IIae, q. 100, aa. 1–2; Germain Grisez, "The First Principle of Practical Reason: A Commentary on the *Summa Theologiae*, 1–2, Question 94, Article 2," *The Natural Law Forum* 10 (1965), 172–5; John Finnis, *Natural Law and Human Rights* (Oxford: Clarendon Press, 1980); *Natural Law Theory: Contemporary Essays*, ed. Robert P. George (Oxford: Clarendon Press, 1994).

122   Ryan, *A Living Wage*, rev. edn., quote 25.

123   Ibid., quote 31.

124   Ibid., quote 33.

125 Ibid., "an explicit," 49; Leo XIII, *Rerum Novarum: The Condition of Labor*, "reasonable and frugal," 31; see Wilhelm von Ketteler, *The Social Teachings of Wilhelm Emmanuel von Ketteler*, trans. Rupert J. Ederer (Washington, DC: University Press, 1981); William Hogan, *The Development of Bishop Wilhelm Emmanuel von Ketteler's Interpretation of the Social Problem* (Washington, DC: Catholic University of America Press, 1946).

126 Ryan, *A Living Wage*, rev. edn., 50; Ryan, *A Living Wage*, 1st edn., 162.

127 Ryan, *A Living Wage*, rev. edn., quote 87.

128 Ibid., quotes 101, 87.

129 William Barry, review of *A Living Wage*, by John A. Ryan, *Catholic Times* (September 14, 1906); Broderick, *Right Reverend New Dealer: John A. Ryan*, 36–7, 45–7.

130 John A. Ryan, "Program of Social Reform by Legislation," Part 1, *Catholic World* (July 1909), 433–44; Ryan, "Program of Social Reform by Legislation," Part 2, *Catholic World* (August 1909), 608–14; Ryan, "The Method of Teleology in Ethics," *New York Reviw* 2 (January–February 1907), 402–29; Ryan, "Moral Aspects of the Labor Union," (1910), *Catholic Encyclopedia*, 15 vols., eds. C. G. Herbermann and others (New York: Robert Appleton Co., 1907–12), 8: 724–8; Ryan, *Social Doctrine in Action: A Personal History*, 107–11; Ryan, "The Fallacy of 'Bettering One's Position," *Catholic World* (November 1907), 145–56.

131 Ryan, *Social Doctrine in Action: A Personal History*, quote 115; see editorial, *Der Wanderer* (February 24, 1910); Edward F. McSweeney, "The Minimum Wage and Other Economic Quackeries," *Columbiad* (April 1913), 3–4; Broderick, *Right Reverend New Dealer: John A. Ryan*, 66–9.

132 Pops Pius X, *Lamentabili Sane*, July 3, 1907; Pius X, *Pascendi Dominici Gregis*, September 8, 1907, *The Papal Encyclicals*, ed. Anne Freemantle (New York: New American Library, 1963), 202–7, 197–201; James F. Driscoll, SS, "Recent Views on Biblical Inspiration," *New York Review* 1 (June–July 1905), 4–11; Francis E. Gigot, "The Higher Criticism of the Bible: Its Constructive Aspect," *New York Review* 2 (November–December 1906), 302–5; Gigot, "The Higher Criticism of the Bible: Its Relation to Tradition," *New York Review* 2 (January–February 1907), 442–4; R. Scott Appleby, *"Church and Age Unite!": The Modernist Impulse in American Catholicism* (Notre Dame: University of Notre Dame Press, 1992), 117–67; Ryan, *Social Doctrine in Action: A Personal History*, 116–17.

133 Morris Hillquit and John A. Ryan, *Socialism: Promise or Menace?* (New York: Macmillan, 1914), 1–38.

134 Ibid., quotes 58, 246, 247, 250.

135 Ryan, *Social Doctrine in Action: A Personal History*, 96; Broderick, *Right Reverend New Dealer: John A. Ryan*, 89; *Fortnightly Review* (June 15, 1914), 359.

136 Ryan, *Social Doctrine in Action: A Personal History*, 96; Broderick, *Right Reverend New Dealer: John A. Ryan*, 89–91.

137 John A. Ryan, *Distributive Justice: The Right and Wrong of Our Present Distribution of Wealth* (New York: Macmillan, 1916; 2nd edn., New York: Macmillan, 1925); see Patrick Gearty, *The Economic Thought of Monsignor John A. Ryan* (Washington, DC: Catholic University of America Press, 1953); Harlan Beckley, *Passion for Justice: Retrieving the Legacies of Walter Rauschenbusch, John A. Ryan, and Reinhold Niebuhr* (Louisville: Westminster John Knox Press, 1992), 176–86.

138 Ryan, *Distributive Justice: The Right and Wrong of Our Present Distribution of Wealth*, quote 147.

139 Ibid., quote 174.

140 Ibid., quote 428.

141 Ibid., quotes 432–3.

142 John A. Ryan, "A Democratic or a Prussian Peace," *America* (November 9, 1918), 103–4; Ryan, *Social Doctrine in Action: A Personal History*, 137–40; Ryan, "Social Aspects of America in the War," *Studies* (March 1918), 80–93; Ryan, "Crippling Germany Forever,"

America (December 14, 1918), 233–5; Ryan, "Militarism for the United States," *America* (November 30, 1918), 175–7; Ryan, "A Substitute for Militarism," *America* (December 7, 1918), 209–11; Broderick, *Right Reverend New Dealer: John A. Ryan*, 102–4.

143   John A. Ryan, *The Church and Socialism and Other Essays* (Washington, DC: University Press, 1919), quotes 5, 22.

144   Broderick, *Right Reverend New Dealer: John A. Ryan*, 96–7; Barbara Miller Solomon, *Ancestors and Immigrants, A Changing New England Tradition* (Cambridge, MA: Harvard University Press, 1956), 195–209; John A Ryan, letter, *Catholic Bulletin* (June 10, 1916).

145   John A. Ryan, "A Catholic Economist and Theologian on Prohibition," *Fortnightly Review* (April 1, 1916), 100–1; Broderick, *Right Reverend New Dealer: John A. Ryan*, 99.

146   Ryan, *The Church and Socialism and Other Essays*, quotes 237, 238, 239.

147   Ibid., quotes 242, 243.

148   John A. Ryan, *Social Reconstruction* (New York: Macmillan, 1920); Ryan, *Social Doctrine in Action: A Personal History*, 144–8.

149   Elizabeth McKeown, *War and Welfare: American Catholics and World War I* (New York: Garland, 1988); Charles E. Curran, "The Reception of Catholic Social and Economic Teaching in the United States," *Modern Catholic Social Teaching: Commentaries and Interpretations*, eds. Kennneth R. Himes, OFM, Lisa Sowle Cahill, Charles E. Curran, David Hollenbach, SJ, Thomas Shannon (Washington, DC: Georgetown University Press, 2005), 469–70; Ralph M. Easley, "Radicals Mislead Churches About Labor," *National Civic Federation Review* (March 25, 1919), 7; Ryan, *Social Reconstruction*, 10–15; Broderick, *Right Reverend New Dealer: John A. Ryan*, 104–8; Easley quote and John A. Ryan to Sister Mary John, May 12, 1919, cited in Broderick, 107, 108; Ryan, *Social Doctrine in Action: A Personal History*, "all such," 149.

150   Ryan, *Social Doctrine in Action: A Personal History*, "this degeneration," 149; *The State and the Church*, eds. John A. Ryan and Moorhouse F. X. Millar (New York: Macmillan, 1922). This book was reprinted in 1924, 1930, 1936, and 1937. In 1940 Ryan and Francis J. Boland, CSC published a revised edition, *Catholic Principles of Politics* (New York: Macmillan, 1940) that retained Ryan's defense of the establishment position; this book was reprinted in 1950.

151   John A. Ryan, "Comments on the 'Christian Constitution of States,'" *The State and the Church*, 26–61, quote 32.

152   Ibid., quotes, 34, 35.

153   Ibid., quotes 36, 37.

154   Ibid., quotes, 38, 39; see Charles A. Ryan, "The End of the State," "Erroneous Theories Concerning the Functions of the State," and "The Proper Functions of the State," *The State and the Church*, 195–207, 208–20, 221–33.

155   John A. Ryan, *Questions of the Day* (Boston: Stratford Company, 1931), 3–53, quote 34.

156   Ryan, Ibid., 57–66, 66–80.

157   Ibid., quotes 83, 63; see Charles A. Ryan, "The End of the State," "Erroneous Theories Concerning the Functions of the State," and "The Proper Functions of the State," *The State and the Church*, eds. John A. Ryan and Moorhouse F. X. Millar, SJ (Washington, DC: National Catholic Welfare Council, 1922; reprinted, New York: Macmillan, 1937), 195–207, 208–20, 221–33.

158   Ryan, *Questions of the Day*, quote 79.

159   Charles A. Ryan, "Religion in the Presidential Election of 1928," *Current History Magazine* (December 1928), reprinted in Ryan, *Questions of the Day*, 91–9, quotes 96, 98, 99; editorial, *Christian Century* 45 (October 18, 1928).

160   Editorial, "A Moral Pestilence," *Nation* (December 25, 1929); Ryan, *Questions of the Day*, 247–55, quotes 252, 253.

161 John A. Ryan, "The End to Hysteria," *N.C.W.C. Bulletin* (June 1924), 24–5; Ryan, *Social Doctrine in Action: A Personal History*, 159–76.

162 John A. Ryan, *The Supreme Court and the Minimum Wage* (New York: Paulist Press, 1923); Ryan, *Social Doctrine in Action: A Personal History*, 218–32.

163 Ryan, *Questions of the Day*, 180–217; Ryan, *Social Doctrine in Action: A Personal History*, 233–41.

164 Ryan, *Questions of the Day*, quotes, 192–3.

165 Ibid., quotes 193, 194, 195.

166 Ryan, *Social Doctrine in Action: A Personal History*, quotes 235; Ryan, *Questions of the Day*, 209–17; John A. Ryan, *A Better Economic Order* (New York: Harper & Brothers, 1935), 1–30; Ryan, "Relief for the Unemployed – Whose Responsibility?" *Catholic Charities Review* (March 1932), 67–70; Ryan, *Seven Troubled Years, 1930–1936: A Collection of Papers on the Depression and on the Problems of Recovery and Reform* (Ann Arbor: Edwards Brothers, 1937).

167 John A. Ryan, "National Responsibility in the Present Crisis," *Catholic World* (November 1932), 169–74; Ryan, *Social Doctrine in Action: A Personal History*, 246–8; see Arthur M. Schlesinger, Jr, *The Age of Roosevelt: The Crisis of the Old Order* (Boston: Houghton Mifflin, 1957).

168 Pope Pius XI, *Quadragesimo Anno: After Forty Years* (1931), *Catholic Social Thought: The Documentary Heritage*, 42–79, quotes 47, 65.

169 Ibid., quotes 65, 66, 67.

170 Ibid., 59–64, quotes 61.

171 Ibid., 63, 66.

172 John A. Ryan, "Some Effects of *Rerum Novarum,*" *America* (April 25, 1931), 58–60; Ryan, *Social Doctrine in Action: A Personal History*, 242–6; Ryan, *A Better Economic Order*, quote 182.

173 Ryan, *Social Doctrine in Action: A Personal History*, 263–5; Broderick, *Right Reverend New Dealer: John A. Ryan*, 211–17.

174 John A. Ryan, "The New Deal and Social Justice," *Commonweal* (April 13, 1934), 657–9; Ryan, *Seven Troubled Years, 1930–1936: A Collection of Papers on the Depression and on the Problems of Recovery and Reform*, 192–5; Ryan, *Social Doctrine in Action: A Personal History*, 249–250.

175 John A. Ryan, "Quack Remedies for the Depression Malady," *Catholic Charities Review* (April 1935), 104–7; Ryan, "Social Justice in the 1935 Congress," *Catholic Action* (September 1935), 7–9; John A. Ryan to Franklin D. Roosevelt, September 24, 1935, cited in Broderick, *Right Reverend New Dealer: John A. Ryan*, 220.

176 Ryan, *Seven Troubled Years, 1930–1936: A Collection of Papers on the Depression and on the Problems of Recovery and Reform*, 295–9; Broderick, *Right Reverend New Dealer: John A. Ryan*, 222–7.

177 Broderick, *Right Reverend New Dealer: John A. Ryan*, 228–9.

178 Ryan, *Social Doctrine in Action: A Personal History*, 250–62, quote 253; Broderick, *Right Reverend New Dealer: John A. Ryan*, 230–3; Ryan, *A Better Economic Order*, 74–115.

179 John A. Ryan, "The Misleading Issue of Neutrality," October 15, 1939, radio address; Ryan, "Confusions About the War," *Commonweal* (March 22, 1940), both cited in Ryan, *Social Doctrine in Action: A Personal History*, 215–17, closing quote 215; Broderick, *Right Reverend New Dealer: John A. Ryan*, 250.

180 Broderick, *Right Reverend New Dealer: John A. Ryan*, 262–3.

181 Ibid., 251; Ryan, *Social Doctrine in Action: A Personal History*, quote 290.

182 Ryan, *Social Reconstruction*, 213–14.

Chapter 4

Christian Realism

Reinhold Niebuhr, H. Richard Niebuhr, John C. Bennett,
and Paul Ramsey

The generation of social ethicists that inherited the social gospel and social ethics had to reinvent social ethics after they turned against the social gospel. What was "social ethics" if one did not believe in redeemed institutions, the progressive character of history, or an idealistic theology of social salvation? In the 1930s Reinhold Niebuhr led a generational attack on the optimism and idealism of the social gospel, all the while taking for granted most of its key assumptions. Social ethics, in his refashioning of it, made much of irony, paradox, and, especially, crisis. It traded the liberal language of process, moral progress, and evolutionary idealism for the orthodox-sounding language of sin, redemption, tragedy, and transcendence. It made "liberal" a sneer word among theologians, despite the fact that Niebuhr belonged to the liberal tradition that he attacked. Some of Niebuhr's disciples strayed into forms of neo-orthodox theology and political neoconservatism that repudiated their roots in the social gospel, but he did not, nor did his closest disciple and colleague, John C. Bennett, who went on to become the dean of the social ethics field for his generation.

Niebuhr's governing intellectual assumptions were liberal; he had few affinities with Karl Barth or the Barthian movement in theology; and he never doubted the social gospel assumption that Christians had a social mission to secure the just ordering of the world. He was a preacher and social ethicist with little formal training in theology and even less taste for formal theologizing. He had no field aside from the social ethical space that the social gospel had cleared for the direct consideration of social questions. Yet he was also a profound theologian who theorized the transcendence of God's mode of being over the contingent, temporal, transient, and fallen being of all creatures. To the generation that experienced two world wars, the Great Depression, and the Cold War, Niebuhr was the one who made sense of the "ought" questions. Always he sought to influence the course of American social and foreign policy from the standpoint of a realistic Christian ethic. By mid-century his influence over American Protestantism was enormous. Niebuhr towered above social ethics to the extent that for many years, when newcomers asked, "What is social ethics?" the usual and most reliable answer was, "That's what Reinhold Niebuhr does at Union Seminary."

Becoming Reinhold Niebuhr

Born in Wright City, Missouri, in 1892, Niebuhr was the son of a German Evangelical Synod pastor, Gustav Niebuhr, who immigrated to the United States from Germany at the age of 18 in 1881. The German Evangelical Synod of North America was a product of the 1817 union of the Reformed and Lutheran Churches of Prussia; Gustav Niebuhr thus considered himself Lutheran and Reformed, as well as evangelical and liberal. He was a vigorous, opinionated, high-minded church leader who read Harnack and Schleiermacher, voted for Teddy Roosevelt, and studied the Bible in Hebrew and Greek. Gustav believed in intellectual freedom and opposed the scholastic dogmatism of orthodox theology, but bitterly opposed liberal modernists who discounted the New Testament miracles. He was deeply committed to the Evangelical Synod, but spurned the cultural and confessional provincialism that prevailed in much of his denomination. Though many German Americans viewed temperance as an Anglo-Saxon plot against German culture, Gustav strongly supported the temperance movement; he also took an ecumenical view toward other Protestant denominations. Socialism was anathema to him, and feminism horrified him; at the same time he urged that the federal government was morally obliged to restrain the excesses of capitalism and that the church had a social mission to promote a good society.

Gustav and Lydia Niebuhr had five children; the oldest was a girl, Hulda; the oldest boy, Walter, was a bit rebellious; a second boy died in infancy; the fourth child – Karl Paul Reinhold Niebuhr – was Gustav's favorite. From an early age Reinhold warmed to his father and tried to be like him. He was exuberant, but disciplined; opinionated and spontaneous, but cooperative. Gustav caught a reflection of himself in his fourth child. He joked and confided with young Reinhold, who took it for granted that he would become a minister like his father: "My father was the most interesting man in our community." In later life Reinhold was shocked to discover that his younger brother, Yale theologian Helmut Richard Niebuhr, carried bitter memories of their father. To outgoing Reinhold, Gustav was a compelling, friendly, and exemplary model: "I have only pleasant memories of my father and the sense of partnership he established with an adolescent boy."[1]

To introverted Helmut he was coldly disapproving and tyrannical. Gustav Niebuhr had little use for his youngest child, who shared little of his spirit; meanwhile he told Hulda to forget about college, since higher education was not to be wasted on girls. Gustav demanded that Hulda be like her mother, whose life as a pastor's wife and helper was a seamless web of domestic and parish tasks.[2] Upon graduating from high school, Hulda took up a succession of parish commitments, just like Lydia Niebuhr; it was only after her father died unexpectedly in 1913, at the age of 50, that she resumed her education and eventually became a seminary professor.[3]

Reinhold Niebuhr was not impressively educated, aside from the theology and Greek that he learned from his father. At the age of 14, in the ninth grade, he took his last science and math classes; the following year he entered the German Synod's "pro-seminary" program at unaccredited Elmhurst College, 15 miles west of Chicago, which amounted to a second-rate boarding school. Elmhurst was a weak version of the German gymnasium; it ignored the sciences and modern history, and its pass at Latin and English was pitiful. Niebuhr rankled at the school's incompetence. He later recalled, a bit blandly, "The little college had no more than junior college status in my day, and I was not interested in any academic disciplines." As a student he organized a protest against the school's Latin and English teachers, which did not endear him to the faculty, especially after Niebuhr's father intervened and the Latin and English teachers were fired. In 1910 Niebuhr enrolled at his father's alma mater, Eden Theological Seminary, which proved to be more of the same, aside from the fatherly influence of Samuel Press, the first native-born member of the Eden faculty and the first who spoke English as his first language. A learned, irenic scholar, Press later served for many years as Eden's president. Raised in a half-English, half-German environment, Niebuhr was deficient in both languages. Under Press's influence he imagined a ministry that transcended his provincial context; he also found his first surrogate father.[4]

Gustav Niebuhr judged that his favored son needed to be trained at a thoroughly American university, preferably one that approximated German university standards of teaching and scholarship. In April 1913, five months before Reinhold enrolled at Yale Divinity School as a third-year Bachelor of Divinity student, Gustav died unexpectedly. The funeral lasted all afternoon, Press gave a memorial address, and for five months Reinhold assumed his father's pastoral chores at St John's Church of Lincoln, Illinois. For many years afterward he felt that he was completing his father's life and work. From the beginning he preached sermons marked by an emphasis on the sin of selfishness and the paradoxical character of Christianity and life. In Niebuhr's rendering, Matthew 10:39 expressed "the paradox of all life: that self-preservation means self-destruction and self-destruction means self-preservation." Only the person who gave up his or her life could be saved, he preached. The essential problem of every human life was every person's captivity to selfishness, and the solution to it was love and self-sacrifice: "The image of God that is still within us will never be satisfied until it is satisfied by the principle that made it – love." Niebuhr confessed that he did not understand the doctrines of the divinity of Christ, the two natures of Christ, the trinity of God, and the communion of the Spirit, and "maybe you don't either." But everyone could understand "the moral and social program of Christ"; on that basis he proposed to preach Christ as the solution to the problem of every human life.[5]

Niebuhr realized that he had no chance of being admitted to Union Theological Seminary and that he was a beneficiary of Yale's relaxed admission standards.[6] He gained admission to Yale Divinity School (then called the Yale School of Religion) only because it was in a rebounding and expanding phase after 20 years of stagnation. Union Seminary and the University of Chicago Divinity School attracted the best students; meanwhile Yale had resisted modern theology, the social gospel, and the ecumenical approach to theological education, clinging to its identity as the seminary of a moderately conservative and declining Congregationalism. As a consequence, class enrollments dropped sharply throughout the 1890s, and by 1906 the entering Bachelor of Divinity class was down to 13 men. That was the nadir of Yale's decline. In 1906 the faculty replaced its core curriculum with an elective system curriculum and added new courses on contemporary issues; the following year the Divinity School declared its independence from the Congregational Church; in 1909 Douglas Clyde Macintosh joined the faculty; and in 1911 the school appointed a therapeutically-oriented theological liberal, Charles Reynolds Brown, as its dean.[7]

Niebuhr's reaction to Yale was typically conflicted. Though grateful to be there and humbled by the learning of his teachers and classmates, he told Press that he learned more from his private reading than from classes. He resolved to "cast my lot with the English," but worried that he was forgetting how to speak German. His dominant feeling was humiliation. "I feel all the time like a mongrel among thoroughbreds and that's what I am," he confessed. It galled him to realize that the culprit was his denominational background:

> The more I see how highly scholarship is prized in other denominations the more the
> penny-wise attitude of our church makes me sore. But what we need more than several

special students is a *college* education for all of our students. The more I look at the thing the more I see that I have been cheated out of a college education. Elmhurst is little more than a high school.

His teenage years had been wasted intellectually, he judged; he especially lacked a decent training in English, philosophy, ethics and science. It made him "boil" to realize that his denomination substituted piety for critical scholarship, and he was finished with "this half-way business" of speaking neither English nor German very well. He had enormous gaps to fill if he was to become "a voice in our church."[8]

For the most part Yale provided what he wanted. The school was too mannered and uppity for his taste – the only professor that Niebuhr really liked was Macintosh, another outsider – but theologically Yale had the goods. Conservatives charged that Yale was Unitarian, Niebuhr observed, but that made sense only if "Unitarian" and "liberal" meant the same thing: "The general tendency of all larger American universities is of course in the general direction of unitarianism. But if this be unitarianism we may give all liberal theology that name, especially German liberal theology." In his experience, the German cast of the new theology taught at Yale was very pronounced: "In the classes one hears nothing but German names referred to: Holtzman, Weizsaecker, Weinel, Gunkel, Weiss, Deissman, Dobschuetz and all of the rest of the tribe are constantly passing in review."[9]

On this count Niebuhr was grateful for his family background. Though he lacked the training and degrees of his classmates, at least he could read German, while most of them could not. His teachers included Macintosh, biblical scholars Benjamin Bacon and Frank Porter, church historian Williston Walker, ethicist Hershey Sneath, and homiletics professor Henry Tweedy. To Niebuhr's understanding, Yale was committed to the liberal, German, history of religions approach to religion, and so was he. In this approach, he explained, "the Bible vanishes as any supernatural authority and Christianity is forced to compete with all religions upon a common basis." There was such a thing as biblical truth, he reasoned, but the content of this truth had to be established by critical reason and experience, not external authority.[10]

Under Macintosh's guidance he read William James, wrote a Bachelor of Divinity thesis on the pragmatic validity of religious knowledge, and appealed to human personality as a privileged realm of spirit not subject to the laws of nature. Niebuhr was slow to notice Walter Rauschenbusch; his two years at Yale were absorbed with the problems of personal belief. With an eye on graduate school and an academic career, he took four courses in the college's philosophy department, but earned mediocre grades and lost his enthusiasm for philosophy, as well as his eligibility for a graduate degree. At the Divinity School, Macintosh's epistemological theorizing confirmed that outcome; Niebuhr later recalled, "This professor meant a lot to me, but I found his courses boring."[11]

Elsewhere he recalled, with typically puckish humor,

> The more I threw myself into these philosophical studies, the more I got bored with all the schools of epistemology that had to be charted – the realists, the idealists, the logical idealists, the psychological idealists, the psychological logical idealists, and the other different kinds of idealists and realists. Frankly, the other side of me came out in the desire for relevance rather than scholarship.[12]

Not so frankly, Niebuhr neglected to explain that his grades disqualified him for doctoral study. His last paper for Macintosh, on the Pauline doctrine of immortality, argued that Paul's concern was the persistence of the individual personality. At the last minute, in June 1915, apparently on Macintosh's urging, Yale surprised Niebuhr by awarding him a Master of Arts degree, but he was finished with graduate education. His two years of Americanizing higher education would have to do.[13]

A few weeks after he graduated from Yale, Niebuhr discovered that his older brother Walter, who had supported the Niebuhr family since Gustav's death, was financially ruined. The responsibility of being the family's breadwinner passed to Reinhold. He confessed to Press that the prospect of entering the ministry as a liberal was unsettling to him: "I am a good deal worried that my liberalism will not at all be liked in our church and will jeopardize any influence which I might in time have won in our church." At the same time, though he craved influence, he could see no alternative to being theologically liberal: "One would have to go to Princeton to escape it."[14]

Niebuhr wanted a progressive, Americanized, reasonably well-paying church for his first pastorate; instead he was sent by synod President-General John Baltzar to a Germanic mission parish on the northwest edge of Detroit, Bethel Evangelical Church. That was deflating and frustrating. For two years Niebuhr had been free to develop his thinking and intellectual skills. Now his life had suddenly turned into a web of unwelcome responsibilities. The Bethel pastorate paid a poor salary; Niebuhr had never had a romantic relationship of any kind; now his mother was living with him; he may have had to help with his older brother's debts; and he did not want to live in Detroit, where the synod ministers impressed him as a "nest of reaction." He groused, "The ministry is the only profession in which you can make a virtue of ignorance." The German synod pastors of Detroit, clinging to the German language and a discredited orthodoxy, represented exactly "the imbecile standpatism" that he loathed. In 1915 they abetted a wave of pro-German nationalism in reaction to America's spreading anti-German sentiments. Niebuhr's pro-Americanism spiked in reaction, as he told Press: "The German propaganda is so hysterical among many of our ministers that largely by default I am getting to be a violent American patriot. There is no real interest in the welfare of this country and no genuine American patriotism . . . To be very candid with you I do not feel at all at home in our church."[15]

His first social cause was to make German-American Protestantism unabashedly American. While Niebuhr's mother conducted Bethel Church's daily business, including the Sunday School program and choir, he wrote a barrage of articles on church reform. While Bethel Church accepted his requests for English hymnals and a weekly English service, Niebuhr clashed with local clerical leaders and brooded that pro-German provincialism was prevailing in the synod. His first article for a national magazine, published in the *Atlantic* in July 1916, was titled "The Failure of German-Americanism." Niebuhr argued that German culture at its best was liberal, cosmopolitan, and forward-looking in politics and religion, but German-American Protestantism typically represented German culture at its worst: conservative, provincial, and stodgy. Americans had good reason to resent the lack of American patriotism recently displayed by German Americans, he implied. German Americans needed to become "less indifferent to the ideals and principles of this nation."[16] If German Americans became better Americans, Niebuhr insisted, they would find that they embraced what was best in their culture of origin.[17]

From the beginning of his career he invoked the Homeric legend of Scylla and Charybdis, the two sea monsters between which Ulysses charted his course: "There is a Scylla and Charybdis in almost every undertaking, two opposite dangers, two extremes, between which one must sail and both of which one must avoid if the undertaking is to be successful."[18] Even the gymnastic altar calls of evangelist Billy Sunday evoked a "yes and no" from Niebuhr, who judged that Sunday's popular revivals contained "a peculiar mixture of good and evil." Though Sunday was often ridiculed for his anti-intellectualism, fundamentalism, and showboating histrionics, Niebuhr observed that he rightly emphasized the "fundamental paradox of Christian faith" that God was both righteous and merciful. If Sunday overplayed the theme of divine wrath, at least his God remained capable of righteous judgment, unlike the sentimentalized deity of liberal Christianity.[19]

Niebuhr worried that liberal theology was too tenderminded, and he envied the freedom and national renown of Sunday, who was not bound to a local congregation or even a denomination. Niebuhr entered the ministry, as he later put it, "with a few thoughts and a tremendous urge to express myself."[20] He felt constrained by his position and denominational ties, though his mother freed him to write attention-claiming articles. He wanted to speak to multitudes, but as a minister he was confined to members of his denomination, and his denomination was puny: "Perhaps if I belonged to a larger denomination this wouldn't irk me so much. I suffer from an inferiority complex because of the very numerical weakness of my denomination."[21]

His deliverance came shortly after Woodrow Wilson declared war against Germany. The Evangelical Synod established a War Welfare Commission to organize pastoral services for its soldiers, and Niebuhr was appointed executive secretary. Synod President-General Baltzar wanted him to operate out of St Louis, but Niebuhr worried that his mother's emotional health depended on her work and security in Detroit. Lydia Niebuhr suffered from depression and anxiety attacks; she needed to be needed at Bethel Church. Thus instead of moving to St Louis, Niebuhr preached on most Sundays and spent the rest of each week on the road, touring military training camps in several states. His sister Hulda moved to Detroit to help their mother manage Bethel Church, and his brother Helmut – a graduate student at Washington University – substituted on Sundays when Niebuhr could not attend. Though the traveling was often exhausting, Niebuhr exulted in his opportunities to tour the country, influence denominational politics, and meet with officials of the Federal Council of Churches. He pressed his Evangelical brethren to believe in the war they were training to enter, or at least, to act as if they believed in the goodness of their country. "When I talk to the boys I make much of the Wilsonian program as against the kind of diplomacy which brought on the war," he observed. He blanched at witnessing a bayonet practice, "yet I cannot bring myself to associate with the pacifists. Perhaps if I were not of German blood I could." Had he not needed to prove his Americanism, he might have chosen pacifism. Niebuhr realized that was not a noble rationale – "that may be cowardly" – but he reasoned that "a new nation has a right to be pretty sensitive about its unity. Some of the good old Germans have a hard time hiding a sentiment which borders very closely on hatred for this nation." For him the real-world choice was between being a good American and romanticizing the Kaiser: "And the Kaiser is certainly nothing to me. I'll certainly feel better on the side of Wilson than on the side of the Kaiser."[22]

The fact that he was not actually *in* the war proved increasingly troubling to him. Niebuhr explained his desire to become a military chaplain to Baltzar, who replied that his War Welfare work was too valuable to give up; the war ended before Niebuhr had a chance to wear a military uniform. Gradually Baltzar became a father figure to him, like Samuel Press, and like several others afterward who supported Niebuhr personally, opened doors for him professionally, and gave him models of social Christian leadership. During the war he and Baltzar were consumed with securing German-American loyalty as a means of victory; Niebuhr urged that a victory aided by American intervention would make possible a new world order based on reconciliation, democracy, free trade, and the League of Nations. The Paris Peace Conference rudely punctured his belief that the war was a means to achieve Wilsonian democratic ideals; before the conference ended, Niebuhr judged that it was a disaster: "Wilson is a typical son of the manse. He believes too much in words." The war victors let Wilson cover their deeds with fine words, he observed, but the deeds were vengeful and wrong. While clinging to the hope that Wilson's democratic faith might still prevail – "words have certain meanings of which it is hard to rob them, and ideas may create reality in time" – Niebuhr worried that liberalism was fatally flawed as a means to create a just world order. He declared in the *New Republic* that liberal idealism "lacks the spirit of enthusiasm, not to say fanaticism, which is so necessary to move the world out of its beaten tracks. [It] is too intellectual and too little emotional to be an efficient force in history." The Versailles Treaty showed the weakness of the liberal alternative to the old order: "We need something less circumspect than liberalism to save the world."[23]

That sentiment eventually made Niebuhr famous, although he still assumed that the purpose of good politics was to save the world. Bethel Church grew tremendously in the early 1920s, feeding off the skyrocketing growth of Henry Ford's Detroit, despite Niebuhr's continued absences. Not coincidentally, the church also voted to worship exclusively in the English language. Americanization was the wave of the future in the Evangelical Synod, and Niebuhr was its apostle. He became a star attraction on the college and church conference lecture circuit, which attracted new members to his congregation. Niebuhr combined a charged intellectual message on an expanding variety of social themes with a constantly animated, whirling, gesticulating style of speaking. In 1922 he caught the attention of Charles Clayton Morrison, who was looking for someone to keep the *Christian Century* interesting while Morrison concentrated on the peace issue. Niebuhr became Morrison's fire hydrant of political and religious opinions, honing his distinctively dialectical, aggressive, ironic writing style in a profusion of *Century* editorials, articles, and reviews. Though Morrison paid him only for unsigned editorials, Niebuhr's were never hard to pick out. Morrison could never get enough of them. "Just send them in," he urged in 1923, "and as many as possible, and as often as possible. You have the right touch."[24]

Morrison became one of Niebuhr's father figures, as did Detroit Episcopal bishop Charles Williams, who pushed Niebuhr toward democratic socialism, and Sherwood Eddy, who founded (with Kirby Page) the Fellowship for a Christian Social Order (FCSO) in 1921. In 1922 Niebuhr and Williams founded a Detroit branch of the FCSO that was strongly pro-labor, though not explicitly socialist. At Williams' urging, Niebuhr studied Rauschenbusch's writings for the first time, which disabused him of the impression that Rauschenbusch's socialism was dangerously utopian. In 1923 Williams died of a heart attack, leaving a stunned Niebuhr with the sense that he was called to complete his mentor's work. "Nowhere have I seen a personality more luminous with the Christ spirit than in this bishop who was also a prophet," he wrote in his diary. "Here was a man who knew how to interpret the Christian religion so that it meant something in terms of an industrial civilization." To Williams' diocese he wrote, "Your diocese has lost a great bishop, but the church universal has lost infinitely more, it has lost a prophet who had the courage to challenge the complacency of a very self-righteous civilization." Increasingly Niebuhr preached and wrote that being a good American had nothing to do with overlooking America's social evils, especially its class divisions.[25]

In 1923 he traveled to Europe on one of Sherwood Eddy's educational tours. Niebuhr was predisposed to the convictions to which the tour led him, "Gradually the whole horrible truth about the war is being revealed. Every new book destroys some further illusion." The war had little to do with battling for or against democratic ideals, he believed; it was simply a struggle for power and economic advantage between two grasping alliances of states. In Europe Niebuhr heard terrible stories about France's mistreatment of Germans in the occupied Ruhr valley, which deepened his resentment of France's punitive attitude toward his ancestral homeland. Upon visiting the Ruhr, in the company of Kirby Page and Episcopal priest Will Scarlett, he witnessed what he called "the closest thing to hell I have ever seen." For three days Niebuhr listened to blood-curdling stories about atrocities and sexual assaults committed by the occupying French forces. He saw severely malnourished German children at the Red Cross centers and families separated by barbed wire. The atrocity stories, atmosphere of hate, and starving children drove him across a line. "This, then, is the glorious issue for which the war was fought!" he bitterly observed. Niebuhr dreamed of sending "every sentimental spellbinder of war days" to the Ruhr. He made a resolution: "This is as good a time as any to make up my mind that I am done with the war business . . . I am done with this business. I hope I can make that resolution stick." Less concerned about proving his Americanism, and having lost his other reasons for not being a pacifist, he vowed "to try to be a disciple of Christ, rather than a mere Christian, in all human relations and experiment with the potency of trust and love much more than I have in the past."[26]

For nearly 10 years he struggled to keep this resolution, all the while objecting that his pacifist colleagues in the FCSO and the Fellowship of Reconciliation were naive and idealistic. Reporting on "the great affliction" in the Ruhr, Niebuhr judged that France's brutal occupation represented the consummation of its "dreams of vengeance." Never an isolationist, he urged that America needed to use its diplomatic leverage to prevent the complete collapse of European civilization. The hopes of Europe rested on England and the United States because the other Western powers were consumed with revenge, "but England is practically powerless because America has withdrawn from European affairs and has left the continent to the tender mercies of French chauvinism." In the 1920s, while serving as national executive council chair of the Fellowship of Reconciliation, Niebuhr argued for an aggressive foreign policy. Somehow pacifism and internationalism had to go together, though he worried in the *Christian Century* that "the principle of nonresistance is too ideal for a sinful human world."[27]

That unsettling impression and the predatory logic of capitalism pushed Niebuhr toward socialism in the 1920s. "There is no Christian basis to modern industry," he wrote in 1923. "It is based upon a purely naturalistic conception of life and cynically defies every spiritual appreciation of human beings. Christianity has had nothing to do with the organization of industrial civilization. It ought therefore to have no pride in it." He was not quite ready to deal with the consequences of calling himself a

Socialist. But Eddy and Page were socialists, the FCSO was socialist in all but name, and in the mid-1920s Niebuhr spent much of his time touring the country as the FCSO's traveling secretary. Increasingly he chided the kind of Christians who "enjoyed their theological liberalism" but were terrified "of even the mildest economic and political heresy."[28]

In 1926 he charged that Henry Ford's reputation as a good employer was a product of self-deception and relentless self-promotion, like that of American capitalism. Ford was both naive and cunning, Niebuhr wrote in the *Christian Century*; he actually believed that as long as he paid the generous wages for which he was famous – which Niebuhr showed he was in fact no longer paying – his workers had no need of unemployment insurance, old-age pensions, and disability compensation. Sarcastically Niebuhr pronounced that Ford was a perfect symbol of American civilization; elsewhere he remarked, "What a civilization this is! Naive gentlemen with a genius for mechanics suddenly become the arbiters over the lives and fortunes of hundreds of thousands." By 1928 Niebuhr was voting for socialist Norman Thomas for president; the following year he joined the Socialist party.[29]

Niebuhr's socialist turn occasioned his first public rift with Morrison. Though Morrison was also a sharp critic of Henry Ford, he steered away from broadsides against American capitalism and concentrated on two issues: peace and temperance. For Morrison, the presidential election of 1928 came down to a choice between Herbert Hoover's foreign policy imperialism and Al Smith's Catholic anti-Prohibitionism, which made it no choice at all, despite Morrison's anti-war fervor. Temperance was a trump for Morrison, who also despised the Catholic Church. To Morrison, anti-militarism and temperance were the heart of the social gospel, and, in 1928, temperance was in trouble. To give up on Prohibition was to give up the social gospel project of morally transforming American society. Smith was in the wrong church, and he seemed to care nothing about the politics of moral community. He dealt with the politically delicate problem of religion by adopting a secular, instrumental approach to politics that ignored religious concerns. The *Christian Century* admonished that that would never create a good society.[30]

Niebuhr did not support Smith, either, and, as late as October 1927, he declared that Smith's "hopelessly wet" opposition to Prohibition was beyond the pale for those who cared about the moral character of America. He could not support a candidate who planned to repeal the Eighteenth Amendment. Smith had no appreciation of "puritan virtues and values," Niebuhr complained, which made democrats like himself politically homeless. But when the election season arrived, Niebuhr criticized Morrison for making temperance the holy grail of American politics. Prohibition was important, Niebuhr affirmed, but not more important than Hoover's right-wing economic policies and imperialist adventures in Latin America. In a choice between Hoover and Smith, Prohibition had to be sacrificed. As usual, liberal Protestantism was too moralistic. To be truly progressive, liberal Protestantism had to give higher priority to economic justice than moral purity. For those who were too timid to vote Socialist, the only morally defensible choice was Smith – a claim that made no moral sense at all to Morrison. This disagreement foreshadowed the break between the liberalism of the postwar social gospel and what came to be called Christian realism.[31]

In the 1920s Niebuhr filled the *Christian Century* with calls for a "robust" faith in human possibilities while warning that all "immediate evidences" contradicted this faith. Modern civilization needed a fusion of reason and religiously inspired good will, he argued; at the same time, liberal Christianity grievously overestimated human virtue. His first book, *Does Civilization Need Religion?* (1927), collected his favorite variations on this double-minded theme. Niebuhr argued that religion was "dying in modern civilization" because it came into conflict with a triumphant modern science and it failed to apply its ethical and social resources to solve "the moral problems of modern civilization." Liberal theology was the answer to the first problem, he averred, and Christian idealism held the key to the second, but it had to change: "If Christian idealists are to make religion socially effective they will be forced to detach themselves from the dominant secular desires of the nations as well as from the greed of economic groups." Any religious idealism that did not forcefully advocate "the equalization of living standards" stood convicted of "insincerity and moral confusion."[32]

Echoing Ernst Troeltsch, Niebuhr reasoned that Christianity was the fate of Western civilization: "Spiritual idealisms of other cultures and societies may aid it in reclaiming its own highest resources; and any universal religion capable of inspiring an ultimately unified world culture may borrow from other religions. But the task of redeeming Western society rests in a peculiar sense upon Christianity." Niebuhr did not claim to know if there was still time to save Western civilization from moral bankruptcy; what he knew was that modern society could not be saved without the inspiring and culture-forming influence of a renewed Christian idealism: "Civilization may be beyond moral redemption; but if it is to be redeemed a religiously inspired moral idealism must aid in the task." The ideal of ethical freedom was implicit in the human character, he asserted, "and awakened personalities will seek to realize that ideal." *Does Civilization Need Religion?* spoke the language of crisis, collapsing civilizations, and human fallibility, yet Niebuhr gave his assurance that old-style, idealistic, spirit-over-nature liberal Christianity was still the answer: "It is the virtue of a vital religious idealism that it lifts life above the level of nature and makes the development of an ethical personality the ultimate goal of human existence." The work of religion was to advance the ideal realm of personality in the face of impersonal social and natural forces.[33]

Niebuhr wrote most of his first book in 1924 and 1925; by the time it was published in 1927 his politics had moved further left. Increasingly he resolved the contradiction between his crisis language and his optimistic idealism by appealing to socialism; to his delight, the book brought a windfall of lecture invitations and new choices. For several years, while Niebuhr kept a foot in the door at Bethel Church, his mentors jockeyed to gain his full-time services. He spoke occasionally for the Evangelical Synod, but disappointed Baltzer by seeking a larger stage. He wrote profusely for Morrison, but declined to join the *Christian Century* as a full-time associate. He spoke frequently for the FCSO, but backed out of an Eddy/Page proposal to join the evangelism team of Henry P. Van Dusen and Samuel Shoemaker. In 1927 Niebuhr was offered a position at Boston University, where his sister Hulda taught Christian education; declining politely, he told Eddy and others that he could be tempted to teach at the right seminary.

Eddy and Page promptly put together a New York package: half-time as an editor at Page's journal, *The World Tomorrow*, and half-time as a teacher of social ethics at Union Theological Seminary. Because Union had no funds for a new position, Eddy promised Union president Henry Sloane Coffin that he would pay Niebuhr's entire salary for the first year. Coffin, then in his second year as Union's president, surmised that Niebuhr might attract ministerial students to the seminary; he believed that during

Arthur McGiffert's presidency, Union placed too much emphasis on graduate research at the expense of training students for the ministry. Except for Harry Ward, the Union faculty was less excited about having Niebuhr as a colleague. Many of Union's starched-collar professors were put off by his excited pulpit behavior, rough manners, and Midwestern twang, and they worried about his lack of academic credentials, which might create the appearance of lowered academic standards. Coffin countered that since Niebuhr's position would cost Union nothing, the seminary had little to lose by approving the appointment. That argument barely prevailed, as the faculty approved Niebuhr's appointment by a single vote. In later life Niebuhr was unable to remember the episode as it happened; he claimed that the faculty called him "to a Chair of Christian Ethics."[34]

Rejecting Social Gospel Idealism

In the company of his mother, who wanted to remain in Detroit, Niebuhr attracted an excited following at Union. His mother lost her partnership with him in the Lord's work, and thus felt abandoned; his students exulted that Niebuhr's engaging personality and brash, electric, opinionated lectures made politics and religion come alive. Students overflowed his classroom and crowded around him in the cafeteria and hallways; to them he was a catalyzing figure who opened Union Seminary to the outside world. To the reserved, scholarly Scots who dominated Union's senior faculty, he was hard to take. Theologically Union was steeped in the social gospel, and William Adams Brown was a major figure in international Christian ecumenism, but the Union faculty was short on figures who addressed secular society. Senior faculty members such as Brown, church historian James Moffatt, and biblical theologian Ernest Scott shuddered at Niebuhr's wild generalizations, his radical friends, his unrefined manners, and the fact that students called him "Reinie." Brown could see Niebuhr exiting Christianity by the same Socialist path that led Union alum Norman Thomas astray. The tremendous student reaction to Niebuhr, however, and the fact that Yale Divinity School tried to steal him in 1929, convinced Coffin that Niebuhr was indispensable to Union; he countered Yale's offer by appointing Niebuhr to the Dodge Professorship in Applied Christianity. Niebuhr felt the irony of his academic success; in later life he confessed that 10 years passed before he did not feel like a fraud in the classroom.

Upon arriving at Union he plunged immediately into New York radical politics. Niebuhr's editorial position at the Christian pacifist/socialist *World Tomorrow* gave him a base of intellectual influence, including access to intellectuals and activist leaders John Dewey, Norman Thomas, John Haynes Holmes, and Edmund Chaffee. He joined the leftist New York Teachers' Union, Paul Douglas' League for Independent Political Action, and Norman Thomas' League for Industrial Democracy. After Thomas received an embarrassing 267,000 votes in the 1928 election, Niebuhr joined the Socialist party. The ascension of Thomas, a former Presbyterian minister, to the top of the Socialist party allowed Niebuhr and other Christian progressives to join it; the anti-clerical types that Rauschenbusch avoided no longer dominated the party. Afterwards the onset of the Great Depression confirmed Niebuhr's fears about the crisis of capitalist civilization. In 1930, along with Eddy, Page, and social ethicist John C. Bennett, he co-founded the radical Fellowship of Socialist Christians, which became Niebuhr's primary organizational outlet. Other members included Roswell Barnes, Buell Gallagher, Francis

Henson, Frank Wilson, and later, Paul Tillich and Eduard Heimann. The leading figures of a new theological generation stopped using euphemisms for socialism and called for the abolition of private industrial property.[35]

Niebuhr believed that his radical turn took him far beyond the boundaries of liberal Christianity. For years he had preached an idealistic religion of pacifism, political reform, and liberal theology while complaining that liberal Christianity was too soft to confront the evils of the world. He called for moral efforts to redeem American society while warning that moral idealism had little power. In the early 1930s these awkwardly mixed feelings and the terrible wreckage of the Great Depression drove him to a sterner creed. In his experience liberal Christianity was moralistic, over-whelmingly bourgeois, enamored with modern progress, sentimental, and naive in its hope for a community of love. Typically it reduced politics to moral striving and religion to moral striving and personal faith. The seeds of this critique of liberal Christianity were scattered throughout Niebuhr's early writings, but in the early years of the Great Depression he came to the verdict that even his socialist friends who remained pacifists or idealists were part of the problem. Many of them were stunned to find the core of their faith ridiculed in Niebuhr's jeremiad, *Moral Man and Immoral Society*. A new era in American theology and social ethics began with the publication of this socio-ethical and political blockbuster in 1932.

In 1932 Niebuhr ran for Congress on the Socialist party ticket and told New Yorkers that only socialism could save Western civilization. He warned readers of *Harper's* magazine: "It will be practically impossible to secure social change in America without the use of very considerable violence."[36] *Moral Man and Immoral Society* was published a month after Niebuhr won 4 percent of the vote. The book drew back from his posturing about considerable violence, but it stressed that politics was about struggling for power. Any progressive politics that failed to acknowledge this truism was stupid. The book's tone was icy, aggressive, and eerily omniscient. It ridiculed the moral idealism of liberal Christianity and marked the end of Niebuhr's calls to build the kingdom of God. It argued that while individuals were occasionally capable of self-transcending virtue or altruism, human groups never willingly subordinated their interests to the interests of others. Morality belonged to the individual sphere of action. Individuals occasionally acted out of self-disregarding compassion or love, Niebuhr allowed, but groups never overcame the power of self-interest and collective egotism that sustained their existence. The liberal Christian attempt to moralize society was therefore not only futile, but desperately lacking in intelligence.[37]

With this book, "stupid" became Niebuhr's favorite epithet. He argued that because liberal idealists failed to recognize the brutal character of human groups and the resistance of all groups to moral suasion, they were always driven to "unrealistic and confused political thought." Secular liberals like John Dewey appealed to reason; Christian liberals appealed to love; both strategies were maddeningly stupid. *Moral Man and Immoral Society* seethed with Niebuhr's anger at the human ravages of the Depression and his frustration at America's aversion to socialism. The book embraced a Christian variant of Marxism, which provided an explanation for the impending collapse of bourgeois civilization and an antidote to the pious moralism of liberal Christianity. "The full maturity of American capitalism will inevitably be followed by the emergence of the American Marxian proletarian," Niebuhr predicted. "Marxian socialism is a true enough interpretation of what the industrial worker feels about society and history to have become the accepted social and political philosophy of all self-conscious and politically intelligent industrial workers."[38]

Like Christianity at its best, Marxism was both realistic and utopian; it had a tragic view of history that was tempered by its hope for the transformation of history. Niebuhr lectured that liberal Christianity needed to regain the realistic Christian sense of the tragedy of life: "The perennial tragedy of human history is that those who cultivate the spiritual elements usually do so by divorcing themselves from or misunderstanding the problems of collective man, where the brutal elements are most obvious. These problems remain unsolved, and force clashes with force, with nothing to mitigate the brutalities or eliminate the futilities of the social struggle." The historical sweep of human life always reflected the predatory world of nature, Niebuhr admonished. For that reason he gave up his vow to follow Jesus as a pacifist, citing Augustine's dictum that to the end of history "the peace of the world must be gained by strife." For the sake of justice *and* peace, modern Christianity was obliged to renounce its sentimental idealism: "If the mind and the spirit of man does not attempt the impossible, if it does not seek to conquer or to eliminate nature but tries only to make the forces of nature the servants of the human spirit and the instruments of the moral ideal, a progressively higher justice and more stable peace can be achieved."[39]

Liberal Protestant leaders howled that Niebuhr ignored the teachings of Jesus, had no theology of the church or the kingdom, and treated his lack of faith in God's regenerative power as a virtue. Norman Thomas and John Haynes Holmes both lambasted Niebuhr's "defeatism," while Yale theologian Robert Calhoun, Union theologian Henry Van Dusen, and World Student Christian Federation leader Francis Pickens Miller complained that Niebuhr's theology relinquished any notion of a socially transformative presence of God in history. University of Chicago chapel dean Charles Gilkey, stunned by Niebuhr's aggressive sarcasm against peace-loving liberal Christianity, declared to his family that Niebuhr had lost his mind. All were friends of Niebuhr's who struggled to fathom what had happened to him.[40]

Most important to Niebuhr, the *Christian Century* mourned that "pessimism can speak no gloomier word." Morrison assigned the book to another friend of Niebuhr's, Chicago pastor Theodore C. Hume, who declared, "To call the book fully Christian in tone is to travesty the heart of Jesus' message to the world." *Moral Man and Immoral Society* contained a "tonic rigor" in its broadside against the social meliorism of liberal Christianity, Hume acknowledged, but the book quickly took on a "darker hue of cynicism" that eventually hardened to "unrelieved pessimism." Hume shook his head at Niebuhr's pronouncement that the religion of Quaker mystic Rufus Jones offered nothing of value to modern Christians who sought to discern the social meaning of their faith. He chided Niebuhr for offering "a fainter sprinkling of theology than might have been expected from a professor of Christian ethics." He worried that Niebuhr's pessimism made him a spiritual bedfellow of religious conservatives; in the meantime, Hume declared, many of Niebuhr's true friends "are still bold enough to believe in the potency of the Christian 'good news,' for society as well as for man's inner life."[41]

The impassioned liberal outcry against his book heightened Niebuhr's sense of alienation from liberal Protestantism and gave him plenty of grist for his attacks upon it. He aggressively defended his position, especially on the sensitive point of his personal faith. "My conclusions are not in accord with liberal Christianity," he observed.

I believe that liberalism has sentimentalized the message of Jesus beyond all recognition. But I fail to see why that should make my book unchristian in tone. I am trying honestly to find the relevance between the message of Jesus and the problems of our day. I may be mistaken in my conclusions, but my conclusions have no unchristian motive or purpose.

It was true that his emphasis on human sinfulness made him sound like a conservative, he allowed, but that was only because liberal Protestantism had forsaken its biblical and classical roots in this subject: "I hold it to be the chief sin of liberalism that it has given selfish man an entirely too good opinion of himself." Liberal theology was wrong in its politics and theology for that reason. Politically it was too comfortable in its moralistic middle-class idealism; theologically it was too humanistic:

> In general my position has developed theologically to the right and politically to the left of modern liberal Protestantism. If such a position seems unduly cynical and pessimistic to the American mind my own feeling is that this judgment is due to the fact that the American mind is still pretty deeply immersed in the sentimentalities of a dying culture."[42]

Niebuhr's liberal critics understood that he attacked liberal Christianity from the socialist political Left. They were less sure what to make of his theology, except that they disliked it. Niebuhr gave comfort to reactionaries and he said hardly anything about God, faith, or redemption. If that was moving "theologically to the right," it seemed a strange form of doing so to liberals who believed in the power of faith and the saving love of God. Repeatedly they protested that Niebuhr showed no faith in divine power of any kind; instead he ridiculed those who had any. The liberal outcry against *Moral Man and Immoral Society* convinced Niebuhr that he had taken the right course in breaking from old friends. It strengthened his determination to reconnect with the evangelical orthodoxy of his youth, as did the penetrating criticism that he received from his brother Helmut, whose critique was loaded with familial weight.

H. Richard Niebuhr, Liberal Religion, and Radical Monotheism

In 1931, Helmut Richard Niebuhr had accepted a theology position at Yale Divinity School and started going by his "American" middle name; the same year, Reinhold suddenly ended his longtime bachelor status by marrying a visiting English fellow at Union, Ursula Keppel-Compton, which deeply wounded Lydia Niebuhr. The following year the two brothers squared off in the only public disagreement of their careers, over the moral responsibility of American Christians to respond to the Japanese invasion of Manchuria. Should American Christians call for an economic embargo against Japan, despite the possibility that such a response might lead to war? In the *Christian Century*, Richard made a case for "the grace of doing nothing," arguing that God had God's own plans for history, and it was not the calling of Christians to make history come out right. Reinhold replied that justice was the highest attainable ideal in politics, and Christians were called to secure justice; there was no grace in doing nothing. Responding to this reply, Richard disclaimed any interest in "demolishing my opponent's position – which our thirty years' war has shown me to be impossible."[43]

For many years Richard had competed with his brother, assisted him, and looked up to him. Sometimes, after a Reinhold sermon or lecture, Richard beamed with approval; on other occasions, upon making eye contact, he looked down and shook his head in disbelief. Outside the public eye they regularly scrutinized each other's writing. Reinhold's marriage was a rare moment of unambiguous celebration; Richard, rejoicing for his brother, offered to take responsibility for Lydia. Meanwhile they argued about Japan privately before allowing it to become a public exception. Richard tried to be a pacifist, though not for liberal reasons. In January 1933, amid the liberal outcry against *Moral Man and Immoral Society*, he seized the chance to dislodge Reinhold from his essentially liberal outlook.[44]

"I have no defense of idealism to offer. I hate it with all my heart as an expression of our original sin," Richard wrote. But Reinhold was still an idealist, in his brother's disapproving opinion. Everything that Reinhold said about human nature and religion took idealism for granted. The ostensible virtue of "moral man" was a key example; Richard asked him to consider the phenomenon of brotherly love: "I hate to look at my brotherly love for you to see how it is compounded with personal pride." First there was the pride of basking in Reinhold's reflected glory, which was painfully mixed, in Richard's experience, with the selfish pride of "trying to stand on my own feet, trying to live up to you, being jealous of you . . . enough to make one vomit." If he could love Reinhold despite the layers of evil pride and jealousy that pervaded their relationship, Richard wrote, "it isn't because any ideal or will to love prevails over my putrid instinct and desire, but because something else which is not my will was at work long before I had a will or an ideal." Human beings had a moral gift of judging right and wrong, not a gift of goodness, he explained. All morally reflective people knew they were bad. Thus, Reinhold was wrong about individual selves being morally superior to their groups:

> The apparently more decent behavior of men in face-to-face relationships is not due at all to any element of reason or of moral idealism, any inclination of the will, but to the fact that there is more coercion, more enlightened self-interest (because the relations are more easily seen) and more possibility of identifying ourselves with the other man and loving ourselves in him or her.

Richard did not deny the existence of ideals; he denied that ideals were effective in influencing human action.[45]

More importantly, Reinhold still conceived religion in thoroughly liberal terms. "You think of religion as a power – dangerous sometimes, helpful sometimes," Richard observed. "That's liberal. For religion itself religion is no power, but that to which religion is directed, God." First Reinhold assumed the liberal idea of the self as a rational agent possessed of a nature-transcending spiritual power of goodwill; then he appealed to the liberal idea that religion was saving and transformative. Richard countered,

> I think the liberal religion is thoroughly bad. It is a first-aid to hypocrisy. It is the exaltation of goodwill, moral idealism. It worships the God whose qualities are "the human qualities raised to the nth degree," and I don't expect as much help from this religion as you do. It is sentimental and romantic. Has it ever struck you that you read religion through the mystics and ascetics? You scarcely think of Paul, Augustine, Luther, Calvin. You're speaking of humanistic religion so far as I can see. You come close to breaking with it at times but you don't quite do it.

Richard admonished that their family's faith was the evangelical religion of Paul, Augustine, Luther, and Calvin. For Reinhold, as for liberal Christianity, religion was an energizing power that served human needs and dictated human responsibilities. Richard implored him to drop this human-centered moralization of Christianity: "I agree wholly with you on the amorality of violence and nonviolence. A pacifism based on the immorality of violence hasn't a leg to stand on. But I do think that an activism which stresses immediate results is the cancer of our modern life." Reinhold's fixation on political issues and his frenetic chasing after causes were spiritually corrupting Richard warned him. "We want to be saviors of civilization and simply bring down new destruction," he told him. "You are about ready to break with that activism. I think I discern that."[46]

At the time Richard Niebuhr's major works lay ahead of him. Born in 1894, he had graduated from Elmhurst College and Eden Theological Seminary, ministered for two years in St Louis, and earned a doctorate at Yale in 1924. He had returned straight to Elmhurst for three years, serving as president, and then served as dean at Eden for four years before returning to Yale as a theology professor in 1931. Yale had tried to lure Reinhold from Union, which responded with a chair; thus Yale settled for the younger brother, who labored for years with the burden of comparisons. Richard Niebuhr won the Yale appointment on the strength of his book *The Social Sources of Denominationalism* (1929), which analyzed the role of race, class, geography, ethnic background, and education in shaping American Protestantism.[47]

His next book, *The Kingdom of God in America* (1937), historicized his critique of American liberal Protestantism. In Richard Niebuhr's telling, liberal theology was the child of a merger between nineteenth-century romantic liberalism and evangelicalism; it was also caught in an inevitably degenerate process. The romantic liberal stream was evolutionary, progressive, immanental, and idealistic, while the evangelical stream was revolutionary, sin-conscious, and conversion oriented. Liberal theologians usually claimed to maintain a balance between these intellectual heritages, he observed, but in fact they whittled away the evangelical one. In the Unitarian Church the gospel died quickly, as William Ellery Channing's Unitarian Christianity gave way to Emersonian Transcendentalism. In mainline Protestantism something similar happened more slowly. Horace Bushnell held together romantic liberalism and evangelical salvation, but the Bushnellians were embarrassed by Bushnell's fixation with atonement and replaced it with evolutionary progress. Niebuhr remarked: "So the process went on. It was not God who ruled, but religion ruled a little, and religion needed God for its support." By the end of Rauschenbusch's era, he judged, the gospel vision of the kingdom beyond had faded into something quite prosaic, the culture and consumer goods of modernity. That verdict yielded a scathing epitaph, soon immortalized by frequent quotation: "A God without wrath brought men without sin into a kingdom without judgment through the ministrations of a Christ without a cross."[48]

Richard Niebuhr thought with Paul, Augustine, Luther, Calvin, and Jonathan Edwards, though on modern terms. His theology had a strong dose of Ernst Troeltsch's historicism and reflected the mood of a rising neo-Reformation movement in theology led by Karl Barth. He believed that instead of adjusting its faith to the changing, relative, temporal aspects of modern culture, the church was supposed to adjust itself, amid the changing aspects of modern civilization, to the eternal. It was called to respond to the crisis of the world in the church, not the other way around. Navigating between

Troeltsch and Barth, he developed a distinctly theocentric, epistemologically perspectival, and ethically relational position. In *The Meaning of Revelation* (1941) he described
revelation as a type of experience akin to reading a single luminous sentence that made
sense of a difficult book. Revelation was about the disclosure of God as a valued reality
that created a basis for practical reasoning about God and the world, Niebuhr argued.
For those who lived within the inner history of the ongoing story of Christ, the event
of Christ bore revelatory meaning, yielding concepts that made the world intelligible:
"Whatever be the case in other human inquires there is no such thing as disinterestedness in theology, since one cannot speak of God and gods save as valued beings or as
values which cannot be apprehended save by a wiling, feeling, responding self." There
was no neutral standpoint from which that which was inseparable from faith could be
approached. A theologian could be wrong, but never neutral.[49]

His most famous book, *Christ and Culture* (1951), established the categories by
which two generations of theologians conceived the relationship of Christianity to
culture. Niebuhr delineated five models: Christ against culture, Christ of culture,
Christ above culture, Christ and culture in paradox, and Christ transforming culture.
Tertullian and Tolstoy exemplified the somewhat admirable, but overly simplistic
"against" model. Liberal Protestantism as a whole, represented by Albrecht Ritschl,
stood for the "of" model, which accommodated the gospel to modern knowledge and
values. Thomas Aquinas epitomized the "above" model, writing for the ages while
taking little notice of his time. The exemplar of the paradoxical model was Martin
Luther, with his doctrine of eschatological tension between the two kingdoms of the
gospel and the Spirit and the law and the sword. Niebuhr respected the complexity
and realism of Lutheran two-kingdoms theology, but criticized its political conservatism, which also showed up in his second example of dialecticism, Søren Kierkegaard.
Augustine and English socialist F. D. Maurice represented the transformer view, which
sought to convert individuals and regenerate culture in the name and spirit of Christ.
In Niebuhr's account, this perspective, at its best, took the world seriously as an object
of redemption without compromising the transcendence of God or the gospel. *Christ
and Culture* stuck as closely as possible to objective description, but its preference for
the transformers came through to decades of seminarians. Briefly it acknowledged that
one did not have to be a Lutheran or even politically conservative to advocate the
paradoxical dualist position; in a footnote, Niebuhr placed his famous brother in the
paradoxical camp.[50]

When Richard Niebuhr typed himself ethically, he called himself a "relational value
theorist." He had in mind, for his later career, a major work on ethics; in 1952 he
wrote an essay, "The Center of Value," that expounded his key ideas. As usual he
began with a typology, distinguishing his perspective from subjectivist and objectivist
ethical theories that abstracted from the relational character of human experience.
Subjectivists reduced the statement "justice is good" to an emotive preference on the
order of "I like justice." Objectivists based the statement on a divine command or a
direct intuition of objective value. Niebuhr agreed with objectivists that "justice is
good" was not merely an emotive preference and he agreed with subjectivists that
moral value had no existence in itself. His alternative was a relational concept of value
as a thoroughly social phenomenon. "Justice is good" was a relational truth, he argued.
The value of justice, like that of all other values, exists in the reciprocal relations that
beings realizing potentiality have to each other. Every good is both a means and an
end; there is no value apart from the relation of selves to each other. When pressed

on whether he really meant to say that the growth of a self in kindness or integrity lacks any value in itself, Niebuhr said yes. There was no virtue apart from relations; value was social and relational without remainder; the virtues could not be called good apart from their goodness for other selves and society. Philosophically, that put him closer to University of Chicago pragmatist George Herbert Mead, who described the self as a social reality, than to Aristotle; theologically, he was closer to Jonathan Edwards, who spoke of the consent of being to being, than to Thomas Aquinas.[51]

The echoes of Augustine, Calvin, and Edwards were strongest in Richard Niebuhr's late work, *Radical Monotheism and Western Culture* (1960), which stressed the perils of idolatry and the transcendent holiness of the One God beyond all names and cultural forms. In radical monotheism the center of value was the principle of being itself, Niebuhr argued: "Its reference is to no one reality among the many but to One beyond all the many." Only One is absolute. Whatever is has being, and is worthy of love, and is good. Niebuhr stressed the latter affirmation. Whatever is must be good, he argued, "because it exists as one thing among the many which all have their origin and their being, in the One." The principle of being is also the principle of value. No finite object, not even a supernatural one, can confer value on the self. Rather, the self attains value through its relation to the One to whom all being is related: "Radical monotheism dethrones all absolutes short of the principle of being itself. At the same time it reverences every relative existent. Its two great mottoes are: 'I am the Lord thy God; thou shalt have no other gods before me" and "whatever is, is good."[52]

Richard Niebuhr intended to write his book on ethics after he stopped lecturing about it. For him, publication was always problematic. The few books that he wrote were short and tightly written; cobbling together his articles, as his brother often did, was inconceivable for him. Richard always dreaded putting his ideas in print, because then he lost the ability to refashion them. An idea, once published, was no longer a fresh object of conversation with students and colleagues; it became public property, something belonging to the past about which others published interpretations. Disliking that loss of immediacy, Niebuhr waited to publish his ethics, but died suddenly in 1962. His lectures at the University of Glasgow in 1960, published posthumously as *The Responsible Self* (1963), had to substitute for a finished work.[53]

The Responsible Self resounded with themes that Niebuhr's students recognized from his lectures. There had to be a better approach to Christian ethics than the usual choice between deontology and teleology, he argued, just as, metaphysically, there had to be something better than "monotheistic idealism" and "monistic deontology." Instead of conceiving the self as a law-ruled citizen (deontology) or goal-oriented maker (teleology), Niebuhr defined it as a responder to other selves and responsibilities. The self existed within various relationships that created and demanded accountability. To be an ethical self was to be a responsible participant in a network of relationships. It followed that instead of conceiving ethics as normative prescription, Christian ethicists did better to disclose the ethos or distinctive character of a Christian community's moral life. Rather than ask "What should we do?" Niebuhr taught his students to ask "What is going on?" and "What is God doing?" Finding the answer was each person's moral responsibility; Christian ethics was merely an aid to Christian self-knowledge within the context of Christian community. That ruled out monotheistic idealism, which organized Christian ethics around the command "Remember God's plan for your life." It also ruled out monistic deontology, the reduction of Christian ethics to moral rules, which demanded: "Obey God's laws in all your obediences to finite rules." His alternative was the ethic of monotheistic responsibility, a modern rendering of Augustine, Calvin, and Edwards: "God is acting in all actions upon you. So respond to all actions upon you as to respond to his action."[54]

That rendering of the theological and social meaning of Christianity shaped a stream of Niebuhr's students at Yale University, notably Paul Ramsey and James M. Gustafson. *The Kingdom of God in America* and *Christ and Culture* were widely read as accounts of how theology and ethics developed; *The Meaning of Revelation* and *Radical Monotheism* helped to shape an American style of neo-orthodoxy that cut loose from Barthian scholasticism; Niebuhr's lectures in ethics taught his students to expound the ethos of the Christian community's distinct life, instead of privileging Reinhold's question of how to exercise power in a morally responsible way.

Richard Niebuhr was wrong about his brother's break from activist religion, something they debated privately for decades afterwards. Liberal Christianity took for granted that religion was supposed to be a power for social good, and so did Reinhold Niebuhr. He had no field apart from the social ethical space that the social gospel created. For Reinhold, as for the liberal tradition, religion was a human construct, grounded in human moral and religious strivings, that was made possible by humanity's unique capacities for transcendence, good, and evil. To the extent that he reflected at all upon nature beyond human nature, Reinhold regarded the natural world as the servant of human need and gratification. He could never embrace a religion that refused to save civilization; for him the social gospel view of religion as energy for the social struggle was a core assumption. He could never say, with his brother, that activism was the cancer of modern life. He must have felt insulted upon reading it, for Niebuhr was consumed with activist passion. His realistic turn was a critique of the way that the social gospelers went about trying to save and transform civilization, not a rejection of the social gospel project. For all the criticism that he took from liberal social gospelers, Reinhold could never turn away from creating a just world order.

But in 1932 Richard Niebuhr may have perceived that his brother was newly open to their evangelical roots, which differed from the evangelical stream of liberal theology. Evangelical liberalism fixated on the religion of Jesus and the social meaning of the kingdom ideal. Richard correctly surmised, even while censuring Reinhold for writing as though Paul and Calvin never existed, that he was ready to reclaim at least part of their family's Lutheran/Calvinist heritage. The closing pages of Reinhold's next book, *Reflections on the End of an Era* (1934), invoked the themes of divine providence and grace in a way that reassured Morrison and Union colleague Henry Van Dusen, who had worried that Niebuhr was losing his faith. In the 1930s his writings became increasingly religious and theological, invoking the classical themes of divine transcendence, grace, providence, judgment, and justification by grace through faith. At the end of the decade Niebuhr reflected, "Even while imagining myself to be preaching the Gospel, I had really experimented with many modern alternatives to Christian faith, until one by one they proved unavailing."[55]

Christian Realism as Socialist Faith

Niebuhr's polemical relation to liberal Protestantism heightened as a consequence of this theological turn and his deepening political radicalism. In *Reflections on the End of an Era*, his most explicitly Marxist work, he declared that liberal Christianity was too soft to provide the emancipatory alternative that was needed. The right combination was radical politics and a theological emphasis on sin. If politics was about struggling for power, Niebuhr reasoned, and radical politics was about struggling for a just redistribution of power, religion could serve the cause of justice only if it took a realistic attitude towards power, interest, and evil. In 1933 he observed,

> Classical religion has always spoken rather unequivocally of the depravity of human nature, a conclusion at which it arrived by looking at human nature from the perspective of the divine. It is one of the strange phenomena of our culture that an optimistic estimate of human nature has been made the basis of theistic theologies. Next to the futility of liberalism we may set down the inevitability of fascism as a practical certainty in every Western nation.[56]

Reflections on the End of an Era expanded this twofold theme with apocalyptic fervor. Niebuhr stressed that modern capitalism, throughout its entire brief reign, exuded an attitude of unqualified optimism. The philosophers of modernity dreamed of progress "almost until the hour of its dissolution." But the ravages of capitalist egotism now confronted modernity's apologists with the deepest and most unpleasant truths about themselves: "The wise men of our era did not realize at all that mind is the servant of impulse before it becomes its master and that the first effect of mind upon impulse is to make man more deadly in his lusts than the brute." If the brute in the forest lived by robbing and destroying other life, there was, at least, a form of harmony in the primitive struggle for survival, because each species survived. In the struggle for survival organized by commercial society, however, human self-consciousness and egotism transmuted "the brute's will-to-survive into the human will-to-power." Niebuhr conceded that capitalism did not create economic imperialism, since every powerful nation was naturally driven into imperialism by its will to live. But capitalism dramatically heightened the imperialism of the major powers and intensified their competition "to exploit the backward portions of the world." A chief cause of the Great War, for example, was the struggle for imperial advantage in Africa.[57]

Modern capitalism was driven by its distinctive will to power to create its own peculiarly insidious forms of imperialism. The problem with capitalism was not a defect in the system or the egotism of individuals who profited from it, but the system itself. "The sickness from which modern civilization suffers is organic and constitutional," Niebuhr declared. "It is not due to an incidental defect in the mechanism of production or distribution but to the very character of the social system . . . Private ownership means social power; and the unequal distribution of social power leads automatically to inequality and injustice."[58]

Niebuhr assumed that capitalism would never generate the degree of mass consumption that mass production required. He assumed that the concentration of economic ownership under capitalism ensured a severe maldistribution of wealth. For only a brief period of its history, he observed, it had been possible to think that the massive disparities of wealth created under capitalism would not engender social anarchy and disintegration. This period was over. Modern capitalism had created economic development of a kind, but at the expense of vulnerable masses in the dominant countries and in the nonindustrialized world. Capitalist society was now disintegrating on the contradictions of a system that required, but could not accommodate, continually expanding markets. "The technique of providing markets for both surplus products and surplus capital by lending surplus capital to permit the purchase of surplus goods has run its course in both English and American imperialism in less than a century," he declared. "Capitalism in short can exist only by attempting to universalize itself but it can live healthily only as long as it fails to do so."[59]

Liberalism and capitalism were finished. No amount of reformist tinkering could stop the world historical drift toward fascism, he contended. The only way to avert a fascist takeover of the entire Western world was for the West to embrace socialism. In 1930 Niebuhr founded the Fellowship of Socialist Christians as a vehicle for his increasingly radical politics. Three years later, shortly before the inauguration of Franklin Roosevelt, Niebuhr announced that capitalism was dying the death it deserved. Capitalism was dying because it was "a contracting economy which is unable to support the necessities of an industrial system that requires mass production for its maintenance, and because it disturbs the relations of an international economic system with the anarchy of nationalistic politics." It deserved to die because it was unable to justly distribute the wealth created by modern technology. "There is nothing in history to support the thesis that a dominant class ever yields its position or privileges in society because its rule has been convicted of ineptness or injustices," he contended. "Those who still regard this as possible are rationalists and moralists who have only a slight understanding of the stubborn inertia and blindness of collective egoism."[60]

Reflections on the End of an Era elaborated Niebuhr's certainties about where history was going. Reformists like Roosevelt were kidding themselves. There was no third way. The chief tragedy of modern life was that modern technology made intranational cooperation and international reciprocity absolutely necessary, but capitalism made justice and cooperation impossible. Injustice, exploitation and imperialism were not byproducts of capitalist modernization, but constitutive in the structure of capitalism itself. Thus, the ravages of capitalist injustice would never be removed by moral effort, political reformism, or even the recognition that capitalism was destroying modern civilization. "If the social injustice which makes modern capitalism untenable is actually rooted in the very nature of capitalism it is not likely that capitalism will be converted to justice by logical and historical proof that social inequality will destroy it," Niebuhr asserted. What was needed was a socialist revolution in which the church played a challenging, inspiriting, and chastening role.[61]

Politically and theologically, liberal Christianity was too soft to do the job. Niebuhr declared, "In my opinion adequate spiritual guidance can come only through a more radical political orientation and more conservative religious convictions than are comprehended in the culture of our era." Liberal Protestantism was too moralistic and middle-class to challenge existing relations of power; the transformative Christianity that was needed would be instructed by Marxism without capitulating to it: "If Christianity is to survive this era of social disintegration and social rebuilding, and is not to be absorbed in or annihilated by the secularized religion of Marxism it must come to terms with the insights of Marxist mythology."[62]

Marx's theory of the class struggle and his critique of the capitalist modes of production and distribution were more valuable than all of the preaching of moral reformers. Like liberal Christianity, however, Marxism betrayed its moral project into an illusion, "for it believes that a kingdom of pure love can be established in history and that its vindictive justice will be transmuted into pure justice." In its own way – which Niebuhr somewhat misconstrued with his references to morality and pure love – Marxism was as naive and as utopian as liberal Christianity. Marxism and liberal Christianity both failed to sustain the dialectical tension between spirit and nature. To collapse the tension between the demands of spirit and the impulses of nature was to open the door to authoritarian hubris. It was to cover the impulses of nature with "the moral prestige of the spiritual" and thus secure moral immunity for a regime or position that operated without moral restraint. Thus did Marxism easily degenerate into a bad religion.[63]

That was Niebuhr's political argument for rejecting liberal Christianity; in *An Interpretation of Christian Ethics* (1935) he blasted it from the religious side, chiding that "liberal Christian literature abounds in the monotonous reiteration of the pious hope that people might be good and loving." Shailer Mathews was a favorite target; Niebuhr ridiculed his "strikingly naive" idealism, which called Christians to be "champions of the underprivileged" and yet rise above the class struggle. For Niebuhr, Mathews epitomized liberal stupidity in politics (through his moralistic idealism) and theology (through his myth-dispensing modernism). The basic defect of liberal theology was its mistaken approach to Christian myth, Niebuhr judged. In effect, liberalism amounted to a reverse-fundamentalism. It rightly contended that the Bible's myths were myths, but reduced Christianity to superficial bromides by failing to appropriate the religious meaning of Christian myth. In Niebuhr's rendering, traditional orthodoxy was wrong because it took Christian myths literally; liberal theology was equally wrong because it refused to take Christian myths seriously: "It is the genius of true myth to suggest the dimension of depth in reality and to point to a realm of essence which transcends the surface of history, on which the cause–effect sequences, discovered and analyzed by science, occur."[64]

His thinking about myth rested heavily on Paul Tillich's, who fled Nazi Germany in 1933 and, on Niebuhr's initiative, joined Niebuhr at Union Theological Seminary. Tillich's approach to the problem was formulated in the 1920s, only a few years after he survived four years of duty as a German chaplain in the Great War. The colossal brutality and evil of the war drove him to two nervous breakdowns and influenced his subsequent preoccupation with the mythic nature of religion. He argued that myth was a symbolic expression of the relation of human beings to that which concerned them ultimately, not merely a prescientific explanation of events in the world. Myth is the essential mode of encounter with the sacred, Tillich reasoned. It is the language of faith, which, as the "universal category of the religious as such," cannot be eliminated without negating faith. Against the liberal attempt to replace the language of myth with a nonmythical religious symbolism or discourse, Tillich taught that myth is an essential element in all cultural and intellectual endeavor, and, in its "broken" form, the key to whatever is true in religion.[65]

For Tillich, as for Niebuhr, myth was a product of human spirituality that symbolically expressed human experiences of sacred power or presence in the natural realm. The Christian myths of divine creation, the fall of humankind, and the double nature of Christ were absurd if taken literally, but if taken as myths, they were religiously deep in meaning. The fall was Niebuhr's bellwether example. Conservative Christianity made absurd claims about the fall as an historical event, he noted, but at least it took seriously the biblical idea that human nature was thoroughly corrupted by sin. On this count traditional orthodoxy tended to be more profound, religiously, than liberal Christianity, which failed to take seriously the defining myths of Christianity. Having dispensed with a literalistic reading of the fall, liberal Christianity degenerated into a culture religion that substituted the Enlightenment myths of progress and human perfectibility for the biblical idea of human fallenness.[66]

In the scriptural story of the fall, Adam and Eve brought sin into a sinless world by defying the command of a jealous God not to eat the fruit of the tree of knowledge. In liberal Christianity, Niebuhr observed, the effort to overcome literalism, anthropomorphism, and supernaturalism reduced the meaning of this story to an expression of the fears of primitive people toward higher powers. Having repudiated a mistaken appropriation of religious myth, liberal Christianity discarded the fall altogether. But the religious truth of the fall was precisely what liberal Christianity lacked, Niebuhr argued. The biblical image of a jealous creator is not a dispensable anthropomorphism but a mythical depiction of the human situation. The root of human evil is the prideful human pretension of being God. As creatures made in the image of God, human beings possess capacities for self-transcendence that enable them to become aware of their finite existence in distinction from, though constitutive with, God's infinite existence. The same awareness moves human beings, however, to attempt to overcome their finiteness by becoming infinite, like God. This was Adam's sin. Fundamentally, evil is always a good that imagines itself to be better than it is. Evil is driven by egotism, which is always wrapped in self-deceit and deceit of others. Thus the biblical myth of the fall was not a dispensable relic of primitive fear and superstition, Niebuhr reasoned, "but a revelation of a tragic reality of life." Every page of human history confirms the truth of the myth.[67]

Niebuhr affirmed that he sought to refurbish the classical doctrine of original sin, though not in any of its classical forms. Rightly understood, the myth of original sin was not an account of the literal origin of evil or a theory of biologically transmitted evil. Augustine's notion that original sin was transmitted through lust in the act of procreation was self-defeating, because it destroyed the basis for moral responsibility.[68] If original sin was an inherited corruption, human beings lacked the freedom to choose not to sin and thus could not be held morally responsible for being in sin. For Niebuhr, the true meaning of original sin was existential, not biological. Its reality was attested by history, but original sin itself was not historical. Just as the myth of the fall was a description of the nature of evil rather than account of the origin of evil, so the reality of original sin was an inevitable fact of human existence but not an inherited corruption of existence. The human capacity for self-transcendence made original sin inevitable. Though it had no history, original sin was a reality "in every moment of existence." Niebuhr fixated on this paradoxical truism; his major theological work, *The Nature and Destiny of Man*, was based upon it: sin is an inevitable existential corruption for which human beings are morally responsible.[69]

An Interpretation of Christian Ethics would have been a defining work merely for delineating Niebuhr's relation to theological liberalism, his understanding of religious myth, and his theory of original sin. But there was more, the heart of the matter: How did he understand the faith and teaching of Jesus? In 1934 Niebuhr resigned from the Fellowship of Reconciliation, dramatically declaring that Christian pacifism was too consumed with its own sense of virtue to make gains toward justice: "Recognizing, as liberal Christianity does not, that the world of politics is full of demonic forces, we have chosen on the whole to support the devil of vengeance against the devil of hypocrisy." He chose to support Marxist vengeance, knowing there was a devil in it, rather than allow the devil of hypocrisy to avoid conflict and preserve the status quo. Those who tried to avoid any traffic with devils simply made themselves accomplices to injustice and potential accomplices to genocide, he judged; moral purity was an illusion.[70]

But these were political arguments, with a very hard edge. Liberal Protestants did not talk about preferring Marxist vengeance to the devil of hypocrisy. Pacifism was ascending in the mainline denominations; it spoke mostly in religious terms; and its leaders included popular religious writers such as Harry Emerson Fosdick, Georgia Harkness, Vida Scudder, Kirby Page, John Haynes Holmes, Walter Russell Bowie, Edmund Chaffee, Richard Roberts, and John Nevin Sayre. All of them appealed to the nonviolent way of Jesus as the normative way of Christian discipleship. Niebuhr surmised that most mainline church members probably did not share the pacifism of their ministers and theologians, but in the mid-1930s nearly every mainline Protestant denomination declared that it would not support another war. Having campaigned for years to bring about this outcome, now Niebuhr was alarmed by it. To challenge the prevailing pacifist ethos of American liberal Protestantism, he had to deal with Jesus, not rest with politics.

Holmes inadvertently helped Niebuhr recognize that necessity. A prominent Unitarian pacifist, Holmes was appalled by Niebuhr's recent turn, especially his Marxist revolutionism. *Reflections on the End of an Era* exhausted his patience with Niebuhr; to Holmes the book was not even slightly Christian. Lashing back at Niebuhr's attacks on liberal Christianity, Holmes repudiated Niebuhr's "growing dogmatism of temper, his flat repudiation of idealism, his cynical contempt for the morally minded, his pessimistic abandonment of the world to its own unregenerate devices, and his desperate flight to the unrealities of theological illusion." Then he got nasty. Holmes was incredulous that Niebuhr still claimed to be a Christian after he dismissed the faith and way of Jesus:

> It is clear enough that Jesus' serene trust in human nature, his stern acclaim of the moral law, his utter reliance upon spiritual forces, his sunny optimism, his radiant passion, would all have seemed a little ridiculous to Niebuhr. The latter would not have opposed the Man of Galilee, but he certainly would have despised him. And with what relief he would have turned to the "cynical and realistic" Pilate. Pilate as the man of the hour![71]

This attack deeply offended Niebuhr, since Holmes was ridiculing his claim to a personal relationship with Christ. Niebuhr protested the "monstrous" unfairness of Holmes' polemic; Holmes replied that he and Niebuhr were still friends; he criticized Niebuhr out of friendship and pastoral concern, not just to score political points. Holmes explained that he sought merely to minister to Niebuhr's "distintegration, confusion, and breakdown." The early Niebuhr was a brilliant writer, but the recent Niebuhr displayed "a tragic instance of intellectual and spiritual bankruptcy" that Holmes, as a friend, offered to name correctly.[72]

Niebuhr told his real friends that he despised Holmes. But this episode helped him clarify what he did not believe about the teaching of Jesus. He did not believe it was socially relevant. Liberals like Mathews got one thing right about the true character of Jesus' teaching, Niebuhr observed. Mathews taught that it was about giving justice, not getting justice; his mistake was to claim that a relevant social ethic could be derived from Jesus' ethic of love perfectionism. Niebuhr put his alternative starkly; many years later he admitted it was too stark:

> The ethic of Jesus does not deal at all with the immediate moral problem of every human life – the problem of attempting some kind of armistice between various contending factions and forces. It has nothing to say about the relativities of politics and economics,

nor of the necessary balances of power which exist and must exist in even the most intimate social relationships.[73]

The teachings of Jesus were counsels of perfection, not prescriptions for social order or justice, Niebuhr argued. They had nothing to say about how a good society should be organized. They lacked any horizontal point of reference and any hint of prudential calculation. The points of reference in Jesus' teaching were always vertical, defining the moral ideal for individuals in their relationship to God. Jesus called his followers to forgive because God forgives; he called them to love their enemies because God's love is impartial. He did not teach that enmity could be transmuted into friendship by returning evil with love. He did not teach his followers that it was their mission to redeem the world through their care or moral effort. Liberal Christianity read these Gandhian admonitions into the teaching of Jesus; Niebuhr countered that Jesus taught an ethic of love perfectionism. The ethic of Jesus was socially relevant as a reminder that there is such a thing as a true moral ideal that judges all forms of social order or rule. But as a perfectionistic ideal, it offered no guidance on how to hold the world in check until the coming of the kingdom. It offered no direct guidance whatsoever on the central problem of politics, which was the problem of justice.

The problem of justice was always the problem of how to gain, sustain, and defend a relative balance of power. "The very essence of politics is the achievement of justice through equilibria of power," Niebuhr argued. "A balance of power is not conflict; but a tension between opposing forces underlies it. Where there is tension there is potential conflict, and where there is conflict there is potential violence." The justice-making work of politics therefore could not disavow all resorts to violence. This was the fact that liberal Christianity could not swallow, Niebuhr observed. Liberal Christian leaders persisted in the illusion that a fully Christianized society would not require coercive violence. Mathews was his favorite example, though Niebuhr failed to note that Mathews was not a pacifist; what mattered was that Mathews had learned nothing since the high tide of the social gospel. He still contrasted the gospel ethic of coopera-tion, peace, and love to the politics of revolutionary coercion. He still claimed that Christianity was committed to a "moral process" of regeneration and not to an eco-nomic philosophy. Niebuhr acidly summarized the liberal gospel of Mathews and his kin: "Christianity, in other words, is interpreted as the preaching of a moral ideal, which men do not follow, but which they ought to."[74]

Niebuhr conceded that the pacifism of the historic peace churches and religious orders could be justified on biblical grounds. The pacifism of the Franciscans, the Mennonites, the Amish, the Brethren and similar groups accepted the love perfection-ism of Jesus' ethic in a literal way – and withdrew from active involvement in the public sphere. These communities grasped the vertical orientation of Jesus' teaching and tried to organize their entire lives in accord with its literal meaning. Under these sectarian circumstances, Niebuhr allowed, some practical teaching might be derived from the teaching of Jesus. Resistance to violence would be forbidden. Rewards for work or service would be eschewed. Resentment toward those guilty of abuse or mistreatment would be forbidden. Love of enemies would be commanded. Niebuhr drove the point home: The love perfectionism of Jesus was a relevant impossibility for each individual in his or her life before God, but no part of Jesus's ethic could be seriously (or at least, directly) applied to the problems of social relationships in a fallen world outside the confines of countercultural sects.[75]

The peace of the world in a fallen world could not be gained by following the way of Christ. Neither could it be gained by turning the perfectionism of Jesus into a social ethic. Peace movements did not bring peace. Niebuhr observed that middle-class professionals led the peace movements – people whose social and economic privileges were made possible by the unacknowledged struggles and violence of others. To insert a perfectionist ethic into public discussion was to imperil the interests of justice.

Christian realism knew that the peace of the world was gained neither by moral absolutism nor by political idealism. Augustine's maxim capsulized the wisdom of Christian realism: the peace of the world is gained by strife. Niebuhr conceded that the teachings of Jesus might be employed to develop the negative or critical side of a Christian social ethic. The teachings of Jesus defined a perfectionist ideal that judged all forms of social order or rule. Because Jesus offered no guidance on how to hold the world in check until the coming of the kingdom, however, no realistic ethic could be drawn from his teaching. The central problem of politics was the problem of justice, which was always the problem of how to gain, sustain, and defend a relative balance of power. Niebuhr explained,

> The very essence of politics is the achievement of justice through equilibria of power. A balance of power is not conflict; but a tension between opposing forces underlies it. Where there is tension there is potential conflict, and where there is conflict there is potential violence. A responsible relationship to the political order, therefore, makes an unqualified disavowal of violence impossible.[76]

The illusions of soft utopians and the violence spawned by hard utopians framed Niebuhr's depiction of the necessary struggle for justice. He blasted the soft utopianism of Mathews, John Dewey, and other liberals "who imagine that the egoism of individuals is being progressively checked by the development of rationality or the growth of a religiously inspired goodwill." *Moral Man and Immoral Society* ridiculed the liberal faith that "with a little more time, a little more adequate moral and social pedagogy and a generally higher development of human intelligence, our social problems will approach solution." Soft utopianism was soft because it failed to accept the inevitability of collective egotism and the necessity of using violence to make gains toward social justice. Because they refused to recognize the brutal character of all social relationships and the violence that permeated all forms of political rule, liberals confused and often impeded the historical struggle for justice, despite their glowing words of tribute to it.[77]

The hard utopians renounced these illusions. Marxism was instructively realistic about the inevitability and necessity of violence, Niebuhr observed. Marxism clung to its own illusion, however, that communism was bringing about the end of history. In current Marxist mythology, the Soviet state was the incarnation of the absolute. To a critical mind, Niebuhr observed, this element of Marxist faith had no more credibility than Dewey's willful faith in Progress. Niebuhr respected the Marxist illusion more than Dewey's rationalism, however. The closing sentences of *Moral Man and Immoral Society* explained why. While Soviet utopianism was indeed mistaken, Niebuhr argued, it was, nevertheless, "a very valuable illusion for the moment; for justice cannot be approximated if the hope of its perfect realization does not generate a sublime madness in the soul." Niebuhr conceded that the sublime madness of Communist utopianism was dangerous because it promoted terrible fanaticisms. Hard utopianism needed to be brought under the control of reason. However, he hoped "that reason will not destroy it before its work is done." Communist utopianism had important work to do in advancing the world-embracing struggle for justice.[78]

In the early 1930s Niebuhr worried that his departmental colleague Harry Ward was becoming a true believer in the Marxist myth and Soviet incarnation. In the mid-1930s, chastened by the terrorism of Stalin's dictatorship, Niebuhr began to grasp that Communist utopianism was not a harmless illusion, either. Letting go of his hope of a liberalized Soviet regime, he wrote in 1935, "Here lies the root of Marxian utopianism and all the nonsense connected with it. The state will wither away!" In the Soviet Union this utopian faith was enforced by a repressive state. Niebuhr acknowledged, "I once thought such a faith to be a harmless illusion. But now I see that its net result is to endow a group of oligarchs with the religious sanctity which primitive priest-kings once held."[79]

That was the seed of what became a principled anti-Communist politics. For most of the 1930s, however, Niebuhr continued to defend the Soviet revolution's "progressive" gains, disputing typical American attitudes about "Communist violence." To Niebuhr, communism was dangerous because its understanding of the social problem was mistaken, not because it promoted violence. The Communists wrongly assumed that political democracy was merely an instrument of class rule. Niebuhr replied that even though modern democracy grew out of the bourgeois revolutions, it did not follow, necessarily, that democracy was simply a ruse to control the masses: "The fact is that democratic principles and traditions are an important check upon the economic oligarchy, even though the money power is usually able to bend democracy to its uses."[80]

Niebuhr did not doubt that democracy was overmatched in America and Europe by the power of what he called "the financial oligarchs," but he urged that democratic political power offered at least some kind of check on economic power. His evidence was that whenever the rule of the capitalist class was imperiled by democratic demands, the capitalists always sought to abrogate democracy. Germany offered a telling example. What made fascism so deeply ominous, Niebuhr warned, was that it promoted a radical and absolute cynicism toward democratic institutions.

Liberal idealism was no match for the cynical evils of fascism or the enormous savageries of Stalinism and capitalism. That was Niebuhr's untiring refrain in the 1930s and early 1940s. Terrible things were happening in the world, yet liberals like Mathews and Dewey claimed to believe that reason and good will could solve the world's problems. In 1936, showing his exasperation, Niebuhr summarized the tenets of the liberal faith. Liberals apparently believed, he wrote:

a. That injustice is caused by ignorance and will yield to education and greater intelligence.
b. That civilization is becoming gradually more moral and that it is a sin to challenge either the inevitability or the efficacy of gradualness.
c. That the character of individuals rather than social systems and arrangements is the guarantee of justice in society.
d. That appeals to love, justice, good-will and brotherhood are bound to be efficacious in the end. If they have not been so to date we must have more appeals to love, justice, good-will and brotherhood.
e. That goodness makes for happiness and that the increasing knowledge of this fact will overcome human selfishness and greed.
f. That wars are stupid and can therefore only be caused by people who are more stupid than those who recognize the stupidity of war.[81]

To Niebuhr it was astonishing that such a faith could survive the terrors of the twentieth century. He poured out a torrent of words to refute it, charging that liberalism was blind to "the inevitable tragedy of human existence, the irreducible irrationality of human behavior and the tortuous character of human history." Repeatedly he blasted Dewey, in particular, for purveying liberal nonsense, notwithstanding that he and Dewey had nearly the same politics. Both believed that authentic democracy required democratic socialism. Both believed that to secure existing democratic gains, democracy had to be extended into the economic system. Both believed that only democratic socialism could achieve social justice, which Niebuhr defined as "a tolerable equilibrium of economic power." Both used the rhetoric of progress in claiming that socialism was the next logical step for history to take. In 1936 Niebuhr explained that "Socialism is the logical next step in a technical society, just as certainly as capitalism was a logical first step. First private enterprise developed vast social progress. Then history proved that the private possession of these social processes is incompatible with the necessities of a technical age." For Niebuhr, as for Dewey, modern civilization had to choose between retrogression and progress.[82]

By this reckoning, fascism was not a genuine historical alternative, but "a frantic effort to escape the logic of history by returning to the primitive." Whatever victories it might win, it would produce only "pathological perversities" with no staying power. The real choice was between retrogression and socialism Niebuhr urged: "Socialism means the next step forward. That next step is the elimination of the specific causes of anarchy in our present society. The basic specific cause of anarchy and injustice is the disproportion of social power which arises from the private possession of social process."[83] For Niebuhr, as for Dewey, social ownership of the means of production was "a minimal requirement of social health in a technical age."[84]

He favored the metaphors of health and sickness to describe America's choice. In Niebuhr's rendering, socialism was "a primary requisite of social health," which made the New Deal ridiculous in its half-hearted measures to save a dying patient. Besides the obvious fact that capitalism was destroying itself, Niebuhr contended, it was equally certain that capitalism had to be destroyed before it reduced the Western democracies to barbarism.[85] Even after it became apparent, in the late 1930s, that capitalism was not disintegrating after all, Niebuhr continued to scorn the New Deal. Taking for granted that socialism meant government ownership and control, he insisted that only socialism could save Western civilization, without bothering to analyze socialist economics. Niebuhr did not apply his penetrating analysis of ruling group egotism to his own solution, ignoring the immense power that state socialism would place in the hands of a self-interested, technocratic planning elite. Instead he invoked a dogma that history would move forward to socialism or backward to an unregulated capitalism.

That dogma secured another one, about the nature of capitalism. In the 1930s and early 1940s, Niebuhr assumed that without a socialist revolution capitalist rationality defined reality. Thus he warned repeatedly, in the face of contrary evidence, that Roosevelt's budget deficits were ruining any chance of an economic recovery. The New Deal reduced national unemployment from 25 to 14 percent in Roosevelt's first term, and only once, in 1936, did Roosevelt's budget deficit exceed $4 billion. Niebuhr, taking for granted that the serious choice was between nationalizing the means of production and balancing the federal budget, urged Roosevelt to raise taxes during the recession of 1937–8 – a move that would have exacerbated the recession and undercut Roosevelt's employment efforts. As it was, Roosevelt's anxiety about deficits caused him to reduce spending on employment in 1937, which helped to send unemployment soaring to 19 percent the following year. Roosevelt was never committed enough to a Keynesian, social-investment approach to generate a full economic recovery in the 1930s. By 1940, seven years after he took office, his employment programs had reduced unemployment only to 14.5 percent.[86]

Niebuhr regarded even Roosevelt's cautious economic interventionism as futile and potentially dangerous. By the end of the 1930s he was willing to say that radicals had to defend the New Deal against its "reactionary critics," but he also contended that Roosevelt's deficit spending was a form of insulin "which wards off dissolution without giving the patient health." The New Dealers were quacks, he grew fond of saying, who pretended not to realize that their cure worked only for a little while: "This quackery must be recognized and exposed."[87] Roosevelt's "whirligig reform" was a stopgap at best. There was no point in trying to reform capitalism, because capitalism was not to be played with or improved. It could only be accepted on its own terms or abolished. Niebuhr exclaimed in 1938, "If that man could only make up his mind to cross the Rubicon! A better metaphor is that he is like Lot's wife. Let him beware lest he turn into a pillar of salt." Most of Niebuhr's metaphors, during this period, dramatized the either/or. Arthur Schlesinger Jr later remarked aptly, however, that Roosevelt's task was not to cross the Rubicon, but to navigate his nation's way up the Rubicon.[88]

Despite believing that Roosevelt wasted his opportunity to save America, Niebuhr began voting for him in 1936. The Socialists had a better platform, but Roosevelt carried out much of it. Increasingly Niebuhr acknowledged the futility of sticking with the Socialist party, which accomplished nothing, instead of joining the Democrats who got (some) things done. As he put it in 1940, "Socialism must come in America through some other instrument than the Socialist Party." With an eye on the British Labour party, Niebuhr assured that the emergence of a genuine farmer-labor party was one of the "inevitabilities of American politics." But organizing an alternative national party would take at least four to eight years, he cautioned.[89]

In the meantime, realistic radicals had to hold their noses and vote for Democrats. In 1939 Niebuhr contended that Roosevelt's reforms were mere palliatives for a dying patient and that Christian Socialists needed to support the better parts of the New Deal, especially the Wagner Act. By the fall of 1941 he began to concede that Roosevelt's reforms were more than palliatives, and that "social justice will depend increasingly upon taxation schedules in the coming years." A few months later he retreated further from the Marxist either/or, declaring that taxation schedules "will have more to do with the kind of justice we achieve in our society than any other single factor." Long after he got used to voting for Roosevelt, however, Niebuhr continued to insist on the necessity of a socialist alternative. In 1943 he explained that while he had given up much of his Marxism, it remained "quite obvious that these forms of 'private' property which represent primarily social power, and the most potent social power of our day at that, cannot remain in private hands. The socialization of such power is a *sine qua non* of social justice."[90]

Thus, the semi-Keynesian policies of the New Deal had their place, but merely as a holding action on inexorable social forces. In the long run, Niebuhr still believed, history would move either forward to Socialism or backward to a purer capitalist barbarism. In the early 1940s Niebuhr conceded that the New Deal secured part of the prize – genuine political control over the economy – but it was only near the end of Roosevelt's life, after World War II took care of America's unemployment problem, that Niebuhr gave up his Marxist either/or.

In the meantime he had to give up another conviction on which he hammered Roosevelt relentlessly – that the president was terribly wrong to prepare for war. Niebuhr's position on this issue was sufficiently ironic that later it became difficult to remember, even by historians. He became a towering figure in American life on the basis of his contention that liberal idealism was no match for the civilizational crises of the Great Depression or the cynical evils of fascism. Later his fame increased when he applied a similar argument to the Cold War. In the 1930s the reputation of *Moral Man and Immoral Society* heightened as the rise of Nazi fascism made Niebuhr's dark vision seem prophetic. For a younger theological generation that no longer believed the world was getting better, *Moral Man and Immoral Society* marked a turning point. The age of religious idealism had passed, and with it had passed the politics of moral community. Old-style liberals attacked Niebuhr's realist turn as a betrayal of Christianity, but chastened younger liberals like John C. Bennett and Walter Marshall Horton declared that Niebuhr defined reality for a new generation. The liberal language of process, ideals, cooperation, personality, and progress lost its credibility and currency, while Niebuhr took American theology in a different direction.

But a great deal of the social gospel remained in Niebuhr's assumptions and spirit, including its postwar repugnance for war. Though he spent the mid-1930s blasting pacifist idealism, Niebuhr still shared the revulsion of his generation for the last war and its determination not to be stampeded into another one. Thus he came late to conceding the necessity of Roosevelt's rearmament campaign against fascism. In 1937, while blasting Roosevelt for propping up capitalism, Niebuhr also condemned Roosevelt's naval buildup as a "sinister" evil, declaring, "this Roosevelt navalism must be resisted at all costs."[91] The following year he wailed that Roosevelt's billion-dollar defense budget "cries to heaven as the worst piece of militarism in modern history." That was a remarkable declaration, considering that modern history included Hitler's military build-up and the specter of a murderous Nazi tyranny. Until the Munich crisis, Niebuhr still shared enough of his generation's anti-war sentiment to make hysterical charges about the evil of countering the Nazi threat. Roosevelt's response to fascist militarism, Niebuhr claimed, was "the most unjustified piece of military expansion in a world full of such madness." It was not too late to remember the lesson of the last war: the best way to avoid war was not to prepare for one. Collective security was the realistic alternative to war. Niebuhr wanted the USA to enact neutrality legislation and voluntarily support sanctions imposed by the League of Nations.[92]

That assumed the viability of existing structures of collective security, however, a notion that Hitler shredded in March 1939 when the German army invaded Czechoslovakia. Germany had obtained the Sudetenland through the Munich appeasement pact of 1938; on September 1, 1939 Germany invaded Poland and rebuffed an ultimatum from Britain and France to withdraw; on September 3 Britain and France formally declared war against Germany. Niebuhr bitterly judged that the Munich accords whetted Hitler's appetite for conquest and fed his contempt for international law. "Munich represented a tremendous shift in the balance of power in Europe," he observed. "It reduced France to impotence . . . it opened the gates to a German expansion in the whole of Europe." In 1940 he confessed that Roosevelt "anticipated the perils in which we now stand more clearly than anyone else." Though Roosevelt was often too cunning for America's good, Niebuhr believed, his re-election in 1940 was imperative for America and the world; it was time to prepare for war against an intolerable tyranny.[93]

Niebuhr wrote the first part of his theological *magnum opus* during the fateful months that he faced up to the inevitability of World War II. His Gifford Lectures, titled *The Nature and Destiny of Man*, were delivered at Edinburgh in the spring and fall of 1939. In April his friend, German theologian Dietrich Bonhoeffer, told him that German army sources were whispering about a September invasion of Poland; in October, while Niebuhr lectured on human destiny, German planes bombed an Edinburgh naval base a few miles away. Niebuhr fretted that his abstract theological lectures were sadly irrelevant in the crisis of the moment, but for the most part he kept to the high road. For three afternoons per week he lectured on "man's most vexing problem," the problem of how human beings should think of themselves. In the form of a reinterpretation of classical Christian teaching, *The Nature and Destiny of Man* asserted that biblically rooted Christianity possesses distinctive spiritual, moral, and intellectual resources to help modern people think about themselves and their world. These resources were desperately needed in a world plagued by various kinds of cynical militarism and nihilism, on the one hand, and a variety of naive idealisms on the other hand. "The fateful consequence in contemporary political life of Hobbes's cynicism and Nietzsche's nihilism are everywhere apparent," he admonished. Only Christianity had the resources to save Europe from fascist barbarism, but it had to be a Christianity that believed in the Christian doctrine of sin.[94]

Niebuhr always thought in terms of a dialectic between one hand and another. In *The Nature and Destiny of Man* one hand was the cluster of views that variously derived from the view of humankind promoted in the Graeco-Roman world of classical antiquity; the other hand was what Niebuhr called the biblical view. The classical view, represented by Platonist, Aristotelian, and Stoic conceptions of human nature, emphasized the primacy and uniqueness of human rationality. Human beings are unique within nature because they are spiritual beings gifted with the capacity for self-reflective thought and reason. The biblical view emphasized the unity of a human self as a created and finite existence in both body and spirit, Niebuhr argued. The biblical view is dialectical in its insistence on the essential relation of body and soul; it opposes the idealistic notion that mind is essentially good or eternal, as well as the romantic notion that the good is to be sought in humanity's "natural" state of embodiment.

In Niebuhr's reading, classical Christianity represented a series of attempts to synthesize the views of scripture and classical antiquity, most importantly in the theologies of Augustine and Aquinas. Modern culture represented, and began with, the destruction of the classical Christian synthesis, as the artists and philosophers of the Renaissance dispensed with the biblical elements and the preachers and theologians of the Reformation dispensed with the elements of classical antiquity. Niebuhr interpreted modern liberal Protestantism as an attempt to reunite the Graeco-Roman and biblical worldviews, but this project was doomed to failure, especially after modern thought adopted a naturalistic interpretation of human nature and destiny. Even in their pre-modern forms, Niebuhr observed, the worldviews of biblical Christianity and classical antiquity had little in common; with the modern turn to naturalism, the classical view of humanity's spiritual nature was negated as well. Modern people believed in a naturalized version of the Graeco-Roman view of themselves. Niebuhr urged that it was precisely the poverty and triumph of this "modernized classical view of man" that made modern life so confused and nihilistic. *The Nature and Destiny of Man* made an argument for the recovery of the biblical and Reformationist view of the self, though, unlike the Barthians, Niebuhr contended that the freedom–cherishing humanism of the Renaissance had a role to play in realizing the fullness of biblical religion.[95]

Liberal Christianity came in for a vigorous drubbing. The liberal impulse in theology was humanistic, deeply indebted to modern culture, and therefore religiously superficial, Niebuhr judged; liberal Christianity made "the central message of the gospel, dealing with sin, grace, forgiveness and justification, seem totally irrelevant." In order to maintain some point of contact with traditional Christianity, he remarked, liberal Christians generally affirmed "that Jesus was a very, very, very good man." But this credo raised the unsettling question "What if a better person should appear?" Would modern Christians be obliged to transfer their loyalties? Niebuhr admonished, "These moderns do not understand that they cannot transcend the relativities of history by the number of superlatives which they add to their moral estimate of Jesus." In their ultimate freedom and self-transcendence, he argued, human beings stand beyond time and nature. Therefore they cannot find a true religious norm "short of the nature of ultimate reality."[96]

He scolded liberal Christianity for selling out the deep mythical meanings of Christian teaching. Albrecht Ritschl, "the most authoritative exponent of modern liberal Christianity," taught that the gospel offers salvation from the contradiction of finiteness and freedom. This problem underlies all religion, Niebuhr allowed, but the gospel subordinates the problem of finiteness to the problem of sin. Biblical religion seeks redemption from sin, which is the disruption of the harmony of creation by human pride and will-to-power. In the biblical view, human beings seek to overcome their insecurity by a will-to-power that overreaches the limits of human creatureliness. Religiously, Niebuhr explained, sin is rebellion against God; morally and socially it is expressed as injustice. The ego that sinfully makes itself the center of existence inevitably subordinates other people to its will and does injustice to them.[97]

Niebuhr's idea of "biblical religion" was thus essentially Reformationist in its language and content, though in his second volume he made room for what he called "a Renaissance version of the answer to the cultural problem." The Barthians simply returned to the self-authenticating revelation of the Reformers and told modern people to like it or lump it, Niebuhr judged: "The theological movement initiated by Karl Barth has affected the thought of the church profoundly, but only negatively; and it has not challenged the thought outside of the church at all. It defied what was true in Renaissance culture too completely to be able to challenge what was false in it." The Renaissance was not wrong to cherish intellectual freedom and personal experience, he believed. On issues pertaining to religious authority and the sources of theology, Niebuhr preferred the real-world, heterogeneous humanism of the Renaissance to the cramped Reformationist principle of *sola scriptura*. He also leaned toward Renaissance humanism on the relation of thought and grace.[98]

His thinking on the latter issue was deeply influenced by Tillich. In *The Interpretation of History* (1936), Tillich argued that there is a type of thought that transcends all conditioned and finite thought and which proves its transcendence by its realization of the finiteness of thought. Subjective thinking can never reach the unconditioned truth, Tillich reasoned, but this judgment is itself independent of its forms of expression: "It is the judgment which constitutes truth as truth." The ultimate self-transcendence of the human spirit is revealed in the self's capacity to understand its own finiteness. Niebuhr embraced this argument as a formulation of the problem of finiteness. Sin is rebellion against God, the root of which is the refusal to admit finiteness. This refusal is sinful because the human spirit has the capacity to recognize its finiteness. When the self refuses out of its sinful pride to recognize its finiteness, its self-glorification can be broken only by the convicting gift of grace. Christianity is a religion of redemption and grace, Niebuhr and Tillich affirmed, not a religion of the universality of spirit. It is not about the realization of self-transcendence as universal spirit, as in philosophical and Christian idealism; Christianity is about the redemptive shattering of the ego's sense of self-sufficiency.[99]

Niebuhrian neoliberalism, usually called neo-orthodoxy, was a religion of the dialectic of divine transcendence and relation. For Niebuhr, transcendence referred to the divine realm beyond all finite experience; to the principle or ground of reality, meaning, judgment, and hope; and to the capacity of the human spirit to transcend itself and relate to God. God is beyond society, history, and the highest ideals of existence, Niebuhr argued, yet God is also intimately related to the world. The human spirit finds a home and grasps something of the stature of its freedom in God's transcendence, yet the self also finds in the divine transcendence the limit of the self's freedom, the judgment spoken against it, and the mercy that makes judgment bearable. Langdon Gilkey aptly observed that "the dialectical ontological presence of God as absolute and yet related – one of Niebuhr's many 'paradoxes' – forms the necessary presupposition for all of his theology." Epistemologically, Niebuhr posited a divine ground of meaning and coherence beyond all finite notions of meaning and coherence; ontologically, he asserted the transcendence of God's being over all contingent and temporal being while affirming that God is continually present to God's creation in the workings of providence, the history of judgment, the grace of renewal, and the stirrings of individual moral conscience. "Insofar as man transcends the temporal process he can discern many things in life and history by tracing various coherences, sequences, causalities and occurrences through which the events of history are ordered," Niebuhr observed in *Faith and History*. "But insofar as man is himself in the temporal process which he seeks to comprehend, every sequence and realm of coherence points to a more final source of meaning than man is able to comprehend rationally."[100]

These were the dominant themes of the Niebuhrian "neo-orthodoxy" that overtook American theology in the 1930s and 1940s. Though Niebuhr was never neo-orthodox in the manner of American Barthians and many Niebuhrians, he effected a transformation of American theological consciousness. His emphasis on sin and tragedy was chastening to liberals such as Fosdick, Georgia Harkness, and Edgar S. Brightman; his whirling dialecticism proved overpowering even to many liberals, such as Gregory Vlastos, who worried that Niebuhr practically made paradox a criterion of truth. Reviewing *The Nature and Destiny of Man*, Vlastos marveled and winced at Niebuhr's "high record for being at home in the paradoxical, the ultra-rational, the irrational." He tried to resist Niebuhr's intellectual power, but confessed, "We read his books with affectionate wonder, like the ideas of our other self, but a self endowed with volcanic energy, capable of out-thinking and out-talking our ordinary self ten times to one."[101]

Niebuhr later recalled that his turn against a regnant liberal idealism was the key to his career: "When I came here [to Union], this was absolutely a paradise of Social Gospel liberalism." Elsewhere he reflected: "It was in full swing when I arrived at the seminary in 1928. The Social Gospel was creative in redeeming American Protestantism from an arid Calvinistic or pietistic individualism. But it was defective in identifying the Christian faith with a mild socialism and a less mild pacifism all encased in an overall utopianism." Tillich observed that Niebuhr transformed the American theological scene with the same suddenness and force that Barth upended liberal German theology after World War I. Having played a role in the Barthian revolt against the Ritschlian and Troeltschian schools in Germany, Tillich arrived in New York just in time to witness a similar transformation: "When I remember what happened here, it was similarly astonishing. When I came [to America in 1933], everybody asked only one question – whatever was discussed theologically – namely the question, 'What do you think about pacifism?'" As a newcomer to America and not a pacifist, Tillich hesitated to address the question. Niebuhr changed the question by transforming the social climate of American theology he observed, saying, "This disappeared after Reinie made his tremendous attack. I believe it was absolutely necessary, and I tried to support him as much as I could in my lectures and early writings, but he was the man who changed the climate in an almost sudden way."[102]

Niebuhrian Realism, World War II, and the Cold War

Niebuhr's climactic blast against the pacifist idealism of American liberal Christianity took place between the outbreak of World War II in September 1939 and America's entry into the war in December 1941. He worried that the democracies seemed "almost defenseless against the concentrated fury which the totalitarian powers are unleashing." He judged that Roosevelt grasped the reality of the fascist threat to democratic civilization, but that most Americans did not, especially American church leaders. He condemned the "burst of hysterical self-righteousness which now consumes the energies of the American churches."[103]

Morrison especially offended him. After supporting Roosevelt in 1936, *The Christian Century* opposed his reelection in 1940, charging that Roosevelt was an American-style fascist who played to the working class and militarized a peaceable nation. In May 1940 Morrison claimed it was not too late for America to broker an armistice; the following month he claimed that it was too late for America to affect the course of the war by intervening against Hitler; repeatedly he held out for neutrality and called for efforts to slow down Roosevelt's march toward war. As late as December 10, 1941, in an issue that went to press just before Japan attacked Pearl Harbor, the *Christian Century* insisted that "Every national interest and every moral obligation to civilization dictates that this country shall keep out of the insanity of a war which is in no sense America's war."[104]

Morrison's pacifism was practical, not absolute, which infuriated Niebuhr all the more. Against the *Christian Century's* apparent conviction that Christians were virtuous to the extent that they avoided conflict, Niebuhr proclaimed that America was obliged to "prevent the triumph of an intolerable tyranny":

> Most of our pacifism springs from an unholy compound of gospel perfectionism and bourgeois utopianism, the latter having had its rise in eighteenth century rationalism. This kind of pacifism is not content with martyrdom and with political irresponsibility. It is always fashioning political alternatives to the tragic business of resisting tyranny and establishing justice by coercion. However it twists and turns, this alternative is revealed upon close inspection to be nothing more than capitulation to tyranny. Now capitulation to tyranny in the name of non-resistant perfection may be very noble for the individual. But it becomes rather ignoble when the idealist suggests that others besides himself shall be sold into slavery and shall groan under the tyrant's heal.

In the name of social gospel idealism, the *Christian Century* was advocating connivance with tyranny and preaching that slavery is better than war; Niebuhr countered that a genuinely moral American Christianity must fight Nazi fascism, "lest we deliver the last ramparts of civilization into the hands of the new barbarians."[105]

To a "very, very sick" civilization, liberal Protestantism preached weakness and purity; Niebuhr acidly observed that it was a dogma of American Christianity "that any kind of peace is better than war." He countered that no morally worthy peace could be brokered with a Nazi regime that was fed by genocidal ambitions and a "pagan religion of tribal self-glorification." To their shame, he admonished, Americans were trying to ignore the fact that the Nazi government intended to abolish Christianity, that it defied all universal standards of justice and moral law, that it "threaten[ed] the Jewish race with annihilation and visit[ed] a maniacal fury upon these unhappy people which [went] far beyond the ordinary race prejudice which is the common sin of all nations and races," that it explicitly vowed to subject all other races of Europe "into slavery to the 'master' race," that it sought "a monopoly of military violence" and colonizing imperial force throughout Europe, and that it was already destroying and enslaving Poland and Czechoslovakia.[106]

The appeasing moralism of America's dominant liberal culture made the world safe for this fascist nightmare Niebuhr admonished: "It imagines that there is no conflict of interest which cannot be adjudicated. It does not understand what it means to meet a resolute foe who is intent upon either your annihilation or enslavement." He warned that America would pay dearly for its self-deception and cowardice if Hitler conquered Europe and then invaded South America, where the Nazis could easily erect a colonized slave economy. As "an American of pure German stock," he pleaded with Americans to recognize that fighting Germany was more tolerable than submitting to it, and he pointedly denied that his thinking was swayed by his well-known affection for England: "I thought Britain was much too slow in understanding or challenging the peril which nazi imperialism presented to both our common civilization and the vital interests of Britain." In his darker moods Niebuhr fretted that American democracy did not deserve to survive: "The fact is that moralistic illusions of our liberal culture have been so great and its will-to-power has been so seriously enervated by a confused pacifism, in which Christian perfectionism and bourgeois love of ease have been curiously compounded, that our democratic world does not really deserve to survive."[107]

Since the *Christian Century* epitomized what was wrong with American Protestantism, Niebuhr resolved to create an alternative to it. Mainline Protestantism needed a journal that renounced the prevailing liberal Christian sentiment that anything was better than war. Niebuhr already had one journal, the Fellowship of Socialist Christians' magazine *Christianity and Society* (which was named *Radical Religion* until 1940), but it was too politicized and socialistic to have many clerical readers. In February 1941 he launched *Christianity & Crisis* as an antidote to the *Century*'s isolationism, enlisting the support of liberal Christian friends who agreed that the *Century*'s isolationism had become an embarrassment to mainline Protestantism. They included Bennett, Sherwood Eddy, Francis McConnell, William Adams Brown, Will Scarlett, Henry Sloane Coffin, Henry Van Dusen, and John R. Mott. The format of *Christianity & Crisis* was cloned from the *Century*, but its editorial line spoke the Christian realist language of tragic necessities, group interests, power politics, lesser evils, and internationalism. Niebuhr and Bennett plunged into the day-to-day business of realigning

American liberal Protestantism; at the same time, Niebuhr took a large step toward the liberal mainstream of the Democratic party by assuming the leadership of a national labor–socialist organization called the Union for Democratic Action (UDA).

He was just as concerned about isolationist trends in American secular politics, especially American progressivism, as about parallel developments in the churches. The Union Seminary liberals who supported *Christianity & Crisis* – especially Coffin, Brown, and Van Dusen – were chastened about war and idealism, but they could never rub elbows with Niebuhr's friends in the trade union and socialist movements. The Union liberals represented one segment of the progressive interventionist movement that he envisioned; Niebuhr conceived the UDA as the key to the other part. Ultimately he wanted to build a national farmer-labor party, but that goal was out of reach in 1941. Under Niebuhr's leadership, the UDA enlisted intellectuals, political activists, and union leaders such as Lewis Corey, Murray Gross, George Counts, and A. Phillip Randolph into a common struggle for justice and democracy; the group's core consisted of New York social democrats and Marxists who were disgusted by the Socialist party's isolationism. At Niebuhr's insistence, the UDA renounced the traditional socialist denigration of religion, excluded Communists from membership, and exhorted Americans to face up to the necessity of fighting fascism. A generation of left-wing activists and intellectuals found their way into the Democratic party establishment by this route; in 1947 Niebuhr folded the UDA into a new organization dominated by establishment liberals, the Americans for Democratic Action (ADA).

After the USA entered World War II, the *Christian Century* accepted that it had lost the argument: "We, too, must accept the war. We see no other way at the moment but the bloody way of slaughter and immeasurable sacrifice. Our government has taken a stand. It is *our* government." Though Morrison still wished that Roosevelt kept the USA out of the war, brokering "an adjustment in the Pacific," he accepted that America had chosen "the way of unimaginable cost and of doubtful morality." All Americans were implicated in the acts of their government, he counseled: "Those who approved and encouraged the policy which has brought us to this tragic hour and those who have resisted this policy whether on moral or prudential grounds are one people . . . We stand with our country. We cannot do otherwise."[108]

To Niebuhr, the war was strictly a lesser-evil affair; he did not believe in just wars, and he worried that "the stupid children of light" would not content themselves with fighting to thwart a greater evil. The USA had barely entered the war against Japan when he began to complain that American Christianity's pro-war pronouncements were nearly as insufferable as its earlier isolationism. "Many of the sermons which now justify the war will be as hard to bear as the previous ones which proved it was our 'Christian' duty to stay out," he cautioned. The purpose of the war was to stop fascism, not to create a new international order in which war would be abolished. Niebuhr's wartime book, *The Children of Light and the Children of Darkness* (1944), expounded a realist-leaning dialectic of idealism and realism, arguing that America needed to find a moral balance between the cynical amorality of the fascist and Stalinist "children of darkness" and the sentimental idealism of the modern liberal "children of light."[109]

Niebuhr believed that Stalinist-style communism was nearly as evil as Nazi fascism, though he downplayed this judgment while America and Russia were linked as wartime allies. In 1939 he wrote in the *Christian Century* that he felt "genuinely sorry for my friends who seem to be under a spiritual necessity to deny obvious facts about Russian tyranny." In the same year he told Bennett and other friends that the tyrannical evil of Soviet communism was "almost, though not quite" as bad as that of Nazi Germany. Niebuhr muddled the latter judgment in the wartime *Children of Light and the Children of Darkness*, but as soon as the war was over he painted a harsh light on Soviet brutality. Like the Nazis, he charged, the Stalinist children of darkness were wise because they grasped the power of self-interest and they were evil because they recognized no law beyond themselves. Conversely, the children of light were virtuous because they recognized the existence of a moral law beyond their own will, but they were dangerously foolish in their underestimation of the power of self-will. "The excessively optimistic estimates of human nature and human history with which the democratic credo has been historically associated are a source of peril to democratic society," Niebuhr warned. *The Children of Light and the Children of Darkness* thrashed Adam Smith, Thomas Jefferson, and John Dewey as theorists of the liberal illusion of social harmony, but Niebuhr made only glancing references to the sentimental idealism of liberal Christianity. By 1944, there was much less of it to condemn. The Protestant mainstream spoke increasingly like Niebuhr, while in his politics, he became comfortable in the liberal mainstream of the Democratic party.[110]

In 1947 the Fellowship of Socialist Christians changed its name to Frontier Fellowship, reflecting Niebuhr's acceptance of welfare state capitalism and the politics of anti-Communist "Vital Center" liberalism; four years later Niebuhr changed the group's name to the even more innocuous Christian Action. He was testy with those, including the *Christian Century*, who worried that his politics were veering toward a middle-of-the-road conformism. Niebuhr countered that the middle ground did not have to be a "dead center," for, throughout the world, the struggle for the middle ground was a fight for democracy. This fight necessarily included a long-term battle against the spread of communism, he insisted, for "we are fated as a generation to live in the insecurity which this universal evil of communism creates for our world."[111]

In the early 1950s Niebuhr provided much of the ideological scaffolding for the "containment" strategy of Cold War liberalism. He warned that communism, though tactically flexible, was inherently fanatical, "with its simple distinctions between exploited and exploiter, its too-simple conception of the class structure of society, its too-simple derivation of all social evil from the institution of property, and its consequent division of every nation and of the whole world into friends and enemies 'of the people.'" Traditional *realpolitik* failed to grasp the "noxious demonry" of this predatory movement, Niebuhr admonished, for Soviet communism was not merely "the old Russian imperialism in a new form." At the same time, in the name of realism, he counseled against a crusading hot war. America's battle against communism needed to walk a fine, patient, vigilant line between treating the Soviet state as a geopolitical Great Power rival and as a Nazi-like enemy that had to be frontally attacked. Communism was morally utopian, he argued, not morally cynical like Nazi fascism, but this fact made it more threatening to the cause of democratic civilization than fascism had ever been, because it made a universalist appeal to the disinherited masses of the Third World.[112]

Niebuhr explained that in power politics, a perverted moralism was always more dangerous than explicit evil. The moral utopianism of the Communist movement gave it greater drawing power than the Nazi movement ever possessed. For this reason communism was capable of creating greater and longer-lasting evils in the world than fascism. Repeatedly he counseled that the best analogy for the Communist threat to the West was not the Third Reich, but the rise of militant Islam in the high Middle

Ages: "Moslem power was consolidated in the Middle Ages and threatened the whole of Christendom much as Communist power threatens Western civilization today." Just as militant Islam brandished a quasi-universal ideology that transcended nationalism while being rooted in the Arab world, the Communist movement wielded a pseudo-universal creed that served Russian imperial ambitions. Moreover, the Islamic concept of a holy war against infidels was "analogous to the Communist conception of the inevitable conflict between capitalism and Communism."[113]

The Niebuhr later revered by neoconservatives was the Niebuhr of this period, whose masculine rhetoric of power, duality, and realism promoted an aggressive anti-Communist politics. When neoconservatives later claimed that they became conservatives only because "real" liberalism no longer existed, it was Niebuhr, above all, whom they invoked as the prototype of real liberalism. Real liberalism was not the feminized progressivism of Jane Addams, Eleanor Roosevelt, George McGovern, and most liberal church leaders. Real liberalism did not blur the line between private and public spheres, or imagine that conflict and violence could be eliminated, or struggle for justice on the basis of moral appeals. Real liberalism would never proclaim that the personal was the political or that cooperation could replace competition. Most importantly, real liberalism would never shrink from fighting against communism, which Niebuhr defined in 1953 as "an organized evil which spreads terror and cruelty throughout the world and confronts us everywhere with faceless men who are immune to every form of moral and political suasion." Through his realistic insistence on the pervasiveness of sin, the inevitability of conflict, the limits of political action, and the necessity of a militarized anticommunism, Niebuhr defined and epitomized, for neoconservatives, the kind of liberalism that was still needed. This rendering of Niebuhr's work and career was reinforced by Christian leftists who viewed Niebuhr chiefly as the figure who turned American Christian ethics into a form of Cold War apologetics. In John Swomley's typical indictment, it was Niebuhr who provided "the religious rationale for the military foreign policy that created the contemporary American empire and the policy of global intervention culminating in the war in Vietnam."[114]

But these ideologically driven critiques assigned a fixed position where none existed. To Niebuhr, Christian realism was not an ideology or even a method; it was a dynamic orientation, chastened by the awareness of sin and interest, that responded to social challenges of the moment. In the early 1950s, while America was convulsed over McCarthyism and FBI agents dug for incriminating details about Niebuhr's radical past, he portrayed "communism" as a devouring totalitarian monolith committed to world domination. Like many of his liberal ADA friends, especially Bennett and Schlesinger, Niebuhr detested Joseph McCarthy and was determined not to allow him to monopolize the anti-Communist issue. In the early 1950s, under the pressure of his concern to prove that ADA liberals weren't soft on communism, Niebuhr demonized Communists and implicitly condoned parts of McCarthy's campaign to smoke Communists out of American government, education, and religion. Niebuhr strongly supported the government's execution of the Rosenbergs for stealing atomic secrets and, in a 1953 article for *Look* magazine, he carelessly and mistakenly claimed that McCarthy's assistant J. B. Matthews had accurately identified more than a dozen pro-Communist fellow travelers in the churches.[115]

But he later apologized for these excesses, and even at the height of Niebuhr's anti-Communist fervor – which lasted until McCarthy self-destructed in 1954 – he was never the kind of Cold Warrior who insisted that America must fight anti-Communist wars around the world. Unlike many professional anti-Communists, he did not back away from attacking McCarthy's viciousness or from denouncing the militaristic hubris of conservatives who wanted to "roll back the Soviet empire." He opposed the kind of anticommunism that conceived the Cold War primarily in military terms. Niebuhr's writings on the cold war emphasized, rather, that Soviet communism needed to be understood and resisted primarily as a religious phenomenon. As he explained in 1953, the evil of communism flowed "from a combination of political and 'spiritual' factors, which prove that the combination of power and pride is responsible for turning the illusory dreams of yesterday into the present nightmare, which disturbs the ease of millions of men in our generation." The following year he phrased the matter more pointedly, in a statement that capsulized his perception of the Cold War: "We are embattled with a foe who embodies all the evils of a demonic religion. We will probably be at sword's point with this foe for generations to come."[116]

This view of Soviet communism as a perverted religion shaped Niebuhr's understanding of how the Cold War should be waged. Confident that the fundamental flaw of the malevolence of the Nazi creed not only left it open to frontal attack but would ultimately lead to its spontaneous failure he pursued the insidious appeal of communism's idealism to the poor of the world as the greater and more enduring agency for evil. This truism could only be understood, Niebuhr argued, "if it is realized how much more plausible and dangerous the corruption of the good can be in human history than explicit evil."[117] As such the rise of militant Islam in the high Middle Ages followed for him as the obvious comparison, and he pressed this religiously objectionable analogy as a strategically astute argument for realist anticommunism; his implication that militant Islam was a demonic religion did not make him pause. The mistakes of the crusaders needed to be taken into account in figuring out how to fight off communism, he urged; precisely because communism was a demonic religion, anti-Communist containment was not a job for ideologues or religious crusaders. Like the Islamic power of the Middle Ages, the Communist movement was deeply entrenched, threatening, and ideologically driven; like the Islamic power it was much more likely to disintegrate from its inner contradictions and corruptions than from external force by its enemies. Niebuhr recalled that the sultan of Turkey was unable to sustain his double role as spiritual leader of the Islamic world and head of the Turkish state. Stalin had essentially the same role "in the world of Communist religion," and thus the same problems.[118]

Like his friend George Kennan, Niebuhr believed that the Soviet regime would eventually self-destruct on the contradictions and failures of its unworkable system. The purpose of containment strategy was to keep enough diplomatic and military pressure on the Soviets to accelerate the implosion of the Soviet state. Kennan was the putative architect of American containment strategy but, like Niebuhr, an opponent of militarized approaches to anticommunism. In 1947, he argued that if the United States kept the pressure on for perhaps 10 to 15 years and showed itself to be a more attractive alternative, the monolithic discipline of the governing Soviet party could be undermined. "And if disunity were ever to seize and paralyze the Party, the chaos and weakness of Russian society would be revealed in forms beyond description," he wrote. "Soviet Russia might be changed overnight from one of the strongest to one of the weakest and most pitiable of national societies."[119]

Niebuhr's early formulations of this belief were less eerily prophetic than Kennan's, but prescient nonetheless. He argued in 1952 that militaristic anti-Communists misunderstood the nature of the enemy, writing,

If we fully understand the deep springs which feed the illusions of this religion, the nature of the social resentments which nourish them and the realities of life which must ultimately refute them, we might acquire the necessary patience to wait out the long run of history while we take such measures as are necessary to combat the more immediate perils.

Soviet communism was an evil, conspiratorial, universalist religion that would eventually self-destruct if the West maintained a self-respecting and patient strategy of containment.[120]

The emergence of a more pragmatic Soviet regime in the late 1950s moved Niebuhr to reconsider both ends of this argument. In 1958, faced with the apparent success of Soviet economic reconstruction and the Soviet Union's unarguable achievements in science, technology, and military expansion, Niebuhr began to doubt that Soviet communism was incapable of sustaining itself indefinitely. At the same time, he began to question the inevitability of the Cold War. If he was no longer certain that communism would eventually self-destruct, he also no longer believed that a state of warfare between the two superpowers was inevitable or sensible. In 1958, "as a kind of trial balloon to initiate discussion," Niebuhr's coeditor and closest colleague, John Bennett, proposed that America should give up its "perpetual official moral diatribe" against world communism. "We should accept the fact that communism is here to stay in at least two great countries, that in them it is a massive human experiment which will have its chance," Bennett urged. The Communist turn was irreversible, but not unchangeable.[121]

To the surprise of many, Niebuhr was moving to the same view. He endorsed the thrust of Bennett's editorial with a declaration of his own. The fate of the world "depends upon our capacity to leaven the lump of our own orthodox conceptions of a changeable Communist orthodoxy," he asserted. Though the Communists still officially believed that the logic of history assured their eventual triumph, Niebuhr insisted that "we had better, for the sake of the world, recognize that this belief is not tantamount to a policy of plotting for world domination by any possible means." Soviet communism was not an immutable monolith, nor an overpowering enemy, nor a world-threatening conspiracy, nor an enemy with which America could not learn to coexist. The following year, in *The Structure of Nations and Empires*, Niebuhr made a case for American/Soviet coexistence, urging that foreign policy realism in the current world situation required greater flexibility in America's attitude toward the Soviet government. What was needed, he wrote, was "a less rigid and self-righteous attitude toward the power realities of the world and a more hopeful attitude toward the possibilities of internal development in the Russian despotism."[122]

Christian realists sharply debated these issues in the 1950s. Many of Niebuhr's followers disputed his arguments for coexistence and his insistence that communism was capable of making internal reforms. Some of them clung to his earlier belief that Soviet communism was an evil but self-destructive religion that had to be waited out; others claimed that both positions were too passive. Kennan influenced Niebuhr's turn toward coexistence, while contending that the Soviet system was inherently unstable. Kennan and Niebuhr protested that "containment" acquired an overly militarized meaning in American policy, that American policymakers overestimated Soviet political, economic, and military strength, and that John Foster Dulles, in particular, mythologized the Cold War into a holy war.

The latter development was especially troubling to Niebuhr, because his writings were often quoted to support America's hardening Cold War mythology. He recoiled at Dulles's doctrine of massive nuclear retaliation and his unctuous description of the Cold War as a struggle between good and evil. Dulles had come into national prominence during World War II, when he chaired the Federal Council of Churches' Commission for a Just and Durable Peace. He and Niebuhr worked together (unsuccessfully) to urge the fledgling World Council of Churches (WCC) to adopt a policy of forgiveness toward the defeated Axis powers. But Niebuhr despaired of Dulles' idea of Cold War realism after he became Secretary of State in the Eisenhower administration. Though Dulles was adept at quoting Niebuhr, Niebuhr felt that Dulles over-moralized the Cold War and relied too much on the threat of retaliatory nuclear force, causing him to ignore the 1956 Suez crisis and other challenges to international stability. In Niebuhr's view, genuine Christian realism did not indulge in nuclear brinkmanship, mythologize the Cold War, or arrogantly dismiss the power struggles in smaller nations. It did not use the nuclear threat as a substitute for aggressive, imaginative, persistent diplomacy. He told friends that Eisenhower and Dulles were too stupid to be entrusted with America's fate, a judgment that Niebuhrians frequently debated. Some of them did not share Niebuhr's partisan dislike of Republicans. On the morning after Eisenhower was elected in 1952, an acutely distressed Niebuhr told his daughter Elisabeth, "You poor girl, you've never lived under a Republican administration, you don't know how terrible this thing is going to be." Dulles's simultaneously threatening and passive approach to foreign affairs confirmed Niebuhr's feelings about Republicans.[123]

The Eisenhower years were otherwise short on drama and divisive issues, however. To the Niebuhrians, bipartisan containment was a good thing, as was America's overall foreign policy consensus. Niebuhr supported the US intervention in Korea and its policy of nuclear deterrence, as did Niebuhrian realists Schlesinger, Kennan, Bennett, Hans Morgenthau, Kenneth W. Thompson, and Paul Ramsey. The Soviet invasion of Hungary in 1956 confirmed Niebuhr's belief that the USA had no other choice regarding nuclear policy. Nuclear disarmament was impossible, he wrote, because the Soviets would accept only an agreement that drove America out of Europe. These were consensus positions among Christian ethicists in the 1950s, not least because of Niebuhr's influence over the field.[124]

But Christian realism became more difficult to define in the turbulence of the succeeding decade. Shortly after Christian realists celebrated the election of a Niebuhr-quoting Democrat in 1960 – John Kennedy – they began to splinter on strategic and tactical issues. Some Kennedy officials, notably McGeorge Bundy, lauded Niebuhr as the one who showed how to combine Christianity with political realism. A few figures from Niebuhr's personal circle, including Schlesinger and Paul Nitze, played prominent roles in the Kennedy administration. Niebuhr supported Kennedy and praised his warnings about the burdens of power, while harboring misgivings about Kennedy's depth and personal morality. Kennedy's maneuvers against Cuba subsequently gave him deeper misgivings. Niebuhr denounced the Bay of Pigs fiasco and Kennedy's subsequent embargo on Cuban products, protesting that his militaristic blundering inflamed anti-US sentiment throughout the hemisphere.[125]

The Berlin crisis heightened Niebuhr's feeling that Christian realism needed a policy overhaul. The Soviets walled off East Berlin in 1961, forcing Kennedy to decide whether to let the wall stand. American policymakers feared that destroying it would spark a Soviet nuclear or conventional-force attack. Niebuhr and Bennett agreed that if the Soviets launched a nuclear attack, America would have to reciprocate. The question was whether the USA should respond to a conventional-force attack with nuclear weapons.

In 1950 Niebuhr and Bennett had defended America's right to use nuclear weapons in a first strike to destroy invading Russian tanks. In 1961 they reconsidered the morality of nuclear deterrence. Bennett took the lead, noting that American ethicists rarely addressed the possibility of a nuclear holocaust set off by the USA. The reason that American ethicists had so little to say about nuclear policy, he judged, was that for them, no genuine moral choices seemed to exist. In this area, the foreign policy consensus was a species of fatalism. Ever since the obliteration bombings of World War II, American ethicists had accepted the premise that moral questions had to be subordinated to strategic questions during war. This assumption was commonly identified with Niebuhrian realism, but Bennett questioned the premise and its morally fatalistic consequences. He urged that Christian realism had to address the moral dilemmas of American nuclear policy: "The idea of nuclear retaliation raises moral problems that have not been given enough attention." It was one thing to grant the moral legitimacy of nuclear weapons as a deterrent, but that did not necessarily sanction any particular doctrine about retaliation, first use, countervalue warfare, or the use of tactical weapons. Bennett offered an opening proposal:

> For us to attack the cities of Russia would be a great atrocity. No moral commitment can oblige us to perpetrate such an atrocity. But it would be almost as evil a deed to take the step that might initially involve the use of tactical nuclear weapons, knowing that it would be almost sure to result in the total conflict in which we would be both the destroyers and the destroyed.[126]

That pushed Christian realism into new territory, against tactical first use, but Niebuhr quickly took a further step, declaring, "The first use of the nuclear weapon is morally abhorrent and must be resisted." He doubted that a democratic society could survive a nuclear triumph: "Could a civilization loaded with this monstrous guilt have enough moral health to survive?" Remarkably, though typically for the time, he ignored the fact that America democracy had already "survived" Hiroshima and Nagasaki; Niebuhr left the question hanging. The following year he declared that it might be time "to take some risks for peace comparable to our ever more dangerous risks in the game of deterrence." The USA needed a more flexible position on disarmament. He proposed to begin by taking certain unilateral initiatives, such as dropping America's unrealistic insistence on foolproof inspection.[127]

The Niebuhr/Bennett shift on nuclear policy set off a round of position-taking among Niebuhrians. Paul Ramsey argued that only conventional weapons could be used in retaliation. Paul Tillich supported the Niebuhr/Bennett arguments against nuclear first use while defending the moral right to retaliate with tactical weapons against a tactical attack. Hans Morgenthau declared "without qualification" that no resort to nuclear weapons could ever be morally justified. Norman Gottwald contended that nuclear weapons could be used morally, but only against military targets. Others expressed their stunned disbelief that Niebuhr sanctioned any form of this debate. Kenneth Thompson warned,

> If we declare we shall not use thermonuclear weapons except in the ultimate defense, we have assisted the Soviet Union in plotting a campaign of expansion and imperialism.

I would prefer the moralist to master a strategy of restraint, silence where policy dictates, and self discipline rather than merely to protest with all right-thinking men the grave hazards of the nuclear age.

Carl Mayer went further, warning that the danger of a nuclear war would increase if the USA came out against first use and the targeting of cities. The only way to peace was to prepare for war he reminded the realists:

It seems that the days of what came to be known as Christian realism are about over in America. But it is somewhat ironical that the very magazine that used to be the staunchest champion of such a realism should today, in the matter of the most crucial political problem of the age, espouse views that hardly differ from those of *The Christian Century*.

Although Niebuhr continued to affirm that nuclear weapons were a deterrent to world war, his revisionism about nuclear policy muddied the realist line in this area and on containment strategy as a whole. Conceding that his new position was inconsistent, he explained that he was driven to it by his fear that the current balance of terror was unsustainable.[128]

But the deeper split between Niebuhrians was still to come. For more than 20 years, since the Chinese revolution, Niebuhr had opposed US intervention in Asian civil wars. He did not think of his stance on Korea as an exception to this policy, because the Korean War was launched by a Soviet-backed invasion. But Vietnam was a tougher case, in Niebuhr's view, because it was both a civil war and a Soviet proxy war. In the early 1960s he agonized over what America should do about Vietnam. He accepted the prevailing domino theory that Communists would conquer Southeast Asia if the USA withdrew from Vietnam. However, the American-backed Diem regime in South Vietnam was a repressive dictatorship. The moral choices were deeply ambiguous to him. He reminded his Kennedy-circle followers that Christian realism had a moral dimension, fearing that they reduced it to amoral manipulation. Meanwhile he waffled on Vietnam, not anticipating that it would become the acid test of America's moral realism, and of his.

In 1964 the new president, Lyndon Johnson, awarded Niebuhr the Medal of Freedom, the nation's highest civilian honor. Later that year Niebuhr supported Johnson's election, partly because he promised not to escalate America's involvement in Vietnam. The following year Johnson invaded the Dominican Republic, which Niebuhr strongly opposed, protesting that force was creative only as the tool "of a legitimate authority in the community"; in the Dominican Republic the Marines incurred resentment from their ostensible beneficiaries. In Vietnam, Niebuhr looked for a third option after Johnson massively escalated in 1965. Niebuhr doubted that the USA could win a military victory in Vietnam, but losing the region to communism seemed intolerable. Thus he urged Johnson to persuade Thailand to offer asylum to all the region's anti-Communist warriors, "and then defend this asylum with massive military power." This bizarre plan, besides exposing Niebuhr's ignorance of the region's history and politics, showed the extent of his concern that the USA needed to stand tall, reminding other nations of its superior military might and will.[129]

In early January 1966 Niebuhr was still exhorting Johnson to "take a stand" in Thailand, but by the end of the month he began to deal with reality. Niebuhr shook his head sadly as Vice President Hubert Humphrey, a treasured friend, gamely defended the war; Niebuhr, embarrassed for his friend, began to turn the other way. Vietnam was not really an important test of America's containment policy, he contended, contradicting Humphrey: "We are in fact dealing with the nationalism of a small nation of Asia." Vietnam failed the tests of national security and economic interest, and it was a futile enterprise anyway. Above all, the carnage of the war was sickening to Niebuhr. On moral and political grounds he denounced America's use of chemical weapons; on strategic grounds he added that bombing North Vietnam was pointless too: "We are making South Vietnam into an American colony by transmuting a civil war into one in which Americans fight Asians. By escalating the war we are physically ruining an unhappy nation in the process of 'saving' it." The following year Niebuhr called for the USA to withdraw from Vietnam; in *The New York Times* he called for a public outcry "against these horrendous policies." Vietnam was an example of the "illusion of American omnipotence," he judged, telling friends that his lack of patriotic feeling frightened him: "For the first time I fear I am ashamed of our beloved nation."[130]

That reaction stunned and angered many Niebuhrians. Ramsey spoke for them, protesting that in the bizarre 1960s, "even Reinhold Niebuhr signs petitions and editorials as if Reinhold Niebuhr never existed." The real Niebuhr would not have supported unilateral disarmament initiatives or getting out of Vietnam, Ramsey suggested. Certainly, the real Niebuhr would not have legitimized the antiwar opposition with emotional rhetoric against his nation's policy. To Ramsey, as to the stream of "Niebuhrians" that came to be called neoconservatives, it was all very sad.[131]

But the right-Niebuhrians had not taken Niebuhr seriously enough when he criticized America's fantasies of omnipotence and righteousness; hence they were too surprised when he applied this critique to America's disastrous venture in Vietnam. In *The Irony of American History* Niebuhr had exhorted, "We cannot simply have our way, not even when we believe our way to have the 'happiness of mankind' as its promise." In *The Structure of Nations and Empires* (1959) he put it more ruefully: "We are tempted to the fanatic dogma that our form of community is not only more valid than any other but that it is more feasible for all communities on all continents." That grandiose self-image led to the jungles of Vietnam, Niebuhr later judged, where the USA committed indefensible evils. He regretted having signed on for the misleading idea of "containment," which soon acquired a simplistic military meaning that he did not support. In 1969 he confirmed that he had followed Kennan in shifting away from containment "to the partnership of the two superpowers for the prevention of a nuclear war." Like Kennan, he disavowed "any simple containment of Communism." Later that year, while images of America's incineration of Vietnam burned in his mind, Niebuhr confirmed that he had changed again:

> I must now ruefully change that decade-ago opinion of mine in regard to Barth's neutralism. While I do not share his sneer at the 'fleshpots of Germany and America,' I must admit that our wealth makes our religious anti-Communism particularly odious. Perhaps there is not so much to choose between Communist and anti-Communist fanaticism, particularly when the latter, combined with our wealth, has caused us to stumble into the most pointless, costly, and bloody war in our history.

Schlesinger later explained that his friend grew increasingly alarmed, during the Cold War, over "the delusions generated by excessive American power." The critic of group egotism recognized that his own country had become a reactionary world power through its arrogance of power.[132]

The later Niebuhr also reconsidered the religious meaning of Christian realism, especially its relationship to theological liberalism. On several occasions he remarked that his attempts to refurbish the classical rhetoric of original sin had been mistaken: "I made a rather unpardonable pedagogical error in *The Nature and Destiny of Man*. My theological preoccupation prompted me to define the persistence and universality of man's self-regard as 'original sin.' This was historically and symbolically correct. But my pedagogical error consisted in seeking to challenge modern optimism with the theological doctrine which was anathema to modern culture." Now he regretted that he had been so "proud and heedless" about the effect of his rhetoric: "These labors of modern interpretation of traditional religious symbol proved vain. The reaction to my 'realism' taught me much about the use of traditional symbols." No matter how vehemently he criticized religious conservatives or stressed his theory of religious myth, he could not retrieve the language of orthodoxy without appearing to endorse a regressive authoritarianism. Since Niebuhr assumed the liberal idea of what modern theology was about, he took the problem very seriously; his intellectual autobiography put it plainly: "My avocational interest as a kind of circuit rider in the colleges and universities has prompted an interest in the defense and justification of the Christian faith in a secular age, particularly among what Schleiermacher called Christianity's 'cultured despisers.'"[133]

Niebuhr took for granted that theology in a modern context had to be apologetic, taking on the arguments of skeptics and secular critics. The old liberals were right to privilege the critical challenges of Christianity's cultured despisers. In Niebuhr's case, the key despisers were nonreligious academics who shared his politics. Some of them, notably Harvard historian Morton White, called themselves "atheists for Niebuhr." Niebuhr was highly attentive to the atheists for Niebuhr. In his last substantive book, *Man's Nature and His Communities*, he disclosed that their criticism was the chief influence on his later career. The reactions of political philosophers to *The Nature and Destiny of Man* were especially significant to him; they applauded his discussions of human nature, but spurned the theology. Niebuhr's last books – *The Structure of Nations and Empires* (1959), *Man's Nature and His Communities* (1965), and *The Democratic Experience* (1969) – were pitched to his secular admirers. *Man's Nature and His Communities* reworked his familiar arguments about realism, politics, and human nature in secular language, resorting to what Niebuhr called "more sober symbols" of analysis. He had the same theology as before, but reached for a larger impact on secular audiences, reasoning that theologians would not be given much of a hearing without making similar adjustments.[134]

This adjustment was keyed to his prolonged struggle to keep his "morbid" doctrine of sin from buttressing conservative resignation or indifference. Niebuhr taught that evil is always constitutive in the good; no human act, no matter how loving or seemingly innocent, is devoid of egotism; purity of any kind is an illusion. From this deeply Lutheran and Reformed doctrine he moved to the judgment that a realistic understanding of sin must be a dialectic of interpenetration, not merely a dialectic of two forces held in tension. Good and evil are always part of each other. Niebuhr keenly understood that this doctrine seemed "morbidly pessimistic to moderns," especially its implication that any gain toward a good end simultaneously creates greater opportunities for evil. Every movement that engenders greater democracy, equality, freedom, or community also engenders new opportunities to create tyranny, squalor, or anarchy. Every effort to make the public sphere more humane heightens the possibility of producing unintended evil consequences. Democratic gains increase the possibilities for greater numbers of people to do evil things. Thus, movements for political reform or transformation are most dangerous when they are oblivious to or claim to be innocent of the harmful possibilities they create. Niebuhr observed, "The conclusion most abhorrent to the modern mood is that the possibilities of evil grow with the possibilities of good, and that human history is therefore not so much a chronicle of the progressive victory of the good over evil, of cosmos over chaos, as the story of an ever-increasing cosmos, creating ever-increasing possibilities of chaos."[135]

The distinct challenge of Christian realism was to hold together the Reformation view of human sinfulness and the social gospel view that Christians are called to transform the structures of society in the direction of justice. Thus the crucial Niebuhrian axiom for the politics of Christian realism was the one from *The Children of Light and the Children of Darkness*: the human capacity for justice makes democracy possible, but the human capacity for evil makes democracy necessary. Any social ethic that took moral responsibility for advancing the cause of justice had to begin with a realistic assessment of the evils within and without. Justice would be gained not by those who believed in progress, but by those who struggled for democracy as a brake on human greed and will to power.

It helped to be religious, Niebuhr advised, because religion was about "the vertical dimension in human life," which revealed "the ultimate possibilities of good and the depths of evil in it." The relevance of an impossible ethical ideal – the law of love – was that it reminded Christians that there was an ideal, even if sin made it unattainable. For Niebuhr, the cross was the ultimate symbol of this fundamental Christian truth: "The message of the Son of God who dies upon the cross, of a God who transcends history and is yet in history, who condemns and judges sin and yet suffers with and for the sinner, this message is the truth about life." His theology of the cross combined elements of the Anselmic idea of atonement as a dialectic of divine justice and divine mercy with an overriding Abelardian doctrine of the spiritual effect of Christ's sacrifice. The cross of Christ revealed the deepest mythic truth of Christianity, that Christ took on the suffering of the world in order to redeem it through his fellow-suffering love. Thus, the cross was the ultimate symbol of sacrificial love, and Christ's law of love was the orienting reality that directs Christian behavior, as far as possible, toward this compassionate moral ideal.[136]

The Niebuhrian Method and Legacy

Niebuhr's later works were written under the shadow of failing health. In 1952 he suffered a devastating stroke that paralyzed much of his left side and left him depressed, physically drained, and unable to speak without slurring his words. In the 1960s his declining health left it to Bennett to sort out the disagreements among Niebuhrians. Between these episodes Niebuhr struggled mightily to regain his health and influence. He coped bravely with his illness, marshaled his physical resources, regained much of his ability to write and perform, and concentrated on the politics of anticommunism, all with the indispensable help of his wife Ursula, who taught religious studies at Barnard College. His view of his country's political situation in the 1950s was more approving than later on. In 1952 Niebuhr enthused, "We have equilibrated power. We have attained a certain equilibrium in economic society itself by setting organized power against organized power. When that did not suffice we used the more broadly based political power to redress disproportions and disbalances in economic society." Welfare state capitalism attained as much of the democratic socialist ideal as appeared to be attainable, he believed. By creating a system of countervailing labor, capitalist, and governmental power, American civilization vindicated the dreams of the social gospelers and progressives without resorting to (much) economic nationalization.[137]

On racial justice Niebuhr was better than most theologians, repeatedly describing white racism as America's worst remaining social problem. He never featured this problem in his major writings, however, and in the 1950s he was overly optimistic about his country's progress toward racial justice, a topic this book takes up in its concluding chapter.[138] For much of Niebuhr's career he believed that England was the best country of all, but by the 1950s he inclined to the proud conclusion that his own country had become the model of the liberal democratic idea, its racial pathologies notwithstanding. In his later career he also judged that his attacks on liberalism were too sweeping and polemical. Liberal Christianity was a richer and more complex tradition than he had acknowledged, and his own thinking was obviously a type of liberal theology. He had spent most of his career fighting for a kind of liberalism that did not view the world entirely through its idealism. Unfortunately, in his zeal for polemical victories, he had usually not put it that way.[139]

In 1960 he put it ruefully: "When I find neo-orthodoxy turning into a sterile orthodoxy or a new Scholasticism, I find that I am a liberal at heart, and that many of my broadsides against liberalism were indiscriminate." He had never been theologically neo-orthodox, he explained; liberalism was his tradition, despite its faults; in politics and religion he believed in a chastened liberal empiricism: "On the whole I regret the polemical animus of my theological and political activities and am now inclined to become much more empirical, judging each situation and movement in terms of its actual fruits." Elsewhere he explained that as a youthful product of the social gospel he was predisposed to approach theology as a polemical enterprise, which he lived to regret: "There is no need for polemics today, and there was no need for them when I wrote. My polemics were of an impatient young man who had certain things to say and wanted to get them said clearly and forcefully."[140]

Niebuhr's last writings commended Christian realism in a cooler voice, disavowing the "rather violent, and sometimes extravagant" polemics of his youth. Against conservative Niebuhr-quoters he admonished: "A realist conception of human nature should be made the servant of an ethic of progressive justice and should not be made into a bastion of conservatism, particularly a conservatism which defends unjust privileges." Sadly, he judged, the Johnson Administration's "fantastic involvement in Southeast Asia" was a symptom of America's peculiar weakness for utopianism, although Niebuhr's opposition to the Vietnam War did not redeem Christian realism in the eyes of a radical-turning younger generation. Liberationist critics charged that Christian realism was part of the problem.[141]

From a liberationist standpoint, Niebuhrian realism was part of the problem because it viewed the world from the standpoint of American political and economic interests. In his prime Niebuhr advised government officials, appeared on the cover of *Time* magazine, attracted a large following of religious and secular admirers, and dominated his field to the point where, as Protestant ethicist Alan Geyer observed, he seemed "an omnipresent figure in theology and ethics." In his last years he lost his field-dominating stature in Christian ethics on the grounds that his realism was an American ideology that served the interests of American power. Latin American liberationist Rubem Alves aptly summarized the liberationist charge: "Realism is functional to the system, contributes to its preservation and gives it ideological and theological justification." By the time that Niebuhr died in 1971, Christian ethics had taken a sharp left turn under the influence of liberation theology, feminism, and the idealism of the sixties generation. The reign of Christian realism in the social ethics field was over.[142]

Niebuhr's stature among the giants of modern theology was anomalous. He created an approach to Christian ethics that dominated its field in his time and which remains a major theoretical option and tradition in the field, but he rarely defined his terms with precision, he gave little attention to methodological problems, and his ethical thinking was very short on a theory of justice or a positive vision of a good society. Bennett remarked of the latter problem: "I think you get at Niebuhr negatively so much better than you do positively. That's the reason that there's lack of vision in a way, lack of a positive vision. It's the criticism of inequality that's more obvious than the actual vision of what an equal world would be like."[143] Niebuhr interpreters Dennis McCann and Karen Lebacqz emphasized the dispositional character of his ethic, arguing that it provided few criteria for distinguishing between just and unjust uses of power. In their view, Niebuhr's conceptions of liberty, order and equality as principles of justice were never systematized clearly enough to yield criteria for distinguishing between moral and immoral uses of power. Other interpreters, notably James Gustafson, Robin W. Lovin, Harlan Beckley, and Merle Longwood, countered that Niebuhr's ethical thinking contained, at least implicitly, the elements of a workable theory of justice, though none of them disputed that Niebuhr's ethic was highly dispositional and intuitive.[144]

Niebuhrian realism was a variant of Max Weber's distinction between the ethics of conscience and the ethics of responsibility. In the prefaces to the later editions of his major works, Niebuhr revised his dichotomy between the ethics of love absolutism and political responsibility, but a qualified version of this distinction remained essential to his ethical perspective. Realism negotiated between the ideal and the actual. The task of a responsible political ethic informed by the love absolutism of Christianity was to pursue the highest attainable social good, which is justice. In his early career he equated justice with equality, arguing that equality is the only regulative principle of justice. *An Interpretation of Christian Ethics* referred to both freedom and equality as principles of justice, but Niebuhr gave clear preeminence and regulative significance to equality. In 1938 he was still arguing that only equality has regulative force as a principle of justice, but in the early 1940s his disenchantment with Marxism moved him to adopt a more pluralistic understanding of justice. The second volume of *The Nature and Destiny of Man* described equality, liberty, and order as regulative principles of justice, giving priority to equality. After Niebuhr gave up on socialism too, he stopped giving priority to equality; in the 1950s he described liberty, order, and equality as equally regulative principles of justice. Sometimes he implied that liberty is more important than order and equality, but on other occasions he used "justice" and "balance of power" as interchangeable terms.[145]

For Niebuhr, justice was a relational term that had no meaning apart from the provisional meaning given to it through its dependence on love. He conceived the rules of justice as "applications of the law of love" which do not have any independence from the law of love. Justice is an application of the law of love to the socio-political sphere, and love is the motivating energy of the struggle for justice. The struggle for justice is regulated by the middle axioms of freedom, equality, and order (or balance of power), but the concrete meaning of justice in any given situation cannot be taken directly from these principles. Thus the meaning of justice can be determined only in the interaction of love and situation, through the mediation of the principles of freedom, equality, and order. When pressed by Ramsey to ground these principles in a modern version of natural law theory, Niebuhr replied that he believed "in an 'essential' nature of man," but did not believe there was any formulation of this essential nature that escaped the ambiguities and biases of historical relativity.[146]

Thus he took no interest in developing a normative theory of justice. Christian realism dealt with proximate problems, seeking always to bring about a greater balance of power and further gains in freedom and equality. The task of theological ethics was to bring the intuitive and pragmatic insights of prophetic Christianity to bear on pressing social problems, not to construct a normative account of justice. Christian realism was more concerned with immediate obstacles to freedom and equality than with the relationships between freedom and equality in a just society. More importantly, Niebuhrian realism privileged intuitive discernment over method because it was fundamentally a love ethic. Niebuhr insisted that only love empowered by divine grace could prevent the struggle for justice from degenerating into a war among interests. Without the formative and redeeming power of love in historical struggles for justice, "the frictions and tensions of a balance of power would become intolerable."[147]

Niebuhrian realism did not claim to resolve the tension between the love ethic ideal and the responsibilities of power. It did not resolve the fundamental paradox of Christian morality, but embraced it. Niebuhr began and ended with the paradox that Christians must assume moral responsibility for the consequences of their acts while taking moral inspiration and guidance from a consequence-disregarding ethic of love. As Beckley observes, "a fully adequate conception of justice requires acts of love that disregard consequences, because the consequences of such uncalculating acts are necessary to preserve and extend justice." Yet Niebuhr believed that the consequences of acting from heedless love were only rarely beneficial. Practically responsible action required paying attention to consequences. Thus he was left with a consequential justification for self-transcending, sacrificial acts that could be performed, as Beckley puts it, "only by agents who could ignore consequences."[148]

No conceivable theory of justice could map out general rules for how a consequence-disregarding sacrificial ethic should inspire particular justice-bearing consequences; thus Niebuhr did not aspire to a theory of justice. For him, love was an indispensable but inherently paradoxical source for obtaining justice. Love is a generative and formative force in struggling for justice, but it also reminds us that every gain toward justice is corrupt. Because he conceived justice as a strategy for approximating an impossible ethical ideal, Niebuhr was left with only provisional and intuitive judgments about what justice required. He used mediating principles of justice to discern how power might be wielded in a morally responsible way, but did not elaborate the regulative functions of these principles. His ethic emphasized, instead, the deeper paradox built into any attempt to take the Christian love ethic seriously in a fallen world.

Thus, the major Christian ethicist of the twentieth century and dominant figure in American social ethics offered remarkably little vision of what a good society should look like. In general terms, Niebuhr identified justice with an approximate balance of power, but his dialectic of sin militated against any illusion that distributive justice necessarily led to a good society. For any scheme that merely redistributed power was likely to produce an evil balance of power. Niebuhr's ethic offered a prophetic criticism of inequality, a warning about the limits of political solutions, an outline of a tri-dimensional understanding of justice, an appeal to the redemptive power of heedless love, and a witness to the ever-gracious providence of a sovereign God. But on theological and political grounds it did not offer a positive vision of a good society, the very thing that social ethics had previously been about.

Just as he took little interest in formal methodological questions, Niebuhr took little interest in formal theology. His thinking was theologically profound and not lacking in systematic coherence, yet he was keenly aware that he lacked the training and temperament of a professional theologian. With powerful religious force he urged Christians to take seriously the "permanently valid" myths of Christianity as living symbolizations of Christian experience. The cross was the center of his faith, holding together his religious and ethical commitments. Religiously, it was the means by which God established God's mercy and judgment on human sin; ethically, it was the ultimate symbol of the importance and unattainability of the law of love. Niebuhr had much less to say about the resurrection, though he described Easter faith as "the very genius of the Christian idea of the historical." He interpreted the idea of the resurrection as a symbol "from our present existence to express concepts of a completion of life which transcends our present existence," adding that the idea of bodily resurrection "can of course not be literally true, but neither is any other idea of fulfillment literally true."[149]

He was reasonably clear about various things that he did not believe about Christian symbols. "There are very few theologians today who believe the Resurrection actually happened," Niebuhr observed, siding with the majority: "There is a progressive retrogression in the New Testament. I mean, there are more and more details about Christ's appearance." In reply to Catholic theologian Gustave Weigel, who accused him of abandoning orthodox Christian teaching, Niebuhr declared with a whiff of incredulity, "I do not know how it is possible to believe in anything pertaining to God and eternity 'literally.'" Niebuhr reasoned that Christian myths were permanently valid symbols, but declined the theological task of explaining exactly how modern Christians should understand the mythical character of Christian teaching. What is the nature of a myth or symbol? What kind of reality lies behind the symbols of the incarnation and resurrection? Are they merely regulative principles in the Kantian sense? Do they have a more substantive reality? Is the resurrection more symbolic than the truth symbolized in the cross? Niebuhr waved off such questions; he was a social ethicist, he explained, not a theologian: "I have never been very competent in the nice points of pure theology; and I must confess that I have not been sufficiently interested heretofore to acquire the competence." By his reckoning, he reflected "the strong pragmatic interest of American Christianity," leaving it to "the stricter sects of theologians in Europe" to systematize Christian concepts. In American seminaries, as Tillich sadly discovered in the 1930s, theology was a handmaiden of social ethics.[150]

Niebuhr taught at Union Seminary until 1960 and wept openly at his retirement dinner, feeling deeply the loss of a vital bond. On that occasion Union announced the creation of an endowed Reinhold Niebuhr Professorship of Social Ethics. Contributors included W. H. Auden, Sherwood Eddy, T. S. Eliot, Hubert Humphrey, Walter Lippmann, Jacques Maritain, Adlai Stevenson, Norman Thomas, Paul Tillich, and Arnold Toynbee. The first Niebuhr professor was obvious: John Bennett, Niebuhr's longtime collaborator, who spoke for himself and many others in December 1959 in remarking that for his generation there were two guides to the necessary remaking of theology: "Reinhold Niebuhr and the catastrophic history of the period."[151]

Making Sense of Niebuhrian Realism: John C. Bennett and Paul Ramsey

One year after Niebuhr died, Michael Novak, a former liberal Niebuhrian who was on his way to becoming a neoconservative, wrote that it seemed like 10. The Democratic realists who came to power in 1960 had created a catastrophe in Vietnam and fueled an explosion of new social movements that challenged the legitimacy of what was invariably called "the system." The voices of a new political generation denounced Niebuhr's vital center liberalism for accommodating the system, especially an overgrown military–industrial complex. The cultural revolutions of the 1960s produced a powerful antiwar movement and a radicalized civil rights movement, as well as new social movements for women's rights, sexual liberation, Black Power, environmentalism, and economic redistribution. They also unleashed a mighty backlash that accomplished what the New Left had started – turning the word "liberal" into an epithet – on its way to building a dominant Republican Right in American politics. At the moment that Novak reflected on the disappearing legacy of Niebuhr's work, an idealistic politician straight out of the Methodist social gospel tradition, George McGovern, was the Democratic party's presidential candidate.[152]

To the original neoconservatives, the nomination of an antiwar progressive by America's dominant political party was a catastrophe for American liberalism and the USA as a whole. Often they lamented that American liberalism had betrayed everything that Niebuhr represented.[153] That verdict had ample resonance, in contrasting ways, on both sides of the debate over Niebuhr's legacy. In his prime Niebuhr reached a dizzying height of acclaim within and outside the field of theology. Foreign policy realist Hans Morgenthau declared that Niebuhr was "the greatest living political philosopher of America, perhaps the only creative political philosopher since Calhoun." In his last years Niebuhr had the strange experience of garnering similar accolades from Arthur Schlesinger, Jr, Hubert Humphrey, and George Kennan while seeing his work spurned by theologians and social ethicists. The new generation of theologians seemed to share none of his assumptions. Often he was summarily dismissed as a nationalist and Cold Warrior. Union Seminary theologian Tom Driver judged in 1968 that Niebuhr's work was "essentially defensive or conservative." For Driver, Niebuhrian realism was too defensive in spirit and too compromised by its connection to established power to be helpful, relevant, or even interesting.[154]

Princeton Seminary theologian Richard Shaull offered a liberationist version of that judgment, contending that Niebuhr's realist paradigm had to be replaced by an alternative theology drawn from the experiences of Third World, Black American, and other marginalized Christian communities. Shaull, a former Niebuhrian, had converted to liberation theology as a missionary in Latin America. Latin American liberationists Gustavo Gutiérrez and Rubem Alves agreed that Christian realism was not only functional to the dominant order, but an ideology of it. Alves put it bluntly: "Realism has not yet recognized that it is an American ideology and yet proceeds to pass universal judgment over the other 'regional' theologies."[155]

That was the kind of frontal assault that felled the social gospel in the 1930s; now it was happening to Niebuhrian realism. The zeitgeist is often a vengeful spirit. John Bennett, having tried to restrain Niebuhr's polemics in the 1930s, tried to play a similar role from the opposite side in the 1970s. In 1936 he observed that each generation attacked its predecessors beyond all fairness while exaggerating the novelty of its own wisdom. Bennett took a different tack, defending Niebuhr's realism without duplicating his stigmatizing exaggerations. A generation later, when the tide turned against Christian realism, Bennett made sense of what it had been and how it needed to change.[156]

Born in 1902 in Kingston, Ontario, educated at Williams College and Oxford University, Bennett completed his divinity and master's degrees at Union in 1926 and 1927, where he began his teaching career just as Niebuhr arrived there. Niebuhr, anxious for allies on a faculty that viewed him suspiciously, found one in Bennett. He later recalled that Henry Van Dusen recommended Bennett to him as a young ethicist "uncommonly endowed with wisdom and common sense." Bennett married Anne McGrew in 1931 and was ordained to the Congregational ministry in 1939. He taught at Auburn Theological Seminary in New York from 1930 to 1938 and at Pacific School of Religion from 1938 to 1943 before returning to Union in 1943 to be Niebuhr's colleague as the Dodge Professor of Applied Christianity.[157]

From the beginning of their relationship, Bennett and Niebuhr compared their misgivings about the old liberalism and a rising Barthian movement. In 1930 Niebuhr wrote to Bennett while traveling in Germany that he tried to debate with a group of Barthians and found it pointless: "A positivism which stands above reason is not debatable so what's the use? It is really hopeless to argue with Barthians." The experience confirmed for Niebuhr that his premises were liberal. The Barthians renounced the spiritual authority of reason and experience; to Niebuhr that was ridiculous. Barth and his followers took the way of revelation and faith alone, armed with a neo-Reformation doctrine of the Word of God; Niebuhr believed that faith and salvation were intimately connected to moral, social, and spiritual experience. But Niebuhr and Bennett agreed that some alternative to liberal idealism and humanism was needed. Niebuhr broke the news with his stunning, sarcastic *Moral Man and Immoral Society*; the following year, 1933, Bennett offered a more temperate rendering of the relationship between social gospel liberalism and Niebuhrian realism.[158]

In the sense of being a coherent structure of belief and practice, Bennett reasoned, liberal theology was breaking apart. But that did not mean that all the pieces of the shattered liberal system were discredited. Some were crucial to good theology; Bennett identified four major ones. The first was that liberalism was "a cleansing force" in modern Christian history: "It has removed a great deal of excess baggage, especially all that went with biblical literalism. It has taken the emphasis off doctrine and ecclesiasticism and put it on those things which are most essential for the Christian life." Bennett and Niebuhr remained straightforward liberals in maintaining that Christianity is a life, not a doctrine, by which they meant primarily the spiritual and ethical life of the individual, not the life of the church. Bennett's second point was closely related to the first. The ultimate authority in religion must be God or the Truth, he acknowledged, and all knowledge is contextually influenced, but from the standpoint of the seeker of religious truth, "the ultimate authority in religion must rest with the insight of the individual." The liberal appeal to the privileged authority of individual reason and experience could not be overthrown without doing immense harm to Christianity: "Any attempt to override the insight of the individual by appealing to obedience to any external authority leads to unreality in religion, breaks up the unity of the personality, and destroys the right relation to God as the God of truth."[159]

That was the keystone, despite their polemics against liberalism; there was no alternative to it on the authority question. By accepting the authority of reason and experience, Bennett observed, liberal theology stripped away the church's mythology about Jesus and gained a clearer grasp of the Jesus of history, which was its third major contribution. The historical Jesus enterprise yielded some faulty Jesuses, but overall it strengthened the intellectual integrity of modern Christianity and aided its spiritual health: "There has been a wholesome simplification of Christianity as a result of the liberal criticism of tradition." Bennett contrasted this enduring liberal achievement to the obfuscating Christologies of the Barthian movement, in which theologians dismissed the historical Jesus as an unknowable enigma while appealing to the eternal Christ of faith. That strategy was a loser for modern theology and Christianity: "We have here a flat contradiction of the Christian belief in the incarnation usually in the name of a reassertion of it. It is only in the human life of Jesus, in his personality and his teaching that the word is revealed to men in its fullness." Liberalism was right to play up the incarnation, he judged. Instead of drawing a line between the human and the divine on the other side of everything that is human, liberalism gave "full weight to the values which are present in humanity as our clue to those aspects of God which are most important for our lives." Barthian theology dismissed the historical Jesus while making the Christ of faith an isolated figure set apart from humanity; liberalism had a better idea, viewing Jesus as the highest revelation of God.[160]

The fourth major contribution of liberal theology followed from the third. Liberal Christianity was a religion of continuity between God and humankind, grace and nature, revelation and natural religion, faith and reason, and Christianity and other religions. Bennett and Niebuhr censured liberal Protestantism for exaggerating divine immanence and the continuities of the sacred and profane orders; however, Barthian neo-orthodoxy lurched too far in the opposite direction, stressing transcendence and discontinuity. Bennett rejected Barth's assertion of a radical discontinuity between revelation and reason:

> It is at this point that the attack from the Barthian theologians seems to me to be most unsound. Revelation which is purely arbitrary, which is beyond rational defense, which has nothing to do with the experiences of God which come to men in mere religion or in secular idealism is itself a precarious foundation for faith and it excludes too many of us from any approach to faith which is possible for us.

The new theology had to be open to revelation *and* guided by reason and common experience. *Sola scriptura* was too limiting: "The roots of faith are many and various, and I can't believe that any theology is the sounder for beginning its task by cutting away all but one."[161]

If Niebuhr's theology was still so deeply liberal, what was all the anti-liberal fuss about? Bennett pointed to four things: Niebuhr's realistic view of human nature, his sense of humanity's dependent relationship on a transcendent God, his socialist belief in the self-destructiveness of capitalism, and the hope of a Christian movement that spoke "a decisive word to the spiritual confusion of the world." All these themes had a history in liberal theology, Bennett allowed, but recent liberalism had little to say about human evil and the systemic evils of capitalism, and as a structure of themes the

Niebuhrian theology amounted to a new departure: "The great contribution of Reinhold Niebuhr's much criticized book, *Moral Man and Immoral Society*, is that it challenges in an inescapable way our illusions about men in society." Much of the social gospel was unsalvageable after Niebuhr's attack upon it; moreover, "Niebuhr is also important because through him more effectively than through any one else the European criticism of liberalism is being mediated to American Christianity, and the dose is mild enough to be taken without too much risk of complications." Niebuhr was the American Barth, but unlike Barth he was grounded in the real world. Bennett promised, "We will never again be even tempted to substitute humanity for God. We will look elsewhere than to enthusiasm for a social goal for our dynamic. We will be forced by our experience to find a deeper basis for living in faith in a God who transcends history."[162]

Liberal theologians at the University of Chicago taught that God was another name for the social process; Niebuhr and Bennett countered that God was transcendent, personal, and really active. Barth taught that theology merely explicated revelation; Niebuhr and Bennett found that amazingly narrow and provincial. Fired by Niebuhr's brilliance and Bennett's cooler analysis, Niebuhrian realism seized the field of social ethics in the 1930s, though in a way that Bennett always found a bit unsettling. Undiscriminating dismissals of the liberal tradition were commonplace; many of Niebuhr's followers adopted his polemical slogans and exaggerations, especially that liberals "didn't believe in sin." Repeatedly Bennett objected to this caricature. In 1939 he protested that he did not recognize the liberal theology of his youth in "most of the tirades against theological liberalism which have become the commonplaces of current discussion." Already there were "Niebuhrians" streaming into the field who lacked Niebuhr's grounding in the social gospel. Bennett later emphasized the difference; in 1939 he urged, "I still believe that we cannot afford to depart far from the spirit and the method of liberalism. As for the conclusions of liberals ten years ago, they must be modified but not entirely rejected."[163]

Niebuhrian theology, as Bennett understood it, held fast to core liberal convictions: God was not cut loose from the highest moral standards. God was not restricted to one channel of revelation. Nothing was settled by a word from an external authority. The figure and teaching of Jesus were emphasized. At the same time Bennett stressed that Niebuhr shredded liberal sentimentality; because of Niebuhr, theology spoke again of the tragedy of sin permeating all existence. Niebuhr taught that the death instinct in human beings often served the life impulse (as when people killed to defend themselves, their loved ones, or their civilization) and that the possibilities for evil expanded with the possibilities for good; Bennett put it poignantly: "The sense that there is no social choice, especially in international relations, which is not intolerably evil, is the thing that haunts me constantly."[164]

In that Niebuhrian mood, but also with Niebuhr's passion for attainable gains toward justice, Bennett wrote the signature works of the Christian realist upsurge that were not by Niebuhr. His first book, *Social Salvation* (1935) presented Christian realism as a corrective variant of social gospel liberalism. "Social salvation belongs to the heart of Christian thought," Bennett declared, explaining that his work was to be understood as "a theological preface to social action." It was not necessary to choose between Rauschenbusch and Niebuhr, although Bennett preferred Niebuhr. Appropriating Rauschenbusch on the kingdom of evil and the class struggle, he toned down Rauschenbusch on the kingdom of God, recalling, somewhat wistfully,

A few years ago it was all so clear. The Social Gospel was regarded as a rediscovery of the original gospel of Jesus. Its charter was the teaching of Jesus concerning the Kingdom of God. The social task of the Christian was to apply the principles of Jesus to the social order. The Christian who believed in the Social Gospel faced the future with a clear sense of direction and with the confidence that the authority of Jesus was behind him.[165]

But these certainties had disintegrated. In Bennett's telling, biblical scholarship was confused and deeply split over the kingdom language of the New Testament, it was impossible to identify the Spirit of Christ with any particular social movement, and the absolute love ethic of Jesus was "far removed from anything which is now possible in the world." The love ethic was not directly relevant to modern Christians: "Glib talk about applying the principles of Jesus has become unreal. We can no longer speak of a 'Christian' social order. The best that we can hope to achieve in this world will involve a compromise with the ideal of Jesus." That was not to disavow Christianity, Bennett cautioned, but only a rather recent and idealistic version of it:

> It has never been characteristic of Christianity to think that the Christian ideal could be fully embodied in human life. Rather has it been taught that man never loses the status of sinner; at best he becomes a forgiven sinner. Realism about the stubbornness of human evil is no strange heresy but is in line with the main trends of historic Christianity.[166]

That was an echo of Niebuhr's recent theological mapping in *Reflections on the End of an Era*. Bennett did not dispute Rauschenbusch's claim that Christian orthodoxy eclipsed the kingdom idea of the gospels; like Niebuhr, he disputed only that true Christianity was concerned with bringing about the reign of God. The kingdom was more elusive, difficult to define, and ultimately, transcendent, than the social gospelers believed. Yet the main thrust of the social gospel was right, Bennett argued. It was neither alien nor novel, but "an inevitable development of the teachings of Jesus." It recovered Jesus' compassion for the poor and his passion for justice: "If we are to have his concern for the real welfare of persons we must take whatever measures are necessary to overcome the evils which crush persons now." Just as Jesus was deeply concerned with the problems of bread and economic distribution, the church had to care about distributive justice.[167]

Political solutions to the problem of justice were unimaginable in first century Palestine; modern Christians followed Christ in a very different context: "Today the problem of bread cannot be solved without a new economic system. Our integrity as Christians depends upon our efforts to overcome the injustice which is the other side of our own privileges." Bennett stressed that the social gospelers got that part right, recovering, as they claimed, the spirit of original Christianity. The question of social compassion was not a secondary or dispensable aspect of Christianity, but the moral heart of Christian faith, as in the parable of the last judgment in Matthew 25. Bennett wrote:

> Did not Jesus separate the sheep and the goats on the basis of their attitude toward the economic needs of others? While the earlier Social Gospel may have been wrong in identifying the Kingdom of God with a new social order, entrance into the Kingdom does depend in our time upon the struggle to remove the obstacles to human welfare in history.[168]

Whether Christians should speak of "building the kingdom" was ultimately irrelevant. The social gospel took hold of the essential obligation, which was to live out, as far as possible, the moral and spiritual meaning of the kingdom faith. The reign of

God was always coming. "Whether it is to be gradual or a series of crises God will not do our work for us," Bennett wrote. "The catastrophes about which we talk so much with rather academic detachment will have no virtue in themselves, for unless we do our part they will mean punishment without redemption for the countless souls who are in their way." It was tempting to get tied up in academic debates about whether Jesus was eschatological, apocalyptic, mystical, or ethical, but it was imperative not to do so. However the academic debates turned out, the church was morally obligated to take Matthew 25 seriously.[169]

Bennett was careful not to identify the gospel with any system of political economy, which was a practical issue, not a dogmatic one. He stressed, however, that the social gospel was revolutionary in putting American Protestantism on the right track. In his view, Ernst Troeltsch's study of Christian social teaching got this point exactly right: until the Christian Socialists came along, the church had never considered structural change toward justice to be part of its mission. Bennett was mindful that without the social gospel, there would have been no social ethics for him to teach. If the social gospel took its kingdom rhetoric too literally and invested too much faith in progress, these were small faults by comparison with its revolutionary achievement.[170]

Christian realism built upon this achievement while eschewing the illusions, optimism, near-pantheism, and pacifism of the social gospel tradition. It was dedicated to social salvation without enshrining any particular ideology with divine sanction. It denounced the ravages of the prevailing order without prescribing any alternative system as a *Christian* solution. It distinguished more clearly than the social gospel between dogmatic and practical issues. On practical grounds, Bennett judged that capitalism was plainly not working and that some form of democratic socialism would better serve the common good: "In other words, it seems clear that a more just society, in which poverty and insecurity are abolished and in which there is more co-operation for the common good, is entirely possible, and that it is the present system which has turned out to be impractical."[171]

On the latter count, *Social Salvation* was more radical than anything Bennett wrote for the succeeding 30 years. Like Niebuhr, he moved rather comfortably into the Democratic party's New Deal mainstream during World War II. Otherwise his first book was like his later ones, identifying with Niebuhr's perspective while avoiding Niebuhr's polemical spirit, adopting Niebuhr's theological anthropology while eschewing his characterization of Christian teaching as mythical, and criticizing social gospel optimism while identifying with the social gospel movement. Christian realism sought to maximize the possibilities for good, he stressed, but always with the tragic Niebuhrian awareness that the possibilities for evil expand with them.

Bennett's signature work on the Niebuhrian departure in social ethics, *Christian Realism* (1941), played up the recent expansion of evil. The horrors of another world war drove many people to speculate about superhuman forces of evil. Bennett sympathized, but cautioned against resorting to the ancient idea of supernatural evil. To account for the nearly apocalyptic evils of the twentieth century, it was enough to consider the ravages of human egotism, the vicious circles of hatred and fear inherited from the past, the culture-shattering pace of modern social change, the power madness of overly-powerful modern rulers, the ease with which ordinary patriotism was manipulated into nationalistic hatred and cruelty, and the destructive capabilities of modern technology. These were the means by which ordinary people committed extraordinary evil, Bennett argued: "If we ascribe our plight to superhuman devils, we shall either neglect our real enemies or yield to the spirit of fatalism." Christian realism recognized the pervasive and indistinguishable character of social evil without giving in to it or mythologizing it or making it an excuse for social indifference or injustice.[172]

He joined Niebuhr's campaign to get the USA. into the war, with caveats on theological points. Bennett judged that Niebuhr exaggerated the love perfectionism of Jesus, which unfortunately reduced the love ethic to the sphere of personal relations. Niebuhr went too far in stripping Jesus' teaching of its social meaning; on the other hand, his rendering of the moral problem of violence and coercion was essentially correct. The moral pronouncements of the New Testament were not laws that Christians applied to their situation, Bennett argued. For example, "When violence is already in progress and the question at issue is not that of violence or no violence but whether one side is to be able to dictate to the other terms of surrender, then those who are responsible for public policy may be obliged to continue to use force to prevent such a result."[173]

Bennett allowed that Quakers, Mennonites, and other Christian pacifists had a strong claim to the true way of Christ as long as they recognized that they simplified the moral choices by taking a sectarian option. For Christians who accepted moral responsibility for order, justice, and the protection of the innocent, the moral choices were more complex: "No nation as a nation can be expected to have the moral discipline to live according to the pacifist faith, paying the price of the cross rather than defending itself or preparing to defend itself." That did not really address the specifically religious objection to killing, however. Even if the state made plausible claims about the necessity of repelling aggressors, how could the way of the cross be reconciled with those claims? Bennett offered a Niebuhrian answer: "I do not believe that pacifists, especially in America, face the problem that arises when they themselves do not bear the brunt of the suffering to which their policy of non-violence may contribute." Though American pacifists spoke about the way of the cross, they were not the ones who were crucified by European and Japanese fascism. Some American pacifists undoubtedly would divert the world's suffering to themselves if they could do so, Bennett acknowledged, but the crucial point was that no such way was open to them. They could not suffer in place of the actual victims of fascism: "When there is no redemptive way of the cross open to Christians in a situation, it is important for them not to disguise their responsibility for the increase of the sufferings of others by the use of words that suggest falsely that they are the ones who suffer."[174]

Unlike Niebuhr, Bennett did not castigate the churches for resisting the current war. *Christian Realism* was an argument for facing up to the necessity of fighting fascism, but Bennett did not find it shameful that the churches, in 1941, were slower than Niebuhr to make the transition. American Protestantism had been right to nurture a deep revulsion for war after World War I, he believed, which had a constructive role to play in the immediate days ahead: "The disillusionment about war which has been so pervasive may have led many to a moral indifferentism concerning the issues involved in this war, but there is genuine moral insight in that disillusionment which must not be lost." Bennett's model on this subject was Abraham Lincoln, who waged a tragically necessary war without hubris or bad faith. Lincoln pressed to victory in a just war without assuming that his side was righteous or that God was on his side. To Bennett that was "the only attitude – other than the position of the pacifist – which has any right in the Christian church."[175]

Like Niebuhr, he hoped for a new party that united progressives against the big business and segregationist interests; in the meantime Bennett drifted with Niebuhr toward Roosevelt's liberal pragmatism. In 1939 he confessed, "It is uncomfortable to have no political movement in which one can have much faith, and to be left with the bare hope that out of the New Deal and the new political consciousness of labor a coherent progressive movement may come into existence." Afterwards he judged that the "Vital Center" Democratic liberalism of Schlesinger and Niebuhr marked the limit of America's political possibilities at the national level. The dream of a farmer/labor/progressive coalition was too wild for the USA, although in New York State Bennett played a leadership role in the Liberal party from 1955 to 1965. Exactly in tandem with Niebuhr, he concluded that America's individualism, weak democratic traditions, and antipathy for trade unionism nullified any serious hope for economic democracy. In 1954 Bennett put it prescriptively, advocating "an experimental modification of capitalism to meet particular needs." He thought he was finished with challenging the capitalist system at its center.[176]

To Bennett and Niebuhr it was frustrating, but also chastening and instructive that churchgoing Protestants opposed even mild economic reforms. Protestant leaders managed to get reasonably progressive statements on peacemaking, race relations, and ecumenical cooperation passed at denominational assemblies, but trade unions and economic democracy were beyond the pale. For decades the Federal Council of Churches inveighed against the economic conservatism of its own congregations, to little effect. Bennett observed: "This situation reflects a persistent problem within Protestantism. Local churches do reflect the interests and the opinions of those economic groups that are dominant among their members. They do not often bring to their members a distinctively Christian social ethic that counteracts the influence of prevailing opinion in the community." Niebuhr and Bennett scaled back their economic ambitions, partly as a consequence of belonging to denominations in which the upwardly mobile laity still did not accept the New Deal, much less the dream of economic democracy.[177]

More than Niebuhr, Bennett was deeply involved in the church's institutional life and work, especially the ecumenical movement. For all of Niebuhr's fame and lecture touring, he did very little speaking in churches, being rarely invited to them. The mainstay of his lecture touring was the college chapel circuit. His reputation for way-out radicalism and over-politicized activism made him a cautionary figure to pastors long after he moved to the ideological center. Niebuhr and Bennett both spoke at ecumenical conferences, but Bennett had more access to local congregations, partly because he was deeply involved in organizational aspects of the ecumenical movement. Bennett played active roles in the 1937 Oxford Conference, the 1948 founding convention of the WCC at Amsterdam, and the WCC assemblies at Evanston (1954), New Delhi (1961), and Uppsala (1968), as well as at the 1966 WCC-sponsored World Conference on Church and Society in Geneva. For two decades, he led the WCC's Department of Church and Society and shaped much of the social witness of world ecumenical Christianity. His commitment to the church's institutional life also motivated him to accept administrative tasks at Union Seminary. In 1955 he succeeded Niebuhr as Dean of the Faculty; in 1960 he was appointed to the new Reinhold Niebuhr chair in social ethics; and in 1963 he assumed the presidency of Union, which he served until his formal retirement in 1970.[178]

More than any figure of his time, Bennett shaped and was persistently engaged with the project of making mainline Protestantism relevant to the modern world. Repeatedly he made the case for a progressive Christian realism that sustained the better parts of its social gospel past. Often he cautioned that whenever Christian realism was stripped of its social gospel roots it took on a cynical and/or conservative appearance. For 25 years he and Niebuhr co-edited *Christianity and Crisis*, which made them keenly aware that many Niebuhrians lacked Niebuhr's passion for social justice and dissatisfaction with Cold War orthodoxy. In each case in which Niebuhr provoked opposition from his right flank – on Cold War ideology, Soviet – American coexistence, nuclear policy, and the Vietnam War – he and Bennett pushed and prodded each other to a new position.

In 1959, shortly before Christian realism began to be pilloried for its ties to the corporate/military establishment, Bennett urged that the primary business of Christian realism was no longer to deflate Christian idealism; that generational necessity had past. The new crisis was very nearly the opposite of the old one. American Protestantism was threatened not by too much idealism, but its lack, having lost "the radical sense of social responsibility which the Social Gospel brought to American Protestantism." A one-sided Niebuhrian corrective had gone too far, Bennett judged. It was wrong for the churches to be complacent in a country where blacks were still denied basic rights as citizens. It was wrong for churches to sanctify the American Way when it showed so little concern for the poor, the vulnerable, and the common good. Moreover, Bennett no longer believed it was enough for Christian realists to uphold the welfare state:

> Today I am convinced that our country is handicapped by the fact that there has been so little of the socialist impulse in our tradition. We seem singularly unable to do well those things that cannot be done for profit and which depend upon the initiative of the state or of the community working through the state; we adhere to the half-conscious dogma that those things which can only be done effectively by the community are in some way on a lower level than those which are effectively done for profit by individuals and private groups. This assumption is the source of the great American inhibition which prevents us from ever doing enough toward education, toward urban renewal and housing, toward making medical care available to all families without bankrupting them.[179]

It seemed to Bennett that the very concept of a public good was dropping out of American consciousness and politics. He implored church leaders to challenge their society's preoccupation with private interests: "I am appalled by the degree to which our great nation is rendered almost helpless to solve many of its urgent problems because of the individualistic dogma which it has inherited from an earlier period." Theologians had no business prescribing economic policies on Christian grounds, he allowed; on the other hand, it was certainly their business to oppose the reigning "unchristian individualistic ideology" that sanctioned American selfishness and contempt for the common good. American society celebrated its growing private wealth while ignoring its deepening public poverty. It grew rich while looking away from under-funded schools, inadequate health care, worsening air and water pollution, a deteriorating infrastructure, and a widening gap between the prospering and working classes. On foreign policy, Christian realism still stood for repelling Communist aggression, but "a considerable change of emphasis" was needed, turning away from America's "generalized hostility toward communism as a monolithic and unchanging adversary." Bennett wanted a more pragmatic, less ideological, and much less self-righteous approach to the Soviet Union. He wanted the USA to acknowledge its mounting public squalor and renounce the reactionary policies in the Third World that made the USA the world's foremost counterrevolutionary power.[180]

The last point touched a nerve among Christian realists. In 1966, while Bennett served as president of Union Seminary and joined the antiwar movement, he was the chief organizer and co-chair of the WCC-sponsored World Conference on Church and Society in Geneva. Except for the WCC assemblies, this was the most influential and broadly representative of the ecumenical conferences, bringing together 410 Protestant and Orthodox delegates. Under Bennett's careful guidance the conference addressed the Vietnam War, adopting a resolution, authored chiefly by Bennett, which censored America's intervention. It declared:

> We would suggest that the churches have a special obligation to question continually the wisdom and rightness of the present Vietnam policies of the belligerents. The massive and growing American military presence in Vietnam and the long-continued bombing of villages in the South and of targets a few miles from cities in the North cannot be justified . . . In view of the dangers created by this situation, we urge that all hostilities and military activity be stopped and that the conditions be created for the peaceful settlement of the Vietnam problem through the United Nations, or the participants in the Geneva Conference, or other international agencies.[181]

This rather mild declaration set off a firestorm of controversy in the USA. Bennett managed to prevent the Geneva Conference from calling for immediate US withdrawal from Vietnam, but he offended many Americans by helping to produce an international denunciation of US policy. One conservative Niebuhrian, Paul Ramsey, expressed the bitter feelings of many Americans from a privileged vantage point.

A native of Mendenhall, Mississippi and doctoral protégé of H. Richard Niebuhr's at Yale, Ramsey was a prolific ethicist who joined the faculty of Princeton University in 1944. In the 1960s he specialized in hard-edged articles on just war; at the end of the decade he branched out to medical ethics, founding the field of bioethics, to which he devoted most of his later career. By 1966 he was renowned in the field for his rigorous scholarship and big personality. Voluble, extroverted, and quick-witted, with a penchant for coarse expression, Ramsay was a formidable debater who had bruised Bennett on several occasions. Yet Bennett accommodated Ramsey's request to attend the conference, where, as a nonvoting member, he predictably took offense at the speeches and proceedings.

Ramsey blasted Bennett and other church leaders for taking specific stands on controversial issues. Moreover, he did not like the social action types that produced ecumenical spectacles like the Geneva Conference. The early ecumenical movement was a high-minded affair that stuck to its subject, ecumenism, and thus deserved its name, he judged, but now it was dominated by social action types who declaimed on things they knew almost nothing about:

> By and large, the American participants, composed too largely of the social action curias, clergymen and academics, brilliant youth one rarely met at the Methodist Youth Fellowship, and with no Christian laymen whose vocation it is actually to share in policymaking executive leadership in the aspired responsible society, did not come to startling new awareness. By and large, they saw or thought they saw their own reflections in the mirror.[182]

On Vietnam, Bennett and the conference criticized America's terrorizing and indiscriminate destruction of Vietnamese villages, culture, and infrastructure. Ramsey replied: "No one ever said that the military destruction taking place in the South is contributing anything positive to political stability or to solving the problems which have produced a revolutionary situation in that country." This was a counterrevolutionary war, not a construction project or relief mission. The object of the war was to smash the Vietcong, which required horrific violence and destruction. The serious question was not whether American intervention required massive destructive force, but whether the USA was able and willing to prevent a Communist takeover of South Vietnam. Scathingly, Ramsey remarked that a smattering of church leaders with moral qualms about "excessive destruction" was not exactly competent to address the serious question:

> The real determiners of United States policy have to estimate the *degree* of danger of escalation into world conflict; and, having done so, they have to compare this with the danger of world conflict if some other course of action is taken or if there is no military action at all in South Vietnam or in the rest of Southeast Asia. Doubtless this depends on the political picture one has of the world, but what accredits the churchmen's picture against that of the government's as a justifying reason?[183]

In Ramsey's view, the ecumenical movement had more important and appropriate work to do. He was a modern Christian who believed in the ecumenical enterprise, he explained. He was not to be confused with fundamentalists or right-wingers who thought that ecumenism was some kind of conspiracy to usher in a world government or the Anti-Christ. Ramsey wanted there to be an ecumenical movement, but not one that took positions on divisive social and political issues. Good ecumenism strove for a consensus on theological foundations before it issued statements of any kind on controversial issues.[184]

Bennett's reply was characteristically respectful and discriminating. He agreed with Ramsey that the churches and ecumenical agencies should devote most of their attention to areas on which some kind of consensus was possible. Dialogue leading to theological agreements was the lifeblood of the ecumenical movement. He had no interest in replacing the movement's central theological concern with pronouncements on every social issue. Bennett cautioned, however, that in a "highly pluralistic theological situation" it was extremely difficult, if not impossible, to obtain ecumenical agreements on fundamental theological beliefs. It was much more difficult to attain agreements on certain doctrinal issues than upon certain pressing social issues. But Ramsey's approach prohibited the movement from addressing any controversial social problem: "Ramsey wants to wait until there is a position in the church that is beyond significant debate, but this would involve a strong inhibition against speaking at all about specific decisions." That stripped the church of its prophetic mission, Bennett protested, nullifying even the church's culture-forming role in the public square. Ramsey denounced *Christianity and Crisis* for opposing Barry Goldwater in the 1964 presidential election; Bennett replied that *Christianity and Crisis* had no reason to exist if it couldn't manage a clear "no" against Goldwater, whose reactionary politics contradicted everything that liberal Protestantism claimed to believe about justice, freedom, and peace: "It would have been a scandal if no agencies of the church had called attention to this situation."[185]

But the breakpoint issue was Vietnam. Bennett conceded that most political issues did not rise to the level of moral urgency that compelled the churches to take a stand; Vietnam was a rare exception. Even in the case of Vietnam, he reasoned, it was possible to leave room for several policy options. Bennett did not believe that church leaders should insist on immediate US withdrawal from Vietnam; that was too specific and ethically questionable. What he believed was that the tragedy of Vietnam had been forced upon American churches in a way that required them to make assessments, draw lines, and speak out. This was undeniably a subjective judgment, and Bennett pressed it subjectively: "I am concerned about the cumulative effect of the bombing of many villages, the saturation bombing with napalm of large areas of jungle because of the suspicion that they contain Vietcong, and I have never understood why these things worry Mr. Ramsey so little."[186]

A New Liberal Consensus?

By then the Niebuhrians were deeply split. In Bennett's view, the later Niebuhr mystified Ramsey-type realists because he took seriously the tensions between Christian morality and American power politics and they did not. Bennett implored of Ramsey: "Why does he never say anything in criticism of the American stance in the world today? He gives the impression that there is no conflict between the Christian perspective and the American stance in the world."[187] Ramsey countered that Bennett, Niebuhr, Roger Shinn, and other *Christianity and Crisis* regulars were obliterating Christian realism. He traced the downfall of Christian realism to the early 1960s, when *Christianity and Crisis* began to search for a "new liberal consensus" in social ethics: "Christian realism is to be found in the sound articulations of the early Niebuhr in *The Nature and Destiny of Man* or in those of the late Niebuhr in *The Structure of Nations and Empires*. It is missing from the genial, quasi-pacifist pragmatism of many of his disciples today." To Ramsey, that was a sad and bizarre turn of events: "Reinhold Niebuhr himself can be quoted in support of the liberal consensus!" The spectacle of Niebuhr making alliances with old-style liberals, progressives, and antiwar protestors marked the occasion, as Ramsey put it, to say "Farewell to Christian Realism."[188]

The right-Niebuhrians invoked Niebuhr's response to fascism to support their position on Vietnam; Bennett and Niebuhr replied that the analogy was spurious. Communism was not primarily a military threat, as Nazism had been, and the Asian situation was more complicated than the German threat to Europe had been. Bennett remarked, "Those who speak with most conviction in favor of our Vietnam policy seem to us to be blind to many intangible factors in the Asian situation that could cause military successes to lead to political and moral defeats."[189] Ramsey's attack on the Geneva Conference moved Bennett to summarize what Christian realism meant to him in the late 1960s:

> I think that the basic theological and ethical teaching in the church should encourage a critical attitude toward the following elements in the US stance: the hangover of capitalist ideology that causes us to drag our feet in relation to socialistic experiments abroad; our absolutistic, crusading anti-Communism in relation to Asia and Latin America; a counter-revolutionary bias that seems unwilling to allow nations in Asia and Latin America to have their own experiments with a revolution; a habit of over-stressing military solutions because we are competent in this field and have the hardware but do not understand the people in some other cultures enough to grasp the political aspect of their struggles; tendencies of a more idealistic sort that mask illusions, especially the tendency to assume

that if we try hard enough we will compensate for all the evil that we do by producing a democratic or quasi-democratic solution.[190]

This agenda marked a significant change in the consciousness and politics of Christian realism, which had paid little attention to the moral underside of American anti-Communism in the Third World. Bennett's new emphasis on curtailing American imperialism in the Third World came from his revulsion at the Vietnam War and his determination to redefine Christian realism. Although he and Niebuhr had occasionally criticized aspects of American imperialism in the past, their stress on the national interest, the struggle for power, and the limitations of morality had set a firmly nationalistic framework for their moral and political analyses. What mattered was America's national interest and the moral conflicts that it posed for American policymakers, not the perspectives of those affected by American policy. Niebuhrian realism addressed the question of how to exercise national power in a morally responsible way, while assuming that any nation's foreign policy reflected the demands of its economic and security interests. Combining Christian moral concern with a nationalistic realism in politics, it tried to tame the excesses of American presumption while assuming that American foreign policy would be shaped by some concept of America's national interest, not a moral or ideological concern.

That was the realism that Ramsey, Kenneth Thompson, Carl Mayer, Ernest Lefever, and other Right-leaning Niebuhrians still defended, as well as future neoconservatives like Irving Kristol and Jeane Kirkpatrick. It was also the realism of the atheists for Niebuhr, who tended to share his recent views about the Cold War and Vietnam. As Ramsey explained, it was an approach that "nudged Christians toward the need to assist in preserving the equilibrium of political power while 'that man in Washington' did the same for the nation as a whole." Ramsey believed that Niebuhr, in his "sober" moments, still understood that "this nation has inherited both power and responsibility in imperial proportions." In its heyday, Christian realism did not try to absolve itself of the moral responsibilities of empire; Ramsey admonished that genuine Christian realism still did not:

> This means simply that we are one of the nations that has the power significantly to influence events beyond our borders. Whether we do or don't, we *do*. There is need for more, not less, Christian realism in our premises. It is the premises the Church is "competent" to affect. The decisions of political prudence upon those premises are another matter.[191]

The real thing accepted the moral and political burdens of American power. Ramsey perceived, however, that Niebuhrians like Bennett, Roger Shinn, Ronald Stone, Robert McAfee Brown, and Charles West no longer viewed America's imperial inheritance as a moral responsibility. Confronted with the Vietnam debacle and an explosion of domestic and international dissent against American imperialism, they became critics of the provincial and nationalistic aspects of Christian realism and its tendency to justify American capitalism, militarism, and anti-Communism. Christian realism had the best understanding of politics and human nature, they argued, but its exclusionary Euro-American purview was very problematic. It had a record of pronouncements that took little or no account of the perspectives of non-Western, non-white peoples affected by American policies. Bennett's participation in the WCC and, especially, his discussions with Third World Christians at the Geneva Conference convinced him that American Christian realism had to change on that score.

Nearly half of the conference participants came from churches in Asia, Africa, and Latin America. Bennett later recalled that it was a transforming experience for him to spend two weeks discussing world events with Third World Christians who did not share his language or assumptions. He referred to it afterwards as "the Geneva experience," remarking: "American churchmen who have had the Geneva experience need not take over any other country's ideology, but they may gain some freedom from our own. A succession of experiences of this type should enable the American churches to provide some corrective for the vision of the magistrates who now control our destinies."[192]

This was the breakpoint for Christian realism. Niebuhr's legacy was complex and variegated, absorbing repentant social gospelers, former radicals, future neoconservatives, neo-orthodox theologians, secular realists, Lutherans who interpreted Niebuhr as a good Lutheran, and many others. In the 1960s a sharp Right/Left division opened up over the politics of anti-Communism. But now a deeper internal critique was on the table. To call for a more open-ended, multicultural corrective to Niebuhr's Euro-American framework was to challenge Christian realism at a deeper level than the running disagreements over national policy. Bennett was by no means a radical proponent of bringing Christian realism into dialogue with liberation theology. Richard Shaull and M. M. Thomas already outflanked him, criticizing their inherited realism from liberationist standpoints. Former students of Niebuhr such as Robert McAfee Brown and Beverly Harrison soon moved in a similar direction, embracing liberationist paradigms that Bennett continued to regard as "other."[193]

As the field swung sharply left, Bennett cautioned old friends that realism was an anti-utopian impulse. It opposed not only the facile optimism of progressives, but also the facile revolutionism of liberationist rhetoric. "Nothing has happened to refute the realistic analysis of the stubbornness of evil in society or the tragic side of history," he declared in 1968. "No return to a pre-Niebuhrian optimism is possible."[194]

Bennett strove to keep his balance, while opening Christian realism to new challenges and perspectives. He specialized in middle-ground formulations that he called "middle axioms," adopting J. H. Oldham's term for statements covering the middle ground between principles and specific policies. General statements of principle about peace or justice had little use, and Bennett judged that it was perilous for Christian ethicists to advocate specific policies or get bogged down in policy details. The place for social ethics was the middle ground. Middle axioms stated the general direction that social policies should take, drawing on Christian principles and empirical evidence. It was unfortunate that he and Oldham called them "axioms," because they were not logical deductions from a fixed premise. By a better name, however, middle axioms were the natural language of Christian realism, just as Bennett contended. They were normative for a given time, but not indefinitely or universally applicable. As a foreign policy discourse, Niebuhrian realism arose as a response to a Euro-American security crisis; thus it emphasized American interests, especially order and security. But in a post-colonial context, Bennett observed, the need was "to encourage forces for radical change, especially in Latin America where our tendency is the opposite." Instead of the old Niebuhrian focus on how American power should be used to promote democracy and justice, Christian realism needed to be realistic about the harm that American power was likely to do "when we try to police the world."[195]

Besides its practical bent, Christian realism was more naturally suited than most ethical discourses to the language of middle axioms because it was not a self-contained theory. Bennett stressed that it was a "corrective" perspective, not a self-standing position like Thomism or personalism. At its best, Christian realism incorporated the spirit of the social gospel and the early Niebuhr's socialism; unmoored from these sources, it amounted to a conservative American ideology, exactly as the liberationists charged. What was needed was a realistic theology that enabled the "powerless victims of injustice" to gain power. Bennett recalled that in its most creative period, this theme was familiar to Christian realism. It resounded in *Moral Man and Immoral Society* and *Social Salvation*. But realism had grown complacent, which led to the liberationist upsurge. Bennett wanted Christian realism to be known again as a theology of solidarity with the oppressed. The major work of his later career, *The Radical Imperative* (1975), expounded this conviction that the best impulses of Christian realism could be recovered through a serious engagement with liberationist criticism.[196]

"I see the need to transform the use of American power in the world," Bennett declared.

> This would involve abandonment of the role of the United States as guardian of the *status quo* for the sake of our economic interests, of being the habitual opponent of revolutions abroad, of being the great power that is the special friend of cruel rightist tyrannies in the interest either of 'anti-Communism' or of maintaining stability as the value of highest priority.

To accent anti-imperialism was to return to the original mode of Christian realism, he wrote:

> I recognize in myself a too bland acceptance of national trends in the 1940s and 1950s. The fact that there was considerable harmony between my ethical convictions and the policies of the United States Government during the Second World War and during the early years of the cold war contributed to this, as did my tendency to be overly optimistic about the effects of the "mixed economy."

The Radical Imperative was closer to the spirit of *Social Salvation* than to his other books.[197]

To make itself realistic to a new situation, Christian realism had to be more ecumenical in spirit and more willing to learn from Latin American, African-American and feminist theologies. Stretching ecumenism to include Catholics was something of a revolution, Bennett acknowledged: "So long as I assumed that my church, the church to which I looked for inspiration and guidance, was limited to worldwide Protestantism, my church was sadly truncated. This was actually true of me until the late 1950s, and I doubt if I was exceptionally bigoted in such matters." Like Niebuhr and most Protestant leaders, Bennett had viewed the Catholic Church as a reactionary monolith that prohibited self-criticism. Like Niebuhr, he developed a positive interest in Catholicism only after learning, in the 1950s, that Jacques Maritain and John Courtney Murray were developing theories of modern democracy and religious freedom from a distinctly Catholic standpoint. The rise of modernizing tendencies in the Catholic Church and its capacity to sustain organic communities of memory drove Bennett to re-think his inherited anti-Catholicism, a process that accelerated after he became Union's president in 1963 and Pope John XXIII convened the Second Vatican Council.[198]

At Union Bennett worked out an exchange program with Fordham University and helped to bring Woodstock Theological Seminary to New York, where it had close ties with Union. As an ethicist and seminary president he became a major proponent of Protestant – Catholic dialogue and cooperation. For many Catholics, he observed, the reforms of Vatican II brought about "debilitating confusion and something close to a loss of religious identity." For many Protestants the same reforms were hard to believe. Bennett took a hopeful view, urging that a more open and revitalized Catholicism was likely to emerge from the church's current disputes over authority, moral teaching, and holy orders, and that provincial ecumenism was a thing of the past.[199]

Three forms of liberation theology – Latin American liberationism, black theology, and feminist theology – burst forth during Bennett's last years at Union, where he hired the leading proponent of black liberation theology, James Cone. By the time that Bennett published *The Radical Imperative*, five years after his retirement from Union, liberation theology was at its peak of creativity and influence. Its seminal texts were published between 1969 and 1973: Cone's *Black Theology and Black Power* (1969) and *A Black Theology of Liberation* (1970); Gustavo Gutiérrez's *Teología de la liberación* (1971; English edition, *Theology of Liberation*, 1973); Rosemary Radford Ruether's *Liberation Theology* (1972); and Mary Daly's *Beyond God the Father* (1973). Bennett ignored Daly, who was already moving to a post-Christian perspective, but *The Radical Imperative* otherwise responded to the radical challenges of liberationist criticism.[200]

He admitted that feminist theology, which arose after the other two, took him by surprise. Ruether wrote that the oppression of women was "undoubtedly the oldest form of oppression in human history." Bennett acknowledged that only recently had that sort of claim begun to make sense to him:

> If I had read that statement five years ago, I would have doubted its validity. I would have thought the word 'oppression' an overstatement for a phenomenon considered so universal. I was too much impressed by the privileges enjoyed by middle-class and upper-class women, and by the informal and indirect forms of power often exercised by them, and by the fact that so many women seemed satisfied with their condition. Today I am more impressed by the extraordinary burden of an imposed status of inferiority and subjection from which women have suffered through the ages and by the injustices and the indignities from which they still suffer even after they have won many rights and opportunities formerly denied them.

Feminist scholarship stressed the patriarchal bias of the Bible; highlighted the misogyny of Jerome, Augustine, Aquinas, and other Church Fathers; blasted the chauvinism of Luther, Calvin, and other Protestant reformers; and denounced the anti-feminism of modern theologians. Bennett acknowledged that, taken together, the rise of feminist consciousness and criticism posed a revolutionary challenge for Christianity.[201]

A new epoch in Christian history had arrived for which there were no precedents and few resources. The predominant images and language of Christian Scripture, tradition, theology, and liturgy were judged to be crucial components of an identity-forming cultural system that demeaned women and gave religious sanction to patriarchy. Christian teaching sanctified Father-ruling concepts of creation, nature, ontology, history, authority, and social roles. Bennett remarked that he knew many women "who feel that everything about the worship of the church leaves them out and they wonder if they can take it much longer." Many others had already left the church. To Bennett, feminism offered the most urgent liberationist challenge to the mainline Protestant churches, because it was the liberationist movement closest to them.[202]

Since the "mainline" churches were white, the black American experience was more remote to them, much more so Cone's radical black theology. Cone stressed that no white theologian had ever taken the oppression of African Americans as a point of departure for theology. Bennett observed that, even worse, white American church leaders usually ignored the oppression of African Americans, and Christian realism largely shared this failing. The Niebuhr/Bennett corpus had some articles opposing racial discrimination, but nothing that privileged black oppression and white supremacy as interpretative categories. Bennett accepted that black theology was long overdue; on the other hand, he had misgivings about Cone's separatism and inflammatory rhetoric. Cone wrote, "What we need is the destruction of whiteness, which is the source of human misery in the world." Bennett worried that Cone indulged a "passionate self-righteousness" that exempted itself from moral and intellectual criticism. He sympathized with Cone's passion to make white people "feel the lash of his rhetoric against whiteness as such." When Cone wrote that it was impossible to think of Christ as non-black in the twentieth century, Bennett surmised that he used "black" as a metaphor for all oppressed people. In that case, black theology stood on the biblical principle that Christ was present especially in the sufferings of the poor, the weak, and the oppressed. Bennett concluded that in a racist culture like the USA, black liberation required something like the Black Power perspective that Cone expressed, except that Cone veered into a separatism that isolated Black Power. Bennett hoped for a black theology of liberation that forged alliances with progressive whites.[203]

Latin American liberationism, being further away, proved easier for white liberals to embrace. Bennett warmly praised Gutiérrez for his biblical grounding, theological learning, emphasis on experience, critique of economic modernization strategies, and deep concern for the sufferings of the Latin American poor. He reported that he had not been convinced by neo-Marxist dependency theory until he read Gutiérrez's version of it, which showed that the economic development strategies devised by US and European elites fostered economic, political, and cultural dependency that locked Latin American nations into cycles of debt and structural poverty. Bennett liked Gutiérrez's selective use of Marxism, which stressed the reality of the class struggle and the illusion of class neutrality while spurning Marxist dogmatism. The concept of institutionalized violence was also helpful, distinguishing between overt forms of repressive and revolutionary violence and the systemic forms of violence at the structural level.

To Bennett, Gutiérrez's *Theology of Liberation* was remarkably reminiscent of *Moral Man and Immoral Society* as a seminal work of prophetic criticism. In his view, it stood to gain from Niebuhrian criticism on two counts. Gutiérrez did not explain how counterrevolutionary violence against oppressive power could be morally controlled, and his rhetoric was unabashedly utopian. *A Theology of Liberation* resounded with the utopian assurance that a new society and "a new kind of man" were coming into being. Bennett granted that political revolutions required revolutions in human consciousness. There was a real danger, however, that liberation theology might sanction new forms of political and religious tyranny under the mandate of revolutionary transformation. Bennett remarked, "My question is the familiar question of Christian realism, the question as to how soon new forms of egoism will appear which will distort the new structures." But he was confident that Gutiérrez understood the danger of absolutizing political movements or of underestimating the pervasiveness of human sin, including revolutionary egotism. Gutiérrez disavowed revolutionary messianism, and he seemed to have a Niebuhr-like awareness of the ambiguity of politics. In the form represented by Gutiérrez, Latin American liberationism was a powerful and compelling form of social Christianity that Bennett hoped would inspire a revival of progressive Christian commitment in the United States.[204]

Could Christian realism stretch this far? Bennett envisioned a progressive theology that kept a realistic grip on the morally ambiguous character of human striving while taking inspiration, correction, and instruction from the new liberation theologies. It would operate out of the liberal tradition of theology while subjecting this tradition to liberationist criticism. It would be ecumenical in spirit, drawing various denominational traditions into a dialogue that diminished longstanding barriers to mutual recognition and cooperation. It would resist utopian ideologies while keeping alive the Christian socialist vision of a democratized social order. It would recognize that politics was a struggle for power while seeking to maximize the regenerative power of nonviolence, cooperation, and ecumenical dialogue. It would thus create the "new liberal consensus" in mainline Christianity that Ramsey had foreseen and decried, forging alliances between realist and various progressive and liberationist movements.

The Right-leaning Niebuhrians and newly named neoconservatives found that development distressing. By the mid-1960s *Christianity and Crisis* was deeply alien to them. The magazine embraced liberationist causes and opened new discussions on feminist, ecological, and economic ethics. In the mid-1970s American Protestant thinkers Robert McAfee Brown, Harvey Cox, Paul Lehmann, Gayraud S. Wilmore, Letty Russell, J. Phillip Wogaman, Beverly Harrison, and Preston Williams renewed progressive theology in something like Bennett's fashion, as did Catholic scholars Ruether, Leslie Dewart, Gregory Baum, David Tracy and Daniel Maguire, and a stream of progressive realists led by Ronald Stone, Roger Shinn, Alan Geyer, Larry Rasmussen, Charles West, and Kermit Johnson. The Christian socialist tradition was revived by liberation theology and German political theology. At the same time, the environmental movement inspired new ecological theologies that criticized modern theology for its anthropocentrism and its capitulation to market economics.

American liberal Protestantism had always taken pride in its critical spirit, tolerance, and comparative openness to new challenges. At its best it was distinguished by its intellectual creativity and social idealism. This self-image was developed, however, in a religious and academic culture in which the predominance of a liberal Protestant worldview could be assumed. The social gospelers, for all their celebrations of freedom, democracy, and even denominational pluralism, never questioned that America needed to remain a Protestant nation. That took for granted that if the cultural hegemony of Protestantism had begun to erode in American life, it had to be restored, albeit in a new form. Long after liberal Protestantism relinquished the dream and rhetoric of Christianizing America, its leaders continued to assume that America belonged to them. Niebuhr, like his colleagues, routinely invoked the "we" of American Protestantism interchangeably with the "we" of America. For mainline Protestantism, there was little need to distinguish between Protestant and American obligations in determining whatever needed to be redeemed or restored or created. America was a Protestant project that other groups were invited to join as long they accepted the authority and governing ethos of America's Anglo Saxon/Germanic Protestant culture.

With the rise of social movements and the acceleration of socioeconomic trends that directly challenged American Protestantism's cultural authority, liberal Protestant theology was thrown into a new situation. The disestablishment of mainline

Protestantism was effected partly through the erosion of its membership base and largely through the rise of new social, religious, and economic forces that eroded the cultural power of the Protestant mainline denominations. Long after Niebuhr was gone, mainline Protestants puzzled that none of their number reached his level of influence. But the trend lines caught up to mainline Protestantism just before Niebuhr died. The Protestant mainline had never outgrown its ethnic families of origin, demographically it failed even to reproduce itself, it spurned evangelism and conversion, and it was too accommodated to secular culture and commercial society to stand out from either. The elite media lost interest in theological trends and the college chapel circuit on which Niebuhr built his fame disintegrated. In that context, the generation of ethicists that carried on the cause of Christian realism had quite different realities to negotiate.

Notes

1   Reinhold Niebuhr, *The Reminiscences of Reinhold Niebuhr* (New York: Columbia University, Columbia Oral History Research Office, 1953), February 14, 1953 interview with Harlan B. Phillips, 1–9, quotes, 1, 3. *The Reminiscences of Reinhold Niebuhr* is a transcript of tape-recorded interviews conducted by the Oral History Research Office at Columbia University. This chapter is adapted from Gary Dorrien, *Soul in Society: The Making and Renewal of Social Christianity* (Minneapolis: Fortress Press, 1995), 84–181; and Dorrien, *The Making of American Liberal Theology: Idealism, Realism, and Modernity* (Louisville: Westminster John Knox Press, 2003), 435–83.

2   See Carl E. Schneider, *The German Church on the American Frontier* (St Louis: Eden Publishing House, 1939); William G. Chrystal, *A Father's Mantle* (New York: Pilgrim Press, 1982), 3–13; 3), Richard Wightman Fox, *Reinhold Niebuhr: A Biography* (Ithaca: Cornell University Press, 1996), 3–12.

3   In his February 14, 1953 interview with Harlan B. Phillips, the single "regret" about Gustav Niebuhr that Reinhold Niebuhr expressed was that his father opposed higher education for Hulda. Niebuhr emphasized that his father was much less patriarchal in his family relations than most German immigrant fathers, however; *The Reminiscences of Reinhold Niebuhr*, 5–7.

4   Reinhold Niebuhr, "Intellectual Autobiography of Reinhold Niebuhr," *Reinhold Niebuhr: His Religious, Social, and Political Thought*, eds. Charles W. Kegley and Robert W. Bretall (New York: Macmillan, 1956), 3–23, quote, 3; *Young Reinhold Niebuhr: His Early Writings, 1911–1931*, ed. William D. Chrystal (St Louis: Eden Publishing House, 1977), 27–29; Fox, *Reinhold Niebuhr*, 13; see Reinhold Niebuhr, "Religion: Revival and Education," (1913), *Young Reinhold Niebuhr*, 46–52; Walter Brueggemann, *Ethos & Ecumenism, An Evangelical Blend: A History of Eden Theological Seminary, 1925–1975* (St Louis: Eden Publishing House, 1975), 1–7.

5   Reinhold Niebuhr, Union Service Sermon, August 17, 1913, Reinhold Niebuhr Papers, Library of Congress, 1–6; Fox, *Reinhold Niebuhr*, 22–3.

6   Niebuhr, *Reminiscences of Reinhold Niebuhr*, 26 February 1953 interview with Harlan B. Phillips, 12–18.

7   Roland Bainton, *Yale and the Ministry* (New York: Harper & Row, 1957), 198–211; Charles Reynolds Brown, *The Social Message of the Modern Pulpit* (New York: Scribner's, 1906).

8   Reinhold Niebuhr to Samuel D. Press, March 3, 1914, Reinhold Niebuhr Papers.

9   Reinhold Niebuhr, "Yale – Eden," *The Keryx* (December 1914), reprinted in *Young Reinhold Niebuhr*, 53–8, quotes, 54, 55.

10 Ibid., 56, 57; see Benjamin W. Bacon, *Jesus the Son of God* (New York: Henry Holt, 1930); Bacon, "Enter the Higher Criticism," *Contemporary American Theology: Theological Autobiographies*, 2 vols., ed. Vergilius Ferm (New York: Round Table Press, 1932), 1: 1–50; Williston Walker.

11 "This professor meant," Patrick R. Granfield, OSB, "Interview with Reinhold Niebuhr," *Commonweal* (December 16, 1966), reprinted in Granfield, *Theologians at Work* (New York: Macmillan, 1967), 51–68, quote, 65.

12 "The more I threw," Niebuhr, *Reminiscences of Reinhold Niebuhr*, February 26, 1953 interview with Phillips, quote, 16.

13 Reinhold Niebuhr, "The Validity and Certainty of Religious Knowledge," Bachelor of Divinity Thesis, Yale Divinity School, 1914, Reinhold Niebuhr Papers; Niebuhr, "The Contribution of Christianity to the Doctrine of Immortality," Master's thesis, Yale University, 1915, Yale University Library; see Niebuhr, "Yale – Eden," 57; Fox, *Reinhold Niebuhr*, 34–8.

14 Reinhold Niebuhr to Samuel D. Press, July 1, 1915, Reinhold Niebuhr Papers.

15 Quotes in Reinhold Niebuhr to Samuel D. Press, November 3, 1915, Reinhold Niebuhr Papers; "virtue of ignorance" quote in Reinhold Niebuhr, *Leaves from the Notebook of a Tamed Cynic* (1st edn., 1929, New York: Meridian Books, seventh printing, 1966), 30; see Fox, *Reinhold Niebuhr*, 41–3.

16 Reinhold Niebuhr, "The Failure of German-Americanism," *Atlantic* (July 1916), 16–18.

17 Reinhold Niebuhr, "An Anniversary Sermon," October 15, 1915, *Young Reinhold Niebuhr*, 59–63.

18 Reinhold Niebuhr, "The Scylla and Charybdis of Teaching," *The Evangelical Teacher* (May 1916), *Young Reinhold Niebuhr*, 74–8.

19 Reinhold Niebuhr, "Billy Sunday – His Preachments and His Methods," *Detroit Saturday Night* (October 14, 1916), 3.

20 Reinhold Niebuhr to Will Scarlett, June 23, 1960, Reinhold Niebuhr Papers.

21 Niebuhr, *Leaves from the Notebook of a Tamed Cynic*, 26.

22 Ibid., 32–3; see Reinhold Niebuhr, "A Message from Reinhold Niebuhr, *The Keryx* (October 1918), reprinted in *Young Reinhold Niebuhr*, 95–100.

23 "Typical son" and "words have certain" quotes, Niebuhr, *Leaves from the Notebook of a Tamed Cynic*, 40, 41; "spirit of enthusiasm" and "less circumspect," Reinhold Niebuhr, Letter to the Editor, "The Twilight of Liberalism,"*The New Republic* (June 14, 1919), 218.

24 "Just send them in," quoted in Charles C. Brown, *Niebuhr and His Age: Reinhold Niebuhr's Prophetic Role in the Twentieth Century* (Philadelphia: Trinity Press, 1992), 25.

25 "Nowhere have I seen," Niebuhr, *Leaves from the Notebook of a Tamed Cynic*, 93; Williams died in February 1923, but this entry was mistakenly published under the heading, "1924"; "your diocese has lost," quoted in Fox, *Reinhold Niebuhr*, 76.

26 Niebuhr, *Leaves from the Notebook of a Tamed Cynic*, quotes, 61, 67, 68, 69; Reinhold Niebuhr, "A Trip Through the Ruhr," *The Evangelical Herald* (August 9, 1923), reprinted in *Young Reinhold Niebuhr*, 124–7.

27 "Great affliction" and "dreams of vengeance," Niebuhr, "A Trip Through the Ruhr," 128; "practically powerless," Reinhold Niebuhr, "Germany in Despair," *The Evangelical Herald* (September 13, 1923), reprinted in *Young Reinhold Niebuhr*, 128–31, quote, 130; "too ideal," Reinhold Niebuhr, "Wanted: A Christian Morality," *The Christian Century* 40 (February 15, 1923), 202; see Niebuhr, "The Despair of Europe," *The Evangelical Herald* (September 20, 1923); and Niebuhr, "America and Europe," *The Evangelical Herald* (November 1, 1923); Niebuhr, "The Dawn in Europe," *The Evangelical Herald* (August 7, 1924); Niebuhr, "Is Europe on the Way to Peace?" *The Evangelical Herald* (September 25, 1924), reprinted in *Young Reinhold Niebuhr*, 132–6, 141–4, 151–3, 157–9.

28 "No Christian basis," Niebuhr, "Wanted: A Christian Morality," 202; "economic and political heresy," Niebuhr, *Leaves from the Notebook of a Tamed Cynic*, 83.

29 Reinhold Niebuhr, "Henry Ford and Industrial Autocracy," *Christian Century* 43 (November 4, 1926), 1354; Niebuhr, "How Philanthropic Is Henry Ford?" *Christian Century* 43 (December 9, 1926), 1516–1517; "What a civilization" quote, Niebuhr, *Leaves from the Notebook of a Tamed Cynic*, 181; see *Reminiscences of Reinhold Niebuhr*, February 28, 1953 interview with Harlan B. Phillips, 21–39.

30 Editorial, "Independents and the Election," *Christian Century* 45 (September 13, 1928), 1098.

31 Reinhold Niebuhr, "Puritan and Democrat," *Christian Century* 44 (October 20, 1927), 1224; Niebuhr, "Governor Smith's Liberalism," *Christian Century* 45 (September 13, 1928), 1107–8; see Reinhold Niebuhr, "Protestantism and Prohibition," *New Republic* (October 24, 1928), 266–7.

32 Reinhold Niebuhr, *Does Civilization Need Religion?: A Study in the Social Resources and Limitations of Religion in Modern Life* (New York: Macmillan, 1927), quotes, 220, 229, 231.

33 Ibid., quotes, 235, 238–9.

34 Fox, *Reinhold Niebuhr*, 105–6; Phelps Noyes, *Henry Sloane Coffin: The Man and His Ministry* (New York: Scribner's, 1964), 192; Brown, *Niebuhr and His Age*, 34; Niebuhr, "Intellectual Autobiography of Reinhold Niebuhr," quote, 8.

35 See Reinhold Niebuhr, "Why We Need a New Economic Order," *World Tomorrow* 11 (October 1928), 397–8; Niebuhr, "Anglo-Saxon Protestant Domination," *World Tomorrow* 11 (November 1928), 438–9.

36 Reinhold Niebuhr, "Catastrophe or Social Control?" *Harper's* 165 (June 1932), 118.

37 Reinhold Niebuhr, *Moral Man and Immoral Society: A Study in Ethics and Politics* (1932, reprint: New York: Charles Scribner's Sons, 1947).

38 Niebuhr, *Moral Man and Immoral Society*, quotes, xx, 144.

39 Ibid., 256.

40 Norman Thomas, review of *Moral Man and Immoral Society*, by Reinhold Niebuhr, *The World Tomorrow* 15 (December 14, 1932), 565, 567; John Haynes Holmes, review of ibid., *Herald Tribune Books* (January 8, 1933), 13; Charles Gilkey quoted in Langdon Gilkey, "Reinhold Niebuhr as Political Theologian," *Reinhold Niebuhr and the Issues of Our Time*, ed. Richard Harries (Grand Rapids: Eerdmans, 1986), 182; see Fox, *Reinhold Niebuhr*, 142–3. Gilkey recalled that his father later changed his estimate of Niebuhr's book.

41 Theodore C. Hume, "Prophet of Disillusion," *Christian Century* 50 (January 4, 1933), 18–19.

42 Reinhold Niebuhr, "Dr. Niebuhr's Position," *Christian Century* 50 (January 18, 1933), 91–2.

43 H. Richard Niebuhr, "The Grace of Doing Nothing," *Christian Century* 49 (March 23, 1932), 379; Reinhold Niebuhr, "Must We Do Nothing?" *Christian Century* 49 (March 30, 1932), 416–17; H. Richard Niebuhr, "The Only Way into the Kingdom of God," *Christian Century* 49 (April 6, 1932), 447; see [Reinhold Niebuhr] "The League and Japan," *World Tomorrow* 15 (March 1932), 4; *Remembering Reinhold Niebuhr: Letters of Reinhold and Ursula M. Niebuhr*, ed. Ursula M. Niebuhr (San Francisco: HarperSanFrancisco, 1991).

44 See H. Richard Niebuhr, *The Social Sources of Denominationalism* (New York: Henry Holt, 1929); H. Richard Niebuhr, *The Kingdom of God in America* (New York: Harper & Row, 1937).

45 H. Richard Niebuhr to Reinhold Niebuhr, n.d. [mid-January, 1933], Reinhold Niebuhr Papers; Fox, *Reinhold Niebuhr*, 144–5.

46 Ibid.; see Fox, *Reinhold Niebubr*, 145–6.

47 H. Richard Niebuhr, *The Social Sources of Denominationalism* (New York: H. Holt, 1929).

48 H. Richard Niebuhr, *The Kingdom of God in America* (New York: Harper & Row, 1937), quotes 195, 193.

49 H. Richard Niebuhr, *The Purpose of the Church and Its Ministry* (New York: Harper & Row, 1956); H. Richard Niebuhr, *The Meaning of Revelation* (New York: Macmillan, 1941), quote 37.

50 H. Richard Niebuhr, *Christ and Culture* (New York: Harper & Row, 1951). Reinhold Niebuhr citation, 183.

51 H. Richard Niebuhr, "The Center of Value," in *Moral Principles of Action*, ed. Ruth Nanda Anshen (New York: Harper & Brothers, 1952), reprinted in Niebuhr, *Radical Monotheism and Western Culture* (1st edn., New York: Harper & Row, 1960; 2nd edn., Harper Torchbook, 1970; Library of Theological Ethics edn., Louisville: Westminster John Knox, 1993), 100–13; see George Schrader, "Value and Valuation," in *Faith and Ethics: The Theology of H. Richard Niebuhr*, ed. Paul Ramsey (New York: Harper Brothers, 1957), 173–204.

52 H. Richard Niebuhr, *Radical Monotheism and Western Culture*, quotes 32, 37.

53 See Richard R. Niebuhr, preface to H. Richard Niebuhr, *The Responsible Self: An Essay in Christian Moral Philosophy* (New York: Harper & Row, 1963), 1–5.

54 H. Richard Niebuhr, *The Responsible Self: An Essay in Christian Moral Philosophy*, quotes 126; see James M. Gustafson, Introduction to ibid., 6–41.

55 Reinhold Niebuhr, "Ten Years That Shook My World," *Christian Century* 56 (April 26, 1939), 546.

56 Reinhold Niebuhr, "After Capitalism – What?" *The World Tomorrow* (March 1, 1933), 204.

57 Reinhold Niebuhr, *Reflections on the End of an Era* (New York: Scribner's, 1934), 17–18.

58 Ibid., 24.

59 Ibid., 27–8.

60 Niebuhr, "After Capitalism – What?" 203.

61 Niebuhr, *Reflections on the End of an Era*, 30.

62 Ibid., 135; see Reinhold Niebuhr, "Is Religion Counter-Revolutionary?" *Radical Religion* 1 (Autumn 1935), 14–20.

63 Niebuhr, *Reflections on the End of an Era*, 136.

64 Reinhold Niebuhr, *An Interpretation of Christian Ethics* (1935, reprint: San Francisco: Harper & Row, 1963), quotes, 105, 108, 7.

65 Paul Tillich, *Religionsphilosophie*, in *Lehrbuch der Philosophie*, ed. M. Dessoir (Berlin: Ullstein, 1925), reprinted in Tillich, *What Is Religion?* trans. James Luther Adams (New York: Harper & Row, 1969), 101–5.

66 Niebuhr, *An Interpretation of Christian Ethics*, 7.

67 Ibid., 54; see Reinhold Niebuhr, *The Nature and Destiny of Man: A Christian Interpretation*, 2 vols. (New York: Charles Scribner's Sons, 1941, 1949), 1:265–80.

68 Niebuhr, *An Interpretation of Christian Ethics*, 55; Reinhold Niebuhr, *Faith and History: A Comparison of Christian and Modern Views of History* (New York: Charles Scribner's Sons, 1949), 120–3; Niebuhr, *The Self and the Dramas of History* (New York: Charles Scribner's Sons, 1955), 12–19.

69 See Niebuhr, *The Nature and Destiny of Man*, 1: 178–86.

70 Reinhold Niebuhr, "Why I Leave the F.O.R.," *Christian Century* 51 (January 3, 1934); reprinted in Reinhold Niebuhr, *Love and Justice: Selections from the Shorter Writings of Reinhold Niebuhr*, ed. D. B. Robertson (1957, reprint: Louisville: Westminster John Knox, 1992), 254–9.

71 John Haynes Holmes, "Reinhold Niebuhr's Philosophy of Despair," *Herald Tribune Books* (March 18, 1934), 7.

72 Fox, *Reinhold Niebuhr*, 153.

73 Niebuhr, *An Interpretation of Christian Ethics*, 23, 105.

74 Ibid., 106–7, 116.

75 Ibid., 114–15.

76   Ibid., 116.
77   Niebuhr, *Moral Man and Immoral Society*, xii, xiii.
78   Ibid., 276–7.
79   Reinhold Niebuhr, "Religion and Marxism," *Modern Monthly* 8 (February 1935), 714.
80   Niebuhr, *An Interpretation of Christian Ethics*, 117.
81   Reinhold Niebuhr, "The Blindness of Liberalism, *Radical Religion* 1 (Autumn 1936), 4.
82   Ibid., "the inevitable," 4; Reinhold Niebuhr, "The Idea of Progress and Socialism,"
      Radical Religion, 1 (Spring 1936), "tolerable" and "socialism is," 28. Niebuhr's "tolerable
      equilibrium" phrase appeared frequently in his writings, as in Niebuhr, "Ten Years That
      Shook My World," 545.
83   Niebuhr, "The Idea of Progress and Socialism," 28.
84   Reinhold Niebuhr, "The Creed of Modern Christian Socialists," *Radical Religion*, 3
      (Spring 1938), 16.
85   See Arthur M. Schlesinger, Jr, "Reinhold Niebuhr's Role in Political Thought," in *Rein-
      hold Niebuhr: His Religious, Social, and Political Thought*, 140; and John C. Bennett, "Rein-
      hold Niebuhr's Social Ethics," in *Reinhold Niebuhr: His Religious, Social, and Political
      Thought*, 73.
86   See Arthur M. Schlesinger, Jr, *The Coming of the New Deal* (Boston: Houghton Mifflin,
      1958).
87   Reinhold Niebuhr, "New Deal Medicine," *Radical Religion*, 4 (Spring 1939), 1–2.
88   Reinhold Niebuhr, "Roosevelt's Merry-Go-Round," *Radical Religion*, 3 (Spring 1938), 4.
      Schlesinger comment in Schlesinger, "Reinhold Niebuhr's Role in Political Thought,"
      142.
89   Reinhold Niebuhr, "The Socialist Campaign," *Christianity and Society*, 5 (Summer 1940),
      4.
90   Reinhold Niebuhr, "Crisis in Washington," *Radical Religion*, 4 (Spring 1939), 9; Niebuhr,
      "Taxation and the Defense Economy," *Christianity and Society*, 6 (Fall 1941), 5; Niebuhr,
      "Better Government Than We Deserve," *Christianity and Society*, 7 (Spring 1942), 10;
      Niebuhr, postscript to A. T. Mollegen, "The Common Convictions of the Fellowship of
      Socialist Christians: A Suggested Statement as the Basis for Discussion," *Christianity and
      Society*, 8 (Spring 1943), 28.
91   Reinhold Niebuhr, "Brief Comments," *Radical Religion* 3 (Winter 1937), 7.
92   Reinhold Niebuhr, "Brief Comments," *Radical Religion* (Spring 1938), 7.
93   Reinhold Niebuhr, "The London Times and the Crisis," *Radical Religion* 4 (Winter
      1938–9), 32; Niebuhr, "Willkie and Roosevelt," *Christianity and Society* 5 (Fall 1940),
      "anticipated" quote, 5.
94   Niebuhr, *The Nature and Destiny of Man*, 1:25; see Fox, *Reinhold Niebuhr*, 187–91.
95   Niebuhr, *The Nature and Destiny of Man*, quote, 1:5.
96   Ibid., 1:145, 146.
97   Ibid., quote, 178.
98   Ibid., quote, 159.
99   Paul Tillich, *The Interpretation of History* (New York: Charles Scribner's Sons, 1936),
      169–71; Niebuhr, *The Nature and Destiny of Man*, 1:217–18.
100 Niebuhr, *Nature and Destiny of Man*, 1: 126–7; Langdon Gilkey, *On Niebuhr: A Theological
      Study* (Chicago: University of Chicago Press, 2001), 16–28, quote, 19; Reinhold Niebuhr,
      Faith and History: A Comparison of Christian and Modern Views of History (New York:
      Charles Scribner's Sons, 1949), 49.
101 Gregory Vlastos, "Sin and Anxiety in Niebuhr's Religion," *Christian Century* 58 (October
      1, 1941), 1202–4.
102 Reinhold Niebuhr, "Professor's Column," *Union Seminary Tower* (May 1960), "when I
      came here," 3, cited in Brown, *Niebuhr and His Age*, 37; Ronald H. Stone, *Professor
      Reinhold Niebuhr: A Mentor to the Twentieth Century* (Louisville: Westminster John Knox
      Press, 1992), "it was in," 84; Paul Tillich, "Sin and Grace in the Theology of Reinhold

Niebuhr," *Reinhold Niebuhr: A Prophetic Voice in Our Time*, ed. Harold R. Landon (Greenwich, CT: Seabury Press, 1962), 32–3.

103 Reinhold Niebuhr, *Christianity and Power Politics* (New York: Charles Scribner's Sons, 1940), 71; Niebuhr, "Christian Moralism in America," *Radical Religion* 5 (1940), 16–17; see Niebuhr, "An Open Letter," *Christianity and Society* 5 (Summer 1940), 30–3.

104 [Charles C. Morrison], "No Third Term!" *Christian Century* 57 (October 16, 1940), 1273; [Charles C. Morrison], "Defending Democracy," *Christian Century* 57 (June 5, 1940); [Charles C. Morrison], "Why We Differ," *Christian Century* 58 (December 10, 1941), 1534–8, quote, 1538; see [Charles C. Morrison], "The Neutrality Act Is Discarded," *Christian Century* 58 (November 26, 1941), 1459; Morrison, *The Christian and the War* (Chicago: Willett, Clark & Co., 1942).

105 Reinhold Niebuhr, "To Prevent the Triumph of an Intolerable Tyranny," *Christian Century* 57 (December 18, 1940), 1580; see Niebuhr, "Editorial Notes," *Christianity and Society* 5 (Spring 1940), 10.

106 Niebuhr, *Christianity and Power Politics*, 44, 68; Niebuhr, "To Prevent the Triumph of an Intolerable Tyranny," 1579; different versions of the same statements.

107 Reinhold Niebuhr, "Notes," *Christianity and Society* 5 (Autumn 1940), 12–13; "pure German stock" and "I thought Britain," Niebuhr, "To Prevent the Triumph of an Intolerable Tyranny," 1579; "moralistic illusions," Niebuhr, *Christianity and Power Politics*, 47.

108 [Charles C. Morrison], "An Unnecessary Necessity," *Christian Century* 58 (December 17, 1941), 1565–7, quotes, 1565.

109 Reinhold Niebuhr, "Editorial Notes," *Christianity and Society* 7 (Winter 1941–2), quote, 9; Niebuhr, *The Children of Light and the Children of Darkness: A Vindication of Democracy and a Critique of Its Traditional Defense* (New York: Charles Scribner's Sons, 1944).

110 "Genuinely sorry," Reinhold Niebuhr, "Ten Years That Shook My World," *Christian Century* 56 (April 26, 1939), 542–6, quote, 543; "Almost, though not quite," Niebuhr quoted in John C. Bennett, "Tillich and the 'Fellowship of Socialist Christians,'" *North American Paul Tillich Society Newsletter* 16 (October 1990), 3; "excessively optimistic," Niebuhr, *The Children of Light and the Children of Darkness*, x; see Niebuhr, *Christian Realism and Political Problems* (New York: Charles Scribner's Sons, 1953), 33–42; Donald Meyer, *The Protestant Search for Political Realism, 1919–1941* (2nd edn.: Middletown, CT: Wesleyan University Press, 1988).

111 Reinhold Niebuhr, "Frontier Fellowship," *Christianity and Society* 13 (Autumn 1948), 4; Niebuhr and others, "Christian Action Statement of Purpose," *Christianity and Crisis* 11 (October 1, 1951), 126; Niebuhr, "Superfluous Advice," *Christianity and Society* 17 (Winter 1951–2), 4–5; Niebuhr, *Christian Realism and Political Problems*, "we are fated," 33; see Niebuhr, "The Organization of the Liberal Movement," *Christianity and Society* 12 (Spring 1947), 8–10.

112 Reinhold Niebuhr, "The Change in Russia," *The New Leader* 38 (October 3, 1955), "with its simple distinctions," 18–19; Niebuhr, "Communism and the Protestant Clergy," *Look* 17 (November 17, 1953), 37; Niebuhr, *Christian Realism and Political Problems*, "noxious demonry," and "old Russian imperialism," 34.

113 Niebuhr, "The Peril of Complacency in Our Nation," *Christianity and Crisis* 14 (February 8, 1954), "we are embattled," 1; Niebuhr, "The Change in Russia," quotes on Islamic analogy, 18–19.

114 See Michael Novak, "Needing Niebuhr Again," *Commentary*, 54 (September 1972); Novak, "Reinhold Niebuhr: Model for Neoconservatives," *The Christian Century*, 103 (January 22, 1986); James Nuechterlein, "The Feminization of the American Left," *Commentary*, 84 (November 1987); Niebuhr quote in Reinhold Niebuhr, *Christian Realism and Political Problems* (New York, Scribner's, 1953), 34; Swomley quote in John M. Swomley, Jr, *American Empire: The Political Ethics of Twentieth Century Conquest*, (London: Macmillan, 1970), 34. For a similar critique of Niebuhr's legacy, see Bill Kellermann, "Apologist of

Power: The Long Shadow of Reinhold Niebuhr's Christian Realism," *Sojourners*, 16 (March 1987), 15–20.

115 Reinhold Niebuhr, "Communism and the Protestant Clergy," *Look* (November 17, 1953), 37.

116 Niebuhr, *Christian Realism and Political Problems*, 42; Niebuhr, "The Peril of Complacency in Our Nation,"*Christianity and Crisis*, 14 (February 8, 1954), 1.

117 Reinhold Niebuhr, *The Irony of American History* (New York: Scribner's, 1952), 128.

118 Ibid., 110.

119 "X," (George F. Kennan), "The Sources of Soviet Conduct," *Foreign Affairs* 25 (July 1947), 579–80.

120 Niebuhr, *The Irony of American History*, 129.

121 John C. Bennett, "A Condition for Coexistence," *Christianity and Crisis*, 18 (April 28, 1958), 53–4.

122 Reinhold Niebuhr, "Uneasy Peace or Catastrophe,"*Christianity and Crisis*, 18 (April 28, 1958), 54–5; Niebuhr, *The Structure of Nations and Empires: A Study of Recurring Patterns and Problems of the Political Order in Relation to the Unique Problems of the Nuclear Age*, (New York: Charles Scribner's Sons, 1959), 282.

123 Elisabeth Sifton, "Remembering Reinhold Niebuhr," *World Policy Journal*, 10 (Spring 1993), 87.

124 Reinhold Niebuhr, "Our Moral Dilemma," *The Messenger* (November 5, 1957), quote 5; see George F. Kennan, *The Nuclear Delusion: Soviet – American Relations in the Atomic Age*, (New York: Pantheon Books, 1982), ix–xxx; Walter LaFeber, *America, Russia and the Cold War, 1945–1966*, (New York: John Wiley & Sons, 1967). I am grateful to John C. Bennett for his insights and recollections regarding this period of Niebuhr's career: author's interview with Bennett, January 2, 1993.

125 Reinhold Niebuhr, "Drama on the Cuban Stage," *The New Leader*, (March 5, 1962), 11; quoted in Fox, *Reinhold Niebuhr*, 276.

126 John C. Bennett and Reinhold Niebuhr, "The Nuclear Dilemma: A Discussion," *Christianity & Crisis*, 21 (November 13, 1961), 200–2; see Bennett, *Nuclear Weapons and the Conflict of Conscience* (New York: Charles Scribner's Sons, 1962).

127 Reinhold Niebuhr, "Logical Consistency and the Nuclear Dilemma," *Christianity & Crisis*, 22 (April 2, 1962), 48.

128 Paul Ramsey, "Dream and Reality in Deterrence and Defense," *Christianity and Crisis*, 21 (December 25, 1961), 228–32; Paul Tillich, "The Nuclear Dilemma: A Discussion," *Christianity and Crisis*, 21 (November 13, 1961), 203–4; Hans J. Morgenthau, "The Nuclear Discussion: Continued," *Christianity and Crisis*, Vol. 21 (December 11, 1961), 223; Norman K. Gottwald, "Moral and Strategic Reflections on the Nuclear Dilemma," *Christianity and Crisis*, 21 (January 8, 1962), 239–42; Kenneth W. Thompson "The Nuclear Dilemma: A Discussion,"*Christianity and Crisis*, 21 (November 13, 1961), 203; Carl Mayer, "Moral Issues in the Nuclear Dilemma," *Christianity and Crisis*, 22 (March 19, 1962), 38.

129 Reinhold Niebuhr, "Caribbean Blunder," *Christianity and Crisis*, 25 (May 31, 1965), 113–14; Niebuhr, "Consensus at the Price of Flexibility," *The New Leader* (September 27, 1965), 20.

130 Reinhold Niebuhr, "The Peace Offensive," *Christianity and Crisis*, 25 (January 24, 1966), 301; Niebuhr, "Escalation Objective," *The New York Times* (March 14, 1967); Niebuhr, Foreword to *Martin Luther King, Jr., John C. Bennett, Henry Steele Commager, Abraham Heschel Speak on the War in Vietnam* (New York: Clergy and Laymen Concerned About Vietnam, 1967), 3; closing quote in Fox, *Reinhold Niebuhr*, 285.

131 Paul Ramsey, "How Shall Counter – Insurgency War be Conducted Justly?" Paper presented at American Society of Christian Ethics Meeting, January 21–2, 1966, reprinted in Ramsey, *The Just War: Force and Political Responsibility* (1968; reprint, Lanham, MD: University Press of America, 1983), 458. For Bennett's response, see John C. Bennett, "From

Supporter of War in 1941 to Critic in 1966," *Christianity & Crisis*, 26 (February 21, 1966), 13–14.

132   Niebuhr, *The Irony of American History* (New York: Scribner's 1952), quote 74; Niebuhr, *The Structure of Nations and Empires*, quote 295; Ronald H. Stone, "An Interview with Reinhold Niebuhr," *Christianity & Crisis*, 29 (March 17, 1969), 48–9; Reinhold Niebuhr, "Toward New Intra-Christian Endeavors," *The Christian Century*, 86 (December 31, 1969), 1662–3; Schlesinger quoted in Matthew Berke, "The Disputed Legacy of Reinhold Niebuhr," *First Things*, 27 (November 1992), 39; see Niebuhr and Alan Heimert, *A Nation So Conceived: Reflections on the History of America from Its Early Visions to Its Present Power* (New York: Charles Scribner's Sons, 1963), 123–55.

133   Reinhold Niebuhr, *Man's Nature and His Communities: Essays on the Dynamics and Enigmas of Man's Personal and Social Existence*, (New York: Scribner's, 1965), 23, 24.

134   Reinhold Niebuhr, "Intellectual Autobiography," in Kegley and Bretall, eds., *Reinhold Niebuhr: His Religious, Social, and Political Thought*, 3; on the "atheists for Niebuhr" phenomenon, see Perry Miller, "The Influence of Reinhold Niebuhr," *The Reporter* 18 (May 1, 1958), 40; Niebuhr, *Man's Nature and His Communities*, 24; Bennett quote in Harold R. Landon, ed., *Reinhold Niebuhr: A Prophetic Voice in Our Time*, (Greenwich, CT: Seabury Press, 1962), 88.

135   Niebuhr, *An Interpretation of Christian Ethics*, 59–60.

136   Reinhold Niebuhr, *Beyond Tragedy: Essays on the Christian Interpretation of History* (New York: Charles Scribers Sons, 1937), 20–1.

137   Niebuhr, *The Irony of American History*, 101.

138   See Reinhold Niebuhr, "The Confession of a Tired Radical," *Christian Century* 45 (August 30, 1928), reprinted in *Love and Justice: Selections from the Shorter Writings of Reinhold Niebuhr*, ed. D. B. Robertson (Philadelphia: Westminster Press, 1957), 120–4; Niebuhr, "The Sin of Racial Prejudice," *The Messenger* 13 (February 3, 1948), 6; reprinted in *A Reinhold Niebuhr Reader: Selected Essays, Articles, and Book Reviews*, ed. Charles C. Brown (Philadelphia: Trinity Press International, 1992), 70–1; Niebuhr, "Christian Faith and the Race Problem," *Christianity and Society* (Spring 1945); and Niebuhr, "The Race Problem," *Christianity and Society* (Summer 1942), reprinted in *Love and Justice*, 125–9, 129–32; Niebuhr, *Pious and Secular America* (New York: Charles Scribner's Sons, 1958), 76.

139   Reinhold Niebuhr, "Coherence, Incoherence, and Christian Faith," *The Journal of Religion* 31 (July 1951), 162; Niebuhr, "Reply to Interpretation and Criticism," *Reinhold Niebuhr: His Religious, Social, and Political Thought*, 441–2; see Daniel D. Williams, "Niebuhr and Liberalism," in *Reinhold Niebuhr: His Religious, Social, and Political Thought*, 196.

140   Reinhold Niebuhr, "The Quality of Our Lives," *Christian Century* 77 (May 11, 1960), quotes, 568; "there is no need" quote, Granfield, *Theologians at Work*, 55.

141   Reinhold Niebuhr, *Man's Nature and His Communities: Essays on the Dynamics and Enigmas of Man's Personal and Social Existence* (New York: Charles Scribner's Sons, 1965), quotes, 21, 25; "fantastic involvement" quote, Granfield, *Theologians at Work*, 54–5.

142   Alan Geyer, quoted in symposium on "Christian Realism: Retrospect and Prospect," *Christianity and Crisis* 28 (August 5, 1968), 178; Rubem A. Alves, "Christian Realism: Ideology of the Establishment," *Christianity and Crisis* 33 (September 17, 1973), 176; see M. M. Thomas, "A Third World View of Christian Realism," *Christianity and Crisis* 46 (February 3, 1986), 8–12.

143   Bennett quote, 1961 colloquium discussion, *Reinhold Niebuhr: A Prophetic Voice in Our Time*, 92–3.

144   Dennis P. McCann, *Christian Realism and Liberation Theology: Practical Theologies in Creative Conflict* (Maryknoll, NY: Orbis Books, 1980), 80–93, 103; Karen Lebacqz, *Six Theories of Justice* (Minneapolis: Augsburg Press, 1986), 83–99; James M. Gustafson, "Theology in the Service of Ethics: An Interpretation of Reinhold Niebuhr's Theological Ethics," *Reinhold Niebuhr and the Issues of Our Time*, 24–45; Robin W. Lovin, *Reinhold Niebuhr*

and Christian Realism (Cambridge: Cambridge University Press, 1995), 198–234; Harlan Beckley, *Passion for Justice: Retrieving the Legacies of Walter Rauschenbusch, John A. Ryan, and Reinhold Niebuhr* (Louisville: Westminster John Knox Press, 1992), 312–43; Merle Long-wood, "Niebuhr and a Theory of Justice," *Dialog* 14 (Fall 1975), 253–62.

145   See Reinhold Niebuhr, "Christian Faith and the Common Life," in Nils Ehrenstrom, M. G. Dibelius, et. al., *Christian Faith and the Common Life*, (Chicago: Willett, Clark & Co., 1938), 85; Niebuhr, *An Interpretation of Christian Ethics*, 132–6; Niebuhr, *The Nature and Destiny of Man*, Vol. 2, 255–6; Niebuhr, "The Limits of Liberty," *The Nation*, 154, (January 24, 1942), 86–8; Niebuhr, *Faith and History: A Comparison of Christian and Modern Views of History* (New York: Scribner's, 1949), 189; Niebuhr, "Christian Faith and Social Action," and "Liberty and Equality" in Niebuhr, *Faith and Politics*, ed.Ronald Stone (New York: George Braziller, 1968), 131, 186–92.

146   Paul Ramsey, "Love and Law," *Reinhold Niebuhr: His Religious, Social, and Political Thought*, 80–123; Niebuhr, "Reply to Interpetation and Criticism," quotes, 435.

147   Niebuhr, "Reply to Interpretation and Criticism," 435.

148   Beckley, *Passion for Justice*, 322–3.

149   Niebuhr, *The Nature and Destiny of Man*, 2: 55–99, "very genius," "not be literally true," 2: 294–5; Reinhold Niebuhr, *Beyond Tragedy: Essays on the Christian Interpretation of History* (New York: Charles Scribner's Sons, 1937), 20–1.

150   Ved Mehta, *The New Theologian* (New York: Harper & Row, 1965), quote, 39; Gustave Weigel, "Authority in Theology," *Reinhold Niebuhr: His Religious, Social, and Political Thought*, 368–77; Niebuhr, "Reply to Interpretation and Criticism," reply to Weigel, 446; Emil Brunner, "Some Remarks on Reinhold Niebuhr's Work as a Christian Thinker," *Reinhold Niebuhr: His Religious, Social, and Political Thought*, 28–33; Niebuhr, "Intellectual Autobiography of Reinhold Niebuhr," 3.

151   John C. Bennett, "How My Mind Has Changed," *Christian Century* 76 (December 23, 1959), 1500; see Reinhold Niebuhr, "John Coleman Bennett: Theologian, Churchman, and Educator," *Theology and Church in Times of Change: Essays in Honor of John Coleman Bennett*, ed. Edward LeRoy Long Jr and Robert T. Handy (Philadelphia: Westminster Press, 1970), 233–6.

152   Michael Novak, "Needing Niebuhr Again," *Commentary*, 54 (September 1972), 52.

153   See ibid., 52–3.

154   Hans J. Morgenthau, "The Influence of Reinhold Niebuhr in American Political Life and Thought," in *Reinhold Niebuhr: A Prophetic Voice in Our Time*, 109; Tom Driver, Symposium on "Christian Realism: Retrospect and Prospect," *Christianity and Crisis* 28 (August 5, 1968), 179.

155   Richard Shaull participated in the 1968 *Christianity and Crisis* symposium on Christian realism, along with Driver, Alan Geyer, John C. Bennett, Harvey Cox, and Roger Shinn; Rubem A. Alves, "Christian Realism: Ideology of the Establishment," 176; see Shaull, "Christian Faith as Scandal in a Technocratic World," *New Theology*, 6, eds. Martin E. Marty and Dean G. Peerman, (New York: Macmillan Company, 1969); Shaull, *Heralds of a New Reformation: The Poor of South and North America*, (Maryknoll, NY: Orbis Books, 1984).

156   John C. Bennett, "The Social Interpretation of Christianity," *The Church Through Half a Century: Essays in Honor of William Adams Brown*, eds. Samuel Cavert and Henry Van Dusen (New York: Charles Scribner's Sons, 1936), 113.

157   Niebuhr, "John Coleman Bennett: Theologian, Churchman, and Educator," 235; see Robert Lee, *The Promise of Bennett* (Philadelphia: Lippincott, 1969); Henry Pitney Van Dusen, Preface to *Theology and Church in Times of Change: Essays in Honor of John Coleman Bennett*, 9.

158   Reinhold Niebuhr to John C. Bennett, June 10, 1930, Reinhold Niebuhr Papers, Library of Congress, Washington, DC; see Niebuhr, "Barth – Apostle of the Absolute," *Christian Century* 45 (December 13, 1928), 1523–4.

159   John C. Bennett, "After Liberalism – What?" *Christian Century* 50 (November 8, 1933), 1403.
160   Ibid., 1403–4.
161   Ibid., 1404.
162   Ibid., 1404–5.
163   John C. Bennett, "A Changed Liberal – But Still a Liberal," *Christian Century* 56 (February 8, 1939), 179–81, quotes, 179; see John C. Bennett, "A Critique of Paul Ramsey," *Christianity and Crisis* 27 (October 30, 1967), 247–50; Bennett, "How My Mind Has Changed," 1501–2.
164   Bennett, "A Changed Liberal – But Still a Liberal," quote, 179; Niebuhr, *An Interpretation of Christian Ethics*, 59–60.
165   John C. Bennett, *Social Salvation: A Religious Approach to the Problems of Social Change*, (New York: Charles Scribner's Sons, 1935), quotes vii, 69.
166   Ibid., 81.
167   Ibid., 90.
168   Ibid., 91.
169   Ibid., 91–2.
170   Ibid., 105–6; Ernst Troeltsch, *The Social Teaching of the Christian Churches*, 2 vols., trans. Olive Wyon (German edn. 1912; 1st English edn. 1931; Louisville: Westminster John Knox Press, 1992), 1: 728.
171   Bennett, *Social Salvation*, 133.
172   John C. Bennett, *Christian Realism* (New York: Charles Scribner's Sons, 1952), 33.
173   Ibid., 102; see John C. Bennett, "A Christian Perspective of the War," *The Friend* (March 1942), 29–31; Bennett, "The Churches and the War," *Christianity and Crisis* 2 (September 21, 1942), 1–2; Bennett, "American Christians and the War," *The Student World* 36 (First Quarter, 1943), 81–9; Bennett, "Being a Christian in Time of War," *The Church School* 2 (March 1943), 129–30, 189.
174   Bennett, *Christian Realism*, 104, 108.
175   Ibid., 110; see John C. Bennett, "The Hardest Problem for Christian Ethics," *Christianity and the Contemporary Scene*, eds. Randolph C. Miller and H. H. Shires (New York: Morehouse-Gorham, 1943), 119–31; Bennett, "The Christian as Soldier," *Christians Face War* (New York: Association Press/National Intercollegiate Christian Council, 1944), 25–30; Bennett, "The Christian Basis for Enduring Peace," *Approaches to World Peace*, ed. Lyman Bryson (New York: Harper & Brothers, 1944), 740–54.
176   Bennett, "A Changed Liberal – But Still a Liberal," 181; John C. Bennett, "Christian Ethics in Economic Life," in *Christian Values and Economic Life*, eds. Bennett, Howard R. Bowen, William Adams Brown, Jr and G. Bromley Oxnam (New York: Harper & Brothers, 1954), 213.
177   Bennett, "Christian Ethics and Forms of Economic Power," 238; John C. Bennett, "A Theological Conception of Goals for Economic Life," *Goals of Economic Life*, ed. A Dudley Ward (New York: Harper & Brothers, 1953), 397–429.
178   John C. Bennett, "The Oxford Conference," *The Chapel Bell* 16 (September 1937), 1–2; Bennett, "Church Unity and the Small Community," *Commonwealth Review* 22 (May 1940), 32–7; Bennett, "The Forms of Ecumenical Christianity," *Toward a World-wide Christianity*, ed. O. Frederick Nolde (New York: Harper & Brothers, 1946), 59–77; Bennett, "The Involvement of the Church," *Man's Disorder and God's Design*, Amsterdam Assembly Series (London: SCM Press, 1948), 91–102.
179   Bennett, "How My Mind Has Changed," 1501.
180   Ibid., 1501–2; see John C. Bennett, "Our Distorted View of Asia," *Christianity and Crisis* 15 (April 18, 1955), 41–2; Bennett, "Approaches to Communism," *Christianity and Crisis* 16 (June 11, 1956), 74–5; Bennett, "Beyond the 'Cold War'?" *Christianity and Crisis* 17 (June 24, 1957), 81–2; Bennett, "A Condition for Coexistence," *Christianity and Crisis* 38 (April 28, 1958), 53–4; Bennett, "Balancing the Risks in Nuclear Testing," *Christianity*

and Crisis 20 (April 18, 1960), 47; Bennett, "Beyond Frozen Positions in the Cold War," *Christianity and Crisis*, 24 (January 11, 1965), 269–70.

181 John C. Bennett, "The Geneva Conference 1966," *Christianity and Crisis* 26 (July 11, 1966), 153–4.

182 Paul Ramsey, *Who Speaks for the Church?: A Critique of the 1966 Geneva Conference on Church and Society* (Nashville: Abingdon Press, 1967), 84.

183 Ibid., 100, 90.

184 Ibid., 21.

185 John C. Bennett, "A Critique of Paul Ramsey," *Christianity and Crisis* 27 (October 30, 1967), 247.

186 Ibid., 248; see John C. Bennett, "Christian Realism in Vietnam," *America* (April 30, 1966), 616–17; Bennett, "It is Difficult to Be an American," *Christianity and Crisis* 26 (July 25, 1966), 165–6.

187 Bennett, "A Critique of Paul Ramsey," 249.

188 Paul Ramsey, "Farewell to Christian Realism," 1966, reprinted in Ramsey, *The Just War: Force and Political Responsibility* (1968; reprint, Lanham, MD: University Press of America, 1983), 487; Ramsey, "How Shall Counter-Insurgency War Be Conducted Justly?" 1966, reprinted in Ramsey, *The Just War*, 458.

189 John C. Bennett, "From Supporter of War in 1941 to Critic in 1966," *Christianity and Crisis* 26 (February 21, 1966), 14.

190 Bennett, "A Critique of Paul Ramsey," 249.

191 Ramsey, "A Farewell to Christian Realism," 488.

192 Bennett, "A Critique of Paul Ramsey," 249.

193 See Robert McAfee Brown, *Theology in a New Key: Responding to Liberation Themes*, (Philadelphia: Westminster Press, 1978); Beverly Wildung Harrison, *Making the Connections: Essays in Feminist Social Ethics* (Boston: Beacon Press, 1985).

194 Bennett, "Christian Realism: Retrospect and Prospect," 176.

195 John C. Bennett, *Christian Ethics and Social Policy* (New York: Scribners, 1946); Bennett, "Christian Realism: Retrospect and Prospect," quote 176.

196 John C. Bennett, "Continuing the Discussion: Liberation Theology and Christian Realism," *Christianity and Crisis* 33 (October 15, 1973), 197.

197 John C. Bennett, *The Radical Imperative: From Theology to Social Ethics* (Philadelphia: Westminster Press, 1975), 7–8, 9–10.

198 Ibid., 91; John C. Bennett, "A Protestant Looks at American Catholicism," *Facing Protestant – Roman Catholic Tensions*, ed. Wayne H. Cowan (New York: Association Press, 1960), 21–38; Bennett, "Church and State," *New Frontiers of Christianity*, ed. Ralph C. Raughley, Jr (New York: Association Press, 1962), 174–200.

199 Bennett, *The Radical Imperative: From Theology to Social Ethics*, 94.

200 James H. Cone, *Black Theology and Black Power* (New York: Seabury Press, 1969); Cone, *A Black Theology of Liberation* (Philadelphia: J. B. Lippincott Co., 1970); Gustavo Gutiérrez, *Teología de la liberación, Perspectivas* (Lima: CEP, 1971); Gutiérrez, *A Theology of Liberation: History, Politics and Salvation*, trans. and ed. Sr Caridad Inda and John Eagleson, (Maryknoll, NY: Orbis Books, 1973); Rosemary Radford Ruether, *Liberation Theology: Human Hope Confronts Christian History and American Power* (New York: Paulist/Newman Press, 1972); Mary Daly, *Beyond God the Father: Toward a Philosophy of Women's Liberation* (Boston: Beacon Press, 1973).

201 Ruether, *Liberation Theology*, 95; Bennett, *The Radical Imperative*, 109.

202 Bennett, *The Radical Imperative*, 109–19, quote 118.

203 Ibid., 119–31; Cone, *A Black Theology of Liberation*, 19.

204 Bennett, *The Radical Imperative*, 131–41, quotes 140.

Chapter 5

Social Christianity as Public Theology

Walter G. Muelder, James Luther Adams, John Courtney Murray, and Dorothy Day

For 30 years, Christian realism was nearly as dominant in social ethics as the social gospel had been for the previous 50 years. Yet for all its influence in defining an American theological generation, Christian realism did not have the field to itself as a general approach or even as a public theology. Old-style liberals continued to play an important role in shaping the field of social ethics, and Catholic theologians interpreted the social-ethical meaning of Christianity from different standpoints and relationships to the American story than the Niebuhrian realists.

For the liberals who held out against a tidal wave of polemics against their tradition, it helped if they were rooted in a version of liberalism that knew its own mind and felt no temptation to change course. That was the case with Walter G. Muelder, who was raised in "Boston personalism" and became its leading social ethicist, and James Luther Adams, who struggled to keep at least part of his Unitarian Universalist tradition in the Christian fold. Both were major contributors to the building of social ethics as an academic discipline, while also playing active roles in the church and public spheres. Both of them tempered liberal optimism with a chastened awareness of personal and collective evil, but did so as liberal descendants of the social gospel.

Roman Catholics, meanwhile, came slower to social ethics as a discipline, but developed distinct discourses expressing the social meaning of Catholic faith in modern, capitalist, individualistic, historically Protestant America. John Courtney Murray, a Jesuit priest and academic, was censured by the Vatican for his controversial theory of religious freedom, but was vindicated at Vatican II. Murray's role in changing Catholic doctrine on religious freedom made him a historic figure in the Catholic Church; more broadly, his creative and provocative thinking about religious pluralism made him a bellwether figure in Christian ethics as a whole. Dorothy Day was also a bellwether figure, and, to her annoyance, an icon. She belonged to no religious order, was not an academic, and wrote no books on social ethics, yet her contribution to Catholic social ethics was immense as the founder of the radical, theologically orthodox, pacifist Catholic Worker movement. In her work the understanding of Christianity as enemy-loving hospitality was renewed in the modern church.

The generation that advanced the social-ethical enterprise in the middle decades of the twentieth century took for granted that Christian morality cannot be divorced from politics and the public debate over the goals of a good society. It also agreed that Christian social ethics lacked a distinct method, while debating the desirability of having one.

Socializing Personalist Theory: Walter G. Muelder

Walter George Muelder was the leading proponent of a third generation tradition, the school of personalist idealism centered at Boston University, and one of the mid-century's four leading proponents of social ethics as a discipline, along with Niebuhr, Bennett, and James Luther Adams. To Muelder, personalism and social ethics fit perfectly together, especially after he improved personalist theory. After he retired from Boston Univesity, however, personalist theology and philosophy faded, while social ethics flourished.

As a theory and school of thought, so-called Boston personalism was founded in the late nineteenth and early twentieth centuries by Boston University philosopher Borden Parker Bowne, who taught that the soul is essentially active, it is known immediately as the experience of consciousness, and self-consciousness is the necessary presupposition of all thinking and the world of objects. The key to Bowne's system was the principle that personality is the single reality that cannot be explained by anything else. Personalist idealism was a theory of the transcendent reality of personal spirit and the organic unity of nature in spirit. Because science is necessarily mechanistic, Bowne argued, it cannot account for the reality or unity of consciousness. It is possible to move from mind to matter, but matter cannot be the ultimate or sufficient cause of mind. Bowne took experience as a whole as his datum, questioning how reality should be thought of on the basis of particular experiences as interpreted by thought. In major works on epistemology, metaphysics, ethics, and theism, he argued that while the reality of personal consciousness cannot be explained on impersonal grounds, everything can be accounted for by the reality of consciousness.[1]

Bowne told his students that Kant's demonstration of the primacy of the creative powers of mind over the things of sense was his greatest and permanent contribution to philosophy. With Kant he emphasized the creative role of mind in producing experience, the notion of the person as an ethical end-in-itself, and the reality of the world of things external to consciousness. At the same time, he rejected Kant's noumenal "thing-in-itself," because it failed to describe or secure the reality of an external world, and he insisted against Kant that purpose is constitutive in theoretical reason. Bowne allowed that purpose, because it plays little role in prereflective experience, does not quite belong on the same plane as the (Kantian) categories of being, space, time, and causality. But purpose is indispensable to reflective thought and is constitutive of it, he argued. The Kantian transcendentals by themselves leave us cut off from things and events. It is purpose – a higher category of thought – that unifies our fields of experience. Purpose is causality raised to the level of intelligent and volitional agency. In its higher forms, Bowne contended, thought has no basis of maintaining itself or of gaining systematic completeness without meaning. There is no knowing without intelligence, and intelligence is nothing without purpose.

With an air of victory he exhorted his students to proclaim the primacy of spirit over the things of sense and the superiority of metaphysics over other forms of understanding. Theologically Bowne was a liberal Methodist who affirmed a Schleiermacherian view of self-authenticating religious experience, a Schleiermacherian understanding of the divinity of Christ, and the Abelardian moral-influence theory of atonement. Ethically he was a strong voluntarist and neo-Kantian moralist whose individualism made him allergic to most social gospel causes. Bowne affirmed the social gospel principle that true religion is ethical without remainder and he supported feminism as a movement for individual rights. But he disdained trade unions, showed little feeling for people beneath his social class, showed no sense of outrage against racial injustice, and had no use for sociological perspectives.

His disciples were a bit slow to acquire the infrastructure and movement-momentum of a school, but by 1925, 15 years after Bowne's death, his brand of ideal-ism had an institutional center, a journal, a Borden Parker Bowne Chair at Boston University, and a movement consciousness. Like Bowne, Boston personalism was epistemologically dualistic, metaphysically pluralist, and ethical in orientation; unlike Bowne, it was a deeply social gospel phenomenon. In its second generation the per-sonalist school was led by prominent Methodist bishop Francis J. McConnell, who earned his doctorate under Bowne in 1899; Boston University theologian Albert Cornelius Knudson, who earned his doctorate under Bowne in 1900; University of Southern California (USC) philosopher Ralph T. Flewelling, who earned his doctorate under Bowne in 1909; and Boston University philosopher Edgar Sheffield Brightman, who studied under Bowne near the end of Bowne's life and earned his doctorate in 1912. McConnell championed the Methodist social gospel, introducing a large popular audience to personalist ideas; Knudson served as dean of the Boston University School of Theology, writing the personalist school's seminal theological texts; Flewelling led a contingent of West Coast personalists, publishing the school's journal, *The Personalist*; Brightman served as the Borden Parker Bowne Professor of Philosophy at Boston University, developing an influential neo-Hegelian version of personalist philosophy.

The second-generation personalists built and sustained an impressive school. Under Bowne's influence, the personalist language of "personality" and "personal spirit" was appropriated by a wide variety of American liberal theologians and pastors, and in its second generation, Bowne-style personalism made significant gains in the church and academy. It became a dominant force in American Methodist seminaries, changed American Methodist theology, and won new respect in the philosophical field, the latter mostly on Brightman's account. Philosophically, personalism was a patchwork of idealist philosophies centered on the metaphysical primacy of consciousness; theologi-cally, it synthesized the distinctive trademarks of the Kantian, Schleiermacherian, Hegelian, and Ritschlian streams of liberal theology, although it was a bit short on Ritschlian historical consciousness. With Kant it affirmed the ethical character of true religion; with Schleiermacher it proclaimed that spiritual experience is the basis of religion; with Hegel it insisted that religion is meaningless without metaphysical claims; with the Ritschlian school it embraced the social gospel and the liberal picture of Jesus. After two generations it gave the appearance of theological permanence. Brightman's writings made personalism respectable in philosophy, and Knudson's works in apolo-getics, systematic theology, and ethics were foundational for modern Methodism.[2]

Just as the second generation of personalist leaders remembered Bowne with glow-ing praise, always paying tribute to his brilliant and inspiring classroom performances and writings, the third generation of Boston personalists lauded the rigor, piety, and success of their teachers, Knudson and Brightman. Two years after Walter Muelder assumed the deanship of Boston University's School of Theology, in 1947, he wrote that it filled him with awe "to stand in the chancel of Robinson Chapel where Knudson and the others have preached and prayed." His third-generation colleagues – theologian L. Harold De Wolf, theologian S. Paul Schilling, and philosopher Peter A. Bertocci – shared that feeling. All were Brightman protégés for whom it was difficult to resist the verdict that personalist thought was already thoroughly well formulated. Muelder came to be the leading personalist of his generation by strengthening its theory in its weakest area.[3]

Born in Boody, Illinois, in 1907, Muelder was fond of saying that he came to personalism and the social gospel by birth. His father, Epke Hermann Muelder, was a German-speaking immigrant and Methodist pastor who hauled his wife and three young children to Boston University in 1908 to clarify his religious beliefs. Having been taught to loathe liberal theology, Epke Muelder studied under Bowne and Knudson, earned his divinity degree in 1909, witnessed Bowne's fatal stroke during class in 1910, and completed his doctorate in 1913. At Boston University he found what Walter later called "a gospel he could preach without fear or favor and with compassion to his generation." Epke Muelder embraced Bowne's philosophy and the social gospel of Walter Rauschenbusch. He and his wife Minnie added four more children to their family during Walter's youth, moving repeatedly from one small Methodist parish assignment to another in Illinois, Iowa, and Wisconsin, barely eking out a living. Walter Muelder later recalled that notwithstanding his family's warmth and liberal spirit, "it was a very difficult life." Because of his family background "it was almost natural for me to walk in the way of personalistic philosophical theology and of social Christianity."[4]

He earned his college degree at Knox College in 1927 and followed his father to Boston University's School of Theology, where Muelder earned a divinity degree in 1930, moved straight into the doctoral program, earned a Borden Parker Bowne fellowship, took a year of study at Frankfurt, wrote a dissertation under Brightman on Ernst Troeltsch's philosophy of history, and graduated in 1933. For six years he taught at Berea College, then taught for five years at USC before returning to his alma mater in 1945 as Dean and Professor of Social Ethics.[5]

Muelder's return to Boston University was very much an intellectual and personal homecoming. He was already a full-fledged social gospeler, personalist, pacifist, and Socialist before he arrived at Boston University the first time, as a student. In 1928 he represented the seminary at a biennial meeting of the Federal Council of Churches and was thrilled to meet church leaders whose social gospel fervor matched his own. On the ethics of war Muelder's guides were Mohandas Gandhi, Harry Emerson Fosdick, and Kirby Page. On social ethics he was devoted to Rauschenbusch, like his father. On the religious life he treasured William James' *Varieties of Religious Experience*, Rudolf Otto's *The Idea of the Holy*, and James Bissett Pratt's *The Religious Consciousness*, which valorized mystical experience. On social theory he was deeply influenced by Troeltschian liberalism and the neo-Marxist socialism of the Frankfurt Schoolers with whom he studied in 1930–1 – Paul Tillich, Karl Mannheim, and Max Horkheimer. Philosophically and theologically he was a straightforward disciple of Bowne, Knudson, and especially Brightman.

Muelder affirmed Bowne's emphasis on the self as conscious experience, the epistemological dualism of idea and object, and the interrelation of faith and reason. On issues that divided Brightman and Knudson – especially Brightman's theories of divine temporality and finitude, and his Hegelian thesis that truth is the whole – Muelder sided with Brightman, who had been a classmate of his father's. He also accepted Brightman's beliefs that synoptic method includes and is superior to the analytical, coherence is the best criterion of truth when it includes empirical and rational coherence, the ideal moral laws are objectively real, and reality is an organic personal monism qualified by the pluralism of finite persons. These positions remained foundational for Muelder's thought. By the time that he graduated from Boston University, however, he already had a vague sense of the convictions that would distinguish him from his teacher.[6]

Muelder wrote his doctoral dissertation on the problem of wholes in Troeltsch's philosophy of history, which helped him discern what was lacking in Brightman's theory of personality. Brightman charged that Bowne's theory of the self was short on psychological facts, but Brightman's debt to social science stopped at psychology. Muelder, studying Troeltsch's historicism, realized that Bowne and Brightman were both ahistorical and individualistic in their focus on the self as conscious experience. Troeltsch theorized that history consists fundamentally of "individual totalities" – *wholes* that synthesize psychical processes and natural conditions. Historical wholes are original, partly unconscious, integral unities of meaning and value that possess a common spirit or mind; his examples included families, social classes, states, cultural epochs, revolutions, and schools of thought. Against Hegel's statism and absolute monism, Troeltsch taught that social analysis must take individual persons seriously as empirically given totalities, for all historical wholes reverberate with creative personality. Though people interact with impersonal forces in physical environments, personality is the bearer of common spirit – the relation of individual and society – and the key to meaning and value.[7]

Muelder adapted Troeltsch's personalism and study of social wholes to his own more evangelical theology, which strengthened his rejection of positivism and belief in organic pluralism. In personalist terms, he reasoned, personality is a principle of individuality, human community, and ultimate reality. Because the category of "personality" applies univocally to both divine reality and the individual person, the essential problems of Christian ethics are those of the self's relation to oneself, other finite persons, and ultimate personality. Theology and theological ethics read off from that which is given, which is the social bond between finite persons and divine reality, as well as the problems of ideal ends and their realization. Christian morality is not Christian if it is not directed toward ideal ends that are aspects of ideal personality, Muelder taught. The heart of any genuinely Christian ethic is the teaching of Jesus that human beings have infinite value as children of God.[8]

Troeltsch's project was essentially a philosophy of history, but Bowne, Knudson, and Brightman had little historical consciousness. Under Troeltsch's influence, Muelder developed a historical-communitarian theory of personality. Development is temporal, practical, inherently teleological, and loaded with meaning and value, he reasoned. All experience is mediated and historical; there is no such thing as pure contemplation or an impartial bystander. Thus theory and practice are necessarily related, as Marx and James insisted; religious thinkers must take seriously the historical conditionedness of all experience and reason. This did not mean that theologians had to follow Troeltsch into historical relativism. In his later career Troeltsch surrendered the idea of personality as a universal principle, arguing that personality is a Christian concept and that Christianity is merely the best religion for the West. In Muelder's view, that was historicism run amok. It was not necessary to give up the metaphysical principle of personality merely because some cultures and civilizations did not appeal to personality, or because some religions sought redemption by escaping from personality. Muelder stuck with Troeltsch's early vision of historical development as the shaping of future community life in accordance with universal and ideal norms, upholding personalism as a brake against the later Troeltsch's relativism. It is possible to make room for relativity without falling prey to relativism, he reasoned. This was precisely the achievement of Brightman's organic and pluralistic personalism, though Brightman unfortunately paid little attention to history.

Muelder proposed that personalist theory was not necessarily ahistorical. The ideal of individual fulfillment transcends every historical epoch, but personality is not a static phenomenon. Because human experience is temporal, it is always implicated in the historical process; because human experience is always social and historical, there is such a thing as a social mind. Countering Bowne's exaltation of the individual mind as the repository of personality, Muelder argued that the "social mind" – a concept that he borrowed from sociologist John Elof Boodin – exists on the same level as that of personal minds. The social mind is the total content of objective spirit. It is not distinct from personal minds, Muelder reasoned, but exists within them. The total content of the social mind transcends the limitations of individual minds, which participate in the social mind and achieve awareness of each other through it.[9]

This theory of the social mind, which Muelder usually called "the communitarian dimension of personality," was his original contribution to personalist theory. He developed it in the 1930s and refined it throughout his career. For years he puzzled over Boodin's claim that intersubjective continuity is substantive. Did the social mind contain a real compounding of will and consciousness? If it contained a real fusion of wills, what happened to the integrity of the individual person? How was one to understand or secure the consciousness of personal privacy? Muelder settled on the view that the social mind consists of energy fields that interact with each other and within which persons interact. Social interaction takes place on both levels, below consciousness and on the level of shared meanings. But these were secondary issues; however the intersubjective continuities of the social mind should be theorized, what mattered was that experience is social. The consciousness of objective spirit exists in individual minds, which participate in it and achieve awareness of each other through it. The self is not an individual center of experience that is merely influenced by its social environment, as Bowne imagined; it *is* its social experience and unique individual experience. The self is conscious, the individual person is self-conscious, and both are historical and therefore temporal.

This did not mean, for Muelder, that the self is merely a collection of social relations. In his theory the self was a real subject – he called it "a *socius* with a private center." A self develops and becomes known by sharing its experiences and meanings with others. With Bowne and Brightman, Muelder affirmed that each person acts from a creative center, personality means freedom, and the highest virtue of personality is love. Beyond them he contended that because "personality" is always a social whole with an individual center, it must be conceived as a historical-communitarian category. Because personality is the most concrete category of existence and value, it is in personality that existing wholes and the highest existing value are both apprehended.[10]

Muelder's early writings crackled with prophetic passion and youthful idealism. For six years he taught in the midst of Appalachian poverty at Berea College and played a leadership role in the local Socialist party; during his five years at USC he chaired the Los Angeles Church Federation's Commission on Race Relations and protested against America's wartime internment of Japanese Americans. After he became a middle-aged seminary dean and theorist of "the responsible society," his writings lost their prophetic crackle, but Muelder remained a committed pacifist and democratic socialist. In December 1944, nine months before he returned to the School of Theology as its dean, he wrote a fervent piece on the need of a revolutionary pacifism, "A Philosophy for Post-War Pacifism," that raised the hackles of Methodist conservatives. Muelder urged fellow pacifists to prepare for a postwar postcolonial world. The West was not prepared for the revolutionary challenges of postcolonialism, he warned; for that matter, neither were American Christian pacifists:

> Unless the revolutionary energies unleashed around the world in the last half decade are permitted to find creative and constructive expression in terms of rapidly expanding freedoms, self-government, and human equality, the remainder of the present century is bound to resemble a downward spiral, a maelstrom sucking into its vortex of violence more and more of the institutions of civilization.[11]

American pacifism was at a low point, Muelder acknowledged. America's intervention in World War II had broad popular support, pacifists felt defensive, and the civil rights of conscientious objectors were often violated. Many pacifists felt additionally defensive because the US government's provision of alternative service for conscientious objectors raised serious questions about the ethics of supporting the war in alternative ways. Moreover, the pacifist movement lacked a unifying philosophy. It was a grab-bag of Gandhian sentiments, sayings of Jesus, and bits and pieces of various radical philosophies and traditions that often conflicted with each other. Muelder noted that anarchist and collectivist pacifism had almost nothing in common, and both contradicted most Christian pacifisms. American pacifism was therefore weak, demoralized, defensive, and morally confused.

From a practical standpoint, he allowed, it was a good thing to have many kinds of pacifism. People committed themselves to nonviolence in different ways and for various reasons. But Muelder had a higher ambition for Christian pacifism than accepting the eclectic status quo. The antiwar movement needed a "synoptic and coherent philosophy" that unified nonviolent theory and practice; for Muelder that was a Christian mission. What was needed was a unifying Christian philosophy that compellingly theorized God's loving nature, the human person, and the social order, as well as the ethical implications of gospel ideals, the reality of personality, and the methods of social change. To the objection that theology and metaphysics were inherently divisive and abstract, Muelder replied that the movement needed good first principles. The evils of communism and fascism were rooted in morally repugnant cosmologies: "First principles function as long-time purposes, and the conceptions inevitably canalize the resources of energy and power."[12]

Christian pacifists were obliged to proclaim the reality of religious truth, Muelder admonished, for Christianity was the living of Christ's way; it was a way of life that said "yes" to the light. Besides believing that Christian pacifism was the true way of life, Muelder believed in the transformational potential of the world's antiwar movements. In 1944 he judged that pacifists already showed distinctive concern over "the conflicts of race, their implications in economic exploitation, imperialism, culture, distance and the like." If religious pacifists allowed the light to open into "wider and wider vistas," it might yet save the world, penetrating "deeper and deeper" into the hearts of people and the chaos of the world: "The movement must be fearlessly mystical, fearlessly practical, and fearlessly intellectual."[13]

Muelder subsequently toned down his rhetoric, but not his principled commitments to pacifism, democratic socialism, racial justice, the social gospel, and the flourishing of personality. Church conservatives bitterly protested his appointment as seminary dean in 1945; five years later they erupted again when *Reader's Digest* published an exposé on "Methodism's Pink Fringe." Written by Stanley High, a member of the Federal Council of Churches' Commission on International Relations and a former liberal, the article identified Muelder as a leader of "a powerful and growing" left-wing movement in American Christianity that represented "a serious liability for Protestant-ism as a whole." High warned of sinister motives: "That such a left-wing minority is officially tolerated is, in itself, an indication of the success of their tactics in concealing their real aims behind a humanitarian facade." The controversy over Muelder's appoint-ment and the article made life difficult for him. At a personal low-point he submitted his resignation to university president Daniel L. Marsh, who refused to accept it. For many years Muelder kept a copy of the letter in his pocket as a reminder that no position was worth compromising his integrity. Often he counseled students to make sure that if they got fired, make it for good reasons. During his tenure the School of Theology increasingly reflected his theology and politics.[14]

Boston personalism had a spotty record on racial justice, owing especially to Bowne's and Knudson's underwhelming interest in it, but during Muelder's tenure the School of Theology became a leading educational force for integration. Muelder taught that American race prejudice was a culturally generated evil that could be overcome by integrating American society and providing equal opportunity to social goods. He was slow to conceive racism in structural terms, since Muelder reasoned there was only one race and the doctrines of creation and redemption had no barriers; moreover, as a socialist he tended to subsume racial injustice under class exploitation. Muelder changed his mind upon reading Gunnar Myrdal's *An American Dilemma* and witnessing the struggles of the early civil rights movement. Racism was structural, he concluded; ideas about racial superiority and inferiority were separable, individual totalities welded into multiple layers of culture, economy, and society. Following Myrdal and political sociologist Robert M. MacIver, Muelder began to say that racism was a distinct problem with multiple and cumulative causes, and to take it seriously as a moral problem was to give high priority to racial integration.

To Muelder, integration was not about adopting uniform cultural manners and beliefs. It was about the rights and opportunities of individuals and social groups to participate as equals in society; thus it required accepting cultural difference. Segregated America equated community with identity, discriminating against African Americans to maintain the integrity of white American culture. Following MacIver, Muelder countered that difference and separateness were not the same thing. The acceptance of difference led to true community, not separatism. Moreover, American Christians were called to show that integration worked. Muelder admonished that in this area especially, actions were more important than words. The most important thing that Christians could do to advance the cause of racial justice was to practice integration in their innermost fellowship.[15]

To an unusual degree he combined prophetic fervor and institutional realism. Muelder was disciplined, rigorous, and charitable in his thinking and personal bearing. He advocated social gospel ideals, but always with an institutionalist's wary eye for selfishness, collective egotism, structural evil, and inertia. To Muelder, America's racial pathology was the supreme example of evil reproduced in social structures with multiple and cumulative causes. Myrdal's *An American Dilemma* taught him how to talk about it beyond the language of moral ideals that he learned from the social gospel, but to Muelder, taking structural evil seriously was a major reason to stick with the social gospel.

He stressed that Rauschenbusch showed the way, holding together gospel ideals and social structural realities. Though Rauschenbusch appealed to the creative possibilities of human nature, Muelder observed, he also recognized the limitations of bourgeois moralism and the harsh realities of the class struggle: "He had neither a merely optimistic view of human nature, nor a belief in inevitable progress, nor a lack of understanding of what Marx so realistically stated." Rauschenbusch was a pioneer, championing important truths that others neglected, including the terrible reality of collective evil. Muelder liked him on cooperation, responsibility, and competition, especially his insistence that competition created a reign of fear that thwarted the values of the kingdom. Rauschenbusch was a salvation preacher, Muelder stressed; he proclaimed the power of the gospel to redeem individuals and the social order, which earned him a host of insults: moralist, idealist, sentimentalist, utopian. Muelder replied that Rauschenbusch made gospel claims and he was neither sentimental nor utopian. Neo-orthodoxy may have scored a few points against him, but it did wrong in disparaging the greatest social gospeler, and it certainly did not improve on him. To Muelder, "Rauschenbusch was undoubtedly working along the correct line," one to which modern Christianity needed to return with sharper social scientific tools.[16]

Two generations after Rauschenbusch wrote sizzling prose and spoke of Christianizing the social order, Muelder wrote workmanlike prose and spoke of "the responsible society." Both sought to persuade and inspire, but in very different times. At its inaugural assembly in Amsterdam in 1948 the World Council of Churches (WCC) condemned the denial of freedom under Communism and the denial of social justice under *laissez-faire* capitalism, calling for an ethic of "the responsible society" that mediated between the Communist and non-Communist worlds. Muelder embraced the spirit and language of this call. In 1952 he joined the WCC's Faith and Order Commission, which he served for 23 years. "The conception of a responsible society commands respect when seen in contrast to ideologically extreme positions," he wrote in 1953. Against the dogmatism and one-sidedness of ideological extremism, responsible thinking was constructive, morally reflective, and moderate. It accepted the dialectical unity of accommodation to reality and prophetic criticism.[17]

There were two governing, rival ideologies in American politics, Muelder observed: *laissez-faire* capitalism and welfare state capitalism. The former heralded the virtue of economic freedom and worshipped at the shrine of the free market; the latter called for social justice and sometimes made an idol of cradle-to-grave security. Muelder's writings featured pro and con classroom analyses of both ideologies, favoring the welfare state. Repeatedly he supported his position with statements by the WCC and other ecumenical assemblies. Just as the early church grappled with the tensions between its pacifist/egalitarian ethic of love and its responsibilities as a social institution, he observed, the modern labor movement had to negotiate between the socialist ideal and the accommodations of business unionism. Similarly, the modern church struggled in new ways with the dialectic of the early church. What was needed was a reasonable, ethical politics of the common good that took seriously the infinite value of personality. Drawing on theology, ethics, and the social sciences, especially Ashley Montagu's cultural anthropology, Muelder marshaled a case for a constructive politics of cooperation: "If we believe that man is more basically cooperative than he is competitive, as science and social experience seem to confirm, then that fact ought to inspire us with faith that practical realism is on the side of mutuality."[18]

That was the tone and theme of his signature work, *Religion and Economic Responsibility* (1953), which called for "new instruments of cooperation and the development of trade and national economies." Muelder repeated the WCC's strictures against Communist dogmatism, materialism, determinism, and atheism, adding that "the ruthless methods used by Communists in dealing with their opponents violate the most elementary principles of personal dignity." The Communist distortion of socialism was "shallow and self-defeating," he judged. In the Soviet Union, communism established a vast prison of "totalitarian state slave-labor," rejected God and objective spiritual laws, and erected a tyrannical dictatorship. At the same time he shared and helped to shape the WCC's opposition to Cold War militancy. Muelder cautioned that Communist ideology derived much of its animating egalitarian core from Christianity, and the Soviet Union had to be dealt with constructively as a major world power. There was no alternative to forging cooperative relations with Soviet communism and its client states, and Christianity had a vital role to play in creating a responsible world community: "Christians everywhere are called upon to evolve a social program which will unite the Christian resources of the world in a constructive and vital community which combines both the truth in collectivist philosophies and the truth in the philosophies of freedom, with *Christian criticism of all economic and political orders*."[19]

The founding of the WCC provided ballast for Muelder's ambitions for world Christianity; it also gave him a way to speak as a moderate institutional ethicist without forsaking his personal commitments to pacifism and democratic socialism. In 1954 he served as a consultant to the WCC's Second Assembly in Evanston, Illinois, and co-chaired its Commission on the Co-operation of Men and Women in Church and Society. His major work, *Foundations of the Responsible Society* (1959), laid the groundwork for his vision of the responsible society by appealing to WCC statements at the Amsterdam and Evanston assemblies. In a responsible society, the WCC declared at Amsterdam, people were allowed to control, criticize, and change their government; power was "made responsible by law and tradition"; power was distributed "as widely as possible through the whole community"; and all citizens possessed the rights to equality of opportunity and economic justice. Muelder allowed that this formulation reflected the Western, democratic, Christian backgrounds of WCC leaders, but he contended that freedom and democracy were not exclusively Western ideals which stood in judgment over all societies. In his characterization, the idea of the responsible society was "a Gestalt or a dynamic moral pattern" that applied critically to the entire world community. At Amsterdam, he conceded, the WCC was not as even-handed as it presumed, since it paired its condemnation of something that actually existed (communism) with something that existed only in the imagination of ideologues (*laissez-faire* capitalism). The WCC was in no position to come out against welfare state capitalism.[20]

Muelder expected the WCC to become less Western-dominated, but no less committed to freedom and democracy as it fulfilled its pledge to "speak boldly in Christ's name both to those in power and to the people, to oppose terror, cruelty and race discrimination, to stand by the outcast, the prisoner and the refugee." In his rendering the idea of a responsible society entailed being morally and spiritually responsible to God, respecting persons as intrinsically valuable, recognizing personality as the ground of all values, upholding freedom as the free and full development of personality, and making freedom responsible for social justice. Though he acknowledged that the ecumenical movement had little chance of agreeing on the meaning of socioeconomic freedom, Muelder enthused that it stood on the side of justice and equality. Between 1925 and 1939 the ecumenical conferences that laid the groundwork for the WCC called for distributive economic justice, cooperation between labor and capital, and progressive policies on social issues. Postwar ecumenism was more cautious on economics, he allowed, and it recognized that establishing efficient production was as important as economic distribution, but it continued to affirm that the state alone held the power and authority "to act as trustee for society as a whole." The ecumenical movement could make its peace with mixed capitalism, but not libertarian ideology.[21]

Muelder believed that social democracy and modern ecumenical Christianity were helping to create responsible state governments in the West; for a pacifist he could be remarkably sanguine on this theme. The state needed power to secure justice, and justice was unattainable without mercy and humility, he argued. The gold standard was a dialectic that held justice, power, mercy, and humility together. The best solution to the problem of justice was a responsible state, which already existed in the West's most advanced democracies. The responsible state was responsible to God and the people, and it encouraged people to use the state and other instrumentalities to advance the cause of social responsibility. Though the ecumenical movement lacked a normative theory of the state, it took for granted the state's practical necessity. Karl Barth, for example, railed against the WCC's policy-oriented ethical positions, arguing that ethicists like Muelder and Reinhold Niebuhr spent too much time trying to influence government policy. Yet Barth was a democratic socialist who assumed the necessity of a strong state. Muelder admonished that powerful ideological and corporate forces did not make that assumption; ecumenical Christianity had to address the fear-driven opposition to government and state power that fueled sizable currents in Western politics, especially in the US dictatorial abuses of state power had to be condemned, he affirmed, "but a generalized fear reinforces certain tendencies toward misanthropy." Simply to fear government power without distinguishing between good and bad uses of it simply increased the power of fear.[22]

Muelder envisioned a world ecumenical movement and an interdisciplinary field of Christian social ethics that promoted good government: "An overemphasis on the idea of power and the negative function of the state in using physical force inhibits creative thought on how the state, conceived as a limited but responsible association, can be constructively developed as a servant of justice and freedom, perhaps even love." With Plato, Aristotle, and Hegel he reasoned that because human beings were communitarian by nature, the subordination of individuals to social institutions could not be evil in principle. The state was a social construct and, ideally, a responsible association that upheld the rights of individuals and enabled their self-realization. It needed to be as powerful as its responsibilities for the general welfare required. On policy particulars Muelder advocated racial integration, progressive income taxes, expansion of the cooperative sector, responsible consumption, and the right to collective bargaining: "It is an irresponsible social policy to seek to destroy the integrity of labor unions under the guise of the so-called 'right to work.'"[23]

In foreign affairs he called for an antimilitarist, liberal–international policy that respected human rights and secured cooperative agreements on trade and security issues. He lauded the WCC for stressing the peacemaking common ground between pacifist and non-pacifist Christian ethics. The ecumenical movement declared repeatedly that violence in war had become indiscriminate, war created worse problems than it solved, the moral bounds of just war theory were eviscerated by modern weapons and warfighting strategy, and war was always a manifestation of evil. Muelder, while cautioning against duping for deceptive peace fronts, urged Christians to support the rights of genuine conscientious objectors to war and blasted McCarthy-style anti-Communism for whipping up a frenzy of fear and persecution: "In our time the worst public injustices are perpetrated in the name of anti-Communism and rooting out subversives. At the moment in America many people are afraid to be openly and honestly engaged in constructive peacemaking which is critical of the nation's foreign policies." A decent society did not make its citizens afraid to dissent from government policy, Muelder admonished.[24]

Moral Theory, Culture, and Christian Social Ethics

In the mid-1950s Muelder served on the WCC's Commission on the Cooperation of Men and Women in Church and Society, which provided a forum for his view that social justice applied to women. Bluntly he denounced "the present pattern of male domination" in American church and society. In secular culture, he observed, important questions about sex roles in family structure and society were being raised – "The right relation of men and women has become radically problematic in today's world." The churches, however, dodged the issue. One culprit was the regnant neo-orthodoxy in theology, Muelder noted; Barth treated Ephesians 5 as the last word on the subject, as did neo-orthodox biblical scholar Floyd V. Filson. Even liberal scholars tried to wring as much progressive content as they could from the biblical motif of mutual submission. Muelder had limited patience with exegetical exercises of that sort – "I am always suspicious when this process takes place." Since the question was a phenomenon of cultural change, it troubled and amazed him that theologians ignored social scientific analysis of it.[25]

"Scientific studies of culture have shown that significant changes in one aspect of culture have effects in all other aspects of culture," he observed. "No one aspect of culture is always the cause of changes elsewhere. Causation in a complex cultural whole is pluralistic and tends to be cumulative." Since cultural change was always caused by dependent variables of differing intensities and power, Muelder argued, no particular factor related to biblical teaching, economic interest, social convention, or anything else was ever fully definitive or determinative. To make intelligent judgments about the rights of women and the relations of women and men, Christian theologians had to address "the whole range of cultural expression." It was ridiculous to settle disputes over women's rights by quoting Christian scripture and tradition, because Christian scripture and tradition were culturally conditioned and Christian claims addressed the total culture, not merely the Christian community: "The Church must be aware of the extent to which its Scriptures, tradition, and life reflect culture if it is to take creative initiative in transforming its own institutional life, the family, the work world, and society as a whole."[26]

Centuries of Hebrew tribalism, patriarchy, Hellenistic dualism, and asceticism lay behind traditional Christian thinking about sexuality, Muelder stressed; in his view, modern Christianity had to sweep away much of it: "Now that we have approached a period of radical reconception it is amazing how little the centuries have to contribute to the concrete analysis of masculinity and femininity and the formulation of responsible relations of men and women to each other." The point was not merely that modern Christianity had new answers to old problems. More important were the new questions: What should the church do to help men recognize and cooperate with women as equals? What should it do to foster men's acceptance of women as equals or superiors in positions of authority? What assumptions should women and men make about each other in interpersonal relations? How should the church address the fact that ambitious women often internalized masculine values? Muelder worried that the church was failing to address these questions because, as in other professions, not many women were training to enter positions of authority. Thus, women exerted little pressure to reform the church's teaching and practices. In 1958, he observed, the proportion of women enrolled in graduate professional schools was no greater than in 1918, although absolute figures were higher. Muelder blamed the regnant culture of early marriage and a popular tendency to ignore the culture-changing implications of social changes that had already taken place. Speaking for his gadfly WCC commission on gender roles, he urged the church to play a leading role in facilitating social and religious reform: "It is imperative that we draw upon the redemptive resources of our faith in order to achieve the full benefit of the mutual responsibility and fellowship within the Church and at the same time contribute to better interpersonal relationships in the family, the work situation, and society in general."[27]

Muelder stuck to ideal principles, but was sensitive to cultural relativity, always ready to rethink the meaning of his principles for new issues or circumstances. He treasured his work for the WCC, yet regretted that the churches united only for functions that they could not perform separately: "They institutionalize their disunity by organized cooperation." He wanted Christian social ethics to develop into a coherent discipline, yet admitted that his work reflected the eclectic and issue-oriented character of the field as it had developed thus far. Like the field in general, Muelder blended theology, the social sciences, and philosophy, drawing on disciplines that possessed a relative autonomy. At the same time, like most of the third generation personalists, only more so in his case, Muelder's commitment to personalist idealism gave his thinking a steady anchor. He stuck with his core positions, went through no phases, and made no major changes of mind. He epitomized the pragmatic progressivism of mid-century ecumenical Protestantism, specializing in middle axioms that mediated between the universality of moral principles and the relativity of particular needs. Unlike John Bennett, Muelder did not appeal to a moral consensus or common ground. For him, middle axioms were moral laws of choice that the ethicist invoked after establishing their coherence with Christian moral belief. Middle axioms were more concrete than ultimate norms and less concrete than specific decisions in particular situations. They provided guidelines for action, allowing Muelder to take seriously the relativity of experience and history without falling into relativism.[28]

Muelder was passionately committed to Bowne's personalist idealism, though he socialized and historicized Bowne's theory of the self. He was equally committed to Brightman's theory of moral laws, though he embraced Harold DeWolf's communitarian additions to it. To Brightman, ethics was "the normative science of morals." Like any science, ethics assumed the existence of its object; in this case the object was the existence of universal moral truths. There were three types of moral laws, Brightman reasoned – formal, axiological, and personalistic. The formal laws described the norms to which a reasonable will must conform; the axiological laws described the values (ends) that a reasonable will should seek to realize; the personalistic laws described the higher values that derived from regarding personality as an intrinsic value without which no other values exist.[29]

Brightman's theory was unapologetically rationalistic. Reason is open to Christian experience and revelation, he assured, but Christian claims had to be established by the same rational norms that adjudicated claims of other kinds. Moving from the abstract to the concrete, and in a progressive fashion that made each law dependent upon and inclusive of the laws that preceded it, his system described two formal principles (the laws of logic and autonomy), six axiological principles (the laws of value, consequences, best possible, specification, most inclusive end, and ideal control), and culminated with three personalistic principles (the laws of individualism, altruism, and the ideal of personality).

The first formal law was that all persons ought to will logically; the second was straight from Kant, that only rationally derived, self-imposed moral laws are imperative. Of Brightman's axiological laws, the law of value posited that all persons ought to choose self-consistent and coherent values; the law of consequences asserted that the foreseeable consequences of an act must always be considered; the law of best possible declared that all persons ought to will the best possible values in every situation; the law of specification was about developing the values that are specifically relevant to particular situations; the law of most inclusive end commended living in a way that realizes the widest possible range of value; and the law of ideal control was about controlling one's consequence-regarding empirical values by ideal values such as "love your enemies." To Brightman, all the moral laws were imperatives that reason discovered in moral experience taken as a whole, but the personalist laws were foundational for all moral existence and the highest of the moral laws. The law of individualism was about realizing in one's own experience the maximum value of which one is capable in harmony with moral law; the law of altruism stated that all persons ought to respect other persons as moral ends-in-themselves and cooperate with others in the realization of shared values; the law of the ideal of personality stated that all persons ought to be guided by their ideal conception of personality as an individual and social reality, in harmony with the other moral laws.[30]

Brightman's disciples were deeply influenced by this scheme, even though it made little impact in his time, unlike his theorizing on personality and divine finitude. DeWolf featured Brightman's system in his courses on ethics, added communitarian principles to it, and presumably taught it to Martin Luther King, Jr. To Muelder, Brightman's moral philosophy was a nearly perfect blend of rationalistic philosophical idealism and modern theology. It held together a rational approach to ethics, an insistence on the existence of universal moral truths, recognition of contextual relativity, and the personalistic content of Christian morality. Like Brightman, Muelder used the terms "law" and "principle" interchangeably, while DeWolf and Peter Bertocci favored the more fluid term "principle," reasoning that Brightman's references to moral laws gave a misleading impression of rigidity. On the issue that separated them from their mentor, Muelder and DeWolf acknowledged that Brightman's thinking was not completely lacking in social consciousness. Brightman had strong personal commitments on peace and social justice issues, and he recognized that personality has social dimen-

sions. He formulated his personalist moral laws, especially the law of the ideal personality, to do justice to the social aspects of morality and personality.

But his emphasis was overwhelmingly on the individual person as the center of
consciousness and will. Brightman worried that Muelder's communitarianism elevated
groups to a status that belonged to personal centers of experience alone; Muelder and
DeWolf judged that this concern made personalist idealism too individualistic. Thus
they amplified the social implications of Brightman's personalist moral laws. DeWolf's
lectures on ethics added three communitarian principles and a culminating metaphysical
principle to Brightman's system, which Muelder adopted. The first "additional" law,
which DeWolf called the "principle" of cooperation, made a self-standing principle
of the second half of Brightman's law of altruism, stating that "all persons ought as far
as possible to cooperate with other persons in the production and enjoyment of shared
values." Muelder noted that this principle, like the ecumenical movement, lifted
human interdependence and community to the level of a primal human need and a
spiritual unity. The second communitarian principle, the law of social devotion, was
that all persons ought to serve the best interests of the group and "subordinate personal
gain to social gain." This principle simply rephrased Brightman's laws of the best possible and ideal control, but in a way that put the key point more plainly. Muelder
explained that the highest good, which Christians called the kingdom of God, is
morally higher than the interest of any self. In the language of British idealist T. H.
Green, each person's real self is higher than his or her bare individuality. Noting that
the law of social devotion lifted up "the principle of the sensitized social conscience
at work everywhere in society," Muelder remarked, "It may at times command
revolution."[31]

The last moral law was the ideal of community. Expanding on Brightman's ideal
of personality, it stated that persons ought to stand for values and ideals that promote
the ideal of community. Thus it brought out the communal content of Brightman's
laws of the best possible, most inclusive end, and ideal control. "This is the principle
of inclusive responsibility, personal and communitarian, at once pluralistic and organic,"
Muelder observed. "In itself it is neither centralist nor decentralist, socialist nor capitalist, and it decides for neither world federalism nor any one political instrumentation.
Yet it does confirm and emphasize the supremacy of personal worth and the idea of
responsible society." Moral theory at the level of moral science did not answer the
question of whether nonviolent resistance was always the best response to the problem
of violence; on the other hand, he believed, it provided the best system of ethical
reflection within which this question and others like it were to be addressed. Society
is concretely interpersonal, for social life has essentially the same relation to personality
that language has to thought. If the human person is a "socius" with a private center,
Muelder reasoned, all human problems have a social dimension and a personal one.
The social gospelers were right: salvation is always personal and social, or it is not
saving. The ultimate ground of salvation is always beyond the personal and social
spheres, for the principles of moral science point beyond themselves. That was the
point of DeWolf's extra-moral principle, the metaphysical principle, which stated that
all persons ought to seek personal knowledge of the transcendent source of the moral
order's coherence. Moral science rightly reaches down with increasing concreteness in
making its formulations, Muelder observed, but the moral principles and choices of
moral theory also reach upward toward their ultimate context.[32]

Personalism Against the Current

The third generation personalists were more concerned about training pastors and theologians than producing original theory. DeWolf taught his communitarian laws for many years before publishing them; they passed from the classroom to public discussion through Muelder's work; when DeWolf finally published his ethical principles he stressed that they described how moral decisions should be made. They did not prescribe rules or commands, it was better not to call them moral laws, and they were not the center of his ethical system. Muelder featured the Brightman/DeWolf moral principles, but to DeWolf they were of secondary significance even for ethics. Muelder and DeWolf had essentially the same theology, philosophy, and ethics, but Muelder was more radical politically, and he wore personalism as a badge of honor and essential identity. In his later career DeWolf stressed that evangelical liberalism was his touchstone, not personalism; Muelder never put it that way. DeWolf and Muelder both disliked neo-orthodoxy, but DeWolf allowed that it had some good points; to Muelder, the Barthian ascendancy was an unqualified disaster, even when it raised legitimate points against liberal theology.

Liberal theology, he conceded, was sometimes idealistic in a mushy, sentimental sense that underestimated the reality of evil; some of it was semi-Christian in its rationalism and historicism; its Ritschlian mainstream disastrously rejected metaphysical reason; and the Chicago School gave up the idea of a cosmic God. But the neo-orthodox onslaught against it had only bad answers. The neo-Reformationists denigrated metaphysics and natural theology, blasted liberal theology for selling out the faith, conceived theology as the explication of revelation, and played up the paradoxical aspects of revelation. Muelder lamented, "I am sorry that this movement ever happened." There were problems with Troeltsch's historical relativism, but neo-orthodoxy was much worse: "Neoorthodoxy made me plain angry because it seemed to beg all the basic questions and to sidestep the painstaking work of epistemology, value-theory, ethics, and metaphysics." To Muelder, neo-orthodoxy was a positivist dead end. Instead of dealing with historical, scientific, and philosophical problems, the Barthians played a smoke-and-mirrors game with a non-objective "Word of God." Niebuhr's version made greater contact with reality, but it was seriously flawed too. "I had some patience with Reinhold Niebuhr's attacks on reformist liberals and sentimental 'parlor pinks,'" Muelder later reflected. "I appreciated his Marxism and his realistic appraisal of communism, but I disliked his failure to do his philosophical homework as he put forward a Neo-Augustinian view of persons, politics, and power." Moreover, Muelder stuck to Christian pacifism, chiding that Niebuhr was the kind of ethicist who opposed war only between wars.[33]

Niebuhr blasted liberal theology for depending on philosophical idealism, but he depended on the idealistic concepts of self, consciousness, transcendence, self-consciousness, self-transcendence, spirit, will, and personality. He faulted liberal theology for watering down the "biblical" faith, but he interpreted original sin, the deity of Christ, and Christ's resurrection as religious symbols. Muelder objected that Niebuhr's mythical interpretation of doctrine left no denotative meaning. Above all, despite the fact that Niebuhr's doctrine of human nature was usually lauded as the strongest part of his theology, Muelder found it disastrously wrong. Niebuhr conceived self-transcendence only as the occasion of sin, not as love, Muelder observed; he abstracted one type of self-transcendence (egocentric will-to-power) and ignored the redeeming power of mutuality and communitarian solidarity in human life. To Niebuhr, love had no saving power except as an abstract ultimate demand and as God's grace beyond history. Muelder countered that redemption *in* history was fundamental to Christianity: "If we assume that man's will is essentially self-contradictory and egocentric, it is impossible to unite such inevitably sinful willing in love. Even God cannot get out of man what is not there. He must work with man's power to love in self-conscious freedom."[34]

Muelder found more of Thomas Hobbes than the New Testament in Niebuhr's account of human nature. Niebuhr began with an isolated will, which led to a dismal Hobbesian end, "the war of all against all." His purported "realism" was not real at all, because it fixated on one dimension of the self's reality. Muelder countered that persons are fundamentally social beings. Self-transcendence of every kind takes place within the larger whole of nature and society, he reasoned; human maturation is a process of advancing to higher levels of sociality. Theology needed to begin where people actually begin, in the reciprocity of social existence. The communitarian personality was an empirical fact, not merely an ideal. Though Niebuhr's picture of the isolated egotist described a real problem, Muelder allowed, "it is not the essential clue to the whole communitarian reality of personal existence."[35]

Though he used the same categorical language of disaster in rejecting Barthian positivism, Niebuhrian pessimism, and Chicago School naturalism, Muelder did not quite mean it that way. Neo-orthodoxy had field-dominating power and prestige; thus its errors had to be forcefully exposed. Muelder did not dread it, however, with the depth of feeling that he held for Chicago naturalism. Historically and theoretically, personalist idealism was based on the denial that physical nature is all there is. Bowne, Knudson, and Brightman argued that "impersonalist" naturalism could not account for the reality of spirit; a bit more puckishly, Brightman sometimes called his position "more inclusive naturalism." The third generation personalists, despite having to deal with a dominant neo-orthodoxy, took for granted that "impersonalist naturalism" posed the greatest challenge to liberal theology. They countered that mechanistic forms of naturalism were not as rational or explanatory as personalist idealism. "The two basic concepts in religion are personality and value," Muelder explained. "Can naturalism do justice to these concepts, as they reveal themselves in prophetic religious experience, within the frames of reference of natural science, social behaviorism, and non-theistic social idealism?"[36]

Doggedly the personalists contended for a negative verdict. In Muelder's generation the major philosophical naturalists were John Dewey, Ernest Nagel, Morris Cohen, Roy Wood Sellars, and George Santayana. Dewey identified naturalism with the continuity of simple and complex processes and the exclusion of any outside force as a cause of change. Nagel emphasized that the human agent is simply part of the flux of natural events: "There is no cosmic plan which aims at man's survival or at his achieving his ideals, for to his lot the universe is morally indifferent." Cohen remarked, "From a naturalistic point of view the whole life of the human species is a minor episode in the history of a tiny speck of cosmic dust." Sellars defined naturalism as the belief "that nature is an all-inclusive, spatio-temporal system and that everything which exists and acts in it, is a part of this system. In short, naturalism is the expression of the desire for explanation in terms of objects which can be handled and studied in accordance with scientific methods."[37]

Muelder distinguished between Santayana's "broken-backed" naturalism and Dewey's humanistic naturalism. Santayana contended that human beings were alienated from nature because of its indifference to human values and ideals; Dewey countered that human values and ends were rooted in nature, which provided "possibilities" for the realization of ideals. Muelder allowed that progressive Christianity was closer to Dewey than to Santayana, but neither of them came close to accounting for personality or affirming the theistic principle. To the naturalists, scientific reason was the sole means to knowledge; nothing existed apart from the natural order; nature was indifferent to ideals, aside from the moral strivings of human beings; and the good life was achievable through some combination of heroic despair, aesthetic appreciation, and social reform.[38]

Muelder appreciated that his generation of naturalists tended to be less reductionist than the mechanistic philosophers that Bowne opposed. James's protest against "medical materialism" made an impact on twentieth-century philosophy, as did the emergent evolutionism of Hegel, Henri Bergson, Samuel Alexander, C. Lloyd Morgan, and Alfred North Whitehead. Emergence theorists recognized the unique role of mind in nature, taught a doctrine of levels that did not reduce all natural relations to physical relations, and pictured the universe as an organic whole of wholes. To Muelder these were welcome ideas that strengthened the twentieth-century picture of reality as a temporal, developmental, and historical process. Eighteenth- and nineteenth-century naturalism was ahistorical, absorbing persons in a mechanical order of nature that made history unimportant. The subsequent emphasis on temporal process restored the importance of history as a category, replacing the Enlightenment picture of nature as a non-temporal machine set against history.[39]

Muelder believed that Troeltschian historicism and Whiteheadian-style organicism set the stage for more constructive dialogues with naturalists than Bowne was able to pursue. Scientific fundamentalism was in retreat; at least, most naturalists now felt obliged to disavow reductionism. Moreover, some naturalists were Muelder's allies in the struggle for social justice – especially Dewey, Cohen, and Sidney Hook. But naturalism was still a false theory, even if it had become more sophisticated. Aside from a few naturalistic Platonists, who had little influence, and naturalistic theists like Henry Nelson Wieman and Bernard Meland, who constituted a special case, most naturalists rejected the objectivity of value, claiming that moral values were subjective and the universe was indifferent to them. Moreover, naturalists continued to identify their philosophy with scientific method, even while claiming to have given up reductionism. Muelder objected: "It is presumptuous to assume that scientific method as such can resolve ultimate metaphysical issues or that any one philosophy has a special claim on scientific work."[40]

In addition, naturalists emphasized the principle of continuity from lower to higher orders of being; Muelder replied that certain discontinuities were just as real in emergent evolution as the principle of continuity. The emergence of mind in nature, for example, was a novelty, something discontinuous with the past. Dewey, determined to erase novelty and discontinuity, played down the differences between mind and body, individual and society, and higher and lower orders of being. To Muelder Dewey was very good on individual freedom and social justice, but his naturalism submerged the self in its environment and obscured personality: "His whole method of continuity has militated against a clear and coherent conception of the self as individuality." Dewey's reductionist approach to personality struck Muelder as a showcase example of what Hegel called "the night in which all cows are black."[41]

Naturalism rested uneasily on shifting tides of natural science, Muelder cautioned. For more than a century naturalists based their case on a physics-oriented mechanistic metaphysics; more recently they took refuge in semantics or Viennese positivism, giving up metaphysical reason. Muelder warned that to give up metaphysics was to abandon much of reality, especially the phenomenon of personality and its value experience. Naturalists contended that no one knew what a personality was; Muelder replied that it was "consciousness capable of reason and ideal values." He added that a tougher question would be, "What is nature?" From a naturalistic perspective, the meaning of "nature" fluctuated with every scientific turn; thus "nature" was equated with whatever science thought at the time. Without personality and metaphysical knowledge, Muelder argued, there were no real values, in which case historical process had no meaning, and naturalistic positivism could not provide one.[42]

It appalled him that the Chicago School tried to do theology under the naturalistic presumption that naturalism equaled philosophy. Though Wieman and Meland held out for the objectivity of value, they conceived God in naturalistic categories as the concrete reality of historical process, rejecting any appeal to a transhistorical realm of spirit. Some Chicago schoolers were even more reductionistically naturalistic. Edward Scribner Ames wrote at length about God and religion, but exclusively in the categories of social psychology. For Ames, Muelder observed, prayer was the therapeutically beneficial practice of talking things over with oneself. Ames had a concept of God as ideal value, but no concept of God as a cosmic metaphysical reality. Muelder shook his head: "Ames has substituted devotion to the highest social values for prophetic religion with its objective reality of God. There is a basic difference between loyalty to an ideal and loyalty to God. Ames is a reductionist in that religion is reduced to social psychology."[43]

To Muelder it was pointless to call that Christian thought; the Chicago School simply gave up the Christian worldview in all but name. His counterpart in building the social ethics discipline, James Luther Adams (widely known as JLA), had a Tillichian affinity for Muelder's side of the argument, but did not draw the line so doggedly. One reason was that Adams was a Unitarian (later, Unitarian Universalist) who had to fight for the right to God-language of any sort in his denomination. Another was that he was in the Chicago School, if not quite of it fully, and built up its program of social ethics.

Boston personalism had a hand in giving Martin Luther King Jr to the world and it produced other notable social ethicists such as Paul Deats Jr, J. Philip Wogaman, Alan Geyer, C. Eric Lincoln, Tex Sample, Joseph D. Stamey, Norman Faramelli, Carol S. Robb, and Rufus Burrow Jr. It had a strong career in the church through its influence on Methodist pastors, and its greatest distinction was its connection to King, who studied principally under DeWolf. But philosophical idealism was already an embattled tradition in the academy when Muelder studied under Brightman, and afterward it became more so. By the 1960s the Chicago School of process theology and empiricism was a stronger force in the theological field than Boston personalism, although the Chicago School lost its institutional home at the University of Chicago. Long before that Chicago became a major player in social ethics because it got 20 years out of JLA before he returned to Harvard for 10 more.[44]

James Luther Adams and Unitarian Christianity

James Luther Adams was a twentieth-century champion of a liberal tradition that the twentieth century nearly left behind, Unitarian Christianity. Though rather isolated as a Christian theist in the Unitarian (later Unitarian Universalist) denomination, he was the most connected, ecumenical, activist-oriented, and least lonely of theologians. An advocate of constructively using power for the public good, he built up the social ethics discipline wherever he went.

He was born in Ritzville, Washington in 1901 to devoutly fundamentalist parents. Adams' father, James Carey Adams, was an itinerant Baptist minister and farmer who joined the Plymouth Brethren when Adams was 13 years old, partly as a protest against the liberalization of the Northern Baptist Convention. James Carey Adams condemned all forms of worldliness, prayed for the Second Coming, and often told his family during bedtime prayers that their next meeting might be with Jesus in the air. After he became a Darbyite Plymouth brother he refused to vote (on religious principle), gave up his life insurance policy (to show his trust in God), refused payment for preaching the gospel (following Paul's example), and drilled his son in the dispensational plan of salvation taught by J. N. Darby and the Scofield Reference Bible. Adams later recalled, "My father was always reminding us that the culture was unregenerate, and that salvation consisted in God's snatching the brand from the burning."[45]

When Adams was 15 his father caught typhoid fever, which permanently ruined his health. Adams worked at various jobs to support his parents and two sisters, including a well-paying position with the Northern Pacific Railway. Seeking to advance "beyond the horizons of the country bumpkin," he enrolled at the University of Minnesota and switched to a nighttime job with the railroad. His parents protested that double shifts of studying and working would destroy his health, he would not be able to support them, and the university would undermine his faith; on the last item they were right. Adams shuttled tiredly between the railroad and classroom, deepened his love of literature, and struggled to stay awake on Sundays while listening to sermons by fundamentalist W. B. Riley, liberal Baptist Norman Henderson, and Unitarian humanist John Dietrich. Gradually he turned against the dogmatic religion of his parents, but shortly after breaking from it he turned against organized religion altogether. Anticipating a career as an anti-clerical lawyer, in his senior he took a speech class and railed constantly against religion until his professor, Frank Rarig, gently observed that religion was obviously the great passion of his life; he could not stop talking about it. To Adams' astonishment, Rarig advised him to enroll in a liberal seminary; on his walk home Adams decided to try it. He asked Dietrich and Henderson about denominations. Dietrich told him that Unitarian ministers were free to preach about whatever they valued; Henderson cautioned that Unitarianism might not be the most religiously satisfying choice for a former fundamentalist, but confided that he would have switched to it had he not felt too old to do so. Adams enrolled at Harvard Divinity School with the hope of making a religious home in the Unitarian Church.[46]

In the 1920s Harvard Divinity School was called the Theological School in Harvard University, not the Divinity School, to signify its recent affiliation with Andover Theological Seminary. Adams studied theology under William Wallace Fenn, New Testament under Henry Cadbury, Old Testament under George Foot Moore, and

Christian history under Kirsopp Lake and George LaPiana. One of his Divinity School classmates was Virgil Thomson, who was already publishing compositions. Enrolling at the Graduate School of Arts and Sciences, Adams also took courses from Alfred North Whitehead and Irving Babbitt. He admired his Divinity School teachers, but chafed at their pretensions to objectivity; Whitehead's naturalistic theism made a formative impression; Babbitt's opinionated, high-powered lectures enthralled him. Babbitt pored over Rousseau's *Confessions* line by line, blasting its romantic individualism as the triumph of stupidity. He told students that Rousseau's celebration of spontaneity, naturalness, and individuality gave the modern age the philosophy it deserved: "If you want to find wisdom, do not look to this Romantic period, and least of all to Jean Jacques Rousseau." Babbitt revered the classical authors of antiquity, especially Sophocles, but he fixated on Rousseau. In self-defense he explained that it was important to see what had gone wrong in modern thought; moreover, Rousseau wrote great prose.[47]

Babbitt believed in a universal humanism that had no need of theology or metaphysics. Religions interested him to the extent that they taught humanistic values and the "saintly" virtues of renunciation and peace; by his reckoning the best religions were Roman Catholicism, Buddhism, and Confucianism. He dissuaded Adams from his leftover Paulinism on the bondage of the will and taught him to appreciate the Catholic doctrine of original sin for its realism. To Babbitt, humanism was about the triumph of the disciplined "higher will" over triviality and ignorance; the higher will was his analogue for divine grace. A Burkean conservative in politics, he disdained the Hebrew prophets, which Adams later held against him. But Adams began his intellectual career as a disciple of Babbitt's literary humanism. Babbitt told him that teaching was better than the ministry because teachers gave exams. Every year he selected four or five students with whom he worked intensely, creating disciples who deeply absorbed his ideas. No minister could do that, he assured Adams. For the rest of his life Adams was grateful to have been one of Babbitt's elect.[48]

Adams continued to support his mother and sisters after his father died, this time by taking ministry and teaching positions, although Lella Mae Adams could not bring herself to attend the "wicked" churches in which her son preached. Often she grieved that heaven would not be eternally blissful for her because her son would be in hell. In 1927 Adams had his first taste of Germany at a summer language course in Heidelberg, although Babbitt warned him that "you can't get anything but Romanticism out of a German. They're all infected." Adams gave six years to the Second Unitarian Church of Salem, Massachusetts, where he settled on a liberal Christian version of Unitarianism; he ministered for two years in Wellesley Hills, Massachusetts, where Vida Scudder became a treasured friend; he consumed the spiritual writings of Friedrich von Hügel, which taught him to respect Catholic mysticism and sacramentalism; he served as editor of the Unitarian weekly magazine *The Christian Register*, where he tried to broaden the theological horizon of Unitarians; and in 1935 he won an academic position at the Meadville Lombard Theological School in Chicago.[49]

He was not quite ready to become a professor. Postponing his appointment for a year, Adams conducted research in England on Bishop Richard Hurd and became friends with T. S. Eliot, with whom he swapped tales about Babbitt. He went to France, visited Benedictine monasteries, and undertook spiritual direction at the seminary of Saint Sulpice in Paris. In Switzerland he interviewed Karl Barth, Emil Brunner, and Willem A. Visser 't Hooft and witnessed Barth's rude performance at a conference.

Returning to Germany with a bulky movie camera, he acted on Visser 't Hooft's urging to make contact with the Confessing Church. Adams lived with Confessing Church leader Peter Brunner (a friend and recent inmate at Dachau Concentration Camp), met Confessing Church leader Martin Niemoller, and collected enough information to earn a nervewracking visit from the Gestapo. He also interviewed philosophers Edmund Husserl, Martin Heidegger, and Karl Jaspers, theologian Rudolf Otto, and religious historian Joachim Wach. Husserl told him that he greatly disliked Barth's theology but was grateful for Barth's opposition to so-called German Christianity. Jaspers told him that religious and political liberalism meant nothing in Germany and that only the Barthian dogmatists had the *Zwang* (guts) to stand up to the Nazis. Adams asked the founder of the German Faith Movement, Wilhelm Hauer, to explain why Germans were so obsessed with racial purity. The Germans mixed Prussian, Swabian, and Bavarian blood, Adams noted, but they were far more racialist than the racially purer British. Hauer explained that the British were too stupid to emphasize their racial identity and that Americans owed their stupidity about race to their British blood. For the rest of his life Adams showed students his home movies of German theologians and philosophers, always reminding them that liberals offered hardly any resistance to Hitler.[50]

Adams was still working on his doctorate when he accepted the call to Meadville, which forced him to drop out of Harvard's doctoral program. He asked the seminary to call him "Professor of Christian Institutions and Liturgies," but before he arrived school officials changed his title to "Chair in the Psychology and Philosophy of Religion." Ernest Cadman Colwell, Dean of the University of Chicago Divinity School, took care of his degree problem, giving him advanced standing toward a doctorate in historical theology at the Divinity School. Working with Wilhelm Pauck in historical theology, Adams made himself competent to teach psychology of religion, basked in the academic ecumenism of the Federated Theological Faculty, and took nine years to write a dissertation on Tillich's philosophy of culture and religion. The Federation of Theological Schools consisted of the University of Chicago Divinity School, Chicago Theological Seminary, Meadville Theological School, and Disciples Divinity House. Two years before Adams completed his doctorate, in 1943, he became the Divinity School's first chair of Ethics and Society. Though he worried that he was unqualified for his position, he found a home in social ethics and became one of its mainstays.[51]

During his years at Harvard Divinity School Adams had been frustrated by the scholarly remoteness of his teachers. In a student address at the school's graduation ceremony he remarked that he had no idea if the divinity professors were committed to anything besides scholarship. He remembered that frustration when he designed Chicago's Ethics and Society program. Adams talked about current social and religious issues in class, required doctoral students to pass examinations in four social sciences, and appropriated sociologist Karl Mannheim's theory of "middle principles" for religious ethics, teaching students to apply general principles or norms to particular situations by discerning the "middle-range" factors that contributed to particular situations. "It was a question of reducing abstractions and coming closer to reality," he later reflected. Knowing the scholarly literature on Amos and Isaiah was a good thing; knowing social theory was good too; the best kind of religious thinking fused prophetic theology and social theory to understand and change the world.[52]

His models of how to think religiously in the modern context were Tillich, Whitehead, Troeltsch, and Otto. To Adams the exemplary religious thinkers were religiously and philosophically deep, broad in their intellectual vision, and had a sense of transcendent mystery. He loved his acquired Unitarianism, but lamented that twentieth-century Unitarianism was intellectually and religiously lethargic and its intellectually vibrant wing was stuck in the shallow waters of anti-theistic religious humanism. The Humanist Manifesto of 1932 was a notable example. It declared that "the time has passed for theism, deism, modernism, and the several varieties of 'new thought' . . . In the place of the old attitudes involved in worship and prayer the humanist finds his religious emotions expressed in a heightened sense of personal life and in a co-operative effort to promote social well-being." Originating among Chicago humanists, the manifesto was signed by 34 intellectuals including Harry Elmer Barnes, John Dewey, Albert C. Diefenbach, John Dietrich, John Herman Randall, Jr, and Roy Wood Sellars. To many Unitarians the humanistic naturalism of the Humanist Manifesto was the wave of the future in religion. Adams owed his appointment at Meadville to his dissent from his denomination's increasingly anti-theological bias.[53]

Theologically he leaned on Pauck during his early years in Chicago, and also Shailer Mathews and Henry Nelson Wieman. Pauck was a refugee from Germany who had studied under Tillich at the University of Berlin in 1921, knew Tillich and Troeltsch personally, and was prone to spend three-quarters of a survey course lecturing on Martin Luther. Adams was a sponge for Pauck's encyclopedic knowledge of the Reformation and modern theology. He also admired the social scientific theologizing of Mathews, who took a fatherly interest in him, and appreciated Wieman's empirical descriptions of divine behavior, though Adams judged that Wieman's empiricism was too narrow and ahistorical. Like Tillich, Mathews, and Wieman, Adams believed that modern theology needed to develop a new language of spiritual meaning and social transformation. By his reckoning Tillich's language of theonomy, ultimate concern, kairos, religious socialism, and the Unconditioned offered the best example. Tillich's theology was distinctly creative and relevant because, as Adams emphasized in his dissertation, he understood that modern churches defeated "their own proper ends" when they recycled the religious language of previous generations.[54]

In 1940, seven years after Tillich fled Germany to join the faculty of Union Theological Seminary, Adams met him for the first time. Tillich was still struggling to convey his ideas in a foreign language and culture; it delighted him to meet an American who knew his German writings. Afterward it occurred to Adams that he was uniquely suited to make Tillich's thought available to Americans. Tillich's subsequent fame would not have been possible without Adams, Pauck, and John Dillenberger. Adams published an influential volume of Tillich's German and American essays titled *The Protestant Era*; he and Pauck guided Tillich's adjustment to American culture and politics; and Dillenberger played a crucial role in helping Tillich produce the first two volumes of his *Systematic Theology*. Tillich's first attempt to introduce himself to Americans, a poorly translated volume titled *The Interpretation of History,* attracted little notice apart from quiet guffaws by colleagues at Union Seminary. Thanks to Adams, Tillich's second attempt was far more successful. *The Protestant Era* offered an expertly translated and edited collection of some of Tillich's most provocative essays. Adams deferred to Tillich's anxieties when he balked at including a neo-Marxist essay, "The Class Struggle and Religious Socialism"; Tillich told Adams and Ernst Fraenkel that it would kill him in capitalist America. *The Protestant Era* helped Tillich find his American voice and audience. Years later he confessed that without Adams

> I would not be what I am, biographically as well as theologically . . . He knows more about my writings that I do myself; he made the first translations into English of articles

I had written in German; he helped me to get a publisher; and I have reasons to suspect that he did many more things for me than I have ever known.[55]

Though he was drawn to systematic thinkers who wrote on a vast scale, Adams's work consisted of thematic and situational essays. He expounded his beliefs about free religion, the primacy of will, prophetic social concern, and voluntary associations in scattered articles, prefaces, lectures, and reviews that he left for others to collect as books. Repeatedly he lamented that theological liberalism as a whole, and especially his beloved Unitarian tradition, lacked the power of world-changing commitment that came from decision and spiritual conversion. To Adams, the Judeo-Christian tradition at its best was an integrative alternative to Apollonian intellectualism and Dionysian voluntarism. The Apollonian tradition exalted reason as the fundamental principle of creation and highest human faculty, interpreting the cosmos as a unified and harmonious structure. The Dionysian tradition exalted vitality over rational form, emphasizing the creative and destructive power of will and the large role of fate. Jewish and Christian thought resembled Greek intellectualism by playing up the God-given rational coherence of the world and Greek voluntarism by emphasizing moral obedience to the divine law. But Adams noted that the classic expressions of Judaism (the prophetic, wisdom, and rabbinic literatures) and Christianity (Jesus, Paul, John, the Greek Fathers, and Augustine) placed a divine valuation on existence that neither of the Greek views contained. The Judeo-Christian tradition taught that the world was good because it was God's creation, nothing in existence was absolutely anti-divine, and even suffering could be a means of grace; in Christianity, the cross was the highest revelation of the divine character.[56]

Adams emphasized that modern liberalism germinated as an intellectualist enterprise. Born as a revolt against Catholic and Protestant forms of dogmatism, it defended the freedom of mind and rejected "total depravity" forms of voluntarism that distorted the Christian doctrine of original sin. His appreciation was immense; Adams believed that the magnificence of the Enlightenment and its humanitarian legacy could "scarcely be overemphasized." But Enlightenment-style liberalism accentuated the saving power of reason to the point of distorting personality, he argued. The Augustinian emphasis on the will and the affections was thrown aside, neglecting the psychic depths of human experience "and of reality itself." Instead of standing for the ideals of prophetic religion, liberal Protestantism provided religious sanction for the values of middle-class respectability. Unitarian liberalism was decidedly middle-class, not prophetic, Adams stressed.[57]

Nineteenth-century Unitarian James Freeman Clarke epitomized the type, describing liberal religion as believing in the Fatherhood of God, the Brotherhood of man, the Leadership of Jesus, Salvation by Character, and "the Progress of Mankind, onward and upward forever."[58] Clarke took it for granted that continuous and inevitable progress was the very purpose of creation; Adams replied with Troeltsch that historical forces were given and not inherently logical. History does not repeat itself in the logical manner of organic nature, he explained, citing Whitehead's thesis that history generates novelty. Though human beings are constrained by various conditioning factors, Adams observed, "humanity is fated also to be free." Religious liberalism had faith in humanity not because of reason alone, but because human beings possessed the relative, volitional, dangerous power to participate in the divine creativity.[59]

The will to mutuality and the will to power are always intertwined, thus history is tragic: "When we say that history is tragic, we mean that the perversions and failures in history are associated precisely with the highest creative powers of humanity and thus with our greatest achievements." Adams noted that people rightly treasured the heritage and customs of their country, but nationalism was also a destructive force. Gains in mobility liberated millions from economic and social deprivation, but also produced a community-destroying rootlessness and instability. Human freedom as the will to mutuality was redemptive, but freedom was also used to dominate and oppress. Adams argued that the old liberalism was unrealistic because it underestimated the tragic contradictions in human nature and history. The next liberalism had to empha-size the necessity of a converted will and the fact that no amount of good will alone could solve the problems of statecraft and social justice. Liberal theology needed to shift from a rationalist orientation lacking a tragic dimension to a voluntarist orienta-tion emphasizing the fate and primacy of will. Modern liberalism neglected the gospel emphasis on conversion, he protested, "and that is the prime source of its enfeeble-ment." Modern liberals had to relinquish their respectable lukewarmness and be con-verted by a convicting love that made spiritual and ethical demands: "And when that has taken place, we shall know that it is not our wills alone that have acted; we shall know that the ever-living Creator and Re-creator has again been brooding over the face of the deep and out of the depths bringing forth new life."[60]

Human beings possessed the freedom of choice as their fate and birthright. To Adams, that was the key to a renewed liberalism. Every attempt to escape from freedom and its responsibilities was an act of freedom; thus the burden of moral responsibility could not be relinquished. To defer to the authority of scripture or the church was no escape from the moral responsibility of having chosen to do so. Every faith was a faith of the free, but many faiths were unworthy of being chosen. Adams called his religious ideal "faith for the free," which had three tenets. The first was a blend of Whitehead's lure of divine love and Tillich's principle of ultimate concern. Human beings depend for their being and freedom upon a creative power and process that are not of their own making, Adams argued; moreover, God is the "commanding reality" that sustains and transforms all life. To Adams, God was the commanding, creative power that provided the structure and process of life-sustaining existence, lured self-actualizing subjects to richer existence, and worked on and through subjects to achieve truth, beauty, and goodness. Tillich taught that God was a name for the infinite and inexhaustible depth and ground of all being. Thus, to speak of God was to refer to the depths of one's life or one's ultimate concern. Atheism was the strange notion that life has no depth; life is shallow. Adams described it as the denial that any reality sustained meaning and goodness; in Whiteheadian parlance, authentically free religion put its faith in "a creative reality that is re-creative."[61]

The second tenet of free religion was that divine reality finds its "richest focus" when human beings cooperate for the common good. Freedom rightly used seeks freedom and social justice for others, Adams contended; any other use of freedom is unsustainable and morally unworthy. He was fond of the saying that "faith is the sister of justice." A faith that was not the freedom-bearing sister of justice cheated people of their spiritual birthright, produced warped religious communities, and worshiped a factional idol: "That way lie the grinding rut and tyranny of the Vatican line, the Nuremberg line, and the Moscow line, different though these lines are from each other in their fear and obstruction of freedom." Adams described the commanding and transforming reign of God as the reign of love, "a love that 'cares' for the fullest personal good of all." The divine love was healing and forgiving, but not removed from suffering: "It drew Jesus up Golgotha to a cross. Thus Jesus was not only a martyr dying for his convictions, but also the incarnation of the affirmative power of love transforming life, even in death, and creating a transforming community."[62]

The third tenet was that freedom in community could not be achieved without "the power of organization and the organization of power." Adams despaired of the kind of religious liberalism that encouraged individuals to believe whatever they wanted. Individualistic liberals dropped the first principle of good religion, the existence of a commanding divine reality. Treating relativistic liberty as the only spiritual truth, they got stuck in a halfway house to nihilism. Some individualistic liberals declined to join a community of faith; Adams admonished that genuinely free religion is always about life-giving community and it necessarily takes place within one: "The free church is that community which is committed to determining what is rightly of ultimate concern to persons of free faith." Other liberals held that churches should avoid controversial issues in order to protect the principle of freedom of belief; Adams countered that free religion had a moral content and character. It could not abide a social evil such as racial discrimination and be genuinely free: "A faith that creates no community of faith and a faith that assumes no definite form is not only a protection against any explicit faith, it is probably also a protection for a hidden idolatry of blood or state or economic interest, a protection for some kind of tyranny."[63]

Because he was not a writer of books, Adams tended to attract students who knew more about him personally than about his disparate writings. Every year he surprised new ones by describing himself as a cautious proponent of natural law. Adams had no use for natural law theorizing that underwrote a parochial interest or buttressed a dogmatic one. No one actually knows the law of nature, he cautioned; to approach it, one must be patient, humble, keep an open mind, root out one's prejudices, be aware of one's context, and remember that every interpretation is fallible. But however difficult it was to grasp the one that may exist within and among the many, the value of trying was not to be denigrated. At least, ethicists should be open to the possibility that the moral life has a universal ground. And if one was a Christian ethicist, Adams contended, the "should" needed to be stronger, because the idea of an objective moral order is built into the monotheistic worldview of Christianity.[64]

Adams considered his thinking about freedom to be reflection of a partial and contextual, yet commonly moral sort, to which he added a theory of power as a twofold reality. To him it was crucially important as a theologian, ethicist, and social activist to affirm the ethically positive and constructive character of power. Power has a theological ground and a human sphere of action, he argued. It is firstly the expression of God's law and love, and secondarily the exercise of human freedom. Power is grounded in divine reality, the very power and ground of being, and as human freedom it is a response to the possibilities of being. Henry Adams declared that power is poison; Jacob Burckhardt assured that power is evil by its nature, no matter who wields it; Lord Acton famously warned that power is corrupting, and absolute power corrupts absolutely. Adams replied that these judgments captured only part of the picture, with disastrous results for social action. Whenever human power was sundered from its ground in the law and love of God it became poisonous, evil, and corrupting. Deracinated modern selves lacking a conscience rushed into politics and the destructive exercise of power, while sensitive types avoided politics and its corrupting influence. Adams admonished that one does not become moral by fleeing from the exercise of power, for the very decision to reject power is an exercise of it, and power "is in no way alien to religion." To be good and do the good, one must exercise power in a manner that is enabled and limited by its divine ground.[65]

All forms of social action are responses to the possibilities of being, Adams reasoned. One cannot understand religion without dealing with power, nor understand power without dealing with religion, because power is the fundamental category of being and of social action. As the creative element of power serving the flourishing of life, power is divine; as the exercise of power cut off from its energizing and limiting divine ground, power is destructive. Armed with this conception of power as the exercise of human freedom under God's law and love, Adams sorted out the relations between two ultimate poles of power within human experience. Plato taught that Being is power, the creative condition and limit of existence expressed as law; Stoicism and Christianity transmuted the Platonist law of being into God's law, *logos*; modern philosophy reduced power to the capacity to exercise influence. Adams observed that modern secularism stayed in the Platonist and Christian line by stressing the power of freedom to control one's self and influence others, but it lost the Platonist/Christian emphasis on power as the capacity to be influenced. Rightly understood, power always has a dual character, while remaining one: "There is no adequate conception of power as freedom except as it is simultaneously conceived of as law and except as it is viewed in a context of interaction ultimately grounded in the divine power of being with its possibilities in terms of free and also ambiguous response."[66]

Just as God is not merely a lawgiver, human beings are not merely free. There are dialectics between and within God and humanity, Adams explained. Plato taught that power is both active and passive; in the Christian worldview, the active and passive powers are dialectically related within God, within human beings, and between God and human beings. God is creative, redemptive, active power (Adams tweaked his Unitarian readers with Trinitarian flourishes) that is influenced by human beings by virtue of taking satisfaction in their free obedience to the divine good. Human beings, for their part, possess active power by virtue of their freedom to influence themselves and others, and passive power by virtue of being affected by God's power of being and the agency of other persons. Adams remarked: "Where mutuality of influence appears, both active and passive power operate; and ideally, coercive power is employed primarily for the maintenance of mutuality."[67]

Power always involves some relation to change; more plainly, Adams wrote, power *is* always a relation of some sort between law and freedom. To perceive, know, imagine, will, or feel is to express freedom as the power of choice, but each expression implies an object that is the necessary condition of the expression. Otherwise perception would be mere self-projection. Perception is an expression of freedom and necessity that shows the character of power as an active and passive relation. Moving from abstraction to modern politics, Adams liked the nineteenth-century British theologian William Whewell on the ethics of democratic power, who argued that every rights-bearing citizen *is* one of the powers that be. To take moral responsibility for one's power is to improve the capacity of the state and law to serve the public good while protecting both from rash innovations. Adams added that while the Christian community undoubtedly had interests that made sense only in the context of the Christian community, the work of using power constructively to create a good society was not one of them: "The theological and ethical principles of Christian social action that are appropriate for the church are ultimately the criteria for judging and transforming society. The Christian looks for a society in which all may be treated as persons potentially responsive to God's redemptive purpose for history. And in working for it, we must perforce use that kind of community today called the voluntary association – where, within the church and outside it, consensus is formed and social action is undertaken."[68]

Adams wrote often about voluntary associations, but he made most of his impact through personal relationships, teaching, and his involvement in voluntary associations, not by writing about them. In the 1930s he helped to revitalize the American Unitarian Association, which produced new programs and outreach efforts that led to the founding of the Unitarian Universalist Association in 1961. In 1944 he threw himself into Chicago politics, helping to found and co-chair a powerful reform organization, the Independent Voters of Illinois (IVI), which campaigned for international cooperation, racial integration, civil liberties, and liberal politicians. One of the latter was Illinois governor and two-time presidential candidate Adlai Stevenson, whom Adams befriended, and through whom he also made connections to the national Democratic Party. One IVI project was refuting Charles Coughlin's radio broadcasts; members took turns on Sunday afternoons immediately after Coughlin aired. Immersed in civic and political activism, Adams often had to explain that "democratic socialism" was not what it sounded like to many Americans; the tradition that he shared with Rauschenbusch and Tillich was something very different from Communism. After the *Chicago Tribune* branded him a Communist anyway, Adams was asked by Stevenson to introduce him at a campaign appearance. Adams later recalled, "I thought this showed that he had a lot of starch." Elsewhere he recalled that there was nothing "intrinsically unusual" about his many years of precinct organizing and electoral campaigning: "It was only unusual for the Protestant churchman or clergyman."[69]

In 1956 he accepted the Edward Mallinckrodt, Jr Chair of Divinity at Harvard Divinity School, ending 20 years of intense activism in Chicago. The following January approximately 20 activist organizations sponsored a farewell reception for him; Adams later called the event "a complete escape into hyperbole." Admirers thanked him for struggling for racial integration, better schools, world peace, and better politics; Adams experienced the reception as an absolution: "It helped to assuage my guilt for having devoted so much time to politics when I was supposed to be a scholar."[70]

Harvard Divinity School had declined in the 1930s, 1940s, and early 1950s. In 1933 it went back to calling itself the Divinity School, but was barely kept alive by the university administration. From 1941 to 1953 the school's only theology professor was an anti-theistic Humanist, Johannes A. C. F. Auer, and its total faculty fell to 15 professors. The Divinity School's enrollment surged after World War II, however, especially by attracting chaplains on the GI Bill of Rights, and in 1947 a special commission led by Ernest Cadman Colwell and Reinhold Niebuhr urged the university to revamp the school's faculty and curriculum. Six years later a new university president, Nathan Marsh Pusey, committed Harvard to fulfilling the commission's recommendations. In 1955 Pusey brought Tillich to Harvard as a University Professor; the following year Adams, theologian Paul Lehmann, and biblical scholars Krister Stendahl and Frank Moore Cross, Jr joined the Divinity School faculty. Adams announced in his inaugural address that the special vocation of a divinity school was to facilitate critical analysis of the nature of faith. A good university divinity school did not teach any particular theology or denominational perspective as a dogma, but neither did it teach a lowest common denominator ecumenism. It opened the "way to enrichment," living on questions more than answers, and renewing itself through passionate engagement.[71]

He preached, taught, wrote, and practiced that association is the central freedom. For 15 years after Adams returned to Cambridge he served as chair of the Committee on Church and State for the Massachusetts branch of the American Civil Liberties Union (ACLU). He was also a cofounder of the Fellowship for Racial and Economic Equality, taught seminars at Harvard Law School and Harvard Business School, served as a consultant for the National Association for the Advancement of Colored People (NAACP), chaired the advisory board of Beacon Press, and cofounded the Society for the Scientific Study of Religion. Often he traced his passion for voluntary associations to having witnessed the nazification of Germany, where freedom of association was abolished. Democracy was about the freedom to form groups that democratically determine public policy, he argued; totalitarianism began with the extinction of that freedom. Thus, voluntary associations were indispensable for any democratic society: "Only through the exercise of freedom of association can the citizen in a democracy participate in the process that gives shape to public opinion and to public policy."[72]

Adams loved to quote Alexis de Tocqueville on the American devotion to associations. In Tocqueville's telling, Americans treasured associations in the same way that the French prized government and the English prized social class. That explained why the USA had the world's healthiest democracy; it was "a nation of joiners." Adams stressed that unlike the state and family, voluntary associations were voluntary, and unlike the nations from which America derived, the USA made religion voluntary. Modern voluntary associations originated in the Radical Reformation, "especially the aggressive sects of the left wing Puritanism," which insisted that religion could not be a matter of free choice if the churches were not free of state control. But the deeper roots of voluntary associations grew out of early Christianity, he argued. Christianity was distinctly suited to develop a civilization that separated religion and the state, for the early church prefigured the modern voluntary association by dispersing power and responsibility, transcending the ethnic boundaries of Judaism, welcoming people of all social classes, raising the status of women, and giving common people the opportunity to learn organizational skills. Early Christianity carried out "a great social revolution" that laid the cultural groundwork for modern democracy.[73]

Adams distinguished between the voluntary associations that he liked, which promoted the common good, and the kind that had to be resisted, which promoted special interests. If members hoped to make personal gains by participating in an association, he argued, it did not belong to the first type. Groups like the ACLU and NAACP existed to make democracy work for all people, advancing the general welfare and defending the rights of excluded minorities. To Adams, the future and health of democracy depended on the capacity of general welfare associations to prevent special interest groups from dominating the political process. Organizationally, a pluralist society needed both kinds of voluntary associations, but general welfare associations advanced and protected genuinely democratic pluralism.[74]

Adams usually described voluntary associations in political terms, but he appreciated that many of them centered on expressive interests such as gardening, photography, painting, literature, music, and other hobbies. In this arena he preferred music and literature, himself being a singer, violinist, and Bach enthusiast who prized the "mysterious, almost fantastic" art of creating and appreciating music. He mused that music is a nonobjective, nonverbal world of its own, "almost a *creatio ex nihilo*, an occasion for immediacy of experience, a nonreducible mode of beauty, of contrast and resolution, of order and of ecstasy rooted in order." With its unique immediacy and inwardness that illumines, orders our experience, and reveals a transcendent source of meaning, he reflected, music is ultimately "not a human achievement but a gift of grace."[75]

He was a critical and comparative thinker, not a systematizer. Max Stackhouse noted that instead of developing the reflective or logical implications of a given point of departure, Adams thought "vis-a-vis other minds, external evidence, or objective events." Even his protégés, Stackhouse and James Gustafson, could not find a unifying center to his thought. Gustafson observed, "I do not have a settled answer to what holds the work together . . . I think the center of gravity is more personal; it combines his moral and intellectual passions, his native brilliance, his insatiable curiosity, his learning, and his powers of articulation." If Adams had a center, Gustafson surmised, it was something like "free women and men put their faith in a creative reality that is re-creative."[76]

That put it very well. Adams drank deeply from big-picture religious thinkers, but always in a way that left their systems in the background. His faith in a "creative reality that is re-creative" smacked of Whitehead, but Whiteheadian scholasticism was foreign to him; he could not have written for *Process Studies*. He loved to expound Tillich's theory of ultimate concern, Otto's theory that the kingdom is already present and not yet fulfilled, and Troeltsch's theory that the meaning of Christianity is social and historical, but his unique contribution to theological liberalism was associational, not theoretical. He zigged and zagged between options, finding his way through comparing alternatives, and brought people together.

He tended to speak his most direct words to Unitarian Universalist audiences. Adams could be painfully direct on the topic of liberal failure. He never forgot that German liberalism rolled over for the Nazis; thus, when recounting the down side of humanistic liberalism, he dropped the zig and zag. Often he lamented that his tradition showed a pronounced tendency to shrink down to humanistic moralism, took little interest in theology, took a very dim view of Christology, and was often religiously shallow. Adams cringed at friends who claimed that only weak-minded conformists still bothered with theology: "This kind of 'religion' is neither liberal nor Christian. It is a superficial provincial backwash of 'progress,' impotent to deal intellectually and responsibly with the deeper, ultimate issues of life." But that was never his last word: "Happily, there are countervailing tendencies among liberal Christians."[77]

He reached Harvard's mandatory retirement age in 1966, but retiring was alien to JLA. He taught at Andover Newton Theological School and Meadville Lombard after retiring from Harvard, returned to Cambridge in 1978, and lost his beloved wife of 50 years, Margaret, shortly afterward. In his last years Adams marveled at the industry of his former students Stackhouse, J. Ronald Engel, and George Kimmich Beach in publishing collections of his essays. He never explained why he had not done it himself, and his chief publicist, Beach, who wanted to ask, shied away from doing so. But Beach was undoubtedly right in surmising that Adams was always too busy with his next project to look back.[78]

Rethinking Religious Freedom and Pluralism: John Courtney Murray

John Ryan notwithstanding, there was not much contact between socially-minded Protestants and Catholics before 1960, and even Ryan was a staunch defender of the

Catholic state ideal that kept the impasse in place. John Courtney Murray, as a Jesuit seminarian, believed that the chasm between Protestantism and Catholicism was so deep and wide that dialogue between them was pointless. Protestantism had lost or rejected so much of classical Christianity that there was no basis even for analogical discussion. At the time Murray had similar feelings about the Anglo-American tradition and the fate of Catholicism within it. But to his surprise, in his early career Murray found himself drawn to the problem of religious freedom, which led him to an unexpected standpoint and career. Murray became the first major American Catholic theologian by rethinking the problem of religious freedom, which led him to think creatively about religious pluralism, and to develop a keen appreciation of the Anglo-American tradition, and to offer a new model of public theology.[79]

He was born in New York City in 1904 to a Scottish-born father (a lawyer) and an Irish mother, both Roman Catholics. In his youth Murray aspired to a medical career, but gave it up for financial reasons; at the age of 16 he joined the New York province of the Society of Jesus. Studying classics and philosophy, he earned a bachelor's degree from Weston College in 1926 and a master's degree from Boston College the following year. For his teaching experience in the Jesuit system he was sent to the Philippines in 1927, where he taught English literature and Latin for three years at Ateneo de Manila. Returning to the USA in 1930 he studied theology for four years at Woodstock College in Woodstock, Maryland; was ordained to the priesthood in 1933; and resumed his studies at the Gregorian University in Rome, where he completed his doctorate in theology in 1937, writing a dissertation on Matthias Scheeben's theology of faith. In 1937 Murray returned to Woodstock as a professor of theology, specializing in the doctrines of grace and the Trinity, where he remained for his entire career, not always to his liking, until his death in 1967.[80]

The Jesuit theologate at Woodstock was a good place to launch Murray's unusual career, although for years he pleaded for something else. His timing was also fortunate, at the beginning of a generational renewal of American Catholic scholarship, although Murray had early doubts about that too.

The first stirrings of theological modernization in the USA had ended badly. In the 1890s Notre Dame chemistry and physics professor and Holy Cross priest John A. Zahm, a popular speaker on the Catholic summer-school circuit, taught that Catholicism was compatible with Darwinian evolution. Paulist priest William Sullivan urged Catholic clergy to take a stand against Vatican authoritarianism. For three years the American church had a scholarly journal, *New York Review*, that published modernist theologians and took a cautiously historicist line. But in 1907 Pope Pius X condemned liberalism, modern science, historical criticism, and modern culture in withering detail, crushing the possibility of a Catholic modernism, and in 1910 the Vatican instituted an anti-modernist oath for all clerics and theology professors. Zahm was forced to disavow his book *Evolution and Dogma*; Sullivan angrily left the church; in 1908 the coeditors of *New York Review*, James Francis Driscoll and Francis Patrick Duffy, were punitively assigned to parishes and the journal folded.[81]

For 30 years afterwards there was nothing like the *New York Review* in American Catholicism. The church's best journal, *Commonweal*, founded in 1921, was possible only under lay direction; neo-scholasticism reigned in the seminaries; and the development of Catholic thought outside the social policy venue of Ryan and *Catholic World* editor John J. Burke was frozen. Even the mild historicism of John Cardinal Newman was too revisionist for a Vatican orthodoxy that overcame history with dogma and deductive principles.

Murray began his academic career just as the dogmatic ice began to melt. American biblical scholars struck first, launching the *Catholic Biblical Quarterly* in 1939; four years later Pope Pius XII's encyclical *Divino afflante spiritu* removed the papal prohibition on historical critical tools in biblical scholarship. Murray's religious order had published *America* since 1909, but that was a newsweekly; for the Jesuits, the key to theological renewal was creating a successor to the *New York Review*. The church's leading scholarly journal, the *American Ecclesiastical Review*, was rigidly conservative, and soon became intransigently conservative. Founded in 1889, it was published in Philadelphia until 1927 and housed at Catholic University of America afterward. In 1940 the Jesuit faculties of the USA combined to produce an alternative, *Theological Studies*. Francis X. Talbot, the journal's first editor, who also edited *America*, observed that the church "badly needed" a journal that addressed contemporary concerns and scholarship. That was a judgment on the stodgy conformism of *American Ecclesiastical Review*. The following year Murray was appointed editor of *Theological Studies* and, shortly afterward, religion editor of *America*; meanwhile Catholic University opted for aggressive conservatism by appointing theologian Joseph Fenton as editor of *American Ecclesiastical Review* in 1944.[82]

The rivalry between Murray/*Theological Studies* and Fenton/*American Ecclesiastical Review* shaped Murray's career and burnished his reputation as an important public theologian and formidable polemicist. In the early going, however, it was not the career that he wanted. Murray had published only two articles when he took over *Theological Studies*, which did not enhance his sense of the journal's importance or potential. He had similar feelings about teaching at Woodstock, which intensified after the USA entered World War II. Murray sought an army chaplaincy, but his Jesuit provincial superior James Sweeney refused. After the war Murray took another shot at getting himself relocated, or at least repositioned, telling his Jesuit provincial Francis McQuade that he was capable of doing a good job with *Theological Studies* or *America*, but not both. *Theological Studies* was a journal aimed at scholars, while *America* was a magazine pitched to general readers, he observed. These were "not only two distinct jobs, but two distinct 'careers,' two different ways of life." The assumption that he could handle both assignments was mistaken, especially because his primary interests had changed.[83]

Writing in 1946, Murray explained to McQuade that in the past four years he had drifted "away from technical theology as such into the field of what I have called 'religion and society.'" He found himself thinking mostly about religious freedom, church and state, liberalism, and the peace issue, and he expected to do most of his writing on those topics. That was an argument for *America* over *Theological Studies*, although Murray pressed it gently; what mattered was to be freed from one of them. The following month he asked McQuade to let him take a position with the National Catholic Welfare Conference as a director of student congresses and conferences. McQuade turned him down rather brusquely; Murray, burning with embarrassment, apologized for "a rather ghastly mistake," confessed that he was "too inclined to take personal initiatives," and apologized again: "Apparently, whenever I do start something, it is a mistake." By the end of the year Murray was exhausted from overwork and unhappiness, even though McQuade allowed him to drop *America*; on one occasion Murray suffered a physical collapse. In February 1947 he pleaded to be relieved of *Theological Studies* too; for that matter, Murray told McQuade, he really wanted a different assignment altogether. He was not suited for the laborious tasks of a scholarly journal; he wanted to feel more useful as a priest and scholar; and he wanted to teach at a university, ideally Fordham, where he would have graduate students: "I want to be a student (and there might be an advantage in having a student over students). And I want to write (my main 'want'); and I want to do a bit of teaching (but not here)."[84]

To Murray's superiors, all of that was beside the point. They appreciated the importance of *Theological Studies*, even if he did not, and Murray was the best they had for the job. Thus he stayed at Woodstock and *Theological Studies* for the rest of his life, where he made a greater impact than he might have managed elsewhere.

In 1942 he began writing about religious freedom. Murray admired philosopher Jacques Maritain, who supported practical ecumenism, and in the early 1940s Murray became an active member of the National Conference of Christians and Jews, which sparked his interest in religious freedom. Buoyed by his collegial relationships with Protestant and Jewish members of the conference, Murray wrote a hopeful article for *Theological Studies* on the prospect of ecumenical cooperation on common concerns, especially the peace issue. He vowed to devote substantial attention to the historical, theological, and canonical aspects of ecumenism in succeeding issues of the journal, which he did, in articles by himself and several others. The following year Murray coauthored one of the National Conference's signature documents, "The Catholic, Jewish, Protestant Declaration on World Peace," which exhorted Christian and Jewish communities to create alternatives to war.[85]

His early writings in this area were cautious, vaguely positive, and careful to distinguish between ecumenical cooperation and Christian reunion. Murray played up the benefits of cooperation without claiming that equal breakthroughs were possible at the doctrinal level. He coined a term, "intercredal," to describe the project of ecumenical dialogue, but soon dropped it as a concession to critics that the word was misleading and overly ambitious. To the *American Ecclesiastical Review*, even cautious cooperation was a dubious enterprise at best. Prominent conservative Francis Connell admonished that the distinction between practical cooperation and doctrinal accommodation was misleading because one kind of leniency led to another, and upholding Catholic orthodoxy was far more important than making friends across religious lines. The very emphasis that *Theological Studies* placed on ecumenism showed that some Catholics were "becoming unduly tolerant" of Protestant churches and doctrines, he judged. Admittedly, charitableness was better than bigotry, but "Is not the pendulum swinging from bigotry to indifferentism?"[86]

Connell cited the National Conference of Christians and Jews as a prime example of the kind of enterprise that lured Catholics into indifferentism. Murray replied that "indifference" to Catholic doctrine did not remotely describe him. He was firmly committed to "Catholic exclusivism," but also believed in practicing "the principle of charity" on practical matters. Not only was it possible to combine these attitudes; in a religiously pluralistic context it was imperative to do so: "I am inclined to think that the purpose and significance of Christian co-operation will not be grasped, nor the danger of indifferentism obliviated, unless the movement is seen by the people against a larger doctrinal background, and in the light of a genuine appreciation of the realities of the present world crisis."[87]

That complex enterprise became Murray's wedge into the broader and more tangled work of rethinking the relation of Catholic faith to modern pluralism. *Theological Studies* teemed with "religion and society" articles; along the way Murray became something of a policy guru to church officials. In 1945 he urged his Jesuit superiors to take a stand against racial discrimination by encouraging African Americans to enter the order. He also wanted Jesuit schools and universities to be known for their non-discriminatory admission policies. On the other hand, Murray shook his head at Jesuits who censured segregated social practices as sinful. Responding to a controversy over an integrated dance at St Louis University, which intensified a public controversy over the school's recent admission of blacks, Murray opined that no moral value was at stake in the question of segregated social functions. The question of racial discrimination in admissions rose to the moral level, he believed, and there was undoubtedly a social value at stake in the policy concerning social functions, but not a moral one: "I would be quite at a loss to detect any grounds for 'sin' in the exclusion of Negroes from the dance. The issue is not between right and wrong, but between tact and stupidity in handling a delicate social situation." In his view, Jesuit officials at St Louis opted for stupidity in allowing black couples to attend the dance, which created unnecessary controversy for the school.[88]

That was private counsel on an issue on which Murray fell woefully short of prophetic spirit. In the public arena he fought a three-sided battle against Catholic traditionalists, Protestant critics, and secular critics about how religious liberty should be understood. Secular critic Paul Blanshard wrote popular books attacking Catholicism as an enemy of American democracy and freedom, and in 1947 a group named Protestants and Other Americans United for Separation of Church and State (POAU) was founded, aggressively reviving the old anti-Catholic nativism in a more secular and ideological form.[89]

Murray charged that the "new nativism" of Blanshard and the POAU was even more repugnant than the old one, because of its ideological bigotry. At least the old nativism did not turn Americanism into an ultimate value. For the old nativists, he explained, it was enough to fixate on the foreignness of Catholics, who were un-American because America was Protestant. The new version charged that Catholicism was un-American because it did not bow to democratic majoritarianism and scientific naturalism. The old Protestant chauvinism had strong tendencies toward cultural monism, exclusive valorization of the democratic state, and national self-righteousness, but at least its devotion to God and transcendent values checked this troika of bad things. The new nativism had nothing to check the bad aspects of Americanism, which it turned into a creed. Recognizing no moral authority in social life besides political will, it had no category besides power to interpret the church, and thus demanded that the church, to be a legitimate social organization, had to be subjected to the will of the democratic state.[90]

Even the most respectable liberal Protestant versions of Americanism were at least implicitly anti-Catholic, Murray stressed. Moreover, Protestantism had a disastrous tendency to degenerate into secularism. Worse yet, atheistic rationalism and post-Protestant secularism were on the rise in the USA. In 1949 Murray recycled these complaints in a debate with Union Theological Seminary dean Walter Russell Bowie that was published in the *American Mercury* magazine. The debate caught the attention of *Time* magazine and many national newspapers, giving Murray his first broad public exposure. To him, Bowie represented an insidiously respectable version of the old nativism. Being a liberal Protestant, Bowie had good manners, believed in God, and was careful to mention several things that he admired about Catholicism. But he confessed that certain things about Catholicism concerned him as a believer in freedom and democracy: "The clearly stated Roman Catholic purpose 'to make America

Catholic' would jeopardize the religious and civil liberties which have been the glory of Protestant countries and of Protestant culture." The Catholic Church did not regard itself as part of a larger Christian fellowship, Bowie explained. Rather, it taught that it was the only Christian Church, which alone possessed the truth, and that because error had no rights, the church had a right to "dominance, wherever it can assert and maintain its claims."[91]

Bowie cited the *Syllabus of Errors* and Leo XIII's *Immortale Dei*, recent troubles in Italy, Argentina, and Spain, and recent statements by Fiorelli Cavalli in the Vatican-vetted *Civilta Cattolica* and Francis Connell in the *American Ecclesiastical Review*. He leaned especially on Cavilli's 1948 article, because it was current and authorized by the Vatican. Cavilli wrote,

> The Roman Catholic Church, convinced, through its divine prerogatives, of being the only true church, must demand the right to freedom for herself alone, because such a right can only be possessed by truth, never by error. As to other religions, the Church will certainly never draw the sword, but she will require that by legitimate means they shall not be allowed to propagate false doctrine. Consequently, in a State where the majority of the people are Catholic, the Church will require that legal existence be denied to error, and that if religious minorities actually exist, they shall have only a *de facto* existence, without opportunity to spread their beliefs.

Where circumstances put this principle out of reach, "the Church will require for herself all possible concessions." The church "adapted" to religious pluralism in certain contexts, Cavilli observed, but it could not accept that error had the same rights as truth without betraying itself and its faith. To Protestants, Cavilli acknowledged, this principle was a "great scandal"; he asked them to understand that it was actually a non-negotiable question of faithfulness to the truth: "The Church cannot blush for her own want of tolerance, as she asserts it in principle and applies it in practice."[92]

In the spirit of "I rest my case," Bowie cited these passages and others at length. Murray replied with a blistering polemical barrage. American Catholics had an ample historical record of democratic participation and constructive citizenship in the USA, he observed, but somehow that never factored into Protestant and secular accounts of what American Catholics really wanted in their country. Did people like Bowie really believe that American Catholics posed some kind of threat to American democracy? How could they believe it if they knew any? Bowie, he said, fixed on papal statements, not the American experience, and he tried to be respectful, but in the end he simply recycled the usual "generalizations," "historical nonsense," "theological nonsense," and "epistemological and ethical nonsense," not to mention the usual prejudices. Murray charged that it was ludicrous to build a freedom-devouring monster out of a few bones scattered in papal statements. Instead of aspiring to scholarly sophistication, Bowie settled for "Sunday-supplement" archeology. It was equally ludicrous to suggest that Catholicism in Spain had any relevance to Catholicism in the American context, Murray scolded. Bowie leaped to scary archaeology and ridiculous analogies because he perceived Catholicism through an American Protestant lens. His argument, so typical in its emotionally unmoored anxiety, reflected "that hostility to the Catholic Church [which] is profoundly lodged in the Protestant collective unconscious, in consequence perhaps of some natal trauma." Murray, asking himself why Protestants were always on the defensive, answered that they lacked a constructive basis or principle. Protestantism existed only as a protest against Catholicism; otherwise it had no concept of what it was for. To Murray, that explained what Bowie and American Protestants really feared. What set off their anxiety was not the doctrine of the Catholic state, but the Catholic claim to be the true religion, because that made Protestantism a "second-class religion."[93]

That cheeky salvo set off an enraged reaction, in which Murray's more thoughtful and prophetic conclusion tended to be overlooked. "It is always a bit difficult to convince anyone that a bogeyman does not exist," he concluded. The difficulty heightened in this case because "Dr. Bowie does indeed have his few scattered bones." Murray was not quite sure how to prove "that it is impossible or illegitimate to construct out of them his fearsome monster." What he knew for certain was that fear, anxiety, and prejudice fueled the whole business, not an understanding of Catholic thought or any threat to American democracy. Papal statements from the past were not "crystal balls" that disclosed "the exact shape of things to come," he admonished. Although Protestants and secular critics claimed to fear otherwise, the church was not stuck forever with an *American Ecclesiastical Review*-style fossilization of *Immortale Dei*. The Catholic legacy was more complex than that; Murray understood the tradition better than its critics; and he had a prediction: "If I were to venture a prophecy, it would be that the development of the genuinely Catholic and democratic state will mean the end of the concept, 'religion of the State' (or the Spanish or Cavilli model), as the constitutional form in which the doctrinal idea of the 'freedom of the Church' has historically found its expression."[94]

That was Murray's project, to help make his prediction come true. Soon he realized that his inflammatory rhetoric did not serve this purpose and was not a good model of public theology. The *American Mercury* sent him 52 letters of response to the debate – all were negative. Chastened that he came off as flippant, arrogant, and evasive, Murray vowed to restrain his penchant for polemical metaphors. He wanted to start a nuanced, complex, intellectually serious discussion of religious liberty, but his polemics against Protestantism made it seem otherwise. They also distracted from the polemical enterprise for which he did not apologize, combating the rising secular tide. The lingering anti-Catholic anxieties of Protestants were a sad phenomenon, he judged, but not something with which Catholics could not cope. The real menace was the new nativism, "which they call evolutionary scientific humanism." Blanshard-style bigotry meant the repudiation of transcendent truth and the end of any robust notion of religious freedom. "Here, I think is the enemy," Murray wrote in a reply that the *American Mercury* declined to publish. "In the presence of this enemy I consider Catholic–Protestant polemic to be an irrelevance."[95]

It was one thing, however, to disavow flippancy and arrogance; the charge of evasiveness belonged to a different category. Murray winced at the many respondents who protested that instead of directly addressing the church–state issue, he danced around it, resorting to name-calling. He replied that his glosses on the complexity of the church–state issue were the true answer, not an evasion. The problem to be overcome was that simple understandings prevailed. Connell and Cavalli clung to a simple orthodoxy, boasting simplistically about the "unblushing intolerance" of the church, which confirmed Protestant fears that Catholicism was simply intolerant. A crucial example was the axiom, "Error has no rights," on which the *American Ecclesiastical Review* settled the entire issue. Murray decried the "false simplicity" of this axiom, which was "politically inoperative" at best (settling nothing about how governments were supposed to correct error) and "ethically meaningless" at worst (adding nothing to the tautology that error is error). He also rejected all simplistic proof-texting from papal statements, especially the *Syllabus of Errors*, which was a "notoriously difficult document," and the entire tradition of simplistic sloganeering about the ideal of the Catholic state. It could not be that Catholic thought was reducible to these slogans or stuck with them.[96]

By contrast, Murray's writing on this subject was richly layered, nuanced, and eventually coherent, although he had to drop a few positions to achieve a settled view, which was then censured by the Vatican. Always he argued out of the Scholastic tradition of natural law theory, but in the 1950s he transformed this tradition by integrating it with Western constitutional theory. Murray argued that any theory or defense of religious liberty had to include a prudential or practical component, a philosophical component, and a theological component. Civil law, a product of prudential reasoning, was a coercive and external restraint on the actions of individuals and groups. Rightly administered, it never contradicted natural law, which was a product of theoretical (philosophical) reasoning. Murray stressed the philosophical component (in his case, Thomist natural law) and the task of practically applying principles developed in the theoretical realms. The natural law was established by theoretical reason, but the moral agent moved from it to civil law by using prudential reason. Any sound prudential judgment had to have theoretical foundations in nature, natural law philosophy, revelation, and/or Catholic doctrine. Following Aquinas, Murray distinguished among four levels of moral discernment, the first three of which were open to all reasonable people. The first was the ethical a priori that good is to be done and evil avoided; the second was the breakthrough to ethical reflection, in which the moral agent began to reflect on how to do good and avoid evil; the third was the establishment of natural law principles that described universal human obligations; the fourth level, which Aquinas and Murray reserved for moral philosophers, applied the precepts of natural law to complex problems in economics, law, medicine, and the like.[97]

Murray insisted that natural law was universal, describing the moral experience of humankind. He bridled when people called it a Catholic theory or said that one had to accept Catholic presuppositions to believe in it, since, in his telling, it had no specifically Catholic presuppositions. If one believed that human beings were intelligent, reality was intelligible, and reality as discerned by human intelligence imposed certain ethical obligations on the will, then one was some kind of natural law theorist. Even these conditions were not really presuppositions, he argued, since all of them could be verified. Murray never stopped believing that natural law was the basis on which common discussion and moral reasoning should be pursued. He did not call it public theology, because that suggested something he rejected – either theology not rooted in church doctrine, or parading church doctrines in public discussion – and the term was not yet established. He did not call it ecumenical theology, either, because while that category flourished, he did not believe in Christian commonality across denominational lines. In his early writings Murray took for granted that the church's internal theological justifications did not belong in public discussion and it was pointless to look for a common basis of symbols or doctrines on which Christians might do public theology ecumenically.[98]

Theologically and spiritually, Protestantism was deeply alien to him; moreover, Murray knew the feeling was mutual even among the agreeable Protestants with whom he discussed ecumenical cooperation. Thus he held no brief for ecumenical theology, overlooking that in modern theology and culture, theology had greater ecumenical and public potential than natural law. Although Murray stuck to his convictions about the ecumenical and universal significance of natural law, he played a major role in changing what Catholic doctrine took natural law to be, and he came to realize that theological considerations were not so easily excluded. At Vatican Council II he also accepted that Protestants were part of the true church.

For him the consuming problem was that religious freedom needed better justifications. Armed with the theory of "Gelasian Dualism," sometimes called "the Gelasian Dyarchy" or "Christian Constitutionalism," Murray sought to provide them. Pope Gelasius I ascended to the papacy just after the fall of the Roman Empire in the West. In 492, embroiled in disputes with emperor Anastasius I, Gelasius told him in a letter, "Two there are, august emperor, by which this world is chiefly ruled, the sacred authority of the priesthood and the royal power." The pope boldly declared that the greater responsibility lay with the priests, because they were stewards of the divine things, while the secular rulers were in charge of public discipline. The priestly class had a higher dignity because the realm of the sacred was higher than that of political rule. But the rulers were also bound by the divine law and received their authority directly from God, not through the church. Gelasius taught that the church and state needed each other to fulfill the divine will and manage the public good. Thus there were two sources of moral authority in society, the Church and State, a principle deeply grafted into Catholic moral and political philosophy. Murray called it the "Gelasian thesis," describing it as the "Magna Carta" of religious liberty and the spiritual health of society: "In a true sense, the whole of Catholic theory and practice had taken the form of a speculative interpretation and practical application of this text."[99]

Murray's first attempt to securely ground a Catholic doctrine of religious freedom did not work out; in the meantime he became more ecumenical. His first articles on religious freedom stuck closely to the idioms of the moral manuals and the 1917 code of canon law, proposing to establish a basis for religious liberty in natural law: "We are supposing that the problem is posited in what Catholic thought calls 'the order of pure nature'; we are moving in the universe of discourse characteristic of Scholastic ethics, the natural science of morals, whose single architect is human reason." Dividing his subject into an ethical problem, a theological problem, and a political problem, he argued that the contingency of civil law was sufficient to ensure the protection of religious freedom on natural law and Catholic grounds, thus denying that establishment (the Catholic state) and intolerance were ideals. Protestants and atheists had natural rights in public expression based on the right of conscience.[100]

But the most that Murray could wring from canon law was grudging political tolerance of a temporary sort. From a natural law and Catholic standpoint, he affirmed, atheism was tolerable only on a temporary basis, because tolerance accepted a lack of harmony between the public and the highest good. Tolerance was justifiable only temporarily for the sake of a lower good, public peace. Murray bought a bit of peace, in theory, by stressing the individual right to conscience, but that left him with a deeper dualism than his "Gelasian" cover. Instead of spelling out the theological and political aspects of his argument, Murray started over, by questioning the canonical tradition with historical tools.

In his early career he blasted the historicist approach to the church–state issue as Protestant foolishness. In 1948 Murray declared, in effect, "Never mind." Any discussion of the church's rights and duties in the temporal order had to proceed from a historical standpoint, he decided: "Nothing is more unhelpful than an abstract starting point." That change of direction was a product of Murray's belated study of the history of Catholic ethical teaching. It surprised him to find that the meaning of natural law in church teaching shifted in relation to changing circumstances. Some natural law principles that he had treated as definitional and timeless had an unexpectedly malleable history. The line between prudential argument (as in politics) and philosophical argument (as in natural law) blurred for Murray, though never to the point of giving up on natural law. There had to be such a thing, he reasoned, but laying hold of it was a more slippery and fallible enterprise than canon lawyers presumed.[101]

Newly absorbed in historical study, Murray acknowledged that much of the church's "philosophical" infrastructure was as enmeshed in historical contingency as the political realm. The crowning example was the church's doctrine of the ideal state, which was a product of a historical emergency – the collapse of the Roman Empire – when the church filled a vacuum left by the state's disintegration. That was the right project for its time, Murray judged, but from a natural law standpoint it was a temporary concession to a crisis, not the realization of an ideal. Something similar occurred during the Middle Ages, when institutions governing the use of physical coercion, especially the law, decayed badly. To restore the rule of law, the church deposed several despotic rulers, employing some tools of temporal rule. In both cases, Murray argued, the church came to the rescue of a battered social order in order to produce something better, a "mature state." That was the true end in matters political. In the context of temporal disorder, the church had done well to stop the breakdown of political, legal, and social institutions. But in the modern context, the goal of nature and reason in the political sphere was a mature state in which popes did not crown political rulers of any kind. Though Murray still tried to place theological doctrines outside the relativizing gaze of historical criticism, he acknowledged that even here, historical circumstance was a causal factor to some degree. For him, the crucial task was to mine the implications of doctrinal change concerning the relation of church and state. If the church's definitional principles had changed in the past, they could change again. The next Catholic doctrine of the state needed to support mature states; toward that end Murray's dualism of church and state yielded to a tripartite theory of church, state, and society.[102]

In the early medieval period the church was forced to assume direct care for the common good, which it did by forming feudal relationships with immature governments. Murray reasoned that in the modern period states regained their capacity to assume their natural responsibilities. A mature state maintained sole custody of coercive power, upheld the rule of law, and took responsibility for the common good. Moreover, a mature state was itself a "perfect society" with its own finality and autonomy. Like the church, the state was prohibited from acting outside its own finality, and like the church, it rightly used its powers as instruments only to its own proper ends. The state was ethically prohibited from using its coercive power for the sake of a religious end, and the church could not demand that the state do so; in Murray's words, "The Church has no right to demand of the state what the state is not required by nature to give." Admittedly, he wrote, during the medieval period the state used its police power to advance religious unity, but that was not necessarily a violation of natural law. The state, when true to its nature, served only the temporal common good. As long as the state promoted religious unity for a temporal reason, to strengthen political unity or the social order, its persecution of heretics passed the test of natural law. But the age of temporal unity based on religion was over, Murray observed; the religious basis of political unity was invalidated by the "progressive differentiation of the political community from the religious community, and its consequent growth in autonomy through the perfection of its own institutions for its own self-direction."[103]

Murray realized where this argument was taking him – straight into a confrontation with the *American Ecclesiastical Review*, although he hoped not the Vatican. George Shea, an *Review* stalwart, used the phrase "Catholic society" instead of the historically overloaded "Catholic state," which prompted Murray to stress differences that Shea did not have in mind. Shea took establishment (the Catholic state) for granted as the normative ideal; Murray replied that "society" and "state" were not interchangeable terms. The concept of "civil society" designated the "total complex of organized human relationships on the temporal plane," of which the political realm was a subset organized "for the common good, in distinction from private goods." To Murray, the common good was not merely the sum total of individual goods, but also included the good of the body politic, the "people" as a social whole. The state was the agency of the body politic responsible for public order and service. As such it was the highest "subsidiary function of society," but Murray stressed its subsidiary status. The state was merely one functional agency of the people, which was a living, historical, social reality – civil society – organized through a total complex of institutions, customs, and beliefs: "'We the people' is a human thing, of flesh and blood, ensouled by a community of ideas and purposes; it has a common life, organized into myriad interlocking institutions, slowly built up in time, which impart to this life a structure and a form."[104]

Murray was aiming at the weakest link of the establishment argument – the notion that a "Catholic majority" was obligated to achieve the ideal of a Catholic state. Civil society and political society were two very different things, he contended, the state was a mere agency of civil society, and even when the society was overwhelmingly Catholic, there was no reason why the faith had to be established in the state. Establishment was an act of reason – an order of positive law – not an act of faith. Even where establishment still existed, it was merely a recognition of the social fact of a people's faith, not a dogma that Catholics needed to believe or an act of faith by the state, "least of all on the part of Citizen Bonaparte," as in the 1803 Concordat. That was a flash of Murray's cutting humor, which occasionally enlivened his many pages of abstract argument. Establishment made sense in the sixteenth century as a way of coping with exploding nationalism and religious diversity, he acknowledged, but it did not make sense in highly developed modern societies that institutionalized the differences between state and society.[105]

Francis Connell replied that church teaching on this subject was plainly contrary. The church taught that political rulers, when persuaded of the truth of the Catholic faith, were obligated to establish Catholicism as the religion of the state. Murray countered that in that case, the state made itself the judge of who had the right theology and who would be permitted to preach the gospel. The *American Ecclesiastical Review* held out for the notion of the state as a faithful personality. Murray replied that in that case, the church was tied to monarchical or dictatorial forms of government – the only kind that could be personified – thereby vitiating the church's independence from the temporal order. The crux of the matter was that so-called Catholic orthodoxy made the state the judge of religious truth, subordinating the sacred realm to the political. Murray put it sharply: "Fr. Connell's effort to exalt the Kingship of Christ over civil rulers results in an exaltation of the civil ruler over Christ the King, whose doctrine is made subject to judgment by the civil power."[106]

By then a great deal was at stake for Murray in the question of whether Catholic orthodoxy was sufficiently flexible to include him. His polemical thrusts at Shea, Fenton, and Connell hurt him at the Vatican, where the *Review* was esteemed for defending the faith in a difficult environment. Leo XIII had invoked the phrase "religion of the state" – though Murray stressed that he used it only once – and it had canonical standing in more than a dozen Concordats from Pius VII to 1929. In the aftermath of his heated exchange with the journal, Murray realized that to clarify his thinking and prevail in the argument, he had to deal with the special problem of Leo XIII. On the one hand, Leo had revived Thomist philosophy, including natural law reasoning and the principle of Gelasian dualism, and had launched the modern tradition of Catholic social thought. On the other hand, he defended religious intolerance, condemned Americanism by name, called for coercive restraints on freedom of speech and assembly, and argued for establishment. Murray, in his typically probing, sifting, testing, sometimes polemical style, went to work on the Leonine legacy, writing six long articles for *Theological Studies* that tried to make sense of Leo's context, thinking, and inheritance. The sixth article, however, "Leo XIII and Pius XII: Government and the Order of Religion," written in 1955, was not published in *Theological Studies* or anywhere else, because Murray was silenced by the Vatican.

The "Leonine Series," so named by J. Leon Hooper, SJ, in his excellent reader on Murray, *Religious Liberty*, and his analysis of Murray's career, *The Ethics of Disclosure*, would not have made an absorbing book, unlike Murray's later collection *We Hold These Truths* (1960). Murray set off in various directions, sometimes promised and failed to return to arguments, and repeated certain points many times, sometimes unavoidably. Always he pressed on the distinction between state and society, recasting Leo's church–state argument in terms of his own.

In "The Church and Totalitarian Democracy," (1952) and "Leo XIII: Separation of Church and State" (1953) Murray examined the Vatican's understanding of political power during the Leonine period. Leo, coping with the dissolution of the Papal States and his imprisonment in the Vatican, restored the Gelasian idea of the church's freedom to the level of a fundamental principle. The French Third Republic, meanwhile, appalled him. At best it struck Leo as a form of majoritarian totalitarianism; at worst it was a more sinister totalitarianism in which a Jacobin elite imposed its atheism as a new anti-religion of the state. In reaction, Murray explained, Leo stressed the necessity of a dualistic scheme that preserved human freedom and the Christian basis of a good society.[107]

In "Leo XIII on Church and State: The General Structure of the Controversy," (1953) Murray explored Leo's reading of the social, national, and ideological forces that threatened the church's existence. Stressing the pope's sense of embattlement, Murray described his outlook as conspiratorial. Leo believed that French and Italian secular leaders stood behind a sprawling network of Masons, Communists, anarchists, sectarians, and others conspiring to erect an atheistic world order. In two articles titled "Leo XIII: Two Concepts of Government" (1953, 1954) Murray argued that Leo was primarily concerned with society, not the state, and that his view of the relation between government action and society (especially the economy and general culture) better fit Murray's triad of church, state, and society. *Rerum Novarum* made a clear distinction between the state and the economic order, but unfortunately Leo did not maintain it anywhere else, and he reaffirmed the church's endorsement of establishment and intolerance. Murray stressed the upshot of his historical investigations. If the church's defense of establishment and intolerance rested on timeless theological and natural law grounds, it was hard to make an argument for the development of doctrine in this area. But, in fact, the church's teaching in this area was shaped profoundly by changing historical realities.[108]

His last article in the series, "Leo XIII and Pius XII: Government and the Order of Religion," (1955) was supposed to be the capstone. Dropping previous hedges and caveats, Murray argued for a clear distinction between society and the state, claiming that it carried forward and made sense of Leo's opposition to continental democratic monism. Advocates of establishment and intolerance usually appealed to Leo's teaching that society was subject to the sovereignty of God, the state was subject to the divine law, and society was subject to the law of Christ. Murray countered that if one took seriously the distinction between society and state, this threefold Leonine argument cut against the Christian state idea. Leo had a concept of public religion that derived from the principle of the subjection of society to the divine sovereignty, but collective public faith was a free act of faith, not something to be established by juridical law. The same thing was true of society's subjection to the law of Christ; if compelled by law, it was not really religious faith. As for the state's subjection to divine law, Murray reasoned that this principle worked only as an expression of Christian constitutionalism, in which the state was limited by the divine law, yet also an instrument of it. Implicitly, Leo had a version of the society–state distinction, but he failed to grasp it because he equated Catholic nations with Catholic peoples and was consumed by the need to protect Catholic peoples from their enemies. Thus he contended that tolerance was an evil. Murray, believing that he had Pope Pius XII on his side, sought to improve on the legacy of that notion. Tolerance was a civic virtue under the conditions and limits of civil power, not an evil, he argued.[109]

In March 1953 an outspoken Curia leader, Alfredo Cardinal Ottaviani, created a media stir with a provocative speech on the church–state issue. Only two months before he had been elevated to cardinal and appointed Pro-Secretary of the Holy Office of the Roman Curia; in later years Ottaviani served as Secretary and Pro-Prefect of the Curia. Rephrasing a typical Curia formulation, he described the legal intolerance of the Spanish state as the "thesis," the approximation of the Catholic ideal, while the legal tolerance of the American system was a mere "hypothesis." Murray heard through the Jesuit grapevine that Pius XII was unhappy with this formulation, and in December the pope gave a speech to a group of Italian jurists, *Ci riesce*, that seemed to undercut Ottaviani's argument. Ottaviani described establishment as an immutable teaching of the church, but Pius asserted that he, as pope, had the ultimate say on this issue. Murray took that to mean the Vatican door was open to the development of doctrine on this issue, especially because Pius also emphasized the limits of law for spiritual and political ends. In the pope's teaching, Murray explained, "tolerance and intolerance are alternative modes of legal action, each of which must find its justification in terms of identically the same set of principles and norms." Murray did not aspire to a Vatican endorsement of the American idea over the Spanish one; it was enough for the church to say that both were legitimate. Ottaviani's "thesis-hypothesis" was a Curial version of what Murray called the "disjunctive" approach; Murray's alternative was a "unitary theory" that applied the same set of principles to various circumstances: "You would therefore more correctly say that both tolerance and intolerance are 'hypotheses,' subsumed under the one complex but unitary thesis. Each of the alternative hypotheses is an application of this unitary thesis to divergent circumstances. Both of them are legal decisions; neither of them is a dogma."[110]

It followed that the Spanish and American models had to appeal for their validity to the same ideal of religious unity and the common good. One was not necessarily better than the other; Murray quipped that any boasting of that sort was as stupid as the drunken argument about whether St. Patrick or the Fourth of July was greater. Each of these systems was a possible ideal "for the circumstances for which it was designed." The real "thesis" was not Spain or the U.S., but the ideal of a Christian society, which endorsed tolerance in some contexts and intolerance in others. The question of tolerance naturally arose with greater intensity in religiously plural societies, Murray acknowledged, but even in an overwhelmingly Catholic society, legal intolerance was not necessarily the ideal: "Before this institution can be validated a question of fact has to be resolved. The thesis itself does not answer such questions of fact; it simply presents the principles to be applied in answering them."[111]

By the time that Murray wrote these words in the late fall of 1954, however, he knew that his capstone article might not get past the Roman censors. Having come rather late to the realization that he was in trouble with the Vatican, he put his cards on the table, in an article that occasioned the message that he was officially silenced.

The key to his silencing was that he offended Ottaviani; moreover, it didn't help that Murray had an admiring Catholic and Protestant audience. In 1950 he was appointed as a consultant for the US government in the Public Affairs Section of the Office of the US High Commissioner of Germany, in which, for three months, he lectured Germans on how their postwar democracy should arrange its church–state relations. The following year he became the first Catholic to be named as a visiting professor at Yale University, an honor that Murray treasured, although he alternated between affirming and denying it. It was important for a Catholic to make such a breakthrough at a prestigious secular university, he explained; on the other hand, he wished it could be someone else. He was too tired and overworked; on the other hand, he pressed his Jesuit provincial John McMahon to approve the appointment and expressed enthusiasm and gratitude for it. One of Murray's graduate students during his year at Yale, George Lindbeck, later recalled watching him prepare for a lecture, "tense yet courtly, driven by a perfectionist urge, and trapped by his own difficulty in scheduling his work into a major loss of sleep." Another graduate student at Yale, James Shannon, who became a bishop, recalled gratefully that he came to know Murray's "great kindness, his enormous erudition, his wholeness as a person, and his subtle, perceptive, often devastating wit."[112]

Murray wrote the Leonine articles after returning from Yale, collecting rebukes from his usual critics. Joseph Fenton was a frequent correspondent; back and forth he and Murray debated the legitimacy of Murray's project. Through 1953 Murray felt secure in his position and standing. His friend John Tracy Ellis, managing editor of the *Catholic Historical Review*, was a strong supporter, as were Murray's Jesuit superiors in the USA and Rome. Murray wished for some strong-minded bishops on his side, but judged that he could get by without them. Responding to an article by Ellis on the American Catholic tradition, he complained that the present church lacked "any American Catholic bishops." Murray explained to Ellis that in a previous generation he could have counted on the support of real American bishops, like John Carroll, but the current bishops were Vatican stooges. That was a very sad state of affairs, he reflected, yet he did not feel endangered. If he claimed that America was the ideal, not Spain, that would be trouble; but he never said that. Murray's feeling of safety strengthened when, in his reading, Pius XII contradicted Ottaviani.[113]

But it was a perilous thing in the 1950s to offend a Curia leader, and Fenton, too, had real influence at the Vatican, especially through Ottaviani. Fenton insisted that Murray read too much assurance into the pope's speech, which did not contradict Ottaviani. In February 1954 Fenton admonished against any presumption that the term "Catholic state" lacked intelligibility or a clear meaning. Moreover, it was time to cease all objections to the principle of "error has no rights," which was deeply established in Catholic doctrine. Finally, it was not feasible "to reprove the teaching that, objectively, a complete separation of Church and State is an evil." Murray had been warned. The following month he gave a forceful reply in a speech at Catholic University of America, stressing that the problem of religious freedom was not merely an American issue. Ultimately it was about humankind's search for political unity: "Political unity may possibly, in God's providence, be the preparation for religious unity." In dealing with religious pluralism, he stressed, the highest good was "a peaceful life for the Church and for divided humanity – the good of world harmony." As for Ottaviani's claim that Spain approximated the Catholic ideal, Murray argued that American Catholics did not represent a mere hypothesis, and he praised Pius XII for taking leave of Ottaviani on that point.[114]

That sealed Murray's fate; nobody in his corner had enough influence at the Vatican to overcome his public chastisement of Ottaviani. The following week Ottaviani complained to Francis Cardinal Spellman, who promised to look into the matter. Meanwhile Fenton blasted Murray for an "utterly baseless and incorrect" attack on Ottaviani that misrepresented the pope's speech and took a "fantastic" line against Catholic doctrine. It was simply ridiculous to pretend there was any difference between Ottaviani and the pope, Fenton declared. They believed the same thing, which was the longstanding orthodoxy of "the great body of manuals in theology and in public ecclesiastical law which deal with this particular subject, the teaching of the *magisterium* itself." The notion that Catholic thought was changing in this area was simply a Murray conceit. One issue later the *American Ecclesiastical Review* ripped Murray again, as Giuseppe Di Meglio called his argument "devoid of foundation" and "disrespectful." Vincent McCormick, SJ, American assistant to the Jesuit Generalate in Rome, advised Murray not to reply, but by then the Vatican had a sufficient supply of incriminating quotes from Murray. At the end of 1954 Murray submitted to the Roman censors his capstone article in the Leonine series; the following July he got a negative verdict. The article could not be published because he was officially silenced on this subject. McCormick, informing Murray that his Jesuit superior agreed with the final verdict, advised him not to fight it. His time had not yet come, and there was no point in "provoking those who will not be appeased."[115]

Murray took it hard. He told McCormick that he was pessimistic to begin with, but had not expected anything this bad: "The whole thing represents a defeat and a failure of the first order." McCormick told him not to give up; he was far from finished; time would bring changes. Murray replied that he had no hope of that. He had already cleared his room of all books on the subject, "in symbol of retirement, which I expect to be permanent." He was finished with the church–state issue, on which the reactionary Right had prevailed. The *American Ecclesiastical Review* responded to its vindication, Murray's silencing, and another papal speech by declaring victory; Fenton announced that the matter was settled "for all future teaching and writing on Church–State relations." Murray resolved to forget the whole business. For some, he told McCormick, the matter still boiled, but to him it had become "a nuisance and a bore.

I couldn't care less." He was willing to take any assignment that McCormick had for him; meanwhile Murray shifted to an aspect of his subject that promised to be safer from an ecclesiastical standpoint: the role of Catholicism in the USA.[116]

The American Idea and the Catholic Presence

Losing the battle for religious freedom was discouraging, but at least it freed him to explore topics related to it. Murray started with an article on Catholics as a creative minority in the USA, moved next to the Christian view of education, and wrote three articles dealing with aspects of censorship, freedom, and law. By 1958 he was ready to un-retire from the church–state issue, sending to the censors an article for *Civilta Cattolica* that distinguished his "unitary" theory from the regnant "disjunctive" one. Murray played down his conviction that Catholic doctrine had something to learn from Anglo-American political philosophy, which smacked of "America better than Spain." The best approach was to have one theory that applied to a diversity of contexts, he argued. But the article was rejected, and the following year he submitted it again, this time dressed up with supportive Latin and Italian quotations, which was also rejected. Between rejections McCormick told Murray to stop annoying his opponents: "We must be patient; some people never forget." If the political situation in the USA were to put the Vatican on the defensive, McCormick reflected, things could change in Murray's favor. In the meantime he was barred from the game: "Be content to stay on the sidelines, unless the hierarchy forces you into play: deepen and clarify your own position, and be ready with your solution approved, when the opportune time comes. That is not coming in the present Roman atmosphere." Two months later, in October 1958, the atmosphere began to change, as Pius XII died and was succeeded by the affable "interim pope," Angelo Cardinal Roncalli, Pope John XXIII.[117]

McCormick's reference to American political winds was a knowing allusion to the presidential aspirations of John F. Kennedy, who had already reached out to Murray for advice on the Catholic constitutional problem. The following year John XXIII stunned the world by calling for a new ecumenical council, a surprise the Curia did its best to deflate. Ottaviani became Secretary of the Curia in 1959, and for three years after John XXIII's announcement the Curia kept a firm grip on the Holy Office, battling to keep Vatican II from modernizing anything. In the meantime Murray revisited his plan for an essay collection. The Vatican rebuke had terminated his proposed collection on the church–state issue, but in 1959 he switched to a book with the same publisher, Sheed and Ward, on the problem of American religious pluralism. *We Hold These Truths: Catholic Reflections on the American Proposition* was published the following year, to immediate acclaim that landed Murray on the cover of *Time* magazine. Although most of its chapters had been published with little notice between 1950 and 1958, in the historic election year of 1960 the book was a sensation.[118]

We Hold These Truths was an exercise in public philosophy and a plea for it. To a vast audience for whom Murray's themes and style were new, he declared that America was indeed, as Abraham Lincoln famously asserted, a nation dedicated to a proposition. The "American Proposition" was both doctrinal and practical, Murray argued. As a philosophical proposition it was the statement of a truth to be demonstrated; like mathematical propositions, it stated an operation to be performed. The American Proposition was a structure of thought making a claim to truth and a political project aimed at historical success. In neither sense was it ever a finished thing; the demonstration was ongoing, and the project decayed if it was not continually renewed. Every American schoolchild knew its content, the Declaration of Independence written by Thomas Jefferson:

> We hold these truths to be self-evident: that all men are created equal; that they are endowed by their Creator with certain inalienable rights; that among these are life, liberty, and the pursuit of happiness; that to secure these rights, governments are instituted among men, deriving their just powers from the consent of the governed; that whenever any form of government becomes destructive of these ends, it is the right of the people to alter or to abolish it, and to institute new government, laying its foundation on such principles, and organizing its powers in such form, as to them shall seem most likely to effect their safety and happiness.

Murray noted that Lincoln, in a moment of national crisis, lifted up the "imperiled part" of the proposition, "All men are created equal," and thus gave impetus to it. To Murray, the American Proposition was the basis of America's public consensus or public philosophy.[119]

He acknowledged that to the eighteenth-century founders, many things were self-evident that were not always self-evident to later Americans. But one thing was not to be doubted: the American Proposition rested on a realist epistemology. Murray explained, "The sense of the famous phrase is simply this, 'There are truths, and we hold them, and we here lay them down as the basis and inspiration of the American project, this constitutional commonwealth." To the founders, the structure of the state and the rules of politics were founded on a structure of objective truth, "universal in its import, accessible to the reason of man, definable, defensible." In many respects the American Proposition was pragmatic, but its philosophy was not pragmatism, for pragmatism knew only results, not truths. In the American Proposition there were truths to be known, accepted, and worked out. Murray sought to discern what truths religiously pluralistic America still held, while he took it for granted that Catholic teaching was "superior to, and in control of, the whole order of civil life." Noting that Americans sometimes asked whether Catholicism was compatible with American democracy, Murray advised that the question was invalid and impertinent, "for the manner of its position inverts the order of values." The pertinent question was whether democracy was compatible with the truth, Catholicism.[120]

But Murray acknowledged that the American Proposition posed special challenges to the Catholic faith, because it was a doctrine of, and experiment in, pluralism – the coexistence within a single political community of groups holding divergent and incompatible views about religious matters. A pluralist society was inevitably one characterized by disagreement and dissension; on the other hand, it implied a community of agreement and consensus, otherwise there was no single political community. If there was to be a nation at all, some set of principles had to be held in common. But in a pluralistic context these principles had to be held in a fashion that did not violate the integrity of the groups within the society. This was a practical problem requiring civic virtue, Murray noted, but it was also theoretical, requiring "some sort of doctrine."[121]

By virtue of its unique history the USA was a novel experiment in pluralism. In Europe the revolutions of modernity disrupted a previous religious unity, Murray noted, but in America pluralism was "the native condition." Thus, in America a new problem was put to "the universal Church," meaning the Catholic Church. Murray reassured his readers that this problem was not impossibly difficult for "the Catholic intelligence," though it required "some nicety" in the exercise of the church's conceptual equipment.[122]

We Hold These Truths displayed Murray's growing admiration for the Anglo-American tradition and his concern that American society was turning away from "the essential contents of the American consensus," which he stressed were congenial to Catholics. Because the USA was conceived in the tradition of natural law, he argued, it was never divided like modern France, Italy, and Spain. Americans as a whole embraced a constellation of ancient ideas, "deeply implanted in the British tradition," about the rule of law, government as an empire of laws, and sovereignty as a purely political reality limited by law. There was no real controversy in American history about the general features of the American ideal; nearly all Americans wanted "a free people under a limited government," a Whig phrase that Thomas Aquinas would have liked. The founders and builders of the American order did not conceive government as a phenomenon of force (as in positivism), a historical category (as in Marxism), or merely the power to coerce (as in realism). For Americans, government was the right to command with an authority derived from law.[123]

Murray stressed that the American founders took these ideas from their British heritage and made only one major addition to them, the written constitution. But the addition was crucial, for the American Constitution was explicitly an act of the people established through constitutional convention and popular ratification, not something granted by the king or prince-president. In the American tradition the principles of consent and popular participation in government were joined together: "Americans agreed that they would consent to none other than their own legislation, as framed by their representatives, who would be responsible to them." This consensus required a quite remarkable degree of faith in the capacity of people to govern themselves and included an outspoken passion for freedom, but Murray argued that it was not unrealistic. Americans never supposed that everybody had to be an expert on the details of government; they took for granted the premise of medieval society that the people possessed an inherent sense of justice; their stress on the rule of self-legislated law was a bulwark against libertine excess; and they rightly preached that only a virtuous people could be free. In the American consensus, freedom was an ethical ideal ordered by discipline. The American founders were individualists who, as descendants of the English tradition, also understood the social nature of human beings. The roots of the English tradition of freedom "were not in the top of anyone's brain but in history," especially the English medieval notion that freedom rested on a natural law in which human nature was expressed.[124]

Murray worried that Americans were losing the capacity to speak this language of ethical and political principles. American academics spurned the very notion of an American consensus because it rested on natural law ideas about moral truths held in common. In place of the old consensus rhetoric of inalienable rights, popular sovereignty, consent, separation of powers, and limited government, Americans increasingly assumed, and were told by the intellectual class, that politics was about groups, class conflict, public opinion, the circulation of elites, and public administration. The American idea of law as an expression of reason had been overtaken by the positivist idea of law as an expression of will. Murray judged that the American consensus was not completely dissolved, but its decay was far advanced: "Perhaps one day the noble many-storied mansion of democracy will be dismantled, leveled to the dimensions of a flat majoritarianism, which is no mansion but a barn, perhaps even a tool shed in which the weapons of tyranny may be forged." He shuddered to think that before long, most Americans would take for granted what their secular academics told them. Instead of believing that government had a moral basis, the foundation of society was the universal moral law, the state was subject to a natural law inhering in human nature, the ultimate origin of law was the divine mind, and the nation lived under God, Americans would believe that government had no moral basis, there was no universal moral law, the legal basis of society was merely statistical, and God was a private preference at best. Murray argued that America's growing Catholic population was an antidote to this trend line of decay.[125]

In 1948 *Christian Century* editor Charles Clayton Morrison contended aggressively that the USA would never have become a pluralistic liberal democracy had it been settled by Catholic pioneers. Morrison was an ardent ecumenist, but strictly within Protestantism. He shook his head at liberal Protestant searches for common ground with the Catholic Church, chiding that the two movements had "radically different conceptions of the Christian religion." Catholicism and liberal Protestantism had a few phrases in common, but contrasting ideas of religion and forms of it. When seen as a whole, Catholicism was an "irresponsible power system" based on hierarchy and dogmatism: "Protestantism cannot cooperate ecclesiastically with a dictatorship. It must make a clear-cut decision to accept its task of winning Christ to America without any illusion that it has a collaborator in Roman Catholicism."[126]

That insulting polemic burned in Murray's craw for years afterward, reinforcing some of his feelings about Catholic–Protestant incommensurability, but also representing a prejudice that had to be challenged. Murray was sensitive to the irony of Morrison's argument that liberal Protestantism wrongly accommodated secular liberal culture and thus lost spiritual and public power. Like Murray, Morrison believed that American Christianity was in a life or death struggle with secular disbelief. For Morrison, as for Murray, nearly everything precious in the American experiment was at stake in the secularization of American culture. Defending the Christian character of the American republic, Morrison sought to renew it through a vigorous ecumenical Protestantism that dropped all denominational encumbrances. On most political issues he was well to the left of Murray, but Morrison typified the last generation of Christianizing liberal Protestants for whom diversity eroded the nation's soul. To Morrison, Luther Wiegle, William Bower, and F. Ernest Johnson the crucial thing was to save a common American faith in the face of hostile secularizing and pluralizing trends.[127]

Murray countered that the way to hold off a rising tide of secular destruction was to make a more creative response to religious pluralism. Whenever Americans spoke their historic language of unalienable rights, constitutionalism, and limited government, he argued, "the Catholic joins the conversation with complete ease. It is his language. The ideas expressed are native to his own universe of discourse." The strongest hope of a renewed American consensus was for more Catholics to join the conversation. Murray stressed that the Catholic Church spoke the universal language of moral rights and responsibilities long before the USA existed, and it would go on speaking it even if non-Catholic Americans settled for the thin soup of positivism, majoritarianism, and disbelief. In that case, "it would be for others, not Catholics, to ask themselves whether they still shared the consensus which first fashioned the American people into a body politic and determined the structure of its fundamental law."[128]

We Hold These Truths did not rest, however, with this account of America's eroding public faith or its table-turning pitch for Catholic Americanism. The book owed much of its public impact to its centerpiece chapter, "Civil Unity and Religious Integrity," which took aim at a quite specific problem, the First Amendment to the Constitution. This chapter, along with another that became the opening chapter of *We Hold These Truths*, had been written as a lengthy article in 1954 titled "The Problem of Pluralism in America." Murray published it four times before including it in *We Hold These Truths*, on one occasion toning down its affirmation of American society. Thus by 1960 it had had an ample career, but to a new audience pondering John Kennedy's presidential candidacy, Murray's treatment of the First Amendment problem was a revelation.[129]

He observed that non-Catholics often raised the issue with a question they assumed to be embarrassing: Did Catholics really believe in the First Amendment? Murray replied that the question seemed embarrassing only because misunderstanding abounded on this subject. The American Constitution was not an object of faith. It prescribed law, not dogma, containing articles of civil peace that Americans were required to observe, not articles of faith they were required to believe.

Three groups dominated the discussion on this topic, he judged, and all of them invested the Constitution with an authority of some type that compelled belief. The first group interpreted the Constitution as prescribing distinctly Protestant religious or cultural beliefs rooted in free-church Puritanism. For them the articles of the First Amendment were articles of faith with a definite religious content. The second group, descendants of early American deism and rationalism, interpreted the Constitution in terms of Enlightenment secular liberalism. For them the articles were invested only with the rationality that attached to law, not any religious meaning, and rationality was the highest value of law. The third group, the "secularizing Protestants," melded its religious faith with American secular culture, trying to bridge the differences between America's Puritan and rationalist traditions. For them, religion was true and relevant to the extent that it embraced the norms of modern secular culture, including its concept of freedom.[130]

Murray took no interest in judging the relative historical merits of these interpretive traditions. What mattered was that all three were deeply rooted in American history, all of them viewed the Constitution as expressing a worldview or ideology, each of them contradicted the other two, and all were wrong in assuming that the Constitution called for some kind of assent. Americans did not have to believe in the First Amendment in the way that Christians assented to the Nicene Creed, he contended. Otherwise the Constitution became a religious test, and in that case "the Federal Republic has suddenly become a voluntary fellowship of believers either in some sort of free-church Protestantism or in the tenets of a naturalistic humanism." To Murray, all three versions of this notion were "preposterous." The USA was "a good place to live in," he acknowledged: "Many have found it even a sort of secular sanctuary. But it is not a church, whether high, low, or broad. It is simply a civil community, whose unity is purely political." The USA was a pluralistic republic that had no business insinuating religious teaching of any kind into its law. Any attempt to do so was "prima facie illegitimate and absurd."[131]

The Constitution offered articles of peace, not faith, which compelled only civil obedience, not religious assent. A bit uncomfortably for Murray, this formulation put him closest to his least favorite group, the secular rationalists, who also expounded the "articles of peace, not faith" view. But the secular Enlightenment types routinely treated their rationalism as a semi-religious creed, he noted, which made them disastrously inept in dealing with religion, especially religious pluralism: "This school of thought, which is of relatively recent growth in America, thrusts into the First Amendment its own ultimate views of truth, freedom, and religion." To the secular rationalists, religion had no value except as private comfort, and Catholicism was a "disvalue." In their reading, the Constitution supported the enlightened view – their own – that the highest form of law was civil law, the highest rights were civil rights, the state was purely an instrument of the popular will, and voting was the highest governing principle of statecraft.[132]

To impose that cramped worldview on the Constitution was to rationalize the mistreatment of religion and religious believers, Murray protested. At best, the secular rationalist view tolerated the church only as a private association, not as a society in its own right, because secular rationalism had room for only one society, civil society: "In this view, separation of church and state, as ultimately implying a subordination of church to state, follows from the very nature of the state and its law; just as religious freedom follows from the very nature of freedom and of truth." Murray observed that even if Protestants found this an acceptable arrangement, Catholics did not: "The Catholic rejects the religious position of Protestants with regard to the nature of the church, the meaning of faith, the absolute primacy of conscience, etc.; just as he rejects secular views with regard to the nature of truth, freedom, and civil society as man's last end. He rejects these positions as demonstrably erroneous in themselves."[133]

Therefore the American democracy needed to take its religious pluralism more seriously. If the First Amendment was a religious test, 35 million American Catholics were officially dissenters. If the First Amendment meant what the secularists said, Catholics were officially denigrated. Murray contended that it was not enough, in a religiously diverse democracy, to have a pluralistic political and legal philosophy. America was overdue to respect the existence of non-Protestant faiths in American society, making good on the acceptance of diversity implied in the Declaration of Independence.

His bellwether example, in a later chapter, was the public school system. Were America to take seriously its religious pluralism, Murray argued, all four of its major concepts of public education would have to be repudiated. These were the historic concept of the public school as a vaguely Protestant enterprise, the rival concept of the school as purely secular, the Deweyan view of the school as an incubator of democracy, and the non-sectarian view of the school as a transmitter of spiritual and/or moral values. None of these views fitted the "present facts of American life," he contended: "American society is neither vaguely Protestant nor purely secular. The religion of America is not 'democracy,' nor is it some generalized faith in 'values.' Religion in America has a form, a precisely defined form, a pluralistically structured form. This is the fact."[134]

That was the point, to respect the existing diversity of religions in the USA. To move in that direction was to reject the usual options of watering down Protestantism, stripping religion from the public square, treating democracy as a substitute for religion, or reducing religion to values. In the USA only public schools received public support, while church schools were denied it. Murray protested that this policy was a vestige of nineteenth-century Protestant America, when mainline Protestants straightforwardly regarded the public schools as transmitters of America's common (Protestant) faith.

Murray did not disparage the role of public schools in incubating a common American culture, he wanted them to take that function more seriously. But the segregated structure of American education was plainly unjust and a relic of the past, he argued. In the existing system, religion was segregated "in the concrete pluralist sense" from public schools, while religious schools were segregated from public assistance. Murray pressed the analogy to racial segregation. Morally, racial discrimination had always been reprehensible, but only recently had (white) American society reached a point at which "the public conscience" had risen above deeply rooted prejudices. Murray wanted religious segregation to end the same way.[135]

It had always been morally unjust to deny public funds to certain schools merely because they taught a particular religion, he contended. According to the moral canon of distributive justice, the moral obligation of government was to care for the needs, merits, and capacities of society's various groups and of society in general. What was needed now was "a growth in moral insight, assisted by a realistic grasp of socio-religious reality." Murray acknowledged that transforming American policy in this area would take a while, involving considerable practical difficulties. But religious discrimi-nation was morally reprehensible, and its sociological support structure was crumbling: "Here again, a true appreciation of sociological change serves to clarify a moral prin-ciple. The denial of aid to the religious school does not square with the fact of our pluralist social structure."[136]

We Hold These Truths was hailed as a historic contribution to American civilization and the 1960 presidential election. Timed to appear a few months before the election, the book was widely cited in the media as a definitive discussion of "the Catholic problem," helping to make Kennedy's case that there wasn't one. Though Murray was more conservative politically than Kennedy, he advised Kennedy on the reli-gion–state issue and conferred with his campaign assistants Arthur Schlesinger, Jr and Theodore Sorensen. Kennedy told Schlesinger that he admired Murray and appreciated his book. Sorensen, who wrote Kennedy's famous church and state speech to the Houston Ministerial Association, read it to Murray over the telephone while standing next to a plane just before leaving for Houston. Murray thought the speech was well done, though he complained that hearing it over the phone was less than ideal. Years later *Newsweek* aptly recalled: "Murray demonstrated in theory what John F. Kennedy demonstrated in practice: that Americanism and Roman Catholicism need no longer fear each other."[137]

Murray's sudden renown felt like vindication to many of his admirers, although at the time the Curial right still controlled the machinery of Catholic orthodoxy. The *American Ecclesiastical Review* was not impressed by *We Hold These Truths* or Murray's magazine cover fame; Fenton blasted the book as a careless, sloppy abandonment of Catholic teaching and a capitulation to liberalism, a reaction that held some danger for Murray. Would the Vatican tell him to lay off these topics too? For a while that was a serious possibility. In 1961 several prominent liberal-leaning theologians were excluded from the preparatory meetings for Vatican II. Murray was invited to attend the first session of Vatican II, but then rudely "un-invited" by Archbishop Egidio Vagnozzi, the Vatican's Apostolic Delegate in Washington, DC. To Murray this "dis-invitation" was deeply disappointing. The following year, after the council's prepara-tory commission produced two competing, mediocre drafts on religious freedom and the issue was dropped from the council's official agenda, Murray implored Baltimore archbishop Lawrence Shehan to take a stand against Ottaviani's disjunctive model:

"Few seem to realize how dreadfully weak their position is . . . We have a heaven-sent opportunity to effect a genuine development of doctrine in this matter."[138]

The Declaration on Religious Freedom began as a chapter in what became the Decree on Ecumenism *(Unitatis redintegratio,* 1964), both of which emerged from a torturous struggle at Vatican II. At the council's first session a reform group led by Augustin Cardinal Bea clashed with the Curial right, led by Ottaviani, over the Catholic state and the desirability of a separate statement on religious freedom. By the end of the first session the old guard had lost control of the debate, new commissions were set up, and the curialists campaigned to squelch the subject. Murray's invitation to the second session arrived in April 1963; ironically, it came at the insistence of Cardinal Spellman, a staunch traditionalist, who recognized that Vatican II was destined to break new ground in this area. Murray rallied the American bishops to put religious freedom back on the agenda, giving a speech at a commission meeting attended by Ottaviani and Fenton that voted overwhelmingly to address the issue on its own. At session three in September 1964 Murray was asked to write the Declaration on Religious Freedom, working from a draft begun in the second session, in collaboration with Monsignor Pietro Pavan. The reformers had prevailed, chiefly because the American bishops supported Murray, though various compromises were struck throughout the process. By November 1964 the Declaration was a self-standing document bearing the marks of its principal author, though Murray regretted compromises that weakened its position and clarity. A penultimate round of opposition pushed final approval of the text to the fourth session in 1965.[139]

Most of the criticism of the first two drafts came from the right, but not all; Murray adeptly negotiated all of them. Critics charged that the early drafts were too legal and political, insufficiently theological and biblical, too explicit that Catholic doctrine had changed, overly fixated on the rights of conscience, and too American. Murray replied that religious freedom was a juridical ideal formally, its scriptural roots were remote at best, the development of doctrine was a Catholic doctrine, and the declaration merely legitimized the American approach, not idealizing it. He agreed, however, that the first two drafts, like liberalism generally, relied too much on the dictates of conscience. The first draft rested on the individual's right to exercise religion according to the dictates of conscience, but stumbled over the extent to which one's sincere conscience established an obligation for others to act in accordance with it. The second draft explicitly declared, in the face of significant opposition, that the foundation of the individual's right to religious freedom was that person's conscience and its sincerity, even if it was in error. Both sides in the dispute agreed that no one should be forced to act against their conscience, but the conservatives insisted that the person who was in error, sincerity notwithstanding, lacked any right to religious freedom or the public manifestation of their error, either in action or public teaching. The right to religious freedom had to be based on the "objective order of truth," not the subjective call of individual conscience.[140]

To get a conciliar declaration on religious freedom, this impasse had to be resolved. It helped that Murray felt pulled in both directions. The liberal reliance on conscience was too simplistic, he reasoned, and it lacked a clear tradition in church teaching, while the conservative position was too simplistic and repressive. There would be no change or even development of church teaching if the "error has no rights" position prevailed, yet the conservatives were right to insist on a natural law basis for religious freedom. Murray's third draft strengthened the juridical foundation of the text in response, describing religious liberty as freedom from coercion. The right at issue was simply a type of immunity, with a negative content, he argued. Historically, this idea was of recent origin – the First Amendment to the US Constitution – but it was rooted in the dignity of the human person, a concept with a rich history in Catholic thought. In the American system, the political and civil freedoms of the First Amendment were protections against coercive action by government, not claims on government and society for positive action, although in his subsequent account of the conciliar debate, Murray wrongly added the words "and society" to the protection clause. The First Amendment protects persons from coercive action only by government, not society. At the council he stressed the limits of government. Murray's third draft emphasized that government was obliged to act in a way that respected the inviolability of the human person. Good government recognized its lack of competence to judge religious belief and action. That did not mean that government should be indifferent to the truth or social value of religion; it meant only that government was not the judge of either. As the protector of human rights, government protected the inviolability of the individual person, including the right to religious freedom, understood as the right to immunity from coercion.[141]

That was the basis of what became the council's Declaration on Religious Freedom, which added that divine scripture, despite saying nothing explicitly about religious freedom, strongly affirmed the dignity of the human person. The third draft went through three revisions, for the last of which Murray was not present, having suffered a collapsed lung. Vatican II rested the right to religious freedom on the dignity of the human person – an objective natural goal of civil society – not the subjective right of conscience. But it did not develop the former idea or the difference; it made a strong appeal to conscience; and the American flavor of the document was unmistakable. Murray's vindication was made possible by the support he received from a majority of the American bishops. In the spirit of the American Constitution, he and they contended that freedom, besides its negative meaning as freedom from coercion, was a byproduct of the limits of juridical power. On December 7, 1965, at the very end of the fourth session, the council endorsed the Declaration on Religious Freedom; the following day Vatican II ended.

Murray's biographer, Donald Pelotte, justly remarked that the best parts of the declaration were the ones where Murray's text was left alone. The opening paragraph of chapter one, in Murray's translation, was one of them:

> This Vatican Synod declares that that the human person has a right to religious freedom. This freedom means that all men are to be immune from coercion on the part of individuals or of social groups and of any human power, in such wise that in matters religious no one is forced to act in a manner contrary to his own beliefs ... This right of the human person to religious freedom is to be recognized in the constitutional law whereby society is governed. Thus it is to become a civil right.[142]

Pope Paul VI celebrated the declaration at a festive mass at St Peter's Basilica, accompanied by Murray and other theologians, the sweetest vindication for which Murray could have hoped. Afterward he enthused that the statement marked a major turning point in Catholic history: "From now on, the Church defines her mission in the temporal order in terms of the realization of human dignity, the promotion of the rights of man, the growth of the human family towards unity, and the sanctification of the secular activities of this world." On other occasions he put it more prosaically, judging that the church merely and belatedly caught up with "the common consciousness of mankind" about the rights belonging to the dignity of the human person. In 1964 Murray suffered two heart attacks; when the council ended the following year he had less than two years remaining, dying in a New York taxicab in August 1967. In the little time that remained to him after Vatican II he wrote a flurry of articles about the declaration, defended it with little equivocation, translated it for a popular edition of the council statements, *Documents of Vatican II*, and wrote an introduction and extensive annotations for the latter book that had something like a canonical effect, conveying his view of the declaration to two generations of readers.[143]

For decades afterward traditionalists hotly disputed some of these renderings, charging that Murray's annotations described his own views, not the vaguer statements of the final text, and that his book *The Problem of Religious Freedom* (1964), published near the end of the council's third session, stampeded the council into endorsing a flawed document. Commenting on Article 13 of the declaration, Murray declared that the church made no claim to be the religion of the state: "Her claim is freedom, nothing more." Traditionalists replied that the latter statement was Murray's fantasy of the Catholic Church and Vatican II, not the reality. Commenting on Article 6, Murray stated that it was beyond the right or competence of government to judge "the truth or value of religious propaganda." Traditionalists countered that political authorities were still obliged in principle to discern and reflect the unique truth of Catholicism; not even Vatican II denied that "age-old Catholic thesis." In *The Problem of Religious Freedom* Murray aggressively defended the American formula of freedom for the church without legal or juridical privileges; traditionalists charged that that was the real Murray – a hardcore Americanist who only pretended in certain contexts not to advocate the American approach as a universal norm.[144]

But Murray's cause prevailed in the church to such an extent that by the early 1970s it was taken for granted, and hard to remember. His writings were neglected, his influence waned, and, when remembered at all, he was usually tagged as a transitional figure who used a worn-out mode of thought and discourse to change a worn-out Catholic doctrine. Reinhold Niebuhr, debating Murray on the viability of natural law, had allowed there was a basis for a general concept of natural law in the acknowledgment of human dignity. But as soon as one moved to the particular, Niebuhr cautioned, "you find the whole question about the historical relativity of reason." Many Catholic ethicists moved in that direction after Vatican II, while the rise of radical Catholic pacifism and liberation theology made Murray seem stodgy and conservative by comparison. Garry Wills, in his popular book *Bare Ruined Choirs* added that Murray was curmudgeonly too.[145]

Charles Curran offered a typical assessment. Against Murray's contention that the American consensus rested solely on natural law, Curran objected that Murray made civic unity depend on a dubious theory of epistemological and metaphysical unity. Against Murray's Gelasian diarchy of church and state, which conceived the individual person as the integrating factor between the spiritual and temporal orders, Curran replied that liberation theology had a better idea, conceiving salvation history as a unity embracing all reality. Murray's dualism left in place all the problems of classic supernaturalism, just as his reliance on natural law perpetuated the classic Catholic failure to recognize the ravages of sin in the sphere of human rationality. Instead of giving faith its biblical priority in the process of salvation, Curran objected, Murray offered a rationalistic harmony of faith and reason. Instead of validating the static notion of being inscribed in natural law theory, Murray should have taken historical consciousness more seriously. Instead of using historicism only to criticize theologies he disliked, he should have acknowledged his own biases and interests. Instead of making Leo XIII look remarkably like Murray, Murray should have acknowledged that his theological opponents had a strong basis in Leo's teaching for their position. And instead of lining up with American conservatives on the Cold War and economic policy, he should have helped the church find its way to a social ethic of peace and social justice.[146]

But Murray was too interesting and instructive to remain forgotten for his weak points. In the mid-1980s, as the fields of theology and social ethics became increasingly preoccupied with the problems of pluralism and the role of religion in public discourse, a Murray renaissance occurred. Lutheran scholar Martin Marty, Catholic theologian Richard P. McBrien, and Lutheran (later, Catholic) social critic Richard John Neuhaus wrote popular books on the role of religion in American public life that made use of Murray's insights. Catholic ethicists John Coleman and David Hollenbach and Methodist ethicist Robin Lovin argued that Murray was an important and still relevant public philosopher, although all of them judged that he was not a public theologian, because his position rested on philosophical arguments. Coleman argued that Murray wrongly traded the rich power of religious symbolism for the conceptual clarity of philosophy, mistakenly ruling out the use of biblical imagery in public discourse.[147]

Catholic ethicist Robert McElroy agreed that Murray's work lacked evocative or inspirational qualities, partly because he shunned biblical imagery. But that was merely a tactical decision that did not disqualify Murray from the title, public theologian, McElroy argued. In his view, Murray was an exemplary public theologian who used natural law to "project the strongest realizable theological assertions onto the national stage." Having sought to make Catholic social thought intelligible to Americans suspicious of Catholic authoritarianism, Murray "succeeded admirably." He was right to use a public language that did not depend on sectarian warrants, because sectarian claims were divisive and illegitimate as public discourse in a pluralistic society. And Murray was right to mediate religious symbols by the precepts of natural law. Had Murray used biblical imagery more directly, McElroy judged, he might have inspired a larger following, but he would not have been a better public theologian. The best foundation for American public theology was natural law.[148]

Richard John Neuhaus and Catholic political philosopher William R. Luckey agreed that Murray was the indispensable public theologian because he used natural law arguments to modernize the church's teaching on religious freedom and theorize an American public philosophy. Neuhaus played up Murray's liberalism – "As a liberal, he was very much opposed to illiberalism, whether of attitude or regime." Luckey stressed that Murray was never guilty of liberalism – "He was a thoroughly orthodox Catholic – no liberal (in any sense of the term) and certainly no indifferentist." Yet they described and treasured the same Murray, who made Catholic sense of the American experience in the language of a public philosophy. It was easy to criticize Murray for making too much of a dubious "American consensus," Luckey argued, but Murray keenly recognized that the consensus was dissolving. He stressed the consensus because he believed the American project was a good and rather novel thing that needed further improvements. To improve on the American improvements of the Western natural law tradition, it was necessary to keep faith with both. In Murray's time, Luckey observed, the onus of defending, preserving, and advancing this dual tradition had already begun to fall on American Catholicism. Luckey and Neuhaus stressed that afterward, the onus fell harder on Catholicism; Neuhaus, just before converting to Catholicism, called it "the Catholic moment."[149]

Murray's acquaintance and interpreter, Francis Canavan, SJ, shared his convictions about religious freedom and the American consensus, but emphasized the problems with both. In 1966 he and Murray spoke at a conference on religious freedom at Bellarmine School of Theology in North Aurora, Illinois. Murray gave his seminal account of what happened at Vatican II, admitting that the Declaration on Religious Freedom merely invoked its objective ground, and certainly did not develop it. Canavan regretted that deficiency. Vatican II barely suggested the theory of constitutional government that derived from Murray's argument, Canavan noted. More importantly, even the final product was still anchored by an appeal to conscience, which moved "directly from the obligation to follow conscience to the right to do so." Did not the declaration hang a heavy line of rights on the assertion of an obligation to follow conscience? Afterward Murray told Canavan that his critique was too kind, for the declaration merely took a pass at its ostensible basis, resting instead on the assertion of conscience.[150]

Twenty-six years later Canavan judged that history had not been kind to Murray's project. Murray located religious freedom in the free exercise of religion, not the nonestablishment of religion. As Vatican II put it, "The right of all citizens and religious bodies to religious freedom should be recognized and made effective in practice." For Murray, the American nonestablishment of religion was merely a means to the end, free exercise; nonestablishment was ancillary to the true end of religious freedom. But a great deal of subsequent American jurisprudence treated the nonestablishment clause as an end in itself, with no definite relationship to free exercise. Canavan judged that Murray's understanding of the First Amendment, though a worthy cause, was an embattled and losing one, and that other foundations of the American Proposition were also disintegrating. Murray believed that religious freedom was a universal right resting on principles derived from the unchanging nature of human beings; otherwise its existence and intelligibility rested merely on the relative and unstable will to be free. But Murray understood that religious freedom was historical, not merely a timeless principle, Canavan noted. The realization of religious freedom depended on a difficult and unusual combination of historical factors: favorable legal and political traditions, a popular will to freedom, and a favorable balance of particular kinds of religious, social, and cultural forces. That described America's past, Canavan wrote wistfully, but the trend lines were unpromising for America's future.[151]

The dean of Murray studies, J. Leon Hooper, was more appreciative than Curran, more critical than McElroy, Neuhaus, and Luckey, and less dire than Canavan. A senior fellow at Georgetown University's Woodstock Theological Center (Woodstock Seminary moved to New York in 1969 and closed in 1974), Hooper sided with Curran and Coleman about the religious deficiencies of Murray's approach. The language of natural law was "much too thin" to foster the rich public discussion of values that Murray wanted, Hooper judged. Instead of "muzzling his faith," Murray should have used the language of faith creatively to challenge the individualism, superficiality, and materialism of American culture, developing explicitly theological warrants for his position. To Hooper, that was the essential task of public theology after Murray, to which Murray made four enduring contributions.[152]

First, Murray's sharp distinction between church and society relieved Catholic thought of its paternalist concept of the state. In place of a fatherly state that corrected and directed the immature masses, Murray embraced the modern notion that human dignity had something to do with allowing human beings to correct and direct themselves. Besides placing limitations on the state for the sake of human dignity, Hooper noted, this idea vested great significance in the development of a richly conversant civil society, which in turn required robust civic virtues. Second, Murray urged that public schools had no right to ignore the religious concerns of Americans. For Murray, the public school was a crucial meeting ground for the state, family, and church. Just as families and the state had a stake in how future generations were shaped through schooling, so did the church. Murray stood for the abolition of religious segregation in American schools, and he wanted public schools to teach the theologies of America's living faiths, because students had a right to religious literacy. Third, after Vatican II recognized the validity of Protestantism as a path of Christian salvation, so did Murray, but he argued that Catholicism better understood the assumption of reason in Christian salvation. The key Catholic contribution to ecumenical discussion was to overcome faulty Protestant notions about the relation of faith and reason. Because Christ redeemed human intelligence, reason and public argument were never to be feared. Fourth, Murray upheld the social ethical conviction that the church is morally obligated to create a good society; Hooper added that after Murray, this imperative included the obligation to present the church's best theological arguments for its social commitments.[153]

In Murray's work Catholic social ethics found its most impressive intellectual expression in the generation leading up to Vatican II. He thought deeply about religious freedom and pluralism, helped to effect a major change in Catholic doctrine, helped Catholicism make sense to a large audience of Catholics and others, and anticipated a communitarian age of pluralistic public theology in which various faiths pursued conversations that reshaped the public sphere. Murray denied that the religion clauses of the Constitution grew out of a Christian worldview. Had he concluded otherwise, he would have contradicted his "articles of peace" assurance that the clauses depended on no religious presuppositions and contained no religious content. Yet, ironically, he paved the way for public theologians and legal scholars who resisted the juridical privatization of religion by stressing the Christian background of the religion clauses. He paved the way for others who resisted the theological thinness of Murray-style apologetics by making more robust religious arguments in the public square. He paved the way for others who practiced public theology in his style. And he paved the way for the entire field of advocates of theology as pluralistic public conversation. Murray spoke to and in the academy, church, and general public with nearly equal ease, benefiting from his daily regime, which he called "ambiguous, inasmuch as I am half-scholar and half-operator." Though he never got the academic perch that he wanted, modern theology and social ethics were better off for it.[154]

Dorothy Day and the Catholic Worker Movement

Dorothy Day was the symbol and spark of a different model of Catholic orthodoxy and public religion. She was born in Brooklyn, New York in 1897, the third of five children, to a mother she described as caring and a father she described as shallow, selfish, and unsympathetic, although not completely lacking. Grace Satterlee Day, a native of Marlboro, New York, told entertaining stories about sea-faring ancestors, many of them whalers, while John Day was a Scotch–Irish native of Tennessee who tired easily of children, drank a lot of whiskey, and disliked foreigners, blacks, and radicals. An itinerant sportswriter, his true home was the racetrack. He wrote sports journalism that showed off his knowledge of the Bible and Shakespeare, though he was a nominal Episcopalian at most; in later life he co-founded a racetrack in Florida. In 1904 he moved his family to San Francisco, but lost his job in the earthquake of 1906. Dorothy Day got her first taste of urban poverty in the family's next move, to a tenement flat on the south side of Chicago. She later recalled gratefully that unlike many nearby fathers, John Day believed in protecting the innocence of his children. Thus she was raised on Dickens, Hugo, and Poe, not the usual "trash" of popular culture, though she acquired a taste for trashy novels too, especially after the family moved to a comfortable home on Chicago's north side. Four of John Day's children followed him into journalism, but he was appalled by the religion and politics of his third child. Dorothy recalled that in later years, when the children were grown and the family gathered for a Sunday dinner, there were no gestures of affection, gloomy silence prevailed, and the siblings could hear each other swallow.[155]

By 1914 she was intensely interested in radical politics and eager to leave home. Enrolling at the University of Illinois, she devoured the writings of Upton Sinclair and Jack London, resolved to become a writer like them, exposing the ravages of poverty and oppression, and took little notice of her courses. The war in Europe was remote to her, while the class war became a consuming passion. Day later recalled, "In my reading I must have absorbed a scorn of religion at that time, a consciously critical attitude toward religious people who were so comfortably happy in the face of the injustices of the world." To her surprise, she took up swearing and found herself sneering against religion, especially that it held down the poor. Radical politics satisfied her religious streak. She fell in love with "the masses," or at least her idea of them, as invoked in the speeches of Eugene Debs and other radical Socialists: "I do not remember that I was articulate or reasoned about this love, but it warmed and filled my heart. The poor and oppressed were going to rise up, they were collectively the new Messiah, and they would release the captives. Already they had been persecuted, they had been scourged, they had been thrown into prison and put to death, not only in other parts of the world, but right here in the United States."[156]

In that mood she quit college after two years, joined her family in moving to New York, and resolved to become a radical writer. To her regret she was not as free of her family, emotionally, as she had thought; Day could not bear to have them move away from her. But she clashed with her father, spent five months looking for a job, and felt a cold blast of what she called "the long loneliness." The enormous size, density, noise, poverty, anonymity, and stench of New York overwhelmed her; 36 years later Day confessed that she never got used to the stench:

> I have lived with these smells now for many years, but they will always and ever affront me. I shall never cease to be indignant over the conditions which give rise to them. There is a smell in the walls of such tenements, a damp ooze coming from them in the halls. One's very clothes smell of it. It is not the smell of life, but the smell of the grave.

Upon finding work with a Socialist newspaper, the *Call*, she left her family anyway, as her father would not support a daughter with a job and she could not take any more of his narcissistic bullying.[157]

Living on the Lower East Side of Manhattan, Day wrote indignant stories about strikes, picket lines, evictions, peace rallies, and factional maneuverings of the Socialists, Industrial Workers of the World (IWW) syndicalists, and anarchists. Since the *Call* was a Socialist paper, it slighted the anarchists, but Day debated whether she was a Socialist, a Wobblie, or an anarchist. When she read Tolstoy, she was an anarchist, but she also liked the IWW solidarity theme of one big union. In the end it came down to anarchism or syndicalism, because Socialism was too doctrinaire for her, and Marx was impenetrable.

Day joined the Wobblies, because they had an immediate program that seemed to make sense in the American context. At the time she paid no attention to John Ryan or the Catholic Church – "Catholics were a world apart" – although remarkably, the *Call* explained Catholic social teaching quite fairly, eschewing the usual Socialist anti-religious fare. Burning for revolution, Day reasoned that she could serve it best as a radical journalist: "I wanted to go on picket lines, to go to jail, to write, to influence others and so make my mark on the world." Leon Trotsky, just before returning to Russia, chided Day in an interview that New York Socialists were naive, making a fetish of parliamentarianism; three months later she joined a celebration of the Russian Revolution at Madison Square Garden. She also wrote about Emma Goldman, though privately Day reproved Goldman's promiscuity and, especially, her flaunting of it. Real revolutionaries didn't prattle about their affairs and personal lives, Day judged: "Men are the single-minded, the pure of heart, in these movements. Women by their nature are more materialistic, thinking of the home, the children, and of all things needful to them, especially love. And in their constant searching after it, they go against their own best interests."[158]

Resigning from the *Call* in April 1917 after a personal dispute, Day worked briefly for the Anti-Conscription League, but it folded after the USA entered World War I, and she moved on to the *Masses*, the most famous and stylish of the Left magazines. Floyd Dell and Max Eastman were its luminaries, and Day idolized John Reed, the *Masses* writer who counted Lenin as a friend and soon wrote a celebrated account of the Russian Revolution. Later she remarked of him: "Wherever there was excitement, wherever life was lived at high tension, there he was, writing, speaking, recording the moment, and heightening its intensity for everyone else." By the summer Day was putting out the monthly *Masses* nearly by herself, as Dell worked on a novel and Eastman plied the lecture circuit; by November the federal government had shut down the magazine, after months of harassment and postal refusals. Since Day was new on the masthead, she escaped being among the five editors and two contributors who were charged with sedition. Feeling unexpectedly liberated from having a job, and perhaps a bit guilty at not being arrested, she promptly got arrested for another cause – solidarity with a group of suffragists. In November 1917 she was arrested in front of the White House for protesting the treatment of suffragists, spending 30 days in jail, 10 on a hunger strike. For Day, it was a soul-searing experience, nothing like the rush of heroic feeling she expected. She felt crushed and desolate, losing all sense of carrying on a nonviolent revolution. The prospect of being released meant nothing to her: "I would never be free again, never free when I knew that behind bars all over the world there were women and men, young girls and boys, suffering constraint, punishment, isolation and hardship for crimes of which all of us were guilty."[159]

Returning to New York she drifted from one rooming house to another, freelanced for Left papers and magazines not shut down by the government, especially the *Liberator*, and floundered personally. The revolution lost its glow, although Day still believed in it. She became a close friend of Eugene O'Neill, who was on the rebound from losing Louise Bryant to John Reed and the Bolshevik Revolution, and whose recent first play, *Bound East for Cardiff*, was a huge success. Day threw herself into O'Neill's social whirl of playhouse rehearsals, parties, and heavy drinking at taverns, often delivering him safely at home, although they were not lovers; their friendship was based on a mutual recognition of loneliness and religious longing. Day's longing pulled her into Catholic churches, where she took comfort in the ambience of worship and the presence of praying congregations.

Feeling deeply her lack of a spiritual center or even selfhood, she took a job as a nurse in Brooklyn, where she fell disastrously in love with a hospital orderly, Lionel Moise, of dangerous charm. Moise did not believe in marriage, but did believe in controlling his romantic partners. Day's fateful attraction to him led to a pregnancy and abortion that traumatized her for years. She wrote a thinly fictionalized account of her life thus far, *The Eleventh Virgin*, which culminated with her abortion. Drifting into a rebound marriage with an older man whom she did not love, Day got divorced the following year, saw her novel panned as an embarrassing piece of exhibitionism, but sold the film rights to a Hollywood company, and so was lifted temporarily out of poverty. The movie was never made, to her eventual relief; years later she shuddered at the book's existence and tersely told Catholic Workers not to waste their time on it. "How much time I wasted during those years," she wrote. The waste included years of traveling, lounging at bars, sleeping around, working at dead-end jobs, idle bantering about revolution, and being subject to a bogus arrest for prostitution at an IWW flophouse in Chicago. Her social circle included several notables – Malcolm Cowley, Kenneth Burke, Allen Tate, Hart Crane – and a dubious assortment of others; Cowley later recalled that his gangster acquaintances admired Day because "she could drink them under the table."[160]

For all of her tavern socializing and sexual carousing, Day was intensely lonely until she met Forster Batterham, a nature-loving anarchist and atheist with whom she fell deeply in love. Entering a common law marriage with Batterham, she seemed to have found her way to a happier, healthier existence, until she became pregnant. Day's life turned a corner when she realized in 1925 that she was again expecting a child. This time, she vowed, she would make a different choice: she would have the baby and raise it in the Catholic faith, notwithstanding that she belonged to no church and converting to Catholicism was sure to destroy her relationship with Batterham. "I knew that I was going to have my child baptized, cost what it may," she later recalled. "I knew that I was not going to have her floundering through many years as I had done, doubting and hesitating, undisciplined and amoral. I felt it was the greatest thing I could do for my child. For myself, I prayed for the gift of faith. I was sure, yet not sure. I postponed the day of decision." She did not want to be alone at the time of her daughter Tamar's birth; her own conversion seemed less important than her daughter's home in the church; and she loved Batterham dearly. So she waited until her daughter was born and baptized. Batterham was pessimistic, extremely individualistic, and a thoroughgoing rationalist; religion was anathema to him, especially Catholicism. After Tamar was born, Day realized that she didn't know any practicing Catholics, so she stopped a nun on the road and asked how to arrange her daughter's baptism. The nun, Sister Aloysia, a longtime grade school teacher, took Day under her wing, instructing her on Catholic doctrine and practices. The sister's understanding of Catholic teaching was pure Baltimore Catechism orthodoxy, which was fine with

Day. In July 1927 Tamar was baptized; the following December Day was baptized conditionally, in case her Episcopal baptism didn't count. Afterwards she mourned the loss of her husband and her connection to radicalism. She had no concept of social Christianity and had never heard of the encyclicals. To her it was obvious that the church was reactionary; her wager was that, nonetheless, it had what she needed: "I was just as much against capitalism and imperialism as ever, and here I was going over to the opposition, because of course the Church was lined up with property, with the wealthy, with the state, with capitalism, with all the forces of reaction." She joined the church with no thought that it might change or might not be as bad as she thought; the point was simply that she wanted to follow Christ and be obedient to him.[161]

Her conversion was very much a solitary affair; no friends were present at her baptism except her godparent, Sister Aloysia. At the time Day was still working for a Communist front, the Anti-imperialist League; to her confessor she explained that she still agreed with the Communists about imperialism and capitalism. Father Zachary gently quoted Lenin that atheism was essential to Marxism, but advised Day to keep her Communist job until she found a better one. Reading her articles, he took a harder line on her style, complaining that she had none; Day's unadorned realism was too grim and dull to hold a reader's interest. For the rest of the 1920s Day wondered if that explained why her career as a novelist never took off. She worked for the pacifist Fellowship of Reconciliation, but felt isolated as the only Catholic on staff; she also worked for the MGM film company, writing summaries of new novels, but that was drudgework. By 1930 she alternated between reminding herself to be grateful for any job during the Depression and fretting that she was growing small. Often she groused that radicalism was thriving everywhere except the group she had joined: "How little, how puny my work had been since becoming a Catholic, I thought. How self-centered, how ingrown, how lacking in sense of community!" In December 1932 she reported for *Commonweal* and *America* on the Hunger March in Washington, DC. Day noted that the protesters called for jobs, unemployment insurance, old age pensions, child welfare, and housing, and that, as usual, the organizers were Communists, not Catholics. After the march she went to the National Shrine of the Immaculate Conception at Catholic University, on the Feast of the Immaculate Conception, and prayed in anguish "that some way would open up for me to use what talents I possessed for my fellow workers, for the poor." When she returned to New York, Peter Maurin was waiting for her at her apartment.[162]

Maurin had learned about Day through a *Commonweal* editor and an Irish Communist in Union Square; both had advised him to introduce himself. He was a short, stocky, middle-aged man with a thick French accent wearing a rumpled suit and tie. Maurin's face and clothes were weather-beaten from decades of manual labor, study, tramping around the country, and sleeping in barns and flophouses, yet Day was struck by his intense liveliness. He did not have the manner of an impoverished man who had been defeated by life. Maurin exuded kindness and intellectual energy, pouring out ideas with an animated expression, although Day strained to understand him through his accent. On their first meeting she was too tired to absorb his message; the following day he returned to expound his theory of a "green revolution" and his vision of her as the next St Catherine of Siena. Maurin had been born into a family of peasant farmers in southern France, the eldest of 22 children. For nine years he had taught in the Christian Brothers religious order in France; later he left the order, emigrated to Canada, and worked for many years in brickyards, steel mills, and coal mines, adopting a Franciscan attitude toward money and life: poverty was his bride, in which he took joy. He had never married; he was a voracious reader and talker; and he believed that the saints were the key to history, not the rise and fall of empires. What really mattered was sanctity, he urged Day; thus, the revolution that was needed would be based on sanctity and community.[163]

"He was a man of tremendous ambition, in spite of his simplicity, or perhaps because of it," Day later recalled. "He wanted to make a new synthesis, as St Thomas had done in the Middle Ages, and he wanted to enlist the aid of a group of people in doing this." Maurin believed that the seeds of a new order already existed in the shell of the dying one, and the IWW was right about one thing: the point was to make a society in which it was easier for people to be good. He envisioned a synthesis of "cult, culture, and cultivation" in which people sought the divine good and built a new social order based on the common good. Day noticed that he did not begin like most radicals, with a searing critique of misery and oppression: "Instead, he aroused in you a sense of your own capacities for work, for accomplishment. He made you feel that you and all men had great and generous hearts with which to love God. If you once recognized this fact in yourself you would expect and find it in others."[164]

Day's articles for *America* and *Commonweal* had convinced Maurin that she was the apostle he had been seeking. Realizing that her understanding of Catholic thought and history was skimpy at best, he set out to "indoctrinate" her, as he put it straightfor-wardly. To Day, his devotion to seeing Christ in others was both familiar language and a revelation of a life-changing possibility. Maurin had a spiritual vision and a program, which he described to anyone who would listen: round-table discussions, houses of hospitality, agronomic universities, and a newspaper. He had no idea how to launch any of it; that would be Day's concern. His role was to "enunciate the principles." In the history of the saints, he told her, God provided the money for saintly enterprises. St Francis de Sales published leaflets and distributed them at gatherings, just like modern radicals. Instead of stressing what the state or the church should do, Christians needed to focus on what they could do themselves to be their brother's keeper. Day fixed on the newspaper idea, which seemed more doable than an agronomic university, espe-cially since she was a journalist. Converting her kitchen to an editorial office, and enlisting her brother John to help with production, she spent her rent and utility money to produce an eight-page tabloid called the *Catholic Worker*.[165]

Maurin wanted to call it the *Catholic Radical* and fill it entirely with his writings, which Day's brother called "easy essays." Maurin wrote in phrased sentences broken up to look like free verse, and his style had a singing, rhythmic quality that resembled advertising jingles. He recited these bits of poetic manifesto on buses, street corners, and amateur nights at theaters, undaunted by unfavorable receptions. Day, his first disciple, replied that the paper should refer to the class of its readers, not the viewpoint of its editors, and it would be a real newspaper containing articles about strikes and unemployment, not merely Maurin's orations. On May 1, 1933, she brought the first issue of the *Catholic Worker* to a May Day rally in Union Square, selling it for one cent. It announced:

> For those who are sitting on park benches in the warm spring sunlight.
> For those who are huddling in shelters trying to escape the rain.
> For those who think there is no hope for the future, no recognition of their plight –
>   this little paper is addressed.

It is printed to call their attention to the fact that the Catholic Church has a social program – to let them know that there are men of God who are working not only for their spiritual but for their material welfare.

It was possible to be radical without being an atheist, Day affirmed, and it was time for a Catholic paper that stood for that possibility, advocating for the unemployed. She did not know if the paper would be a monthly, a fortnightly, or a weekly, nor if she would have an office by the next issue. That didn't matter, for Jesus "wandered this earth with no place to lay his Head." A bit later in the same issue, Day printed six of Maurin's jingles, including one on the church's morally paralyzing wealth:

> Christ drove the money changers
> out of the Temple.
> But today nobody dares
> to drive the money lenders
> out of the Temple
> because the money lenders
> have taken a mortgage
> on the Temple.[166]

To Maurin, however, the first issue was a crushing disappointment, because Day filled it with standard radical fare about strikes, trials, and economic exploitation. For months he had lectured her daily about the saints and the green revolution, stressing the importance of a positive vision of a good society. Maurin was fond of saying "strikes don't strike me," and he wanted nothing to do with standard radical protest. The old order was dying anyway; criticizing it was a waste of time. The *Catholic Worker* needed to expound his vision of artisans and worker-owned factories coming together in decentralized agricultural communes, where workers and scholars forged a new synthesis. Eventually he conceded that not every article had to be written by him; however, the paper had to expound his vision, otherwise he could not be associated with it. For weeks after the first issue Maurin shunned personal contact with Day. Removing his name from the masthead, he announced in the second issue that he would be responsible only for the material under his name.

Day, caught up in the demands of producing the paper, barely noticed his absence. Yet she moved the *Catholic Worker* in his direction, striking a balance between his spiritual vision and her belief that a worthwhile newspaper had to pay attention to real-world injustices. Maurin called his vision "Christian communism" and he experienced his poverty as a liberating force. He was a product of a foreign culture and a non-stop talker who rejected the wage system, fixated on rural communes, and, to put it mildly, had eccentricity issues. For the next 20 years Day negotiated her relationship to him, while their followers debated the differences between them. Day unfailingly credited Maurin as the founder and theorist of the Catholic Worker movement, but it was emphatically her enterprise, shaped by her worldview and sensibility.[167]

Later she recalled, "I could not blind myself to the conflict between us, the conflict that would continue between one or another who came to join in the movement later." But Day was not the only one to adjust; Maurin adjusted to her after the

Catholic Worker made an explosive impact. Young followers hawked the paper in the streets; parishes subscribed in bundles of 500; letters poured in from readers throughout the country, enthusing that a radical Catholic newspaper was overdue; Day struggled to meet the demand for it. In the paper's first seven months its circulation soared to over 100,000; by 1936 it was 150,000. Catholic high school teachers sent their students to help produce and distribute the paper, and homeless people began to knock at Day's apartment on 15th Street, both of which raised the question of a Catholic Worker community. Day's apartment became the first House of Hospitality, open to all comers, which led to two more in the winter of 1933–4, which the community outgrew, leading to Day's leasing of two large buildings on Mott Street in Chinatown in 1936. By then there were 33 Catholic Worker houses across the country. The success of the newspaper financed the original rentals, which prompted followers in other cities to establish houses of their own. Sixteen years later Day was nostalgic for the movement's "early zeal, that early romance, that early companionableness," which she viewed in emphatically movement terms: "It is a permanent revolution, this Catholic Worker Movement."[168]

From the beginning the Catholic Worker houses were different from street missions catering only to the "deserving poor" or those willing to be evangelized. The Hospitality Houses welcomed anyone needing a refuge, allowing people to stay as long they wanted. Homeless newcomers were considered members of the community – brothers and sisters in Christ – not guests or clients. John C. Cort, who joined the Mott Street house in 1936, later recalled, "What we had there was a form of anarchist dictatorship. There wasn't any democratic, participatory decision-making. Dorothy made all the decisions. She was the abbess, as we called her. She made the rules." Day enjoyed arguing with argumentative types like Cort and, years later, Michael Harrington and Ammon Hennacy, but her word prevailed. In 1935 the movement launched its first farming commune, on Staten Island, which was followed by several others, although Day judged eventually that in rural areas, the Catholic Worker worked best as a ministry of hospitality, not farming. In 1950 she lost the lease at Mott Street and bought a five-story, redbrick house at 223 Chrystie Street, St Joseph House, which anchored the movement for decades, and subsequently added houses on First Street and Third Street.[169]

Much of the paper was newsy, chatty, and personal, but also political. On occasion Day admonished that because the class war was terribly real, the paper could not restrict itself to celebrations of God's love. Communists put Catholics to shame in carrying out the moral commands of the gospel, yet "most Catholics speak of Communists with the bated breath of horror." Day put the matter sharply, warning that Communists stood a better chance with God than the Catholics who did nothing for the poor and vulnerable. On the other hand, the *Catholic Worker* did not approve of the New Deal's solution for the poor and vulnerable. Dramatically expanding the role of the federal government in American life could not be a good thing, Day protested, echoing a Maurin theme. The *Catholic Worker* supported worker ownership and the responsibility that came with it, not the Welfare State, which it usually called the Servile State, adopting Hilaire Belloc's phrase. Day complained, "The state entered in to solve these problems by dole and work relief, by setting up so many bureaus that we were swamped with initials."[170]

The ideology of the *Catholic Worker* was insistently Catholic, communal, anti-capitalist, personalist, and inclusive. In 1935 Day disclosed that it was also pacifist. The vehicle of the latter disclosure was an article by Paul H. Furfey, a priest and sociologist associated with the movement, which imagined a dialogue between Jesus and a typical patriot. The patriot loved peace, but held that possessing a strong defense was the best way to assure peace; Jesus replied that all who took the sword perished by it. The patriot urged Jesus to be practical, because Japan and Russia were arming against the USA; Jesus replied that one should love one's enemies and do good to them. That was noble, the patriot allowed, but common sense called for a policy of self-defense. Jesus replied that love divine called for turning the other cheek. The patriot countered that life and death were at stake; only a strong defense could prevent the killing of innocent people. Jesus told him not to be afraid of those who killed merely the body. Finally the patriot appealed to the just war doctrine of the church; Jesus replied, "You have heard it was said, an eye for an eye and a tooth for a tooth, but I say to you not to resist evil."[171]

That was exactly what Day meant by being obedient to Christ, even if she had no word from the church to that effect. The Furfey article stirred little reaction in 1935, but the following year the *Catholic Worker's* stout defense of absolute pacifism caused an uproar in American Catholicism after Spain erupted into civil war. Virtually the entire American Catholic hierarchy and Catholic press supported Franco; Day warned that Franco was a dubious candidate for Catholic support, because fascism was virulently anti-Semitic. In the face of nearly monolithic Catholic support for Franco, the *Catholic Worker* refused to support either side in the war. Furious responses poured in to the *Catholic Worker* office, protesting that Franco defended the church from the murderous destruction of Spanish Communists and anarchists. Day replied that if Catholics followed Jesus, they were not supposed to believe, with the Fascists and Communists, that victory came by shedding the blood of others. Catholics were supposed to be willing "to shed every drop of their own blood, and not take the blood of their brothers." To claim that the church was mortally threatened in Spain was to think like the world, not like Jesus. Just as Jesus had not wanted Peter to defend him in Gethsemane, he did not want the church to defend itself by violence in Spain or anywhere else.[172]

To defend Christianity by killing people was absurd; Day compared it to the crowd that taunted Jesus to prove his divinity by coming down from the cross: "But Christ did not come down from the Cross. He drank to the last drop the agony of His suffering, and was not part of the agony the hopelessness, the unbelief, of His own disciples?" She identified with the "littlest ones" in Christian history who followed Jesus to the cross instead of killing for a cause, their nation, or in self-defense. She prayed that all Christians would be given the courage to suffer, making Christianity a spectacle of the way of Jesus. That position cost the *Catholic Worker* dearly. Subscriptions and bundle orders were canceled, the mail was vitriolic, and in several dioceses, bishops banned the paper from all churches and parish schools. When the war began in 1936, the paper's circulation stood at 160,000; by the time the Spanish fascists prevailed in March 1939, the *Catholic Worker* was down to 50,000.[173]

Repeatedly Day exhorted readers that there was nothing to add to "love your enemies, do good to those who persecute you." The hard sayings were essential to the way of Jesus; one could not follow him by taking leave of them. Moreover, the works of mercy could not be separated from the works of peace. The gospel command was to feed the hungry and comfort the afflicted, but the murderous violence of war caused destruction, starvation, and untold misery. Day was not the kind of pacifist who played down the evil of Nazism. From the beginning of Hitler's rise to power she picketed the German embassy, protesting against fascist anti-Semitism. In 1939 she helped found the Committee of Catholics to Fight Anti-Semitism, which lobbied to lift immigration quotas for European Jews and denounced Charles Coughlin's anti-Semitic radio screeds. Coughlin ranted to a vast audience that commercial banking Jews and Communist Jews somehow conspired to take over the world; Day's group launched a paper, *The Voice*, to counter Coughlin's propaganda. Between 1939 and 1941 the *Catholic Worker*'s circulation rebounded by 25,000, partly because Day's campaign against anti-Semitism had become more respectable.[174]

But joining the war against fascism was out of the question for her, even as this contention split the Catholic Worker movement. In January 1942 Day published an editorial titled, "Our Country Passes from Undeclared to Declared War; We Continue Our Pacifist Stand." In the wake of Pearl Harbor and an American intervention that closed even most of the Catholic Worker houses, Day went straight to the point: "We are at war, a declared war, with Japan, Germany, and Italy. But still we can repeat Christ's words, each day, holding them close in our hearts, each month printing them in the paper." This was a time to remember St Francis, she wrote, and to quote other saints and the pope, and to continue publishing articles that opposed war unconditionally:

> We are still pacifists. Our manifesto is the Sermon on the Mount, which means that we will try to be peacemakers. Speaking for many of our conscientious objectors, we will not participate in armed warfare or in making munitions, or by buying government bonds to prosecute the war, or in urging others to these efforts. But neither will we be carping in our criticism. We love our country and we love our President.[175]

But even most of the Catholic Workers went off to war, causing most of the houses of hospitality to close. Day insisted that the remaining communities had to distribute the *Catholic Worker*, even if they rejected its pacifist stand, which caused further dissension and losses. Day conceded that this war was morally different than others of her lifetime, yet that made her inveigh against it all the more, imploring her readers not to make an exception for any war. Her spiritual director, pacifist priest John Hugo, was a regular in the *Catholic Worker* until Cardinal Spellman silenced him in 1943. Christian anarchist Ammon Hennacy, a non-Catholic beyond the reach of Spellman, was another mainstay on the pacifist imperative. Day received special attention from J. Edgar Hoover, who recommended before Pearl Harbor that in the event of a national emergency she should be placed in custodial detention. Later, the FBI demoted her to its "restriction of activities" list. Before Pearl Harbor, Day published articles on the immorality of proscription; afterwards she took the next step, urging men not to register for the draft, which earned a summons to the chancery office of the New York Archdiocese, where an aide to Spellman told her to stand corrected. "I was not quite sure what that meant, but I did assent," she recalled, reasoning that it was not her place to tell others how to follow their consciences. "We had to follow our own consciences, which later took us to jail; but our work in getting out a paper was an attempt to arouse the conscience of others, not to advise action for which they were not prepared."[176]

Negotiating a perilous relationship with Spellman, she laid off on the draft, but pressed hard on the immorality of war. Day spoke to student groups and Catholic

Worker communities throughout the country, declaring that the gospel had nothing to do with starving whole populations, bombarding open cities, or killing anyone. The gospel was about laying down one's life for one's friends. Living as she did, in harsh conditions, and ministering to the most destitute and forsaken of America's urban poor, Day had some immunity from the usual complaint that Christian pacifists lived off the privileges of the system and the sacrifices of others. On occasion she spent her social capital on this point. After Pearl Harbor a Catholic paper made a patronizing reference to the "sentimentality" of Christian pacifists; Day's reply was blistering. To all who imagined that she was sentimental, she wrote:

Let them come to live with the criminal, the unbalanced, the drunken, the degraded, the perverted. (It is not the decent poor, it is not the decent sinner who was the recipient of Christ's love.) Let them live with rats, with vermin, bedbugs, roaches, lice. (I could describe the several kinds of body lice.)

Let their flesh be mortified by cold, by dirt, by vermin; let their eyes be mortified by the sight of bodily excretions, diseased limbs, eyes, noses, mouth.

Let their noses be mortified by the smells of sewage, decay, and rotten flesh. Yes, and the smell of the sweat, blood and tears spoken of so blithely by Mr. Churchill, and so widely and bravely quoted by comfortable people.

Let their taste be mortified by the constant eating of insufficient food cooked in huge quantities for hundreds of people, the coarser foods, so that these will be enough to go around; and the smell of such cooking is often foul.

Then, when they have lived with these comrades, with these sights and sounds, let our critics talk of sentimentality.

She was fond of quoting Dostoyevsky's Father Zosima: "Love in practice is a harsh and dreadful thing compared to love in dreams."[177]

For Day, the war years were a desert experience, spiritually and politically; later she put it simply, "Somehow we got through it on Mott Street." In the wake of Hiroshima and Nagasaki she wrote a horrified response that took aim at President Truman's reported elation:

Truman is a true man of his time in that he was jubilant. He was not a son of God, brother of Christ, brother of the Japanese, jubilating as he did. He went from table to table on the cruiser which was bringing him home from the Big Three conference, telling the great news; 'jubilant' the newspapers said. *Jubilate Deo.* We have killed 318,000 Japanese.

On the other hand, she never managed much of a response to the question that divided Christian progressives: Knowing that Hitler was slaughtering the Jews, how could she stick with pacifism? Day replied that winning the war had not saved many Jews.[178]

She wearied of labor activists and even Catholic Workers who said they preferred the *Catholic Worker* before it turned pacifist or fixated on pacifism. Writing in 1952 during another American war, Day remarked on the strangeness of this complaint: "Here we had been writing about pacifism for fifteen years and members of two of our groups were just beginning to realize what it meant. We had been pacifist in class war, race war, in the Ethiopian war, in the Spanish Civil War, all through World War II, as we are now during the Korean war." Every reader knew that her guide was the Sermon on the Mount, Day reflected. She had no problem receiving cancellations from people who, at wartime, turned out not to agree. "But there were a very great many who had seemed to agree with us who did not realize for years that the *Catholic Worker* position implicated them; if they believed the things we wrote, they would be bound, sooner or later, to make decisions personally and to act upon them." The works of mercy went together with the works of peace; the gospel was about more than works of mercy.[179]

It was true, however, that in the 1940s and 1950s, the *Catholic Worker* featured writers for whom pacifism and anarchist opposition to the state were consuming passions, especially Hennacy, Eric Gill, and Robert Ludlow. Ludlow was so dogmatic on the theme of "war is the health of the state" that Day sometimes had to smooth things over with readers. Though her favorite writers for the paper wore the anarchist label as a badge of honor, she preferred the term "libertarian" as less apt to confuse or offend. The *Catholic Worker* made much of its connection to G. K. Chesterton and Hilaire Belloc, who opposed the "servile state" in the name of a pre-capitalist, communitarian "distributism." To Day, the name and image of the paper were serious matters. Unfailingly she stressed her great respect for the bishops, which won some indulgence from them, but her friendships with prominent Communists Mike Gold and Elizabeth Gurley Flynn caused heartburn at the New York Archdiocese, as did her picketing at St Patrick's Cathedral in 1949 in solidarity with a gravediggers' union. Spellman told the press that the gravedigger strike was Communist-inspired; two years later his aide, Msgr Edward Gaffney, told Day to either change the paper's name or shut it down. The archdiocese could no longer abide the appearance of being associated with a pro-Communist newspaper.[180]

Day replied that it wasn't *her* paper and she had to consult with others. A few days later she told Gaffney she was willing to change the name, but then took it back, pleading against a "grave scandal" that would embarrass the church. The archdiocese backed down, pausing at Day's emphasis that the *Catholic Worker* had a worldwide reputation and audience. The following year her autobiography, *The Long Loneliness*, put Day on the road to icon status, beyond the punitive reach of media sensitive church officials. Among the book's many rave reviews, it garnered an admiring two-part one by Dwight MacDonald in the *New Yorker*.[181]

The Long Loneliness emphasized Maurin's role in founding the Catholic Worker movement, lovingly described his five years of invalidism and death in 1949, and revealed that he had always regarded himself as an anarchist, but only privately. In later life he dropped "Christian Communist" as hopelessly confusing, settling for "communitarian." For years Day admonished young Catholic Workers to show more respect for Maurin, though some contended that she gave mixed messages on this point and that he made only one significant convert: Dorothy. In her autobiography, Day stressed that Maurin was routinely underestimated and insulted. On one occasion, having been invited for dinner, he was left in a basement, mistaken for a plumber. Another time an upstate pastor demanded a refund, having sent Maurin's carfare to the *Catholic Worker*, only to be greeted by someone he took to be "a Bowery bum." Day tried to set the record straight: Maurin was the John the Baptist of his generation, "a voice crying in the wilderness, and a voice too, saying, 'My little children, love one another.'" Michael Harrington, who joined the *Worker* shortly after Maurin died, had a different reading. As one of Day's favorites, he knew her well, but judged that whenever she talked about Maurin, she got boring. That made Harrington suspect that he was hearing a line.[182]

In later life Day had to struggle with the contradiction of being famous, admired, and taken no more seriously than before. She was dead serious about becoming a saint, but hated being dismissed politically for being one. In the 1950s she grieved over the execution of Julius and Ethel Rosenberg for atomic spying, protested repeatedly against civil defense drills, which got her two jail terms, and greeted the civil rights movement with elation and a declaration of solidarity. In 1957 she confessed, "Whenever I am invited to speak at schools around the country and receive praise for talking about the problems of destitution in this rich country, I feel guilty." Why heap praise on spiritual celebrities instead of changing the system? Catholic Workers idolized her as a saint, yet also gossiped about her past, wondering which of her literary and political acquaintances were former lovers. Staffer Ed Egan recalled, "Everybody revered Dorothy and told terrible stories about her." Jim Forest, who played a major role in the *Catholic Worker* and the peace movement, recalled that when he met Day in 1960, she was extremely formidable and on the verge of becoming venerable.[183]

In 1960 Day spent some of her "venerable" capital by welcoming the Cuban Revolution, which enraged many Catholics. How could she support atheistic Communists? Day replied that Communists were better known for caring about the poor. She agreed with Fidel Castro that if the Catholic Church could live under the Roman Empire, feudalism, monarchy, competing empires, republicanism, and democracy, it surely could live under a Socialist state. Though she rejected Marxist socialism and violent revolution, she believed that resorting to revolutionary violence was better than capitulating to oppression. Day put it plainly, to the astonishment of many readers: "We do believe that it is better to revolt, to fight, as Castro did with his handful of men, than to do nothing. We are on the side of the revolution. We believe there must be new concepts of property, and that new concept is not so new."[184]

That was the theory of revolutionary pacifism usually associated with A. J. Muste and the War Resisters League, which some Catholic Workers denounced as a betrayal of pacifism. Day replied that she knew something about living up to the ethical test of nonviolence; the "betrayal" accusation was utter nonsense. She had always been a revolutionary pacifist, combining pacifism with the right to the revolutionary overthrow of oppression. Moreover, that right was especially relevant in the post-colonial nations of the Third World. In addition, Muste was a longtime comrade. The Catholic Worker and War Resisters League organizations worked closely together, and for decades Day had admired Muste's capacity to sustain a peaceable integrity in the midst of angry, posturing, self-dramatizing leftisms. In November 1965, deeply embroiled in a budding movement against the war in Vietnam, she treasured her last public appearance with Muste, at a demonstration in Union Square where young men burned their draft cards. Muste was calm and exemplary to the end, showing a tense crowd how to keep the right tone; that was how Day wanted to be remembered too: "You listened to what he had to say, not to how he said it."[185]

Repeatedly she made the case for the Cuban revolution, sometimes romanticizing Castro's government, other times making excuses for it. "Of course I know that the island is an armed camp, that all the people make up the militia," she wrote in September 1962, shortly before going there. "It is too late now to talk of nonviolence, with one invasion behind them and threats of others ahead." Later she eulogized that despite being racked by war, boycotted by the mighty USA, and drained by the flight of its professional class, the Cuban government made enormous efforts in health and education, and the Cuban people were so united that the nation was no longer ravaged by delinquency, violence, addiction, and unemployment.[186]

Three times in the 1960s she traveled to Rome on behalf of Catholic pacifism. In 1963 Day joined a group of 50 women calling themselves "Mothers for Peace" that sought to thank Pope John XXIII for his recent encyclical, *Pacem in Terris* ("Peace on Earth," 1963). The group failed to achieve a private meeting with the pope, but he thanked them indirectly in a public message at St Peter's Basilica. In September 1965, at the outset of the third session of Vatican Council II, Day returned to Rome with Eileen Egan, director of Catholic Relief Services in South Asia, to urge a council declaration on the centrality of nonviolence to the gospel. She met with bishops, fasted with female peace activists, and lobbied for a strong statement on nuclear weapons. The following month the council came remarkably close to the statement she wanted, declaring in the *Pastoral Constitution on the Church in the Modern World*,

> Every act of war directed to the indiscriminate destruction of whole cities or vast areas with their inhabitants is a crime against God and humanity, which merits firm and unequivocal condemnation. The hazards peculiar to modern warfare consist in the fact that they expose those possessing recently developed weapons to the risk of perpetuating crimes like these and, by an inexorable chain of events, of urging men to even worse acts of atrocity.

The council urged nations to make legal provision for conscientious objectors to war, declared that the harm inflicted on the poor by the arms race "is more than can be endured," and exhorted, "Providence urgently demands of us that we free ourselves from the age-old slavery of war."[187]

For Day that was an answer to prayer, although she lamented that the statement contained equivocating asides. Press coverage of the pastoral constitution described it as a vindication of the Catholic peace tradition and especially the Catholic Worker movement. Two years later the International Congress of the Laity, meeting in Rome, affirmed that reading of the document's significance, honoring Day as a distinguished guest. At St Peter's Basilica she was one of two Americans invited to receive the Eucharist from Pope Paul VI. Afterwards she was asked how she felt about this honor. Day replied that she felt nothing except concern for the pope, who looked ill, and concern for the many nonviolent persons who were in prison, and concern about "this terrible Vietnam war in which we are now engaged."[188]

By then the *Catholic Worker* had regained all the momentum, numbers, and influence it had lost during the Spanish Civil War and World War II. Catholic Worker pacifism rebounded in the 1960s because America's war in Vietnam went badly and the *Worker* played a leading role in founding and building the movement against it. The antiwar movement began in the summer of 1963, when Catholic Worker activist Tom Cornell invited leaders of several peace groups to discuss a joint protest against US policy in Vietnam. Since there was no Vietnam consulate in New York, the group settled on the apartment of the Saigon Government Observer to the United Nations, protesting for 10 days. Two years later the movement was still small, but gaining attention, especially for its draft-card burnings.

A turning point occurred on November 6, 1965, when Day and Muste addressed a large demonstration at Union Square. Five peace activists led by Cornell and Jim Wilson tried to burn their draft cards, but a protester soaked them with a blast from a fire extinguisher while a group of counter-demonstrators shouted, "Burn yourselves, not your draft cards!" Wilson later recalled that he half-expected the liquid to be gasoline, to set the card-burners on fire. Buddhist monks in Vietnam had set themselves on fire, and a week before the Union Square demonstration, American Quaker Norman Morrison immolated himself in front of the Pentagon. Three days after the Union Square rally, 22-year-old Roger LaPorte doused himself with gasoline in front of the US Mission to the United Nations and lit a match. He told rescue workers before lapsing into a coma: "I am a Catholic Worker. I did this as a religious action. I am anti-war, all wars." LaPorte had joined the Catholic Worker community in 1963, devoted himself to the poor, and been present at Union Square.[189]

Day went into crisis mode while LaPorte lay dying, determined to prevent a pandemic of suicide protests. Asking Cornell to write a careful statement for her, she prohibited all other Catholic Workers from speaking to the media. Her message honored LaPorte's sacrifice while pleading for different forms of protest and penance. Later she reflected that LaPorte had shown no sign of mental illness; he was, instead, "deeply sensitive to the sufferings of the world" and persuaded of the necessity to break the spell of propaganda and an indecent order.[190]

Day shared the rage and revulsion of young peace activists for America's carnage in Vietnam, which was a bond between her and them even as she recoiled from the indulgent craziness of the 1960s. She was deeply bitter about Vietnam, she wrote in 1967, yet she felt equally bitter about South Africa, Nigeria, the Congo, Indonesia, and Latin America. Most of all she felt revulsion at America and being an American: "Woe to the rich! *We* are the rich! The Works of Mercy are the opposite of the works of war, feeding the hungry, sheltering the homeless, nursing the sick, visiting the prisoner. But we are destroying crops, setting fire to entire villages and to the people in them." There was something commendable about the way Cardinal Spellman traveled the globe to visit American troops, she observed: "But oh, God, what are all these Americans, so-called Christians, doing all over the world so far from our own shores?" Neither could she fathom, from a Christian, Spellman's terrible words about the imperative of winning a total victory in Vietnam, words "as strong and powerful as bombs." On occasion Day declared, and was often quoted as declaring, that she would keep silent if Spellman silenced her; in the meantime she pleaded openly for bishops and cardinals who believed in the way of Jesus.[191]

The 1960s were thrilling and appalling to her, with emphasis shifting from the former to the latter. The leadership network of the antiwar movement was loaded with Day's disciples and friends, notably Daniel Berrigan, Phillip Berrigan, Elizabeth McAllister, Tom Cornell, Jim Forest, Jim Miller, James W. Douglass, Kathe McKenna, John McKenna, Eileen Egan, Karl Meyer, and Chuck Matthei. Surveying an antiwar protest, Catholic Worker Betty Bartelme remarked, "All Dorothy's children are here." Jim Miller later recalled,

> The presence of young Catholics in the movement was pretty awesome. Dorothy knew this was creating confusion within the church. She would chuckle about it, because she understood the paradox. This was the message she'd been preaching for a long time, finally getting to a much larger audience. I sensed a real crossing of generations and a mutual respect with Dorothy.[192]

Day appreciated the contrast between the 1930s, when "Catholic pacifism" seemed an oxymoron, and the 1960s, when it stood at the center of a mass movement. She took delight in the fame of the Berrigan brothers – while disliking some of their theatrical protests – and the rise of a powerful farm workers movement led by Cesar Chavez, which she supported heartily. At the same time, she lamented that much of the Catholic Left lacked her reverence for the sacraments and church authority. In an affectionate public letter in 1972 to Daniel Berrigan, a Jesuit priest who had recently spent 17 months in prison, Day gave thanks for his charisma ("Thank God, how the young love you") and his dedication ("Thank God, you are truly bearing the cross, giving your life for others") and also that of his brother Phillip ("I cannot tell you how I love you both") before complaining that many young peace activists had dreadful views on divorce, birth control, and abortion. "The teaching of Christ, the Word, must be upheld," she admonished. "I believe in the Sacraments. I believe Grace is conferred through the Sacraments. I believe the priest is empowered to forgive sins." Having been saved by the Church from her own moral confusion and spiritual aimlessness, she recoiled at a generation that scoffed at the Church's sexual morality.[193]

She got a close look at the escalating craziness of the time. By 1969 Day was accustomed to being screamed at by radicals who thought the peace movement needed a strong dose of revolutionary violence. Pacifism had failed to change the system or stop the war, they railed, sometimes hysterically. Day heard it even at Catholic Worker houses. Tom Cornell, her mouthpiece to the New Left movements, recalled the feeling of siege: "People storm into her room using every foul word in the book. Why hadn't she stopped the war? 'You're a fake. You're a phony. All you do is go flying around to see the fucking pope'." For decades Day's sensibility had prevailed at the *Worker*. Routinely she told new arrivals that the point of joining the *Worker* was to become a saint and that anti-Catholic sneers would not be tolerated. Ammon Hennacy, who wanted to marry her, joined the Catholic Church just to qualify, but kept disqualifying himself with cheeky remarks about Catholic dogma. Day was able to sustain the *Catholic Worker* through its crises because she blended rock-hard convictions about pacifism and the Catholic faith with a genuine affection and respect for co-workers that helped them accept her personal authoritarianism.[194]

But in the late 1960s she acquired comrades who lurched far beyond sneering at the Catholic Church and Catholic Worker pacifism. Contempt for church authority was freely expressed; mock Masses were performed; loud anathemas prevailed. All of it repulsed her deeply. Day fought off a barrage of free-floating hostility against the church and authority in general, insisting there would be no Catholic Worker that was not truly Catholic. At the time, in the late 1960s and early 1970s, she tried to assure Cornell that the craziness had not really escalated to new heights; there had always been a lot of it, which came with the work of ministering to the homeless and mentally challenged. Near the end of her life she admitted that of course, it had gotten much worse in the late sixties; for her it was a "terrible" period.[195]

In the 1970s she faded from public view, dividing her time between a beach cottage on Staten Island, the Catholic Worker farm on the Hudson River (Tivoli), St Joseph House on Chrystie Street, and Maryhouse (a shelter for homeless women). She hated adulation and could be cutting with those who fawned upon meeting her. It annoyed her when people came to St Joseph House wanting to meet the spiritual celebrity instead of helping those in need. Some of her annoyance was rooted in humility, and some in moral passion. There was also her embarrassment at knowing that her autobiographies created an idealized image of her, yet she hated researchers digging for details about her past or mentioning *The Eleventh Virgin*. In 1972 Day allowed the University of Notre Dame to award her the prestigious Laetare Medal; four years later she gave her last public address. In 1980 she died; three years later the American Catholic bishops, in *The Challenge of Peace*, lauded her for renewing the Catholic pacifist tradition.[196]

One of Tamar Hennessy's nine children, Kate Hennessy, recalled fondly that her grandmother Dorothy was never a comforting type with whom one cuddled, but always a passionate type who stirred one's soul and juiced up one's psyche: "To have known Dorothy means spending the rest of your life wondering what hit you." Day assured Catholic Workers for decades that marriage and hospitality work did not go together, and she was very tough on friends who divorced or remarried. For many years she severed her friendships with anyone who entered a marriage forbidden by church law; James Douglass, a noted theologian, became a prominent example of the shunning treatment. Near the end of her life, however, Day softened on the shunning business. She told Daniel Berrigan that she missed the friends she had cast aside on this account, including his brother Phillip, and she wanted them back. She wished she had been more compassionate with her friends instead of standing on church law. In letters to Phillip Berrigan and others she apologized for not being a good friend. Daniel Berrigan reasoned that like many converts, Day was zealous about the letter of the law; thus it took decades for her immense humanity to overcome her theology.[197]

In March 2000 the Vatican officially accepted Day as a candidate for canonization, declaring her a "servant of God." Undoubtedly her official status in the church will some day catch up with the one she carried unofficially for the last 25 years of her eventful life.

Notes

1   The biographical and theological sections of this section on Muelder are adapted from Gary Dorrien, *The Making of American Liberal Theology: Crisis, Irony, and Postmodernity* (Louisville: Westminster John Knox Press, 2006), 14–7, 26–7. The discussions of Muelder's social ethics and method are new to this volume. See Borden Parker Bowne, *Theory of Thought and Knowledge* (New York: Harper and Brothers, 1897); Bowne, *Metaphysics* (New York: Harper and Brothers, 1898); Bowne, *Theism* (New York: Harper and Brothers, 1887); Bowne, *Personalism* (Boston: Houghton, Mifflin, and Co., 1908).

2   See Edgar S. Brightman, *The Problem of God* (New York: Abingdon Press, 1930); Brightman, *Personality and Religion* (New York: Abingdon Press, 1934); Brightman, *A Philosophy of Religion* (New York: Prentice-Hall, 1940); Brightman, *Person and Reality: An Introduction to Metaphysics*, eds. Peter A. Bertocci, Janette G. Newhall, and Robert S. Brightman (New York: Ronald Press, 1958); Albert Cornelius Knudson, *Present Tendencies in Religious Thought* (New York: Abingdon Press, 1924); Knudson, *The Philosophy of Personalism: A Study in the Metaphysics of Religion* (New York: Abingdon Press, 1927); Knudson, *The Doctrine of God* (New York: Abingdon-Cokesbury Press, 1930); Knudson, *The Doctrine of Redemption* (New York: Abingdon-Cokesbury Press, 1933); Knudson, *The Validity of Religious Experience* (New York: Abingdon Press, 1937); Knudson, *The Principles of Christian Ethics* (New York: Abingdon-Cokesbury Press, 1943); Knudson, *Basic Issues in Christian Thought* (New York: Abingdon-Cokesbury Press, 1950); see Gary Dorrien, *The Making of American Liberal Theology: Making Christianity Modern, 1900–1955* (Louisville: Westminster John Knox Press, 2003); *The Boston Personalist Tradition in Philosophy, Social Ethics, and Theology*, eds. Paul Deats and Carol Robb (Macon, GA: Mercer University Press, 1986); Rufus Burrow, Jr, *Personalism: A Critical Introduction* (St Louis: Chalice Press, 1999).

3 Walter G. Muelder, "Report from the Dean: The School of Theology," *Bostonia* 20 (April 1947), 13.

4 "A gospel," Walter G. Muelder, "Christian Social Ethics Looks Forward," *Nexus* 21 (May 1964), 3–4; Bogumil Gacka, *Interview with Emeritus Dean Walter Muelder* (Stockbridge, MA: Marian Press, 1996), 2–3, "difficult life," 3; Walter G. Muelder, "Communitarian Christian Ethics: A Personal Statement and a Response," *Toward a Discipline of Social Ethics: Essays in Honor of Walter George Muelder*, ed. Paul Deats, Jr (Boston: Boston University Press, 1972), "almost natural," 296.

5 Walter G. Muelder, "Individual Totalities in Ernst Troeltsch's Philosophy of History," PhD dissertation (Boston University, 1933).

6 Walter G. Muelder, "Communitarian Dimensions of the Moral Laws," *The Boston Personalist Tradition in Philosophy, Social Ethics, and Theology*, 237–9; *Interview with Emeritus Dean Walter Muelder*, 15; Muelder, "An Autobiographical Introduction: Forty Years of Communitarian Personalism," in Muelder, *The Ethical Edge of Christian Theology: Forty Years of Communitarian Personalism* (Lewiston, New York: Edwin Mellen Press, 1983), 6, 22.

7 Ernst Troeltsch, *Der Historismus und seine Probleme* (Tübingen: J. H. Mohr, 1922); Troeltsch, *Gesammelte Schriften*, 4 vols. (Tübingen: J. C. B. Mohr, 1912–25), 3: 118–21; Muelder, "Individual Totalities in Ernst Troeltsch's Philosophy of History."

8 Walter G. Muelder, "Personality and Christian Ethics," *Personalism in Theology: A Symposium in Honor of Albert Cornelius Knudson*, ed. Edgar Sheffield Brightman (Boston: Boston University Press, 1943), 187; Muelder, "Individual Totalities in Ernst Troeltsch's Philosophy of History"; Muelder, "Communitarian Dimensions of the Moral Laws," 240–1; Muelder, "Religion and Postwar Reconstruction," *World Affairs Interpreter* (Autumn 1942), 275–85.

9 Troeltsch, *Gesammelte Schriften*, 3: 118–21; Muelder, "Communitarian Dimensions of the Moral Laws," 240–2; Muelder, *Moral Law in Christian Social Ethics*, 32–4; Walter G. Muelder, "Norms and Valuations in Social Science," *Liberal Learning and Religion*, ed. Amos N. Wilder (New York: Harper and Brothers, 1951); Muelder, "Theology and Social Science," *Christian Social Ethics in a Changing World*, ed. John C. Bennett (New York: Association Press, 1966); Muelder, "Religion and Postwar Reconstruction," 275, 280; John E. Boodin, *The Social Mind* (New York: Macmillan, 1939).

10 Muelder, "Personality and Christian Ethics," 200–3; Muelder, "Communitarian Dimensions of the Moral Laws," 240–42; Muelder, "An Autobiographical Introduction: Forty Years of Communitarian Personalism," "a *socius*," 7; Walter G. Muelder, *Moral Law in Christian Social Ethics* (Richmond: John Knox Press, 1966), 23–47.

11 Walter G. Muelder, "A Philosophy for Post-war Pacifism," *Fellowship* (December 1944), 200.

12 Ibid., 200–1.

13 Ibid., 201; see Walter G. Muelder, "Pacifism and Politics: A Reply to Felix Greene," *Fellowship* (June 1947), 93–4; Michael Dwayne Blackwell, *Pacifism in the Social Ethics of Walter George Muelder* (Lewiston, NY: Edwin Mellen Press, 1995), 253–82.

14 Stanley High, "Methodism's Pink Fringe," *The Reader's Digest* (February 1950), 134–8, quotes, 135; C. Eric Lincoln and Paul Deats, Jr, "Walter G. Muelder: An Appreciation of His Life, Thought, and Ministry," *Toward a Discipline of Social Ethics: Essays in Honor of Walter George Muelder*, 3; Muelder, "Autobiographical Introduction: Forty Years of Communitarian Personalism," 34. The School of Theology's pacifist contingent during Muelder's era included Schilling, church historian Richard B. Cameron, psychologist of religion Paul E. Johnson, registrar Wayne Jones, and librarian Jannette E. Newhall.

15 Walter G. Muelder, "Minorities Can Be Integrated," *Intercollegian* (February 1953), 16–17; Muelder, "Communitarian Dimensions of the Moral Laws," 249–50; Gunnar Myrdal, *An American Dilemma*, 2 vols. (New York: Harper and Brothers, 1944); Robert M. MacIver,

The More Perfect Union (New York: Macmillan Co., 1948), 9–10; MacIver, *The Web of Government* (New York: Macmillan, 1947).

16 Walter G. Muelder, *Religion and Economic Responsibility* (New York: 1953), 156–8; see Muelder, "New Theology and Old Social Gospel," *New Christian Advocate* (October 1958), 26–8.

17 Muelder, *Religion and Economic Responsibility*, quote, xi; Amsterdam Assembly, World Council of Churches, "The Church and the Disorder of Society (Amsterdam: World Council of Churches," 1948).

18 Muelder, *Religion and Economic Responsibility*, 6–31, 92–6, 97–116, quote, 95.

19 Ibid., "new instruments," 249; "the ruthless methods," 13; 237–42, "Christians everywhere," 242.

20 Walter G. Muelder, *Foundations of the Responsible Society* (New York: Abingdon Press, 1959), 15–38; Amsterdam Assembly, World Council of Churches, "The Church and the Disorder of Society," 192.

21 Amsterdam Assembly, World Council of Churches, "Message"; Muelder, *Foundations of the Responsible Society*, 18–38, quote, 36.

22 Muelder, *Foundations of the Responsible Society*, 101–61, quote 108.

23 Ibid., quotes, 108, 191; see *'Right-to-Work' Laws: Three Moral Studies by an Oblate Father, an Eminent Rabbi, and a Methodist Dean* (Washington, DC: International Association of Machinists, 1954), 43–55.

24 Muelder, *The Responsible Society*, 258–80, quote, 261.

25 Walter G. Muelder, "The Togetherness of Men and Women," (1958), in Muelder, *The Ethical Edge of Christian Theology*, 321–36, quotes, 321, 322.

26 Ibid., 328–29.

27 Ibid., 331–5, quotes, 330, 333.

28 Muelder, "Autobiographical Introduction: Forty Years of Communitarian Personalism," 25–7, 38, quote 38; Muelder, "Communitarian Dimensions of the Moral Laws," 251; Muelder, *Moral Law in Christian Social Ethics*, 9–10, 61; see John C. Bennett, *Christian Ethics and Social Policy* (New York: Charles Scribner's Sons, 1946); Nils Ehrenstrom and Walter G. Muelder, eds., *Institutionalism and Church Unity* (London: SCM Press), 1963.

29 Edgar S. Brightman, *Moral Laws* (New York: Abingdon Press, 1933), quote, 13.

30 Ibid., 98–242; see Muelder, *Moral Law in Christian Social Ethics*, 61–112.

31 Muelder, *Moral Law in Christian Social Ethics*, 113–19, quotes, 116, 117, 119; DeWolf's lectures were unpublished when Muelder wrote *Moral Law in Christian Social Ethics*, and Muelder quoted from DeWolf's class syllabi and lecture notes. DeWolf's subsequently revised version of the moral principles was published in L. Harold DeWolf, *Responsible Freedom: Guidelines to Christian Action* (New York: Harper & Row, 1971), 144–78; see T. H. Green, *Prolegomena to Ethics*, 5th edn. (Oxford: Clarendon Press, 1906).

32 Muelder, *Moral Law in Christian Social Ethics*, 119–25, quote, 119–20.

33 Muelder, "Communitarian Dimensions of the Moral Laws," quotes, 242, 242–3.

34 Walter G. Muelder, "Reinhold Niebuhr's Conception of Man," *The Personalist* (Summer 1945), reprinted in Muelder, *The Ethical Edge of Christian Theology*, 103–15, quotes, 105, 109.

35 Ibid., quotes, 109.

36 Walter G. Muelder, "Naturalism Versus Prophetic Religion," *Crozer Quarterly* (October 1939), reprinted in Muelder, *The Ethical Edge of Christian Theology*, 43–57, quote, 43.

37 Muelder's quotations of Dewey from G. Adams and W. P. Montague, eds., *Contemporary American Philosophy* (New York: Macmillan, 1930), 23–4; of Nagel from Horace A. Kallen and Sidney Hook, eds., *Philosophy Today and Tomorrow* (New York: L. Furman, 1935), 388–9; of Cohen from Adams and Montague, *Contemporary American Philosophy*, 247; of Sellars from Roy Wood Sellars, "Religion Faces Naturalism," *Religion in Life* (Autumn 1937); Muelder, "Naturalism Versus Prophetic Religion," 45–6.

38 Muelder, "Naturalism Versus Prophetic Religion," 46–8.
39 See Samuel Alexander, *Space, Time and Deity*, 2 vols. (New York: Macmillan Co., 1920); Alexander and C. Lloyd Morgan, *Emergent Evolution* (New York: Henry Holt, 1923); Alfred North Whitehead, *Inquiry into the Principles of Natural Knowledge* (Cambridge: Cambridge University Press, 1919); Whitehead, *The Concept of Nature* (Cambridge: Cambridge University Press, 1920).
40 Muelder, "Naturalism Versus Prophetic Religion," 47–51, quote, 51.
41 Ibid., 51–2; see John Dewey, *Experience and Nature* (LaSalle, IL: Open Court, 1929).
42 Muelder, "Naturalism Versus Prophetic Religion," 53.
43 Ibid., 53–4; see Edward Scribner Ames, *The Psychology of Religious Experience* (Boston: Houghton Mifflin, 1910); Ames, *The New Orthodoxy* (2nd edn., Chicago: University of Chicago Press, 1925); Ames, *Religion* (New York: Henry Holt and Co., 1929).
44 See Paul Deats Jr, "The Quest for a Social Ethic," *Toward a Discipline of Social Ethics: Essays in Honor of Walter George Muelder*, 21–48; J. Philip Wogaman, *A Christian Method of Moral Judgment* (Philadelphia: Westminster Press, 1976); Wogaman, *Christian Perspectives on Politics* (Louisville: Westminster John Knox Press, 2000); Alan Geyer, *Ideology in America: Challenges to Faith* (Louisville, KY: Westminster John Knox Press, 1998); C. Eric Lincoln, *Race, Religion and the Continuing American Dilemma* (New York: Hill and Wang, 1984); Tex Sample, *Blue Collar Ministry: Facing Economic and Social Realities of Working People* (Valley Forge, VA: Judson Press, 1984); Carol S. Robb, *Sexuality and Economic Justice: Where Economic and Sexual Ethics Meet* (Boston: Beacon Press, 1990); Rufus Burrow Jr, *Personalism: A Critical Introduction* (St Louis, MO: Chalice Press, 1999); Burrow, *God and Human Dignity: The Personalism, Theology, and Ethics of Martin Luther King Jr.* (Notre Dame: University of Notre Dame Press, 2006).
45 James Luther Adams, *Not Without Dust and Heat: A Memoir* (Chicago: Exploration Press of the Chicago Theological Seminary, 1995), quote 16; Adams, "Taking Time Seriously," *Christian Century* 61 (6 September 1939), reprinted in Adams, *The Prophethood of All Believers*, ed. George K. Beach (Boston: Beacon Press, 1986), 33. The biographical and theological sections of this discussion of Adams are adapted from Gary Dorrien, *The Making of American Liberal Theology: Crisis, Irony, and Postmodernity* (Louisville: Westminster John Knox Press, 2006), 134–43.
46 Adams, *Not Without Dust and Heat*, 48–61, quote 49; Adams, "Taking Time Seriously," 34.
47 Adams, *Not Without Dust and Heat*, 73–111, quote 99; see Irving Babbitt, *Rousseau and Romanticism*.
48 Adams, *Not Without Dust and Heat*, 94–111.
49 Ibid., 119–128, quotes 128, 120; see James Luther Adams, "The Sacred and the Secular: Friedrich von Hügel," *The Christian Register* (11 October 1934), reprinted in Adams, *The Prophethood of All Believers*, 61–70.
50 Adams, *Not Without Dust and Heat*, 155–209; James Luther Adams, "The Evolution of My Social Concern," *The Unitarian Universalist Christian* 32 (1977), 12–4, reprinted in *The Essential James Luther Adams: Selected Essays and Addresses*, ed. George Kimmich Beach (Boston: Skinner House Books, 1998), 115–20; Adams, *An Examined Faith: Social Context and Religious Commitment*, ed. George Kimmich Beach (Boston: Beacon Press, 1991), 36–7.
51 Ibid., 220–5; see James Luther Adams, *Paul Tillich's Philosophy of Culture, Science, and Religion* (New York: Harper & Row, 1965).
52 Adams, *Not Without Dust and Heat*, 82, 225–7, 318–19, quote 319; see James Luther Adams, "Our Responsibility in Society," *Authority and Freedom*, eds. Adams, J. J. van Holk and A. V. Murray (Delft, Netherlands: W. Gaade, 1953), reprinted in Adams, *The Prophethood of All Believers*, 151–64; Adams, "The Study of Christian Social Ethics at the Divinity School," *Harvard Divinity Bulletin* 36 (April 1962), 13; Adams, "Theological Bases of Social Action," *Journal of Religious Thought* 8 (Autumn/Winter 1950–1), 6–21.

53 "The Humanist Manifesto," (1932), *The Humanist* 8 (March–April 1953), 58–61.

54 Adams, *Paul Tillich's Philosophy of Culture, Science, and Religion*, 1–64, quote 7.

55 Paul Tillich, *The Protestant Era*, trans. and ed. James Luther Adams (Chicago: University of Chicago Press, 1948); James Luther Adams, "Tillich's Concept of the Protestant Era," ibid., 273–316; Wilhelm and Marion Pauck, *Paul Tillich: His Life and Thought* (San Francisco: Harper & Row, 1989), 220–1; Adams, *Not Without Dust and Heat*, 368, 376–7; Paul Tillich, *The Interpretation of History* (New York: Charles Scribner's Sons, 1936); Tillich, Foreword to *Voluntary Associations: A Study of Groups in Free Societies*, ed. D. B. Robertson (Richmond, VA: John Knox Press, 1966), quote 5.

56 James Luther Adams, "The Changing Reputation of Human Nature," 1941 Berry Street Conference Address, reprinted in *The Essential James Luther Adams*, 51–78, and reprinted in Adams, *Voluntary Associations: Socio-Cultural Analyses and Theological Interpretation*, ed. J. Ronald Engel (Chicago: Exploration Press of the Chicago Theological Seminary, 1986), 14–61.

57 Adams, "The Changing Reputation of Human Nature," *The Essential James Luther Adams*, quotes, 58, 59.

58 James Freeman Clarke, *Vexed Questions in Theology* (Boston: G. H. Ellis, 1886), 10–16; see David Robinson, *The Unitarians and the Universalists* (Westport, CT: Greenwood Press, 1985), 234–5.

59 Adams, "The Changing Reputation of Human Nature," 63–6, quote 65.

60 Ibid., quotes 67, 78.

61 James Luther Adams, "A Faith For the Free," *Together We Advance*, ed. Stephen H. Fritchman (Boston: Beacon Press, 1946), reprinted in Adams, *The Prophethood of All Believers*, 43–56, quotes 48, 50; also reprinted in *The Essential James Luther Adams*, 21–44.

62 Adams, "A Faith for the Free," quotes 50, 51, 52.

63 Ibid., quotes 52, 54.

64 James Luther Adams, "The Law of Nature: Some General Considerations," *Journal of Religion* 25 (April 1945), 88–95.

65 James Luther Adams, "Theological Bases of Social Action," *Journal of Religious Thought* 8 (Autumn/Winter 1950–1), reprinted in Adams, *On Being Human Religiously*, 102–19, quote 103.

66 Ibid., quote 105; see James Luther Adams, "Blessed are the Powerful," *Christian Century* 86 (June 18, 1969), 840.

67 Adams, "Theological Bases of Social Action," quote 105.

68 Ibid., quote 118.

69 Adams, *Not Without Dust and Heat*, "I thought," 271; Adams, "The Evolution of My Social Concern," "it was only," 129.

70 Adams, *Not Without Dust and Heat*, 282–3.

71 Levering Reynolds, Jr, "Chapter IV. The Later Years (1880–1953)," *The Harvard Divinity School: Its Place in Harvard University and in American Culture*, ed. George Huntston Williams (Boston: Beacon Press, 1954), 194–8, 210–29; James Luther Adams, "The Uses of Diversity," *Harvard Divinity Bulletin* 23 (1958), 47–64, reprinted in Adams, *An Examined Faith*, 290–300, quote 293.

72 James Luther Adams, "The Indispensable Discipline of Social Responsibility," (1962), *Journal of the Liberal Ministry* 6 (Spring 1966), 80–6, reprinted in Adams, *Voluntary Associations: Socio-Cultural Analyses and Theological Interpretation*, 153–9, and reprinted in *The Essential James Luther Adams*, 179–94, quote 182–3; Max L. Stackhouse, "James Luther Adams: A Biographical and Intellectual Sketch," *Voluntary Associations: A Study of Groups in Free Societies*, 333–57.

73 Ibid., quotes 183, 184, 187; James Luther Adams, "The Voluntary Principle in the Forming of American Religion," *The Religion of the Republic*, ed. Elwyn Smith (Philadelphia: Fortress Press, 1971), 217–46, reprinted in Adams, *Voluntary Associations: Socio-Cultural Analyses and Theological Interpretation*, 171–200.

74   Adams, "The Indispensable Discipline of Social Responsibility," quote 191; James Luther Adams, "Voluntary Associations," *The Westminster Dictionary of Christian Ethics*, ed. Jamers F. Childress and John Macquarrie (Philadelphia: Westminster Press, 1986), 651–2; Adams, "Voluntary Associations in Search of Identity," *Journal of Current Social Issues* 9 (1971), 15–22.

75   James Luther Adams, "Music as a Means of Grace," *Crane Review* 10 (1967), 42–5; reprinted in Adams, *On Being Human Religiously: Selected Essays in Religion and Society*, ed. Max L. Stackhouse (Boston: Beacon Press, 1976), 151–4, quotes 153, 154; also reprinted in *The Essential James Luther Adams*, 79–84.

76   Stackhouse, "James Luther Adams: A Biographical and Intellectual Sketch," 333, 334; James M. Gustafson, Review of *The Prophethood of All Believers*, by James Luther Adams, *The Unitarian Universalist Christian* 43 (Spring 1988), 53, cited in George Kimmich Beach, "Introduction," Adams, *An Examined Faith*, 8.

77   James Luther Adams, "The Liberal Christian Holds Up the Mirror," *The Unitarian Universalist Christian* 32 (Spring/Summer 1977), reprinted in Adams, *An Examined Faith*, 308–22, quotes, 316; see Adams, "The Liberalism that is Dead," *Journal of Liberal Religion* 1 (1940), 38–42; Adams, "Liberal Religion in a United World," *Christian Register* 63 (1944), 54–5; Adams, "The Ages of Liberalism," *Journal of Religious Thought* 14 (Spring–Summer 1957), 101–17.

78   George Kimmich Beach, "Introduction," *The Essential James Luther Adams*, 11; see George Kimmich Beach, *Transforming Liberalism: The Theology of James Luther Adams* (Boston: Skinner House Books, 2004).

79   John Courtney Murray, SJ, "Crisis in the History of Trent," *Thought* 7 (December 1932), 463–73; J. Leon Hooper, SJ, "General Introduction," in John Courtney Murray, *Religious Liberty: Catholic Struggles with Pluralism*, ed. J. Leon Hooper, SJ, (Louisville: Westminster John Knox Press, 1993), 17.

80   John Courtney Murray Papers, Archives of the Woodstock College Library, Georgetown University, Washington, DC; John Courtney Murray, *Matthias Ccheeben on Faith*, ed. D. Thomas Hughson (1937 dissertation; Lewiston, NY: Edwin Mellen Press, 1987); Donald E. Pelotte, SSS, *John Courtney Murray: Theologian in Conflict* (New York: Paulist Press, 1975), 3.

81   See John A. Zahm, *Evolution and Dogma* (reprint, New York: Arno Press, 1978); William L. Sullivan, *Letters to His Holiness Pope Pius X* (Chicago: Open Court Publishing Co., 1910); R. Scott Appleby, *"Church and Age Unite!": The Modernist Impulse in American Catholicism* (Notre Dame, IN: University of Notre Dame Press, 1992), 117–67.

82   Editorial, "Comments," *America* 62 (March 9, 1940), quote 591; see Pelotte, *John Courtney Murray: Theologian in Conflict*, 5–7; "Founding of the *American Ecclesiastical Review*," CatholicHistory.net, www.catholichistory.net, accessed August 24, 2006.

83   John Courtney Murray to James P. Sweeney, SJ, March 17, 1943; Murray to Francis A. McQuade, SJ, April 22, 1946, Archives of the New York Province of the Society of Jesus, New York, New York; both cited in see Pelotte, *John Courtney Murray: Theologian in Conflict*, 7–8.

84   Murray to McQuade, April 22, 1946, "away from"; John Courtney Murray to Francis A. McQuade, SJ, May 8, 1946, "rather ghastly"; Murray to McQuade, February 20, 1947, "I want"; Pelotte, *John Courtney Murray: Theologian in Conflict*, 8–13.

85   John Courtney Murray, "Current Theology: Christian Co-operation," *Theological Studies* 3 (September 1942), 413–31; American National Conference of Christians and Jews, "The Catholic, Jewish, Protestant Declaration on World Peace," reprinted in *The Pattern for Peace and the Papal Peace Program* (Washington, DC: Catholic Association for International Peace/Paulist Press, 1944), appendix to pamphlet; see Murray, "Current Theology: Co-operation: Some Further Views," *Theological Studies* 4 (March 1943), 100–11; Murray, "Current Theology: Intercredal Co-operation: Its Theory and Its Organization," *Theological Studies* 4 (June 1943), 257–86.

86 Francis Connell, "Catholics and 'Inter-faith' Groups," *American Ecclesiastical Review* CV (November 1941), 336–53, cited in Murray, "Current Theology: Christian Co-operation," 414.

87 Murray, "Current Theology: Christian Co-operation," 416.

88 John Courtney Murray to Zacheus J. Maher, SJ, April 30, 1945, John Courtney Murray Papers, Woodstock College Archives, Woodstock, Maryland; cited in Pelotte, *John Courtney Murray: Theologian in Conflict*, 11.

89 Paul Blanshard, *American Freedom and Catholic Power* (Boston: Beacon Press, 1949); Blanshard, *Communism, Democracy and Catholic Power* (Boston: Beacon Press, 1951); Blanshard, *The Irish and Catholic Power* (Boston: Beacon Press, 1953); Protestants and Other Americans United for Separation of Church and State, "Separation of Church and State: A Manifesto by 'Protestants and Other Americans United,'" *Christian Century* 65 (January 21, 1948), 79–82.

90 John Courtney Murray, "Reversing the Secularistic Drift," *Thought* 24 (March 1949), 36–46; Murray, review of *American Freedom and Catholic Power*, by Paul Blanshard, *The Catholic Mind* 169 (June 1949), 233–4; Murray, "Paul Blanshard and the New Nativism," *The Month* 5 (April 1951), 214–25.

91 W. Russell Bowie, "The Catholic Position: Protestant Concern Over Catholicism," *American Mercury* 69 (September 1949), 261–73, quotes 262; see Francis J. Connnell, "Preserving the Faith Inviolate," *American Ecclesiastical Review* 114 (January 1946), 34–47.

92 Fiorelli Cavilli, "La Condizione dei Protestanti in Spagna," *La Civilta Cattolica* 2 (April 1948), 29–47; cited in Bowie, "The Catholic Position: Protestant Concern Over Catholicism," 264.

93 John Courtney Murray, "The Catholic Position: A Reply," *American Mercury* 69 (September 1949), 274–83, quotes 274, 276, 281.

94 Ibid., quotes 281, 282.

95 John Courtney Murray, Letter to the Editor of *American Mercury*, September 9, 1949, Woodstock College Archives, cited in Pelotte, *John Courtney Murray: Theologian in Conflict*, 19.

96 Ibid., 20; see Murray, "The Catholic Position: A Reply," (September 1949), 281–3; John Courtney Murray, "The Catholic Position: A Reply," *American Mercury* 69 (November 1949), 637–9.

97 John Courtney Murray, "The Natural Law," *Great Expressions of Human Rights*, ed. R. M. MacIver (New York: Harper, 1950), 72–5; Murray, "Natural Law and the Public Consensus," *Natural Law and Modern Society*, ed. John Cogley (Cleveland: World Publishing Co., 1963), 62–3; Charles E. Curran, *American Catholic Social Ethics: Twentieth-Century Approaches* (Notre Dame: University of Notre Dame Press, 1982), 178–83; Hooper, "General Introduction," 21–5; Robert W. McElroy, *The Search for an American Public Theology: The Contribution of John Courtney Murray* (New York: Paulist Press, 1989), 53–60.

98 Murray, "Natural Law and the Public Consensus," 62; Murray, "Current Theology: Christian Co-operation," 413–31; Murray, "Current Theology: Intercredal Co-operation: Its Theory and Organization," 257–86.

99 Pope Gelasius I, "Letter to the Emperor Anastasius," Brian Tierney, *The Crisis of Church and State* (Englewood Cliffs, NJ: Prentice-Hall, 1964), 13–15; John Courtney Murray, "Contemporary Orientations of Catholic Thought on Church and State in the Light of History," *Theological Studies* 10 (June 1949), quote 196; see John Courtney Murray, "The Yale University Lectures," 1951, I, 12–15, John Courtney Murray Papers; McElroy, *The Search for an American Public Theology: The Contribution of John Courtney Murray*, 20–1; Robert Carlyle and A. J. Carlyle, *A History of Medieval Political Theory in the West* (Edinburgh: William Blackwood and Sons, 1930).

100 John Courtney Murray, "Current Theology: Freedom of Religion," *Theological Studies* 6
      (March 1945), 85–113; Murray, "Freedom of Religion, I: The Ethical Problem," *Theologi-
      cal Studies* 6 (June 1945), 229–86, quote 242. These arguments are dissected in detail by
      J. Leon Hooper, SJ, *The Ethics of Discourse: The Social Philosophy of John Courtney Murray*
      (Washington, DC: Georgetown University Press, 1986), 30–50.

101 John Courtney Murray, "Government Repression of Heresy," *Proceedings of the Third
      Annual Convention of the Catholic Theological Society of America* (Bronx, NY: Catholic Theo-
      logical Society of America, 1948), 26–98, quote 33.

102 John Courtney Murray, "St Robert Bellarmine on the Indirect Power," *Theological Studies*
      9 (December 1948), 491–535; Murray, "Contemporary Orientations of Catholic Thought
      on Church and State in the Light of History," *Theological Studies* 10 (June 1949), 177–234;
      Murray, "Current Theology: On Religious Freedom," *Theological Studies* 10 (September
      1949), 409–32; Hooper, "General Introduction," 29–30; Hooper, *The Ethics of Discourse:
      The Social Philosophy of John Courtney Murray*, 51–2.

103 Murray, "Government Repression of Heresy," quotes 75, 72; Hooper, *The Ethics of Dis-
      course: The Social Philosophy of John Courtney Murray*, 57–8.

104 John Courtney Murray, "The Problem of 'The Religion of the State,'" *American Ecclesi-
      astical Review* 124 (May 1951), 327–52, quotes 344, 351; George W. Shea, "Catholic
      Doctrine and 'The Religion of the State,'" *American Ecclesiastical Review* 123 (September
      1950), 161–74; Hooper, *The Ethics of Discourse: The Social Philosophy of John Courtney
      Murray*, 61–2.

105 Murray, "The Problem of 'The Religion of the State,'" quote 345.

106 Francis J. Connell, "Reply to Fr. Murray," *American Ecclesiastical Review* 126 (January
      1952), 49–59; John Courtney Murray, "For the Freedom and Transcendence of the
      Church," *American Ecclesiastical Review* 126 (January 1952), 28–48, quote 32; Hooper, *The
      Ethics of Discourse: The Social Philosophy of John Courtney Murray*, 63; see Connell, "Does
      Catholic Doctrine Change?" *American Ecclesiastical Review* 117 (November 1947),
      321–31.

107 John Courtney Murray, "The Church and Totalitarian Democracy," *Theological Studies* 13
      (December 1952), 525–63; Murray, "Leo XIII on Church and State: The General Struc-
      ture of the Controversy," *Theological Studies* 14 (March 1953), 1–30.

108 John Courtney Murray, "Leo XIII: Separation of Church and State," *Theological Studies*
      14 (June 1953), 145–214; Murray, "Leo XIII: Two Concepts of Government," *Theological
      Studies* 14 (December 1953), 551–67; Murray, "Leo XIII: Two Concepts of Government:
      Government and the Order of Culture," *Theological Studies* 15 (March 1954), 1–33.

109 Murray, "Leo XIII and Pius XII: Government and the Order of Religion," 1955, in
      Murray, *Religious Liberty: Catholic Struggles with Pluralism*, 49–125; see Hooper, *The Ethics
      of Discourse: The Social Philosophy of John Courtney Murray*, 70–2.

110 Alfredo Cardinal Ottaviani, "Church and State: Some Present Problems in the Light of
      the Teachings of Pope Pius XII," *American Ecclesiastical Review* 128 (May 1953), 321–34;
      Pope Pius XII, "*Ci riesce*: A Discourse to the National Convention of Italian Jurists,"
      Vatican Press Office English Translation, *American Ecclesiastical Review* 130 (February 1954),
      129–38; "Alfredo Cardinal Ottaviani: Prefect Emeritus of *Doctrine of the Faith*," *Catholic
      Hierarchy*, www.catholic–hierarchy.org.bishop, 1, accessed September, 12 2006; Murray,
      "Leo XIII and Pius XII: Government and the Order of Religion," quote 112.

111 Murray, "Leo XIII and Pius XII: Government and the Order of Religion," quotes
      112.

112 George A. Lindbeck to Rev. Thomas Ambrogi, September 6, 1967, Woodstock College
      Archives; James Shannon, "Tribute to John Courtney Murray," *Catholic Bulletin*, Archdio-
      cese of Minneapolis–St. Paul Minnesota Weekly (September 7, 1967), 3; both cited in
      Pelotte, *John Courtney Murray: Theologian in Conflict*, 31.

113 John Courtney Murray to John Tracy Ellis, July 20, 1953, Woodstock College Archives,
      cited in Pelotte, *John Courtney Murray: Theologian in Conflict*, 37–8; see John Tracy Ellis,

"Church and State: An American Catholic Tradition," *Harper's* 207 (July–December 1953), 63–7. This article described the following bishops as "American" in the sense to which Murray alluded in reply: John Carroll, John England, John Hughes, James Gibbons, John Lancaster Spalding, John Ireland, John J. Keane, Richard J. Cushing, and John T. McNicholas.

114   Joseph C. Fenton, "The Teachings of *Ci riesce*," *American Ecclesiastical Review* 130 (February 1954), 114–23, quotes 122–3; Pelotte, *John Courtney Murray: Theologian in Conflict*, 45–6. Murray never prepared a full text of this address, but he left a nine-page typewritten transcript and a longhand manuscript (Woodstock College Archives).

115   Pelotte, *John Courtney Murray: Theologian in Conflict*, 44–52; Joseph C. Fenton, "Toleration and the Church–State Controversy," *American Ecclesiastical Review* 130 (May 1954), 342–3; Guiseppe Di Meglio, "*Ci riesce* and Caardinal Ottaviani's Discourse," *American Ecclesiastical Review* 130 (June 1954), 384; Vincent McCormick to John Courtney Murray, July 9, 1955, Woodstock College Archives, cited in Pelotte, 52.

116   John Courtney Murray to Vincent McCormick, July 15, 1955, "the whole thing" and "in symbol," Woodstock College Archives; Murray to McCormick, January 22, 1956, "a nuisance," Woodstock College Archives, cited in Pelotte, *John Courtney Murray: Theologian in Conflict*, 53–4; Pope Pius XII, "Vous avez voulu," Address to the Tenth International Congress of Historical Sciences, September 7, 1955, *American Ecclesiastical Review* 133 (November 1955), 340–51; Joseph C. Fenton, "The Holy Father's Statement on Relations between the Church and State," *American Ecclesiastical Review* 133 (November 1955), 323–31.

117   John Courtney Murray, "Catholics in America – A Creative Minority?" *Catholic Mind* 53 (October 1955), 590–7; Murray, "The Christian Idea of Education," *Eight Views of Responsibility in Government, Business, Education and the Church* (St Louis: St Louis University, 1955), 372–84; Murray, "Special Catholic Challenges," *Life* (December 1955), 144–6; Murray, "The Bad Arguments Intelligent Men Make," *America* 96 (November 3, 1956), 120–3; Murray, "Freedom, Responsibility, and Law," *The Catholic Lawyer* 2 (July 1956), 214–23; Murray, "Questions of Striking a Right Balance: Literature and Censorship," *Books on Trial* 14 (June–July 1956), 393–5, 444–6; Murray, "Church and State: The Structure of the Argument," 1958, unpublished; Murray, "Unica Status Religio," 1959, unpublished; Vincent McCormick to John Courtney Murray, August 5, 1958, Woodstock College Archives, cited in Pelotte, *John Courtney Murray: Theologian in Conflict*, 59.

118   John Courtney Murray, *We Hold These Truths: Catholic Reflections on the American Proposition* (New York: Sheed and Ward, 1960); see Douglas Auchincloss, "City of Man and God," *Time* (December 12, 1960), 64–70.

119   Murray, *We Hold These Truths: Catholic Reflections on the American Proposition*, vii–viii; Thomas Jefferson, "A Declaration by the Representatives of the United States of America, in General Congress Assembled," *Life and Selected Writings of Thomas Jefferson*, ed. Adrienne Koch and William Peden (New York: Random House, 1993), 24; see Pauline Maier, *American Scripture: Making the Declaration of Independence* (New York: Vintage Books, 1997).

120   Murray, *We Hold These Truths: Catholic Reflections on the American Proposition*, viii, ix.

121   Ibid., x.

122   Ibid., xi.

123   Ibid., quotes, 28, 32.

124   Ibid., quotes 33, 38.

125   Ibid, 42.

126   Charles Clayton Morrison, *Can Protestantism Win America?* (New York: Harper & Brothers, 1948), 85, 87.

127   See John Courtney Murray, "Dr. Morrison and the First Amendment," *America* 78 (March 6, 1948), 627–9; Murray, "Dr. Morrison and the First Amendment, II," *America* 78 (March 20, 1948), 683–6; Morrison, *Can Protestantism Win America?* 87–97.

128   Murray, *We Hold These Truths: Catholic Reflections on the American Proposition*, quotes 41, 43.

129   See John Courtney Murray, "The Problem of Pluralism in America," *Thought* 24 (Summer 1954), 165–208; reprinted in *Catholicism in American Culture* (New Rochelle, NY: College of New Rochelle, 1955), 13–38; short version reprinted in *Commonweal* 60 (August 1954), 463–8; less pro-American version titled "Church, State, and Religious Liberty," *The Catholic Mind* 57 (May–June 1959), 201–15; chapters 1 and 2, "E Pluribus Unum: The American Consensus" and "Civil Unity and Religious Integrity: The Articles of Peace," in *We Hold These Truths*, 27–43, 45–78.

130   Murray, *We Hold These Truths: Reflections on the American Proposition*, 48–9.

131   Ibid., 54.

132   Ibid., 52, 53.

133   Ibid., 53–4,

134   Ibid., 144.

135   Ibid., 145–6.

136   Ibid., 148.

137   Pelotte, *John Courtney Murray: Theologian in Conflict*, 76–7; Arthur M. Schlesinger, Jr, *A Thousand Days: John F. Kennedy in the White House* (Boston: Houghton Mifflin, 1965), 108; Theodore C. Sorenson, *Kennedy* (New York: Harper and Row, 1965), 190; "The Voice of Reason," *Newsweek* (August 28, 1967); John F. Kennedy, "Remarks on Church and State," *Church and State in American History*, ed. John Wilson (Boston: C.C. Heath and Co., 1965), 188–90.

138   Joseph C. Fenton, "Doctrine and Tactic in Catholic Pronouncements on Church and State," *American Ecclesiastical Review* 135 (October 1961), 274; Robert B. Kaiser, *Pope, Council and World* (New York: Macmillan, 1963), 65; Pelotte, *John Courtney Murray: Theologian in Conflict*, 79–80, quotes 80.

139   See Richard J. Regan, SJ, *Conflict and Consensus: Religious Freedom and the Second Vatican Council* (New York: Macmillan, 1967); Michael Novak, *The Open Church: Vatican II, Act II* (New York: Macmillan, 1964); Pelotte, *John Courtney Murray: Theologian in Conflict*, 92–4; Francis Canavan, SJ, "Religious Freedom: John Courtney Murray and Vatican II," *Faith & Reason* 8 (1987), reprinted in *John Courtney Murray and the American Civil Conversation*, eds. Robert P. Hunt and Kenneth L. Grasso (Grand Rapids: Eerdmans, 1992), 167–80; Vatican Council II, "Decree on Ecumenism, *Unitatis redintegratio*, November 21, 1964), *Vatican Council II: The Conciliar and Postconciliar Documents*, ed. Austin Flannery (Northport, NY: Costello Publishing Co., 1998), 452–553.

140   John Courtney Murray, "The Declaration on Religious Freedom: A Moment in Its Legislative History," *Religious Liberty: An End and a Beginning*, ed. John Courtney Murray (New York: Macmillan, 1966), 15–42, quote 22.

141   Ibid., 27–9, 37–8; Canavan, "Religious Freedom: John Courtney Murray and Vatican II," 175.

142   Vatican Council II, "Declaration on Religious Freedom," (*Dignitatis Humanae*, December 7, 1965"), trans. John Courtney Murray, *The Documents of Vatican II*, eds. Walter M. Abbot, SJ and Joseph Gallagher (New York: America, 1966), 678–9; see *Vatican Council II: The Conciliar and Postconciliar Documents*, 799–812; Pelotte, *John Courtney Murray: Theologian in Conflict*, 99.

143   John Courtney Murray, "The Issue of Church and State at Vatican Council II," *Theological Studies* 27 (December 1966), 580–606, quote 601; Murray, "The Declaration on Religious Freedom," *Vatican II: An Interfaith Appraisal*, ed. John H. Miller, CSC (Notre Dame: University of Notre Dame Press, 1966), 565–77, "common," 565; see Murray, "Religious Freedom," *Freedom and Man*, ed. John Courtney Murray (New York: P. J. Kenedy, 1965), 131–40; Murray, "This Matter of Religious Freedom," *America* 112 (January 9, 1965), 40–3; Murray, "Conference on the Development of the Doctrine of Religious Liberty,"

Council Day Book, ed. Floyd Anderson (Washington, DC: NCWC Press, 1966), 14–17; Murray, "La Déclaration sur la Liberté Religieuse," *Concilium* 15 (1966), 7–18; Murray, "The Declaration on Religious Freedom: Its Deeper Significance," *America* 114 (April 23, 1966), 592–3; Murray, "Freedom, Authority, Community," *America* 115 (December 3, 1966), 734–41; Murray, "Declaration on Religious Freedom: Commentary," *American Participation at the Second Vatican Council*, ed. Vincent A. Yzermans (New York: Sheed & Ward, 1967), 668–76; Murray, "Religious Freedom," *The Documents of Vatican II*, 673–4, text with commentary, 674–96.

144 Murray, text with commentary, *The Documents of Vatican II*, "the church," 693; ibid., 684; John Courtney Murray, *The Problem of Religious Freedom* (Westminster, MD: Newman Press, 1964); see Brian W. Harrison, "John Courtney Murray: A Reliable Interpreter of *Dignitatis Humanae?*" *Living Tradition: Organ of the Roman Theological Forum* (January 1991), www.rtforum.org, accessed August 7, 2006.

145 Niebuhr's seminar remark at the Center for the Study of Democratic Institutions recorded in "Two Faces of Federalism," ed. Robert M. Hutchins, 1961, Archives of the Center for the Study of Democratic Institutions, Santa Barbara, California; cited in McElroy, *The Search for an American Public Theology: The Contribution of John Courtney Murray*, 156; Garry Wills, *Bare Ruined Choirs: Doubt, Prophecy, and Radical Religion* (Garden City, NY: Doubleday, 1972). From 1953 onward, Murray served on the board of the Center for the Study of Democratic Institutions.

146 Curran, *American Catholic Social Ethics: Twentieth Century Approaches*, 223–32.

147 See Martin E. Marty, *Religion and Republic: The American Circumstance* (Boston: Beacon Press, 1987); Richard P. McBrien, *Caesar's Coin: Religion and Politics in America* (New York: Macmillan, 1987); Richard John Neuhaus, *The Naked Public Square: Religion and Democracy in America* (Grand Rapids: Eerdmans, 1984); "Theology and Philosophy in Public: A Symposium on John Courtney Murray's Unfinished Agenda," *Theological Studies* 40 (December 1979), 702–14; David Hollenbach, "Public Theology in America: Some Questions for Catholicism After John Courtney Murray," *Theological Studies* 37 (December 1976), 300–1; John A. Coleman, *An American Strategic Theology* (New York: Paulist Press, 1982), 193–8;

148 McElroy, *The Search for an American Public Theology: The Contribution of John Courtney Murray*, 143–83, quotes 153, 154.

149 William R. Luckey, "The Contribution of John Courtney Murray, S.J.: A Catholic Perspective," *John Courtney Murray and the American Civil Conversation*, 19–43, quote 42; Richard John Neuhaus, "Democracy, Desperately Dry," ibid., 3–18, quote 5; Neuhaus, *The Catholic Moment: The Paradox of the Church in the Postmodern World* (San Francisco: Harper & Row, 1987).

150 Francis Canavan, SJ, "Murray on Vatican II's Declaration on Religious Freedom," *Communio* 9 (Winter 1982), 404–5; Canavan, "The Catholic Concept of Religious Freedom as a Human Right," *Religious Liberty: An End and a Beginning*, 78–9; Canavan, "Religious Freedom: John Courtney Murray and Vatican II," *John Courtney Murray and the American Civil Conversation*, quote 176.

151 "The Declaration on Religious Liberty," *Documents of Vatican II*, quote 685; Canavan, "Religious Freedom: John Courtney Murray and Vatican II," 177–80.

152 J. Leon Hooper, SJ, "John Courtney Murray, S.J., and Religious Pluralism," *Woodstock Report* 33 (March 1993), 1–7, quotes 2; see Hooper, *The Ethics of Discourse: The Social Philosophy of John Courtney Murray*, 195–225.

153 Ibid., 3–7; see John Courtney Murray, "The Religious School in a Pluralistic Society," *Catholic Mind* 54 (September 1956), 502–11; Murray, "State University in a Pluralist Society," *Catholic Mind* 57 (May–June 1959), 242–52; Murray, "On the Future of Humanistic Education," *Humanistic Education and Western Civilization*, ed. Arthur A. Cohen (New York: Holt, Rinehart and Winston, 1964), 231–47.

154   John Courtney Murray to John J. McMahon, "Memorandum for Very Rev. Father Pro-
      vincial with Regard to Visiting Professorship at Yale University," June 12, 1951, quote,
      Archives of the New York Province of the Society of Jesus, cited in Pelotte, *John Courtney
      Murray: Theologian in Conflict*, 33; see Gerald V. Bradley, "Beyond Murray's Articles of
      Peace and Faith," *John Courtney Murray and the American Civil Conversation*, 181–204;
      Bradley, *Church–State Relationships in America* (Westport, CT: Greenwood Press, 1987).

155   Dorothy Day, *The Long Loneliness* (New York: Harper & Row, 1952; reprinted, San
      Francisco: HarperSanFrancisco, 1997), 15–36; Jim Forest, *Love is the Measure: A Biography
      of Dorothy Day* (Mahwah, NJ: Paulist Press, 1986; reprinted, Maryknoll, NY: Orbis Books,
      1994), 3–10; William R. Miller, *Dorothy Day: A Biography* (New York: Harper & Row,
      1982), 3–12.

156   Day, *The Long Loneliness*, quotes 41, 46.

157   Ibid., quote 51.

158   Ibid., quotes 60, 62.

159   Ibid., quotes, 68, 78; see Forest, *Love is the Measure: A Biography of Dorothy Day*, 24; John
      Reed, *Ten Days That Shook the World* (New York: Boni and Liveright, 1919).

160   Day, *The Long Loneliness*, 83–132, quote 85; Dorothy Day, *The Eleventh Virgin* (New
      York: A. & C. Boni, 1924); Malcolm Cowley, *Exile's Return: A Literary Odyssey of the
      1920s* (New York: Viking Press, 1951), 69.

161   Day, *The Long Loneliness*, quotes 136, 149.

162   Ibid., 151–66, quotes 165, 166.

163   See Peter Maurin, *Easy Essays* (New York: Sheed and Ward, 1936); Marc Ellis, *Peter
      Maurin: Prophet in the Twentieth Century* (New York: Paulist Press, 1981); Day, *The Long
      Loneliness*, 169–70; Forest, *Love is the Measure: A Biography of Dorothy Day*, 56–7.

164   Day, *The Long Loneliness*, quotes 170, 171; Dorothy Day, *Loaves and Fishes* (New York:
      Harper & Row, 1963; reprint, Maryknoll, NY: Orbis Books, 1997), 3–11.

165   Day, *The Long Loneliness*, quote, 173.

166   *The Catholic Worker* (May 1, 1933), 1, 3.

167   Day, *The Long Loneliness*, 178–81; Forest, *Love is the Measure: A Biography of Dorothy Day*,
      60–3; Miller, *Dorothy Day: A Biography*, 227–80.

168   Day, *The Long Loneliness*, quotes, 180, 186.

169   Rosalie G. Riegle, *Dorothy Day: Portraits by Those Who Knew Her* (Maryknoll, NY: Orbis
      Books, 2003), quote 3.

170   Dorothy Day, "Why Write About Strife and Violence?" *The Catholic Worker* (June 1934),
      reprinted in *Dorothy Day: Selected Writings*, ed. Robert Ellsberg (Maryknoll, NY: Orbis
      Books, 1992), 62–3; Day, *The Long Loneliness*, "the state entered," 222.

171   See Paul H. Furfey, *Fire on the Earth* (New York: Macmillan, 1936); Furfey, *Three Theories
      of Society* (New York: Macmillan, 1937); Furfey, *This Way to Heaven* (Silver Spring, MD:
      Preservation of the Faith Press, 1939), Furfey, "From Catholic Liberalism to Catholic
      Radicalism," *American Ecclesiastical Review* 166 (1972), 678–86.

172   Dorothy Day, "The Use of Force," *Catholic Worker* (November 1936), reprinted in
      Dorothy Day: Selected Writings, 77–8; see Forest, *Love is the Measure: A Biography of Dorothy
      Day*, 72–3.

173   Day, "The Use of Force," 78.

174   Robert Ellsberg, Editor's Introduction, *Dorothy Day: Selected Writings*, xxxii; Forest, *Love
      is the Measure: A Biography of Dorothy Day*, 73–4.

175   Dorothy Day, "Our Country Passes from Undeclared to Declared War; We Continue
      Our Pacifist Stand," *Catholic Worker* (January 1942), 1.

176   *American Catholic Pacifism: The Influence of Dorothy Day and the Catholic Worker Movement*,
      eds. Anne Klijment and Nancy L. Roberts (Westport, CT: Praeger, 1996), "custodial"
      and "restriction," 26; Mark and Louise Zwick, "Dorothy Day and the Catholic Worker
      Movement," Introduction to Dorothy Day, *On Pilgrimage* (Grand Rapids: Wm. B.
      Eerdmans, 1999), 46–7; Day, *Loaves and Fishes*, quote, 63.

177 Dorothy Day, Editorial, *Catholic Worker* (February 1942), reprinted in Day, *Dorothy Day: Selected Writings*, 263–64.

178 Day, *Loaves and Fishes*, "somehow," 63; Day, *Catholic Worker* (September 1945), reprinted in Day, *Dorothy Day: Selected Writings*, 266–9, "Truman," 266; Zwick, "Dorothy Day and the Catholic Worker Movement," 50; Miller, *Dorothy Day: A Biography*, 364–5.

179 Day, *The Long Loneliness*, 264.

180 See Hilaire Belloc, *The Servile State* (London: T. N. Foulis, 1912); G. K. Chesterton, *What's Wrong with the World* (New York: Dodd, Mead & Co., 1910).

181 Forest, *Love is the Measure: A Biography of Dorothy Day*, 88–96; Miller, *Dorothy Day: A Biography*, 426–431.

182 Day, *The Long Loneliness*, 263–81, quote 279; Riegle, *Dorothy Day: Portraits by Those Who Knew Her*, 117.

183 Dorothy Day, "We Plead Guilty," *Commonweal* LXVII (December 27, 1957), 330–33, "whenever," 330; Interview with Edmund J. Egan, October 1968, Dorothy Day – Catholic Worker Collection, 15, Marquette University Archives, cited in Maurice Isserman, *The Other American: The Life of Michael Harrington* (New York: PublicAffairs, 2000), 84; Forest, *Love is the Measure: A Biography of Dorothy Day*, 147–8.

184 Dorothy Day, "A Revolution near Our Shores," *Catholic Worker* (July–August 1961), reprinted in Day, *Dorothy Day: Selected Writings*, 299–302, "we do," 302.

185 Dorothy Day, "A.J.," *Commonweal* 86 (March 24, 1967), 14–16, quote 16; see A. J. Muste, *Essays of A. J. Muste*, ed. Nat Hentoff (Indianapolis: Bobbs-Merrill, 1967).

186 Dorothy Day, Editorial, *Catholic Worker* (September 1962), (December 1962), reprinted in Day, *Dorothy Day: Selected Writings*, 306–8, 310–11, "of course," 307.

187 "Pastoral Constitution on the Church in the Modern World," *(Gaudium et spes*, December 7, 1965), *Vatican Council II: The Conciliar and Post Conciliar Documents*, 903–1001, quotes 990, 991.

188 Forest, *Love is the Measure: A Biography of Dorothy Day*, 112–13.

189 Riegle, *Dorothy Day: Portraits by Those Who Knew Her*, 72, 75; Forest, *Love is the Measure: A Biography of Dorothy Day*, 114–15.

190 Tom Cornell, "Catholic Worker Pacifism: An Eyewitness to History," *Catholic Worker Home Page*, www.catholicworker.com, accessed September 22, 1906, 1–6; Forest, *Love is the Measure: A Biography of Dorothy Day*, 114–15.

191 Dorothy Day, "In Peace is My Bitterness Most Bitter," *Catholic Worker* (January 1967), reprinted in Day, *Dorothy Day: Selected Writings*, 337–8.

192 Riegle, *Dorothy Day: Portraits by Those Who Knew Her*, quotes 69, 75.

193 Dorothy Day, Open Letter to Fr Daniel Berrigan, SJ, *Catholic Worker* (December 1972), reprinted in Day, *Dorothy Day: Selected Writings*, 3346–8.

194 Riegle, *Dorothy Day: Portraits by Those Who Knew Her*, quote 71.

195 Ibid., 71–2.

196 National Conference of Catholic Bishops, *The Challenge of Peace: God's Promise and Our Response; A Pastoral Letter on War and Peace*, May 3, 1983 (Washington, DC: United States Catholic Conference, 1983).

197 Riegle, *Dorothy Day: Portraits by Those Who Knew Her*, ix, 26, quote ix.

Chapter 6

Liberationist Disruptions

Martin Luther King Jr, James H. Cone, Mary Daly,
and Beverly W. Harrison

In the early 1970s a third major paradigm in theology and ethics emerged: liberation theology. The social gospel and Niebuhrian realism took pride in their establishment status, but liberation theology was about the experiences and interests of excluded people. Progressive theology in both of its main ethical streams tried to make Christianity credible and socially relevant to modern, educated, secularized, middle-class communities, taking for granted the cultural centrality of liberal Protestantism; liberation theology was devoted to liberating oppressed people from dependency and oppression.

Formally, liberation theology emerged in the USA in the aftermath of the assassination of Martin Luther King Jr, but there were glimmerings of it in modern America's greatest liberation movement, the civil rights movement. The founder of black liberation theology, James Cone, later judged, rightly, that King was a liberation theologian "before the phrase was coined" and the most important theologian in American history. As for liberation theology itself, Cone and Mary Daly were the originators in the USA, forging theologies that gave rise to new social ethical perspectives, although in both cases the lag between theology and ethics was significant.[1]

Unlike the social gospel and Christian realism, in which social ethical convictions dominated and theology trailed behind, the liberationist departure spoke theologically from the beginning. The social gospel movement was already fading before Rauschenbusch provided its theology in *A Theology for the Social Gospel*; Niebuhr's perspective was driven and shaped primarily by ethical concerns; in Catholicism, natural law theorizing was predominant. Liberation theology, in its own way, was essentially ethical, but its pioneers were theologians – Cone and Daly – who privileged the interests, respectively, of oppressed blacks and women.

The personal legacies of Cone and Daly for Christian theology were dramatically different. Cone's sense of his Christian theological vocation deepened as he trained a generation of black theologians, while Daly eventually repudiated Christianity. The theological trajectories diverged as well. Black liberation theology kept faith with the black church emphasis on the omnipotence and moral perfection of God, while feminist theology as developed by Daly, Rosemary Radford Ruether, Carter Heyward, and Beverly W. Harrison conceived the divine as immanent, not omnipotent, and in process. But black liberationism and feminist theology also overlapped considerably and to some extent influenced each other, as illustrated in the work of Cone and Harrison.

Martin Luther King Jr and the Beloved Community

The greatest figure in the story of American Christian social ethics so vastly transcended that story that placing him in it is incongruous. The legacy of Martin Luther King Jr was enormous, overwhelming the boundaries and topics of a work on social ethics. His story is too well known to bear repeating, and I have described his theological development in a previous book. But an interpretation of modern Christian social ethics must say something about its greatest figure.

Martin Luther King Jr was born on January 15, 1929 to a Baptist ministerial father, Martin Luther King, Sr ("Daddy King"), whom he always described as forceful and self-confident, and a nurturing mother, Alberta Williams King, whom he described as warm, soft-spoken, and easy-going. Daddy King had grown up poor as a sharecropper's son in Stockbridge, Georgia, while Alberta Williams grew up in a middle-class environment as the daughter of a successful pastor; both of King's parents stressed that he was "somebody." In 1944 he graduated from Booker T. Washington High School in Atlanta, having skipped the ninth and twelfth grades; four years later he graduated from Morehouse College, where, not ready for college, he was a mediocre student; his next stop was a white liberal school, Crozer Theological Seminary, where he flourished; in 1955 he completed a doctorate in theology at Boston University, where he studied under L. Harold DeWolf and wrote a dissertation on Paul Tillich's and Henry Nelson Wieman's concepts of God.

When King moved to Montgomery, Alabama in 1955 to assume the pastorate of Dexter Avenue Baptist Church, he had no premonition of a skyrocketing civil rights movement and only a slight acquaintance with Gandhi's strategy of nonviolent resistance to tyranny. But he had a profound conviction, burnished by his background in the black church and an education in social gospel personalism, of God's personal reality and the infinite value of human personality. This credo had a negative corollary that confirmed King's deepest feeling: if the worth of personality was the ultimate value in life, segregation was one of the world's most terrible evils. Evil was precisely that which degraded and nihilated personality. King's background and academic training fused at this point – that salvation included the fulfillment of one's moral and spiritual personality through a personal relationship with Jesus Christ. Segregation was designed to humiliate, exclude, and degrade the personhood of African Americans as a class; King, knowing that he was "as good as anybody," preached that racism was anti-Christian.

He joined the National Association for the Advancement of Colored People (NAACP) promptly upon moving to Montgomery, and, in August 1955, received a letter informing him of his selection to the group's executive committee, which was signed by Rosa L. Parks, branch secretary. On December 1 Parks was arrested for refusing to move to the back of the Cleveland Avenue bus in downtown Montgomery, and King emerged as a protest movement leader. Repeatedly he gave the assurance that Parks had acted on her own; the NAACP had not put her up to it. Responding to a whirlwind of events, King assembled in his mind the fragments of gospel religion, personalist philosophy, Thoreauian protest, and Gandhian resistance strategy that spoke to him personally and gave him a vision of how the movement's boycott of the Montgomery bus system needed to proceed.[2]

In its early days the Montgomery movement led by King, minister Ralph Abernathy, and Pullman porter E. D. Nixon did not speak the language of noncooperation and nonviolent resistance. Contrary to King's subsequent account, it did not center on Christian love and self-sacrifice, either. His first major speech as a movement leader, at Holt Street Baptist Church on December 5, inspired a packed house with a series of enthralling declarations about justice.

King proclaimed that people had grown tired "of being trampled over by the iron feet of oppression" and of being "thrown across the abyss of humiliation." The crowd exploded with deafening shouts and applause. King calmed the crowd, admonished against violence, and assured, "We are Christian people. We believe in the Christian religion. We believe in the teachings of Jesus." There would be no crosses burned at Montgomery bus stops and no white people lynched on "some distant road." King took a second run at justice-centered oratory, declaring that if they were wrong, so were God, Jesus, and the US Constitution. It was not enough to talk about love; King asserted boldly that justice and love worked together. Justice stood beside love, as "love in calculation," correcting whatever stood against love in society. The crowd exploded again, but King surprised his audience by failing to take a climactic third run. History would be written in Montgomery, he vowed, where American blacks would show their moral courage "to stand up for their rights." Ending abruptly, he asked the crowd merely to "think of these things," which evoked a brief, puzzled silence before the crowd applauded. Having lacked time to prepare, King didn't know what else to say. In the succeeding weeks he pulled together a philosophy and strategy, helped by movement professionals Bayard Rustin, a black socialist and veteran of the War Resisters' League, and Glenn Smiley, a white Methodist associated with the Fellowship of Reconciliation.[3]

From the beginning King emphasized the Christian character of the struggle for civil rights. After his home in Montgomery was bombed, he urged his attitude on an angry crowd:

> We cannot solve this problem through retaliatory violence. We must meet violence with nonviolence. Remember the words of Jesus: "He who lives by the sword will perish by the sword." We must love our white brothers no matter what they do to us. We must make them know that we love them. Jesus still cries out in words that echo across the centuries: "Love your enemies; bless them that curse you; pray for them that despitefully use you." This is what we must live by. We must meet hate with love. Remember, if I am stopped, this movement will not stop, because God is with the movement. Go home with this glowing faith and this radiant assurance.[4]

King was almost superhumanly magnanimous, and, without using the word, he called the movement to practice magnanimity. To follow Christ is to accept hardship with grace, suffer mistreatment for the sake of others, and forgive oppressors without demonizing them, he preached. From his graduate school training he knew, and took seriously, the writings of Anders Nygren and Paul Ramsey on the self-sacrificial character of divine love (agape), especially Nygren's emphasis that divine love is disinterested and Ramsey's ethical analysis of "enemy-neighbor" love. But King rejected the Nygren/Ramsey contention that agape applies directly to God alone. Nygren and Ramsey conceived agape as the outpouring of God's gracious love on behalf of human subjects, enabling them to practice more qualified forms of altruism. To King, that smacked of theological exclusivism, shortchanging the infinite value of the human soul. "There must be a recognition of the sacredness of human personality," he insisted. "Deeply rooted in our political and religious heritage is the conviction that every man is an heir to a legacy of dignity and worth." Religiously and politically, his theme was the universality of God's image in human souls. Human beings are divinely endowed with infinite value apart from any particular religious conviction that one may hold or any special grace that one may have received: "This innate worth referred to in the phrase *image of God* is universally shared in equal portion by all men."[5]

This creed was the bedrock of King's social activism. From the Montgomery boycott, to the creation of the Southern Christian Leadership Conference in 1957, to the sit-ins and freedom rides of the early 1960s, to the great campaigns in the early 1960s for civil rights in Albany (Georgia), Birmingham (Alabama), St Augustine (Florida), and Selma (Alabama), to his later campaigns for domestic and international social justice, he urged that persons were always to be treated as divinely spirited ends-in-themselves and that the rights claimed by black Americans were simply the rights of freedom and justice to which all people were entitled:

> In an effort to achieve freedom in America, Asia, and Africa we must not try to leap from a position of disadvantage to one of advantage, thus subverting justice. We must seek democracy and not the substitution of one tyranny for another. Our aim must never be to defeat or humiliate the white man. We must not become victimized with a philosophy of black supremacy. God is not interested merely in the freedom of black men, and brown men, and yellow men; God is interested in the freedom of the whole human race.[6]

He modeled his favorite sermon, "The Dimensions of the Complete Life," on a homily by Phillips Brooks, "The Symmetry of Life." In 1954 King preached it as a pastoral candidate at Dexter Avenue Baptist Church; in 1958 he preached it at Purdue University, addressing the first National Conference on Christian Education of the newly formed United Church of Christ; in 1964 he preached it in Westminster Abbey, London, on his way to accept the Nobel Peace Prize. Invoking the geometric perfection of the city of God as described in Revelation 21, King analogized that, like a cube, the complete life possesses three dimensions of length, breadth, and height. The length of a life is its inner drive to achieve personal ends; the breadth of a life is its outward moving care and concern for the well being of others; the height of a life is its upward-moving desire for God. The good life is about the flourishing of personality, he urged, which is "something of a great triangle," creatively integrating personal, social, and ultimate concerns: "At one angle stands the individual person, at the other angle stand other persons, and at the top stands the Supreme, Infinite Person, God. These three must meet in every life if that life is to be concrete."[7]

Always he preached the religion and politics of believing that human beings are children of God made in God's image. "Man is a being of spirit," King taught. "He is God's marvelous creation. Through his mind he can leap oceans, break through walls, and transcend the categories of time and space. The stars may be marvelous, but not so marvelous as the mind of man that comprehended them." Yet human beings misused their freedom and marred the image of God within them:

> See how we treat each other. Races trample over races; nations trample over nations. We go to war and destroy the values and the lives that God has given us. We leave the battlefields of the world painted with blood, and we end up with wars that burden us with national debts higher than mountains of gold, filling our nations with orphans and widows, sending thousands of men home psychologically deranged and physically handicapped.[8]

King's name for the social hope of the kingdom – a regenerated society – was "the beloved community." The phrase origined with American neo-Hegelian Josiah Royce and was familiar to King's personalist teachers at Boston University. For Royce and the personalists it expressed the ethical meaning of the kingdom of God. King taught that the foundation of the beloved community is the divine indwelling that equally graces all people: "There is no graded scale of essential worth; there is no divine right of one race which differs from the divine right of another. Every human being has etched in his personality the indelible stamp of the creator." Human life is infinitely valuable because every human being possesses God's spirit and is valued by God: "Whenever this is recognized, 'Whiteness' and 'Blackness' pass away as determinants in a relationship, and 'Son' and 'Brother' are substituted." It followed that racial prejudice is an assault on the divine spirit within despised races: "Segregation stands diametrically opposed to the principle of the sacredness of human personality. It debases personality."[9]

During his graduate training at Boston University, King took one course from Edgar Brightman, who fell ill and died in 1953. He knew Brightman barely long enough to catch his admiration for the Hegelian theme that progress occurs through dialectical struggle. Just as Hegel theorized that Spirit uses the passions of individuals to fulfill its own nature and realize its goal, King saw the Spirit acting in Rosa Parks' act of tired defiance:

> She was not 'planted' there by the NAACP, or any other organization; she was planted there by her personal sense of dignity and self-respect. She was anchored to that seat by the accumulated indignities of days gone by and the boundless aspirations of generations yet unborn. She was a victim of both the forces of history and the forces of destiny. She had been tracked down by the *Zeitgeist* – the spirit of the time.

That was also how he thought of himself.[10]

In the last years of King's tragically shortened life he urged that the next phase of the civil rights movement had to emphasize economic justice. Equality of individual opportunity had little meaning for oppressed people if it was not accompanied by social policies that created greater equality of condition, he contended. He called for a "revolution of values" that refused to accept massive disparities in economic condition as inevitable. "The time has come for an all-out war against poverty," he declared in 1967. "The rich nations must use their vast resources of wealth to develop the underdeveloped, school the unschooled and feed the unfed." In domestic policy he called for living wage legislation and a minimum guaranteed income for all households; in foreign affairs he called for an end to the USA's economic exploitation of the Third World and its support of reactionary governments in Asia, Africa, and South America. He disputed that America needed to support military dictatorships as a bulwark against Communism:

> We must not engage in a negative anti-Communism, but rather in a positive thrust for democracy, realizing that our greatest defense against Communism is to take offensive action in behalf of justice. We must with affirmative action seek to remove those conditions of poverty, insecurity and injustice which are the fertile soil in which the seed of Communism grows and develops.[11]

For two years after President Johnson signed the Civil Rights Act of 1965 and massively intervened in Vietnam, King agonized over the politics of opposing America's war. In 1967 he declared at Riverside Church in New York that he felt morally obliged "to break the betrayal of my own silences and to speak from the burnings of my own heart." For a brief time he believed in Johnson's anti-poverty program, but

> then came the build-up in Vietnam, and I watched the program broken and eviscerated as if it were some idle political plaything of a society gone mad on war, and I knew that America would never invest the necessary funds or energies in rehabilitation of its poor so long as Vietnam continued to draw men and skills and money like some demonic, destructive suction tube.

Confronted by liberal allies and civil rights leaders who claimed that a civil rights leader had no business taking controversial positions on foreign policy, and confronted by Black Power advocates claiming that King's nonviolence had become irrelevant, King declared that he "could never again raise my voice against the violence of the oppressed in the ghettos without having first spoken clearly to the greatest purveyor of violence in the world today – my own government." The war was poisoning America's soul, he pleaded: "It can never be saved so long as it destroys the deepest hopes of men the world over."[12]

Sadly he declared that America was on the wrong side of anti-colonialist movements throughout the world. King still believed in the American dream that he famously expressed at the March on Washington, DC, in 1963, that America had an opportunity to realize the revolutionary democratic promise of its Declaration of Independence. But by 1967 he felt compelled to accentuate that America was rich, privileged, short on compassion, and morbidly afraid of communism. Thus the first modern country had become the world's foremost counterrevolutionary power. What was needed was a spiritual reawakening to the revolutionary democratic ideals of a better America: "Our only hope today lies in our ability to recapture the revolutionary spirit and go out into a sometimes hostile world declaring eternal hostility to poverty, racism, and militarism."[13]

Many years after King was gone, it was revealed that he had been sexually promiscuous and had extensively plagiarized many of his graduate papers and published writings, including his doctoral dissertation. Further revelations detailed his chauvinistic treatment of women in general, and of Ella Baker and Coretta Scott King in particular. King's moral failings were terribly real, and not lacking in people hurt by them. They tarnished his moral image, but not his iconic standing as an historic figure of the magnitude of Abraham Lincoln and Mohandas Gandhi. King was an exemplar of his theme that freedom has no reality apart from power: power is integral to hope and liberation, he taught; integration requires equal access to political and economic power; freedom is participation in power. In *Where Do We Go From Here: Chaos or Community?* King declared that the goal of the civil rights movement was to transform the powerlessness of American blacks "into creative and personal power." He insisted that "there is no salvation for the Negro through isolation" and that the problems of Americans blacks could not be solved unless "the whole of American society takes a new turn toward greater economic justice." All could be free, but only if all were empowered to participate. Freedom and integration went together to build the beloved community.[14]

For many, King also epitomized the ethic of self-sacrificial love and nonviolent resistance to oppression as a way of life not merely a method, though that reading of his legacy was problematic for many liberationists. In the aftermath of King's assassination in 1968, James Cone took for granted that King was a major source and inspiration of the prophetic theology that was needed. But the King valorized by white liberals struck Cone as the exemplar of a white liberal ideal, not a symbol of black liberation. Cone respected King, but felt some ambivalence toward him; he hated what white liberals made of King, even more so other whites. In that conflicted brew of feelings and reactions black liberation theology was born.

James H. Cone and Black Liberation Theology

If not for the summer riots of 1967, James Cone might not have been a theologian by the time that King was murdered the following year, and black liberation theology might not have been founded. Cone was in the library during the climactic years of the civil rights movement, earning a doctorate in theology. Then he taught theology during the rise of the Black Power movement. By 1967 the ironies were galling to him. He savored the writings of James Baldwin, Richard Wright, and LeRoi Jones (later, Amiri Baraka), which pulsated with existential meaning, but he was stuck Barth, Tillich, and Niebuhr, who epitomized the culture of whiteness without noticing it. Cone decided he was in the wrong field. He would have to get another doctorate, this time in a field that spoke to him, black literature: "How could I continue to allow my intellectual life to be consumed by the theological problems defined by people who had enslaved my grandparents?" To have something worthwhile to contribute to the new black consciousness, and to keep himself from falling into despair, he had to get out of theology. But then Detroit erupted in race riots, as did other American cities; Cone decided that he lacked time for another doctorate. He would have to make do with the education he had already, to say something on behalf of the struggle of oppressed American blacks for freedom.[15]

He was born in Fordyce, Arkansas in 1938 and raised in nearby Bearden, a rural community of 400 blacks and 800 whites, which made an indelible imprint upon him, along with his parents Charlie and Lucy Cone. Cone's mother was a faithful church-goer and believer in God's righteousness; his father was a guardian of the family's dignity who often said that blacks could not survive white oppression without constant struggle and that "no black should ever expect justice from whites." After Cone had become a renowned theologian, he remarked that all his writing and speaking amounted to mere "dim reflections of what my parents taught and lived." If his father, lacking any social protection, could fearlessly oppose the evils of white society, how could he, protected by doctorate and tenure, dare to do less?[16]

In the early 1950s, while Cone attended high school, his father filed a lawsuit against the Bearden School Board, protesting against school segregation. Cone later recalled that "absolute madness seemed to enter the minds and hearts of the white folks in Bearden at the very idea of blacks and whites going to the same schools." In 1954, when Cone graduated, the Supreme Court decision in *Brown v. Board of Education* made his father's suit a key local case for school integration. There were rumors of a lynching plan; Charlie Cone assured his sons James, Cecil, and Charles that if it happened, several lynchers would die in the process. For two years Cone attended an unaccredited African Methodist Episcopal Church (AME) school in North Little Rock, Shorter College, transferring to Philander Smith College in Little Rock in 1956, where he first heard of Martin Luther King Jr and witnessed the gut-wrenching integration of a large urban high school: "Those were very rough and tense days," he later recalled. Every black person that he knew opposed "the satanic force of white supremacy" and took for granted "that God was on our side," while every white person, as far as he could tell, was too blinded by hate and privilege even to comprehend that justice was God's will.[17]

At Philander Smith, a Methodist college, Cone discovered the world of scholarship, taking special interest in black history. The writings of Frederick Douglass, Booker T. Washington, and W.E.B. Du Bois were exciting to him; on the other hand, in disciplinary terms they belonged to history, while Cone wanted to change the world through religion. The past interested him only as a clue to how things came to be the way they were; he did not want to live there. At the age of 16 he had started preaching at his brother's AME congregation in Spring Hill; during his college years he ministered to two AME congregations, taking for granted that ministry would be his vocation. On that assumption Cone and his brother Cecil enrolled at Garrett Biblical Institute (later, Garrett-Evangelical Theological Seminary) in 1958. Both were immediately disillusioned. Northern relatives had told them for years that things were better for blacks in the North; it took Cone a single day to conclude differently: "I was rudely awakened to the fact that white America is the same everywhere."[18]

A local barber told him to get out of his shop; an ethics professor told racist jokes; in every way Evanston and Garrett felt "hostile and strange" to Cone, constantly communicating to him that blacks were inferior. At least in the South racism was widely acknowledged, because many white Southerners were proud of it; in Evanston Cone felt the same ethos of racism without the acknowledgment. White students and faculty dehumanized blacks routinely while considering themselves free of racial bigotry. Cone's older black classmates assured him that a grade of "C" was the best he could expect from Garrett's faculty, which drove Cone to a degree and career he had not expected. Excelling in his studies, he found a mentor in theologian William Hordern, completed his divinity degree in 1961, and enrolled in Garrett's joint doctoral program with Northwestern University. Garrett's graduate advisor told Cone not to bother applying for the doctoral program; Hordern told him he would resign if Cone were not admitted; for Cone that was a realized impossibility, "the first time that any white person ever put himself on the line for me."[19]

Thus he found himself in the library, studying European theology, while many black classmates including Cecil Cone threw themselves into civil rights activism. Cone felt the contradiction deeply, telling himself he had to seize the opportunity to become a theologian. From the beginning he was surprised at what theologians took to be important. The reward structure of North American theology was geared to learning German, studying in Germany, and mastering German debates; meanwhile American Christian racism had no standing as a theological topic. "The failure to discuss it as a central problem in theology appeared strange and racist to me," he later recalled. "Most North American theologians identified their task as keeping up with the problems defined by European theologians." Reading James Baldwin, King, and Malcolm X on the side, Cone found it tormenting to sit through lectures on European topics. On one occasion he erupted in protest, calling his teacher a racist, which terminated the class for that day. The professor, a close acquaintance of Cone's, was devastated to be called a racist; Cone later explained that he "had no capacity for understanding black rage." After that Cone made the best of a bad situation at Garrett, which he later described as a little better than average for liberal white seminaries: "I hardly knew who I was as a theologian; I was a graduate student who mimicked white male Europeans and Americans." Keeping his feelings mostly to himself, he got his degree in 1965 with a dissertation on Barth's theological anthropology.[20]

His first teaching post was at Philander Smith, where he stewed over the irrelevance of his training. Cone wrote articles that meant nothing to him and were rejected anyway. Alienating the school's trustees, he left after two and a half years and moved to Adrian College in Adrian, Michigan in 1966, where his intense feeling of isolation proved to be something of a spur to find his own subject and voice. After a lonely year in Adrian, Cone told himself it was not too late to change fields, but changed his mind abruptly after Detroit exploded. Whatever he had to say, he would have to say as a theologian. He later recalled that upon hearing white theologians and pastors admonish blacks to follow Jesus instead of resorting to violence he found his voice: "I was so furious that I could hardly contain my rage. The very sight of white people made me want to vomit. 'Who are they,' I said, 'to tell us blacks about Christian ethics?'" How did whites muster the gall to lecture oppressed blacks about love and nonviolence? "My rage was intensified because most whites seemed not to recognize the contradictions that were so obvious to black people."[21]

That was the wellspring of emotion and conviction that produced his electrifying first book *Black Theology and Black Power* (1969). Alone in Adrian aside from his first wife Rose and a white friend, Lester Scherer, who remained a trusted ally, Cone took heart at learning he was not alone in the field: a militant group called the National Committee of Negro Churchmen (later, the National Conference of Black Churchmen [NCBC]) had been founded in 1966. By then Cone identified with Stokely Carmichael's Black Power alternative to integrationist ideology and strategy. In early 1968 Cone met Carmichael and prominent religious historian C. Eric Lincoln and took his first pass at writing a theological manifesto for Black Power radicalism. Lincoln's support and influence were crucial for Cone, opening doors to lecture invitations, job offers, and publishers; eventually he smoothed the way for Cone to become his colleague at Union Theological Seminary.[22]

On April 4, 1968 King was assassinated. Cone later recalled, "Although I had already embraced Black Power before King's murder, that event intensified my conviction and made me more determined to write an extended essay equating Black Power with the Christian gospel." Cone expected to be charged with reducing the gospel to an ideology; as a Barthian, part of him even agreed. On the other hand, Barth had ferociously attacked liberalism in his appeal to the transcendent Word, and Barthian theologians did nothing to abolish racism. Cone told himself he was closer to Barth than the Barthians; in any case, what mattered was to destroy white supremacism: "By the summer of that year, I had so much anger pent up in me I had to let it out or be destroyed by it." King's murder was merely the last straw, one added to the killing of Malcolm X and many Black Power militants: "My anger stretched back to the slave ships, the auction block, and the lynchings. But even more important were my personal encounters with racism in Bearden, Little Rock, Evanston, and Adrian."[23]

If theology was to be his work, he would not do it in a way that compromised his integrity. More precisely, Cone vowed to himself, he would never compromise with the evils of white racists: "Racism is a deadly disease that must be resisted by any means necessary. Never again would I ever expect white racists to do right in relation to the black community." In that spirit of angered resolve, but also ecstatic emancipation he wrote *Black Theology and Black Power* in four weeks, later describing it as a conversion experience: "It was like experiencing the death of white theology and being born again into the theology of the black experience."[24]

Malcolm X's phrase, "by any means necessary," was fundamental to Cone's definition of his object, Black Power: "Complete emancipation of black people from white oppression by whatever means black people deem necessary." Black Power used boycotts when necessary, he explained, demonstrations when necessary, and violence when necessary. Cone's first book contained the liberationist principle of responding to a world that defined the oppressed as non-persons; however, neither personhood nor the word "liberation" were key concepts for him as yet. He focused on why Black Power rejected white liberalism and black reformism. White liberals took pride in their liberality toward blacks, Cone observed, and they howled with wounded defensiveness when Black Power advocates like him and Carmichael placed them "in the same category with the George Wallaces." Cone told them to deal with it. Invoking Malcolm's analogy of the rapist asking his victim to like him, Cone said it was pathetic for white liberals to ask blacks to like them. Some whites protested that it was unfair to lump them with racists; others told Cone that things were better in their town because they supported the civil rights movement. Cone replied that all whites were responsible for white oppression and American whites had always had "an easy conscience."[25]

Black Power was an announcement that all whites were responsible for white oppression. Cone reflected that King, by the end of his life, represented the "least threatening" option; thus many whites claimed to admire him. But in his time King was hated for threatening white supremacy, until greater threats emerged: "What whites really want is for the black man to respond with that method which best preserves white racism." Cone preferred Malcolm on the basic problem of American society, who was "not far wrong when he called the white man 'the devil.'" American society was gripped by demonic forces, Cone explained, which so controlled the lives of white racists that they seemed incapable of distinguishing themselves from the alien power.[26]

Was that racism in reverse? Was there such a thing as "black racism," which triggered the "white backlash" feared by liberals? Cone replied: "While it is true that blacks do hate whites, black hatred is not racism." Racism had a two-fold structure, he observed. It assumed that biological race was a determinant of psycho-cultural traits and capacities, which supported the belief that one race was superior over others and thus possessed a right to dominance over them. Black Power, by contrast, made no assertion of racial superiority or right to dominance. It was simply an assertion of the right to liberation from white oppression. Cone allowed that Black Muslim theology offered a partial exception, describing blacks as a superior race and whites as devils, but even there, Black Muslims claimed no right to enslave whites, and the Nation of Islam was hardly a serious threat to white American hegemony. The Black Muslim movement, a "justifiable reaction to white racism," did not represent the Black Power movement, which focused on black empowerment and self-identity: "Black Power seeks not understanding but conflict; addresses blacks and not whites; seeks to develop black support, but not white good will."[27]

Black Power was against integration, especially its humiliating assumption that white institutions were superior. The last thing that black people needed was to be assimilated into white culture, Cone argued. White liberals, to the extent that they acknowledged white racism, sought to cure their culture of it by integrating blacks into it. They claimed to believe that race should not matter; the Christian ones added that Jesus was above race. Cone replied that race mattered everywhere in real-world America, assimilation was deadly for blacks, and in the American context of black oppression, Christ was a black liberator.

Black Power was a declaration of emancipation from seeking or depending on the good will of whites. White people in general had amazingly short memories, Cone noted. They persecuted blacks viciously for centuries, but puzzled over the feelings of hostility that sparked urban riots. White liberals, in particular, wanted to be morally innocent of racism while enjoying the privileges of whiteness. Cone remarked that the white liberal was a "strange creature" who often said "the right things," intellectualized the race problem "beautifully," and was even capable of defending Carmichael or allowing his daughter to marry a black man: "But he is still white to the very core of his being. What he fails to realize is that there is no place for him in this war of survival." The humiliating phase of linking arms with white liberals was over. The black struggle for liberation would get nowhere if blacks got tied up with the anxieties and superiority complexes of white liberals, Cone argued. There was a place in the justice struggle for white radicals – the John Browns who burned with hatred of white racism. They didn't get in the way of black liberation or presume to tell black radicals what to do, and they risked their lives for freedom. In conversation Cone sometimes allowed that some of the Freedom Riders belonged in that category. But a theology of Black Power had to repudiate the white liberal quest of innocence, its bogus "solidarity" with black freedom, and its myth of a "raceless Christ."[28]

"White liberal preference for a raceless Christ serves only to make official and orthodox the centuries-old portrayal of Christ as white," Cone explained. That was an idol that sanctified oppression. If Christ was really the redeemer and liberator of the scriptural witness, in the American context he had to be black, "working though the activity of Black Power." Cone's next book developed that thesis; in the meantime he enunciated the basic principles of liberation theology, condemned white churches for perpetuating white oppression, and took an ambivalent view of black churches, emphasizing the negative. The historic black churches offered a social haven to blacks, but also facilitated white oppression. King and the civil rights movement offered the beginning of a corrective, but only a beginning. The next step was for the black church to become relevant "by joining Christ in the black revolution."[29]

Cone admonished black pastors to stop being "'nice' to white society." The riots threw many pastors on the defensive, activating their moralizing impulse. Cone urged that a relevant black church had to *fight* racism, taking a rebellious attitude: "It cannot condemn the rioters. It must make an unqualified identification with the 'looters' and 'rioters,' recognizing that this stance leads to condemnation by the state as law-breakers. There is no place for 'nice Negroes' who are so distorted by white values that they regard laws as more sacred than human life. There is no place for those who deplore black violence and overlook the daily violence of whites. There is no place for blacks who want to be 'safe,' for Christ did not promise security but suffering." Instead of draining the black community of its rebellious spirit, trying to become like the white churches, black churches needed to embrace the new era of Black Power: "It is an age of rebellion and revolution. Blacks are no longer prepared to turn the other cheek; instead, they are turning the gun." The black revolution was already happening; the only question was whether black churches would join it.[30]

Black Theology and Black Power was a sensational debut that won a large readership and changed Cone's life. A prime example of late-1960s revolutionary oracle, it was published in March 1969, a month before civil rights leader James Forman presented his galvanizing "Black Manifesto" to the National Black Economic Development Conference in Detroit, which embraced it. Forman demanded a $500 million program of reparations for slavery and racial discrimination, called for the seizure and "total disruption" of church agencies, and urged blacks to "fight our enemies relentlessly." On May 4 he interrupted the Sunday service at Riverside Church in New York, dramatically repeating his demands. The Black Manifesto prompted an explosion of media coverage that stressed Forman's attack on white churches and often mentioned his similarity to Cone. Besides sweeping Cone's book into the media spotlight, the manifesto impacted on Cone's career institutionally. At Union Theological Seminary, a group of approximately 70 students pressed Union president John Bennett to respond to Forman's demands. Several days of demonstrations and hurried board meetings produced a twofold response: Union Seminary contributed $100,000 to black enterprise development in Harlem, promised to raise an additional $1 million, and created a new faculty position that it offered to Cone, who had several offers to consider. Cone chose Union Seminary, joined the NCBC, forged relationships with several black nationalist groups, and accepted Amiri Baraka's invitation to play a leading role in the Congress of African People (CAP), a major nationalist group.[31]

The latter experiences were chastening, however, helping him clarify that his center was Christian liberation theology, not black nationalism. Speakers at the 1970 CAP conference in Atlanta ridiculed religion and the black church unsparingly, sneering that the church had no place on its own terms in the struggle for black liberation. The conference abounded in hostility and name calling, which taught Cone a bitter lesson: "The mere agreement that white people are devils is not enough to attain our freedom." He had similar experiences with other black revolutionary groups, including the Black Panthers. At an NCBC conference in Oakland, Panther leader David Hilliard insulted black preachers with vulgar and threatening invective, telling them to choose between shooting white police officers and being shot by the Panthers. That reordered Cone's strategic priorities. Threatening to harm black people was beyond the pale; he shuddered at the "twisted" minds of Hilliard and other revolutionary leaders, which showed the destructive force of white oppression. Neither did Cone want any revolution that excluded his Christian mother. He was willing to support nationalist and Marxist organizations on a secondary basis, but resolved that his primary loyalty was to the liberationist wing of black Christianity.[32]

Organizationally that meant the NCBC, not a denominational home. At Philander Smith, Cone had joined the United Methodist Church because he failed to win a teaching position at an AME college. To many later observers that was a puzzling move, if not self-contradictory; to Cone it was analogous to teaching at Union Seminary. As a sharp critic of the AME Church's lack of episcopal accountability and what he called its "moral corruption," Cone was met with frosty treatment in the church and was not recognized as a theological leader. He joined the United Methodist Church, notwithstanding that he called it the anti-Christ, because it offered a workable base for him to develop liberation theology. In that respect, the Methodist Church was much like Union Seminary. Cone wanted the AME Church to support black liberation and him, but when it did neither, he reasoned that he was better off in a place that provided a "meaningful context" for doing liberation theology. Being half-accepted in the AME Church was galling, because it should have supported black liberation; being half-accepted in the Methodist Church was more tolerable, since it was not founded on the idea of black self-determination and had no prospect of moving in that direction. Yet in that context he was recognized as a leading theologian.[33]

Shortly after Cone joined the faculty at Union, he explained the logic to Bennett, who inquired about Cone's description of the white church as the anti-Christ. "Jim, you don't mean that literally, do you?" Bennett asked. Cone replied that he was dead serious; he was not spinning metaphors. From a black liberationist perspective, the white church was the enemy of Jesus Christ. Bennett asked, "But why did you choose to teach at Union if you mean it literally?" Cone explained that his father cut billets and logs for a living, and he taught at Union. Neither situation was very agreeable, but as long as he had to make a living, he might as well do it at Union: "Living in a racist society, every black person has to assume that his job may not meet all the requirements for which he or she may have been called." In 1973 Cone rejoined the AME Church, persuaded by a group of AME bishops that they earnestly wanted him back.[34]

His epochal work, *A Black Theology of Liberation* (1970), launched the North American tradition of liberation theology by expounding what it meant to interpret Christianity from a black liberationist perspective. At the time Cone was unaware of similar stirrings in Latin America and South Africa, but he defined "blackness" as a symbol of oppression extending beyond the North American context. The object of black theology, he declared, was "liberation from whiteness." Black theology was "theology of and for the black community, seeking to interpret the religious dimensions of the forces of liberation in that community." Cone stressed that whites were "in no position whatever" to make judgments about the truth claims or legitimacy of black theology. The very point of black theology was to "analyze the satanic nature of whiteness" and offer a liberating alternative to it. No white theologian had ever taken white America's oppression of blacks as the point of departure for theology: "Apparently white theologians see no connection between whiteness and evil and blackness and God." Even white theologians who wrote about racial injustice failed to attack white racism in its totality. Thus, white theology was not Christian theology at all, but its enemy. Every Christian theology worthy of the name was a liberation theology, and in a North American context, Christ was black.[35]

Cone stressed that black theology was of and for the black community, declaring that it was "accountable only to the black community." Black theology did not claim a universal starting point or aim. It was intrinsically communal, refusing to be separated from the black community of faith; it identified liberating activity with divine action; and it rejected all abstract principles of right and wrong. It lived by a single principle, liberation, which was always partial and contextual: "There is only one principle which guides the thinking and action of black theology: an unqualified commitment to the black community as that community seeks to define its existence in the light of God's liberating work in the world." The test of truth in black theology was whether a statement or action served the end of black liberation.[36]

Identifying six sources of black theology – black experience, black history, black culture, revelation, scripture, and tradition, Cone did not ontologize blackness, or at least, he did not intend to do so. But some of his statements came close enough to attributing qualities of being to race that many readers – critics and sympathizers alike – mistakenly took him to say that whites and blacks were different kinds of human beings. "The black experience is possible only for black persons," he declared. White musicians tried to play like Johnny Lee Hooker or B. B. King, but could never replicate black soul: "Black soul is not learned; it comes from the totality of black experience, the experience of carving out an existence in a society that says you do not belong." The black experience was about struggling for survival under racist oppression, loving "the spirit of blackness," and hearing soaring sermons on God's love in black congregations. It was also, Cone wrote, the rush of feeling that one got from bombing a white-owned building "and watching it go up in flames. We know, of course, that getting rid of evil takes something more than burning down buildings, but one must start somewhere."[37]

Cone did not claim to start, theologically, with revelation in the Barthian manner. The sources of theology were, in fact, interdependent even if one claimed to start with revelation. What mattered about revelation was its content, not its methodological priority: "As a black theologian, I want to know what God's revelation means right now as the black community participates in the struggle for liberation. *Revelation is a black event* – it is what blacks are doing about their liberation." Affirming that black theology took seriously the shaping authority of the scriptural witness, Cone lifted up the scriptural themes of exodus from slavery and liberation from oppression. In scripture and revelation, he stressed, God was disclosed as a partisan, liberating power. The God of the Bible called blacks to liberation, not redemptive suffering: "Blacks are not elected to be Yahweh's suffering people. Rather we are elected because we are oppressed against our will and God's, and God has decided to make our liberation God's own undertaking." To the black militants who turned from God because they loathed the "Uncle Tom approach of black churches," especially its "deadly prattle about loving your enemies and turning the other cheek," Cone was entirely sympathetic. But there was another Christianity that fought the enslavement of African Americans in the name of God's blackness and liberating will: "The blackness of God means that God has made the oppressed condition God's own condition. This is the essence of the biblical revelation."[38]

Because liberation was the very essence of the divine nature, God was black. Cone drew the sharpest contrast between his theology and that of his teachers at this point: "White religionists are not capable of perceiving the blackness of God, because their satanic whiteness is a denial of the very essence of divinity. That is why whites are finding and will continue to find the black experience a disturbing reality." For blacks, evil was anything that arrested or negated liberation; salvation was liberation. For whites, evil was normal life, benefiting from the privileges of whiteness; salvation was the abolition of whiteness. White theologians, preferring their privileges, pleaded that color should not matter. Cone replied, "This only reveals how deeply racism is embedded in the thought forms of their culture." Black liberation was not a relative option in theology: "Those who want to know who God is and what God is doing must know who black persons are and what they are doing." That did not mean joining the "war on poverty" or making other "sin offerings" promoted by white liberals to assure themselves of their goodness, Cone admonished, "Knowing God means being on the side of the oppressed, becoming one with them, and participating in the goal of liberation. *We must become black with God!*"[39]

And how could whites do that? Cone did not claim to take the question seriously: "This question always amuses me because they do not really want to lose their precious white identity, as if it is worth saving." But salvation was not moral anyway, he cautioned, equating blackness and salvation. The solution was spiritual, not moral, for blackness was a work of God, not a moral achievement. Blackness, like salvation, had to be received as a divine gift: "God comes to us in God's blackness, which is wholly unlike whiteness. To receive God's revelation is to become black with God by joining God in the work of liberation." Elsewhere he put it existentially, observing that Christian redemption had "nothing to do with black people being nice to white people as if the gospel demands that we ignore their insults and their humiliating presence."[40]

The latter statement, published in 1975, sought to clarify Cone's perspective on violence. He got off to a bad beginning: "With Marcus Garvey, we say: 'Any sane man, race or nation that desires freedom must first of all think in terms of blood.'" That seemed to cross the line into treating race as biologically significant, though Cone subsequently explained that he did not mean to cross it literally. Moving to a potent critique of the white concern about violence, Cone observed that white people cared only about the violence that harmed them: "Why did we not hear from the 'non-violent Christians' when black people were *violently* enslaved, *violently* lynched, and *violently* ghettoized in the name of freedom and democracy?" For whites, he noted, violence was a threat to personal safety in what was supposed to be a white world; for blacks, violence was systemic and pervasive. At lectures, whites asked Cone if he really supported violence; he replied: "Whose violence? What the hell are you talking about?" Sometimes violence was an instrument of liberation and reconciliation, just like the Bible said. Cone remarked, "According to the Bible, reconciliation is what God does for enslaved people who are unable to break the chains of slavery." Reconciliation was the divine gift of being set free from bondage, participating in God's liberating activity. Thus, for black theology, reconciliation with white people had to mean one thing before it could mean anything else: "Destroying their oppressive power."[41]

Many white reviewers complained that Cone's books were emotional, intellectually thin, obsessed with race, infatuated with violence, and dependent on the accusative mode. Sometimes they accused in return, calling him a racist; Catholic sociologist Andrew Greeley won the prize for invective, describing Cone as a racist with a "Nazi mentality." Cone alternated between brushing off his white critics and raging in reply. In his brushing off mode, he recalled Malcolm's observation that whites were skilled at making "the victim look like the criminal and the criminal look like the victim." In both cases Cone seethed inside: "I could barely contain my rage whenever I read their books or found myself in their presence. They were so condescending and arrogant in the way they talked about black theology, always communicating the impression that it was not genuine theology, because it was too emotional and anti-intellectual."[42]

But liberation theology was too profound in its critique and constructive import even for defensive white critics to dismiss it. Why did racial justice disappear from the agenda of white American theology after slavery was abolished? How was one to account for the stupendous silence of white American theologians through decades of segregation and racist lynching? What did it mean that Latin America was almost entirely enslaved by Christian colonizers? How should the Enlightenment be viewed if one took seriously that Europe was deeply involved in the slave trade throughout the eighteenth century? What would it mean if theology interpreted history from the standpoints of oppressed and excluded peoples?

Cone was the apostle of the revolutionary turn in American theology that privileged liberationist questions. He had become that way by reading Du Bois, Baldwin, Malcolm X, Frantz Fanon, and King, not his theological teachers, and he pressed hard on the point that white theology had bad priorities. In Cone's early career several white theologians recognized the historic and normative significance of his critique, notably Paul Lehmann, Frederick Herzog, William Hordern, Peter C. Hodgson, Helmut Gollwitzer, and John Bennett. Lehmann and Herzog were, for Cone, especially significant interlocutors. Lehmann, a Union Seminary ethicist, debated with Cone at length, mostly privately, on the perils of conflating Christian faith with an ideology. Hordern, Bennett, and Gollwitzer echoed the same concern, while Bennett added that Cone's work smacked of self-righteousness and wrongly claimed immunity from public criticism. All of them acknowledged, however, the importance of Cone's indictment of the white liberal failure to focus on racial oppression; Herzog, a Duke Divinity School theologian, did something about it, offering the first theological work by a white American to take up Cone's challenge.[43]

Lehmann agreed with Cone that black theology was the crucial point of departure for exploring the truth of Christian theology; on the other hand, he argued that Cone identified too unqualifiedly the truth of Christian theology with the concrete reality of blackness. Black theology was certainly Christian theology, but Christian theology was not black theology without remainder, for the ultimate object of Christian theology was the transcendent divine mystery that could not be grasped. Lehmann allowed that such a statement had to be suspended as soon as it was set down, or put in scare quotes; otherwise it became an excuse to ignore Cone's criticism. But Cone's position was faulty for erasing the distinction between God's story and the black story of liberation.[44]

Herzog praised Cone for offering the first American theology devoted to the liberation of oppressed people. The social gospel was a liberal reform project lacking a real theology, Herzog judged, and neo-orthodoxy was devoted to alleviating middle-class anxiety. Cone was the first American theologian to base his theology on God's question: "Your neighbor is oppressed. What is your responsibility?" Instead of attending to modern intellectuals, Cone attended to the needs of blacks and other oppressed peoples. That was the way to a better theology, Herzog argued, although he urged Cone to develop a systemic economic critique. As for white American supporters of liberation theology, what mattered was to change white America. Herzog backed off on integration and the beloved community. The task for white radicals was to change the values of white society, he argued, not to work in or with black communities.[45]

Cone's first reaction to feminist theology was that it was a farcical attempt to change the subject. Two early feminist judgments on his project, however, outlasted in memory those of his white male colleagues. Mary Daly, in 1973, panned Cone's theology as a fiercely patriarchal and vindictive "cry for vengeance." It had biblical support, but was bad for women. It transcended religion as a crutch, but settled for "religion as a gun." Daly argued that Cone's simplistic either/ors and "will to vindication" never went beyond the dualistic, sexist models internalized by Western selves and societies. Thus he had a one-dimensional solution that never reached to the root of racism.[46]

Rosemary Radford Ruether, in 1972, criticized Cone on two points, the first of which she applied subsequently to Daly. It was terribly important for a liberation theology not to denigrate or deny the humanity of any group, she argued. For a theology to be liberating, it had to condemn the demonic powers that possessed oppressive groups, but always in the name of an emancipating community reality that lay beneath the alienating power. Liberation lost its moral basis when it dehumanized the oppressor. Ruether acknowledged that Cone occasionally suggested the possibility of a universal salvation. But his constant rhetoric of destroy-the-oppressor gave "the overwhelming impression that theological categories have been wedded to racial identities in such a way that denies the humanity, as well as the false power, of white people." Identifying whiteness with the demonic, Cone failed to distinguish between whiteness as the nature of white people and whiteness as the destructive power possessing white society.[47]

The second problem with Cone was closely related to the first, Ruether judged: his theology was not very "black" in a cultural sense. The idioms, theology, and preaching of the black church were rooted deeply in African-American experience, but Cone was alienated from the black church. Black church preaching was hopeful, unselfconscious, involved in ordinary politics, and universalistic, but Cone was none of these things. He represented a "black intelligentsia in theology" that lacked a living relation to black culture, which left him with no communal basis for doing black theology. Ruether argued that although Cone condemned white theology, he lived in it and through it, promoting an abstract theory of blackness that had more to do with German theology than the black experience: "The result of this reversal in the thought of a man like Cone is that his 'blackness' and 'whiteness' are peculiarly flat and 'formal' in character. There is little living black culture reflected in Cone's sense of blackness." Just as black people were more than the oppressed, white people were more than oppressors.[48]

Similar critiques of Cone were commonplace among black clergy, which Ruether heard while teaching at Howard University, and were echoed even in the black theology movement. J. Deotis Roberts, a major figure in the movement, protested repeatedly that Cone's preeminence was undeserved because he represented only himself and gave the movement a bad image. In his view, Cone was wrong to denigrate racial reconciliation, his language was too violently anti-white, his theology was too Barthian, his thinking as a whole was narrow and exclusive, and he was disastrously cut off from black culture, the black church, and the African sources of black religion. Roberts exhorted in *Liberation and Reconciliation* (1971), "The narrowness that Cone has sought to impose upon Black Theology must be rejected. This must be done for the sake of Black Theology itself." Against Cone he insisted that liberation and reconciliation were equally indispensable. Roberts wanted a black liberation theology that did not give up on integration; sadly, he judged that the trend was toward militant separatism: "I am aware that some blacks have elected themselves judges and executioners of whites for their evil deeds. For these prophets of hate, revenge and revolt have become their only creed. My understanding of the Christian faith leads me to reject this path." Black liberation was a precondition for racial reconciliation, Roberts argued, but blacks had to be willing to advance the cause of black–white fellowship and cooperation.[49]

Elsewhere he blasted Cone for "reckless and irresponsible statements" that made black theology appear "anti-white, racist, separatist." Complaining that white theologians identified black theology with Cone's version of it, Roberts was offended especially by the apparent moral nihilism of Cone's "any means necessary" rhetoric. On this issue, as on movement politics, Roberts had a schoolmaster's sense of accountability. He denounced Cone's "ethic of no ethic," observing ruefully, "Young angry black militants were seeking guidance. They asked for bread; he cast them a stone. A moral paralysis remains inherent in Cone's theological method."[50]

Roberts implied, like Ruether, that Cone denied the humanity of whites, a reading that missed the significance of Cone's disillusionment with radical black nationalists. Cone had strained relations with certain nationalists precisely because he did not deny the humanity of whites. To him, "whiteness" was an ideology, an evil force in white society, not something biological. Never a hater, his combination of moral passion and vibrant friendliness drew overflow crowds to his courses, where he taught that no race could denigrate another without degrading itself. On several points related to his narrowness and lack of roots in black culture, Cone eventually shifted his position, but not as a concession to Roberts. He and Roberts managed a respectful relationship in leading the black theology movement, but continued to disagree on major issues, especially reconciliation. To Cone, the Roberts rendering of liberation/reconciliation was contradictory nonsense. In *God of the Oppressed* (1975) he put the matter plainly: "If liberation is the precondition of reconciliation, why then should enslaved blacks assure white oppressors that we are ready to be reconciled when the latter have no intention of loosing the chains of oppression?" Cone told Roberts that he needed to decide whether he was a liberationist or a reformist. In liberation theology, liberation was the uncompromised normative principle. For Cone, the acid test was interracial cooperation. Liberation was about blacks defining for themselves the meaning of liberation and reconciliation. If Roberts wanted to work with white people on religious and political causes, he was still a liberal. "Reconciliation and liberation on white terms have always meant death for black people," Cone exhorted. Cooperation or fellowship with whites always led to further oppression. Virtually all whites were oppressors, and even progressive whites wanted to tell blacks what racial justice meant. Thus the Black Power radicals were right to expel white liberals from the civil rights movement. Black liberation was the defining objective of black theology and was definable only by black liberationists.[51]

Cone realized that trailblazers had to deal with critics from all sides; thus he kept telling himself to take his critics in his stride. He regarded his ostensible narrowness and militancy as indispensable strengths in the face of a hostile racist society. Whites criticized him in defense of their racial privileges; Cone noted that even his friend Lehmann could not overcome the vast gulf between them, "which can be best summed up with the terms 'black' and 'white.'" If one did not share the "black context" defined by slavery and colonization, one was in no position to assess black theology, even in sympathy. Similarly, Cone's disagreements with black pastors and liberal black academics were predictable to him. Many black pastors were conservatives, while theological critics like Roberts, Major Jones, and Preston Williams essentially continued the social gospel liberalism of the civil rights movement. Jones, a longtime associate of King's, misinterpreted Cone as a human-centered ideologue, missing his insistence on the *divine* initiative and imperative for liberation. Williams, a Harvard ethicist, criticized Cone for denigrating the role of reason and the temperate weighing of evidence in theology; Cone shook his head that Williams "could be so grossly misguided" as to take white rationality seriously.[52]

But there emerged another group of critics that Cone took far more seriously. Religious historians Charles H. Long and Gayraud S. Wilmore and theologian Cecil Cone pressed hard on the problem of Cone's lack of a basis in African and African-American culture. Long opposed the very idea of a black *theology*, arguing that theology was inherently the discourse of a privileged class to define cultural categories. Wilmore, a leader of the NCBC, argued for a non-theological Christian culturalism; Cone's brother Cecil argued for a theology of African theism. All of them argued that black religious thought was a deeper, richer, older, and more fruitful tradition than black Christian theology, and that Cone's liberationism was too dependent on European theology and Black Power radicalism. His conceptual categories were European, not African; he substituted radical politics for black religion; and his position was too reactive, overdefined by white racism, which left him with a concept of liberation as the mere negation of whiteness.[53]

Coming from thinkers whom he respected, and with whom, in the cases of Wilmore and Cecil Cone, he was closely associated, Cone puzzled for two years over his options: "I was embarrassed by this critique, because no one had been more critical of white theology than I. To find out from my black colleagues that I was still held captive by the same system that I was criticizing was a bitter pill to swallow. What then was I to do? Deny the obvious or give up in despair?" Finally he decided to do neither, taking the third option of deepening the historical and cultural basis of his thought. Theology could be liberating, and liberation was the central motif of the gospel, but he had to pursue black liberation theology as a more thoroughly African/African-American enterprise. Cone's first try at establishing a deeper cultural ground for his thought, *The Spirituals and the Blues* (1972) expounded the spirituality of African-American music. His major constructive work, *God of the Oppressed* (1975) mixed his characteristic stress on the biblical narrative of liberation with evocative discussions of African-American history and culture. He retained his emphasis on the priority of divine action and his thesis of a single narrative line from the Bible to liberation theology, which Cone described as the story of God's liberating revelation. But he cut back on the Barthian warnings against beginning with human questions or cultural forms, in light of his own deepening immersion in African-American history.[54]

Cone still believed that black theology worked best as a form of radical neo-orthodoxy. Liberalism deconstructed too much of the biblical witness, while religious conservatism was beyond the pale. Neo-orthodoxy preserved the authority of the biblical witness and the centrality of Jesus Christ, the central religious elements of black Christianity. But with *God of the Oppressed*, Cone began to hold his revelationist and cultural motifs in tension, stressing that the truth of the black story could be tested only by categories derived from the black experience. Black religion is biblical, he argued, which is antithetical to the values of white culture. One cannot be white (culturally) and think biblically, for biblical thought is driven by the liberating interest of the oppressed.[55]

In his later career Cone's commitment to the liberating interest of the oppressed opened his thought to additional influences and critiques. Christian socialists and Third World liberationists challenged his silence on political economics, pressing the question of whether black theology wanted a new economic system or merely a bigger slice of the American capitalist pie. Cone agreed that black theology could not establish solidarity with Third World revolutionary movements if it did not acquire a stronger economic message. Moreover, economic oppression in the USA cried out for economic correctives. Thus he affirmed that he stood "against capitalism and for democratic socialism, for Karl Marx and against Adam Smith, for the poor in all colors and against the rich of all colors, for the workers and against the corporations." In 1980, influenced by his Union Seminary colleague Cornel West, Cone suggested that a blend of Marxist criticism and prophetic black religion might provide the emancipatory vision that was needed: "Together black religion and Marxist philosophy may show us the way to build a completely new society."[56]

That suggested a politics of democratic socialism within multiracial organizations such as Democratic Socialists of America, in which West played a leading role. Cone never crossed that line, however, and wrote only occasional asides about political economics. His engagements with Third World liberation movements kept to a theological plane, including addresses to the Pan-African Conference of Third World Theologians in 1977 and the Ecumenical Association of Third World Theologians in 1981. In the former speech he took aim at African theologians Harry Sawyerr, Edward W. Fashole-Luke, and especially John Mbiti, all of whom stressed their differences from American black theology. Mbiti judged that black theology was "full of sorrow, bitterness, anger and hatred," and too absorbed by radical politics. Cone replied that his African critics were too otherworldly and that Jesus died on the cross to overcome human suffering, not merely to transcend it. The politicized radicalism of black theology was not alien or irrelevant to Africa, he urged, pointing to the liberation movement in South Africa. Cone noted that South Africans Desmond Tutu, Manas Buthelezi, and Allan Boesak approached theology in his fashion as a discourse of social and political liberation, which he commended to other African theologians. Meanwhile he rethought his opposition to feminism.[57]

His first reaction to feminism was dismissive: "I rejected it as a joke or as an intrusion upon the legitimate struggle of black people to eliminate racism." As a youth he had feared to be in the presence of a white woman, "because her word alone could get a person lynched, legally electrocuted, or confined to prison for life." Years later the feminist movement's rhetoric of violation reminded him of the racist fearmongering of his youth. White feminist complaints about male supremacy struck him as frivolous at best:

> Unfortunately, my early reflection on women's liberation was so completely controlled by black males' fears that I could not think straight regarding the complexity of the problem. It was easy for me to say that if white women are oppressed by their men, it is not the fault of black men. We black men certainly are not oppressing white women.[58]

But at Union Seminary Cone encountered white feminist colleagues and students who forced him to recognize the parallels between racist and sexist injustice. More importantly, black women admonished him to recognize the damage caused by sexism within the black community. Cone later recalled,

> Black women's silence began to end at Union and other places, because black men misused their silence by refusing to even consider that sexism was a real problem in the black community. Black men continued to claim that "black women have always been free." As I listened to black women articulate their pain, and as I observed the insensitive responses of black men, it became existentially clear to me that sexism was a black problem too.[59]

Realizing the necessity of feminist criticism, Cone became a critic of discrimination against women, although he did not incorporate feminist or womanist theory into his writings. As a teacher he supported black female students in their quests for ordination and mentored black female scholars, importantly aiding the development of womanist theology. As a teacher, speaker, and writer of prefaces to the works of others, he opposed injustices to women and supported black women in the field without adopting a feminist or womanist perspective on gender as a category of analysis.

Cone's later work deepened in his thought and scholarship the primary sources with which he began, Malcolm X and Martin Luther King Jr. His major work of the 1990s, *Martin & Malcolm & America* (1991), parsed the differences between Malcolm X's separatist Muslim nationalism and King's Christian universalism, while accenting the commonalities between them. Citing the black tradition of viewing the two men as "kind of a team," Cone stressed that Malcolm and King complemented each other positively *and* served as necessary correctives to each other. Malcolm corrected King's dangerous and emotionally unhealthy fixation with blacks loving their white enemies, while King corrected Malcolm's narrow fixation with black versus white: "We need both of them and we need them *together*. Malcolm keeps Martin from being turned into a harmless American hero. Martin keeps Malcolm from being an ostracized black hero." Standing with both of them, Cone declared: "We must declare where we stand on the great issues of our time. Racism is one of them. Poverty is another. Sexism another. Class exploitation another. Imperialism another. We must break the cycle of violence in America and around the world."[60]

Having begun with a blend of Black Power politics and radical neo-orthodox theology, Cone's thought grew into a multi-stranded liberationist perspective that outstripped, without negating, its origins in black revolutionary nationalism. He remained a theologian, but accepted that black theology had to be grounded in the history and culture of black American religion. For many years he lamented that black theology was largely an academic phenomenon, but in his later career he expressed surprised delight at its considerable inroads in the churches. In the academy black theology had a vital existence, producing generations of liberationist and womanist theologians, Bible scholars, ethicists, and historians. Some of Cone's students became prominent figures in these fields, notably Kelly Brown-Douglass, Jacquelyn Grant, Dwight Hopkins, Linda E. Thomas, and Josiah Young. Reflecting on his legacy in 1999, Cone noted that people often asked him whether he remained as angry as when he wrote *Black Theology and Black Power*: "When I hear that question I smile to contain my rage." How could he be any less angry when America remained so violently unjust to most blacks?[61]

Cone's anger deepened when he reflected that, for all the success of black theology and womanism in the academy, it made little impact on the work of white theologians. With few exceptions, he judged, progressive white theologians at the end of the twentieth century still managed to treat white racism as a low priority concern. American historians increasingly recognized the central importance of slavery, colonialism, segregation, and white supremacy for their subject, but in theology, scholars remained "virtually mute." Cone found the silence astonishing and infuriating, protesting that theology should have been prominent in the cause, not chasing after intellectual and cultural fads: "White supremacy is one of the great contradictions of the gospel in modern times. White theologians who do not oppose racism publicly and rigorously in their writings are a part of the problem and must be exposed as the enemy of justice." Elsewhere he put it more personally, admonishing whites that destroying white supremacy had to be their daily commitment, not an occasional conference topic: "No day passes in which blacks don't have to deal with white supremacy. It is found everywhere – in the churches, seminaries, publishing houses, in government, all around the world. There is no escape. If whites get tired talking about race, just imagine how people of color feel."[62]

As for his protégés and colleagues in black theology, Cone judged that virtually all of them were too mild and accommodating: "We have opposed racism much too gently. We have permitted white theological silence in exchange for the rewards of being accepted by the white theological establishment." That was a pitiful bargain, he scolded. Theology needed a "truly radical race critique" far more than it needed postmodern musings, token appointments for blacks, or another quest of the historical Jesus. What black theology needed most of all was to lift Malcolm X to the level of Martin King, in theory and practice: "We did not wrestle with Malcolm long enough. We quickly turned to Martin King. The mistake was not in moving toward King but rather in leaving Malcolm behind. We need them both as a double-edged sword to slay the dragon of theological racism." Cone was fond of saying that Martin King taught him how to be a Christian and Malcolm X taught him how to be black. It was true, he allowed, that black theology needed to move beyond the dialectic of nationalism and integration represented by Malcolm X and King. But the best way to do it was to work with the best that the African-American heritage had to offer. In his last years at Union, Cone returned to the secular black writers who had nearly lured him from theology at the outset of his career, asking why they were stronger critics of lynching than black theologians, who rarely discussed it, and white theologians, who hardly ever mentioned it. His forthcoming book, *The Cross and the Lynching Tree*, promised an answer.[63]

Black theology was something new that worked hard at claiming historical roots in Africa, the Bible, and African-American history. In Cone's case it pressed the questions of separatism and black nationalism, but always in a way that sought to claim continuity with previous generations that had no clue of liberation theology. The other main stream of liberation theology to emerge from the late 1960s and early 1970s, radical feminism, was less novel, yet also less concerned with claiming a historic heritage. Black liberation theology treasured the biblical themes of exodus and liberation, the sovereignty of God, Jesus as redeemer, and the kingdom of God as the sign of Christ's resurrection. Feminist theology, from the beginning of its modern rebirth, was more conflicted about retrieving much of anything from the past. The founding theorist and oracle of modern radical feminist theology, Mary Daly, took little interest in her nineteenth-century predecessors, did not lay claim to biblical themes, and pressed the separatist logic of radical feminism, which eventually caused her to repudiate Christianity. But the fact that she abandoned her theological career does not obviate her historical significance as the progenitor and first catalyzing theorist of feminist liberation theology.

Beyond Patriarchal Religion: Mary Daly and the Rebirth of Feminism

A century before Daly, radical feminist theology had its first airing in the writings and speeches of suffragist leader Elizabeth Cady Stanton, especially her iconoclastic book *The Woman's Bible*. But for decades afterward feminist theology of any kind barely existed in the Protestant churches, flaring only as an argument over the right of women to exercise lay leadership. Women argued for the right to serve on the church council, official board, session, or vestry, and to represent the church at regional or national meetings. Upon winning these rights, feminist pioneers Anna Howard Shaw, Georgia Harkness, Edna Baxter, M. Madeline Southard, Nannie Helen Burroughs, and Ida Robinson pressed for women's right to ordained ministry, stressing the moral unfairness of treating women differently from men. That argument prevailed in the Congregational and Methodist Protestant churches in the 1850s and 1860s, respectively; it was defeated in most churches for decades, with exceptions in some evangelical and holiness groups; it made some small gains in the social gospel era and larger ones in the mid-twentieth century. A major breakthrough occurred in 1956, when the Presbyterian Church USA began ordaining women to the ministry. But when fully-fledged feminist theology – the kind that privileged gender as a category of analysis and activism – re-emerged in the late 1960s, its leading figures were Roman Catholic women who had benefited from none of this history.[64]

The book that launched the feminist theology movement was Daly's *The Church and the Second Sex* (1968), a searing attack on Christian misogyny that soon seemed mild by Daly standards. Born in 1928 in Schenectady, New York to working-class Roman Catholic parents, Mary Daly graduated from the College of St Rose in Albany, New York in 1950, where her teachers were sisters of Saint Joseph of Carondelet.

Daly appreciated that St Rose displayed the possibility that women could be college professors, although she later judged that hers were "stunted" and "tamed" women. In her rendering the college offered a perfect example of patriarchal suffocation. Her philosophy classes raised issues that she found intensely interesting, notwithstanding that only priests were permitted to teach philosophy, and they taught very badly: "They taught with abominable incompetence, and they could not have cared less." Some of them opined that philosophy was wasted on females. Since the college lacked a philosophy major, Daly majored in English, which qualified her for graduate study in English, not philosophy. She earned a master's degree in English at Catholic University in 1952, applied to a new doctoral program in religion at St Mary's College in Notre Dame, Indiana, and completed the degree in two years. Daly quenched her desire for philosophy by reading Thomas Aquinas on her own, which turned her into a Thomist of sorts, despite his appalling verdict that females were misbegotten.[65]

Her first doctorate won little respect on the job market, however, and Daly still wanted one in philosophy. Thus she applied to Notre Dame, which did not accept women, taught unhappily at Cardinal Cushing College in Massachusetts, applied to Catholic University, which did not bother to reply – "the crude bigotry of that wretched institution was blatant in this case" – and had an inspiration. She was too Catholic to consider anything besides Catholic schools, but being female excluded her from them. Her inspiration was that Catholic institutions in Germany and Switzerland would be open to her because the German and Swiss governments outlawed discrimination against women. Daly enrolled at the University of Fribourg, a Dominican school in Switzerland, where she stayed for seven years and two doctorates, leaving behind "the smog of dullness that hung over life in America." She loved the natural beauty of Europe, its old world charms, and the freedom of being an alien; to her it was thrilling not to be trapped by the soul-killing sameness of America and the "alienation of 'belonging.'" The Bible and church history were boring to her, but Daly loved metaphysics, philosophy of religion, and speculative theology, completing her doctorate in theology in 1963. Her dissertation focused on the debate over theology as speculative wisdom (Thomism) or faith-based practice (neo-Augustinianism), passionately defending Thomist speculation: "My Lust was for the Life of the Mind. I had no desire to be a priest or to minister to anyone."[66]

She was saved by her femaleness from having to disqualify herself for the degree. In 1963 the Vatican's oath against modernism was still in place for all priests and doctors of theology; Daly and the Fribourg Dominicans were slow to consider what that meant for her. Shortly before commencement, Daly realized that she had a problem. She desperately wanted the degree, but could not perjure herself by claiming to repudiate intellectual freedom and other modernist ideas. The Dominicans came to her rescue, unwittingly, by deciding that while it was acceptable for a woman to be a Doctor of Theology (Daly was the first), no woman could be allowed to take the Anti-Modernist Oath, because that would qualify her to teach in a Pontifical Faculty of Theology such as Catholic University of America. She later recalled, "I almost exploded with relief and laughter in the face of the professor who pompously announced this solemn decision."[67]

But even her second doctorate was just another step to the one she really wanted, in philosophy. Having taken philosophy courses in her theology program, Daly needed only a few seminars and a dissertation — on the natural theology of Jacques Maritain — to complete a philosophy doctorate at Fribourg in 1965. Maritain was her model of a good religious philosopher, especially his conviction that intuition and rationality were essential to each other. Daly argued for the possibility of a natural knowledge of God, rooted in a Maritain-style rational intuition of being. "I loved both modes of knowing," she later recalled. Intuition was indispensable, but so was arduous reasoning rooted in it.[68]

Daly did not think of herself as a feminist pioneer or reformer, though she was repelled by the sexism of her teachers and repulsed when her friends married. She had not gone to Fribourg to blaze a path for women; she wanted to learn and teach philosophical theology. The cultural lag between culture and theology, however, proved to be very short in the case of feminist theology. In December 1963, a few months after Betty Friedan's *The Feminine Mystique* sparked the women's movement by interrogating "the problem that has no name," *Commonweal* magazine published an article by St John's University philosopher Rosemary Lauer that called for women's equal rights in the Catholic Church.[69]

Lauer observed that the church's discrimination against women was deeply rooted in ancient Semitic culture, where "no man would deign to speak with a woman in public, not even his own wife." It was powerfully reinforced by Aquinas's appropriation of Aristotelian biology, which posited that women were merely passive in human generation, unable to reason, and thus not fully human. For Aquinas it followed that "man is the principle and end of woman . . . woman exists for the man, not man for the woman." Lauer urged that the church's understanding of women was overdue for an overhaul:

> It seems very clear that the entire question of woman's position in society and in the Church needs desperately to be reconsidered in the light of the most recent findings of Scripture scholars, biologists, sociologists, anthropologists, and historians. Great strides have been made in all these areas, but it remains to synthesize the results and present a new picture of women and a corresponding program of action.[70]

To Daly this article was inspiring, a bit shaming, and a wake-up alarm. Why had women like her kept silent about their "semi-human" status in the church? In a letter to *Commonweal* she commended Lauer for breaking the silence – "there should be a barrage of such essays, and of scholarly books which treat the history of the problem" – and vowed that her own silence was over: "The beginnings of these articles and these books (how badly we need these books, especially!) are already in the minds and on the lips of many of us. And – this is both a prophecy and a promise – they will come."[71]

In January 1965 Daly wrote an article for *Commonweal* that caught the attention of a publishing consultant; shortly afterwards she wrote another that urged the Second Vatican Council to address the status of women in the church. In the fall of 1965 she sneaked into a major session of Vatican II. Daly caught the hopeful spirit of the council, which she later called "one great carnival of an event." For a moment she shared the ebullient feeling in the streets that historic changes were taking place. Her peek inside, however, was deflating:

> The contrast between the arrogant bearing and colorful attire of the 'princes of the church' and the humble, self-deprecating manner and somber clothing of the very few women was appalling. Watching the veiled nuns shuffle to the altar rail to receive Holy Communion from the hands of a priest was like observing a string of lowly ants at some bizarre picnic.

Daly tried to listen to the speeches at the session, "but the voices were all male, senile, cracking whines of the men in red." In that mood she took up the publishing consultant's invitation to turn her article, "A Built-in Bias," into a book.[72]

The invitation felt like a summons, she later recalled, "and I knew clearly that the time was right for the First Coming of *The Church and the Second Sex*." Nearly 20 years later she likened the summons to "a Call from the cosmos itself – an unrelenting Call . . . beckoning me on to further Be-Speaking." Published in 1968, *The Church and the Second Sex* took its bearings from Simone de Beauvoir's feminist classic *The Second Sex*. De Beauvoir contended that Christianity, especially Roman Catholicism, was a major instrument of the oppression of women. Specifically, church leaders turned their misogynistic fears of female sexuality into moral norms that harmed women; Catholicism sealed the enslavement of women by enshrining in dogma and ritual the image of a Virgin Mother kneeling before her son; and the church reinforced inferiority feelings in women by excluding them from the priesthood. To Daly, this account conveniently summarized the problem.[73]

Her book made liberal feminist arguments about Christianity that Elizabeth Cady Stanton and Anna Howard Shaw would have recognized, but which seemed radical after a half-century of feminist dormancy in American society. Daly played up the differences between the Yahwist and Priestly creation stories in Genesis, stressed that the Priestly story contained no hint of sexual subordination, and decried sexist interpretations of the Fall. She noted that Jesus treated women as persons, often in defiance of prevailing customs. She quoted Galatians 3:28 ("there is neither male nor female, for you are all one in Christ Jesus") against the quasi-Pauline tradition of Ephesians 5:22 ("wives, be subject to your husbands"), contending that Paul occasionally transcended the sexism of his culture. She described patristic Christianity as a retrogression from the woman-respecting ethic of Jesus, quoting Jerome, Ambrose, Augustine, and Clement of Alexandria on the moral superiority of males. "In the mentality of the Fathers, woman and sexuality were identified," Daly explained. "Their horror of sex was also a horror of woman." The Fathers projected their guilt feelings about sex and temptation onto women, making them the guilty party; Christian women for centuries were forced to pay for the Fathers' misogyny.[74]

Catholic tradition passed down the wisdom of Peter Lombard, who declared that woman was sensuality itself, and Bonaventure, who taught that females represented the inferior part of the soul, and Thomas Aquinas, who invoked Aristotle on the natural defectiveness of females, and Ignatius of Loyala, who compared women to Satan, and Pope Pius XII, who stressed the principle of male headship in marriage. Daly admired Teresa of Avila, who regretted that the obstacle of sex prevented her from preaching, and Ursuline founder Angela Merici, who wanted her order to live as uncloistered apostles, and Mary Ward, who founded the English Ladies as a Jesuit-like institute of educators devoted to the emancipation of women. But the Ursulines were driven back to the cloister by ecclesiastical authorities after Merici's death, and the Vatican suppressed Ward's institute for undertaking manly work. Not until Vatican II did the Catholic Church offer a genuine word of respect for women. Daly enthused that the council's *Pastoral Constitution on the Church in the Modern World* condemned discrimination based on sex, dropped the old biologism in discussing marriage, eschewed the usual insults concerning women's inferiority, and generally spoke the language of modern personalism. Although Vatican II said very little about women, everything that it said was better than what the church had said for centuries, and the tone was better. Daly reasoned that it was probably just as well that the council said very little: "From the liberal's point of view, a minimum of official statements is usually preferable to too many."[75]

She mentioned two other Catholic women of her generation who were beginning to make a mark as feminist scholars, Rosemary Radford Ruether (whom Daly called "Mrs. Ruether") and Elisabeth Schüssler. Schüssler was then a graduate student in New Testament at the University of Münster, where she completed her doctorate in 1970 and made her early reputation as an interpreter of the book of Revelation. Ruether had earned her doctorate in Classics and Patristics at Claremont Graduate School in 1965 and begun her teaching career at Howard University. By 1968 she was a prolific essayist, although her early work contained little hint of a feminist perspective. Ruether's first post-dissertation book, a collection of essays on ecclesiology titled *The Church Against Itself* (1967), contended in the "secular city" spirit of the time that the church had to learn how to live "with radical cultural insecurity." The church as triumphant colossus and sacramental fortress was disintegrating, she argued. Her first glimmer of feminist consciousness was a critique of the Catholic prohibition of artificial contraception. In 1964 Ruether noted that as a graduate student and mother of three children she experienced the church's command as a psychological impossibility. In effect, the church told her to abandon her academic dreams in order to have an unlimited number of children. That amounted to "a demand that I scuttle my interests, my training, and in the last analysis, my soul." Ruether admonished that the hardness of Catholic teaching in this area was not a virtue; she respected moral rigor when it served worthy moral values, but the church's position yielded merely "weariness and disgust." Daly observed that that reaction was spreading rapidly in the Catholic Church.[76]

In 1968 the cause of women's ordination was important to Daly; it was even important to her that the cause had clerical supporters such as Bernard Häring, Gregory Baum, and Joseph Fichter. Some Catholic ecumenists strangely warned that Catholicism would jeopardize its relations with Protestant churches if it ordained women;

Daly countered that the very opposite was true. Most American mainline Protestant denominations ordained women as ministers and took a "realistic" view of divorce, she observed. The Catholic Church's ecumenical standing was harmed by its exclusivism; even the Episcopal Church was moving toward women's ordination. Daly was tough on the "pedestal peddlers" who urged women to rise above emancipation through spiritual purity. The pedestal ideal of the "eternal feminine" rendered women publicly nonexistent, she protested. It taught women to surrender their personhood, hide behind veils in semi-cloistered communities, and obey male superiors – or opt for the lower version of the same thing by identifying with the roles of wife and mother. The feminist upsurge was precisely a rejection of self-effacing femininity, she argued. It was about the development of authentic, self-creative, publicly active female persons who claimed the same opportunities and responsibilities as men.[77]

"The Church has been wounded in its structures, for it has deprived itself of the gifts and insights of more than half of its members," Daly wrote. More importantly, the church impaired the flourishing of women and men, "for in a society which welcomes and fosters prejudice, not only is the human potential of the subject group restricted, but the superordinate group also becomes warped in the process." The solution for Catholic women was the one that de Beauvoir commended for all women: to be inspired to self-liberation by the examples of brave, independent, self-actualizing women. Daly urged that those who understood the problem of female subordination and also possessed the "required creative vigor" had a responsibility to offer examples of liberated existence to others, chiefly by "raising up their own image." For Catholic women that required a renunciation of the spiritual idealization of powerlessness; on a theological level it also required a demythologization of the reigning male God. Officially the church taught that God had no sex, Daly allowed, but implicitly the church's theology and spiritual practices conveyed the impression that God was male. The church's language about God was overwhelmingly male; female pronouns could not be substituted without causing "shock and embarrassment"; and the church's theology was explicitly static and hierarchical, conceiving God as an immutable, all-powerful being.[78]

Daly enthused that liberal theologians were providing the groundwork of a better theology. Catholic theologian Gabriel Moran conceived revelation as an event, which Daly liked for its "openness to the facts of contemporary experience." French Jesuit Teilhard de Chardin offered a vision of cosmic process that reinterpreted the incarnation in evolutionary terms, which Daly commended for breaking the backward-looking Catholic fixation with reparation and expiation. Liberal feminist theology needed to understand Christianity as "the religion of the absolute future," Daly believed, invoking German theologian Karl Rahner's phrase. Male-dominated orthodoxies were inevitably preoccupied with defending structures of authority inherited from the past, but a rising women's movement aligned with a rising theological liberalism sought to make the Catholic Church a genuine agent of human flourishing.[79]

Daly had several "modest proposals" toward that end. The problem of discrimination had to be raised on all levels of the church's life and eliminated, she argued. Token appointments were nearly worthless; women had to be represented proportionally on all parish, diocesan, and national councils; and women had to be ordained to the priesthood. Daly cited a potentially door-opening statement by Pope John XXIII that "human beings have the right to choose freely the state of life which they prefer, and therefore the right to establish a family, with equal rights for man and woman, and also the right to follow a vocation to the priesthood or the religious life." Why would the pope endorse equal rights for women, in a carefully vetted encyclical, if he meant something else? Catholic feminists and liberals had to find the courage of self-assertion, she exhorted. Having asked for too little, they made little progress. Having been "too timid in affirming their worth and their rights," they were put down by male hierarchs who denied they had any rights: "Until they have the clear-sightedness and courage to reject discrimination totally, it is to be expected that women will be the losers on all levels."[80]

The problem of the nun was a category unto itself. Daly observed that nuns embodied the pedestal ideal of the eternal feminine, yet also transcended it to a greater degree than most married women. Nuns spent little time in the company of men, often they were only indirectly subject to the rule of males, and the leaders of women's communities were sometimes powerful figures. Nuns were paradoxical figures, especially after Vatican II; Daly called them walking paradoxes. She noted that nuns contributed no feminist leaders to the church, because they internalized the eternal feminine ideology. Until recently, Catholic religious orders had been highly skilled at breaking down the self-assertiveness of nuns, isolating them from the world, but Vatican II and the zeitgeist of the 1960s loosened the orders' totalizing grip. Nuns were enrolling at secular universities, adopting contemporary dress, and working in professional roles; many others renounced their vows. Daly's assured response was that these secularizing trends were healthy for the nuns and the church. What mattered was the flourishing of Catholic women, not the survival of women's religious orders: "The risk of an individual's losing her commitment to 'the religious life' is incomparably less grave than the risk of foreshortening her potential as a human being." The church of the future would be reformed, humanized, and democratized, she argued. It would replace the caste system with a declericalized liberalism that respected the spiritual gifts of all men and women. It would invite married and celibate men and women to the ordained ministries, and as soon as the church became a healthy institution, it would have no difficulty attracting them.[81]

By Daly's reckoning the church was breaking into two Catholicisms; one was liberal and open-minded, the other clung to a static orthodoxy: "This fundamental division between liberal and conservative cuts across all others. A liberal Christian feels more at home talking to an open and honest agnostic than to his conservative fellow believers." To her, the instructive example was de Beauvoir, who rejected Christianity, yet showed the way that theology needed to take. De Beauvoir revealed the sins of church and society against the second sex, but allowed that religion could be a transforming power. She admired Teresa of Avila for transcending the sex role system of her time; Daly agreed that feminism was about transcending sexual differentiation: "In the exercise of self-transcending creative activity, inspired and driven forward by faith and hope, sustained by courage, men and women can learn to 'set their pride beyond the sexual differentiation.'" With God's help, men and women could overcome the alienating ravages of gender duality, achieving a "higher order of consciousness and being" that created integral, androgynous human beings.[82]

The Church and the Second Sex drew wide attention to Daly and Catholic feminism, as well as unwanted attention to her employer, Boston College. She made publicity appearances on television programs, sparred with William F. Buckley, Jr on his program *Firing Line*, was featured in a *Time* magazine article on Catholic feminism, and lectured extensively. Catholic icon Thomas Merton contributed a laudatory jacket blurb to her book, calling it "a hard-hitting, highly original, and even revolutionary little book unmasking the latent anti-feminism in so much Catholic thinking and practice." Ruether noted that Daly's book combined solid historical research with "a breezy, readable style" and was "not unduly profound." Myrtle Passantino, writing in *America*, called the book "thoughtful, honest, [and] provocative," observing that Daly opened some windows that Vatican II overlooked. *Time* magazine, noting that Daly was unmarried, deemed the book "a lively polemic" by "an avowed suffragette for female rights within the church." The *Library Journal Book Review* described it as "a call to action for Roman Catholics to end the discrimination against women in the church," observing that Daly wrote "as a loyal Catholic who wishes to reform the church from within." Psychologist of religion Don Browning wrote in the *Christian Century* that Daly's book was "well worth reading," although exaggerated. Daly wrongly assumed there were no significant differences between men and women, lumped "relationality" with "passive" and "submissive" as scorn-words, and ignored biological and social scientific evidence that women were more contextual, interdependent, and relational than men: "It appears that, in her view, to be human is to be free to be technological, functional and specialized, but being human apparently has little if anything to do with being male or female."[83]

Most reviewers took the book seriously as an intellectually responsible polemic, and Daly soon made it clear that she saw very significant differences between females and males. The reviewers that mattered most, however, were the administrative and faculty guardians of Boston College, a Jesuit university, who were not pleased to be associated with a media-hyped popular book that blasted the Catholic Church. They responded by firing her, in the form of a terminal one-year contract. This decision eventually radicalized Daly, but at first it chastened her. She became the symbol of a campus furor over academic freedom, spoke across the country about feminism – which brightened the spotlight on Boston College – and vowed to stay in the Catholic Church. For months she labored on a manuscript titled "Catholicism: Death or Rebirth?" arguing for rebirth, but not very well. The question mark was hers. Daly struggled with the book, couldn't finish it, consulted with her publisher, and was told not to bother finishing it. Losing the book contract battered her self-confidence, but in June 1969 Boston College relented to an escalating public controversy over her firing by granting Daly promotion and tenure. "It was a strange victory," she later recalled. "Apparently the book which had generated the hostility which led to my firing had generated the support which forced my rehiring."[84]

Five months after making tenure, Daly still plugged for liberal reformism. Writing about theologian Charles Davis, a priest who had left the church, she reasoned that it was better to change the church from within than choose the isolated ineffectuality of leaving. "I am still willing to work in my own way (lazily) at a mutually transforming confrontation with my own heritage," she wrote. But that was self-denial, for Daly was on a come-out path. During her "terminal" year at Boston College she had received little support from colleagues, which wounded and angered her. She especially resented being judged by academics who had never published a book nor bothered to read hers. "Something had happened to the meaning of 'professor,' to the meaning of 'university,' to the meaning of 'teaching,'" she later recalled. Her colleagues called each other "Doctor" but addressed her as "Miss Daly." Some made patronizing remarks about her teaching, urging students not to take her courses. Daly learned from female colleagues at other colleges and universities that they experienced similar mistreatment; Boston College was merely typical. Later she reflected: "It was the universalist quality of this personal 'revelation' that was important. I began to under-stand more of the implications of the feminist insight that 'the personal is political.'" More importantly: "I understood more clearly the nature of the beast and the name of the demon: patriarchy."[85]

Daly's path-breaking efforts to name the problem played a leading role in reshaping the discourse of theology in mainline seminaries and divinity schools. In 1971 she blasted liberal theologian Gregory Baum for describing God as the divine Father under whom all people were sons, not strangers, outsiders, or alienated persons: "A woman whose consciousness has been aroused can only say that such language makes her aware of herself as a stranger, as an outsider, as an alienated person, not as a daughter who belongs or is appointed to a marvelous destiny. She cannot belong to this without assenting to her own lobotomy. Language intended to signify transcendence is in fact functioning to inhibit her self-transcendence."[86]

Daly's writings made a difference, teaching theologians and pastors to speak the faith inclusively, but she lost interest in reforming Christianity. Liberal reformism was not enough if the problem was global patriarchy. By 1970 Daly found herself strug-gling to indulge liberal followers who admired her as a pioneer: "The 'I' who was then standing before the friendly audiences and tossing out the familiar phrases was already disconnected from the words, already moving through a new time/space. I often heard the old words as though a stranger were speaking them – some personage visiting from the past." Increasingly, the liberal agenda of seeking equality in church and society seemed misguided to her. It was pointless to liberalize Christianity or modern society if both were inherently misogynist. In the early 1970s the conviction deepened in Daly that they were. Liberal theology was about muddling through, not real transcendence; the antiwar movement was just as sexist as the dominant culture; what was needed was a real leap forward in female consciousness.[87]

Strengthened by her friendships with radical feminists Janice Raymond and Eliza-beth Farians, Daly left her liberal Catholic self behind.[88] On September 14, 1971, she became the first woman to preach a sermon at Harvard's Memorial Chapel, ending with a dramatic walk-out. Feminism was a revolution of true sisterhood against the "world-wide phenomenon of sexual caste," she declared. The false sisterhoods of the past and present were "in fact mini-brotherhoods, serving male interests and ideals" that perpetuated the global caste system of male tyranny. Daly proclaimed: "The new sisterhood is the bonding of women for liberation from sex role socialization. The very word itself *says* liberation and revolution." Sisterhood was an exodus community of women freed from the Fatherland; it was a counter-world to the existing global religion of patriarchy.[89]

Two years later Daly's book *Beyond God the Father* took leave of Christianity and stopped just short of treating males as enemies. Christianity and Judaism, she argued, like the Bible they cited, taught women to hate themselves, defer to men, feel guilty for the evils of the world, and keep silent. The Genesis myth of the Fall was a show-case example. For thousands of years, theologians managed not to notice the absurdity of portraying men as the givers of life and women as the progenitors of the world's evil. In the modern age theologians noticed that biblical myths were mythical, so they interpreted the Fall as symbolic of the universal human condition of estrangement, with no specific meaning for male–female relations. Daly charged that the latter turn was demonic, because it conveyed the lie that sexual oppression was not at issue. The

Bible's malignant image of women was still "deeply embedded in the modern psyche," no matter what modern scholars said the Genesis story was "really" about.[90]

Reinhold Niebuhr taught that the myth of the Fall was a crucial corrective to liberal Protestant optimism; Daly replied that it was a crucial example of "false naming." Because Genesis misnamed the mystery of evil, it was a source of evil to women, cultivating a backward-looking consciousness that typed women as primordial scapegoats. That was the primordial lie of patriarchy, she wrote: "Together with its offspring – the theology of 'original sin' – the myth reveals the 'Fall' of religion into the role of patriarchy's prostitute." In this fundamental sense, Daly argued, the medium of biblical myth was itself the message, for the myth of the Fall was an instrument of patriarchal evil.[91]

Daly spurned the Equal Rights Amendment, "equal pay for equal work," and other liberal reforms, warning that assimilation was deadly. Mere politics held little interest for her; what mattered was the real leap forward in female consciousness. On ethics she was a Nietzschean minus Nietzsche's misogyny, calling for a "transvaluation of values." Against the Christian idealization of charity, meekness, humility, self-sacrifice, and service, which she suspected was a guilty reaction to the greed and violence of Christian males, Daly wanted an ethic of ecstatic emotional potency and liberation. The Christian ethic of self-giving was disastrous for women, she judged, because they took it seriously. Negatively, feminism was about smashing the pious, humble, hypocritical, herd-following morality of Christianity. Positively, it was hard to know exactly what it meant ethically. Daly judged that it was too soon, in 1973, to know what a feminist ethic would be. Women had just begun to think out of their own experience. Even feminists like her had male voices and theories in their heads that drowned out the inner speaking of female spirit. *Beyond God the Father* was an argument for rebellion, woman-space, and the emancipation of female spirit. The new ethic would be created "in the manner of outlaws" by rebellious women "whose awareness of power of being is emerging in refusal to be cast into a mold."[92]

From there Daly veered to a separatist "Hag-ographic Gynocentrism," declaring in her book *Gyn/Ecology* (1978) that "patriarchy is itself the prevailing religion of the entire planet, and its essential message is necrophilia." In her rendering, Buddhism, Hinduism, Islam, Judaism, Christianity, Freudianism, Jungianism, Marxism, and Maoism were "essentially similar" varieties of male tyranny; all were "infrastructures of the edifice of patriarchy," treating women as objects of terror. Radical feminism was the theory and practice of anti-gynocidal rebellion, she argued. It was "absolutely Anti-androcrat, A-mazingly Anti-male, Furiously and Finally Female." Halfway between Daly's coming out book, *Beyond God the Father*, and the "Positively Revolting Hag" Gnosticism of *Gyn/Ecology* she looked back at the book that launched feminist theology and her career, *The Church and the Second Sex*.[93]

Besides its oblivious use of "man" and "he" as generic terms, she noted, the book used the word "discrimination" a great deal, which signaled its reformist character. She found it comical that the early Daly thought it important to distinguish between the J and P creation stories, and took seriously Paul's statement that in Christ there was neither male nor female. Since "Christ" was an exclusively male symbol, the statement was literally meaningless. Worse yet was the early Daly's enthusiasm for John XXIII, who vaguely acknowledged, in the later Daly's rendering, "that women are human." The later Daly remarked: "The enthusiasm of our author snatching at these crumbs tossed from on high speaks volumes about the desolation of the culture in which she struggled to survive." Unfortunately, she noted, the early Daly apparently knew nothing of Elizabeth Cady Stanton, Sojourner Truth, Matilda Joslyn Gage, and Virginia Woolf; thus she needed many quotes from male writers. As for the early Daly's hope of "dialogue and cooperation between men and women," the later Daly replied: "The rapism of males and of male institutions is not easily unlearned." The early Daly believed that Catholic opponents of women's ordination were wrong to emphasize Christ's maleness instead of his humanity; the later Daly recanted: "She was trying to transcend the untranscendable, that is, the message of male supremacy contained in the medium itself." But that was futile, because Christianity was a form of phallicism that symbolically and literally compelled worship of maleness, seeking to extinguish female spirit.[94]

The later Daly sought to reawaken female spirit/be-ing by inventing a soaring language of "Wicked Wiccan Women," "Be-Witching Websters," "Nag-Gnostic Voyagers," and "Spinning Crones," drawing on occult literature. Her books ventured into what she called "the Realm of the Wild," describing her experiences with auras and other occult phenomena, and summoned women to break free from every form of phallic morality: "Norns know our Hour is arriving. Nags announce the resurgence of female powers. Wild women will to shift the shapes of words, of worlds. Naming Elemental sources/forces, Sirens call women to a metapatriarchal journey of exorcism and ecstasy."[95]

This lyrically powerful, Gnostic, conspiracy-minded vision of spiritual deliverance from a patriarchal anti-cosmos inspired part of the feminist theology movement to take Daly's "Cronespace" option. Other feminists adopted her separatist ideology without the Crone-spinning. Many others used her books to calibrate their own versions of feminism, judging variously that she had gone too far by the time of *Beyond God the Father* (1973), or *Gyn/Ecology* (1978), or *Pure Lust: Elemental Feminist Philosophy* (1984). Many feminists drew the line at Daly's dehumanizing denigrations of males as a class, most women, and feminist pastors. For those who had entered the ordained ministry after being inspired by *The Church and the Second Sex* or *Beyond God the Father*, it was sad to read Daly's slashing description of female pastors as patriarchal co-conspirators "serving dead symbols and serving these up to starving congregations of bamboozled believers who are doubly tricked by the incorporation of females into the processions of priestly predators." That seemed far afield from their reality, in which progressive Christianity and a deep commitment to feminist liberation went together.[96]

Christian Feminist Liberation Ethics: Beverly W. Harrison

The leading theologian of the latter option was Ruether, who wrote a classic systematic theology and major works on eco-theology and female redemption. In social ethics, however, the leading feminist thinker was Cone's colleague at Union Theological Seminary, Beverly Wildung Harrison, whose influence in the field vastly exceeded her published output.[97]

Born in 1932 and raised in the repressed blandness of small town Minnesota, the white middle class, and mainline Presbyterianism, Harrison had no feminist consciousness until the late 1960s, and little consciousness of white privilege until the 1980s. She grew up in a prosperous, racially homogeneous Minnesota farming town (Luverne), where her father developed a successful business after losing two in the Depression before she was born. On her mother's side her family was German Lutheran, with an embedded streak of anti-Semitism; politically it was Republican, because Abraham Lincoln had freed the slaves and Minnesota statesman Harold Stassen, a political liberal on racial integration, was a family favorite.

Harrison later recalled that like virtually all white feminist scholars of her generation, she was slow to comprehend her inculpation in white racism. Elsewhere she recalled that by virtue of being middle class, Midwestern, and a child of the Depression era, she entered adulthood and career "without the least awareness" that there had ever been a feminist movement in the USA or a need for one. To her it was "an unspeakable impoverishment" to have known nothing, for so many years, about the feminists of the abolitionist and suffrage generations, Elizabeth Cady Stanton, Susan B. Anthony, Sojourner Truth, Anna Julia Cooper: "How much easier my life would have been had I known of this earlier challenge to the social conventions that enshrouded my life, conventions that taught me that I was by 'nature,' by virtue of my genitals, especially suited to be a wife and mother, that my 'femininity' meant that professional work, if I did it at all, should and would be only a transitional or secondary phase of my existence." As it was, Harrrison nearly settled for queen bee status in an eroding male liberal Protestant world, until the feminist movement changed her life and world.[98]

Her early moral agency had much to do with her mother and something to do with the Presbyterian Church. Harrison's mother, a widow with five children, taught her to prepare for the contingency of not being supported by a husband; Harrison's participation in church youth groups provided leadership opportunities. In 1950 she enrolled at Macalester College in St Paul, Minnesota, where young Robert McAfee Brown taught during her sophomore and junior years. Brown urged Harrison to study theology beyond the college level, specifically at Union Theological Seminary, which in 1953 turned out to be his next career stop. Unlike most women who considered seminary in the early 1950s, Harrison found several supportive pastors, and she had a role model – Elizabeth Heller, a campus minister at the University of Minnesota. Since campus ministers did not have to be ordained, the Presbyterian Church did not ordain women, and Harrison knew a female campus minister, she settled on campus ministry as a career. At Union she studied under Niebuhr, Bennett, and Brown and embraced Niebuhr's theology, which she called, following convention, neo-orthodoxy. In later life Harrison usually described herself as a thoroughgoing Niebuhrian in seminary, although she sometimes recalled having entertained doubts about Niebuhr's realism and individualism. Enrolled in the Master of Religious Education program, she gave little thought to ordination and had no real conviction that it should be open to her. In 1956 the door opened anyway in the United Presbyterian Church, but she stuck to her plan, entering campus ministry that year at University of California Berkeley with a Union religious education degree and no ordination.[99]

Years later Harrison stressed that at every step she was supported by the teachers and clergy she knew; hers was not a story of exclusion or belittlement. At Union and Berkeley, where she served as an associate Presbyterian university pastor for five years, she found unexpected success in male domains. Intellectually, her friendships with social scientists at Berkeley proved to be formative, inspiring her interest in social theory. But Harrison's professional success came at a price that she was slow to comprehend. Often she was complimented for being different from most women, approaching her work like "one of the boys." For the next decade she told herself that being man-like was her strength. Many of her female contemporaries floundered in ministry, finding it too demanding, humiliating, or confusing to endure. Harrison reasoned that she was tougher and smarter than they were. They were needy, while she was strong and successful. They got hurt feelings and nursed personal slights, while she took her lumps like a man. Prizing the admiration of her male clerical peers, Harrison felt superior to other women, and alienated from them: "I was impatient with their 'weakness' and the ease with which *they* became discouraged. Stoical by family background and culture, I was quick to dismiss their 'emotionality,' as men often do."[100]

But that imperiled her gender identity and self-confidence: "A sense of superiority and a deep uneasiness that something was terribly wrong with me as a woman operated in my soul." If femininity was something to be disparaged, what did that make her? If she could be successful only by not being womanly, what kind of woman was she? "I was simultaneously a professional success and a 'failed' woman," Harrison later recalled. Since her success depended on not being what she was, a woman, it felt phony to her, not being really hers. She could not own the power she possessed. Rather, she achieved results by imitating something she was not: "The result was that though I evidently performed well enough to fool everyone else, I never felt quite 'good' about what I did or who I was."[101]

Meanwhile, her male colleagues told her she was too gifted intellectually not to get a doctorate and pursue a theological career. Harrison had even more trouble picturing herself as an academic; on the other hand, "if others said that I could, I would try." For a year she worked for the Presbyterian Church's Commission on Ecumenical Mission and Relations; in 1963 Harrison returned to Union Seminary, where she studied ethics under Roger Shinn and John Bennett and felt acutely the fall of Niebuhrian realism. Union Seminary in the mid-1950s had seemed powerful, important, and self-confident to her; a decade later her teachers seemed defensive and dispirited, caught in the grip of a malaise that shrank from strong convictions and bold action. The new Union had no idea what came after neo-orthodoxy. Death-of-God theology was the media fad in divinity schools; Niebuhr's muscular Christian language seemed quaint in that context; and Union Seminary shared in the apprehensiveness of a declining liberal Protestantism. Harrison found it unnerving to begin studying for a theological career at the very moment when theology lost its bearings. The Niebuhrian language of transcendent divinity and purpose was no longer plausible to her, but she had nothing to replace it with, lacking any inkling of feminist consciousness or liberation theology.[102]

In 1966, instead of replacing a retiring dean of women at Union, Bennett named Harrison as assistant dean of students and instructor in Christian ethics, notwithstanding that she was still a doctoral student. Years later, Harrison remembered that she joined the administration and faculty "toward the end of my Ph.D. program," which was true in terms of course requirements, but not the degree; she did not complete her doctorate until 1975. Performing capably as a dean and instructor, in 1969 she was rewarded with a dual appointment as assistant professor and acting dean of students.[103]

In her capacity as an administrator, Harrison spoke with female students about their concerns and struggles, which at first confirmed her belief about them: many were too feminine and needy to survive the rigors of seminary. Harrison eased them out of Union, consoling them that graduate education and ministry were not for everyone.

Near the end of her second year of advising, however, she caught enough of the feminist uprising to rethink her administrative role. Betty Friedan's gripping description in *The Feminine Mystique* of the "problem that has no name" struck a chord of recognition in Harrison, despite Friedan's focus on suburban housewives. Looking further into feminism, Harrison began to apply feminist criticism to her own situation. Was it possible that the women who dropped out had a more humane or healthy idea of what seminary education should be? What were Harrison's judgments against them, if not a form of sexism? "Slowly I recognized how much I disvalued women, myself included, and made a connection between my own conformity and my lack of a sense of my power in my work." Two specific realizations swept over her: she had not supported the personal concerns of women who sought her counsel, and every time she eased a woman's departure from Union, "I was cutting myself off from my sisters and weakening the base of support for my own work."[104]

In a difficult period at Union, where enrollment dropped from over 700 in the late 1960s to 456 in 1975, Harrison became a faculty mainstay, chairing its long-range planning committee and establishing a women's counseling team and women's center, which reflected the seminary's growing commitment to feminism. In 1973 she was granted tenure, a year before finishing her dissertation on H. Richard Niebuhr's moral theology, which set off some faculty muttering. Brushing off the mutters, Harrison devoted herself to mentoring female students and building up the women's center. "My identification with feminism had begun in a deep intellectual loneliness," she later recalled. "During my first years as a faculty member at Union, I had felt the pain of real invisibility." Knowing that feminist scholars at other institutions felt the same thing, and wanting to build up feminist ethics, Harrison helped launch a new organization, the Feminist Ethics Consultation, which supported the intellectual and personal development of feminist scholars in religious ethics. For the most part she gave preference to movement and solidarity work over her own scholarship, which led to a seminary controversy over her faculty standing.[105]

In 1978 Union's committee on appointments, a group of tenured faculty, voted not to recommend Harrison for promotion to full professor to the board of trustees. That verdict set off 10 months of protests, meetings, demonstrations, and a commencement replete with pro-Harrison armbands. At the time Harrison had authored a few articles on sexism, but no books. Faculty members opposed to her promotion contended that a full professor had to be a book author. Some added that the problem began when Harrison was awarded tenure before she had a doctorate, setting a bad precedent. Others countered that Harrison's scholarship was promising, she devoted extraordinary time to students, and she was an excellent teacher. In January 1979 the committee on appointments reaffirmed its decision after a thorough review, but the following month Union's board of trustees promoted Harrison to full professor, an unprecedented action that enraged many faculty and left bitter feelings on both sides for years.[106]

In that embattled context Harrison became the mother of feminist social ethics. On April 15, 1980 she gave her inaugural address as a full professor at Union, speaking on "The Power of Anger in the Work of Love." The next day biblical scholar Phyllis Trible gave her inaugural address. Brightly garbed female scholars from many institutions came to Union to celebrate the achievements of Harrison and Trible. Speaking to them, Harrison began with a tribute to Mary Daly, noting that Daly described procession as the first of the eight deadly sins of Phallocracy. Religious and academic processions celebrated male privilege and control, expressing the same fixation with maleness that produced the Christian Trinity. As usual, Harrison declared, Daly was right: "We have very far to go before Christianity acknowledges adequately its complicity in breeding and perpetuating the hatred and fear of the real, full, lived world power of female persons! Misogyny, as Daly claims, is hydra-headed, having as many forms as there are cultures, languages, and social systems." What men feared above all was women's assertion of their own power, exactly as Daly claimed, although Harrison cautioned that Daly's scholarship was sometimes sloppy in making her case. What mattered was that Daly got the big things right and paved the way for feminist theology and ethics: "Only Mary Daly's profound rage has produced a feminist critique strong enough to ensure that some minimal attention must be given it within ecclesiastical and academic circles."[107]

No one in that audience could have missed the unspoken analogy, that Mary Daly was the James Cone of feminism. Only a militant confrontationalist could have established feminist or black liberation theology. But the separatist impulses of Cone and Daly played out very differently, because Daly mythologized the journey to a spiritual Otherworld. Harrison wanted to believe, with Daly, that patriarchy could be destroyed by the refusal of woman-identified women to take part in patriarchal processions of all kinds. She did believe that Daly's "joyful world of Womanspace" could be, on occasion, a useful sanctuary for women. But Daly's leap into Otherworldly Womanspace was too otherworldly and segregated to be realistic, ethical, or healthy, Harrison judged: "In contrast to Daly, my basic ethical thesis is that women, and other marginated people, are *less* cut off from the real, material conditions of life than are those who enjoy the privileges of patriarchy and that, as a result, an otherworldly spirituality is far removed from the life experience of women."[108]

Harrison's early feminism shared the exuberance of white feminist "sisterhood is powerful" rhetoric; in 1980 she was still urging her audiences to celebrate the worldwide explosion of the revolutionary spirit of sisterhood. "'Woman-spirit rising' is a *global* phenomenon," she declared, it was the ultimate and therefore "longest" revolution, and it would be fulfilled sooner "if we celebrate the strength that shines forth in women's lives." Methodologically, she conceived feminist ethics as a type of liberation theology: "What is authentic in the history of faith arises only out of the crucible of human struggle." Feminist liberation was about the struggle of women and feminist-supporting men to accept and live deeply into the gift of life, which was the locus of divine revelation. Like other forms of liberation theology, it made use of the power of anger in the work of love, learning the meaning of love through immersion in the struggle for social justice.[109]

Philosophically, Harrison was a dialectical materialist who believed, with Marx, that history and consciousness emerged from the historical struggle for life. She treasured Daly's roar for feminist revolution, but not her subjective idealism or her grounding of feminism in biological gender. Daly's idealism lacked a strategy for action and a strong critique of collective practices, Harrison judged; essentially, it was a critique of concepts. Although Daly was right to favor process over static being, she never overcame the abstract rationalism of her Catholic background. She seemed not even to notice that process could be the basic structure of a philosophy of being. Harrison urged feminists to challenge the classic ontology of Be-ing more radically than Daly, by taking seriously Marx's insistence that the power of nature passes through the "species-being" of human nature. The world is created and shaped through human action. Instead of operating exclusively with naturalistic metaphors that eschewed historical categories and reproduced a binary essentialism of female and male natures, Harrison rooted feminist ethics in the real-world doings of moral creativity: "We dare not minimize the very real historical power of women to be architects of what is most authentically human."[110]

Harrison had a place for anger in feminist ethics, and a place for males, and a place for love, understood as radical mutuality and reciprocity. She did not have a place for sacrifice as moral virtue, except as something to be endured in a hostile world for the cause of radical love. "Like Jesus, we are called to a radical activity of love," she asserted. Christian feminist ethics was about deepening relation, building community, and passing on the gift of life. It was not about acquiring virtue through sacrifice. Jesus opposed the distortions of power and wrong relationship out of love, not because he wanted to be a martyr. In the cause of radical love he ended up having to accept martyrdom, a foreseeable consequence. But his virtue was that he sought right relationship and the ends of justice. The point was to stop the trail of crucifixions, not to idealize being crucified. Harrison put it positively: "We are called to express, embody, share, celebrate the gift of life, and pass it on!" To pass on the power of love was to gift others as one had been gifted, keeping the power of relationship alive in the world.[111]

As a moral theorist Harrison refused to choose between deontological and teleological ethics, a position she commended to liberation ethicists. Deontological theories determined the moral rightness or wrongness of acts by appealing to established principles; teleological theories evaluated the morality of acts by appealing chiefly or exclusively to consequences; Harrison opted for a mixed model in which rules and consequences corrected each other. Exclusive deontology led to ethical rigidity, she argued, while teleological or utilitarian approaches to ethics tended to compromise moral values too quickly, as when the utilitarian calculus of "the greater good for the greater number" justified unjust treatment of a minority population. Each perspective needed the correction of the other: "The truth is that *both* deontological and utilitarian moral reasoning carried to their logical conclusions, without the corrective of the other, can lead to actions that offend moral intuitions." Harrison's version of mixed theory took its methodological bearings from liberation theology, in which a fundamental commitment to the liberation of oppressed persons shaped one's selection of topics, ethical priorities, and appropriation of the past. From a liberationist standpoint, she contended, social justice had to take precedence and priority over the morality of specific individual acts. In this respect Catholic natural law theory had the right logic, though not the right content.[112]

For most of her career Harrison expounded her idea of the right content in essays and conference papers, writing only one book that was not an essay collection. The exception was a book on the ethics of abortion, *Our Right to Choose* (1983), which she began during the turmoil over her promotion to full professor. In the late 1970s an upsurge of violent attacks on abortion clinics occurred, motivating Harrison to write about abortion. A further motive was that Christian ethicists tended to abstract the issue out of its lived context in women's lives. Putting it strongly in an article published shortly before the book, Harrison charged that most of the literature on this subject betrayed "the heavy hand of misogyny, the hatred of women." A further motive was that supporters of the right to abortion usually made a sharp distinction between politics and morality, stressing the political right to individual privacy. Harrison judged that the usual defense was a loser. Feminists had to stop ceding the moral ground to opponents of the right to abortion. Instead of treating abortion as a "discrete deed" that was morally meaningful in itself, context notwithstanding, feminists needed to raise a more basic and prior moral question: "What am I to do about the procreative power that is mine by virtue of being born female?"[113]

The abortion issue was not merely a private matter of individual choice, she argued. More broadly and deeply, it was about the capacity of women as a class to shape their procreative power instead of being controlled by forces hostile to women's moral agency. Harrison observed that financially privileged women were not at risk of losing their procreative power of choice, even if abortion were to be outlawed again. Abortion services always would be available to women of means. The moral imperative was to guarantee that all women had the same "taken-for-granted option." For Harrison, the morality of the act of abortion itself was a secondary issue. From a feminist standpoint, the primary moral question was to determine what constituted a humane social policy on abortion. On the former question she respected a diversity of views; on the latter question, "I am not in the least a pluralist." The right of women to shape their procreative power was "a social good that all women require."[114]

Harrison stressed that there was no distinctively Protestant rational tradition of opposition to abortion. Historically and culturally, anti-abortion was a Catholic fixation. Historically, Protestant cultures did not make a great issue of abortion, partly because Protestant ministers were married and often poor, and thus were not removed from the social realities of compulsory childbirth. When Protestants opposed abortion, she noted, they did so either on Catholic natural law grounds or on biblicist grounds. But biblicism was irrational; it was pointless to reason against a biblicist argument, since biblicist positions were not based on reason. Thus, to argue for the right to abortion on moral grounds, feminists had to challenge the moral legitimacy of Catholic natural law reasoning in this area.

In the category of "moral consensus," Harrison agreed with Catholic ethicists and Protestant opponents of abortion that human life had intrinsic value and that unjustified killing was evil. But the moral status of fetal life was uncertain and contested, she argued. Before the morality of abortion itself could be assessed, two central moral assumptions had to be established. The first was the right of women to full moral agency. The second was that bodily integrity was a fundamental condition of moral agency and human well-being. Women had no dignity without freedom from bodily invasion, and their dignity was inherently social. Harrison wrote: "The fact of women's biological fertility and capacity for childbearing in no way overrides our moral claim to the 'right' of bodily integrity, because this moral claim is inherent to human well-being. No society that coerces women at the level of reproduction may lay claim to moral adequacy." As for the personhood of the fetus, Harrison stressed that "person" was a moral category implying participation in a moral community, not something reducible to any particular level of biological maturation. Human existence was intrinsically social and relational without remainder. There was no personality apart from one's participation in a world of social relations and moral actions.[115]

That was not quite an argument for infanticide or abortion on demand, as Harrison recognized that the fetus had some humanlike value in the later stages of gestation. She drew the line at viability, arguing that until that point, the fetus lacked anything like a woman's right to freedom from bodily invasion, freedom for bodily integrity,

and self-direction. With a mixture of ethical arguments she urged that a morally adequate society must organize its life to support procreative choice. On teleological
grounds she asserted the primacy of women's well-being; on deontological grounds
Harrison defended women's right to choose; as a relational theorist she stressed
women's experiences of pregnancy and embodiment; as a pragmatic realist she tried
to negotiate the volatile politics of abortion.[116]

"If those who condemn all acts of abortion are successful, women's lives will be
drastically altered for the worse," Harrison warned. At the same time, she took seriously the moral desirability of making the resort to abortion more rare. There were
four main groups of females who faced unwanted pregnancies, she observed. The first
group did not understand contraception; the second did not use contraception because
of carelessness, strange ideas, or a partner's opposition; the third group used contraceptives unsuccessfully; and the fourth consisted of victims of sexual violence. Harrison
argued that the first two groups were large because much of society denigrated
women's sexuality and the need for contraception, resulting in large numbers of people
who did not understand contraception or held irrational or self-destructive ideas about
it. Conjecturing that the largest group was number three, she argued that expanded
economic opportunities for women would reduce the number of abortions in this
category and that better contraceptives were needed. As for sexual violence, the
primary culprit again was hatred of women. If contempt for women and violence
against them were dramatically reduced, the number of abortions in all four categories
would dramatically decline. In a better world, with better social support, women
would be able to choose or avoid motherhood: "Only uncompromising, extensive
support for a feminist agenda of social justice for women can hold out any hope of
reducing the need for abortions in this society."[117]

Our Right to Choose was a milestone in feminist social ethics, especially for its development of hermeneutical and moral principles out of women's experience. Rosemary
Ruether, in a jacket endorsement, called the book "an indispensable contribution to
contemporary ethical thought about abortion." *Christian Century* reviewer Judy
Weidman was noncommittal about Harrison's position, but judged that the book
"added a forceful argument to the ongoing debate." *Journal of Religion* reviewer Jean
Lambert remarked with equal reserve that Harrison offered "fruitful resources for reflection on religious perception and theological interpretation." *Theological Education*
reviewer Peter Paris made a stronger statement about the book's disciplinary importance, calling it "a major contribution to the discipline of Christian ethical studies."
Journal of the American Academy of Religion reviewer Nathan Kollar did not like Harrison's
"preachy and repetitious" style, but judged that the book was an important addition
to the social ethical literature on human rights. *Horizons* reviewer Lisa Sowle Cahill
was more specific about her qualms, wondering how a fetus could acquire rights after
viability if it possessed none before. She also worried that Harrison's stress on relationality and sociality conflicted with the trump value she gave to the liberal ideal of individual autonomy for women. But Cahill applauded "Harrison's attempt to develop a
nuanced perspective on a hard dilemma," especially her emphasis that moral agency
had meaning only within the social, historical web of interpersonal relations.[118]

Having the field of pro-choice feminist Christian ethics nearly to herself, Harrison
accepted her leadership role on this issue while refusing to be confined to it. She
wanted more company on abortion and lamented feeling equally alone on radical
political economy, on which she felt a deep kinship with Harry Ward. To Harrison
it was terribly important for Christian social ethics to make the best possible use of

social theory, especially on political economics. That required coming to terms with Weberian sociology and neo-classical economics, but above all, it required overturning Niebuhr's influential critique of Marxism.

Her own introduction to Marx had occurred in Niebuhr's classroom. As a student Harrison had admired Niebuhr greatly, arriving at a "total identification with his viewpoint," yet she soon realized that Niebuhr knew only a fraction of Marx's corpus, and he tended to generalize on the basis of a few fundamental ideas about Marxism. He drew his understanding of Marx from Old Left Marxists, not from a close study of Marx. Years later Harrison urged Christian ethicists to stop hiding behind Niebuhr's critique of Marx, which was "misinformed and substantially inaccurate."[119]

Niebuhr described Marx as a scientific positivist with a dogmatic, historical determinist agenda: Science provided objective, non-relational knowledge, and the task of social theory was to gain rational control over society by applying scientific knowledge to it. Harrison replied that Niebuhr missed the double edge of Marx's critique. Niebuhr grasped Marx's attack on philosophical idealism, that ideas are not autonomous realities divorced from historical context and conditioning, but he missed completely Marx's attack on scientific objectivism because it did not square with his presumption that Marx was a positivist. Harrison's Marx did not believe that that he knew, on the basis of science, where history was going. Marx sought merely to describe "the concrete social relations of the particular historical epoch in which he lived." The real positivists, Harrison argued, were the apologists for the new capitalist order who described the laws of exchange value as the universal essence of economic activity. Marx showed that the essential element of economic activity was work, not exchange value, and that every economic system was subject to change through collective historical action. The very idea of economic laws, including capitalist "laws of the market," flunked the test of historical understanding. Social science was about critically interpreting whatever existed, not about providing scientific or predictive knowledge about the future.[120]

Ironically, Harrison judged, Marx and Niebuhr believed the same thing about constructive social change: its wellspring was political courage, not historical inevitability. But Niebuhr routinely misconstrued Marx on this point, and he compounded the problem by interpreting Marx as a (bad) philosopher of history. In Niebuhr's rendering, Marx was primarily the theorist of a utopian and optimistic philosophy of history. Harrison replied that Marx lacked any philosophical ambition of that sort. For Marx, the very idea of a philosophy of history was a speculative waste of time and a species of ahistorical mystification. Marx's critique of religion was not free of prejudice, Harrison allowed, but Marxism made a stronger claim to historical concreteness than Niebuhrian realism, which always found the same dynamic of power-seeking self-aggrandizement within and between groups and nation states. On Niebuhrian grounds, it was hard to find a moral ground for choosing between sides in a struggle for power. To Harrison, that was one of the larger ironies of Niebuhr's project, "that the empirically oriented Niebuhr actually opened religious ethics to an anti-empirical, and probably the most antihistorical, social theory available in his time or in ours." To do better than that, social ethics had to disown "the Niebuhr-engendered 'marxophobia' of religious ethicists," which had turned out to be "an ideological impairment of staggering proportions."[121]

On the whole Harrison judged that Max Weber had a more constructive impact on Christian ethics than Niebuhr, although Weberian sociology shared with Niebuhrian realism the fault of being easily hijacked by conservatives. Weber's focus on the interaction of "ideal" and "real" factors in social process was invaluable to social ethicists, and his descriptions of the macrosocial level of the social world, especially politics and the bureaucratic modes of social organization, were deservedly famous. But Weber's concept of "value-free" sociology was more value-laden and interested than he acknowledged, and his emphasis on "ideal types" tended to obscure historical particularities. Harrison cautioned that moral reasoning was inherently evaluative and prescriptive; it could not rest with Weberian claims to causal/predictive understanding or even critical description. When social ethicists typified social relations in Weberian style they lost the focus on historical particularities that gave moral reasoning its power and necessity. Moreover, Weber was like Niebuhr in bequeathing a certain theoretical evasiveness to social ethics, which owed much to his (and Niebuhr's) centrist bourgeois ideology and interests: "Just as Reinhold Niebuhr placed realism at the service of middle-of-the-road reform, so Weber used *verstehen* sociology to legitimate emergent liberal bureaucratic forms of social organization." Weber had a stronger interest than Niebuhr in the interaction of cultural and economic forces, Harrison allowed, but like Niebuhr, he made a premature peace with triumphant welfare state capitalism. Both of them evinced a bourgeois fascination with the state as a balancer of economic power, and Weber's claim to "value-free" objectivity put a misleading, positivistic spin on his analysis of bureaucratic administrative structures.[122]

Like Niebuhr, Weber missed the dialectic in Marx's dialectical materialism, describing Marx as an economic determinist or reductionist. Marx's polemics against allies who really were economic determinists were lost on Weber, as on Niebuhr. Not coincidentally, Harrison observed, both of them settled for the liberalism of the welfare state. As long as the state had the trappings of parliamentary democracy and assumed some responsibility for taming capitalism, it passed the test of realism (Niebuhr) or scientific "multifactor indeterminism" (Weber). Harrison protested that social ethics desperately needed to do better than that. Weber and Niebuhr were too impressed by modern state liberalism, which they treated as politically normative, "even optimal morally." Whenever social ethics took a Niebuhrian and/or Weberian line, which was most of the time, it masked "the very existence of the modern economy" by taking it for granted.[123]

In 1986 the US Roman Catholic bishops issued a historic pastoral letter titled *Economic Justice for All: Catholic Social Teaching and the U.S. Economy*. Authored principally by Jesuit social ethicist David Hollenbach, the bishops' statement steered a careful path between an "unfettered free-market economy" and an unnamed system at the other end of the ideological spectrum. Advocates of unfettered capitalism, the bishops observed, claimed that the laws of exchange defined economic rationality, while extremists of the other sort claimed that capitalism inherently bred inequality and an exploited underclass. Unfettered capitalists wanted as little government intervention in the economy as possible, while "others" wanted to abolish private property and the market system. The former view was an ideology of enlightened self-interest; the latter view was an anti-capitalist ideology; the bishops stood between them, while disavowing any specific ideology or policy prescription: "Catholic social teaching has traditionally rejected these ideological extremes because they are likely to produce results contrary to human dignity and economic justice." The church's approach was "pragmatic and evolutionary," they taught. It recognized that the economy was created by human beings and could be changed by them, which ruled out capitalist positivism, but it also respected private property and markets, which ruled out the other extreme.

The best approach was to work within the prevailing mixed economic system to make it more just, struggling for reforms in a variety of economic and political contexts. The church had lived under a variety of socio-economic systems and would continue to do so, evaluating each by the ethical principles of human dignity: "What is the impact of the system on people? Does it support or threaten human dignity?"[124]

Harrison respected the communitarian, personalist, and rationalist aspects of Catholic teaching. Occasionally she remarked that Catholic social thought had a stronger social conscience and theoretical basis than most of the Protestant tradition. She appreciated the US bishops' emphasis on poverty and inequality, but she hated the fact that they perpetuated stereotypes about the political Left. At the risk "of turning some people off," Harrison confessed to being "one of these extremists referred to" who believed that capitalism was inherently predatory and unjust. Yet she had never met a fellow extremist who advocated the abolition of private property and the market. So why did the bishops keep beating a dead horse?[125]

Mistakenly, Harrison claimed that this "caricature of left-wing politics" was originated by Niebuhr and later picked up by Catholics, forgetting *Rerum Novarum*. In any case, she asked the bishops to stop misrepresenting "the views of the political left." Socialists like her were not against personal private property or the limited use of markets; their goal was to bring the means of production (by which the wealth of society was produced) under the direction of society and its people. Socialism was about popular ownership of the means to acquire wealth. Under late capitalism it was quite common for people to have significant personal wealth and virtually no social power, Harrison observed. Christian ethics could not give up on socialism, because it was the only strategy that delivered social power to the many.[126]

Harrison judged that Marx got the main things right in political economy. Marx taught that capitalism could never be a means to economic democracy because capitalism was about exploiting the many to produce wealth for the owners of productive capital. He showed that capitalism commodified everything it touched, beginning with land, natural resources, human labor, and machines. In a capitalist society exploitation became the dominant mode of social interaction between the ownership class and the many, who survived by selling their labor. Ultimately the many lost even the use of their labor as an expression of their lives and dignity. Marx did not invent the idea of the class struggle, Harrison noted; every important economist of the late eighteenth and nineteenth centuries addressed the heightened social conflicts that accompanied the rise of capitalism. Like Adam Smith and David Ricardo, Marx was motivated to invent an economic science that relieved modern society of its staggering violence. Though Marx got some things wrong – he was too admiring of capitalist productivity and may have had a reductionist view of nature – he perceived exactly why capitalism was degrading.[127]

Speaking as a Socialist who did not equivocate about the real thing – social ownership of the major means of production – Harrison advised the bishops and other Christian ethicists to stop calling the USA a mixed economy. This convention, favored by Niebuhr and adopted by Catholics, was "a perfectly preposterous assertion." The Tennessee Valley Authority was a significant socialist venture by the US government, but Harrison could not think of a second example. In the USA, socializing basic productive functions was politically off the map. Under the New Deal the USA moved "very grudgingly," after bitter political struggle, to a regulatory state system in which the state restrained the most antisocial effects of capitalism by administrative rule. It also developed a minimal system of social insurance at the federal level and a degrading set of welfare policies for children and indigent mothers at the state level. That was nothing like a mixed economy, Harrison admonished: "Our solution to capitalist political–economic crisis always has been to use the state to shore up or strengthen existing patterns of the private ownership of the means of production at whatever price to the wider society."[128]

To Harrison, socialism was still the answer, despite its defeats: "I submit that Christian intellectuals need to be clear that whether we like it or not, the historical direction in which we must move is the line originally staked out historically by European socialism." As a concession to typical confusions it was all right to use the phrase "democratic socialism," although in fact the phrase was redundant; Harrison stressed that Western socialism had always been about the democratization of economic life. She urged social ethicists to "have enough integrity to challenge the Red-baiting always going on." If the Left backed down from socialism, it would have to back down from liberalism and feminism too: "We are living in a profoundly repressive political climate."[129]

To the extent that she remained hopeful, it was because liberation theology had become a significant movement. In the third world the problem of capitalism was terribly obvious, Harrison observed, and so liberation theology was virtually always socialist. In the US, where socialism had almost no history, even liberation theology hesitated at opting for it, but Harrison expected that to change. The same logic of capitalism that ripped apart cultures and societies in the third world was beginning to wash back from the periphery of the capitalist world order – "for that is what the third world is" – to its base powers, especially the USA. State governments in the USA and even regulative sectors of the federal government were losing the ability to manage powerful economic forces. Poverty and inequality were escalating, and big business was scouring the globe for low-tax, cheap-labor havens, destroying communities in the process. Harrison stressed that the liberationist struggle for socialism and women's rights in the third world was inseparable from the same struggle in the USA: "We must find our way to a situation in which people have some direct say in how social wealth is used."[130]

As her standing grew in the social ethics field in the 1980s and 1990s, Harrison recognized that many feminist ethicists did not share her feeling of kinship to liberal Christianity or her socialist commitments. On the former issue she was sympathetic, judging that liberal churches and seminaries were overly preoccupied with survival and depressed by nostalgic memories of past glory. In the face of declining social influence, she observed, "fixation on fantasies of a golden past has set in." Some theologians sought to recover a lost Christian grandeur by retrieving a favored tradition; others retreated to an ecclesial subculture; Harrison urged liberals to be braver than that, fusing the best of the liberal tradition with liberation theology. A tradition that included Harry Ward, James Luther Adams, Martin Luther King, Jr, and Reinhold Niebuhr was nothing to sneer at.[131]

Harrison admired Ward's fervent anti-capitalism and his feisty, brave, good-spirited persistence in the face of "unrelenting controversy and vilification." She taught a course on his work, stressing that Ward's admiration for Soviet communism should not have disqualified him from an honored place in the history of social ethics. To Harrison, Ward was a precursor of what liberalism needed, which was what had happened to her: to be radicalized by responding to injustice and oppression. Just as Ward exemplified the radical potential of the social gospel, Harrison wanted to sustain and transform the best of the social gospel, Christian socialist, and Christian realist traditions. Though she still thought of herself as a liberal Protestant social ethicist, it was not liberal theology that helped her decide which aspects of liberalism to retain. "By the early eighties, I was very clear," she later recalled. Liberation theology gave her the means to sort out what was worth keeping and what was worth struggling for.[132]

That set her against feminist ethicists who dropped socialism as an outmoded or unattractive project. "In a fundamental sense, I see my primary interest as the ethics of political economy," Harrison observed. "My primary interests have always been in examining how politics and economics interact." In some areas and situations, she reasoned, a democratic political process was the best way to coordinate a productive system; in other cases, markets were more efficient than politics. The ideal was to build an economic democracy that made the best use of politics and markets, combining political planning with market coordination. Harrison tired of the objection that democratic socialism did not exist after 125 years of trying. The reason it did not exist was that a socialist state could not survive in a capitalist world economy without selling out socialism: "Capitalism requires that you go with the existing global capitalist system of market exchange. And because current elites insist upon market-centered decision making, political considerations always get short shrift, so the 'economy' does not produce for people's well-being." In a capitalist world economy, any nation that did not compete on predatory capitalist terms made itself a candidate for economic starvation:

> We're in the midst of a huge moral dilemma because everybody tells us there is only one way to go and that capitalism will do what the impoverished globe needs. We who love democracy need to begin to create alternative political constraints on a now global productive system that does not have to give a damn bit of attention to what people need.[133]

Harrison's idea of what it meant to make liberation theology feminist was influenced profoundly by her participation in the Mud Flower Collective, a racially and ethnically mixed group of theological educators that included Katie G. Cannon, Carter Heyward, Ada María Isasi-Díaz, Bess B. Johnson, Mary D. Pellauer, and Nancy D. Richardson. Formed in 1982, the group explored what feminism meant if it was not merely the white, middle-class, universalistic rhetoric of gender equality proclaimed by white feminists in the late nineteenth-century and the 1960s and 1970s. Presenting its individual and collective perspectives in 1985, the group declared, "Contemporary feminism has inherited both the courage of the feminist abolitionists and the racism of the white women who sold out black people in a futile attempt to climb the ladders of success put in place by white men of privilege."[134]

The Mud Flower Collective agreed that contemporary feminists needed to oppose white supremacy and economic injustice as well as gender oppression. It did not agree on the core meaning of feminism. For Pellauer, feminism was "simply the struggle against sexism." For Heyward it was also the refusal "to compromise the well-being of women." For Cannon, feminism did not have "anything to do with women; it's the commitment to end white supremacy, male domination, and economic exploitation." For Isasi-Díaz, feminism was the understanding of sexism as "the paradigm of all oppression." For Johnson, feminism made no sense if it was not "preceded by the word black," and if it did not oppose "the trinity of sexism, racism, and classism."

For Richardson, feminism began with women's experience and contended for the well-being of all women. For Harrison, feminism began with a woman's assertion of her power: "It's not, in the first instance, a theory, but a very personal act."[135]

For several years the group compared and reflected on the variable weight that its members ascribed to the oppression of women in its interaction with racial and economic injustice. Harrison found the experience of interrogating her own whiteness to be painful and liberating. She recalled her family's anti-Semitism, its lack of conscience about the extermination of Native Americans – despite living less than 30 miles from the Pipestone Reservation – and heard Cannon and Isasi-Díaz describe their experiences of racist exclusion and invisibility as doctoral students at Union Seminary. Years later Harrison recalled, "Initially I felt trapped by these terrible contradictions. I was ashamed and confused. I think many white women start where I started. Our silence about racism is maintained because of an agonizing guilt about it."[136]

Harrison's Mud Flower experience helped her perceive that guilt thwarted revolutionary change; what was necessary was to work through the guilt that came from interrogating whiteness. In her case, that included interrogating white Protestantism. Harrison realized that she had absorbed from white Presbyterianism the lesson that she needed God as a substitute for her own life and powers. God's will was to be found in self-denial; Christians were supposed to deny themselves to do God's will. From her "somber, sad religion" she had learned to look for God in that which was not herself or in her experience: "I learned that so deeply – God would be what I was not!" Alice Walker's description of finding God in herself and the color purple helped Harrison claim her own powers of being. More important was Harrison's experience of feminist community with women who knew what Walker meant: "Finally, of course, that's precisely where I found God – in myself/my community." For Harrison, the experience of spiritual connection with other feminists was transforming: "Women's community has been the place where honesty, pain, and struggle have drawn me into a sense of God . . . Increasingly in my life it has been women who were really struggling to live, women who would not let their lives be denied, who have been the deep source of the grace I've experienced."[137]

Reflecting on annual denominational battles over gay and lesbian rights, Harrison argued that Christians routinely projected onto gays and lesbians their unacknowledged anxieties about sexuality. Traditional Christian teaching on sexuality was repressive and patriarchal, its harm to women was immense, and in some ways it harmed gays and lesbians even more harshly. As a Christian ethicist Harrison grieved at the self-loathing and fearfulness that Christian ethics instilled in many gays and lesbians. Appealing for a different Christian ethic, she urged, "We must find our way to valuing, celebrating, and making normative all deep, respectful, sensuous, empowering relationships, which, wherever they exist, ground our well-being and the bonds of mutual respect." One's sexuality is one's embodied sensuous capacity for relationship, she observed. There was such a thing as coming to terms with one's sexuality that allowed one to enjoy sex and be freed from compulsion and control by it, and yet also to accept that sexuality had "a dimension without our self-control." A church that repressed or evaded sexuality was bound to be lifeless, boring, and unable to stir people's souls, she judged: "I see too much banality, superficiality of feeling, and a lack of deep sensibility and emotional responsiveness in our churches. We are out of touch with the depth of life and with the concrete sufferings and vulnerability of people."[138]

Harrison's partner, theologian Carter Heyward, expounded this theme in several books, advocating what she called "touching our strength" and "coming into our power." Harrison warned that as long as Christians failed to claim their powers of sexuality, they lacked vital powers of relation and attractive religious communities: "Racial and ethnic people who struggle for justice for their communities, strong women, gay people, and all those who have left sexual repression behind, do *not feel welcome in our churches*, and these are the ones who are 'coming of age,' critically, in our social world, no longer willing to 'please' the established powers in society." A church that repelled the passionate types had no future worth pursuing.[139]

In Harrison's later career a different style of feminist theorizing emerged, one that spoke the language of deconstruction and postmodernity. Repeatedly Harrison, Ruether, Daly, Heyward, Letty Russell, and other feminists of their generation were tagged as modernists or foundationalists who made essentialist claims, overgeneralized their own experiences, did not appreciate the importance of cultural difference, and imposed binary categories on the fluid phenomenon of sexual identity. Harrison shook her head at postmodern feminist criticism. It was wrong to suggest "that we worked from such assumptions and that our work is, for that reason, at best deeply flawed, at worst no longer tenable." In her view, the early feminists, except Daly, were better remembered as historicists. Even if their early writings appealed to "sisterhood" and "experience" too uncritically, the charge of foundationalism was overwrought. They construed theological statements as historical-cultural constructs, not as transcendental claims. Moreover, it was ridiculous to tag as a "reformist" any feminist who did not repudiate Christianity, though that usage was standard fare among post-Christian feminists. Harrison protested that she and Ruether were more radical politically than the academic feminists who typed them as reformists.[140]

The whole business of applying political terms to feminists on the basis of their relation to religious communities was wrongheaded, as was the postmodern sport of denigrating Christian socialist feminists as "essentialists." Harrison struggled to find the right tone of reply, especially to feminists who identified primarily with the academy and devoted comparatively little time to social justice movements. In her view, postmodern feminists prized style at the expense of depth, and mistreated their feminist forerunners: "The currently fashionable 'trashes' of 'liberationist' approaches to theology, rooted in sometimes subtle and sometimes crass deconstructions of what is and what is not possible in our appeals to historicity and our efforts for change, can be dangerous if they celebrate resistance without the determination to *struggle* for such change continuously." It was not terribly admirable to reduce feminist praxis to snooty performances at academic conferences. The early feminists, now derided as old-fashioned, tried to change the world, and they practiced a dialogical style that respected disagreement. Sometimes they may have fallen short of appreciating diversity at the level of theory, Harrison allowed, but they produced a more diverse academy by creating an ethos of dialogue. The feminists of her generation looked out for each other, spurning the ethos of predatory competition. That was not something to deride.[141]

Harrison appealed for a feminist movement that was generous toward women of all colors and ferocious in opposing patriarchy, white supremacism, and economic injustice. Feminist theory and practice had no fixed starting point and no final end, she argued. To struggle for feminism was to take up, in the phrase of Letty Russell and Shannon Clarkson, "the wonderfully messy business of encouraging women's theologies." Harrison commended that untidy commitment to solidarity as an alternative to competitive rivalries: "Today more than ever before, it needs to be remembered that those of us who adopted the term *feminist liberation theology* for our work did so because we shared the epistemic conviction that theory is a movement *within* praxis, and that theory is to be judged by the practice it engenders." The first generation of feminists learned by doing, speaking for the rights of the excluded gender. It practiced a politics of inclusion that brought new voices to the discussion as a condition of better knowledge. If it tended to worry more about inclusive practices than refining new theories, that was a point in its favor.[142]

To the extent that Harrison felt compelled to defend a theoretical orientation, she opted for the broad middle ground of "standpoint" theory, eschewing Daly's transcendentalism and Judith Butler's gender-bending deconstruction of female identity. Harrison-style feminism was a principled standpoint with a history, a capacity to recognize its own relativity, and a transformational agenda. It was always engaged in networking, constantly building new forms of solidarity. Harrison worried that if Butler-style postmodernism won the day in feminist theory, not much of an ethic or praxis would be left. The most vital feminist truths remained to be created, Harrison urged, but extreme postmodernists renounced the claim to possess or even search for moral truths, much less create new ones. In that case the transformational agenda was abandoned. Postmodern academic feminism, consumed with its maze of self-referential literary tropes, lost sight of the feminist vision of a better world. Harrison countered that the relational, networking, liberationist approach to feminism already represented the epistemic challenge to malestream thought that was needed: "It is a legacy no one should challenge. Networking has been and must continue to be our the(a)ological mode of practice par excellence."[143]

Feminist theory began with the activism of ordinary women, Harrison insisted. To pursue feminist thought in some other way was "suicidal." There was no feminism worthy of the name apart from the struggles of women for the right to their personal and collective power: "These movements, grounded in the discourse of justice and human rights, do not share the total moral and religious skepticism characteristic of Western epistemic skepticism." Harrison was not opposed to postmodern criticism; to a considerable degree she felt at home in its rhetoric of subversion and transgression. Much of it was an outgrowth of the same hermeneutic of suspicion that fueled liberation theology. By virtue of being a liberationist, she had much in common with postmodern critiques of authority, rationality, cultural homogeneity, ascribed meaning, and meta-narrative. But postmodern criticism had an undeniable nihilist tendency, she cautioned, and nihilism never liberated anybody. Confronted with "the ever-growing lists of things that the academically sophisticated tell us we cannot claim to know or have no warrant to say," Harrison countered that knowledge is everywhere, everyone can learn, truth is inexhaustible, and the most truth is found when everyone teaches and learns.[144]

She realized how that sounded to postmodernized audiences: "If all this makes me sound 'premodern' or 'modernist,' so be it." If believing in liberation meant that she had to swallow the unfair charge of modernist essentialism, she was willing. But she would not take from postmodern feminists or nihilists the charge that her commitment to feminist liberation was a colonial impulse or a desire for control. Feminist liberation theology was about living towards freedom, refusing to settle for anything less than the claiming of personal and collective female power, she urged. If that conflicted with the spirit of the postmodern age, something was wrong with the spirit of the age.[145]

Harrison roared with passion and anger; at Union Seminary most of the lore about her had something to do with both. She could be rough on colleagues, declaring that most of them were geeky types who started studying "at about age six, when they realized they weren't going to be the football players." Most academics had a "very narrow" sense of being that was confined to the sterile, intellectual, competitive culture of the academy, she judged. But Harrison was known also for building friendships with colleagues, nurturing students, standing up for beleaguered colleagues and students, and enabling a stream of feminist ethicists to enter the field. Having taken 12 years to complete her doctorate, she was usually the last member of the Union faculty to give up on a struggling doctoral student. Her problems with self-organization also entered local lore, as students helped her find her syllabuses and photocopied articles amid the papered chaos of her office. Characteristically, most of Harrison's writing consisted of conference lectures on assigned topics, which she revised for subsequent conferences with little thought of publication; her two essay collections were collected by others.[146]

The first collection, *Making the Connections*, began as an assemblage known as the "Blue Book," which Carol Robb put together in her role as a research associate in women's studies at Harvard Divinity School. The Blue Book circulated among feminist ethicists for several years before growing into a published book. The second collection, *Justice in the Making*, published five years after Harrison retired from Union Seminary in 1999, was produced by six of her former students (Elizabeth M. Bounds, Pamela K. Brubaker, Jane E. Hicks, Marilyn J. Legge, Rebecca Todd Peters, and Traci C. West), all of them active in social ethics. Characteristically, Harrison balked at fashioning a second collection of her scattered articles and lectures. Her former doctoral advisees, knowing the importance of teaching her perspective to the next generation, produced a model collection interwoven with interviews.

Her ethics colleague at Union Seminary, Larry Rasmussen, speaking on the occasion of Harrison's retirement from Union, aptly summarized her legacy with what he called "an audacious claim": that after Harrison, "Christian ethics is a different discipline." Before Harrison, Rasmussen observed, women were excluded from the guild of Christian ethics, as were African Americans. The story of North American social ethics was a litany of white male academics. Even the larger story of North American Christian ethics was a litany of the same figures plus some more white males. Rasmussen noted that Stanley Hauerwas, having recently abandoned his plan to publish a history of the field, had realized belatedly there was something wrong with his manuscript, which consisted entirely of the usual white males. On the one hand, Hauerwas decided against writing a different story; on the other hand, he allowed that the field's historic exclusion of women and African Americans might have indicated "the impoverishment of what it means to be a discipline."[147]

"Impoverishment" was exactly the point, Rasmussen observed. After Beverly Harrison, the field of Christian social ethics was no longer impoverished. It was, instead, a more "robust discipline" than the one she entered.[148]

Notes

1 James H. Cone, *Risks of Faith: The Emergence of a Black Theology of Liberation, 1968–1998* (Boston: Beacon Press, 1999), xvii.

2 Rosa L. Parks to Martin Luther King, Jr, August 26 1955, *The Papers of Martin Luther King. Jr.*, 5 vols., eds. Clayborne Carson, Ralph E. Luker, Penny A. Russell (Berkeley: University of California Press, 1992–2005), 2: 572. This discussion of King adapts material

from Gary Dorrien, *The Making of American Liberal Theology: Crisis, Irony, and Postmodernity* (Louisville: Westminster John Knox, 2006), 143–61. See Martin Luther King, Jr *Stride Toward Freedom: The Montgomery Story* (New York: Harper & Brothers, 1958); King, "Pilgrimage to Nonviolence," *Christian Century* 77 (April 13, 1960), 439–41; Taylor Branch, *Parting the Waters: America in the King Years, 1954–63* (New York: Simon and Schuster, 1988); Kenneth L. Smith and Ira G. Zepp, Jr, *Search for the Beloved Community: The Thinking of Martin Luther King Jr.* (Valley Forge, PA: Judson Press, 1998); Lewis V. Baldwin, *There is a Balm in Gilead: The Cultural Roots of Martin Luther King, Jr.* (Minneapolis: Fortress Press, 1991); Baldwin, *To Make the Wounded Whole: The Cultural Legacy of Martin Luther King, Jr.* (Minneapolis: Fortress Press, 1992); Garth Baker-Fletcher, *Somebodyness: Martin Luther King, Jr., and the Theory of Dignity* (Minneapolis: Fortress Press, 1993); James H. Cone, *Malcolm & Martin & America: A Dream or a Nightmare* (Maryknoll, NY: Orbis Books, 1991); Walter E. Fluker, *They Looked for a City: A Comparative Analysis of the Ideal of Community in the Thought of Howard Thurman and Martin Luther King, Jr.* (Lanham, MD: University Press of America, 1989); David J. Garrow, *Bearing the Cross: Martin Luther King, Jr., and the Southern Christian Leadership Conference* (New York: Quill, 1999); William D. Watley, *Roots of Resistance: The Nonviolent Ethic of Martin Luther King, Jr.* (Valley Forge, PA: Judson Press, 1989); Keith D. Miller, *Voice of Deliverance: The Language of Martin Luther King, Jr., and Its Sources* (New York: Free Press, 1992; reprint, Athens, GA: University of Georgia Press, 1998.

3   Martin Luther King, Jr, "MIA Mass Meeting at Hold Street Baptist Church," December 5, 1955, *The Papers of Martin Luther King Jr.*, 3: 71–4, quotes 72, 73, 74; see Branch, *Parting the Waters: America in the King Years, 1954–63*, 136–42.

4   King, Jr, *Stride Toward Freedom*, 137–8.

5   Martin Luther King, Jr, "The Ethical Demands of Integration," *Religion and Labor* (May 1963), 4; see Anders Nygren, *Agape and Eros*, trans. Philip S. Watson (Philadelphia: Westminster Press, 1953), 75–81; Paul Ramsey, *Basic Christian Ethics* (New York: Charles Scribner's Sons, 1950), 2–3, 13, 94–105; Smith and Zepp, Jr, *Search for the Beloved Community*, 61–6.

6   King, Jr, *Stride Toward Freedom*, 220–1; see Martin Luther King, Jr, "The Power of Nonviolence," "An Experiment in Love," and "Nonviolence: The Only Road to Freedom," in *A Testament of Hope: The Essential Writings and Speeches of Martin Luther King, Jr.*, ed. James Melvin Washington (New York: HarperSanFrancisco, 1986), 12–15, 16–20, 54–61.

7   Martin Luther King, Jr, *The Measure of a Man* (Philadelphia: Pilgrim Press, 1968), 41–59, quotes, 43; see Robert Michael Franklin, *Liberating Visions: Human Fulfillment and Social Justice in African-American Thought* (Minneapolis: Fortress Press, 1990), 104–9. On the relation of "Three Dimensions" and Brooks's sermon, see Miller, *Voice of Deliverance: The Language of Martin Luther King, Jr., and Its Sources*, 75.

8   King, Jr, *The Measure of a Man*, quotes, 26–7, 31.

9   Martin Luther King, Jr, "Man in a Revolutionary World," (July 6, 1965), *Minutes of the Fifth General Synod of the United Church of Christ* (Chicago: United Church of Christ, 1965), 237–8; cited in Ansbro, *Martin Luther King, Jr.: Nonviolent Strategies and Tactics for Social Change*, 22; see Josiah Royce, *The Problem of Christianity*, 2 vols. (New York: Macmillan, 1913), 1:30 172; Rufus Burrow Jr, *God and Human Dignity: The Personalism, Theology and Ethics of Martin Luther King Jr.*, (Notre Dame, IN: University of Notre Dame Press, 2006), 161–2.

10   See Ansbro, *Martin Luther King, Jr.: Nonviolent Strategies and Tactics for Social Change*, 76–86; Burrow, Jr, *Personalism*, 218–22; King, Jr, *Stride Toward Freedom*, 44.

11   Martin Luther King, Jr, *Where Do We Go From Here: Chaos or Community?* (New York: Harper & Row, 1967), quotes, 178, 188, 189.

12   Martin Luther King, Jr, "Declaration of Independence from the War in Vietnam," 4 April 1967, reprinted in *Two, Three . . . Many Vietnams: A Radical Reader on the Wars in Southeast*

Asia and the Conflicts at Home, eds. Banning Garrett and Katherine Barkley (San Francisco: Harper & Row, 1971), 206–15, quotes, 206, 207, 208.

13 Martin Luther King, Jr, "I Have a Dream," 28 August 1963, *The Essential Writings and Speeches of Martin Luther King, Jr.*, 217–20; King, Jr, "Declaration of Independence from the War in Vietnam," 215.

14 See Ralph Abernathy, *And the Walls Came Tumbling Down: An Autobiography* (New York: Harper & Row, 1989); Lewis V. Baldwin, "Abernathy Book Controversial, Marred by Claim," *Nashville Banner* (18 November 1989), D15; Jimmie Lewis Franklin, "Review Essay: Autobiography, the Burden of Friendship, and Truth," *Georgia Historical Quarterly* 74 (Spring 1990), 83–98; Georgia Davis Powers, *I Shared the Dream: The Pride, Passion, and Politics of the First Black Woman Senator From Kentucky* (Far Hills, NJ: New Horizon Press, 1995); David Thelen, "Becoming Martin Luther King, Jr.: An Introduction," *Journal of American History* 78 (June 1991), 13–14; Theodore Pappas, "A Doctor in Spite of Himself: The Strange Career of Martin Luther King, Jr.'s Dissertation," *Chronicles* 15 (January 1991), 25–9; Pappas, *Plagiarism and the Culture War: The Writings of Martin Luther King, Jr., and Other Prominent Americans* (Tampa, FL: Hallberg Publishing Corporation, 1998), 85–103; Martin Luther King, Jr, Papers Project, "The Student Papers of Martin Luther King, Jr.: A Summary Statement on Research," *The Journal of American History* 78 (June 1991), 23–31; David Levering Lewis, "Failing to Know Martin Luther King, Jr.," ibid., 81–5; David J. Garrow, "King's Plagiarism: Imitation, Insecurity, and Transformation," 86–92; Clayborne Carson, with Peter Holloran, Ralph E. Luker, and Penny Russell, "Martin Luther King, Jr., as Scholar: A Reexamination of His Theological Writings," ibid., 93–105; John Higham, "Habits of the Cloth and Standards of the Academy," ibid., 106–10; Bernice Johnson Reagan, " 'Nobody Knows the Trouble I See': or, 'By and By I'm Gonna Lay Down My Heavy Load,' " ibid., 111–19; Keith D. Miller, "Martin Luther King, Jr., and the Black Folk Pulpit," ibid., 120–3; Miller, "Composing Martin Luther King, Jr.," 70–82; Miller, *Voice of Deliverance: The Language of Martin Luther King, Jr., and Its Sources*; David J. Garrow, "The Intellectual Development of Martin Luther King, Jr.: Influences and Commentaries," *Martin Luther King, Jr.: Civil Rights Leader, Theologian, Orator*, 3 vols., ed. David J. Garrow (New York: Carlson Publishing, 1989), 2: 443; Walter G. Muelder, "Philosophical and Theological Influences in the Thought and Action of Martin Luther King, Jr." *Debate & Understanding* 1 (Fall 1977), 179–89; King, *Where Do We Go From Here: Chaos or Community?* quotes, 43, 55.

15 James H. Cone, *My Soul Looks Back* (Maryknoll, NY: Orbis Books, 1986), 42–3.

16 Ibid., quotes 20, 22.

17 Ibid., quotes 21, 25.

18 Ibid., quote 29.

19 Ibid., quote 34.

20 Ibid., "the failure," 37; Cone, *Risks of Faith: The Emergence of a Black Theology of Liberation, 1968–1998*, "devastated," xv; James H. Cone, "*Martin & Malcolm & America*: A Response by James Cone," *Union Seminary Quarterly Review* 48 (1994), 52–7, "I hardly," 53.

21 Cone, *My Soul Looks Back*, 44.

22 Cone's first publication, an essay on "Christianity and Black Power," was rejected by the *Christian Century* and *Motive* magazines before Lincoln published it in his book *Is Anybody Listening to Black America?* ed. C. Eric Lincoln (New York: Seabury Press, 1968), 3–9; see Cone, *My Soul Looks Back*, 140, n.2.

23 Cone, *My Soul Looks Back*, quotes 46, 47; see "Statement by the National Committee of Negro Churchmen," July 31, 1966, reprinted in *Black Theology: A Documentary History*, 2 vols., eds. James H. Cone and Gayraud S. Wilmore (2nd edn., revised, Maryknoll, NY: Orbis Books, 1993), 1: 19–26; Gayraud S. Wilmore, *Black Religion and Black Radicalism: An Interpretation of the Religious History of African Americans* (3rd edn, rev., Maryknoll, NY: Orbis Books, 1998), 226–30. Wilmore was one of the 48 original signatories of the National Committee statement.

24 Cone, *My Soul Looks Back*, quotes 47, 48.

25 James H. Cone, *Black Theology and Black Power* (New York: Harper & Row, 1969; 2nd edn., 1989; reprint, Maryknoll, NY: Orbis Books, 2005), quotes 6, 22, 23.

26 Ibid., quotes 56.

27 Ibid., quotes 15–16.

28 Ibid., 27–8, 68.

29 Ibid., quotes 68, 48, 111.

30 Ibid., 113–14.

31 James Forman, "The Black Manifesto," adopted by the National Black Economic Development Conference, Detroit, Michigan, April 26, 1969, reprinted in *Black Theology: A Documentary History*, 1: 27–36, quotes 33, 35; Robert T. Handy, *A History of Union Theological Seminary in New York* (New York: Columbia University Press, 1987), 280–3. The Black Manifesto was originally called "Manifesto to the White Christian Churches and the Jewish Synagogues." Most of the additional $1 million was raised by 1974.

32 *African Congress: A Documentary of the First Modern Pan-African Congress*, ed. Amiri Baraka/ LeRoi Jones (New York: Morrow, 1972); Cone, *My Soul Looks Back*, quotes 55, 57; see James H. Cone, "Black Theology and the Black College Student," *Journal of Afro-American Issues* 4 (Summer/Fall 1976), 420–30.

33 Cone, *My Soul Looks Back*, 72.

34 Ibid., 73.

35 James H. Cone, *A Black Theology of Liberation* (Philadelphia: J. B. Lippincott, 1970; 20th anniversary edition, Maryknoll, NY: Orbis Books, 1990), quotes 5, 7, 8, 9.

36 Ibid., 10.

37 Ibid., quotes 25.

38 Ibid., quotes, 30, 56, 57, 63.

39 Ibid., 64, 65.

40 Ibid., 65, 66; James H. Cone, "Black Theology on Revolution, Violence, and Reconciliation," *Union Seminary Quarterly Review* 31 (Fall 1975), 5–14, "nothing to do," 13.

41 Cone, "Black Theology on Revolution, Violence, and Reconciliation," quotes 5–6, 10, 13, 14.

42 Andrew M. Greeley, "Nazi Mentality in this Country," *Inter/Syndicate* (1971), 1971; *Malcolm X Speaks*, ed. George Breitman (New York: Grove Press, 1966), 165; James H. Cone, "Preface to the 1986 Edition," *A Black Theology of Liberation*, xii–xiii, quote xiv.

43 See Paul Lehmann, *The Transfiguration of Politics* (New York: Harper & Row, 1975), 259–75; James H. Cone and William Hordern, "Dialogue on Black Theology," *Christian Century* 88 (September 15, 1971), 1079–82; Frederick Herzog, *Liberation Theology* (New York: Seabury Press, 1972); Peter C. Hodgson, *Children of Freedom: Black Liberation in Christian Perspective* (Philadelphia: Fortress Press, 1974); Hodgson, *New Birth of Freedom: A Theology of Bondage and Liberation* (Philadelphia: Fortress Press, 1976); Helmut Gollwitzer, "Why Black Theology?" *Union Seminary Quarterly Review* 31 (Fall 1975), 38–58; John C. Bennett, *The Radical Imperative: From Theology to Social Ethics* (Philadelphia: Westminster Press, 1975), 126–8.

44 Paul Lehmann, "Black Theology and 'Christian' Theology," *Union Seminary Quarterly Review* 31 (Fall 1975), 31–7.

45 Frederick Herzog, "Theology at the Crossroads," *Union Seminary Quarterly Review* 31 (Fall 1975), 59–70, quote 61.

46 Mary Daly, *Beyond God the Father: Toward a Philosophy of Women's Liberation* (1973, reprint, Boston: Beacon Press, 1985), 25.

47 Rosemary Radford Ruether, *Liberation Theology: Human Hope Confronts Christian History and American Power* (New York: Paulist Press, 1972), 134–7, quote 137.

48 Ibid., 137–9, quotes 137, 138.

49 J. Deotis Roberts, *Liberation and Reconciliation: A Black Theology* (Philadelphia, PA: Westminster Press, 1971; 2nd edn., Maryknoll, NY: Orbis Books, 1994), quotes 5, 75–6.

50 J. Deotis Roberts, *Black Theology Today: Liberation and Contextualization* (New York: Edwin Mellen, 1983), 39.

51 James H. Cone, *God of the Oppressed* (San Francisco: HarperCollins, 1975), 239–40; Cone, "'Let Suffering Speak': The Vocation of a Black Intellectual," in *Cornel West: A Critical Reader*, ed. George Yancy (Oxford: Blackwell, 2001), 111; author's conversation with James H. Cone, April 5, 2006.

52 James H. Cone, "Black Theology and Ideology: A Response to my Respondents," *Union Seminary Quarterly Review* 31 (Fall 1975), 71–86, quotes 72; Major Jones, *Christian Ethics for a Black Theology* (Nashville: Abingdon Press, 1974), 72; Preston Williams, "James Cone and the Problem of a Black Ethic," *Harvard Theological Review* 65 (October 1972), 485–8; Cone, *God of the Oppressed*, "could be," 203.

53 Charles H. Long, "Perspectives for a Study of Afro-American Religion in the United States," *History of Religion* 11 (August 1971), 54–66; Long, "Structural Similarities and Dissimilarities in Black and African Theologies," *Journal of Religious Thought* 32 (Fall/Winter 1975), 9–24; Gayraud S. Wilmore, *Black Religion and Black Radicalism* (Garden City, NY: Doubleday, 1972); Cecil Cone, *Identity Crisis in Black Theology* (Nashville: African Methodist Episcopal Church, 1975); Cecil W. Cone; "The Black Religious Experience," *Journal of the Interdenominational Theological Center* 2 (Spring 1975), 137–9; James H. Cone, *For My People: Black Theology and the Black Church* (Maryknoll, NY: Orbis Books, 1984), 78–98.

54 Cone, *My Soul Looks Back*, "I was," 60–1; James H. Cone, *The Spirituals and the Blues* (1st edn., 1972; reprint, Maryknoll, NY: Orbis Books, 1991).

55 Cone, *God of the Oppressed*, 97, 124.

56 James H. Cone, "The Black Church and Marxism: What Do They Have to Say to Each Other?" (pamphlet) (New York: Institute for Democratic Socialism, 1980), 9–10; see Cone, "Black Theology and Third World Theologies," *Chicago Theological Seminary Register* 73 (Winter 1983), 3–12.

57 James H. Cone, "A Black American Perspective on the Future of African Theology," Pan-African Conference of Third World Theologians, December 17–24, 1977, Accra, Ghana, reprinted in *Black Theology: A Documentary History*, 1: 393–403; Cone, "Black Theology and Third World Theologies," Fifth International Conference of the Ecumenical Association of Third World Theologians, August 17–29, 1981, New Delhi, India, reprinted in *Black Theology: A Documentary History*, 2: 388–98; John Mbiti, "An African Views American Black Theology," *Worldview* 17 (August 1974), reprinted in *Black Theology: A Documentary History*, 1: 379–84, quote 380; see Mbiti, *African Religions and Philosophy*(2nd edn., Gaborone, Botswana: Heinemann Educational Books, 1990).

58 Cone, *My Soul Looks Back*, quotes, 115–16.

59 Ibid., 118.

60 James H. Cone, *Martin & Malcolm & America: A Dream or a Nightmare* (Maryknoll, NY: Orbis Books, 1991), 246–71, quotes, 316, 318.

61 Cone, *Risks of Faith*, "When I hear," 130; see Gayraud S. Wilmore, "A Revolution Unfulfilled, but not Invalidated," postscript to Cone, *A Black Theology of Liberation*, 20th anniversary edition, 145–63.

62 Cone, *Risks of Faith*, 136; James H. Cone, "Theology's Great Sin: Silence in the Face of White Supremacy," *Union Seminary Quarterly Review* 55 (2001), 1–14, "no day," 12.

63 Cone, *Risks of Faith*, quotes 135–6; adapted from James H. Cone, "Looking Back, Going Forward: Black Theology as Public Theology," *Black Faith and Public Talk: Critical Essays on James H. Cone's Black Theology & Black Power*, ed. Dwight N. Hopkins (Maryknoll, NY: Orbis Books, 1999), 246–59; Cone, *Martin & Malcolm & America: A Response by James Cone*," 56; James H. Cone, "Strange Fruit: The Cross and the Lynching Tree,"

Harvard Divinity Bulletin 35 (Winter 2007), 47–55; author's discussion with Cone, September 12, 2007.

64   See Elizabeth Cady Stanton, et. al., *The Woman's Bible, Part 1, Comments on Genesis, Exodus, Leviticus, Numbers and Deuteronomy* (New York: European Publishing Company, 1895); *The Woman's Bible, Part 2, Comments on the Old and New Testaments from Joshua to Revelation* (New York: European Publishing Co., 1898); (reprint, parts 1 and 2, New York: Arno Press, 1972); 142; Barbara Brown Zikmund, "The Struggle for the Right to Preach," *Women and Religion in America; Volume 1; The Nineteenth Century*, eds. Rosemary Radford Ruether and Rosemary Skinner Keller (San Francisco: Harper & Row, 1981), 193–241; Zikmund, "Winning Ordination for Women in Mainstream Protestant Churches," *Women and Religion in America; Volume 3; 1900–1968*, eds. Rosemary Radford Ruether and Rosemary Skinner Keller (San Francisco: Harper & Row, 1986), 339–48; Constant H. Jacquet, Jr, *Women Ministers in 1977* (New York: Office of Research, Evaluation and Planning, National Council of Churches, March 1978); Virginia Lieson Brereton and Christa Ressmeyer Klein, "American Women in Ministry: A History of Protestant Beginning Points," *Women of Spirit: Female Leadership in the Jewish and Christian Traditions*, eds. Rosemary Radford Ruether and Eleanor Mclaughlin (New York: Simon and Schuster, 1979), 301–32.

65   Mary Daly, *Outercourse: The Be-Dazzling Voyage* (San Francisco: HarperCollins, 1992), 42–53, quotes 42, 48.

66   Ibid., 55–70, quotes 55, 58, 59, 67, 60; see Mary Daly, "Autobiographical Preface to the Colophon Edition," Daly, *The Church and the Second Sex* (New York: Harper & Row, 1975), 8–10, reprinted as "Autobiographical Preface to the 1975 Edition," Daly, *The Church and the Second Sex* (Boston: Beacon Press, 1985).

67   Daly, *Outercourse: The Be-Dazzling Voyage*, quote 70.

68   Ibid., quote, 74; Mary Daly, *Natural Knowledge of God in the Philosophy of Jacques Maritain* (Rome: Catholic Book Agency, 1966).

69   Betty Friedan, *The Feminine Mystique* (London: Victor Gollancz, 1963); Rosemary Lauer, "Women and the Church," *Commonweal* 79 (December 20,1963), 365–8.

70   Lauer, "Women and the Church," quotes 365, 368.

71   Mary Daly, letter on "Women and the Church," *Commonweal* (February 14, 1964), quote 603.

72   Mary Daly, "A Built–in Bias," *Commonweal* 81 (January 15, 1965), 508–11; Daly, "Catholic Women and the Modern Era," *Wir schweigen nicht länger! – We Won't Keep Silence Any Longer!* ed. Gertrud Heinzelmann (Zurich: Interfeminas Verlag, 1965), 106–10; Daly, *Outercourse: The Be-Dazzling Voyage*, 77–9; Daly, "Autobiographical Preface to the 1975 Edition," quotes, 9, 10.

73   Daly, "Autobiographical Preface to the 1975 Edition," "and I knew," 11; Daly, *Outercourse: The Be-Dazzling Voyage*, "like a Call," 78; Simone de Beauvoir, *The Second Sex*, trans. H. M. Parshley (New York: Alfred A. Knopf, 1953); Daly, *The Church and the Second Sex*, 56–69.

74   Daly, *The Church and the Second Sex*, 74–90, quote 88.

75   Ibid., 74–123, quote 121.

76   Elisabeth Schüssler, *Priester für Gott: Studien Zum Herrschafts- und Priestermotiv in der Apokalypse* (Münster: Aeschendorff, 1972); Rosemary Radford Ruether, *The Church Against Itself: An Inquiry into the Conditions of Historical Existence for the Eschatological Community* (New York: Herder and Herder, 1967), quote 235; Rosemary Radford Ruether, "A Question of Dignity, A Question of Freedom," *What Modern Catholics Think about Birth Control*, ed. William Birmingham (New York: New American Library, 1964), 233–40.

77   Daly, *The Church and the Second Sex*, 123–65, quote 134.

78   Ibid., quotes 176, 177, 180.

79   Ibid., quotes 184, 186; Gabriel Moran, F.S.C., "The God of Revelation," *Commonweal* 85 (February 10, 1967), 499–503.

80 Daly, *The Church and the Second Sex*, 192–219, quotes 205; the encyclical was John XXIII's "*Pacem in Terris*" (Peace on Earth, 1963).

81 Daly, *The Church and the Second Sex*, quote 212.

82 Ibid., quotes 220–1, 223.

83 Rosemary Ruether, review of *The Church and the Second Sex*, by Mary Daly, *Sexuality and Moral Responsibility*, by Robert P. O'Neill and Michael A. Donovan, and *Beyond Birth Control, The Christian Experience of Sex*, by Sidney C. Callahan, *Theology Today* 26 (April 1969); Myrtle Passantino, review of *The Church and the Second Sex*, by Mary Daly, *America* (May 11, 1968), 646; review of *The Church and the Second Sex*, by Mary Daly, *Time* 91 (April 19, 1968), 71; Genevieve Casey, review of *The Church and the Second Sex*, by Mary Daly, *Library Journal Book Review 1968* (New York: R. R. Bowker, 1969), 391; Don Browning, review of *The Church and the Second Sex*, by Mary Daly, and *Beyond Birth Control: The Christian Experience of Sex*, by Sidney C. Callahan, *The Christian Century* 85 (July 24, 1968), 944–5.

84 Daly, *Outercourse: The Be-Dazzling Voyage*, 102; Daly, "Autobiographical Preface to the 1975 Edition," "it was," 13.

85 Mary Daly, "Mary Daly on the Church," *Commonweal* 91 (November 14, 1969), "I am still," 215; Daly, *Outercourse: The Be-Dazzling Voyage*, 93–7; Daly, "Autobiographical Preface to the 1975 Edition," "something had" and "it was" quotes, 13.

86 Mary Daly, "The Courage to See: Religious Implications of the New Sisterhood," *Christian Century* 88 (22 September 1971), 1108–11; see Gregory Baum, *Man Becoming* (New York: Herder & Herder, 1970).

87 Daly, "Autobiographical Preface to the 1975 Edition," "the I," 14; Daly, *Outercourse: The Be-Dazzling Voyage*, "I had," 103.

88 Daly, *Outercourse: The Be-Dazzling Voyage*, "by 1970," 104.

89 Mary Daly, "The Women's Movement: An Exodus Community," *Religious Education* 67 (September–October 1972), 327–33, quotes 330, 331, 332; Daly, "After the Death of God the Father," *Commonweal* 94 (March 12, 1971), 7–11.

90 Daly, *Beyond God the Father: Toward a Philosophy of Women's Liberation*, 45–6.

91 Ibid., 47.

92 Ibid., 98–131, quotes 131.

93 Daly, *Gyn/Ecology: The Metaethics of Radical Feminism* (Boston: Beacon Press, 1990), quotes 39, 29.

94 Mary Daly, "Feminist Postchristian Introduction: A Critical Review of *The Church and the Second Sex*, written from the perspective of 1975 A.F. (Anno Feminarum)," in Daly, *The Church and the Second Sex*, 15–51, quotes 22, 25, 41–2, 43, 49.

95 Mary Daly, "Original Re-Introduction," preface to the 1985 edition of Daly, *Beyond God the Father*, quotes xii; see Mary Daly, *Pure Lust: Elemental Feminist Philosophy* (Boston: Beacon Press, 1984).

96 Daly, "Original Re-Introduction," quote xviii; see Daly, *Gyn/Ecology*, 27–9.

97 See Rosemary Radford Ruether, *Sexism and God-Talk: Toward a Feminist Theology* (2nd edn., Boston: Beacon Press, 1993); Ruether, *Gaia & God: An Ecofeminist Theology of Earth Healing* (San Francisco: HarperSanFrancisco, 1992); Ruether, *Women and Redemption: A Theological History* (Minneapolis: Fortress Press, 1998).

98 Beverly W. Harrison, interview with Traci C. West, "Making Connections: Becoming a Feminist Ethicist," in Beverly Wildung Harrison, *Justice in the Making: Feminist Social Ethics*, eds. Elizabeth M. Bounds, Pamela K. Brubaker, Jane E. Hicks, Marilyn J. Legge, Rebecca Todd Peters, and Traci C. West (Louisville: Westminster John Knox Press, 2004), 6; Beverly Wildung Harrison, "Keeping Faith in a Sexist Church: Not for Women Only," (1977, 1979) in Harrison, *Making the Connections: Essays in Feminist Social Ethics*, ed. Carol S. Robb (Boston: Beacon Press, 1985), 206–34, quotes 207.

99 Harrison, "Keeping Faith in a Sexist Church: Not for Women Only," 208–9; Vita of Beverly (Jean) Wildung Harrison, Office of Communication, Union Theological

Seminary, New York; see Robert McAfee Brown, *Reflections over the Long Haul: A Memoir* (Louisville: Westminster John Knox Press, 2005), 73–80.

100   Harrison, "Keeping Faith in a Sexist Church: Not for Women Only," 209–10.

101   Ibid., 210.

102   Ibid., 211.

103   Ibid., 212; Vita of Beverly (Jean) Wildung Harrison; Handy, *A History of Union Theological Seminary in New York*, 260.

104   Harrison, "Keeping Faith in a Sexist Church," 212–13.

105   Harrison, interview with West, "Making Connections: Becoming a Feminist Ethicist," "my identification," 7; see Beverly W. Harrison, "H. Richard Niebuhr: Towards a Christian Moral Philosophy," Ph.D. dissertation, Union Theological Seminary, New York, 1974.

106   Handy, *A History of Union Theological Seminary in New York*, 322–3; see Beverly W. Harrison, "Sexism and the Contemporary Church: When Evasion Becomes Complacency," *Sexist Religion and Women in the Church: No More Silence!* ed. Alice L. Hageman (New York: Association Press, 1974), 195–216; Harrison, "The Early Feminists and the Clergy," *Review and Expositor* 72 (1975), 41–52. I was one of the armbanded pro–Harrison protesters at Union's 1978 commencement.

107   Beverly W. Harrison, "The Power of Anger in the Work of Love: Christian Ethics for Women and Other Strangers," *Union Seminary Quarterly Review* 36 (1981), 41–57, reprinted in Harrison, *Making the Connections: Essays in Feminist Social Ethics*, 3–21, quotes 5; see Phyllis Trible, "A Meditation in Mourning: The Sacrifice of the Daughter of Jephthah," *Union Seminary Quarterly Review* 36 (1981), 59–73.

108   Harrison, "The Power of Anger in the Work of Love: Christian Ethics for Women and Other Strangers," 5–6.

109   Ibid., 7–8; see *Sisterhood is Powerful: An Anthology of Writings from the Women's Liberation Movement*, ed. Robin Morgan (New York: Random House, 1970).

110   Harrison, "The Power of Anger in the Work of Love: Christian Ethics for Women and Other Strangers," 10–11, quote 11; on Daly's subjective idealism, Harrison agreed with the analysis of Carter Heyward, "Speaking and Sparking; Building and Burning," *Christianity and Crisis* 39 (April 2, 1979), 69.

111   Harrison, "The Power of Anger in the Work of Love: Christian Ethics for Women and Other Strangers," 18–19.

112   Beverly W. Harrison, *Our Right to Choose: Toward a New Ethic of Abortion* (Boston: Beacon Press, 1983), quote 14.

113   Beverly W. Harrison, with Shirley Cloyes, "Theology and Morality of Procreative Choice," adapted version of articles published in 1981 and 1982 (*The Witness* 64 [July and September, 1981] and *Abortion: The Moral Issues*, ed. Edward Batchelor [New York: Pilgrim Press, 1982]) in Harrison, *Making the Connections: Essays in Feminist Social Ethics*, 115–134, "the heavy," 115; Harrison, *Our Right to Choose: Toward a New Ethic of Abortion*, "what am," 9. On the problems of "discrete deed" approaches to ethics, see H. Richard Niebuhr, "The Christian Church and the World's Crisis," *Christianity and Society* 6 (1941), 1–7, cited by Harrison; see Andrew H. Merton, *Enemies of Choice: The Right-to-Life Movement and Its Threat to Abortion* (Boston: Beacon Press, 1981).

114   Harrison, *Our Right to Choose: Toward a New Ethic of Abortion*, quotes 3, 16.

115   Ibid., 154–230, quotes 198–9.

116   Ibid., 197, 216.

117   Ibid., 226–259, quotes 229, 249.

118   Judy Weidman, review of *Our Right to Choose: Toward a New Ethic of Abortion*, by Beverly W. Harrison, *Christian Century* 100 (November 16, 1983), 1056; Jean Lambert, review of ibid., *Journal of Religion* 66 (January 1986), 90–1; Peter J. Paris, review of ibid., *Theological Education* 24 (Autumn 1987), 134–6; Nathan Kollar, review of ibid., *Journal of the American*

Academy of Religion 54 (Spring 1986), 175–6; Lisa Sowle Cahill, review of ibid., *Horizons* 11 (Spring 1984), 202–3.

119 Beverly W. Harrison, "The Role of Social Theory in Religious Social Ethics: Reconsidering the Case for Marxian Political Economy," original edition presented as a paper to a social ethics section of the American Academy of Religion, 1980; revised edition in Harrison, *Making the Connections: Essays in Feminist Social Ethics*, 54–80, quotes 60.

120 Ibid., 61–2.

121 Ibid., quotes 63, 60.

122 Ibid., 63–7, quote 65.

123 Ibid., 66–7.

124 US Conference of Catholic Bishops, *Economic Justice for All: Catholic Social Teaching and the U.S. Economy* (1986), reprinted in *Catholic Social Thought: The Documentary Heritage*, eds. David J. O'Brien and Thomas A. Shannon (Maryknoll, NY: Orbis Books, 2004), 572–680, quotes 609.

125 Beverly W. Harrison, "Theology, Economics, and the Church," lecture at Episcopal Divinity School, May 5, 1986, reprinted in Harrison, *Justice in the Making: Feminist Social Ethics*, 172–184, quotes 175.

126 Ibid., quotes 175.

127 Ibid., 175–7; see Beverly W. Harrison, "Socialism–Capitalism," *Dictionary of Feminist Theologies*, eds. Letty M. Russell and J. Shannon Clarkson (Louisville: Westminster John Knox Press, 1996), 264–6, and Harrison, *Justice in the Making: Feminist Social Ethics*, 162–5.

128 Harrison, "Theology, Economics, and the Church," quotes 177.

129 Ibid., quotes 182, 183.

130 Ibid., quotes 181, 182.

131 Beverly W. Harrison, interview by Elizabeth M. Bounds, "Working with Protestant Traditions: Liberalism and Beyond," in Harrison, *Justice in the Making: Feminist Social Ethics*, 79–84, quote 80.

132 Beverly W. Harrison, review of *Labor–Religion Prophet: The Times and Life of Harry F. Ward*, by Eugene P. Link, *Union Seminary Quarterly Review* 39 (1984), 316–22, reprinted in Harrison, *Justice in the Making: Feminist Social Ethics*, 92–7, "unrelenting," 96; Harrison, "Working with Protestant Traditions: Liberalism and Beyond," "I was," 81.

133 Beverly W. Harrison, interview by Rebecca Todd Peters, "Reflecting on the Relationship between Politics and Economics," in Harrison, *Justice in the Making: Feminist Social Ethics*, 157–61, quotes 157, 159.

134 Mud Flower Collective, *God's Fierce Whimsy: Christian Feminism and Theological Education* (New York: Pilgrim Press, 1985), quote 10.

135 Ibid., 14–15.

136 Ibid., 90; Harrison, "Making Connections: Becoming a Feminist Ethicist," quote 8.

137 Mud Flower Collective, *God's Fierce Whimsy: Christian Feminism and Theological Education*, 111–12.

138 Beverly W. Harrison, "Human Sexuality and Mutuality," in *Christian Feminism: Visions of a New Humanity*, ed. Judith L. Weidman (San Francisco: Harper & Row, 1984), 141–57, reprinted in Harrison, *Social Justice in the Making: Feminist Social Ethics*, 53–65, quotes 63.

139 Ibid., 63.

140 Beverly W. Harrison, "Feminist Thea(o)logies at the Millennium: 'Messy' Continued Resistance or Surrender to Postmodern Academic Culture?" in *Liberating Eschatology: Essays in Honor of Letty M. Russell*, eds. Margaret A. Farley and Serene Jones (Louisville: Westminster John Knox Press, 1999), 156–71, reprinted in Harrison, *Social Justice in the Making: Feminist Social Ethics*, 113–28, quote 115; see *Horizons in Feminist Theology: Identity, Tradition, and Norms*, eds. Rebecca S. Chopp and Sheila Greeve Davaney (Minneapolis:

Fortress Press, 1997); Mary McClintock Fulkerson, *Changing the Subject: Women's Discourses and Feminist Theology* (Minneapolis: Fortress Press, 1994); *Transfigurations: Theology and the French Feminists*, eds. C. W. Maggie Kim, Susan M. St Ville, and Susan M. Simonaitis (Minneapolis: Fortress Press, 1993); Daphne Hampson, *Theology and Feminism* (Cambridge, MA: Basil Blackwell, 1990); *Woman-Spirit Rising: A Feminist Reader in Religion*, eds. Carol Christ and Judith Plaskow (New York: Harper & Row, 1979).

141 Harrison, "Feminist Thea(o)logies at the Millennium: 'Messy' Continued Resistance or Surrender to Postmodern Academic Culture?" quote 117.

142 Ibid., quotes 117, 116, Harrison quoted a remark by Russell and Clarkson at the publication party for their book *Dictionary of Feminist Theologies*, eds. Letty M. Russell and J. Shannon Clarkson (Louisville: Westminster John Knox Press, 1996) at the 1997 American Academy of Religion meeting in San Francisco.

143 Ibid., quote 118; see Judith Butler, *Gender Trouble: Feminism and the Subversion of Identity* (New York: Routledge, Chapman & Hall, 1990); Butler, *Excitable Speech* (Berkeley: University of California Press, 1998).

144 Harrison, "Feminist Thea(o)logies at the Millennium: 'Messy' Continued Resistance or Surrender to Postmodern Academic Culture?" quotes 122, 123.

145 Ibid., quote 125.

146 Harrison quote, *God's Fierce Whimsy: Christian Feminism and Theological Education*, 93.

147 Larry Rasmussen, "A Different Discipline," *Union Seminary Quarterly Review* 53 (1999), 29–51, quote 29; see Stanley Hauerwas, "Christian Ethics in America (and the *Journal of Religious Ethics*): A Report on a Book I Will Not Write," *Journal of Religious Ethics* 25 (1998), quote 72; reprinted in Hauerwas, *A Better Hope: Resources for a Church Confronting Capitalism, Democracy, and Postmodernity* (Grand Rapids, MI: Brazos Press, 2000), 55–69.

148 Rasmussen, "A Different Discipline," quote 30.

Chapter 7

Disputing and Expanding
the Tradition

Carl F. H. Henry, John Howard Yoder, Stanley Hauerwas,
Michael Novak, and Jim Wallis

Liberation theology was the first movement in the leading seminaries and divinity schools to radically question whether modern theology and ethics had been working with the right topics. Yet even liberation theology was essentially continuous with the social gospel and Christian realist traditions, not a fundamental break from them. Otherwise it would not have found a home in leading seminaries and divinity schools. Liberation theology took for granted the tools of liberal criticism, and much of the liberationist critique of oppression, structural evil, and social redemption came straight from the social gospel and Christian realist traditions, drawing from the same liberal, radical, and socialist wellsprings that inspired the social gospelers and Niebuhrians.

But for evangelicals and neoconservatives the continuities of the dominant social ethical tradition were more problematic. For Carl F. H. Henry, a conservative evangelical, modern theology and ethics were misguided betrayals of Christian orthodoxy. For John Howard Yoder, an Anabaptist evangelical, the social ethics tradition was a seriously mistaken offshoot of liberal theology and the magisterial Reformation. For Stanley Hauerwas, an evangelical Methodist provocateur, Yoder's Radical Reformationist critique was basically right, though Hauerwas had a more complex relationship with mainline social ethics. For Michael Novak, a Catholic neoconservative, the problem was essentially ideological; Niebuhrian realism in its mid-century phase was a salutary development, but the social gospel was a disaster, post-1965 liberalism was worse, and liberation theology was worse yet. Neoconservatism was a political corrective to the leftist biases of social ethics. For Jim Wallis, a progressive evangelical activist, the social ethical tradition was problematic for excluding evangelicals and for lumping evangelical pacifists with the "Christ against culture" category, but the greater problem was that evangelicals betrayed their own prophetic heritage in their lurch to the political Right.

In the late 1940s a group of young fundamentalists proposed to reclaim Christianity and American society for a renewed Protestant orthodoxy. Carl F. H. Henry, Edward J. Carnell, Harold J. Ockenga, and Billy Graham were foremost among them. They took it for granted that modern theology and its social ethical offshoot were heterodox; on the other hand, they were determined to overcome the anti-intellectual and separatist spirit of fundamentalism. The "new evangelicals," as they sometimes called themselves, sought to restore Protestant orthodoxy to a place of respect in American culture and reclaim the gospel mandate to redeem society. They allowed that the social gospel had been right to claim that Christianity had a social mission; otherwise liberal Protestantism was a colossal mistake that had to be overturned.

Carl F. H. Henry and the New Evangelicalism

Carl Henry was the leading theologian and social ethicist of the new evangelicalism. The son of German immigrants who settled in New York and changed the family name from Heinrich during World War I, he converted to evangelical Protestantism at the age of 20 while working as a journalist. Afterwards Henry attended Wheaton College, where he met Graham and Carnell and was influenced by philosophy professor Gordon Clark. He earned a doctorate in philosophy at Boston University and began his teaching career at Northern Baptist Theological Seminary in Chicago, where he dreamed of an upgraded fundamentalist orthodoxy.

Henry and Carnell knew from close acquaintance that America's elite theological schools ignored the intellectual heroes of American fundamentalism. Barely a generation after Benjamin B. Warfield, Reuben A. Torrey, and J. Gresham Machen waged an epochal battle for the mainline Protestant churches, they were not taken seriously enough even to be dismissed. Henry and Carnell got the message: to the academy, "fundamentalist intellectual" was an oxymoron. They vowed to change that impression. In 1945 a group of evangelicals led by Ockenga founded the National Association of Evangelicals as an alternative to the Federal Council of Churches. The following year they founded Fuller Theological Seminary in Pasadena, California, where Henry and Carnell joined the faculty. In 1947, only a few weeks before Fuller Seminary opened its doors, Henry published a manifesto for a new fundamentalism, calling off his movement's generational retreat from the world.[1]

American fundamentalism derived from the conservative reaction against liberal Protestant trends of the late nineteenth and early twentieth centuries. By name it was an inter-denominational movement to uphold the literal truth of "fundamental" Christian doctrines. In 1875 conservative evangelicals launched the Niagara Bible Conference, the prototype for hundreds of conferences at which conservatives defended the fundamentals. Three years later the Niagara Conference listed 14 fundamentals, one of which, dispensational eschatology, was of very recent vintage in Christian history. From the beginning the fundamentalist movement asserted that all Christian doctrines rested on the doctrine of biblical inerrancy: if the Bible contained any errors, it could not be God's Word; and if it was not God's verbally inspired Word, it could not be a secure source of religious authority. A few fundamentalist theologians, notably James Orr, rejected inerrancy doctrine, but the movement as a whole opted overwhelmingly for it; by 1910, inerrancy doctrine defined fundamentalism. Some fundamentalists denied that premillennial eschatology, or at least its dispensational version, belonged on the list of fundamentals, but they became a distinct minority in early twentieth-century fundamentalism.[2]

Millennialism is the idea of a utopian kingdom of God on earth, usually lasting 1,000 years. Historically, Christian eschatology had three streams of thought in this area: amillennialism, premillennialism, and postmillennialism. The dominant Christian tradition, amillennialism, denied or lacked millennial expectation. Augustine taught that the kingdom of God was spiritual, not social or political, which convinced Pope Gregory I, most of the papal tradition, Thomas Aquinas, Martin Luther, and John

Calvin. Augustine developed his view against the premillennial eschatology of the early church, especially its Greek-speaking Eastern theologians. Premillennialists taught that Christ would return to earth to establish an earthly kingdom. The Radical Reformation went back to this chiliastic view of the kingdom, as did most of the Puritans who settled New England, although neither tradition prescribed a detailed scheme. The postmillennial view interpreted the kingdom of God as a historical utopia in which the world would be Christianized through evangelism and social transformation. In this interpretation the reign of God was realized before Christ returned; thus the return of Christ was postmillennial. A good many in the Calvinist tradition were postmillennial, notably Jonathan Edwards, as were John and Charles Wesley, and the Methodist and social gospel traditions.

In the nineteenth century many groups proclaimed that the world was in its last days. People could be saved in history, but history had no future and was not worth saving. This sense of worldly futility and darkness fueled the preaching of John Nelson Darby (1800–82), an Irish sectarian and former Anglican priest who preached in the American midwest and northeast, converting the Plymouth Brethren movement to his spiritual vision. Darby taught that God had one plan of salvation for an earthly people (Israel) and a separate plan for a heavenly people (the Christian church). To read the Bible rightly was to "rightly divide" it between these two programs, interpreting every passage literally in terms of its dispensational context. The Bible described seven dispensations in which God tested humanity, each of which ended with a catastrophic divine judgment for humanity's failure to meet the test. The first dispensation ended with the human Fall from sin and expulsion from Eden, the second with the Flood, the third with the Tower of Babel, the fourth with the end of the Hebrew exodus from Egypt, the fifth was the period of the Law from Exodus 12 to Acts 1 (Pentecost), and the sixth was the age of the church. The seventh dispensation was the millennial reign of Jesus in Jerusalem.[3]

For Darby, the Bible was a kind of secret code containing divine messages about the future of the world. To read the Bible truly was to crack its code, perceiving that a seemingly obscure passage in Daniel 9 actually contained a precise prediction of the end of the fifth dispensation, the inauguration and history of the church, and the arrival of the future messianic age. Daniel 9:24–7 referred to a 70-week period "to put an end to sin and to atone for iniquity." Reasoning that "70 weeks" actually meant 70 weeks of years (that is, 490 years, or 70 "sevens"), Darby calculated that Christ's crucifixion happened at the end of the 69th week. Then the clock stopped. Darby's "postponement theory" accounted for the age of Christianity, which had no prophecies of its own, but existed in a kind of time warp or "great parenthesis" that interrupted the fulfillment of God's promise to Daniel. Because God worked with only one people at a time, Darby taught, Christians would be "raptured" from the earth before God resumed dealing with Israel. The Great Tribulation was foretold in Daniel 9:24–7, while the proof text for the rapture was Paul's remark in 1 Thessalonians 4:16 that living believers in Christ would be caught up in the clouds together with the dead in Christ after Jesus descended from heaven. Since the church existed in non-historical time, Darby reasoned, the pretribulational rapture could occur at any moment. Before the tribulation Christ would come to rescue his saints; after the tribulation he would return with his saints to defeat the Antichrist and establish his millennial kingdom.[4]

Much of this scheme was common to millennial movements, but Darby's eschatology was original in its two-track dispensationalism and its doctrine of the "any moment" second coming. His successors debated the precise timing of the rapture and the placement of dispensational lines, sometimes disavowing their connection to Darby, but they stressed what Darby and C. I. Scofield called "rightly dividing the Word of Truth." Dispensationalism decentered the incarnation, death and resurrection of Christ by consigning these events to the period of the Law. It nullified centuries of biblical interpretation, fixating on a novel leap of imaginative deduction, the rapture. Because God worked with only one people at a time, the church had to be removed from the scene before God could resume dealing with Israel. The beginning of the tribulation marked the resumption of Daniel's seventieth week. Biblical history resumed after the prophecies of Daniel and Revelation were fulfilled: the appearance of the "anti-Christ," the rise of the nation-uniting Beast foretold in Daniel 2: 1–49, the return of the Jews in unbelief to Palestine, the conversion of some Jews, the terrible persecution of converted Jews during the first three-and-a-half years of the great tribulation, and the triumphant return of Christ to earth foretold in Revelation 19: 11–21.

This rendering of Christian eschatology had a powerful hold over most of the fundamentalist movement, as Henry acknowledged. Even many leaders of the new evangelicalism took it for granted. Wilbur Smith, Henry's colleague at Fuller Seminary, was a leading dispensationalist who blended its apocalyptic scheme with lurid warnings about the Soviet Communist drive to conquer the world. Billy Graham preached dispensational doctrine at his crusades and lauded Smith as "the greatest evangelical leader of our day." The namesake of Fuller Seminary, evangelist Charles Fuller, was an ardent dispensationalist. Henry realized that a frontal attack on dispensational exegesis would be futile. Instead, in a book that announced the advent of a new fundamentalism, *The Uneasy Conscience of Modern Fundamentalism* (1947), he criticized the sectarian bunker-mentality of his tradition.[5]

Fundamentalists rarely preached against "such social evils as aggressive warfare, racial hatred and intolerance, the liquor traffic, exploitation of labor or management, or the like," Henry observed. Ignoring centuries of Christian theology, biblical scholarship, and spiritual practice, they replaced the great hymns of the past with "a barn-dance variety of semi-religious choruses" and turned the world-changing gospel of Christ into "a world-resisting message" of apocalyptic deliverance. Henry called for a different kind of fundamentalism, one that reclaimed the social mission of the gospel and discarded shibboleths that "cut the nerve of world compassion." Treading lightly on a chief cause of the shibboleths, dispensationalism, he described his position as "broadly premillennial." That placed him with the Puritans, not the sectarian dispensationalists. Henry respected the sober amillennialism of Lutheran orthodoxy and much of the Reformed tradition. He wanted fundamentalists to stop obsessing about signs of the end time, but more importantly and practically, he wanted them to permit a modest range of views on this subject.[6]

Thus he proposed a truce between premillennialists and amillennialists that ruled out the postmillennial fantasy of a Christianized world. The parties of orthodoxy needed to make room for each other on eschatology, Henry argued. They also needed to acknowledge that the postmillennial tradition was right about one thing: the church had a mission to transform society. Postmillennialists got this theme from the Bible, even though they misconstrued it. The gospel was relevant to every world problem while the Lord tarried: "The main difference between the kingdom of God *now* and the kingdom of God *then* is that the future kingdom will center all of its activities in the redemptive King because all government and dominion will be subjected to Him. This difference overshadows the question, however important, whether the future kingdom involves an earthly reign or not."[7]

The Uneasy Conscience of Modern Fundamentalism accomplished all three of Henry's objectives: it showed that a fundamentalist could criticize fundamentalist sectarianism without being expelled from the movement; it opened some breathing room on eschatology; and it announced the existence of a new, aggressive, intellectually engaged evangelicalism. For 10 years Henry chaired the theology department at Fuller Seminary, which took a strict line on inerrancy doctrine and basked in its close association with Graham, who skyrocketed to fame after the Hearst press publicized his 1949 crusade in Los Angeles.

On occasion the new evangelicalism distanced itself slightly from the reactionary politics of the old fundamentalism. Graham and the new evangelicals sometimes spoke a cautious word against racial prejudice; in the early 1950s, after years of preaching to segregated audiences, Graham went back and forth on the morality of doing so, and in 1954, after the *Brown* decision, he began to preach only to non-segregated audiences. Graham also cultivated personal relationships with Harry Truman (which failed disastrously) and Dwight Eisenhower (which succeeded), and Fuller Seminary practiced integration to some degree in its admission policies. Otherwise the new evangelicalism was not much different in the sociopolitical arena from the old one. The new evangelicals railed against communism in apocalyptical style and opposed King's civil rights campaigns after he asked for church support.[8]

In 1955 Graham, Sun Oil millionaire J. Howard Pew, and Graham's father-in-law Nelson Bell founded a new magazine, *Christianity Today*, as an outreach to liberal clergy. For many years all three founders were deeply involved in the magazine's editorial and financial affairs; from the outset it was Bell's personal ministry and passion; both facts had a major impact on Henry, the magazine's founding editor. Bell's and Graham's desire to reach liberal clergy made Graham doubt at first that Henry would make a good editor for it. Graham worried that Henry was too fundamentalist and intellectual to reach spiritually unsatisfied readers of *The Christian Century*. The idea was to provide a Bible-believing alternative to mainline pastors who might be open to a skillfully presented evangelical message.

Graham wanted the magazine to disclose its theological position only gradually; Henry disagreed vehemently, contending that *Christianity Today* had to come on strong from the beginning. Protestantism was in a crisis of belief without realizing it, he argued. The major Protestant denominations had fallen for ecumenism, half of church-going American Protestants favored a united Protestant church, and nearly 40 percent of the clergy believed that scripture contained legends and myths. Henry urged Graham and Bell to let him speak clearly to that crisis of belief, offering an alternative to mainline Protestantism.[9]

He won the magazine's editorship by converting the founders to this vision for it. In his inaugural issue Henry announced that *Christianity Today* originated "in a deep-felt desire to express historical Christianity to the present generation." The Protestant establishment had prestige and institutions, but no gospel substance. Fundamentalism had Bible colleges, radio ministries, and a wealth of conviction, but no intellectually respectable magazines. The faithful evangelical remnant needed better representation, he proposed: "Neglected, slighted, misrepresented, evangelical Christianity needs a clear voice to speak with conviction and love, and to state its true position and its relevance to the world crisis. A generation has grown up unaware of the basic truths of the Christian faith taught in the Scriptures and expressed in the creeds of the historic evangelical churches." He pledged "to be both salt and light in a decaying and darkening world."[10]

Henry built *Christianity Today* into a powerhouse, while clashing with his bosses for 12 years. Theologically he stood for a transdenominational evangelicalism that took a hard line on inerrancy doctrine without making it the basis of excommunicating theologians who were soft on inerrancy. Politically he advocated militant anti-communism, took a dim view of trade unions, opposed minimum wage legislation, railed against big government, opposed involuntary integration, and condemned the civil rights demonstrations. Behind the scenes he clashed with his employers, usually on personal and professional grounds, sometimes on public issues.[11]

Christianity Today hammered constantly on the apostasy of the mainline churches and theologians. In Henry's telling, liberal Protestant theologians lost confidence in "the distinctive supernaturalism of Christian redemption," then "dissolved" the confidence of others. Walter Rauschenbusch was a major dissolver. Rauschenbusch retained a gospel of personal regeneration, Henry allowed, but he "encouraged new political attitudes hitherto alien to American Protestantism." Afterwards liberal Protestantism dropped personal regeneration, transmuting the gospel to politicized idealism. Henry explained that the social gospel construed political activism not merely as a means of upholding justice, "but of actually transforming society." Setting aside the gospel emphasis on spiritual renewal, the social gospel placed its hopes on "other agents of change such as education and legislation." It distorted the kingdom of God, which became a worldly concept with social and political meaning. Social gospel rhetoric about Christianizing society was about transforming social structures, not about saving souls or even effecting social reforms: "Soon 'social evangelization' became synonymous with idealistic political action, and centered increasingly in ecclesiastical pressures inspired by denominational hierarchies and implemented by their political lobbies."[12]

Theologically, Henry argued, the Protestant abandonment of Christian teaching began in the eighteenth century, but in social ethics, it began with Rauschenbusch; he seemed to forget Gladden and Peabody. On Rauschenbusch's urging the church began "to participate directly in political affairs even to the extent of ecclesiastical lobbying for specific political objectives." Theologically, the social gospel was a disaster for the church; social ethically, it was a disaster for the church and nation:

> Whenever the Church considers itself the conscience of the State, or the pulsebeat of the body politic, the damage it incurs by thus directly merging its interests with those of the world or the surrounding culture is no less serious than that inflicted on a political order by the Church's legislation of her patterns of social behavior upon society in general.

That was a typically clunky sentence on a point that Henry subsequently refrained from applying to his group. In his telling, Judaism and Catholicism had a theocratic ideal, but American Protestantism had a better idea until the social gospel came along. Classic Protestantism embraced the New Testament idea of the kingdom of God, which was spiritual, not political. American Protestantism forged the best Protestant legacy in this area until the social gospel came up with a liberal version of the Catholic idea. Henry explained that Catholic doctrine supported the coercion of free persons for the sake of an ostensible "common good." American Protestantism stood for freedom in politics and society until liberal Protestantism, by methods far more "subtle" than Catholicism ever managed, insinuated the idea of the common good into American national life.[13]

Federal Council of Churches official S. Parkes Cadman declared that the church had an "imperative duty" to pursue world peace; Henry replied that the peace of Christ had nothing to do with pursuing world peace. Like most Protestant liberals, Cadman spoke "in utter disregard of Jesus' contrast of Christian peace with world peace." Before the social gospel, Henry stressed, no American Protestant – not even a liberal one – looked to the state as an instrument of redemption and the social good. Afterwards liberals carried on as though "Christianization" was a mainstream goal in the Protestant tradition, not a sectarian one: "These churchmen, who claimed to stand in the Protestant tradition, seemed to have forgotten the example of Luther, who opposed vigorously the attempt of certain Anabaptists to impose Christian ideals on the whole order of society." Instead of rooting themselves in historic Protestantism and the New Testament, Henry protested, liberal Protestant leaders baptized the idealism of Anglo-Saxon progressives. This apologetic move, made to buy off an overpowering modernity, had a disastrous inheritance. Having forged an alliance with secular progressives, religious progressives helped pave the way to the ascendance of secular liberalism. Henry lamented that the secular, managerial, big government ethos of the New Deal was triumphant in American politics and society. The language of individual duty had been cast aside; aggrieved individuals and groups clamored for their rights, increasingly by mob pressure; every interest group vied for legislative social change of some kind; even "erstwhile advocates of free enterprise" no longer believed in free enterprise, demanding government favors.[14]

Henry asserted that only an "apostate" Christianity relied on idealism, education, legislation, and government compulsion. Faithful Christians relied on the supernatural power of God to transform sinners into evangelists and good citizens. The church had a stake in legislation and social change, but changing society was not the church's primary business. Distinguishing among four strategies of social change – revolution, reform, revaluation, and regeneration – Henry advocated evangelical regeneration. Revolutionaries sought to destroy ultimate norms pertaining to marriage, property, and the state. Reformers advocated gradual amendments of particular abuses. Reevaluators sought to change things by conceptualizing them differently. For Henry, revolution was out because it denied the existence of God-given norms. Reform strategies placed too much faith in evolutionary development and were usually materialistic and humanistic. Reevaluation had the virtue of taking ideas seriously, emphasizing transcendent values discoverable in human experience, but it lacked a cosmic ground for its norms and values.

The business of the church, Henry argued, was to pray for and give witness to the regenerative power of God in human souls. God's very Spirit was the answer to the world's trouble, not government, education, or an unregenerate conscience. The regeneration approach proclaimed the kingdom of God as a new order transcending the world order and the power of the Holy Spirit to deliver sinners from spiritual bondage:

> The Holy Spirit sunders the shackles of human sin, requiring men first to recognize social evils in the light of personal wickedness. While personal sin often finds its occasion in

the prevailing community situation, the Christian pulpit and personal witness encourage effective solution of social evils by calling out a race of renewed men united in devotion to God's purpose in creation and redemption.[15]

The regenerative standpoint had a distinct view of work, he taught. Other approaches superficially criticized the "drudgery" of the assembly line or the powerlessness of the modern "wage slave." The regenerative approach stressed the spiritual condition of the worker. The "real drudgery" of modern work derived from "a distaste for work itself" in modern society, Henry explained. Unbelievers, lacking any concept of work as a calling from God, took a bad attitude towards work. They wallowed in the worst their jobs demanded, often mimicking union propaganda. Henry countered, "The joylessness, the depressing drudgery of monotonous toil, are caused more by the worker than by the character of his work." To abide in Christ was to be lifted above fatigue and dissatisfaction, finding spiritual fulfillment in dull or onerous work, rejoicing in the opportunity to witness for Christ. Henry put it negatively: "As a disciple of Christ, the believer knows that if work is mere drudgery it is in the grip of sin." He also put it positively: "While the unbeliever is on the assembly line in bondage, the believer is free." Christians were happy in their work, because they were in Christ. If Paul could say that being enslaved should not matter to a Christian, evangelicals could say that grueling work should not matter to a Christian. Henry allowed that there was ample reason to tag Protestantism as the religion of the middle class; Protestant preaching often failed to reach "the laboring masses" because not many Protestants were numbered among them. But that was a point in favor of the Protestant ethic, which spurred Protestants to work their way out of the working class: "It must not be forgotten how many have been lifted to new incentive and achievement through the power of regenerative religion."[16]

The best thing the church could do for the social order was to bring sinners to Christ, Henry urged. Salvation was for individuals, and society was a beneficiary of Christian salvation. As for government, Henry argued that civil government held God-given responsibilities to maintain a just order. The historic Western liberal emphasis on liberty was mistaken, because only Christ could make a person free. Justice, however, was something that governments could handle, even apart from the gospel, although Henry cautioned that there was no moral law apart from its divine ground. The divine law was the ultimate ground; the moral law was knowable to all rational beings; justice stood on the moral law. Henry reasoned that one did not have to be a Christian to recognize the universal validity of the moral law, and therefore of justice. Because the moral law was universally valid, Christians had no right to reserve just dealing to Christians. In a just order, he argued, every person was a subject of rights and an object of duties, "the same rights and duties that qualify all other persons under the same circumstances." Justice was expressed in general laws that applied without respect of persons. There were no exemptions from it and no exceptions to being protected by it. Civil laws were just to the extent that they protected the rights of all. Government was God's means of preserving justice in a fallen order, for Christians and all others.[17]

To Henry, these were arguments for opposing the civil rights movement, even as he acknowledged that racial prejudice was morally wrong. *Christianity Today* blasted the demonstrations and civil disobedience campaigns, claimed that King's integrationist goal was implicitly Communist, condemned the 1963 March on Washington as a mob spectacle, denounced interracial marriage, supported "voluntary segregation," and applauded the University of Mississippi for refusing to admit James Meredith as a student. The magazine also skewered liberal church leaders for supporting King and desegregation. Henry protested that just as liberals supported minimum wage legislation and compulsory unionism with no thought of the rights they infringed, they thought nothing of enlisting government power to impose racial integration on white communities. Most galling of all, liberals took these positions in the name of Christian morality, as though the Bible agreed with them.[18]

By 1964, however, Henry began to say that his group had unfortunate priorities in this area; he had begun to realize that *Christianity Today* would not look very good to historians on this issue. Never one to apologize, he took nothing back but did say that he wished (unnamed) evangelical leaders had taken a stand against racial discrimination. Conservative church leaders had a better grasp than liberals of the relevant principles, he claimed. Conservative Christians were appalled by lawbreaking; they knew that liberals routinely misused the language of rights; and they understood that the gospel could not be transmuted into a program of social justice. Confronted with "the constant liberal appeal to 'the gospel' to justify political programs," conservative Christians understandably fell back on evangelization. Moreover, they were right to be repelled when liberal church leaders "encouraged local law-breaking as a means of law-changing." Evangelicals were not wrong to oppose the tactics and goals of the civil rights movement. But Henry allowed that evangelicals should have spoken against racial prejudice. In the crucial ministry of preaching that racism was wrong, "the evangelical churches ought to have been *in the vanguard*." The fact that they rarely mustered a public word against racial bigotry hurt the evangelical cause, he acknowledged: "In the absence of relevant preaching, indignation over statute-breaking ran deeper in the Bible Belt than a sense of guilt concerning the injustice of their own local laws." Henry called it a "defeat" for Christianity that liberal Christians got the transcendent question right while defying biblical principles and community laws, while conservative Christians were the reverse.[19]

Under Henry's skillful direction *Christianity Today* found a large audience, one exceeding the expectations of the magazine's founders. Yet he was constantly reminded that it was their magazine and not his. His editorial authority was undermined by board members, especially Pew, who insisted on their right to preview all editorials and controversial articles, especially about capitalism. Henry fought these encroachments on his authority, but Bell circumvented him by passing advance galley proofs to Pew and others. Bell's dual role was the heart of the problem for Henry. Bell was an executive editor on the magazine staff and the secretary-treasurer of the board, which gave him a seat on the board's executive committee, chaired by Ockenga. Henry protested that this arrangement was patently unfair and unprofessional.[20]

The bosses countered that Henry was not very likable, which made him inept at social functions and fundraising. Despite the magazine's extraordinary success they clashed with him repeatedly, complained that he published too many academic articles, found him unpleasant company, and resented his chafing at their authority. In later years they also complained that Henry was more committed to far-flung lecturing and his own writing than to the magazine. These complaints got Henry fired in 1967. With no warning or consultation, the executive committee manipulated him into resigning, partly by leaking that *Christianity Today* was looking for a new editor.

Henry was infuriated. To a vast audience he was the second most important figure in the evangelical movement, behind Graham, whose role in the episode cut him deeply. Henry observed at the time: "After ten years of service [actually 12], my relationship to the magazine was not only summarily ended without consultation or reason, but in the absence of a resignation and without agreement on public announcement." A few weeks later, while noting that the committee's plotting against him (especially Ockenga) hurt him personally, Henry remarked that the worst part was being dumped without warning, which gave him no chance to land a better position "while I still had a prestigious base." Had the evangelical bosses treated him decently, he might have won a position at a state university, directed the religion division of a major publishing house, or at least returned to seminary teaching. Nineteen years later his autobiography still seethed at the slights and insults he received from what he called "the evangelical establishment."[21]

Only after he resigned did Henry learn that his bosses would have let him stay had he agreed to reduce his outside speaking engagements and activities. He felt betrayed by the evangelical establishment. In his view, which Carnell shared, evangelicalism had tremendous potential in American society, but the provincialism and small-mindedness of evangelical leaders prevented the movement from fulfilling its regenerative cultural mission. Henry put it starkly in *Evangelicals at the Brink of Crisis* (1967), warning that American evangelicalism was in danger of becoming "a wilderness cult in a secular society." He took no interest in settling for sub-cultural status. A culturally marginalized evangelicalism was a failure. Evangelicalism continued to grow in the 1970s, but Henry was hard to impress, complaining that evangelicals had little to show for their membership gains. It was not enough just to grow; evangelicals needed to change the direction and character of American culture. *Newsweek* magazine dubbed 1976 as the "Year of the Evangelical"; Henry demurred: "It is time that the evangelical movement sees itself for what it is: a lion on the loose that no one today seriously fears."[22]

That changed the following year, as a rising Christian right began to earn fear and political respect. In the mid-1970s Jerry Falwell, Cal Thomas, and other old-style fundamentalists decided that Henry and Graham had been right about the necessity of taking back the dominant culture. The ascension of a liberal evangelical, Jimmy Carter, to the presidency in 1976 spurred right-wing evangelicals to create organizations that opposed Carter, liberalism, and the erosion of Christian America. The first three organizations were founded in 1977: National Christian Action Council, Focus on the Family, and the American Family Association. Two subsequent organizations, Christian Voice and Concerned Women for America, were founded in 1979; another, Religious Roundtable, arose in 1980. Most importantly, Falwell launched the Moral Majority organization in 1979, which propelled thousands of evangelicals into right-wing electoral politics.[23]

From the beginning Henry was viewed by Christian Right leaders as a father and guru of the movement, although sometimes as a distant, hard to please father. Earning his living as a lecturer for World Vision International, he wrote a massive six-volume apologetics, provided intellectual firepower for the Christian Right, and accepted the role of senior counselor to it, sometimes with a whiff of disapproval. Repeatedly he warned that America became increasingly corrupt and unstable as it become more secular; sometimes he added that the Christian Right was a bit too shallow for its mission and his taste.[24]

America's secular establishment in the academy and media had a belief system, Henry argued, and it was terribly wrong. It was especially wrong in its pieties about itself. One pious illusion was that democracy was secure as long as individual rights were preserved; Henry replied that any democracy lacking shared moral and spiritual values was on the road to anarchy and destruction. Another was that Americans were essentially good-hearted; Henry replied, "Shall we call a nation 'good' if most of its unwed teenagers indulge in premarital intercourse, if it has a million or more abortions each year, if it has a 40 percent divorce rate and an epidemic of venereal disease?" Another was that America's commitment to capitalism assured continued prosperity; Henry replied that capitalist selfishness became self-destructive when it was cut loose from God and morality. Another was that poverty was a terrible evil that government should eliminate; Henry replied that the Bible took poverty for granted and did not endorse wealth redistribution. Another was that preventing a nuclear holocaust was morally imperative; Henry replied, "There is no moral virtue in selective murder." If Americans could murder millions of unborn babies, what was the virtue in fretting about nuclear war? Another was that the mass media should reflect current personal and social values; Henry replied that only a blighted society "waiting to be plowed under by its own delinquency" could be so stupid.[25]

He was not shy about claiming his place in American religious history. Henry drew a straight line from the Puritans to the nineteenth-century evangelical abolitionists to the early twentieth-century evangelical Prohibitionists to *The Uneasy Conscience of Modern Fundamentalism* to the Moral Majority. He later recalled that his movement-launching book had put the crucial point precisely, "That public affairs not be left to nonevangelical political forces." Had there been no *Christianity Today*, there would have been no Moral Majority or Christian Right. Some evangelicals preferred to say that *Christianity Today* stood up for a despised evangelical orthodoxy, but for Henry that was never enough. In the 1970s evangelicals waged ugly battles over inerrancy that made evangelicalism look bad at the very moment that it gained mass media attention. Henry believed in inerrancy, but not in expelling evangelicals who did not believe in it. To him, inerrancy was not worth poisoning the evangelical well or hurting the cause of evangelical growth. The point had always been to reclaim American culture for Protestant orthodoxy: "*Christianity Today* recognized from its beginnings the importance of social as well as personal ethics and of the application of biblical principles to the whole sociocultural arena, even if its energies were often exhausted in challenging ecumenical conceptions."[26]

Long after the Christian Right became a religious and political juggernaut, taking over much of the Republican party, Henry admonished that the movement's success was terribly limited. It was a good thing to control the social agenda of the Republican party, but that was a far cry from a third Great Awakening that restored America's Christian identity. In 1986 he declared that he still dreamed of "the movement's profound potential," but admitted that he found it increasingly difficult to distinguish his dream of an evangelical Christendom from a hallucination: "I remain profoundly convinced that evangelicals are now facing their biggest opportunity since the Reformation, and yet are forfeiting it. Unless soon enlarged, the present opening, at least in the United States, may not long remain." Evangelicals stood at a crossroads, he announced, exactly as he had claimed repeatedly for decades. Evangelicals would either mobilize their energies to transform the world or be driven by the world into a reactionary ghetto. Holding on to the status quo was not an option, because Western societies were hostile to Christianity. Evangelicals would either "penetrate" the modern world or be defeated by it.[27]

More than ever, evangelicalism needed fervent convictions and a mobilized army of Christian activists. Yet even that was not enough, for the Christian Right was long on both, yet the battle for America's soul was still being lost. Henry never doubted that his friend Carnell had been right about the crucial inadequacy of American evangelicalism: it needed prestige desperately. Wielding political power and gaining respect did not necessarily go together. If evangelicalism did not gain respect in the academy, it had no chance of fulfilling its social mission. At the very least, it had to be respected by scholars of religion at elite universities; more ambitiously, it needed to build new Christian universities and win back many that it had lost.

That preoccupation, plus the personal factors, had cost Henry his perch at *Christianity Today*. In 1963, already concerned that Henry took more interest in theologians than in running a mass circulation magazine, his bosses reluctantly granted him a nine-month sabbatical, which he spent interviewing European theologians. The interviews led to a series of articles in *Christianity Today* and a book, *Frontiers in Modern Theology*, in which Henry showed the disarray of neo-orthodoxy. Since the 1920s, neo-orthodoxy had ruled Protestant theology; Henry showed that it was in decline, reduced to competing revisionisms that won little following. Some theologians relinquished any appeal to revelation, leaving them with empty religious relativism. Others appealed to a nonobjective Word, which left them at the mercy of post-Bultmannians who demythologized "the Word" down to nothing. Henry declared that the decline of neo-orthodoxy was a precious opportunity for evangelicals: "If Christianity is to win intellectual respectability in the modern world, the reality of the transcendent God must indeed be proclaimed by the theologians – and proclaimed on the basis of man's rational competence to know the transempirical realm." That was the project he pursued in his six-volume apologetics, while evangelical activists built a political empire.[28]

For many years Henry brushed off the obvious objection that his attacks on the social gospel applied to his own cultural and political ambitions for evangelicalism. He replied that evangelicals did not politicize the gospel by turning the kingdom of God into a sociopolitical goal or by advocating specific legislation. Up to the mid-1970s that was a dubious claim; afterwards it would have been laughable, and Henry backed off from it. Occasionally he offered a cautionary word about taking politics too far, but always he contended that the Christian Right had been driven into politics by outrageous provocations. It was not the evangelical Right's "long-smoldering" resentment of liberal ecumenism or its conscious adoption of a right-wing political ideology that caused evangelicals to surge into political activism, he explained. Evangelicals took up politics in outraged reaction to the Supreme Court's legalization of federal funding for abortions in 1973 and the Internal Revenue Service's imposition of "racial tests on Christian schools" in 1978. Once the government invaded the moral space of the church and Christian consciences, Henry contended, conservative evangelicals had no choice but to build a politicized Christian Right.[29]

He bridled at the media "double-standard" that questioned the political campaigning of Christian Right Republicans but saw nothing wrong with the "glaring politicization" of the black churches. Henry claimed that conservative evangelicals were usually careful to channel their political activism through political organizations, not through congregations or denominational agencies. He gave his assurance that they understood that the church had to refrain from imposing its theological convictions on society; thus, the Moral Majority denied it was a theological organization. Yet the Moral Majority and its chief successor, the Christian Coalition, could not have been more explicit in claiming a religious basis and working for Republican electoral victories. How were they not guilty of politicizing Christianity in a nakedly partisan fashion? Henry struggled to take the question seriously. To him it was obvious that evangelicals were far from dominating American society, they were driven into politics in the first place, and the usual fuss about "theocracy" was an invention of secular humanists, who grew hysterical upon learning that some Americans still believed in eternal ethical standards.[30]

But on occasion Henry gave indications of taking the question more seriously, if only because rising anxiety about it threatened his dream of an evangelical America. The mission was to win America to Christ, he cautioned, not merely to gain political power. If evangelicalism stood merely for the winning side of an electoral struggle, it would fail. That raised the question of where the line between politics and religion should be drawn. If the evangelical answer had changed, what was it now? In 1984, speaking to a Christian Right organization, the Institute for Religion and Democracy, Henry waited until his final sentence to allow that there was a problem in this area. The problem had two parts, he observed, and evangelicals needed new answers to both: how were Christians to "encapsulate in legislation moral values that are not merely sectarian"? and what language were they to speak if theological language was ruled out?[31]

He did not claim to have the answer to either part, leaving that crucial business to the next generation of evangelicals. In the meantime, Henry scolded, evangelicalism had bigger problems. Its leaders were shallow types with a talent for television punditry. It found a large audience, but not really a new audience; rather, evangelicalism lived "on the margin of the already existing churches." Featuring "idolized spokesmen" who specialized in polemics and soundbites, not theological depth, it relied more on public relations and "team patriotism" than the power of theological conviction. That was not the regeneration movement Henry had envisioned. Having struggled to lift American evangelicalism above its barely-literate fundamentalist past, he was grieved to see evangelical publishers catering "to the pitch-it-low mentality," hawking stupid potboilers. He admonished that evangelical literature was often as dumbed-down and sensually overdriven as the mindless popular culture surrounding it. Catching himself in full scold-mode, he joked that, being a "supposed" premillennialist, he might be expected to believe that everything was getting worse. But Henry never stopped dreaming of the massive spiritual revival that fell just short of the postmillennial kingdom.[32]

Though his confessional loyalty was primarily to transdenominational evangelicalism and only secondarily to the Baptist tradition, Henry stressed that the Baptist tradition was a branch of Reformed Protestantism, not the radical Reformation. The seeming kinship between "Baptist" and "Anabaptist" was misleading, aside from a shared rejection of infant baptism and trans-congregational polity. When Henry mentioned the social ethical witness of the radical Reformation churches, he stressed that real evangelicalism went back to Luther and Calvin, not to the Müntzerites, Swiss Brethren, Hutterian Brethren, Mennonites, Moravians, South German Anabaptists, and Hoffmanites. To Henry it was something of an embarrassment that the Reformation immediately sprouted theologies of pacifism, radical dissent, communism, separatism, and apocalyptic perfectionism. When he referred to "the Reformation," he meant the magisterial one.

That was commonplace in the American evangelical establishment, which had a storehouse of historic epithets on this subject. Dutch Calvinists had a stern sixteenth-century confessional statement, the Belgic Confession, on the evils of Anabaptism: "We detest the Anabaptists and other seditious people, and in general all those who reject the higher powers and magistrates and would subvert justice, introduce community of goods, and confound that decency and good order which God has established among men." The Lutheran Formula of Concord (1580) was detailed in its condemnations, listing intolerable Anabaptist heresies (nine, including that unbaptized children were righteous and innocent), intolerable Anabaptist beliefs about politics (five, including prohibitions on government service, war, oaths, and capital punishment), and intolerable Anabaptist ideas undermining domestic society (three, including prohibitions on private property and working as a merchant or inn-keeper). The Second Helvetic Confession, a sixteenth-century product of Swiss–German Reformed Protestantism, similarly condemned Anabaptists for opposing infant baptism, capital punishment, war, swearing oaths, serving as magistrates, "and such like things," concluding: "We condemn also the Anabaptists in the rest of their peculiar doctrines which they hold contrary to the Word of God. We therefore are not Anabaptists and have nothing in common with them."[33]

By the mid-twentieth century American evangelicals and liberal Protestants usually did not claim to have *nothing* in common with Anabaptists, but the divisions remained very deep, and Anabaptists took pride in their own storehouse of epithets. The major figure to bride the gap, and to make an important contribution to Christian social ethics, was Mennonite theologian John Howard Yoder.

John Howard Yoder and the Politics of Jesus

Yoder was highly conscious of belonging to a minority tradition. In fact, his belonging to a dissenting Christian community that confessed and indwelled God's nonviolent kingdom meant everything to him. He wrote extensively on ecumenism, partly because he wished that the entire Christian church had more of the Mennonite spirit, and he became a prominent theologian by saying so. But Yoder knew well that the prospect of Christianity turning pacifist was approximately zero, and he did not worry about his legacy. Reserved, exacting, not very sociable, and a bit arch, he had an unlikely personality for a major social ethicist. Asked in 1978 to comment on his growing prominence in theology, he replied: "Oh, time has passed me by. I won't strategize making sure I get my monument." He took no interest in introspection either. Asked if he were happy, Yoder replied, characteristically, "I haven't found it very useful to ask that question." But he conceded that he was grateful for his family and academic tenure, "and I don't think I'll run out of Anabaptist sources."[34]

He was born in 1927 in Smithville, Ohio, where his father ran a greenhouse business. Yoder attended College of Wooster in Ohio for two years and graduated from Goshen College, a Mennonite school in Indiana, in 1947. From 1949 to 1954 he directed postwar relief efforts in France for the Mennonite Central Committee; he married Anne Marie Guth there in 1952. Staying on for a doctorate at the University of Basel (Switzerland), he studied under luminaries Walter Eichrodt (with whom he took 11 courses), Oscar Cullmann (nine courses), and Karl Barth (five courses), and consumed local Anabaptist sources. To the extent that Yoder had a specific field, it was historical theology, in which he wrote a dissertation on debates between the sixteenth-century Swiss Magisterial Reformers and Swiss Anabaptists.[35]

Thus he was not really a protégé of Barth, who was not his doctoral adviser or even in the same field. But Barth influenced Yoder more than any modern theologian.

Yoder wrestled with Barth's writings, identified with his theology to a considerable extent, and attended five of his doctoral colloquia in addition to course work. In 1957 Yoder wrote a critical 47-page essay on Barth's view of war; five years later, on the night before he defended his doctoral dissertation, he delivered to Barth an expanded version of his critique of Barth's position.[36]

Barth argued that the Decalogue's absolute command of Exodus 20:13, "You shall not kill," was better rendered, linguistically and culturally, as "You shall not murder," which meant more constructively "You shall respect life." In the Bible and the church, he contended, "You shall respect life" sometimes meant, "You shall sometimes kill out of respect for life." Yoder accepted that "murder" was more correct than "kill." The problem was Barth's "quasi-mathematical logic," which moved from "do not kill" to "respect life" to "do kill out of respect for life." Yoder protested that Barth's abstract principle about respecting life did not have the same meaning in the two imperatives, for the quantities that were supposedly equal to a third quantity (respecting life) were not equal to each other. More importantly, Barth's procedure reduced the command of God to a dubious, general, abstract principle.[37]

Barth justly regarded himself as passionately antiwar. He told his students that pacifism was "almost infinitely right" and that when nations went to war, 99 times out of 100 they lacked sufficient moral justification for doing so. In the late 1930s, however, he believed that his nation and others confronted the exception. In 1938 he declared that when Czechoslovakian soldiers resisted Hitler's invasion, they fought for Christ and his church; the following year he defended Switzerland's program of military preparedness; two years later he exhorted British Christians to remain steadfast in their nation's resistance to Nazi Germany. Barth admonished pacifists that God might command war; to deny the possibility was to sin against God's freedom. Six years after World War II ended he invoked the same argument in *Church Dogmatics*, discussing the ethics of war.[38]

Yoder allowed that the latter argument at least held the promise of a proper Barthian claim, one that construed a divine command for the time. But Barth did not deliver one. He presented no scriptural word or even an ethical intuition or mystical vision to justify his contention that Switzerland had to prepare for battle; Barth merely described a political situation "in which he saw nothing else for Switzerland to do." Yoder sympathized that Switzerland's political situation had been dire indeed. Listening to Barth lecture retrospectively on the subject in 1951, he appreciated that Barth spent most of his time shredding bad arguments for Christian warfare. But the theological question was that of the divine command. What was it in 1939? When Barth addressed that question, he switched from the divine command to a bare assertion of political necessity. Yoder protested, "The Christian theologian can never permit this kind of shifting of concepts to take place." The business of the theologian was to listen for and obey the divine Word – that was the basis of Barthian theology. "When, however, we ask him for the case in which God has spoken, we are confronted with the freedom of Switzerland."[39]

Yoder's argument and his graduation package to Barth were characteristic of him, although he waited until 1970 to publish *Karl Barth and the Problem of War*. He gave six years to the Mennonite Board of Missions and a year to his father's greenhouse business in Wooster, Ohio before beginning his teaching career in 1965 as a theology professor at Goshen Biblical Seminary; two years later Yoder took a second job as a part-time theology professor at the University of Notre Dame. He taught at Goshen until 1984, where he served as president from 1970 to 1973; and he taught at Notre Dame until his death in 1997.

In his early career Yoder caught the wave of radical counterculturalism in American theology and society, which embarrassed him. His essay collection *The Original Revolution* (1971) had a title perfectly suited to the time, which Yoder disavowed in his opening sentences. "In the late sixties an enormous proliferation of interest and imagery around the concern of Christians for social change became evident," he observed. Books on revolutionary theology appeared "almost every week." Yoder promised that his book belonged to no fad, appearances notwithstanding. Some of its contents preceded the fad, which was likely to be over before the book's faddish title hit the market. *The Original Revolution* had a sense of audience, however; Yoder explained that rigorous theological defenses of Christian pacifism had become rare, while the bookshelves were filled with impressionistic writings on pacifist heroes such as Gandhi and King. He wrote for readers who were ready for rigorous theological pacifism.[40]

He cautioned that moral options did not change as much over time as modern people tended to presume. The options for displaced persons born under foreign occupation and puppet governments were not significantly different for Palestinians in the time of Jesus, Pennsylvanians in the 1770s, Algerians in the 1950s, and contemporary Vietnamese peasants. Jesus had four choices, like the others. One was realism, beginning with the existing situation and aiming for the best possible outcome within it. For Yoder, what mattered most about realism was that it ruled out the possibility of a "brand new start." There was nothing to talk about except variations on what already was. In modern times, progressive realists sought to infiltrate the establishment to end the Vietnam War or to abolish apartheid in South Africa. Yoder replied that of the four options, realism was the one farthest from the mind of Jesus, who never gave a moment's consideration to sanctioning the existing order in order to change it. One could not serve the establishment, even as a reformer or house prophet, and be with Jesus, for the house prophet that stayed in the house remained with Herod.[41]

Revolutionary violence was the second option. In the time of Jesus the Zealots preached holy warfare against the empire; Yoder stressed that Jesus was close enough to the Zealots for many observers to have taken him to be one, and the Romans executed him for it: "He used their language, took sides with the poor as they did, condemned the same evils they did, created a disciplined community of committed followers as they did, [and] prepared as they did to die for the divine cause." But Jesus opposed the path of revolutionary violence because it did not create a new order. Violent revolution preserved the self-righteousness of the mighty and denied "the new peoplehood Jesus announces."[42]

The desert was the third option, withdrawing to a life of isolated communal purity. Yoder sympathized with this, with a nod to his Amish cousins, but noted that Jesus set out "quite openly and consciously for the city." The fourth option was conventional religion, which identified faithfulness with spiritual matters and left social-ethical problems to the politicians and professional experts. Yoder acknowledged the appeal of truncated religion to many people, as eliminating much perplexity; on the other hand, it was ethically bankrupt. To stay out of military or political concerns "is to give one's blessing to whatever goes on."[43]

Jesus rejected all the usual options to inaugurate something new, Yoder argued, "a new peoplehood and a new way of living together." The gospel alternative was about creating "a new, voluntary, covenanting community in which the rejection of the Old is accredited by the reality of the New which has already begun." The new aeon of the kingdom come was the point. The cross of Christ was not a new revelation, Yoder observed, for the path of the suffering servant was foretold in Isaiah 53. Even the resurrection of Christ was not something essentially new, for biblical faith affirmed God's victory over evil from the beginning. What was new was the incarnation of these ideas in Christ and his inauguration of the new aeon, the power of God revealed as sacrificial divine love. In the old order, sin and death ruled under the signs of vengeance and the state; in the new aeon of Christ's victory over sin and death, the rule of vengeance and the state were overthrown. Yoder explained that the essential change did not take place within the realm of the old order nor abolish it. It took place in the new aeon of the partially manifest kingdom of God, which existed simultaneously with human history. After Christ, the state and vengeance still existed, but their rule was broken. The old aeon pointed backwards; it manifested itself socially in the world and society in general, and its most intense manifestation was in the ordering violence of the state. The new aeon pointed to the fulfillment of the kingdom, of which the church was a foretaste. In the coming of the kingdom, the doom of the old order was set in motion, awaiting the final triumph of God in the consummation of history: "It is in the light of this promised fulfillment that life in the new aeon, which seems so ineffective now, is nevertheless meaningful and right."[44]

It seemed to Yoder that biblical scholars should want to make their scholarship useful to theological ethicists and that ethicists should want a biblical basis for what they did. In his major work, *The Politics of Jesus* (1972), an essay collection that put Yoder on the map of modern theology, he observed that neither group shared his opinion on this. Writing from a hermeneutical perspective that he called "biblical realism," which took account of historical criticism while claiming the entire scriptural witness as the church's canon, Yoder lamented that biblical scholars wrote for each other, laboring over "vast systems of crypto-systematics," while social ethicists seemed to feel no poorer for it, preferring conversation with social scientists and philosophers. The problem cut much deeper, however, than a mere lack of interdisciplinary conversation between biblical scholars and theological ethicists. In social ethics, Yoder argued, the problem was that ethicists took it for granted that the substantive norms of Christian ethics had to be found outside the gospel.[45]

The story of modern Christian ethics, in Yoder's telling, was a tale of reasons not to make Jesus the norm of Christian ethics. Jesus was an apocalyptical sermonizer who believed that the world would soon pass away; thus his teaching paid no attention to problems concerning the building and defense of a just social order (Reinhold Niebuhr). Or, Jesus was a simple rural figure who personalized all ethical issues (Tolstoy). Or, slightly differently, Jesus lived in a world over which he had no control; thus he dealt only with simple moral situations of interpersonal conflict (Paul Ramsey). Or, Jesus was indifferent to social and political issues, being concerned solely with the spiritual condition of individuals (Roger Mehl). Or, Jesus was a radical monotheist who pointed people away from all local and finite values (H. Richard Niebuhr). Or, Jesus entered the world to die for the sins of humankind, which lifted him beyond the category of teacher or exemplar (Catholic and Protestant orthodoxy).[46]

Yoder countered that the gospels supported none of these verdicts. If, as modern ethicists claimed, Jesus was not the norm of Christian ethics, it was doubtful there was such a thing as *Christian* ethics. But the gospels presented a figure possessing a quite definite politics. *The Politics of Jesus* moved straight through the gospel of Luke to explicate its subject, remarking on the politics of the Annunciation, the temptation narrative, the "platform" declaration of Luke 4:14, the reaffirmation of the platform in Luke 6:12, passages on the cost of discipleship, the Epiphany in the Temple, the Last Renunciation of Luke 22, and the cross and resurrection. Yoder noted that Jesus' platform was taken from Isaiah 61, where "the acceptable year of the Lord" may have referred to the deliverance of the Babylonian captives or an event at the end of the age, or both. In rabbinic Judaism it stood for the jubilee year of Leviticus 25 and Deuteronomy 15, when the soil was left fallow, slaves were liberated, all accumulated debts and inequities were cancelled, and mortgaged property was returned. Jesus' platform was a message of good news to the poor, deliverance to captives, recovery of sight, liberation for the oppressed, and the jubilee cancellation of debt and enslavement. It was the proclamation of a new order of emancipation and equality. After Jesus was killed the disciples despaired that apparently he was not the one to redeem Israel, as they had hoped. He appeared to them with a rebuke: "Was it not necessary that the Messiah should suffer these things and then enter into his glory?" (Luke 24:26) Jesus did not rebuke the disciples for focusing on the kingdom, Yoder argued, nor did his "glory" statement refer to the ascension. He wanted the disciples to grasp that his suffering inaugurated the kingdom: "The cross is not a detour or a hurdle on the way to the kingdom, nor is it even the way to the kingdom; it is the kingdom come." Jesus called people to a radically new ethic and order marked by the cross of Calvary, "a cross identified as the punishment of a man who threatens society by creating a new kind of community leading a radically new kind of life."[47]

Yoder left aside most historical-critical debates about the historicity of gospel narratives; it was enough to present the gospel picture of a social-ethical Jesus and its understanding of the cross. In agreement with S. G. F. Brandon, he argued that Jesus was socially close to the Zealots, he was executed for sedition, and his memory was somewhat depoliticized in early Christianity for apologetic reasons. Against Brandon he argued that Jesus was not a Zealot and the New Testament contained plenty of clues to his politics, because most of it survived in the life and memory of the New Testament church. Concerning the imitation of Christ theme, Yoder noted that the New Testament took little interest in it, with one enormous exception. Unlike subsequent church lore, the New Testament did not commend Christians to imitate Jesus the celibate, itinerant, or companion of fishers. The exception was the way of the cross, the crucial theme of the gospels and epistles. The New Testament persistently commended Christ's passion and death as the divine way of responding to the world's powers; Paul described his ministry as sharing in the death and resurrection of Christ (2 Cor.4:10–11). Christians were to be "like Jesus" in one way, that of radical servanthood, in which Christians opened their arms to their enemies, absorbing hostility with forgiveness and love divine. Yoder cautioned against individualistic or spiritualizing interpretations, for the cross was not about dealing with illness, failure, stress, or the like; it was the price that Christians paid for following the way of Christ's social nonconformity. Unlike illness or failure, the cross was entirely avoidable: "It is the end of a path freely chosen after counting the cost."[48]

In Yoder's interpretation, Jesus called his followers to a messianic ethic of the kingdom that radically restructured all social relationships. One chapter of *The Politics of Jesus* compiled scripture passages expounding the radical, social-ethical, pacifist, fellow-suffering way of Christ. Yoder noted that Christians had to ignore and/or spiritualize a great deal of the Bible to make it fit the religion they wanted; Carl Henry was a prominent example. Henry completely disregarded Jesus' social humanity as a model for social ethics, Yoder observed. When Henry dealt with Jesus, he focused on motivational virtues such as unselfishness and obedience, not on ethical specifics pertaining to poverty or resistance to imperial rule. Yoder judged: "Henry thus represents faithfully the tradition that has been able to appropriate much of the New Testament idiom without catching its central historical thrust."[49]

That was the dominant tradition in Christian history, Yoder stressed. Protestant and Catholic orthodoxies set aside the social ethic of Jesus in favor of orthodox doctrines about him; modern scholars denied that Jesus had a social ethic; Yoder ignored thinkers who did not fit this picture, such as Rauschenbusch. Most Christian leaders did not want the social ethic that Jesus proclaimed, Yoder argued, so they brushed it aside, sometimes with pious explanations, often without taking seriously the possibility that it was meant to be taken seriously. Since *The Politics of Jesus* was an essay collection, the chapters did not really build on each other, but it had an overall coherence. In the first half Yoder made the case that Jesus had a radical politics. In the second half he stressed that Jesus and the early church were not radical in the modern liberal or liberationist senses, for the gospel was not about rebellion, individual emancipation, or self-determination.

The ethical instructions of the "household codes" made telling examples of the difference. German scholars, following Martin Luther, described Colossians 3:18–4:1, Ephesians 5:21–6:9, and 1 Peter 2:13–3:7 as *Haustafeln*, a distinct literary form adopted by the early church. Colossians instructed wives to be subject to their husbands as to the Lord, husbands to love their wives, children to obey their parents, parents not to provoke their children in a discouraging way, and slaves to obey their earthly masters. Ephesians was very similar, adding the instruction to "be subject to one another out of reverence for Christ." References to parents and children were omitted from 1 Peter, but the author added that Christians were to obey "every human institution."

Yoder contended that modern scholars misconstrued the household codes out of ideological bias and confusion. Many scholars viewed the codes as an advance on the overheated eschatology of Jesus; later, the scholarly trend swung against the codes because of their ostensibly reactionary content. In both cases scholars took the usual assumption for granted, that the church had to derive a social ethic from somewhere, since it lacked one from Jesus that could be followed. The household codes must have been imported. Martin Dibelius, a pioneer of form criticism, explained that as the early church gradually came to grips with the everyday world, it adopted the proverbial wisdom and moral codes of local sources. Dibelius referred vaguely to the family codes of popular Greek philosophy and Jewish *halakah*; for decades after Dibelius, scholars contended that Stoicism was the more likely source. Yoder seized on recent critiques of the Stoicism thesis, noting that the household codes lacked the signature Stoic emphasis on the dignity of the addressed prince, freedman, or father. The New Testament addressed the subjects first, and thus had a subversive element not found in Stoicism; it addressed wives before husbands, children before parents, and slaves before slavemasters.[50]

That showed the revolutionary spirit of the ethic of Jesus, addressing the subordinated person as a moral subject, Yoder contended. Early Christianity assigned personal and moral responsibility to people who had no legal or moral standing in their culture. In the Christian community, even women, children and slaves were regarded as decision makers. Stoicism was about the freedom of dignified males not to be subordinate to anybody or anything except God and the state; Christianity instructed Christian partners to be willingly subordinate to each other. Yoder stressed the importance of Christian subordination, which was not about subjection (implying oppression) or submission (implying passivity). Christian subordination was about willingly, lovingly accepting one's place in the old order as it gave way to the new one inaugurated by Christ in his death and resurrection. There would have been no centuries-long tradition of Christian pacifism without this attitude of acceptance, Yoder cautioned. The church needed instruction on this matter because the memory of Jesus threw into question whether subordination still carried any ethical meaning. If the new age had begun, did slaves still have to obey their masters, or children their parents? Yoder remarked, "For the apostles to encourage slaves and women to be subordinate, there must have been some specific reason for them to have been tempted to behave otherwise."[51]

Christianity was, in fact, liberating in something like the modern sense of the term; hence the question arose. Did the apostles' response betray the radical ethic of Jesus? Many years later, Yoder wished he had said, "Yes, but . . ." At the time he gave no hint of "yes." Instead he blasted those who did say it, which evoked hostile reviews. Yoder panned "progressive Protestants" for complaining that Paul had "a low view of women" and that he failed to attack slavery "head-on as we now know he should have." Barthians, he noted, sometimes took a different tack toward the same end, rejecting the household codes as a relapse into natural theology. Yoder replied that it was not an option for him, as a committed Christian, to mock or ignore the teaching of Paul and the early church. New Testament scholar Krister Stendahl offered an influential solution that Yoder ripped as "condescending" and clueless. In Galatians 3:28, Paul declared that in Christ there were no differences between "Jew and Greek, slave and freeman, male and female." Stendahl called this statement a "breakthrough" text that set the Christian standard against other statements of Paul and the early church. Yoder replied: "Paul still gets the credit for finally reaching that height, which we can recognize as a height by its modern sound; and thus we can credit the New Testament with a personalistic view which by implication was to undermine slavery and subordination; but in order to be thus indulgent with the apostle we must forgive his retention of the vestiges of the subordination idea and (for our purposes) cut them out of the canon."[52]

There had to be a better way to make room for female ministers in the Church of Sweden than to mutilate the Bible, Yoder admonished. What if the "doctrinaire egalitarianism" of modern Western culture was wrong? To modern Westerners the very idea of "woman's place" had become "either laughable or boorish," while "subordination" seemed insulting. But what if it turned out, either by revelation or experience, that modern views on this subject were "demonic, uncharitable, destructive of personality, disrespectful of creation, and unworkable?" What if the liberated self so prized by modern society turned out to be a colossal disaster? Were modern people so consumed with their individuality that they could not comprehend Paul's teaching about the Christological basis of mutual subordination? Yoder chided that the "egocentric modernity" of readers like Stendahl distorted the texts they liked as much as the ones they disliked. Galatians 3:28 was about the complementary unity of all Christians in the body of Christ, not the equality of individuals.[53]

Subordination was not a bad idea that Paul or the early church borrowed from elsewhere, Yoder insisted. It was not something that Paul or the early church failed to overcome after realizing that the Jesus ethic of Galatians 3:28 was too radical to apply to the real world. The ethic of subordination was a true application of the ethic of Jesus, applying the central theme of Christology to the universal human problem of estrangement and bondage to sin: the way of Christ was the way of suffering to the cross. For a Christian, the law of life was Jesus' suffering.

Modern liberals, conservatives, moderates, and liberationists wanted Christianity to be about something else, Yoder argued. Thus, many denied that Jesus had a social ethic, and some read their own politics into Jesus. Yoder allowed that the early church might have depoliticized Jesus to some degree, compromising his radicalism, but not on this point. The church's call to reciprocal subordination was a revolutionary proclamation, not a relapse, one reflecting the complementary unity of the gathering kingdom. It was ethically constitutive of the way of Christ, who came to serve and to give his life, emptying himself in the form of a slave (Mark 10:45, Philippians 2:7). Against the Lutheran tradition, which identified the household codes with the divine orders of creation, Yoder contended that the early church did not have a conservative social ethic and did not consecrate the existing social order. When the household codes exhorted subordinated persons to accept their subordination, the point was to undercut the social order by reversing the imperative:

> For a first-century husband to love (*agapan*) his wife or for a first-century father to avoid angering his child, or for a first-century master to deal with his servant in the awareness that they are both slaves to a higher master, is to make a more concrete and more sweeping difference in the way that husband or father or master behaves than the other imperative of subordination would have made practically in the behavior of the wife or child or servant.[54]

Since the upshot of the household codes was actually revolutionary, unlike Greek, Roman, or Jewish sources, Yoder judged that they must have had a Christian origin. He noted that 1 Peter employed no reversal in the political realm, inviting the king to the servant role. Many interpreters reasoned that the author of 1 Peter expected no royal readers; Yoder suspected that the real reason went back to Jesus' instruction to the disciples to reject the role of governance as unworthy of a disciple's servant calling (Mark 10:42–3, Matt.20:25, Luke 22:25). There was no contradiction between accepting the radical ethic of Jesus and accepting subordination within the structures of the old world, for Christians were free from needing to smash the old structures, which were crumbling anyway.[55]

The Politics of Jesus made Yoder a notable theologian and gave the Anabaptist vision a new prominence in theology. Brethren theologians Vernard Eller and Dale W. Brown and Mennonite reviewer George R. Edwards expressed gratitude for both developments. Eller called Yoder "a brother of the Brethren [who] now has performed a most valuable act of brotherly counsel in giving us this book." He rejoiced that Yoder spelled out the contrasts between genuinely *Christian* radicalism, which accepted subordination as an act of fidelity and discipleship, and the "current varieties of radical 'liberation politics,'" which made a virtue of insubordination. Subordination allowed the believer to become an instrument of God's purpose, Eller explained; it rose above and negated the violent clash of adversaries. Insubordination was a form of violence even in the cause of liberation. Eller wished that Yoder had written the book instead of collecting one, which would have strengthened his argument, and he regretted that

Yoder often stopped short of the resurrection. Yoder described the politics of Jesus as the way of the cross; Eller admonished that Calvary stood only for death and rejection apart from the resurrection. But, for Anabaptists, *The Politics of Jesus* was a break-through: "I am convinced that it is the most important book that Brethren (conserva-tives, liberals, and radicals) can read today."[56]

Some responses were cooler. Jesuit theologian John R. Donahue found the book a generally competent rendering of Christian pacifism, but criticized Yoder for ignor-ing crucial historical-critical problems and lacing his ahistorical argument with proof texts. He also judged that Yoder flirted with a formal ethic of suffering in which pacifist affliction became self-justifying. Teresa M. DeFerrari, writing in the *Catholic Biblical Quarterly*, put a common criticism more tartly, remarking that it was "easy for a man in the twentieth century to tell slaves and women that Christ wanted them to fully accept their subjection." She doubted that Yoder would have been so enthusiastic about pacifism or revolutionary subordination had he been a slave or a woman. There was also Yoder's Pauline theme that the church was the one entity in which the world's social boundaries had no force; in DeFerrari's experience the truth was pretty much the opposite: "Secular society is overcoming artificial and unjust socio-cultural boundaries while the church continues to maintain them."[57]

The Politics of Jesus had a fervent admirer in Baptist theologian James William McClendon Jr, who declared that the book changed his life and theology. It had a respectful critic in Methodist social ethicist J. Philip Wogaman, who admired Yoder's forceful presentation but judged that his eschatological perfectionism abandoned the church's responsibility to maintain a just order: "Can we so easily disclaim responsibil-ity for the factual course of history? Is there no point at which the Christian is driven to be the instrument of God's factual victory over specific injustices?" And it had a sharp critic in Elisabeth Schüssler Fiorenza, who protested that Yoder's supposed radi-calism endorsed female subjection all the same, urging "Christian slaves and women to accept 'things as they are.'" Yoder waved off Wogaman's critique as the sort of thing that Constantinian liberals always said. To Schüssler Fiorenza he was anxious to set the record straight, because she misconstrued his argument. Revolutionary subor-dinationism was not about accepting "things as they are," he explained, otherwise it would not have been revolutionary. When he referred to "things as they are," he had in mind the transcendence of male and female that was a spiritual reality in the body of Christ. He agreed with Schüssler Fiorenza that the early church lost some of the emancipatory vision of Jesus; thus it became a place that extinguished female leadership and its memory. To Yoder, that meant that the church lost some of the transformative moral meaning of subordination.[58]

Yoder's friends and Anabaptist colleagues, desiring his theological leadership, urged him not to settle for essay collections. On that point he disappointed them, sticking to the essay format. There were always developments in ecumenism, current events, special topics in Anabaptist history, problems in ecclesiology, and theological trends to which he wanted to respond. Also, lectures converted more readily to essays than to books. Having made a mark in his early career as an advocate of Anabaptist pacifism, Yoder wearied of seeing his position described in Troeltschian and Niebuhrian catego-ries that were alien to him. On the one hand, he allowed, he was openly, respectfully, repentantly, and doxologically aware that his Mennonite identity shaped his theological position; on the other hand, he considered his work a biblical and ecumenical call to faith addressed to Christians of every communion. He believed that the Free Church, pacifist, biblical faith of the Radical Reformation was "closer to the gospel and more properly to be recognized as the imperative under which Christians stand than are the major alternatives." But he did not write as a sectarian, because he rejected the othering presumptions that labeled him as one. Neither did he write as a celebrant of a minority ethnic cultural tradition; Yoder could be rough on fellow Mennonites who took that tack. "Christ against culture" was not really the point, because Richard Niebuhr rendered "culture" as an autonomous and monolithic category, presenting skewed options. Neither did Yoder write as a non-Catholic or even a Mennonite, because he was serious about challenging the whole church to consider the claims of the Anabaptist traditions. For Yoder the point was always to present the Radical Reformation model as "a paradigm of value for all ages and communions," not to lionize his denomination.[59]

Applying that objective to social ethics, he conceived the kingdom of God *as* a social ethic. A great deal of US American social ethics asked questions that came naturally to a church that found itself in the majority, Yoder observed. Some social ethicists, in the manner of Stanley Hauerwas, asked questions that assumed or prized a minority status for the church. The best approach was to ask for what things the entire Christian community should stand. Theologically Yoder wanted all Christian churches to seek Christian unity on the basis of Christ himself as Christ was revealed in scripture, putting aside the authority of all church traditions, councils, and confessional statements. Ethically he wanted Christian churches to find their unity in the kingdom of Christ.[60]

That project, in his rendering, required relinquishing Constantinian questions. Yoder stressed that for three centuries before Christianity joined the empire, the church existed on a free church basis, opposing violence, oath-taking, private wealth, and serving in high imperial government. Then the ethical message of the gospel was turned "into its opposite." Under Constantine, the machinery of doctrinal repression and ethical cooptation began to be built. Under Theodosius, it became a civil offense not to be a Christian. A bit later, Augustine sought to raise the bar, making it criminal to be the wrong kind of Christian. Yoder remarked, "The meaning of the decision to confess Christ was thereby not simply warped or fogged over but structurally reversed, i.e., denied."[61]

In Yoder's telling, the church of the Middle Ages extended the ethical corruption of Christianity, identifying the church "with the sword, with wealth, and with hierarchy." Unfortunately, the magisterial Reformation made only small adjustments to that legacy. The Lutheran, Calvinist, and Anglican reformers took no interest in recovering the ethical spirit of the early church; moreover, they assigned to ethical questions in general only a secondary importance. The Reformers of the magisterial traditions focused on "selected matters of faith and order," retained baptismal practices that identified "an entire population with the church," and fortified civil control of the church, retaining compulsory membership in the church for all citizens except Jews and the church's moral approval of government violence.[62]

Yoder emphasized that the Radical Reformation was a more thoroughgoing affair. The Anabaptists changed "not simply the definition of certain ministries or churchly practices, but also the entire understanding of what it means to be Christian." In the Anabaptist traditions the kingdom-oriented, pacifist, free church ethic of the early church was reclaimed. The radical reformers restored the standards of the New Testament, refusing the sword, which was left to pagan Caesars, restoring the simplicity of life and the sharing of wealth, and treating all believers as equal within the body of Christ. In other words, Yoder explained, to the radical reformers the ethical issues were the crucial ones. If any Christian ethical tradition deserved to be called orthodox, it was the one that Christians held in common in the age of the New Testament church and pre-Nicene Christianity, which the radical reformers restored.[63]

To Yoder the ethical issues were still the crucial ones at stake, although he did not anticipate much ecumenical progress with liberal pacifist Christians who shared his politics. If one gave up the authority of Christ as attested in scripture, what was the point? In formal terms, he argued, American liberal Protestantism was no better than Catholicism. The Catholic Church assumed a centuries-long structure of doctrine and institutional superstructure that was not open to outside criticism and so did liberal Protestantism: "The only difference is that this evolution has gone down another track for four or five centuries." In Catholicism the Counter-Reformation, papal infallibility, and the Assumption of Mary were not debatable; in Protestantism the Renaissance, the Reformation, the Enlightenment, idealism, and the scientific worldview had the same status, along with Greco-Roman ideals of equity and due process and Occidental ideals of democracy. Yoder judged: "Built as it is on layer upon layer of ideological alluvium that it dares not submit to too close a scrutiny, this theological position is just as incapable of talking across the fence as is Rome." Admittedly, liberal Protestantism had no pope, but, Yoder remarked edgily, the outdated opinions of popular theologians in the prestige divinity schools served as a functional equivalent.[64]

As for ethics, he admonished with only slightly less edge, "There are other ways to do Christian ethics than to ask, 'How can we help to move the total social system?'" The social gospelers and Niebuhrians assumed a situation of majority control; thus, when something happened in American society, they felt "responsible" for it, even for results that were partly evil. Yoder judged that Reinhold Niebuhr differed from the social gospelers chiefly in acknowledging that some of the things they took responsibility for were hurtful to others and to some degree selfish. That didn't stop Niebuhr from hitching Christian ethics to violence and selfishness, Yoder protested. For Niebuhr, moral responsibility required one to employ as much violence and self-interest as necessary to bring about the lesser evil. For Yoder, the way of Christ was a different way, one that accepted the consequences of the suffering love of Christ in bad situations, disposing no capacity to impose one's preference: "Most pacifists accept the fact that nonpacifists will be running the world violently. They interlock their own rejection of violence with the knowledge that others will keep on killing and coercing." Instead of trying to tip the scale toward a lesser evil, Yoder urged, a Christian should ask: "In a situation where I cannot tip the scales, on what other grounds might I decide what to do?"[65]

Just as he rejected the other-ing label "sectarian" and its implication that "sectarians" like him took no ethical responsibility for society, Yoder rejected the notion that "absolutists" like him paid no attention to practical consequences. It was simply untrue that Niebuhrian realists and Catholic just warriors had utilitarianism on their side while all he had was religious deontology. "By categorizing the pacifist as an absolutist, the nonpacifist tends to dispense himself from hard realism in his own case," Yoder observed. What were the long-term consequences of resorting to force? How was one to know that violence would achieve the posited ends? When the just-war principle of "last resort" was invoked to justify resorting to violence, how was one to know that a sufficient time frame had been taken into account? If violence was the means to a better end, how could the end result not include the violence of the means? How was one to know that, in the long run, establishing a new regime by armed force was better than taking the slower, non-violent, democratic approach to social change from below? Yoder contended that pacifists usually pressed these pragmatic questions more carefully and seriously than proponents of war, from which he drew a twofold conclusion: pacifists were more pragmatic than realist and just-war advocates of warfare, and the latter groups needed to take the tests of just-war doctrine more seriously.[66]

Taken seriously, he argued, just-war doctrine contained rigorous tests of the moral right to war and the moral conduct of it. Regarding the moral right to fight (*jus ad bellum*), the just-war tradition taught that war may be waged only by a legitimate ruler, fought only for a just cause, fought only with a right intention in the objective sense (*finis operis*) and fought only with a right intention in the subjective sense (*finis operantis*). The criterion of legitimacy excluded tyrants, war by private citizens (except in emergency defense), and war by criminal gangs or privateers. For a just cause, the offense had to be actual (not merely possible), intentional, of substantial importance, objective and verifiable, and unilateral (not provoked). To pass the test of right intention in the objective sense, a war could be fought only to restore peace. National honor, territorial gain, commercial aggrandizement, and weakening or destroying one's enemies were not valid ends, and unconditional surrender was not a morally justified demand. Right intention in the subjective sense excluded hatred, vengefulness, cruelty, desire for power or fame, and material gain as motivating intentions. Positively it included love for the victims of aggression, trust in God, willingness to face risk or sacrifice, love for the enemy, humility, regret at the necessity of fighting, and, in many formulations of just-war doctrine, the demonstration of mercy after victory. Yoder noted that the American Catholic bishops added a new category to subjective right intention, "comparative justice," in their 1983 pastoral letter *The Challenge of Peace*, which recognized that both sides often believed they had a just cause.[67]

Classical formulations of just war doctrine distinguished between the moral right to fight (*jus ad bellum*) and the right way to fight (*jus in bello*), lacking the modern notion of "due process," which applied to both categories. Since modern formulations of just-war doctrine grouped classical tests of cause, intention, authority, and means under the category "due process," and because procedural issues applied to both types of justification, Yoder argued that tests of procedural integrity were best grouped in a separate heading between the two main types. These tests included the procedural rules that war must be a last resort after exhausting all possible means of negotiation, mediation, and arbitration and recourse to international tribunals. The "last resort" criterion also required a "cooling off" provision of time for an enemy to back down, a formal declaration of war preceded by a warning and sufficient time to sue for peace, a statement of war goals, and the recognition of an enemy's right to sue for peace on the stated terms at any time. Other principles under the category of due process stated that enemies never lost the right to sue for peace, unconditional surrender was not a valid war goal, international law and treaties were to be respected, the entire war had to cause less harm than the harm it sought to prevent (the principle of proportionality), and the war had to be winnable.[68]

In the second traditional category, *jus in bello*, just-war doctrine taught that to fight rightly the means of war must be necessary (indispensable), proportional, respectful of the immunity of the innocent, discriminating, respectful of the dignity of humankind, and not forbidden by positive law or treaties. The necessity principle ruled out unnecessary combat and killing and wanton destruction. The proportionality principle ruled out any destruction greater than the damage prevented or the offense being avenged, any punishment greater than the guilt of the offender, and disproportionate violence of any kind in tactics, strategy, or use of a weapon. The immunity principle applied to all innocent persons constituting no threat, traditionally consisting of women, children, the aged, the infirm, clergy, religious, foreigners, unarmed persons engaged in ordinary tasks, neutral third parties, soldiers on leave, surrendered soldiers, and prisoners. The principle of discriminating means required every weapon, strategy, and military unit to be subject to measured control. The dignity principle forbade slander, mutilation, torture, treason, perjury, lying (with exceptions), pillage, poisoning the environment, fighting on holy days or during a proclaimed truce, and profaning churches or cemeteries; it also respected sanctuary and the giving of quarter to surrendered enemies. In medieval times the prohibitions of positive law and treaties were part of canon law and civil law; in modern times the Hague Convention of 1907 prohibited poison or poisoned weapons, killing surrendered enemies, refusing quarter, and making improper use of a flag of truce.[69]

Yoder wanted nation states and just-war churches to take these restraints on going to war and fighting wars more seriously. That seriousness needed to include the development of tools to make just-war principles operational. Towards that end, he held back from a definite answer to the usual pacifist questions: Has any war ever met the just-war requirements? Has any ruler, government, or general ever rejected an advantageous tactic or strategy on the grounds that it violated a rule of just war? For any system of thought, Yoder cautioned, it was always a worthy test to ask whether it applied to real life. Citing John Courtney Murray he observed, a bit vaguely, that there were few examples in history where a major party to a conflict actually adhered to the restraints of just-war doctrine. Most wars were fought for naked national interest and/or religious or ideological idolatry. Even when leaders claimed to respect the rules, they did not develop the requisite instrumentalities to abide by them. The same thing was true of the just-war churches, which, in Yoder's telling, devoted extensive resources to moral problems they cared about, especially sexuality, but pitifully little to the implications of just-war doctrine.[70]

Just-war doctrine had problems on every level, he stressed. There were problems of conceptual adequacy that made it difficult to apply general criteria to specific cases. There were problems concerning the institutional requirements of the system, since decisions had to be made by competent agencies that often did not exist. There were problems on the attitudinal level, since common opinion was often prejudiced or self-serving. But just-war thinking and pacifist thinking were not diametrically opposed, Yoder urged. Most of the time they agreed on the pertinent questions and answers, against other views. Yoder believed that just-war doctrine had some value as an instrument of moral discussion. At least, he wanted to believe it. He explained that for the sake of the "integrity of my interlocutors," he wanted political officials and the just-war churches to take what was purportedly their belief about war more seriously.[71]

Yoder put it sharply, noting that most politicians, church leaders, and theologians claimed they were "not idolaters sacrificing their fellow creatures to the absolute value of national interest, not frenzied murderers killing without any discipline, not crusaders identifying their cause with God." He tried to give them the benefit of the doubt, explaining that some were his friends and colleagues. In theory, it was not impossible to accept responsibility for the minimum evil necessary in order to establish a decent world order or even a just peace. The just-war tradition offered a theory and practice for doing so. "But for me to take them seriously does demand that I ask of them how they are making that moral claim operational," Yoder wrote. "How do they live up to its demands or even plan to do so?"[72]

In his later career Yoder became more adamant that he was not a sectarian. The term had always made him cringe; belatedly he said so. From the beginning he smoldered at the presumption of Troeltsch and the Niebuhr brothers to decide who belonged to the mainstream "church type" and who were sectarians. Later he winced when his friend and Notre Dame colleague Stanley Hauerwas burnished his own credentials as a dissenter by playing up the "sectarian" aspects of Yoder's stance. On occasion Yoder acquiesced to being described as a "purist" or an advocate of "Mennonite withdrawal from society," then regretted the acquiescence. Fuller Seminary theologian Richard Mouw, a friendly critic, treated Yoder as the epitome of a good sectarian, which Yoder found hard to take. Worst of all, many Anabaptists really did acquiesce, regarding themselves as withdrawn, sectarian outsiders to the Protestant establishment.[73]

Years later Yoder reflected that for many years he resigned himself to "having no choice but to play by other people's rules." He had told himself that he was like a Jew in Babylon in 500 BCE, speaking Chaldean, or like Martin Buber in Germany in 1920, speaking German. But that didn't really help, and the misrepresentations mounted. It did not help that he taught at Notre Dame, where things Catholic pervaded the atmosphere and stereotypes about Mennonites prevailed. Finally he began to protest that "sectarian" was an inherently pejorative term that marked some Christians as outsiders to a presumed establishment. The "establishment" did not refer to a majority or even to those representing one; it referred to a minority in dominant social roles that presumed the authority to speak for everyone. Yoder was reasonably comfortable with "Anabaptist," "evangelical," and "Radical Reformationist" as markers of his Christian identity; above all he identified with "catholic." His normative testimony applied to Christianity as a whole and all Christians; moreover, he refused to concede that any Christian communion had stopped reforming.[74]

On one occasion Yoder and Hauerwas introduced themselves to an incoming class of graduate students in theology at Notre Dame. Yoder explained that he fell back on theology after botching his attempt at the greenhouse business. He had no field to speak of, but dabbled in Reformation history, biblical studies, theology, and ethics. For many years he wrote mostly in defense of Christian pacifism, but as far as he knew, he had convinced only one person to become a pacifist. That was Hauerwas. After Yoder died of an aortic aneurysm in 1997, Hauerwas reflected, "In truth I know I was a burden for John. In speech and writing John was exacting. He had the kind of exactness only an analytic philosopher could love. He never said more or less than needed to be said."[75]

Yoder shared more of Hauerwas' polemical temperament than this remembrance let on, but they were indeed contrasting types on the matter of exactness and excess. As Hauerwas put it,

I, on the other hand, love exaggeration. Why say carefully what can be said offensively? I know that John, committed as he was to the ministry of careful speech, found exasperating how I said what I thought I had learned from him. Yet he was patient with me – which is an indication that he knew he had to treat even me nonviolently.

Yoder was a major influence on Hauerwas, but just as Yoder was more complex than the typical rendering of him as a Mennonite sectarian suggested, Hauerwas was complex and idiosyncratic to the point of being inimitable.[76]

Thinking Christian Pacifism Through: Stanley M. Hauerwas

Stanley Hauerwas was a leading proponent of virtue ethics, a pioneer of narrative theology, a sharp critic of political liberalism, a commentator on medical ethics, an admirer of Karl Barth, a sharp critic of liberal theology, a leading exponent of the centrality of ecclesiology, a provocative and brilliant interpreter of biblical themes, and the most renowned theological ethicist of his generation. He was already launched on virtue ethics when he converted to pacifism early in his career, so he might have become prominent even without converting. Becoming a pacifist, however, forced him to rethink everything he believed about Christian ethics, leaving nothing untouched and sending him in surprising directions. Afterwards his trademark convictions never changed or even wavered.

Born in 1940, Hauerwas grew up in Pleasant Grove, Texas, where his father, Coffee Hauerwas, laid bricks for a living. He slept in the living room of a three-room house and later recalled that he had not realized his family was poor until he went to college. Hauerwas inherited his father's colorful Texas profanity, which he retained after becoming a theologian. From his parents and community he also inherited a Texan identity, which taught him how to be different, and an upbringing in Methodist evangelical revivalism, which gave him salvation anxiety. Belonging to Texas made a deep imprint on Hauerwas's psyche and personality. Years later he stressed that Texas protected him from being claimed entirely by the USA or another larger story. He also noted that being a (white) Texan usually required repressing certain local memories and often led to making virtues of one's worst sins, such as the town that for years featured a banner over its main street: "Welcome to Greenville: The Blackest Land, the Whitest People."[77]

As a youth Hauerwas's salvation anxiety peaked every Sunday night at church, where he waited for an urging of the Spirit that never came. Wanting to be saved, at the age of 15 he compensated at a sweaty Sunday night service, on the tenth singing of "I Surrender All," by joining a group at the altar that dedicated their lives to the ministry; Hauerwas reasoned that God would have to save him if he became a minister. During high school he had second thoughts, puzzling over his religious choice. Did he really know enough about Christianity to accept it or reject it? Hauerwas swung toward rejection after reading B. David Napier's *From Faith to Faith*, which mentioned factual errors in the Bible, and Nels Ferré's *The Sun and the Umbrella*, which compared the church to an umbrella blocking out the divine light of the sun. As a college student at Southwestern University in Georgetown, Texas, however, he found a Methodist mentor, religion and philosophy professor John Score, who convinced him that he still did not know enough to make a decision about Christianity. That was just enough to carry Hauerwas to Yale Divinity School in 1963.[78]

Impressed by R. G. Collingwood's *The Idea of History*, Hauerwas thought he would study historiography and the problem of divine action, not realizing that H. Richard Niebuhr had spent much of his career at Yale reflecting on that tangle of problems.

Niebuhr died the year before Hauerwas arrived. At Yale Hauerwas studied under Julian Hartt, Hans Frei, and James Gustafson, and read a great deal of Barth and both Niebuhrs. Hartt and Barth convinced him that he had the wrong idea about theology; instead of aspiring to a system, it was better to approach theology as an *ad hoc* discipline of the church that addressed practical implications of faith and belief. That verdict led Hauerwas to ethics and a doctoral degree at Yale after completing his divinity degree, where he acquired his first stock of theological templates: Barth on Christology and dogmatic method, H. Richard Niebuhr on moral experience and revelation, Reinhold Niebuhr on ethical realism, John Wesley on Christian experience, Aristotle and Aquinas on virtue and character, and Ludwig Wittgenstein on philosophy as practical discourse.[79]

Hauerwas assumed that Reinhold Niebuhr was right that Christians had to be willing to use violence to secure the good; in later life he sometimes recalled that he held foremost in mind the annihilation of Europe's Jews. The only alternative to Christian realism, he judged, was a sectarian or individualistic retreat to an ethic of intention, where the controlling point of ethical concern was one's righteousness, not the needs of others. To his surprise, Hauerwas liked Aristotle and Aquinas, mainly because their stress on virtue gave him the first glimmer of an alternative to the currently fashionable "situation ethics," which reduced ethics to deciding for the "loving choice" in an ethical quandary. He took equal delight in Wittgenstein's thesis that philosophy was essentially therapeutic, not a battle of theories and positions. Reading Yoder's pamphlet on Barth, Hauerwas admired the penetrating analysis, but judged that Yoder's ecclesiology was "crazy." Sectarianism held no lure for Hauerwas; he wanted to work within mainline Protestantism because that was where serious theology was done. In 1968 he began his teaching career at Augustana College in Rock Island, Illinois; two years later he joined the faculty at Notre Dame.[80]

He made his first mark as a virtue ethicist. Having chafed at the sterility of textbook approaches to ethics and the shallowness of situation ethics, Hauerwas judged that contemporary ethicists were too fixated on a narrow concept of moral experience. The prevailing concern of Christian ethics was to analyze how particular actions might be justified. Ethics was about solving moral dilemmas; teaching ethics was about showing how ethical theories differently solved dilemmas. To Hauerwas, that preoccupation lost sight of the gospel concern with the self that did the deciding. If ethics inhered in moral character and its development, Christian ethicists needed to give at least as much attention to the formation of moral virtues as they gave to the justification of moral decisions. Instead of fixing on how to solve dilemmas, they needed to ask how moral selves were developed and which virtues were central to Christian living.[81]

How should Christian convictions shape the moral lives of Christians? In his first book, *Character and the Christian Life* (1974), Hauerwas took his initial pass at that question, stressing (Methodist) sanctification and his graduate school reading list. His first essay collection, *Vision and Virtue* (1974), added the novels and philosophical writings of Iris Murdoch to his canon, featuring her emphasis on vision as the hallmark of moral living. From there he moved to the story of the moral agent, adding another trademark Hauerwas theme, the narrative character of Christianity and theology, which he expounded in *Truthfulness and Tragedy* (1977). As an advocate of virtue ethics and narrative theology, Hauerwas helped to launch significant theological trends. Ethical systems designed to solve moral quandaries had very limited usefulness, he argued. No deontological theory of moral obligations substituted for the thing that mattered most in the moral equation – the development of a sound moral character within a substantive moral community. Situation ethics was no better, since it employed a single theory (act-utilitarianism) to account for and justify all moral acts and practices. Hauerwas countered that ethical reality was embedded in and enlivened by historical experience. In ethics, the crucial matters were the practices, habits, and virtues instilled in individuals by moral communities.[82]

What kind of Christian community best nurtured Christ-following moral selves? Hauerwas puzzled over that question in his first year at Notre Dame, and found himself drawn surprisingly to Yoder. At the time Yoder was little known, having published only a handful of essays and pamphlets and a pamphlet-length book, *The Christian Witness to the State*. Hauerwas began with Yoder's pamphlet on Niebuhr, which impressed him for defending Christian pacifism without falling into Niebuhr's either/or of liberal idealism or sectarian irrelevance. Next he re-read the pamphlet on Barth, which now seemed less impossible ecclesiologically, because it provided a basis for a communally thick, Christological ethic. Arranging a meeting with Yoder, Hauerwas found him rather stiff, even forbidding: "He did nothing to try to ingratiate himself." But Yoder gave him a stack of mimeograph papers, an early version of *The Politics of Jesus*. By then Hauerwas was hooked, though still resisting pacifism; he was too ornery and Niebuhrian to feel any natural attraction to it. In 1971 he wrote an article, rejected by six journals, which contended that Yoder's position deserved to be taken seriously; the journal editors did not concur. To be published in the USA, "The Non-resistant Church: The Theological Ethics of John Howard Yoder" had to wait for Hauerwas' first essay collection, but it laid the groundwork for all that was to come.[83]

For Christian ethicists, Hauerwas observed, it was conventional wisdom to say that Christians had to employ violence to secure the good. Ethicists routinely legitimized violence or even took it for granted that violence was ethically necessary. In his view, it was time for Christian ethicists to "feel the oddness" of that situation. Yoder helped modern readers feel it by stating plainly that the church's business was to obey God, whose will was revealed and exemplified in Christ. God sought to bring the kingdom of the world into God's realm by letting Christ be killed on the cross. Just as Christ did not resist evil with violence in carrying out God's will, Christians were called to follow Christ nonviolently. Hauerwas stressed Yoder's dualism between the nonviolent, self-giving norm of Christ and the coercive, grasping way of the world: "The kind of life assumed by the faithful Christian is not the same as the secular man of good will. The Christian's duties are not the same as those laid upon him by the modern welfare state. This means that there are simply some aspects of society in which the Christian will not be called to participate."[84]

Hauerwas harbored a few misgivings. Yoder based Christian ethics exclusively on revelation, which smacked of Barthian positivism. His dichotomy between the believing Christian and the unbelieving world seemed unrealistically sharp, and he exaggerated the Christian's freedom from moral principles and ideal patterns. Hauerwas was not ready to say that revelation, unlike other forms of human knowing, was not subject to historical relativity. He doubted that there was always a clear line of demarcation between living faithfully and not doing so, and he questioned Yoder's ethic of the state. If, as Yoder acknowledged, the state was responsible for protecting the innocent from the guilty, how was one to determine innocence from guilt without appealing to moral principles that applied to believers and unbelievers alike? Hauerwas judged that Yoder needed some justice principles, like it or not, which would help him determine which forms of justice were more intimately connected to Christian faith than others.[85]

But these were secondary matters. On the main things, Yoder had already convinced Hauerwas that mainstream social ethics had the wrong objectives. The social mission of the church was not to directly challenge and transform the social structures of society. It was for the church to be itself, a nonviolent communal witness to the existing and coming kingdom of God. The church had no business speaking to the state on every public issue, and when it spoke, it needed to do so in a way that did not violate its Christian integrity. Hauerwas assured that the church had every right to appeal to liberty, equality, and democracy, for these were the highest standards that the "world of unbelief" was capable of recognizing. In the same way, the church rightly appealed to cultural values bearing a close relation to Christian faith, such as honesty, hard work, mutual respect, unselfishness, and tolerance. But in all such speaking, Hauerwas argued, following Yoder, the church had to remember that such matters fell under the ethical categories of prudence and self-preservation. The state had no higher ethic or calling, but the church, whenever it spoke directly to the state, had to make sure never to compromise its higher calling.[86]

Hauerwas began to say that he was a pacifist of Yoder's type; increasingly his essays on virtue, narrative, politics, and personal ethics showed the difference. His third collection of essays, *A Community of Character* (1981), ranged widely in subject matter yet featured a core theme, that the church was a distinct society holding "an integrity peculiar to itself." Too many Christians justified Christianity by appealing to its work for social justice "or some other good effect." That strategy was a loser even when it convinced nonbelievers to accept the "social benefits" standard, Hauerwas urged. The only reason to be a Christian was that one believed Christian convictions to be true, "and the only reason for participation in the church is that it is the community that pledges to form its life by that truth." Social ethics was not something that the church acquired after getting its theology straight, nor something that the church "applied" to society. The church itself *was* a social ethic: "Our theological convictions and corresponding community are a social ethic as they provide the necessary context for us to understand the world in which we live."[87]

Because he stressed the role of the church as a distinct, counter-cultural, identity-forming agency of the kingdom, Hauerwas allowed that questions about his confessional identity were fair game. He was a mainline Methodist who rejected mainline Protestantism, an evangelical with little connection to American evangelicalism, a pacifist in a mostly non-pacifist denomination, and a Protestant theologian in a Catholic institution. He believed that the Anabaptist peace churches were the best exemplars of the Christian witness, but did not belong to one. Reaching for a concise moniker, Hauerwas called himself "a high-church Mennonite," skirting the problem that such an entity existed only in his head. In the real world he worshipped at a Lutheran church during his two years at Augustana College, attended Sacred Heart parish on the Notre Dame campus for several years (on occasion Hauerwas was refused communion, whereupon he got in a different line), and considered joining the Catholic Church. Often he wrote on the necessity of church authority and the ecclesial matrix of scriptural meaning, which raised the question of converting to Rome. Hauerwas struggled with the question for years, imagining himself as a Catholic. His fascination with the power of sacramental practice in Catholic life caused him to add the importance of church practices to his stock themes. His wife Ann, however, threatened to divorce him if he converted to Catholicism, so Hauerwas joined a Methodist church in South Bend, where he found a spiritual home for the remainder of his years at Notre Dame. Methodist pastor John Smith, unimpressed by Hauerwas's theological renown, made him attend a membership class for a year. That impressed Hauerwas, who rejoiced at finding a Methodist community that saved him from the tyranny of his willful individualism.[88]

That did not settle the issue for him, however. Hauerwas's tortured marriage ended in divorce, and in 1983 he confessed that he could not say whether he wrote as a Protestant or Catholic. He was a lifelong evangelical Methodist who did not intend to disavow that identity; on the other hand, he was influenced by Catholic sacramentalism and ecclesiology, and regarded his work as catholic theological ethics. In the same year, Notre Dame's administration furnished additional clarity on the matter by making its theology department more intentionally Roman Catholic. New department chair Richard McBrien, a liberal Catholic theologian, did not care for Hauerwas or his "sectarian" perspective. Hauerwas, holding McBrien in equally low regard, suddenly felt unwelcome at Notre Dame, his Catholic yearnings notwithstanding. In 1984 he moved to Duke University, expecting to put the Catholic option behind him, but he grappled with it again there. Though he joined a local Methodist Church, Hauerwas questioned anew whether he should convert to Rome, until he married a Methodist minister, Paula Gilbert, in 1989. That settled the Catholic question, eventually, regardless of the divorce issue. He explained that if the Catholic Church did not recognize the priesthood of his wife, he could not be a Catholic, which brought him to a final contradiction. Hauerwas believed in the priestly ordination of his wife, despite the fact that she and the Methodist Church did not, since Methodism had no ordained priesthood.[89]

His relationship to mainline social ethics was similarly conflicted. Hauerwas kept saying that his field took a wrong turn from the beginning, yet he sustained a lover's quarrel with it for decades. He taught the history of the field, battled with it constantly, and blasted it for treasuring the wrong things, but hoped for a course correction. The social gospelers who invented social ethics sought to formulate the means "for Christians to serve their societies, particularly American society," he observed. Niebuhr and his disciples attacked the social gospel, but Nieburian realism was merely a shrewder and more sophisticated version of it: "For Niebuhr and the social gospelers the subject of Christian ethics was America." They agreed that social ethics was about creating a just American society and disagreed mainly on the theological and practical efficacy of moral idealism.[90]

That was the core of the social ethical mistake, Hauerwas argued. The social gospel and Niebuhrian realism both had a liberal Constantinian concept of Christianity. In effect, their church was America. Both traditions reduced the theology in theological ethics to activist utilitarian ends. H. Richard Niebuhr changed the subject slightly, seeking to account for moral activity within the relativities of history, but his theocentric historicism relativized Christianity even more than liberalism and Niebuhrian realism. For him and James Gustafson, God was the absolute, ineffable Maker of heaven and earth that relativized all claims to the good. Catholic social ethics took a different route to the same problem. Catholicism was Constantinian without apology, and its most celebrated American ethicist – Murray – tailored Catholic teaching to fit the American circumstance. Thus, Catholic social ethics and H. Richard Niebuhr shared the crucial failing of the social gospel and Reinhold Niebuhr: all surrendered the particularity of the gospel to a construct or methodology purporting to establish common ground with unbelievers.

Social ethics was always about accommodating American society, seeking a place at the table of public conversation. In every version except the witness of the Anabaptist peace churches, Hauerwas judged, social ethics accommodated the gospel to the demands of liberal society. Instead of emphasizing the particularity of the Christian witness, social ethicists translated Christian claims into the ostensibly inclusive languages of philosophy or sociology: "Theologians and religious thinkers have largely sought to show that the modes of argument and conclusions reached by philosophical ethicists are no different from those reached by ethicists working with more explicit religious presuppositions. The task of Christian ethics, both socially and philosophically, was not revision but accommodation."[91]

Because the story of American social ethics, in this telling, was one of working out the problems "bequeathed to us by the social gospel and the Niebuhrs," it was virtually synonymous with compromising the church's Christian identity and embracing the moral problems of Caesar. Since it was not very Christian, it did not sustain the distinctive gospel ethic. Hauerwas explained that social ethicists puzzled over how to attain and exercise power in a morally responsible way, which was not a Christian question. That question was unthinkable to pre-Constantinian Christianity, which never asked under what circumstances Christians should kill to serve a relative political good. Citing Yoder for support, he admonished: "Something has already gone wrong when Christians think they can ask, 'What is the best form of society or government?'" It was asked, and could only be asked, after the church accepted Caesar as a member: "This question assumes that Christians should or do have social and political power so they can determine the ethos of society. That this assumption has long been with us does nothing to confirm its truth."[92]

Constantinianism and accommodation fit together logically and historically, but just as the gospel should not have been distorted to accommodate Caesar, it should not have been cut to fit liberal society. Hauerwas charged that modern theologians were far too impressed by liberal democracy. When they sought to make Christianity relevant to it, repeatedly they translated Christian claims into a non-theological idiom, "But once such a translation is accomplished, it becomes very unclear why they need the theological idiom in the first place." Lacking any message of their own, modern theologians perpetuated theology and themselves by claiming linkages with non-Christian philosophical and sociopolitical perspectives. To Hauerwas, that was self-defeating. Theologians who tried to convince unbelievers that Christianity was still relevant merely confirmed the secular assumption that theology was a form of special pleading: "The more theologians seek to find the means to translate theological convictions into terms acceptable to the nonbeliever, the more they substantiate the view that theology has little of importance to say in the area of ethics."[93]

Hauerwas stressed that the idea of a self-standing "ethics" began with the Enlightenment, specifically Immanuel Kant. The idea was to dispense with theological claims lacking credibility, staking Christianity on credible, universal, moral truths. For Hauerwas, there was no cure for social ethics that did not repudiate this faulty starting point. Christianity was not a perennial philosophy, a world-embracing universal faith, or even a particular system of beliefs. The center of Christianity was not any particular belief about Jesus constructed by the church, nor did Christian ethics assume moral responsibility for organizing the world. The center of Christianity was the community-forming way of Christ that inspired a new kind of corporate spiritual existence in an alien world. To say that the early Christians believed in God was not very interesting, Hauerwas observed, "What is interesting is that they thought that their belief in God as they had encountered him in Jesus required the formation of a community distinct from the world exactly because of the kind of God he was."[94]

Gospel Christianity was narrative dependent and community oriented. It created an embodied ethic that could not be abstracted from the Christian community or translated into idioms shared by outsiders. Hauerwas explained, "As Christians we believe we not only need a community, but a community of a particular kind to live well morally. We need a people who are capable of being faithful to a way of life, even when that way of life may be in conflict with what passes as 'morality' in the larger society."[95] With Yoder, Hauerwas described Christianity as the messianic faith of believers inhabiting the new aeon, the kingdom of God, in the face of the principalities and powers. With coauthor (and at the time, Duke University chaplain) William Willimon he put it more starkly: "Christianity is an invitation to be part of an alien people who make a difference because they see something that cannot otherwise be seen without Christ."[96]

With Yoder and Willimon he stressed that his ecclesiology was not a form of sectarianism and did not advocate "withdrawal" from the world: "How can the church possibly withdraw when it, by necessity must always find itself surrounded? There is no place to which it can withdraw. I am not asking the church to withdraw, but rather to give up the presumptions of Constantinian power, particularly when those take the form of liberal universalism."[97] To the objection that he abandoned the church's moral responsibility to keep society from disintegrating into chaos, Hauerwas replied that there was no shortage of liberal Constantinians who wanted to manage the world in a "good" way.[98] America's policy institutes and universities overflowed with people seeking power to make the world a better place. Christianity had no business reinforcing any part of that Constantinian disposition, he urged. The church remained deeply addicted to Constantinianism because modern Christians thought they could do good things by attaining power and because "all our categories have been set by the church's establishment as a necessary part of Western civilization."[99]

To attain power in the past, the church had to betray Christianity. That trade-off did not change significantly when the power structure was managed by liberal and democratic procedures, Hauerwas argued. In the past the church made peace with the war-making state by selling out Christ's commands to love one's enemies, do good to one's persecutors, resist not evil, and turn the other cheek. The liberal state made the same demand. Modern theologians, seeking to make Christianity relevant or palatable to the modern age, surrendered the heart of Christian faith. In the name of "applying" Christianity to society, they followed Niebuhr in turning salvation into something "fundamentally individualistic, if not gnostic."[100]

Hauerwas played up the irony that the deeply political Niebuhr had to de-politicize Christology to be a social ethicist. For Niebuhr, Christianity was a useful myth for the task of reorienting American society, and salvation was otherworldly deliverance from the human condition, "not the sanctifying possibility within history of a political alternative that is saving." Hauerwas countered that the church was supposed to live faithfully in the light of Christ's proleptic kingdom:

> There's an important difference between what I mean by 'kingdom' and what Niebuhr means by it. For Niebuhr the kingdom is always an ideal that stands over against any

possible realization in history. What that means is that he doesn't have any concrete manifestation of God in history. He just has the ideal standing over against historical realities. And I don't know if you need Jesus for that project.[101]

Hauerwas believed in a Christian ethic that made no sense without Jesus. For him, as for Yoder and Rauschenbusch, the reign of God was a community-making social order within history as well as an ideal at the end of history and beyond it. Apart from Christ's kingdom-inaugurating resurrection from the dead, there was no ethic of the kingdom and no point in rehabilitating Christianity. The kingdom was a spiritual reality, not merely an ethical or religious idea. Without the faith that Christ inaugurated a new era within history, there was not enough reason to follow Christ, much less any reason to salvage Christian ethics. To Hauerwas, the problem with Christian realism was displayed in Niebuhr's discomfort with the language of Easter faith and the biblical theology of the kingdom. Niebuhr salvaged a social role for modern churches without disputing the skepticism of modern culture toward Christian beliefs. He contributed to the demise of modern Protestantism by defending it as a religious philosophy or mythology that served social purposes, confirming the modern prejudice that theology had no work of its own to do. For Niebuhr, the "love perfectionist" nonviolent way of Christ was a serious option only for sectarians who opted out of the social struggle for justice. For Hauerwas, the biblical ethic of nonviolence was "incumbent on all Christians who seek to live faithfully in the kingdom made possible by the life, death, and resurrection of Jesus." Nonviolence was the "hallmark" of Christian ethics, not a minority option among better possibilities.[102]

To the extent that Hauerwas found himself choosing between Rauschenbusch and Niebuhr, he preferred Rauschenbusch, who at least held fast to the kingdom faith. Christian ethicists needed to unlearn their Niebuhrian lessons, he urged: "Niebuhr taught us how to think. He gave us the categories that we've thought with for years. But I've slowly tried to train myself out of thinking in those categories. That's a very hard task, because when you let someone set the problem, oftentimes you keep getting their answer. So the challenge is how not to let them set the problem anymore."[103] Leaning on Barth and Yoder for his answer, Hauerwas affirmed that the church existed to witness to Christ, not to baptize or reform modern culture. In his Gifford Lectures of 2001 he stressed that Niebuhr viewed the incarnation and resurrection of Christ as myths, had no doctrine of the church to speak of, had no doctrine of sanctification at all, and stripped the kingdom of its social-ethical meaning. Niebuhr still spoke to liberal Christians who could not imagine accepting Christianity on stronger terms, but that fateful strategy sold out most of what mattered: "Anyone who would put Niebuhr on the side of the angels must come to terms with the extraordinary 'thinness' of his theology. Niebuhr's god is not a god capable of offering salvation in any material sense."[104] Elsewhere Hauerwas put it more personally: "I can only think the way I think because Reinhold Niebuhr made such important mistakes."[105]

By the mid-1990s Hauerwas seemed to have embraced his reputation as a theological provocateur and entertainer. The jacket blurbs for his book, *Dispatches from the Front* (1994), emphasized its entertainment value. Cornel West praised his "idiosyncratic" and "cantankerous" style; Robert Bellah enthused that Hauerwas was never boring; literary critic Frank Lentricchia declared, "There's no one I'd rather be reading." Hauerwas confirmed that he aspired to entertain, his writing was a "form of gossip generally known as journalism," and he hoped that readers would find his "up-yours attitude" to be interesting and challenging. Every chapter delivered these goods, sparkling with opinionated jolts that only Hauerwas would have written. He did not want his students to make up their own minds, "because most of them do not have minds worth making up." Egalitarianism was "the opiate of the masses." Religion professors liked their subject "if it is dead or they can kill it." Niebuhr's theology was "a gnostic account of Christianity." Hauerwas had "a deep distrust of the family, since for Christians the family is one of the great sources of idolatry." Political theorist Amy Guttmann's defense of liberal democracy was so filled with "sheer arrogance" as to be "almost beyond belief." Finally: "From my perspective 'public' and 'pluralism' are simply words of mystification that some people use when their brains are on automatic."[106]

Hauerwas enjoyed writing in this way, and he took pride in the contrasts between his irreverent independence and the ingratiating, self-censoring correctness of academic theology. Yet he often expressed anger or annoyance at not being taken seriously. *Dispatches from the Front* set the record straight on which came first. Colleagues and peers dismissed him long before he started writing polemically, he explained; his "polemical, if not violent" style was a response to not being taken seriously. It made him "angry as hell" that theologians sold out Christianity to liberal culture and then derided him for mentioning it. In the name of pluralism, openness, and academic respectability, theologians routinely underwrote their presumptions of superiority and suppressed "all strong positions" like his.[107]

The charge of "sectarianism" was a prime example. Richard McBrien, James Gustafson, and many others dismissed Hauerwas for giving in to the "sectarian temptation." Theologically, Gustafson explained, Hauerwas was a fideist who did not bother to justify his claims or the credibility of his favored biblical texts; ethically he was a "sociological tribalist" and pacifist who wrote off the broad moral responsibilities of modern Christians. In 1985 Gustafson put it strongly, in a statement frequently cited afterward, that Hauerwas isolated Christianity "from taking seriously the wider world of science and culture and limits the participation of Christians in the ambiguities of moral and social life."[108]

Later that year he put it more sharply, after Hauerwas wrote that Gustafson resolved the tensions between historicism and universalism by opting for an unreal universalism. Hauerwas contended that Gustafson's quest for the universal caused him to make Christianity secondary, which was a disastrously wrong option:

> I remain stuck with the problem of history in a way different from Gustafson because I remain stuck with the claim that through Jesus' resurrection God decisively changed our history. Therefore I believe we must continue to begin with the 'particular,' with the historical, not because there is no other place to begin but because that is where God begins.

Gustafson replied that he did not know who "our" was supposed to be in the statement about God changing "our" history. As for beginning where God began: "I say, harshly, that I find that sentence, even in context, to be ludicrous."[109]

Where was God before the Easter appearances? To the extent that Hauerwas made sense, Gustafson judged, he had become a sectarian, "a twentieth-century version of Marcion." To Hauerwas, nature had no theological significance, natural science was irrelevant, and God was "the tribal God of a minority of the earth's population." Hauerwas achieved notoriety by advocating "an intellectual and moral sectarianism of the most extreme sort," one fueled by simplistic either/ors, such as the choice between historicism and universalism. Gustafson countered that in the real world, ideas like historicism and universalism held graded relevance within a continuum of interrelated possibilities. Moreover, Hauerwas was not merely a sectarian, but an incoherent word-spinner. His slippery use of words such as "history" and "particularism" resembled "a greased pig at the country fair contest," and he appeared to believe that he could do theological ethics without making philosophical claims. Gustafson admonished his former student that, having made a name for himself, he needed to clarify what he was talking about.[110]

For years Hauerwas tacked back and forth between explaining himself and blasting variations of Gustafson's critique. He assumed a qualified epistemological realism, was not aware of any scientific conclusion that refuted his theological perspective, disputed the right of liberal academics to decree which theologies were sectarian, described himself as a deeper historicist than Gustafson, and denied that he denied that Christians should support civic republicanism. It was only when the state resorted to violence "to maintain internal order and external security" that Christians were obliged not to support it. Modern theologians, feeling at home in modern societies, actually believed that "the societies are our creations," Hauerwas observed. He replied that it was a terrible illusion to think that liberal democracy changed the moral equation. Just as Constantinianism was a form of apostasy, so was any business about democracy legitimizing state violence. The right to vote did not make killing for the state any less odious or anti-Christian. Contending that justice was "a bad idea for Christians," Hauerwas urged American Christians to be "alien citizens." He refused to say that following Christ involved struggling for the right ordering of the world: "Because when people say that, they always become Constantinian. They want you to play the game of responsibility. 'Aha,' they say, 'you're not being responsible!' But, because of Niebuhr, responsibility carries a whole set of presumptions that I don't want to accept."[111]

For Hauerwas, the "real world" was not the social order of ubiquitous violence described by Niebuhr and other social ethicists that liberalism sought to manage. The real world, for a Christian, was the kingdom-disclosing social reality inaugurated by the resurrection of the crucified Christ. Modern theology sought to convince its diminishing audience that Christianity was adaptable to the "real world" of modern culture and experience, but this spiritually impoverished strategy failed by succeeding.

That was to be the thesis of his magnum opus, a critique of American Christian ethics from Rauschenbusch to Gustafson, which would conclude by explaining why Yoder offered a better option. For many years Hauerwas taught a course titled "Christian Ethics in America" that covered Rauschenbusch, both Niebuhrs, Murray, Catholic ethicist Charles Curran, Ramsey, Gustafson, and Yoder. Training doctoral students in ethics, he took for granted the necessity of teaching the history of the field. By the 1970s it was no longer customary for students to have earned a seminary degree before they applied to doctoral programs; thus Hauerwas recognized that doctoral students could not be expected to have already studied Rauschenbusch and Niebuhr. Moreover, at Notre Dame the Protestant tradition was largely unknown anyway. After he moved to Duke Hauerwas kept teaching the course, and kept planning a major work that devoted separate chapters to each of his eight subjects.

He assumed that the book, despite sharply criticizing the social ethics tradition, would defend the integrity and significance of modern Christian ethics as a discipline. Hauerwas planned to argue that the American tradition began with Rauschenbusch's

Christianizing the Social Order and petered out with Gustafson's *Can Ethics Be Christian?*
These titles framed the book's central question. Having begun with the ambition of
transforming the entire social order in the name of Christ's kingdom, how did American Christian ethics decline to the point where transformation was forgotten and ethicists like Gustafson were not even sure they should call their work Christian?[112]

The answer, as Hauerwas had argued for years, was that America had always been
the subject of American Christian ethics. Instead of upholding the distinct identity of
the church as a Jesus-following spiritual community, Christian ethicists identified
Christian ethics with liberal democracy, worried about their standing in the American
academy, and internalized other values of modern liberal culture. They succeeded to
a considerable extent, Hauerwas assured his students, a record he respected, in a way.
He told them that it was important to understand the fathers of American Christian
ethics, even if they were terribly wrong.

By the time that Hauerwas began to write the book in the mid-1990s, however,
the latter assurance rang hollow to him. He realized that he no longer believed in
Christian ethics as a field. His critique of American Christian ethics had eviscerated
what remained of his determination to teach and preserve it. If Kant established a
faulty basis for Christian ethics, and the social gospel provided a flawed one for social
ethics, and Christian ethicists after Rauschenbusch put Christian ethics out of a job,
making Christianity "unintelligible to itself," what was there left to defend? Instead of
offering a grand tour that ended with Yoder's corrective to the entire story, Hauerwas
lost his appetite for the project. It seemed more plausible to say that Christian ethics
should not have been invented than to suggest it could be fixed by a strong dose of
Yoder. As an academic enterprise, he observed, Christian ethics had morphed into a
religious studies hodgepodge called "religious ethics," which was not a discipline and
barely qualified as an area of study. Christian ethics, by contrast, had once been a
discipline, but its meltdown into religious ethics confirmed that it should not have
branched off on its own in the first place.[113]

There were additional factors causing him to let go of the book, if not the field.
Harlan Beckley and I wrote books covering much of the story that Hauerwas had
planned to tell. Beckley's *A Passion for Justice* dealt with Rauschenbusch, Niebuhr, and
Ryan; my *Soul in Society* featured detailed accounts of the social gospel, Christian
realism, and liberation theology. Hauerwas wrote generous reviews of both works and
ruminated, subsequently, over my discussions of black liberation theology, white feminism, womanism, and neoconservatism. These subjects played no role in the history
he had taught and planned to write. He reflected that liberation themes obviously
played a large role in contemporary Christian ethics, but because they did not "comport
with the theological and ethical frames of the Niebuhrs, Ramsay, and Gustafson," he
did not include them. In 1980 Hauerwas had argued that the crucial influence on
Christian ethicists was where they went to graduate school, not their religious tradition: "We are where we went." By the mid-1990s he realized in a new way that for
him, for better and worse, "Christian ethics" stood for the sort of thing he learned at
Yale under Gustafson. He had trouble relating liberation themes to what he considered
Christian ethics. He also realized that he did not want to write a long polemic against
his teachers and role models. So he wrote an article "on a book I will not write,"
affirmed that some of his best friends were Christian ethicists and even religious ethicists, and warned that what remained of theology in religious ethics was being crowded
out by the yearning of ethicists for academic respectability.[114]

Persistently he railed against the liberal Enlightenment myths of objectivity and story-less reason. Postmodernism was supposed to represent the death of Enlightenment mythology, so how could the religious studies denigration of theology be advancing when everyone agreed there was no such thing as rational neutrality? Bitterly he protested that the great theologians of the past could not have taught in American universities, because they had religious beliefs. Hauerwas told his first-year students that he was out to convert them to pacifism; meanwhile most of his doctoral students were Christian pacifists like himself. It galled him that universities trained graduate students to have no opinions, so they could win jobs and teach their own students to have no opinions. He wanted the academy to support strong convictions and stand for something besides unreal rationality and commercial success. He did not mind having been pushed out at Notre Dame, because Notre Dame was supposed to be Catholic, just as Brandeis was supposed to be Jewish and Duke was supposed to be Methodist.

His critique of liberal culture extended to its capitalist selfishness and materialistic avoidance of suffering. Hauerwas admired communities like the Amish, Jehovah's Witnesses, and orthodox Jews that had large families and a low view of the corrupting outside world. He admired the refusal of traditional communities to structure their childrearing and care of the elderly around the material and professional needs of modern achievers, a recurrent theme that set off accusations of antifeminism. On the ethics of life he was consistently antiwar, anti-capital punishment, anti-abortion, and anti-euthanasia, which heightened his sense of isolation in the Methodist church. He wrote movingly of the ways that physically and emotionally disabled people interrupted the success-arrangements of their families, helping them to slow down, count their blessings, and experience salvation. Disabled people freed others from the false expectation of needing to be strong and in control, Hauerwas observed. Usually they set off fear in others, but they also provided invaluable opportunities to let go of controlling self-management and discover the possibility of shared needs, burdens, and joys. On a related theme he argued that modern medicine kept people from absorbing or even naming the silences of suffering and mortality through which the voice of God might be heard. Hauerwas wanted churches to be spiritual communities that practiced the virtues of caregiving and faithfulness, resisting the culture of success, materialism, and denial of mortality.[115]

He was famously contrarian on these themes. Debating an advocate of medical experiments on fetal tissue, Hauerwas asked, "What if it were discovered that fetal tissue were a delicacy; could you eat it?" The stunned researcher was forced to admit that logically, his answer would have to be "yes." Speaking at a rally against the death penalty, Hauerwas could not resist baiting part of his audience, declaring that he made an exception for stock-fraud, for which there needed to be a guillotine in the middle of Wall Street. Usually on such occasions he did not bother to explain what he meant, letting his audience figure it out. During the controversy in 1993 over whether gays should be allowed to serve in the military, Hauerwas argued for "yes" with a polemical twist, writing in the *Charlotte Observer* that Catholics should have been far more threatening to the military than gays, because Catholics were supposed to take seriously the strictures of just-war theory. Although Hauerwas supported equal rights for women in church and society, he provoked feminists repeatedly. On one occasion he found himself sharing an elevator with a feminist critic, Gloria Albrecht. Hauerwas shook her hand and remarked, "I guess you and I don't really have much to say to one another." Albrecht agreed, and the ride continued in silence; for Hauerwas and

Albrecht, it was better to acknowledge the conflict than to make nice-talk. Upon meeting his junior colleague in theological ethics at Duke, Amy Laura Hall, Hauerwas told her, "I'm a ball scratcher." Hall, a fellow Texan, assured Hauerwas that she would scratch hers if she had any. Later she told a reporter that she tried to help Hauerwas understand why his sexualized barnyard language was threatening to many women: "The gender stuff with him is so tricky – and at his best, Stanley knows that."[116]

In 2001 Hauerwas gave the prestigious Gifford Lectures at the University of St Andrews in Scotland, where he used Barth, Yoder, and John Paul II to help expound his concept of sacred politics – the building of Christian communities that embodied Christian claims. Barth gave a "stunning intellectual performance" that challenged the accommodation of Christian theology to modern culture, he argued, but the hope of a sacred politics also needed outward-reaching, church-identified witnesses, not mere intellectual performers. Yoder and the pope were witnesses of that sort, "representative figures of churches that have challenged the presumptions of modernity." Hauerwas was not representative of anything, but in his own way he aspired to the category of witness.[117]

Later that year *Time* magazine anointed him one of sorts, naming him "America's Best Theologian." Jean Bethke Elshtain, profiling Hauerwas for the magazine, described him as "a volatile, complex person with an explosive personality and high-energy style." She also noted his penchant for "rough speech." That unleashed a flood of media attention, much of which told of prim evangelical audiences being flabbergasted by his stream of expletives. Hauerwas stoked the media blaze with a profanity-laced interview for *Lingua Franca* that rocketed around the Internet. A year later, sensitive to local egos, he told *Duke Magazine* that if he were any other member of the Duke faculty, "I would be very tired of 'Hauerwas.'" In fact, he was tired of Hauerwas too: "I have no idea how I have suddenly become famous, but I am not happy about it. Indeed, when a theologian, particularly in the kind of world we live in, becomes famous, you have an indication that a mistake has been made. Our subject after all is God." Trying to escape narcissism was very difficult under these circumstances, he allowed, especially because the very effort to escape only increased one's self-fascination: "My only hope is having friends who remind me of what I am supposed to be about." That hope was well founded, for Hauerwas had many friends and a gift for friendship.[118]

For years he sloughed off complaints of social ethicists that he condemned liberal society too indiscriminately, legitimized Christian indifference to social justice struggles, and weakened Christian support for American democracy. In *Soul in Society*, I argued that Hauerwas's polemic against social justice politics was unbiblical and ethically unacceptable, and that he wrongly disparaged the social ethical concern for the "right ordering of the world." The core of the problem, I argued, was his sharp dichotomy, borrowed from Yoder, between the church and the unredeemed:

> This insistence on dichotomizing the world between Christians and pagans marks the essential difference in spirit between Hauerwas's theology and progressive social Christianity. For the social gospelers, as for contemporary liberationists and ecofeminists, the moral core of Christianity compels cooperative efforts with unbelievers, in whom the Spirit also dwells. Hauerwas's emphasis on the Christian–non-Christian dichotomy produces an unacceptable position regarding the Christian struggle for a just social order, as well as a way of speaking about non-Christians that smacks of religious arrogance. The premodern church that dichotomized the world into these categories believed that all other religions

are false, that Christ is the only way to salvation, and therefore, that only Christians can escape eternal damnation. Modern Christianity cannot pretend to aspire to this worldview or seek to rescue some aspect of it for other purposes. To believe in the reality of the indwelling kingdom of Christ does not require that one regard the rest of the world as unregenerate or deprived of grace.[119]

Gloria Albrecht pressed a similar critique. Hauerwas's entire scheme rested on problematic Western dualisms of self and world, one's group and the others, church and world, and resident alien versus secular culture, she argued, saying,

> From his worldview of violent dualisms, he yearns for a loving, nonviolent unity. His proposal of "resident alien" status for the church in society seems to assume that Christians and the church can be part of society while not being fundamentally shaped by society. As resident aliens, we are to be firmly but nonviolently "us" in relation to "them." Womanist and feminist critiques of the church have revealed the violence to women and others that such "unity" has masked.

Despite writing prolifically about Christian nonviolence, Albrecht protested, Hauerwas offered no acknowledgment of "relationships of domination within 'the Christian narrative' and its tradition, nor the multiplicity of voices, nor the silencing throughout history of many Christians' stories."[120]

Critiques of this sort rolled off Hauerwas for years with little effect on his position until 2004, when political philosopher Jeffrey Stout criticized him for undermining Christian support of American democracy. Stout praised Hauerwas for putting Christian pacifism, not his critique of liberalism, at the center of his social ethic. However, it was not clear to Stout that anything much came of this position. The USA lacked a military draft, and Hauerwas did not advocate military tax avoidance, civil disobedience, or anything else that might have any real consequences. More importantly to Stout, Hauerwas wrongly conflated liberal theory with democratic practice, putting down the importance of maintaining democracy by ridiculing aspects of liberal political philosophy that he rejected. Stout challenged Hauerwas to acknowledge that liberal theory and democratic practice were not the same thing, and that strengthening American democracy was a morally worthy enterprise for Christians.[121]

At first Hauerwas replied in the usual way: Stout overestimated his influence, the first political responsibility of Christians was to be the church, the first political loyalty of Christians was to God, and whatever contributions Christians made to the social order had to be made one witness at a time.[122] On second consideration, he switched gears. It was probably true, Hauerwas allowed, that he skewered democracy too easily by poking holes in liberal theory. For him, liberal democracy was bankrupt and uninteresting. Liberalism was about having no story and not needing one. Hauerwas held no brief for the kind of democracy that rested on the bare rights of an unencumbered, deracinated, liberal self. But there was such a thing as radical democracy, he observed. Until now, he had not quite grasped how to talk about it, and so he had left the impression of believing that Christians should be indifferent to the fate of democracy. Leaning on Yoder and political theorist Sheldon Wolin, Hauerwas came out for radical democracy.[123]

He recalled that when he converted to Christian pacifism, he considered Yoder's work deficient for not developing a theory of legitimacy by which states could be judged. But later he found Yoder's realism about the state to be perfectly apt. The state needed no theoretical justification; it simply existed, exactly as the New Testament assumed in its references to the principalities and powers. Instead of contriving a theory of legitimacy, Yoder adhered to the Pauline understanding of government authority as God's instrument in a process leading to its defeat. The Pauline church did not expect governments to renounce violence. Existing between the two aeons, it asked governments only to be just, to care for widows and orphans, and to use the least violent means possible to secure order. For Hauerwas, as for Yoder, ecclesiology was a form of politics, the politics of redemption and eschatology. The church was political to the extent that it followed Jesus, refusing to be assimilated into civic nationalism. It had time to be political, refusing to be hurried, because to the church, reality was eschatological.[124]

Wolin similarly stressed the importance of time in the Christian outlook. Before Christianity, he observed, time was a closed circle; in Christianity history was transformed into an eschatological drama of deliverance. The early Christians were able to eschew their ostensible political obligations under the empire because they followed the teaching of Jesus, an alternative politics geared to the end of the age. Hauerwas declared that he was a radical democrat in this sense of embracing an alternative politics with a long memory of origin and plenty of time for practice and engagement. The most deeply political things he had ever written, by this standard, were his reflections on being the church with mentally handicapped persons: "A community that has the time and can take the time, the patience, to be constituted by practices represented by those 'slower' than most of us, is a community that may provide an alternative to the politics of speed that currently shapes our lives."[125]

He took delight in being impossible to peg on the usual ideological grid. Hauerwas held conservative positions on various ecclesiastical and moral issues and sat on the board of *First Things*, a neoconservative journal, yet he denounced neoconservatives ferociously and could be rough on traditional conservatives too. He blasted liberation theology and progressive Christianity, denying that the metaphor of liberation deserved to be "central or overriding as a description of the nature of Christian existence," but he outflanked most of the Christian Left on anti-imperial and antiwar issues. When neoconservatives attacked liberal theology or the National Council of Churches, they often cited Hauerwas for support. Neoconservatism, however, was something very different from Hauerwas and Yoder.[126]

Ideological Americanism:
The Neoconservative Reaction

The neoconservative phenomenon was essentially political and ideological, not religious, but it had a religious component and made a significant impact on social Christianity. It arose in the early 1970s as a reaction against the social movements of the time and the liberalization of the Democratic Party. Unlike previous forms of American political conservatism, what came to be called "neoconservatism" harbored no nostalgia for Tory England, the Old South, *laissez-faire* capitalism, or the nativist–isolationist "normalcy" of the 1920s. When it took a religious form, it did not hanker for pre-modern orthodoxies, either. For neocons, the Fall had occurred only recently, with the rise of radical social movements in the USA.

The original neocons were former leftists who hated the antiwar, feminist, black liberationist, and counter-cultural aspects of what Paul Ramsey called "the new liberal consensus." Some were veterans of the Socialist anti-Stalinist wars of the 1930s, such as Emanuel Muravchik, Arnold Beichman, Arch Puddington, John Roche, and Harry Overstreet. Others were mainstream political types and intellectuals such as Henry Jackson, Daniel Patrick Moynihan, Daniel Bell, Nathan Glazer, Max Kampelman, Jeane Kirkpatrick, and Ben Wattenberg. A few were conservative Niebuhrians who spurned the recent progressive turn in Christian realism, such as Paul Ramsey, Ernest Lefever, and Kenneth Thompson. A few were politically homeless conservatives who found their way to the neocon Right, notably Irving Kristol, Peter Berger, and James Q. Wilson, and there were also a few refugees from the New Left, especially Richard John Neuhaus, Norman Podhoretz, and Michael Novak.[127]

Neoconservatism marked the last stage of the old Left, being the last movement in American politics to define itself principally by its opposition to communism. It was a generational phenomenon launched by mostly Jewish intellectuals and activists, which caused many to regard "neoconservatism" as mere code for "Jewish conservatism," and which fueled bitter controversies over the militant Zionism of most neocons. From the beginning, however, the movement attracted many prominent non-Jewish proponents, including William Bennett, Peter Berger, Francis Fukuyama, Zalmay Khalilzad, Jeane Kirkpatrick, Ernest Lefever, James Nuechterlein, Daniel Patrick Moynihan, Michael Novak, Richard John Neuhaus, Paul Ramsey, Kenneth Thompson, George Weigel, and James Q. Wilson.

At first the neocons bristled at their label, disputing that they had become conservatives of any kind. Often they protested that they had not changed; thus, they were not the ones that needed to be labeled. It was liberalism that had changed, having turned culturally radical and antiwar. Many of the neocons had not known any conservatives personally when they began to be called neoconservatives. But the neocons grew into their name by objectively aligning with the US political Right. For a while they tried to revive the militant Cold War wing of the Democratic Party, but failing with that, in the mid-1970s they began to trickle into the Republican Party. They were attracted not so much to the party as to a particular Republican: Ronald Reagan. In 1980 the neocons streamed into his presidential campaign, and when Reagan won the presidency, more than a dozen of them won high-ranking positions in his administration. By then the neocons had accepted their name, which legitimized their place in the Republican party while distinguishing them from other kinds of conservatives.

Michael Novak and Democratic Capitalism

For Michael Novak, neoconservatism represented a return – after a radical detour – to the values of an upwardly mobile, working-class Pennsylvania childhood. In one of his periodic attempts to explain his transformation he recalled, "If I had been knocked from a horse by a blinding light on a single memorable day, it would be easier to say. Instead, it was quite gradual, through examining my own left-wing presuppositions one by one. Underneath this questioning, perhaps, lay a pursuit of self-knowledge, a drive to be faithful to my family and roots, to be myself."[128] Having been urged by his father never to bet against Notre Dame or the United States, Novak had a brief career as a New leftist, decided that his friends in progressive church circles "were simply not my people," and moved to the political Right as a celebrant of American capitalism.[129]

He was born into an ethnic, working-class neighborhood in the downtown section of Johnstown, Pennsylvania in 1933. Novak's grandparents came to the USA from villages in the Tatra Mountains in Slovakia, not far from the southern Polish border. His father worked for an insurance company, and in 1940, the family moved uptown to Morrellville, "where the Americans lived." Several moves later – following the elder Novak's promotions – they resettled in Johnstown, shortly before Novak went off to seminary. Against the opposition of his father, who did not want his sons to become priests, he entered the junior seminary program at Notre Dame's Holy Cross Seminary. Novak was uncertain of his call to the priesthood, but determined to put his religious vocation to the test. He was 14 years old.

He gave 12 years to the question, studying at Stonehill College, the Gregorian University, and Catholic University of America before deciding against ordination in 1960, six months before he was scheduled to be ordained. The celibacy requirement was the main reason; in addition, Novak worried that being a priest would stunt his writing career. "Chastity was difficult for me; obedience even more so," he later explained. "I've always believed that a priest should teach and defend church doctrine. The problem for me was that I also wanted to be a writer, which required a degree of intellectual independence I couldn't have as a priest."[130] Choosing independence, he wrote to *Commonweal* magazine, telling the editors that he hoped to be "introduced to the world" when he visited their offices. James Finn later recalled that before they decided how to respond to this overture, Novak showed up, "young, quietly energetic, openly inquiring, interested – it seemed – in everything."[131] He started writing books the following year, beginning with a novel, published shortly before he enrolled in Harvard University's graduate program in philosophy, about the ordination of a young seminarian.[132]

Not realizing that philosophy at Harvard meant logic and language analysis, Novak pictured himself as a socially engaged philosopher/novelist in the tradition of Mauriac, Sartre, and Camus. It stunned him to discover that Harvard's philosophical positivism was even more lifeless, narrow, and uninteresting than the Thomist scholasticism in which he was trained. Turning to church politics, he enrolled at Harvard Divinity School, married artist Karen Loeb, and went to Rome to report on the second session of Vatican Council II. His honeymoon produced articles for *Commonweal* and *Time* magazines and an influential book, *The Open Church*, on the significance of the council.

The Open Church argued that Roman Catholicism was stuck in a non-historical memory of its past and needed to open its windows to the modern world. Catholic theology recycled a frozen neo-Thomism that was impervious to developments in modern science, history, and philosophy. In Novak's telling, Catholic social doctrine failed to grasp or appreciate the achievements of modern industrialism, democracy, and pluralism, largely because the church had been ghettoized by the overweening influence of its Italian and Spanish traditions. Roman Catholicism needed to learn from the experiences of Catholics who knew the blessings of modernity. It especially needed to learn from the American experience. America was the first modern country, the harbinger of the world's future. Not for the last time, Novak argued that the success of the American Experiment necessitated corrections in Catholic teaching.[133]

At Vatican II he became friends with ecumenical Protestant theologian Robert McAfee Brown, who subsequently helped Novak win a teaching position in the Special Program in Humanities (later called the Religion Department) at Stanford

University. Despite lacking a doctorate – Novak failed his comprehensive exams at Harvard Divinity School – he became the first Catholic to teach in Stanford's Religion Department, and later, the first to serve on the editorial boards of *The Christian Century* and *Christianity & Crisis*.

He supported America's war in Vietnam until 1967, when, surrounded by friends at Stanford who "abhor the war and oppose it vociferously," he declared that he opposed it too, because America's mass destruction was self-defeating. In the 1968 Democratic primary season Novak worked for Eugene McCarthy, unhappily, and switched to Robert Kennedy after the Nebraska primary. After Kennedy was assassinated, Novak gave up on liberal reformism. He hated McCarthy's effete style; Hubert Humphrey's support for the war was beyond the pale; so Novak became a radical. For the next two years, when such attitudes were most fashionable, he epitomized the social type of the liberal-bashing New leftist. Upping the ante on Tom Hayden's declaration that the real evil of America rested in its "liberal way of life and mind," Novak declared in *A Theology for Radical Politics* (1969): "The enemy in America, then, is the tyrannical and indifferent majority: the good people, the churchgoers, the typical Americans."[135]

In his telling, the pathetic mediocrity and hollowness of the majority showed through in "the vacant eyes watching television and drinking beer; the tired eyes of the men on the commuter train; the efficient eyes of the professor and the manager; the sincere eyes of the television politician." Novak explained that Americans were bored, apathetic, manipulated, and violent, knowing not what they were but only what they were useful for: "One could cry out in anguish that the suffering and sacrifices of past generations have come to this. A grown man with a can of beer finds his chief fulfillment in a televised game, watched by thirty million others, and believes our land free, brave, and just." Novak proposed to "bring a radical Christian theology to the support of the student movement." He flirted with revolutionary violence: "Against armed ranks of policemen, a grenade is more serious and effective than calling names." The moment for armed revolution had not quite arrived, but "those who serve now in the Army may one day be grateful to have learned military skills."[136]

In 1968 Harris Wofford, a cofounder of the Peace Corps and subsequently US Senator (Pennsylvania) launched a new branch of the State University of New York, SUNY-Old Westbury. An experimental college, Old Westbury was conceived in the spirit of the time. Wofford invited Novak to join the faculty, who considered his acceptance an act of commitment to the Revolution.

Instead it ended his radical phase. Of the first 100 students admitted to Old Westbury, all but one told a surveyor that electoral politics was a bourgeois fraud. Novak assured them he agreed; Humphrey was not worth supporting, even if that put Richard Nixon in the White House. However, he soon had second thoughts about his radical turn. Classes had barely begun when students and faculty began to demonstrate against Wofford. Novak was shocked when a faculty member smashed the door of the bourgeois bookstore to allow students to steal from it. Another professor proved his thoroughgoing egalitarianism by holding his seminar classes underneath a classroom table. "Think of this as childish vulgar Marxism," Novak later recalled. "The grown-up version has uncannily repeated itself in every Communist Party victory." His five years at Old Westbury tamed his passion for a revolution of consciousness.[137]

By 1970 Novak had found his way back to mainstream liberalism, working for Wofford's former Peace Corps mate, Sargent Shriver, as a speechwriter in a national campaign for Democratic congressional candidates. Novak spent the summer traveling with Shriver, meeting thousands of the vacant-eyed Americans he had ridiculed. He later recalled that the humanity and generosity of the people he met across the country made him ashamed of the literary snobbery that filled his writings about them: "Comparing the actual American people to the vision of America cherished in the literary culture I then took part in, I was subverted. I came to think there was more health in the people than in their literary elites, including me."[138]

In a mood of confused uncertainty about his moral, political, and religious beliefs he wrote about disillusionment, the loss of faith, and small consolations. A semi-autobiographical novel, *Naked I Leave* (1970), chronicled the sexual odyssey of a Slavic ex-seminarian from a Pennsylvania steel town. A philosophical meditation, *The Experience of Nothingness* (1970), proposed that the experience of being "empty, alone, without guides, direction, will, or obligations" provided the opportunity to create oneself. An introduction to religious studies, *Ascent of the Mountain, Flight of the Dove* (1971), appealed to myth and symbol, urging that religious forms of story making and openness to mystery hold creative possibilities for alienated modern selves. Novak obscured the "what" of religious belief, ruminating vaguely about making one's story the subject of religious meaning. *Ascent of the Mountain* recommended a long list of theologians; shortly after, Novak began to attack nearly all of them.[139]

He turned a corner without really meaning to in his next book *The Rise of the Unmeltable Ethnics* (1971). Feeling alienated from the white Anglo-Saxon Protestants and Jews that, in his telling, dominated academic culture, Novak declared that the American melting pot was a WASP myth designed to reinforce the values and social dominance of WASPs. Homogeneity was not a reality in America, or even a worthy goal, he argued; rather, it was an instrument of domination that forced ethnics to turn themselves inside out to be accepted as Americans.

WASP culture was repressed, rationalistic, moralistic, reformist, obsessed with cleanliness, and above all, individualistic, Novak explained. It loosened the bonds of family ties to enable individuals to become successful. Devoted to material success, it controlled self and society through reason: "In all God's world, is there anything as cool as a Yale lawyer across the carpeted office of a major philanthropic fund? How could any other race ever fashion its psyche to that style?" Unfortunately, WASPs universalized their cultural eccentricities and Lockean politics. They were "the soap and water experts of the world," self-righteously imposing their antiseptic sterility and individualism on ethnic minorities, who resented the imposition. Novak declared that for ethnics, to be Americanized was to be humiliated, fashioning their psyches to a suffocating style: "Immigrants from southern and eastern Europe had to learn order, discipline, neatness, cleanliness, reserve. They had to learn to modulate emotion, to control passion, to hold their hands still, to hold the muscles of their face placid, to find food and body odors offensive, to quieten their voices, to present themselves as cooly reasonable."[140]

America assaulted the natural earthiness, passion, and blood-rich culture of its ethnic immigrants. Novak wrote that ethnic immigrants retained thicker family and kinship ties than WASP Americans, which were a bulwark against utopianism and other deracinated WASP enthusiasms. The blood-thick family-style politics of American ethnics was usually called machine politics, but wrongly; in the USA, reform politics was machine-like: impersonal, procedural, abstract, moralistic, governed by rules. Novak warned that WASP conceits were stirring a backlash. Ethnic minorities preferred their own value systems and weren't buying the melting pot anymore. Thus a new cultural pluralism was needed. Most liberals worried a great deal about prejudice against blacks and very little about prejudice against ethnics, Novak argued; meanwhile, the WASP elite pitted blacks and Catholic ethnics against each other. A different cultural politics was the answer to this sorry picture: "Ethnics can understand the strategic interests of blacks. Hence, to place costs and needs on a frank trading basis would no doubt constitute a step forward." Novak wanted blacks and ethnic groups to establish "a decent quid pro quo," struggling against a common enemy: "The enemy is educated, wealthy, powerful – and sometimes wears liberal, sometimes radical, sometimes conservative disguise. The enemy is concentrated power." Instead of spurning the values and interests of ethnic working-class communities, the Democratic party needed to spurn the snobbish liberalism of its leaders, attacking the real enemy by affirming the new cultural pluralism.[141]

The following year Novak worked on George McGovern's presidential campaign staff, with mounting distress. He hated McGovern's idealist whining and the Democratic party's cultural liberalism, which alienated working-class constituencies. One incident on the 1972 campaign trail was symptomatic. At the Homestead steel mill in Illinois, campaigning for the McGovern–Shriver ticket, Novak noticed that steelworkers were giving Shriver a frosty reception. Looking around to see why this largely Slavic crowd treated Shriver so coldly, he discovered that the local advance person was "a young woman wearing a miniskirt, high white boots, and a see-through blouse, with a large proabortion button on her collar." By then, Novak's book was controversial; he told friends that the steel mill scene confirmed everything he had warned about.[142]

The Rise of the Unmeltable Ethnics refashioned Novak's radicalism, pointing to the WASP establishment's "hegemony of economic power." The WASP ideology of economic growth was "monstrous," he charged; it conceived the earth as "a planet to be conquered and despoiled" and subjected working people to "a constant stream of silent contempt." A new progressive politics was needed, one that attacked the WASP elite's ideology of modernization. WASP reformism was guilt-oriented, Novak observed, but white ethnics were like American blacks in disdaining guilt: "White ethnics refuse to feel guilty. Guilt is not their style. They react to guilt feelings with anger. They do not imagine life as an effort to live up to abstract ideals like justice, equality, fairness, reasonableness, etc.; but as a struggle to survive." Novak founded the Ethnic Millions Political Action Committee (EMPAC) to mobilize ethnics into a progressive political force, and served as editor of *Slovakia*, the annual publication of the Slovak League of America.[143]

The Rise of the Unmeltable Ethnics had a very rough reception, especially for its antifeminism, electoral opportunism, appeals to envy and resentment, cultural conservatism, and sweeping generalizations about blacks and ethnics. Citing Novak's self-description as the intellectual voice of disaffected ethnic Democrats, cultural critic Garry Wills replied in the *New York Times Book Review*: "So quickly does listening to one's blood become a matter of sniffing around after loose votes." Wills lamented that a moral man could write such an "immoral book," in which "bright aphorisms and seductive phrases" made a case for the "social uses of hatred." The apparent purpose of the book, Wills observed, was to teach Archie Bunker new hatreds and thus "extend the already vast repertoire of American resentments." In a crowning achievement of sorts, Novak showed that civility was an Anglo-Saxon deceit. His book invented new hatreds and resentments as he went along, "working his gentle soul into Zorba-the-Greek exhibitionism."[144]

That set the tone. Many reviewers piled on, adding insults that drove Novak to his bed. He later described the experience as an excommunication. For months he protested that he was still a progressive, until the presidential election helped him accept that he was not. The enormity of McGovern's defeat confirmed Novak's warnings about the alienating conceits of Democratic liberalism. Middle America was wiser than the intellectuals. Neoconservatism as an organized movement began in the wake of McGovern's defeat with the formation of the Coalition for a Democratic Majority, a group that tried to recapture the Democratic party from the liberals and radicals who had ruined it. Novak was a charter member. He joined the neoconservative reaction at the moment that it became a political phenomenon worth naming.

Intellectually, however, Novak was unprepared for the transition. Years later he recalled, "Though I slowly was becoming deradicalized, the information in my head during these years was very often exclusively derived from writers of the far left."[145] In *Choosing Our King* (1974) he resumed his polemic against corporate capitalism, complaining that it made room for blacks, but not ethnics. Novak opposed affirmative action mainly because it discriminated against ethnics. He still opposed capitalism, ostensibly, for the same reason, but really because he didn't know anything else. For several years he cast about in search of a new intellectual mentor or guide.[146]

The first figure he considered was Reinhold Niebuhr, whose once-towering work, Novak observed in 1972, now seemed remote and irrelevant. Novak urged that Niebuhr's message was as relevant as ever: "The new moralism we see all around us is all too like the old moralism, against which Niebuhr directed the central energies of his life. In many ways it is as if he had lived and worked in vain." The new moralism, like the old one, preached that gains toward the common good were attainable through rationality or religiously inspired goodwill. Invoking Niebuhr, Novak warned that progressivism was a species of bad faith. He especially disliked the new emphasis on racial justice, complaining that liberals had turned "white racism" into the ultimate smear term, replacing "McCarthyism." Under the pressure of the new moralism, even Niebuhrians like John Bennett were caving in, urging *Christianity & Crisis* to give a platform "to those who push the white man hardest, for we see that white racism is a deeper cultural sickness than we realized in the early 60's." Novak told Bennett to get hold of himself instead of wallowing in guilt and moralistic illness. Niebuhr in his prime would have known how to quash the new moralism; however, by the 1960s he was fading, and liberal Protestantism had no one else like him. Moreover, the new moralism was more potent than the old one, because it was not confined to mainline Protestants. This time Jews and Catholics were equally afflicted.[147]

To explain how that happened, Novak turned to the concept of the New Class. This notion had a colorful history in Marxist thought; sociologist David Bazelon had recently revived it; American socialist Michael Harrington had recently used it strategically. The idea of the New Class, in its various permutations, was that organizational position mattered more than private ownership in managerial societies. Harrington argued that the baby boom generation then graduating from college was in a position to forge alliances with working-class, unionized, and poor people or to become their sophisticated enemy. The New Class could use its education to create a good society or to protect its new privileges. Harrington urged the children of the '60s to become the "conscience constituency" of American society, building a new liberal majority that supported equality and peace.[148]

That was exactly the idealism that turned Novak's stomach. "There is something beguilingly deceptive in this self-flattery of educated professionals," he wrote. Harrington was supposed to be a Marxist, yet he trafficked in the squishy moralism that

Niebuhr demolished. To a Niebuhrian, Novak noted, the notion of a conscience constituency was laughable. Harrington's vision was coming true, but not for the reasons he thought. Novak allowed that liberal concerns about civil rights, poverty, and the Vietnam War were morally legitimate. The problem was that liberals concealed their selfish interests under the cloak of moral righteousness. In the name of compassion, he explained, liberals got cushy jobs for themselves administering poverty programs. They abolished the local patronage jobs of the old machine politics, always in the name of reform and moral righteousness, but really to do something meaningful with their college degrees. They specialized in reforms that others paid for, such as school busing, exempting their own children from social engineering. They also had special psychic interests. Novak observed that the New Class "somehow feels it must exorcise its complicity in various social evils: white racism, militarism, imperialism, male chauvinism, consumerism, affluence." Meanwhile the rest of the country paid for the psychic need of liberals to escape the moral ambiguities of life and "be thoroughly good." For Novak, Niebuhr was the corrective to liberal self-deception: conscience was an individual phenomenon; the moralities it produced were for individuals; groups appealed to morality only to cover their collective interests. Liberal moralism produced unhealthy individuals and worse politics.[149]

For years Novak had compared capitalist reality to an unrealized socialist ideal; now he struggled to purge himself of his acquired idealism. "It wasn't until the mid-'70s that I became able to think of the issue in empirical terms at all," he later recalled. "My religious background and my lack of background in economics made it difficult for me to keep the actual comparative factors in focus."[150] Like too many social ethicists, he had conceived political economics as a choice between rival moral visions, and thus found it impossible not to choose democratic socialism. Novak lamented that his religious background had filled his imagination with solidaristic, communal images of the good society. This predisposition was reinforced by his aversion to liberal theory, which offered images of atomized individuals forming contracts and compacts. The narrowly empirical, pragmatic, individualistic ethos of capitalism seemed to him "not only foreign but spiritually *wrong*."[151]

But realism compared existing systems, not moral visions, he reflected. If democratic socialism was so desirable, why were there no democratic socialist societies? Novak reasoned that the lack of a historical example of democratic socialism revealed something about the worthiness of socialism even as an ideal. Democratic socialism did not exist, and the existing socialisms were totalitarian prisons. If the struggle to attain the ideal always failed, it was not worth pursuing. As this conclusion took hold of Novak in the mid-1970s he was afraid to write about it or even discuss it with his wife and friends. Avoiding the subject, he wrote a book on sports, stewed for two years over his right-turning politics, and finally announced in 1976 in the *Wall Street Journal* that he no longer believed in social democracy. At the time many neocons were still conservative social democrats; Novak told them that if a democratized socioeconomic order was actually unattainable, it was pointless to invoke it as an ideal.[152]

He conceded that social democracy seemed to hold moral advantages over its rivals. The democratic socialist language of freedom, equality, community, and the common good appeared to be more consistent with Christian and Jewish moral values than capitalism. To refute that verdict, he had to undermine the moral appeal of democratic socialism. In economics, Novak turned to Ludwig von Mises and Friedrich A. Hayek for instruction, but they were no help on the moral level. Niebuhr was unhelpful too, since his socioeconomic writings were Marxist and his later writings avoided the capitalist/socialist debate. Novak resolved to deal with the moral issue on his own, reformulating Hayek's position "in highly moral terms." It was not enough merely to forsake socialism, like Niebuhr, for the only way to get rid of a powerful idea was to replace it with an even more powerful one.[153]

Novak later recalled that he felt a profound inner emptiness over the loss of his socialist vision, until "fortunately, there fell into my hands, among other writings, some of the essays of Irving Kristol, recalling me to an intellectual tradition I had hitherto avoided: that of the American Framers and that of the British and French liberals of the early nineteenth century." Kristol, a neoconservative social critic, commended the Whig tradition of the Anglo-Scottish Enlightenment, especially Adam Smith. Novak's more powerful idea was already forming in his mind. His identification with the Whig tradition strengthened its hold over him. The idea was democratic capitalism.[154]

Leaving Old Westbury, Novak served as director of humanities at the Rockefeller Foundation, supported Henry Jackson in the 1976 Democratic primaries, and rooted privately for Gerald Ford against Jimmy Carter in November. After the election, Republican party chair William Brock presented Novak with the Republicans' Favorite Democrat Award. Two years later, while teaching at Syracuse University, Novak won a perch as a resident scholar at the American Enterprise Institute (AEI), where he developed his thinking on democratic capitalism, his "stronger" idea.[155]

His first AEI book, *The American Vision* (1978), asserted that most discussions of American capitalism focused too narrowly on the economic system as a mechanism for exchange. Since academics were specialists, they stuck to the areas of their expertise. Novak countered that American capitalism existed only as part of an interlocking political, cultural, and economic system; thus, when academics wrote about it, they missed the essence of the system. Democratic capitalism, as a system, was uniquely dynamic because it originated in the convictions "(1) that both elites and those at the economic bottom will circulate; and (2) that there is equality for all, whatever their starting place, not only to better their positions but also to go as far as imagination, work, and luck will take them." The key to America's success was its creation of an opportunity society. In the American vision, what mattered was to seize entrepreneurial opportunities, not to fret over one's starting place or wait for the leveling hand of government. Novak's idea of a tripartite society, which he borrowed from Harvard sociologist Daniel Bell, laid the groundwork of his defense of democratic capitalism.[156]

In 1980 he joined the neocon stampede to the Reagan camp, though Novak still called himself a Democrat. He shared the aggressive militarism of the neocons, claiming that Richard Nixon, Gerald Ford, and especially Jimmy Carter made the world safe for communism. America needed a bigger military and a forceful policy of repelling communism. Novak did not compete with other neocons, however, for influence on this subject. He concentrated on democratic capitalism, and in 1982 published his major work, *The Spirit of Democratic Capitalism*, which reformulated Bell's theory of the tripartite society.[157]

In *The Cultural Contradictions of Capitalism* (1976) Bell rejected all interpretive frameworks that conceived modern societies as structurally interrelated unitary wholes. His pluralistic alternative to Marxist Hegelianism, Durkheimian functionalism, and other unitary models distinguished among society's techno-economic structure, polity, and culture. A distinctive axial principle and structure established the foundation for institutions belonging to each realm. Bell argued that America's three realms were not congruent with each other and that each contained its own distinctive norms, types of behavior, and dynamics of change. American capitalism was plagued with contradictions because there were discordances between the political, economic, and cultural spheres.[158]

Bell pointed to commercial advertising, credit cards, and an expanding economy as chief causes of the discordances. America was built on hard work, prudence, thrift, deferred gratification, familial loyalty, and a sense of the sacred, he argued, but capitalism undermined these virtues by manipulating consumers to crave unnecessary goods and services and demand immediate gratification. Capitalism subverted the very ties of family, community, religion, and moral habit on which American society was founded and still depended.

Thus, Bell's tripartite model was a descriptive framework for his thesis about the cultural ravages of capitalism. He did not claim the three realms were mutually supportive; his point was that they were not. But Novak adopted the model as a norm. He described the three realms, acknowledged his dependence on Bell while ignoring Bell's critique, and claimed that only democratic capitalism generated and secured a pluralistic coexistence of realms. In Novak's hands, Bell's critique of modern capitalism was turned into a normative ideal identified with it.[159]

He explained, "In the conventional view, the link between a democratic political system and a market economy is merely an accident of history. My argument is that the link is stronger: political democracy is compatible in practice only with a market economy." That was a false choice, because Novak's rendering of the "conventional" view was rarely expounded by anyone, and his own position was equally extreme. Tracing the origins of modern democracy and capitalism to "identical historical impulses," he argued that both had moral form "before institutions were invented to realize them." These impulses limited the state's power and thus liberated the energies of individuals and independent communities. Two revolutions were linked in theory and historical practice, as reflected in Marx's phrase, bourgeois democracy. For Novak, the phrase was apt, regardless of Marx's attitude toward it. Novak argued that democratic capitalism was coherent because modern democracy and capitalism sprang "from the same logic, the same moral principles, the same nest of cultural values, institutions, and presuppositions." The causal link was logical, not merely historical. On occasion capitalism flourished without democracy, he allowed, but "the natural logic of capitalism leads to democracy." Capitalism created a bourgeoisie that demanded political rights; thus it was the engine of democratic expansion. Put together, capitalism and democracy created a pluralistic society; more importantly, it was the only social system that did.[160]

That turned Bell's argument on its head. Just as Novak twisted Bell's framework into a normative model called democratic capitalism, he ignored Bell's thesis that America's political and cultural realms were overmatched by the power of its organized economic interests. Bell was a socialist in economics, a liberal in politics, and a conservative in culture. He denied that democracy and democratic pluralism could be sustained only by a capitalist economy. Although capitalism and democracy arose together, he observed, and although both were justified by liberal theory, "there is nothing which makes it either theoretically or practically necessary for the two to be yoked." For Bell, pluralism was safeguarded politically by liberalism, subordinating the needs of the community to the rights of the individual. In the economic realm, pluralism was best protected by democratic socialism, in which "the community takes precedence over the individual in the values that legitimate economic policy." Far from claiming that only capitalism nourished a pluralism of realms, Bell argued that social democratic gains in the economic realm were needed to preserve the pluralism of realms otherwise undermined by commercial society.[161]

For Bell, the capitalist principle was empty. He wrote in *The Winding Passage* that capitalism, upon losing its original justifications, took over "the legitimations of an anti-bourgeois culture to maintain the continuity of its own economic institutions." Citing Irving Kristol and Joseph Schumpeter on the capitalist lack of a transcendental justification, Bell argued that capitalism was "simply instrumental and rational, and creates no values of its own." Novak made his claim to originality on this point, claiming that Bell, Schumpeter, and virtually all intellectuals who described capitalism got it wrong. Intellectuals, even pro-capitalist ones, took for granted that capitalism had no spiritual basis. That prevented them from grasping the essence of capitalism, Novak argued. "It is simply not true," he wrote, "that capitalism 'creates no values of its own.' Capitalism is intrinsically related to some core values – to liberty in the sense of self-discipline; to invention, creativity, and cooperation, the root of the corporation; to work, savings, investment in the future; to self-reliance, etc." In Novak's view, capitalism had an "underlying spiritual power" that even its defenders missed. It was not merely utilitarian. It taught the disciplines of thrift and hard work, prevented "moral abuses," and held unique "capacities for self-renewal." Above all, it had a "powerfully self-transforming, creative, and inventive" spirit.[162]

To receive the kind of advocacy and respect it deserved, capitalism had to be defended as a faith. Most intellectuals were far from helpful to this task, Novak allowed, but there was one intellectual tradition that offered real help. Irving Kristol had led him to it; Friedrich von Hayek explained it to him. In his essay, "Why I Am Not a Conservative," Hayek identified with the Whig tradition of Macaulay, Tocqueville, Acton, Burke, and Madison.[163] Upon reading it, Novak exulted that he had found a home, recognizing himself in Hayek's description of the Whig sensibility. For years afterward his books offered lists of Whig intellectual heroes, sometimes adding Aquinas, Bellarmine, Hooker, Montaigne, Smith, Montesquieu, Mill, Cobden, Jefferson, Hamilton, and Lincoln to the roll, plus many modern thinkers. John Courtney Murray and Irving Kristol were usually on the modern list; Jacques Maritan was always on it, notwithstanding that during his radical phase Novak claimed him for radical theology, giving the assurance that Maritain was "more New Left than liberal."[164]

Novak's tendency to pad the roll with thinkers who didn't belong there caused some critics to doubt his seriousness, but his identification with Whiggery had a serious point, as he explained: "One of the great achievements of the Whig tradition was its new world experiment, *Novus Ordo Seclorum*. Its American progenitors called that experiment the commercial republic. The Whigs were the first philosophers in history to grasp the importance of basing government of the people upon the foundation of commerce. They underpinned democracy with a capitalist, growing economy." That is, the Whigs invented democratic capitalism, which was the connection between Novak's neoconservatism and the Whig tradition.[165]

Whiggery derived from the twin revolutions behind bourgeois democracy. In eighteenth-century Europe, the Whigs played their aristocratic and working-class enemies off against each other. English Whigs and French liberals opposed the ruling aristocracies of their time, winning support from workers and small property owners, but they also opposed the workers and petit-bourgeois when they demanded the right to vote through the Reform Act and July Charter. Politically, Whiggery was a way station between traditionalism and democracy, advocating constitutional monarchy and limited suffrage. That strategy was problematic in the USA, however, which lacked aristocratic and proletarian forces. American Whigs lacked their needed enemies. As Louis Hartz explained in *The Liberal Tradition in America*,

> Here there are no aristocracies to fight, and the Federalists and the Whigs are denied the chance of dominating the people in a campaign against them. Here there are no aristocracies to ally with, and they cannot use their help to exclude the people from political power. Here there are no genuine proletarian outbursts to meet, and they cannot frighten people into fleeing from them.

The American Whigs were isolated, "put at the mercy of a strange new giant" they could not control. In a liberal society they were deprived of their liberal veneer. Their haughty diatribes against "the mob" were not only politically suicidal, but absurd, since in the USA they were no more liberal than the commoners. Belatedly, the Whigs compensated in the 1840s by discovering democratic capitalism.[166]

Novak's relation to Whig history and appropriation of it had a few oddities. He appealed frequently to the wisdom of Whig trimmers Smith, Burke, Macaulay and Montesquieu, but ignored their opposition to democracy. His version of Whig liberalism was decidedly American, yet he did not mention the Whigs closest to his position – the American democratic capitalists of the 1840s. In his telling the Whigs were the cautious, chastened, empirical party of republican liberty, and nearly all the American founders were Whigs. They were forward-looking, but respected the wisdom of the past. They respected the dim view toward commerce taken by moralists, but perceived that commerce itself had changed with the rise of capitalism. Preoccupied with checks and balances, they crafted a prudential approach to politics "more suited to the middle-aged mind than to the youthful mind."[167]

Novak celebrated democratic capitalism before he knew much about its history, and he was slow to claim the Whig tradition. *The American Vision* made no mention of the Whig background, and *The Spirit of Democratic Capitalism* noted only that Hayek was probably correct in tracing democratic capitalism to the Whigs. Afterwards Novak rejoiced that he had found something better than socialism, though he fretted that the term "Whig" bore "the faint sense of the attic about it." Style and temperament were important to him; having a homeland tradition was even more important; the keystone was democratic capitalism.[168]

This idea was rooted in the later history of the American Whig Party. In the early 1840s Whig leaders Thurlow Weed and Daniel Webster, stung by their party's repeated defeats, began to accept the realities of American politics, especially that it was politically stupid to disdain the common people in a democracy. Their alternative was a Jeffersonian form of capitalism. Hartz recounted that the Whigs let go of aristocratic frustrations and exaggerated proletarian fears, accepted America's liberal unity "with a vengeance," and developed the notion of democratic capitalism. Calvin Colton, campaigning on this theme, declared: "Every American laborer can stand up proudly, and say, I AM THE AMERICAN CAPITALIST."[169]

It was a novel strategy. The Whigs went beyond stealing the Democrats' best issue, egalitarianism; they also transformed it. Hartz explained,

> For if they gave up Hamilton's hatred of the people, they retained his grandiose capitalist dream, and this they combined with the Jeffersonian concept of equal opportunity. The result was to electrify the democratic individual with a passion for great achievement and

to produce a personality type that was neither Hamiltonian nor Jeffersonian but a strange mixture of both: the hero of Horatio Alger.[170]

The mid-nineteenth-century Whigs concocted America's triumphant ideology of self-made capitalist individualism, out of which they fashioned the myth of Americanism, a classless melting pot of self-made individualists. Long after the Whig party was gone, Whig "Americanism" stigmatized even the mildest progressivism as un-American. Hartz characterized this legacy as a form of ideological terrorism, observing that the myth of democratic capitalism "tried to frighten the American democrat with his own absolute liberalism." It denigrated the state and stigmatized whoever turned to it to gain or protect their rights: "And the best way of doing this was to call him a 'socialist' which, of course, was to make him perfectly 'un-American.'"[171]

Novak knew very little about the nineteenth-century American Whigs when he wrote his signature works on democratic capitalism. In the early 1990s, when I pressed him on the subject, he was surprised and delighted to learn of his connection to the American Whigs of Harrison's generation. This connection extended beyond democratic capitalism, to the myth of Americanism, for upon turning to the right, Novak made his peace with Americanism. The once unmeltable ethnic jumped into the pot. The Anglo-Saxon apologists he had denounced as imperialists became his heroes. Novak later explained that he had not meant his harsh attacks on WASP America to be taken literally. *The Rise of the Unmeltable Ethnics* was a pitch for status recognition, speaking for Burke's little platoons of (ethnic) families and neighborhoods. He had not wanted the WASP establishment to be pulled down: "I can still recall the astonishment I felt at the time when a fortress I thought both admirable and impregnable was suddenly surrendered without a fight." It amazed and appalled him to see America's cultural establishment "surrender" to Black Power, feminism, and the new moralism. That spectacle heightened his resolve to defend the Whig vision against the ravages of the New Class.[172]

The Whigs celebrated the material achievements of capitalism and the moral virtues that entrepreneurialism engendered. Novak shared these enthusiasms and surpassed them, writing a "theology" of the corporation that described seven sacramental ways in which corporations "mirror the presence of God." *Toward a Theology of the Corporation* (1981) lauded the "communal focus" of modern capitalism, "the rise of communal risk taking, the pooling of resources, the sense of communal religious vocation in economic activism." Corporations, by virtue of their communal-religious character and independence from the state, provided "metaphors for grace, a kind of insight into God's ways in history." Novak cautioned that for corporations to mirror God's presence, the state's power to control rights and goods had to be strictly limited. Fortunately, this attitude toward the state was "the distinctively American way of thinking about private property."[173]

Irving Kristol offered two cheers for capitalism, with a bit of hedging about its cultural aftershocks; Novak offered seven, with no hedging. Kristol stressed that capitalism was productive and tolerant; Novak added that it was also spiritual and virtue producing, explaining that "With the invention of democratic capitalism in America, new demands were made upon the citizens, for which new virtues were required."[174]

The first new virtue created by American capitalism was civic responsibility, in which individual initiative and community cooperation blended equally to form a distinctive political culture. To Novak, political theorist C. B. Macpherson's critique of "possessive individualism" did not apply to the USA because American self-reliance, community-building, and self-government produced a "new kind of human being," the communitarian individual. Under American capitalism the ambitions of free individuals – especially the "most imaginative and able members" – were channeled to build new communities and lay the groundwork for new enterprises.[175]

These enterprises required and engendered the second virtue, the "peculiarly capitalist virtue" of enterprise itself. Novak observed that the spirit of enterprise preceded capitalism, but under capitalism it became "the red-hot center, the dynamo, the ignition system, of development. It is the very principle of economic progress." This virtue disclosed new needs of communities, or at least, new markets for consumption. The "moral moment" of enterprise consisted "in the effort, ingenuity, and persistence required to bring that insight into reality."[176]

The third virtue was the central one, entrepreneurial creativity, which defined capitalism, Karl Marx notwithstanding. Marx stressed that capitalism used private property, markets, and profit incentives in a distinctive way. Novak agreed that private property, market exchanges, and accumulation of profit were central to capitalism; however, the essence of the system lay elsewhere. Fundamentally, capitalism was about creativity, powers of mind, not institutions. It began and thrived on invention, discovery, and enterprise, activities of creative mind. Novak explained that modern capitalism was the system "designed to nourish the creativity of the human subject or to nourish, in Smith's phrase, 'skill, dexterity, and judgment.'"[177]

This redefinition was crucial to Novak because it permitted him to distinguish "capitalism" from pre-capitalist economies of biblical times, eighteenth-century British mercantilism, and, of particular concern at the moment, Latin American mercantilism. To have real capitalism, he argued, a society had to have intellectual property rights, as in the US Constitution's patent and copyright clause.[178] Any society lacking protection of intellectual creativity did not deserve to be called capitalist, even if it featured private property, markets, and profit incentives. Novak wrote: "Capitalism is a new order in history precisely because it is centered more than any other system on the creativity of the human mind." The material world became "more and more mind" wherever capitalism took root and flourished.[179]

The fourth virtue was "a special kind of communitarian living." Capitalist societies abounded "in many varieties of frank and friendly association, in a great deal of teamwork, in habits of openness and easy companionship that are marvelous to see and to experience." Novak conceded that capitalism broke down communal, family, ethnic, and religious ties, and he acknowledged that there was "said to be much loneliness" in commercial societies. But modern business was long on committees, meetings, and consultations, he observed; the more capitalist a society became, the more it engendered new forms of association.[180]

The last virtue was competitiveness. Rescuing the competitive spirit from moral suspicion, Novak contended that Americans' lingering wariness of it was a hangover prejudice from Christian morality and nineteenth-century English novels. Capitalist competitiveness was actually a virtue because it fostered economic fairness and protected societies from monopolistic collusion. It thwarted the concentration and abuse of economic power. In his telling, it was a distinctly capitalist virtue. European social democracies mixed competitiveness and democratization, but they tried to prevent economic concentration by politicizing the economic sector. That was the wrong prescription, for which the corrective was to view competitiveness as a genuine virtue, not something to be restrained or merely tolerated.[181]

Critics noted that Novak's "democratic capitalist" alternative to liberal moralism and ideology was not exactly lacking in moralistic and ideological fixations of its own. Catholic conservative Russell Kirk, Catholic liberal Peter Steinfels, and Catholic socialist John C. Cort stressed that capitalism was undemocratic in its essential structure and practice; sometimes they quoted Novak on this point. Since the adjective "democratic" did not modify, describe, or define the noun "capitalist," what sense did it make to speak of democratic capitalism? Novak replied that "democratic capitalism" was real even if democracy and capitalism conflicted. Democratic capitalism was a fitting name for the merger of a democratic polity and a capitalist economy. Steinfels countered that putting two words together did not prove that they represented anything in reality. Novak was tall and balding, but that did not establish "tall baldingism" as a meaningful concept. Neither did the existence of societies like the USA and Canada establish the existence of "democratic capitalism." Cort put it more harshly, contending that "democratic capitalism" made no more sense than "the democratic Mafia," as the Mafia also existed in politically democratic societies.[182]

Both analogies were exaggerated, appearing to take the "accident of history" view of the relationship between capitalism and democracy. There was no significant connection between being tall and balding, or between democracy and the Mafia, but there was an important connection between the historical emergence of capitalism and the rise of modern democracy. The pertinent question was, what kind of connection? Was capitalism the economic precondition of democracy? Was it a main cause or a necessary one? Did capitalism and democracy maintain the same relationship through all stages of their development? Novak's false choice between "accident of history" and "absolute necessity" allowed only dogmatic simplicities about complex social and historical relationships.

The link between capitalism and democracy was the liberal state. It appeared first in eighteenth-century England, in response to the interests of an expanding capitalist class. There was nothing democratic about the liberal state, but it was liberal, protecting freedom of speech, association, and enterprise. The Whigs were the ideological guardians of pre-democratic liberalism. They needed the commoners to break the aristocracy's grip on political power, but were determined to prevent democratic rule. As Novak's defense of capitalism became increasingly aggressive and ideological, he played down the fact that democracy grew through the struggles of social justice movements and was usually resisted by the capitalist class. By sheer repetition, "democratic capitalism" took on a life of its own in his writing, becoming the subject of active verbs and even personified. But the complex interaction between capitalism and democracy had not changed; only Novak's politics had changed. Since he no longer supported social justice movements that strengthened the bargaining power and rights of disenfranchised groups; "democratic capitalism" became an object of faith, standing in place of movements that won the rights of universal suffrage, collective bargaining, racial nondiscrimination, social insurance, and the progressive income tax.

On occasion Novak admitted that he coined the phrase "democratic capitalism" as an alternative to "democratic socialism," not realizing that it already had a colorful history. But the adjective in "democratic socialism" described and defined the noun; in this case, the goal was to democratize society's political and economic realms, as the phrase denoted. Novak conceded the difference, taking satisfaction that he found wealth and renown by switching to the winning side just before it turned the world economy into a single capitalist one.[183]

Interrogating Liberation Theology and the Catholic Bishops

As the expert on things Catholic at the AEI, Novak sustained a running debate with liberation theology, and, for several years, the American Catholic bishops. For many years he dismissed liberation theology as a semi-Christian fad infatuated with Marxist slogans. When the fad persisted, he explained in the *New York Times Magazine* that liberation theology was a popular front phenomenon, originating in Latin America, which gained its excitement from flirting with Marxism and bashing capitalist America.[184] Elsewhere he put it more precisely, explaining that liberation theologians relied on neo-Marxist dependency theory and that Latin Americans as a whole "do not value the same moral qualities North Americans do."[185]

Dependency theory ranged from the unicausal neo-Marxism of Andre Gunder Frank and Samir Amin to the multicausal social democracy of Raul Prebisch and Fernando Henrique Cardoso. In every version it stressed the vulnerability and dependence of comparatively weak "periphery" nations. Dependency theorists cited unfavorable trade agreements, the promotion of cash crops for export, exploitative policies of transnational corporations, aid to corrupt and repressive governments, and large external debts contracted with these governments as examples of the dependent relationship.[186] Peru's Catholic bishops, in 1969, offered a poignant expression of the dependency perspective: "We are the victims of systems that exploit our natural resources, control our political decisions, and impose on us the cultural domination of their values and consumer civilization . . . Foreign interests increase their repressive measures by means of economic sanctions in the international markets and by control of loans and other types of aid."[187]

Novak replied that the bishops and their intellectual mentors needed to be liberated from the attitudes and habits of victims: "They accept no responsibility for three centuries of hostility to trade, commerce, and industry. They seem to imagine that loans and aid should be tendered them independently of economic laws." Instead of wailing about imperialism and exploitation, the bishops needed to look in the mirror. The real source of their sense of grievance, Novak claimed, was that "others, once equally poor, have succeeded as they have not."[188] Latin America, in the early 1950s, could have taken the same path as Japan, Singapore, and Taiwan: "They did not, in part because of the influence of Raul Prebisch, tradition, culture, and well-meaning Americans. They have reaped what they have sown." Latin America, "a continent with a dependent frame of mind," was its own worst problem. Dependency theory was true only as a reflection of the victimization complex of Latin Americans themselves. Latin American programs for economic modernization failed because Latin Americans were culturally backward and always looked for outsiders to blame for their problems. To become less miserable, Novak admonished, Latin American societies had to modernize economically, politically, and culturally. Whining about imperialism would never get them there.[189]

But dependency theorists opposed dependency and whining, too, even as they documented Latin America's considerable experience with modernization strategies.

By the mid–1980s, every Latin American nation struggled with debt service obligations rivaling or outstripping incoming credits. Most of the debts were structured like variable rate mortgages, with interest percentages tied to fluctuations in the US prime rate. Loans taken out at 4 percent interest in the early 1970s became repayable at 15 to 20 percent rates after the inflation of the late 1970s. More than half of Latin America's external debt thus reflected the compounding of inflated interest rates rather than original principal. The debt burden debased Latin American currencies, deprived the USA of Latin American markets, undermined prospects for new investment, and, in some cases, set off vicious campaigns of military repression.[190]

Faced with the historical fact that Latin America's large foreign-owned banana and mining companies, banks, and agribusinesses controlled their markets and opposed democratic reforms in the name of capitalist liberty, Novak replied that democratic capitalism did not exist in Latin America; thus capitalism was not the problem. A system was capitalist only if it featured "a predominantly market economy; a polity respectful of the rights of the individual to life, liberty, and the pursuit of happiness; and a system of cultural institutions moved by ideals of liberty and justice for all." By that standard, there were no capitalist nations in Latin America.[191]

Many of Novak's specific proposals were sound. He advocated new legal structures to permit cheap incorporation of small businesses, restructured banking institutions and laws to permit universal availability of credit to the poor, copyright and patent protections to foster economic creativity, and investments in universal education. Rightly he admonished liberationists not to treat commerce itself as the enemy, which harmed the poor. By inserting subjective cultural variables into his definition of capitalism, however, he eliminated the possibility of empirical refutation. That was a variant on the apologetic he claimed to forsake when he turned against social democracy. In Latin America, capitalist development yielded crushing debts, legacies of environmental and economic exploitation, military repression, and economies based on export dependence. But in Novak's rendering, capitalism existed in Latin America only as a promise; it had no history.[192]

Repeatedly he blasted liberation theology while ignoring its theology. In *Will It Liberate?* (1986) Novak scored points against liberationist hyperbole and justly warned against the simplistic Marxism of leading liberationists, especially José Miranda. Yet his attacks on what he called liberationist "rubbish" were ultimately chauvinistic and unfair. In its most representative forms, liberation theology was a rejection of the cultural legacy of Latin American authoritarianism and a call for community self-determination, economic democracy, and political freedom. Theologically, the movement's mainstream was deeply rooted in scriptural teaching and the spiritual traditions of the church, reflecting the spiritual experiences of grassroots base communities. Politically, the movement was characterized mainly by a democratic, cooperative, community-oriented praxis that Novak completely overlooked. He misrepresented liberation theology as a whole, which concentrated on community development, establishing health care services and schools, founding consumer and producer cooperatives, and resisting imperialism, by stressing the Marxist pronouncements of a few intellectuals, especially from the movement's early years. When Novak lectured against liberation theology in Sao Paulo in 1985, a protester held up a sign that read, "Liberation theology is ours." That was the point.[193]

In 1982 Novak and Notre Dame philosopher Ralph McInerny founded a monthly magazine, *Catholicism in Crisis* (later shortened to *Crisis*) as a vehicle for neoconservative criticism of modern Catholicism. At the time the American Catholic bishops were preparing a pastoral letter on the ethics of nuclear deterrence. Alarmed at the growing influence of a church peace movement that he called "widespread, well-organized, and well-financed," Novak inveighed against it. It was ridiculous to call for a nuclear freeze after the USA had fallen behind the Soviet Union in military might, he contended; the USA needed a military build-up in every category. In the meantime, Catholic bishops needed to resist the peace movement.[194]

The second draft of the bishops' pastoral letter, *The Challenge of Peace*, authored principally by Jesuit ethicist J. Bryan Hehir, nearly rejected the deterrence system. The final draft was more cautious, but only slightly; it condemned the nuclear targeting of cities, called for a halt to the nuclear arms race, and accepted the moral legitimacy of the deterrence system only as long as serious negotiations leading to disarmament were taking place.[195]

Novak fought against the whole business, later recalling that he nearly lost his faith along the way. In August 1982 he hit bottom after a bruising appearance at a bishops' meeting. Bitterly he reported in *National Review* that dealing with the bishops was like dealing with the Moonies. It was pointless to argue with them because, like the Moonies, the bishops were impervious to factual evidence. They had fallen for an innocent vision of peace that was not to be dispelled by reality. For two years Novak warned against a looming catastrophe in Catholic teaching, drawing slight consolation when the final draft was toned down. *The Challenge of Peace*, despite last-minute alleviations, worsened the crisis in Catholicism. Of the Moonie-like spell that led the bishops to criticize the arms race and the ethics of deterrence, Novak concluded, "One can only hope for them to be deconverted, as once they were converted." Given the spell under which they had fallen, the bishops' "positively Gnostic" and irresponsible "glorification" of the peace movement was inevitable.[196]

From there he turned to the bishops' forthcoming letter on political economics. Novak warned, "Judging by my own education in American Catholic seminaries and in Rome, and judging by the current political climate, I think they may be tempted to emphasize the negative. That, certainly, is the Catholic reflex on this subject."[197] He implored the bishops to keep their reflexes in check by facing the historical facts: "In the world of fact, the American social system is morally superior to any historical Catholic social system, whether of the Vatican or of any Catholic state. In the world of theory, American social teaching, in all its rich pluralism and radical depth, is both morally superior and far more highly developed than Catholic social teaching."[198]

This time Novak and former US Treasury Secretary William Simon organized a corporate-dominated Lay Commission to instruct the bishops. Anticipating a very unwelcome pastoral letter, the group issued a manifesto, *Toward the Future*, shortly before the bishops' first draft was released in November 1984. Written by Novak, the statement celebrated the material blessings of capitalism, proclaimed the superiority of American social teaching, and declared against advocates of economic planning, "The condition of inventiveness is liberty."[199]

To the Novak group, the bishops' first draft was as bad as feared. Authored principally by Jesuit ethicist David Hollenbach, it criticized America's maldistribution of wealth, endorsed steps toward economic democracy, and called for the recognition of basic economic rights for all American citizens. Providing justice for the poor, the bishops argued, was the "single most urgent claim on the conscience of the nation." Thus, the nation's investment process should be directed specifically toward meeting the economic needs of the poor. Basic economic rights were "as essential to human dignity as are the political and civil freedoms granted pride of place in the Bill of

Rights of the U.S. Constitution." Citing the USA's long struggle to secure civil and
political rights for all Americans, the bishops declared, "We believe the time has come
for a similar experiment in securing economic rights: the creation of an order that
guarantees the minimum conditions of human dignity in the economic sphere for
every person."[200]

To Novak, the new letter was a disaster. Besides being "whiney and ungenerous,"
it confirmed and extended the worst aspects of Catholic social teaching on economic
rights and the moral duties of the state. Without denying that the bishops had official
Catholic teachings on their side, he urged them to reconsider what they were doing.
The doctrine of economic rights undermined the American idea of the limited state.
Did they really want to call for greater state power in the name of Catholic morality?
The doctrine also undermined the social structure of economic incentives, because it
shifted basic moral obligations to provide for one's family from the individual to the
state. Novak noted helpfully that the bishops needed to define economic rights more
carefully, distinguishing the notion as a claim in justice from constitutional or legal
claims. It was unclear whether they advocated a constitutional amendment or a new
class of legal entitlements.[201]

In either case, he insisted, the idea of economic rights was unnecessary and dangerous. It was unnecessary because the USA already had equal opportunity for individuals,
which satisfied the practical objectives of the 1948 United Nations Declaration of
Human Rights. It was dangerous because the notion sanctioned greater state power,
especially since the bishops also endorsed economic democracy, which he called "a
democratic socialist battlecry." Novak later recalled, "After I explained to the bishops
that 'economic democracy' was a wedge for democratic socialism, they stopped using
the phrase."[202]

In October 1985, shortly before the bishops dropped economic democracy, Novak
renewed his attack on economic rights. By enclosing economic rights within the
concept of human rights, he explained, liberals sought "to gain for the former the
prestige won by the latter through the horrors of World War II." First they weakened
the concept of political rights by describing them as "claims," which made political
rights seem analogous to economic rights. Then they vested economic goals with moral
content. Finally they advocated a preferential option for the state "as the final and
normally the chief bearer of responsibility."[203]

That was a somewhat prejudicial summary of Hollenbach's strategy in his book
Claims in Conflict: Retrieving and Renewing the Catholic Human Rights Tradition. Novak
implored the bishops not to commit Catholic teaching to Hollenbach's interpretation
of human rights theory: "The extensive effort underway to commit the church to
'economic rights' has the potential to become an error of classic magnitude. It might
well position the Catholic Church in a 'preferential option for the state' that will more
than rival that of the Constantinian period."[204]

He charged Hollenbach and others with misusing Pope John XXIII's endorsement
of economic rights. In *Pacem in Terris*, John XXIII asserted that human beings possessed
a right to sustainable income, food, shelter, medical care, and social services, listing
these essential needs under the category of "rights to life." Novak cautioned, however,
that the pope did not declare these rights to be universal: "He confined them explicitly
to the person who cannot meet his own responsibilities to provide for these basic
needs 'through no fault of his own.'" That was an endorsement of limited welfare
rights, not Hollenbach's universalism. Catholic social doctrine was already problematic,

to Novak. It sanctioned anti-capitalist sentiments and overemphasized the value of community and solidarity. The bitter irony was that *American* bishops were now proposing to extend the claims of Catholic natural law theory. Their letter revealed an utter failure "to grasp the full power of the American legacy."[205]

Novak admonished the bishops that in the vocabulary of *American* politics, "solidarity" was a dangerous notion. It did not carry the moral glow for most Americans that it obviously held for the bishops. Solidarity was "a more proper term for the hive, the herd, or for the flock than for the democratic community." The bishops, whatever they thought they were doing, were imposing "the Marxist definition of 'economic rights' upon the Western tradition of civil and political rights." That led them to sanctify other un-American concepts such as solidarity, participation, marginalization, and economic democracy. These were terrible words, utterly foreign to the American experience, Novak claimed. Worse yet, the bishops used "horrible words" to describe the American system. His example: "The concentration of privilege that exists today results far more from institutional arrangements that distribute power and wealth inequitably than from differences of talent or lack of desire to work."[206]

To Novak, that statement capsulized the tragedy of the entire pastoral letter. It used phrases, such as "concentration of privilege," that had nothing to do with America: "Where is this 'concentration'? Which American inherits 'privilege'? This sentence is an outrage. It is wholly unsupported by evidence, because it cannot be. It is a species of 'blaming America first.'"[207]

It could not be that America had concentrations of wealth or privilege. That was a literary convention lacking any basis in fact. America showed why economic rights were unnecessary, by offering equal opportunity to everyone. The American alternative was superior to the statist concepts of economic rights promulgated in social democratic and Catholic social theory.

But did not actual equality of opportunity require some degree of equality of condition? And if the USA did, in fact, possess extreme disparities of condition, with massive concentrations of wealth and privilege, did that not refute the claim to equality of opportunity? Novak denied both propositions. Equality of opportunity was real, equality of condition was unnecessary, and America had no concentrations of wealth anyway.[208]

Ultimately he was forced to concede that the doctrine of economic rights was too firmly established in Catholic teaching to be dislodged. Novak still argued that economic rights should be interpreted as a moral obligation, not a political one. But he granted that the obligation in question was a matter of justice, not mere charity. Thus, goods such as food, housing, employment, and medical care were, according to Catholic theory, "goods indispensable to a full human life." Vaguely, Novak tried to distinguish between rights inhering in the nature of persons, which merited state protection, and economic rights, which did not merit state protection and yet deserved "in justice to be provided."[209]

These reluctant concessions lost the argument. If economic security was a morally obligatory question of justice, it followed that state power should be used, when necessary, to obtain it. If basic economic goods were indispensable to a full human life, as Novak conceded, then economic needs were as important as civil and political rights. Hollenbach replied to Novak that since the provision of economic goods was indispensable to a full human life, it followed that these needs qualified as rights inhering in the nature of human beings. They were not to be regarded only as worthy goals of the individual moral life. In *Economic Justice for All*, the bishops asserted that rights to security and freedom were equally important.[210]

Novak became a hero to Catholic political conservatives by leading the conservative opposition to the bishops. His later career was devoted to corporate apologetics and the company that came with it. From his position at the AEI he contended for an infusion of Whig realism into Catholic thought, wrote a column for *Forbes* magazine, won the million-dollar Templeton Prize in 1994, and settled into the lifeworld of big business seminars and conferences. Often he lectured that Catholic social teaching had much to learn from the classical liberalism of the Whigs, who taught the virtue of enterprise and defined the American experiment:

> When was the last time we heard in church, or learned from a text of moral theology, that personal economic enterprise is a necessary moral virtue? Or received instruction in how to practice it? Or learned to criticize social systems in the light of how well, or how badly, they nourish and promote personal economic enterprise? Does our catechism teach us even so much as the basic conceptual definition of this virtue?[211]

Often he protested that Catholicism modernized in the wrong ways. Catholic thinkers adapted to trends in liberal and postmodern thought, but clung to traditional ways of thinking about human nature, wealth, and materialism. Since Novak otherwise admired the strong papacy of John Paul II, he had to play down the pope's occasion-ally blistering words about consumerism and the social mortgage on property. On the other hand, Novak commended the Catholic conscience to libertarian disciples of Milton Friedman and John Hospers, and he complained that Catholic ethicists rou-tinely confused the Whig tradition with its libertarian stream. To Novak, Hayek was the model Whig, because he emphasized social order, law, legislation, and tradition. Hayek rejected the egotistical self of libertarian theory and did not reduce self and society to economistic interchanges.[212]

But Novak protested too much, for Hayek's repudiation of social justice was no less emphatic or categorical than Friedman's. In *The Mirage of Social Justice*, Hayek contended that "the common good" was an atavistic concept inherited from the col-lectivistic consciousness of tribal societies, in which hunters derived emotional benefits from providing food for their tribal dependents. To Hayek, the common good was a tribal hangover, and so was social justice. Both were infantile sentiments that tried to compensate for the loss of fellowship experienced within tribal societies, and both were overdue to be left behind.[213]

Novak was too Catholic to go that far, but he sought to limit the social justice impulse in Catholicism. For him, the crucial test of the economic system was whether it created wealth; for Catholic moral theory, the test was how the system produced and distributed wealth. Novak's zealous protection of the economic sphere from poli-tics and rights conflicted with the Catholic emphasis on social justice and the organic connections between the political, economic, and cultural spheres. He found an appre-ciative and remunerative audience in the big business wing of conservative Catholi-cism, but resented his lack of an academic following. Often he bridled at being dismissed by theologians and ethicists, complaining that they were prejudiced against him because of his politics and corporate connections. While most academics ignored his later writings, he took flack from theological conservatives for prizing the American experience over Catholic teaching. Novak hoped to be remembered for making a historic corrective to Catholic thought, or at least, for anticipating the direction that Catholic teaching had to take.[214]

He was a true-believing neoconservative in every sense of the term. Novak wrote less about foreign policy than many neocons, but he stressed the missionary component of democratic capitalism and made the neocon transition to "unipolarism" after the Soviet bloc imploded. In the waning months of the Cold War, shortly before an expiring Soviet Union finally disintegrated, neoconservatives began to argue that the moment had come to create an American-dominated world order. Instead of reducing military spending, the USA needed to expand its military reach to every region of the world, using America's tremendous military and economic power to prevent any nation or group of nations from becoming a great power rival. Some neocons called it "American global dominion," others favored "unipolarism" or "full spectrum dominance." The governing idea, by whatever name, was to secure and extend America's unrivaled military and economic preeminence. Charles Krauthammer explained in 1989, "America's purpose should be to steer the world away from its coming multipolar future toward a qualitatively new outcome – a unipolar world." Ben Wattenberg, with a lighter touch, gave the assurance that "a unipolar world is a good thing, if America is the uni."[215]

Novak quickly adopted the unipolarist view, in his case as a democratic globalist. From the beginning there were key differences between neoconservatives over democratic idealism. Nationalistic realists such as Krauthammer and Irving Kristol distinguished between defending American superiority, which they supported, and pursuing global democracy, which they eschewed. Novak belonged to the movement's larger faction, which called for an aggressive policy of exporting democracy and building a global Pax Americana. Leading democratic globalists included Wattenberg, Novak, Paul Wolfowitz, Richard Perle, Norman Podhoretz, Midge Decter, Joshua Muravchik, Zalmay Khalilzad, and Catholic theologian George Weigel. In both cases neoconservatism became identified with the view that US foreign policy had to be committed to sustaining America's unrivaled global military and economic dominance.

Besides calling for an enhanced global American military, Novak stressed that America increasingly remade the world in its image by non-military means. Most of the world was tuning in to American culture and trying to emulate America's political and economic systems, he enthused. The former Soviet bloc nations, in particular, were looking in the right direction: "Regarding pluralism, the smaller, more homogeneous nation-states of Europe have less to teach than America does. And about enterprise, initiative, and risk, do Western European socialists or Americans have more to teach?"[216]

His chief theme in this area was that the USA had a defining commitment to construct a *Novus Ordo Seclorum*, a new order of the ages. Throughout its history, Novak contended, America was an exception to history. It combined liberty and democracy, invaded only to liberate, cared nothing for conquest, and aspired only to help other nations become free and democratic. Thus the world had nothing to fear, and everything to gain, from the USA becoming an unrivaled superpower. Most importantly, America's greatest power was spiritual, not military:

> Call this mysticism, if you like, or 'soft' power. But as you have watched Chinese students in Shanghai carry a replica of the U.S. Statue of Liberty, listened to a brewery worker in Prague quoting from Jefferson and watched dissidents in the fifteen republics of the

U.S.S.R. voice dreams of new democracies, free economies and liberties of conscience, surely you have been tempted to think that this is the one kind of power most consistent with the purposes for which the U.S. was founded.[217]

Novak was prolific on this theme, celebrating the universal, Godly force of the American idea in the world. His claim to realism vanished when he warmed to the subject of America the greatest. He blasted critics of American military overreach, calling them "declinists," and exulted that the American idea and nation were ascending, not declining. After the USA defeated Iraq in the Gulf War of 1991, Novak proclaimed, "This is the end of the decline. This is the decline of the declinists. The mother of all battles turned into the daughter of disasters for the declinists. For years, people are going to cite the lessons of the Persian Gulf." Twelve years later, he supported the US invasion of Iraq to finish the business of the first Gulf War and strike a blow in America's global war on terrorism.[218]

For the most part Novak was a typical neocon on foreign policy, always contending the need for larger defense budgets and an aggressive use of American military force. What distinguished him somewhat in this company was his mystical emphasis on the godly power of the American idea. Neocons agreed that the crucial question was the degree to which one believed in America; for Novak, believing in America folded into believing in God's will for the world. In 2003, a few weeks after neocons had the invasion of Iraq for which they had pleaded, Novak observed jubilantly of the neocon phenomenon, "Neocons are on the whole cheerful folk, always ready for new battles, who fight with a certain joy and gusto, nourished by a real hope." The ultimate source of that hope was spiritual, he asserted: "We really do believe that God created this cosmos for the blossoming of liberty."[219]

In his book *The Universal Hunger for Liberty* (2004) Novak stressed that economic globalization was making the world look more like the United States. Global conglomerates like Coca-Cola and Barclay's were "important sources of moral teaching" that trained ever-larger swaths of humanity in the virtues of democratic capitalism, offering "horizon expanding opportunities" to previously undeveloped areas. Moreover, globalization was also political and cultural. Novak offered a "Neocon Creed" for a globalizing world: economic realism was a necessity, which meant democratic capitalism; good politics was more important than economics, which meant a Whiggish politics of limited government; and conservative culture was the most important thing of all.[220]

But that evoked the problem with which Novak started. For years he wrote columns in *Forbes* that peeked out amid massive advertising sections and the magazine's updates on junk bonds and leveraged buy-outs. Usually Novak rejoiced in the spread of things American throughout the world. Sometimes he enthused that God was at work in the expansion of American capitalism. But on occasion he flashed an undertow of anxiety about exporting American culture. Reflecting on the power of advertising and the values of the commercial media, Novak lamented, "We are besieged by ideas, ideals, and solicitations that on reflection we find morally repulsive." In *National Review* he reported that he and his wife often felt overwhelmed by the media tidal wave, "which we could hardly hold back by ourselves." America's public moral culture as expressed in television, music, and cinema was "a disgrace to the human race."[221]

Novak realized that these judgments comported oddly with his claim for integral American capitalism; he had never really disposed of the cultural contradictions problem. He coped with the problem by calling for culture war. To the extent that America had moral and spiritual problems, he argued, they belonged to the moral-cultural realm. Capitalism was not a primary cause of the rot and vulgarity in American life; the culprit was a dysfunctional moral-cultural realm. For Novak, the moral-cultural realm was a system that paralleled the political and economic realms. Its primary function was to shape and control the forces unleashed in the other realms. To the extent that capitalism assaulted the ties of family, community, and tradition, it was up to families and faith communities to nurture deeper values. Churches and other institutions in the moral-cultural realm had to do their jobs, shaping the moral culture in which capitalism operated, counteracting the egotism and materialism of the market. Novak reported that if America's moral-cultural communities tried to fulfill their proper role, and then failed in the effort, he would concede that capitalism bore some responsibility for the problem. In the meantime he conceded nothing, instead blaming those who shaped American culture. In politics and economics, the political Right had prevailed, but the Left still controlled the heights of American culture. To really put American society on the right track, conservatives needed to gain control of the television networks, movie industry, universities, and religious denominations.[222]

That was the basis on which neocons first joined forces with the Christian Right; foreign policy alliances came later. The main thing was the culture war against feminism, gay rights, abortion, affirmative action, and other forms of cultural degeneracy. When Novak explained why progressive Christianity had become repugnant to him, he singled out the feminist factor. In his telling, feminism infected modern Christianity with a Gnostic virus, an irrational rage against the natural order. In the natural order the female principle was oceanic, blurring crucial differences, while the male principle provided necessary distinctions. Catholic orthodoxy, highly attuned to the natural order, conceived God in masculine images, played up the maleness of the redeemer, and "fenced in" the sacraments with male images. But feminism was an assault on Catholicism and the natural order. Novak urged that the church needed strong male leaders who repudiated feminist nonsense; instead it had meek leaders:

> If men and non-feminist women were to respond as feminists allege that they do – with decisiveness, competitiveness, and repression – these absurdities would long since have been laughed out of currency. But in the presence of feminists, most men are meek, humble, and submissive. They scrutinize feminism seriously, seeking some possible way, absurd as it seems, in which the will of God might actually be expressed in it.[223]

The church was plagued with vengeful feminists because it tried to appease their absurd anger, he argued: "The rage of feminists is partly to be explained by the weakness of the males they encounter. Men find it more difficult to stand up to the fury of a woman than to any other thing on earth; nothing so tests their manhood." Failing the test, the church found itself besieged by self-hating feminists demanding a world made over. To Novak, feminism was a declaration of war against nature, experience, and tradition. The feminist revolution was not progressive, humane, or even radical, but total: "That is why the hatred they manifest is so unbelievably intense." By the third century, he observed, the church fathers figured this out; thus they stopped allowing women to take prophetic, priestly, and episcopal roles. Catholic orthodoxy showed its wisdom by suppressing female voices. Novak urged that priests and bishops had to be male, not because the church had anything against women, but because the integrity of the church's tradition had to be protected from the oceanic confusions of female experience.[224]

Modern Catholicism still had no female priests, he allowed, but it made a mockery of the ancient Mass: "I normally leave the contemporary liturgy in a state of numbness. I think of the progressive Church as 'progressive bourgeois Christianity,' and its sentiments of peace, love, community, solidarity and the like remind me of the saccharine holy cards of an earlier form of bourgeois Christianity, which I also did not like." Instead of celebrating the ancient liturgy, Catholic congregations turned the Mass into "a celebration of our being together. It's awful."[225]

Novak judged that modern Christianity suffered awful distortions of what it was supposed to be because it trembled at appearing not to be progressive. Tellingly, virtually every major Christian theologian of the twentieth century was a socialist. Novak noted the point ruefully many times, sometimes calling the roll of socialist theologians. He added that organizations like the Society of Christian Ethics imparted "a democratic socialist vision of reality."[226] Quoting Madison, he admonished that "the rage for equality is a wicked project." Unfortunately, American liberal Protestantism and mainstream Catholicism were tragically "hooked into this project." That left him with much to oppose and overcome.[227]

Progressive Evangelicalism: Jim Wallis

The Christian Right received enormous media coverage because of its power in the Republican party, and it excelled at conveying its social message through the media appearances of Jerry Falwell, Pat Robertson, James Dobson, and political operative Ralph Reed. But in social ethics it was a minor player. It produced no distinguished social ethical thinkers (Henry won his prominence as an apologist and religious journalist), and the evangelicals who achieved academic distinction (such as Yoder, Hauerwas, and Glenn H. Stassen) did not support the Christian Right.

Even in the public square the Christian Right faced significant competition from evangelicals of other traditions. For over 30 years *Sojourners* magazine rekindled the memory of nineteenth-century America's radical evangelical movements. In the 1990s *Sojourners* editor Jim Wallis achieved public prominence as a voice of the progressive evangelical alternative. And in 2005 Wallis broke through to a higher order of renown that accomplished his long-sought objective of ending the Christian Right's monopoly on religious discourse in American national politics.

Wallis was born in 1948 and raised in a conservative evangelical (Plymouth Brethren) family in Detroit, where his father, a Detroit Edison engineer, was a lay minister. As a teenager he underwent an intense conversion to racial justice activism that alienated him from his church. As a college student at Michigan State University in the late 1960s his intense opposition to the Vietnam War deepened his alienation. In both cases he was told by church acquaintances that political issues like racism and war had no place in the church. Wallis burned with righteous indignation at this assurance. When Detroit erupted in 1967, almost no one from his congregation fathomed the black rage on display; to the local Plymouth Brethren, blacks had no cause to be angry at whites. Wallis was mortified by the racism and nationalism of his church community. It struck him deeply that Christians could rationalize any social evil by dichotomizing between religion and politics. That experience fired his passion for bringing together religion and politics for regenerative ends.[228]

As a college student he made a religion of antiwar activism during the turbulent election year of 1968, the moratorium marches of 1969, and the national student strike of spring 1970. He thought he had left Christianity behind. But Wallis was too religious to settle for an activist substitute for the faith he had lost. In his senior year he started reading the Bible again, concentrating on the gospels, trying to decide what to do with his life. The gospel picture of Jesus and the call to follow the radical way of Jesus came through to Wallis. Graduating from college in 1970, he enrolled at Trinity Evangelical Divinity School in Deerfield, Illinois. Wallis wanted a seminary that took the Bible seriously; he had a low view of political liberalism and figured that liberal theology was its first cousin. Immediately at Trinity he met a handful of students who shared his excitement and perplexity at being simultaneously evangelical, antiwar, and committed to racial justice.[229]

The group's immediate problem was existential. Evangelical seminaries had a very low tolerance for civil rights activism of any sort, and one could not oppose the Vietnam War on an evangelical campus without being branded a Communist. To Wallis the monolithic conservatism of evangelical leaders was strange and appalling. He organized antiwar protests and prayer vigils on campus, prompting outraged alumni to demand his expulsion. Kenneth Kantzer, dean of the seminary, upheld Wallis's right not to be expelled, but told him he was hurting the seminary financially, especially by publishing a newspaper. In the spring of 1971 Wallis's group formed a residential community and launched a cheeky 16-page tabloid, *The Post-American*. Describing themselves as products of student radicalism and the evangelical church, they urged readers to choose between the cross of Christ and the American flag. The group struggled to hold together for four years, Wallis never graduated, the *Post-American* upgraded to a magazine, and in 1975 the group moved from Chicago to Washington, DC, changing the magazine's name to *Sojourners*. Two original members of the group, Joe Roos and Bob Sabath, moved to Washington with Wallis; others joined the community along the way.[230]

Sojourners was best known as a magazine, but it was also the name of Wallis's Christian community, an ecumenical fellowship located in a poor neighborhood 20 blocks from the White House, which sponsored a variety of ministries. From the beginning the magazine emphasized that the Bible emphasized justice and serving the poor. The early *Post-American/Sojourners* featured dogmatic pleas for anarcho-Christian pacifism in virtually every issue, until even the editors found them boring. By the late 1970s *Sojourners* had switched to a topical format, spruced up its appearance, and eased up on self-righteous didacticism, sometimes cautioning against left-wing self-righteousness. It attracted an eclectic audience of Catholics, mainline Protestants, secular activists, religiously unmoored seekers, and various kinds of evangelicals, attracting interns and new members from the same groups, which raised identity questions. At various times in the 1980s and 1990s the non-evangelicals outnumbered professed evangelicals, and Wallis had to deal with demands to blur or shed the community's evangelical identity. Persistently he insisted that Sojourners was an evangelical fellowship, *Sojourners* was an evangelical magazine, and the primary mission of both was to the evangelical world, no matter how ecumenical the community became nor how alienated it felt from the dominant forms of US American evangelicalism. The payoff for that stubborn conviction was hard for many insiders to see in the 1980s; 20 years later it was obvious.

In the 1980s Wallis's group was deeply involved in campaigns opposing the Reagan administration's policies in Central America, especially its battles against the Sandinista government in Nicaragua and the revolutionary movement in El Salvador. *Sojourners* was the main force behind Witness for Peace, an ecumenical group that organized support for Central American social justice movements. It was a main venue of liberation theology, featuring writings by theologians and missionaries. It supported the sanctuary movement for Central Americans fleeing political persecution and was a major sponsor of the "Pledge of Resistance," which organized campaigns of protest and civil disobedience to be carried out in the event that the USA invaded Nicaragua. It was equally involved in the Nuclear Freeze and other movements for nuclear weapons disarmament and in the movement to abolish apartheid in South Africa. A decade later, in 1995, Wallis founded Call to Renewal, a coalition of religious groups that campaigned for a living wage, tax reform, and other measures designed to combat poverty.[231]

Much of Wallis's writing chronicled his involvements in these movements and campaigns. He was fond of saying that he specialized in the two subjects that were off limits in polite society, politics and religion. Often he wrote about the slippery relationships between religious faithfulness and being involved in political movements. Being comfortable with evangelical language opened unlikely doors for him; for Wallis, the revival language of sin and conversion was second nature. He preached for revival unabashedly, conducting evangelistic campaigns that blended personal and social salvation. He always stressed the biblical link between personal salvation and social justice, urging that God was personal, but never private. Liberal Christianity wrongly depersonalized God and religion, he contended, while conservative Christianity wrongly restricted both to private space, until it bolted into public space. Linking himself to the abolitionist and social justice preaching of nineteenth-century evangelicals, Wallis enlisted modern evangelicalism against war, violence, poverty, racism, inequality, male chauvinism, abortion, and capital punishment, invoking what Joseph Cardinal Bernadin called the "seamless garment ethic" or "consistent ethic of life."[232]

From the beginning, *Sojourners* was soaked in politics, but mostly of the protest variety. Its original "post-American" pacifism was long on peace church nonconformity and "speaking truth to power." Wallis and the Sojourners community practiced civil disobedience, commended tax resisters, organized teach-ins for peace, boycotted predatory corporations, and demonstrated against US military policies. On the lecture circuit Wallis often objected that *Sojourners*-style social ethics had no place in divinity school renderings of social ethics because it was evangelical and it refused to be consigned to Niebuhrian Christ-against-culture irrelevance. That raised the question of the *Sojourners* line on government, on which it conveyed mixed messages for many years. *Sojourners* published scores of articles demanding government programs for social insurance and economic redistribution, and it blasted the Reagan administration for cutting government aid to the poor. It also published anarcho-pacifists for whom government was the enemy. Wallis could be quoted either way, and the magazine's dominant language of resisting the powers often conveyed a misleading impression. In the 1980s outsiders were sometimes surprised to learn that Wallis, Joyce Hollyday, Danny Collum, and other *Sojourners* mainstays assumed the necessity of national governments and of reform movements to make them work better.

In the 1990s, however, the magazine recalibrated its language and social vision, if not its heart. Faced with a resurgent Christian Right in a new organization, the Christian Coalition, Wallis concentrated on building up an ecumenical alternative to it. He grew more political in the ordinary sense of the term, seeking to influence both political parties. For years Wallis had refused to be labeled with any "ism" or political tag, mostly to avoid the appearance of mere politicking. He was not a liberal or a conservative, he argued, and he did not fit the mold of any existing political party. He did not want to belong to a party anyway. He prized his outreach to Democrats, Republicans, independents, and other political types. He was a throwback to the nineteenth-century evangelicals, which made him a misfit in contemporary American politics.

But in the mid-1990s Wallis began to pitch this claim a bit differently, presenting himself as a harbinger of an untried third way in American politics and religion. His ambitions became grander as he made his peace with ordinary politics and the mass media. Now his claim to be neither liberal nor conservative morphed into a positional framing point, serving a political objective. In his book *The Soul of Politics* (1994) Wallis urged that the USA needed to find a third way between the religious Right and the secular Left, and that it was happening. *Sojourners* was no longer merely an outpost of protest politics and an ignored religious option, progressive evangelicalism. It stood in the vanguard of a sweeping transformational movement that US American politics, religion and culture desperately needed.[233]

Conservative religion was preoccupied with words and dogma, Wallis explained. Its piety had no energy for social justice, and its politicized wing was "bizarre and frightening." Conservative American Christianity, living in the most materialistic culture in history, preached a gospel of prosperity. Faced with obscene disparities of wealth and fantastic military budgets, it defended the privileges of the rich and advocated global military hegemony. It was also, Wallis observed, a white religion, which lacked a conscience for racial justice, fueled a backlash against women's rights, and denigrated gays and lesbians with blatant caricatures.[234]

Liberal religion, on the other hand, was a weak and dispirited pushover for secular liberal culture. Wallis contended that liberal clergy and denominations were too secularized to preach about personal regeneration; thus they lacked any transformative power. They had a social conscience, but one usually cut off from its religious wellspring. When religious liberals spoke in public, the words sounded bureaucratic and ideological, not spiritual. Instead of prizing prophetic integrity, they worried about their political correctness and ideological conformity. To Wallis they appeared to be "captive to the shifting winds of the secular culture." Liberal religious types deferred constantly to secular thinkers and authorities, he judged, which was a sure path to being ignored. Somebody besides fundamentalists had to challenge the soul-killing sterility and moral emptiness of liberal culture, but religious liberals were unlikely candidates for the job. American society and politics, and in fact the entire world, needed the saving power of justice-seeking gospel faith.[235]

Wallis claimed to see it happening in religiously based protest movements, grassroots Christian organizing campaigns, spiritually revitalized churches, new Christian communities, the evangelical upsurge, the growth of the *Sojourners* network, and the crowds at his lectures:

> A real alternative in American religious life has emerged, unrecognized by the media. While the press has focused on the loud voices of the Religious Right and limited its field of vision to the conservative tenor of the last several years, a prophetic spiritual movement for social change has been steadily growing and is making a difference in the institutions of both religion and society.

He stressed that the next great awakening had begun in the 1960s, before the Christian Right existed. It was an uprising of spiritual conviction expressed variously in liberation theology, the social justice currents of a burgeoning evangelicalism, the environmental movement, and the spiritually vital streams of progressive Christianity. Wallis enthused,

The effects of this progressive spirit are being felt in virtually every constituency of the American churches and in the Jewish community. This spiritual movement reaches out in respectful partnership with other faith traditions beyond the religious mainstream of the society. And it invites a new dialogue between the religious and nonreligious about the shape of social and political morality.[236]

There was such a thing as a morally and spiritually regenerative approach to politics, he urged, and *Sojourners* was a laboratory for it: "*Sojourners* is working to change the 'soul of politics.'" Protest politics were no longer enough: "What has often been expressed as 'prophetic protest' now has the capacity to be a vital source of 'prophetic vision' as well. Out of religious values and moral concerns, new social and economic alternatives are emerging." The next great religious awakening, which was already burgeoning, needed to heal modern people of their addiction to materialism, convert them to being stewards of God's creation, replace the "ethic of profit" with an "ethic of community," atone for racism and sexism, put an end to "our wasteful and destructive militarism," and strengthen the bonds of connection in the entire global human family.[237]

The mass media, looking to balance out Falwell or Robertson, turned increasingly to Wallis for balancing quotes. Wallis played the game assiduously, winning extensive media coverage, but he insisted that his project was not to build up a religious Left as an antidote to the religious Right. That was a crass convention of the media, which conceived politics reductively as a struggle for partisan influence and power. Wallis believed that he stood for something grander than a status pitch for equal time. He was not trying to build a left-wing version of the nakedly partisan, power-oriented Christian Coalition. The Christian Right, besides holding bad theology and politics, had the wrong strategy. Instead of building a culture-changing movement it opted for power politics, trying to take over the Republican party. To Wallis, the civil rights movement was a better model, because it took the long view, building up a mass movement for change that persuaded by moral argument. Repeatedly he denied that his goal was to win a place for the religious Left in the Democratic party. His evangelical revivalism and opposition to abortion put him at odds with Democratic party operatives, and in any case, merely grabbing for political power was spiritually corrupting, as it proved to be for the Christian Right. Wallis wanted a culture-changing spiritual revival that transformed both political parties and the culture of politics as a whole.

He sought to persuade readers in two more books, *Who Speaks for God?* (1996) and *Faith Works* (2000), that it was not so wild a dream. *Who Speaks for God?* urged that faith and citizenship went together, and that a new politics of spiritually-based compassion and community was gathering force in US American society. Wallis pointed to the ecumenical activism of Call to Renewal, enthusing that "the phone hasn't stopped ringing." He described the Call to Renewal and the wider upsurge of ecumenical activism as "an alternative to the Religious Right," which convinced many observers that his project really was to build up a politicized Christian Left, his denials notwithstanding. *Faith Works* recycled the same argument with a stronger personal dimension and sermonic touch, helping readers see the everyday sources of his optimism. Few people saw what Wallis experienced on a weekly basis, constantly meeting grassroots organizers and a younger generation of evangelicals who cared about poverty, racism, sexism, and militarism. Wallis stressed that they existed in growing numbers.[238]

He drew hope from meeting people who shared his faith and vision. His books told stories about them, recounting his experiences, repeatedly invoking the same framing argument about the religious Right and secular Left. In the election year of 2004, however, Wallis detected something new as he labored almost daily on television, radio, and the Internet, commenting on the election campaign. He sensed a heightened anxiety about America's moral culture, especially the moral state of its politics. There seemed to be a new opportunity for his usual themes. His publisher at Harper Collins agreed; Wallis's next book was likely to hit a gusher. After the election, a flood of commentary about the "values voter" and the Democratic party's religion problem forced Wallis to finish writing in a rush to seize the moment; *God's Politics: Why the Right Gets It Wrong and the Left Doesn't Get It* (2005), was perfectly timed. Wallis put it personally in the opening sentence of his breakthrough book: "I have one of the best jobs in the world because I get to know some of the most faith-inspired people everywhere who are doing some of the most important things anywhere."[239]

Wallis agreed with the conventional media view that Republicans excelled at the politics of moral values and that Democrats needed to learn how to talk about religion and morality. But there were serious problems with Republican religion, he argued, and Democrats had a deeper problem than their awkwardness about discussing religion in public. Both parties needed a better vision than the truncated one they settled for. Wallis explained, "My vision – a progressive and prophetic vision of faith and politics – was not running in this election. George Bush and John Kerry were, and John Kerry lost – not progressive religion." Neither candidate addressed poverty as a burning moral issue, Wallis observed. Neither candidate treated the war in Iraq as "a clearly religious matter" or upheld a consistent ethic of life. Both parties failed the crucial tests of moral politics. People of faith needed to create a better politics and political culture: "That can best be done by reaching into both the conservative Christian communities who voted for George Bush and more liberal Christian communities who voted for John Kerry."[240]

Wallis contended that if either party got truly serious about moral politics, it would transform the political landscape. Neither party deserved to call itself "pro-family" or "pro-life." Every week he met evangelicals and Catholics who blanched at the bullying tactics of the Christian Right and at the pro-abortion dogmatism of the Democratic party. At every lecture somebody asked him, "How can I vote for what I've just heard?" Wallis told them it should be possible: "If there were ever candidates running with a strong set of personal moral values *and* a commitment to social justice and peace, they could build many bridges to the other side."[241]

In his reading there were three main options in contemporary US politics: conservative on everything, liberal on everything, and libertarianism. Conservatives had a few differences on economics and foreign policy, he allowed, but the differences were slight, and the Right dominated American politics. Liberals had their own range of slight differences that mattered even less, since they usually lost. To Wallis, the ascendancy of libertarianism in American culture and politics was worrisome, because it stood for selfishness at both ends: amoral on social issues and right wing on economics. Wallis called it the "just leave me alone and don't spend my money option."[242]

That was a bad alternative to the tired debate of conservative versus liberal, he urged. A better option was the one that progressive evangelicals shared with many Catholics, black church Protestants, ecumenical Jews and Muslims, and spiritually energized liberal Protestants. It affirmed personal responsibility *and* social justice, family values *and* just treatment of gays and lesbians, the sanctity of life *and* equal rights for women. "At the heart of the fourth option is the integral link between personal ethics and social justice," Wallis explained.

> It is traditional or conservative on issues of family values, sexual integrity, and personal responsibility, while being very progressive, populist, or even radical on issues like poverty and justice. It affirms good stewardship of the earth and its resources, supports gender equality, and is more internationally minded than nationalist – looking first to peacemaking and conflict resolution when it comes to foreign policy questions.[243]

On abortion he challenged Democrats to change their party line and work pragmatically with Republicans to reduce the number of abortions. On gay and lesbian rights he supported civil unions but not marriage. On foreign policy he stepped gingerly into unfamiliar territory. Wallis was still a pacifist at heart and still regarded peacemaking as the heart of the Christian witness. But he had taken the path of prescribing policies for the state, there was no such thing as a pacifist state, and in the wake of the terrorist attacks of September 11, 2001, he could not claim to believe that the USA should renounce the use of force.

Shortly after 9/11, Hauerwas admitted to Wallis that he was having trouble finding his public voice. Hauerwas resented being told that pacifists should shut up during wartime. He believed that pacifists had a right to commend policies that reduced violence, and he accepted that global police action and international courts were morally legitimate.[244]

Wallis realized that he and Hauerwas had the same problem in making a policy argument. He had opposed every war since Vietnam, but resisting terrorism was not necessarily equivalent to war. Like most pacifists he accepted that police action to protect families and neighborhoods was morally legitimate. In the wake of 9/11 Wallis took the same tack as Hauerwas, extending Yoder's distinction between police action and war. Yoder taught that police action was structurally and ethically different from war because it was directed only at an offending party, it was subject to review by higher authorities, and usually the preponderance of police power made violent resistance to it futile. That gave Wallis just enough of a basis to say that he still opposed war, but not state police action to stop terrorism: "Terrorists must be found, captured, and stopped. And their violent plans must be disrupted *before* they are carried out. All this involves using some kind of force." These words were hard for him to choke out, he admitted: "To accept any use of force is a very difficult thing for those committed to nonviolent solutions." *Sojourners* opposed the war in Iraq, but made its peace with global policing; Wallis found himself saying: "Perhaps it is time to explore a theology for global police forces, including ethics for the use of internationally sanctioned enforcement – precisely as an alternative to war."[245]

Persistently, seemingly without tiring of airports or repetition, Wallis urged that religion and politics needed to go together; bad things happened when they did not; a deadly combination of bad theology and bad politics was very powerful in American life; and the answer to bad theology was good theology, not secularism. In the presidency of George W. Bush he found a toxic combination of bad theology and bad politics, lamenting that Bush's personal faith made him arrogantly confident of his mission to rid the world of evil by overthrowing governments in the Muslim world. In good theology, Wallis admonished, empire was understood to be morally repugnant, believers were not told that God was on their side, and nations were not commissioned to rid the world of evil. In good theology, nations were understood to be too consumed with hubris and will to power to be agents of redemption. Banishing evil was God's business. On the other hand, that did not mean that religion had no rightful place in the public utterances of a president or movement leader. The USA needed more presidents like Abraham Lincoln, who got the dialectic right, and the world needed more witnesses like Martin Luther King Jr, Oscar Romero, and Desmond Tutu, who showed the way.[246]

For 35 years Wallis was the unchallenged guardian and symbol of progressive evangelicalism, until *God's Politics* launched him to another level of renown. His book tour became a movement whirlwind of overflowing auditoriums, media appearances, and book signings that morphed into town meetings and revivals. The book stayed on the *New York Times* bestseller list for four months, lending credence to Wallis's decade-long thesis of a rising progressive evangelical tide. Explaining the reaction, Wallis told his audiences that there were three great hungers in the modern world. People yearned for spiritual integrity, social justice, and the connection between the two. Later he remarked,

> *God's Politics* became the right book at the right time, and revealed what was already there waiting to be expressed. Many people of faith felt their voice was not being heard in the national debate over faith and politics and found something to point to. I soon realized the large numbers of people were not just coming to hear my voice, but also to express *their* voice.[247]

Some of his former comrades preferred the early Wallis. Catholic pacifist writer Colman McCarthy protested that the later Wallis placed his faith in government and wasted his time on mundane politics. Many critics derided Wallis's denial that he wanted to be the liberal version of Jerry Falwell, angling for political influence as an advocate of a religious Left centered on progressive evangelicalism. Since that was the basis of his media fame, why did he insist on denying it? Wallis adeptly replied, however, that he had a larger ambition, to change the culture of US American politics as a whole. At *Sojourners*, he noted in 2005, all the talk was about building the movement, not about selling his book or gaining political access:

> This is about how to build a movement on the back of a book tour. The story now is not the book, but the tour. Why are so many people at bookstores? We're getting 400 in Dayton, Ohio, and Austin, Texas, and Wichita, Kansas. Also in Philadelphia and Boston. They're sitting on the floor. In Los Angeles, it was pouring rain. A thousand people showed up. It's this buzzing thing, which means that something is needing to be expressed.

The Christian Right's monologue on faith and politics was over, he declared, and a better version of religiously inspired moral politics was coming.[248]

Notes

1   See George M. Marsden, *Reforming Fundamentalism: Fuller Seminary and the New Evangelicalism* (Grand Rapids: Eerdmans, 1987), 16–17; Harold Lindsell, *Park Street Prophet: A Life of Harold John Ockenga* (Wheaton, IL: Van Kampen Press, 1951); Harold John Ockenga, "Can Fundamentalism Win America?" *Christian Life* (June 1947), 13–15; Gary Dorrien, *The Remaking of Evangelical Theology* (Louisville: Westminster John Knox Press, 1998), 52–3.

2   See James Orr, *Revelation and Inspiration* (New York: Charles Scribner's Sons, 1910), 197–218. This introductory section on Henry and conservative evangelicalism adapts

material from Gary Dorrien, "Niebuhr and Graham: Modernity, Complexity, White Supremacism, Justice, Ambiguity," in *The Legacy of Billy Graham*, ed. Michael G. Long (Louisville: Westminster John Knox Press, 2007); and Dorrien, "Evangelical Ironies: Theology, Pluralism, Politics, and Israel," *Evangelicals and Jews in Dialogue*, ed. Nancy Isserman (Philadelphia: Temple University Press, 2008), and Dorrien, *The Remaking of Evangelical Theology*.

3 See J. N. Darby, *The Collected Writings of J. N. Darby* 35 vols., ed. William Kelly, Doctrinal No. 1 (reprint, Sunbury, PA: Believers Bookshelf, 1971), 3:1–43; Darby, *The Collected Writings of J. N. Darby*, Prophetic No. 4 (reprint: Winschoten, The Netherlands: H. L. Heijkoop, 1971), 11:110–67; C. I. Scofield, *Rightly Dividing the Word of Truth* (Westwood, NJ: Revell, 1896); William E. Blackstone, *Jesus is Coming* (New York: Revell, 1908).

4 See Darby, *The Collected Writings of J. N. Darby*, 3: 1–43; Ernest R. Sandeen, *The Roots of Fundamentalism: British and American Millenarianism 1800–1930* (Chicago: University of Chicago Press, 1970); George M. Marsden, "Fundamentalism as an American Phenomenon," *Reckoning with the Past: Historical Essays on American Evangelicalism from the Institute for the Study of American Evangelicals*, ed. D. G. Hart (Grand Rapids: Baker Bok House, 1995), 303–21; Nathan O. Hatch, "Millennialism and Popular Religion in the Early Republic," in Leonard I. Sweet, ed., *The Evangelical Tradition in America* (Macon, GA: Mercer University Press, 1984), 112–14; C. Norman Kraus, *Dispensationalism in America: Its Rise and Development* (Richmond: John Knox Press, 1958); Ruth A. Doan, *The Miller Heresy, Millennialism, and American Culture* (Philadelphia: Temple University Press, 1987); Nathaniel West, *The Thousand Year Reign of Christ* (Grand Rapids: Kregel Publications, 1993, 1st edn. 1899).

5 Carl F. H. Henry, *The Uneasy Conscience of Modern Fundamentalism* (Grand Rapids, MI: Eerdmans, 1947), 18–19; see Wilbur Smith, *The Atomic Age and the Word of God* (Boston: W. A. Wilde, 1948); Smith, *World Crises and the Prophetic Scriptures* (Chicago: Moody Press, 1951); Smith, *Therefore Stand: A Plea for a Vigorous Apologetic in the Present Crisis of Evangelical Christianity* (Chicago: Moody Press, 1945); Graham quoted in Marsden, *Reforming Fundamentalism*, 72.

6 Henry, *The Uneasy Conscience of Modern Fundamentalism*, 29–30.

7 Ibid., 29–34, 52–7, quote 54.

8 See Harold Lindsell, "The Bible and Race Relations," *Eternity* (August 1956), 43–4; Marsden, *Reforming Fundamentalism*, 252–5; John Oliver, "A Failure of Evangelical Conscience," *Post-American* (May 1975), 26–30; Donald W. Dayton, *Discovering an Evangelical Heritage* (New York: Harper & Row, 1976), 2–3; Michael G. Long, *Billy Graham and the Beloved Community* (New York: Palgrave Macmillan, 2006), 79–142.

9 Carl F. H. Henry, *Confessions of a Theologian: An Autobiography* (Waco, TX: Word Books, 1986), 141–3.

10 Unsigned editorial, "Why *Christianity Today*?" *Christianity Today* 1 (October 15, 1956), 1.

11 See Henry, *Confessions of a Theologian*, 182–4.

12 Carl F. H. Henry, *Aspects of Christian Social Ethics* (Grand Rapids: Eerdmans, 1964; reprint, Grand Rapids: Baker Book House, 1980), quotes 110, 111.

13 Ibid., quotes 112–13; see Carl F. H. Henry, *Frontiers in Modern Theology: A Critique of Current Theological Trends* (Chicago: Moody Press, 1964).

14 S. Parkes Cadman, *Christianity and the State* (New York: Macmillan, 1934), 331; Henry, *Aspects of Christian Social Ethics*, quotes 113, 116, 117.

15 Henry, *Aspects of Christian Social Ethics*, 9–30, quotes 9, 25.

16 Ibid., 31–71, quotes 60, 61, 62.

17 Ibid., 72–104, quote 92.

18 Christianity Today; closing quote, *Aspects of Christian Social Ethics*, 122.

19 Henry, *Aspects of Christian Social Ethics*, 122–3.

20 Henry, *Confessions of a Theologian*, 182–4.

21 Ibid., 276, 281.

22 Carl F. H. Henry, *Evangelicals at the Brink of Crisis* (Waco, TX: Word Books, 1967), 3; Henry, *Evangelicals in Search of Identity* (Waco, TX: Word Books, 1976), 96.

23 See Allen D. Hertzke, *Representing God in Washington* (Knoxville: University of Tennessee Press, 1988); Matthew C. Moen, *The Christian Right and Congress* (Tuscaloosa, AL: University of Alabama Press, 1989); William Martin, *With God on Our Side: The Rise of the Religious Right in America* (New York: Broadway Books, 1996); John C. Green, Mark J. Rozell, and Clyde Wilcox, *The Christian Right in America* (Washington, DC: Georgetown University Press, 2003).

24 Carl F. H. Henry, *God, Revelation, and Authority*, 6 vols. (Waco, TX: Word Books, 1976–83).

25 Carl F. H. Henry, *Christian Countermoves in a Decadent Culture* (Portland, OR: Multnomah Press, 1986), 31–40, quotes 32, 36, 37.

26 Ibid., quotes 117; see Henry, *Evangelicals in Search of Identity*, 55, 67; Harold Lindsell, *The Battle for the Bible* (Grand Rapids: Zondervan, 1976); Lindsell, *The Bible in the Balance* (Grand Rapids: Zondervan, 1979).

27 Henry, *Confessions of a Theologian*, 402; see Carl F. H. Henry, *The Christian Mindset in a Secular Society: Promoting Evangelical Renewal and National Righteousness* (Portland, OR: Multnomah Press, 1984), 9–25.

28 Henry, *Frontiers in Modern Theology*, 154–5.

29 Henry, *Christian Countermoves in a Decadent Culture*, 116–17.

30 Ibid., 118–19.

31 Ibid., 119.

32 Ibid., quotes 123, 126, 138.

33 "The Belgic Confession," *Reformed Confessions of the 16ᵗʰ Century*, ed. Arthur C. Cochrane (Philadelphia: Westminster Press, 1956); "The Formula of Concord," 1580, *The Book of Concord: The Confessions of the Evangelical Lutheran Church*, ed. Theodore G. Tappert (Philadelphia: Fortress Press, 1959), 498–9; "The Second Helvitic Confession," *The Constitution of the Presbyterian Church, U.S.A.: The Book of Confessions* (Louisville: Westminster John Knox Press, 2004), quotes 101, 116.

34 Stanley Hauerwas, "Remembering John Howard Yoder, December 29, 1927–December 30, 1997," *First Things* 82 (April 1998), 15.

35 John Howard Yoder, *Täufertum und Reformation in der Schweiz: I. Die Gespräche zwischen Täufern und Reformatoren 1523–1538*, Schriftenreihe des Mennonitischen Geschichtsvereins, no. 6 (Karlsruhe: Buchdruckerei und Verlag H. Schneider, 1962); see Yoder, *Täufertum und Reformation iim Gesprach: Dogmengeschichtliche Untersuchung der frühen Fesprache zwischen Schweizerischen Tüfern und Reformatoren* (Zurich: EVZ–Verlag, 1968).

36 John Howard Yoder, *Karl Barth and the Problem of War* (Nashville: Abingdon Press, 1970); reprint, with additional essays, *Karl Barth and the Problem of War and Other Essays on Barth*, ed. Mark Thiessen Nation (Eugene, OR: Cascade Books, 2003).

37 Karl Barth, *Church Dogmatics: The Doctrine of Creation*, 3: 4, trans. A. T. Mackay, T. H. L. Parker, Harold Knight, Henry A. Kennedy, John Marks (Edinburgh: T. & T. Clark, 1961), 324–564; Yoder, *Karl Barth and the Problem of War and Other Essays on Barth*, 9–100.

38 See Karl Barth, *This Christian Cause: A Letter to Great Britain from Switzerland* (New York: Macmillan, 1941); Barth, *Church Dogmatics: The Doctrine of Creation*, 3: 451–70; John Howard Yoder, *The Original Revolution: Essays on Christian Pacifism* (Scottdale, PA: Herald Press, 1971), "almost" quote, 83.

39 Yoder, *Karl Barth and the Problem of War and Other Essays on Barth*, 17–34, 61–71, 84–9, quotes 85; Yoder, *The Original Revolution: Essays on Christian Pacifism*, 83–4.

40 Yoder, *The Original Revolution: Essays on Christian Pacifism*, quotes 8; see Yoder, *Nevertheless: The Varieties and Shortcomings of Christian Pacifism* (Scottdale, PA: Herald Press, 1971).

41 Yoder, *The Original Revolution: Essays on Christian Pacifism*, 19–21, quote 19.

42 Ibid., quotes 22–3, 24.

43 Ibid., quotes 25, 26.

44 Ibid., quotes 31, 32, 60; see John Howard Yoder, *The Christian Witness to the State* (Newton, KS: Faith and Life Press, 1964; reprint, Scottdale, PA: Herald Press, 2002), 9–10.

45 John Howard Yoder, *The Politics of Jesus* (Grand Rapids: Eerdmans, 1972; 2nd edn., 1994), quote 3.

46 Ibid., 4–8; see Reinhold Niebuhr, *An Interpretation of Christian Ethics* (New York: Harper and Brothers, 1935); Leo Tolstoy, *The Kingdom of God is Within You* (New York: T. Y. Crowell, 1899); Paul Ramsey, *Basic Christian Ethics* (New York: Scribner, 1950), 166–71; Roger Mehl, "The Basis of Christian Social Ethics," in *Christian Social Ethics in a Changing World*, ed. John C. Bennett (New York: Association Press, 1966), 44–6; H. Richard Niebuhr, *Radical Monotheism and Western Culture* (New York: Harper & Row, 1960).

47 Yoder, *The Politics of Jesus*, 21–53, quotes 51, 53.

48 Ibid., 93–109, quote 96.

49 Ibid., 112–31, quote 128.

50 Ibid., 162–92; see Heinz-Dietrich Wendland, "Zur Sozialethischen Bedeutung der Neutestamentlichen Hausfateln," in *Die Leibhaftigkeit des Wortes: Festgabe Adolf Köberle*, eds. Otto Michel and Ulrich Mann (Hamburg: Furche Verlag, 1958), 34–7; Eduard Schweizer, "Die Weltlichkeit des Neuen Testamentes: die Haustafeln," in *Beiträge zur Alttestamentlichen Theologie: Festschrift für Walther Zimmerli*, eds. Hertert Donner, Robert Hanhart, and Rudolf Smend (Göttingen: Vandenboeck, 1977), 402–5. Yoder relied heavily on the unpublished dissertation of David Schroeder, "Die Haustafeln des Neuen Testaments, Ihre Herkunft und ihr theologischer Sinn," Evangelical Theological Faculty, University of Hamburg, 1959.

51 Yoder, *The Politics of Jesus*, quote 173.

52 Ibid., quotes 167, 174; see Krister Standahl, *The Bible and the Role of Women* (Philadelphia: Fortress Press, 1966).

53 Yoder, *The Politics of Jesus*, 174, 175.

54 Ibid., quote 178.

55 Ibid., 179–87.

56 Vernard Eller, review of *The Politics of Jesus*, by John Howard Yoder, *Brethren Life and Thought* 18 (Spring 1973), 107–8; see Dale W. Brown, review of ibid., *Post American* (January 3, 1974), 3; George R. Edwards, review of ibid., *Mennonite Quarterly Review* 48 (October 1974), 534–8.

57 John R. Donahue, SJ, review of ibid., *Theological Studies* 35 (March 1974), 180; Teresa M. DeFerrari, review of ibid., *Catholic Biblical Quarterly* 36 (January 1974), 150.

58 James William McClendon, Jr, *Systematic Theology: Ethics* (Nashville: Abingdon Press, 1986), i, 73–5; J. Phillip Wogaman, *A Christian Method of Moral Judgment* (Philadelphia: Westminster Press, 1976), 123–9, quote 128–9; Elisabeth Schüssler Fiorenza, *Bread Not Stone: The Challenge of Feminist Biblical Interpretation* (Boston: Beacon Press, 1984), 83; Yoder, *The Politics of Jesus*, 192; see Fiorenza, *In Memory of Her: A Feminist Theological Reconstruction of Christian Origins* (New York: Crossroad, 1983).

59 John Howard Yoder, *The Priestly Kingdom: Social Ethics as Gospel* (Notre Dame, IN: University of Notre Dame Press, 1984), quotes 81, 4–5; see Yoder, *The Royal Priesthood: Essays Ecclesiological and Ecumenical*, ed. Michael G. Cartwright (Grand Rapids: Eerdmans, 1994), 231–41; Yoder, "How H. Richard Niebuhr Reasoned: A Critique of *Christ and Culture*," in Glen H. Stassen, D. M. Yeager and John Howard Yoder, *Authentic Transformation: A New Vision of Christ and Culture* (Nashville: Abingdon Press, 1996), 31–89.

60 Yoder, *The Priestly Kingdom: Social Ethics as Gospel*, 80–5; Yoder, *The Royal Priesthood: Essays Ecclesiological and Ecumenical*, 222–30.

61 Yoder, *The Royal Priesthood: Essays Ecclesiological and Ecumenical*, 242–61, quotes 245–6; Yoder, *The Priestly Kingdom: Social Ethics as Gospel*, 105–22.

62 *The Priestly Kingdom: Social Ethics as Gospel*, quotes 106, 107; Yoder, *The Royal Priesthood: Essays Ecclesiological and Ecumenical*, 260–1.

63 Yoder, *The Priestly Kingdom: Social Ethics as Gospel*, quote 107; Yoder, *The Royal Priesthood: Essays Ecclesiological and Ecumenical*, 243–8.

64 Yoder, *The Royal Priesthood: Essays Ecclesiological and Ecumenical*, 224.

65 Yoder, *The Priestly Kingdom: Social Ethics as Gospel*, 96–101, quotes 96, 100, 101; see Yoder, *The Christian Witness to the State*, 5–8, 66–71, 84–90.

66 Yoder, *The Priestly Kingdom: Social Ethics as Gospel*, quote 115; John Howard Yoder, *When War Is Unjust: Being Honest in Just–War Thinking* (Maryknoll, NY: Orbis Books, 1996; 2nd edn., Eugene, OR: Wipf & Stock, 2001).

67 See Yoder, *When War Is Unjust: Being Honest in Just-War Thinking*, 147–54; James Turner Johnson, *The Just War Tradition and the Restraint of War* (Princeton, NJ: Princeton University Press, 1981); LeRoy Brandt Walters, *Five Classic Just-War Theories: A Study in the Thought of Thomas Aquinas, Vitoria, Suarez, Gentili, and Grotius* (New Haven: Yale University Press, 1974); Michael Walzer, *Just and Unjust Wars* (New York: Basic Books, 1977); Yoder, "How Many Ways Are There to Think about the Morality of War?" *Journal of Law and Religion* 11 (Summer 1995), 83–107; National Conference of Catholic Bishops, *The Challenge of Peace: God's Promise and Our Response* (Washington, DC: United States Catholic Conference, 1983).

68 Yoder, *When War Is Unjust: Being Honest in Just-War Thinking*, 154–5; see John A. Ryan and Francis J. Boland, CSC, *Catholic Principles of Politics* (New York: Macmillan, 1947), 256–62.

69 Yoder, *When War Is Unjust: Being Honest in Just-War Thinking*, 156–60.

70 Ibid., 1–7, 50–64, 78–9; see John Courtney Murray, SJ, "Theology and Modern War," *Theological Studies* 20 (1959), 40–61.

71 Yoder, *When War Is Unjust: Being Honest in Just-War Thinking*, 19–80, quote 5.

72 Ibid., quote 5.

73 John Howard Yoder, *For the Nations: Essays Evangelical and Public* (Grand Rapids: Eerdmans, 1997), 3–7; Richard Mouw, *Politics and the Biblical Drama* (Grand Rapids: Eerdmans, 1976), 90–2. Yoder pointed to Hauerwas' polemical style and dramatic book titles.

74 Yoder, *For the Nations: Essays Evangelical and Public*, 4–8, quote 4; see Yoder, "How H. Richard Niebuhr Reasoned: a Critique of *Christ and Culture*," 31–89.

75 Hauerwas, "Remembering John Howard Yoder, December 29, 1927–December 30, 1997," 15–16.

76 Ibid., 16.

77 Stanley M. Hauerwas, "A Tale of Two Stories: On Being a Christian and a Texan," *Perkins Journal* 34 (Summer 1981), 1–15, reprinted in Hauerwas, *Christian Existence Today: Essays on Church, World and Living In Between* (Durham, NC: Labyrinth Press, 1988), 25–45; see William Cavanaugh, "Stan the Man: A Thoroughly Biased Account of a Completely Unobjective Person," in Stanley Hauerwas, *The Hauerwas Reader*, eds. John Berkman and Michael Cartwright (Durham: NC: Duke University Press, 2001), 17–32.

78 Stanley Hauerwas, *The Peaceable Kingdom: A Primer in Christian Ethics* (Notre Dame: University of Notre Dame Press, 1983), xix; Hauerwas, "A Tale of Two Stories: On Being a Christian and a Texan," 39; Cavanaugh, "Stan the Man: A Thoroughly Biased Account of a Completely Unobjective Person," 19; see B. David Napier, *From Faith to Faith* (New York: Harper & Brothers, 1955); Nels F. S. Ferré, *The Sun and the Umbrella* (New York: Harper & Brothers, 1953).

79 Hauerwas, *The Peaceable Kingdom: A Primer in Christian Ethics*, xxi.

80 Stanley Hauerwas, "Why *The Politics of Jesus* Is Not a Classic," in Hauerwas, *A Better Hope: Resources for a Church Confronting Capitalism, Democracy, and Postmodernity* (Grand Rapids: Brazos Press, 2000), 129–36, "crazy," 133; Hauerwas, *The Peaceable Kingdom: A Primer in Christian Ethics*, xxi–xxii; author's conversation with Stanley Hauerwas, March 5, 2004.

81   See Stanley Hauerwas, *Character and the Christian Life* (San Antonio: Trinity University Press, 1974); Hauerwas, *Vision and Virtue: Essays in Christian Ethical Reflection* (Notre Dame, IN: Fides Publishers, 1974); Hauerwas, with Richard Bondi and David B. Burrell, *Truthfulness and Tragedy: Further Investigations into Christian Ethics* (Notre Dame: University of Notre Dame Press, 1977).

82   See Hauerwas, "Toward an Ethics of Character," and "The Self as Story: A Reconsideration of the Relation of Religion and Morality from the Agent's Perspective," *Vision and Virtue: Essays in Christian Ethical Reflection*, 48–67, 68–92; Hauerwas, "From System to Story: An Alternative Pattern for Rationality in Ethics," and "Story and Theology," *Truthfulness and Tragedy: Further Investigations into Christian Ethics*, 15–39, 71–81.

83   Stanley Hauerwas, "The Nonresistant Church: The Theological Ethics of John Howard Yoder," *Journal of Religious Studies* (India), 1971, reprinted in Hauerwas, *Vision and Virtue: Essays in Christian Ethical Reflection*, 197–221; Hauerwas, "Why *The Politics of Jesus* is Not a Classic," quote 134; author's conversation with Stanley Hauerwas, March 5, 2004; see John Howard Yoder, "Reinhold Niebuhr and Christian Pacifism," (Pamphlet), *Concern* (1968).

84   Hauerwas, "The Nonresistant Church: The Theological Ethics of John Howard Yoder," quotes 198, 205.

85   Ibid., 217–21.

86   Ibid., 212–13.

87   Stanley Hauerwas, "Introduction," "A Story-Formed Community: Reflections on *Watership Down*," and "The Church in a Divided World: The Interpretive Power of the Christian Story," in Hauerwas, *A Community of Character: Toward a Constructive Christian Social Ethic* (Notre Dame, IN: University of Notre Dame Press, 1981), 1–6, 9–35, 89–110, quotes 1, 109.

88   Hauerwas, "Introduction," and "The Virtues and Our Communities: Human Nature as History," *A Community of Character: Toward a Constructive Christian Social Ethic*, 5–6, 11–128, quote 6; see Stanley Hauerwas, "The Ministry of a Congregation: Rethinking Christian Ethics for a Church–Centered Seminary," in Hauerwas, *Christian Existence Today: Essays on Church, World, and Living In Between*, 111–31; Cavanaugh, "Stan the Man: A Thoroughly Biased Account of a Completely Unobjective Person," 22; *Why Narrative? Readings in Narrative Theology*, eds. Stanley Hauerwas and L. Gregory Jones (Grand Rapids: Eerdmans, 1989); Hauerwas, "The Church as God's New Language," in *Scriptural Authority and Narrative Interpretation*, ed. Garrett Green (Philadelphia: Fortress Press, 1987), 179–98.

89   Stanley Hauerwas, *The Peaceable Kingdom: A Primer in Christian Ethics* (Notre Dame, IN: University of Notre Dame Press, 1983), xxvi; Stanley Hauerwas to author, May 8, 1996; author's conversation with Stanley Hauerwas, October 12, 1998; see Hauerwas, "The Importance of Being Catholic: Unsolicited Advice from a Protestant Bystander," *First Things* 1 (March 1990), 21–30, reprinted in Hauerwas, *In Good Company: The Church as Polis* (Notre Dame, IN: University of Notre Dame Press, 1995), 91–108.

90   Stanley Hauerwas, "On Keeping Theological Ethics Theological," *Revisions: Changing Perspectives in Moral Philosophy*, eds. Stanley Hauerwas and Alasdair MacIntyre (Notre Dame, IN: University of Notre Dame Press, 1983, 16–42, quotes 24, reprinted in Hauerwas, *Against the Nations: War and Survival in a Liberal Society* (Notre Dame, IN: University of Notre Dame Press, 1992), 23–50.

91   Ibid., 31–2; Stanley Hauerwas, "A Christian Critique of Christian America," *Community in America: The Challenge of Habits of the Heart*, eds. Charles H. Reynolds and Ralph V. Norman (Berkeley, CA: University of California Press, 1988), 250–65, reprinted in Hauerwas, *Christian Existence Today: Essays on Church, World and Living In Between*, 171–90; see H. Richard Niebuhr, *Radical Monotheism and Western Culture* (New York: Harper & Brothers, 1943); James Gustafson, *Ethics from a Theocentric Perspective*, 2 vols. (Chicago: University of Chicago Press, 1981, 1984). This section of the Hauerwas discussion adapts material from Gary Dorrien, *Soul in Society: The Making and Renewal of Social Christianity* (Minneapolis, MN: Fortress Press, 1995), 351–8.

92   Hauerwas, "A Christian Critique of Christian America," 260.

93   Hauerwas, "On Keeping Theological Ethics Theological," 30, 31–2.

94   Ibid., 34; see Stanley Hauerwas, "On Doctrine and Ethics," *Cambridge Companion to Christian Doctrine*, ed. Colin Gunton (Cambridge: Cambridge University Press, 1997), 21–40, reprinted as "How 'Christian Ethics' Came to Be," in Hauerwas, *The Hauerwas Reader*, 37–50.

95   Hauerwas, "On Keeping Theological Ethics Theological," 35.

96   Stanley Hauerwas and William H. Willimon, *Resident Aliens: Life in the Christian Colony* (Nashville: Abingdon Press, 1989), 24.

97   Stanley Hauerwas, *After Christendom? How the Church is to Behave if Freedom, Justice, and a Christian Nation are Bad Ideas* (Nashville: Abingdon Press, 1991), 18.

98   Hauerwas, "A Christian Critique of Christian America," 263.

99   Hauerwas, *After Christendom*, 18–19.

100   Stanley Hauerwas, "When the Politics of Jesus Makes a Difference," *Christian Century*, 110 (October 13, 1993), quote 983; Hauerwas, "Why *The Politics of Jesus* Is Not a Classic," 131.

101   Hauerwas quoted in Paul T. Stallsworth, "The Story of an Encounter," *Reinhold Niebuhr Today*, ed. Richard John Neuhaus (Grand Rapids: Eerdmans Company, 1989), 104, 114.

102   Ibid., 114; Hauerwas, *The Peaceable Kingdom*, "hallmark," xvi; Stanley Hauerwas, *With the Grain of the Universe: The Church's Witness and Natural Theology* (Grand Rapids, MI: Brazos Press, 2001), 87–111.

103   Quoted by Stallsworth, "The Story of an Encounter," 103.

104   Hauerwas, *With the Grain of the Universe: The Church's Witness and Natural Theology*, 113–40, quote 138; see Stanley Hauerwas, "Walter Rauschenbusch and the Saving of America," in Hauerwas, *A Better Hope: Resources for a Church Confronting Capitalism, Democracy, and Postmodernity* (Grand Rapids, MI: Brazos Press, 2000), 71–107.

105   Stanley Hauerwas, "Christian Ethics in America (and the *Journal of Religious Ethics*): A Report on a Book I Will Not Write," in Hauerwas, *A Better Hope: Resources for a Church Confronting Capitalism, Democracy, and Postmodernity* (Grand Rapids, MI: Brazos Press, 2000), 55–69, quote 56.

106   Stanley Hauerwas, *Dispatches from the Front: Theological Engagements with the Secular* (Durham, NC: Duke University Press, 1994), quotes 5, 8, 14, 23, 158, 196, 190. The discussion of this book adapts material from Gary Dorrien, review of *Dispatches from the Front*, by Stanley Hauerwas, *Journal of Religion* (October 1995).

107   Hauerwas, *Dispatches from the Front: Theological Engagements with the Secular*, 24–5.

108   James M. Gustafson, "The Sectarian Temptation: Reflections on Theology, the Church, and the University," *Proceedings of the Catholic Theological Society* 40 (1985), 83–94, quotes 84.

109   Stanley M. Hauerwas, "Time and History in Theological Ethics: The Work of James Gustafson," *Journal of Religious Ethics* 13 (Spring 1985), 3–21, quote 19; James M. Gustafson, "A Response to Critics," *Journal of Religious Ethics* 13 (Fall 1985), 185–209, quotes 191.

110   Gustafson, "A Response to Critics," 191, 195.

111   Hauerwas, "Introduction," *Christian Existence Today*, 1–19, "to maintain," "in the name," 15; edited version reprinted as "Why the 'Sectarian Temptation' is a Misrepresentation: A Response to James Gustafson," in Hauerwas, *The Hauerwas Reader*, 90–110; Hauerwas, *After Christendom? How the Church is to Behave if Freedom, Justice, and a Christian Nation are Bad Ideas*, "bad idea," 45–68; Stallworth, "The Story of an Encounter," "because when people," 113–14; see Stanley Hauerwas, "Should Christians Talk So Much About Justice?" *Books and Religion* 14 (May/June 1986); Hauerwas, "On the Right to be Tribal," *Christian Scholars Review* 16 (March 1987), 238–41.

112   Hauerwas, "Christian Ethics in America (And the *Journal of Religious Ethics*): A Report on a Book I Will Not Write," 64–5; author's conversation with Hauerwas, October 12, 1998.

113   Hauerwas, "Christian Ethics in America (And the *Journal of Religious Ethics*): A Report on a Book I Will Not Write," quote 64.

114 Ibid., 64–9, quote 68; Hauerwas to author, October 23, 1997; author's conversation with Hauerwas, November 20, 1997; see Harlan Beckley, *Passion for Justice: Retrieving the Legacies of Walter Rauschenbusch, John A. Ryan, and Reinhold Niebuhr* (Louisville: Westminster John Knox, 1992); Gary Dorrien, *Soul in Society: The Making and Renewal of Social Christianity* (Minneapolis: Fortress Press, 1995). At the 1980 American Academy of Religion Meeting in New York, Hauerwas gave a paper making the graduate school argument; this paper was folded subsequently into his article, "Christian Ethics in America (And the *Journal of Religious Ethics*): A Report on a Book I Will Not Write," quote 59.

115 See Stanley Hauerwas, *Suffering Presence: Theological Reflections on Medicine, the Church, and the Mentally Handicapped* (Notre Dame: University of Notre Dame Press, 1986); Hauerwas, *God, Medicine, and Suffering* (Grand Rapids: Eerdmans, 1994); Hauerwas, "How Christian Ethics Became Medical Ethics: The Case of Paul Ramsey," in Hauerwas, *Wilderness Wanderings: Probing Twentieth Century Theology and Philosophy* (Boulder, CO: WestView Press, 1997), 124–40; Hauerwas, "Suffering the Retarded: Should We Prevent Retardation?" *The Deprived, the Disabled, and the Fullness of Life*, ed. Flavian Dougherty (Collegeville, MN: Michael Glazier, 1984), reprinted under the title, "Should Suffering Be Eliminated: What the Retarded Have to Teach," *The Hauerwas Reader*, 556–76.

116 Cavanaugh, "Stan the Man: A Thoroughly Biased Account of a Completely Unobjective Person," 27, 29; Stanley Hauerwas, "Onward Christian Soldiers," *Charlotte Observer* (May 31, 1993), reprinted as "Why Gays (As a Group) are Morally Superior to Christians (as a Group)," *The Hauerwas Reader*, 519–21; Mark Oppenheimer, "For God, Not Country: The un-American Theology of Stanley Hauerwas," *Lingua Franca* (September 2001); author's conversation with Gloria Albrecht, May 30, 2007; see Gloria Albrecht, *The Character of Our Communities: Toward an Ethic of Liberation for the Church* (Nashville: Abingdon Press, 1995), 29–61.

117 Hauerwas, *With the Grain of the Universe: The Church's Witness and Natural Theology*, 216–17.

118 Jean Bethke Elshtain, "America's Best: Christian Contrarian," *Time* (2001), *Time.com*, www.cnn.com/SPECIALS/2001,americasbest/TIME/society, accessed February 9, 2007; Oppenheimer, "For God, Not Country: The un-American Theology of Stanley Hauerwas," *Lingua Franca*; "Faith Fires Back: A Conversation with Stanley Hauerwas," *Duke Magaazine* 88 (January–February 2002), www.dukemagazine.duke.edu/dukemag/issues, accessed January 25, 2007.

119 Dorrien, *Soul in Society: The Making and Renewal of Social Christianity*, 355–61, quote 359.

120 Albrecht, *The Character of Our Communities: Toward an Ethic of Liberation for the Church*, 103–37, quotes 100, 101.

121 Jeffrey Stout, *Democracy and Tradition* (Princeton: Princeton University Press, 2004), 140–79.

122 "Homiletics Interview: Stanley Hauerwas," *Homiletics Online* (2004), http://www.homileticsonline.com/subscriber/interviews, accessed January 25, 2007; see Stanley Hauerwas, *Performing the Faith: Bonhoeffer and the Practice of Nonviolence* (Grand Rapids: Brazos Press, 2004), 215–41.

123 Stanley Hauerwas, "Democratic Time: Lessons Learned from Yoder and Wolin," *Cross Currents* 55 (Winter 2006), 534–52.

124 Ibid., 538–42; Yoder, *The Christian Witness to the State*, 12, 42, 78; John Howard Yoder, "The Christian Case for Democracy," in *The Priestly Kingdom: Social Ethics as Gospel*, 151–71.

125 Hauerws, "Democratic Time: Lessons Learned from Yoder and Wolin," 543–7, quote 547; Sheldon Wolin, *Politics and Vision* (lst edn., 1960; 2nd edn., Princeton: Princeton University Press, 2004), 38–69; Wolin, *The Presence of the Past: Essays on the State and the Constitution* (Baltimore: Johns Hopkins University Press, 1989), 142–9.

126 Hauerwas, *After Christendom? How the Church is to Behave if Freedom, Justice, and a Christian Nation are Bad Ideas*, quote 55.

127 This section on Michael Novak and neconservatism adapts material from Gary Dorrien, *The Neoconservative Mind: Politics, Culture, and the War of Ideology* (Philadelphia: Temple University Press, 1993), 1–18, 207–64; and Dorrien, *Imperial Designs: Neoconservatism and the New Pax Americana* (New York: Routledge, 2004), 7–25.

128 Michael Novak, "Errand into the Wilderness," in *Political Passages: Journeys of Change Through Two Decades, 1968–1988*, ed. John H. Bunzel (New York: The Free Press, 1988), quote 248.

129 Author's interview with Michael Novak, March 20, 1990, quote; see Novak, "Engagement But No Security," *Commonweal* 108 (January 30, 1981), 45; Novak, "The Game's Not Over," *Forbes*, 146 (August 20, 1990), 56; Novak, *Confession of a Catholic* (San Francisco: Harper & Row, 1983), 12.

130 Author's interview with Novak, March 20, 1990, quote; see Michael Novak, "Orthodoxy vs. Progressive Bourgeois Christianity," in *Once a Catholic: Prominent Catholics and Ex-Catholics Discuss the Influence of the Church in Their Lives and Work*, ed. Peter Occhiogrosso (Boston: Houghton Mifflin Co., 1987), 121–4.

131 James Finn, "The Evolving Thought of Michael Novak," *National Review*, 38 (December 31, 1985), 109.

132 Michael Novak, *The Tiber Was Silver: A Novel of Spiritual Adventure in Modern Rome* (New York: Doubleday, 1961).

133 Michael Novak, *The Open Church: Vatican II, Act II* (New York: Macmillan, 1964); Novak, "Catholic Education and the Idea of Dissent," *Commonweal*, 76 (April 27, 1962).

134 Michael Novak, *A Time to Build* (New York: Macmillan, 1967), 405–12, quote 421; Novak, "Stumbling Into War and Stumbling Out," in Robert McAfee Brown, Abraham J. Heschel, and Michael Novak, *Vietnam: Crisis of Conscience* (New York: Association Press, 1967), 38, 47.

135 Michael Novak, *A Theology for Radical Politics* (New York: Herder & Herder, 1969), 25, 79.

136 Ibid., 28, 60, 74, 81.

137 Novak, "Errand into the Wilderness," 251.

138 Novak, "Engagement But No Security," 44.

139 Michael Novak, *Naked I Leave* (New York: Macmillan, 1970); Novak, *The Experience of Nothingness* (New York: Harper & Row, 1971); 51; Novak, *Ascent of the Mountain, Flight of the Dove: An Invitation to Religious Studies* (New York: Harper & Row, 1971).

140 Michael Novak, *The Rise of the Unmeltable Ethnics: Politics and Culture in the Seventies* (New York: Macmillan, 1971), 126, 249.

141 Ibid., 115, 285.

142 Novak, "Errand into the Wilderness," 257.

143 Novak, *The Rise of the Unmeltable Ethnics*, 248, 254.

144 Garry Wills, review of *The Rise of the Unmeltable Ethnics*, by Michael Novak, *New York Times Book Review* (April 23, 1972), 27–8.

145 Novak, "Errand into the Wilderness," 258.

146 Michael Novak, *Choosing Our King: Powerful Symbols in Presidential Politics* (New York: Macmillan, 1974), 291; see Novak, "Against 'Affirmative Action,'" *Commonweal*, 100 (April 5, 1974), 102, 118; Novak, "Errand into the Wilderness," 260.

147 Michael Novak, "Needing Niebuhr Again," *Commentary* 54 (September1972), 52.

148 David T. Bazelon, *Power in America: The Politics of the New Class* (New York: New American Library, 1967); Michael Harrington, *Toward a Democratic Left: A Radical Program for a New Majority* (New York: Macmillan, 1968), 282–91, quote 289.

149 Novak, "Needing Niebuhr Again," 60–1.

150 Author's interview with Novak, March 20, 1990.

151 Michael Novak, *The Spirit of Democratic Capitalism* (New York: American Enterprise Institute/Simon & Schuster, 1982), 24.

152 Michael Novak, "A Closet Capitalist Confesses," *Wall Street Journal* (April 20, 1976); Novak, *The Joy of Sports* (New York: Basic Books, 1976); see Novak, *The Guns of Lattimer* (New York: Basic Books, 1978); Novak, *In Praise of Cynicism (or) When the Saints Go Marching Out* (Bloomington: Poynter Center, 1975); Novak, "Orthodoxy vs. Progressive Bourgeois Christianity," 130; Novak, "Capitalism, Socialism, and Democracy: A Symposium," *Commentary* 65 (April 1978), 63–4.

153 Novak, "Errand into the Wilderness," 260.

154 Ibid., 254.

155 Michael Novak, "A Switch to Reagan: For a Strong America," *Commonweal* 107 (October 24, 1980), 588–91.

156 Michael Novak, *The American Vision: An Essay on the Future of Democratic Capitalism* (Washington, DC: American Enterprise Institute, 1978), 1, 24.

157 Novak, "A Switch to Reagan," 589–91; Novak, "Errand into the Wilderness," 260.

158 Daniel Bell, *The Cultural Contradictions of Capitalism* (New York: Basic Books, 1978), 10.

159 Novak, *The Spirit of Democratic Capitalism*, 14–16, 49–67; Michael Novak, "Seven Theological Facets," in *Capitalism and Socialism: A Theological Inquiry*, ed. Michael Novak (Washington: DC: American Enterprise Institute, 1979), 112–13.

160 Novak, *The Spirit of Democratic Capitalism*, 14–15.

161 Bell, *The Cultural Contradictions of Capitalism*, xii.

162 Michael Novak, "Class, Culture & Society," review of *The Winding Passage: Essays and Sociological Journeys, 1960–1980*, by Daniel Bell, *Commentary* 72 (July 1981), 72.

163 Friedrich A. Hayek, "Why I Am Not a Conservative," postscript to *The Constitution of Liberty* (Chicago: University of Chicago Press, 1960), 400–ll.

164 Novak, *Confession of a Catholic*, 115–18; Novak, "Errand into the Wilderness," 254–5, 269–72; Michael Novak, *Freedom with Justice: Catholic Social Thought and Liberal Institutions* (San Francisco: Harper & Row, 1984), 16–17; Novak, "Free Persons and the Common Good," in *The Common Good and U.S. Capitalism*, eds. Oliver F. Williams and John W. Houck (Lanham, MD: University Press of America, 1987), 238–40; Novak, *Will It Liberate? Questions About Liberation Theology* (New York: Paulist Press, 1986), 35; Novak, "The Return of the Catholic Whig," *First Things* 1 (March 1990), 38; Novak, *This Hemisphere of Liberty: A Philosophy of the Americas* (Washington, DC: AEI Press, 1990), 9; Peter Steinfels, "Michael Novak and his ultrasuper democraticapitalism," *Commonweal* 110 (January 14, 1983), 13.

165 Novak, *This Hemisphere of Liberty*, 11.

166 Louis Hartz, *The Liberal Tradition in America: An Interpretation of American Political Thought Since the Revolution* (New York: Harcourt Brace Jovanovich, 1955), 93.

167 Novak, *This Hemisphere of Liberty*, 8; Novak, "Free Persons and the Common Good," quote 240.

168 Novak, *The Spirit of Democratic Capitalism*, 89; Novak, *Confession of a Catholic*, quote 117.

169 Hartz, *The Liberal Tradition in America*, 110; Arthur M. Schlesinger, Jr, *The Age of Jackson* (Boston: Little, Brown and Company, 1945), Colton quote 271; see Michael Novak, "Not Only the Rich Are Capitalists Now," *Forbes*, 144 (September 4, 1989); Novak, "Capitalist Liberation," *Forbes* 144 (September 18, 1989).

170 Hartz, *The Liberal Tradition in America*, 111–12.

171 Ibid., 205–8, quote 208.

172 Michael Novak, "The Old Virtues," review of *The Way of the WASP: How It Made America, and How It Can Save It, So To Speak*, by Richard Brookhiser, *Commentary* 91 (March 1991), 54.

173 Michael Novak, *Toward a Theology of the Corporation* (Washington, DC: American Enterprise Institute, 1981), 41–3; Novak, *The Spirit of Democratic Capitalism*, 359.

174 Irving Kristol, *Two Cheers for Capitalism* (New York: Basic Books, 1978); Michael Novak, "Business Should Speak Up," *Forbes*, 143 (May 1, 1989); Novak, *This Hemisphere of Liberty*, 10; Author's interview with Novak, March 20, 1990; Novak, "Boredom, Virtue, and Democratic Capitalism," *Commentary*, 88, (September 1989), 35.

175 Novak, "Boredom, Virtue, and Democratic Capitalism," 35; Novak, "Mediating Institutions: The Communitarian Individual in America," *The Public Interest* 68 (Summer 1982); Novak, "Habits of the Left-Wing Heart," *National Review* 37 (June 28, 1985), 36; C. B. MacPherson, *The Political Theory of Possessive Individualism* (Oxford: Oxford University Press, 1962).

176 Novak, "Boredom, Virtue, and Democratic Capitalism," 35.

177 Michael Novak, "Defining the U.S. System," *The Washington Times*, April 28, 1989; Novak, *This Hemisphere of Liberty*, 28.

178 Novak, "Boredom, Virtue, and Democratic Capitalism," 36; Michael Novak, "'Built Wiser Than They Knew': The Constitution and the Wealth of Nations," *Crisis* 5 (May 1987); Novak, "The Mind-Centered System," *Forbes* 143 (February 6, 1989).

179 Novak, *This Hemisphere of Liberty*, 44.

180 Novak, "Boredom, Virtue, and Democratic Capitalism," quote 36; Michael Novak, "The Virtue of Enterprise: The Discovery of a 'Right to Economic Initiative' Could Revolutionize Catholic Social Thought," *Crisis*, 7 (May 1989).

181 Novak, "Boredom, Virtue, and Democratic Capitalism," 36.

182 Steinfels, "Michael Novak and his ultrasuper democraticcapitalism," 14–15; John C. Cort, "The Social Thought of Michael Novak: At Odds With the Principles of Catholic Social Thought," *New Oxford Review* (November 1988), 8–9; Russell Kirk, "The Neoconservatives: An Endangered Species," *The Heritage Lectures* No. 178 (Washington, DC: The Heritage Foundation, 1988), 6–7; Michael Novak, "Defining the U.S. System," *The Washington Times* (April 28, 1989); Novak, letter to *New Oxford Review*, July/August 1988.

183 Novak, letter to *New Oxford Review*; Michael Novak, "A Phrase With a Winning Ring," *Forbes* 144 (August 7, 1989); Novak, *This Hemisphere of Liberty*, 106.

184 Michael Novak, "The Case Against Liberation Theology," *New York Times Sunday Magazine* (October 21, 1984), 51; Novak, *Will It Liberate?* 13–32; Novak, "Liberation Theology on the Move," *National Review*, Vol. 37 (September 20, 1985); Robert McAfee Brown, review of *Will It Liberate? Questions About Liberation Theology*, by Michael Novak, *Christianity & Crisis* 47 (April 6, 1987), 124.

185 Novak, *The Spirit of Democratic Capitalism*, 299–307.

186 See Raul Prebisch, *The Economic Development of Latin America and its Principal Problems* (New York: The United Nations, 1950); Andre Gunder Frank, *Capitalism and Underdevelopment: Historical Studies of Chile and Brazil* (New York: Monthly Review Press, 1967); Andre Gunder Frank, *Dependent Accumulation and Underdevelopment* (New York: Monthly Review Press, 1979); Fernando Henrique Cardoso and Enzo Falleto, *Dependency and Development in Latin America* (Berkeley: University of California Press, 1979); Gabriel Palma, "Dependency: A Formal Theory of Underdevelopment or a Methodology for the Analysis of Concrete Situations of Underdevelopment?" *World Development* (July–August 1978), 881–924.

187 Cited in Novak, *The Spirit of Democratic Capitalism*, 279.

188 Ibid., 279.

189 Novak, *Will It Liberate?* 129; Michael Novak, "Why Latin America Is Poor," *Forbes*, 143 (Nov. 8, 1989; Novak, "Liberation Theology in Practice," *Thought* 59 (June 1984).

190 See Walden Bello and Stephanie Rosenfeld, "Dragons In Distress: The Crisis of the NICS," *World Policy Journal* 7 (Summer 1990), 431–68; Andre Gunder Frank, "Can the Debt Bomb Be Defused?," *World Policy Journal*, 1 (Summer 1984), 723–43; Hugo Assmann, "Democracy and the Debt Crisis," *This World* 14 (Spring/Summer 1986), 83–98; Robert E. Wood, "Making Sense of the Debt Crisis," *Socialist Review* 81 (1985), 7–33; James S. Henry, "Where the Money Went: Third World Debt Hoax," *The New Republic* (April

14, 1986), 20–3; Fernando Fajnzylber, *Estrategia Industrial y Empresas Internacionales: Posicion relativa de America y Brasil* (Rio de Janeiro: United Nations, CEPAL, November 1970); Richard J. Barnet and Ronald E. Muller, *Global Reach: The Power of the Multinational Corporations* (New York: Simon & Schuster, 1974); Peter Evans, *Dependent Development: The Alliance of Multinational, State and Local Capital in Brazil* (Princeton: Princeton University Press, 1979).

191 Novak, *The Spirit of Democratic Capitalism*, 14; Michael Novak, "Public Theology and the Left: What Happens After Reagan?" *The Christian Century* 105, (May 4, 1988), quote 454; Novak, "Why Latin America is Poor."

192 Novak, *This Hemisphere of Liberty*, 55–6; see Novak, *Will It Liberate?* 5.

193 See Paul Sigmund, *Liberation Theology at the Crossroads: Democracy or Revolution?* (New York: Oxford University Press, 1990); Arthur F. McGovern, *Liberation Theology and Its Critics: Toward an Assessment* (Maryknoll: Orbis Books, 1989); Jose Miranda, *Marx and the Bible: A Critique of the Philosophy of Oppression*, trans. John Eagleson, Maryknoll (Maryknoll, NY Orbis Books, 1974); Miranda, *Communism in the Bible*, trans. Robert R. Barr (Maryknoll, NY: Orbis Books, 1982); John R. Pottenger, *The Political Theory of Liberation Theology: Toward a Reconvergence of Social Values and Social Science* (Albany, NY: State University of New York Press, 1989); Michael Novak, "Are You Sleeping Well, Fidel?," *Forbes*, Vol. 145 (February 5, 1990); Novak, "Liberation From Liberation Theology," *Forbes* 143 (May 15, 1989); Novak, *Will It Liberate?* 13–32; Novak, "Liberation Theology – What's Left," *First Things* (June/July 1991); 10–12; George V. Pixley, *God's Kingdom: A Guide for Biblical Study* (Maryknoll, NY: Orbis Books, 1981); Jon Sobrino, *Christology at the Crossroads: A Latin American Approach*, trans. John Drury (Maryknoll, NY: Orbis Books, 1978); Sobrino and Juan Hernandez Pico, *Theology of Christian Solidarity*, trans. Phillip Berryman (Maryknoll, NY: Orbis Books, 1985); Gustavo Gutierrez, *We Drink from Our Own Wells: The Spiritual Journey of a People*, trans. Matthew J. O'Connell (Maryknoll, NY: Orbis Books, 1984); Leonardo Boff, *Ecclesiogenesis: The Base Communities Reinvent the Church*, trans. Robert R. Barr (Maryknoll, NY: Orbis Books, 1986); Alvaro Barreiro, *Basic Ecclesial Communities: The Evangelization of the Poor*, trans. Barbara Campbell, (Maryknoll, NY: Orbis Books, 1982); Guillermo Cook, *The Expectation of the Poor: Latin American Basic Ecclesial Communities in Protestant Perspective* (Maryknoll, NY: Orbis Books, 1985).

194 Michael Novak, "Making Deterrence Work," *Catholicism in Crisis* (November 1982); Novak, "Moral Clarity in the Nuclear Age," *Catholicism in Crisis*, 1 (March 1983); reprinted in *National Review* 35 (April 1, 1983); J. M. Cameron, *Nuclear Catholics and Other Essays* (Grand Rapids, Eerdmans, 1989), 60–74; Novak, *Moral Clarity in the Nuclear Age* (Nashville: Thomas Nelson, 1983).

195 National Conference of Catholic Bishops, *The Challenge of Peace: God's Promise and Our Response* (Washington, DC: United States Catholic Conference, 1983).

196 Michael Novak, "Born-Again Bishops," *National Review* (August 6, 1982), 960; author's interview with Novak, March 20, 1990; Novak, "Why the Church Is Not Pacifist," *Catholicism in Crisis* 2 (June 1984); Novak, *Moral Clarity in the Nuclear Age*, quote 121.

197 Michael Novak, "On Democratic Capitalism," *National Review* 34 (October 29, 1982), 1351; see Novak, "Price–Bishop Economics," *National Review* 35 (March 4, 1983), 260; Novak, "Theology & Economics," *National Review* 36 (February 10, 1984), 40.

198 Novak, "The Twilight of Socialism," 2.

199 Lay Commission on Catholic Social Teaching and the U.S. Economy, *Toward the Future* (New York: Lay Commission, 1984), 58.

200 National Conference of Catholic Bishops, *Economic Justice for All: Catholic Social Teaching and the U.S. Economy* (Washington, DC: United States Catholic Conference, 1986), reprinted in *Origins* (Washington, D.C.: National Catholic News Service, November 27, 1986), 85–94.

201 Michael Novak, "Toward Consensus: Suggestions for Revising the First Draft," *Catholicism In Crisis* 3 (March 1985), 9–10.

202 Ibid., 5; author's interview with Novak, March 20, 1990, "after I explained."

203 Michael Novak, "Economic Rights: The Servile State," *Catholicism in Crisis*, 3 (October 1985), 8.

204 David Hollenbach, *Claims In Conflict: Retrieving and Renewing the Catholic Human Rights Tradition* (New York: Paulist Press, 1979); Novak, "Economic Rights: The Servile State," 10; Novak, "Socialists Circle Bishops," *National Review*, 37 (April 5, 1985), 46; Novak, "Polarizing Catholics?" *National Review* 37 (November 15, 1985), 46; Novak, "Blaming America: A Comment on Paragraphs 202–4 of the First Draft," *Catholicism in Crisis* 3 (July 1985), 12–16.

205 Novak, "Economic Rights: The Servile State," 8, quotes 10.

206 Michael Novak, "The Christian Vision of Economic Life," *Catholicism in Crisis* 3 (December 1985), 27, 29.

207 Ibid., 29.

208 Ibid., 29; author's interview with Novak, March 20, 1990.

209 Novak, "Economic Rights: The Servile State," 13.

210 David Hollenbach, "The Growing End of an Argument," *America* (November 30, 1985), 365; see Michael Novak, *Free Persons and the Common Good* (Lanham, MD: Madison Books, 1989), 155.

211 Novak, "The Virtue of Enterprise," 21.

212 Novak, *This Hemisphere of Liberty*, 38; Novak, "A papal 'yes' to capitalism," *Forbes* 147 (May 27, 1991); Novak, *Free Persons and the Common Good*, 86; Milton Friedman, *Capitalism and Freedom* (Chicago: University of Chicago Press, 1962); John Hospers, *Libertarianism* (Los Angeles: Nash, 1971).

213 Friedrich A. Hayek, *Law, Legislation and Liberty, Volume 2: The Mirage of Social Justice* (Chicago: University of Chicago Press, 1976).

214 Novak, "The Return of the Catholic Whig," 42; Novak, *Free Persons and the Common Good*, 80; Michael Novak, "The Rights and Wrongs of 'Economic Rights': A Debate Continued," *This World* 17 (Spring 1987), 47; Novak, "St. Thomas For the Twenth–First Century," *Catholicism in Crisis* 2 (March 1984); Novak, "Dissent in the Church," *Catholicism in Crisis* 4 (January 1986); Novak, "Not Yet: Biblical Realism and Power Politics," *Catholicism in Crisis* 2 (July 1984); see David Schindler, "The One, True American Religion," *Thirty Days* (June 1989).

215 Charles Krauthammer, "Universal Dominion: Toward a Unipolar World," *National Interest* 18 (Winter 1989), 48–9; Ben J. Wattenberg, *The First Universal Nation: Leading Indicators and Ideas about the Surge of America in the 1990s* (New York: Free Press, 1991), 54; see Krauthammer, "The Unipolar Moment," *Foreign Affairs* 70 (1991), 23; Wattenberg, "Neo-Manifest Destinarianism," *National Interest* 21 (Fall 1990), 54.

216 Michael Novak, "The Game's Not Over," *Forbes* 146 (August 20, 1990), 56.

217 Ibid., 56; see Michael Novak, *On Two Wings: Humble Faith and Common Sense at the American Founding* (San Francisco: Enounter Books, 2002).

218 Peter Applebome, "At Home, War Healed Several Wounds," *New York Times* (March 4, 1991), Novak quote; Michael Novak, "Pax Americana," *Forbes* 147 (April 29, 1991), 121.

219 Michael Novak, "Neocons: Some Memories," *National Review Online* (May 20, 2003), www.nationalreview.com/script/printpage, accessed January 30, 2007.

220 Michael Novak, *The Universal Hunger for Liberty: Why the Clash of Civilizations is Not Inevitable* (New York: Basic Books, 2004), "important sources" and "horizon-expanding," 226, 227; Novak, "Neocons: Some Memories," neocon creed.

221 Michael Novak, "Changing the Paradigms: The Cultural Deficiencies of Capitalism," in *Democracy and Mediating Structures: A Theological Inquiry*, ed. Michael Novak (Washington, DC: American Enterprise Institute, 1980), 199; Novak, "The Revolt Against Our Public Culture," *National Review* 36 (May 4, 1984), 48.

222 Author's interview with Michael Novak, March 20, 1990; Michael Novak, "The Left Still Owns American Culture," *Forbes* 145 (March 5, 1990), 118.

223 Michael Novak, "Woman Church Is Not Mother Church," *Catholicism in Crisis* 2 (February 1984), 20–1; see Novak, *Confession of a Catholic*, 13, 193–8.

224 Novak, "Woman Church Is Not Mother Church," 21; see Elaine Pagels, *The Gnostic Gospels* (New York: Vintage Books, 1979).

225 Novak, "Orthodoxy vs. Progressive Bourgeois Christianity," 127.

226 See Michael Novak, "New Questions for Humanists," in *The Denigration of Capitalism: Six Points of View*, ed. Michael Novak (Washington, DC: American Enterprise Institute, 1979), 57; Novak, "Changing the Paradigms: The Cultural Deficiencies of Capitalism," 193; Novak, *Confession of a Catholic*, 178–81.

227 Novak, *Confession of a Catholic*, 180; Novak, *Free Persons and the Common Good*, 158, 161.

228 This section reflects my experience with the Sojourners community. I wrote extensively for *Sojourners* in the 1980s, had friends in the Sojourners community, and heard Wallis speak many times.

229 See Jim Wallis, *Revive Us Again: A Sojourner's Story* (Nashville: Abingdon Press, 1983), 72–7.

230 Ibid., 77–108.

231 See Jim Wallis, ed., *Waging Peace: A Handbook for the Struggle to Abolish Nuclear Weapons* (San Francisco: Harper & Row, 1982); Wallis, ed., *Peacemakers: Christian Voices from the New Abolitionist Movement* (San Francisco: Harper & Row, 1983); Wallis and Joyce Hollyday, eds., *Crucible of Fire: The Church Confronts Apartheid* (Maryknoll, NY: Orbis Books, 1989); Wallis and Hollyday, eds., *Cloud of Witnesses* (Maryknoll, NY: Orbis Books, 1991); Wallis, *Faith Works: Lessons from the Life of an Activist Preacher* (New York: Random House, 2000).

232 Jim Wallis, *The Call to Conversion* (New York: Harper & Row, 1981, 2nd edn. 1992; Wallis, *Agenda for Biblical People* (New York: Harper & Row, 1976, 2nd edn. 1984).

233 Jim Wallis, *The Soul of Politics: A Practical and Prophetic Vision for Change* (New York: New Press; Maryknoll, NY: Orbis Books, 1994).

234 Ibid., quote 36.

235 Ibid., 36–7.

236 Ibid., 39.

237 Ibid., quotes 278, 44, 46.

238 Jim Wallis, *Who Speaks for God? An Alternative to the Religious Right – A New Politics of Compassion, Community, and Civility* (New York: Delacorte, 1996), quote 31; Wallis, *Faith Works: Lessons from the Life of an Activist Preacher* (New York: Random House, 2000).

239 Jim Wallis, *God's Politics: Why the Right Gets It Wrong and the Left Doesn't Get It* (New York: HarperCollins, 2005), xiv, quote xiii.

240 Ibid., quotes xxiiii.

241 Ibid., quotes 73, xxiii.

242 Ibid., quotes 74.

243 Ibid., quote 74.

244 Ibid., 167; see "Interview with Stanley Hauerwas," *Religion and Ethics Newsweekly* (September 6, 2002), www.pbs.org/wnet/religionandethics/week601, accessed July 28, 2007.

245 Wallis, *God's Politics: Why the Right Gets It Wrong and the Left Doesn't Get It*, quotes 164; Yoder, *The Politics of Jesus*, 204.

246 Jim Wallis, "Dangerous Religion: George W. Bush's Theology of Empire," *Sojourners* 32 (September 1, 2003), 20–7.

247 Wallis, *God's Politics: Why the Right Gets It Wrong and the Left Doesn't Get It*, quote 386–7.

248 Colman McCarthy, "Jim Wallis Tells a Tired Tale: The Faith-based Politics of a Liberal Activist Are as Suspect as Bush's," *National Catholic Reporter* 41 (February 18, 2005), 16; Michael Lumsden "God's Politics: An Interview with Jim Wallis," *Mother Jones* (March 10, 2005), www.motherjones.com, accessed July 28, 2007.

Chapter 8

Dealing with Modernity
and Postmodernity

Charles Curran, James M. Gustafson, Gibson Winter,
Cornel West, Katie G. Cannon, and Victor Anderson

For decades the field of social ethics had a modest range of subjects and theoretical orientations. Then Vatican II modernized the Catholic Church, neo-orthodoxy fell off its pedestal in Protestant theology, liberation theology and feminism gave voice to marginalized communities, modernity became old-fashioned, evangelical Protestantism rushed into the public square, the concept of "mainline Protestantism" lost its socio-logical coherence, and postcolonial theorists attacked all appearances of essentialism. Social ethics exploded, in response, into a profusion of subjects and orientations. By the early twenty-first century the field's chief professional society, the Society of Christian Ethics (SCE), featured working groups on African and African-American ethics, Anglican ethics, biblical ethics, business ethics, Catholic moral theology, Christian–Islamic ethics, church and academy, comparative religious ethics, covenantal ethics, Enlightenment ethics, environmental ethics, ethical issues in higher education, ethics and law, ethics and literature, ethics and political economy, ethics and sexuality, evangelical ethics, families and the social order, health care ethics, international affairs, Latino(a) ethics, lesbian and gay issues, liturgy and ethics, monetary policy, moral and religious psychology, pedagogy, professional ethics, realist ethics, and restorative justice, in addition to numerous caucuses and denominational groupings.

Diversity, especially self-consciousness about it, prevailed. Every meeting of the SCE evoked complaints about issue proliferation and protests about issues lacking an interest group. Postmodernity – the phenomenon of cultural fragmentation, instability of meaning, and incredulity toward metanarrative – became the contested text and context of social ethics. For some ethicists the postmodern condition nullified the possibility of making credible claims about the common good. For most it dramatized the necessity of refashioning the language of interrelationality to address and reflect radical heterogeneity.

The thinkers who refashioned social ethics in the context of late twentieth-century postmodernity included theologians who identified with the modern tradition of social ethics and social critics less connected to it. Charles Curran, the most controversial and renowned American Catholic ethicist of the post-Vatican II period, challenged the regnant Catholic understanding of natural law. James M. Gustafson, a prominent ethicist and theocentric theologian, trained many ethicists in his long career at Yale University and the University of Chicago Divinity School. Gibson Winter, an equally prominent teacher and advocate of melding social ethics with social science, wrote the field's most important programmatic text. Cornel West, a social critic and religious philosopher, was the greatest public intellectual associated with progressive Christianity since Reinhold Niebuhr. Katie Cannon, trained in black liberation theology and feminist ethics at Union Theological Seminary, founded womanist ethics as a response to a social ethical field in which all the blacks were men and all the women were white. Victor Anderson, a social ethicist and cultural critic, was a leading proponent of deconstructing essentialist claims in ethics and cultural criticism, especially regarding race and sexuality.

Moral Theology and the Curran Controversy

For decades American Catholic ethicists enjoyed higher standing in ecumenical Protestant circles and greater intellectual freedom than their counterparts in Catholic theology and biblical scholarship. John Ryan worried briefly that the Vatican would apply its condemnations of modernism and liberalism to his area and positions, but it did not, which allowed Ryan and a succession of Catholic ethicists to have active public careers. John Courtney Murray crossed the line with the Vatican in the 1950s, but his timing was fortunate, and Protestant ecumenists admired him long before his position was vindicated at Vatican II. Dorothy Day was radical on some topics, but like Ryan, Murray, and later, Michael Novak, she gave the Vatican no trouble on topics pertaining to sexual ethics and women's equality. On these topics, public criticism of the church's teaching by Catholic theologians did not arise until Vatican II was underway. The moral theologian who pressed the issue, Charles Curran, was an unlikely rebel.

Born in Rochester, New York in 1934, Curran was a product of the college-seminary system of the 1950s, and, in his early career, an example of its passive, churchly piety. His Irish father (an insurance adjuster) and Irish-German mother were second-generation Americans. In 1955 Curran graduated from the local diocesan seminary college, St. Bernard's, and was promptly sent off to the North American College in Rome, where he studied at the Gregorian University. Ordained a priest of the Rochester diocese in 1958 and granted a licentiate in sacred theology from the Gregorian the following year, he later recalled only two issues on which he quibbled with an instructor. The church's teaching on religious liberty and the fate of unbaptized infants made him shudder a bit; otherwise he was docile and accepting.[1]

The Gregorian was not demanding for anyone who could handle Latin. Most of Curran's courses featured a single exam, no term papers, no discussion, lectures read in Latin, and many absent students. He, however, rarely missed a lecture. In 1958 his bishop told him to prepare for a career as a moral theologian at St Bernard's Seminary – "naturally I had no say whatsoever in the matter." Curran had sought parish ministry, was not interested in teaching, and would have preferred canon law to moral theology. As it was, he took his doctorate in "very traditional moral theology" from the Gregorian in 1961 and completed a second doctorate the same year in less traditional moral theology at the Academia Alfonsiana in Rome before returning to St Bernard's.[2]

For him the Alfonsia was the crucial stop. At the Gregorian he wrote a typical casuistical dissertation on the prevention of conception after rape. At the Alfonsiana, a Redemptorist institution specializing in moral theology, he branched out to a historical topic, "Invincible Ignorance of the Natural Law in Saint Alphonsus." The Redemptorists were founded in the eighteenth century by the patron saint of moral theologians,

Saint Alphonsus Liguori, who taught that some humans might be invincibly ignorant of the natural law. This theory, which offended eighteenth-century rigorists, appealed to the repressed rebel in Curran. He preferred the Alfonsia program because it was more demanding and scriptural, the Redemptorists were good teachers, and Bernard Häring taught there. Häring's major work, *The Law of Christ* (1954), offered a scriptural, life-centered alternative to manual casuistry, which reduced moral theology to confessional practice. Manual casuistry arranged the confession of sins according to number and species, training confessors to calibrate degrees of sinfulness. Häring taught that moral theology and spiritual theology belonged together, and both needed to be soaked in scripture, otherwise moral theology degenerated to mechanics. Moral theology was primarily about living in Christ, "the nonviolent but also powerful unmasker of all false images of God, of every religious falsification, the perfect worshiper in spirit and in truth." Curran embraced Häring's approach to moral theology, especially his emphasis on growth and change in the spiritual life and the centrality of following Jesus.[3]

He returned to Rochester just before Vatican II. American Redemptorist Francis X. Murphy (the renowned "Xavier Rynne" who reported on Vatican II for the *New Yorker*) advised Curran to cover up his revisionism by teaching in Latin; Curran took a pass at lecturing in Latin, using a textbook, and blending into St Bernard's faculty. But his Latin lecturing typically stopped three weeks into the semester, his "introductions" stretched to six months before taking up the textbook, he was barely older than most of his students, and he was fortunate to find some friendly colleagues, some of whom had been his teachers. In 1964 Curran told a convention of the Canon Law Society that both parties in a mixed marriage should not be required to raise their children in the Catholic faith, which earned a warning from the diocese to get back in line. The same year he questioned whether the Catholic Church had the right position on birth control, a topic that had begun to attract scholarly attention. In 1959 the contraception pill had entered the market; three years later one of its key developers, Catholic physician John Rock, argued in his book *The Time Has Come* that the pill was perfectly natural because it operated in the same manner as the body's endocrine system; in 1963 a handful of Catholic clerics and academics began to question the church's prohibition on artificial contraception.[4]

Curran joined this tentative and very fledgling dissent in August 1964. From his weekend experiences in parish confessional boxes he knew that many couples were tormented by the contraception ban. Why was it wrong to use contraception, especially if the rhythm method was unreliable? One young couple told him tearfully of another pregnancy; they lived on a teacher's salary and already had nine children. What were they supposed to do? Curran reported that whenever he talked with other priests, they asked each other the same thing. In his first article on the subject he asserted that contraception was wrong on an objective level and he opposed a "contraceptive mentality." The rhythm method was better than contraception because rhythm required the virtues of self-control and loving self-sacrifice. But from pastoral experience Curran believed that many who practiced contraception did not sin on a subjective level. They were not onanists who selfishly closed themselves to the service of life, as the manuals put it; they lacked the intention of sexual sin. Moreover, undermining his opening assurance, Curran had doubts about the objective wrongfulness of contraception. The rhythm method used time to prevent conception, while contraception used a spatial device; what was the moral difference? Citing Yale religious philosopher Louis Dupré, who argued that no individual act was absolute and that procreation was valuable only in relation to other values, not as a self-subsisting telos, Curran stopped just short of saying that the church had to change its teaching on contraception.[5]

Three months later, speaking to the Catholic Club of Harvard, he crossed the line. As soon as Curran became known for advocating a change in church teaching, he had to acknowledge that the pastoral problem also cut the other way. Laypersons told him that if the church removed its ban they would feel betrayed, having suffered illness, frustration, financial hardship, and even the threat of death out of obedience to church authority. Priests told him they would not be able to face parishioners whom they had exhorted to obey the church. Curran admitted that the fallout from a change in church teaching would be substantial; however, it could not be right to cling to a wrong position. Drawing on his doctoral studies on conception and natural law casuistry, he historicized the problem, tentatively at first. Curran argued that the church prohibited contraception on the authority of its own tradition and the natural law, lacking a scriptural warrant, but "natural law" meant different things and was used mainly to rationalize prevailing positions. Banning contraception was not the only verdict consistent with natural law. Catholic tradition was a stronger force than the logic of natural law. The church appealed to natural law to buttress the view that happened to prevail in Catholic teaching, albeit with the help of natural law theory. Later Curran stressed that the tradition was unfortunately dependent on medieval biology. At the time that the church's teaching on contraception was formed, theologians believed that the seed was the only active element in human reproduction. It followed, for them, that every act of intercourse was open to procreation. Curran believed that Catholic moral theology was overdue for an update.[6]

This verdict inspired his signature argument about the right to dissent from specific moral teaching. Although church officials dispensed with medieval biology, they clung to natural law and the church's authority. Regarding church authority, Curran argued that there had to be room for the individual's right to dissent from noninfallible church teaching. Because church teaching on specific moral issues was never infallible, he contended, Catholics had a right to dissent from it. The right of conscientious dissent was meaningful only if it was not purely formal, and it extended to moral issues on which the church did not possess absolute certainty. Regarding natural law, Curran gradually sharpened his critique. He liked the realist aspect of natural law – morality had to correspond to reality – but warned that natural law theorizing was a slippery enterprise with a troubled history.

The prevailing concept of natural law in Catholic ethics echoed the third-century Roman lawyer, Ulpian, who defined it as that which is common to all human beings and animals, such as procreation and the education of offspring. Thomas Aquinas employed this definition many times, citing Ulpian specifically. Curran observed, however, that natural law sometimes referred to the "right reason" of human beings. In this usage, which Aquinas occasionally employed, it distinguished between rationally guided human actions and animal processes or the physical structure of acts. Unfortunately, Curran noted, Aquinas usually used the Ulpian-type concept; more importantly, the manualists codified it. For the most part Catholic moral theology identified the "natural" with the biological and physical. Curran judged that that was the wrong choice; theologians would have done better to validate the "natural" right of reason to interfere in natural processes: "A proper understanding of man should start with that which is proper to man. Rationality does not just lie on top of animality, but rationality characterizes and guides the whole person." Had the church not adopted an Ulpian-type understanding of natural law, its moral theologians would not have identified the human act with its physical structure (which Curran called "physicalism"), and modern Catholics would not have to struggle with mistaken moral problems. Years later Curran developed a sharper historicist critique of natural law, but for many conservatives his early writings were already beyond the pale of permissible reassessment.[7]

In 1965 he was dismissed from St Bernard's for being too liberal and controversial. Curran took his first firing in stride, because Catholic University of America was bidding for him and the diocese of Rochester had previously refused to let him take another position. Now he was free to develop his thinking in more cosmopolitan company. Faculty dean Walter Schmitz and religious educationist Gerard Sloyan viewed Curran as the church's most promising young ethicist, one who would heighten Catholic University's relevance and academic prestige. University officials, on the other hand, had misgivings about him from the outset, and soon objected to his revisionism about mixed marriages, natural law, contraception, and masturbation. Curran told the Catholic Theological Society of America that Catholic theology had to change its three-centuries-old teaching that the "misuse of the sexual faculty" was always a grave and serious moral evil. The church's sexual teaching was overly biological, fossilizing a faulty understanding of the importance of human semen. At best the church allowed that sexual misuse might not be as grave subjectively as it was objectively, but by challenging the manualist axiom that in sexual matters "there is no parvity of matter," Curran sought to move beyond the subjective–objective distinction. His book *Christian Morality Today* (1966) gave wide currency to his views on these subjects, which enraged the Catholic Right and alarmed many cardinals, archbishops, and bishops on Catholic University's board of trustees. At the time every archbishop in the USA was an *ex officio* member of the university board. The Vatican's apostolic delegate to the United States, Archbishop Egidio Vagnozzi, pressed for Curran's dismissal, and in April 1967 the university tried to fire him.[8]

Informed that he had been fired, Curran told a few friends and colleagues, which set off a firestorm of faculty and student protest. A public rally took place the next day; the *Washington Post* described it on page one; students went on strike; the mass media descended on Catholic University; the *New York Times* ran the story on the front page for several days; and the entire university faculty endorsed the strike. Curran's friend and colleague Daniel Maguire told a packed house at McMahon Auditorium, "If there is no room for Charlie in the Catholic University of America, there is no room for the Catholic University *in* America." Faced with a sweeping strike and embarrassing publicity, the university capitulated, giving Curran a new contract and promotion. His victory struck a blow for intellectual freedom at Catholic institutions, though Curran understood that it had little to do with him personally. He was new, little known, and did not teach undergraduates, yet they picketed for him: "The time was ripe. My incident just ignited the immense mound of tinder that had been accumulating over the years." Years later he reflected that notoriety and theological leadership came too quickly for him. He was too young to be a lightening rod for conservatives and reactionaries: "I was thirty-three years old at the time, but all of this gave me a kind of stature and position that I was not really prepared for." Surrounded by older colleagues who didn't know how to retool their thinking after Vatican II, he accepted speaking invitations across the country, spoke to the media about situation ethics, and defended the liberalization of Catholic theology: "They offered no leadership, so there was a void that pushed me into the position of the public leader of progressive American theologians."[9]

To Curran, contraception was not the most important ethical issue facing the church, and he did not want to be known only for his position about it; thus he accepted the speaking invitations and addressed additional subjects. He also hoped that Paul VI would soon defuse the issue. For years Curran told lecture audiences that the mere existence of a papal birth control commission showed that a change in church teaching was conceivable. In 1968 his hope soared after a majority of the pope's commission favored a change, until Curran learned that the pope was leaning the other way. Through the media Curran and others appealed to the pope, urging that issuing no encyclical would be better than the catastrophe of reaffirming the contraception ban. On July 27, 1968 *Time* magazine informed Curran that the pope had answered, showing him an advance copy of *Humanae vitae*. Two days later it was published; in the meantime Curran organized an unprecedented protest.[10]

The pope declared that spouses "must conform their activity to the creative intention of God, expressed in the very nature of marriage and of its acts." The unitive and procreative meanings of the sexual act were inseparable in the divine and natural law. Ten theologians at Catholic University met to formulate a response, drafted by Curran and Daniel Maguire, which emphasized that Catholic doctrine recognized the right to dissent from noninfallible teaching. Releasing their statement to the media on July 30, with endorsements from 87 American Catholic theologians, Curran's group announced its dissent at a press conference. The statement set off a barrage of condemnations, praise, and puzzled commentary that such a thing was possible. Nothing like an organized public dissent from papal teaching had ever occurred in American Catholicism. Twenty Catholic University professors supported the dissent, including theologians Bernard McGinn, Roland E. Murphy, and David Tracy; eventually more than 600 Catholic scholars signed it. For Curran, establishing the right to dissent was more important than the arguments about contraception: "No faithful Catholic can lightly dismiss the authoritative teaching of the papal or hierarchical teaching office in the Church. Great respect is due to such teaching. However, this does not mean that the teaching itself is always correct. The papal and hierarchical teaching offices must be seen in the whole context of a theology of the church."[11]

Humanae vitae offered no scriptural argument, appealing to natural law and church tradition. Curran replied that for Christian ethics, natural law could not be a self-standing entity to which scriptural or theological considerations might be added. The theological basis of natural law was the Christian doctrine of creation, and natural law made theological sense only within the context of the Christian understanding of creation, sin, incarnation, redemption, and eschatology: "Christian ethics cannot absolutize the realm of the natural as something completely self-contained and unaffected by any relationships to the evangelical or supernatural." In a Christian worldview, he argued, nature and creation were supposed to be relativized by redemption and eternal life. The realm of nature was provisional within the total history of salvation; thus "natural law" was meaningful only within the context of salvation history, not as something integral in itself.[12]

Curran lamented that modern popes had a pronounced tendency to absolutize natural law conclusions, especially about sex; *Humanae vitae* was the crowning example. Sexual morality was not the only casualty of this trend, he noted. Aquinas stressed the social function of property, but Leo XIII committed Catholic ethics to a naturalistic defense of private property. Catholic moral theology did not always define human acts by their physical structure, Curran observed; when dealing with killing, theft, and lying, Catholic orthodoxy paid attention to context. But in the sexual area, the physical structure of the act prevailed: Masturbation was intrinsically disordered, assisted abortion to save the life of a mother did not merit the casuistical nuances of just war, and contraception interfered with the act of sexual intercourse. The interpersonal, familial, and social circumstances counted for nothing; the morality of the act was defined by its physical and biological structure. Curran protested that Catholic moral theory needed to advance beyond the pre-scientific and pre-technological circumstances in which it arose: "In a pre-technological civilization, man found happiness by conforming himself to the rhythms of nature. But through science and technology contemporary man must interfere with the laws of nature to make human life more human."[13]

His deepest concern was pastoral, to assure Catholics they could reject the pope's teaching on birth control and remain good Catholics. Aided by a New York law firm, the Catholic University theologians spent a year defending themselves to a university board of inquiry, which absolved them of violating their professional responsibilities. Afterward Curran and coauthor Robert E. Hunt denied that the dissenting theologians replaced the pope's authority with their own, explaining that the church's teaching function was not exhausted by its Petrine and hierarchical offices: "The primary teacher in the Church always remains the Holy Spirit; but no one person or office in the Church – pope or bishop, theologian or dissenter – has a monopoly on the Holy Spirit."[14]

Having judged that the deontological and teleological models were inadequate, Curran also ruled out a simple utilitarianism or consequentialism that reduced ethics to the greatest good for the greatest number. In Catholic ethics, proportionalism was a major alternative, stressing intentionality, circumstances, and the distinction between physical and moral evil. Notre Dame ethicist Richard McCormick was the dean of proportional theory. He contended that while no intention or circumstance justified a wrong moral object, some physical evils could be justified for the sake of a higher moral end. Curran often made proportional judgments on hard cases, such as that one should commit a physical evil (cutting off a gangrenous leg) for a proportionate reason (saving a life). He appreciated McCormick's ability to criticize conservative Catholic positions on sexual and medical ethics more or less on their own terms. But proportionalism was too close to manualist casuistry for Curran. He did not want to say that contraception was a physical evil that could be excused for a proportionate reason. That smacked too much of anti-sexual stigmatizing, exemplifying the proportionalist tendency to identify as evil something that was merely finite. No human action was perfect, but the inability to be perfect was a function of finitude, not evil. To Curran, proportional theory was helpful in solving various moral quandaries, but he wanted a more expansive, fluid, life-centered model that reflected the complexity and wholeness of moral living.[15]

He found it in H. Richard Niebuhr's idea of the "responsible self" that responded relationally to other selves and responsibilities. The natural law conceptuality of *Humanae vitae* viewed nature as a principle of operation within every existing thing and the self as a substantial entity that properly lived according to the principle of being embedded within the self. Following Niebuhr, Curran defined the self as a participant in a network of relationships: "Man is not a being totally programmed by the nature he has. Rather, man is characterized by openness, freedom, and the challenge to make himself and his world more human in and through his many relationships." Selfhood was constituted in and through relationships. To Curran, the relational-responsibility model incorporated the best elements of the deontological and teleological models while averting their absolutist tendencies: "One cannot absolutize what exists in terms of relationships."[16]

He treasured Vatican II primarily for legitimizing the transition from classicism to historical consciousness. In Curran's view, the relationality model showed how to take the next step in the field of moral theology, taking historical consciousness seriously. Unlike classicism, historical consciousness emphasized the particular and contingent, paid special attention to human subjectivity, and employed an inductive method. It aimed for the best hypothesis instead of absolute certainty. Unlike extreme forms of existentialism and nominalism, it also insisted on the real connections of the self to other human beings, the world, the past, and the future. Repeatedly Curran contended that despite the Catholic Church's reputation for self-importance and making its followers feel guilty, most Catholic moral theology paid little attention to the church and did not take sin seriously enough.

Both faults reflected the church's longstanding ahistorical dogmatism. The church stressed its importance to salvation, but taught a philosophically based moral theology that ignored the particular, historical, ecclesial context of Christian living. It heaped moral censure on acts it considered immoral, but adhered to a natural law optimism that underestimated the ravages of sin against reason, human nature, and creation. Sin is a power that distorts and harms humanity and nature, Curran admonished; it is not merely an act. To some observers, Curran's criticism of natural law methodology and optimism, his reliance on Richard Niebuhr's relational model, and his debt to Reinhold Niebuhr's analysis of sin showed that he was more Protestant than Catholic. Curran replied that his home was the Catholic Church and that Protestantism and Catholicism needed to learn from each other.[17]

Despite his Protestant debts, Curran was deeply devoted to the renewal of specifically Catholic moral theology. Most of his work tracked the post-Vatican II development of his field, and in 1974 he made a conscious decision to emphasize social ethical issues. Writing widely on the history of Catholic social thought, he analyzed Catholic unionist and peace movements, made a detailed case for progressive tax policy, and supported liberal feminist critiques of society and the church. Assessing the two lodestars of American Catholic social ethics, Ryan and Murray, he favored Ryan's political liberalism over Murray's conservatism and "very limited state." On the social issue that exploded into public prominence in 1973 – abortion – Curran cautioned against Catholicizing American law. It was regrettable, he allowed, that "a great number of people do not believe the fetus is a human being." But because so many Americans did not believe it, the Supreme Court made the right ruling in *Roe v. Wade*. Catholics had no business overturning the decision with a constitutional amendment: "I wish the reality were otherwise, but in the light of the situation I understand why the Court came to its conclusion." As a belief issue, Curran added, abortion and euthanasia were not categorically different from contraception and sterilization: "Legitimate dissent in these areas remains a possibility because of the complexity and specificity of the material with which we are dealing and the fact that one cannot obtain the degree of certitude that excludes the possibility of error."[18]

In 1979 Curran and McCormick launched a series of theme-based readers titled *Readings in Moral Theology*. Featuring essays on moral norms, the magisterium, the use of scripture in moral theology, social teaching, dissent, natural law, feminism, and other topics, this series became an indispensable sourcebook for North American Catholic moral theology, redefining its mainstream and range of topics. Curran and McCormick coedited the first nine volumes; they teamed with Yale Divinity School ethicist Margaret A. Farley for the ninth volume, on feminism; later Curran continued the series on his own. Curran found much to appreciate and oppose in the teaching of Pope John Paul II; however, he was in trouble with the Vatican well before John Paul II became pope in 1978.[19]

Persistently he contended that the church had more than one magisterium and that a plurality of magisteria were needed as a brake on the Vatican's belief in its absolute certainty: "There are many magisteria in the Church – papal and episcopal magisteria, the authentic magisterium of laity and the magisterium of theologians. Each of these has a creative service in the Church." All faithful Catholics recognized the God-given role of the hierarchical magisterium, but its "teaching on specific moral questions cannot absolutely exclude the possibility of error." Curran disliked the church's tone of dogmatic certainty in claiming that human life began at conception (he believed it began at least 14 days after conception) and that euthanasia was always an abhorrent evil. On these subjects he dissented, "but my dissent is not all that great. Others might propose a more radical solution." In his view premarital sex was usually, but not always, morally wrong; gay and lesbian sexual acts in the context of a committed relationship striving for permanency were objectively good, although short of the ideal; and the church needed to end its prohibition of divorce. Curran wanted to reconcile divorced Catholics to their church and curtail the pain and hypocrisy of the annulment traffic.[20]

His provocations on these themes and presence at a pontifical university (one granting academic degrees accredited by the Vatican) moved the Vatican to discredit him. Church officials, noting that many American Catholics believed they could ignore *Humanae vitae* and still be good Catholics, pointed an accusing finger at Curran, as did conservative Catholic tabloids. Curran's stellar personal reputation and scholarly prominence heightened his value as a disciplinary example, although he later learned that the Vatican file on him began in 1966, when his career had barely begun. In 1979 the Sacred Congregation for the Doctrine of the Faith, headed by Franjo Cardinal Seper, informed him that it had launched a formal investigation of his work. Seper charged that Curran minimized or denied the authority of the papal magisterium, propagated a "mistaken concept of pluralism in Catholic theology," promoted "public dissent" from the teachings of the magisterium, taught a non-Catholic view of sin as destruction of the objective moral order, exaggerated the physicalist orientation of Catholic sexual morality, denied the possibility of true knowledge of moral absolutes, turned scriptural absolutes into mere ideals or goals, opposed the church's prohibition of divorce, failed to uphold church teaching on abortion and euthanasia, contradicted church teaching on masturbation, premarital sex, homosexuality, contraception, and sterilization, and publicly challenged the authority of *Humanae vitae*.[21]

For three years Curran corresponded with Seper and his deputy Jerome Hamer, OP, disputing their claims that his positions had no rightful place in the church. The congregation's lengthy delays before responding to Curran frustrated him greatly, as did its tendency to settle arguments by appealing to its own authority. In 1982 the investigation took a fateful turn for Curran when theologian Joseph Cardinal Ratzinger became prefect of the congregation. Curran pressed Ratzinger to state the terms and conditions under which the congregation would recognize any right to public dissent; Ratzinger ignored the question, rejected Curran's arguments with little discussion, and told him to retract his positions. Curran offered to change his departmental position, switching from theology (an ecclesiastical faculty granting pontifical degrees and subject to Vatican regulations) to the university's department of religion and religious education, but the Vatican was not impressed. Richard McCormick, Richard McBrien, and David Tracy drafted a letter of support for Curran that was signed by nine former presidents of the Catholic Theological Society of America; eventually 750 theologians signed it. The statement pleaded that the academic reputation of Catholic universities would be damaged greatly if the Vatican punished Curran, and also noted that no American Catholic theologian was more liked or admired than Curran. But Ratzinger already knew that many theologians identified with Curran and liked him. For Ratzinger, the point was to break the "circular method of contestation" by which theologians quoted each other in defiance of authoritative church teaching. In a tense meeting with Ratzinger at which Häring served as Curran's advocate, Curran complained about the unfairness of being singled out. Ratzinger replied that he would be happy to investigate anyone that Curran named; Curran responded that he had no interest in fueling Ratzinger's enterprise.[22]

In 1986 Ratzinger informed Catholic University that because Curran rejected the authority of the magisterium and took unacceptable positions on contraception, sterilization, masturbation, divorce, and homosexuality, he was neither "suitable nor eligible" to teach Catholic theology. Two years later the university's board of trustees fired Curran from his tenured position; the following year Curran lost a civil case to regain it. He taught briefly at Cornell University and the University of Southern California, continued to write on trends in Catholic moral theology, and in 1991 accepted a university chair at Southern Methodist University. Curran treated the entire episode as a "teaching moment" for the church. To enhance its own credibility, he argued, the magisterium needed to recognize the right of dissent; he also reminded himself that to make this argument effectively he had to refrain from anger and questioning anyone's motives.[23]

His firing, however, gave him the freedom to say things more plainly. Curran's critiques of the Vatican acquired an edgier tone, and he responded frankly to the encyclicals of John Paul II. Curran appreciated that *Laborem exercens* (1981) and *Centesimus annus* (1991), appropriated personalist ideas, usually took progressive positions, and showed at least a bit of historical consciousness. But when John Paul II wrote about sexual and medical ethics, historical consciousness disappeared and dogma prevailed. *Veritatis splendor* (1993) blended natural law and the divine will, contending that natural law participates in the eternal law, which is God's very wisdom. The pope plainly stated his central theme: "The reaffirmation of the universality and immutability of the moral commandments, particularly those which prohibit always and without exception intrinsically evil acts." In *Evangelium vitae* (1995) he gave special attention to the intrinsic evil of euthanasia and abortion, declaring that direct abortion "is always gravely immoral." Repeatedly John Paul II and the Sacred Congregation for the Doctrine of the Faith condemned contraception, masturbation, artificial insemination, homosexuality, in vitro fertilization, and sterilization.[24]

Curran replied that natural law can be variously interpreted, nature has no normative character anyway, and papal teaching on sexual and medical ethics needed to deal with real-life situational problems, limits on human knowledge, modern criticism, and exceptions to moral norms. There was something sadly ironic about the papacy of John Paul II, he judged. The pope brandished proof texts from Vatican II, claiming to defend the council's teaching and legacy, but he repudiated the historical consciousness that inspired its reforms. In social ethics the pope creatively applied church doctrine to a changing world, but on sexual and medical ethics he made the world stand still. Curran countered that historical consciousness changed the way one looked at reality. To think inductively and pay attention to the particular was to relinquish the view of scripture and tradition as storehouses of immutable propositions. To him the situation in Catholicism amounted to "historical consciousness meets the immutable." John Paul II treated the decalogue as a univocal record of divine commands; Curran replied that biblical scholarship interpreted the second tablet of the decalogue as arising from the experiences of the Hebrew tribes. Moreover, it was absurd for the Vatican to insist that the church had never erred in its teaching; to Curran, the claim was disingenuous "at best." The Vatican opposed democracy until the 1940s and it condemned religious liberty right up to Vatican II. With a sharper edge he noted that Häring's top examples included the torture and burning of witches, condemnations of interest taking, justifications of slavery, and condemnations of religious liberty.[25]

As a devoted Catholic, Curran took consolation that the Vatican censured him only on issues that did not belong to the church's religious teaching, at least as he construed the matter. Moral truth was based on reason and experience, he reasoned, not revelation; only truths of faith were based on revelation. Everything on which he dissented from church teaching belonged to the category of fallible discourse. Although the Vatican disputed this interpretation, Curran found implicit endorsement of it in the fact that Ratzinger made no judgment against his faith or priestly status. In 1999, six years before Ratzinger ascended to the papacy as Pope Benedict XVI, Curran reflected: "I write as a person deeply committed to the Catholic Church and to the Catholic moral tradition. I have a few disagreements with the hierarchical teaching on some specific issues, but these disagreements are part of living in the Catholic Church today and do not put me outside the pale of Roman Catholicism."[26]

His notoriety notwithstanding, Curran was a moderate liberal who affirmed absolute moral norms. He did not press the relativity of knowledge or the moral value of diversity to the point of denying the existence of universal truths: "The challenge for us as church is to recognize greater particularity and diversity while also maintaining some universality and unity." Catholic moral theology was right to insist on the universality of commutative, distributive, and social justice, he argued, and also right to recognize political/civil rights (such as freedom of religion and speech) and social/ economic rights (such as basic necessities for life) as universal human rights. Curran believed that the Aristotelian/Thomist tradition was amenable to modern and postmodern criticism. General principles were always obliging. Murder, injustice, adultery, rape, torture, and the violation of someone's right to truth were always wrong. These norms were certain; the problem was to determine what constituted murder, adultery, or injustice in given situations.[27]

As Curran saw it, the church did not undermine its absolute norms by taking relationality and historical consciousness seriously. But the church did undermine its norms by being rigidly dogmatic, just as fundamentalist views of the Bible undermined scriptural authority. Curran wore his notoriety with kindly modesty and humor, often acknowledging that he was hardly the rebel type and was outflanked considerably to the left by his friend Daniel Maguire. Although he had hoped to finish his career at Catholic University, Curran flourished at Southern Methodist University, gaining the Elizabeth Scurlock University Professorship. Unlike Maguire and David Tracy, who wrote for a broad academic audience, he wrote in a distinctly Catholic idiom, practicing the ecclesial self-consciousness that he prescribed for Catholic ethicists. For Curran, the Catholic Church was decidedly the primary context of his scholarship and personal life.[28]

Msgr George A. Kelly of New York, lamenting the liberalization of American Catholicism, described Curran as the main culprit: "On a day that now seems long ago, April 24, 1967, a young priest, not ten years ordained, changed the course of Catholic development in the United States. He confronted American bishops and won. He challenged a pope and was promoted . . . The U.S. hierarchy has not recovered since." Responding in his memoir, Curran wrote simply that he hoped and prayed that history would bear out that he played "a positive role in the life of the church."[29]

Naturalistic Theocentrism: James M. Gustafson

Curran had ample company in owing more to the Niebuhr who was not a social ethicist than to the Niebuhr who was one. Richard Niebuhr influenced much of the ethics field, especially through his doctoral students. His most notable protégé, James M. Gustafson, cast a lengthy shadow of his own through his books and many doctoral students. Exacting, scholarly, a bit dour, and known for acerbic judgments, Gustafson shared Niebuhr's dislike of liberal subjectivism, a feeling that intensified in his later career. He taught that theology was supposed to be about God, not about making God serve human ends, a belief that limited his interest in social varieties of theological ethics.[30]

His father, John O. Gustafson, was a minister and immigrant from Sweden who shared the typical northern Swedish love of forests and rivers. Having found his way to the Upper Peninsula of Michigan, which reminded him of home, John Gustafson passed his love of nature and theology to his son James, who was born in Norway, Michigan in 1925. Gustafson attended North Park Junior College from 1942 to 1943, served in the Army Corps of Engineers in Burma and India from 1944 to 1946, completed his undergraduate degree at Northwestern University in 1948, and obtained a bachelor of divinity degree from Chicago Theological Seminary and the University of Chicago Divinity School in 1951. Earning his doctorate under Niebuhr at Yale in 1951, he taught at Yale for 17 years, moved to the University of Chicago Divinity School in 1972, moved to Emory University in 1988, and retired in 1998.

For many years Gustafson was essentially a tool-sharpener, analyzing approaches to ethical decision-making and ways of relating theology to ethics. In *Treasure in Earthen Vessels* (1961), he took aim at the World Council of Churches Commission on Christ and the Church, blasting its neo-orthodox triumphalism; Gustafson countered that the church was a natural and social phenomenon like other institutions. A major analytical work, *Christ and the Moral Life* (1968), examined the moral significance of Christ as creator, redeemer, sanctifier, justifier, pattern, and teacher. Gustafson surveyed and categorized, mapping ways that believing in Christ made in the lives of Christians.[31]

Most of his early work took essay form. Two essay collections, *The Church as Moral Decision Maker* (1969) and *Christian Ethics and the Community* (1971) analyzed Christian attitudes toward technology, patterns of Christian social activism, perspectives on the church as a community of moral discourse, and the relation of Christian ethics to social problems. Another collection, *Theology and Christian Ethics* (1974) featured essays on moral education, the role of scripture in Christian ethics, views on the relationship of the empirical sciences to ethics, and issues in biomedical ethics. In his book, *Can Ethics Be Christian?* (1975), Gustafson gave a nuanced, qualified, but affirmative answer to the title question, arguing that the apprehension of God's reality through the hearing and living of the Christian story made possible a distinctively Christian moral character.[32]

He taught his students to do ethics in his manner, by acquiring pertinent technical information and making rigorous arguments. Gustafson featured thick descriptions, surveyed methodological options, and was usually short on answers. Paul Ramsey was his model of a rigorous ethical analyst, though Gustafson was more liberal and rela-tivistic than Ramsey. In the 1970s Gustafson acquired similar debts to Charles Curran and Richard A. McCormick, using their interpretations of Catholic moral casuistry as foils for his own thinking. Critics protested that Gustafson's work was tedious, knit-picking, and merely academic. Some wished for stronger normative judgments and not so much analytical twisting and turning. Some wanted Christian ethics to be as relevant and decisive as the new liberationist and feminist theologies. Gustafson held out against them, preaching the disciplinary virtue of thick description and analysis. Christian ethics had no future as an academic discipline if it merely chased after the latest fad in politicized religion, he argued, sometimes acidly.[33]

By the late 1970s, however, Gustafson began to weary of tool-sharpening labor. He did not like a great deal of what passed for theology and ethics, a normative judg-ment he was ready to expound. More importantly, he was ready to expound his own theological ethic. He later reflected that he did not regret his many years of analyzing patterns of moral reasoning, but did regret that it took him so long to spell out his corrective to a field that had lost its way in self-absorbed concerns.[34]

Gustafson disliked the indifference to science that he found in most theologies, and the tendency even of liberal theologians to cite "the biblical message" or "revelation" as important sources of knowledge. Like Richard Niebuhr, his theological sensibility was neo-Calvinist and radically monotheistic. It disturbed him to see theology psy-chologized and politicized as though neo-orthodoxy had never happened. Barth and the Niebuhrs overthrew the liberal strategy of making religion instrumental to moral ends, Gustafson contended, but by the 1970s the field was rife with "vulgar" forms of politicized religion that treated God as a means to subjective ends. Liberal theology and the new political theologies were about human feelings, arrangements, and goals, not honoring God. They reduced the moral meaning of Christianity to human needs, redemption to an assurance of acceptance, and God to a support system.[35]

Richard Niebuhr had the right idea, but even he did not see it through. Gustafson pushed it through in two volumes, *Ethics from a Theocentric Perspective* (1981, 1984), blending Christian piety, themes of the Christian tradition, scientific data on the natural world, and ethical reasoning. He argued that the humanization of religion was a plau-sible, though unfortunate reaction to the decline of supernaturalism under modernity. When theologians stopped believing in a supernatural God and began to doubt the reality of life after death, they turned religion into an answer to personal and social problems. Freedom from guilt and anxiety were promised; cheap grace abounded; middle-class readers of popular theology were assured of their acceptance; and the great doctrines of the Bible were "theologically castrated to assure people that whatever seems to bring them happiness is what they ought to do."[36]

Liberation theology had "morally legitimate" concerns, but it reduced God to a partisan player and theology to an ideology of moral and political causes. Gustafson countered that good theology was always theological, not utilitarian. It understood God's power as "more sovereign, thus ruling nature as well as social experience, and thus qualifying the certainty of his identification with one cause or one course of action." By that standard, Richard Niebuhr's theology was the best of the modern tradition. It described God as the creator, governor, and redeemer of the universe, affirmed that the universe is present in every particular, had a keen sense of the historical relativity of human beings and the sovereign transcendence of God, and did not issue precise moral principles and rules.[37]

Virtually all of modern theology and ethics were too humanistic by comparison, Gustafson argued. Even Barth was too anthropocentric, teaching that God's commands were given primarily to serve the needs of human beings. Gustafson replied that the book of nature is terribly instructive on God's solicitude for human needs: the universe began without human beings and will end without them. At the level of feeling and self-identity, modern theology remained pre-modern, refusing to absorb the scientific picture of reality. But the Christian tradition, especially its Reformed branch, did not lack resources for the task of demythologizing anthropocentrism. Selectively appealing to Calvin, Gustafson gave highest importance to a "sense of a powerful Other," the centrality of piety in the religious life, and an understanding of human life as dependently related to the powers and purposes of God.[38]

Calvin esteemed piety as an appropriate response to an all-powerful God, teaching that God's providence ruled over the course of history and all particular events within it; Gustafson refashioned that as the sovereignty of a "powerful Other" on which all things ultimately depend and to which all things and beings are ultimately related. Piety is not a passing emotion, he cautioned, "It is a settled disposition, a persistent attitude toward the world and ultimately toward God." In the religious life, piety is more inclusive than faith, and its chief characteristics are awe and respect. Faith was often contrasted with reason and unfaithfulness, but piety could not be contrasted with faith and did not trust (like faith) in the benevolence of God to fulfill human needs. Gustafson explained that to be faithful was to be trusting, free of fear, and slow to anger. Faith as faithfulness was crucial to piety, but piety had a wider affective range, encompassing the aspect of awe that was expressed in fear, and it sometimes showed anger toward God.[39]

Gustafson's four-stranded rope of Christian piety, Christian themes, scientific data, and ethical reasoning stressed piety and "the way things are" in explicating its concept of divine reality: God is the power that "bears down" upon and sustains humanity, arranges an order of relationships, and provides the preconditions for human activity and a sense of direction. He protested that "even liberal theologians" found it impossible not to moralize and humanize this description. Even Gordon Kaufman refused to let go of a moral God, describing "God" as the symbol of "a life-policy of humanizing and personalizing the world." Gustafson replied that divine humanizing and pluralizing were "shibboleths" left over from the myths of Genesis. There was a "deep incongruity" between what was known about the world and what theologians said about God's moral stewardship of it. Gustafson allowed that it was not necessary to derive one's ultimate values from a scientific understanding of the way things are, but it was absolutely necessary to assess ultimate values in light of the way things appear to be.[40]

"My argument radically qualifies the traditional Christian claim that the ultimate power seeks the human good as its central focus of activity," he wrote. The good, after all, was always contextually relative. Tornadoes and cancer were not good for anything, but true piety did not look for a beneficent divine intention in every harmful event. Gustafson counseled that piety took the form of fear or anger as well as gratitude: "Piety stands in awe of the powers that bear down on us and sustain us; it does not trust them to fulfill all our perceptions of the human good." Richard Niebuhr taught that God acted in all actions upon creation; for Gustafson that was a bit too strong. It was better to say that human beings possessed the capacity to respond interactively to persons and events, "and that through those actions we respond to the divine governance."[41]

As an ethical perspective, theocentrism was a theology of piety and complexity. Life is too complex to yield moral absolutes or specific ethical guidelines on difficult moral problems, Gustafson argued; at the same time, the theocentric framework provided a larger and more substantive context for ethical reflection than the nominalist individualism of situation ethics. He stressed the moral necessity of accepting suffering as a primary fact of existence and the moral responsibility of helping others cope with suffering and find sources of hope. Gustafson described family life as a school for learning the senses of dependence, gratitude, and obligation, emphasizing the importance of building moral character through the acceptance of finitude, suffering, and forgiveness.[42]

"We are to relate all things in a manner appropriate to their relations to God, but there are no divinely initiated or infallibly revealed prescriptions of proper actions," Gustafson argued. The rules of moral responsibility could not be directly read off the complex interrelationships of the natural world. He had no harmonic vision in which all things worked together for the human good. Neither was there an immutable hierarchy of moral norms that settled problems of norm conflict or other ethical dilemmas: "But the theology backs certain ends and values, and sets the significance of human life within the larger context of the ordering of life in the world. It provides signals or indications of points to be taken into account in making personal and social choices."[43]

Gustafson's prominence as a religious ethicist assured that other prominent ethicists would respond to him. Daniel Maguire set the tone for a barrage of negative reviews by objecting that "Gustafson gives us more badspel than gospel . . . In no meaningful way can this theocentric and not a little eccentric God say: 'I have called you friends!'" The essence of Gustafson's position, Maguire judged, was to transfer humanity's egocentric predicament to God, who was definitely a male potentate, whose plan for humankind was ultimate extinction, and who wanted his grandeur to be glorified and celebrated. Gustafson did not believe in eternal life and he barely mentioned Jesus; Maguire replied, "What's to celebrate?" With less of an edge, but a similar list of objections, Candler School of Theology ethicist Jon P. Gunnemann observed that Gustafson had no doctrine of revelation, Christ and grace played minor roles, and he was too deferential to scientific positivism.[44]

Four of Gustafson's friends and prominent colleagues – Paul Ramsey, Stanley Hauerwas, Catholic ethicist Lisa Sowle Cahill, and Richard McCormick – wrote lengthy critiques that, for Gustafson, hit too many of the same notes. All of them commended his erudition and exacting analysis, but strongly rejected his theology. Ramsey lamented that Gustafson took so little from the Bible and Christian tradition that he was left with almost no basis for saying that human beings belonged to God as their creator and savior. Hauerwas, a former student of Gustafson's, judged that

Gustafson's quest for universality caused him to make Christianity secondary, which was the wrong option.[45] Cahill, another former student of Gustafson's, objected that he minimized the role and status of Jesus, described a barely Christian or even theistic God, and misused Calvin, who did not conceive piety as courageous resignation to an overpowering cosmos. McCormick shook his head that a prominent Christian ethicist would ignore the Johannine and Pauline writings and reduce Jesus to an inspiring religious leader. Moreover, he admonished, the inaccessible remoteness of God was not a fundamental Christian belief.[46]

For Gustafson it was unsettling and a bit alienating to be criticized so roundly by leading colleagues in his field, including protégés. He was long accustomed to influencing theological ethics through his students at Yale and Chicago. Somewhat sadly he noted that many of his former students carried on his ethical concerns, but none embraced "my own systematic position." In that context and mood he made a late career move in 1988, accepting an invitation from a former protégé – Emory University president James T. Laney – to teach seminars at Emory for faculty members from all schools and departments. Gustafson still regarded himself as a theological ethicist, but judged that most theologians were homebodies, too easily content with their familiar world of Christian texts and ideas. At Emory he welcomed the opportunity to focus on what he called "intersections with nontheological materials." Instead of speaking out of a self-referential liberalism, liberationism, or postliberalism, he argued, it was more interesting and vital to explore problems in medical ethics and social policy from the standpoint of real world "actuality." Theologians should draw upon Christian experience, but not speak on its authority or be enveloped by its categories.[47]

His later writings urged that the root of the human problem was "contraction of our thinking and our affections, of our loyalties and concerns." Contemporary theology exemplified the problem, in his view. Liberationists identified divine reality with their own ideology; postliberals like Hauerwas and George Lindbeck turned theology into a ghettoizing language of in-house claims; nearly all theologians insisted that God is perfectly moral and the good is destined to triumph. Gustafson countered that theology and ethics needed to become more real and true, overthrowing every form of provincialism. The provincial mindset is invariably despotic, he warned, and anthropocentrism is a form of provincial despotism, claiming human self-sufficiency in place of the patterns and processes of relational dependence in which life actually takes place. Theocentrism recognized the ambiguities of the "many relations of multiple values" that things have for each other in nature; it perceived that human goods and the goods of the nonhuman world are always relative to various purposes and subjects.[48]

That was a reformulation of Troeltsch's sociohistoricist liberalism. Gustafson allowed that, like Troeltsch, he absorbed relational relativity so deeply that he risked losing any sense of the distinctiveness of Christianity. But Gustafson aspired to Troeltschian integrity in seeing the matter through: "The ideas, myths, and practices of other religious traditions, the implications of historical relationalism for Christian life and thought, and the impingement of the sciences and other secular discourse on traditional Christian beliefs have to be faced by theologians, institutional religious leaders, pastors and others." There was no credible alternative to the old liberal project of facing up to the implications of modern knowledge: "The 'agenda' of classic liberal theology is unavoidable; the 'liberal' spirit which takes seriously critiques of received Christianity is essential for the well-being of its life." Every modern Christian is an intersection of Christianity and modernity, he urged; thus the liberal question of how to accommodate modernity was still the right one.[49]

Elements for a Social Ethic: Gibson Winter

Gustafson ended up with a theological ethic that perfectly reflected his training at Yale and the University of Chicago Divinity School and his subsequent career at both institutions. Essentially he blended a thoroughgoing form of Richard Niebuhr's theocentrism with the naturalist empiricism of the Chicago School.

For three generations Chicago School theologians taught their students to search for moral norms within the variegated life of society. In the early twentieth century, Gerald Birney Smith was emphatic that theology had to become as scientific as chemistry, or at least sociology. In the 1930s and 1940s, Henry Nelson Wieman taught a rigorous version of process empiricism that had something like Peabody's idea of an underlying unity in nature. From the mid-1940s to the early 1960s, Bernard Meland taught Chicago students to search for clues to the hidden moral and religious basis of what he called "America's spiritual culture." These three theologians, plus historical theologian Shailer Mathews and philosopher Charles Hartshorne, were the principal definers of the Chicago approach to theology.

But the Chicago School also had prominent social-ethical proponents. The early symbols of Chicago-style social ethics were Graham Taylor and Jane Addams. A generation later, when the Divinity School launched a formal social-ethics program, the key figure was James Luther Adams. A generation later, Gibson Winter and Alvin Pitcher carried forward the Chicago tradition of discerning the soul in the social order. The Chicago School, being a school, had a certain ingrown ethos that calcified over time, and it favored its own when making faculty appointments. But its leading ethicists, Adams and Winter, were never quite "of" the Chicago School in the manner of its leading theologians. Adams had come from Harvard and later returned to it; Winter had come from the Episcopal ministry and later moved to Princeton Seminary. Both made their mark principally at Chicago, however, where each trained a generation of social ethicists to forge theoretical and practical ties to the social sciences.[50]

Gibson Winter began his professional career as a pastor and community organizer, moved to the academy as an ethical analyst of the US American church and metropolis, wrote one of the classic texts of social ethics, *Elements for a Social Ethic* (1966), during his transition from sociology to philosophy, and spent most of his later career reflecting on the disclosure of meaning in history. His early work analyzed the social organization of power, giving unusual attention to the social impact of religious congregations. Later he stopped writing and teaching about religious congregations, reinforcing a trend in the field, and delved into ontology and hermeneutical theory. Throughout his career he was a major proponent of tying together social ethics and the social sciences.

He was born in Boston in 1916, graduated from Harvard College in 1938, and earned a seminary degree from Episcopal Theological School in 1941. Ordained to the Episcopal priesthood, from from 1941 to 1944 Winter served parishes in Waterbury, Connecticut and Belmont, Massachusetts before giving two years of wartime service as a US navy chaplain, where he served in the Pacific theater and attained the rank of lieutenant junior grade. After the war he served an Episcopal parish in Foxboro, Massachusetts for three years, moving to Brighton, Michigan in 1949, where he and Francis Ayres founded the Parishfield Community, a training center for lay ministry. For seven years he taught laypersons how to relate their faith to social problems, an experience that shaped his early scholarship; afterward he served on the Parishfield board for many years. Completing a doctorate at Harvard in 1952 during his Parishfield ministry, where he studied under sociologist Talcott Parsons, Winter began his teaching career at the University of Chicago Divinity School in 1956. He still thought of himself primarily as an activist, but wanted to develop his ideas. Two years later the books began, starting with a meditation on the problems of modern families, *Love and Conflict: New Patterns in Family Life* (1958).[51]

Winter's first book was an exercise in pastoral counseling and social commentary. Ruminating on the social pressures faced by families, he offered an optimistic, therapeutic gospel of healing and integral living, advising that open communication was the key to both. Years later he blushed at the book's lack of feminist consciousness. But *Love and Conflict* raised the issue on which Winter made his early mark as a social ethicist. Throughout Christian history, he wrote, churches concerned themselves primarily with directing and renewing communities that already existed as layered, rooted, social organisms. But socially thick *neighborhoods* were disappearing from US urban centers: "There is no longer a fabric of community to penetrate. There is a loose network of relationships centering around broad interests, but there is little that could be described as community in residential areas."[52]

That disturbing judgment gave rise to Winter's breakthrough book, *The Suburban Captivity of the Churches* (1961), which conveyed its argument in the title. From 1870 onward, he observed, the white Protestant churches fled from America's urban centers to the suburbs, where they became even more homogeneous than before they fled. Native born white Protestants, upon moving upward in social rank from manual labor to white collar work, left behind an urban cycle of demolition and blight, and worshipped with people just like themselves – until they had to move again to flee an expanding circle of urban blight. These churches usually had friendly manners and warm rhetoric, he noted. They were also deeply exclusive; in fact, exclusiveness was their defining characteristic: "The style of life, manner of dress, form of worship, appointments, windows, clerical garb, and even the coffee hour serve to include some and exclude others." The mainline churches that remained in the cities were deformed by their lack of a social basis; in the suburbs they flourished, but as exclusive enclaves; in both cases they lacked a strong biblical message. Many things were wrong with this picture, Winter argued; the main thing was that suburban Protestantism lost the gospel faith of radical inclusion: "How can an inclusive message be mediated through an exclusive group, when the principle of exclusiveness is social-class identity rather than a gift of faith which is open to all?"[53]

Winter stressed the racial divide. The upwardly mobile white Protestants who fled to the suburbs were prejudiced against blacks; otherwise they might not have fled. But they were usually less prejudiced than the (usually less educated) white Protestants they left behind, who came into contact with blacks more frequently. Winter summarized the sorry story of the Protestant exodus. In the 1870s Protestants began fleeing the cities to get away from Catholic immigrants. By the turn of the century they were also fleeing Jewish and foreign-born Protestant immigrants to metropolitan areas. Then the Great Migration of American blacks to northern cities set off a tidal wave of suburbanization. By 1950 white mainline Protestantism was thoroughly identified with the success dream and consumption style of suburban privilege: "The major White denominations have moved toward exclusive identification with the White middle classes; in fact, they are insulating themselves geographically from the working-class people of the metropolitan areas. The net effect of population change has been an upgrading of the major denominations through social and physical insulation from the working classes."[54]

The Suburban Captivity of the Churches ended on a hopeful note, however, which Winter continued in *The New Creation as Metropolis* (1963). The source of his optimism was that white Protestants increasingly acknowledged that their lives in the suburbs were sterile and hollow. "The problem of emptiness is the pressing issue of modern life," he declared. White Protestants had a bad case of it when they moved to suburbia, then it got worse: "In the final analysis, the overdeveloped society discovers emptiness and despair at the end of its struggle for productivity. Productivity without meaning is empty." In Winter's telling, mainline Protestantism was beginning to fight off the spiritual lethargy and hollowness of its suburban decline. Neo-orthodox theology had made its way into Sunday School curricula, recovering the language of the Bible for Christian education programs without disregarding modern scholarship. Pastors learned depth psychology, "enabling the churches to respond magnificently to the infinite problems created by industrial development." Most denominations had experienced a liturgical renewal that enhanced the aesthetic and spiritual power of worship. Many denominations encouraged greater lay leadership, which democratized the practice of ministry. New ministries to hospitals, universities, industries, and other nonresidential structures of society were emerging. And some churches were looking for ways to get plugged back into the metropolis.[55]

Winter urged his readers that the congregational or parish-based model for organizing church life was not the best way for the church to re-engage the metropolis. In *The New Creation as Metropolis* he enthused that a new society was "taking shape before our eyes," one filled with democratic promise. However, to help fulfill the promise, the churches needed to reorganize themselves as regional centers that ministered to the needs and institutions of urban communities. Instead of centering the church in a homogeneous residential congregation and treating laypersons as supporters of clerical ministry, the church had to reverse the usual ecclesiological and ministerial priorities, conceiving the church as the servant of society and clergy as servants of the laity: "The residential sphere deliberately encloses man in a private morality. The historical task in the metropolitan area is the creation of an interdependent metropolis."[56]

The church as residential community was reasonably effective at dealing with emotional adjustment issues, personal equilibrium, the care of children, and family life, Winter allowed. These were important matters, "the matrix from which personality emerges in health or disorder." Every church had to take them seriously. But the residential congregation could not be the basis on which a servant church struggled for a good society, for its very idea was to be a private, consumer-based enclave insulated against the metropolis. Winter acknowledged that the residential congregation did not lack means of connection to the wider society and a sense of moral responsibility for it. But the private character of every congregation curtailed its public outreach. By its nature as a private residential organization, the church looked out for its own, mostly. In the servant church the main fields of ministry were the public spheres of social, political, economic, and educational life. The servant church built structures of public ministry within the metropolis that struggled for racial justice, social and economic equality, and better schools. Winter stood for addition and a reversal of priorities, not substitution or subtraction. The residential congregation had its place, its ministerial functions, even its necessity; without it there would be no urban ministries. But the prophetic call of the church was outward, public, and other-directed. It worried more about saving the metropolis than about sustaining suburban congregations: "To engage in such an apostolate means freedom from the fear of loss, participation in the New Mankind to which we belong, and risk of the position that we now possess. The servant Church in the churches and latent in the society is that community which manifests this freedom as sacrifice."[57]

With these books Winter seemed to be launched on a latter-day social gospel career, accenting the positive, counseling Christians not to fear secularization and the secular city, and playing up the psychic, ethical, and social rewards of social service. Many pastors read him for guidance on how to sustain the church and its social ministries in the face of a rising secular tide. But *The New Creation as Metropolis* contained the seed of Winter's turn away from the church. He had dropped his neo-orthodoxy and started reading French phenomenologists, especially Maurice Merleau-Ponty and Paul Ricoeur. This philosophical turn, at first, buttressed his ecclesiological focus. In *The New Creation as Metropolis* he described the church as the historical mediator of the new humanity and new creation: "The Church's identity in the world involves a continuity with the past; her future as the New Mankind is eternally present through the divine initiative. This tie of future to past is mediated through *forms* which point to an eternal being or identity, yet they take on new concrete expressions in each particular age." Winter stressed that the communion of God and humanity promised in "the New Mankind" was mediated by the church's cultic celebration of the Eucharist. Moreover, in the servant church the cultic moment took on greater depth, as it became an expression of the servanthood of the laity: "We have frozen the cultic moment in the congregational assembly. When the cultic life of the servant Church becomes integral to the ministry of the laity, we shall see celebration of the Lord's Supper in the contexts of our communal life."[58]

But the church as cultic mediator turned out to be the mediator of Winter's transition from a practical, theologically neo-orthodox church and community centered project to one preoccupied with phenomenology and social scientific method, and from that to one preoccupied with hermeneutical theory. While critics debated the practicality of the servant model and Winter's optimism about the benefits of secularization on church life, he found his attention drifting elsewhere. Years later he told me that he went to conferences that his books inspired, but found the debates too "churchy" and ephemeral. Winter judged that his early books dealt with the symptoms of America's social crisis – the suburban exodus, continuing racism – not the structural forces underlying it. He sustained a hopeful mood mostly on the gains of the civil rights movement and the charismatic leadership of Martin Luther King Jr. But the gains stopped with the civil rights bills, the mood changed, Black Power challenged King's moral authority, and King struggled to develop a movement response to the structural causes of oppression. In addition, Winter found the secular tide more troubling and spiritually devitalizing than his early books let on. To get at the underlying structural alienation within American life, he decided, he had to adopt a different kind of analysis.[59]

His doctoral students at Chicago were caught in the transition. Robert Benne, the product of a conservative Nebraska Lutheran background, had barely come to terms with Winter's early books when he started writing his doctoral dissertation in 1966. By then Winter had moved on to phenomenology and insisted that Benne move with him. The end of the Chicago School at the University of Chicago created similar problems for Benne's classmates. William Dean, trained under Bernard Loomer and Bernard Meland, clashed with his new adviser in 1965, Langdon Gilkey, over his right to complete a dissertation on Alfred North Whitehead. Gilkey told Dean to find a better subject; the Chicago tradition of process thought was finished. Dean, Benne, and others fought for their right to complete their programs. To Benne, Winter's new interests were forbiddingly abstract, formal, inscrutable, and unappealing. He later called the experience "a nightmare." For many of Winter's later students at Chicago and Princeton Seminary, however, his later work established what social ethics was about.[60]

For Winter, social ethics needed to be grounded in social science, just as Peabody, Taylor and the early Chicago Schoolers claimed, but both disciplines needed a more sophisticated understanding of social science. In essence, his new project was a forerunner of what came to be called "hermeneutic phenomenology." More than ever, Winter argued, social ethics and social science needed each other. At their birth in the 1880s, social science was rather full of itself, and social ethics, while rightly defending itself against the dogmatic positivism of the social sciences, never really let go of its a priori religious worldview, especially the reality of a transcendental moral order. For 40 years, social ethicists paid more attention to social scientists than the other way around, while disappointments and resentments mounted, mostly on the social ethical side. Then the whole idea of a social scientific discipline of social ethics was washed away in most divinity schools by the neo-orthodox reaction. Instead of tying together social ethics and social science, neo-orthodoxy reasserted the independence of theology.[61]

Winter observed that as long as neo-orthodox positivism prevailed in theology, there was no hope of a serious conversation between social ethics and the social sciences. However, by the mid-1960s neo-orthodox hegemony was crumbling; for Winter it had already crashed:

> Thus, the time is ripe for a new openness to anthropological concerns within the field of social ethics. However much the theologians may have contributed to the barriers which separated social science and social ethics, they are now disenchanted with their biblical theologies and antiphilosophical orthodoxies. The doors are open, although not much traffic is moving through at the present time.[62]

Winter's major work, *Elements for a Social Ethic* (1966) sought to start traffic moving in both directions. On both sides there were longstanding prejudices and turf battles to overcome, he argued. In the USA, social science began with a mechanistic, evolutionary model of humanity, social Darwinism, which stressed the competitive struggle for survival, interpreting social customs exclusively as the environmental adaptations of developed natural organisms. In this scheme the task of social science was to formulate laws of the adaptive process, such as competition and division of labor, which bore a telling resemblance to the principles of *laissez-faire* economics. Just as economists commended free market policies that shipped food out of Ireland while human beings starved in the streets of Ireland, sociologists obliterated the human subjects of their analysis in the name of science. Winter remarked, "Dogmatism about the form of science became a substitute for scientific inquiry into social realities." For William Graham Sumner, sociology had the same relationship to society that physics had to physical nature, never mind that social reality included free human subjects. Instead of increasing human freedom through knowledge, social Darwinism restricted freedom in the name of science. Sociology showed that human beings were enslaved to societal forces.[63]

Winter recalled that the first sociologist, French theorist Auguste Comte, was only slightly better than the social Darwinists. Comte at least recognized that people had to be persuaded to obey the laws of nature, but his positivism obliterated the human subject all the same, like a great deal of sociology after him. In Winter's telling, the breakthrough challenge to sociological determinism came from the American pragmatists Charles S. Peirce, William James, John Dewey, and George Herbert Mead, who viewed the self as an active and creative subject within evolutionary process. Instead of a mechanistic model of externally related elements, the pragmatists offered a social process model of internal relations, restoring the agency of the human subject. Early social science treated intersubjective realities such as language, understanding, and social organization as products of external forces, keeping evolution simple and mechanical. By contrast, pragmatism fixed on the evolution of mind within evolution. Against the scientific rationalist picture of an objective scientist standing on neutral ground lifted above space, time, and interest, the pragmatists stressed that reason is situated, perspectival, and interested.[64]

For a great deal of Chicago School theology, especially Meland, the crucial pragmatist was James, for his stress on the relationality of experience. For Edward Scribner Ames it was Dewey, for his social pragmatic approach to religion. For Winter's social ethical purpose the crucial pragmatist was Mead, for his emphasis on the social character of the self. Mead taught that the self *is* a social structure, or, more personally, that one becomes a self by participating in the social process. At some point in the evolutionary process, he wrote, a radical change occurred that made it possible for human beings to think, communicate, symbolize, and use language. Mead did not claim to understand how it happened, when, or whether the change was quantitative or qualitative. The part that he knew something about involved what he called "gestures" and the social construction of meaning. In his interpretation, one became a self by interpreting the responses of others to one's gestures, such as pointing to something. Selfhood rested on one's internalization of the responses of others to oneself. Even the meaning of one's gestures was determined by the response of others to them. To be a self was to receive self-awareness through one's coming to awareness through the response of others to oneself. Self-consciousness and gesturing went together, each developing with the other as the self was given to itself in the reflexive process of interpreting the interpretation of the self's acts by others. In essence, Winter observed, Mead offered a social theory of the internal relations of self and other, "an intersubjective matrix through which selfhood emerges." The conversation of gestures began as an external phenomenon, as in mechanistic theories of external relations, but the crucial matter was an internal, intersubjective, albeit thoroughly social phenomenon of emerging self-consciousness.[65]

That was a huge step forward, Winter believed. Building on insights from Peirce, James, and Dewey, Mead offered a valuable account of the social self – the "me." He was not as good on the self as a centered being – the "I," partly because he never broke away from the ambiguities of behaviorism. The "I" was the self through which the gesture initiated. Winter noted that Mead took for granted the desire and need of the "I" to communicate and the relation of the "I" to the "other" that such a desire presupposed; thus he saw beyond the external relations of mechanistic theory. But he took for granted the role of the "I" in the phenomenon that interested him, the emergence of the "me." That was not good enough, Winter judged. If the "me" came to be only through its reflexive awareness of its response to the other, it could not be the source of the initiating gesture. The "I" could not be presupposed in accounting for the social self without reducing it to the social "me." But that was how Mead and his symbolic interactionist and social pragmatic successors rendered the self. In effect, if not by intention, Mead reduced the "I" of self-consciousness to the "me" of social experience. Thus he provided an inadequate account of the internal relations of sociality to which he pointed. Mead taught that selves emerged in social experience through communication, and that the social process of communication presupposed selves. Selves and social process were necessary presuppositions for each other. For Winter that was too paradoxical; he dissolved the paradox by taking Merleau-Ponty's phenomenological option. There was no contradiction if one construed the "I" as central to the emergence of the social "me," Winter judged. Instead of taking social theory further down the path of reductionism, Continental phenomenology progressed beyond behaviorism, conceiving the self as a finite freedom of embodied subjectivity or intentionality. For Merleau-Ponty and the phenomenological tradition, consciousness was the totality of being coming to awareness in the thoughts, symbols, and actions of a self, and the self was a body-subject sharing in the process from which it emerged as self-transcending freedom.[66]

Elements for a Social Ethic offered a grand tour and critique of the philosophical foundations of contemporary social science, unmasking social scientific claims to value-free objectivity. Every social scientific account of human behavior contained normative assumptions about the nature, limits, capacities, and/or motives of human beings, Winter contended, but these assumptions were usually unacknowledged or at least unexamined. Moreover, every social scientific mode of analysis featured an organizing scheme that predetermined to some extent its findings, its claims to objectivity notwithstanding. Four models dominated contemporary social science: behaviorism, functionalism, voluntarism, and a variously named "intentionalist," interactionist, or aesthetic model. Each had a style, a dynamic structure, a principle of unification, and an ordering principle that shaped its findings.

In behaviorist theory, the physical sciences were literally the model for the human sciences, the structure focused on pleasure/pain impulses, the principle of unification was a mechanistic model of exchanges, and the ordering principle was adjustment to external conditions. In functionalist theory, the style was that of a vital organism, the dynamic structure focused on the needs of a social self, the principle of unification was social equilibrium, and the ordering principle was adaptation by internal and external transformation. Voluntarist theory privileged the master–slave dialectic of domination–liberation, focused structurally on competing interests, treated conflict and compromise as the principle of unification, and found its ordering principle in domination and rationalization. In theories based on an aesthetic or symbolic interactionist model of harmony, the dynamic structure was the intentional self, the principle of unification was order, and the ordering principle was continuity of meaning.

There was much to be said for and against the behaviorist focus on conditions, the functionalist focus on adjustments, the voluntarist focus on conflicts, and the aesthetic focus on continuity or symbolic interactions, Winter judged. And in every case claims to value-free objectivity were unwarranted. Every social scientific model imputed some end or goal to the social process, "even if this end is merely the extension of what has already been determined by previous states of the society. Each style of social science has an explicit or implicit understanding of the meaning of the social process, since social process cannot be thought or ordered without some implication of meaning or directionality."[67]

Winter confirmed that he had strong ethical concerns; he wished only that social scientists were more reflective and forthcoming about their own. Science and ethics had different work to do, he allowed; each clarified different aspects of the everyday world; and social science had precedence in determining the logic of its models. But science and ethics intersected as they defined the course of human fulfillment, and the task of evaluating the implications of scientific findings for everyday life was primarily an ethical one. Following Richard Niebuhr, Winter asserted that value had no existence in itself. Because value existed only in the flourishing or crippling relations of existent selves, ethical reflection did not begin in a vacuum. Values were the "pregiven stuff of social process," although Winter did not go as far as Emile Durkheim, for whom society was the only reality. Winter believed that God was the ultimate source of humankind and reality, not society; however, Durkheimian sociology was right to stress that the social world of human beings had a given moral structure. Winter explained: "The social world is a valued world of meanings. It is moral through and through, since it is from first to last a world of demands, claims, rights, approvals, punishments, imputations, and obligations."[68]

Science and ethics intersected at the point of human intentionality, where science met its limit and judgment. Winter reasoned that science sought to explain the conditioning of intentionality by the past, while ethics was concerned with intentionality in itself, the moral quality of human intentionality in its relationships and direction. Each of the dominant social science models had an ethical character, or at least, structures that differently named the social problem and the norms of justice. In the behaviorist model of mechanistic balance, the alienation described was exploitation and the appropriate norm of justice was equal access and reward for effort. In the functionalist model of organic equilibrium, the problem was exclusion and the norm of justice was equal participation in the social process. In the voluntarist model of master and slave, the problem was domination and the norm of justice was equal freedom as power and consent. In the aesthetic or intentional model of unity, the problem was assimilation and the norm of justice was harmony of creative freedom.[69]

For Winter, each of these models had ethical value, though some were more limited than others. Behaviorism was very limited ethically, because it considered only the functioning of the system, not the just allocation of values. Unfortunately, mainstream economists contented themselves with behaviorist reasoning, skipped ethical evaluation, and applied their models directly to social policy. The functional model dealt with the allocation of values, but treated the problem of social unity on "too low a level," trusting the social process to overcome injustice and estrangement. The voluntarist model was the best one for dealing with interest and power, Winter judged. Essentially a political model, it recognized the incompatibility of interests and values in society, the inequality of access to opportunity, the will to power of every group, and the excluding or discriminating downside of every value consensus. Reinhold Niebuhr was primarily a voluntarist, for better and worse; on the negative side, Winter noted that voluntarists tended to overgeneralize, applying a politicized doctrine of social struggle to everything. Social process did not always reduce to the politics of oppression and justice. In the aesthetic or intentional model of striving for harmony, other dimensions of social experience were illuminated. Intentional theory dealt with freedom as power, but also as transcendence. It dealt with problems of equal rights and opportunity, but across the entire range of the social process, not giving exclusive priority to the political: "Its principal contribution to the other models is its emphasis on man's constituting freedom as he struggles with value and meaning."[70]

In Winter's view, the major intentional theorist thus far was German social phenomenologist Alfred Schutz, who sought to provide a philosophical basis for the fundamental concepts of social science. Winter regretted that Schutz wedded his intentional analysis to Max Weber's voluntarism, obscuring his own disclosure of the intentionality of the everyday world. To Winter, intentional theory was valuable for illuminating aspects of social reality that voluntarism ignored and for providing an antidote to functionalist reductionism. Intentional theory and functionalism were structurally similar. Both models started with the value-consensus of a common culture and centered on the unification of the social process. But functionalism minimized or denied human creativity and self-transcendence; it treated cultural values as givens and conceived human beings as constituted wholly by the social process. Functionalists were right to stress the given character of social identity, Winter allowed; however, social theory had to recognize the importance of human creativity, including the constituting reality of personal freedom and the openness of the future. Because the intentional phenomenological approach came closest to approximating the lived experience of the everyday world, it was the only one that was not reductionist.[71]

Favoring intentional phenomenology and sociology among the social scientific options, Winter called his social-ethical position "historical contextualism." Ethical reflection was no substitute for social scientific analysis; on the other hand, analysis without ethical norms yielded only bad ethics – either the prejudices of mere subjective interests or the assumed conventions of a given culture. To his account of the historical conditions and given structures identified by social science, Winter added a brief exploration of "new values and possibilities amid competing and complementary interests." In his case the ethic had a Christian basis and grammar, focusing on the work of love in advancing justice, though Winter was careful not to call it a Christian ethic. In his telling, love universalized the relatedness of humanity's being; the fact that Christianity said so was not the point. "The unifying principle of the social world is love," he asserted. In the social world, love expressed itself as freedom and community. Love was the lure to relation and community that accounted for people caring for each other, the pain they experienced when community was damaged or broken, and the thirst they felt and expressed for freedom: "Our informing perspective is that love as the power of giving, openness, and reconciliation shapes the natural, social, and cultural world toward enriched interdependence and harmony, luring man to freedom as particular being in an interdependent world."[72]

Winter envisioned an era of cooperation between social scientists and social ethicists that helped to build what he called a "responsible society." Citing Richard Niebuhr's notion of the "responsible self" as a moral agent involved in, responsive to, and accountable for a social world, Winter urged responsible selves on both sides of the science/ethics divide to provide guidance to policymakers. Social scientists and social ethicists had no business actually making policy, he cautioned. Historical contextualism was about creating a social world that enabled human flourishing. One of its planks was that ultimate responsibility for policy rested in the hands of elected and professional policymakers. In Winter's view, social science had become too preoccupied with abstract models to help policymakers make good decisions, and social ethicists were ignored because they contributed nothing useful to the policymaking process. Both problems could be mitigated if social scientists and social ethicists worked together. He envisioned think tanks, policy centers, and other "centers for collaborate research" toward that end. Winter acknowledged that serious collaboration was out of reach as long as social scientists harbored anxieties about their scientific status and ethicists fretted about becoming "entangled in mere facts." If social scientists wanted to help build a just society, they had to come to terms with the ethical aspects of their work.

If social ethicists wanted a place in the policymaking conversation, they had to speak the language of social science. Winter put it plainly: "Social ethics can develop as a significant factor in the shaping of social policy only if it comes to terms with the work of social science and collaborates in the scientific enterprise."[73]

That was a strong and updated rendering of an old argument, reinvigorating the stream of social ethics that had always taught that social ethics had to have a close kinship with social science if it wanted to be a respectable field. Winter became a prominent figure in the field by championing that option. He gave only a brief foot-note to the major trend of thought counter-factual to his position. In the text of *Elements for a Social Ethic* he declared, "The failure of social ethics to contribute significantly to an understanding of societal identity can be attributed largely to its isolation from the human sciences." In a footnote he allowed that Reinhold Niebuhr was, of course, the notable exception to the "failure" statement; Niebuhr made a huge contribution to America's "societal identity."[74]

But Niebuhr did it by spurning the social science imperative. Winter acknowledged that Niebuhr made his impact through "independent political observation." That was mild and vague compared to Niebuhr's explanation. In *Moral Man and Immoral Society* Niebuhr blasted social scientists for betraying middle-class prejudices "in almost every-thing they write" and for refusing to recognize the class interests that shaped their sociological conclusions. Liberal educators like Dewey understood very little about the struggle for justice, he judged, and "the sociologists, as a class, understand the modern social problem even less than the educators." Niebuhr drew on sociology, anthropol-ogy, and political science when it suited his purpose, and years later he toned down his attacks on social scientists and the theologians who admired them. But his mode of doing social ethics remained straightforwardly political without apology. Winter reasoned that Niebuhr succeeded because the subject on which he concentrated, poli-tics, was "the most appropriate field of social ethics for nonsystematic interpretation." For prophetic types, social ethics as political advocacy remained an option of at least minimal viability. But to save the field and make a valuable social contribution, social ethicists needed to forge alliances with social scientists, because social ethics needed systematic research and intelligibility. The primary task of social ethics was the Durkheimian and phenomenological work of bringing to light the moral accomplish-ments and failures of a given society, not creating a new ethic.[75]

Winter's encyclopedic blend of social science and phenomenology made *Elements for a Social Ethic* the major work of its kind – foundational and programmatic – in the field of religious social ethics, constructing a framework for social ethical evaluation of public issues. Because the book ended with an appeal to social scientists and social ethicists to make a united contribution to policymaking, it gave the appearance that Winter's subsequent work would head in that direction. His students knew better, for Winter was more reflective than practical, and his plunge into phenomenology and hermeneutical theory took him into deeper philosophical water.

For 15 years he pondered the second installment of his foundational project, even-tually producing a slim, dense meditation on the root symbols of human dwelling, *Liberating Creation: Foundations of Religious Social Ethics* (1981). A generation of social ethicists entered the field under his tutelage during that period, studying the social scientific literature that he synthesized, and absorbing his philosophical interlocutors – Mead, Merleau-Ponty, Ricoeur, Schutz, Gadamer, Dewey, and Martin Heidegger. Winter told his students at Chicago and Princeton Theological Seminary (where he moved to in 1976) that the deepest religious social ethics was a species of hermeneutics. The point was not to create ethical truth or even analyze it but to indwell it with interpretive insight, uncovering the moral ethos of society. One of his students at Chicago, John A. Coleman, SJ, later recalled that *Elements for a Social Ethic* was a graduate education in itself for him, forcing him to rethink his understanding of social science and social ethics. Coleman judged, however, that as Winter plunged deeper into philosophical hermeneutics, he lost his way. Social ethics would not flourish on a diet of Heidegger and Gadamer. Some of Coleman's classmates felt the same way, as did some of mine a few years later; others pursued cultural hermeneutics in Winter's fashion; in the meantime Winter sought to make sense of the racial explosion of the late 1960s.[76]

As he saw it, the civil rights movement of 1954–66 rode the crest of a rising "techno-society" in which racial differences lost their previous social significance. An increasingly technocratic society of interdependent technical functions found it bothersome and disruptive to pay attention to race. Winter reasoned that government, industry, and the military needed competent workers to handle technical functions, and segregation was a hindrance to getting things done. So the federal government and corporate class signed on for racial integration: "The racial issue would soon be obliterated. Let bygones be bygones! Black and White together! We are all members of the producer-consumer world, thanks to the techno-society, so let's march into that promised land hand in hand."[77]

White liberals, believing that race should not matter, actually believed that passing a few bills would make race irrelevant, Winter observed. Meanwhile, white Americans as a whole were genuinely surprised to learn that blacks were scarred by centuries of oppression and not ready to let bygones be bygones. In the summer of 1966, the demand for Black Power sounded the death knell of the civil rights movement and white cluelessness about it. "White liberals had bought the universal promise of the techno-society," Winter recalled. They were attracted to the dream of whites and blacks joining together at work, school, and play, and were very attracted to not having to feel guilty anymore about segregation: "Black Power crushed this White liberal dream. It thought the unthinkable – that color did make a difference. Black Power laid down one, non-negotiable condition for participation in the new society – Blacks would participate as Blacks!" Drawing from his experience in Chicago, Winter reflected that Black Power obliterated integration as a guiding moral norm and "crushed the hopes of the urbanologists" who had envisioned cosmopolitan cities lacking ethnic or racial boundaries: "Integrative proposals for urbanization ran head-on into Blackness." For decades the "urban juggernaut" had demolished ethnic neighborhoods and melted ethnic individuals into a bland Americanism; Black Power, however, "raised up a community which refused to be programmed into extinction."[78]

White urbanization was a specter of psychic and cultural genocide for blacks that promised only "brainwashing for the Black consciousness," Winter remarked. It obscured the fact that there were two societies in the USA, one white and the other black, which were separated from each other in a hierarchy of domination: "The White system is an Overclass controlling access to the techno-society. The Black system is an Underclass living on the edge of that White urbanization – participating marginally in its economic opportunities, spatially excluded from its day-to-day intercourse and culturally excluded from its hopes." Black Americans, living downstream from the white Overclass, got a flood of information about whites from teachers, police, ward politicians, and the media, Winter observed. Whites, on the other hand, knew much less about blacks, who lacked the power to distribute and filter information, and what they "knew" was largely screened by the media through stereotypes. Winter argued that this grim picture would improve only after American blacks acquired the voice and power to articulate their experience and be heard: "Communication between the two worlds is broken. Until communication opens, the White Overclass is trapped in its own ignorance."[79]

In the 1970s he moved back and forth in the classroom between hermeneutical theory and liberation theologies, teaching black liberation theology, Latin American liberationism, and feminist theology sympathetically while working on a book that operated quite differently. For liberationists, eschatology was the central theological symbol; for Winter the central symbol was creation, or more precisely, co-creation with the immanent divine Creator. In the company of friends he would say that he wanted to believe that liberation theology was the answer to the modern crisis of theology and belief, but despite his sympathy for liberationist ends, he did not believe it. He believed that modernity had erased "the experiential base of religious faith." In 1978 he put it plainly for publication, declaring that modern people in their everyday mode of thinking lived without any real sense of the religious. The lack was real whether they admitted it or not: "We live in a post-religious age in process of becoming a new religious age. In this interim period we are experiencing a crisis of religious faith and religious thought, a crisis at the very moment in history when humankind is teetering precariously on the brink of environmental and political disaster."[80]

In that mood and conviction he wrote _Liberating Creation_, which had nowhere near the impact of _Elements for a Social Ethic_ but which meant more to him. For Winter, living in a post-religious age necessitated a postmodern poetics of dwelling. Transcendental idealists, following Kant's lead, tried to salvage a religious referent by rendering the divine mystery as a datum of consciousness. Positivists elevated data-things to ultimate status, bowing to science as a final authority. To Winter, postmodernism marked the end of the modernist search for an ultimate referent. Whatever else it meant, "postmodernism" stood for the repudiation of all extra-historical realities. Human beings are cultural and linguistic without remainder, immersed in their histories all the way down. There are no trans-historical norms to guarantee rightness of any sort; all guarantees are actually fictions that legitimate a particular tradition. Winter accepted these verdicts without equivocation; he had moved to a full-fledged postmodernism with regard to ultimate referents and epistemic foundations. He cautioned, however, that experience was a teacher about things that enhanced life and things that destroyed it. The bloodbath called the twentieth century taught a great deal about militarism and imperialism. To find out how to enhance the flourishing of life, Winter argued, people needed to learn from their historical experience, their dwelling in the world. Beginning there, _Liberating Creation_ contended that human dwelling was essentially an artistic process of interpreting symbols. Metaphoric insights in the social sciences, art, philosophy, and ethics opened vistas of human flourishing. Thus, Winter proposed, the most illuminating approach to social ethics conceived it as disclosure of the foundational symbols of human dwelling.[81]

The traditional metaphors of human dwelling were organic; modernity represented the triumph of a mechanistic metaphor; Winter argued that salvation lay with a third possibility, the artistic. In a "techno-scientific" age dominated by the shallow instrumentalism of technique and capitalist rationality, the liberating spark of artistic imagination was the key to a better future. *Liberating Creation* stuck very closely to its philosophical sources, weaving a tight mosaic of authorities on Winter's themes. From Heidegger he took the root metaphor of dwelling and the critique of technology. From Ricoeur he took the notion of human dwelling as an analogue to the written text and the strategy of interpreting dwelling by reading society as a text. With Gadamer he argued that art is always performance (never an object in isolation) and the essence of an artistic event is the representation of what it *is* in its true being. From Dewey he took the idea of the continuity of artistic process with all levels of human experiencing and the description of artistic process as interplay of creativity and environment. With Schutz he turned to symbolization to solve the problem of intersubjectivity (how can one experience the presence of another as an immediate datum?), arguing that selves are mediated to each other in symbolization, not as empirical entities in apperception. And he adopted Clifford Geertz's hermeneutic anthropology, including Geertz's claim that ideology, besides its Marxist meaning as false consciousness (the legitimation of repressive force), can also be a metaphoric projection of an alternative future.[82]

Liberating Creation was mostly metaphysics, written in the arcane style of Continental hermeneutics. It ended, however, with a chapter on social ethics, which contended for ideology in its positive sense. Describing the crisis of Western spirituality, Winter observed that Western technocracy concealed its spiritual foundations behind a mask of calculating rationality, yet its symbols were familiar and taken for granted: "The central symbol is progress. Progress is expansion. The frontier or the underdeveloped nation is good because it is a place for extending human powers to develop, to advance, to conquer, to gain dominion, to increase control." Other prominent symbols of Western spirituality included individuality ("the ultimate reality in this world"), human rights ("the rights of individuals in their system, not the rights of whole peoples") and power ("the organizing symbol of the techno-society"). Western techno-societies prized individuality in property as well as people, rallied heroically to save a single individual trapped in a cave while oppressing entire populations, and treated land as a commodity, "an exploitable resource."[83]

Winter replied that the notion of infinite progress or development was a curious distortion of the biblical heritage, which stressed human finitude. What seemed to have happened was that the radical transcendence of the Calvinist God delivered earthly history to "the mastery of the saints," which subsequently gave way to the mastery of industrial capitalism. Winter proposed an ethic of dwelling in its place, marked by the overarching symbol of justice. On the political level, justice enabled the "creative responsibility of a people for its history, including the control of its economic life for the preservation of all species life and the well-being of future generations." Justice took care of the natural environment and provided for the economic needs of people. Though Winter was vague and brief as ever in the policy area, he ended with the judgment that religious social ethics was "essentially a critique and proposal of ideology." It was a critique of ideological false consciousness and an ideological vision of a humane and ecological future. If there was such a thing as a value-free sociology, he noted with a touch of wistfulness, "there might be a way through the morass of ideologies." But the morass was unavoidable for a social ethic that tried to do anything worthwhile. Winter still believed that the justice-making work of social ethics would advance only as teams of ethical and scientific workers pulled together in a common task. But this time he ended on a stronger voluntarist note. Established moralities always legitimized the established powers of a society, he warned. The primary work of social ethics was to open the "horizon of possibilities in a people's struggle for justice and peace."[84]

Most reviewers remarked on the book's obscure style and its relation to *Elements for a Social Ethic.* Richard A. Hoehn wrote that *Liberating Creation* was insightful, obscure, and "asks questions it does not fully answer." Drew Christiansen, SJ judged that Winter's "oracular style obscures as much as it reveals" and that his long-awaited sequel, despite offering "a line of continuous development" in its argument, was unlikely to have much impact on the field. John Coleman took back his graduate school critique of Winter's hermeneutical turn, enthused that it bore fruit for religious ethics, and lauded the book as a splendid "culmination of his scholarly work." Franklin Gamwell judged that the book was hard to read but worth the effort, "a challenging illustration of this mode of thought." Dennis McCann wearied of "Winter's demon-ology of technocratic capitalism" and judged that his work suffered "from a lack of persuasive socio-economic analysis," but also noted that Winter had rare patience and skill, and hoped for a third book that worked out the criteria by which Winter adju-dicated conflicting interests.[85]

Winter had no plans for a third major work, but in later life he wrote occasionally on social-ethical topics and taught as an adjunct professor at Temple University. He had moved to Princeton Seminary from Chicago in the hope of building up its doc-toral program in social ethics, but Winter's postmodern Left-liberalism did not fit there and he was pushed into early retirement, which bruised him deeply. Compassionate, courtly, and kind, he inspired devoted friendship among his students. In 1984, grieved by the Reagan administration's military aid to El Salvador and counter-revolutionary war in Nicaragua, he delivered what amounted to a creedal statement:

> We are living out our real American "faith" in domination and violence. Our only hope is that the nothingness yawning before this path of violence may lead to a turning, to a recognition that true security and violence do not belong together. The Holy in dwelling is a quality of life, a quality of fairness, respect, of listening as well as speaking, of caring as well as exchanging. I respect this tradition of holiness, just as I respect the tradition of science that can bow to new data and accept new insights. This is the way toward a post-modern faith which seeks Shalom for all peoples.[86]

Though he paid little attention to churches in his later work, Winter sustained a deep interest in the theory and practice of building civic organizations, activist net-works, and communities of moral memory. He was fond of saying that politics was community work of the most comprehensive sort and that America needed a national politics that supported communities on every level. In his later years he also made clear that while he did not believe in a God that transcended history or that held power over being and non-being, he had never stopped believing in God the Divine Mystery and matrix of history: "If we share with the creator in the genesis of the cosmos, the world is open and God is freely limited by sharing our partnership and our freedom. God, too, dwells with a future that *is not.* Further, we are not separate from God. We are inwardly bonded with the Mystery as we are with all of life . . . We dwell within the spiritual creativity of the Mystery, even as the Spirit dwells within us."[87]

Cornel West applauded Winter's opposition to Western mechanism and his com-mitment to radical democracy. But Winter defined the problem too narrowly and was vague about the relation of Heideggerian dwelling to political praxis, West judged. If soul-killing technological reason was truly the sum and substance of the modern problem, Winter's deep investment in Heideggerian poetics might have been justified. But there were other problems besides mechanistic will-to-power, West argued, and the organicist tradition contributed to them. At its best (Herder, Hegel, Heidegger), organic thinking offered sophisticated visions of harmony; at its worst (Hitler, Heidegger), it was horrid; overall, it had a history of authoritarianism, mystification, and totalizing visions. West cautioned that even the most attractive visions of organic harmony led to "premature closures" expressing the Western will to power. Winter's organic myth of participatory communitarianism was not really an exception, despite his exemplary politics. Instead of blending historicism and radical politics with romantic naturalism, he should have opted for a thoroughgoing historicism and developed a concrete radical politics. That was West's option, which favored the historicist tradition of Marx, Nietzsche, and Gramsci over its mechanistic and organic rivals, always from the standpoint of a Christian prophetic criticism that privileged the existential human struggle with death, courage, and love.[88]

Prophetic Public Criticism: Cornel West

Gibson Winter loved and taught liberation theology, but did not consider himself a liberation theologian because he was too deeply postmodernist to believe in the liberationist God. Cornel West had a similar relationship to liberation theology that played out very differently. A philosopher by training and social and cultural critic by vocation, he left specifically theological claims to others. Yet his thought was essentially liberation theology in the form of philosophical and social criticism, a mode of witness through which he became the leading religious public intellectual of his generation.

He came to Christian social criticism through his upbringing in an African-American Christian family and church and his exposure to the civil rights and Black Panther movements. His grandfather C. L. West was a Baptist minister in Tulsa, Oklahoma, where West was born in 1953. Both of his parents were raised in Louisiana; his father was a civilian air force administrator, which necessitated moving around when West was young; eventually the family settled in a segregated section of Sacramento, California. West later recalled that he was a beneficiary of California's version of Jim Crow because he did not have to deal with white people or struggle for a place in the world: "Whiteness was really not a point of reference for me because the world was all black . . . That was a very positive thing, because it gave me a chance to really revel in black humanity." Because he grew up relatively free of direct experiences with whites, he reflected, he was able in later life to perceive whites as human beings without being affected by negative experiences or preconceptions: "I didn't have to either deify them or demonize them . . . I could just view them as human beings, and I think that was quite a contribution of my own context."[89]

As a youth he reveled in the preaching of Shiloh Baptist Church pastor Willie P. Cooke, admired Martin Luther King Jr, was hooked by Søren Kierkegaard's struggle with melancholia and mortality, and came to political consciousness by listening to Black Panther meetings. From Kierkegaard he took the lifelong conviction that philosophy should be about the human experiences of living, suffering, and finding hope. From the Panthers he took the lifelong conviction that politics should combine the best available theory with concrete strategies: "They taught me the importance of political philosophy *and* strategy."[90]

At the age of 17 he graduated from John F. Kennedy High School in Sacramento and enrolled at Harvard. Aside from Kierkegaard, West's knowledge of philosophy rested on Will Durant's *Story of Philosophy* and other popular histories; philosopher Robert Nozick assured him that Harvard would expose him to more "high-powered" fare, especially in the analytic tradition. In more important ways, however, West already knew who he was and what he aimed to do: "Owing to my family, church, and the black social movements of the 1960s, I arrived at Harvard unashamed of my African, Christian, and militant decolonized outlooks." He was determined to shape his own image, not have it shaped for him by Harvard University: "I've always wanted to be myself, and, of course, that is a perennial process." At Harvard he studied philosophy under Nozick, John Rawls, Hilary Putnam, and Stanley Cavell, history under Samuel Beer, H. Stuart Hughes, and Martin Kilson, and social thought under Talcott Parsons, Terry Irwin, and Preston Williams, all in addition to his major, Near Eastern languages and literature, which he undertook so he could read ancient religious texts in their original languages and also graduate in three years.[91]

That made him 20 years old when he began his doctoral program in philosophy at Princeton University. West worried that Princeton philosophers would undermine his Christian faith, disabuse him of his attraction to Wittgenstein, and look down on his equally strong attraction to Frankfurt School neo-Marxism. Instead, his teachers took no interest in religion, which allowed him to keep Kierkegaard and African-American mystic Howard Thurman close to his heart. His mentor, Richard Rorty, took a pragmatic historicist turn that reinforced West's commitment to Wittgensteinian anti-foundationalism, while Sheldon Wolin encouraged him to plunge deeper into the Hegelian Marxist tradition. West started with a dissertation on English idealist T. H. Green's neo-Hegelianism, switched to one on Aristotelian aspects of Marxist thought, and settled on one that explored Marx's ethical commitments. He argued that Marx's appropriation of historical consciousness and critique of capitalism were informed by ethical values of individuality and democracy, notwithstanding his attacks on moral reason. By the mid-1970s West was already acquiring a reputation as an intellectual spellbinder. The first time that I saw him, in 1975, he had attracted a sidewalk crowd of a dozen people at Harvard Divinity School and was expounding exuberantly on the varieties of black nationalism. The crowd grew larger as passersby stopped to ask, "Is that Cornel West?" Two years later he began his teaching career at Union Theological Seminary, which seemed to him the perfect home for his broad intellectual and activist interests.[92]

"You know, my aim was always to teach at Union Seminary," he recalled many years later. "Union Seminary, for me, was the real institutional site that brought together all of my interests. It was a Christian seminary, it was deeply shaped by progressive politics, Marxism, feminism, antihomophobic thought and black liberation theology." Elsewhere he put it more precisely:

> I decided to teach at Union Seminary for three reasons: It was (and still is) the center of liberation theology in the country; it was one of the best places for black theological education in the country; and it allowed me to teach and read widely in philosophy, social theory, history, literary criticism and cultural thought. Union was the perfect place to become a broadly engaged cultural critic with a strong grounding in the history of philosophy and criticism.

At Union he formed friendships with colleagues James Cone, James Forbes, Beverly Harrison, Tom Driver, Dorothee Sölle, and especially James Washington. Equally significant for West's intellectual trajectory were his friendships with socialists Stanley Aronowitz and Michael Harrington, his involvement with Aronowitz's journal *Social Text*, which related leftist thought to the cultural politics of difference, and his collaboration with cultural theorists associated with the editorial collective *Boundary 2: An International Journal of Literature and Culture*, especially Paul Bové, William Spanos, Michael Hayes, Donald Pease, and Nancy Fraser.[93]

For West it was crucial to get his bearings about the kind of socialist he was, the kind he was not, and the kinds with which he could work collaboratively. Michael Harrington's Democratic Socialist Organizing Committee, formed in 1973 after the break-up of the Socialist party, smacked too much of its anti-Communist, social democratic background to be something that West could join. In 1982, however, Harrington's organization merged with the New American Movement (NAM) to form Democratic Socialists of America (DSA). NAM, a socialist offshoot of the New Left, emphasized cultural politics, anti-anti-Communism, and radical democracy. Most of its leaders were veterans of the 1960s social movements, including Aronowitz and social critic Barbara Ehrenreich. Black studies scholar Manning Marable joined DSA, as did West, though both of them battled for years with DSA's social democratic mainstream, especially its right flank of Old Left anti-Communists. DSA described itself as a "multi-tendency" organization. West held it to that claim, contending for his Gramscian, anti-imperialist, black liberationist socialism as an alternative to social democratic gradualism. For seven years he served on DSA's political committee; afterwards, following Harrington's death in 1989, West served as DSA's honorary co-chair.[94]

He argued that, unfortunately, democratic socialism was like liberal theology, a valuable project that had outlived its usefulness. Though West always cautioned that he was not a theologian, to the extent that he identified with a theological tradition, it was liberation theology. Democratic socialism was too compromised by its historic identification with middle-class electoral reformism to provide the emancipatory vision that was needed, he argued. Like liberal theology, democratic socialism was a creative project of the past that represented, at best, a "crucial stepping-stone" to something better: a Marxist, feminist, Garveyist, ecological, and antimilitarist revolutionary vision.[95]

West delineated six types of Marxism – Stalinism, Leninism, Trotskyism, Gramscianism, Social Democracy, and revolutionary Councilism – assigning a theological analogue to each. Stalinism, a total perversion of its founding symbols, was the Ku Klux Klan of Marxism. The Leninist and Trotskyist traditions were fundamentalist, marshalling proof texts for truncated versions of Marxist norms. West admired the Left-romanticist tradition of Italian theorist Antonio Gramsci, especially his emphasis on cultural forms of hegemony, but acknowledged that Gramsci was only slightly democratic. Gramsci defended freedom on strategic grounds, not principle; thus his version of socialism was still essentially Leninist. To West, that made Gramscian Marxism analogous to theological neo-orthodoxy, "an innovative revision of dogmas for dogmatic purposes." As for European social democracy, it was too much like the social gospel. One could get an impressive critique of capitalism from it, but not a revolutionary praxis. Though social democracy retained the Marxist concepts of the class struggle and the dialectic of history, it sold out revolutionary consciousness, concentrating on electoral reformism and anti-Communism. Like the social gospel, it accommodated bourgeois modernity too deeply not to be compromised by it.[96]

For West the real thing was the Councilist Marxism of Rosa Luxemburg, Anton Pannekoek, and Karl Korsch, which he viewed as analogous to liberation theology. Against the class collaborationism of Social Democracy and its anti-Communist animus, the Councilist tradition was revolutionary and pre-figural. Instead of viewing workers as wage earners, voters, and consumers, it viewed workers as collective, self-determining producers who prefigured the coming Socialist order. Councilist Marxism was about workers seizing power through revolutionary organizations that already prefigured a Socialist society. Because the Councilist tradition was anti-collaborationist and internally democratic, West prized it as the authentic expression of revolutionary Marxism: "Councilism is to Marxism what liberation theology is to Christianity: a promotion and practice of the moral core of the perspective against overwhelming odds for success."[97]

Since the point was to actually change society, however, not merely to adopt a position, the overwhelming odds were a serious problem. As theory, revolutionary councilism was an important tradition of Socialist thought. As anything else, it barely existed. The social democratic tradition that West dismissed at least had actual parties and worked in solidarity with actual trade unions; Councilism, on the other hand, represented solidarity with an imaginary movement. In two books I argued for an updated guild socialist idea of economic democracy, contending that if democratic socialism was too defeated to be worth considering, that did not speak well for the utility of revolutionary Councilism, which existed only as the fantasy of Left intellectuals.[98]

That was a majority view in DSA, which West battled against. On short-term practical grounds, he allowed, democratic socialists had a strong case; on the other hand, since that option would never build real socialism, it was a loser. Democratic socialism stood for the betrayal of revolutionary consciousness and the very idea of radical democracy. Instead of building a true alternative to capitalism it settled for electoral reformism, extending the welfare state, and denouncing communism. I replied that West's radical democratic vision was unattainable on Councilist terms, he was wrong to identify liberation theology with a single form of Marxism, and democratic socialism was not identical with welfare state social democracy. Democratic socialism also included a guild socialist stream that was closely related, structurally and historically, to the Councilist tradition. Councilism needed democratic socialism in the same way that liberation theology needed to be informed and limited by earlier forms of Christian socialism, especially those in the guild socialist tradition.[99]

To a considerable degree West moved in that direction without giving up his preferences for the Councilist revolutionaries of an earlier generation. He drew increasingly on current theories of "market socialism," especially by Branko Horvat, Wlodzimierz Brus, and Alec Nove, which acknowledged the necessity of market mechanisms and establishing mixed forms of ownership. Any feasible model of socialism had to get prices right just as surely as it abolished racial, sexual, and economic hierarchies, he argued. In the name of "wholesome Christian rejection of such hierarchies," he advocated a mixed-model democratic socialism featuring "a socio-economic arrangement with markets, price mechanisms, and induced (not directed) labor force, a free press, formal political rights, and a constitutionally based legal order with special protections of the marginalized." In structural terms that entailed an economy with five major sections:

1   state-owned industries of basic producer goods (electricity networks, oil and petrochemical companies, financial institutions);

2   independent, self-managed, socialized public enterprises;
3   cooperative enterprises controlling their own property;
4   small private businesses; and
5   self-employed individuals.[100]

Harrington argued that the future, inevitably, would be collective; the question was whether the collectivism of the future would be democratic or authoritarian. West, joining Harrington in lecture tours for DSA, found himself adopting Harrington's signature theme. Centralization was as inescapable in modern society as the market, he argued; the struggle was to democratize collective structures. In 1986 West put it programmatically: "The crucial question is how are various forms of centralization, hierarchy, and markets regulated – that is, to what extent can democratic mechanisms yield public accountability of limited centralization, meritorious hierarchy, and a mixture of planned, socialized, and private enterprises in the market along with indispensable democratic political institutions?"[101]

Elsewhere he put it more plainly, noting that for Harrington the choice was not between the bureaucratic collectivism of command economies and the "free enterprise" competition of capitalism: "Rather, the basic choice in the future will be between a democratic, or 'bottom-up' socialization, and corporate, or 'top-down,' socialization." The point for Harrington, and eventually for West, was to broaden the participation of citizens in the economic, political, and cultural dimensions of the social order so that they would "thus control the conditions of their existence." By the end of the 1980s West believed that Harrington's focus on democratizing the process of investment was exactly right and even that his democratic socialism was inspiring, "indeed visionary." On the other hand, West still preferred revolutionary Councilism and he found Harrington ironically lacking at the cultural level. Despite having begun his career as a chronicler of American poverty, in *The Other America*, Harrington's later work fixed doggedly on structural economic analysis, social theory, and political strategy. He lived too far above the everyday, grasping, vacuous, nihilistic, television-watching, sometimes violent culture of ordinary consumers to write about it. Harrington was eloquent about the structural injustices of capitalism, but he passed over its equally devastating operations on the cultural level.[102]

That was never true of West, who emphasized cultural criticism. West wrote about popular music, television, sexuality, identity politics, black culture, white supremacism, the culture of nihilism, and the cultural limitations of progressive organizations dominated by whites. For DSA he wrote a pamphlet on racism, "Toward a Socialist Theory of Racism," that the organization featured for over 20 years. Most socialist theorizing about racism, he argued, focused on the Afro-American experience from a Marxist perspective, of which there were four main types. The first viewed racism as an epiphenomenon of the class struggle, subsuming racial injustice under the general rubric of working-class exploitation. Eugene Debs, an icon of this approach, had a simple answer to the question of what socialism offered blacks: "Nothing, except socialism." Debs took it for granted that racism was a divide-and-conquer ruse of the ruling class. To him, a socialist revolution was the only solution to racial injustice and all other social evils; any solution outside the labor framework was racism in reverse. West acknowledged that Debs, having fought racism bravely, was an honorable example of the color-blind strategy; nonetheless, socialist reductionism was not the answer, since it ignored the complexity of the problem.[103]

The second approach, usually taken by the socialist wing of the union movement, stuck to the class exploitation thesis while acknowledging that blacks were subjected to a second dose of exploitation through workplace discrimination and exclusion. This acknowledgment of racism as "super-exploitation" marked an improvement on Debs-style color-blindness, West allowed, but it still limited the struggle against racial injustice to the workplace.

The third approach was the "Black Nation" thesis propounded by the Garveyite movement of the 1920s, the American Communist Party, various Leninist organizations, and a variety of black nationalist organizations and individuals including, most recently, James Forman. Contending that blacks constituted an oppressed nation within the United States, proponents usually cited Joseph Stalin's definition of a nation in *Marxism and the National Question* (1913): "A historically constituted, stable community of people formed on the basis of a common language, territory, economic life and psychological make-up manifested in a common culture." In the case of Marcus Garvey, the Black Nation thesis led to a powerful "back to Africa" movement. West commended the Garveyite and Communist traditions for taking the cultural dimension of the freedom struggle more seriously than other socialist approaches; in this respect, most black nationalists were "proto-Gramscians." But as theory it was shot through with ahistorical special pleading, and as practice it was backward looking, if not reactionary.[104]

The fourth socialist approach, identified chiefly with W. E. B. Du Bois and neo-Marxist Oliver Cox, arose as an alternative to the Black Nation thesis. It argued that racism was a product of class exploitation and of xenophobic attitudes not reducible to class exploitation. For Du Bois and Cox, West explained, racism had a life of its own, depending on psychological factors and cultural practices that were not necessarily or directly caused by structural economic injustices. Du Bois and Cox had the right project, West argued; they pointed to the capitalist role in modern racism while stressing psychological and cultural aspects of the problem. The contemporary struggle against racism needed to move further in that direction, stressing that the roots of racism lay in conflicts between the civilizations of Europe, Africa, Asia, and Latin America before modern capitalism arose, while retaining the Marxist emphasis on class exploitation. Moreover, all four of the dominant Marxist approaches operated largely or exclusively on the macrostructural level, concentrating on the dynamics of racism within and between social institutions. But a full-orbed theory of racism also had to deal with the genealogy of racism, the ideological dimensions of racism, and microinstitutional factors.[105]

In other words, the best socialist theory of racism would be Gramscian, stressing culture and ideology, while extending beyond Gramsci's particular formulations. It would assume that cultural practices of racism had a reality of their own that did not reduce to class exploitation; that cultural practices were the medium through which selves were produced; and that cultural practices were shaped and bounded by civilizations, including the modes of production of civilizations. It would offer a genealogical account of the ideology of racism, examining the modes of European domination of non-European peoples. It would analyze the microinstitutional mechanisms that sustained white supremacism, highlighting the various forms of Euro-centric dominance. And it would provide a macrostructural analysis of the exploitation and oppression of non-European peoples, tracking the variety and relationships between the various types of oppression.

That was a project for theorists of a scholarly bent, a title that West declined. He was an intellectual freedom fighter, not a scholar, theologian, or professional philosopher, he explained. For 20 years he averaged over 150 lectures per year, speaking to academic and non-academic audiences on his broad range of topics. To social activists he often waxed on the cultural limitations of progressive organizations dominated by whites. DSA was, for him, a primary case in point. Since African Americans and other people of color usually perceived progressive white organizations as racially and culturally alien, West observed, they did not join them, which ensnared these organizations in a vicious circle. Even when white progressives made serious attempts to diversify, they failed because of their geographical and cultural remoteness from the everyday lives of people unlike themselves. This failure desensitized white organizations to the necessity of struggling against white supremacism, further widening the cultural gap between people of color and white activists.

West urged that the only way to break this vicious circle was for progressive organizations to privilege the issues of people of color, taking the liberationist option of siding with the excluded and oppressed. Strategies based on white guilt were paralyzing, both psychologically and politically, while strategies based on making white organizations more attractive to racial minorities had little effectiveness. The answer was for activist organizations and progressive religious communities to make a commitment of will to the specific struggles of people of color. It was pointless for progressive organizations to pursue diversity campaigns if they did not make the struggle against white supremacism their highest priority, he argued. There had to be a transformation of consciousness, one that was practical, convinced of the priority of racial justice, and not overburdened with useless guilt: "What is needed is more widespread participation by predominantly white democratic socialist organizations in antiracist struggles – whether those struggles be for the political, economic, and cultural empowerment of Latinos, blacks, Asians, and North Americans or anti-imperialist struggles against U.S. support for oppressive regimes in South Africa, Chile, the Philippines, and the occupied West Bank."[106]

In liberation theology, West explained, this transformation of consciousness was called "conscientization." It occurred only through an act of commitment that brought about a new awareness of marginalization, exclusion, or oppression from the perspective of those victimized by it. Only by taking the liberationist option would white activists comprehend or sustain their awareness of the crucial importance of struggling against racism in all its forms. Bonds of trust across racial lines would be forged only within contexts of struggle in which white activists privileged the concerns of people of color. West cautioned:

> This interracial interaction guarantees neither love nor friendship. Yet it can yield more understanding and the realization of two overlapping goals – democratic socialism and antiracism. While engaging in antiracist struggles, democratic socialists can also enter into a dialogue on the power relationships and misconceptions that often emerge in multiracial movements for social justice in a racist society. Honest and trusting coalition work can help socialists unlearn Eurocentrism in a self-critical manner and can also demystify the motivations of white progressives in the movement for social justice.[107]

West's involvement with DSA evoked a range of reactions that he encountered weekly on the lecture trail. White liberals blanched that he limited his effectiveness by identifying so explicitly with a socialist organization. Conservatives Red-baited him for it. Black nationalists heaped scorn on him for doing so. Radicals of various kinds chided him for hanging out with social democrats. West replied, "I've got to be organized with some group." Socialism alone would never eradicate racism, and anti-racist struggle was fundamental to any progressive politics worth pursuing: "Yet a democratic socialist society is the best hope for alleviating and minimizing racism, particularly institutional forms of racism." He chose DSA because it was multiracial, multi-tendency, and comprehensive, standing for racial justice, economic democracy, feminism, environmentalism, and anti-imperialism: "We need the groups highlighting connection and linkage in a time of balkanization and polarization and fragmentation. There's got to be some group that does this."[108]

In his early career he shared the black radical and conventional Left assumption that Martin Luther King Jr was, at best, "a grand example of integrity and sacrifice," and not much more. Malcolm X was the more inspiring figure: "Malcolm X's voice was as fresh as ever. We were all convinced that Malcolm X would hold *our* position and have *our* politics if he were alive." In the 1970s King was not someone to be claimed for the road ahead, West recalled, "King was for us the Great Man who died for us – but not yet the voice we had to listen to, question, learn from and build on."[109]

That began to change in the 1980s as West, Cone, David Garrow, and others played up King's socialism and anti-imperialism. West rediscovered in King an exemplar of most of the things he cared about:

> King's thought remains a challenge to us principally in that he accented the anticolonial, anti-imperialist, and antiracist consequences of taking seriously the American ideals of democracy, freedom, and equality. He never forgot that America was born out of revolutionary revolt and subversive rebellion against British colonialism and imperialism and that while much of white America viewed the country as the promised land, black slaves saw it as Egypt; that just as Europe's poor huddled masses were attracted to America, the largest black mass movement (led by Marcus Garvey) was set on leaving America! Through his prophetic Christian lens, King saw just how far America had swerved away from its own revolutionary past.[110]

In 1986, speaking at a King symposium at the US Capitol, West disavowed the conventional underestimation of King, observing that he embodied "the best of American Christianity." King was an exemplary organic intellectual, nonviolent resister, prophet, and egalitarian internationalist, West told listeners, declaring,

> As an organic intellectual, he exemplifies the best of the life of the mind involved in public affairs; as a proponent of nonviolent resistance he holds out the only slim hope for social sanity in a violence-ridden world; as an American prophet he commands the respect even of those who opposed him; and as an egalitarian internationalist he inspires all oppressed peoples around the world who struggle for democracy, freedom, and equality.[111]

In 1984 West moved to Yale Divinity School, where he won a joint appointment in American Studies, took part in campus protests for a clerical union and divestment from apartheid in South Africa, and was arrested and jailed. As punishment for his jailing the university cancelled his leave for spring 1987, forcing him to spend the semester commuting between Yale and the University of Paris. The following year he returned to Union Seminary, but in 1988 he moved to Princeton University as

Professor of Religion and Director of Afro-American Studies. Princeton asked what it would take to get him; West replied that it would take a serious commitment to build a premier black studies program. He gave six years to building one centered on novelist Toni Morrison, then moved to Harvard in 1994 to join its black studies program, with a joint appointment at the Divinity School; literary theorist Henry Louis Gates, Jr, the architect of Harvard's program, famously called it the "Dream Team" of black studies.

West's renown in the academy ascended with each of these moves. Fundamentally he was a liberationist critic, but to the extent that he hung his reputation on familiar academic categories he did so as a religious/philosophical proponent of "prophetic pragmatism." His chief academic work, *The American Evasion of Philosophy* (1989), argued that the task of a revolutionary intellectual was to develop a counternarrative to the hegemonic texts and narrative of the prevailing order. In the US American context, he contended, the best resources for this project were the pragmatist, Marxist, and Christian intellectual traditions. West prized pragmatism as the distinctive American contribution to Western philosophy; more importantly, it underwrote historicist social criticism pressing toward social transformation.

In West's rendering of the American pragmatic tradition, Peirce was the founder and methodologist, concerned chiefly with the pragmatic rendering of clear and distinct ideas; James was an Emersonian moralist preoccupied with the powers and anxieties of individuals; and Dewey was the theorist of pragmatic historical consciousness and creative democracy. Following Rorty, West embraced a historicist neo-pragmatism that rejected all reductionist claims to objective knowledge. Unlike Rorty, however, West was religious, and unlike Gramsci, who took religion seriously only for political reasons, West's political reasons were trumped by existential concerns. He explained that the central narratives of the Bible and the insights of Christian thought into "the crises and traumas of life" were indispensable for his sanity. Christian narrative and insight held at bay, for him "the sheer absurdity so evident in life, without erasing or eliding the tragedy of life." As a pragmatist, he focused on transient and provisional matters, not believing in extra-historical justifications or in defending faith with rational arguments. Yet as a Christian pragmatist his hope transcended the transient matters. Logical consistency mattered, West allowed; however, in the realm of faith, the ultimate issue was life or death, not the risk of logical inconsistency.[112]

At the level of practical politics, where solidarity with the oppressed was at issue, it also helped to be religious. West allowed that one did not have to be religious to appreciate how oppressed people coped with their situation, "but if one is religious, one has wider access into their life-worlds." Similarly, he was a pragmatist without claiming that one had to be such to be effective. Some of his favorite thinkers were pragmatists, especially Du Bois, Gramsci, Dewey, James, Reinhold Niebuhr, sociologist C. Wright Mills, literary critic Lionel Trilling, and political philosopher Roberto M. Unger. But some of the greatest modern prophets had no truck with pragmatism: King, Rauschenbusch, Sojourner Truth, Elizabeth Cady Stanton, and Dorothy Day. That didn't matter, West held; what mattered was to struggle against oppression everywhere: "Prophetic pragmatism worships at no ideological altars. It condemns oppression anywhere and everywhere, be it the brutal butchery of third-world dictators, the regimentation and repression of peoples in the Soviet Union and Soviet-bloc countries, or the racism, patriarchy, homophobia, and economic injustice in the first-world capitalist nations."[113]

For all of his success, and to some degree because of it, despair was a real option for West. He wrote constantly about "keeping faith" and "sustaining hope" partly as an admonition to himself. In 1993, the year before he moved to Harvard, he published two books that differently registered his deepening gloom about US American culture and democracy, the condition of black America, and his deepening unease about both. One of these books, *Keeping Faith: Philosophy and Race in America*, collected his recent articles on pragmatism, Marxism, racial justice, and progressive politics. The other book, *Race Matters*, launched him into the realm of American public celebrity just as he began to talk about taking leave of the USA.

Keeping Faith disclosed that West felt increasingly exiled from the black community and despairing about American society. To be a black American intellectual was to be caught "between an insolent American society and an insouciant black community," he lamented. White America as a whole was not willing to learn much of anything from people of color, while black America took little interest in the life of the mind. Thus, "the African American who takes seriously the life of the mind inhabits an isolated and insulated world." West cautioned that the problem was objective, not something that anyone could avoid with sufficient sincerity or skill. Because America was racist, and because there was no African-American intellectual tradition to support black intellectuals, the ones that came along were condemned to "dangling status." Black America had only two organic intellectual traditions, he explained: musical performance and black church preaching. Both were oral, improvisational, histrionic, and rooted in black life. Both traditions contained canons for assessing performance and models of past achievement. The intellectual field had no comparisons. West allowed that black America managed to produce a few remarkable intellectuals – Du Bois, Baldwin, Zora Neale Hurston, E. Franklin Frazier, and Ralph Ellison – but they were exceptions, and did not compare to the best black preachers and musicians. The only great black American intellectual thus far was novelist Toni Morrison. Aside from the handful of exceptions, black American intellectuals either capitulated to the white academy or catered to the "cathartic provincialism" of a black community that had no use for real intellectuals.[114]

This dreary picture was getting worse West warned: "As we approach the last few years of this century, black literate intellectual activity has declined in both quantity and quality." Integration merely integrated black youths into decaying public high schools, bureaucratized universities, and "dull middlebrow colleges" that cared nothing about developing black intellectuals. More broadly, West found it "depressing and debilitating" to realize that race still mattered tremendously in virtually every sphere of US American life. The "decline and decay in American life" seemed irreversible to him, making him grateful for his refuge in Addis Ababa, Ethiopia, the homeland of his wife Elleni Gebre Amlak. West reported that he was strongly tempted to make Ethiopia his home, not merely a refuge: "Not since the 1920s have so many black folk been disappointed and disillusioned with America. I partake of this black zeitgeist; I share these sentiments. Yet I try to muster all that is within me, including my rich African and American traditions, to keep faith in the struggle for human dignity and existential democracy."[115]

With the same mixture of gloom and willful hope he wrote a cry from the heart for the trade market, *Race Matters*, that made him famous far beyond the academy. Many of West's new readers must have expected a sermon on the evils of white racism – instead he barely mentioned it, spending much of the book showing how the "decline and decay in American life" applied to black America. West took a hard line on what he called "nihilism in black America" and the shortcomings of contemporary black leaders. America as a whole shared the problem of nihilism, he assured readers, but it applied with a special vengeance to black America. Two sentences in the book's introduction prepared readers for the jeremiad that followed: "We have created rootless, dangling people with little link to the supportive networks – family, friends, school – that sustain some sense of purpose in life . . . Post-modern culture is more and more a market culture dominated by gangster mentalities and self-destructive wantonness."[116]

Capitalist culture bombarded its youthful consumers with titillating images designed to stimulate self-preoccupation, materialism, and antisocial attitudes, West contended; moreover, most American children lacked adequate parental guidance: "Most of our children – neglected by overburdened parents and bombarded by the market values of profit-hungry corporations – are ill-equipped to live lives of spiritual and cultural quality." In a word, postmodern capitalist culture was deeply nihilistic. Philosophically, nihilism was the doctrine that there are no credible grounds for truth statements or standards; at the street level, it was the experience of "horrifying meaninglessness, hopelessness, and (most important) lovelessness." In West's telling, the culture of nihilism was especially toxic in poor black urban neighborhoods. It was the "major enemy of black survival in America," more destructive than oppression or exploitation. The black American struggle against nihilistic despair was hardly new, he acknowledged. It was as old as the slave ships and auction blocks that ripped apart black families and condemned blacks to chattel servitude. Yet as recently as the early 1970s, black Americans had had the lowest suicide rate in the USA. A generation later, young black Americans had the highest rate. What had changed? What accounted for "this shattering of black civil society"?[117]

West was not sure how much to blame the bitter ironies of racial integration or the collapse of black optimism after the King years had passed. He was more certain about two factors: "I believe that two significant reasons why the threat is more powerful now than ever before are the saturation of market forces and market moralities in black life and the present crisis in black leadership." The flood of violence and sexual titillation that poured through the culture industries of television, radio, video, and music was disastrous for black America, he argued. All Americans were influenced and degraded by the decadence of the media, which bombarded them constantly with images of depravity. The black underclass, however, facing special threats to its survival in the first place, was especially vulnerable to being damaged by it: "The predominance of this way of life among those living in poverty-ridden conditions, with a limited capacity to ward off self-contempt and self-hatred, results in the possible triumph of the nihilistic threat in black America."[118]

More than ever, West argued, black America needed compelling black leaders; unfortunately, contemporary black leaders were grasping and morally unimpressive: "The present-day black middle class is not simply different than its predecessors – it is more deficient and, to put it strongly, more decadent. For the most part, the dominant outlooks and life-styles of today's black middle class discourage the development of high quality political and intellectual leaders." In fact, the worst aspects of America's general cultural decadence were "accentuated among black middle-class Americans."[119]

The great black leaders of the past carried themselves with moral dignity, West explained. They wore suits and white shirts, conveyed a serious moral purpose, treated ordinary blacks with humble respect, and projected a bold, gut-level anger at the condition of black America. "In stark contrast, most present-day black political leaders appear too hungry for status to be angry, too eager for acceptance to be bold, too self-invested in advancement to be defiant." On occasion they took a stab at prophetic speech, but that was "more performance than personal, more play-acting than heart-felt." Like other new entrants to the middle-class culture of consumption, they were obsessed with status and addicted to self-gratification. Instead of raging against "the gross deterioration of personal, familial, and communal relations among African-Americans," they looked away from it, knowing they were poorly suited to condemn it.[120]

Contemporary black political leaders sorted into three types, West argued: race-effacing managers, race-identifying protest leaders, and race-transcending prophets. The first type, epitomized by Los Angeles mayor Thomas Bradley, relied on political savvy and personal diplomacy to claim a place at the establishment table. The second type confined their attention to "black turf" and assiduously protected their hold over it. West cited Nation of Islam leader Louis Farrakhan as an extreme example, but also assigned black nationalists and most leaders of the civil rights organizations to the second category. The third type was the ideal, which stood boldly for racial justice while transcending race as a category of personal identity and collective loyalty. Harlem civil rights leader Adam Clayton Powell, Jr was one; more recently, Harold Washington, Chicago's mayor in the mid-1980s, was another; Jesse Jackson tried to be one in his 1988 presidential race, but never quite overcame his opportunist past; West judged that his own generation had yet to produce one.

Black intellectuals sorted into similar types, by his account: race-distancing elitists, race-embracing rebels, and race-transcending prophets. The first type, impressed by their own cultivation and accomplishments, held themselves above other blacks; West cited the "mean-spirited" cultural critic Adolph Reed, Jr as an example. The second type rebelled against the snobbish insularity of the white academy by creating a black-space version of it headed by themselves; West put most Afrocentrists in this category. The ideal, the race-transcending prophets, courageously fused the life of the mind with the struggle for justice without paying heed to social standing, career advancement, or intel-lectual fashions. West's exemplar was James Baldwin; neo-Marxist social critic Oliver Cox also qualified; on the contemporary scene, only Toni Morrison deserved to be called a race-transcending prophetic intellectual. West stressed the negative: "This vacuum continues to aggravate the crisis of black leadership – and the plight of the wretched of the earth deteriorates."[121]

Anticipating the charge that he was too harsh, ungenerous, or opportunistically playing to a white audience, West admonished, "The crisis in black leadership can be remedied only if we candidly confront its existence." He was not calling for a Messiah figure to replace Malcolm or King, for that was not the point, and there were always problems with messiah figures anyway. Malcolm said nothing about "the vicious role of priestly versions of Islam in the modern world," and King was sexist and homo-phobic. West did not even believe that the answer was to build an organization dedi-cated to race-transcending prophetic politics, although he still hoped to see one emerge. What really mattered was to develop "new models of leadership and forge the kind of persons to actualize these models." Black America needed race-transcending prophets who raged for racial justice and social justice for all: "To be a serious black leader is to be a race-transcending prophet who critiques the powers that be (including the black component of the Establishment) and who puts forward a vision of fundamental social change for all who suffer from socially induced misery."[122]

Race Matters brought West such a crush of national and international publicity that he moaned to friends about the ravages of over-exposure. The book's paperback edition of 1994 was adorned with gushing reviews from major media outlets. *Newsday* called it "exciting," "illuminating," and filled with "profound and unsettling thoughts." *The New York Times* applauded its "ferocious moral vision and astute intellect." *Newsweek*, describing West as "an eloquent prophet with attitude," enthused that his book was "devoted to kicking butt and naming names." In a single sentence that placed West in the highest company imaginable, the *Washington Post Book World* declared that his book was as moving as any of King's sermons, as profound as Du Bois's *The Souls of Black Folk*, and as exhilarating as Baldwin's early work. *Time*, in a quotable estimate that somehow did not make the book's cover, declared,

> Cornel West is one complex dude: brilliant scholar, political activist, committed Christian and soul brother down to the bone. At 40 he has become one of the most insightful and passionate analysts of America's racial dilemma to emerge in recent years, the architect of a post-civil rights philosophy of black liberation that is beginning to be heard across the country.[123]

From there West climbed to higher levels of public renown, attaining fixture status in the mass media through countless profiles, interviews, and guest appearances while confining his writing, for nearly a decade, to coauthored books on topical themes. He seemed to be too busy to write them on his own. A book that he coauthored with liberal rabbi Michael Lerner, *Jews & Blacks: Let the Healing Begin* (1995), which called for a new alliance between progressive Jews and blacks, got a whopping $100,000 advance. A book that he coauthored with Harvard economist Sylvia Ann Hewlett, *The War Against Parents: What We Can Do For America's Beleaguered Moms and Dads* (1998), made a trade-market pitch for liberal economic and social policies while urging parents to strengthen their marital commitments. Meanwhile West appeared regularly on C-SPAN and other television networks, commented weekly on Tavis Smiley's National Public Radio program, served as a senior advisor to presidential candidate Bill Bradley in the 2000 Democratic primaries, campaigned for Ralph Nader in the 2000 presidential election, supported Al Sharpton's brief presidential bid in 2004, cut two rap CDs, *Sketches of My Culture* (2001, Artemis) and *Street Knowledge* (2004, Roc Diamond), and played the role of Councilor West, a member of the Council of Zion, in two of the *Matrix* movies, *The Matrix Reloaded* and *The Matrix Revolutions*.[124]

He obviously enjoyed being famous, yet West was mindful of its perils. He was wary of being corrupted by adulation and enrichment. He winced at the obvious conflict between social justice militancy and celebrity success. And he understood that the more famous he became, the more *he* became the subject instead of anything that he said. Often he became an object of jealousy or resentment. Having stressed the shortcomings of others on his way up, West got a stream of tart responses in reviews and on the lecture circuit. Sometimes it happened during the introduction of the speaker, after he had put himself out to speak at somebody's conference or group; often it happened in the discussion period after a lecture. Black nationalists and black radicals charged that he sold out his race; in 1993 the African United Front tagged West as an "Uncle Tom," claimed that he was "far more favorable to Jews than to Blacks," and protested that he never presented "the Black side" of the conflict between American blacks and Jews. On the Right, where West's blistering critiques of white supremacism were noticed, he was often charged with epitomizing the radicalization and corruption of the academy. Meanwhile the hazards of his fame were noted by figures closer to him. One of his friends told *Time* magazine that part of West really wanted to be "the next H.N.I.C. [Head Negro in Charge, a satiric acronym with a long history]. It's not just white folks holding him up." James Cone told the same reporter that his friend's celebrity was spiritually perilous: "One of the best ways to destroy someone is to expose and promote him. It's very hard to be critical of a system that makes a hero out of you."[125]

Friendly reviewers more or less in West's intellectual orbit mixed critical jabs with the compliments. African-American studies scholar Randal Jelks, in the *Christian Century*, considered *Race Matters* an effective "popularization of West's thought," but protested that West was too gloomy, showed no sense of humor, and put a misleading title on the book; *Race Matters*, the title, smacked of racial essentialism. Womanist theologian Delores Williams, in *Theology Today*, lauded West's "brilliant analysis" before criticizing his claim to speak the truth to power with love. It was one thing for King to talk about loving white people into repentance, Williams admonished, but King had millions of supporters to back up his challenge to white supremacy. Who was West, and what did he have, to compare with that? And if West really cared about ordinary people, why were his writings loaded with Latin terms and academic jargon?[126]

Friends and foes alike questioned the quality of West's scholarship. Stanley Aronowitz, one of his closest friends and collaborators, was fond of saying in the 1990s that West's scholarship had not started yet. *Time* magazine echoed a common complaint that his writings were vague and utopian. In 1995 *New Republic* literary editor Leon Wieseltier put it much worse, declaring that West's work was "noisy, tedious, slippery . . . sectarian, humorless, pedantic and self endeared." In Wieseltier's telling, West did not make arguments, he merely declaimed. He was not a philosopher, but merely cobbled together snatches of philosophies. West's eccentricity was surpassed only by his vanity, which was enormous, Wieseltier opined. His books were monuments "to the devastation of a mind by the squalls of theory." In sum, in a quote immortalized by repeated citation: "They are almost completely worthless."[127]

This attack was delivered by a prominent neoliberal in the flagship journal of neoliberal politics. Its parade of mean-spirited exaggerations made West more vulnerable to attacks not deriving from the political Right, usually without citation. It also inspired and fueled ferocious ridicule from the Right, where Wieseltier was nearly always cited gleefully. Conservative activist David Horowitz offered a typical rendering. In 1999, reviewing the *Cornel West Reader*, Horowitz invoked Wieseltier's charges, added a few of his own about West's "intellectual superficiality" and "blasts of hot air," and condemned West's friendships with Sharpton and Louis Farrakhan. In the 1990s West had cultivated friendships with Farrakhan and other black nationalist leaders in an attempt to build bridges between them and other groups. He was especially concerned about the hostility between black nationalists and Jews. To Horowitz, that was the key to West's eminent stature: his oxymoronic capacity to pose simultaneously as a racial healer and a "bedfellow of racial extremists." West got away with it, Horowitz contended, only because no one took him seriously – "He is the quintessential non-threatening radical, an African American who can wave the bloody shirt to orchestrate the heartstrings of white guilt, while coming to dinner at the Harvard faculty club and acting as a gentleman host."[128]

Horowitz's right-wing activism was beyond the pale for anyone in West's intellectual orbit. However, many of West's usual allies concurred that he took his mission of racial reconciliation a step too far in courting influence with Farrakhan. In his early writings West condemned Farrakhan's characterization of Judaism as a "gutter religion" as "despicable." Later he spoke more guardedly about the "underdog resentment and envy" that fueled black anti-Semitism, and in 1995 he supported Farrakhan's Million Man March. Trading on his public prominence, West told black nationalists that overcoming white supremacism was something they could not do by themselves. He urged Farrakhan to repudiate anti-Semitism and acknowledge the equal humanity of all persons. Michael Lerner, discussing with West the possibilities of reconciliation between blacks and Jews, drew the line at Farrakhan, calling him a "racist dog." West replied characteristically, "I wouldn't call the brother a racist dog but a xenophobic spokesperson when it comes to dealing with Jewish humanity."[129]

If racial healing was to extend beyond the ranks of liberals, the humanity of persons on all sides of the conflict had to be acknowledged as a first principle. Stepping straight into the crossfire between black nationalists and Jews, West urged friends on both sides to stop the vicious cycle of vituperation, realizing that he risked his reputation and his efficacy as a racial healer by doing so. Ironically, he took his greatest risk during the same period in which he received a barrage of criticism for selling out.

Conservative magazines regularly complained that only conservatives and a smattering of (usually Jewish) neoliberals like Wieseltier had the nerve to criticize Cornel West. That was a plausible impression if one relied on television and conservative magazines for information. In the academy and political Left, however, criticizing West was a favorite pastime. Many scholars blasted him for blaming the victim in his critique of black nihilism. Cultural critic Nick De Genova protested that West sounded "like the classic example of a colonized elite, trapped in an existential condition of self-hatred and shame because he has come to view his own people as undignified, indecent, backward, and uncouth." Social critic Eric Lott similarly ripped West for coming perilously close to denying the humanity of poor blacks; Lott contended that West's entire "lexicon of urban savagery" was disastrously wrongheaded, frightening, and reactionary, as well as unsupported by evidence.[130]

Political scientist Floyd W. Hayes III, black studies scholars Lewis Gordon and Peniel E. Joseph, and philosophers Charles Mills and Clevis Headley concurred that West's critique of Afro-nihilism was hard to distinguish from blame-the-victim conservatism. Hayes protested that instead of stressing the ravages of white supremacism and capitalist exploitation, West recycled the old "culture of poverty" elitism that blamed "impoverished Black Folk for their own predicament and for being unable to rid themselves of it." Gordon added that West underestimated Du Bois and denigrated the black Marxist tradition, especially C. L. R. James and Walter Rodney. Joseph put it more hotly, blasting West for his "victim-blaming and excoriation of contemporary Black leadership." West's account of black intellectualism rested on a method of "demonization and invocation," Joseph argued. He lifted Toni Morrison above all others by invocation, with no argument, put down everyone else, and did not bother even to mention the radical black humanist tradition of Angela Davis, Huey Newton, Fred Hampton, and Vicki Garvin.[131]

Headley admonished that West's evasion of philosophy was literal and not something to be proud of. West never developed a serious argument, Headley contended, he merely patched together "various rhetorics of liberation for the purpose of building progressive coalitions." In Headley's judgment, West's writings amounted, at best, to "an impressive collage of political slogans" that infused pragmatism with his magnetic personality: "He substitutes intellectual seduction in place of rational persuasion." Adding to the objections of Hayes, Gordon, Joseph, Mills, and Headley that West spent much of his breakthrough book blaming blacks for their nihilism, feminist theorist Iris M. Young protested that West and Hewlett stooped to a similar antifeminism in their critique of American family life. It was offensive enough when conservatives made alarmist statements about the downfall of marriage, Young contended, "but coming from supposed progressives, they are frightening! Privileging marriage and genetic ties of parenting in this way is heterosexist and insulting to adoptive parents, and wrongfully supports continued stigmatization of single mothers."[132]

Philosopher John Pittman chided West for conjuring a pragmatic ethical Karl Marx remarkably like Cornel West. Philosopher George Yancy worried that West relied too heavily on religion, which in his case rested on a terribly thin crypto-fideism. Since West's claims for religion were merely pragmatic and historicist, how could much of a religion come from that? Comparative literature scholar Nada Elia advised West to stop complaining about feeling exiled. For one thing, he exaggerated his suffering; for another, to the extent that he was truly marginalized, he was free to do the work of criticism that radical intellectuals were supposed to do. Political philosopher Lucius Turner Outlaw, Jr suggested, disapprovingly, that West criticized Du Bois for failing to deal with major European thinkers because West wanted to lift himself above Du Bois.[133]

West endured the attacks from the Right with as little response as possible. There was little to be gained by defending himself from ridicule or by debating with people with whom he shared nothing. He engaged his other critics wholeheartedly, without noting the irony of the personal offense that his writings of the early 1990s caused. No one was more generous with praise or charitable affection than West. He wrote effusive blurbs for dozens of fellow authors, constantly praised colleagues as the "greatest" this or that, and routinely greeted acquaintances as long-missed sisters and brothers. Often he explained that public intellectualism and original scholarship were different things. Contrary to Aronowitz's implication, West had no plans for a scholarly phase. The Gramscian task of engaging the dominant culture from a left-intellectual standpoint was vocation enough for him.

On most points of criticism he was a model of respectful engagement, though West made an exception for the charge that he blamed the victim in *Race Matters*. To him, this charge was a "bizarre," "sophomoric," and "leftist knee-jerk" myth that somehow survived his many writings on white racism, a response that ignored the point of his critics that *Race Matters* vastly outsold his other writings. As for the black intellectual tradition, he respected it greatly, but not to the point of indulging Gordon's filiopiety. Du Bois produced outstanding work in historical sociology, West acknowledged; on the other hand, Du Bois was a Victorian elitist and Enlightenment rationalist who did not compare intellectually to the great musical geniuses of black America. Moreover, most of the black Marxists extolled by Gordon were Leninists. As for Joseph's charge that West dismissed black nationalism, West replied, "ludicrous." *Prophesy Deliverance!* lauded the black nationalist tradition, and West's comradely friendships with black nationalist leader Maulana Karenga, Afrocentric theorist Molefi Asante, and "the beloved Minister Louis Farrakhan" were matters of public record. He added that his $10,000 contribution to the Black Radical Congress surely said something about his respect for black nationalism; to Joseph he appealed, "please do more homework."[134]

To academic critics of his improvisational style, he gave short shrift. West told Headley that obviously he did not share Headley's devotion to philosophical professionalism, cognitive models, formal analysis, and the positivist distinction between reason and emotion. Thus it was not surprising that Headley and others like him did not comprehend West's intellectual style, though West wished they would recognize its legitimacy. To Young he replied that it should be possible to defend the progressive possibilities of heterosexual marriage from a feminist and egalitarian standpoint without being accused of bigotry against gays, lesbians, and single parents. Repeating a central argument of his book on the family, West contended that children did best when raised by two biological parents who were married to each other. The empirical evidence on this point was terribly clear, and important, he urged. To set progressivism against it was disastrous for progressivism and for children: "We make it clear that this does not stigmatize single mothers and fathers, disqualify loving gay or lesbian parents, or preclude successful adoption of children." He took no interest in bolstering discrimination against gay or lesbian parents. Progressivism had to be against that, just as it had to "put a premium on the well-being of children."[135]

To Pittman he replied that every insightful interpretation of Marx had background premises. Georg Lukacs described a neo-Hegelian Marx, Alexandre Kojeve described a Heideggerian Marx, and Louis Althusser described a structuralist Marx. It would have been odd if ethical pragmatist West had not played up the ethical aspects of Marx's thought. To Yancy he acknowledged that he tended to be silent about the philosophic and religious "more" beyond utility and politics. To pursue the more was to lapse into metaphysics or onto-theology, which he eschewed. That did not make him a pragmatic reductionist, West cautioned. He treasured the irreducible mystery of being and emphasized the tragicomic "funk" of living, suffering, struggling, and dying. West prized Anton Chekhov above all thinkers, often calling himself a "Chekhovian Christian." To him, Chekhov was the greatest literary artist of the modern age because he was "the pre-eminent poet of the funk of life, its tragicomic darkness, mystery, and incongruity, with a blues conclusion: keep lovin' and fightin' for justice anyway, i.e., regardless of the situation." Chekhov inveighed against evil while spurning the aid of religion; as a Chekhovian Christian, West held to a "blues-ridden gospel" of resistance to evil that trusted in the possibility of divine goodness: "Ours is in the trying – the rest is not our business."[136]

To Elia he replied that he reveled in his marginality from the Black community and American culture while feeling estranged from neither. To Outlaw he denied that he was driven by his considerable "notoriety" or even his ambivalence about it to place himself above Du Bois. West criticized Du Bois only because Du Bois deserved it, not to make himself number one: "My Chekhovian Christian voice simply cuts deeper and thereby is more truthful than Du Bois's Goethean Enlightenment view that undergirded his marvelous scholarship."[137]

Repeatedly, realizing that being exalted made him a target, West admonished friendly critics not to judge him by an inflated standard of expectation. In particular he asked them not to imagine that he aimed "to save American civilization or achieve greatness owing to white recognition." He did not expect to be remembered as a historic figure, and he doubted there was a "Westian" ideology or position. Intellectually, he was someone who looked at the world through various lenses, not a grand theorist. He was keenly aware that his prominence had much to do with having come along at the right moment: "My sheer level of privilege and scope of exposure is unprecedented."[138]

West's immense good will and generous spirit helped him get on with academics who thought they better deserved to be famous. By 1999, when he annotated and published *The Cornel West Reader*, he was long practiced at explaining that he rejected the narrowly academic view of academic work. He believed that the academy needed to address audiences and topics outside the academy, a view that he featured prominently in the reader. In 2001, however, he acquired a president at Harvard who had a narrow idea of what a Harvard professor should be and an amazingly obtuse understanding of West's value to the university.

West had never met Harvard's new president, economist Lawrence Summers, before being summoned to a fateful meeting with him in October 2001. Though Summers had not read West's books, he had strong opinions about them that closely resembled the Wieseltier genre of ridicule. He blasted West for producing a rap CD that embarrassed Harvard, reproached him for missing classes to campaign for Bradley, opined that "no one in his right mind" could have supported Sharpton, admonished him to write a major scholarly work that established him as a real academic, chastised him for giving too many A grades to students, and exhorted West to start writing the kind of books that academic journals would review. In other words, West needed to legitimize his appointment as a distinguished university professor. Summers proposed to have regular meetings with West to monitor his progress. In reality, West had not missed any classes while campaigning for Bradley or anyone else, one of his courses had an enrollment of 700 students, and he had already written a scholarly tome, *The American Evasion of Philosophy*, and published a collection of academic essays, *Keeping Faith*.[139]

Feeling attacked and insulted, West decided to resign quietly from Harvard and return to Princeton. It seemed pointless to fight with Summers, nor did he relish the prospect of a media spectacle. For two months he refused to speak to reporters about the rumored episode, but the story exploded into a page one spectacle anyway. As West later recalled, the dominant story line was of a principled president "upholding standards and refusing to give in to an undeserving and greedy professor." Though many Harvard students defended West, *The Harvard Crimson*, a student newspaper, fed the press frenzy by recycling Wieseltier's polemic and mocking West's purported vanity and hypocrisy. Recalling his attack on the hedonism of the black middle class, the paper found a contradiction "between West's prophetic contempt for material gain and his exquisitely tailored suits, comfortably tenured lifestyle, lucrative speaking gigs and fancy cars." Fareed Zakaria piled on in *Newsweek*, recycling Wieseltier's litany yet again; *Newsweek* readers were assured that "noisy, self-endeared, completely worthless" and all the rest had been on target and still were. *The New Republic* added that West was the epitome of the contemporary mutation of the public intellectual: a celebrity master of public relations. Brilliantly packaging himself as a brand, the magazine explained, West kept himself in the news and choreographed his controversy with Harvard. Instead of producing serious scholarship, he offered "tossed-off books, rap CDs, and shallow public disputes over the respect due to him."[140]

The Summers episode set up West for a media bashing far beyond his collective past experience, a point West made vividly in his second meeting with Summers. By then Summers realized that the media controversy was bad for Harvard and his presidency; he thanked West for not playing the race card. West replied that in the USA "the whole deck was full of race cards," but there were additional issues at stake. He would have welcomed a serious exchange about academic freedom and the public responsibilities of the academy. As it was, he found himself pilloried in the media, because Summers "had authorized every xenophobic and conservative or neoliberal newspaper writer in the country to unleash pent-up hostility toward me." In West's telling, Summers apologized to him for setting off a damaging "misunderstanding," then told a reporter he had not apologized, then told West the reporter misquoted him. West, after learning otherwise from the reporter, blasted Summers on the Tavis Smiley Show as "the Ariel Sharon of American higher education," an arrogant bully unsuited for his position. That set off another media explosion, this time featuring the charge that West had to be anti-Semitic for linking Harvard's first Jewish president with Sharon. West later recalled ruefully that most of his Harvard colleagues sat back and said nothing while he was roasted in the media, which showed the typical "spine-lessness in the academy." Undergoing surgery for cancer, he waited for the controversy to burn itself out and returned to Princeton.[141]

To West the entire episode was pathetic and damaging. He later reflected that it should have been possible for him to disagree with Summers "without being subjected to slightly veiled threats and overt disrespect." Harvard was supposed to stand for academic freedom. Having sought to facilitate greater mutual respect between American blacks and Jews, West regretted the symbolism of having clashed with Summers. Above all, he regretted that for all of his fame as a public intellectual, the controversy offered a chastening warning to others who shared his belief in the necessity of academic engagement with popular culture. In a sequel to *Race Matters* titled *Democracy Matters* (2004), he put it with a slightly defiant edge:

> As one who is deeply committed to the deep democratic tradition in America and to engaging youth culture, I have no intention of cutting back on my academic and outreach activities, because the effort to shatter the sleepwalking of youths who are shut out of the intellectual excitement and opportunity of the academy is such a vital one for our democracy.[142]

Race Matters was about the social ravages of white supremacy, West remarked; *Democracy Matters* was about the degradation of American democracy in the age of American empire. Writing against the background of the Bush administration's imperial disaster in Iraq, but also implicitly reflecting his vigorous opposition to Al Gore in the 2000 presidential election, West declared: "The rise of an ugly imperialism has been aided by an unholy alliance of the plutocratic elites and the Christian Right, and also by a massive disaffection of so many voters who see too little difference between two corrupted parties, with blacks being taken for granted by the Democrats, and with the deep disaffection of youth." Since the Republican and Democratic parties were both owned by corporate money and interests, choosing between them was like choosing between "the left-wing and right-wing versions of the Dred Scott decision."[143]

Three dogmas of modern American life played the leading roles in degrading American democracy, he contended. Capitalist fundamentalism (the glorification of unfettered markets and market rationality) cast aside the public good while delivering the world to the corporations. Aggressive militarism (the pursuit of global military empire) imposed the will of American elites on other nations. Escalating authoritarianism (the diminishment of individual rights) betrayed hard-won liberties in the name of national security. Taken together, West argued, "we are experiencing the sad American imperial devouring of American democracy," which amounted to "an unprecedented gangsterization of America."[144]

In West's view, the Republican party was myopically mendacious in promoting capitalist fundamentalism, aggressive militarism, and authoritarianism, while the Democratic party was pathetically spineless in promoting weaker versions of the same thing.

"The saturation of market forces in American life generates a market morality that undermines a sense of meaning and larger purpose," he wrote. Capitalist fundamentalism reduced all values to market value, pitting government institutions against each other in a race to the bottom that shredded social safety nets and corrupted societies "all the way up." Worst of all, 15 years after the end of the Cold War, America was more deeply and pervasively militaristic than ever.[145]

Nihilism in America was a two-sided coin, West observed. On one side it was the despair of worthlessness and believing in nothing that afflicted Americans of all races and classes, which was especially devastating in poor communities. On the other side it was the ruthless abuse of power that nihilistic elites waged on a daily basis, which also fell heaviest on America's most vulnerable communities: "Political nihilism now sets the tone for public discourse, and market moralities now dictate the landscape of a stifled American democracy." For West the administration of George W. Bush was the showcase example, serving up fear and greed, tax cuts for the rich, and imperialism:

> A political nihilist is one who is not simply intoxicated with the exercise of power but also obsessed with stifling any criticism of that exercise of power. He will use clever arguments to rationalize his will to power and deploy skillful strategies, denying the pain and suffering he may cause, in order to shape the world and control history in light of the pursuit of power.[146]

In theory, the Democratic party existed to "fight the plutocracy," exacting concessions from the corporate class that benefited the majority. In fact, West lamented, contemporary Democratic leaders fell woefully short of Franklin Roosevelt and even Lyndon Johnson. At least Johnson recognized and cared that poor whites and most blacks had the same fundamental interests. By contrast, current Democrats like John Kerry and Hillary Clinton were "paternalistic nihilists," slick professionals who spoke blandly for democracy with no heart-felt rage at the injustices of the system.[147]

West had a version of American exceptionalism that contrasted with America's self-congratulatory versions. The American democratic experiment was unique only in the sense that most Americans refused to acknowledge "the deeply racist and imperial roots of our democratic project," he argued; "no other democratic nation revels so blatantly in such self-deceptive innocence, such self-paralyzing reluctance to confront the nightmare of its own history." Despite having grown huge and powerful, American civilization refused to grow up. It was stuck in an adolescent refusal to face painful truths about itself, which made America unable to negotiate tempting options that were bad for itself and others. West put it bluntly: "Race has always been the crucial litmus test for such maturity in America. To acknowledge the deeply racist and imperial roots of our democratic project is anti-American only if one holds to a childish belief that America is pure and pristine, or if one opts for self-destructive nihilistic rationalizations."[148]

Though he was often accused of selling out racial justice to further his own celebrity, or of imagining that he was the only "race-transcending prophet" of his time, West was emphatic that ignoring or minimizing the matter of race would not make anything better. There were many issues to address in struggling for social justice, he urged, but race was nearly always intertwined with them: "Niggerization in America has always been the test case for examining the nihilistic threats to America. For so long niggerization has been viewed as marginal and optimism central to America. But in our time, when we push race to the margins we imperil all of us, not just peoples of color."[149]

Democracy Matters received his usual mix of praise and brickbats. *The Village Voice* lauded West as "a thinker of dazzling erudition, whose critiques are inevitably balanced by an infectious optimism and magnanimity of spirit." *The Seattle Times* called him "a compelling and sought-after deep thinker in a nation weaned on five-second sound bites." Womanist ethicist Cheryl Sanders enthused in the *Christian Century* that the book was an inspiration and blessing to her: "What I love about his new book, *Democracy Matters*, is how deeply motivated and illuminated I felt when thinking through his formulation of democratic solutions to the problem of American imperialism." *Daily Princetonian* arts writer Hamid Khanbhai lauded West as "a polemicist with all the pizzazz of a passionate gospel preacher," though he worried about West's eagerness to implant democracy in the Middle East. Historian Daniel Levine, writing in *America*, commended West's politics, but criticized his "platitudinous" style, "outright banality," and "sloppy thinking." *New Criterion* reviewer Mark Bauerlein, upholding a conservative tradition, recycled Wieseltier yet again before asserting that West's latest book was no better. West never reasoned his way to conclusions or even appealed to empirical evidence, Bauerlein complained; he simply made charges and declared things with overheated language. In Bauerlein's judgment, *Democracy Matters* showed what happened when an intellectual was hailed by the mass media, "courted by rival universities, and invited, interviewed, and idolized without end. The process is fatal to the scholarly intelligence."[150]

As a writer West sometimes did not get through; the torrential riffs that made him a sensational speaker often did not sing as well on the page. Many of his reviewers would have done better, however, had they acknowledged that they did not know what to make of someone who glided effortlessly from Matthew Arnold to C. L. R. James to Socrates to John Coltrane to Kierkegaard to Michel Foucault to Toni Morrison to Dostoyevsky to Alain Badiou to Jay-Z and Outkast, finding juxtapositions that only he would have perceived. There was simply no one to compare to West, until his protégé Michael Eric Dyson made a similar splash. West enthralled lecture audiences like no other intellectual of his time, taught in prisons, wrote about hip-hop, and recorded CDs that sought to convey the greatness of the black tradition to youths who would not have touched his books. Most reviewers who chastised him lacked even a fraction of his intellectual range. Somehow, reviewers who knew nothing of postcolonial theory knew that his use of it was worthless because he spurned academic conventions.

On the Right, the need to disparage West was an ideological necessity; for many others, the jealousy factor played a role; in addition, his dramatic expansiveness made him easy to caricature. He persistently overdressed in informal contexts while criticizing other black intellectuals for wearing "shabby" clothes. Sometimes a serious point became lost in his maze of allusions. *In These Times* writer Salim Muwakkil noted that there was "something excessive about him." But in a generation that produced excessive wailing about the decline of public intellectualism, the lack of engagement between the academy and public, and the loss of a progressive Christian voice in the public square, Cornel West was the towering exception. He made himself a target for criticism by achieving what others claimed was no longer possible.[151]

He never really changed, notwithstanding the Left critics who liked his early writings and claimed that he sold out later. From the beginning West was committed to a Christian liberationist vision of social justice and reconciliation, though some readers wrongly took his early writings to be Marxism dressed up as Christian thought. West was not "really" a Marxist who used Christianity; it was more the other way around. He began as a liberationist social critic committed to building progressive multiracial coalitions and he remained one. He moved easily among groups that had little in common with each other and that sometimes could not stand each other: *Monthly Review* Marxists, postmodern deconstructionists, black nationalists, civil rights leaders, anti-imperialist activists, conservative and liberal academics, DSA social democrats, black church pastors and congregants, churchgoing white Protestants and Catholics.

But West was not satisfied with bringing together likeminded progressives from different backgrounds. He worked at the boundaries of his wide-ranging social existence, struggling, above all, to bring black nationalists and black radicals into dialogue and solidarity work with white progressives. West realized that he jeopardized his favored standing with white progressives and some black civil rights leaders by cultivating bonds of trust with Farrakhan and the Nation of Islam. That he took the risk was typical of him. "The tensions between blacks and Jews are so volatile and our national discourse regarding difficult issues is so stunted that thoughtful dialogue is nearly impossible," he lamented. By playing close to the edge of the field, he jeopardized his capacity to be a racial healer. For West, however, the spiritual principle at issue trumped the questionable politics of the situation. The love ethic of Christianity compelled him to appeal to the humanity of anti-Semitic black nationalists just as it compelled him to look for it in the racist beneficiaries of white supremacism.[152]

Political theorist Rosemary Cowan, in a discerning interpretation of West's thought, rightly characterized him as fundamentally a Christian liberationist. But Cowan called his approach "the politics of redemption," missing West's reticence about salvation language. The social gospel had a theology of social salvation, as did black liberation theology. West was more chastened, treading lightly in the area of theology and refusing to speak of redemption as anything that human beings had any part in effecting. He believed in rendering service, and in "trying to alleviate and attenuate the hell that we are catching," but cautioned that only God can redeem. In a similar spirit of emphasizing real-world survival and toning down the liberationist language of eschatological deliverance, black feminists launched their own tradition of liberation theology and ethics.[153]

Union Seminary was known for its prominent black scholars and female scholars, but during West's years there it had none that were both. In that environment Katie G. Cannon pondered what a black feminist ethic would be. The key to her answer appeared in 1983, when Alice Walker published *In Search of Our Mothers' Gardens: Womanist Prose*.[154]

Womanist Ethics: Katie Geneva Cannon

Katie G. Cannon was the first African-American woman to earn a doctorate at Union Theological Seminary and the first African-American woman to be ordained in the United Presbyterian Church, USA. In her early career she taught at Episcopal Divinity School in Cambridge, Massachusetts; later she taught at Temple University in Philadelphia; later, moving closer to home, she taught at Union Theological Seminary and Presbyterian School of Christian Education in Richmond, Virginia. Born and raised in Kannapolis, North Carolina, she came to Presbyterianism by family heritage, came to her "firsts" through an urgent desire to grow beyond her roots, and came to her mature spiritual perspective by reclaiming her Southern, poor, extended family heritage.

In Kannapolis, a segregated rural town near Charlotte where the Ku Klux Klan was an oppressive force, Cannon began at an early age to plot her escape. Her mother, Corine Lytle Cannon, worked as a domestic; her father, Esau Cannon, was a truck driver; in addition to their seven children, the Cannons lived among large groups of relatives. Corine Cannon was the nineteenth of 20 children, each of whom had at least seven children, and her husband's family was almost as large. The slave tradition dichotomy between house servants and field hands was a palpable reality to them. The Lytle family was churchly, literate, and inclined to look down on the field laboring, hard partying, less religious types from which Esau Cannon came. The Lytles lamented that Corine married beneath herself, while the Cannons regretted that Corine was dark skinned. Cannon later recalled that she knew little of her father, however, because her mother claimed him exclusively: "That was her man. 'He's mine, get your own man,' she'd say. We were appendages to their marriage; we could never come between them."[155]

Elsewhere she recalled with slight exaggeration, "We all live there . . . We dominate the place . . . There are thousands of us." Cannon coped with the sprawling chaos of her family situation, which included many alcoholic relatives, by embracing the rules of school and church, finding comfort in institutional structures. "I liked the rules," she remarked of her early attraction to school, which extended to church: "I was overendowed with Christianity. This was linked with education." In her world, black women worked as domestics or teachers; later they were also allowed to work in the mills. Cannon aspired to be a teacher, but also fantasized about saving blacks from self-destructive behavior. For most of her youth she judged that blacks were poor and backward because they were promiscuous: "I figured this whole thing out – the curse of blackness had to do with SEX . . . We drink, we party, we dance, we have children out of wedlock – all of this animalistic behavior – no wonder we are enslaved."[156]

If that was the problem, salvation was deliverance from licentiousness. Cannon resolved to be a missionary, perhaps a nun: "The energy needed to be controlled . . . I'd go to Africa . . . I'd save us!" In high school, however, she discovered to her astonishment that white youths got drunk and formicated just like her black classmates: "That is when I became a militant." If whites behaved the same way with no apparent social consequences, there had to be another reason why blacks suffered "so brutally." Cannon's remembrance of November 22, 1963 was, for her, a telling marker of the difference. On the day that President John Kennedy was assassinated, Cannon was a ninth grader at George Washington Carver High School. "It was a *comical* day at Carver," she recalled. Her civics class, watching the television coverage of Kennedy being whisked to a Dallas hospital emergency room, laughed at the attempts of "these white people to . . . do this resurrection thing on Kennedy." Cannon and her classmates were not candidates for the great national grieving over Kennedy: "Our lives were worth nothing to these white people. In ninth grade, we were already working on organically critiquing society. We knew the country was evil and violent. None of us really mourned Kennedy's death." Social criticism had begun to trump moralistic reproach.[157]

Five years later she was a first-year student at Barber-Scotia College (a liberal arts college seven miles from her home) when Martin Luther King Jr was assassinated. Infuriated at the government, Cannon and her classmates took it for granted that King was killed by a conspiracy, not a lone assassin: "Naivete has never been our privilege." Swiftly she converted to Black Power radicalism: "I had on my dashiki. I had my Black Power fist dangling from my neck . . . It was like a transfusion of blackness. I was high on it. I *loved* it." She consumed Black Power literature, but fell into depression and had a second transforming experience as a college intern at Ghost Ranch in Sante Fe, New Mexico, a Presbyterian retreat. Luxuriating in the beauty of the ranch's 23,000 acres, Cannon became physically active for the first time in her life, met friendly white people for the first time, and realized that getting out of Kannapolis was a genuine possibility for her: "The ranch is what gave me hope . . . It opened up the horizon and pushed it toward the sun."[158]

During her college years Cannon was recruited by James Costen, a Presbyterian minister and president of Johnson C. Smith Seminary in Atlanta, to study for the ministry. Cannon had never known a female pastor; Costen helped her imagine herself as one. Enrolling at Interdenominational Theological Center in Atlanta, she discovered a ministerial vocation, majored in Old Testament, and undertook an archaeological dig in Israel, which bruised her enthusiasm for the land of the Bible. The Israelis she met were virulently racist, hurling epithets at her that she had never heard directly in the USA. Stunned at the bigotry she encountered, Cannon felt intensely lonely, driven to the wilderness: "You know, you give up your slave experience and depend upon God." She returned to seminary still wanting to study Hebrew scripture, though with conflicted feelings.[159]

Her next academic stop was the doctoral program at Union Theological Seminary in New York, where Cannon eventually, painfully relinquished her ambition to be a biblical scholar. Her searing experience in Israel had been hurtful and alienating, but not too humiliating to overcome. Her first encounter with the white academy was thoroughly humiliating. Enrolling at Union in 1974, Cannon felt completely out of place. To her, Union was impossibly arid, erudite, white, and elitist. Even the black students seemed unreal to her. At Interdenominational Theological Center the free-wheeling, high-spirited unpretentiousness of black culture had prevailed; at Union, Cannon's awkward attempts to deflate scholarly decorum elicited eye-rolling embarrassment and disapproval: "All I was trying to do was cut through the bullshit. I'd come from all-black schools, and whenever anybody was talking this highfalutin kind of stuff, people would say, 'Come on, let's be real. Be real!'" Union Seminary did not confirm her sense of what was real, nor indulge her aversion to abstract theory; it only made her feel loud and frivolous. At ITC she had been the gatekeeper of student study groups, deciding who got in: "I had *controlled* them. I dominated." At Union students shunned her, excluding her from study groups. Moreover, the Hebrew Bible division at Union was noted for its air of academic seriousness. "It's only by grace that I didn't crack," Cannon later recalled. "I mean, suddenly the ground was opening up and I was falling down into the descent into Hell."[160]

It did not help that she felt guilty about being there, supported by scholarships that exceeded the combined incomes of her parents. Cannon anguished over the contradictions between her privileges and the hard-pressed lives of her parents and relatives. Often her mother told her that if she really hated Union so much, she could return to Kannapolis and work in the mill. Otherwise, Corine Cannon exhorted, "You must do it for all of us!" Failing to win a mentor in Hebrew Bible, Cannon switched reluctantly to social ethics, where she found mentors in Roger Shinn and Beverly Harrison.[161]

An East Side therapist helped Cannon realize that she was too traumatized by white people to see any differences between them: "I would say, 'All white people,' and she would say, 'Well, wait a minute, Katie. Not *all* white people.' Our work together helped me start to make sense out of this big ball of whiteness that was scaring the hell out of me." White society was a menacing world to her; Union's culture of academic whiteness seemed doubly menacing. Cannon had to learn "to make the white world more liveable." The white feminism of her therapist helped Cannon make the transition. To Cannon's surprise, the feminist rhetoric of individual freedom and equal rights for women struck chords of recognition. Warming up to feminism, she loosened her exclusive identity with blackness. Cannon's black male classmates, by disliking her dramatic persona and challenging her right to ordination, caused further loosening. She responded by joining the seminary's Women's Caucus, becoming, in her telling, "an honorary white person." On the one hand, it troubled and perplexed her to find her primary community of support among white women; on the other hand, at least they respected her right to be at Union: "I had been trained all my life to deal with race and white supremacy . . . but nobody had conscientized me in terms of what it meant to be born a female, a black female."[162]

The writings of Zora Neale Hurston and Alice Walker helped Cannon find her social ethical bearings on what it meant to be a black female. In 1983 Walker provided the concept of "womanism," which Cannon called "the new gatekeeper in my land of counterpain." Meanwhile Cannon's doctoral dissertation featured Hurston's life and work. The dissertation came first, in 1983, but its book version had a Walkeresque title, *Black Womanist Ethics* (1988).[163]

Walker offered a four-part definition of a womanist. First, she was a serious, morally responsible adult, as in the black folk expression of mothers to female children, "You acting womanish." A womanist was a black feminist or feminist of color; the term was also interchangeable with the folk expression, "You trying to be grown." Second, a womanist loved other women, "sexually and/or unsexually," preferred women's culture and the personal qualities of women, and sometimes loved individual men. She was committed to survival and the wholeness of people, and was not a separatist, "except periodically, for health." Third, a womanist loved music, dancing, the moon, the Spirit, love, food, roundness, struggle, and herself. Lastly, Walker wrote, "Womanist is to feminist as purple to lavender."[164]

Walker's previous writings, especially *The Color Purple*, were already important to Cannon and other black women who had recently entered the theological field. Then Walker offered "womanism," which for Cannon was "philosophically medicinal." It named the elements and contours of her black, female, Southern, spiritual, overcoming sensibility, expressing her preference for the company and folkways of black women. For many black women who entered the American Academy of Religion and the Society of Biblical Literature in the 1980s and 1990s, the idea of womanism was personally and collectively definitive. Cannon was the first to explain it as a type of theological ethics.[165]

African-American women needed and possessed distinctive virtues, she argued. White Americans prized self-reliance, frugality, and industry, and white ethicists provided philosophical and religious reasons for doing so, because these virtues worked for whites, facilitating their success. But they did not work for black Americans, Cannon argued. To subscribe to white values was to legitimate the power that whites held over blacks, thereby worsening black humiliation. In racist America, the game was rigged against blacks who tried to acquire finance capital or climb a career ladder. Even when blacks adopted white individualism and frugality, they were put down anyway, which was humiliating, adding to the "evidence" of their supposed inferiority. Cannon remarked: "Racism does not allow Black woman and Black men to labor habitually in beneficial work with the hope of saving expenses by avoiding waste so that they can develop a standard of living that is congruent with the American ideal."[166]

Cannon stressed that black women worked for lower wages than men and white women, doing jobs that others refused to do. For them, to embrace work as a prime value was to risk their emotional and physical health. Moreover, the range of their moral agency was severely limited by racism and poverty. White theologians described a self with a wide capacity for moral agency, taking for granted that each person is free and self-determining. The assumption that each person holds self-determining power underwrote the white Christian idea of Christian virtue, which prized the choice of bearing one's cross. White Christian ethics treated voluntary suffering as a moral norm. The virtuous Christian chose to follow Jesus to the cross, making personal sacrifices as a voluntary commitment. The Christian followed Christ by choosing to suffer for the sake of others.

Cannon replied that for blacks, however, suffering was not a choice or a desirable moral norm – it was a repugnant everyday reality to overcome: "The vast majority of Blacks suffer every conceivable form of denigration. Their lives are named, defined and circumscribed by whites." Since black Americans lacked the moral agency and freedom of whites, it was wrong to apply the ethic of voluntary suffering to them. Moreover, it was also obscene, because blacks owed their lack of moral agency and freedom to the oppression they suffered at the hands of whites. For Cannon, black faith and liberation ethics were responses to these conditions, helping blacks "purge themselves of self-hate" and throw off the judgment of an ethic that did not rightly apply to them:

> The ethical values that the Black community has construed for itself are not identical with the body of obligations and duties that Anglo-Protestant American society requires of its members. Nor can the ethical assumptions be the same, as long as powerful whites who control the wealth, the systems and the institutions in this society continue to perpetuate brutality and criminality against Blacks.[167]

Repudiating the myth of black inferiority and the application of white ethical standards to black people, Cannon argued that black folk culture, as described by Walker and Hurston, possessed a distinct ethical character. Womanist ethics began with the experiences of black female survivors, deriving its moral norms from the study of black female culture and experience. *Black Womanist Ethics* did not get to the business of ethical construction, pointing merely to how it might be done. "For too long the Black community's theological and ethical understandings have been written from a decidedly male bias," Cannon declared. Womanist thought was a type of black libera-tionism, but one that privileged the distinctive experiences and moral agency of black women.[168]

Cannon walked a fine line between stressing the objective ravages of racism and denying that black women were emotionally stunted by it. To a degree she lauded Hurston on the latter theme, though Cannon would never say, as Hurston insisted of herself, that she lacked any interest in "the race problem." Hurston famously wrote in 1928, "I am not tragically colored. There is no great sorrow damned up in my soul, nor lurking behind my eyes. I do not mind at all. I do not belong to the sobbing school of negrohood who hold that nature somehow has given them a lowdown dirty deal and whose feelings are hurt about it." Cannon had a different voice, but she loved Hurston's saucy flair and her portraits of complex, psychologically integral black women.[169]

Hurston's characters labored long hours, held families together, danced and partied, had affairs, protected vulnerable black males, and loved and raged at them, all with little sense of being defeated or victimized. Since Hurston did not experience black people or herself as humiliated or degraded, she did not portray blacks in that way. Subtly refuting the white supremacist slander of black inferiority, she portrayed emotionally healthy characters who did not think of themselves as a "problem" and gave almost no thought or time to white people. Adopting critic Mary Burgher's description of black female novelists as a whole, Cannon praised Hurston for showing that black women turned their lost innocence into "invisible dignity," sustained a "quiet grace" despite being refused the possibility of feminine delicacy, and converted their unchosen responsibilities into "unshouted courage."[170]

For Hurston, as for black women generally, Cannon argued, suffering was an everyday reality, not something to be prized as a moral value. Virtue was not about experiencing suffering, or even enduring it. To be virtuous was to sustain a robust, self-respecting, feisty affirmation of one's life and life itself. Borrowing a term favored by Walker, Cannon noted that Hurston was long on "unctuousness," the virtue of taking the good and bad together in the same stride; Hurston called it "soaking up urine and perfume with the same indifference."[171]

The invisible dignity of black women enabled them to maintain self-respect despite being treated as the "mules of the world." Their quiet grace enabled them to persist against forces that denied their humanity. Their unshouted courage enabled them to calibrate the effects of human wills besides their own and to accept accountability for occurrences beyond their control. In all this persisting and resisting, Cannon stressed, black women acquired a wily sense of the relativity of truth, using whatever means they found to hold off the threat of violence and death: "For Black people the moral element of courage is annexed with the will to live and the dread of greater perpetrations of evil acts against them."[172]

Cannon allowed that Hurston ended badly, lapsing into reactionary politics and isolation in her last years. But her finest work offered the best depiction of the folk wisdom of black women: "Across the boundaries of her own experience, Hurston wrote about the oppressive and unbearable, about those things that rub Black women raw. Her richness and chaos, her merits and faults witnessed to an ethic that can be lived out only in community."[173]

Cannon was fond of Hurston's self-description, that she tried "to hit a straight lick with a crooked stick." Cannon wrote womanist ethics in the same manner. On the one hand, as a Christian social ethicist, she spoke to and about "the universality of the human condition," transcending her blackness and femaleness. On the other hand, as a womanist liberation ethicist, her blackness and femaleness were very much in play; womanist liberation was determinately situated, deconstructive, and perspectival: "In other words, my role is to speak as 'one of the canonical boys' and as 'the non-canonical other' at one and the same time." Canonical notions about ethical scholarship had "nothing to do with the realities of Black women," she judged. To qualify for membership in the scholarly guild of Christian ethicists, one had to demonstrate proficiency in abstract theory, philosophy, and the classical canon of ethical texts and problems. Cannon put it ruefully: "To prove that she is sufficiently intelligent, the Black woman as Christian ethicist must discount the particularities of her lived experiences and instead focus on the validity of generalizable external analytical data."[174]

The dilemma was obvious and perplexing. If she spoke the canonical language of abstraction and Euro-American concerns, she risked betraying black women. But if she spoke as a pure liberationist, she risked being devalued by the guild as "a second-class scholar specializing in Jim Crow subject matter." It was one thing to include black women in the field, Cannon observed; it was a further thing to recognize black women's moral reasoning as an important aspect of the field. Both ideas were new, but the field resisted the second more than the first. The experience of black women was routinely ignored, even in black theology. On the rare occasions when black women were mentioned, their moral agency was hardly ever respected or accurately described.[175]

Cannon conceived womanist ethics as a corrective enterprise that worked within and outside the guild, interpreting traditional paradigms from the perspectives of the black, female noncanonical other. As a critical enterprise, womanist ethics pointed to the silencing and denigration of black women, including the sexist content of black male preaching; as a constructive enterprise, it described the genius of black women in creatively shaping their destinies. "The womanist scholar stresses the role of emotional, intuitive knowledge in the collective life of the people," studying the consciousness of black women as reflected in their literature and institutions.[176]

The womanist alternative for which Cannon called in the 1980s was already a blooming garden by the end of the decade. When Cannon started seminary in the early 1970s, the total number of African-American women enrolled in a seminary doctoral program was one. By 1990 womanist theology and ethics was a rising movement led by Cannon, M. Shawn Copeland, Jacquelyn Grant, Cheryl A. Kirk-Duggan, Cheryl Townsend Gilkes, Clarice Martin, Marcia Riggs, Cheryl Sanders, Emilie Townes, and Delores S. Williams. Cannon remarked of their road to academic recognition,

> Even with the requisite credentials for matriculation in hand, we were constantly barraged with arrogance and insults, suspicion and insensitivity, backhand compliments and tongue-in-cheek naivete. The worlds of divinity school, denominational headquarters, regional adjudicatory offices, and local parishes, between which we negotiated, demanded different and often wrenching allegiances. But we continued to study, struggling for our rightful places in the church and in the academy.[177]

As the womanist community grew in size and productivity, Cannon defended her inside–outside concept of womanist method from criticism. Cheryl Sanders, in 1989, enthused that womanist scholars relied on their own experience and sources. Womanist scholarship focused commendably on black women and womanist scholars, Sanders observed; in fact, nearly all the footnotes in womanist scholarship cited the writings of black women. To Sanders, that showed that most womanists were free of self-hatred, needing no approval from outside authority figures: "To see black women embracing and engaging our material is a celebration in itself."[178]

Cannon took that as a direct challenge. Unlike many womanists, she observed, her writings often cited white scholars, especially Harrison and Elisabeth Schüssler

Fiorenza. Did that make her a self-hater? Worse yet, "Did it make me a fraud?" Cannon exhorted womanists to avert the path of exclusion and insularity. If womanism was to remain a liberationist discourse that supported the emancipation of "a whole people," it could not cut itself off from white feminist thought. The same thing was true of its relation to black theology, though Cannon mentioned only feminism: "As one of the senior womanist ethicists, I am issuing advance warning to new womanist scholars, both actual and potential, that Sanders's devaluation of credibility consequent on such a conservative framework of Black-sources-only encourages guesswork, blank spots, and time-consuming busy work, the reinvention of the proverbial wheel over and over again." Womanism would not flourish as an intellectual or spiritual departure if it imposed purity tests on the sources that womanists could cite. Cannon urged womanists to take the long view, and an open one: "Staying open-minded as heterogeneous theoreticians may prove to be the most difficult ethical challenge in securing and extending the legacy of our intellectual life."[179]

In her early career she wearied of being told to choose between blackness and womanhood; later she tried not to be defensive when a postmodernized generation resisted her essentialism; in both cases she protested against being marginalized in the academy. Being black was no more and no less important to her than being female, Cannon asserted. Womanism was the refusal to make this false choice. Womanist ethics refused to surrender to either/or dichotomies that spurned the necessary, difficult, messy work of appropriation and reciprocity. Attending always to the interrelationships of race, gender, and class, it drew on the "rugged endurance of Black folks in America" to fulfill new possibilities of human flourishing. Cannon protested that after 20 years of womanism, the academy was just as rife with "androcentric, heteropatriarchal, malestream, white supremacist culture" as ever: "From 1983 until now, storms of opposition, bigotry and suspicion mount." The mere legitimacy of the womanist enterprise had to be defended daily from academics who "experience our very presence as colleagues as a cruel joke." Thus the existence of the womanist tradition was not something to be taken for granted, she cautioned.[180]

As for postmodernism, Cannon respected the fact that young black feminist scholars often found womanism to be too essentialist in its stress on "blackness" and too identified with Southern folk wisdom to speak for them. If black women who came of age in the 1990s favored hip-hop, an iconographic aesthetic, and hybrid identities, Cannon would not tell them they had a moral obligation to be womanists. Womanism was a "self-naming sensibility," not something handed down by coercion, she assured them. On the other hand she cringed at the term "post-womanist," asking young scholars not to spurn 20 years of labor:

> Those of us who have been busy doing womanist work from the moment that we enrolled in seminary believe we have built a solid womanist foundation. We officially began constructing this womanist house of wisdom in 1985, and as intellectual laborers we continue to work day in and day out so that our scholarly infrastructure is built on solid rock instead of shifting sand.

It was a serious thing to erase the liberationist work of previous generations, she cautioned. If womanism seemed too stodgy and smacked too much of 1970s polemics, that could be fixed; it did not have to be stuck in the 1970s or 1980s. The womanist house of wisdom was an ongoing project: "The real challenge before us is not to become 'post-womanist' but to investigate feasible ways to actualize the definition of *womanism."* The idea of building on the wisdom of ordinary black women could not be wrong and was not outdated, she believed. It was the ultimate example of taking liberation theology seriously in a North American context.[181]

Taking Postmodernity Seriously: Victor Anderson

Cannon doubted that the postmodern animus against essentialism was really much of an advance, but she respected that it resonated with many younger scholars. Cornel West spoke to the latter feeling in his lectures on postmodernity and race-transcending prophecy. In the social-ethics field the leading proponent of postmodern anti-essentialism as an approach to race, gender, sexuality, and cultural criticism was West's former student Victor Anderson, a Vanderbilt ethicist of Cannon's generation.

Born in 1955 and raised in conservative Baptist evangelicalism, Anderson made his way to religious naturalism, pragmatic anti-essentialism, and gay rights activism without letting go of a theological center. He was educated at Trinity Christian College in Chicago, from where he graduated in 1982, and served as an associate pastor of a Baptist church before and during his college years. His next stop was Calvin Theological Seminary in Grand Rapids, Michigan, where he earned two master's degrees, won the Calvin College Minority Faculty Recruitment Fellowship for Graduate Studies, taught for two years at Calvin College, and ministered to a Christian Reformed church. In 1988, a year before he resigned his ordination, Anderson took his Calvin College fellowship to Princeton University, where he studied under Jeffrey Stout, Cornel West, Malcolm Diamond, and Victor Preller, won an Andrew Mellon scholarship, took a one-year exchange fellowship to Yale University, and became a pragmatist. He completed his doctorate in 1992 with a dissertation on the pragmatism of D. C. Macintosh, H. Richard Niebuhr, and James M. Gustafson that formed the basis of his second book. Joining the faculty of Vanderbilt University, where he taught religious ethics at the divinity school and African-American studies at the college of arts and sciences, Anderson established primary teaching and research interests in modern American theology, American empiricism and pragmatism, black theology, cultural criticism, social ethics, and sexual ethics. He was also deeply involved in community education concerning HIV/AIDS.[182]

At Princeton he caught the high tide of the postmodern renewal of American pragmatism. (Former) Princeton philosopher Richard Rorty was the prophet of the new pragmatism. In *Philosophy and the Mirror of Nature* (1979) and *Consequences of Pragmatism* (1982) Rorty rejected the entire Western philosophical quest for secure foundations, advocated a revision of Deweyan pragmatism that dropped Dewey's optimism about human progress, and contended that theology was too enmeshed in Western "Philosophy" (Rorty's term for foundationalism generally) to have a viable future. In his telling the great traditions of philosophy, including the Platonist wellspring of theology, had outlived their usefulness – therefore, so had theology. "Neopragmatism," a postanalytic movement led by Harvard philosopher Hilary Putnam and Rorty's protégés at Princeton, Jeffrey Stout and Cornel West, rejected the positivist dichotomy between facts and values. Stout and West developed neopragmatism into a social philosophy and critique of theology; their student, Anderson, contended that theology needed a strong dose of neopragmatism to regain its academic identity and public relevance.[183]

He began his career, in the spirit of Rorty's Heideggerian critique of Western onto-theology, with a critique of racial essentialism in black theology and black identity politics. Employing a genealogy of Western racial discourse in the manner of French postmodernist Michel Foucault, Anderson's first book, *Beyond Ontological Blackness* (1995), turned the dismantling tools of poststructuralist theory on modern representations of "blackness." The essentialized "blackness" of black theology and identity politics was a mirror image of the colonialist "othering" that gave birth to modern racism in the eighteenth century, he argued. The Enlightenment and post-Enlightenment imperialists mythologized their own world conquering genius, inventing whiteness as a superior category, which gave birth to a reactive defense called blackness.[184]

Anderson called for a pragmatic, postmodern, culturally fluid alternative to black essentialism. Instead of reifying race as though it actually existed independently of historical particularities and subjective intentions, he contended, black intellectuals needed to break free of the totalizing, unresolved, binary dialectics of slavery and freedom, black and white, insider and outsider, and struggle and survival. Like black identity politics as a whole, black theology held back the flourishing of African Americans by treating race as something real, central, and consuming. Anderson favored a "grotesque" Nietzschean subversion of the confining, conformist black cult of the heroic. "When black identities are justified primarily in terms of ontological blackness, too many of the differences that genuinely signify black life and culture recede into the background," he wrote. "Too often the heroically representational qualities of racial genius, the cult of black masculinity, and its often brutal forms of conformity gain ascendancy."[185]

He judged that all three phases of the black theology movement ontologized blackness, practicing forms of "racial apologetics" that fostered a conformist cult of "heroic genius." Cone essentialized the black revolutionary consciousness of the 1960s, climaxing in what Anderson called the "absurd" contention that only black people can share in the black experience. Anderson stressed that Cone was alienated from the "evangelical gospel" of the black churches and that his early work depended on white theologians whom he otherwise condemned. More importantly, by defining blackness as the unitary experience of suffering and rebellion against whiteness, Cone made white racism the ground and necessary condition of blackness. Blackness was created and defined by its enemy, whiteness; there was no black theology or "new black being" without it. Anderson observed, "In this way, black theology renders whiteness identifiable with what is of ultimate concern . . . When race is made total, then ontological blackness is idolatrous."[186]

The second phase of black theology championed by Dwight Hopkins, James H. Evans, Jr, and Peter Paris took an Afrocentric narrative turn, but Anderson judged that it perpetuated the consuming reification of blackness in a milder voice. The movement's third phase, womanism, did the same thing in a different way. Womanist writers Katie Cannon, Delores Williams, and Jacquelyn Grant heralded a tradition of suffering, surviving, "sassy" female figures – "the mirror image of black masculinity" – though Anderson acknowledged that womanists emphasized the complexity of black women's experience and commendably supported gays and lesbians. But the pro-lesbian motif in womanist writing contradicted the womanists' claim to fidelity with black Christian experience, he objected; ironically, that put Anderson on the side of Cheryl Sanders, a prominent critic of womanist pro-lesbianism, against other womanists. On the one hand, he argued, the womanist movement held fast to the "aporias of ontological blackness," upholding "the black faith" as an ideological totality and identity claim. On the other hand, it advocated "transcending openings" regarding sexual orientation. Anderson urged womanists to break free from the victimized consciousness of identity politics:

> If suffering and resistance continue to have a totalizing function in womanist theological discourse as they do in classical black theology and Afrocentric theologies, on what does transcendence depend? At what point do thriving and flourishing enter the equation of suffering and resistance? An existence that is bound existentially only by the dimensions of struggle and resistance or survival, it seems to me, constitutes a less than fulfilling human existence.[187]

The flourishing that all people want should be the point, Anderson contended. The actual oppression of many blacks was trivialized by "the absurdity that anyone who is black is also oppressed." Identifying with West's call for a "race-transcending prophetic criticism," Anderson cited Houston Baker, Jr, Madhu Dubey, Michael Eric Dyson, Henry Louis Gates, Jr, Darlene Clark Hine, bell hooks, Toni Morrison, Adolph L. Reed, and Joe Wood as African-American intellectual allies in this cause. He liked hooks' remark, "We eschew essentialist notions, epistemologies, habits of being, concrete class locations, and radical political commitments." Wood was another favorite of Anderson's, especially for his declaration "I am a multitude of names, masks, community memberships. Denying this is tyranny – 'race' is not my only state . . . I make new communities all the time." Anderson put it bluntly: "Talk about liberation becomes hard to justify where freedom appears as nothing more than defiant self-assertion of a revolutionary racial consciousness that requires for its legitimacy the opposition of white racism . . . The identification of ontological blackness with *ultimate concern* leaves black theology without the hope of cultural transcendence from the blackness that whiteness created."[188]

He did not blame the founders of black theology for adopting an essentialist ideology, but urged the understanding that it was no longer effective toward its best ends. The defining dialectic of race had to be transcended in the direction of the good that is common to all people, the flourishing of every person. Howard Thurman and Martin Luther King, Jr called it the beloved community. Cornel West called it radical democracy. Anderson called it cultural fulfillment. To him the subverting power of the grotesque was more liberating than the usual varieties of radical politics, though he was not apolitical. The aesthetic critique of culture displaced the heroic by the grotesque, breaking the grip of the black church's heterosexist moralism.

Elsewhere he put it more bluntly. Anderson did not attend the Million Man March of October 16, 1995 in Washington, DC, which celebrated the very model of moralistic heroism that he found alienating and oppressive. He described the march as "abominations of a million men." It was repugnant to lionize black manliness, strength, self-determination, and racial loyalty while ignoring the sins of homophobia: "No gay or lesbian representative addressed the crowds, no public affirmation of black homosexual love was commended, and no overt sign of acceptance was shown, except the silence of a million men. That is an abomination." Anderson did not expect black religious leaders to advocate theological justifications of gay and lesbian rights; it was enough to stand for justice and peace, he argued. What was needed was that they recognize the human rights of gays and lesbians. The church had to speak against "the plight of black gays and lesbians who suffer abuse, murder, and alienation within the community that gave them life and regards them as abominations." *Beyond Ontological Blackness* put it more formally, calling for a new cultural politics of difference that showed "how African Americans can *take each other* in public life with aesthetic sensibilities that resist eclipsing individuality under collectivity."[189]

Anderson's first book made a mark in religious and cultural criticism, where its interpretation of black theology was sometimes granted too much authority. Contrary to Anderson, Cone and other black theologians did not straightforwardly ontologize race; they treated blackness and whiteness as cultural tropes. However, Anderson's critique of essentialism and heroic masculinism had a strong basis, and were powerfully rendered. Duke Divinity School ethicist Willie James Jennings called the book a "groundbreaking" analysis that represented "a moment of clarity and adjustment in Afro-American philosophical and religious thought." J. Deotis Roberts protested that Cone was not the sole founder or representative of early black theology – "it was more of a movement than a project" – and that Anderson wrongly portrayed it as a monolith. Still, Roberts was deeply impressed: "Anderson has dealt a devastating blow against classical African-American life and thought. But will he be able to build on the ruins he has heaped on us?" Others suggested that Anderson-style cultural criticism might take black theology in a new direction; Dwight Hopkins, despite being criticized by Anderson, noted that his own work increasingly drew upon the tools of postmodern cultural criticism.[190]

Beyond Ontological Blackness featured Anderson's regulative ideals of cultural fulfillment and transcendence, but gave little hint of his theological position. He reasoned that the goods and ends that contribute to human flourishing are relevant for every field of cultural studies, not merely religion. Thus his critique of black essentialism was not the place for his theology. His next book, *Pragmatic Theology* (1998), put forward his position, followed his teachers, and defied them.

The teacher of Anderson's teachers, Richard Rorty, to the extent that he took notice of theology, opined that it was no longer a relevant form of academic or public discourse. Theology was like metaphysics, he explained, in accounting for human actions in transhistorical terms. Theologians used a priori logic, believed in an order "beyond time and chance," and usually held antidemocratic sentiments. Modern consciousness, however, disarmed theology of its self-justifying pretensions. Theology had no work to do after the world was stripped of its transhistorical meanings; in Rorty's view, pragmatism was the best replacement for it. The secular, historical, practical outlook of pragmatism offered a credible and useful alternative to discourses presuming to answer ultimate questions. By this definition William James was not a model pragmatist, Rorty judged. James betrayed pragmatism by defending the religious hypothesis that the best things are eternal; Rorty explained that James got stuck at the second of Dewey's three stages of religious consciousness, retaining the idea of something non-human that is on the side of human beings.[191]

To Anderson, Rorty's dismissal of theology was too casual to be upsetting. Rorty did not bother to acquaint himself with modern theology before sweeping it aside. Content with his "dispositional hostilities," Rorty appeared not to notice that a good deal of modern theology was pragmatic and naturalistic. Stout's critique of theology was more interesting. For Rorty, theology was too meaningless to be worth opposing; for Stout, theology was still the "other" that secular moral philosophy needed to replace. Stout shared Rorty's general view of the pragmatic displacement of theology, especially that all claims about universal or transhistorical moral truths were fictional reifications of subjective states. But Stout recognized that the old humanist and positivist debunkers of theology were often reactionary, not to mention badly mannered. The new pragmatism had to transcend its oppositional relationship to theology.[192]

On that basis Stout sought dialogues with theological and religious ethicists; on the other hand, he could not find any worth debating with. In his telling, liberals appropriated the themes, catch phrases, and methods of other disciplines and intellectual trends, but they lacked a distinctively theological message. Other theologians spoke with greater religious authority on the basis of a common religious identity, but they made claims that failed the tests of public warrant and relevance. Dogmatists repeated the dogmas of their groups, disdaining the ground rules of public conversation. Unfortunately, no contemporary theologian offered distinctively religious thought that was also publicly relevant and warranted.[193]

Anderson replied that his teacher was more polemical than he presumed. By Stout's rules, theologians were not allowed to play if they did not leave their dogmas behind, but as soon as they took the field they were dismissed for abandoning theology. If they opted for a universal foundation they were hopelessly backward; if they played without foundations they had nothing to say that was not better said by others. Academic theology could not win if disciplinary distinctiveness was the fundamental rule of the game. Anderson observed that Stout identified real theology, normatively, with classical theism and functionally, with the communication of sacred doctrine. But there was no reason to let Jeffrey Stout define what theology was, especially since he had a prejudiced and narrow view of it, just like Rorty. Anderson observed that historically, theology functioned variably as the doctrine of God, the matrix of historical processes directed toward a consummate telos, or the cultural identity of a community. Viewed that way, it was quite possible for theologians to have fruitful conversations with pragmatists. Instead of prizing the distinctiveness of a past orthodoxy, theologians were better advised to pragmatically reconstruct theology.[194]

His model was the early Chicago School of Shailer Mathews, Gerald Birney Smith, and Edward Scribner Ames, which understood that theological languages were social constructions, but which also took its ideas to be constructions of a reality present in experience that facilitated personal and social transformation. As such, the reality that theology studied was sacred. Early Chicago School pragmatism remained the best model for doing public theology, Anderson urged, explaining,

> The Chicago theologians did not see it as their task to duplicate and transmit the inherited materials of doctrine and theology that once shaped American higher learning. They saw an opportunity for a pragmatic theology among the human studies. They saw their task as discovering the vital significance of religious life and disclosing the ways that theological ideas contribute to the advancement of human fulfillment.[195]

For the Chicago School, as for James, Dewey, and Anderson, reality was "the totality of undifferentiated matrices of experience." Human self-consciousness occurs in a socializing process and is based on the awareness of others in experience, Anderson observed. Unlike Rorty and Stout, the founders of pragmatic philosophy and theology did not view incommensurability as the framing issue between pragmatism and theology. For them, theology was a distinctive interpretation of a shared human reality, and the pragmatic test of theology was whether it advanced human understanding and flourishing. Naturalism and supernaturalism were incompatible, but not pragmatism and theology. To Anderson, the early Chicago School got it exactly right, before lapsing into Whiteheadian metaphysics: modern theology needed to be a form of pragmatic secularization, and the "controlling theme" for understanding modern theology was naturalism, not the incommensurability between pragmatism and theology.[196]

Just as pragmatism was compatible with theology, so was naturalism. Moreover, Anderson argued, it was crucial not to equate naturalism with pragmatism, because pragmatism is only one of the critical discourses that are compatible with naturalism. Materialistic naturalists deny that the physical evolutionary processes and necessities of life exhibit any unitary intentions or end; philosophical naturalists ascribe to the evolutionary processes and necessities a formal unity construed as fortune or fate; pragmatic naturalists view reality as thoroughly processive and open to novelty. In place of a world of independent substances known by the correspondence between ideas and external objects, Anderson-style pragmatic naturalism pictured a radically interdependent and changing web of concrete entities. Its keynotes were process, openness, and relationality. It viewed the processes, necessities, values, and meanings of the world as circumscribed by the dynamic interrelation of all things to each other, and was compatible with belief in religious meaning. Pragmatic naturalism interpreted religious symbols primarily in moral and expressive terms, leaving a role for theology as the interpretation of religious experience.[197]

That reduced theology and social ethics to value studies, a strategy that, Anderson recognized, left many readers feeling empty: "Few American theologians have been satisfied with treating theological ideas as if they are only aesthetic or moral in meaning." But the advantages were also considerable, he urged. His approach fit into the critical ethos of the academy, minimizing conflicts between theology and other disciplines. It made room for the explanation, not merely description, of religious experience. It oriented theology and social ethics toward the flourishing of life, underwriting a metaphysic of finitude and transcendence (understood as limits to action and the experience of transformation). Anderson's doctrine of God was an echo of the Chicago School: "God is conceptually disclosed as that structure of experience that gives meaning and value to the whole of experience, because it transcends every particular experience in a unity of experience." Just as reality is the undifferentiated totality of experience, the divine symbolizes the unity of reality; pragmatically, "God" is a symbol for the totality of meaning and value.[198]

Pragmatic naturalism was not yet a movement, Anderson acknowledged, but it had impressive theological advocates, notably James Gustafson and Gordon Kaufman. Gustafson practiced theology as a way of construing the world. Kaufman recovered the theme of mystery for religious naturalism, theorizing the unity of transcendence and finitude. For Anderson, the future of theology and social ethics as credible academic disciplines took that line.[199]

He liked West's description of "prophetic pragmatism," which wedded the social justice ethic of biblical prophecy to philosophical pragmatism. Though Anderson disliked the hero cult of Martin Luther King, Jr, he agreed with West that King and Reinhold Niebuhr were the best exemplars of public theology. Both used theological categories in their critiques of American society, recognized the moral limits of human beings, and struggled to advance the common good. Anderson signed on for all three, despite his poststructuralist affinities; social ethically, he argued, the common good was an indispensable idea. Admittedly, it smacked of ideological totalitarianism, Eurocentric domination, and God. But none of that negated the necessity of a common good, he urged. The conflicted, diverse moral culture of contemporary North American life ought to be common to all: "This is the only moral culture that we have in North America. It is our moral habitat both for philosophical and for theological reflection."[200]

In the face of everyday struggles that gays, lesbians, immigrants, and African Americans endured against prejudice and discrimination, he acknowledged, "common good" talk seemed unreal: "I admit that conflicts between gays and lesbians with the dominant heterosexual mainstream, bilingual advocates versus English only, family values versus homosexual unions, blacks versus white separatists and their paramilitary ideologies all seem to render our democratic form of life fragile, perhaps even fragmented." The Deweyan task of attending to the common good was especially difficult if one was a member of an excluded group. But despite the fragmentation of contemporary life, Anderson refused to resign himself to radical incommensurability or cynicism. The common good, though never realized, had to be struggled for.[201]

Notes

1 Charles E. Curran, "Growth (Hopefully) in Wisdom, Age, and Grace," *Journeys: The Impact of Personal Experience on Religious Thought*, 87–116, quote 90; Curran, *Faithful Dissent* (Kansas City, MO: Sheed & Ward, 1986), 3–8; Currran, *Loyal Dissent: Memoir of a Catholic Theologian* (Washington, DC: Georgetown University Press, 2006), 1–26; Paul Collins, *The Modern Inquisition: Seven Prominent Catholics and Their Struggles with the Vatican* (Woodstock, NY: Overlook Press, 2002), 48–9.

2 Curran, "Growth (Hopefully) in Wisdom, Age, and Grace," 90.

3 Charles E. Curran, "The Prevention of Conception After Rape," (doctoral dissertation, Rome: Pontifical Gregorian University, 1961); Curran, "Invincible Ignorance of the Natural Law According to Saint Alphonsus," (doctoral dissertation, Rome: Academia Alfonsiana, 1961); Bernard Häring, *Das Gesetz Christi: Moral theologie dargestellt für Priester und Laien* (Freiburg I. Br.: Erich Wewel, 1954); Charles Curran, "Bernard Häring: A Moral Theologian Whose Soul Matched His Scholarship," *National Catholic Reporter* (July 17, 1998), quote; Curran, "Growth (Hopefully) in Wisdom, Age, and Grace," 90–1.

4 John Rock, *The Time Has Come: A Catholic Doctor's Proposal to End the Battle for Birth Control* (New York: Knopf, 1962); Josef Maria Reuss, "Eheliche Hingabe und Zeugung," *Tübinger Theologische Quartalschrift* 143 (1963), 454–76; William van der Marck, "Vruchtbaarheidsregeling," *Tijdschrift voor Theologie* 3 (1963), 386–413; Louis K. Dupré, "Toward a Re-examination of the Catholic Position on Birth Control," *Cross Currents* 14 (Winter 1964), 63–85; Curran, *Faithful Dissent*, 6–7, 48; Curran, "Growth (Hopefully) in Wisdom, Age, and Grace," 92–3.

5 Charles E. Curran, "Christian Marriage and Family Planning," *Jubilee* 12 (August 1964), 12–18, revised in Curran, *Christian Morality Today* (Notre Dame: Fides Publishers, 1966), 47–66.

6 Charles E. Curran, "Personal Reflections on Birth Control," *Current* 5 (Spring 1965), 5–12; Curran, "The Birth Control Issue," *The Lamp* 64 (March 1966), revised in Curran, *Christian Morality Today*, 85–91; Curran, "Natural Law and the Teaching Authority of the Church," *The Lamp* 64 (March 1966), revised in *Christian Morality Today*, 79–91; Curran, "The New Morality," *Commonweal* 86 (February 18, 1966), 581–2.

7 Curran, "Absolute Norms and Medical Ethics," *Absolutes in Moral Theology?* ed. Charles E. Curran (Washington, D.C.: Corpus Books, 1968), 108–53, quote 118; Curran,

Christian Morality Today, 80–4; Curran, "The Sacrament of Penance Today," *Worship* 43 (November–December 1969), 510–31, 590–610; Curran, "Growth (Hopefully) in Wisdom, Age, and Grace," 93–6; Curran, *Faithful Dissent*, 10–11.

8 Charles E. Curran, "Masturbation and Objectively Grave Matter: An Exploratory Discussion," *Proceedings of the Catholic Theological Society of America* 21 (1966), 95–112; Curran to author, May 12, 2005; Curran, "Theological Foundations for a Spiritual Formation in Freedom and Responsibility," *Proceedings of the Society of Catholic College Teachers of Sacred Doctrine* 9 (1965), 164–76; Curran, *Faithful Dissent*, 14–15; "Interview with Fr. Curran at Catholic University," *Baltimore Catholic Review* 32 (April 28, 1967), 1, 7. Curran's book *Christian Morality Today* went through seven printings and sold over 50,000 copies, by far the biggest seller of his career. See Curran, *Loyal Dissent: Memoir of a Catholic Theologian*, 25–6.

9 Curran, "Growth (Hopefully) in Wisdom, Age, and Grace," "the time" quote, 102; Collins, *The Modern Inquisition*, "I was pushed" and "they offered" quotes, 56; Curran, *Loyal Dissent: Memoir of a Catholic Theologian*, Maguire quote, 36.

10 See Charles E. Curran, "Fulfilling Human Sexuality: Bodily Possibilities," *Commonweal* 88 (June 14, 1968), 386–7; Curran, "Sexuality and Sin: A Current Appraisal," *Homiletic and Pastoral Review* 68 (September 1968), 1005–14, and 69 (October 1968), 27–34.

11 Pope Paul VI, *On the Regulation of Birth: Humanae Vitae* (Washington, DC: United States Catholic Conference, 1968), n. 10, quote 7; Editor's introduction, *Contraception: Authority and Dissent*, ed. Charles E. Curran (New York: Herder and Herder, 1969), "no faithful," 10; Curran, *Loyal Dissent: Memoir of a Catholic Theologian*, 49–69; Charles E. Curran and Robert E. Hunt, *Dissent In and For the Church: Theologians and Humanae Vitae* (New York: Sheed & Ward, 1969), 3–26.

12 Charles E. Curran, "Natural Law and Moral Theology," *Contraception: Authority and Dissent*, 151–75, quote 155; see *The Birth Control Debate*, ed. Robert G. Hoyt (Kansas City: National Catholic Reporter, 1968); Robert J. Kritland, "Just One Minute, Father Curran!," *Catholic World* 208 (January 1969), 152–4.

13 Curran, "Natural Law and Moral Theology," quote 169; Charles E. Curran, "The Morality of Contraception," *Albertus Magnus Alumna* 5 (Winter 1968), 4–6, 14; Curran, *A New Look at Christian Morality* (Notre Dame: Fides Publishers, 1968).

14 Curran and Hunt, *Dissent In and For the Church: Theologians and Humanae Vitae*, quote 219; Charles E. Curran, with John F. Hunt, Terrence R. Connolly, et al., *The Responsibility of Dissent: The Church and Academic Freedom* (New York: Sheed and Ward, 1969).

15 See Richard A. McCormick, *Notes on Moral Theology 1965–1980* (Washington, DC: University Press of America, 1981); McCormick, *Corrective Vision: Explorations in Moral Theology* (Kansas City, MO: Sheed & Ward, 1994); *Moral Theology: Challenges for the Future: Essays in Honor of Richard A. McCormick*, ed. Charles E. Curran (New York: Paulist Press, 1990).

16 Curran, "Natural Law and Moral Theology," "man is not," 172–3; Charles E. Curran, "Moral Theology: The Present State of the Discipline," *Theological Studies* 34 (September 1973), 446–67, "best elements" and "one cannot," 453; see H. Richard Niebuhr, *The Responsible Self: An Essay in Christian Moral Philosophy* (New York: Harper & Row, 1963).

17 Charles E. Curran, "Methodological and Ecclesiological Questions in Moral Theology," *Chicago Studies* 9 (Spring 1970), 59–80, revised in Curran, *Contemporary Problems in Moral Theology* (Notre Dame: Fides Publishers, 1970), 242–68; Curran, "Is There a Distinctively Christian Ethic?," *Metropolis: Christian Presence and Responsibility*, ed. Philip D. Morris (Notre Dame: Fides Publishers, 1970), 92–120; Curran, "Responsibility in Moral Theology: Centrality, Foundation, and Implication for Ecclesiology," *Who Decides for the Church?*, ed. James A. Coriden (Hartford, CT: Canon Law Society of America, 1971), 113–42; Curran, *Ongoing Revision: Studies in Moral Theology* (Notre Dame: Fides Publishers, 1975);

Curran, *Themes in Fundamental Moral Theology* (Notre Dame: University of Notre Dame Press, 1977); Curran, *Transition and Tradition in Moral Theology* (Notre Dame: University of Notre Dame Press, 1979); Curran, *Critical Concerns in Moral Theology* (Notre Dame: University of Notre Dame Press, 1984).

18 Curran, *Ongoing Revision in Moral Theology*, 210–28; Charles E. Curran, "Human Life: The Fifth Commandment," *Chicago Studies* 13 (Fall 1974), 279–99; Curran, *American Catholic Social Ethics: Twentieth-Century Approaches* (Notre Dame: University of Notre Dame Press, 1982), 26–91, 172–232, "very limited," 232; Curran, *Issues in Sexual and Medical Ethics* (Notre Dame: University of Notre Dame Press, 1978), "a great" and "I wish," 220, "legitimate dissent," 155; Curran, "Civil Law and Christian Morality: Abortion and the Churches," *Conversations* (Spring 1975), 1–19; Curran, "How My Mind Has Changed, 1960–1975," *Horizons* 2 (Fall 1975), 187–205; Curren, "American and Catholic: American Catholic Social Ethics 1880–1965," *Thought* 52 (March 1977), 50–74.

19 See Charles E. Curran and Richard A. McCormick, eds., *Readings in Moral Theology No. 1: Moral Norms and Catholic Tradition* (New York: Paulist Press, 1979); *No. 2: The Distinctiveness of Christian Ethics* (1980); *No. 3: The Magisterium and Morality* (1982); *No. 4: The Use of Scripture in Moral Theology* (1984); *No. 5: Official Catholic Social Teaching* (1986); *No. 6: Dissent in the Church* (1988); *No. 7: Natural Law and Theology* (1991); *No. 8: Dialogue About Catholic Sexual Teaching* (1993); Curran, McCormick, and Margaret Farley, eds., *Feminist Ethics and the Catholic Moral Tradition: Readings in Moral Theology No. 9* (1996); Curran, ed., *John Paul II and Moral Theology: Readings in Moral Theology No. 10* (1998); Curran, ed., *The Historical Development of Fundamental Moral Theology in the United States: Readings in Moral Theology No. 11* (1999); Curran and Leslie Griffin, eds., *The Catholic Church, Morality, and Politics: Readings in Moral Theology No. 12* (2001); Curran, ed., *Change in Official Catholic Moral Teachings: Readings in Moral Theology No. 13* (2003); Curran, ed., *Conscience: Readings in Moral Theology No. 14* (2004).

20 Charles E. Curran, "Ten Years Later: Reflections on the Anniversary of *Humanae Vitae*," "*Commonweal* 105 (7 July 1978), 425–30, "there are many," 427; Curran, *Ongoing Revision: Studies in Moral Theology*, "teaching on specific," 64, "but my dissent," 157; Curran, *Themes in Fundamental Moral Theology*, 180–4, "involve the person," 132; Curran, "Homosexuality and Moral Theology: Methodological and Substantive Considerations," *Thomist* 35 (July 1971), 447–81; Curran, *Catholic Moral Theology in Dialogue* (Notre Dame: Fides Publishers, 1972), 65–110; Curran, "Abortion: Law and Morality in Contemporary Catholic Theology," *Jurist* 33 (Spring 1973), 162–83; Curran, "Sterilization: Roman Catholic Theory and Practice," *Linacre Quarterly* 40 (1973), 97–108; Curran, "Divorce: Catholic Theory and Practice in the United States," *American Ecclesiastical Review* 168 (January 1974), 3–34.

21 Franjo Cardinal Seper, Prefect of the Sacred Congregation for the Doctrine of the Faith, "Observations of the Sacred Congregation for the Doctrine of the Faith on Some Writings of Father Charles Curran," (July 1979), reprinted in Charles Curran, *Faithful Dissent* (Kansas City: Sheed & Ward, 1986), 118–37, quotes 118, 121.

22 Joseph Cardinal Ratzinger to Charles E. Curran, February 10, 1983, reprinted in Curran, *Faithful Dissent*, 196; Ratzinger to Curran, May 10, 1983, ibid., 197–8; Joseph Cardinal Ratzinger, "Observations of the Sacred Congregation for the Doctrine of the Faith Regarding the Reverend Charles E. Curran," April 1983, ibid., 200–8, "circular method," 203; Charles E. Curran, "Response to the 'Observations of the Sacred Congregation for the Doctrine of the Faith Regarding the Reverend Charles E. Curran," August 10, 1983, ibid., 211–22; Ratzinger to Curran, April 13, 1984, ibid., 227–8; Curran, "Response to the Questions Posed in the Letter from Cardinal Ratzinger dated April 13, 1984," August 24, 1984, ibid., 229–45; Ratzinger to Curran, September 17, 1985, ibid., 248–50; Statement of past presidents of the Catholic Theological Society of America and the College Theology Society, ibid., 282–4.

23 Charles E. Curran, "A Teaching Moment Continues," *America* 156 (April 25, 1987), 336–40; Curran, *Tensions in Moral Theology* (Notre Dame: University of Notre Dame Press, 1988), 50–73; Curran, *Faithful Dissent*, 35–6; Curran, *Loyal Dissent: Memoir of a Catholic Theologian*, 107–59; Curran, "Academic Freedom and Catholic Institutions of Higher Learning," *Journal of the American Academy of Religion* 55 (Spring 1987), 108–21; Curran, "Charles Curran: Why I Am Still a Roman Catholic," *National Catholic Reporter* 23 (September 4, 1987), 9–11.

24 John Paul II, *Veritatis Splendor*, n. 51, *Origins* 23 (1993), quote 330; John Paul II, *Evangelium vitae*, n. 57, *Origins* 24 (1995), quote 709; see John Paul II, *Laborem exercens*, n. 15, *Catholic Social Thought: The Documentary Heritage*, eds. David J. O'Brien and Thomas A. Shannon (Maryknoll, NY: Orbis Books, 1992), 373–4; *Centesimus annus*, nn. 49–50, *Catholic Social Thought*, 464–77; Charles E. Curran, "*Veritatis Splendor*: A Revisionist Perspective," *Veritatis Splendor: American Responses*, eds. Michael E. Allsopp and John J. O'Keefe (Kansas City, MO: Sheed & Ward, 1995), 224–43; Curran, "Encyclical is Positive, Problematic," *National Catholic Reporter* 31 (April 24,1995), 4–5.

25 Charles E. Curran, "Two Traditions: Historical Consciousness Meets the Immutable," *Commonweal* 123 (October 11, 1996), 11–13; Curran, *History and Contemporary Issues: Studies in Moral Theology* (New York: Continuum, 1996); Curran, "Destructive Tensions in Moral Theology," *The Church in Anguish: Has the Vatican Betrayed Vatican II?* eds. Hans Küng and Leonard Swidler (San Francisco: Harper & Row, 1987), 273–8; Curran, *Tensions in Moral Theology*, 7–31; Curran, *The Catholic Moral Tradition Today: A Synthesis* (Washington, DC: Georgetown University Press, 1999), "at best," 220; Curran, *Faithful Dissent*, 38; *Change in Official Catholic Moral Teaching: Readings in Moral Theology No. 13*, ed. Charles E. Curran (New York: Paulist Press, 2003).

26 Curran, *The Catholic Moral Tradition Today: A Synthesis*, quote 239.

27 Ibid., "the challenge," 24; Charles E. Curran, "A Century of Catholic Social Teaching," *Theology Today* 48 (1991), 154–69; Curran, "Catholic Social Teaching and Human Morality," *One Hundred Years of Catholic Social Thought: Celebration and Change*, ed. John A. Coleman (Maryknoll, NY: Orbis Books, 1991), 72–87; Curran, "What Catholic Ecclesiology Can Learn from Official Catholic Social Teaching," *A Democratic Catholic Church: The Reconstruction of Roman Catholicism*, eds. Eugene C. Bianchi and Rosemary Radford Ruether (New York: Crossroad, 1992), 94–112; Curran, "Absolute Moral Norms," *Ethics in Crisis?* ed. John Scally (Dublin, Ireland: Veritas, 1997), 25–32.

28 See Daniel C. Maguire, "The Chastity Mask," *Religious Consultation Report* 8 (nd, 2004), 1–2; Maguire, *The Moral Choice* (Garden City, NY: Doubleday, 1978); Maguire, *Death by Choice* (Garden City, NY: Doubleday, 1984); Maguire, *The Moral Core of Judaism and Christianity: Reclaiming the Revolution* (Minneapolis: Fortress Press, 1993); Maguire, *Sacred Choices: The Right to Contraception and Abortion in Ten World Religions* (Minneapolis: Fortress Press, 2002).

29 George A. Kelly, *Keeping the Church Catholic with John Paul II* (New York: Doubleday, 1990), 46–7; Curran, *Loyal Dissent: Memoir of a Catholic Theologian*, 68–9.

30 This section on Gustafson is adapted from Gary Dorrien, *The Making of American Liberal Theology: Crisis, Irony, and Postmodernity* (Louisville: Westminster John Knox Press, 2006), 289–307.

31 James M. Gustafson, *Treasure in Earthen Vessels: The Church as a Human Community* (New York: Harper & Row, 1961); Gustafson, *Christ and the Moral Life* (New York: Harper & Row, 1968).

32 James M. Gustafson, *The Church as Moral Decision Maker* (Philadelphia: Pilgrim Press, 1969); Gustafson, *Christian Ethics and the Community* (Philadelphia: Pilgrim Press, 1971); Gustafson, *Theology and Christian Ethics* (Philadelphia: Pilgrim Press, 1974); Gustafson, *Can Ethics Be Christian?* (Chicago: University of Chicago Press, 1975).

33 James M. Gustafson, *Protestant and Roman Catholic Ethics* (Chicago: University of Chicago Press, 1978), 148; Gustafson, "A Theocentric Interpretation of Life," *Theologians in Transition: The Christian Century "How My Mind Has Changed" Series*, 82–92.

34 Gustafson, "A Theocentric Interpretation of Life," 91–2.

35 Gustafson, "A Theocentric Interpretation of Life," 83–90, "vulgar," 85.

36 James M. Gustafson, *Ethics from a Theocentric Perspective: Theology and Ethics* (Chicago: University of Chicago Press, 1981), 18–19, quote 19.

37 Ibid., 24–5, 54–5, quotes 25.

38 Gustafson, *Ethics from a Theocentric Perspective: Theology and Ethics*, 94–9, 163–4; Karl Barth, *Church Dogmatics: The Doctrine of God*, 2: 2, trans. G. W. Bromiley, et.al., (Edinburgh: T. & T. Clark, 1957), 583–630; see Loren Eiseley, *Darwin's Century* (Garden City, NY: Doubleday, 1961), 96–7.

39 Gustafson, *Ethics from a Theocentric Perspective: Theology and Ethics*, 163–78, 201–4, quote 165.

40 Ibid., quotes 264, 266.

41 Ibid., quotes 271, 272, 274.

42 James M. Gustafson, *Ethics from a Theocentric Perspective: Ethics and Theology* (Chicago: University of Chicago Press, 1984), 153–277, quotes 209, 250.

43 Ibid., quote 275.

44 Daniel C. Maguire, review of *Ethics from a Theocentric Perspective: Theology and Ethics*, by James M. Gustafson, *Commonweal* 109 (July 16, 1982), 408–9; Jon P. Gunnemann, review of *Ethics from a Theocentric Perspective: Ethics and Theology*, by James M. Gustafson, *Interpretation* 40 (July 1986), 330–1.

45 Paul Ramsey, "A Letter to James Gustafson," *Journal of Religious Ethics* 13 (Spring 1985), 71–100; Stanley M. Hauerwas, "Time and History in Theological Ethics: The Work of James Gustafson," *Journal of Religious Ethics* 13 (Spring 1985), 3–21.

46 Lisa Sowle Cahill, "Consent in Time of Affliction: The Ethics of a Circumspect Theist," *Journal of Religious Ethics* 13 (Spring 1985), 22–36; see John Calvin, *Institutes of the Christian Religion*, I, 5, 5; 2 vols., trans. Ford Battles, ed. John T. McNeill (Philadelphia: Westminster Press, 1955), 1: 58; Richard McCormick, SJ, "Gustafson's God: Who? What? Where? (Etc.)," *Journal of Religious Ethics* 13 (Spring 1985), 53–70, quotes 60, 69.

47 James M. Gustafson, *Intersections: Science, Theology, and Ethics* (Cleveland: Pilgrim Press, 1996), quotes ix, x; Gustafson, *An Examined Faith: The Grace of Self-Doubt* (Minneapolis: Fortress Press, 2004); Gustafson, "A Response to Critics," *Journal of Religious Ethics* 13 (Fall 1985), 185–209.

48 James M. Gustafson, *A Sense of the Divine: The Natural Environment from a Theocentric Perspective* (Cleveland: Pilgrim Press, 1996), quotes 86, 47, 48; Gustafson, *An Examined Faith: The Grace of Self-Doubt.*

49 James M. Gustafson, "Doubting Theology: James M. Gustafson Replies," *Christian Century* 121 (June 29, 2004), 32–6, quotes 36.

50 See Henry N. Wieman, *The Source of Human Good* (Carbondale, IL: Southern Illinois University Press, 1946); Bernard E. Meland, *America's Spiritual Culture* (New York: Harper & Brothers, 1948); Dorrien, *The Making of American Liberal Theology: Crisis, Irony, and Postmodernity, 1950–2005*, 58–132.

51 Professor Winter was my friend and mentor at Princeton Theological Seminary in the late 1970s.

52 Gibson Winter, *Love and Conflict: New Patterns in Family Life* (New York: Doubleday, 1958), quote 152.

53 Gibson Winter, *The Suburban Captivity of the Churches: An Analysis of Protestant Responsibility in the Expanding Metropolis* (Garden City, NY: Doubleday, 1961), quotes 29, 39.

54 Ibid., quote 48.

55 Ibid., 161–77, quotes 175.

56 Gibson Winter, *The New Creation as Metropolis* (New York: Macmillan, 1963), quotes 1, 48.

57 Ibid., quotes 58, 88–9.

58 Ibid., quotes 128, 129.

59 Gibson Winter, "Notes for a Socio-Political, Religious Biography," *Religious Studies Review* 10 (October 1984), 328–30.

60 Robert Benne, "Brushes With the Great and Near Great: Fifty Years of Theological Reminiscences," *Dialog* 42 (Spring 2003), reprinted in Benne, *Reasonable Ethics: A Christian Approach to Social, Economic and Political Concerns* (St Louis: Concordia Publishing House, 2005), 30–8, quote 34; see Benne, "The Sometime Prodigal Son: A Theological Autobiography," *Dialog* 35 (Fall 1996), reprinted in ibid., 18–29; see Dorrien, *The Making of American Liberal Theology: Crisis, Irony, and Postmodernity*, 123–32.

61 Gibson Winter, *Elements for a Social Ethic: Scientific Perspectives on Social Process* (New York: Macmillan, 1966), 3–5.

62 Ibid., quote 4.

63 Ibid., 6–10, quote 9.

64 See Charles Sanders Peirce, *Collected Papers of Charles Sanders Peirce*, 6 vols., vol. 5, *Pragmatism and Pragmaticism*, ed. Charles Hartshorne and Paul Weiss (Cambridge, MA: Harvard University Press, 1934); William James, *Pragmatism: A New Name for Some Old Ways of Thinking* and *The Meaning of Truth: A Sequel to Pragmatism* (Cambridge, MA: Harvard University Press, 1978); John Dewey, *The Essential Dewey*, 2 vols., Vol. 1, *Pragmatism, Education, Democracy*, ed. Larry A. Hickman and Thomas M. Alexander (Bloomington: Indiana University Press, 1998).

65 Winter, *Elements for a Social Ethic: Scientific Perspectives on Social Process*, quote 21; see George Herbert Mead, *The Philosophy of the Act* (Chicago: University of Chicago Press, 1938); Mead, *The Social Psychology of George Herbert Mead*, ed. Anselm Strauss (Chicago: University of Chicago Press, 1956).

66 Winter, *Elements for a Social Ethic: Scientific Perspectives on Social Process*, xi–xvi, 22–33; see Maurice Merleau-Ponty, *Phenomenology of Perception*, trans. Colin Smith (London: Routledge & Kegan Paul, 1962); Merleau-Ponty, *The Primacy of Perception and Other Essays on Phenomenological Psychology, the Philosophy of Art, History and Politics*, ed. James M. Edie (Evanston, IL: Northwestern University Press, 1964).

67 Winter, *Elements for a Social Ethic: Scientific Perspectives on Social Process*, 119–212, quote 164–5.

68 Ibid., 215–18, quotes 218; see H. Richard Niebuhr, "The Center of Value," in Niebuhr, *Radical Monotheism and Western Culture, With Supplementary Essays* (1st edn., New York: Harper, 1960; Louisville: Westminster John Knox Press, 1993), 100–13.

69 Winter, *Elements for a Social Ethic: Scientific Perspectives on Social Process*, 215–42.

70 Ibid., quotes 239, 242.

71 Ibid., 241–2; see Alfred Schutz, *The Phenomenology of the Social World*, trans. George Walsh and Frederick Lehnert (Evanston, IL: Northwestern University Press, 1967).

72 Winter, *Elements for a Social Ethic: Scientific Perspectives on Social Process*, quotes 244, 249, 251.

73 Ibid., 254–85, quotes 280, 281.

74 Ibid., 269.

75 Ibid., 269; Reinhold Niebuhr, *Moral Man and Immoral Society: A Study in Ethics and Politics* (New York: Charles Scribner's Sons, 1932), xiv–xv, xvi; see Gibson Winter, preface to *Social Ethics: Issues in Ethics and Society*, ed. Gibson Winter (New York: Harper & Row, 1968), 10.

76 John A. Coleman, SJ, "Gibson Winter's Constructive Social Ethics," *Religious Studies Review* 10 (October 1984), 331; Coleman, review of *Liberating Creation: Foundations of Religious Social Ethics*, by Gibson Winter, *Theology Today* 39 (July 1982), 224.

77 Gibson Winter, *Being Free: Reflections on America's Cultural Revolution* (New York: Macmillan, 1970), 47.

78 Ibid., 47, 48.

79 Ibid., 53, 54, 59.

80 Gibson Winter, "A Theology of Creative Participation," in *Belief and Ethics: Essays in Ethics, the Human Sciences, and Ministry in Honor of W. Alvin Pitcher,* eds. W. Widick Schroeder and Gibson Winter (Chicago: Center for the Scientific Study of Religion, 1978), 277–93, quotes 278, 279; see Winter, "Women's Liberation: The Culture Context," *Theology Today* 34 (January 1978), 410–21.

81 Gibson Winter, *Liberating Creation: Foundations of Religious Social Ethics* (New York: Crossroad, 1981), ix–xiv; Winter, "Notes for a Socio-Political Religious Biography," 328–9.

82 Winter, *Liberating Creation: Foundations of Religious Social Ethics,* 10–91; see Martin Heidegger, *Poetry, Language, Thought,* trans. Albert Hofstadter (New York: Harper & Row, 1971); Heidegger, *The Question Concerning Technology and Other Essays,* trans. William Lovitt (New York: Harper and Brothers, 1977); Paul Ricoeur, *The Conflict of Interpretations: Essays in Hermeneutics* (Evanston, IL: Northwestern University Press, 1974); Ricoeur, *Interpretation Theory: Discourse and the Surplus of Meaning* (Fort Worth, TX: Texas Christian University Press, 1976); Ricoeur, *The Rule of Metaphor: Multi-disciplinary studies of the Creation of Meaning in Language,* trans. Robert Czerny (Toronto: University of Toronto Press, 1977); Hans-Georg Gadamer, *Truth and Method,* trans. Joel Weinsheimer and Donald Marshall (2nd edn., New York: Crossroad, 1989); John Dewey, *Art as Experience* (New York: G. P. Putnam, 1954); Alfred Schutz, *Collected Papers,* 3 vols. (The Hague: Martinus Nijhoff, 1962, 1964, 1971); Clifford Geertz, *The Interpretation of Cultures* (New York: Basic Books, 1973).

83 Winter, *Liberating Creation: Foundations of Religious Social Ethics,* 101–2.

84 Ibid., quotes 117, 122, 127, 129, 134.

85 Richard A. Hoehn, review of *Liberating Creation: Foundations of Religious Social Ethics,* by Gibson Winter, *Journal of the American Academy of Religion* 51 (September 1983), 523; Drew Christiansen, SJ, review of ibid., *Theological Studies* 43 (December 1982), 740; John A. Coleman, SJ, review of ibid., *Theology Today* 39 (July 1982), 224–6; Franklin Gamwell, review of ibid., *Christian Century* 99 (October 20, 1982); Dennis P. McCann, review of ibid., *Journal of Ecumenical Studies* 19 (Fall 1982), 802.

86 Winter, "Notes for a Socio-Political, Religious Biography," 329–30; see Gibson Winter, *America in Search of its Soul* (Harrisburg, PA: Morehouse Publishing, 1996).

87 Gibson Winter, *Community and Spiritual Transformation: Religion and Politics in a Communal Age* (New York: Crossroad, 1989), 121.

88 Cornel West, "Winter in the West," *Religion and Intellectual Life* (Spring 1984), reprinted in West, *Prophetic Fragments: Illuminations of the Crisis in American Religion and Culture* (Grand Rapids, MI: Eerdmans Company, 1988), 246–9, quote 247.

89 Cornel West, "On My Intellectual Vocation," interview with George Yancy, in West, *The Cornel West Reader* (New York: Basic Civitas Books, 1999), 19–20.

90 Author's conversation with Cornel West and Michael Harrington, May 27, 1988.

91 West, "On My Intellectual Vocation," "high-powered" and "I've always," 21; Cornel West, "The Making of an American Radical Democrat of African Descent," Introduction to West, *The Ethical Dimensions of Marxist Thought* (New York: Monthly Review Press, 1991), reprinted in West, *The Cornel West Reader,* 3–18, "Owing to," 5.

92 See West, *The Ethical Dimensions of Marxist Thought;* West, *The Cornel West Reader,* 9–10.

93 West, "On My Intellectual Vocation," "you know," 22; West, "The Making of an American Radical Democrat of African Descent," "I decided," 11.

94 I was a member of the National Board of DSOC and DSA.

95 Cornel West, "Harrington's Socialist Vision," *Christianity & Crisis* (December 12, 1983), 484; reprinted in West, *Prophetic Fragments: Illuminations of the Crisis in American Religion and Culture,* 25–9.

96 Cornel West, *Prophesy Deliverance! An Afro-American Revolutionary Christianity* (Philadelphia: Westminster Press, 1982), 134–7; see West, "Black Theology and Marxist Thought," *Black Theology: A Documentary History, 1966–1979*, ed. Gayraud S. Wilmore and James H. Cone (Maryknoll, NY: Orbis Books, 1979), 552–67.

97 West, *Prophesy Deliverance! An Afro-American Revolutionary Christianity*, 137; on Marxist Councilism, see Serge Bricianer, *Pannekoik and the Workers' Councils* (St Louis: Telos Press, 1978); Stanley Aronowitz, *The Crisis in Historical Materialism: Class, Politics, and Culture in Marxist Theory* (New York: Praeger Publishers, 1981); Rosa Luxemburg, *Selected Political Writings of Rosa Luxemburg*, ed. Dick Howard (New York: Monthly Review Press, 1971).

98 See Gary Dorrien, *The Democratic Socialist Vision* (Totowa, NJ: Rowman & Littlefield, 1986), 129–30; Dorrien, *Reconstructing the Common Good: Theology and the Social Order* (Maryknoll, NY: Orbis Books, 1990), 162–4.

99 Dorrien, *Reconstructing the Common Good: Theology and the Social Order*, 164.

100 Cornel West, "Alasdair MacIntyre, Liberalism, and Socialism: A Christian Perspective," in *Christianity and Capitalism: Perspectives on Religion, Liberalism, and the Economy*, eds. Bruce Grelle and David A. Krueger (Chicago: Center for the Scientific Study of Religion, 1985), reprinted in West, *Prophetic Fragments: Illuminations of the Crisis in American Religion and Culture*, quote 134–5; see Alec Nove, *The Economics of Feasible Socialism* (London: George Allen & Unwin, 1983); Wlodzimierz Brus, *The Economics and Politics of Socialism* (London: Routledge & Kegan Paul, 1973); Branko Horvat, *The Political Economy of Socialism: A Marxist Social Theory* (Armonk, NY: M.E. Sharpe, 1982).

101 Cornel West, "Critical Theory and Christian Faith," *Witness* (January 1986), reprinted in West, *Prophetic Fragments: Illuminations of the Crisis in American Religion and Culture*, quote 122; see Michael Harrington, "Is Capitalism Still Viable?" *Journal of Business Ethics* 1 (1982), 283–4; Harrington, "Corporate Collectivism: A System of Social Injustice," *Contemporary Readings in Social and Political Ethics*, eds. Garry Brodsky, John Troyer, David Vance (Buffalo: Prometheus Books, 1984), 245.

102 Cornel West, "Michael Harrington, Socialist," *Nation* (January 8/15, 1990), reprinted in West, *Beyond Eurocentrism and Multiculturalism: Prophetic Thought in Postmodern Times* (Monroe, Maine: Common Courage Press, 1993), 181–8, quotes 183, 184.

103 Cornel West, "Toward a Socialist Theory of Racism," Institute for Democratic Socialism," (1985), reprinted in West, *Prophetic Fragments: Illuminations of the Crisis in American Religion and Culture*, 97–108; see Ray Ginger, *The Bending Cross: A Biography of Eugene Victor Debs* (New Brunswick: Rutgers University Press, 1949), 259–61; Nick Salvatore, *Eugene V. Debs" Citizen and Socialist* (Urbana, IL: University of Illinois Press, 1982), 225–30.

104 West, "Toward a Socialist Theory of Racism," 98–9, Stalin quote 98; see Marcus Garvey, "Address at Newport News, October 25, 1919," *Negro World* (November 1, 1919), reprinted in *The Marcus Garvey and Universal Negro Improvement Association Papers*, ed. Robert A. Hill (Berkeley: University of California Press, 1983), 1: 112–20; Harry Haywood, *Negro Liberation* (New York: International Publishers, 1948); James Forman, *Self-Determination and the African-American People* (Seattle: Open Hand Publications, 1981).

105 West, "Toward a Socialist Theory of Racism," 99–101; see Oliver C. Cox, *Caste, Class and Race* (Garden City, NY: Doubleday, 1948).

106 West, "Toward a Socialist Theory of Racism," 107–8.

107 Ibid., 108; see Cornel West, "Beyond Eurocentrism and Multiculturalism," in West, *Prophetic Thought in Postmodern Times*, 3–30.

108 Cornel West, "We Socialists," *Crossroads* (July/August 1991), reprinted in West, *Prophetic Reflections: Notes on Race and Power in America* (Monroe, ME: Common Courage Press, 1993), 239–44, "I've got to be" and "We need," 243; West, "Toward a Socialist Theory of Racism," "yet a democratic," 108.

109 West, "The Making of an American Radical Democrat of African Descent," quotes 7.

110 Cornel West, "Martin Luther King, Jr: Prophetic Christian as Organic Intellectual," Address delivered at a King symposium at the U.S. Capital, October 1986, reprinted in West, *Prophetic Fragments: Illuminations of the Crisis in American Religion and Culture*, 3–12, quotes 11.

111 Ibid., 11–12.

112 Cornel West, *The American Evasion of Philosophy: A Genealogy of Pragmatism* (Madison: University of Wisconsin Press, 1989), 42–111, 194–210, 226–39, quotes 233.

113 Ibid., quotes, 233, 235; see Cornel West, *Keeping Faith: Philosophy and Race in America* (New York: Routledge, 1993), 89–105.

114 West, *Keeping Faith: Philosophy and Race in America* (New York: Routledge, 1993), 67–85, quotes 67, 72.

115 Ibid., quotes 73, xv, xvii.

116 Cornel West, *Race Matters* (Boston: Beacon Press, 1993; paperback edition, New York: Vintage Books, 1994), quotes 9, 10.

117 Ibid., quotes 12, 23.

118 Ibid., quotes 24, 27.

119 Ibid., quotes 54.

120 Ibid., quotes 56, 58.

121 Ibid., 57–66, quote 66; see Adolph Reed Jr., *The Jesse Jackson Phenomenon: The Crisis of Purpose in Afro-American Politics* (New Haven: Yale University Press, 1986); Reed, "What Are the Drums Saying, Booker? The Current Crisis of the Black Intellectual," *Village Voice* 40 (April 11, 1995), 31–6; Reed, "Dangerous Dreams: Black Boomers Wax Nostalgic for the Days of Jim Crow," *Village Voice* 41 (April 16, 1996), 24–9.

122 West, *Race Matters*, quotes 69, 70.

123 Jack E. White, "Philosopher With a Mission," *Time* (June 7, 1993), 60–2, quote 60; other quotes cited from book jackets.

124 See Cornel West and Michael Lerner, *Jews and Blacks: Let the Healing Begin* (New York: Putnam, 1995); West and Henry Louis Gates, Jr, *The Future of the Race* (New York: Knopf, 1996); West, *Restoring Hope: Conversations on the Future of Black America*, ed. Kelvin S. Sealey (Boston: Beacon Press, 1997); West and Sylvia Ann Hewlett, *The War Against Parents: What We Can Do For America's Beleaguered Moms and Dads* (Boston: Houghton Mifflin, 1998); West and Gates, *The African-American Century: How Black Americans Have Shaped Our Country* (New York: Free Press, 2000).

125 African United Front, "Open Letter to Cornel West and the Other Uncle Toms," (1993), www.blacksandjews.com/Open_LetterAUF, accessed 3/24/07; White, "Philosopher With a Mission," quotes 61–2.

126 Randal Jelks, review of *Race Matters*, by Cornel West, *Christian Century* 110 (June 30/July 7, 1993), 684–5; Delores S. Williams, review of ibid., *Theology Today* 51 (April 1994), 158–62.

127 Leon Wieseltier, "All and Nothing at All: The Unreal World of Cornel West," *New Republic* 212 (March 6, 1995), 31–6, quotes 31, 32; White, "Philosopher with a Mission," 62.

128 David Horowitz, "Cornel West: No Light in His Attic," salon.com, (October 11, 1999), 1–6, quotes 2–3, www.frontpagemag.com/Articles, accessed March 23, 2007.

129 Cornel West, "Reconstructing the American Left: The Challenge of Jesse Jackson," *Social Text* 11 (1984), 3–19, "despicable," 14; West, *Race Matters*, "underdog," 112; West and Lerner, *Jews and Blacks: Let the Healing Begin*, Lerner quote 191, West quote 212; see *Black Religion After the Million Man March*, ed. Garth Kasimu Baker-Fletcher (Maryknoll, NY: Orbis Books, 1998).

130 Nick De Genova, "Gangster Rap and Nihilism in Black America: Some Questions of Life and Death," *Social Text* 43 (1995), 89–132, quote 95; Eric Lott, *The Disappearing Intellectual* (New York: Basic Books, 2006), 114–15.

131 Floyd W. Hayes III, "Cornel West and Afro-Nihilism: A Reconsideration," in *Cornel West: A Critical Reader*, ed. George Yancy (Oxford: Blackwell Publishers, 2001), 245–60, quote 248; Lewis R. Gordon, "The Unacknowledged Fourth Tradition: An Essay on Nihilism, Decadence, and the Black Intellectual Tradition in the Existential Pragmatic Thought of Cornel West," in ibid., 38–58; Peniel E. Joseph, "'It's Dark and Hell is Hot:' Cornel West, the Crisis of African-American Intellectuals and the Cultural Politics of Race," 295–311, quotes 298, 299; Clevis Headley, "Cornel West on Prophesy, Pragmatism, and Philosophy: A Critical Evaluation of Prophetic Pragmatism," in ibid., 59–82; Charles W. Mills, "Prophetic Pragmatism as Political Philosophy," in ibid., 192–223.

132 Headley, "Cornel West on Prophesy, Pragmatism, and Philosophy: A Critical Evaluation of Prophetic Pragmatism," in ibid., 59–82, quotes 66, 70; Iris M. Young, "Cornel West on Gender and Family: Some Admiring and Critical Comments," in ibid., 179–91.

133 John P. Pittman, "'Radical Historicism,' Antiphilosophy, and Marxism," in ibid., 224–44; George Yancy, "Religion and the Mirror of God: Historicism, Truth, and Religious Pluralism," in ibid., 115–35; Nada Elia, "Cornel West's Representations of the Intellectual: But Some of Us Are Brave?" ibid., 35–345; Lucius Turner Outlaw, Jr, "On Cornel West on W. E. B. Du Bois," ibid., 261–79.

134 Cornel West, "Afterword: Philosophy and the Funk of Life," ibid., 349–50, 356, quotes 358.

135 Ibid., 350, quotes 359.

136 Ibid., 351–5, quotes 351, 352, 353.

137 Ibid., 361, quote 356.

138 Ibid., quotes 350, 360.

139 Cornel West, *Democracy Matters: Winning the Fight Against Imperialism* (New York: Penguin Press, 2004), 193.

140 Ibid., "upholding," 198; Ross Douthat, "Let Us Now Praise Cornel West," *Harvard Crimson* (January 11, 2002), 1; Fareed Zakaria, "The Education of a President," *Newsweek* (January 14, 2002), http://fareedzakaria.com, accessed March 24, 2007; Editorial, "The Pragmatist," *The New Republic* (April 19, 2002), http://www.tnr.com/doc, accessed March 24, 2007.

141 West, *Democracy Matters: Winning the Fight Against Imperialism*, 196, 197; Sam Tanenhaus, "The Ivy League's Angry Star," *Vanity Fair* (June 2002), 201–3, 218–23; Lynne Duke, "Moving Target," *Washington Post* (August 11, 2002), F1, F43.

142 West, *Democracy Matters: Winning the Fight Against Imperialism*, 198, 199.

143 Ibid., 2, 3.

144 Ibid., quotes 8.

145 Ibid., quotes 27.

146 Ibid., 28, 29.

147 Ibid., quotes 33, 35.

148 Ibid., 41.

149 Ibid., 60.

150 *Village Voice* and *Seattle Times* statements published as jacket endorsements for the paperback edition of *Democracy Matters* (Penguin Books, 2004); Cheryl Sanders, review of *Democracy Matters: Winning the Fight Against Imperialism*, by Cornel West, *Christian Century* 122 (July 12, 2005), 36; Hamid Khanbhai, review of ibid., *Daily Princetonian* (November 4, 2004); Daniel Levine, review of ibid., *America* 191 (November 8, 2004), www.americamagazine.org, accessed April 4, 2007; Mark Bauerlein, review of ibid., *New Criterion* (December 29, 2004), 32.

151 See West, *Race Matters*, "shabby," 61; Salim Muwakkil, "Cornel West: Public Intellectual," *In These Times* (November 4, 2004), www.inthesetimes.com, accessed April 4, 2007; Michael Eric Dyson, *Making Malcolm: The Myth and Meaning of Malcolm X* (New York: Oxford University Press, 1995); Dyson, *Race Rules: Navigating the Color Line* (New York: Vintage Books, 1996).

152 West, *Democracy Matters: Winning the Fight Against Imperialism*, quote 199.

153 Rosemary Cowan, *Cornel West: The Politics of Redemption* (Cambridge: Polity Press, 2003); West, "On My Intellectual Vocation," quote 29.

154 Alice Walker, *In Search of Our Mothers' Gardens: Womanist Prose* (New York: Harcourt, Brace & Co., 1983).

155 Katie Geneva Cannon, "Exposing My Home Point of View," in *Hard Times Cotton Mill Girls: Personal Histories of Womanhood and Poverty in the South* (Ithaca, NY: ILR Press, 1986), 26–39, reprinted in Cannon, *Katie's Cannon: Womanism and the Soul of the Black Community* (New York: Continuum, 1995), 162–70, quote 167.

156 Sara Lawrence-Lightfoot, *I've Known Rivers: Lives of Loss and Liberation* (Reading, MA: Addison-Wesley, 1994), quotes 18, 34, 54.

157 Ibid., quotes 54, 59.

158 Ibid., quotes 61, 62, 65.

159 Ibid., quote 90.

160 Ibid., quotes 102, 103.

161 Ibid., quote 104.

162 Ibid., quotes 105, 106, 107.

163 Katie G. Cannon, *Katie's Canon: Womanism and the Soul of the Black Community* (New York: Continuum, 2002), quote, 23; Cannon, "Resources for a Constructive Christian Ethic for Black Women with Special Attention to the Life and Work of Zora Neale Hurston," PhD dissertation, Union Theological Seminary, 1983.

164 Alice Walker, *In Search of Our Mothers' Gardens: Womanist Prose* (New York: Harcourt Brace Jovanovich, 1983), xi–xii.

165 Cannon, *Katie's Canon: Womanism and the Soul of the Black Community*, quote 23; see Alice Walker, *The Color Purple* (New York: Washington Square Press, 1982).

166 Katie G. Cannon, *Black Womanist Ethics* (Atlanta: Scholars Press, 1988), 2.

167 Ibid., 3–4.

168 Ibid., 6.

169 Zora Neale Hurston, "How It Feels to Be Colored Me," *World Tomorrow* (May 1928), 17; Cannon, *Black Feminist Ethics*, 11.

170 Mary Burgher, "Images of Self and Race in the Autobiographies of Black Women," in *Sturdy Black Bridges*, ed. Roseann Bell, et. al. (New York: Anchor Books, 1979), 113; Cannon, *Black Feminist Ethics*, 17; see Zora Neale Hurston, *Dust Tracks on a Road* (Philadelphia: Lippincott, 1942); Hurston, *Moses, Man of the Mountain* (Philadelphia: Lippincott, 1939); Hurston, *Mules and Men* (Philadelphia: Lippincott, 1935); Hurston, *Seraph on the Sewanee* (New York: Charles Scribner's Sons, 1948); Hurston, *Their Eyes Were Watching God* (Philadelphia: Lippincott, 1938).

171 Alice Walker, Foreword to Robert Hemenway, *Zora Neale Hurston: A Literary Biography* (Urbana: University of Illinois Press, 1977), xvii; Hurston, *Their Eyes Were Watching God*, quote 119; Cannon, *Black Feminist Ethics*, 103–5; see Katie G. Cannon, "Unctuousness as Virtue: According to the Life of Zora Neale Hurston," *Zora Neale Hurston Forum* (Fall 1987), 38–48, reprinted in Cannon, *Katie's Canon: Womanism and the Soul of the Black Community*, 91–100.

172 Cannon, *Black Womanist Ethics*, 145.

173 Katie G. Cannon, "Resources for a Constructive Ethic: The Life and Work of Zora Neale Hurston," *Journal of Feminist Studies in Religion* 1 (1984), 37–51, reprinted in Cannon, *Katie's Canon: Womanism and the Soul of the Black Community*, 77–90, quote 90.

174 Katie G. Cannon, "Hitting a Straight Lick with a Crooked Stick: The Womanist Dilemma in the Development of a Black Liberation Ethic," *Annual of the Society of Christian Ethics* (1987), 165–77, reprinted in Cannon, *Katie's Canon: Womanism and the Soul of the Black Community*, 122–8, quotes 122, 123.

175 Ibid., quote 123.

176 Ibid., quote 126.

177 Katie G. Cannon, "Metalogues and Dialogues: Teaching the Womanist Idea," *Journal of Feminist Studies in Religion* 8 (Fall 1992), 125–30, reprinted in Cannon, *Katie's Canon: Womanism and the Soul of the Black Community*, 136–43, quote 137; see *A Troubling in My Soul: Womanist Perspectives on Evil and Suffering*, ed. Emilie M. Townes (Maryknoll, NY: Orbis Books, 1993).

178 Cheryl J. Sanders and others, "Roundtable Discussion: Christian Ethics and Theology in Womanist Perspective," *Journal of Feminist Studies in Religion* 5 (1989), 83–112, quote 111; Katie G. Cannon, "Appropriation and Reciprocity in the Doing of Womanist Ethics," *Annual of the Society of Christian Ethics* (1993), 189–96, reprinted in Cannon, *Katie's Canon: Womanism and the Soul of the Black Community*, 129–35.

179 Cannon, "Appropriation and Reciprocity in the Doing of Womanist Ethics," quotes 131.

180 Ibid., "rugged endurance," 135; Katie G. Cannon, "Structured Academic Amnesia: As If This True Womanist Story Never Happened," in *Deeper Shades of Purple: Womanism in Religion and Society*, ed. Stacey M. Floyd-Thomas (New York: New York University Press, 2006), 19–27, "from 1983," 22, "experience our," 23.

181 Katie G. Cannon, "Response," *Journal of Feminist Studies in Religion* 22 (2006), 96–8; see Cannon, "Sexing Black Women: Liberation from the Prisonhouse of Anatomical Authority," *Loving the Body: Black Religious Studies and the Erotic*, eds. Anthony B. Pinn and Dwight N. Hopkins (New York: Palgrave, 2004), 11–30.

182 Victor Anderson, "The Legacy of Pragmatism in the Theologies of D. C. Macintosh, H. Richard Niebuhr, and James M. Gustafson," PhD dissertation, Princeton University, 1992.

183 See Richard Rorty, *Philosophy and the Mirror of Nature* (Princeton, NJ: Princeton University Press, 1979); Rorty, *Consequences of Pragmatism* (Minneapolis: University of Minnesota Press, 1982); Rorty, *Contingency, Irony, and Solidarity* (Cambridge: Cambridge University Press, 1989); Hilary Putnam, *Reason, Truth, and History* (New York: Cambridge University Press, 1981); Jeffrey L. Stout, *The Flight from Authority: Religion, Morality, and The Quest for Autonomy* (Notre Dame: University of Notre Dame Press, 1981); Stout, *Ethics After Babel: The Languages of Morals and Their Discontents* (Boston: Beacon Press, 1988); Cornel West, *The American Evasion of Philosophy: A Genealogy of Pragmatism* (Madison: University of Wisconsin Press, 1989).

184 Victor Anderson, *Beyond Ontological Blackness: An Essay on African American Religious and Cultural Criticism* (New York: Continuum, 1995), 21–85.

185 Ibid., quote 162.

186 Ibid., 86–94, quotes 16, 89, 91–2, 15.

187 Ibid., 93–117, quotes 110, 116, 112; see Dwight Hopkins, *Shoes that Fit Our Feet: Sources for a Constructive Black Theology* (Maryknoll: Orbis Books, 1993); James H. Evans, Jr, *We Have Been Believers: An African American Systematic Theology* (Minneapolis: Fortress Press, 1992); Peter J. Paris, *The Social Teachings of the Black Churches* (Philadelphia: Fortress Press, 1985); Jacquelyn Grant, *White Women's Christ and Black Women's Jesus* (Atlanta: Scholars Press, 1989); Delores Williams, "A Womanist Perspective on Sin," *A Troubling in My Soul: Womanist Perspectives on Evil and Suffering*, 130–50; Cheryl J. Sanders, "Roundtable Discussion: Christian Ethics and Theology in Womanist Perspective," *Journal of Feminist Studies in Religion*, 5 (1989), 83–91.

188 Anderson, *Beyond Ontological Blackness: An Essay on African American Religious and Cultural Criticism*, Anderson quotes 103, 117, 161; bell hooks, *Yearnings: Race, Gender, and Cultural Politics* (Boston: South End Press, 1990), quote 19; Joe Wood, "The New Blackness," (1992, 15–16), cited in Anderson, op. cit., 141.

189 Victor Anderson, "Abominations of a Million Men," *Black Religion after the Million Man March: Voices on the Future*, ed. Garth Kasimu Baker-Fletcher (Maryknoll: Orbis Books,

1998), 19–26, quotes 22, 24; Anderson, "Deadly Silence: Reflections on Homosexuality and Human Rights," *Homosexuality and Human Rights*, eds. Martha Nussbaum and Saul Olyan (New York: Oxford University Press, 1997); Anderson, *Beyond Ontological Blackness: An Essay on African American Religious and Cultural Criticism*, quote 143; see Anderson, *Divine Grotesqueries: Five Essays in African American Philosophical Theology* (Trinity International Press).

190 Willie James Jennings, review of *Beyond Ontological Blackness: An Essay on African American Religious and Cultural Criticism*, by Victor Anderson, *Theology Today* 53 (January 1997), 527–8; J. Deotis Roberts, review of ibid., *Journal of Religion* 78 (April 1998), 279–80; Dwight N. Hopkins, *Introducing Black Theology of Liberation* (Maryknoll: Orbis Books, 1999), 110–11; see L. H. Mamiya, review of *Beyond Ontological Blackness: An Essay on African American Religious and Cultural Criticism*, by Victor Anderson, *Choice* 33 (April 1996), 1326; Mary Alice Mulligan, review of ibid., *Encounter* 58 (Summer 1997), 331–3.

191 Rorty, *Contingency, Irony, and Solidarity*, quote, xv; Richard Rorty, "Religious Faith, Intellectual Responsibility, and Romance," *Pragmatism, Neo-Pragmatism, and Religion: Conversations with Richard Rorty*, 3–21.

192 Victor Anderson, *Pragmatic Theology: Negotiating the Intersections of an American Philosophy of Religion and Public Theology* (Albany: State University of New York Press, 1998), 13–28, quote 17; Stout, *Ethics After Babel: The Languages of Morals and Their Discontents*, 109–23; Richard Rorty and Gianni Vattimo, *The Future of Religion* (New York: Columbia University Press, 2005).

193 Stout, *Ethics After Babel: The Languages of Morals and Their Discontents*, 163–88; Anderson, *Pragmatic Theology: Negotiating the Intersections of an American Philosophy of Religion and Public Theology*, 17–24.

194 Anderson, *Pragmatic Theology: Negotiating the Intersections of an American Philosophy of Religion and Public Theology*, 22–8.

195 Ibid., quote 67.

196 Ibid., quotes 101, 102.

197 Ibid., 100–4; see Eugene Fontinell, *Toward a Reconstruction of Religion: A Philosophical Probe* (Garden City: Doubleday, 1970).

198 Anderson, *Pragmatic Theology: Negotiating the Intersections of an American Philosophy of Religion and Public Theology*, quotes 104, 106.

199 Ibid., 107–15; see James M. Gustafson, *Ethics from a Theocentric Perspective*, 2 vols. (Chicago: University of Chicago Press, 1981, 1984); Gordon D. Kaufman, *In Face of Mystery: A Constructive Theology* (Cambridge, MA: Harvard University Press, 1993); Kaufman, *God–Mystery–Diversity: Christian Theology in a Pluralistic World* (Minneapolis: Fortress Press, 1996).

200 Anderson, *Pragmatic Theology: Negotiating the Intersections of an American Philosophy of Religion and Public Theology*, quote 129; see Cornel West, *Keeping Faith: Philosophy and Race in America* (New York: Routledge, 1993), 91–139; Victor Anderson, "The Wrestle of Christ and Culture in Pragmatic Public Theology," 19 (May 1998), 133–50.

201 Anderson, *Pragmatic Theology: Negotiating the Intersections of an American Philosophy of Religion and Public Theology*, 129.

Chapter 9

Economy, Sexuality, Ecology, Difference

Max L. Stackhouse, Dennis P. McCann, Lisa Sowle Cahill,
Marvin M. Ellison, John B. Cobb, Jr, Larry Rasmussen,
Daniel C. Maguire, Sharon Welch, Emilie M. Townes,
Ada María Isasi-Díaz, María Pilar Aquino, and David Hollenbach

In the 1990s, after the Cold War had ended and difference and plurality prevailed in social ethics, nearly everything seemed to be up for debate, some things with particular urgency. Was the field's historic sympathy for democratic socialism something to defend, modify, be embarrassed about, or repudiate? What did social ethics contribute to the struggles over gay and lesbian sexuality that divided the denominations? In a field featuring new traditions and markers of cultural difference and identity, what was the value of having a tradition and how should different social-ethical communities deal with each other? And what, belatedly, did social ethics have to say about averting environmental catastrophe and ruin?

Dealing with these questions, social ethicists kept alive the social gospel progressivist, Niebuhrian realist, and liberationist traditions, revised and blended Protestant and Catholic versions of these traditions, nurtured offshoots of them, sustained distinctly confessional approaches, fashioned postmodern critiques of all traditions, and embraced neoconservatism and evangelicalism. Most social ethicists stayed to the left politically, and a bit less so theologically, but the field's right flank grew in both areas. Fluid boundaries and hybrid identities became commonplace, including fusions of conservative and radical perspectives exemplified by Stanley Hauerwas and the "radical orthodoxy" group.[1]

In the early 1970s Lutheran social ethicist Robert Benne joined the traffic to the neoconservative Right and judged that no one with his politics could teach social ethics at a mainline Protestant seminary. Thus he left the Lutheran School of Theology in Chicago for Roanoke College. But Benne kept his membership in the Society of Christian Ethics (SCE), where he found increasing ideological company as American politics swung to the right. Conservative evangelicals joined the SCE and American Academy of Religion, challenging both organizations to broaden their claims to ideological diversity. Neoconservatives and conservative evangelicals surged into the public square and the Republican party, launching "culture wars" against liberal denominations and secular liberalism, and organized the Institute on Religion and Democracy, which raised money from right-wing foundations to attack the policies of the Episcopal, Presbyterian, and United Methodist churches. In the 1990s they blasted the liberal churches for clinging to economic progressivism and for taking seriously liberationist critiques of white, male, and heterosexual privilege.[2]

Neocons and traditional conservatives were not the only ones to say that mainstream social ethics had swung too far to the left or had always been that way. Ecumenical Protestant ethicist Max Stackhouse and Catholic ethicist Dennis McCann forcefully agreed with neoconservatives about economics, which raised, for many, the question of whether Stackhouse and McCann had become neocons too. Stackhouse played a similar role in church debates over sexual justice, though in the latter case he spoke for what he described as an embattled ecumenical consensus barring gays and lesbians from marriage and ordination.

Capitalist Apologetics as Public Theology: Max Stackhouse and Dennis McCann

Stackhouse seemed to exemplify the neoconservative story, having begun his career as a democratic socialist in the mold of his teacher James Luther Adams before drifting rightward on economic and social issues. In the 1970s he was a critic of the American military–industrial complex and an advocate of economic democracy. In the 1980s, while teaching at Andover Newton Theological School, Stackhouse began to hedge on American militarism and capitalism, took a dim view of feminist theology and gay rights, and advocated public theology. His version of public theology stressed human rights and the Calvinist doctrine of common grace, backed by the Tillichian concepts of religion as ultimate concern, religion as the substance of culture, and culture as the form of religion. Deeply influenced by Tillich and Reinhold Niebuhr, Stackhouse featured Tillich's dialectic of sacramental and rationalist consciousness, which Tillich resolved through his concept of theonomy.[3]

But Tillich stressed that his religion and politics made sense as a unity only if there was such a thing as non-utopian socialism, which he called "religious socialism." By the late 1980s Stackhouse had given up on Christian socialism, advising theologians to leave behind the fantasy of a cooperative commonwealth. Good public theology was liberal in its commitment to critical reason, universalistic human rights, regulated capitalism, and political pragmatism, he argued. He resented being lumped with neo-conservatives, which happened frequently after he began writing for neocon journals. To Stackhouse the tag was unjust. He identified with mainline Protestantism, his theology was Tillichian, and he was not a Republican, so how could be a neocon? His increasingly strident pro-capitalism and opposition to gay liberation, however, ended the question for many social ethicists about the appropriateness of the tag.

In 1991 Stackhouse and McCann wrote a manifesto for a post-Communist world and the next era of social ethics: "Public Theology after the Collapse of Socialism: A Postcommunist Manifesto." For social ethics, they declared, the death of Soviet communism was a momentous event, one loaded with things to atone for, because modern theology and social ethics usually espoused some version of the socialist faith: "The Protestant Social Gospel, early Christian realism, much neo-orthodoxy, many forms of Catholic modernism, the modern ecumenical drive for racial and social inclusiveness, and contemporary liberation theories all held that democracy, human rights, and socialism were the marks of the coming kingdom." But modern theology and social ethics were dead wrong about socialism, the authors judged: "The future will not bring what contemporary theology said it would and should."[4]

Theologians described a fantasy, not something real; meanwhile, really existing socialism collapsed under the weight of its own impracticality, tyranny, and corruption.

To Stackhouse and McCann it did not matter that social democracy had a long record of militantly opposing communism; the death of the Communist mistake discredited every form of socialism. Modern theology had already vested far too much of its social hope in the vision of a fully realized democracy. The authors assured their readers that no serious person still believed that the best route to social justice was to gain political control of the marketplace and means of production. The demise of ugly, totalitarian socialism marked the occasion to stop giving theological sanction to the fantasy of a socialist economy blended with democracy and individual rights.

More than that, it was an occasion for repentance. The collapse of socialism was not like other recent crises, Stackhouse and McCann admonished. It was, instead, a judgment on modern theological sin, demanding repentance of theologians and ethicists. They explained that in the recent crisis leading to the Gulf War, the USA had had to face its responsibilities as a great power in the Middle East. In Central America in the 1980s, the USA had to deal with problems that its own paternalism played a role in creating. Before that, the war in Vietnam exposed America's national arrogance, and the civil rights movement demanded the repudiation of white racism. Each of these crises altered the social landscape, but none showed modern Christianity to be guilty of something demanding repentance, they observed. Modern ecumenical Christianity stood for international responsibility, opposition to nationalist arrogance, and the abolition of racism. In these areas, it had a commendable tradition, one that rightly censured American complacency and/or malevolence. In political economics, however, modern ecumenical Christianity had a long record to atone for: "All too many religious leaders still cling to the belief that capitalism is greedy, individualistic, exploitative and failing; that socialism is generous, community-affirming, equitable and coming; and that the transition from one to the other is what God is doing in the world." That dead-wrong presumption had to be confessed and renounced if modern ecumenical Christianity was to be publicly relevant in a globalizing world.[5]

Besides inheriting a socialist bias from the social gospel, Stackhouse and McCann lamented, modern Christianity was rife with claims to epistemological privilege that made its positions impervious to correction and negated its effectiveness in the public square. Varieties of Barthian theology, Wittgensteinian fideism, fundamentalism, dogmatic confessionalism, and liberation theology were prevalent in theology, all of them claiming immunity from outside criticism. Stackhouse and McCann reiterated a central Stackhouse theme, that theology had no genuinely *public* message if it did not "reach beyond confessional particularities, exclusive histories and privileged realms of discourse." The only worthwhile social ethic was public and cosmopolitan. There was a place for theology as the proclamation of personal sin and redemption, the authors allowed; mostly, that place was a church building. Narrative theology had its charms, as did metaphorical theology. Certainly, confessional traditions were not wrong to teach their confessions. There was even "a valid ministry" to be served in the various theologies of special interests: "If theology is primarily the reflected experience of some particular gender or race or support group, let them serve the needs of their sectarian enclaves."[6]

But theology and ethics had more important work than boosting the morale or interests of individuals, confessional groups, and sectarian enclaves. It had to strengthen the intellectual credibility and social relevance of Christianity in the public square. To be publicly relevant in a globalizing social order, Stackhouse and McCann urged, Christianity had to speak the reasonable, testable, non-sectarian language of public theology, developing a social ethic "in which democracy, human rights and a mixed economy are acknowledged as universal necessities." A relevant social Christianity would address an emerging global public linked by new forms of technology and interdependency. It would advocate a "reformed capitalism" that used law, politics, education, theology, and ethics to constrain capitalist exploitation, while spurning inherited illusions about the purpose of economics.[7]

The purpose of economic activity was to maximize production and accumulation, not to build a just order. Stackhouse and McCann put it plainly: "Creating wealth is the whole point of economic activity." Theologians had a long record of ignoring this elementary truism of neoclassical economics; somehow they were even proud of doing so. Christian ethicists needed to get real about economics, the authors judged. If they changed their habits in this area, they stood a chance of being respected by social scientists and the business world; otherwise they made their field look ridiculous. Instead of applying democratic political norms to the economic sphere or imagining ecologically correct economic systems, social ethicists had to accept the real-world superiority of corporate capitalism. They needed to learn "how to form corporations and manage them, how to find markets, how to develop technology, how to work with employees, and how to make profits for the common good." The next great challenge for social ethics was to work with and become relevant to the globalization phase of the capitalist revolution. Social ethicists had to "labor in the vineyards of the world – even when the vineyards reach around the globe in new patterns of corporate capitalism."

That required giving up inherited prejudices about capitalism. Since corporate capitalism was already transforming the world in its image, Christian ethicists needed to appreciate why it was prevailing. Stackhouse and McCann urged that if Christians learned to appreciate the creativity and productive efficiency of corporations, they might "even learn to love them as we have learned to love our churches, neighborhoods, nations, schools and hospitals." The Postcommunist Manifesto ended with a send-up of 1848 and a summons: "Christians of the world, awake! Now that the specter of communism has vanished, cast off the spell of economic dogmatism! There is nothing to lose but ideology and irrelevance."[8]

Stackhouse's prominence in the field, and the manifesto's strident rhetoric, assured an ample response, some of which was favorable. Even some of its boosters winced at the stridency, however. Robert Benne noted that he had taken essentially the same position a decade earlier, when the social punishments for doing so were harsher in the social-ethics guild. He appreciated the support he had received from Stackhouse and McCann, and was tempted, 10 years later as a movement conservative, to give three cheers to the manifesto. But Benne was also a Lutheran who cringed at displays of ardor and political religion. The manifesto made him cringe several times; thus he gave only two cheers. Stackhouse and McCann were too eager to match redemption to the right kind of ideology, and their ambitions for a world-embracing public theology were overreaching: "The tendency to draw a straight line between the Christian Gospel and human action in any economic program, as well as the inordinate claims made for its clericalized model of public theology, deserve criticism." In this area, Benne suggested, it was much easier for neo-Calvinist Stackhouse and Catholic McCann to meld together than it would have been for either with him, even though all three had essentially the same politics: "If Lutherans can't or won't supply the zest for social transformation exhibited by our Calvinist and Catholic colleagues, then perhaps we can provide a bit of ballast for the balloons they send up."[9]

In essence, Benne judged that the manifesto was too ideological and smacked of overreaching neocon imperialism, despite the fact that he claimed the neocon label while Stackhouse and McCann spurned it. Stackhouse and McCann told colleagues that they were not neocons precisely because they were not ideologues or infatuated with American supremacy. Stackhouse pointed to his admonition against neocon triumphalism in *Public Theology and Political Economy* (1987): "Let us not be smug about this. Let us not uncritically celebrate the corporation today when in fact many features of corporate life produce items of little lasting value, distribute them inequitably, consume inordinate quantities of the world's nonrenewable resources, and cooperate with the most exploitative forces present in other lands." Moreover, he did not dismiss "the horror stories of discrimination, pettiness, meanness, and the rat race told by executives and laborers alike." The problem that neocons rightly stressed, he argued, was that modern theology had a "blind spot" for economics. In subsequent years, while sounding increasingly like Novak, Stackhouse asked why, if social ethicists were so adept at distinguishing different kinds of socialism, they couldn't do the same thing for capitalism.[10]

He fashioned theological ethics as a critical resource in the comparative analysis, assessment, and guidance of public life in church and society, publishing books collaboratively with scholars who shared this concept of the field, especially McCann. McCann's early work contrasted the "religious disinterestedness" of Niebuhrian realism with liberation theology, contending that Niebuhr's profound sense of the limits of human effort offered a more critical and pragmatic approach to society than the "revolutionary enthusiasm" of liberationists. Upon teaming up with Stackhouse he described their project as a realistic alternative to anti-capitalist leftism and neocon triumphalism. There had to be a place in social ethics, he argued, for pro-capitalist advocacy that rejected the "abstract and ill-informed denunciations of capitalism" prevailing in the field *and* that stopped short of neocon overreaction. In 1993 Stackhouse moved from Andover Newton to the Stephen Colwell chair at Princeton Theological Seminary; two years later McCann moved from DePaul University to Agnes Scott College, just as his massive reader, coedited with Stackhouse and Shirley J. Roels, *On Moral Business*, was published. McCann, noting that social ethicists usually focused on economic justice at the national and international levels, argued that it also needed to deal with marketing, finance, accounting, human resource management, and other specialized business disciplines. Stackhouse, plugging hard for cosmopolitan public theology, argued that theology had a worthwhile future only if it assessed the relative validity of its doctrines and practices by the highest standards of truth and justice available in rational discourse.[11]

For Stackhouse the difference between political theology and public theology was crucial. Modern theology and ethics abounded in political theologies, which were usually rooted in a particular religious or denominational standpoint, and which usually told the government how it ought to act, although there were also sectarian and separatist political theologies that opted for mere rebellion. For the most part, he stressed, political theology was an enterprise of liberal or conservative church figures focusing on the state. It addressed the public through politics. Genuinely public theology was something else, asserting the priority of the public sphere over its political dimension. Sometimes he put it snappily, that the public was prior to the republic. The public sphere was the entire matrix of schools, law courts, hospitals, communications media, religious organizations, and other institutions of community life and civil society, including the customs, moral values, and everyday living concerns of communities. Public theology reflected critically on all of that, expressing and analyzing the public dimension of faith as it manifested itself in the interlocking threads of social and cultural existence.

To Stackhouse it was sheer folly to discuss globalization without mentioning God; he wanted social ethicists to press the point. His three-volume anthology on "God and globalization" ranged widely over its subject, featuring scholars from a variety of perspectives, organized around the New Testament references to principalities (powers), authorities, and dominions. In the New Testament, he noted, the Greek term for the powers *(exousia)* appeared more than 100 times and was often linked with official leaders, or more often, the symbolic power of offices and roles. In both cases, the powers had a distinct theological dimension. When ordered in right relation to the divine source and norm of all existence, the powers served important ends. When the powers became consumed with their own value or were otherwise cut off from the transcendent source of life, they became enemies of the flourishing of life and the good. Stackhouse urged that globalization without divine order and the divine good was a menace to life, but globalization that helped restore the right ordering of the powers to the divine ground of the good was redemptive.[12]

Right Ordering and Sexual Difference

For Stackhouse, theonomous ordering was not merely the high-flying worldview principle that it was for Tillich and Adams. Applying it to sexuality, he found himself lining up with church conservatives, though he regarded himself as a defender of an under-defended middle ground, not a conservative. Commenting on the many pronouncements of American Protestant denominations on the ethics of sexuality since 1970, Stackhouse contended that mainline churches, despite being chronically embroiled in intense controversies over gay rights, repeatedly found their way to a commendable middle ground. They upheld the human and civil rights of gays and lesbians, but refused to betray fundamental Christian teaching about the privileged moral status of heterosexual marriage. This position deserved to be recognized as the consensus view of the ecumenical churches, he argued. Instead its ecumenical stature was rarely noticed, much less respected, and the controversies raged on.[13]

Repeatedly the ecumenical denominations declared that genital sexual relations should be confined to heterosexual marriage, which was the moral ideal for intimate relationships. Being gay or lesbian did not negate anyone's human rights, the churches agreed; in addition, gays and lesbians deserved not to be discriminated against in housing, employment, and others spheres of civic life. At the same time, the churches did not morally sanction gay sexuality or same-sex marriage. Officially, they excluded sexually active gays and lesbians from ordained ministry, though Stackhouse allowed that some denominations had ambiguous policies on this issue. Further, the churches adopted liberal feminist principles regarding equality of dignity, opportunity, status, and compensation, but rejected radical feminist theories that viewed patriarchy as the root of all evil. Finally, the churches agreed to welcome gay, lesbian, and divorced people into the spiritual fellowship of the church. Modern churches spoke and sang the faith with a mildly feminist tone, Stackhouse observed, but they explicitly reaffirmed "the basic teachings about the normative character of the heterosexual family" whenever they addressed the subject.[14]

In political terms, the mainline churches sought to accommodate feminist, womanist, and gay rights perspectives without rejecting the essential beliefs of most Christians and the classical Christian tradition about the privileged status of heterosexual marriage. More importantly, Stackhouse argued, the churches got it right theologically, despite the clamor for ordaining gays and lesbians and supporting gay and lesbian marriage. Scripture taught that life was about relationships and the relational ideal was fidelity in communion, which had a normative character: "It is an enduring, reasonable, and coherent conviction of those religions born out of the Biblical traditions, that the authors of the Adam and Eve stories of Genesis were inspired to see the human situation with a degree of revealing accuracy." By creating humanity and giving to human beings a "nearly godlike" dignity, Stackhouse argued, God enabled human beings to enjoy communion with God and each other, exercise freedom, and recognize God's laws and purposes. Further, God distinguished human beings into male and female, "a differentiation that both makes possible an interaction between them that is similar to a relationship with the Creator and makes them potential partners in the processes of creation."[15]

One could not get more fundamentally significant than that, Stackhouse implored. In the biblical understanding, there was a created order, and true fidelity occurred only within the framework of this ontological order. The primary patterns and purposes of sexuality were disclosed in God-given norms of a biological and theological nature – fidelity and fecundity. These norms were institutionalized in heterosexual marriage, which Stackhouse acknowledged was more relative, in its shape, to historical context. In Jewish and Christian history the shape of family life was patriarchal, sometimes matriarchal, usually tribal or clannish to some degree, for centuries feudal or manorial, recently bourgeois, and very recently dual-career. As far as family shape was concerned, he reasoned, the modern church was right to accept that there were different kinds of families, most of which should be welcomed into the fellowship of the church, just as the church was right to contend for universal fairness, dignity, human rights, and civil rights. But the church was also right to accept that it had no right to overturn the most fundamental notions taught in scripture about the existence of a created order and the purposes of God for humanity.[16]

Many churches, nonetheless, ordained gays and lesbians to ministry and performed services of union for gay and lesbian couples. Stackhouse allowed that by some appearances the "advocacy movements in the Ecumenical churches" seemed to be winning. Advocates of sexual justice in the two denominations closest to him, the United Church of Christ and the United Presbyterian Church USA, described the pertinent ethical norm in this area as "justice love." Stackhouse called them "false prophets." Beverly Harrison described gay and lesbian sexuality as a liberating break from the religious and societal ethic of "compulsory heterosexuality." Stackhouse replied that Harrison's work in this area was "antitheological, anti-ethical, and anti-intellectual." He advised her to think about how her "projection" charges could be turned against her, instead of charging that her opponents needed therapy for their hang-ups and intolerance.[17]

In 1996 Episcopal bishop Walter C. Righter was accused of heresy for ordaining a gay priest, but was not censured. Afterwards Righter declared that misogyny and homophobia were linked, especially in the anxieties of people who feared change. The struggle over gay sexuality was a fight between the past and the future, he urged, and the church of the present needed to formulate a new social contract. Stackhouse replied that misogyny, homophobia, and fear of change were undoubtedly bad things, but Righter's position undercut "the very prospect of a normative theology and an enduring morality able to assess and guide changing experience in changing societies."

Despite the wide currency that Righter's position held in the academy and liberal congregations, Stackhouse argued, it was not likely to prevail in any mainline denomination, and it definitely would not prevail in any denomination that took seriously its biblical-covenantal basis.[18]

He explained that mainline Protestants did not want to be driven into sectarianism. Mainline Protestants belonged to mainline churches because they believed in civilization and shaping a decent culture. They respected the fundamental truths of Christianity and the foundations of Western civilization. They had no desire to be hostile to culture, exiled from legitimate justice causes, or constantly angry about the secular or pagan character of American society. They wanted to play a role in making American society more just and good. Stackhouse implored that it was a bad thing, neither just nor loving, to denigrate the way that God wanted people to live. Thus it was imperative for the mainline churches to reject the gay rights agenda of making "gay coupling equal to heterosexual marriage," even as the churches upheld the human and civil rights of all people. God created human beings for fidelity, fecundity, and family, Stackhouse argued. True justice and love flowed from being faithful to God's plan: "Sexuality, the formation of households and homes, the nurture of children and the development of ways to aid those in need, ought to take place in the covenanted relationships of a differentiated civil society which recognizes the reality of the basic orders of creation or spheres of life."[19]

Stackhouse's preference for public theology over political theology had something to do with the politics of the two issues for which he was best known. Though his fervent pro-capitalism and strictures on gay and lesbian sexuality were minority views in the social-ethics guild, both made sense to public majorities that would have been surprised to learn what he was up against in the American Academy of Religion, the SCE, and eventually, his denomination. In 2005 the General Synod of the United Church of Christ became the first major Christian deliberative body in the USA to pass a formal statement of support for equal marriage rights for all people regardless of gender. The resolution, supported by approximately 80 percent of the delegates at the synod's meeting in Atlanta, reaffirmed the denomination's support of equal access to civil marriage regardless of gender and explicitly declared the church's support of gay and lesbian marriage. In most ecumenical denominations something like the consensus view described by Stackhouse retained the force of church law, but in several denominations the trend lines were clearly in the direction of liberalization.[20]

In American Catholicism, ethicist Lisa Sowle Cahill was a major proponent of cautiously liberalizing church teaching in this area, leaving open the possibility of gay and lesbian relationships that passed the tests of Christian moral norms. For Marvin Ellison, the leading advocate of gay liberation ethics, the issue at stake was one of sexual justice.

Lisa Sowle Cahill: Sources, Norms, and Moral Reasoning

Lisa Cahill, a social ethicist at Boston College, grew up primarily in northern Virginia, earned her doctorate at the University of Chicago under James Gustafson, and began her teaching career at Boston College in 1976. She wrote widely on sexuality, family, and bioethics from a moderately liberal Catholic and feminist perspective. Deliberate, scholarly, and probing, her writings approached ethical issues through a fourfold grid of sources: foundational texts of the faith community (the Bible), the collective experience of the faith community (tradition), normative accounts of the human (philosophical theories of ideal humanity), and descriptive accounts of the human (natural and social scientific knowledge). In the area of sexuality, she observed, modern ethicists tended to rely most on biblical arguments and scientific descriptions, even though they tended not to be experts in these fields. Ethicists waded into arguments about scriptural interpretation and scientific evidence at their peril, but also necessarily.[21]

Eschewing novel interpretations of her own, Cahill dealt with Genesis by drawing on feminist biblical scholars Phyllis Bird, Sandra Schneiders, and Phyllis Trible. Bird argued that the sexual complementarity theme in Genesis 1 was about the sustainability of nature under divine care, not sexual hierarchy. Schneiders warned against focusing exclusively on the literal sense of a text and limiting the meaning of a text to its original audience. Trible argued that Genesis 2 described a sexually undifferentiated (not androgynous) earth creature (*'ādām*) that God differentiated by a subsequent act into male and female. Cahill judged that Schneiders had the crucial argument, which relieved Christians of needing to find any particular thing in the text, including the egalitarian discoveries of Bird and Trible. In Trible's account, humanity was not intrinsically sexual, which seemed a high price to pay for feminist equality. For Cahill, it was enough to say that difference and cooperation were part of the original creation described in Genesis, the context of sexual differentiation was God's providence for creation, supremacy and subordination were conditions of sin, and modern interpreters appropriated texts with questions not imagined by the scriptural authors.[22]

She acknowledged that the Bible as a whole contained a moral code favoring the institutionalization of sexuality "in heterosexual, monogamous, permanent, and procreative marriage." By treating heterosexual marriage as the place for sexual relations, scripture supported the continuity of family, church, and civic life and nurtured affective commitments between spouses. It specifically condemned adultery, fornication, sexual immorality, and homosexual acts as violations of the covenant community's sexual norm. Undeniably, the Bible prescribed "a certain fundamental norm of human relationships." However, Cahill cautioned, the existence of the norm does not give it undeniable authority. The Bible does not provide a detailed sexual ethic, describe how the general norm should be applied in practice, or explain how sources besides the Bible should be used in formulating moral arguments. In the Bible, heterosexual monogamy is a norm, but so is patriarchy. Moreover, monogamy and patriarchy are both confirmed by Christian tradition, cross-cultural anthropology, and philosophical anthropology. If modern Christians no longer hold out for the authority of the patriarchal norm, what is the basis for insisting on the authority of exclusive heterosexual monogamy?[23]

Cahill observed that it was virtually always a circular basis. Christian ethicists made an exception for heterosexual monogamy by fashioning a "circular construal of central Christian images and human insights," finding in heterosexual monogamy values and safeguards intrinsic to the biblical idea of creation. They defined what was normatively human and Christian, claimed that heterosexual monogamy was demonstrably consistent with the norm, and claimed that sexual hierarchy was not. Cahill stressed that the demonstration consisted of an appeal to a critical norm brought to the Bible by Christian tradition and often supplemented by philosophy or science: "The persuasiveness of the norm depends on a reasonable consensus, based both on immediate experience and on normative reflection employing philosophical categories and central Christian images, that human persons are images of God, and by definition are capable of and are most fully human when enjoying goods such as freedom, rationality, sociality, cooperation, commitment, fidelity, and equality." Socially and interpersonally, the meanings of sexual experience were realized most fully when sex was "pleasurable, reciprocal, affective, unitive, and procreative." Heterosexual monogamy was said to enhance these goods, while sexual hierarchy did not; thus it was reasonable and moral to retain the former biblical norm while dispensing with the other.[24]

But the Bible itself contains numerous exceptions to and loose applications of its norm of monogamous, heterosexual, procreative marriage, Cahill noted. Ancient Israel sanctioned polygamy and concubinage; Levirate marriage augmented the birth of heirs; Deuteronomy allowed divorce at the husband's initiative; and Matthew and Paul permitted divorce. If the Bible allows exceptions of this sort, Cahill argued, it is reasonable for ethicists to make room for exceptions on something – human sexuality – that modern science understands better than the Bible, though she allowed that nobody understands it very well: "Despite the fact that homosexuality remains incompletely understood, we find what appears to be a consensus that most persons discover their sexual orientation as a 'given,' if an ambiguous and confusing given, rather than choosing it. Furthermore, homosexuality is a variation in human sexual orientation that occurs consistently even though with less frequency than heterosexuality." These factors do not establish psychological or biological health, much less moral rightness, Cahill observed; on the other hand, since gay and lesbian sexuality is not chosen and constantly recurs in human societies, every society has a moral obligation to enhance human life as far as possible for gays and lesbians: "The decisive question for Christian ethics is which 'naturally' occurring and even functionally 'healthy' facts, states, and relations also represent moral ideals."[25]

Cahill accepted the church's teaching in this area, that the central Christian norm is a lasting, faithful procreative union between one woman and one man. The ethical challenge was to formulate a moral criterion for exceptions to the norm. Her proposal had two tracks. First, she argued, Christian ethics rightly defined fidelity as faithfulness to the essence of the norm, but it also needed to allow variance in the ways the norm was fulfilled, allowing for "some leeway at the level of practice." Second, Christian ethics had to allow for the possibility of ethical departures from the norm and unusual applications of it. Most ethically justified departures in the second category were creative applications, she argued, and outright departures only rarely qualified for moral approval. But there had to be room for such a possibility. Outright departures from the essential meaning of the norm were not intolerable "if they represent the most morally commendable courses of action concretely available to individuals caught in those tragic or ambiguous situations that agonize the decision maker and vex the analyst."[26]

That opened the door to a sexual justice perspective, if only by a crack. Citing papal and church teaching for support, Cahill defined the marital ideal by two fundamental principles, committed partnership and openness to procreation. To her, the ideal was "an intentionally permanent commitment of partnership and love; and the willingness of the couple to welcome and nurture as a couple any children that result from their union." To accept this standard as the ideal was not to exclude exceptions to it under inappropriate or impossible circumstances, she argued. Cahill mentioned situations involving remarriage after divorce, premarital sex in committed relationships, avoidance of conception, "and even the committed homosexual relationship." In the category of excluded exceptions she mentioned adultery, casual sex, and coercive or abusive sexual relations. Admonishing against simplistic moralizing, she urged that moral reasoning about sexuality is as complex as the ethics of economics or war. In the past it mattered to the moral equation that the basic organization of society depended on kinship, unlimited procreation was a good, marital and familial ties defined the social identity and roles of a person, and there was no concept of a sexual orientation. In modern times it matters to the moral equation that these things are no longer true and that sexual orientation is not controllable.[27]

As an ethicist Cahill sought to be "irenic, ecumenical, and cautious." Conflicts over sexuality were notoriously divisive, causing immense suffering, exclusion, and even hatred, she observed. In the church and society there was a great need for irenic, ecumenical, cautious moral reasoning about sexuality. On the whole, she judged, liberal Protestantism had a better record on women's equality and liberality toward gays and lesbians than the Catholic Church, which remained "persistently captive to patriarchal assumptions." Official Catholic teaching about sex and gender persistently defined women by their reproductive function, tied sexual meanings to the biological structure of sex acts, and focused on the morality of individual acts, excluding the social relationships and contexts in which acts occurred. On the other hand, liberal Protestantism and some liberal Catholic scholars tended to relativize biblical teaching too dismissively, substituting modern values of consent, tolerance, and freedom for supposedly "obsolete" moral prohibitions. Cahill urged Christian ethicists to the hard, complex, integral work of holding together the moral wisdom of the Christian past and present with modern knowledge and experience.[28]

Marvin M. Ellison: Sexual Justice

Marvin Ellison, a professor of Christian ethics at Bangor Theological Seminary and a doctoral protégé of Beverly Harrison's at Union Theological Seminary, was a leading advocate of sweeping away obsolete prohibitions in the name of a covenantal ideal that he called "communal right-relatedness." To be truly ethical, he argued, a sexual ethic must be centered on just relationality. Anything that thwarts or denigrates loving, mutual, equal relationships was, he contended, unjust: "Sexual 'justice-love' of mutuality and respect means honoring the goodness of sexuality, having gratitude for diversity, granting special concern for the sexually abused and violated, and acknowledging accountability for sexual behavior." He described the collective struggle for sexual justice as the "longest revolution," citing Carter Heyward's statement that sexual justice is "the most trivialized, feared, and postponed dimension of social justice in western society and, possibly, the world."[29]

For three years Ellison served on a Presbyterian committee commissioned by the 1988 General Assembly of the Presbyterian Church that was charged with drafting a new statement on sexual ethics for the denomination. His concept of "justice-love," a single standard test of all sexual relationships, was the centerpiece of the group's 200-page report, "Keeping Body and Soul Together: Sexuality, Spirituality, and Social Justice." The report declared, "To do justice-love means seeking right-relatedness with others and working to set right all wrong relations, especially distorted power dynamics of domination and subordination." Submitted to the 1991 General Assembly, the report sparked a national media controversy for its moral endorsement of gay and lesbian relationships.[30]

Social ethicist Karen Lebacqz commended the report warmly. "Justice-love" was an awkward phrase, she allowed, and so was "right-relatedness," but the church needed new language to convey its faith "that God demands nothing more nor less than justice and love intertwined." Any human activity not exhibiting love and justice together was morally wrong; Lebacqz marveled that an official church body had finally said so: "At last a report that places sexuality squarely within the framework of concerns for *justice* in church and society." Theologian Tom Driver dryly gave his assurance that the spectacle of pro-feminist, pro-gay Presbyterians did not presage the collapse of civilization.[31]

Outside the world of liberal seminaries and congregations, the report was subjected to much rougher treatment. Conservatives condemned it as a betrayal of Christianity, repeatedly characterizing the report as an attack on heterosexual marriage. Cultural critic Camille Paglia heaped widely quoted ridicule on "the joy of Presbyterian sex," sneering that liberal Presbyterians remained sexual reactionaries while imagining themselves liberated. *New York Times* religion writer Peter Steinfels, taking the measure of Presbyterian complaints and a media firestorm, predicted that the report would be "virtually dead on arrival" at the General Assembly of 1991, which turned out to be accurate. Presbyterian commissioners opted not to debate the report, offered a word of thanks to the committee members for their work, and added a word of "regret for the cruelties its members have suffered."[32]

Ellison, absorbing the backlash, cautioned sexual justice advocates that their cause was not for the faint of heart. American society routinely denigrated gays, lesbians, bisexuals, and transsexuals, he observed, and stereotypes abounded. Even liberal churches often failed to back up their claims about being inclusive with any deeds of solidarity or genuine hospitality. Ellison remarked, "When a church says, 'all are welcome' but has no track record of anti-racism, anti-sexism, or anti-homophobia action and no history of explicitly gay-affirmative outreach, the message conveyed is a resounding lack of interest in the lives and struggles of gay people." Too often, he observed, churches offered merely grudging acceptance of gays and lesbians. Many settled for a policy of "don't ask, don't tell," which healed nobody. The church needed justice ministries for people of all sexual orientations, restoring dignity to all hurting and wronged persons. The watchwords of justice ministry were solidarity and the joy of shared struggle, Ellison wrote, and something else, "a certain 'moxy,' or moral fearlessness."[33]

Ellison wrote to attract allies to that cause: "The audience I have in mind certainly includes other gay, lesbian, bisexual, and transgender persons, but also feminists of all colors, progressive people on the fringes and in the mainstream of religious communities, and all who are tired of the old sex-negativities and who long for more egalitarian relationships." He supported the right of gay and lesbian couples to marry, arguing that it was a human right; on the other hand, he had mixed feelings about the gay marriage movement, because he had mostly negative feelings about marriage. Historically, he explained, the institution of marriage naturalized male gender privilege, reinforced female subordination, and was the lynchpin of the state's regulation of sex: "By and large the institution is more associated with inequality and oppression than with justice and liberation." Having once been married heterosexually, Ellison did not look forward to being married to his male partner. Some marriages were true partnerships, he acknowledged, and achieving the legal right to marry was an indispensable goal of the sexual justice movement. But the real prize was the "queer notion" of sexual justice and liberation, not making an oppressive institution more inclusive. Stressing that sexual justice was intrinsically connected to other liberation struggles, Ellison drew a line on what that meant negatively; he was finished with progressive movements that did not explicitly welcome him as a gay man: "My participation in political alliances now depends on whether gay, lesbian, bisexual, and transgender people are honored as colleagues and mentors in a common struggle."[34]

Liberals and liberalism usually failed the test, he argued. Though Ellison hesitated to criticize liberal churches that nurtured his moral development, he warned repeatedly that liberals lacked courage on this issue and that liberalism itself was part of the problem. Liberal ideology was based on the individualist dichotomy between public and private and the rationalist dichotomy between reason and feeling, he argued. Both prevented liberals from taking gay liberation seriously as a justice issue. Liberals consigned sexuality to the private sphere, and thus had little room for sexuality as a justice issue. To the extent that they defended sexual freedom they did so on the basis of the right to privacy, not justice. The liberal impulse was to keep personal things personal, free of political interference; to Ellison, that approach was shortsighted, artificial, frustrating, and ultimately reactionary. The liberal wall between the personal and public spheres was an obstacle to justice and liberation, just like the patriarchal dichotomy between thinking and feeling that liberals also embraced. The field of Christian ethics, having been devised by liberals, usually assigned sexuality to personal ethics or moral theology, not social ethics, which was about the public ordering of social, political, and economic relations of power. Ellison urged that feminism had a better idea.

Feminists began by rejecting the split between thinking and feeling, which led them to reject the barrier between the personal and public, which gave rise to their liberating slogan: The personal is the political. Ellison remarked, "Although liberalism professes to value human dignity, its tendency toward individualism places self-regard and other-regard in tension, forever in opposition." Dichotomizing between the harsh world of the public sphere and the private haven of heterosexual family life, liberalism relied on the willingness of women and other socially subordinated peoples to sacrifice themselves for the public good: "In contrast, feminist and gay liberation perspectives encourage self-love as healthy and morally good, especially among marginalized peoples. Self-love is a corrective to internalized oppression and self-hate." Putting it personally, Ellison declared, "As a gay man, although I have been nurtured by liberalism, I have also become vividly aware that this tradition makes no room for receiving me or other nonnormative peoples. Liberalism sees my struggle for self-respect as a private concern, not as a matter of justice or as a problem of disordered power."[35]

Instead of privatizing sexuality as a concern that individuals managed on their own, Ellison wanted social ethicists to view sexualities – the embodied capacities of persons for love and intimacy – as being strengthened or diminished by social structures and relationships. Any society or religious community standing for heterocentrism – the view that heterosexuality alone was normal and ideal – taught everyone not fitting the model to hate themselves. Patriarchy taught that erotic power was dangerous, female sexuality in particular had to be controlled, and the safe place for it was male-dominated heterosexual marriage. Ellison countered, "As progressive people of faith, our calling is to embody *justice-love*, an intimate co-mingling of our longing for personal well-being in our bodies and right-relatedness with others throughout the social order." Unlike the sexual libertarian tradition, gay liberation at its best was profoundly moral, social, and relational. It did not work at the level of isolated individuals. Putting it theologically, Ellison urged that gay, lesbian, bisexual, and transgendered people needed church: "We need communities of spirited resistance, offering relatively safe and secure places to dream dreams of a world without homophobia, racism, sexism, and other oppressions. We need nurturing places to protest against routinized brutalization and moral indifference, to celebrate our survival, and to keep us receptive to justice claims from beyond ourselves."[36]

In every ecumenical denomination movements for sexual justice existed, cracking the ecumenical consensus that Stackhouse lauded. The official church laws and codes to which he pointed were real, but so were moxy-ish dissenting movements that added sexual justice to the lexicon and agenda of progressive Christianity and social ethics. In Stackhouse's denomination, the United Church of Christ, ordinations of gays and lesbians to the ministry were commonplace, as were services of union. In the Presbyterian Church, a rather un-Presbyterian policy of "local option" was adopted after 30 years of fighting over gay rights, in the hope of buying some denominational peace. In the Episcopal Church the election of an openly gay man, Gene Robinson, as a bishop (New Hampshire) in 2003 sent shockwaves through the Anglican communion. By then the ecumenical "consensus" to hold the line against gay and lesbian relationships still existed in theory, but not in practice, and the theory was fading.

Debating Economic Democracy

On political economy Stackhouse made a credible claim to speak for another majority, but not the majority of social ethicists. J. Philip Wogaman, a prominent figure in the social-ethics guild and dean of Wesley Theological Seminary, offered a typical response to Stackhouse-style obituaries for economic democracy. Wogaman recalled that when he wrote his popular textbook on comparative economic ideologies in the 1970s, *The Great Economic Debate*, he nearly eliminated the chapter on *laissez-faire* capitalism. A few years later, during the Reagan ascendancy, Wogaman was grateful not to have prematurely written off an ideology that had seemed, only recently, to be obsolete. In the 1990s it seemed to Wogaman that capitalist boosters were making a similar mistake in writing off the entire Marxist, social democratic, and Christian socialist traditions. There were too many kinds of Christian socialists to be able to say much about them as a whole, Wogaman acknowledged, but three commonalities were significant. In modern Christianity, it was the Christian socialists that cared about oppressed people. Second, it was the Christian socialists who challenged capitalist ideology, especially that the unrestrained market could be trusted to ensure the public good and take care of the poor. Third, it was the Christian socialists who contended that society had a collective moral responsibility to deal with economic problems and serve the common good. Wogaman worried that in the current environment of capitalist triumphalism, Americans were being swayed to ignore "the excesses and brutalities and idolatries of the free market."[37]

Theologian D. Stephen Long, arguing from the "radical orthodoxy" perspective of John Milbank, took aim at the Stackhouse/McCann model of public theology, noting that it was instructively similar to the economic concept of value – something nonparticular that substituted for particular goods while facilitating trade and consumption. Public theology thus conceived had the same shape as global capitalism. Both had a formal character that recognized "value," but lacked any particular or substantive goods. The vision of a capitalist cosmopolitan salvation was not new in Western history, Long observed; it went back to Kant's liberalism. What was new was the spectacle of theologians describing the global market as a redemptive institution. Novak said it brazenly, but Slackhouse and McCann were only slightly less unabashed, as in their statement, "Enhancing the capacity for capitalization in responsible corporations is as much the new name for mission as development is the new name for peace." They also described the business corporation as a "worldly ecclesia," while affirming that it was wrong to make an idol of corporations. Long shook his head; contrary to the Stackhouse/McCann claim to classical "orthodoxy," Christian orthodoxy viewed capitalism as a threat to Christian identity. Economic exchanges were obviously necessary for human flourishing, he allowed, but it was simply wrong to claim that creating wealth was the "whole point of economic activity," as if the cultivation of virtue and the ultimate end of communion with God had nothing to do with economics. It was equally wrong to demand that theologians repent of their tradition's anti-capitalism. Long replied that the real contempt worked the other way around, in the everyday dismissal of Christian values by economists and business corporations. Stackhouse and McCann, having hitched their theology to corporate capitalism, succeeded in being relevant and public, but sacrificed core Christian teaching "for that relevance and publicity."[38]

Some social ethicists took the path of Stackhouse and McCann, usually in the name of public relevance. English social ethicist John Atherton, canon theologian of Manchester Cathedral and secretary of the William Temple Foundation, was a surprising early example. A product of the Anglican socialist tradition of Temple and F. D. Maurice, Atherton declared in 1992 that the downfall of communism marked the end of democratic socialism too. The debate that Christian socialists had sustained about the differences between social democracy and mere liberal democracy no longer mattered to Atherton. What mattered was to get on the right side of the capitalist blowout. Affirming his "conversion" to the pro-capitalism of Novak, Benne, Stackhouse, and McCann, he explained that he had belatedly absorbed "a lesson that most church leaders, official bodies and theologians in the West, and the ecumenical movement, have yet to learn." The lesson was that corporate capitalism had prevailed to the point of achieving a "dominating position in today's world." If Christian ethicists aspired to any public relevance, they had to accept that the victory of an unleashed, global, corporate capitalism changed the rules of the game. Atherton gave his assurance that he had no ideological interest in pressing this argument; he sought merely to make sense of what was happening. He found a dramatic way of putting it, however. Now that communism had expired, "there is no socialist economics, there is only economics."[39]

There was something strange about claiming that the death of communism somehow discredited the vision of social and economic democracy, a thesis I argued in two books, *Reconstructing the Common Good* (1992) and *Soul in Society: The Making and Renewal of Social Christianity* (1995). Democratic socialists were the original anti-Communists. For 60 years nothing was more galling to them than to be lumped with their Communist opponents. Consistently, militantly, and through decades of up-and-down political fortunes, social democrats warned that communism was suffocating and ultimately unsustainable. To them it was incredible to be told, afterward, that the death of communism somehow marked the end of their relevance. The ravages of unfettered capitalism and imperialism that produced socialist movements in the first place had not diminished with the triumph of a more corporate and globalized capitalism. Christian ethicists pressed for gains toward social and economic democracy because their commitments to freedom, equality, and community and their resistance to the predatory logic of capitalism compelled them to seek an alternative to it. To call this entire project a mistake was to resign Christian ethics to a status quo politics that preserved the privileges of the wellborn and fortunate. It was to pretend, wrongly, that concentrations of economic power could be ignored without undermining political democracy and without doing harm to the poor and vulnerable.[40]

It was also to assume, wrongly, that the planet's ecosystem, a finite reality, could withstand another century of the unlimited growth of "modernization," much less the manic logic of post-Cold War capitalist globalization.

Ecology as Political Economics and Theology

American social ethics up to the 1970s was a determinately humanistic tradition that took little interest in nature beyond human nature. From its biblical heritage it assumed that human beings were privileged by divine validation over other species. From its Enlightenment heritage it assumed that Christianity was defensible only as a form of religious humanism. By taking what liberal theologians called "the anthropocentric turn" away from religious orthodoxy, modern Christianity intensified the traditional Christian view that humanity was the center and apex of creation. Aside from an occasional appeal to romantic nature consciousness, for inspiration, the social gospelers rarely referred to the natural world, and Christian realism was even more fixated on history at the expense of nature. American theologians took an instrumental view of the natural world, which left them poorly suited to challenge commercial society's view of nature as a commodity to be conquered and exploited. Beyond the rather weak reminder that Christians were called to be stewards of creation, the major traditions of modern theology and social ethics provided little resistance to a dominant commercial order that valued nature chiefly for its exchange value.[41]

In the early 1970s, however, a few theologians began to interrogate this legacy; in social ethics it took a little longer. The environmental movement of the 1960s caught the attention of theologians John B. Cobb, Jr, H. Paul Santmire, and Joseph Sittler, who called for changes in religious awareness and social policy to halt the destruction of the natural world. Santmire's book, *Brother Earth: Nature, God, and Ecology in a Time of Crisis* (1970), was the first example of what came to be called "ecotheology." By the end of the 1970s only a few examples existed, but in the 1980s the field took off, notably in works by Elizabeth Dodson-Gray, George Hendry, Dieter Hessel, Matthew Fox, Douglas John Hall, Sallie McFague, and Jay McDaniel. All were theologians, while social ethicists were still debating Niebuhr, Vatican II, and liberation theology. Of the first wave of ecotheologians, Cobb was the most significant.[42]

Cobb was already the leading theologian of Whiteheadian process thought when he became an environmentalist in the late 1960s. He had begun his academic career in the early 1950s, found a home at Claremont School of Theology in 1958, and published a major work of process theology, *A Christian Natural Theology*, in 1965. By the end of the decade he felt settled in his thinking. Social issues belonged to social ethics; his ambition was to build up process thought as a major theological and philosophical school. His son Clifford, however, convinced him to read Paul Ehrlich's bestseller *The Population Bomb* (1968), which shook Cobb profoundly. Though he winced occasionally at the book's alarmism, he found its message almost unendurably powerful: "For the first time I saw, vividly, the ways in which increases in consumption and population feed on one another and bring insupportable pressures to bear on the earth's resources. The danger to our future and that of our children struck me with almost unbearable force."[43]

Next he read Lynn White Jr's celebrated critique of nature-harming monotheism "The Historical Roots of the Environmental Crisis," which, together with Ehrlich, shattered Cobb's belief in academic disciplines. White charged that the anthropocentric bias of Christianity was a major cause of the environmental crisis. In a rush of emotion, Cobb judged that if modern civilization was destroying the ecological basis of sustainable life, it was foolish to trudge along in conventional disciplines. Traditional ways of compartmentalizing knowledge and doing theology seemed obsolete to him. During the same period he read Cone, Gutierrez, and Daly, who convinced him that academic theology privileged the interests and standpoints of white, male, middle-class academics. "I watched with admiration as Black theology, liberation theology, and feminist theology all rejected disciplinary boundaries," he later recalled. "And I came to the conclusion that the theological vocation was to think self-consciously about the most important issues of the day. I was persuaded that no problem could be more critical than that of a decent survival of a humanity that threatened to destroy itself by exhausting and polluting its natural context."[44]

More than ever he believed in process thought. Cobb had become an adherent of Alfred North Whitehead's metaphysical system because it provided a credible religious worldview; now he realized it was also an ecological worldview. Whiteheadian thought presented a picture of a divinely-influenced universe oriented toward beauty and the intensification of experience, in which the universe demonstrated an inherent tendency toward increasing complexity, self-organization, and the production of emergent wholes that were more than the sum of their parts. It rejected the dualisms of mind/matter and history/nature that grounded the anthropocentric bias of traditional Christian monotheism; thus, to Cobb, it offered a religious worldview that was not merely credible, but also healing and transformative. Increasingly Cobb noticed environmental asides by Whitehead and Cobb's teacher Bernard Meland that he had previously ignored, and he remembered that his mentor Charles Hartshorne had long been concerned with environmental issues: "It was past time for me to join my teachers in a side of their thought and practice that I had disregarded."[45]

Cobb surpassed his teachers in integrating ecological concern with process thought. He lectured widely on ecology, organized a conference on the "theology of survival," and wrote his first book on environmentalism, *Is It Too Late?: A Theology of Ecology* (1972). Urgently he contended that the ecological crisis was the most fundamental and overwhelming problem facing humankind, it was too severe to be left to policy engineers, population pressures threatened to destroy the world's renewable resources, and a "new Christianity" was needed to meet the crisis. Noting that traditional Christianity fostered a "lack of concern for the subhuman world," he implored that one could believe in the sacredness of human life without reducing the value of other living things to nothing. Existence consists fundamentally of living events, Cobb argued. Events are alive to the extent that they include novelty; all events include aspects of their past; the things that we ordinarily called "living" are societies of events. All things are living and have value in an ongoing creation that is charged with the divine impulse. Cobb urged that this was a better perspective than traditional Christianity and modern humanism, because traditional Christianity viewed only the transcendent creator as sacred, and humanism was barren of spiritual value and even more anthropocentric than Christianity. To believe in God was to have faith that human beings work *with* something greater than themselves, Cobb asserted. Inspired by this faith "our generation is called upon to repent of its self-indulgent ways, to discipline itself, and to accept reductions in the standard of living to which it has grown so quickly accustomed."[46]

Soft-spoken and kindly in personal bearing, Cobb was a whirlwind of activity, writing works of constructive theology, contributing to debates on philosophical theology, speaking at academic and environmental conferences, taking part in Christian–Buddhist dialogues, writing practical theology, and serving as the process theology movement's chief organizer and institutional leader. He gave most of his later academic career to constructive theology and most of his post-academic career to activism; in both cases he poured out lectures, articles, and books, and lectures and articles that turned into books. For 10 years he waited to acquire more than a sprinkling of coworkers in ecotheology. After they emerged he found rays of hope in their work, especially the ecologically centered work of the World Council of Churches (WCC); at the same time he lamented the lack of intellectual vigor in Christian congregations and the decline of ecumenical Christianity as a cultural force.

Cobb wanted the churches to espouse an inclusive and inspiriting ideal, transformation: "Transformation is what happens when God is effectively present in an event. God's presence introduces a novelty that enables a human being to incorporate elements from the situation into experience in a way that is enriching." That was straightforward Whiteheadianism, but Cobb's writings in practical theology often dispensed with references to Whitehead. He argued that many things in the witness of the church needed to be transformed, not merely renewed, and the church was called to be a transforming witness. He did not pretend to see it happening. "I see present trends in the church and in the wider society as self-destructive," Cobb wrote in 1993. "We are on a bulldozer heading for a cliff and overrunning all the obstacles to self-destruction. The few gestures I can make toward slowing down the bulldozer or diverting it in a different direction are all quickly pushed aside."[47]

He tried to be hopeful: "Our churches do not have to function mindlessly as they decay." Elsewhere he was more specific: "The only hope is that people will be grasped by a different vision of what the future might be like, one that is, in the words of the World Council of Churches, 'just, participatory, and sustainable.'" The latter phrase encapsulated his consuming social and religious concerns. Contending that endless economic growth in a finite world was not sustainable, Cobb insisted that there was such a thing as having enough and that intolerable suffering could be avoided only if the world's major powers committed to a serious strategy of sustainable development. In 1981 he teamed with biologist Charles Birch to warn, "The ideology of growth misunderstands the true nature of growth and aims at a monstrosity that will destroy life." Drawing upon economist Herman Daly's pioneering work in "steady state" economic theory, Cobb and Birch called for a "third way" economic strategy that rejected the pro-growth ideologies of socialism and capitalism, which maximized general production, in favor of sustainable welfare rooted in worker and community ownership.[48]

Crucial to this argument was the distinction between general product growth and actual economic improvement. In 1989, the year before Cobb retired from Claremont

School of Theology, he and Herman Daly elaborated this distinction in a major work, *For the Common Good: Redirecting the Economy toward Community, the Environment, and a Sustainable Future.* General product growth was much easier to define and quantify than actual economic improvement, they acknowledged, but some measure of sustainable economic welfare was necessary if economic policymakers were to distinguish between constructive and harmful growth. Working with Daly and Clifford Cobb, and drawing upon studies by economists Xenophon Zolotas and A. Myrick Freeman, Cobb devised an index of national economic and social health that drew a grim picture of American trends: "Economic welfare has been deteriorating for a decade, largely as a result of growing income inequality, the exhaustion of resources, and the failure to invest adequately to sustain the economy in the future." The authors pointed especially to diminishing returns of oil extraction and the ripple effects of rising energy costs upon investment and worker productivity: "As increasing competition lowers the returns to labor, and as returns to scarce capital decrease, the income gap is likely to worsen if actions are not taken to improve equality."[49]

Repeatedly Cobb warned that the global economy generated massive levels of debt, structural dependency, accelerated inequality, and unsustainable environmental destruction. To continue to expand the globally integrated economy without regard for the social and environmental ravages of growth was to invite disaster. He advocated a political economy of worker and community ownership and a politics that rejected the fixation with economic growth fostered by capitalism:

> As long as we collectively suppose that meeting economic needs and having full employment require a growing economy, we will collectively support policies that put greater and greater pressure on an already over-stressed environment. We will also continue to support policies whose results are greater and greater injustice, with the rich getting richer and the poor getting poorer both within each country and among the world's nations.[50]

To Cobb, the Stackhouse/McCann manifesto was terribly wrong and commonplace. It ignored nearly everything that mattered and swallowed neoclassical economic theory as a description of the way the world worked. Instead of addressing the subordination of nature and social needs to economic power under global capitalism, Stackhouse and McCann simply accepted the system and the theory that justified it. Neoclassical doctrine taught that the purpose of economic activity was to maximize wealth; Stackhouse and McCann repeated that maxim as though Christian ethics had nothing to say on the subject. Neoclassical theory was about acquiring as many goods as possible for as little labor as possible, not about building sustainable communities; Cobb noted that Christian anthropology and ethics begged to differ. Neoclassical theory treated labor as a nearly perfect substitute for land, in which "land" denoted the entire physical world; Cobb preferred the Christian doctrine of creation. Stackhouse and McCann accepted the neoclassical picture of the economy as an isolated system through which exchange value circulated between firms and households. Cobb urged that the economy was firmly tied to the physical world and that environmental damage was no mere "externality." Briefly, Stackhouse and McCann lamented that America was addicted to debt, dependent on foreign oil, and faced with ecological disaster, but the rest of their manifesto was a pitch for more debt-driven, dependency-breeding, nature-harming economics.[51]

Cobb recognized that Stackhouse and McCann had realism, of a sort, on their side; maximizing economic growth was apparently a precondition of any feasible politics in the present system. He did not doubt that Stackhouse and McCann wanted a better capitalism that rectified the problems created by actually existing capitalism. He also acknowledged that some of the policy ideas that he and Daly put forth in *For the Common Good* might be wrong; his protectionist proposals were especially dubious. But he firmly opposed dealing with environmental problems by administering larger doses of the same policies that created the problems. To Cobb, achieving sustainable welfare for all people was a moral imperative. Maximizing general production was not the way to do it, because that created larger environmental problems in a world already facing the disastrous problems of global warming, ozone depletion, acid rain, deforestation, land and water pollution, and population growth.

Instead of financing environmental repair from the surplus earnings of nature-harming development, he argued, it was better for societies to build sustainable economies: "Community is served far better by retaining community control over the economy than by first destroying community – as by factory closings – and then responding to the resulting social disruptions with special programs paid for by the extra product generated by the closings." As an educator and Christian he could not content himself with training students to be winners in a predatory economy:

> The whole world has become more and more dependent on a complex system administered by multinational finance and dependent on diminishing resources of energy whose use is environmentally destructive. Fewer and fewer communities will be able to participate in making the decisions that are determining their well-being, since more and more will be dependent on decisions made by those who control capital investments and whose professional commitment is maximization of profit, not well-being.[52]

The specter of eco-apocalypse hovered over much of Cobb's work in ecotheology and sustainable economics. Having come to environmentalism through Ehrlich's searing Malthusian picture of a planet ravaged by overpopulation and consumption, he tended to write out of that framework and feeling, like much of the ecotheology movement that he inspired. Some ecotheologians, however, wrote in a more lyrical, evocative, sometimes poetic voice about the hidden wholeness and interconnectedness of all things, sometimes drawing on process theology. Sallie McFague, Thomas Berry, Brian Swimme, and Jay McDaniel wrote ecotheology of that sort. So did Larry Rasmussen, the leading social-ethical proponent of ecological theology.[53]

Eco-Justice for the Sake of Everything: Larry Rasmussen and Daniel C. Maguire

Like Cobb, Rasmussen was known for other things besides his environmentalism. A lay theologian in the Evangelical Lutheran Church of America, he taught in his early career at Wesley Theological Seminary and for 18 years as the Reinhold Niebuhr Professor at Union Seminary; in both places he wrote widely about theological ethics, the relation of the Bible to ethics, and Dietrich Bonhoeffer. Above all, however, he was known for putting ecology at the top of the social-ethical agenda. For Rasmussen, the eco-apocalyptic tone of much ecological writing was warranted, but not his style.[54]

Insightful, genial, often flashing a gently wry sense of humor, he wrote about possible looming catastrophes with an irenic spirit. Rasmussen was fond of Rabbi Abraham Joshua Heschel's maxim that humankind would not die for lack of information, but was in danger of perishing for lack of appreciation. In Rasmussen's style of ecotheology, appreciation was a main theme and characteristic. He mixed short, crisp sentences, especially in transition, with long evocative ones, peeling his topics layer by layer. Though he spoke often of "the earth and its distress," he rarely referred to "the environmental crisis," which lacked the real-life sense of all things bundled together "from the inside out." The environment, after all, was not unsustainable, he observed; what was unsustainable was the modern way of life. Though he put it more gently than Cobb, Rasmussen shared Cobb's urgency that lacking a fundamental course correction, the earth was condemned to overheat, choke on its waste, exhaust its resources, and turn on its human destroyers.[55]

As a starting point for construing what it meant to respect the integrity of creation, he invoked the theory of "biotic rights" developed by social ethicist James Nash. Nash, in his book *Loving Nature* (1991), elaborated the universal moral implications of loving creation, arguing that "all creatures are entitled to moral consideration." At one end of a dipolar model he placed respect for individual lives; at the other pole he posited a holistic concern with collective connections. In 1993 Nash sketched a doctrine of rights, delimiting the moral responsibilities of human beings to nonhuman life. In his scheme, all creatures possessed the right to participate in the "natural dynamics of existence" (a right to flourish according to nature), the right to healthy and whole habitats, the right to reproduce their own kind without human interference (biodiversity), the right to fulfill their evolutionary potential without human interference, the right not to be abused, the right to reparations or restitution to restore natural conditions disrupted by human abuse, and the right to a fair share of the goods necessary for individuals and species. Rasmussen noted that these were prima-facie claims, not moral absolutes. Nash's "biotic rights" were principles deserving to be honored and upheld, not inviolable absolutes. In some circumstances, overriding moral claims took priority. But the idea that human beings owed principled moral consideration to nonhuman life, not just each other, Rasmussen argued, was indispensable to paying nature its due.[56]

"The integrity of creation," as a phrase, was coined by the WCC, as were the terms "sustainability" and "the sustainable society," though not "sustainable development." Prior to 1974, "sustainability" referred to the sustained yield of forests and fisheries. At a 1974 conference in Bucharest, the WCC expanded the term beyond renewable natural resources to apply to human behavior and society: "The goal must be a robust, sustainable society, where each individual can feel secure that his quality of life will be maintained or improved." In the WCC's first accounting of what that meant, it entailed equitable distribution of scarce supplies, common opportunity to take part in social decisions, ready availability of food, prudent use of non-renewable resources, and adaptability to climate changes. The following year, at the WCC's Nairobi assembly, the council adopted a new program aimed at building "just, participatory, and sustainable" societies that upheld the equal importance of justice, common access, and ecological sustainability. Rasmussen allowed that in the succeeding generation the WCC hurt itself by issuing statements with a stridently anti-capitalist, anti-Western tone. German liberationist Ulrich Duchrow, a neo-Marxist theologian deeply involved in the WCC's Commission on Justice, Peace, [and] Creation, was a major influence on the council's ideology and rhetoric during the 1980s and 1990s.[57]

But Rasmussen was a major player in the commission too, where he exerted a moderating influence, and he stressed that the council's fundamental message in this area was not socialist: "It was that capitalist economics prosper most when labor, technology, and capital are fluid; they are thus driven to international integration at high levels; and this takes place at the expense of local communities, their resources, culture, and ways of life." The WCC condemned the destructive aspect of capitalist "creative destruction," not the capitalist system *per se*, Rasmussen explained. Its critique focused on the devastation of communities at the low end of the neo-liberal development process, the showering of benefits on the privileged and well-connected, and the destruction of the environment. By insisting that sustainability had to be linked with justice and participation, the WCC used the term very differently to the sense in which it subsequently became operative in corporate, development, and Northern national government circles. To the World Bank, "sustainability" meant global economic growth qualified by environmental considerations. To the WCC and other progressive non-governmental organizations it meant economic viability, social equity, and ecological renewability. Rasmussen remarked, "The search, therefore, is for local and regional self-reliance and economic and environmental sustainability, as well as the global institutions needed to serve these on a contracting planet."[58]

Elsewhere he put it more plainly: "I do not think the question is, how do we wrap the global environment around the global economy? I think the proper question is, how do you wrap both economies and environment around healthy community?" The rhetoric of sustainable development took the global economy for granted and tried to sustain it ecologically, he explained. It assumed a 500-year history of globalization in which European tribes scattered across the earth and colonized various parts of it. After World War II, development experts categorized all economies and societies by a single standard of "development" or its lack, measuring social well-being by the level of production and consumption of goods. The third wave of globalization started with the fall of Soviet communism and the rise of a global market. Here the market itself became the model for society, never mind that it destroyed local cultures, substituted commercial monocultures, exacerbated inequality, and ravaged the earth. Rasmussen took no interest in sustaining that: "I want something where folks – all the folks – have a greater say in what their life together will be, and that requires a kind of decentralization that 'community' indicates and 'sustainable development' does not." Thus he spoke of sustainable community, not sustainable development.[59]

Sustainability was the capacity of social and natural systems "to survive and thrive together, indefinitely," he proposed. It required thinking "sideways and around corners," not just up and down hierarchically or forward and backward chronologically. It grasped the interconnections of relevant wholes, not merely the pieces. Rasmussen liked to quote economist Kenneth Boulding's remark that anyone who believed in infinite growth on a finite plan had to be either a madman or an economist. Boulding described the earth as a closed system, spaceship earth, and humankind as the crew. Everything in the capsule recycled with feedback loops; everything went somewhere and nothing went away. Rasmussen cautioned again, however, that earth was not the problem; people were the problem. Instead of spaceship earth, a better image was a day-care center, where children had enough space to be free but were not free enough to kill themselves or others: "The electrical circuits cannot be chewed; dangerous objects are placed out of reach; the schedule allows for the unexpected and unpredictable." In earth as day care, there was a margin for sin and error. People did not have to get it perfectly right, as in a spaceship.[60]

Clarifying sustainable community, Rasmussen began with a story. In April 1994 the Society for International Development held its convention in Mexico City. At a closing plenary grandly titled "Building Partnerships and Collaboration Towards Global Transformation" a representative of the indigenous peoples of Chiapas, the Zapatistas, was allowed to speak. Two hours after the North American Free Trade Agreement (NAFTA) had gone into effect in January, the Zapatistas had declared war on the Mexican government. Chiapas, one of Mexico's richest provinces, possessed vast oil reserves, dams that supplied more than half of Mexico's hydroelectric power, and one-third of Mexico's coffee production. It was also one of Mexico's poorest provinces, afflicted with widespread hunger and disease amidst a sprawling network of economic modernization projects. One third of the population of 3.5 million was Indian. Addressing the development professionals, the Chiapas rebel explained that his people had no interest in seizing state power. They wanted simply to dwell in their land, be recognized as fellow human beings, and govern themselves. Their struggle was to reclaim their community from the government and corporate interests. Rasmussen stressed that the Zapatista rebellion was not a revolt against a lack of development. It was a rebellion against 40 years of outside overdevelopment that had ruined their community, on top of 500 years of oppression.[61]

He called the Chiapas rebellion a "glimpse" of an alternative to neo-liberal development, a "reverse ordering of economy and ecology." In the usual ordering, environments were altered to serve the economy, while profits paid for environmental cleanup. In sustainable community reverse-ordering, economies were altered to serve comprehensive environments. The difference was stark and vast, he emphasized. Neo-liberal development strategies, including the environmentally sensitive ones, began with an open and essentially unlimited physical world. Sustainable community began with a very limited world that operated by borrowing. Development strategies viewed the world as industrial and information systems needing to be managed as human and natural capital; community strategies attended to home environments "in a comprehensive way around basic needs and quality of life." Development professionals spoke pretentiously of managing the planet or even of saving it, while community proponents focused on saving the neighborhood.[62]

Saving the neighborhood projected far beyond any particular neighborhood, however. Rasmussen allowed that certain kinds of problems, such as fixing ozone damage or reducing greenhouse gases, required international treaties to usurp authority from local and regional bodies. Dealing with pollution, global warming, genetic diversity, marine ecosystems, and oceans also required international government cooperation. In all cases the Catholic doctrine of subsidiarity applied to community sustainability: No higher authority or organization should be charged with rectifying a problem that a lower, smaller, or more local organization could solve. The key to subsidiarity in this area was appropriate scale and action, Rasmussen argued. Threats to a shared atmosphere required transnational cooperation. But food, shelter, livelihood, and many other needs were met best on a community and regional basis, not by centralized institutions. Rasmussen judged that most of the norms of sustainable community – participation, solidarity, sufficiency, material simplicity, spiritual richness, responsibility, and accountability – were best served on a subsidiarity basis. To change from the current path of manic destruction to sustainable community entailed operational problems of staggering size and complexity, he acknowledged. Sticking to subsidarity was the best way to do it.[63]

It helped to be religious, he suggested. The seventh assembly of the WCC took place in Canberra, Australia in 1991. Its theme was "Come, Holy Spirit, Renew the Whole Creation!" Section I of the assembly, titled "Giver of Life – Sustain Your Creation!" put a group of delegates to work on specific earth issues; Rasmussen was one of them. In a plenary address, Korean feminist theologian Chung Hyun Kyung electrified the assembly with a syncretistic appeal to move "from anthropocentrism to life-centrism." The speech set off an ecumenical and media controversy over Chung's syncretism and the theological boundaries of WCC discourse. Rasmussen's group stuck to the language of prophetic covenant symbolism, declaring, "The stark sign of our time is a planet in peril at our hands." Later he reflected that the language of prophecy had the advantage of being able to grab people's attention and call "unabashedly" for conversion before it was too late, "turning to God and away from destructive ways of life."[64]

He was fond of saying, "Being with the gracious God means loving the earth." For Rasmussen, that meant that the universe is God's body. God is more than the creaturely, Rasmussen assured, but the creaturely is charged with God's glory and is the only place where the divine fullness is known. In Christian contexts he sometimes added, "Being with the gracious God means loving Jesus." For Rasmussen, as for Luther, the way of the cross was God's ethic. Applied to ecology, it meant that to redeem the planet, "go to the places of suffering and find God and God's power there." Finally, "Being with the gracious God means going home." To experience God's ever-gracious presence, he urged, one should look at one's closest reality: "When you find putrid death there, together with real remnants of life, take heart!" The God of the cross enters death to negate it.[65]

Rasmussen loved the tradition of American social ethics and taught it at Union Seminary, devoting roughly equal attention to the social gospel, Christian realism, and liberation theology. Sometimes he told his students that the next major social-ethical paradigm needed to be eco-justice, because, like it or not, "from here on it's either life together or not at all." That was a variation on the message of his friend and collaborator Daniel Maguire, who declared, "If current trends continue, we will not. And that is qualitatively and epochally true. If religion does not speak to [the threats of militarism and environmental catastrophe], it is an obsolete distraction."[66]

In that spirit Maguire and Rasmussen worked together in the Religious Consultation on Population, Reproductive Health and Ethics, which Maguire served as president. Rasmussen planned a post-academic career book on the eco-justice fourth phase of social ethics, while Maguire wrote on the necessity of a common Christian moral creed. As white, male, progressive products of the social-ethical tradition, they identified readily with the tradition and imagined a creative next stage for it.

Maguire, a prolific writer on justice issues and a former Catholic priest, stressed the "undergoading theme" of male power, "specifically white and Western male power." Males had a "seemingly universal genius for monarchical power, even in countries that are supposed to be democratic," he observed. With the burgeoning of capitalism in the East, male planetary power changed colors to some degree, but it remained firmly male, feminism notwithstanding. In a male-dominated world, thrones were a permanent temptation, at least for males: "You can do a lot on a throne. You can write the script, define reality, determine what and who is sacred; you can have one rule for the 'noble' courtiers and one for the commoners, and you can use people as compost for your privileges." Modern economics was a chief throne of male power: "There we find – surprise! – mostly men – like the pharaohs of old, royally and hegemonically perched." But Maguire judged that theory was even better than economic privilege in sustaining the rule of males. Theory defined the status of things, the earth, and people, conferring and legitimizing power; thus, "Theory is power, and most of Western theological, philosophical, and economic theory has been written by men, royally and hegemonically perched men."[67]

Did that mean that white males like himself and Rasmussen should just shut up and get out of the way? Maguire sympathized with that sentiment, but advised against it. Feminism, he argued, was unfinished business until men became feminists:

> Men must look at what they and their fellows tracing back to antiquity have wrought. The voices of the beleaguered and "wretched of the earth" and the wretched earth itself will continue to cry in pain until they – the victim gender and the victim earth – are joined in common quest with those who have too long basked in the sick aura of purloined privilege.

In a sexist world, maleness was "unjust wealth." But for Maguire that conviction fueled a vision of common radical Christianity and a beloved community beyond Christian borders. The goal was to transform all sexual, racial, and class privileges into common currency. Until males recognized the counterfeit nature of their inherited wealth, "a revolutionary job waits to be done and the earth will continue to die."[68]

An ebullient personality, gifted with sparkling humor despite the jeremiads, Maguire gave scintillating talks on the lecture circuit that galled Marquette University officials and the Catholic Right, especially when he opined against official "pelvic theology." Maguire protested that when Catholic hierarchs talked about war, complex casuistry prevailed, but when the topic was abortion, circumstances meant nothing: "Here they have only a single word to offer us: No! No abortion ever – yesterday, today or tomorrow. No conceivable tragic complexity could ever make abortion moral." Official Catholicism clung to fundamentalism only and whenever women's bodies were involved, he charged, protesting, "I find this situation abhorrent and unworthy of the richness of the Roman Catholic traditions that have nourished me." Maguire chastised Catholic theologians for leaving him and ethicist Christine Gudorf isolated on this issue. Though his colleagues spoke up on contraception, silence prevailed on abortion. Many colleagues agreed with him, often urging him on, but refused to acknowledge it publicly; he called them "uncourageously polite." Later the same thing happened on gay marriage, on which he contended that the right to marry was a human right, not an award for being heterosexual. Maguire insisted that the Catholic tradition was not immutable or uniform on these subjects; unfortunately, he allowed, his lack of public support from Catholic theologians made him look wrong.[69]

He took the same attitude to Catholicism that he took to religion in general: it was deeply implicated in the evils of the human record, yet contained the moral and spiritual core of the world's salvation. Maguire allowed that religion was an "unlikely savior," having sacralized every form of violence and privilege that had to be overcome. But he believed that religion and morality shared the same source in symbolically charged apprehensions of fundamental meaning. The search for meaning, he argued, was universal, an eternal passion, and redemptive. Judaism and Christianity were essentially moral revolutions, explosions of ethical creativity that called for radical transformations of society. In Maguire's telling, all religions were vehicles of transforming moral energy. First came the primal awe at the gift of life; then came the moral and religious responses, which pronounced the gift good and sacred; thousands of years later, the saving powers of the religions were still largely untapped. He pictured religions as an array of radii shooting out from a common source, with atheistic humanism and Hinduism the furthest apart. Religion, despite being so much of the problem, also contained the solution, he contended. Religion, understood as ethically transformative sense of the sacred, was indispensable to the cultural revolutions that were needed to save the world from destroying itself.[70]

To that end he risked seeming old-fashioned in a postmodern age by proposing a common Christian moral creed. There were certain things that every Christian should confess and practice, Maguire argued, which happened to be the most important things in Christianity. His creed began with a profession of faith in the reign of God, which impelled believers to create a world in which oppression gave way to justice, opening to a new heaven and earth. The creed continued that biblical justice (*tsedaqah*) is the hallmark of God's reign, "a justice that sees the ending of poverty and its evils as the prime moral challenge and mission for Christian peoples." It professed that "the only holiness" consists of being in solidarity with the poor and excluded, and that prophecy includes "the art of cherishing the earth and its peoples, joining with the prophetic movements of all the world's religions." It professed that peace is achievable by justice, not by war; that Christians are "missionaries of truth" serving a God of truth; and that God calls all people to freedom, which is a virtue only when married to justice and compassion. It professed hope in the realization of God's plan and belief that the entire law is summed up in love, which compels love of enemies. And it professed that joy is the destiny of God's creatures, but where poverty and prejudice persist, the work of building the reign of God is not done.[71]

A Moral Creed for All Christians (2005) was soaked in biblical sayings and admonitions, pressing hard on the fullness of the Hebrew word for justice, *tsedaqah*. The Bible defined holiness morally, Maguire stressed, and *tsedaqah* was the ultimate expression of biblical morality, although the cold English term "justice" caught only a fraction of its meaning. Western/English justice was avowedly impartial and it assumed a private definition of poverty. It defined rights in terms of sovereign individuality, and it was static and conservative. Biblical *tsedaqah*, by contrast, was biased in favor of the poor and critical of the rich, assumed a social definition of property, defined rights in terms of social solidarity and need, and was evolutionary and revolutionary. Maguire noted that the US American symbol of justice was a blindfolded woman holding a scale that balanced perfectly. In the US, the ideal of justice was neat, mathematically balanced, and disinterested. Biblical justice, being thoroughly moral and social, was very different. Wearing no blindfold, it plunged into the messy business of making things come out right, understanding that the scales never balance otherwise. Maguire favored Heschel's saying that biblical justice was nothing less than "God's stake in history."[72]

Theologies were various, and so was Christianity, Maguire allowed. Not many Christians took their moral creed from the Bible. And yet it was there, waiting to be reclaimed: "There is an exciting, demanding moral creed in the biblical tradition. The religion we call Christianity is a moral classic. At times it has turned civilizations in a humanizing direction. At other times, it has decayed and become little more than comfort food." The role of theology was to call Christians back to the prophetic heart of biblical religion, he urged, sounding like Rauschenbusch. If American churches outside the conservative evangelical fold were struggling, perhaps it was because they had lost the "vision and excitement" of the Bible's essential ethical message.[73]

Maguire was right; it should have been possible to win every Christian's assent to something like the moral creed that he derived from the Bible. He reclaimed the ethical heart and center of prophetic faith. His insistence on speaking in a universal mode laid hold of profound truths: the moral core was real and everything in creation was at stake. As he keenly understood, however, only a small minority of American Christians understood Christianity in anything like his liberationist reading, and most of them did not speak of common creeds. His version of Christian morality was, after all, one particular attempt among others, with historical and cultural blinders like all other attempts. Being white, male, American, and economically privileged had something to do with his confidence in expounding the universal meaning of Christianity and all religions.

Liberation theology usually stuck to its original logic of particularity. If most "theology," it turned out, was really white theology, and male and middle-class too, the grail of universality was probably out of reach. Every theology was a particular vision, having come from somewhere. In liberation theology the fulcrum of knowing was a standpoint of solidarity with particular others, particular oppressed or excluded communities. For Sharon Welch it led to an ethic of risk that let go of Christianity and definitive answers. For Emilie Townes it led to inductive and poetic engagements with culture as a transmitter of evil. For Ada María Isasi-Díaz and María Pilar Aquino it led to the solidarity perspectives of *mujerista* and Latina feminist theology. These theorists ranged outside their primary discourse community to advance the cause of justice for oppressed people, but in ways that accented the consequences of difference.

Sharon Welch: Toward an Ethic of Risk and Conflict

Sharon Welch, the daughter of two social gospel ministers, identified primarily with feminist liberationism and secondarily with the Unitarian Universalist tradition. For most of her career she taught religious studies and women's studies at the University of Missouri; in 2007 she became provost at Meadville Lombard Theological School; throughout her career she pressed a fundamental question: how should one sustain the struggle for liberation, or even decide what it is, if there are no definitive answers?

Her first book, *Communities of Solidarity and Resistance* (1985), which was her doctoral dissertation at Vanderbilt Divinity School, put it boldly. Welch appreciated liberation theology for its radical witness against oppression, but she rejected liberationist claims to truth. Citing Cone's contention that non-liberationist understandings of the gospel were heretical, Welch replied that all such contentions smacked of special pleading. As a female oppressed by every version of Christian orthodoxy, she wanted nothing to do with the language of Christian orthodoxy and heresy. Moreover, her oppressor status as a white American made her doubly skeptical of liberationist truth claims, because she knew from personal experience that Christianity blended easily with structures of oppression. It was naïve and dangerous to say that only liberation theology was "truly" Christian, she argued. To take that line was to claim an exception from the contingent temporality of theological discourse, which was not credible even for something as admirable as liberation theology.[74]

To Welch, liberation theology was an exemplary recent form of the revolutionary strand in Christianity. She identified with it because she identified with its revolutionary consciousness and praxis, not because it appealed to Christian norms. Liberationist faith was true if it liberated oppressed persons, she argued. Nothing was added to the truth of liberationist claims by claiming continuity with biblical or dogmatic norms. Disclaiming any interest in the question of unbelief, she disbelieved in divine transcendence of any sort and regarded every form of orthodoxy as oppressive. To Welch, the feminist movement and parts of the peace movement were truly liberating because they were "intrinsically relative" enterprises devoted to the abolition of domination: "I find in sisterhood a commitment to liberation and an openness to different ways of understanding and reaching liberation." She did not see much liberation occur under Christian auspices:

> In sisterhood there is freedom from a self-securing that requires absolutizing one's perspective. In the Christian tradition, however, I find a pathological obsession with security, an obsession that impels the denial of difference (thus concern with heresy and essences), an obsession that leads to a blinding Christian triumphalism, an obsession that receives symbolic expression in the concept of the sovereignty of God.[75]

On the emancipatory revolution of sisterhood, Welch invoked Mary Daly; on the necessity of repudiating universal languages of morality, she invoked Michel Foucault. All forms of moral discourse contained rhetorical strategies to gain power, she argued, citing Foucault. Liberation theology was most compelling to her when it acknowledged its drive for emancipating power without leaning on dogmatic ethical claims. In Welch's rendering the language of universal values was equally repugnant because it reeked of privilege and masked its struggle for control. Every language of universality was an instrument of privilege and domination, she contended. One needed a privileged education to learn about ontological categories and universal values; universal languages were spoken by ruling groups precisely to avoid having to relinquish their power. When token exceptions from excluded groups spoke a supposedly universal language, they negated their own dignity. The category of "equal rights," for example, had a long history of masking discrimination and rewarding token exceptions. Welch declared, "It would be an act of the greatest folly for me to criticize sexism on the grounds of universally recognized values such as equality, the nature of moral persons, or any other determination of what characterizes the human, and thus women, as such." It seemed "absurd" to her to "use the very categories that masked my oppression in order to denounce it." Warning that the recent entry of women into "the worlds of academia, politics, and the business world" might be "a brief anomaly . . . easily erased," Welch did not believe that equal rights rhetoric was much of an ally in the struggle for permanent feminist gains. What mattered were particular acts of resistance to male domination. Feminism moved forward when women raised their voices, refused to be treated as sexual objects, and smashed patriarchal assumptions.[76]

In her early career Welch gradually let go of her identity as a Christian theologian, gravitated to social ethics, religious studies, and women's studies, and sought to formulate a feminist ethic. In addition, she stopped speaking the language of feminist sisterhood after reading black feminist and womanist critiques of its white supremacist presumptions. "Risk" became her central theme, one that she explicated by drawing on writings by African-American women. Following Emilie Townes, Welch conceived social ethics as the study of social structures, processes and communities, especially "socially shared patterns of moral judgments and behavior." If the shared social structures and patterns of morality were themselves immoral, Welch asked, how did one achieve to something better? Stressing the necessity of taking risks, the lack of a feminist ethic of conflict, and the indispensability of community, Welch fashioned an ethic of community and solidarity. Instead of prizing intellectual justification and universal morality, she argued, feminist social ethics put a premium on accountability and respect. To be accountable was to face up to the existence of harm, wrongdoing, and inequality of power. Townes described accountability as "a respect-filled communal dialogue with a transclass base." Welch added that to be respectful was to recognize the dignity, equality, and independence of others.[77]

A feminist ethic of risk and community was not to be confused with the communal approach of Hauerwas and Yoder, she emphasized. The communal approach rested on a cohesive community sharing definitive principles, rules, and customs. Welch's approach was a version of Jürgen Habermas's communicative ethics, featuring interactions between multiple communities that spoke different moral languages. The Aristotelian polis and the church imagined by Hauerwas were cohesive communities, but neither had room for a feminist understanding of female dignity and freedom. With Habermas, Welch believed in the communicative model of cultivating public conversations among diverse communities; against Habermas, she believed that the communicative model was liberating only if it rested on prior commitments to solidarity or concrete justice-making actions. Habermas, ruling out privileged claims and appeals to tradition or external authority, described an ideal of multiperspectival public conversation bounded by liberal norms of civility and rationality. Previously excluded communities were welcomed as participants; the goal was to achieve consensus. Welch objected that it was not very transformative merely to join an ongoing conversation, and solidarity was a better goal than consensus. Moreover, it was disrespectful to require participants from oral cultures to leave behind all reliance on tradition. Human beings were more than rational actors; mere agreement was less important than mutual transformation toward liberation: "When mutual transformation occurs, there is the power of empathy and compassion, of delight in otherness, and strength in the solidarity of listening to others, bearing together stories of pain and resistance."[78]

Feminist social ethics moved "from critique to action and back to critique," she argued. Lacking a basis in action, critique devoured the critic's hope and energy. Mere criticism led to numbness, a cynical despair at the futility of caring or seeing: "Without working with others on projects geared toward social change, it is impossible to maintain the vision and energy necessary to sustain long-term work." Welch cautioned that middle-class people who hung back from justice struggles were prime candidates for cynical despair. The numbness of middle-class privilege was a deadening byproduct of the luxury of being able to avoid oppressed and excluded people. Lack of engagement with community struggles for justice led to cynicism, a distorted form of rage that reflected the vicious cycle of disengagement. Cynicism viewed victims merely as victims. Welch urged that engaged activists saw larger realities and opportunities: "As long as critique occurs in the context of work for justice, it is possible to experience the essential factor in maintaining resistance – love for oneself, for the oppressed, and for those working against oppression."[79]

She acknowledged that early white feminism universalized the experiences of privileged white women in the name of "women's experience." Mary Daly, Rosemary Ruether, and many others described patriarchy as the fundamental form of oppression and women's liberation as the ultimate revolution, an account sharply rejected by

Audre Lord, Jacquelyn Grant, and Katie Cannon. Welch urged, however, that the corrective was not to denigrate personal experience as a category in the manner of many historicist and poststructuralist critics, notably Sheila Davaney. There was such a thing as referring to experience hermeneutically as a process or discursive strategy, eschewing essentialist presumptions. Moreover, Welch observed, the appeal to experience was a staple of black women's literature, as well as Ada María Isasi-Díaz's *mujerista* theology. Liberationists had serious disagreements to negotiate, including conflicts of interests and interpretation. Rejecting experience as a hermeneutical category would not solve any of them. What was needed, Welch argued, was an ethic of criticism that faced up to the inevitability of conflict between and within liberationist movements.[80]

She offered a recent personal example. In *A Feminist Ethic of Risk*, Welch observed, she had drawn extensively on the writings of black women. The book was ostensibly about the primacy of dialogue in creating feminist ethics, yet her title named only one dialogical partner, feminism, giving no indication of the substantial role played by womanist work in the book's argument. Womanist critics noted the problem; Welch replied that by attempting to write about racism, she had learned "more about how deeply it is embedded in my habits of knowing and naming." The best she could do was learn from her mistakes and try to root them out of her thinking, taking seriously the differences between constructive and dismissive criticism.[81]

She did not doubt that much of the deconstructionist criticism of feminist essentialism was constructive. Yet much of it was also wrongly dismissive, she argued. For example, feminists schooled in French deconstruction repeatedly dismissed Daly as an essentialist, notwithstanding Daly's emphasis on fluidity and change. Daly may have expounded an ontology, Welch allowed, but it was not one of fixed essences. Daly described women's "innate be-ing" as a verb, not a noun, she stated repeatedly that women belonged to different "tribes," and she stressed the diversity among women as individuals. Welch stressed the diversity among feminists, and vowed, "for now," to keep appealing to women's experiences, "an evocation of more stories, more details, more conflicts, coalitions, and relationships."[82]

Townes employed a similar emphasis on experience, stories, and relationships, with no caveats about "for now."

Emilie Townes: Womanism and the Cultural Production of Evil

Emilie Townes, the daughter of two college professors in Durham, North Carolina, surprised herself by becoming an academic. As a youth she marveled at her mother's classroom lectures in biology, but did not aspire to an academic career. Attending segregated schools, she was admonished by teachers not to spurn the opportunities won for her by Harriet Tubman, Frederick Douglass, and Booker T. Washington. Years later, in the published version of her doctoral dissertation, Townes recalled of the heroes framed on her classroom wall, "They became our silent judges, our measure of excellence. They rejoiced with us when we got arithmetic problems right or a new spelling word mastered. They were relentless in their demand for excellence and cheerleaders for our education. I hold those pictures firm in my memory."[83]

Taking her undergraduate degree at the University of Chicago, Townes stayed on for a master's degree at the Divinity School, was ordained to the American Baptist ministry, and completed a Doctor of Ministry degree at the Divinity School, where she was the school's only black woman in residence until her final two years. She coped with her loneliness by vowing to spend part of her ministerial career helping lonely seminarians of color. Afterwards Townes managed a seminary bookstore and taught a course at Garrett-Evangelical Theological Seminary, which, to her surprise, she enjoyed immensely, causing her to consider another degree. She planned to wait a few years before starting a PhD program, but met Katie Cannon at a conference. Cannon urged Townes not to lose any more time, telling her that in the entire USA there were only five black women with earned doctoral degrees teaching in theological education. For Townes, this admonition was another call to accountability. Enrolling at Northwestern University, she worked with historian Josef Barton and Garrett Seminary religious historian Rosemary Skinner Keller, pastored a local Metropolitan Community Church, and wrote a dissertation on Ida B. Wells-Barnett. In her early career she taught at Saint Paul School of Theology in Kansas City; later she taught for six years at Union Theological Seminary in New York; in 2005 she moved to Yale University as the Andrew W. Mellon Professor of African American Religion and Theology.[84]

Townes was mindful as she began her career that Cannon and a generation of older womanists led by Toinette Eugene, Cheryl Gilkes, Renita Weems, and Delores Williams had cleared a path for her. She started to write a book on the womanist approach to evil and suffering, then realized that collecting one would provide a richer account. *A Troubling in My Soul: Womanist Perspectives on Evil and Suffering* (1993) brought together 14 contributors. Organized around Alice Walker's definition of womanism, the book showcased a burgeoning community of scholars. Several contributors amplified Cannon's original critique of the Christian idealization of suffering; Townes put it plainly, rejecting every understanding of suffering as God's will. The main point of a womanist ethic was to eliminate suffering, she argued: "Suffering is outrageous. Suffering does not ennoble, enable, or equip this generation or future generations of Black people. A life based on survival and reaction does not produce healthy minds, bodies, or souls. The fragmentation of the spirit and the witness prevents the Black church from living in the new Jerusalem."[85]

Townes stressed that womanism was "intentionally and unapologetically biased." Disclaiming scholarly objectivity, the womanist approach was emphatically embodied, personal, and communal. Elsewhere she put it more personally, explaining that her work reflected her upbringing in a powerfully formative and loving family and her experience of black church Christianity in several congregations: "Unlike the modernist search for universal truths, I reflect from the particularity of my own faith journey." In a book on the social ethic of womanist spirituality, *In a Blaze of Glory* (1995), Townes struggled at first to express her experience of womanist Christianity as growing into the wholeness of spirit and body. Womanism as she knew it was something lived, not something catalogued in books; on the other hand, books had a role to play. Then came a breakthrough: "In utter frustration, I turned to my own poetic voice to break the silence. Poetry came as a response to a sermon found in Toni Morrison's novel *Beloved*. The way had revealed itself!" Afterwards her writings mixed poetry and prose to express the spirituality of "soulful relationships" that sustained her:

> to be called beloved
> is to be called by God
> to be called by the shining moments
> be called deep within deep.[86]

For Townes, the social conservatism of typical black church preaching was lamentable, but not lacking sympathetic qualities. It had a certain integrity rooted in a history of coping with racial oppression, which she respected even as she opposed the repressive aspects of its approach to gender and sexuality issues. The conservatism of secular social critics like Shelby Steele and Thomas Sowell, however, had no sympathetic qualities. There was nothing to be said for black social critics who specialized in condemning affirmative action programs. Sowell-type conservatism was a species of black self-denigration, she argued – "We have learned to hate ourselves without even realizing the level of our self-contempt. In loving ourselves, developing our hearts, we must become our own best critics and our greatest cheerleaders for justice and hope." Townes judged that Steele and Sowell simply ignored the structural aspects of social inequality in their celebrations of individualism and the opportunities of the global market: "They represent modernist notions of individualism and an ease with systems that promise diversity, but are structured to deny diversity's concrete demands for change."[87]

Another deadly species of self-denigration in the black community, she wrote, was colorism. Discriminatory practices favoring light-skinned blacks had long standing in elite black culture; all but one of the 21 male leaders and two female leaders of Du Bois's "Talented Tenth" (the top 10 percent of the black population by his reckoning) were mulattos. Light-skinned blacks predominated in subsequent twentieth-century black politics and activist circles, and many black businesses discriminated on the basis of skin color. In the 1960s, Townes observed, "Black is Beautiful" rhetoric defied traditional colorism, but its corrective impact on the black community and larger society were limited. Sadly she concluded, "The mournful legacy of colorism is relentless."[88]

In a Blaze of Glory operated mostly in that mood, sometimes as admonition. In person Townes was kindly, generous, and deep-souled; on the page she could seem despairing. In her preacher voice she wrote, "The Black Church of a lived spirituality cannot content itself with protestations of holiness if there is nothing holy present in how we hold one another and act as partners with God in shaping a witness in the lives of those folk who have not yet experienced the transformation of death and grace." A friend admonished Townes in reply, "Em, when are you going to do happy?" Townes replied, "I'm an ethicist – I don't do happy!" On reflection, she realized that was not a very good answer: "It began to haunt me. In parts of the African American faith tradition, being haunted is not considered bad or negative. It simply means that God is trying 'to get a word through' to you, and one needs to be still and listen." In the pulpit Townes spoke of hope and the promise of salvation; in her academic work those themes were in short supply. She vowed to close the gap, even as she wrote about a distressing topic, the crisis of health care in the black community.[89]

Black life in the USA was often painted "in absolutely grim and hopeless colors," she observed. To judge from the dominant media images, there was "nothing healthy or whole" in everyday black existence. Townes appealed for balance and empirical sense. There were more African-American males in college than in prison, "vastly more" self-supporting black mothers than ones on welfare, more black accountants than black athletes, and slightly more black families headed by married couples (47 percent) than by single mothers (46 percent). As for health care, drug addiction was no more a black problem than a white one – "Too much of the rhetoric from pulpit to podium has painted the impact of drugs on Black life as a near-hopeless devastation" – and black infant mortality rates were improving. On the other hand, Townes stressed, the picture in health care service was distressingly bad and unequal. Middle-class black families suffered higher mortality rates than middle-class white families, blacks consistently received less advanced treatment than whites, and 60 percent of the African-American population lived in communities which housed one or more uncontrolled toxic waste sites. Townes implored,

> we are called to love ourselves
> to one another
> *to love God hard*
> if we are to *live* out
> the pouring of God's spirit in our lives
> we must reach out to our brothers and sisters
> and touch creation with our hearts and souls[90]

Her major work, *Womanist Ethics and the Cultural Production of Evil* (2006), explored what she called "the deep interior life of evil and its manifestations." Theological books on theodicy usually trafficked in concepts and theories; Townes observed that she derived more from Toni Morrison, James Baldwin, and the stereotypical storytelling of decidedly lesser writers. Blending Foucault's understanding of imagination and the fantastic with Gramsci's understanding of hegemony as ideological domination, Townes explored how the "fantastic hegemonic imagination" of white Americans played with history and memory to construct five influential stereotypes: Mammy/Aunt Jemima, Sapphire, the Tragic Mulatta, the Welfare Queen, and Topsy.[91]

Foucault celebrated the subversion of Western rationalism and naturalism by imagination, especially the "fantastic" consciousness of other worlds besides the mundane landscape of science. Focused on books and literary consciousness, he described the imaginary as something that grew in the intervals between studying texts, not as something that necessarily opposed reality. Townes added that imagination and the fantastic were at play in everyday experiences of uncertainty about the actuality of a perception or experience. Ghosts and shifted realities were examples of the fantastic; so were structures of domination and subordination. Moreover, the fantastic became an everyday reality for those who lived in it. From Gramsci, Townes took the idea of hegemony as the set of ideas that dominant groups employed to legitimize their rule and secure the consent of subordinated groups. The stereotypes of the American black experience constructed by the "fantastic hegemonic imagination," she argued, exemplified the cultural production of evil.[92]

The Mammy figure, a nineteenth-century fiction invented by Southern slaveholders to show how slaves loved their owners and were loved by them, exemplified the problem of identity as property and commodity. Originally she was invented as a response to abolitionist charges that slave owners exploited their (usually light-skinned) female slaves. Apologists for slavery pictured the slave-owning household as an integral unit that included an old, fat, dark-skinned, desexualized, happy woman whom no slaveholding male would have desired sexually. The "living proof of miscegenation" told a different story, Townes observed; moreover, there was very little evidence for Mammy, since black women rarely lived past 45 and the household servants known to history were nearly always young and light-skinned. After slavery ended, the

Mammy figure soared to new heights of popularity as the perfect counterpoint to the sweet, innocent, white, beautiful Southern Belle, who needed someone fit for household labor; later she morphed into Aunt Jemima, the jolly queen of pancakes. In the early twentieth century various white groups including the United Daughters of the Confederacy sought to build monuments in Washington DC and elsewhere to the "old Black Mammies of the South," despite black opposition. Townes remarked: "Despite the facts, the belief that White owners loved their Mammies became ingrained in U.S. culture."[93]

Townes belonged to the generation that rebelled against Aunt Jemima, Uncle Tom, Topsy, and other white stereotypes that demeaned black identity. Commenting on the protests against Aunt Jemima, Townes recalled, "We thought we had banished her with raised black gloved fists and self-empowerment and affirmative action and an emerging Black middle class." But mere rejection was an inadequate response, she judged. Sixty years of black protests against Aunt Jemima finally yielded an updated pancake queen adorned with pearls and styled hair. Instead of merely rejecting the latest instantiation of Mammy as commodity and property, Townes spoke for countermemory, the reconstitution of history. "Countermemory is the patient and persistent work of mining the motherlode of African American religious life," she explained. It defanged cultural stereotypes like Aunt Jemima by critically interpreting and refashioning them, turning the tables on white prejudices and anxieties. Townes pointed to the black minstrel tradition, which was loaded with stereotypes, yet contained knowing put-downs of white arrogance, indirect protest messages, and ironic spins on the likes of Aunt Jemima. When white minstrel performers recycled some of the same material to ridicule black life and culture, she observed, they usually missed the critical thrusts aimed at white bigotry; thus they ended up lampooning themselves, unknowingly. For Townes, the entire process fell under the category of countermemory, in which an oppressed people exposed and otherwise coped with the cultural production of evil: "The spirituals, gospels, blues, work and protest songs, jazz, R&B, soul, hip hop, all have within them segments that have taken a long, hard look at the nature of subjugations in our lives and have something to say about it and the ways to lessen, if not eradicate, the many wounds inflicted on Black lives on a minute-by-minute basis."[94]

Treating identity as property was a major form of the cultural production of evil. Townes described "uninterrogated coloredness" as another, the tendency to restrict references to race or discussions of racial justice to dark-skinned blacks. Uninterrogated coloredness gave whites a pass from dealing with the privileges and characteristics of whiteness, and it allowed darker-skinned racial ethnic groups to ignore their own color-based caste system. Here Townes's pertinent stereotype was Sapphire, the malicious, loud, bitchy female who emasculated black males. Based on the character Sapphire Stevens in the "Amos 'n Andy" television show of the 1950s, Sapphire was dangerous for the white imagination because whites had no "safe" place for a black woman who spurned white culture and cared for her own family chiefly through her penchant for domineering hostility. As with Mammy, Townes observed, the fact that Sapphire was a creation of the white imagination did not stop many blacks from treating her as something terribly real.

Sapphire became a symbol of blackness lacking any explicitly white counterpart, for whiteness was too dominant to be visible to whites. Townes contended against the white resort to colorblindness, which masked the cultural significance of race and the sheer reality of white privilege: "Avoiding the messiness and complexity of race in the quest for a color-blind stance only serves to make palatable a bootlicking selective engagement with our genuine differences – differences that are assumed to be divisive rather than enriching." To eliminate racist privilege, white society had to acknowledge its existence and struggle morally with it. Whiteness was homeland for the fantastic hegemonic imagination; evocations of neutrality and objectivity simply held the "gigantic superego" of white supremacy in its unacknowledged dominant place: "To ring ourselves around a deadly May pole of uninterrogated coloredness is to dance, literally, with the devil. We fool ourselves if we believe that continuing to obscure whiteness eradicates it or erases its history and deadly effects."[95]

As for countermemory, Townes observed, it was worth remembering that Sapphire was also a precious stone. Sapphire was tough, relentless, and more inclined to demand accountability than to assign blame: "Sapphire urges us to be relentless in our analysis and inclusive in our recovery of history and sociopolitical analysis when prying open and interrogating the previously uninterrogated." The typical womanist trilogy of race, gender, and class critique was fundamental, but so was the imperative of opposing heterosexism, ageism, the color caste system, and all forms of exclusion including "the Pandora's box around issues of beauty."[96]

Part of the beauty issue was the racist favoring of light skin over dark, a prejudice tangled in the USA with empire and miscegenation, which correlated with the stereotype that Townes called "the Tragic Mulatta." Invented by the white abolitionist writer Lydia Maria Child in 1842, the Tragic Mulatta quickly became another stock type in American white and black consciousness. Usually the daughter of an enslaved mother and a slave-owning father, she was nearly always beautiful, virtuous, and culturally refined by white standards. Often she had no consciousness of being black until her father died. In many abolitionist stories she was cast as the heroine, albeit one afflicted by self-hatred, depression, alcoholism, suicidal tendencies, sexual perversion, and often, the death of a white husband. The Tragic Mulatta showed the terrible ravages of slavery in ways that worked on the feelings of white readers. Her whiteness evoked sympathetic identification in white readers, while her pathologies showed what slavery did even to the most sympathetic character. In other renderings, racist white writers depicted her as depraved without qualification; sometimes she was a self-hating nihilist who passed for white. Townes stressed that the Tragic Mulatta was a product and commodity of the white imagination. Lacking any historical basis, she was tragic to white audiences because she was "near White but not White." Her "almostness" made her both pitied and shunned. In the nineteenth century, especially in sentimental abolitionist versions, she represented the tragic deceit of slavery; more recently she represented the tragedy of empire: "Her contemporary siblings in almostness are poor peoples, darker-skinned peoples, peoples who live outside of the West (which means most people), immigrants, and sexual minorities."[97]

As always, Townes's focus was the journey of the black community, but her analysis and subject had fluid boundaries. She stressed that modern Americans lived in many communities, sometimes simultaneously, which made them a deeply historical people, though white American culture pushed all Americans toward ahistoricism and one-dimensionality. Living off the spoils of empire, Americans made false consciousness virtually synonymous with good Americanism:

We live off the bitter fruits of a fantastic imagination that caricatures and pillages peoples', all peoples', lives – our thoughts, our culture, or religion, our isness. We have logoized versions of ourselves: Native Americans are reduced to spiritual, Blacks are reduced to hip-hop, Asians are reduced to intellect, Latinos/as are reduced to salsa, and Whites . . . well, Whites have no culture, no-is-ness, they are simply . . . White.[98]

Townes had a movement sense about womanism, and a caretaker's love of it. She knew that in some corners of theological education it was standard fare to say that womanism was provincial and self-referential, a retreat from real liberation theology: "Some Black male colleagues in the liberationist tradition go about their intellectual work as though womanist discourse is a fad, a passing fancy, or a momentary bout of theological indigestion." Too often, she protested, courses on liberation theology, modern theology, and the black church never mentioned the womanist movement. Others mentioned it only to put it down: "Some lecture on the faddishness and soon-to-be deadness of womanist thought."[99]

These judgments had a way of getting back to those who were being dismissed behind their backs, she noted. Womanism put survival ahead of liberation, which to some was a betrayal of liberation theology. It spoke in the idioms of black, female, Southern culture, which to some made it provincial. Often it spoke with a poetic flare, which to some was a failure of academic seriousness. Townes replied,

> we talk amongst ourselves and listen to what we have to say
> no room of our own
> no solitary mind at work in a concrete world spinning out abstractions
>   who hopes to save
>   but ultimately cannot

As for the future of womanist theology and ethics:

> alice walker sure didn't know what she was fixin' to start
>   but some of us are brave
>   won't you join us?[100]

Latina Feminisms: Ada María Isasi-Díaz and María Pilar Aquino

The womanist option defined by Walker prevailed among US black female religious thinkers, though there were significant dissenters from it, notably social critic bell hooks and social ethicist Traci C. West, who argued that "black feminism" was more open-ended and liberating. West appreciated the womanist movement, having studied under Delores Williams at Union Seminary and entered the social-ethics field as womanism developed into an important perspective. She treasured its achievement of a vital space in the academy that privileged black female subjectivity. But the problem of parochialism was obvious in womanist writing, she judged. It began with the womanist notion that accountability was "exclusively tied to one's own racial/ethnic group" and included the assumption that black women like herself were not supposed to call themselves feminists. West replied: "If there is such a consensus being promoted by womanists, how can they avoid the contradiction of circumscribing conformity and policing black womanhood while claiming to free it from the bondage of too few acceptable forms?"

Remarking on the "narrowing" tendency of womanist thought, West pointed to its repeated conflation of feminism with whiteness, which had the unfortunate effect of "erasing the contributions of a generation of black feminist foremothers." Much as she admired the womanist movement, West refrained from identifying with "this exclusively black community-based tradition of intellectual work."[101]

A similar argument played out rather differently among Hispanic feminists. Theologian Ada María Isasi-Díaz, a Cuban exile, developed a perspective named *mujerista* theology that grew out of her dialogues with Latina women living in the United States. *Mujerista* theology was similar to womanism in key respects, and in the mid-1990s it seemed to be acquiring a stature in liberation theology analogous to womanism. But some Latina theologians in the USA took a different path, judging that the style and ethnographic basis of *mujerista* theology were too narrow. María Pilar Aquino, a Mexican-born Roman Catholic theologian teaching at the University of San Diego, was a leading figure in the movement for a more pluralistic, multivocal "Latina feminism."

For Isasi-Díaz the path to *mujerista* theology included growing up middle class in pre-Castro Cuba and fleeing the country at the age of 18 after the revolution of 1960. Later it included three years of missionary work in Lima, Peru as a member of a religious order before leaving the order in 1970. Later it included becoming a feminist in 1975 and thinking her way to a distinctly Latina feminism while completing her doctorate at Union Theological Seminary in 1990. Isasi-Díaz had a vibrantly friendly personality, a penchant for expressing herself somewhat dramatically, and a deep gratitude to the feminist movement that changed her life. She also stressed that Latina feminism had to be different from the Anglo version she experienced in the United States. Usually she began her story in the middle, with the conversion to feminism that put her on the path to becoming a theologian.

In 1975 Isasi-Díaz was working as a sales clerk at Sears in Rochester, New York and studying for a master's degree in medieval history when a friend more or less dragged her to the inaugural Women's Ordination Conference (WOC), held in Detroit. It amazed her to learn there was such a thing as feminist theology, much less a rising movement of Catholic feminism. Isasi-Díaz was converted by the speeches and, especially, the hopeful excitement pervading the conference. Nearly 30 years later she recalled that the conference transformed her worldview and gave "direction to my life for the rest of my days."[102]

As an activist in the WOC movement she participated in the 1976 "Call to Action" conference of the United Catholic Conference, meeting Yolanda Tarango, whose reluctance to become involved with the women's ordination movement puzzled her. Tarango was a feminist who believed in women's ordination, so what was the problem? Tarango told Isasi-Díaz to pay attention to the movement's racial and ethnic prejudices. Gradually she began to do so, which caused friction in the WOC organization. Isasi-Díaz clashed with the organization's white Anglo leaders, attributing the conflict to cultural differences and her growing Latina identity. For seven years she worked for the WOC; by the fifth year she felt deeply alienated. Two years later she was asked to resign. Later she recalled, "The Euro-American feminists, being part of the dominant culture, deal with Hispanic women – and other racial/ethnic women – differently from the way they deal with each other. They take for granted that feminism in the USA is *their* garden, and therefore they will decide what manner of work racial/ethnic women will do there." Elsewhere she recalled that she was "extremely distraught by what happened" and tried to learn from the experience. The experience left her "wounded and disillusioned," but not disaffected from the struggle for women's liberation: "I simply needed to find new avenues for involvement, new ways of contributing to the liberation of women."[103]

The new way of *mujerista* theology emerged from dialogues that Isasi-Díaz and Tarango conducted with LAS HERMANAS groups – a national organization of Hispanic Catholics – in various parts of the country. Ordinary Latinas living in the USA had ways of living the faith and coping with difficult conditions that deserved to be heard, Isasi-Díaz and Tarango contended. If there was a liberation theology for grassroots Hispanic communities in the USA, it had to come from their experience and their reflections on it, not that of male theologians in Central America or of female Anglo theologians in the USA. In 1988 Isasi-Díaz and Tarango published the first fruit of this conversational enterprise, *Hispanic Women: Prophetic Voice in the Church*, which conveyed the perspectives of LAS HERMANAS groups on faith, family, work, and society. For the coauthors, the objective was to provide a platform for Hispanic women and to enhance their moral agency.[104]

Isasi-Díaz called this project Hispanic women's liberation theology and herself a *feminista hispana*, while puzzling over the inadequacies of both names. The women that she interviewed rarely called themselves Hispanics or Latinas. They described themselves as *cubanas, chicanas, puertorriqueñas*, or the like, identifying with the country of their birth or that of their ancestors. Mexican Americans were exceptions, identifying with a term that indicated their ethnic-national roots and US citizenship. In both cases, Isasi-Díaz judged, most Hispanic women, including those who explicitly criticized sexism, regarded feminism as a preoccupation of Anglo women. The term *feminista* was culturally alien to them. Isasi-Díaz searched for a term that fitted Hispanic culture and opposed sexism, something analogous to "womanism" in the African-American context. She had tired of explaining what *feminista hispana* did not mean and reasoned that Hispanic feminism deserved a name of its own, like womanism. Later she explained: "To be able to name oneself is one of the most powerful acts any person can do. A name is not just a word by which one is identified. A name also provides the conceptual framework, the mental constructs that are used in thinking, understanding, and relating to a person."[105]

In the 1970s a radical feminist group in Peru had coined the term *mujerista* as a name for its movement and ideology, but Isasi-Díaz was unaware of it. As far as she knew, the term was original to her; thus her writings did not mention its ideological lineage. In Hispanic love songs and protest songs, she noted, women were called *mujer*. A song by Rosa Marta Zárate described *mujeres* as women who struggled to liberate themselves; Isasi-Díaz embraced that connotation: "Yes, we are *mujeres*, and those of us who make a preferential option for the *mujeres* are *mujeristas*." Since Christianity was an intrinsic component of Hispanic culture, she argued, *mujerista* liberationism was necessarily a type of theology. Specifically, it was a three-stranded rope of feminist theology, Latin American liberation theology, and cultural theology wrapped together to form "a new reality" expressing the religious and cultural perceptions of Hispanic women. In 1989 she declared, "What we called up to now Hispanic women's liberation theology will henceforth be called *mujerista* theology."[106]

At the time Isasi-Díaz was a doctoral student in social ethics. For her, graduate school was not so much about learning a field as about preparing herself for a career as a movement pioneer. Defining the field on her own, she honed her theological arguments in conversation with her mentor, Beverly Harrison, and her doctoral class-mates at Union Seminary – Katie Cannon, Elizabeth Bounds, Pamela Brubaker, Chung Hyun Kyung, and Marilyn Legge. Isasi-Díaz's connection to Cannon helped her delineate how *mujerista* theology, like womanism, could be closely related to liberation theology while striking out on its own. The published version of her doctoral disserta-tion, *En la Lucha / In the Struggle: Elaborating a Mujerista Theology* announced the birth of a new form of liberation theology.

At the time there was already a current of Latin-American feminist theology, led by Elsa Tamez, and the beginning of a US Latina feminist theological literature, pio-neered by Aquino and Ana María Pineda. *En la Lucha / In the Struggle* had a movement spirit, however, and was distinctly geared to the US context. By the time the book appeared, Isasi-Díaz was four years into her teaching career at Drew University, long enough to have professorial scars to go with her activist and student ones: "As a Latina, I have often experienced ethnic prejudice and sexism: in educational institutions both as a student and as a professor; in women's groups and in organizations where differ-ence is neither understood nor valued; in many diverse situations and places such as stores, conferences, government offices, Latino businesses and organizations." For her, *mujerista* theology was a form of liberationist activism: "To do *mujerista* theology is an effective way to struggle against the prejudices that oppress me and my Hispanic sisters."[107]

Having adopted *mujerista* to dispense with the unwelcome connotations of *feminista*, Isasi-Díaz judged that "Hispanic" and "Latina" were indispensable in referring to Hispanics from various national origins. Instead of favoring either term exclusively, she employed them interchangeably, using "Hispanic" in odd numbered chapters and "Latina" in even numbered ones. Hispanics were racially and nationally diverse, she stressed; the only thing they had in common was the Spanish language (although even that was not really universal). As for *mujerista*, since the inherited terms were prob-lematic, it was worth the trouble of coining a new one: "A *mujerista* is a Hispanic Woman who struggles to liberate herself not as an individual but as a member of a Hispanic community." Unlike many Anglo feminists, she stressed, she was not a sepa-ratist, did not pit women against men, did not denigrate families, and took no interest in the liberal feminist pursuit of equality within oppressive structures:

> A *mujerista* is called to gestate new women and new men – Hispanics who are willing to work for the common good, knowing that such work requires us to denounce all destructive sense of self-abnegation. A *mujerista* is a Latina who makes a preferential option for herself and her Hispanic sisters, understanding that our struggle for liberation has to take into consideration how racism/ethnic prejudice, economic oppression, and sexism work together and reinforce each other.[108]

To Isasi-Díaz, liberation theology had already obliterated the distinctions between systematic/dogmatic theology and ethics/moral theology. She did not think of herself as more of a theologian than an ethicist or the other way around. *Mujerista* theology began with the givens of a social construct, Hispanic ethnicity. The ethnic markers of Hispanic identity, she argued, included so-called natural traits such as language, race, country of origin, and gender, but they also included the various social, eco-nomic, and political factors that brought Hispanics to the United States, the ways that

Hispanics were treated by the dominant culture, the daily struggles of Hispanics to survive and make a better life, and the visions they held of a better life. Interpreted this broadly, Hispanic ethnicity was an organizing tool that helped Hispanics to describe who they were and how they lived, not a conceptual framework based on fixed traits. In theory the term "Hispanic" embraced all Mexicans, Mexican Americans, Chicanos, Puerto Ricans, Cubans, Central and South Americans, and others of Spanish origin. For Isasi-Díaz, however, the broad sense of the term was too diverse and unwieldy for intelligible discussion; thus she used it more narrowly as a signifier for Mexican Americans, Puerto Ricans, and Cubans.[109]

There were three main elements of Hispanic women's ethnicity, she contended: *mestizaje*, survival, and socioeconomic reality. *Mestizaje* was the blending of different races, which, she cautioned, was not the attempt by one race to dominate another race or make it disappear. For Latin Americans, *mestizaje* did not carry the negative connotations that "miscegenation" bore for many whites and blacks in the USA. It was a fusion of different races and cultures into something new that precluded the subordination of one group to another.

Mexican philosopher José Vasconcelos, in the 1940s, described *mestizaje* as a process of creating a new race, the cosmic race – *la raza cósmica*. Mexican-American theologian Virgilio P. Elizondo made extensive use of these concepts, distinguishing between the "first *mestizaje*" (the Spanish-Catholic conquest of Mexico) and the "second *mestizaje*" (the Nordic-Protestant conquest of Mexico). In both cases, Elizondo observed, epochal conquests gave rise to new possibilities that threatened the identities of established groups: "A *mestizo* group represents a particularly serious threat to its two parent cultures. The *mestizo* does not fit conveniently into the analysis categories used by either parent group. The *mestizo* may understand them far better than they understand him or her." To be a *mestizo*, Elizondo wrote, was to live as an "insider-outsider," indwelling both parent cultures while belonging fully to neither. Isasi-Díaz agreed that *mestizaje* involved more than racial and cultural blending; in the USA, Hispanics were a "mostly marginalized people" living in the intersections between countries of origin to which they did not belong and a US society to which they did not fully belong either. *Mestizaje* included the ongoing coming together of different races and cultures in social contexts that had little or no history of it: "For us Hispanic Women, the creation of a new race is a very real part of our daily lives."[110]

She gave equal weight to the struggles of Hispanic women for cultural and socioeconomic survival. Unlike Anglo feminist critiques of the family as the central site of women's oppression, Isasi-Díaz argued, *mujerista* theology shared the strong family orientation of Hispanic culture. For that reason and others reflecting cultural difference, *mujerista* theology held different ideas to Anglo feminists about what constituted appropriate gender behavior: "Maintaining our families is an intrinsic part of our struggle . . . This is precisely the reason why Hispanic Women resist the conception of sexism as defined by Anglo women." Hispanic culture and most Hispanic men were undeniably sexist, she acknowledged, but it was offensive to suggest that Hispanic culture and males were especially sexist relative to other cultures and males. Moreover, it was equally offensive to make Anglo feminist conventions the normative standard of human behavior. In English usage, the former offense occurred every time an Anglo used the term "machismo" instead of "male chauvinism." Isasi-Díaz asserted, "In the struggle against ethnic and racist prejudice, it has to be recognized that the survival of Hispanic Women is directly related to the fate of Hispanic culture." Because

Christianity and family played central roles in Hispanic culture, *mujerista* theology was unequivocally committed to both while rejecting patriarchal, sexist, and exclusively heterosexual versions of them.[111]

Further, it held fast to the communitarian ethos of Hispanic culture against the deracinating and humiliating Anglo emphasis on individualism. Isasi-Díaz observed that in the USA privacy in the personal realm was treasured and individuals strove for success in the global marketplace. She recoiled at both conventions, especially the achievement ideology: "This myth is promulgated constantly in the most pervasive way possible. It contributes significantly to the negative self-image of Latinas who cannot get ahead, not because we do not try hard, but because of socioeconomic realities that militate against us in all areas of life." On the one hand, she argued, the socioeconomic deck was stacked against Hispanic Americans no matter how hard they worked. Most Hispanics who bought into the game were humiliated by it, depriving them of their capacity to understand structural oppression. On the other hand, it was a bad game anyway: "For us the term 'individual' carries a pejorative meaning, a sense of egocentrism and selfishness that we believe to be inherently bad since it works against what is of great value to us, our communities." Instead of buying the Anglo-American lie that the good life was a function of individual achievement, Hispanics needed to strengthen their existing communities and build praxis-oriented new ones, "which bring together personal support and community action, and which have as a central organizing principle our religious understandings and practices as well as our needs."[112]

For Isasi-Díaz, that was a description of communal Christian liberation, which she called "the kin-dom of God." In her early work she used the term sparingly, interchangeably with liberation; later she featured it as a theological concept. The coming of the divine kin-dom "has to do with a coming together of peoples, with no one being excluded and at the expense of no one," she wrote. Thus, *mestizaje* was the heart of the *mujerista* idea of the kin-dom. Beginning with *mestizaje* as a contextual reality and normative ideal, *mujerista* theology understood all racism and ethnic prejudice as evil and the embrace of diversity as divine. Ultimately, *mujerista* theology stood for the flourishing of all coming together within the divine kin-dom. For Isasi-Díaz, the term "kin-dom" was a substitute for the sexist and hierarchical metaphors of "kingdom" and "reign." It also marked the centrality of family and community in Latina culture. Though she was often credited with originating the term, Isasi-Díaz credited her friend Georgene Wilson, OSF with teaching it to her.[113]

Her generalizations about Hispanic women's beliefs and practices were based on her interviews, an ethnographic approach that studied the distinctive characteristics and customs of cultures. Theoretically, informants were the teachers, mediation was minimized, and informants were encouraged to speak in their own words. In practice, Isasi-Díaz acknowledged, she stuck to the first and third principles of the ethnographic approach, but her personality was too strong to be leashed to a research method that kept her silent; she had too much to say to her informants. If she distorted the data in the process, making it come out the way she wanted, there was a way to find out: "If the community fails to recognize itself in the *mujerista* theology that I present, then it is obvious that I have manipulated and changed the voices of Hispanic Women instead of providing a platform for them."[114]

In her telling, her interviews with Hispanic female groups and individuals conflicted with the ways that Latin-American liberationists usually talked about scripture and Jesus. Liberation theologians discussed the Bible at length without mentioning that

Latin Americans took little interest in the Bible. "The Christianity that became and is an intrinsic part of Latino culture is one that uses the Bible in a very limited way, emphasizing instead the traditions and customs of the Spanish church," she observed. Latin-American Catholics did not disavow the Bible, but they rarely referred to it either. "Most of us seldom read the Bible and know instead popularized versions of biblical stories – versions Latins create to make a point." Elsewhere she confirmed, "The Bible per se is extremely peripheral to the lives of Hispanic women." Even priests ignored it, finding scripture of little relevance to their lives or ministry: "When the priests do use the scripture readings, hardly ever do their sermons show any real exegetical work."[115]

Popular religion was more powerful than the Bible in real-world Latin-American spirituality, she stressed. Noting the tendencies of local communities to fuse Catholic, Amerindian, and African religious traditions, and the tendency of liberationists and the Vatican to look down on popular religion, Isasi-Díaz enlisted *mujerista* theology decidedly in its favor, with feminist caveats: "In *mujerista* theology we see popular religiosity as an essential part of popular culture and, therefore, as a part of the identity of and central to the lived-experience of the people. It is an essential part of our deepest constitutive element." Admittedly, popular religion was often laced with sexist and other oppressive aspects that had to be excised, she allowed, but overall, popular religiosity was "one of the most creative and original parts of our heritage and our culture."[116]

As for Jesus, he did not compare remotely to Mary, despite the many books about Jesus. Isasi-Díaz remarked that Latin-American liberationists wrote about Jesus in the same way they carried on about the Bible, trying to help "the common folk" relate to Jesus and the Bible, "but in their work, the fact that the great majority of Hispanics relate very little to Jesus is never confronted. Instead, it is glossed over." Liberation theologians were overdue to stop being embarrassed that Hispanics, especially Hispanic women, overwhelmingly preferred Mary to Jesus. For Hispanics, Isasi-Díaz explained, Mary was an accessible and immanent presence of the divine in their lives, while Jesus was closely bonded to an inaccessible male God. Moreover, Mary fitted more readily into the syncretizing practices of popular religiosity:

> Is Our Lady of Guadalupe the Mother of Jesus, or is she Tonantzin, the Aztec goddess, Mother of the Gods on whose pilgrimage site, the hill of Tepeyac, Our Lady of Guadalupe appeared? In their hearts, and often quite openly, Latinas with Caribbean roots who pray to St. Barbara are identifying her, directly or indirectly, with Chango, the Yoruban God of Thunder.

To grassroots Hispanic communities, she observed, the Vatican's declaration that St Barbara was a legend was completely irrelevant. They understood intuitively that orthodox condemnations of syncretism were about struggles for power, not upholding the faith.[117]

Since *mestizaje* was the heart of the *mujerista* idea of the kin-dom, which Isasi-Díaz equated with salvation/liberation, her theology had a deep investment in the reality, valorization, and language about *mestizaje*. *En la Lucha / In the Struggle* used the term in an expansive sense, citing Vasconcelos and Elizondo, noting the popular saying from Venezuela, "Aqui todos somos café con leche; unos más café, otros más leche" (Here we are all coffee and milk; some more coffee, others more milk). Every Hispanic culture had elements of African culture and race, Isasi-Díaz affirmed. The *mestizaje* concept included the African cultural and racial component; it was not an attempt to "whiten" Hispanic culture. But that assurance did not persuade critics who noted the term's history and common usage, including Elizondo's emphasis on the "two conquests." Instead of highlighting the African and Amerindian elements of Hispanic cultures, the *mestizaje* concept whitened them out. At first Isasi-Díaz resisted this critique, which cast aspersions on a treasured term and her own intentions. Eventually she realized that in the US context it was necessary to emphasize that "whitening" was not the point. Thus she added the term *mulatez* to *mestizaje*, creating the binomial, *mestizaje–mulatez*. In most Hispanic cultures, she explained, *mestiza* and *mulata* were markers of Amerindian and African races and cultures. By using the binomial term, she accented that Amerindian and African races and cultures were integral aspects of all Hispanic cultures.[118]

Mujerista theology was also accused of lacking intellectual rigor; Isasi-Díaz, noting that every liberation theology was accused of being too subjective and ideological, replied bluntly: "*Mujerista* theology denounces any and all so-called objectivity. What passes as objectivity in reality merely names the subjectivity of those who have the authority and/or power to impose their point of view." So-called orthodoxy was merely the religion of the powerful that sustained their domination, she contended, and so were academic claims to intellectual rigor and scholarly objectivity. Instead of prizing or claiming a phantom objectivity, theologians needed to claim responsibility for their subjectivity. That meant situating the subject, showing awareness of one's subjectivity, and taking the risk of self-disclosure before presuming to say anything else.[119]

Isasi-Díaz had Hauerwas's penchant for exaggeration and, like him, a cultural explanation for it. She lamented her embattlement, but also seemed to thrive on it. Sometimes she tried to head off objections by anticipating them. "Because I am Cuban, my language is full of what others consider exaggerations, hyperboles, repetitions," she observed. "What seems hyperbolic to the English reader is to me nothing but a needed emphasis; what seems repetitious is a way of connecting ideas and constantly building on what I consider central in the argument." Since her context was an unknown world to most of her readers, she took for granted the necessity of repeating herself. Since it was imperative to her to be true to herself and resonate with Hispanic readers, she rejected pleas to smoothen her writing style: "My insistence on sounding in English like myself, and not like someone for whom English is her first language, is a way of preserving my identity, of insisting that to contribute to the theological enterprise Latinas do not need to forget our culture or our language."[120]

In the classroom she had numerous encounters with students who treated her disrespectfully. Isasi-Díaz wearied of having to cope with prejudice and point it out. On various occasions she wrote about it: "As a Latina professor of theology I can fill several pages with stories of the demands students make of me, with the negative attitude some have toward me, with their lack of respect for my authority." The majority of students at Drew treated her respectfully, she assured readers; on the other hand, there were enough who did not that the university often felt like a battle zone to her. Many students created "an atmosphere around me and about me that results in weakening my authority and power not only with the students but also with the institution at large." Elsewhere she lamented that no matter what she said about herself or her work, she got "rebuked by someone whose opinion I respect."[121]

But Isasi-Díaz's version of Latina feminist theology dominated the field for several years. At conferences of the American Academy of Religion, *mujerista* theology was routinely cited as the Latin-American form of feminist theology. This status was enhanced by an influential reader on liberation theologies, *Lift Every Voice* (1990, 1998), which represented Latina feminism with two articles, both by Isasi-Díaz. The first expounded her belief that solidarity, the union of kindred persons for a common social purpose, was the best expression of the biblical command to love one's neighbors. The second explained that the Bible had a marginal role in *mujerista* theology because it played a minor role in the lives of Hispanic women. There was a place for using the Bible selectively in *mujerista* theology, she allowed; however, "Hispanic women's experience, not the Bible, are the sources of *Mujerista* theology, a liberative praxis."[122]

Her later writings repeated her central themes, defended the necessity of repetition, and expressed her longing for Cuba. "I have lived feeling that I left my heart there, just as the song says, when I became an *exhiliada* at age eighteen," Isasi-Díaz reflected in 2004. Calling herself "a displaced person," she insisted to disbelieving friends that she was strongly tempted to return permanently to Cuba despite the fact that her family and career were in the USA: "I am not an American; I am a Cuban who lives in New York." Her first visit to Cuba in 1987 confirmed the feeling: "Though I hold American citizenship and live in New York City, I am a Cuban and the city of La Habana inhabits me." From 1997 to 2004 she returned to Cuba every year to teach at a Protestant seminary and work in a Catholic parish.[123]

Though she described herself as "loud and quite expressive by the standards of this society," Isasi-Díaz felt shackled emotionally by the USA. The coldness and guarded relationships of Anglo colleagues saddened her. She longed for the emotional intensity of Cuban society, judging that US Americans were embarrassed by public displays of emotion because they were afraid to be vulnerable and perceived as weak. For several years before she became a feminist she worried that US society had suffocated her passion; afterwards she worried that Anglo society extinguished whatever passions Anglo Americans might feel for social justice.[124]

Her success at winning a place for Latina feminism in the US academy was viewed by some Hispanic intellectuals as a mixed blessing. Anglo feminist theologian Susan A. Ross and Latino theologian Roberto Goizueta commended Isasi-Díaz for rooting *mujerista* theology in the everyday experiences of Hispanic women, though Ross urged her to engage the theological community more widely, especially Catholic social ethics. Cultural theologian Benjamin Valentin, setting himself against the "insular enchantment with matters of culture, identity, and difference" that marked many liberation and postmodern theologies, praised Isasi-Díaz for avoiding insularity. In his view, the strong imprint of US Anglo feminism and womanism on her thought was a decided strength. By engaging more than one community in her approach to social justice, he explained, Isasi-Díaz fashioned a theology with a "wider sense of the public" than often prevailed in liberation theology. A bit more grudgingly, Hispanic religious scholars María Pilar Aquino, Daisy L. Machado, and Jeanette Rodríguez lauded "the important work and contributions" of Isasi-Díaz in gaining recognition for Latina feminism among the academy and public. All scholars in the field were indebted to her work, they acknowledged.[125]

But Aquino, Rodríguez, and other Latina feminists judged that Isasi-Díaz got certain things very wrong. Overgeneralizing from her experience, Isasi-Díaz ignored modern traditions of Latina feminism and wrongly purveyed the "myth" that feminism was alien to Latinas. Critics protested that she said nothing about historical streams of Latina/Chicana feminism that were not inspired by or connected to Anglo feminism;

instead she fashioned an essentialist feminism of her own that reacted to the Anglo type she knew. To Aquino especially, *mujerista* theology had too much in common with the sectarian gynocentrism of the original *mujerista* movement in Peru, even though Isasi-Díaz said nothing about it.[126]

Aquino put it strongly, asserting that genuine Latina feminism stood in the modern historical traditions of Latina/Chicana feminism. "Many of us Latina/Chicana *mestizas* who struggle everywhere for justice and liberation have called ourselves *feminists*," she observed. "The main reason we have chosen deliberately not to call ourselves *mujeristas*, as Ada María Isasi-Díaz does in her theological perspective, is that there are no *mujerista* sociopolitical and ecclesial subjects or movements in the United States or in Latin America." *Mujerista* theology was the invention of Isasi-Díaz, Aguino suggested. It was right about certain things, but it was not rooted in a church tradition or indigenous feminist movement. Citing Puerto Rican theologian Raquel Rodríguez, Aquino noted that *mujerismo* carried negative connotations among feminists in Latin America. Citing feminist anthropologist Marta Lamas, she added that *mujerista* feminism was a sectarian construct that engendered "false oppositions" and weakened the political force of actual feminist movements. Aquino explained, "Throughout the continent and the Caribbean, the *mujerista* position is indisputably understood as an ideology rooted in both the assumption of a homogeneous identity of women and a unitarian and unifying women's strategy for change." Since *mujerista* theology had no actual, self-aware subject in the USA or Latin America, Aquino judged, it fell inevitably into sectarianism and essentialism, notwithstanding Isasi-Díaz's protests that her position was neither sectarian nor essentialist.[127]

It was frustrating for Aquino and other critics that US American theologians identified Latina feminism with Isasi-Díaz. "It is necessary to dispel this myth and to correct this error," Aquino urged. "Given the long-standing political meaning that such ideology has for Latin American feminists, and in view of its countermoving effects, I suggest that our theology must be clearly characterized by a *non-mujerista* orientation." Actual Hispanic feminism was pluralistic, explicitly feminist, rooted in Latina traditions, and had a place in Catholic and mainline Protestant theological traditions, she argued: "The Latina feminist theologian, developing critically the reflective language of faith, wants to use the power of theology with its liberating traditions as a religious force which contributes to personal and social transformation and to the elimination of suffering born of violence and social injustice."[128]

Aquino wore her mainstream theological and feminist status proudly. Born in Nayarit, Mexico and raised near the Sonora border, she was the daughter of Mexican migrant workers, the first Mexican-born Roman Catholic woman to earn a doctorate in theology, and the first Catholic woman since St Theresa of Avila to earn a doctorate at the Pontifical University of Salamanca. She taught theology and religious studies at the University of San Diego, where, like Isasi-Díaz, she endured the doubts of numerous students about her qualifications to instruct them; Aquino was grateful that every year some of them grew to recognize their prejudices. Her professional activities included co-founding the Academy of Catholic Hispanic/Latino Theologians of the United States and serving as its first female president. Comfortable with the idioms of academic theology, she implored Catholic bishops to do something about the church's dearth of female Hispanic theologians and rejected Isasi-Díaz's position on the Bible: "I believe that *la biblia* occupies a central place in our religious identity, and it is important for Latina grassroot women." She also eschewed the liberationist theme, repeated by Isasi-Díaz, that theology was something one *did*, a project: "Theology is not something I do, as if it were an object external to my life. Theology is a central axis of my identity as a Catholic woman, and it is the way I *co*-respond to the mystery of God in my life."[129]

For all of her criticism of *mujerista* theology, however, Aquino agreed with Isasi-Díaz about the centrality of the everyday experiences (*cotidiana*) of Hispanic women for theology, the close kinship between Latin-American liberation theology and Latina feminism, the distinct perspective of Latin-American women and the importance of *mestizaje*. For her, Latina feminist theology was "an attempt to grasp the re-creating work of the Spirit that activates the strength, word, memory, and liberating struggles of women." It affirmed "that we women are starting from our own problems, from ourselves, and the problems we share with other men and women of the oppressed peoples." More cautiously than Isasi-Díaz, but along a similar line, Aquino criticized the church hierarchy and most liberation theologians for denigrating popular religion. Very much like Isasi-Díaz she protested that liberation theology was usually sexist, dismissing feminist theory and ignoring violence against women, and that capitalist neo-liberalism was disastrous for Hispanic communities. On the latter issue she made the same appeal to solidarity and visionary courage as Isasi-Díaz: "Our theology believes that it cannot give up its liberating religious vision. It cannot give up the spiritual strength found in the historical experience of peoples and theologies that have created counter-hegemonic visions – against dominant homogenization, against the fragmentation of peoples, and against the assimilation of their distinct cultural world."[130]

Aquino's version of Latina feminist theology had three foundational principles, all of them explicitly liberationist. It began with the faith of the people, took the liberationist option for the poor and oppressed, and conceived theology as liberating praxis. The first principle privileged the experience of faith in grassroots Christian communities; the second privileged the needs of the downtrodden; the third conceived theology as a sacramental, communal, empowering, and liberating fusion of theory and practice. To modernist intellectuals, she observed, the option for the poor that defined and held together liberation theology was a scandal. To postmodern intellectuals it was madness. To liberationists it was "a fundamental Christian imperative – a required norm for the protection of our rationality."[131]

To Aquino the difference between polycentric and intercultural diversity was crucial. In the 1980s Johannes-Baptist Metz proposed the idea of a "polycentric church" that valorized the cultural diversity already present in Christianity. This notion won a following among theologians, notably Juan José Tamayo and Roberto Goizueta, as the ideal for a liberation theology that dealt creatively with cultural diversity. Metz later decided, however, that the polycentric model was naïve about power and insufficiently pluralistic; Aquino agreed on both counts. The polycentric church retained a self-centered dynamic and it facilitated cross-cultural dialogues among relative equal groups, she noted. What was needed was a genuinely intercultural model that cast aside any notion of a self-centered dynamic, recognized the practical implications of inequality, and opposed the oppressive aspects of all cultures. In the real world, she argued, the possibility of multicultural conversation was negated by massive disparities of power. Neo-liberal economics widened the chasm between rich and poor, assaulting local cultures wherever it spread. Nice words about cultural dialogue masked the overwhelming reality: "The fact is that any theological discourse that takes seriously into account the plural fabric of reality and of knowledge must deal also with the asymmetric character of social power relations at all levels."[132]

"Social power relations" included racial and sexual hierarchies and other oppressive aspects of all cultures. Cultural diversity was not much of an ideal if it legitimized the bad parts of existing cultures, Aquino cautioned. Condemning the "dehumanizing and unhealthy trends in Mexican culture," she declared, "I have always rejected the romanticization of 'family values,' 'the motherland,' and 'motherhood' in the context of such a seemingly intractable patriarchal and sexist Mexican culture. This type of culture has been greatly instigated by a dominant Roman Catholicism."[133]

Instead of idealizing the idea of many cultural versions of the same thing conversing agreeably with each other, Aquino's intercultural approach put a liberationist understanding of multiculturalism at the heart of Christian identity. For her, as for Isasi-Díaz and Elizondo, *mestizaje* was the best symbol of it: "I mean here not only the biological *mestizaje*, which created a new race, but especially the cultural and intellectual *mestizaje* that created a new *intercultural reality* and, consequently, an *intercultural theology*." Citing Elizondo's observation that biological *mestizaje* was "easy and natural," while cultural *mestizaje* was hard and threatening, Aquino exhorted readers to face up to the hard part, adding that the mixture of white and black – *mulataje* – was an intrinsic part of intercultural theology: "*Mestizaje* is a historical fact that still opens up old wounds, just as it is also the opportunity to build an intercommunicative platform with other voices who speak from their own irreducible cultures." *Mestizaje* blending occurred in many ways, but wherever it gave rise to a new people, a new history began with them.[134]

Human Rights and Catholic Social Ethics: David Hollenbach

The liberationist and postmodern emphasis on diversity militated against global claims, but that did not stop some ethicists who took liberation theology and postmodernism seriously from making them. Maguire was a prominent example; Jesuit social-ethicist David Hollenbach was another. A doctoral graduate of Yale and former professor at Georgetown University and Weston School of Theology, Hollenbach held the Margaret O'Brien Flatley chair in Catholic theology at Boston College. His defense of economic rights, discussed in Chapter 7, was an important plank of a larger argument about the ethical necessity and Catholic adoption of modern human rights theory.

To Hollenbach, the Catholic acceptance of human rights doctrine was remarkable to the point of being "astonishing"; it was also too precious to squander. He recalled that historically the Catholic Church opposed the socialist and democratic traditions that gave birth to human rights theory, which predisposed it against human rights. Official Catholicism disapproved right up to the pontificate of John XXIII, who embraced human rights at the very moment that the church began to deal constructively with political and religious pluralism. Hollenbach stressed that these developments belonged together logically and historically. In modern Catholicism, coming to terms with pluralism was not something that militated against the universalistic logic of human rights. The church under John XXIII and Vatican II embraced human rights precisely as a way of coping with political and religious plurality.[135]

Hollenbach judged that the most significant utterance of Vatican II was John Courtney Murray's seemingly innocuous statement in *Dignatatis humanae* that the council sought to "develop" Catholic tradition on "the inviolable rights of the human person and the constitutional order of society." The church had never explicitly acknowledged that doctrine sometimes changed, Hollenbach observed, and *Dignatatis humanae* made a huge change on a major issue, "a reversal of the explicit content of church teaching." Both were stunning breakthroughs. The church not only reversed its position on a major issue at Vatican II, but acknowledged doing so, albeit in the language of "development." By adopting a strong view of human rights, the church was able to change its position on religious freedom:

> At the council the modern Catholic church for the first time was compelled to come to grips in an official way with the realities of the religious, cultural, social, economic, political, and ideological pluralism of the contemporary world. The most obvious effect of this acknowledgement of pluralism was the council's movement from the kind of unitary model of church–state relationships that prevailed through almost all of previous church history to a pluralistic model based on the right of all persons to religious liberty."[136]

Vatican II marked the end of single unitary models that privileged Catholicism, Hollenbach argued. The church broke free from authoritarianism in religion and politics alike, recognizing that the argument for freedom and pluralism applied to both realms. Hollenbach stressed that the implications for Catholic social ethics were enormous. Instead of conceiving society dogmatically as an exigency of natural law, John XXIII and Vatican II made all social structures and models accountable to the standards of human rights: "Basic human rights set limits and establish obligations for all systems and ideologies, leaving the precise form in which these systems will be organized undefined."[137]

That made the Catholic Church remarkably like the United Nations, Hollenbach contended. In his reading, the church was affected profoundly by the founding of the United Nations in 1945 and the UN's adoption of the Universal Declaration of Human Rights in 1948. The UN founders sought to show that it was possible for a diverse community of nation states to affirm cultural and political pluralism *and* a normative basis of justice concerns. Hollenbach noted that the reformist majority at Vatican II had a very similar concern. Admittedly, the UN was dominated by a handful of mostly Western powers in its early years, but it developed into a genuine worldwide community. A generation after the UN was established, the Catholic Church took a similar step toward becoming a global church instead of a European one with missionary outposts.

Hollenbach observed that two main traditions of human rights discourse competed for influence at the United Nations. The liberal tradition of the West emphasized the civil and political liberties of speech, association, press, and religion and the juridical guarantees of habeas corpus and due process. The Socialist and Communist traditions held that the rights to gainful employment and economic security were more important than personal liberties. In Hollenbach's view, the Catholic Church did well not to choose between these competing traditions of rights theory; instead, Catholic social ethics affirmed all the rights enumerated in both traditions. John XXIII's *Pacem in terris* set the standard, affirming the rights to life, bodily integrity, food, clothing, shelter, rest, medical care, and the social services necessary to protect these rights; the rights to education, information, and the freedom of speech and press; the right to religious freedom; the rights to marriage and procreation; the rights to gainful employment, a just wage, humane working conditions, worker participation in management decisions, and ownership of private property; the rights of assembly, association, and the right to organize; the rights to freedom of movement and migration; the political right to participate in public affairs; and the juridical right to constitutional protection of all other rights, including habeas corpus and due process.[138]

Hollenbach sharpened and defended this approach to human rights doctrine. He was critical of the papal tendency under Paul VI and John Paul II to claim a harmonized standpoint far above the fray of competing claims, since the result was often an abstract generalization that accomplished little. The Catholic approach was comprehensive, Hollenbach argued, but it did not have to be vague, abstract, or imperious. Abstract harmonization was not its essential mark, for it had a foundational principle: human dignity as the foundation of all rights. To Hollenbach, this norm was a principle of moral and political legitimacy, not an ideological principle of social organization; it did not focus on institutional means. Catholic thought grounded its claims for universal human rights on the dignity of the person, backed by two warrants: The transcendence of the person over the world of things (a reality evident to all rational beings) and the creation of human beings in the image of God (a doctrine of faith). In Catholic theology, Hollenbach explained, doctrines illuminated general human experience and were themselves illuminated by experience. Boldly, the church dared to integrate theology and philosophy, which enabled a certain boldness on human rights: "The Catholic tradition does not hesitate to claim a universal validity for the way it seeks to ground human rights in the dignity of the human person."[139]

In Catholic moral theology the standard of human dignity called for laws and policies that served human persons as free, needy, relational beings of transcendent worth. Hollenbach acknowledged that the task of determining which policies best protected human freedom, fulfilled human needs, and supported human relationships was contextually relative. "Human dignity" was an empty abstraction without the specifics, but policy specifics were particular and contextual. To determine the implication of the universal principle in particular situations, Catholic ethics relied on its tradition of social and political teaching. Hollenbach recalled that modern Catholic social ethics began with Leo XIII, the living wage, and the limited state; for decades the church railed against anticlerical theories of religious liberty; and during the Cold War it posed as a third way between capitalism and socialism under the banner of corporatism, solidarism, or Christian democracy. Vatican II built on these traditions, he acknowledged, but more importantly, it marked an epochal breakthrough by legitimizing pluralism. After Vatican II, Catholic ethicists were free to serve the cause of human dignity in pluralistic contexts, stressing the ways that civil/political and social/economic rights were trampled by "oppressive power configurations." At its best, Catholic ethics stressed that civil/political and social/economic rights were interconnected and interdependent. Hollenbach explained, "The historical memory of the church is combining with its present historical experience as a community to produce what amounts to a transnational human-rights ideology." By granting what amounted to doctrinal status to human rights ideology, the church placed the full weight of its moral authority on respect for social pluralism, the interdependence of all human rights, and the moral necessity of upholding the rights of all people, especially the oppressed and excluded.[140]

That put Catholic ethics at odds with the individualistic concept of human rights that prevailed in the United States, Hollenbach noted. US American individualism viewed human rights through the paradigm of the right to be left alone, construing private property as the archetype of all human rights. Catholic ethics differed by blending individual liberties and social justice concerns. Hollenbach enthused that the international human rights movement grew steadily throughout the 1970s and 1980s, usually expressing a Catholic-like understanding of human rights as a bulwark of liberty and social justice. In 1993 the World Conference on Human Rights, meeting in Vienna under the sponsorship of the United Nations, gave a telling measure of the movement's global strength. Delegates of 171 nations representing 85 percent of the world's population issued the Vienna Declaration and Programme of Action, which affirmed and expanded all the standards of the 1948 Universal Declaration and declared that "the universal nature of these rights and freedoms is beyond question." Many of the nations supporting the Vienna Declaration had been colonized or oppressed by dictatorships in 1948; thus they had no say in the Universal Declaration. Hollenbach pointed additionally to the "astonishing" growth of nongovernmental organizations devoted to human rights advocacy, such as Amnesty International and Human Rights Watch, and to international judicial bodies devoted to enforcing human rights, such as the International Criminal Tribunal. The empirical case for the universality of human rights was getting stronger, he urged: "Human rights are becoming the core of a truly global common morality."[141]

Hollenbach acknowledged four streams of "countersigns" to his argument. Some Islamic, Confucian, and African critics objected that human rights doctrine was still too Western to speak for them, and Western postmodernists rejected the very idea of a human rights ethic. Muslim critics usually centered on the right to religious freedom, where Shari'ah law forbade conversions away from Islam and limited the religious freedom of non-Muslims in Islamic nations. Confucian critics pointed to the individualism of human rights ideology, which conflicted with normative Confucian ideas about proper relationships between parents and children, ministers and rulers, husbands and wives, and older and younger brothers. Some African intellectuals and political leaders made a similar argument about the incompatibility of human rights individualism and African communalism. Western postmodernists cited these objections in claiming that every so-called common morality was a form of cultural hegemony that legitimized sociopolitical domination.[142]

Hollenbach explicated these arguments respectfully, noted that they were subjects of vigorous debate in Islamic, Confucian, African, and Western academic contexts, and argued gently for the plausibility and ethical necessity of human rights universalism. The jury was out in many Islamic, Confucian, and African contexts as to whether human rights ideology was incompatible with central cultural norms, he observed. No culture was static; the treatment of women and religious minorities varied greatly in Muslim countries; religious and cultural traditions were complex and variously interpreted; and cultural narrowness and insularity were always problematic. Those who insisted that Islamic, Confucian, and African traditions were incompatible with human rights norms were not necessarily the best interpreters of these traditions, he suggested. In any case, their claims had dubious moral consequences, as other interpreters of these traditions contended. Hollenbach cautioned against being oversensitive to accusations of cultural imperialism in this area. One could not defend the idea of human rights without being accused of hegemonic presumption, but in some cases that was simply a cost of standing for the moral good. He stressed that vital movements for human rights existed everywhere:

> There are notable intellectual and activist movements within the Islamic, Confucian, and African traditions that argue for the value of a global human rights ethic in the context

of their own societies. They often do this by proposing that people of their own traditions and societies will be better off if cultural traditions are developed in ways that lead to the affirmation of human rights.[143]

That plea was persuasive to Hollenbach, though he conceded there were serious grounds to doubt the viability of a common ethic. Citing social critic Michael Ignatieff, he stressed the pragmatic arguments for human rights, contending that human rights standards protected the social agency of individuals and communities, especially against oppression. Ignatieff maintained that the obvious diversity of cultural understandings of the good and the controversies over cultural imperialism did not negate the practical value of human rights standards in protecting individuals and communities from outrageous evils. Human rights was about the practical obligation not to inflict insufferable wrong on any human being.[144]

Ignatieff stuck with pragmatism in defending this position. Eschewing foundational theories, he judged that any claim for a theoretical foundation merely weakened support for human rights. For him it was enough to say that human rights standards helped to protect human beings from insufferable harm; thus they were valuable. For Hollenbach that was not enough. He allowed that the drafters of the Universal Declaration opted for pragmatism, since they were able to agree only about the rights, not about the "why." Philosopher John Rawls, in his theory of "overlapping consensus," allowed a larger role for moral reasons without claiming a common moral basis. Rawls argued that people from differing traditions should be able to discover within their traditions their own reasons to affirm overlapping moral principles. Moral reasons had a key role to play in the politics of human rights, though human rights had no common moral basis; it rested on the convergence of incommensurable ways of thinking. Hollenbach replied that Ignatieff's pragmatism lacked moral weight and Rawls' strategy wasn't much better. Neither approach was able to say whether the Universal Declaration or the Vienna Declaration represented a transient overlapping of interests or a genuine moral agreement, because Ignatieff equated moral concern with group interest, and Rawls merely showed that people could have different reasons for moral judgments that they happened to agree about at the moment. In both cases, the overlaps were no more secure than the configuration of circumstances or interests that produced them. If the interests of the parties changed, the overlaps disappeared, negating human rights.[145]

Hollenbach urged that human rights advocates needed a stronger basis for consensus, which would lead to a stronger consensus: "We need to present *reasons* why the human rights ethos should become a more truly *common* morality and a more truly *global* ethic. Unless we know the reasons on which the consensus is based, we will not know whether it is a genuinely moral consensus or merely the result of lucky circumstances." There had to be a third way between hoping for a metaphysical or religious consensus and settling for overlaps that lacked a common moral basis. Following Jacques Maritain, Hollenbach argued that the solution was to exercise common practical reason. There was no prospect of a consensus among Christians, Confucians, Muslims, and secularists about God and human destiny, Hollenbach allowed, but it was not misguided to strive for agreements about the reasons why torture, genocidal violence, and religious compulsion were morally repugnant regardless of circumstance. Disagreements about ultimate convictions did not preclude morally based agreements about the unacceptability of certain practices. The human rights movement needed a common moral basis to have moral force, which was attainable by restricting shared moral reasoning to practical concerns.[146]

Hollenbach took for granted that Rawlsian "overlapping" occurred routinely in discussions of human rights. Christians, Confucians, and Muslims appropriately drew from the wellsprings of their own traditions to justify their support of human rights. But Rawls's strategy rested too quickly with the putative incommensurability of traditions, Hollenbach judged; thus it did not sufficiently challenge moral traditions to grow or change. Contrary to Ignatieff's approach, the most effective versions of human rights doctrine did not exclude foundational arguments; contrary to Rawls's approach, the most important moral reasoning had to be shared across traditions. When moral reasoning was risked across traditions, Hollenbach argued, defenders of particular traditions were sometimes challenged to revise or reinterpret their traditions. Catholics stopped defending religious intolerance; Confucians and Muslims allowed greater latitude for women. Hollenbach remarked that

> A form of practical reason that is essentially an instrumental calculus of self-interest cannot play this role, for it will either simply reinforce what the group from a particular tradition already believes or challenge the group in ways that lack authentic respect for its traditions. In either case, an instrumental rationality of self-interest lacks what is required to bring traditions together on ground that is genuinely shared.[147]

Most religious traditions had a version of the Golden Rule – in Christianity, "Do unto others as you would have them do unto you" – though sometimes the rule was applied only to insiders. Hollenbach emphasized and universalized the reciprocity of moral obligation contained in the rule's many versions. Using practical reason to interpret the Golden Rule as a universal obligation, he acknowledged that this strategy was a variant of Kantian cosmopolitanism. Just as Kant linked the universal reach of moral obligation with the requirement of respect for humanity as such, treating every human being as an end, Hollenbach linked the universality of moral obligation with the intrinsic dignity of persons. Just as Kant described the human race as a moral community bound by reciprocal moral obligations, Hollenbach used practical reason to forge a common morality of human rights, interpreting the Golden Rule as a universal principle. Unlike Kant, however, who looked down on traditions and identified enlightenment with the verdicts of his own reason, Hollenbach took seriously religious and cultural traditions as vehicles of moral truth. He also played up the moral implications of human self-transcendence, contending that every person was morally obligated not to harm any other person's capacity for self-transcendence. To be capable of experiencing moral obligation was to be responsible for ensuring its realization in others, he argued. Every person's capacity for self-transcendence made a claim on someone's capacity for it: "He or she is not confined within the limits of self-consciousness but can genuinely encounter the other as a fellow person. Thus, one human being *is* a kind of *ought* in the face of another."[148]

To Hollenbach, the movement for human rights represented globalization at its best, just as the structural adjustment programs of the World Bank and International Monetary Fund showed globalization at its worst. Globalization that enhanced social solidarity was a good thing, he argued, because solidarity was a precondition of basic justice. In the economic realm there had to be a way to make globalization work for solidarity against worsening poverty, exclusion, and domination, which was the legacy of neo-liberal globalization thus far. What was needed was an economic equivalent to the vision of solidarity and positive interdependence displayed by the human rights movement. Hollenbach suggested that the idea of a worldwide rights-bearing human community might be the answer, a movement toward the globalization of citizenship that placed a higher value on membership in the human community than in belonging to a particular nation state.[149]

He prized his mainstream status in Catholic social ethics, which helped him nudge it to the left. Hollenbach specialized in judicious, scholarly essays that applied the reforming spirit of Vatican II to an increasingly global church and showed the relevance of Catholic social teaching to contentious public issues. Having had the heady experience of writing a pastoral letter for the US bishops early in his career, he was used to brickbats from the Right. When attacked he usually asserted his mainstream status in the field and tradition. In 1996 the Vatican thwarted Hollenbach's promotion at Weston School of Theology, which delighted his conservative critics and prompted him to join a non-pontifical institution, Boston College. A decade before, during the controversy over the pastoral letter on economics, Michael Novak accused Hollenbach of abusing the bishops' trust in him by "secretly smuggling an egalitarian, socialist concept into Catholic thought." Hollenbach replied that Novak's attack was "a symptom of a very real disease in our society" that Murray rightly named barbarism. In barbaric conditions, Hollenbach explained, citing Murray, public debates about justice died from disinterest, or degenerated into "the angry mutterings of polemic," or took flight to "the shrillness of hysteria." Novak was the hysterical type, Hollenbach judged, and it was terribly important for social ethicists to resist being lured into Novak-style barbarism.[150]

That was an atypical revenge-kick for Hollenbach; most of the time he exemplified scholarly civility and reasonableness. At an abstract level he and Novak agreed that Catholic social ethics needed to incorporate aspects of liberal and communitarian moral theories into natural law reasoning; the sharp differences between them were essentially ideological. To Hollenbach, socialism was not a smear term, and the egalitarian impulse in Catholic ethics had to be developed as inherent in social justice, not denigrated as un-Catholic. He noted that in *Economic Justice for All*, the US bishops amplified natural law doctrine; modestly he refrained from noting his role in the process.[151]

From liberal theory, he explained, which taught that the right is prior to the good, the bishops appropriated the language of individual rights and freedoms. From communitarian theory, which taught that the good is prior to the right, they appropriated a modern language of virtue and the common good. Hollenbach judged that liberal theory lacked the corrective Aristotelian and Thomist emphasis on the morally constitutive roles of communities in shaping individual sensibilities. On its own terms, liberalism was incoherent, because it neglected the constitutive role of community in shaping the individual "self" on which liberalism was ostensibly based. On the other hand, modern communitarianism by itself was too much like the old religion. Its emphasis on the cultivation of virtue and the common good needed the liberal passion for individual rights. Without liberalism, communitarian theory was suffocating.[152]

The best option for contemporary Catholicism was the one the US bishops took in *Economic Justice for All*, Hollenbach argued. It was "a liberalism of a strongly revisionist kind" that blended the modern and ancient languages of rights and the common good. Catholic social ethics, at its best, synthesized the Aristotelian/Thomist notion of covenanted community with the liberal commitment to the freedom and equality of all individuals before the law.[153]

In this area, as in his arguments for human rights universalism and the social justice agenda of human rights, Hollenbach exemplified the possibility of a liberal version of

Murray's public theology project. In one sense his attempt to rehabilitate moral universalism was decidedly untimely, sailing against the postmodern impulses of his generation. In another sense his timing was perfect, staking out ethical terms on which different religions and cultures under postmodern circumstances could agree on the good and stand for it.

Notes

1 See *Radical Orthodoxy: A New Theology*, ed. John Milbank, Catherine Pickstock and Graham Ward (London: Routledge, 1999).

2 See Robert Benne, *Reasonable Ethics: A Christian Approach to Social, Economic, and Political Concerns* (St Louis: Concordia Publishing House, 2005), 24; *Hard Ball on Holy Ground: The Religious Right v. the Mainline for the Church's Soul*, ed. Stephen Swecker (North Berwick, ME: Boston Wesleyan Press, 2005).

3 See Max Stackhouse, "Countering the Military–Industrial Complex," *Christianity & Crisis* 31 (February 1971), 14–22; Stackhouse, "Understanding the Pentagon," *Worldview* 14 (July–August 1971), 14–16; Stackhouse, *The Ethics of Necropolis: The Military–Industrial Complex and the Quest for a Just Peace* (Boston: Beacon Press, 1971); Stackhouse, "Toward Economic Democracy," *Colloquy* 6 (October 1973), 28–31; Stackhouse, "An Ecumenist's Plea for a Public Theology," *This World* 8 (1984), 47–79; Stackhouse, *Creeds, Society and Human Rights: A Study in Three Societies* (Grand Rapids: Eerdmans, 1984); Stackhouse, "Religious Freedom and Human Rights: A 'Public Theological' Perspective," *Our Freedoms: Rights and Responsibilities*, ed. W. L. Taitte (Austin: University of Texas Press, 1985), 69–114; Stackhouse, "Theology and Human Rights," *Perkins Journal* (October 1986), 11–18; Stackhouse, "What Tillich Meant to Me," *Christian Century* 107 (January 30, 1990), 99–102; Paul Tillich, *Die sozialistische Entscheidung* (Potsdam: Alfred Protte, 1933); English edition, Tillich, *The Socialist Decision*, trans. Franklin Sherman (New York: Harper & Row, 1977); Tillich, *The Interpretation of History*, trans. N. A. Rasetzki and Elsa L. Talmey (New York: Charles Scribner's Sons, 1936).

4 Max L. Stackhouse and Dennis P. McCann, "Public Theology After the Collapse of Socialism: A Postcommunist Manifesto," *Christian Century* 108 (January 16, 1991), 1, 44–7, quotes 1; see Stackhouse, "From the Social Gospel to Public Theology," *Being Christian Today: An American Conversation*, eds. Richard John Neuhaus and George Weigel (Washington, DC: Ethics and Public Policy Center, 1992), 33–58.

5 Stackhouse and McCann, "Public Theology After the Collapse of Socialism: A Postcommunist Manifesto," 1, 44.

6 Ibid., quotes 44–5; see Stackhouse, "From the Social Gospel to Public Theology," *Being Christian Today: An American Conversation*, 49–58.

7 Stackhouse and McCann, "Public Theology After the Collapse of Socialism: A Postcommunist Manifesto," 45–6.

8 Ibid., 46–7; see Max L. Stackhouse, "The Moral Roots of the Corporation," *Theology and Public Policy* 5 (Summer 1993), 29–39.

9 Robert Benne, "Less Enthusiasm, Please, I'm Lutheran," *Christian Century* 108 (January 23, 1991), reprinted in Benne, *Reasonable Ethics: A Christian Approach to Social, Economic, and Political Concerns*, 181–5, quotes 185.

10 Max L. Stackhouse, *Public Theology and Political Economy: Christian Stewardship in Modern Society* (Grand Rapids: Eerdmans, 1987), quotes 133. This section draws on the author's conversations with Stackhouse.

11 Dennis P. McCann, *Christian Realism and Liberation Theology: Practical Theologies in Creative Conflict* (Maryknoll, NY: Orbis Books, 1981), 178–9; McCann, "A Word to the Reader,"

in *On Moral Business: Classical and Contemporary Resources for Ethics in Economic Life*, eds. Max L. Stackhouse, Dennis P. McCan, and Shirley J. Roels, with Preston N. Williams (Grand Rapids: Eerdmans, 1995), McCann quote 7; see McCann and M. L. Browns- berger, "Management as a Social Practice: Rethinking Business Ethics after MacIntyre," *Annual of the Society of Christian Ethics* (1990), 223–45, reprinted in ibid., 508–13; McCann, "Doing Well and Doing Good: The Challenge to the Christian Capitalist," *Christian Century* 110 (October 6, 1993); *Christian Social Ethics in a Global Era*, ed. Max L. Stack- house (Nashville: Abingdon, 1993); Stackhouse, "The Global Future and the Future of Globalization," *Christian Century* 111 (February 1994), 109–18.

12 See *God and Globalization: Religion and the Powers of the Common Life*, eds. Max L. Stackhouse and Peter Paris (Philadelphia: Trinity Press International, 2000); *God and Globalization: The Spirit and the Modern Authorities*, eds. Stackhouse and Don Browning (Philadelphia: Trinity Press International, 2001); *God and Globalization: Christ and the Dominions of Civilization*, eds. Stackhouse and Diane B. Obenchain (Philadelphia: Trinity Press International, 2002).

13 Max L. Stackhouse, *Covenant and Commitments: Faith, Family and Economic Life* (Louisville: Westminster John Knox, 1997), 13–43.

14 Max L. Stackhouse, "The Prophetic Stand of the Ecumenical Churches on Homo- sexuality," Theology Page, Office of General Ministries, United Church of Christ, www.ucc.org/theology, 1–14, accessed May 13, 2007; Stackhouse, *Covenant and Commit- ments: Faith, Family and Economic Life*, 13–16.

15 Stackhouse, "The Prophetic Stand of the Ecumenical Churches on Homosexuality," quotes 2.

16 Stackhouse, *Covenant and Commitments: Faith, Family and Economic Life*, 15–20; Stackhouse, "The Prophetic Stand of the Ecumenical Churches on Homosexuality," 8–10.

17 Stackhouse, *Covenant and Commitments: Faith, Family and Economic Life*, 34–5, quote 35; see Beverly W. Harrison, "Misogyny and Homophobia," in Harrison, *Making the Connec- tions: Essays in Feminist Social Ethics*, ed. Carol J. Robb (Boston: Beacon Press, 1985), 135–6.

18 Stackhouse, "The Prophetic Stand of the Ecumenical Churches on Homosexuality," quote 11; see "Behind the Charge of Heresy," *Boston Globe* (August 4, 1996), D 1, 3.

19 Stackhouse, "The Prophetic Stand of the Ecumenical Churches on Homosexuality," 10–11.

20 Twenty-fourth General Synod of the United Church of Christ, "Resolutions of the United Church of Christ, 2005," http://en.wikipedia.org/wiki/Resolutions, accessed August 16, 2007; see Richard B. Hays, *The Moral Vision of the New Testament: A Con- temporary Introduction to New Testament Ethics* (San Francisco: HarperSanFrancisco, 1986; Robert A. Gagnon, *The Bible and Homosexual Practice: Texts and Hermeneutics* (Nashville: Abingdon Press, 2001); Gagnon, "Gays and the Bible: A Response to Walter Wink," *Christian Century* 119 (August 14–27, 2002), 40–3.

21 Lisa Sowle Cahill, *Between the Sexes: Foundations for a Christian Ethics of Sexuality* (Phila- delphia and New York: Fortress Press and Paulist Press, 1985), 1–11.

22 Cahill, *Between the Sexes: Foundations for a Christian Ethics of Sexuality*, 45–56; see Phyllis A. Bird, " 'Male and Female He Created Them': Gen.1:27b in the Context of the Priestly Account of Creation," *Harvard Theological Review* 74 (1981), 129–59; Sandra M. Sch- neiders, "From Exegesis to Hermeneutics: The Problem of the Contemporary Meaning of Scripture," *Horizons* 8 (1981), 30–4; Phyllis Trible, *God and the Rhetoric of Sexuality* (Philadelphia: Fortress Press, 1978), 15–21.

23 Cahill, *Between the Sexes: Foundations for a Christian Ethics of Sexuality*, 143–4.

24 Ibid., 144; see Lisa Sowle Cahill, *Sex, Gender and Christian Ethics* (Cambridge: Cambridge University Press, 1996), 121–65.

25 Cahill, *Between the Sexes: Foundations for a Christian Ethics of Sexuality*, 144–8, quotes 147–8; see Lisa Sowle Cahill, "Homosexuality: A Case Study in Moral Argument," in

Homosexuality in the Church, ed. Jeffrey Siker (Louisville: Westminster John Knox, 1994), 61–75.

26   Cahill, *Between the Sexes: Foundations for a Christian Ethics of Sexuality*, 148; see Cahill, *Sex, Gender and Christian Ethics*, 255–7.

27   Cahill, *Between the Sexes: Foundations for a Christian Ethics of Sexuality*, 148–52, quotes 148–9.

28   Ibid., "irenic," 150; Cahill, *Sex, Gender and Christian Ethics*, "persistently captive," "obsolete," 256.

29   Marvin M. Ellison, *Erotic Justice: A Liberating Ethic of Sexuality* (Louisville: Westminster John Knox Press, 1994), "communal," 4; Ellison and Sylvia Thorson-Smith, "Keeping Body and Soul Together, Again for the First Time," in *Body and Soul: Rethinking Sexuality as Justice-Love*, eds. Marvin M. Ellison and Sylvia Thorson–Smith (Cleveland: Pilgrim Press, 2003), "sexual," 7; Carter Heyward, *Touching Our Strength: The Erotic as Power and the Love of God* (San Francisco: Harper & Row, 1989), "the most," 4.

30   General Assembly Special Committee on Human Sexuality, Office of the General Assembly, Presbyterian Church (USA), *Keeping Body and Soul Together: Sexuality, Spirituality, and Social Justice* (Louisville: Office of the General Assembly, 1991), quote 18. This report was subsequently reprinted as *Presbyterians and Human Sexuality 1991* (Louisville: Office of the General Assembly, 1991).

31   Karen Lebacqz, "Sex: Justice in Church and Society," *Christianity and Crisis* (May 27, 1991), 174; Tom F. Driver, "Presbyterians, Pagans, and Paglia," *Christianity and Crisis* (February 3, 1992), 20.

32   Camille Paglia, "The Joy of Presbyterian Sex," *New Republic* (December 2, 1991), 24; Peter Steinfels, "Beliefs," *New York Times* (May 25, 1991); Office of the General Assembly, Presbyterian Church (USA), June 11, 1991; cited in Ellison and Thorson-Smith, "Keeping Body and Soul Together, Again for the First Time," 8–9.

33   Marvin M. Ellison, "Setting the Captives Free: Same-Sex Domestic Violence and the Justice-Loving Church," in *Body and Soul: Rethinking Sexuality as Justice-Love*, 284–97, quotes 296–7.

34   Ellison, *Erotic Justice: A Liberating Ethic of Sexuality*, "the audience," and "my participation," 4; Marvin M. Ellison, *Same Sex Marriage? A Christian Ethical Analysis* (Cleveland: Pilgrim Press, 2004), 147–68, "by and large," 149.

35   Ellison, *Erotic Justice: A Liberating Ethic of Sexuality*, quotes 8.

36   Ibid., quotes 115, 121; see Ellison, *Same-Sex Marriage? A Christian Ethical Analysis*, 165–8.

37   J. Philip Wogaman, "Socialism's Obituary Is Premature," *Christian Century* 107 (May 30–June 6, 1990), 570–2; see Wogaman, *The Great Economic Debate: An Ethical Analysis* (Philadelphia: Westminster Press, 1977).

38   D. Stephen Long, *Divine Economy: Theology and the Market* (New York: Routledge, 2000), 55–6; Stackhouse and McCann, "Public Theology After the Collapse of Socialism: A Postcommunist Manifesto," 45.

39   John Atherton, *Christianity and the Market: Christian Social Thought for Our Times* (London: SPCK Press, 1992), quotes 12, 16, 20.

40   Gary Dorrien, *Reconstructing the Common Good: Theology and the Social Order* (Maryknoll, NY: Orbis Books, 1992), v–vii; Dorrien, *Soul in Society: The Making and Renewal of Social Christianity* (Minneapolis: Fortress Press, 1995), 1–4, 290.

41   This section adapts material from Dorrien, *Soul in Society: The Making and Renewal of Social Christianity*, 308–35, 266–7.

42   See H. Paul Santmire, *Brother Earth: Nature, God, and Ecology in a Time of Crisis* (New York: Thomas Nelson, 1970); Santmire, *The Travail of Nature: The Ambiguous Ecological Promise of Christian Theology* (Philadelphia: Fortress Press, 1985); Joseph Sittler, *Essays on Nature and Grace* (Philadelphia: Fortress Press, 1972); Elizabeth Dodson-Gray, *Green Paradise Lost* (Wellesley, MA: Roundtable Press, 1981); George Hendry, *Theology of Nature*

(Philadelphia: Westminster Press, 1980); Dieter T. Hessel, *For Creation's Sake: Preaching, Ecology and Justice* (Philadelphia: Westminster/Geneva, 1985); Matthew Fox, *Original Blessing: A Primer in Creation Spirituality* (Santa Fe: Bear and Company, 1983); Douglas John Hall, *Imaging God: Dominion as Stewardship* (Grand Rapids: Eerdmans, 1986); Sallie McFague, *Models of God: Theology for an Ecological, Nuclear Age* (Philadelphia: Fortress Press, 1987); Jay McDaniel, *Of God and Pelicans: Theology of Reverence for Life* (Louisville: Westminster John Knox, 1989).

43   John B. Cobb Jr, *Sustainability: Economics, Ecology and Justice* (Maryknoll, NY: Orbis Books, 1992), "for the first," 1; see Paul Ehrlich, *The Population Bomb* (New York: Ballantine Books, 1968). This section adapts material from Gary Dorrien, *The Making of American Liberal Theology: Crisis, Irony, and Postmodernity, 1950–2005* (Louisville: Westminster John Knox Press, 2006), 222–4.

44   John B. Cobb Jr, "Intellectual Autobiography," *Religious Studies Review* 19 (January 1993), quote 10; Cobb to author, October 30, 2002; Lynn White Jr, "The Historical Roots of the Environmental Crisis," reprinted in *The Ecocriticism Reader: Landmarks in Literary Ecology*, eds. Cheryl Glotfelty and Harold Fromm (Athens: University of Georgia Press, 1996).

45   Cobb Jr, *Sustainability: Economics, Ecology and Justice*, quote 3.

46   John B. Cobb Jr, *Is It Too Late?: A Theology of Ecology* (Beverly Hills, CA: Bruce, 1972), quotes 54, 138.

47   John B. Cobb Jr, *Reclaiming the Church: Where the Mainline Church Went Wrong and What to Do about It* (Louisville: Westminster John Knox Press, 1997), "transformation is," 60; Cobb, "Intellectual Autobiography," "I see," 11; see Cobb, *Transforming Christianity and the World: A Way beyond Absolutism and Relativism*, ed. Paul F. Knitter (Maryknoll, NY: Orbis Books, 1999); Cobb, *Lay Theology* (St Louis: Chalice Press, 1994).

48   John B. Cobb Jr, "Autobiography," 1991 lecture, Pacific Coast Theological Society, "our churches," 13; Cobb, "Intellectual Autobiography," "the only hope," 11; Charles Birch and John B. Cobb, Jr, *The Liberation of Life: From the Cell to the Community* (Cambridge: Cambridge University Press, 1981), 239–40, "the ideology," 263–4; see World Council of Churches, *Now Is the Time: The Final Document and Other Texts from the World Convocation on Justice, Peace, and the Integrity of Creation* (Geneva: WCC Publications, 1990).

49   Herman E. Daly and John B. Cobb, Jr, with contributions by Clifford W. Cobb, *For the Common Good: Redirecting the Economy toward Community, the Environment, and a Sustainable Future* (Boston: Beacon Press, 1989), 401–55, quote 455. For an extensive discussion of issues summarized in this section, see Dorrien, *Soul in Society: The Making and Renewal of Social Christianity*, 316–34.

50   Cobb, *Sustainability: Economics, Ecology, and Justice*, "as long as," 5; see John B. Cobb, Jr, *The Earthist Challenge to Economism: A Theological Critique of the World Bank* (New York: St. Martin's, 1999).

51   John B. Cobb Jr, "Sustainable Community," *Christian Century* 108 (January 23, 1991), 81.

52   Ibid., 81–2.

53   See Sallie McFague, *The Body of God: An Ecological Theology* (Minneapolis: Fortress Press, 1993); McFague, *Super, Natural Christians: How We Should Love Nature* (Minneapolis: Fortress Press, 1997); Thomas Berry, *The Dream of the Earth* (San Francisco: Sierra Club Books, 1988); Berry and Brian Swimme, *The Universe Story: From the Primordial Flaring Forth to the Ecozoic Era* (San Francisco: HarperSanFrancisco, 1992); and Jay McDaniel, *With Roots and Wings: Christianity in an Age of Ecology and Dialogue* (Maryknoll, NY: Orbis Books, 1995).

54   See Larry Rasmussen, *Dietrich Bonhoeffer: Reality and Resistance* (Nashville: Abingdon Press, 1972); Rasmussen and Bruce C. Birch, *Bible and Ethics in the Christian Life* (Minneapolis: Augsburg Publishing House, 1976).

55   Larry L. Rasmussen, *Earth Community Earth Ethics* (Maryknoll, NY: Orbis Books, 1996), quotes 9; see Abraham Joshua Heschel, *Who Is Man?* (Stanford, CA: Stanford University

Press, 1965), 83. The phrase "earth and its distress" Rasmussen took from a 1929 lecture by Dietrich Bonhoeffer titled "Song of Songs."

56 James Nash, *Loving Nature: Ecological Integrity and Christian Responsibility* (Nashville: Abingdon, 1991), quote 181; Nash, "Biotic Rights and Human Ecological Responsibilities," *Annual of the Society of Christian Ethics* (1993), 154–7; Rasmussen, *Earth Community Earth Ethics*, 107–9.

57 See Wesley Granberg-Michaelson, *Redeeming the Creation, the Rio Earth Summit Challenge to the Churches* (Geneva: WCC Publications, 1992); World Council of Churches, *Now Is the Time: The Final Document and Other Texts from the World Convocation on Justice, Peace, and the Integrity of Creation;* Ernest Lefever, *Amsterdam to Nairobi: The World Council of Churches and the Third World* (Washington, DC: Ethics and Public Policy Center, 1979); Rasmussen, *Earth Community Earth Ethics*, 138–54; Ulrich Duchrow, "The Witness of the Church in Contrast to the Prevailing Ideologies of the Market," in *Christian Social Ethics: A Reader*, ed. John Atherton (Cleveland: Pilgrim Press, 1994), 285–301.

58 Rasmussen, *Earth Community Earth Ethics*, quote 142.

59 Marianne Arbogast, "The Icon 'Round God's Neck: Toward Sustainable Community – An Interview with Larry Rasmussen," www.thewitness.org/archive/oct2000, accessed May 16, 2007.

60 Rasmussen, *Earth Community Earth Ethics*, quotes 168, 171; see Kenneth Boulding, "The Economics of the Coming Spaceship Earth," in *Environmental Quality in a Growing Economy*, ed. Henry Jarrett (Baltimore: Johns Hopkins University Press, 1968), 3–14.

61 Larry L. Rasmussen, "Introduction to Next Journey," in Daniel C. Maguire and Larry L. Rasmussen, *Ethics for a Small Planet: New Horizons on Population, Consumption, and Ecology* (Albany, NY: State University of New York Press, 1998), 106–9. This essay was the concise version of Rasmussen's *Earth Community Earth Ethics;* for his earlier version of the Chiapas story, see Rasmussen, *Earth Community Earth Ethics*, 127–37. See Gustavo Esteva, "Basta!," *The Ecologist* 24 (May/June 1994), 83–5.

62 Rasmussen, "Introduction to Next Journey," quotes 117; see Larry L. Rasmussen, *Moral Fragments and Moral Community: A Proposal for Church and Society* (Minneapolis: Fortress Press, 1993).

63 Rasmussen, "Introduction to Next Journey," 118–24.

64 Chung Hyun Kyung, "Come, Holy Spirit – Renew the Whole Creation," in *Sings of the Spirit*, ed. Michael Kinnamon (Geneva: WCC Publications, 1991), 43; Section I, "Giver of Life – Sustain Your Creation!," *Signs of the Spirit*, quote 55; Rasmussen, *Earth Community Earth Ethics*, 227–44, unabashedly" and "turning," 243.

65 Larry L. Rasmussen, "Returning to Our Senses: The Theology of the Cross as a Theology for Eco-Justice," in *After Nature's Revolt: Eco-Justice and Theology*, ed. Dieter T. Hessel (Minneapolis: Fortress Press, 1992), 40–56, quotes 41, 50, 54.

66 Daniel C. Maguire, *The Moral Core of Judaism and Christianity: Reclaiming the Revolution* (Minneapolis: Fortress Press, 1993), quote 13; see Rasmussen, *Earth Community Earth Ethics*, 10.

67 Daniel C. Maguire, Preface to Maguire and Rasmussen, *Ethics for a Small Planet: New Horizons on Population, Consumption, and Ecology*, vii.

68 Ibid., vii–viii; see Maguire, *The Moral Core of Judaism and Christianity: Reclaiming the Revolution*, 37–43; Maguire, "Conclusion," in *What Men Owe to Women: Men's Voices from World Religions*, eds. John C. Raines and Daniel C. Maguire (Albany, NY: State University of New York Press, 2001), 281–5.

69 Daniel C. Maguire, "A Question of Catholic Honesty," *Christian Century* (September 14, 1983), 803–7, quotes 803; Maguire, "The 'Pro-Life' Lie," *CommonDreams.org* (February 2, 2005), www.commondreams.org, accessed May 19, 2007, 1–2; Maguire, "Introduction," *Sacred Rights: The Case for Contraception and Abortion in World Religions*, ed. Daniel C. Maguire (Oxford: Oxford University Press, 2003), 3–20; Christine E. Gudorf,

"Contraception and Abortion in Roman Catholicism," in *Sacred Rights: The Case for Contraception and Abortion in World Religions*, 55–78.

70 Maguire, *The Moral Core of Judaism and Christianity*, 3–22, 38–47; Daniel C. Maguire, "More People, Less Earth: The Shadow of Man-Kind," in Maguire and Rasmussen, *Ethics for a Small Planet: New Horizons on Population, Consumption, and Ecology*, 45–9; see Maguire, *The Moral Choice* (New York: Doubleday, 1978).

71 Daniel C. Maguire, *A Moral Creed for All Christians* (Minneapolis: Fortress Press, 2005), 1–2.

72 Ibid., 41–80; Abraham J. Heschel, *The Prophets* (Philadelphia: Jewish Publication Society of America, 1962), 198. Images of Justice in the USA and Europe devolve from the Roman Justitia (who had some but not all of the attributes of the Greek Themis, who personifies the divine right order of things according to law and custom), and as such commonly bear the attributes of scales and sword; the blindfold, which is sometimes depicted and sometimes not, was a later development in the Renaissance period when the image acquired some of the attributes of Fortuna.

73 Ibid., 216–17.

74 Sharon D. Welch, *Communities of Resistance and Solidarity: A Feminist Theology of Liberation* (Maryknoll, NY: Orbis Books 1985), 32–54.

75 Ibid., quotes 72.

76 Ibid., quotes 79, 80.

77 Sharon D. Welch, *A Feminist Ethic of Risk* (rev. edn., Minneapolis: Fortress Press, 2000), 14–37; Emilie M. Townes, *Breaking the Fine Rain of Death: African American Health Issues and a Womanist Ethic of Care* (New York: Continuum, 1998), "socially shared," 26; Townes, *In a Blaze of Glory: Womanist Spirituality as Social Witness* (Nashville: Abingdon Press, 1995), "respect-filled," 138.

78 Welch, *A Feminist Ethic of Risk*, 123–58, quote 135; see Jürgen Habermas, *The Theory of Communicative Action*, 2 vols., trans. Thomas McCarthy (Boston: Beacon Press, 1984, 1987).

79 Welch, *A Feminist Ethic of Risk*, quotes 168.

80 Sharon D. Welch, "Sporting Power: American Feminism, French Feminisms, and an Ethic of Conflict," in *Transfigurations: Theology and the French Feminists*, ed. C. W. Maggie Kim, Susan M. St Ville, and Susan M. Simonaitis (Minneapolis: Fortress Press, 1993), 171–98; see Sheila G. Davaney, "The Limits of the Appeal to Women's Experience," in *Shaping New Vision: Gender and Values in American Culture*, eds. Clarissa W. Atkinson, Constance H. Buchanan, Margaret R. Miles (Ann Arbor: UMI Research Press, 1987), 32–48; Audre Lord, Jacquelyn Grant, *White Women's Christ and Black Women's Jesus: Feminist Christology and Womanist Response* (Atlanta: Scholars Press, 1989), 195–209.

81 Welch, "Sporting Power: American Feminism, French Feminisms, and an Ethic of Conflict," 181–2.

82 Ibid., 190–8, quote 198; see Sharon D. Welch, *After Empire: The Art and Ethos of Enduring Peace* (Minneapolis: Fortress Press, 2004); Mary Daly, *Pure Lust: Elemental Feminist Philosophy* (Boston: Beacon Press, 1984), 2–3, 352–3.

83 Emilie M. Townes, *Womanist Justice, Womanist Hope* (Atlanta: Scholars Press, 1993), quote ix.

84 Author's conversation with Emilie Townes, October 7, 2004; The Fund for Theological Education, "Partners," www.theund.org, accessed May 23, 2007.

85 Emilie M. Townes, "Living in the New Jerusalem: The Rhetoric and Movement of Liberation in the House of Evil," in *A Troubling in My Soul: Womanist Perspectives on Evil and Suffering*, ed. Emilie M. Townes (Maryknoll, NY: Orbis Books, 1993), 78–91, quote 90–1.

86 Emilie M. Townes, "Introduction: On Creating Ruminations from the Soul," in *A Troubling in My Soul: Womanist Perspectives on Evil and Suffering*, "intentionally," 2; Townes,

In a Blaze of Glory: Womanist Spirituality as Social Witness (Nashville: Abingdon Press, 1995), "unlike," 13, "in utter" and "soulful," 11, "to be," 47.

87   Townes, *In a Blaze of Glory: Womanist Spirituality as Social Witness*, 63.

88   Ibid., quote 109.

89   Ibid., "the Black Church," 118; Emilie M. Townes, "Introduction: On Creating Ruminations on the Spirit," *Embracing the Spirit: Womanist Perspectives on Hope, Salvation and Transformation*, ed. Emilie M. Townes (Maryknoll, NY: Orbis Books, 1997), "happy" quotes, xii.

90   Townes, "Introduction: On Creating Ruminations on the Spirit," "absolutely," xii; Emilie M. Townes, "'The Doctor Ain't Taking No Sticks': Race and Medicine in the African American Community," in *Embracing the Spirit: Womanist Perspectives on Hope, Salvation and Transformation*, 179–93, "too much," 186, "we are called," 193; see Farai Chideya, *Don't Believe the Hype: Fighting Cultural Misinformation about African-Americans* (New York: Plume/Penguin Books, 1995); Townes, *Breaking the Fine Rain of Death: African American Health Issues and a Womanist Ethic of Care* (New York: Continuum Books, 1998).

91   Emilie M. Townes, *Womanist Ethics and the Cultural Production of Evil* (New York: Palgrave Macmillan, 2006), quote 5.

92   See Michel Foucault, *Language, Counter-Memory, Practice: Selected Essays and Interviews*, ed. Donald F. Bouchard (Ithaca, NY: Cornell University Press, 1977), 90–1; Antonio Gramsci, *Selections from the Prison Notebooks*, ed. Quintin Hoare and Geoffrey Nowell Smith (New York: International Publishers, 1971), 57–8.

93   Townes, *Womanist Ethics and the Cultural Production of Evil*, 29–55, quotes 32, 36.

94   Ibid., quotes 47, 52.

95   Ibid., quotes 71, 74.

96   Ibid., 76–7.

97   79–110, quotes 88.

98   Ibid., quote 97.

99   Emilie M. Townes, "The Womanist Dancing Mind: Speaking to the Expansiveness of Womanist Discourse," in *Deeper Shades of Purple: Womanism in Religion and Society*, ed. Stacey M. Floyd-Thomas (New York: New York University Press, 2006), 236–47, quotes 240.

100 Emilie M. Townes, "Question of the Day," *Union Seminary Quarterly Review* Festschrift for Delores S. Williams, 58 (2004), 157–62, quotes 160, 162.

101 Traci C. West, "Is a Womanist a Black Feminist? Marking the Distinctions and Defying Them: A Black Feminist Response," in *Deeper Shades of Purple: Womanism in Religion and Society*, 291–5, quotes 293, 294–5, 292; see bell hooks, *Yearning: Race, Gender, and Cultural Politics* (Boston: South End Press, 1990); Traci C. West, *Disruptive Christian Ethics: When Racism and Women's Lives Matter* (Louisville: Westminster John Knox Press, 2006).

102 Ada María Isasi-Díaz, "*La Lucha*: My Story," in *Transforming the Faiths of Our Fathers: The Women Who Changed American Religion*, ed. Ann Braude (New York: Palgrave Macmillan, 2004), reprinted in Isasi-Díaz, *La Lucha Continues: Mujerista Theology* (Maryknoll, NY: Orbis Books, 2004), 11–23, quote 11; see *Women and Catholic Priesthood*, ed. Anne Marie Gardiner (New York: Paulist Press, 1976).

103 Ada María Isasi-Díaz, "A Hispanic Garden in a Foreign Land," in *Inheriting Our Mothers' Gardens: Feminist Theology in Third World Perspective*, ed. Letty M. Russell, Kwok Pui-lan, Ada María Isasi-Díaz, and Katie G. Cannon (Louisville: Westminster Press, 1988), 91–106, reprinted in Isasi-Díaz, *Mujerista Theology* (Maryknoll: Orbis Books, 13–28, "the Euro-American," 18; Isasi-Díaz, "*La Lucha*: My Story," "extremely," "wounded," "I simply," 19–20.

104 Ada María Isasi-Díaz and Yolanda Tarango, *Hispanic Women: Prophetic Voice in the Church* (San Francisco: Harper & Row, 1988).

105 Ada María Isasi-Díaz, "*Mujeristas*: A Name of Our Own," in *The Future of Liberation Theology*, ed. Marc H. Ellis and Otto Maduro (Maryknoll, NY: Orbis Books, 1989),

410–19, quote 410; see Isasi-Díaz, "Toward an Understanding of *Feminismo Hispano* in the U.S.A.," in *Women's Consciousness, Women's Conscience*, ed. Barbara H. Andolsen, Christine E. Gudorf, and Mary D. Pellauer (New York: Winston, 1985), 51–61.

106 Isasi-Díaz, "*Mujeristas:* A Name of Our Own," quotes 411.

107 Ada María Isasi-Díaz, *En La Lucha / In the Struggle: Elaborating a Mujerista Theology* (Minneapolis: Fortress Press, 1994; Tenth Anniversary Edition, Minneapolis: Fortress Press, 2004), quotes xi; see María Pilar Aquino, "Teología y Mujer en América Latina," *Reflexión y Liberación* 15 (1992), 27–40; Aquino, "Santo Domingo: La Visión Sobre las Mujeres Latinoamericanas," *Reflexión y Liberación* 19 (1993), 39–50; Aquino, *La Teologia, La Iglesia y La Mujer en América Latina* (Bogota, Columbia: Indo-American Press, 1994); Elsa Tamez, *Bible of the Oppressed* (Maryknoll, NY: Orbis Books, 1982); Tamez, *Through Her Eyes: Women's Theology from Latin America* (Maryknoll, NY: Orbis Books, 1989); Tamez, *The Amnesty of Grace* (Nashville: Abingdon Press, 1993); Ana María Pineda, "Pastoral de Conjunto," *New Theology Review* 3/4 (1990), 28–34; Pineda, "Evangelization of the 'New World': A New World Perspective," *Missiology* 20 (1992), 151–61; Pineda, "The Challenge of Hispanic Pluralism in a Hispanic Context," *Missiology* 21 (1993), 437–42.

108 Isasi-Díaz, *En La Lucha / In the Struggle: Elaborating a Mujerista Theology*, quotes 23.

109 Ibid., 30–43.

110 Ibid., "mostly," and "for us," 33; José Vasconcelos, *La Raza Cósmica* (11th edn., Mexico City: Espasa-Calpé Mexicana, 1948); Virgilio Elizondo, *Galilean Journey – The Mexican American Promise* (Maryknoll, NY: Orbis Books, 1983), 7–18, quotes 18.

111 Isasi-Díaz, *En La Lucha / In the Struggle: Elaborating a Mujerista Theology*, quotes 36, 37.

112 Ibid., quotes 53, 55.

113 Isasi-Díaz, *Mujerista Theology*, 59–85, quote 65–6.

114 Isasi-Díaz, *En La Lucha / In the Struggle: Elaborating a Mujerista Theology*, 80–96, quote 89.

115 Ibid., "the Christianity" and "most of," 62; Ada María Isasi-Díaz, "The Bible and *Mujerista* Theology," in *Lift Every Voice: Constructing Christian Theologies from the Underside*, ed. Susan Brooks Thistlethwaite and Mary Potter Engel (San Francisco: HarperSanFrancisco, 1990; 2nd edn., Maryknoll, NY: Orbis Books, 1998), 267–75, "The Bible per," "when the priests," 268.

116 Isasi-Díaz, *En La Lucha / In the Struggle: Elaborating a Mujerista Theology*, 63.

117 Ibid., quotes 90, 65.

118 Ada María Isasi-Díaz, "A New *Mestizaje/Mulatez:* Reconceptualizing Difference," in *A Dream Unfinished: Theological Reflections on America from the Margins*, ed. Eleazar S. Fernandez and Fernando F. Segovia (Maryknoll, NY: Orbis Books, 2001), 203–19.

119 Isasi-Díaz, *Mujerista Theology*, 59–85, quote 77.

120 Isasi-Díaz, *En La Lucha / In the Struggle: Elaborating a Mujerista Theology*, quotes 25.

121 Isasi-Díaz, *Mujerista Theology*, "as a Latina" and "an atmosphere," 112, 125; Isasi-Díaz, *La Lucha Continues: Mujerista Theology*, "rebuked," 185.

122 Ada María Isasi-Díaz, "Solidarity: Love of Neighbor in the 1980s," and Isasi-Díaz, "The Bible and *Mujerista* Theology," in *Lift Every Voice: Constructing Christian Theologies from the Underside*, 30–9, 267–75, quote 274. In the second edition of *Lift Every Voice*, Isasi-Díaz's first article was retitled, "Solidarity: Love of Neighbor in the 21ˢᵗ Century."

123 Ada María Isasi-Díaz, "La Habana: The City That Inhabits Me," in *Spirit in the Cities: Searching for Soul in the Urban Landscape*, ed. Kathryn Tanner (Minneapolis: Fortress Press, 2004), reprinted in Isasi-Díaz, *La Lucha Continues: Mujerista Theology*, 122–56, quotes 124, 134.

124 Isasi-Díaz, *La Lucha Continues: Mujerista Theology*, 186–218, quote 215.

125 Susan A. Ross, review of *Mujerista Theology*, by Ada María Isasi-Díaz, *Journal of the American Academy of Religion* (1997), 953–5; Benjamin Valentin, *Mapping Public Theology: Beyond Culture, Identity, and Difference* (Harrisburg, PA: Trinity Press, 2002), 70, quote xiv; María Pilar Aquino, Daisy L. Machado, and Jeanette Rodríguez, "Introduction," in *A Reader in*

Latina Feminist Theology: Religion and Justice, eds. Aquino, Machado, and Rodríquez (Austin, TX: University of Texas Press, 2002), xiv.

126   Aquino, Machado, and Jeanette Rodríguez, "Introduction," xiv, xx; see Martha P. Cotera, *The Chicana Feminist* (Austin, TX: Information Systems Development, 1977); *Chicana Voices: Intersections of Class, Race, and Gender*, ed. Teresa Córdova and Norma Cantú (Austin: University of Texas Center for Mexican American Studies, 1986).

127   María Pilar Aquino, "Latina Feminist Theology: Central Features," in *A Reader in Latina Feminist Theology: Religion and Justice*, 133–60, quotes 138; see Raquel Rodríguez, "La Marcha de las Mujeres: Apuntes en torno al movimento de mujeres en América Latina y el Caribe," Revista *Pasos* 34 (1991), 11.

128   Aquino, "Latina Feminist Theology: Central Features," 139.

129   Ibid., "I believe," 153; María Pilar Aquino, "Theological Method in U.S. Latino/a Theology: Toward an Intercultural Theology for the Third Millennium," in *From the Heart of Our People: Latino/a Explorations in Catholic Systematic Theology*, eds. Orlando O. Espín and Miguel H. Díaz (Maryknoll, NY: Orbis Books, 1999), 6–48, "theology is not," 41.

130   María Pilar Aquino, *Our Cry for Life: Feminist Theology from Latin America*, trans. Dinah Livingstone (Maryknoll, NY: Orbis Books, 1993), "an attempt," 3, "that we women," 95; Aquino, "Theological Method in U.S. Latino/a Theology: Toward an Intercultural Theology for the Third Millennium," "our theology believes," 19; see Aquino, "Directions and Foundations of Hispanic/Latino Theology: Toward a *Mestiza* Theology of Liberation," *Journal of Hispanic/Latino Theology* 1 (November 1993), 5–21.

131   Aquino, "Theological Method in U.S. Latino/a Theology: Toward an Intercultural Theology for the Third Millennium," 27–32, quote 31; see Aquino, *Our Cry for Life: Feminist Theology from Latin America*, 112–21.

132   Aquino, "Theological Method in U.S. Latino/a Theology: Toward an Intercultural Theology for the Third Millennium," quote 36; see Johann-Baptist Metz, "Standing at the End of the Eurocentric Era of Christianity: A Catholic View," in *Doing Theology in a Divided World*, eds. Virginia Fabella and Sergio Torres (Maryknoll, NY: Orbis Books, 1985), 85–90; Juan José Tamayo, *Presente y futuro de la teología de la liberación* (Madrid: San Pablo, 1994), 29; Roberto Goizueta, "United States Hispanic Theology and the Challenge of Pluralism," in *Frontiers of Hispanic Theology in the United States*, ed. Allan F. Deck (Maryknoll, NY: Orbis Books, 1992), 15, 19; Goizueta, *Caminemos con Jesús: Toward a Hispanic/Latino Theology of Accompaniment* (Maryknoll, NY: Orbis Books, 1995); Jean-Baptist Metz, "Perspectivas de un cristianismo multicultural," in *Cristianismo y liberacíon: Homenaje a Casiano Floristán*, ed. Juan José Tamayo (Madrid: Editorial Trotta, 1996), 36.

133   María Pilar Aquino, "Response," *Journal of Feminist Studies in Religion* 21 (2005), 131–6, quote 136; see Aquino, *Our Cry for Life: Feminist Theology from Latin America*, 33–41.

134   Aquino, "Theological Method in U.S. Latino/a Theology: Toward an Intercultural Theology for the Third Millennium," 36–7; Virgilio Elizondo, *"Mestizaje* as a Locus of Theological Reflection," in *Mestizo Christianity: Theology from the Latino Perspective*, ed. Arturo Bañuelas (Maryknoll, NY: Orbis Books, 1995), 7–27, quote 9–10; see Elizondo, *The Future is Mestizo: Life Where Cultures Meet* (New York: Meyer-Stone, 1988); Aquino, Directions and Foundations of Hispanic/Latino Theology: Toward a *Mestiza* Theology of Liberation," 5–21.

135   David Hollenbach, SJ, *Justice, Peace and Human Rights: American Catholic Social Ethics in a Pluralistic Context* (New York: Crossroad, 1988), quote 88.

136   Ibid., "at the council," 89; Vatican Council II, "Declaration on Religious Freedom," (*Dignitatis Humanae*, December 7, 1965), trans. John Courtney Murray, *The Documents of Vatican II*, eds. Walter M. Abbot, SJ and Joseph Gallagher (New York: America, 1966), 677–8.

137   Hollenbach, *Justice, Peace and Human Rights: American Catholic Social Ethics in a Pluralistic Context*, quote 90–1.

138 John XXIII, *Pacem in Terris: Peace on Earth* (1963), reprinted in *Catholic Social Thought: The Documentary Heritage*, eds. David J. O'Brien and Thomas A. Shannon (Maryknoll, NY: Orbis Books, 1992), 131–62; Hollenbach, *Justice, Peace and Human Rights: American Catholic Social Ethics in a Pluralistic Context*, 93–4.

139 Hollenbach, *Justice, Peace and Human Rights: American Catholic Social Ethics in a Pluralistic Context*, quote 96.

140 Ibid., quotes 98.

141 David Hollenbach, SJ, *The Global Face of Public Faith: Politics, Human Rights, and Christian Ethics* (Washington, DC: Georgetown University, 2003), quotes 235.

142 Ibid., 235–7; see *Prospects for a Common Morality*, ed. Gene Outtka and John P. Reeder Jr (Princeton: Princeton University Press, 1993).

143 Hollenbach, *The Global Face of Public Faith: Politics, Human Rights, and Christian Ethics*, quote 239.

144 Ibid., 238–40; Michael Ignatieff, *Human Rights as Politics and Idolatry*, ed. Amy Gutmann (Princeton: Princeton University Press, 2001), 58–77.

145 See John Rawls, *Political Liberalism* (New York: Columbia University Press, 1993), 146–9; Rawls, *The Law of Peoples* (Cambridge, MA: Harvard University Press, 1999), 37–45.

146 Hollenbach, *The Global Face of Public Faith: Politics, Human Rights, and Christian Ethics*, quote 242; see Jacques Maritain, "Introduction," in *Human Rights: Comments and Interpretations*, ed. UNESCO (New York: Columbia University Press, 1949), 9–10.

147 Hollenbach, *The Global Face of Public Faith: Politics, Human Rights, and Christian Ethics*, quote 243.

148 Ibid., quote 247; see Immanuel Kant, *Foundations of the Metaphysics of Morals*, trans. Lewis White Beck (Indianapolis: Bobbs-Merrill, 1959), 39–47; Kant, *Idea for a Universal History with a Cosmopolitan Intent*, in Kant, *Perpetual Peace and Other Essays*, trans. Ted Humphrey (Indianapolis: Hackett, 1983), 29–40.

149 David Hollenbach, SJ, "Christian Ethics and the Common Good," December 12, 2002 lecture to Woodstock Center, http://woodstock.georgetown.edu, accessed July 22, 2007; see Hollenbach, *The Common Good and Christian Ethics: New Studies in Christian Ethics* (Cambridge: Cambridge University Press, 2002).

150 David Hollenbach, SJ, "Justice as Participation: Public Moral Discourse and the U.S. Economy," in *Community in America: The Challenge of Habits of the Heart*, ed. Charles H. Reynolds and Ralph V. Norman (Berkeley: University of California Press, 1988), 217–29, quotes 218; Michael Novak, "McGovernism Among the Bishops," *Washington Times* (October 25, 1985); John Courtney Murray, *We Hold These Truths: Catholic Reflections on the American Proposition* (New York: Sheed and Ward, 1960), 12.

151 David Hollenbach, SJ, "Liberalism, Communitarianism and the Bishops' Pastoral Letter on the Economy," *Annual of the Society of Christian Ethics 1987* (Washington, DC: Georgetown University Press), 19–23; National Conference of Catholic Bishops, *Economic Justice for All: Catholic Teaching and the U.S. Economy* (Washington, DC: United States Catholic Conference, 1986); this section adapts material from Gary Dorrien, *The Neoconservative Mind: Politics, Culture and the War of Ideology* (Philadelphia: Temple University Press, 1993), 254.

152 See John Rawls, *A Theory of Justice* (Cambridge, MA: Harvard University Press, 1971); Bruce A. Ackerman, *Social Justice in the Liberal State* (New Haven: Yale University Press, 1980); Michael J. Sandel, *Liberalism and the Limits of Justice* (Cambridge: Cambridge University Press, 1982); Amitai Etzioni, *The Spirit of Community: Rights, Responsibilities, and the Communitarian Agenda* (New York: Crown Publishers, 1993).

153 Hollenbach, "Liberalism, Communitarianism and the Bishops' Pastoral Letter on the Economy," 20–1.

Chapter 10

Borders of Possibility:
The Necessity of "Discredited"
Social Gospel Ideas

In the beginning social ethics was a social gospel dream of economic democracy, expansive Christian fellowship, and the marriage of Christian ethics and social science. It was housed in the academy, but took its energy and character from America's Third Great Awakening, the social gospel, which transformed American Protestantism. As a social gospel phenomenon, social ethics was a product of evangelical piety, Enlightenment criticism, liberal theology, late Victorian culture, and Progressivism, and it replaced the old moral philosophy with a buoyant blend of religious idealism and social scientific analysis. But above all it was a social gospel solution to the clash between a burgeoning corporate capitalism and a rising labor movement.

For 50 years social ethics remained a social gospel enterprise, even in its non-academic versions, and even in its minority streams that were not white, male, middle-class, or Protestant. In the 1930s the field pushed aside its optimistic social gospel beginnings in favor of Reinhold Niebuhr's sterner language of sin, power politics, transcendence, and realism, which held center stage for 30 years until the same thing happened to Christian realism, with the rise of liberation theology.

All three of these movements held high a vision of social transformation; in the two transitions, the dream of a transformed economic order was resurrected. Niebuhrians judged that the social gospel sold out the struggle for social justice because it was too middle-class and idealistic to be a serious force in power politics. Liberationists judged that Christian realism sold out the struggle for social justice because it was too middle-class, idealistic, white, male-dominated, nationalistic, and socially privileged. But liberation theology was too marginal and radical in US American society to make much of an impact upon it; meanwhile social ethics produced offshoots with small followings in every direction. Today, a century after Ernst Troeltsch praised the Christian Socialists for being the first Christian movement to attempt structural changes toward social justice, the social Christian goal of democratizing economic power is more remote than ever.[1]

The early social ethicists took it for granted that modernity had a stage beyond capitalism. If modernity was a good thing, which they also did not doubt, it had to have a stage beyond capitalism. For over a century of social gospel, Christian realist, and liberationist movements, social ethicists took it for granted that replacing a predatory and community-destroying economic order with something better was a crucial part of modern Christianity's social mission. Protestant and Catholic social Christianity mostly spoke a "third way" language of cooperatives and guilds, while Christian Socialists favored a binary language of moving forward or backward. Even after the Christian realists gave up on socialism and binary choices, they stood for achieving as much of the democratic socialist ideal as possible under American circumstances. Nearly all the great theologians and social ethicists of the twentieth century and late nineteenth century were democratic socialists of some kind, although the kind varied significantly.

For reformers like Washington Gladden, Francis G. Peabody, Shailer Mathews, and John A. Ryan, the ideal of decentralized economic democracy was intrinsic to the social gospel. For social gospelers in the Rauschenbusch line like Justin Wroe Nixon, Dores Robinson Sharpe, and Walter Muelder it was important to call economic democracy "socialist" without embracing state socialism. For state socialists, economic democracy was something serious only if it meant government control of the economy. Harry F. Ward, George Herron, Vida Scudder, Sherwood Eddy, and Kirby Page were prominent in that school long before social ethics turned Niebuhrian; afterwards Reinhold Niebuhr was joined in it by Eddy, Page, John Bennett, Roswell Barnes, Buell Gallagher, Francis Henson, and Frank Wilson. In both cases the state socialists propounded a host of bad ideas. Wrongly, they equated socialization with nationalization; wrongly, they rejected production for profit; wrongly, they claimed that state planners could replicate the pricing decisions of markets; wrongly, they wanted government planners or guild organizations to organize an economy not linked by markets; wrongly, they identified realism and real socialism with themselves, dismissing other models.[3]

On these issues Rauschenbusch ended up looking better than the radical and realist movements that panned him for being too idealistic. He advocated decentralized economic democracy, contended that democratic worker control was the heart of the matter, and recognized that markets could not be abolished in a free society. He had a strong concept of personal and collective evil coupled with an overcoming message of social salvation. On the other hand, even Rauschenbusch recycled the totalizing rhetoric of state socialism, embraced the Marxist theory of surplus value, claimed that prices under socialism would be based entirely on services rendered, and trusted too much in the overcoming tide of social idealism.

To its credit, most of the social gospel movement vested its economic hope in cooperative ownership, mixed forms of worker and community ownership, and profit-sharing strategies. It had a vision of economic justice, but did not treat moral, cultural, and political issues as epiphenomena of economic interests. In the 1930s social gospel liberals like Ryan, Nixon, and Francis McConnell stood for social insurance, public works employment, good government reforms, an expanded cooperative sector and a progressive income tax while Niebuhr claimed these were nothing but Band-aids to make middle-class moralists feel better. It was simply "stupid" to hold on to a moral, community-oriented approach to politics, he judged. The radical ideologies of the 1930s were supposedly more realistic than the reformism of the social gospel, but all of them crashed and burned. Niebuhr, upon giving up on Marxism, adopted a welfare-state realism that put him in the mainstream of liberal Democratic politics. In domestic politics later Christian realism was a strategy of countervailing power relations between capital, labor, and an assertive national government. Internationally it was a theory of countervailing power relations among sovereign states. In both cases, realism emphasized the power of states and the relative balance of power.

Niebuhr took it for granted that theologians had to translate the moral, social, and religious meaning of Christianity into secular terms in order to help Christians play a role in the political sphere and enable secular types to make sense of Christian claims. On this point he was more liberal than the social gospelers, with ambiguous consequences. Instead of moralizing the public square, Niebuhr contended, liberal Christians needed to grasp that politics was a struggle for power driven by interest and will-to-power. The social gospelers thought that a cooperative commonwealth was literally achievable; Niebuhr replied that the very idea of a good society ideal had to be given up because group egotism was inevitable.

This disparagement of the "good society" idea was costly for Christian ethics. The idea of a good society or common good emerges from discussion and is always in process of revision. To let go of it is to undercut the struggle for attainable gains toward social justice, negating the elusive but formative vision of what is worth struggling for. Without a vision of a good society that transcends the prevailing order, ethics and politics remain captive to the dominant order, restricted to marginal reforms. The borders of possibility remain untested.

Moral Man and Immoral Society (1932) drew the lines that are still at issue. Niebuhr's Depression-era blast against liberal idealism repudiated the liberal Protestant belief that the ethos of a moral community could be insinuated into the public realm. In the 1930s that was an argument for his Marxist either/or: the only serious choice was between militant socialism and fascist barbarism. He hammered on this theme throughout the decade. In the 1940s Niebuhr made his peace with the New Deal, but his condemnation of Christian idealism remained intact. Since the liberal Christian quest for a politics of community was an illusion, the only recourse for the church was to strengthen the capacity of the state to act as a secular moral guarantor.[4]

That was the welfare-state version of Christian realism, which underwrote the merger of political liberalism and centralized state power. In the early twentieth century, Progressives like Henry Churchill King and Herbert Croly contended that American democracy would not survive if it did not make its peace with concentrated power. To defend democratic gains from concentrated economic power, the Progressives called for a consolidation of countervailing political power. They supported centralized government, trade unions, and a nationalized politics. America would become more democratic only if it became more of a *nation* in its institutions and spirit. This strategy was consummated with the success of the New Deal, which effectively united liberalism and the national idea. The historic American democracy of small towns and civic republicanism gave way to the democracy of nationalized liberalism. In a society shaped increasingly by corporate economic power, the only effective progressive politics was that of the national republic.[5]

For Niebuhr these were basic political truisms. The Progressives of Theodore Roosevelt's generation had fought for them, sometimes with sentimental flourishes; the New Dealers put them in place, a bit haphazardly; the mid-century liberal realists defended them, emphasizing the need to consolidate state power for relatively good ends. To enlist the church in this enterprise, Niebuhr drove a wedge between the moral identity and social mission of the churches. The social mission was no longer the social gospel project of converting American society to the biblical vision of freedom, justice, community, and peace. Niebuhrian realism was about providing religious support for a secular liberal agenda that served the struggle for freedom and justice.

Niebuhr's attentiveness to irony and paradox, his insistence on the inevitability of collective egotism, and his sensitivity to the complex ambiguities inherent in all human choices made permanent contributions to Christian thought. His passion for justice roared through all his work, through all his changes of position. But his dichotomizing between the moral identity and social mission of the church weakened the church's identity and social agency, helping to strip the public sphere of the language of moral value. The upshot was ironic because no one struggled more brilliantly than Niebuhr to make Christianity relevant to modern society. Near the end of his life, Niebuhr warned Wolfhart Pannenberg and Richard John Neuhaus to steer clear of the kingdom of God. The social gospelers had proved that the kingdom idea was a loser, he urged. Any appeal to the biblical idea of the kingdom as an inbreaking spiritual and historical reality was bound to produce disasters. It made Rauschenbusch incorrigibly naïve about how to relate Christianity to politics. Niebuhr declared that if it were up to him, he would tear the kingdom of God out of the Bible and Christian doctrine.[6]

That was an over-the-top expression of the problem of Niebuhr's realism. By shortchanging the kingdom of God, personal regeneration, the Holy Spirit, and the church as the body of Christ, Niebuhr fashioned a theology with a distinct socio-ethical trajectory. It had room for the sovereignty of a creator God and the redeeming power of divine love mediated through the cross of Christ. But when Niebuhr invoked the authority of "reality" for Christian ethics, he did not mean the reality of God's presence in the spirit of the resurrected Christ or its regenerative power. He was not prepared to cut against the grain of America's reality, and thus he never opposed a real American interest in the name of Christian ethics. Niebuhr ridiculed the social gospel attempt to insinuate the ethos of a moral community into the public sphere as hopeless, sentimental, and confused. The public sphere was not the realm of moral value, but of interest and power. To a paternalistic Protestant culture that worried about its creeping softness, Niebuhr offered a powerful voice. Christian realism tried to save a place for the church in a secularizing society by accepting the liberal bour-geois dichotomy between a virtue-producing private realm and an instrumental/technocratic public realm. This strategy worked for a generation that still lived off the memory of a culturally enfranchised Protestantism.

But it had diminishing returns even in Niebuhr's lifetime, and it rang false to suc-ceeding feminist and other liberation movements that emphasized the presence of the personal in all things political. Mainline Protestantism never outgrew its ethnic families of origin, it failed even to replace itself demographically, and it gave up its hope of transforming the culture. No longer claiming a vision of its own in the public sphere, it was reduced to support work for anti-communism and other causes endorsed by the liberal establishment. But if the meaning of Christian faith can be translated into secular terms, why bother with Christianity? Niebuhr's strategy left progressive Chris-tianity without enough to say or do in its own language, in its own way, and for its own reasons.

Social Ethics and Racial Justice

On racial justice Niebuhr was better than most white theologians. He wrote nearly a dozen articles about it, describing racism as a transcendently evil form of self-worship. But he never featured this subject in his major works or gave it high priority in his activism. In his early career Niebuhr was devoted to social gospel pacifism; in his middle career he burned for socialism and religious realism; in his later career he gave priority to anti-fascism, anti-communism, and vital center realism. In each phase, while he recognized that white liberals tended to be too easy on themselves, his anxiety about the sin of liberal false righteousness was a major factor in keeping him from giving high priority to the struggle against racism.

Niebuhr explained that when white liberal Christians apologized to blacks or Jews for the sins of white America, they won moral points for humility and contrition, but wrongly. Confessions of this sort were dictated by pride; thus they carried a whiff of hypocrisy. Instead of expressing a real confession, the penitent communicated his or her moral superiority. That scruple, plus the social punishments that would have fallen, impeded Niebuhr from saying as much as he should have about white racism. It also troubled him that, in his experience, victims of racial discrimination rarely confessed their own shortcomings, though he allowed that this appearance could be a defensive reaction to the insincerity of white Americans' contrition for racism.[7]

Racism ignored the conditioned character of one's life and culture, Niebuhr reasoned. It fed on the false pretense that one's color, creed, or culture represented the final good. As a liberal Democrat he took for granted that coercive government policies to prohibit racial discrimination and promote racial justice were necessary. But the problem of racial bigotry was ultimately a spiritual issue, Niebuhr argued; it could not be cured by social engineering: "The mitigation of racial and cultural pride is finally a religious problem in the sense that each man, and each race and culture, must become religiously aware of the sin of self-worship, which is the final form of human evil and of which racial self-worship is the most vivid example."[8]

In 1957, three years before Niebuhr retired from Union Seminary, he contended that the USA had solved all of its serious social problems, with one exception. Niebuhr explained that it had solved the problems of liberty and equality "beyond the dreams of any European nation." The New Deal was so successful that even Republicans accepted it. America's only remaining social problem was that of the color line, which, in Niebuhr's view, was "on the way of being resolved." The Supreme Court finally recognized equality as a criterion of justice, and the *Brown* decision redeemed the promise of America for black Americans; "At last the seeming sentimentality of the preamble of our Declaration of Independence – the declaration that 'all men are created equal' – has assumed political reality and relevance."[9]

That is a measure of the bland optimism of the 1950s, that even Reinhold Niebuhr could be naïve in celebrating America the good, even on the politics of the color line. But Niebuhr felt deeply the evil of US American racism, and in 1956 he challenged Billy Graham to do something about it.

Niebuhr had a low opinion of Graham's evangelistic enterprise, which he expressed plainly on several occasions. He was appalled that for millions of Americans Billy Graham represented Christianity. But in 1956, near the end of a typical slam on Graham, Niebuhr switched to moral exhortation, urging Graham to do something ethically useful with his fame. In his early career Graham had preached to segregated audiences, offering the assurance that Jesus had no opinion on the matter. Then for three years he zigged and zagged on segregation, until the *Brown* decision, after which he preached only to integrated audiences. Niebuhr admonished him to go further, preaching against racial prejudice and the everyday racism of his audiences.[10]

For the next several years Graham struggled with Niebuhr's challenge, as he subsequently acknowledged. Graham's record during the period of the civil rights movement was highly ambiguous and loaded with ironic complexity, unlike the whitewashed things he later said about it. But Niebuhr's challenge to him displayed the ironies of the liberal righteousness problem. Niebuhr called out Graham publicly, stressing that the mostly violently racist sections of the country were the ones that had the most revivals. He summoned Graham to an extraordinarily difficult task, one entailing dangers and burdens from which Niebuhr was far removed. Niebuhr had no contact with Graham's audiences and by the 1950s he faced little prospect of confronting angry crowds of any kind. But even within his rarefied world of liberal seminaries and prestige lectureships, Niebuhr did not take the risk that he prescribed for Graham, that of challenging his group to interrogate its white supremacism.

Asking white liberals in the 1950s to acknowledge their casual racism would not have gone well. It would have evoked, for Niebuhr, the kind of hostility that Graham confronted constantly in the South, even as Graham tried not to offend the moral pride of his audience. Liberals took pride in having no racial biases; that was what made them liberals. The goal was to open opportunities for blacks and dispel the social fiction that race mattered. Niebuhr took it for granted that the problem, for whites, was to eliminate racial bias, not to dismantle an entire national culture of white supremacy.

But the race problem in the USA is primarily a white problem, that of white supremacy. In Niebuhr's time, the USA seemed to be making progress toward equality, and significant gains *were* made. The Civil Rights Act of 1964 was enacted three months before that year's presidential election, a year later the Voting Rights Act was passed into law, and affirmative action programs were adopted. But the reaction against these gains was volatile, helping to drive American politics to the right. In 1964 the far right wing of the Republican party made a startling upsurge, winning the party's presidential nomination. Four years later the Republican establishment regained control of the party with a carefully crafted, racially coded, backlash message that won the White House. The Nixon Administration proved highly adept at racial politics, which led to something even worse for racial justice, a triumphant far Right led by Ronald Reagan. By 1980 the far Right held the White House and the party's moderately liberal wing was headed for obliteration. This political swing yielded campaigns coded with racist images of black criminals and welfare queens, xenophobic slurs against Latin-American immigrants, huge military budgets crowding out social investments in human needs, and tax policies that set off the economic equivalent of tectonic plate movements – massive increases in economic inequality.

Wherever white people are dominant, white culture is transparent to them. It is hard to see because it is everything that is not specifically African-American culture, Native American culture, Mexican culture, and so on. More precisely, it is hard for whites to see because white supremacy makes white culture normative. At its extreme, white supremacy is about bigots wearing sheets and burning crosses. But more broadly and normally it is something that bestows privilege on every white person in US American society, some more than others.

White supremacy is a structure of power based on privilege that presumes to define what is normal. If you live in the USA without being constantly reminded of your race, and do not have to worry about representing your race, and can worry about racism without being viewed as self-interested, and do not have to worry about being targeted by police for your race, you are a beneficiary of white supremacy. Its privileges are your daily bread and environment. Today the shape of this inheritance is complicated immensely by the immigration of Asians, Latin Americans and others from every part of the world into the USA. Some of them move right into white privilege; some struggle to get a piece of it; some have no chance of getting any; all are affected by the ravages of America's original sin. White supremacy is deeply entrenched in American society, reinforced by powerful self-interested institutions, and widely denied, if not invisible to its deniers.

Overcoming that legacy at the national policy level requires decently progressive tax policies, living wage legislation, affirmative action programs, single-payer health coverage that extends Medicare to everyone, and a generous immigration policy. At the level of congregational and community practice it requires multiracial organizations that privilege the issues of people of color, exactly as Cornel West contends. The Industrial Areas Foundation (IAF) and Gamaliel Foundation organizations have been doing this since 1940 and 1968 respectively. The IAF, founded by Saul Alinsky in Chicago, has a long history of community advocacy on anti-poverty and housing issues. Most of its leadership, institutional support, and community work have had a Catholic basis. In the 1950s the group's Community Service network in California, led by Cesar Chavez and Delores Huerta, was a powerful organizing tool in Mexican-American communities. In the 1980s the IAF project Texas Interfaith, led by Ernesto Cortes, had similar success. IAF organizations designed and passed the nation's first living wage bill in Baltimore in 1994, got a similar bill in New York in 1996, and by 2006 were conducting living wage campaigns in over 100 communities. They have built thousands of homes in New York, Baltimore, Philadelphia, and the District of Columbia through the Nehemiah homes project and trained thousands of disadvantaged workers for high-technology jobs through the Quest vocational project.[11]

The Gamaliel Foundation was established to support the Contract Buyers League, an African-American organization struggling against discriminatory banking policies affecting blacks in Westside Chicago. A network of interfaith, multiracial, grassroots organizations, it takes its name from Acts 5:38 and currently numbers 60 affiliates in 21 US states and five provinces of South Africa. Gamaliel organizations combat poverty, demand better schools, fight anti-immigrant policies, and address other high-priority needs of marginalized communities. They feature high levels of intentionality and group process. New organizations meet for 12 months or more, building bonds of trust and commitment, before deciding which issues to address. They specialize in bringing together Christian activists from diverse racial, ethnic, and religious communities to empower marginalized groups and make concrete gains toward social justice. Along the way, and not coincidentally, Gamaliel organizations enable white middle-class Christians to see the world from a perspective they would never get from a diet of white church preaching and worship.[12]

Foreign Policy Realism and American Empire

In foreign policy the ironies of Niebuhr's legacy were toxic. For Niebuhr it was difficult to bear the fact that Cold War ideologues like John Foster Dulles and Irving Kristol considered themselves Niebuhrians. In his last years he had similar problems with conservative Niebuhrians closer to him like Paul Ramsey, Kenneth Thompson, Ernest Lefever, and Carl Mayer. His disagreements with the latter group over Vietnam foreshadowed the rise of neoconservatism, where claims to true Niebuhrianism were rampant. One can only wish that Niebuhr's neoconservative admirers had absorbed even half of his realism on their way to becoming Republicans. Had they done so, the world might have been spared the catastrophe of America's invasion of Iraq.

One of the central problems of US American Christian ethics today is to confront the USA's growing militarism and imperialism. In the classic sense of the term, setting aside the Native American reservations, the United States is not an empire. It does not exercise direct dominion over conquered peoples. It does not formally rule an extensive group of countries under a single sovereign authority. In most cases the USA favors democracy and self-determination for other nations. The USA's official colonies have been few and scattered, most of its occupations have been brief, the largest of its 14 dependent entities is Puerto Rico, and its domination of Latin America has been mostly indirect. Most US Americans have little imperial consciousness, and they are not militaristic in the sense of glorying in their wars or military might.

Yet the United States has been on a neo-imperial trajectory since its founding. It conquered nearly an entire continent and waged genocidal violence against Native Americans, colonizing the surviving tribes in reservations. For almost 90 years the USA was a slave state, many of whose leaders wanted to create a Western empire based on the extension of slavery throughout the Caribbean. From the Monroe Doctrine to the Bush Doctrine, presidents have made doctrinal pronouncements about their putative right to dominate or invade sovereign nations. Theodore Roosevelt, who viewed his imperial ambition as a natural outgrowth of the US American story, was fond of saying that his country's entire national history was one of expansion. His corollary to the Monroe Doctrine, announced in 1906, declared that the USA was entitled to invade any Latin American nation that engaged in "flagrant wrongdoing." Latin Americans took that to mean any action that conflicted with US interests.

The USA had an ample record of intervening in Latin America before the Roosevelt Corollary was announced. In 1898 it annexed Cuba and Puerto Rico, along with Guam, the Philippines, and the Hawaiian islands. Afterwards, up to World War II, the USA added interventions in Colombia, Panama, Honduras, the Dominican Republic, Cuba, Nicaragua, Haiti, Mexico, and Guatemala, in addition to "making the world safe for democracy" in World War I; China was another frequent destination of American forces.

In 1945 the USA began to amass a global military empire, beginning with its new military bases in western Germany, Japan, Korea, and the eastern Mediterranean. In 1989, having emerged from the Cold War as the world's only superpower, the USA began to debate what it should do with its unrivaled might. Powerful currents in American politics and the defense industry called for a foreign policy of global supremacy. Neoconservatives put it explicitly, coining the term "unipolarism" for their doctrine of global military hegemony. That was a fittingly odd term for a new kind of empire, one not based on the conquest of territory, that dwarfs all colonizing empires of the past.

The neoconservative doctrine of unipolar hegemony trades on America's long history of exceptionalist supremacy – God's New Israel, the City on a Hill, Manifest Destiny, the Redeemer Nation, Pax Americana, the Leader of the Free World. It offers a vision of what the USA should do with its unrivaled power. In its most rhetorically seductive versions it conflates the expansion of US power with the dream of global democracy, as in President George W. Bush's second inaugural address.

In other words, neoconservatism is merely an explicit, think-tank version of American supremacism, one that defends the USA's routine practices of empire. Since the end of the Cold War, neoconservatism has been defined by its doctrine of "full spectrum dominance," yet this doctrine is not unique to neoconservatives. It was a staple of defense industry and Pentagon literature before George W. Bush won the presidency. The Joint Chiefs of Staff, in their *Joint Vision* statements of 1996 and 2000, declared that the USA is committed to sustaining "full spectrum dominance" on a global scale as a primary military policy. *Joint Vision 2020*, issued on May 30, 2000, put it this way:

> The overall goal of the transformation described in this document is the creation of a force that is dominant across the full spectrum of military operations – persuasive in peace, decisive in war, preeminent in any form of conflict . . . Full spectrum dominance [is] the ability of U.S. forces, operating unilaterally or in combination with multinational and interagency partners, to defeat any adversary and control any situation across the full range of military options.[13]

That put it as plainly as possible, under the Clinton Administration. For eight years, neoconservatives railed against President Clinton for wasting America's dominance. What was the point of having a globally dominant military if one used it only for dubious humanitarian interventions? They wanted a huge military expansion and what they called "creative destruction" in the Middle East. Under the administration of George W. Bush they gained awesome military increases and destruction, however lacking in creativity.

Today the fiasco of Iraq is undeniable, setting off a revival of foreign policy realism. Political writers Anatol Lieven and Peter Beinart advocate returning to Niebuhr's neo-liberal Democratic political realism. Social ethicists Ronald Stone and Robin Lovin uphold the Bennett tradition of Niebuhrian progressive Christian realism. Social ethicist Jean Bethke Elshtain defends neoconservative ideology from a putatively Niebuhrian standpoint. Numerous figures with less explicit connections to Niebuhr advocate returning to a chastened or nationalistic realism. Some are moderately conservative realists with strong anti-imperial convictions, such as Chalmers Johnson and Andrew Bacevich. Some are classic political realists wary of ideology and imperial overstretch, notably Zbigniew Brzezinski, Samuel P. Huntington, James Kurth, Robert F. Ellsworth, and Dimitri K. Simes. Hawkish, right-wing, nationalistic realism has also made a comeback as represented by Daniel Pipes and Dov Zakheim; on cable television it is expounded daily by Pat Buchanan and Tucker Carlson.[14]

This revival of realist sentiment is an ambiguous development, because foreign policy realism is inherently nationalistic and it usually gives short shrift to ethical factors, Reinhold Niebuhr notwithstanding. Since 1950 realism has justified US support for apartheid in South Africa and alliances with dictators in Indonesia, the Philippines, Chile, Argentina, and a long list of others, all in the name of strategic interests. Foreign policy realism is too nationalistic and fixated on power not to conflict with Christian moral principles, and it is very difficult from a realist standpoint, if not impossible, to oppose a genuine national interest on ethical grounds. It took all of Niebuhr's immense dialectical skill to establish that there could be such a thing as a modern theological version of *Realpolitik*. Turning this unlikely combination into a dominant social-ethical standpoint was an achievement of singular genius.

Because of Niebuhr, there is such a thing as progressive realism, and even progressive Christian realism. Today, in the aftermath of a catastrophic American invasion of Iraq, progressives and realists need to find common ground to work together. That common ground includes a deep skepticism about the moral and ideological claims of empires and the selfish interests of all nation states. It distinguishes between international police action and preventive wars against nations. It rejects the fantasy of beneficial transformations flowing from wars of aggression and comprehends that terrorism can only be minimized, not eliminated.

For all the illusions and mistakes of liberal social gospelers in the 1930s and 1940s, they stood for the right things in foreign policy: liberal internationalism and the creation of alternatives to war. Many of them wrongly clung to this agenda as a dogma, overcompensating for the bitter lessons of World War I; thus they failed to face the ethical necessity of stopping fascist aggression. They tended also to be short on anti-imperial solidarity, though Muelder and Howard Thurman were exceptions. Compared to the ethical paralysis of liberal pacifists between 1938 and 1941, Niebuhr's call to prevent the triumph of an intolerable tyranny was a blast of prophetic brilliance, one of the high points of the social-ethical tradition. But 1940 was an emergency situation, not the template for later generations. The liberal internationalist project of facilitating cooperation among states and creating forms of collective security is the right one for every generation that seeks to prevent the next world war.

The liberal internationalist commitments to democracy, cooperative problem-solving and universalistic human rights are indispensable to a constructive foreign policy, as is the commitment to create structures that transcend nationalism and provide collective security. These beliefs are compatible with a realist perspective on the will-to-power of political entities, that all states are self-interested and power seeking. The case for a stronger international community has a realistic basis, that the benefits of multilateral cooperation outweigh the costs and risks of not working together. A superpower that insists on absolute security for itself makes all other nations insecure. All parties are better off when the most powerful nations agree not to do everything that is in their power and nations work together to create new forms of collective security. In an increasingly interdependent world, nation-states have to cooperate with each other to address security issues that transcend national boundaries.

On September 11, 2001, and for weeks following, the USA had a precious opportunity, a moment with new possibilities. Not since the end of World War II had there been such a moment when a huge step forward was possible toward building a community of nations. If the USA had responded to 9/11 by sending NATO and American forces after al Qaeda, rebuilding Afghanistan, and building new networks of collective security against terrorism, it would have gained the world's gratitude. Instead it took a course of action that caused an explosion of anti-American hostility throughout the world, a torrent of bitter feeling that has not abated. To make the United States less hated in the Arab and Muslim worlds, the USA must remove the imprint of the invader that sets off terrorist reactions, and pledge itself to international cooperation, multilateralism, human rights, and creating structures of collective security that transcend nationalism.

Economic Democracy: The Future of a Discredited Vision

Today the USA has no rival as a global superpower, and global capitalism has produced economic powers that are often mightier than the states whose borders they cross. Economic globalization – the integration of national economies into the global economy through trade, direct foreign investment, short-term capital flows, and flows of labor and technology – has "flattened" the world, as political journalist Thomas Friedman puts it, making a mockery of political attempts to channel its predatory impulses. Friedman, a celebrant of global capitalism, calls it "turbo-capitalism." Social critic Mickey Kaus says that progressives should stop trying to tame turbo-capitalism for humane or ecological ends. Global capitalism is too predatory and technocratic to be amenable to government reforms, he contends. Liberals persist in spending their political capital on increasing the minimum wage, restoring progressive taxation, taxing capital gains, and slowing down runaway shops, but these responses do not mitigate the global race to the bottom that exacerbates inequality. In the USA, manufacturing jobs are disappearing, while downsized workers compete for minimum wage jobs in the service sector. At the same time, the global economy is an amazing boon for economic winners. American-based corporations have roughly doubled their wealth since their early 1990s, paying huge rewards to top performers in lucrative industries, and the global economy stokes a culture of celebrity.[15]

Kaus argues that no amount of government engineering will arrest the accelerating inequality trend or the "Hollywood Effect" of lavishing absurd rewards on celebrities and corporate executives. Capitalism is a culture, not merely an economic system. Before capitalism went global, it was possible to keep top performers from earning the full measure of their economic potential. Unions restrained wage disparities, while cultural values of loyalty and trust restrained the predatory impulses of the market. But these restraints have been routed. Turbo-capitalism feeds on inequality and obliterates cultural values and communities that get in the way. Instead of persisting in a hopeless battle for economic justice, Kaus wants liberals to spend their political capital on securing forms of social equality, such as national health insurance and public works projects. Friedman wants the USA to spend more on green technology and science education. Both advise liberals to give up on nostalgic dreams of reforming the wealth machine.[16]

This fashionable and privileged counsel underestimates the potential of another kind of globalization – the activism of non-governmental organizations (NGOs), to influence economic outcomes. NGO-style activism has surged since the early 1990s, forcing corporations and governments to deal with civil liberties issues, social justice causes, and environmental problems, including economic aspects of these issues. Moreover, the counsel to simply accept turbo-capitalism overlooks that some societies do better than others in dealing with the maldistributive logic of the global market.

Governments still play a key role in managing globalization and shaping socioeconomic outcomes. Free trade agreements usually contain clauses dealing with human rights, labor rights, and ecological standards. Industrialized nations have contentious disputes over immigration policy and the control of labor flows. Government policies on technology and direct foreign investment have immense impacts on the kind of economy that a nation develops. And without strong institutions and policies regulating short-term capital flows, turbo-capitalism everywhere is vulnerable to the kind of meltdown that occurred in East Asia in 1997. East Asia's capitalist dynamos achieved model records on the economic fundamentals, sustaining budget surpluses, strong investment and growth rates, low inflation, and low trade deficits. Taiwan, South Korea, Singapore, and Hong Kong racked up phenomenally high rates of productive investment, while Malaysia and Thailand sought to catch up by following the International Monetary Fund's prescription of keeping governments out of financial restructuring business. All of that did not stop these nations and others from crashing to negative growth rates, as a run on short-term capital set off a panic that fed on itself. It didn't help that the International Monetary Fund doled out bad fiscal advice and pushed for unsustainably fast capital market liberalization. The East Asian economic take-off was fueled in the first place by free trade policies managed by state-dominated economies that selected and nurtured key industries. Then a lack of monitoring and regulatory mechanisms allowed the entire "miracle" to collapse in a few months.[17]

Government policies on health care, unemployment insurance, and wages still make significant differences on economic outcomes. In European social democracies everyone receives free health care, unemployment insurance is generous and extended, solidarity wage policies restrain inequality, and no one goes hungry, all because of longstanding social contracts that lessen the predatory impact of the global market. In the 1980s Sweden and Japan had vigorous national debates over the tolerable limits of income inequality. Swedish conservatives argued that the wage differential between corporate executives and laborers permitted by the nation's solidarity wage policy should be increased to eight to one; radicals held out for no more than four to one. In Japan, where worker shareholder plans were commonplace, a similar debate occurred over the tolerability of allowing more than the existing ratio of sixteen to one.

In the United States the ratio climbed to 145 to 1 and there was no debate. The right to attain wealth was exalted over other values. The Reagan administration cut the marginal tax rate for individuals from 70 percent to 28 percent and cut the top rate on capital gains from 49 percent to 20 percent. These policy measures had huge effects on the kind of society the USA chose to become. By the end of the decade, the top fifth of the population earned more than half of the nation's income and held more than three-quarters of its wealth while the bottom fifth received barely 4 percent of its income. Kaus says that holding out for any particular ratio would be arbitrary: "Once we've failed to draw a line between equality and inequality, between 1 to 1 and 2 to 1, what's the basis for so self-confidently taking a stand at 8 to 1 or even 1,000 to 1?" But no particular ratio is the point. The point is that if current trends prevail, the ratio will reach 1,000 to 1 and make a mockery of American democracy.[18]

Kaus allows that a serious case could be made for one economic justice strategy: a strong progressive income tax combined with a serious push for worker ownership and shareholding. He doubts that even a popular movement along these lines would make much of an impact on global capitalism, but for stubborn types who cannot accept the givens of a flat world, it's the best bet.

The goal of democratizing economic power has been left, indeed, to stubborn types who refuse to accept the putative givens. But they are stubborn chiefly for facing certain terribly real problems, not for clinging to fanciful dreams. The economy is physical. There are limits to economic growth. The earth's ecosystem cannot sustain an American-level lifestyle for more than one-sixth of the world's population. One billion people live on less than $1 per day. Neo-liberal development turns diverse and self-sufficient economies in the former Third World into vulnerable, debt-racked monocultures often dependent on single cash crops for export. Corporations that care nothing about equality or community increasingly rule the world, reenacting the tragedy of the commons. In recent decades corporate giants like ExxonMobil have succeeded as businesses and investments while ignoring the impact of their behavior on local communities and the environment. To confront these realities is to face the necessity of democratizing economic power and creating an ecologically sustainable economy. Those who control the terms, amounts, and direction of credit have the largest say in determining the kind of society in which everyone else lives. Therefore the musty, quaint, "discredited" vision of decentralized economic democracy is more relevant than ever.

Economic democracy and ecological sustainability are naturally linked, and have similar problems. Sustainable development requires a dramatically expanded worker-and-community owned sector that is rooted in communities, committed to sufficiency, and prepared to accept lower returns. It begins with the development of social sectors that do not belong wholly to the competitive market or the state. Producer cooperatives take labor out of the market by removing corporate shares from the stock market and maintaining local worker ownership. Community land trusts take land out of the market and place it under local democratic controls to serve the social needs of communities. Community finance corporations take democratic control over capital to finance cooperative firms, make investments in areas of social need, and fight the redlining policies of conventional banks. Community-oriented strategies widen the base of social and economic power by expanding the cooperative and social market sectors, mixing together cooperative banks, employee stock ownership plans, producer cooperatives, community land trusts, and planning agencies that guide investments into locally-defined areas of need such as housing, soft-energy hardware, infrastructure maintenance, and mass transit.

But merely expanding the cooperative and social market sectors is not enough. Because cooperatives prohibit non-working shareholders, they attract less outside financing than capitalist firms. Because they keep low-return firms in operation, cooperatives tend to stay in business even when they cannot pay competitive wages. Because cooperatives are committed to particular communities, cooperative capital and labor are less mobile than corporate capital and labor. Because cooperatives maximize net income per worker rather than profits, they tend to favor capital-intensive investments over job creation. Because cooperative worker/owners often have their savings invested in a single enterprise, they avoid risky innovations. These problems can be mitigated with productivity enhancing tax incentives and regulations, but there are trade-offs, very much like those in environmental economics.

Worker ownership increases economic risks to workers and it privileges workers in more profitable sectors. Moreover, worker/owners in successful firms tend to be biased toward capital-intensive (rather than job-creating) investments, because they don't want to dilute their profits-per-worker ratios. Thus, cooperatives tend to be slower than capitalist firms to expand employment when increasing demand makes job creation possible. To mitigate the problem of capitalization, cooperatives institute internal capital accounts that facilitate reinvestment of savings. Cooperatives are also helped by regulations promoting job expansion, reinvestment, innovation, and bank lending to cooperatives.

Expanding the cooperative sector, however, is of very limited utility for the larger goals of democratizing economic power and achieving sustainable development. Many workers don't want to belong to cooperatives, and a universalized cooperative system would be unable to impose high entry fees. If everyone had to belong to a cooperative, many of them would fail, which would force the state into its familiar capitalist role of socializing the economy's losses. The most successful cooperative networks, such as the renowned Mondragon network in Spain, succeed because they impose high borrowing fees on new members; workers have to buy their way in. That excludes workers lacking the resources or nerve to make a commitment, which does little for equality.[19]

Large-scale economic democracy thus requires a more entrepreneurial and structurally flexible model with a greater capacity for scaling up. The best candidate is the mutual fund (or public bank) model of social ownership developed by social and economic theorists Rudolf Meidner, David Miller, Saul Estrin, David Winter, Julian Le Grand, Alec Nove, Radoslav Selucky, John Roemer, David Belkin, and Thomas E. Weisskopf. A variation of guild socialism, it establishes competing holding companies owned by equity shareholders, the state, or other cooperatives in which ownership of productive capital is vested. The holding companies lend capital to enterprises at market rates of interest and otherwise control the process of investment, including decision-making power to initiate new cooperatives and shut down unprofitable enterprises.[20]

In the largest experiment of this kind yet conducted, the Meidner Plan in Sweden, an annual tax on major company profits was paid in the form of stock to eight regional mutual funds, which were controlled by worker, consumer, and government representatives. As their proportion of stock ownership grew, these groups were collectively entitled to representation on company boards. A 40-percent ceiling was placed on the amount of stock that the eight funds in total could own of any single firm. The Meidner Plan expired in 1990 after eight years of operation. The Social Democrats lost the succeeding election, and when they returned to power they spent their political capital on sustaining the welfare state, not advancing economic democracy. But globalization forced them to scale back the welfare state anyway. Today they face the same decision as other European social democracies, whether to concentrate wholly on saving social welfare gains of the past, or move forward by creating more economic democracy.[21]

The distinct advantage of mutual fund social ownership is that it diversifies forms of risk sharing, promoting economic efficiency by forcing firms to be financially accountable to a broad range of investors. Since the funds represent part of workers' compensation, this model contains a built-in system of wage restraints and facilitates a new form of capital formation. It requires no program of nationalization, and investors still seek the highest rate of return. Most mutual fund or public bank strategies separate risk in production from entrepreneurial risk, assigning production risks to worker-managed enterprises and entrepreneurial risks to the holding companies.

The mutual fund idea offers a way beyond the welfare state, by expanding the base of economic power, while saving the social and political gains of liberalism. It establishes democratic control over the process of investment without resorting to government planning, building on the cooperative principle that people work more efficiently when they have a stake in the company. It promotes economic democracy while checking the growth of both private and public economic power. Thus it sustains and advances beyond the social gospel and guild socialist ideas of economic democracy.

But no model of social ownership should be treated as the next progressive blueprint. From a democratic perspective, the crucial problem with the mutual fund model is that it weakens workers' power at the firm level and empowers the investors of collectively owned social capital. There are slippery trade-offs between the needs of the holding companies and the rights of worker-managed enterprises. To the extent that the holding companies are granted supervisory control over their client enterprises, worker control is diminished; to the extent that the holding companies are kept in a weak position, the crucial advantages of the mutual fund model are traded off as the enterprises essentially become cooperatives.[22]

One way to avoid the trade-off is to institute circular forms of ownership and control modeled on the second-degree cooperatives of Mondragon. Estrin requires the holding companies to bear capital risks while allowing their client firm managements to make critical decisions affecting these risks *and* without being eligible to share in the profits. In this model, cooperative firms become shareholders in the holding companies themselves, thus minimizing the trade-offs between democratic control and efficiency.[23]

The caution against blueprints, however, is more important than any particular proposal to solve the problem of control. Decentralized, economic democracy must be a project built from the ground up, piece by piece, opening new choices, creating more democracy, seeking to build a new economic order that is more egalitarian, cooperative, and ecological than the existing one. It is a project that breaks from the universalizing logic of state socialism. The tests of its efficacy are pragmatic. The point is to provide better choices.

A politics that expanded the cooperative and mutual fund sectors would give workers important new choices. The central conceit of neoclassical economics could be turned into a reality if meaningful choices were created. The neoclassical conceit is that capitalism doesn't exploit anyone, because labor employs capital as much as capital employs labor. But in the real world, the owners of capital nearly always organize the factors of production. To expand the cooperative, mutual fund and other social market sectors would give choices to workers that neoclassical theory promises, but does not deliver. And it would create a political culture that is more democratic, egalitarian, cooperative, and ecologically conscious than the one we have now.

The effort to democratize power today must take place at the point of production (as in Marxism), and the electoral arena (as in liberalism), and in the postindustrial "living place" where people struggle to create environments that are more ecological, culturally diverse and hospitable. Whatever remains of progressive Christianity today requires a multicultural, feminist, ecological consciousness that challenges and transforms the old economism. At the same time, no serious challenge to existing relations of power can ignore the factors of production. We cannot advance the cause of social justice by writing off the seemingly hopeless problem of economic injustice. Those who control the process of investment still play the largest role in determining the kind of society in which we live. Gains toward social and economic democracy are needed today for the same fundamental reason that political democracy is necessary: to restrain the abuse of unequal power. And that is a quintessential social Christian project.

Notes

1   Ernst Troeltsch, *The Social Teaching of the Christian Churches*, 2 vols., trans. Olive Wyon (1st edn., 1912; Louisville: Westminster John Knox Press, 1992), 2: 1011.

2   This chapter adapts material from Gary Dorrien, "Beyond State and Market: Christianity and the Future of Economic Democracy," *Cross Currents* (Summer 1995), 184–204; Dorrien, *Soul in Society: The Making and Renewal of Social Christianity* (Minneapolis: Fortress

Press, 1995), 290–308; Dorrien, "Beyond the Twilight of Socialism: Rethinking Economic Democracy," *Harvard Divinity Bulletin* (Summer 1996); Dorrien, *Imperial Designs: Neoconservatism and the New Pax Americana* (New York: Routledge, 2004); Dorrien, "Rethinking the Theory and Politics of Christian Socialism," *Democratic Left* (January 2000), 23–6.

3 See Justin Wroe Nixon, *The Moral Crisis in Christianity* (New York: Harper & Brothers, 1931); Nixon, *Protestantism's Hour of Decision* (Philadelphia: Judson Press, 1940); Dores Robinson Sharpe, *Walter Rauschenbusch* (New York: Macmillan, 1942); Benjamin E. Mays, ed., *A Rauschenbusch Reader: The Kingdom of God and the Social Gospel* (New York: Harper Brothers, 1957); George Herron, *The New Redemption: A Call to the Church to Reconstruct Society According to the Gospel of Christ* (New York: T.Y. Crowell, 1893); Herron, *The Christian State: A Political Vision of Christ* (New York: T.Y. Crowell, 1895); Vida D. Scudder, "Christianity in the Socialist State," *Hibbert Journal* 8 (April 1910), 562–81; Scudder, *Socialism and Character* (Boston: Houghton Mifflin, 1912).

4 See Reinhold Niebuhr, "Roosevelt's Merry-Go-Round," *Radical Religion* 3 (Spring 1938), 4; Reinhold Niebuhr, "New Deal Medicine," *Radical Religion* 4 (Spring 1939), 1–2.

5 Herbert Croly, *The Promise of American Life* (1909; Boston: Northeastern University Press, 1989); Henry Churchill King, *The Moral and Religious Challenge of Our Times* (New York: Macmillan, 1911); Richard T. Ely, *Ground Under Our Feet* (New York: Macmillan, 1938); Robert LaFollette, *LaFollette's Autobiography: A Personal Narrative of Political Experiences* (1911; Madison: University of Wisconsin, 1960).

6 Richard John Neuhaus, Introduction to Wolfhart Pannenberg, *Theology and the Kingdom of God* (Philadelphia: Westminster Press, 1969), 31–2; Neuhaus, discussion in *Reinhold Niebuhr Today*, ed. Richard John Neuhaus (Grand Rapids: Wm. B. Eerdmans, 1989), 108.

7 Reinhold Niebuhr, "The Confession of a Tired Radical," *Christian Century* 45 (August 30, 1928), reprinted in *Love and Justice: Selections from the Shorter Writings of Reinhold Niebuhr*, ed. D. B. Robertson (Philadelphia: Westminster Press, 1957), 120–4.

8 Reinhold Niebuhr, "The Sin of Racial Prejudice," *The Messenger* 13 (February 3, 1948), quote, 6; reprinted in *A Reinhold Niebuhr Reader: Selected Essays, Articles, and Book Reviews*, ed. Charles C. Brown (Philadelphia: Trinity Press International, 1992), 70–1; see Niebuhr, "Christian Faith and the Race Problem," *Christianity and Society* (Spring 1945); and Niebuhr, "The Race Problem," *Christianity and Society* (Summer 1942), reprinted in *Love and Justice*, 125–9, 129–32.

9 Reinhold Niebuhr, *Pious and Secular America* (New York: Charles Scribner's Sons, 1958), 76.

10 Reinhold Niebuhr, "Proposal to Billy Graham," *Christian Century* (August 8, 1956), reprinted in Niebuhr, *Love and Justice*, ed. D. B. Robertson (Philadelphia: Westminster Press, 1957), 154–8; see Niebuhr, "A Theologian Says Evangelist is Oversimplifying the Issues of Life," *Life* (July 1, 1957), 92; Niebuhr, "Literalism, Individualism, and Billy Graham," *Christian Century* (May 23, 1956), reprinted in Niebuhr, *Essays in Applied Christianity*, ed. D. B. Robertson (New York: Meridian Books, 1959), 123–31; Michael G. Long, *Billy Graham and the Beloved Community* (New York: Palgrave Macmillan, 2006), 79–142.

11 See Saul Alinsky, *Rules for Radicals* (New York: Vintage Books, 1971); Industrial Areas Foundation, *IAF: 50 Years of Organizing for Change* (Franklin Square, New York: Industrial Areas Foundation, 1990); Industrial Areas Foundation, "IAF in Action," www.industrialareasfoundation.org, 2006, accessed August 19, 2007.

12 See Gamaliel Foundation, "History," and "Gamaliel Today," 2006, www.gamaliel.org, accessed August 19, 2007.

13 Joint Chiefs of Staff, US Department of Defense, Army General Henry H. Shelton, chairman, *Joint Vision 2020* (May 30, 2000), quote; www.dtic.mil/jv2020, accessed April 17, 2006; see Bill Murray, "The Joint Chiefs Take Aim at IT," *GCN* (June 5, 2000), www.gcn.com/print, accessed October 19, 2006; "USSPACACECOM Vision for 2020,"

www.fas.org/spp/military, accessed October 19, 2006; see US Department of Defense, *Report of the Quadrennial Defense Review* (Washington, DC: US Department of Defense, Government Printing Office," 1997); US Department of Defense, *Report of the Quadrennial Defense Review* (Washington, DC: US Department of Defense, Government Printing Office," 2001); Andrew Bacevich, *American Empire: The Realities and Consequences of U.S. Diplomacy* (Cambridge, MA: Harvard University Press, 2003); Rahul Mahajan, *Full Spectrum Dominance: U.S. Power in Iraq and Beyond* (New York: Seven Stories Press, 2003); Ellen M. Wood, *Empire of Capital* (London: Verso, 2003).

14 See Anatol Lieven and John Hulsman, *Ethical Realism: A Vision for America's Role in the World* (New York: Pantheon Books, 2006); Peter Beinart, *The Good Fight: How Liberals – And Only Liberals – Can Win the War on Terror and Make America Great Again* (New York: HarperCollins, 2006); Ronald H. Stone, *Prophetic Realism: Beyond Militarism and Pacifism in an Age of Terror* (New York: T. & T. Clark, 2005); Jean Bethke Elshtain, *Just War Against Terror: The Burden of American Power in a Violent World* (New York: Basic Books, 2003); Chalmers Johnson, *The Sorrows of Empire: Militarism, Secrecy, and the End of the Republic* (New York: Henry Holt, 2004); Andrew J. Bacevich, *American Empire: The Realities and Consequences of U.S. Diplomacy* (Cambridge, MA: Harvard University Press, 2002); Zbigniew Brzezinski, *The Choice: Global Dominion or Global Leadership* (New York: Basic Books, 2004); James Kurth, "The Adolescent Empire," *National Interest* 48 (Summer 1997), 3–15; Robert F. Ellsworth and Dimitri K. Simes, "Realism's Shining Morality," *National Interest* (Winter 2004/05), reprinted in *The Right War? The Conservative Debate on Iraq*, ed. Gary Rosen (New York: Cambridge University Press, 2005), 204–11; Daniel Pipes, "Salvaging the Iraq War," *New York Sun* (July 24, 2007); Patrick J. Buchanan, *Where the Right Went Wrong* (New York: St. Martin's Griffin, 2005).

15 Mickey Kaus, *The End of Equality* (New York: Basic Books, 1992), 25–57; Kaus, "For a New Equality," *New Republic* 202 (May 7, 1990), 21.

16 Kaus, *The End of Equality*, 58–77; Thomas Friedman, *The World Is Flat: A Brief History of the Twenty-First Century* (New York: Farrar, Straus and Giroux, 2005).

17 See Padma Desai, *Financial Crisis, Contagion and Containment* (Princeton: Princeton University Press, 2003); Jagdish Bhagwati, *The Wind of the Hundred Days: How Washington Mismanaged Globalization* (Cambridge, MA: MIT Press, 2001); Bhagwati, *In Defense of Globalization* (New York: Oxford University Press, 2004), 199–207; Joseph Stiglitz, *Globalization and Its Discontents* (New York: W. W. Norton, 2003), 89–132.

18 Kaus, *The End of Equality*, quote 13; see Kevin Phillips, *The Politics of Rich and Poor: Wealth and the American Electorate in the Reagan Aftermath* (New York: Random House, 1990), 76–9; Donald L. Barlett and James B. Steele, *America: What Went Wrong?* (Kansas City: Andrews and McMeel, 1992), 4–7; Frederick R. Strobel, *Upward Dreams, Downward Mobility: The Economic Decline of the American Middle Class* (Lanham, MD: Rowman & Littlefield, 1993), 91–102.

19 See H. Thomas and Chris Logan, *Mondragon: An Economic Analysis* (London: Allen and Unwin, 1982); William Foote Whyte and Kathleen King Whyte, *Making Mondragon: The Growth and Dynamics of the Worker Cooperative Complex* (Ithaca, NY: ILR Press, 1988); K. Bradley and A. Gelb, *Co-operation at Work: The Mondragon Experience* (London: Heinemann Educational Books, 1983); Terry Mollner, *Mondragon: A Third Way* (Shutesbury, Mass: Trusteeship Institute, 1984).

20 See David Miller, *Market, State and Community: Theoretical Foundations of Market Socialism* (Oxford: Clarendon Press, 1990); David Miller and Saul Estrin, "A Case for Market Socialism: What Does It Mean? Why Should We Favor It?" in Frank Roosevelt and David Belkin, eds., *Why Market Socialism?* (Armonk, NY: M.E. Sharpe, 1994), 225–40; Saul Estrin and David Winter, "Planning in a Market Socialist Economy," in Julian Le Grand and Saul Estrin, eds., *Market Socialism* (Oxford: Oxford University Press, 1989), 100–38; Estrin and Julian Le Grand, "Market Socialism," in *Market Socialism*, 1–24; Alec Nove, *Socialism,*

Economics, and Development (London: Allen & Unwin, 1986); Radoslav Selucky, *Marxism, Socialism and Freedom* (Oxford: Oxford University Press, 1989); John Roemer, "Market Socialism: A Blueprint: How Such an Economy Might Work," in *Why Market Socialism?* 269–81; Roemer, *Free to Lose: An Introduction to Marxist Economic Philosophy* (Cambridge, MA: Harvard University Press, 1988); Belkin, "Why Market Socialism? From the Critique of Political Economy to Positive Political Economy," in *Why Market Socialism?* 3–47; Thomas E. Weisskopf, "Challenges to Market Socialism: A Response to Critics," in *Why Market Socialism?* 297–318.

21 See Rudolf Meidner, *Employee Investment Funds: An Approach to Collective Capital Formation* (London: George Allen & Unwin, 1978); Meidner, "A Swedish Union Proposal for Collective Capital Sharing," in *Eurosocialism and America: Political Economy for the 1980s*, ed. Nancy Lieber (Philadelphia: Temple University Press, 1982), 25–33; Jonas Pontusson, "Radicalization and Retreat in Swedish Social Democracy," *New Left Review* 165 (September/October 1987), 5–33.

22 See Weisskopf, "Challenges to Market Socialism: A Response to Critics," 303–8; Joanne Barkan and David Belkin, "Comment," in *Why Market Socialism?* 282–8.

23 See Saul Estrin, "Worker's Co-operatives: Their Merits and their Limitations," *Market Socialism*, 183–92; Estrin and Le Grand, "Market Socialism," 18–19.

Index

Abbott, Ezra, 8
Abbott, Lyman, 29–31, 76–7
  Gladden and, 70, 79–80, 82
Abell, Aaron I., 35
Abernathy, Ralph, 391
abolitionist movement, 158–60
  evangelicals and, 457
abortion
  Catholic position on, 539–40
  evangelical outrage over, 458–60
  Harrison's discussion of, 426–8
  Wallis's discussion of, 518
Academia Alfonsiana, 534–5
Academy of Catholic Hispanic/Latino
    Theologians, 655–6
Acton, Lord, 330
Adams, Henry, 330
Adams, James Carey, 324
  theology of, 328–34
Adams, James Luther, 3, 305, 323, 432
  early life and career, 324–34
  personalist theory and, 306
  Stackhouse and, 612
  Unitarian Christianity, 324–34
  University of Chicago Divinity School
    and, 549
Adams, Lella Mae, 325
Adams, Margaret, 334
Addams, Anna Hostetter Haldeman, 170–2
Addams, Jane, 3, 6, 42–4, 46, 49, 263
  black social gospel movement and, 146
  Chicago School and, 549
  early life and career of, 168–75
  Gladden and, 81
  legacy of, 168–9
  Ransom and, 155–7, 168
  religious views of, 184–5

social ethics and, 175–85
Strong and, 76
Ward and, 110–11
Addams, John, 170–1
Adkins v. Children's Hospital, 206
Aeterni Patris, 188
African Americans
  Catholic Church and, 337–8
  liberation theology and, 291–4
  schools for, 78
  social gospel movement and, 3, 30–2, 60–1,
    146–215
  Taylor and, 49–51
  Townes's discussion of, 641–6
  West's discussion of, 569–84
  womanist ethics and, 587–92
  see also black theology; racial justice
African culture, human rights and, 660
African Methodist Episcopal Church
  Cone and, 397, 401–2
  Ransom and, 147–51, 157–8, 160–1,
    163–8
African United Front, 575
Afro-American Council, 154–5, 167
Afro-American League, 154–5
"against" model of liberal theology, 242
Agnes Scott College, 615
Aiken, Charles A., 11
Albrecht, Gloria, 485–7
alcoholism, Ransom's discussion of, 153
Alexander, Samuel, 322
Alinsky, Saul, 680
Allen, Richard, 152, 163
Allen University, 151
Allport, Gordon, 34
Aloysia (Sister), 364–5
Althusser, Louis, 579

Alves, Rubem, 272–3, 276
AME Church Review, 162–5
America (newsweekly), 336, 365-6
American Academy of Religion, 587, 611, 618, 653–4
American Academy of Social and Political Science, 32
American Alliance for International Friendship, 80
American Bible Society, 98
American Board of Commissioners for Foreign Missions, 98
American Civil Liberties Union (ACLU), 125, 128, 206, 333
American Civil War, 104
American Dilemma, An, 312–13
American Ecclesiastical Review, 336–7, 339–40, 343–5, 348, 355
American Economic Association, 18, 23, 32, 70–1
American Encyclopedia, 51
American Enterprise Institute (AEI), 496, 508
American Evangelical Alliance, 76
American Evasion of Philosophy, The, 571, 580
American Family Association, 456
American Friends' Service Committee, 182
American Heroine: The Life and Legend of Jane Addams, 169
American Historical Society, 32
American Home Missionary Society, 74, 98
American ideal, Murray's discussion of, 349–61
American Institute of Christian Sociology, 44, 70
American Ladies' Christian Association, 98
American League Against War and Fascism, 125, 128
American League for Peace and Democracy, 128
American Magazine, The, 98
American Mercury magazine, 338
American Missionary Association (AMA), 78–9
American Missionary Society, 30
American Peace Society, 80
American Red Cross, 182
American Revolutionary War, 104
Americans for Democratic Action (ADA), 261, 263
American Social Science Association, 17–18, 32, 40–1

American society, Rauschenbusch's discussion of, 99–104
American Sociological Association, 32
American Sociological Society, 32
American Statistical Association, 32
American Sunday School Union, 98
American Vision, The, 496, 499
Ames, Edward Scribner, 323, 354, 596
Ames, William, 11
Amin, Frank and Samir, 503
Amlak, Elleni Gebre, 572
"Amos 'n Andy" (television show), 644–5
Anabaptists
 evangelicals and, 459–61
 Hauerwas and, 477
 Yoder and, 461–74
Anderson, Marian, 213
Anderson, Victor, 5, 534
 postmodernism and, 592–8
Andover Newton Theological School, 334, 612
Andover Review, 21–2
Andover Theological Seminary, 21–2, 324
Anglo-Saxon culture
 Murray's discussion of, 350–1
 Strong's embrace of, 61, 74–9
Anthony, Susan B., 422
anti-capitalism, Ward and, 114–20
anti-Catholicism, 186–99, 202–4
 of Morrison, 234
 Murray's discussion of, 338
Anti-Conscription League, 363
anti-imperialism, social gospel movement and, 76
Anti-Imperialist League, 365
Anti-Lynching League, 152, 154
Anti-Modernist Oath, 413
Antioch College, 9
anti-Semitism
 Catholic Church and, 370
 West and, 575–7, 581
antislavery movement, social gospel and, 61
apocalypticism, Rauschenbusch's discussion of, 94–7
Apollonian tradition, 328
apologetics
 capitalist apologetics, 612–16
 Niebuhr and, 270
 social gospel movement and, 10–11
Applied Christianity movement, 18, 61
Applied Christianity: The Moral Aspects of Social Questions, 41

Approach to the Social Question, The, 20, 33
Aquinas, St. Thomas, 256, 341, 351
  Daly's reading of, 412–15
  Hauerwas and, 475
  natural law theory and, 538
  Novak and, 498
Aquino, María Pilar, 405, 637
  Latina feminism and, 646, 655–7
Aristotelianism
  Hauerwas and, 475
  moral philosophy and, 11–12
Armstrong, Samuel Chapman, 30–1
Arnett, Benjamin W., 149, 152–4, 156–8,
  160, 164
Arnett, Benjamin W. Jr., 164
Arnold, Matthew, 26, 583
Aronowitz, Stanley, 565, 576, 578
Asante, Molefi, 578
Ascent of the Mountain, Flight of the Dove, 492
Ashley, W. J., 191
Aspects of Social Christianity, 23
Atherton, John, 625
Atlantic magazine, 230
Auden, W. H., 275
Auer, Johannes A. C. F., 332
Augustine
  millennialism and, 448
  Niebuhr's discussion of, 248, 256
Ayers, Francis, 549–50

Babbitt, Irving, 325
Bacevich, Andrew, 682
Bacon, Benjamin, 229
Bacon, Leonard, 29
Badiou, Alain, 583
Baker, Ella, 395
Baker, Houston Jr., 594
Baldwin, James, 396–7, 404, 572, 574–5,
  643
Baldwin, Roger, 206
Baltzer, John, 230–1, 235
Baptist Church
  evangelicals and, 459–60
  German Americans and, 93–4
Baptist Congress, 90–1
Baraka, Amiri, 396, 401
Barbarism the First Danger, 74
Barbour, Clarence, 108
Bare Ruined Choirs, 358
Barnes, Harry Elmer, 327
Barnes, Roswell, 236, 675
Barnett, Samuel and Henrietta, 172

Barry, William Francis, 187, 194
Bartelme, Betty, 375
Barth, Karl
  Adams and, 325–6
  Bennett and, 277–9
  Cone and, 396, 398, 403, 405
  Gustafson and, 545–6
  Hauerwas and, 474–6, 481, 486
  Muelder and, 315–16
  Niebuhr and, 226, 241–2, 257–9
  Yoder and, 460–2
Barton, Josef, 641
Bascom, John, 23
Batten, Samuel Zane, 91
Batterham, Forster, 364
Bauerlein, Mark, 583
Baum, Gregory, 293, 415
Baxter, Edna, 412
Bay of Pigs crisis, 266
Bea, Augustin (Cardinal), 356
Beach, George Kimmich, 334
Beacon Press, 333
Beardslee, Clark, 41
Beckley, Harlan, 273–4, 484
Beecher, Henry Ward, 21, 41, 158
Beer, Samuel, 564
behaviorist theory, social ethics and, 555–6
Beichman, Arnold, 489
Beinart, Peter, 682
Being a Christian, 64
Belgic Confession, 459–60
Belkin, David, 687
Bell, Daniel, 101–2, 455, 489, 496–8
Bell, Nelson, 451
Bellah, Robert, 481
Bellamy, Edward, 10
Belloc, Hilaire, 368, 372
Beloved, 641
"beloved community," King's concept of,
  394, 594
Benedict XIV (Pope), 198
Benedict XVI (Pope), 543; *see also* Ratzinger,
  Joseph (Cardinal)
Benne, Robert, 552–3, 611, 614–15
Bennett, Anne McGrew, 277
Bennett, John C., 3, 317, 401
  Christian realism and, 276–87
  Cone and, 401–2, 405
  early life and career of, 277–87
  economic democracy and, 675
  emerging liberal consensus and, 287–94
  Harrison and, 422–3

Niebuhr and, 255, 260, 263–7, 276–87
Novak's discussion of, 494
Ramsey and, 285–7
Reinhold Niebuhr and, 226, 236
Bennett, William, 489
Berger, Peter, 489
Bergson, Henri, 322
Berkeley, George, 13
Berlin crisis, 266–7
Berrigan, Daniel, 375–7
Berrigan, Phillip, 375–7
Berry, Thomas, 630
Bertocci, Peter, 318
Beyond God the Father, 291, 419–21
Beyond Ontological Blackness, 593–5
Biblical criticism
    by Aquino, 655–6
    by Cahill, 619–21
    of Gladden, 71–3
    historical approach to, 6
    mujerista theology and, 651–2
    Rauschenbusch on, 85
    Yoder's discussion of gospels, 463–74
    see also inerrancy ideology; New Testament
biblical religion, Niebuhr's ideal of, 257–9
Bibliotheca Sacra, 150–1
Bigelow, Herbert Seeley, 30
Bingham, John A., 147
bioethics
    Cahill on, 618–21
    eco-justice and, 631–7
Birch, Charles, 628
Bird, Phyllis, 619
Birth of a Nation, 168
Bishop, Robert Hamilton, 22
Black, Hugo, 208, 213
black feminism, 646
black intellectuals
    Anderson and, 594–8
    West's discussion of, 571–84
Black International anarchists, 23
Black Manifesto, 401
black nationalism, Ransom's involvement in, 165–8
"Black Nation" thesis, West's discussion of, 568
Black Panther Party, 401
    West and, 563–4
Black Power movement, 395–6, 398–400
    Cannon and, 586
    Winter and, 552, 559–60
Black Radical Congress, 578

black theology
    Anderson's discussion of, 593–98
    Cone's legacy in, 402–11
    liberation theology and, 291–4, 390
    politics and, 458–9
    social gospel movement and, 158–215
    Townes's critique of, 642–6
Black Theology and Black Power, 291, 398–401, 410
Black Theology of Liberation, A, 291, 402–11
Black Womanist Ethics, 587–92
Blaine, James, 186
Blanshard, Paul, 338
Bliss, W. D. P., 45, 70, 88–9, 120
"Blue Book," 437
Boardman, George Dana, 91
Boesak, Allan, 409
Bolshevism, 114–17
    Day's view of, 362–4
Bonaventure, 415
Bonhoeffer, Dietrich, 256, 630
Boodin, John Elof, 310
Boston College, Daly at, 416–19
Boston Guardian, 167
Boston Herald, The, 160
Boston personalism, 305–16
"Boston riot," 157
Boston University
    Henry's career at, 448
    King at, 391, 394
    personalist theology at, 306–8
    Ward at, 113
Boulding, Kenneth, 632
Boundary 2: An International Journal of Literature and Culture, 565
Bounds, Elizabeth M., 437, 649
Bouquillon, Thomas J., 191
Bové, Paul, 565
Bowen, Francis, 14
Bowen, Henry, 64
Bower, William, 352
Bowie, Walter Russell, 249, 338–40
Bowne, Borden Parker, 71, 306–10, 312, 317–18, 321–2
Bradley, Bill, 575, 580
Bradley, Thomas, 574
Briggs, Charles, 9
Brightman, Edgar Sheffield, 258, 307–10, 317–21
    King and, 394
British Labour Party, 201
Brock, William, 496

Brooks, Phillips, 16, 85, 393
*Brother Earth: Nature, God, and Ecology in a
    Time of Crisis*, 626–30
Brotherhood of the Kingdom, 90–2, 94
Brown, Charles Reynolds, 29, 160, 228, 261
Brown, Dale W., 467
Brown, Francis, 8
Brown, John, 158–9
Brown, Robert McAfee, 288–9, 293, 422
Brown, Rome G., 195
Brown, William Adams, 98, 236, 260
Brown-Douglass, Kelly, 410
Browning, Don, 418
Brown v. Board of Education, 396–7, 451, 678
Brubaker, Pamela K., 437, 649
Brunner, Emil, 325
Brunner, Peter, 326
Brus, Wlodzimierz, 566
Bryant, Louise, 364
Bryant, William Cullen, 63
Bryson, Gladys, 35
Brzezinski, Zbigniew, 682
Buber, Martin, 473
Buchanan, Pat, 682
Buckley, William F. Jr., 417
Bukharin, Nikolai, 120
Bundy, McGeorge, 266
Burckhardt, Jacob, 330
Burgher, Mary, 589
Burke, John J., 335
Burke, Kenneth, 364
Burroughs, Nannie Helen, 412
Burrow, Rufus Jr., 323
Burton, Nathaniel, 38
Bush, George W., 516, 518–19, 681–2
Bushnell, Horace, 21, 37–41
    atonement theology of, 85
    Gladden influenced by, 62–3
    liberal theology and, 241
    Manifest Destiny ideology and, 74
Bushnell, Mary, 39–40
Buthelezi, Manas, 409
Butler, Judith, 436

Cabot, Richard Clarke, 34
Cadbury, Henry, 324
Cadman, S. Parkes, 453
Cahill, Lisa Sowle, 4–5, 428, 547–8
    on norms and moral reasoning, 618–21
Cain, Richard H., 151
Calhoun, Robert, 238
Call (socialist newspaper), 362–3

Call to Renewal, 514
Calvinism
    evangelicals and, 455–60
    Gustafson's discussion of, 546
    New England Congregationalism and, 21
Calvin Theological Seminary, 592
Campbell, J. P., 151
Canavan, Francis, SJ, 360
Can Ethics Be Christian?, 484, 545
Cannon, Corine Lytle, 585
Cannon, Esau, 585
Cannon, Katie Geneva, 5, 433–4, 533, 584
    Anderson and, 593
    Isasi-Díaz and, 649
    Townes and, 641
    Welch and, 640
    womanist ethics and, 584–92
Canon Law Society, 535
Capital, 172
capitalism
    capitalist apologetics, 612–16
    Catholic Church and, 188–99, 430–1
    Cobb's ecotheology and, 629–30
    democratic capitalism ideology, 489–512
    eco-justice and, 631–7
    economic democracy and, 683–8
    Gladden's discussion of, 66–7, 69
    Harrison's discussion of, 430–3
    Hauerwas's critique of, 485
    modernity and, 674–7
    Muelder and, 313–14
    Niebuhr's discussion of, 123, 234–9,
        245–59, 262
    Novak's discussion of, 494–503, 511–12
    Rauschenbusch's discussion of, 96–7,
        101–4
    Ryan's discussion of, 197–9, 206–15
    Ward's criticism of, 112–20
    West's discussion of, 573
    Wogaman's discussion of, 624–6
Cardoso, Fernando Henrique, 503
Carlson, Tucker, 682
Carmichael, Stokely, 398–400
Carnegie, Andrew, 76, 80
Carnell, Edward J., 447–8, 456, 458
Carroll, John, 347
Carter, Jimmy, 456, 496
Castro, Fidel, 373–4
Catholic Biblical Quarterly, 336, 468
Catholic Charities Review, 197
Catholic Church
    Addams' views on, 184

American ideal and, 351–61
Bennett's view of, 290–1
Curran controversy and, 534–44
Daly's critique of, 412–21
Day's involvement in, 362–77
democracy and, 349–61
eco-justice and, 633–4
evangelicals and, 452–3
Harrison's discussion of, 427, 430–1
Hauerwas and, 477–9, 483–5
human rights and social ethics in, 374, 657–64
liberation theology and, 503–12
mujerista theology and, 651–7
Murray and, 334–49
Novak and, 489–503
Ryan and, 185–215
social ethics and, 305, 534–44
social gospel movement and, 146, 185–6, 199–215
Spanish Civil War and, 369–70
in United States, 349–61
women's rights and, 62
Yoder's discussion of, 462–74
Catholic Club of Harvard, 536
Catholic Conference on Industrial Problems, 206
Catholic Fortnightly Review, 197
Catholic Historical Review, 347
"Catholicism: Death or Rebirth?", 418
Catholicism in Crisis, 504–5
Catholic Radical, 366
Catholic Relief Services, 374
Catholic Theological Society of America, 537, 542
Catholic Times, 194
Catholic University of America, 190–1, 194, 197, 336
  Curran and, 537
  Daly at, 412–13
  Novak and, 490
Catholic Worker (newspaper), 366–74
Catholic Worker movement, 305, 364–77
Catholic World, 335
Cavalli, Fiorelli, 339
Cavell, Stanley, 564
"Center of Value, The," 242
Centesimus annus, 542
Central America, violence in, 513–14
Century, The, 63–4
Chaffee, Edmund, 236, 249
Challenge of Peace, The, 377, 471, 505–7

Channing, William Ellery, 13, 30, 241
Character and the Christian Life, 475
Chardin, Teilhard de, 416
Charities, 44
Charlotte Observer, 485
Chatauqua Society, 44, 70
Chavez, Cesar, 680
Chekhov, Anton, 579
Chesterton, G. K., 372
Chicago Chronicle, 46
Chicago Civic Federation, 44, 111
Chicago Plan Commission, 44
Chicago School of Civics and Philanthropy, 44
Chicago School theology, 184–5, 320, 323, 549–63
  Anderson and, 596–8
Chicago Theological Seminary (CTS), 326
  social gospel movement and, 44–51
  Taylor's career at, 6, 41–4
Chicago Tribune, 157, 332
Chicago Woman's Trade Union League, 175
Child, Francis J., 8
Child, Lydia Maria, 645
Children of Light and the Children of Darkness, The, 261–2, 271
China, Niebuhr's position on, 267–71
Choosing Our King, 494
Christ and Culture, 242, 244
Christ and the Moral Life, 544
Christian Action, 262
Christian Century, The, 205, 428, 451, 576, 583
  Morrison as editor, 237
  Niebuhr and, 232–5, 239, 259–62
Christian Coalition, 458–9, 514–15; *see also* Christian Right; evangelicalism
"Christian Constitutionalism," 342
Christian Demand for Social Reconstruction, The, 113
Christian Ethics and the Community, 544
Christianity
  Darwinism and, 69–73
  Gladden's discussion of, 66–9
  Manifest Destiny ideology and, 73–9
  social gospel ideal of, 60–1
Christianity and Crisis, 260–1, 284, 287, 293, 494
Christianity and Society, 260
Christianity and the Social Crisis, 45, 94–9, 103
Christianity Today, 451–2, 454–5, 457–8
Christianizing the Social Order, 99–104, 146–7

Christian Morality Today, 537
Christian Natural Theology, A, 62
Christian Nurture, 40
Christian realism
  Bennett and, 276–87
  cold war politics and, 259–71
  dominance of, 305
  evangelical and conservative view of, 447–8
  liberal consensus and, 287–94
  liberation theology and, 276
  Niebuhr's legacy in, 272–6, 675–7
  socialist faith and, 244–59
Christian Realism, 281–7
Christian Register, The, 325
Christian Right
  media coverage of, 512
  neoconservatives and, 458–59, 511–12
  Wallis's progressive evangelicalism and,
    513–19
  see also evangelicals; fundamentalism
Christiansen, Drew, SJ, 562
Christian socialism
  Rauschenbusch and, 88–9, 101–4
  social ethics and, 25–29
  World War I and, 114–20
  see also socialism and social democracy
Christian Sociology, 23
Christian State, The, 45
Christian Voice, 456
Christian Way, The, 64
Christian Witness to the State, 476
Chung Hyun Kyung, 633, 649
Church, Robert L., 35
Church Against Itself, The, 415
Church and the Second Sex, The, 412, 414,
  417–21
"Church and Totalitarian Democracy, The,"
  345
Church as Moral Decision Maker, The, 544
Church Dogmatics, 461
Churchill, J. W., 21
Church Peace Union, 80
Ci niesce, 346
City Club of Chicago, 111
City Missionary Society, 39
civilization, Gladden's belief in, 81–3
Civil Rights Act of 1964, 679
civil rights movement
  evangelical repudiation of, 454–60
  King and, 391
  progressive evangelicalism and, 512–19
  Winter and, 559–60

Civilta Cattolica, 339, 349
*Claims in Conflict: Retrieving and Renewing the
  Catholic Human Rights Tradition*, 506
Clark, Gordon, 448
Clarke, James Freeman, 328–9
Clarke, William Newton, 91
Clarkson, Shannon, 435
class politics
  Addams' discussion of, 176–85
  Day's discussion of, 368
  Gladden's discussion of, 65–9
  Niebuhr and, 246–59
  Rauschenbusch and, 88–9
  social ethics and, 22–4, 43–4
  social gospel movement and, 61
  Ward's involvement in, 109, 115–20
  see also economic democracy
Clay, Cassius Marcellus, 127
Cleveland, Grover, 23, 186
Clinton, Hillary, 582
Clinton, William J., 682
Coalition for a Democratic Majority, 494
Cobb, Clifford, 626, 629
Cobb, John B. Jr., 5, 626–31
Coe, George Albert, 110, 125
Coffin, Henry Sloane, 123–4, 126–7, 235–6,
  260–1
Cohen, Morris, 321–2
Coit, Stanton, 42
Cold War politics, H. R. Niebuhr and,
  259–71
Coleman, John A., SJ, 359, 559, 562
Coleridge, Samuel Taylor, 71, 85
Colfax, Schuyler, 63
College of Philadelphia, 13
College of St. Thomas, 189–90
Collingwood, R. G., 474
Collum, Danny, 514
colorism, Townes's discussion of, 642
Color Purple, The, 587
Colton, Calvin, 499
Coltrane, John, 583
Columbian Exposition of 1893, 152
Columbus and Hocking Valley Coal and
  Iron Company, 65
Colwell, Ernest Cadman, 326, 332
Colwell, Stephen, 10
Commager, Henry Steele, 168
Commission on Ecumenical Mission and
  Relations (WCC), 423
Commission on Justice, Peace, [and]
  Creation (WCC), 631

Committee of Catholics to Fight Anti-
Semitism, 370
"Committee of Six," 49
Committee on Church and State, 333
Commons, John, 111
Commons, The, 44
commonsense realism, at American
Universities, 11–14
Commonweal magazine, 207, 335, 365–6,
413–14, 490
communism, 122–30; *see also* Bolshevism
Adams and, 332–4
Bennett's discussion of, 284–7
capitalist apologetics and, 612–16
Day's involvement in, 362–7
economic democracy and demise of,
625–6
fundamentalist predictions concerning, 450
Garveyite movement and, 568
human rights and, 658
labor movement and, 114–15
Muelder and, 313–14
Niebuhr's view of, 252–72
Novak's discussion of, 496
Rauschenbusch's discussion of, 96–7
social gospelers and, 60–1
Ward and, 113, 120, 122–30
Communities of Solidarity and Resistance, 637
community, Muelder's idea of, 319
Community of Character, A, 477
competitiveness, Novak's embrace of, 501–2
Comte, Auguste, 553–4
Conaty, Thomas, 190–1
Concerned Women for America, 456
Cone, Cecil, 396–7, 408
Cone, Charlie, 396
Cone, James H., 4, 291–2
Anderson's discussion of, 593, 595
Cobb and, 627
Daly and, 405, 411, 425
liberation theology and, 390, 396–411
West and, 565, 570, 576
Cone, Lucy, 396
Cone, Rose, 398
Confessing Church, 326
Confessions (Rousseau), 325
conflict, ethics of, 637–40
Confucianism, human rights and, 660–2
Congregational Church
feminist theologians in, 412
Gladden and, 64–5
Yale Divinity School and, 228

Congregational Pastors' Union, 39
Congress of African People (CAP), 401
Connecticut Bible Society, 39
Connell, Francis, 337, 339, 343, 345
"conscientization," West's concept of,
569–70
consensus, human rights and, 661–3
Consequences of Pragmatism, 592
Constantinian ideology
Hauerwas's discussion of, 478–80
Yoder's discussion of, 469
Constitution of the United States, Murray's
discussion of, 349–61
containment policy, 262, 269
contraception, Catholic prohibition against,
535–44
Contract Buyers League, 680
Conway, Jill Ker, 169
Cook, Joseph, 30
Cooke, Willie P., 563
Cooley, Charles, 71
Coolidge, Calvin, 50, 114
Cooper, Anna Julia, 422
cooperative markets, economic democracy
and, 686–8
Copeland, M. Shawn, 590
Corey, Lewis, 261
Cornell, Tom, 374–6
Cornel West Reader, 576, 579–80
corporate capitalism
capitalist apologetics and, 614–16
economic democracy and, 685–8
Novak's discussion of, 500
see also capitalism; globalization
Corrigan, Michael A., 187
Cort, John C., 368, 502
Cortes, Ernesto, 680
Costen, James, 586
Coughlin, Charles E., 211–12, 332, 370
Councilist Marxism, West's study of, 565–7
Counts, George, 261
Cowan, Rosemary, 584
Cowley, Malcolm, 364
Cox, Harvey, 293
Cox, James M., 50
Cox, Oliver, 568, 574
Crafts, Walter, 65
Crane, Charles, 49
Crane, Hart, 364
Crapsey, Algernon Sidney, 30, 105
Croly, Herbert, 676
Cross, Frank Moore Jr., 332

Cross and the Lynching Tree, The, 411
Crozer Theological Seminary, 391
Cuba
  American invasion of, 162, 266
  Isasi-Díaz and, 654
Cuban Revolution, Day's defense of, 373–4
Cullmann, Oscar, 460
cultural chauvinism, in social gospel
    movement, 60–1
Cultural Contradictions of Capitalism, The, 496–7
cultural criticism
  by Aquino, 656–7
  black liberation theology and, 408–11
  Christianity and, 242–4
  evangelicals and, 611–12
  Hauerwas on religion and, 482–8
  moral theory and, 316–19
  mujerista theology and, 650–2
  Novak's critique of, 491–3, 500–3,
    510–11
  Wallis's discussion of, 517–19
  by West, 567–8, 572–3, 581–4
  womanism and cultural production of evil,
    640–6
Curran, Charles, 4–5, 358, 360, 483, 533
  Gustafson and, 545
  moral theology and, 534–44

Daily Princetonian, 583
Daily Worker, 129
Daly, Herman, 628–9
Daly, Mary, 4, 291
  Cobb and, 627
  Cone and, 405, 411, 425
  feminist theology of, 411–21
  Harrison and, 424–5, 435–6
  liberation theology and, 390
  Welch and, 638–40
Darby, John Nelson, 324, 449–50
Darrow, Clarence, 155
Darwinism
  Catholicism and, 335
  Christian accommodation of, 22
  Manifest Destiny ideology and, 73–9
  Peabody and, 36
  Rauschenbusch and, 84
  reconciliation of Christianity with, 6–7
  social ethics and, 17, 553–63
  social gospel movement and, 69–73
  see also social Darwinism
Daughters of the American Revolution, 183
Davis, Allen F., 169
Davis, Angela, 577

Davis, Charles, 418
Davis, John W., 50
Davis, Richard Harding, 181–2
Dawn (periodical), 70
Day, Dorothy, 4, 305, 361–77, 534, 571
Day, Grace Satterlee, 361–2
Day, John, 362
Day, Tamar: *see* Hennessy, Tamar
Dean, William, 552–3
Deats, Paul Jr., 323
De Beauvoir, Simone, 414, 416–17
Debs, Eugene, 114, 160, 362, 567–8
debt service obligations, 504
Declaration on Religious Freedom, 356–8,
    360
Decree on Ecumenism (*Unitatis redintegratio*),
    356
Decter, Midge, 509
DeFerrari, Teresa M., 468
De Genova, Nick, 577
deism, First Amendment rights and, 353–4
Dell, Floyd, 363
De Meglio, Giuseppe, 348
democracy
  Addams' discussion of, 176–85
  aggressive exportation of, 509–12
  Catholic opposition to, 543
  economic democracy, 624–6
  Hauerwas's discussion of, 479–88
  Murray on Catholicism and, 349–61
  West's discussion of, 581–4
Democracy and Social Change, 128–9
Democracy and Social Ethics, 176–85
Democracy Matters, 581–3
democratic capitalism, 489–512
democratic globalism, 509–12
Democratic Party, 161
  Adams and, 332
  neoconservative reaction to, 488–9
  Ryan and, 186, 208–15
  Wallis and, 516–19
  West's discussion of, 581–2
democratic socialism
  communism's demise and, 625–6
  West's advocacy for, 565–84
  see also economic democracy; socialism
Democratic Socialist Organizing Committee,
    565
Democratic Socialists of America (DSA),
    409, 565–70
dependency theory, liberation theology and,
    503
Derby, Elias Haskett, 7

Der Wanderer, 195
Descartes, Rene, 14
Descent of Man, The, 73, 75–6
Dewart, Leslie, 293
Dewey, John, 34, 71, 236–7
　Addams and, 175, 183–4
　Humanist Manifesto and, 327
　Muelder's discussion of, 321–2
　Niebuhr's critique of, 251–3, 262
　Rorty's discussion of, 592
　West's criticism of, 571
　Winter and, 554, 556, 558–9
DeWolf, Harold, 317–20, 391
Diamond, Malcolm, 592
Dibelius, Martin, 465
Diefenbach, Albert C., 327
Die Religion, ihr Wesen und ihre Geschichte (Religion, Its Nature and Its History), 9
Dietrich, John, 324, 327
Dignatatis humanae, 658
Dillenberger, John, 327
"Dimensions of the Complete Life, The," 393
Dionysian tradition, 328
Disciples Divinity House, 326
Disciples of Christ, 121
Discourses on Religion, 9
Dispatches from the Front, 481–2
dispensationalism, 450
Distributive Justice, 197–8
Divino afflante spiritu, 336
Dixon, Thomas Jr., 30
Dobson, James, 512
Documents of Vatican II, 358
Dodson-Gray, Elizabeth, 626
Does Civilization Need Religion?, 235
Dombrowski, James, 35–6, 123, 126
Dominican Republic, U.S. invasion of, 268
Donahue, John R., 468
Dorcas Federal Labor Union, 175
Döring, Maria, 87
Dostoyevsky, Fyodor, 583
Douglas, Paul, 236
Douglas, William O., 213
Douglass, Frederick, 30, 162, 397, 640
Douglass, Harlan Paul, 30
Douglass, James W., 375, 377
Driscoll, James Francis, 335
Driver, Tom, 277, 565, 622
Drummond, Henry, 71
dualistic religion, Taylor's criticism of, 47
Dubey, Madhu, 594
Du Bois, W. E. B., 30–1, 78–79

Cone and, 397, 404
　Ransom and, 155, 158, 162–3, 167–8
　"Talented Tenth" concept of, 642
　West's discussion of, 568, 571–2, 575, 577–9
Duchrow, Ulrich, 631
Duffy, Francis Patrick, 335
Duke, David Nelson, 111, 129–30
Duke Magazine, 486
Duke University, Hauerwas at, 484–8
Dulles, John Foster, 265–6, 680
Dupré, Louis, 535
Durant, Will, 564
Durkheim, Emile, 556
Dutch Reform Church, Christian sociology and, 36–7
dwelling metaphor, in Winter's work, 559–63
Dyson, Michael Eric, 583, 594

Eastman, Max, 363
Ecce Homo: A Survey of the Life and Work of Jesus Christ, 41
ecology
　economic democracy and, 686–8
　political economics and theology of, 626–30
economic democracy
　social ethics and, 624–6, 674–7, 683–8
Economic Justice for All: Catholic Social Teaching and the U. S. Economy, 430, 508, 663–4
economic rights, Hollenbach's defense of, 505–7, 657–65
economics
　Bennett's discussion of, 283–7
　capitalist apologetics and, 614–16
　dependency theory and, 503–4
　ecotheology and, 628–30
　evangelical-neoconservative critiques of, 612
　King's advocacy for, 394–6
　Muelder's discussion of, 315–16
　mujerista theology and, 650
　Niebuhr's discussion of, 253–9
　Novak's discussion of, 504–6
　Rauschenbusch's advancement of, 101–4
　Ryan's discussion of, 206–15
　social gospel movement and, 5
　Winter's discussion of, 553–63
Economy Act of 1932, 208
ecotheology
　eco-justice and, 630–7
　emergence of, 626–30

Ecumenical Association of Third World
    Theologians, 409
ecumenical movement, 109
    Bennett and, 285–7
    Catholicism and, 337–49
    Daly and, 415–21
    Murray and, 341–9, 352–61
    see also Vatican Council II
Eddy, Sherwood, 109, 117
    economic democracy and, 677
    Niebuhr and, 232–35, 260, 275
Eden Theological Seminary, 227–8, 241
education
    for African Americans, 78–9
    racial justice and, 29–32
    religious pluralism and, 354–61
Edwards, George R., 467
Edwards, Jonathan, 14, 449
Edwards, R. A. R., 184
Edward Waters College, 151
Egan, Ed, 373
Egan, Eileen, 374–5
Ehrenreich, Barbara, 565
Ehrlich, Paul, 626–27
Eichrodt, Walter, 460
Eisenhower, Dwight D., 451
Elements for a Social Ethic, 549, 553–5, 558,
    560–2
Eleventh Virgin, The, 364, 376
Elia, Nada, 578–9
Eliot, Charles William, 8, 16, 34
Eliot, T. S., 275, 325
Elizondo, Virgilio P., 650–3
Eller, Vernard, 467–8
Ellis, George E., 8
Ellis, John Tracy, 347
Ellison, Marvin M., 5, 621–4
Ellison, Ralph, 572
Ellsworth, Robert F., 682
Elmhurst College, 227, 241
El Salvador, 513, 563
Elshtain, Jean Bethke, 486, 682
Ely, Richard
    American Economic Association and, 70–1
    Gladden and, 76
    public image of, 6
    Rauschenbusch and, 88–9
    Ryan and, 189–90, 193
    social gospel movement and, 10, 20, 23,
        61
    on sociology, 6–7, 18, 32, 41, 109–10
Emergency Banking Act, 208

Emerson, Ralph Waldo, 74
Emerton, Ephraim, 16
Emory University, Gustafson and, 546–8
Encyclopedia of Social Reform, 45
Engel, J. Ronald, 334
Engels, Friedrich, 173, 196
*En la Lucha/In the Struggle: Elaborating a
    Mujerista Theology*, 649
Enlightenment
    Hauerwas's discussion of, 479–80, 485
    Kristol's discussion of, 496
Episcopal Church, 121
    evangelical attacks on, 611–12
    gay rights in, 624
    Gibson and, 549–50
    women's ordination in, 416
Equal Rights Amendment, 420
eschatology, Darbyism and, 449–50
Espionage Act (U. S.), 114, 116
Essay concerning Human Understanding, 12–13
Estrin, Saul, 687
ethical religion, Ward's vision for, 122–30
Ethics from a Theocentric Perspective, 545
Ethics of Disclosure, The, 345
ethnic identity
    mujerista theology and, 650–7
    Novak's discussion of, 492–4, 500
Eugene, Toinette, 641
euthanasia, Catholic position on, 540–4
Evangelical Alliance, 70
evangelicals
    neoconservatives and, 611
    new evangelicalism and, 449–60
    politics of Jesus and, 460–74
    progressive evangelicalism, 512–19
    social ethics and, 447
Evangelicals at the Brink of Crisis, 456
Evangelium vitae, 542
Evans, James Jr., 593
Everett, Charles Caroll, 8, 16, 19
Everybody's Magazine, 197
evil
    cultural production of, 640–6
    Niebuhr's discussion of, 248
evolution, Gladden's discussion of, 71–3
Evolution and Dogma, 335
Ewing, Quincey, 30
Experience of Nothingness, The, 492

Fabian Socialists, 91, 116
"Failure of German-Americanism, The," 230
Fairbanks, Charles, 111

Faith and History, 258
Faith and Order Commission, 313
Faith Works, 516
fall, scriptural story of, Niebuhr's discussion
  of, 247–8
Falwell, Jerry, 456, 512, 516, 519
families
  Cahill on, 618–21
  mujerista theology and, 650–1
  Ryan's discussion of, 193–4
  Stackhouse's discussion of, 616–18
  West's discussion of, 575, 579
Fanon, Frantz, 404
Faramelli, Norman, 323
Farians, Elizabeth, 419
Farley, John (Cardinal), 197
Farley, Margaret A., 541
Farrakhan, Louis, 574, 576–7, 584
fascism, H. R. Niebuhr's criticism of, 252–5,
  260
Fashole-Luke, Edward W., 409
Faunce, W. H. P., 29
Federal Council of Churches
  Bennett and, 283
  Commission for a Just and Durable Peace,
    266
  evangelicals and, 453
  Muelder and, 308, 312
  Niebuhr and, 230
  pacifism and, 80
  Ransom and, 161–2
  Rauschenbusch and, 94
  Ryan and, 193, 195
  social gospel movement and, 44, 76, 98
  socialism and, 121–2
  Ward and, 112–13
Federated Theological Faculty, 326
Federation of Labor, 155
Fellowship for a Christian Social Order
  (FCSO), 232–3, 235
Fellowship of Reconciliation, 105, 232–3,
  265, 392
Fellowship of Socialist Christians, 236, 260–2
Feminine Mystique, The, 413, 424
Feminist Ethic of Risk, A, 640
feminist theology
  Addams and, 169–70
  Bowne and, 307
  of Cahill, 618–21
  Christian feminist liberation ethics, 421–37
  Cone's view of, 405–6, 409–11
  Daly and, 411–21

eco-justice and, 634–7
Ellison's critique of, 623–4
Gibson and, 550
of Harrison, 421–37
Latina feminists and, 646–57
liberation theology and, 291, 390
Novak's critique of, 511–12
social ethics and, 5
social gospel movement and, 4
Stackhouse's discussion of, 616–18
Welch and, 637–40
womanism and cultural production of evil
  and, 640–6
womanist ethics and, 587–92
see also womanist ethics; women's rights
Fenn, William Wallace, 324
Fenton, Joseph, 336, 345, 347–8, 355–6
Ferguson, Adam, 13
Ferré, Nels, 474
Fichter, Joseph, 415
Filson, Floyd V., 316
Finn, James, 490
Finney, Charles, 39
Firing Line (television show), 417
First Amendment rights, Murray's discussion
  of, 353, 357
First Things, 488
Fisk, Franklin W., 46
Fiske, John, 72–9
Fleming, Peter, 195–6
Flewelling, Ralph T., 307
Flower, Benjamin Orange, 30
Flynn, Elizabeth Gurley, 128, 372
Focus on the Family, 456
Foerster, Robert F., 34
Forbes, James, West and, 565
Forbes magazine, 508
Ford, Gerald, 496
Ford, Henry, 234
Ford, James, 34
Ford, Munson, 85
foreign policy
  containment and, 262, 264–6, 269, 276
  realism, social ethics and, 680–3
Forest, Jim, 373, 375
*For God and the People: Prayers of the Social
  Awakening*, 98, 104
Forks of the Road, The, 81
Forman, James, 401, 568
*For the Common Good: Redirecting the Economy
  toward Community, the Environment, and a
  Sustainable Future*, 629

For the Right (newspaper), 88–9, 137n.92
Fortune, T. Thomas, 154, 163
Fosdick, Harry Emerson, 79–80, 109, 249, 258
   Muelder and, 308
Foucault, Michel, 583, 593, 638, 643
Foundations of the Responsible Society, 314
Fountain, Charles H., 205
Fourteenth Amendment, "separate but equal"
   doctrine and, 30
Fox, Matthew, 626
Francis, Convers, 8
Frank, Andre Gunder, 503
Frank, Sam, 126
Frankfurter, Felix, 213
Frankfurt School, 308
   West and, 564
Fraser, Nancy, 565
Fraternal Council of Negro Churches, 165
Frazier, E. Franklin, 572
Freeman, A. Myrick, 629
Frei, Hans, 475
Fremantle, William H., 41
Fribourg Dominicans, 412–13
Friedan, Betty, 413, 424
Friedman, Milton, 508
Friedman, Thomas, 684
From Faith to Faith, 474
From the Hub to the Hudson, 62
Frontier Fellowship, 262
Frontiers in Modern Theology, 458
Fukuyama, Francis, 489
Fuller, Charles, 450
Fuller Theological Seminary, 448, 450–1
fundamentalism
   Henry's definition of, 448–50
   see also evangelicals
Furfey, Paul H., 369

Gadamer, Hans, 558–9, 561
Gaffney, Edward (Msgr), 372
Gage, Matilda Joslyn, 421
"Galesian Dualism/Dyarchy," 342, 358
Gallagher, Buell, 236, 675
Gamaliel Foundation, 680
Gandhi, Mohandas K., 308, 391, 395
Gannett, William Channing, 30
Garrett Biblical Institute (Garrett-Evangelical
   Theological Seminary), 397–8
Garrison, William Lloyd, 63, 160
Garrow, David, 570
Garveyite movement, 568
Garvin, Vicki, 577

Gates, Henry Louis Jr., 571, 594
Gelasius I (Pope), 342
General Conference of the Methodist
   Episcopal Church, 111
General Council of Congregational and
   Christian Churches, 121
George, Henry, 84, 88, 187
German-American Protestantism, Niebuhr's
   Americanization of, 229–36
German Christianity, 326
German Evangelical Synod of North
   America, 226–7, 230–1
German Faith Movement, 326
German theology, Peabody's experiences
   with, 8–9
Germany
   Niebuhr and, 255–9
   Rauschenbusch's defense of, in World
     War I, 92–4, 104–9
   war against Soviet Union, 129
Geyer, Alan, 272, 293, 323
Gibbons, James (Cardinal), 187, 197
Gigot, Francis E. C., 195
Gilbert, Paula, 478
Gilkes, Cheryl Townsend, 590, 641
Gilkey, Charles, 237
Gilkey, Langdon, 258, 552–3
Gill, Eric, 372
Gillette, Henry, 39
Gladden, Solomon and Amanda, 61
Gladden, Washington
   Darwinism and, 69–73
   death of, 108
   early life and career, 61–9
   economic democracy and, 675
   evangelicals and, 452
   Manifest Destiny and racial justice
     ideology and, 73–9
   nervous breakdown of, 62–3
   pacifism of, 80–3, 182
   personal life of, 65, 131n.17
   public image of, 6
   racial issues and, 77–9, 134n.55
   Ransom and, 152
   Rauschenbusch and, 105
   Ryan and, 193
   social ethics and, 21, 27–9
   social gospel movement and, 20, 29, 98
   social ministry of, 70–3
   sociology and, 18
   Taylor and, 41, 48
   World War I and, 79–84

Glazer, Nathan, 489
globalization
    Cobb's critique of, 629–30
    democratic globalism, 509–12
    economic democracy and, 683–8
    public theology and, 616
    U. S. imperialism and, 681–3
God in Christ, 62
God of the Oppressed, 407–8
*God's Politics: Why the Right Gets It Wrong
    and the Left Doesn't Get It*, 517–19
Goizueta, Roberto, 654, 656
Gold, Mike, 372
Golden Rule
    Gladden's discussion of, 66
    Ward's statement on, 112
Goldman, Emma, 363
Gollwitzer, Helmut, 405
good society ideology, social ethics and, 675–7
Gordon, Lewis, 577–8
Goshen Biblical Seminary, 461–2
Gospel for a Working World, 114
Graham, Billy, 447–8, 451, 455–6
    Niebuhr and, 678–9
Gramsci, Antonio, 565, 568, 571, 643
Grant, Abram, 157–8
Grant, Jacquelyn, 410, 590, 593, 640
Grant, Ulysses S., 64
Gray, Asa, 8
Gray, John, 110
Great Economic Debate, The, 624
Great Migration
    Ransom's work in Chicago and, 154
    Taylor and, 49
Great Terror (Soviet Union), 126–30
Great War: *see* World War I
Greeley, Andrew, 404
Green, T. H., 319
    West's study of, 564
Gregorian University, 490, 534
Gregory I (Pope), 448
Gross, Murray, 261
Guffey Coal Act, 212
Gulf War of 1991, 510
Gunnemann, Jon P., 547
Gunsaulus, Frank W., 155
Gustafson, James M., 3, 244, 273, 475, 533
    Adams and, 334
    Anderson's study of, 592, 596
    Cahill and, 618–19
    Hauerwas and, 478, 482–4
    naturalistic theocentrism and, 544–8

Gustafson, John O., 544
Guth, Anne Marie, 460
Gutiérrez, Gustavo, 276, 291–3, 627
Guttmann, Amy, 482
Gyn/Ecology, 420–1

Habermas, Jürgen, 639
Hale, Edward Everett, 76
Hall, Amy Laura, 486
Hall, Douglas John, 626
Hall, George C., 49
Hall, Thomas C., 113
Hall, Toynbee, 172
Hampton, Fred, 577
Hampton Institute, 30–1
Hanley, Frank, 111
Hanna, Mark, 153
Harding, Warren G., 50
Häring, Bernard, 415, 535, 542
Harkness, Georgia, 249, 258, 412
Harnack, Adolf von, 94–5, 227
Harner, Jerome, 541
Harper, Frances Ellen, 162
Harper, William Rainey, 42, 45
Harper Collins publishers, 517
Harper's magazine, 74, 237
Harrington, Michael, 368, 372, 494–5
    West and, 565, 567
Harris, George, 21
Harrison, Beverly W., 4, 289, 293,
        390
    Cannon and, 586, 590–1
    Christian feminist liberation ethics of,
        421–37
    Ellison and, 621
    on homosexuality, 617
    Isasi-Díaz and, 649
    West and, 565
Hartford Seminary, 40–2
Hartranft, Chester, 37–41
Hartshorne, Charles, 549, 627
Hartt, Julian, 475
Hartz, Louis, 499–500
Harvard Bulletin, 33
Harvard Crimson, The, 580
Harvard Divinity School
    Adams at, 324–7, 332–4
    Eliot's support of, 16
    Novak at, 490
    Peabody at, 8–10
    Robb as teacher at, 437
    social science and, 34–5

Harvard University (Harvard College)
 chapel requirements abolished at, 16
 Gibson at, 549–50
 moral philosophy at, 11–12
 Peabody at, 8
 West at, 564, 571, 580–4
Hauer, Wilhelm, 326
Hauerwas, Stanley, 4, 447, 469, 473, 512
 Gustafson and, 547–8
 Isasi-Díaz and, 653
 radical orthodoxy movement and, 611
 virtue ethics of, 474–88
 Wallis and, 518–19
 Welch's discussion of, 639
Hayek, Friedrich A. von, 495, 498, 508
Hayes, Floyd W., 577–8
Hayes, Michael, 565
Hayes, Rutherford B., 74, 134n.55
Haymarket riots, social ethics and, 23
Headley, Clevis, 577–9
Healy, Patrick, 211
Hecker, Isaac, 187
Hecker, Julius, 123, 129–30
Hedge, Frederic Henry, 8
Hegel, G. F. W., 307, 309, 322–3, 394
 West's study of, 564
Hehir, J. Bryan, 505
Heidegger, Martin, 326, 558, 561–3
Heimann, Eduard, 237
Heller, Elizabeth, 422
Henderson, Charles, 45
Henderson, Norman, 324
Hendry, George, 626
Hennacy, Ammon, 368, 370, 372, 376
Hennessy, Kate, 377
Hennessy, Tamar (Tamar Day), 364–5, 377
Henry, Carl F. H., 4, 447
 new evangelicalism and, 448–60, 512
 Yoder's discussion of, 464–5
Henson, Francis, 236–7, 675
hermeneutics, social ethics and, 559–61
Herriot, Frank, 126
Herron, George
 economic democracy and, 675
 public image of, 6, 109
 social gospel movement and, 29, 60–1
 socialism and, 120
 Strong and, 76
Herzog, Frederick, 405
Heschel, Rabbi Abraham Joshua, 631
Hessel, Dieter, 626
Hewlett, Sylvia Ann, 575, 578

Heyward, Carter, 390, 433–5
Hicks, Jane E., 437
High, Stanley, 312
Highlander Folk School, 126
Hill, James J., 189–90
Hilliard, David, 401
Hillis, Newell Dwight, 30, 161
Hillquit, Morris, 196–7
Hincks, Edward Y., 21
Hine, Darlene Clark, 594
Hispanic Women: Prophetic Voice in the Church,
 648
historical contextualism, Winter's concept of,
 557–63
historical criticism
 at Harvard, 8
 Tholuck's analysis of, 9
"Historical Roots of the Environmental
 Crisis, The," 627
historicism
 in Murray's work, 342–3, 359
 in Niebuhr's work, 241–2, 246–7
 in Winter's work, 550–63
Hitler, Adolf, 128, 213, 255
Hoar, George F., 76
Hobbes, Thomas, 321
Hobson, John A., 191, 206–8
Hodge, A. A., 152
Hodge, Charles, 149
Hodgson, Peter C., 405
Hoehn, Richard A., 562
Hofstadter, Richard, 71
Hollenbach, David, 4–5, 359, 430, 505–7
 on human rights and Catholic social
 ethics, 657–64
Hollyday, Joyce, 514
Holmes, John Haynes, 81, 236, 238, 249
homosexuality
 Anderson's discussion of, 594–98
 Daly's discussion of, 411–21
 evangelical-neoconservative attacks on, 612
 Harrison's discussion of, 434–7
 sexual justice and, 621–4
 Stackhouse's discussion of, 616–18
 Wallis's discussion of, 518
Hook, Sidney, 322
hooks, bell, 594, 646
Hooper, J. Leon, SJ, 345, 360–1
Hoover, Herbert, 50, 182, 205–8, 234
Hoover, J. Edgar, 370
Hopkins, Dwight, 410, 593
"Hopkinsians," 21

Hordern, William, 397, 405
Horizons, 428
Horkheimer, Max, 308
Horowitz, David, 576–7
Horton, Myles, 126
Horton, Walter Marshall, 254
Horvat, Branko, 566
Hospers, John, 508
Hospitality Houses, 368, 370
Housatonic (ship), sinking of, 82
"household codes" *(Haustafeln)*, Yoder's
    discussion of, 465–7, 522n.50
House Special Committee to Investigate
    Un-American Activities (HUAC), 128
Houston Ministerial Association, 355
Howe, Julia Ward, 160
Howells, William Dean, 63
Huerta, Delores, 680
Hughes, Charles Evans, 167
Hughes, H. Stuart, 564
Hughes, Hugh Price, 109
Hugo, John, 370
Hull House, 172–5, 183–4
Hull House Labor Museum, 175
Humanae vitae, 538–41
humanism, Adams' study of, 325
Humanist Manifesto, 327
human rights, Catholic social ethics and,
    374, 505–7, 657–64
Hume, David, 13
Hume, Theodore C., 238
Humphrey, Hubert, 268–9, 275–6, 491
Hungary, Soviet invasion of, 266
Hunger March in Washington, 365
Hunt, Robert E., 539
Huntington, Samuel P., 682
Hurd, Richard, 325
Hurston, Zora Neale, 572, 587–9
Husserl, Edmund, 326
Hutcheson, Francis, 13–14
Hyndman, H. M., 196

IBW Woman's Club, 155–6
Idea of History, The, 474
Idea of the Holy, The, 308
Ignatieff, Michael, 661–2
Ignatius of Loyola, 415
immigration
    Addams' views on, 183
    anti-Catholicism, 187
    Rauschenbusch's support of, 92–4
    Ryan's discussion of, 200

Immortale Dei, 202, 339–40
imperialism
    Christian realism and, 288–94
    foreign policy realism and, 680–3
    social gospel movement and, 29, 60–1,
        76–9, 156
    West's discussion of, 581
In a Blaze of Glory, 641–2
income inequality, economic democracy and,
    685–8
Independent newspaper, 37, 63–4
Independent Voters of Illinois (IVI), 332
individualism
    Adams' discussion of, 330
    Addams's critique of, 176, 188
    Anderson's discussion of, 595
    Babbitt's discussion of, 325
    Bell's discussion of, 497–8
    Bennett's discussion of, 282–4
    Brightman's discussion of, 318–19
    Cahill on rights of, 620–1
    Cannon's discussion of, 587–8
    capitalism and, 211, 613
    Ellison's discussion of, 623
    Gladden on responsibility and, 63, 66–8
    Gustafson's discussion of, 547
    Hauerwas's discussion of, 475, 478
    Henry's discussion of, 456–7
    human rights and, 659–63
    Latina theology and role of, 649, 651
    Maguire on justice and, 637
    Muelder's discussion of, 309–12, 315, 323
    Murray's discussion of, 350–1, 356–60
    natural rights theory and, 192
    Niebuhr's discussion of, 237, 240, 245,
        251, 258, 422
    Novak's critique of, 492, 495, 500–1, 504
    Rasmussen's ecotheology and, 631
    Rauschenbusch's discussion of, 89–101
    Ryan on rights of, 191, 196, 199, 203–4
    salvation and, 27, 66, 454
    social ethics and, 19–20, 34, 36, 40
    social gospel movement and, 69–70
    Taylor's discussion of, 40, 45–7
    Townes' critique of, 642
    Ward on limits of, 114, 120
    West's discussion of, 564
    Whig ideology and, 499–500
    Winter's discussion of, 559, 561
    Yoder's discussion of, 464–6
Industrial Areas Foundation (IAF), 680
industrialism, Gladden's discussion of, 67–9

Industrial Workers of the World (IWW), 69, 114, 363, 366
inerrancy ideology, 122
    evangelicals and, 457–60
In Place of Profit: Social Incentives in the Soviet Union, 124–5
In Search of Our Mothers' Gardens: Womanist Prose, 584
Institute on Religion and Democracy, 611–12
Institutional Church and Social Settlement, 157
intentional theory, Winter's discussion of, 556–63
Inter-Denominational Congress, 39, 70
Interdenominational Theological Center, 586
International Congregational Council, 44
International Congress of the Laity, 374
International Congress of Women, 180
International Criminal Tribunal, 660
International Monetary Fund (IMF), 662
Inter-Ocean, 46
Interpretation of Christian Ethics, An, 247–59, 273
Interpretation of History, The, 257–8, 327
In These Times, 583
Iraq War, foreign policy realism and, 681–3
Ireland, John (Archbishop), 187, 190, 197
Irish World and American Industrial Liberator, The, 186
Irony of American History, The, 269
Irwin, Terry, 564
Isasi-Díaz, Ada María, 4–5, 433–4, 637
    Latina feminism and, 646–57
Is It Too Late?: A Theology of Ecology, 627–8
Islamic ideology, human rights and, 660–2
isolationism, H. R. Niebuhr's criticism of, 260–1
Issel, Ernst, 26
Ives, Samuel Curtis, 41–2

Jackson, Henry, 489, 496
Jackson, Jesse, 574
Jackson, T. H., 150–1
James, C. L. R., 577, 583
James, Henry, 63
James, William, 322, 554, 571, 595
    Catholic Church and, 19
    Christian sociology and, 36
    Gladden and, 71, 76
    Muelder and, 308
    Niebuhr and, 229
    social gospel movement and, 110

Jaspers, Karl, 326
Jaurés, Jean, 196
Jay-Z, 583
Jefferson, Thomas, 262, 350
Jelks, Randal, 576
Jennings, Willie James, 595
Jesus Christ and the Social Question, 20–1, 25–9, 45
Jews & Blacks: Let the Healing Begin, 575
John Paul II (Pope), 486, 508, 541–3
    Hollenbach's criticism of, 659
Johnson, Andrew (President), 147
Johnson, Bess B., 433
Johnson, Chalmers, 682
Johnson, F. Ernest, 352
Johnson, Georgia Douglas, 162
Johnson, Hugh, 211
Johnson, James Weldon, 162–3
Johnson, Kermit, 293
Johnson, Lyndon, 268, 272, 395, 582
Johnson, Mordecai, 60, 167
Johnson, Reverdy, 147
Johnson C. Smith Seminary, 586
John XXIII (Pope), 290, 349, 374, 506–7
    Daly's discussion of, 416–17, 420–1
    human rights advocacy of, 657–8
Joint Vision 2020, 682
Jones, Jenkin Lloyd, 30
Jones, LeRoi: *see* Baraka, Amiri
Jones, Major, 407
Jones, Rufus, 238
Jones, Theodore, 155
Joseph, Peniel E., 577–8
Journal of Religion, 428
Journal of the American Academy of Religion, 428
July Charter, 498
justice
    eco-justice, 630–7
    economic democracy and, 684–8
    King's fight for, 392–6
    Muelder's discussion of, 314–16
    Niebuhr's discussion of, 242–3, 249–50, 273–6
    Wallis's progressive evangelicalism and, 512–19
    see also racial justice; sexuality and sexual justice
Justice in the Making, 437
"justice-love," Ellison's concept of, 621–4
just-war doctrine, Yoder's discussion of, 471–4

Kampelman, Max, 489

Kant, Immanuel, 13, 192, 560
  capitalism and, 625
  Hauerwas's discussion of, 479–80, 484
  human rights and philosophy of, 662–3
  personalist theory and, 306–7, 318

Kantzer, Kenneth, 513

Karenga, Maulana, 578

Karl Barth and the Problem of War, 461–2

Kaufman, Gordon, 546, 596

Kaus, Mickey, 684–6

Keane, John (Bishop), 190

Keating, Edward, 211

"Keeping Body and Soul Together:
  Sexuality, Spirituality, and Social
  Justice," 621–14

Keeping Faith: Philosophy and Race in America,
  572, 580

Keller, Rosemary Skinner, 641

Kelley, Florence, 173

Kelly, George A. (Msgr), 544

Kennan, George, 264–6, 269, 276

Kennedy, John F., 266–7, 349, 353, 355,
  585

Kent, William, 49

Keppel-Compton, Ursula, 123–4, 239, 271

Kerby, William, 191, 197

Kerry, John, 516, 582

Khalilzad, Zalmay, 489, 509

Khanbhai, Hamid, 583

Khruschev, Nikita, 129

Kierkegaard, Søren, 242–3
  West's reading of, 563–4, 583

"Killing Wrong-Doers as a Cure for Wrong-
  Doing," 82

Kilson, Martin, 564

kin-dom, Isasi-Díaz's concept of, 650–3

King, Alberta Williams, 391

King, Coretta Scott, 395

King, Henry Churchill, 676

King, Martin Luther Jr., 2, 4, 167, 318, 323,
  519
  Anderson's discussion of, 597
  "beloved community" of, 394, 594
  Cannon and, 585–6
  Cone and, 396–7, 404, 410–11
  evangelicals' criticism of, 454–5
  liberation theology and, 390–6, 432
  West's discussion of, 563, 570–1
  white evangelicals and, 451
  Winter and, 552

King, Martin Luther Sr. ("Daddy King"), 391

Kingdom (periodical), 70

kingdom of evil concept, Rauschenbusch's
  discussion of, 107–8, 241

Kingdom of God in America, 241, 244

Kingdom of God is Within, The, 177–8

Kingsley, Charles, 25, 193

Kirk, Russell, 502

Kirk-Duggan, Cheryl A., 590

Kirkpatrick, Jean, 288, 489

Knights of Labor, 22–4

Knudson, Albert Cornelius, 307, 312, 321

Kojeve, Alexandre, 579

Kollar, Nathan, 428

Korean War, Niebuhr's support of, 266, 268

Korsch, Karl, 566

Krauthammer, Charles, 509

Kristol, Irving, 288, 489, 496, 498, 500, 509,
  680

Kropotkin (Prince), 71

Ku Klux Klan, 168

kulaks, Stalin's liquidation of, 124–6

Kurth, James, 682

Laborem exercens, 542

labor movement
  Addams' involvement in, 174–5
  Gladden and, 65–69
  Ransom's involvement in, 155
  Ryan and, 186, 191–9, 201–2, 206–15
  social ethics and, 23
  social gospel and, 10–14
  in Soviet Union, 124
  World War I and, 114–15

Labor Movement in America, The, 23

Labor Question, The, 68

laissez-faire ideology, 51
  Gladden and, 71
  Muelder's discussion of, 313

Lake, Kirsop, 325

Lamarckian developmental theory, 71

Lamas, Marta, 656

Lambert, Jean, 428

Lamentabili Sane, 195

Laney, James T., 548

LaPiana, George, 325

LaPorte, Roger, 375

Lasalle, Ferdinand, 196

LAS HERMANAS groups, 648

Lathrop, Julia, 173

Latina feminists, social ethics and, 646–57

Latin America
  dependency theory concerning, 503–4

Latin America (*cont'd*)
  liberation theology in, 276–7, 291–94,
    402, 503
  U.S. intervention in, 681–3
Lauer, Rosemary, 413–14
Law of Christ, The, 535
Lawson, Victor, 46
Lay Commission, 505
League for Independent Political Action, 236
League for Industrial Democracy, 236
League of Nations, 50, 114–16, 163, 182
  Niebuhr and, 232
  Ryan's support of, 199
League to Enforce Peace, 80–1
Lears, T. J., 169
Lebacqz, Karen, 273, 622
Lectures on Theology, 85
Lefever, Ernest, 288, 489, 680
Legge, Marilyn J., 437, 649
Le Grand, Julian, 687
Lehmann, Paul, 293, 332, 405
Lentricchia, Frank, 481
"Leonine Series," 345–9
Leo XIII (Pope), 187–9, 193, 202, 339,
    345–6, 359, 538
  Hollenbach's discussion of, 659
"Leo XIII: Separation of Church and State,"
    345
"Leo XIII and Pius XII: Government and
    the Order of Religion," 346
"Leo XIII on Church and State" The
    General Structure of the Controversy,"
    345–6
Lerner, Michael, 575
Leverett, John, 12
Levine, Daniel, 168–9, 583
liberal theory
  Adams's discussion of, 328–34
  capitalism and, 246–59
  Catholicism and, 335–49
  Daly's discussion of, 416
  emerging consensus on, 287–94
  evangelical repudiation of, 452–60
  Gustafson's discussion of, 545
  Hauerwas's critique of, 482–8
  Muelder's discussion of, 320–3
  Niebuhr and, 226, 231–9, 279
  Novak's critique of, 494–5
  racial justice and, 31
  Ransom's embrace of, 150–1
  Richard Niebuhr and, 241–63, 277–87
  sexual justice and, 623–4

  social ethics and, 4–7, 20–4, 226–7
  Wallis's discussion of, 513–19
Liberal Tradition in America, The, 499
*Liberating Creation: Foundations of Religious
    Social Ethics*, 558–62
Liberation and Reconciliation, 406
liberation theology
  Catholicism and, 503–12
  Christian realism and, 289–94
  Cone and, 396–411
  Daly's feminist theology and, 411–21
  eco-justice and, 637
  emergence of, 390
  Gustafson's discussion of, 545–8
  Harrison's Christian feminist liberation
    ethics, 421–37
  Hauerwas's discussion of, 484
  King's legacy in, 391–96
  Latina feminist theology and, 647–57
  legacy of, 447
  Niebuhrian legacy and, 276–87
  Welch's discussion of, 637–40
  West and, 563–84
  Winter and, 560
  womanist ethics and, 588–92
Liberation Theology, 291
Liberator (magazine), 363
libertarianism, Wallis's discussion of, 517–18
Library Journal Book Review, 418
Lieven, Anatol, 682
Lift Every Voice, 654
Liguori, Alphonsus (Saint), 535
Lincoln, Abraham, 170, 349–50, 395, 519
Lincoln, C. Eric, 323, 398
Lincoln, Robert L., 157
Lindbeck, George, 347, 548
Lindsay, Ben, 111
Lingua Franca, 486
Link, Eugene, 126–27
Lippmann, Walter, 275
Living Wage, A, 190–5
Lloyd, Henry Demarest, 10, 30
Locke, John, 12–13
Loeb, Karen, 490
Lombard, Peter, 415
London, Jack, 362
Long, Charles H., 407–8
Long, D. Stephen, 624–5
Long, Huey P., 211
Long Loneliness, The, 372
Longstreth, Thaddeus, 65
Longwood, Merle, 273

Look magazine, 263
Loomer, Bernard, 552
Lord, Audre, 640
Los Angeles Church Federation's
    Commission on Race Relations, 310–11
Lott, Eric, 577
Lotze, Rudolf Hermann, 110
Love and Conflict: New Patterns in Family Life,
    550
Lovin, Robin W., 273, 359, 682
Loving Nature, 631
Lowell, A. Lawrence, 34
Luckey, William R., 359–60
Ludlow, Robert, 372
Lukacs, Georg, 579
Lusitania, sinking of, 113, 180
Luther, Martin, evangelicals and, 455–60, 465
Lutheran Formula of Concord, 460
Lutheranism
    social ethics and, 23–4
    two kingdoms theology of, 242
Luxemburg, Rosa, 566
Lyon, David Gordon, 16
Lyons, Eugene, 126

MacDonald, Dwight, 372
MacDowell, Mary, 155
Macfarland, Charles S., 98, 109, 113
Machado, Daisy L., 654
Machen, J. Gresham, 448
Macintosh, Douglas Clyde, 228–40, 592
MacIver, Robert M., 312
Macpherson, C. B., 501
Madison, James, 14
magisterial authority, Curran's rejection of,
    539–44
magisterial Reformation, evangelical view of,
    459–60, 468–74
Magrude, J. W., 111
Maguire, Daniel C., 4–5, 293, 537–8, 543,
    547–8
    eco-justice and, 630–7
Making the Connections, 437
Malcolm X, 397, 399, 404, 410–11, 570
Malthusian population theory, 71
Mammy figure, Townes's discussion of,
    643–4
Manassa Society, 154
Manifest Destiny ideology
    German Americans and, 93–4
    social gospel movement and, 60–61, 73–9,
    162–3

Mannheim, Karl, 308, 327
Man's Nature and His Communities, 270
manual/moral casuistry, 535, 545
Marable, Manning, 565
Maritain, Jacques, 275, 290, 413, 498
market socialism, West's discussion of, 566–7
marriage
    Cahill's discussion of, 619–21
    sexual justice and, 621–4
    Stackhouse's discussion of, 616–18
Marsh, Daniel L., 312
Marshall, Charles C., 204–5
Martin, Clarice, 590
Martin & Malcolm & America, 410
Marty, Martin, 359
Marx, Karl
    Addams' study of, 172
    Cone's discussion of, 408–9
    Harrison's analysis of, 429–31
    liberation theology and, 503–4
    Niebuhr and, 237–38, 244–9, 251–9
    Novak's discussion of, 496–7, 503
    Rauschenbusch and, 102–4
    socialism and, 196–8
    West's study of, 564–8, 578–9, 583–4
Marxism and the National Question, 568
Masses (magazine), 363
Mather, Increase, 12
Mathews, Shailer
    Adams and, 327
    Chicago School theology and, 549, 596
    economic democracy and, 675
    Niebuhr's attack on, 247, 249–50, 252
    public image of, 6
    social gospel movement and, 20, 29, 61,
    82, 98, 109
Matrix Reloaded, The, 575
Matrix Revolutions, The, 575
Matthei, Chuck, 375
Matthews, J. B., 263
Maurice, Frederick Denison, 25, 193, 242
Maurin, Peter, 365–8, 372
Mayer, Carl, 268, 288, 680
Mays, Benjamin E., 60, 167
Mazzini, Giuseppi, 172
Mbiti, John, 409
McAllister, Elizabeth, 375
McBrien, Richard P., 359, 478, 482, 542
McCann, Dennis P., 4–5, 273, 562, 612,
    624–5
    capitalist apologetics of, 612–16
    Cobb's critique of, 629–30

McCarthy, Colman, 519
McCarthyism, 263–4
McClendon, James William Jr., 468
McConnell, Francis J., 109, 112, 260, 307
  economic democracy and, 675
McCormack, John, 208
McCormick, Richard, 539–42, 545, 547–8
McCormick, Vincent, SJ, 348–9
McCormick Reaper Manufacturing
    Company, strike against, 23
McDaniel, Jay, 626, 630
McDowell, Mary, 49, 173
McElroy, Robert, 359–60
McFague, Sallie, 626, 630
McGiffert, Arthur, 236
McGinn, Bernard, 538
McGlynn, Edward (Fr.), 88, 187
McGovern, George, 263, 276, 493–4
McGowan, R. A., 210
McInerny, Ralph, 504–5
McKelway, Alexander, 30
McKenna, John, 375
McKenna, Kathe, 375
McKinley, William, 153, 156
McMahon, John, 347
McQuade, Francis, 336
McQuaid, Bernard J., 187
McSweeney, Edward, 195
Mead, George Herbert, 111, 554, 558
Meadville Lombard, 334
Meadville Theological School, 326
Meaning of Revelation, The, 242
media coverage
  evangelicals and, 458–9, 486
  Wallis's critique of, 516–19
Medulla Theologica, 11
Mehl, Roger, 463
Meidner, Rudolf, 687
Meidner Plan, 687–8
Meland, Bernard, 322, 549, 552, 554
  ecotheology and, 627
Men and Religion Forward Movement, 44
Mennonite Board of Missions, 461–2
Mennonite Central Committee, 460
Mennonite Church
  Hauerwas and, 477
  Yoder and, 462–74
Men's Sunday Club, 154
Meredith, James, 455
Merici, Angela, 415
Merleau-Ponty, Maurice, 552, 555, 558
Merriam, Charles, 49

Merton, Thomas, 417–18
mestizaje, mujerista theology and, 650–3, 657
"Methodism's Pink Fringe," 312
Methodist Book Concern, 113, 116–17
Methodist Church, 121
  Cone and, 401
  evangelical attacks on, 611–12
  feminist theologians in, 412
  Hauerwas and, 478, 485
  see also African Methodist Episcopal
    Church
Methodist Federation for Social Service,
    111–12, 116, 125
Methodist Social Creed of 1908, 98
Metz, Johannes-Baptist, 656
Mexico, in World War I, 82
Meyer, Donald, 130
Meyer, Karl, 375
"middle axioms" theory, 3
Milbank, John, 624–5
military power
  neoconservative unipolarization and,
    681–3
  Novak's praise of, 509–10
Mill, James, 13
Mill, John Stuart, 33, 103
Millar, Moorhouse F. X., 201
millennialism, 448–51
Miller, David, 687
Miller, Francis Pickens, 238
Miller, Jim, 375
Miller, Kelly, 162
Million Man March, 577, 594
Mills, C. Wright, 571
Mills, Charles, 577–8
Mirage of Social Justice, The, 508
Miranda, José, 504
modernity, social ethics and, 674–7
Moffatt, James, 236
Moise, Lionel, 364
Molotov, V. M., 124, 126
Mondragon cooperatives, 688
Monroe Doctrine, 163, 681
Montagu, Ashley, 313–14
Montgomery bus boycott, 391–2
Moody, Dwight, 37, 39
Moore, George Foot, 324
Moral Creed for All Christians, A, 636–7
Moral Majority organization, 456, 458–9
Moral Man and Immoral Society, 60, 237–40,
    251, 255, 277, 279, 290, 292, 558,
    676

moral philosophy
  culture and, 316–19
  philosophical origins of, 10–14
  social ethics and, 15–20
moral politics, progressive evangelicalism and, 515–19
moral reasoning, social ethics and, 618–21
moral theology
  Catholic Church and, 658–64
  Curran and, 534–44
Moran, Gabriel, 416
Morgan, C. Lloyd, 322
Morgenthau, Hans, 266–7, 276
Morris, Edward H., 49, 155
Morris Brown College, 151
Morrison, Charles Clayton, 259
  as *Christian Century* editor, 205, 232–4, 237
  Murray and, 352
  Niebuhr and, 259
  social gospel movement and, 109
Morrison, Norman, 375
Morrison, Toni, 571–2, 574, 577, 583, 594, 641, 643
"Mothers for Peace," 374
Mott, John R., 260
Mouw, Richard, 473
Moynihan, Daniel Patrick, 489
Mozley, J. B., 41
Mud Flower Collective, 433–4
Muelder, Epke Hermann, 308
Muelder, Minnie, 308
Muelder, Walter G., 3, 120, 683
  early life and career, 308–16
  economic democracy and, 675
  moral theory and culture and, 316–19
  neo-orthodoxy and, 320–3
  personalist theory and, 306–16, 320–3
  social ethics and, 305
mujerista theology, 647–57
Munger, Theodore, 65
Municipal Voters' League, 44
Münsterberg, Hugo, 33
Muravchik, Emanuel, 489
Muravchik, Joshua, 509
Murphy, Edgar Gardner, 30
Murphy, Francis X., 535
Murphy, Roland E., 538
Murray, John Courtney, 4, 290, 305
  Catholicism and, 349–61, 534, 540
  early life and career, 335–49
  Hauerwas's discussion of, 478, 483

Novak and, 498
on religious freedom and pluralism, 334–49
Yoder's discussion of, 472
Muste, A. J., 373–5
mutual fund social ownership model, 687
Muwakkil, Salim, 583
Myrdal, Gunnar, 312

Nader, Ralph, 575
Nagel, Ernest, 321
Naked I Leave, 4492
Napier, B. David, 474
Nash, James, 631
National Association for the Advancement of Colored People, The, 161
  Adams and, 333
  King's involvement with, 391
National Association of Evangelicals, 448
National Association of Manufacturers, 69
National Black Economic Development Conference, 401
National Catholic War Council, 201
National Catholic Welfare Conference, 201–2, 206, 210, 213, 336
National Catholic Welfare Council (NCWC), 202
National Christian Action Council, 456
National Civic Federation Review, 201
National Committee of Negro Churchmen, 398
National Conference of Back Churchmen (NCBC), 398, 401
National Conference of Charities and Corrections, 32
National Conference of Christians and Jews, 337
National Conference of Unitarian Churches, 8
National Congregational Council, 44
National Council of Churches, neoconservative attacks on, 488
National Council of the Congregational Churches, 70
National Equal Rights League (NERL), 158–60, 167–8
National Federation of Churches and Christian Workers, 44
National Industrial Recovery Act of 1933, 211
nationalistic realism, 682–3
National Labor Relations Act, 212

National Prison Association, 32
National Recovery Administration (NRA),
    208, 211–12
National Review, 505, 510
National War Labor Board, 201
Nation magazine, 80, 204
nativism, Catholic Church and, 338
naturalistic theocentrism, 544–8
natural law theory
    Anderson and, 597
    Catholic Church and, 191–2, 341–9,
        351–2, 358–9, 538–44
    Curran and, 534–44
    evolution of, 11–12
    Muelder's discussion of, 321–3
natural rights theory, 191–2
Nature and Destiny of Man, The, 248, 256–9,
    270, 273, 287
Nazism
    Adams's experiences with, 326, 333
    Catholic Church and, 370
    H. R. Niebuhr's criticism of, 252–5, 260
Neander, August, 85
*Negro: The Hope of the Despair of Christianity,
    The*, 167–8
*Neighborhood Guilds: An Instrument of Social
    Reform*, 42
neoclassical theory, Cobb's critique of, 629
neoconservatives
    Catholicism criticized by, 504–5
    Christian realism and, 276–94
    democratic capitalism and, 489–503
    evangelicals and, 611–12
    Hauerwas's criticism of, 488
    ideological Americanism and, 488–9
    Niebuhr's influence on, 263, 680
    Novak and, 494–503, 508–12
    social ethics and, 447
    Stackhouse and, 612–16
    unipolar hegemony ideology of, 681–3
neoliberalism
    eco-justice and, 633
    West's critique of, 576–7
neo-orthodoxy
    evangelicals' criticism of, 458
    Harrison and, 422–3
    Muelder's discussion of, 320–3
    Niebuhr and, 258–59
    of Winter, 549–51, 553
Neuhaus, Richard John, 359–60, 489, 677
New American Movement (NAM), 565
New Class, Novak's discussion of, 494–5

New Creation as Metropolis, The, 551–2
New Criterion, 583
New England Congregationalism, 21
New Era, or, The Coming Kingdom, The, 76
Newer Ideals of Peace, 177–8
new evangelicalism
    emergence of, 447–8
    Henry and, 448–60
New Left, 276
    Day's criticism of, 375–7
    Novak and, 489
Newman, John (Cardinal), 335
New Masses, 129
New Redemption, The, 45
New Republic, 80, 232, 576, 580
Newsday, 575
New Social Order: Principles and Programs, The,
    114–16
Newsweek magazine, 456, 580
New Testament
    public theology and, 616
    Yoder's discussion of, 464–74
New Themes for the Protestant Clergy, 10
Newton, Huey, 577
Newton, Isaac, 11–12
New York Christian Advocate, 116
New Yorker magazine, 372
New York Review, 195, 335–6
New York Teachers Union, 236
New York Times, 537, 622
New York Times Book Review, 493, 519
New York Times Magazine, 503
Niagara Bible Conference, 448
Niagara Movement, 158–60, 167
Nicaragua, political unrest in, 514
Niebuhr, Elizabeth, 266
Niebuhr, Gustav, 226–28
Niebuhr, Helmut Richard, 2, 226–7, 230
    Anderson's study of, 592
    Curran and, 539–40
    early life and career of, 241–4
    Gustafson and, 544–6
    Harrison's study of, 424
    Hauerwas and, 474–5, 478–83
    legacy of, 271–6
    liberal theology of, 239–44
    Medal of Freedom awarded to, 268
    Winter and, 556–58
    World War II and Cold War politics and,
        259–71
    Yoder's view of, 463, 469. 473
Niebuhr, Hulda, 227, 230, 235, 294n.3

Niebuhr, Lydia, 227, 229–30, 236, 239
Niebuhr, Reinhold, 1–3, 110, 227, 294n.3
  Anderson and, 597–8
  Beckley's discussion of, 484
  Cone and, 396
  Curran and, 540
  Daly and, 420
  early life and career, 226–36
  economic democracy and, 675–7
  foreign policy influence of, 680, 682–3
  Harrison and, 422–3, 429–31
  Harvard Divinity School and, 332
  Hauerwas and, 475–6, 478–83
  liberal theology and, 226, 320–1, 432
  McCann and, 615
  Murray and, 358
  Novak and, 494–6
  personalist theory and, 306
  racial justice and, 677–8
  social gospel criticized by, 60–1, 236–9
  Ward and, 122–30
  West and, 571
  Winter's discussion of, 558
  Yoder's view of, 463, 470, 473
Niebuhr, Walter, 227, 230
Niemoler, Martin, 326
Nietzsche, Friedrich, 420
"nightwatchman state," Locke's concept of, 13
nihilism, West's discussion of, 572–3, 577–8, 582–4
Nitze, Paul, 266
Nixon, E. D., 391
Nixon, Justin Wroe, 109, 675
Nixon, Richard, 491, 496
Nobel Peace Prize
  Addams as recipient of, 168
  King as recipient of, 393
non-governmental organizations (NGOs), 684–8
"Non-resistant Church: The Theological Ethics of John Howard Yoder," 476
norms, social ethics and, 618–21
Norris, George, 211
North, Frank Mason, 98, 111–12
North American Free Trade Agreement (NAFTA), 633
Northern Baptist Convention, 131, 324
Northwestern University, Ward at, 109–10
Norton, Charles Eliot, 76
Notre Dame, University of
  Hauerwas at, 475–8, 482–3, 485

  Novak at, 489–90
  Yoder at, 461–2, 472–3
Novak, Michael, 4, 276, 447, 534
  democratic capitalism and, 489–503, 625
  Hollenbach and, 663
  on liberation theology, 503–12
  neoconservatism and, 489
  Stackhouse and, 615–16
Nove, Alec, 566, 687
Novus Ordo Seclorum, 509–10
Noyes, George Rapall, 8
Nozick, Robert, 564
nuclear deterrence
  Niebuhr's views on, 266–8
  Novak's opposition to, 504–5
Nuclear Freeze, 514
Nuechterlein, James, 489
Nygren, Anders, 392

Oberlin College, 150
Ockenga, Harold J., 447–8, 456
Ogden, Robert, 30–1
O'Grady, John (Fr.), 201
"Oh Master Let Me Walk with Thee" (hymn), 63
Oldham, J. H., 289
One Hundred Percent Americanism, 183
O'Neill, Eugene, 364
On Moral Business, 615
Open Church, The, 490
Original Revolution, The, 462
Osgood, Howard, 84
Other America, The, 567
Ottaviani, Alfredo (Cardinal), 346–9, 355–6
Otto, Rudolf, 308, 326–7, 334
Our Country, 41, 74
Our Right to Choose, 426–8
Outkast, 583
Outlaw, Lucius Turner Jr., 578–9
Outlook (periodical), 31, 76
"overlapping consensus" concept, human rights and, 661–2
Overstreet, Harry, 489
Oxford Conference, 283

Pacem in Terris (Peace on Earth), 374, 658
pacifism
  Addams' involvement in, 180–5
  Bennett's discussion of, 282–7
  Day's defense of, 368–77
  evangelicals and, 453
  Gladden and, 80–3, 182

pacifism (*cont'd*)
  Hauerwas and, 474–88
  Muelder and, 310–16, 378n.14
  Niebuhr's criticism of, 248–60
  Protestant churches' embrace of, 121
  of Rauschenbusch, 105
  Wallis's commitment to, 512–19
  Ward's involvement in, 122–30
  Yoder's view of, 461–74
Page, Kirby, 109, 121, 232–5, 249
  economic democracy and, 677
  Muelder and, 308
Palmer, A. Mitchell, 114
Pan-African Conference of Third World
    Theologians, 409
Pannekoek, Anton, 566
Pannenberg, Wolfhart, 677
Paris, Peter, 428, 593
Parishfield Community, 549–50
Paris Peace Conference, 168, 232
Parker, Edwin Pond, 38, 48
Parker, Theodore, 21, 30
Parkhurst, Charles H., 30
Parks, Rosa, 391
Parsons, Talcott, 550, 564
Pascendi Dominici Gregis, 195
Passantino, Myrtle, 418
Passion for Justice, A, 484
*Pastoral Constitution on the Church in the
    Modern World*, 374, 415
patriarchal religion, Daly's feminist critique
    of, 411–21
Pattison, Thomas Harwood, 85
Patton, Carl S., 70
Patton, William, 38
Pauck, Wilhelm, 326–27
Pauline theology, Yoder's discussion of,
    464–74, 488
Paulist order, 187
Paul Quinn College, 151
Paul VI (Pope), 357, 374, 538, 659
Payne, Daniel A., 149–52, 151
Payne, Henry, 153
Payne Institute, 151
Payne Theological Seminary, 149, 151
Peabody, Ephraim, 7, 30, 110
  vocational education and, 29–30
Peabody, Francis Greenwood
  Applied Christianity movement and, 18
  early life and career of, 7–10
  economic democracy and, 675
  evangelicals and, 452

founding of social ethics and, 2, 6–7,
    16–22, 25–9, 32–5
  Gladden and, 76
  legacy of, 35–6, 51, 549
  racial justice and, 30–2
  "Social Museum" of, 32–3
Peabody, Mary Ellen Derby, 7
Peaden, Catherine, 184
Pease, Donald, 565
Peirce, Benjamin, 8
Peirce, Charles S., 554, 571
Pellauer, Mary D., 433
Pelotte, Donald, 357
Perkins, Frances, 208, 211
Perle, Richard, 509
Perry, Ralph Barton, 34–5
personalism, 305–16, 320–3
Personalist, The, 307
personalist theory, Muelder and, 306–19
personality, social gospel movement and
    importance of, 47
Peters, Rebecca Todd, 437
Pew, J. Howard, 451, 455
Pfleiderer, Otto, 9
Philander Smith College, 396–8, 401
Phillips, Harlan, 294, n.3
Phillips, Wendell, 158
Phillips Academy, 21
Philosophiae Naturalis Principia Mathematica,
    11–12
Philosophy and the Mirror of Nature, 592
"Philosophy for Post-War Pacificism, A,"
    311
piety, Gustafson's discussion of, 546–8
Pilgrimage of Harriet Ransom's Son, The, 147
Pineda, Ana María, 649
Pitcher, Alvin, 549
Pittman, John, 578–9
Pius IX (Pope), 188
Pius X (Pope), 195, 335
Pius XI (Pope), 208–11
Pius XII (Pope), 336, 346–9, 415
Platonic theory, Adams's discussion of, 331
"Pledge of Resistance," 514
Plekhanoff, Georges, 196
Plessy v. Ferguson, 30, 154
pluralism
  American ideal *vs.*, 350–61
  Hauerwas's discussion of, 480–2
  Novak's rejection of, 509–10
  public school system and, 354–61
Plymouth Brethren, 324, 449, 512